DK CHILDREN'S ILLUSTRATED ENCYCLOPEDIA

NEW EDITION

DK CHILDREN'S ILLUSTRATED ENCYCLOPEDIA

LONDON, NEW YORK,
MELBOURNE, MUNICH, AND DELHI

FIRST EDITION 1991

Senior Editor Ann Kramer
Senior Art Editor Miranda Kennedy
Editors Christiane Gunzi, Susan McKeever, Richard Platt, Clifford Rosney
Art Editors Muffy Dodson, Debra Lee, Christian Sévigny, Val Wright
Picture Research Anne Lyons
Additional Research Anna Kunst, Deborah Murrell
Picture Manager Kate Fox
Production Manager Teresa Solomon
Editorial Director Sue Unstead

SEVENTH EDITION 2010

Editor Ashwin Khurana
Senior Art Editor Sheila Collins
Project Editor Jenny Finch
Managing Editor Linda Esposito
Managing Art Editor Diane Thistlethwaite
Publishing Manager Andrew Macintyre
Category Publisher Laura Buller
Picture Researchers Myriam Megharbi, Karen VanRoss
DK Picture Library Martin Copeland
Senior Cartographic Editor Simon Mumford
Production Controller Angela Graef
Production Editor Marc Staples
Jacket Designer Natalie Godwin
Jacket Editor Mariza O'Keeffe, Joanna Pocock
Jacket Manager Sophia Tampakopoulos

First published in Great Britain in 1991
This abridged edition published in 2010 by
Dorling Kindersley Limited,
80 Strand, London WC2R 0RL
Reprinted 1991, 1992 (twice), 1993
Reprinted with revisions 1992
Second edition 1993
Third edition 1995
Fourth edition 1996, reprinted 1997
1998, 1999
Fifth edition 2000
Sixth edition 2006
Seventh edition 2010

Copyright © 1991, 1993, 1995, 1996, 2000, 2006, 2010 Dorling Kindersley Limited
A Penguin Company

2 4 6 8 10 9 7 5 3
176244 - 05/10

A CIP catalogue record for this book is available from the British Library.

ISBN: 978-1-40535-372-4

Hi-res workflow proofed by Colourscan, Singapore
Printed and bound by Hung Hing, China

Discover more at
www.dk.com

CONTENTS

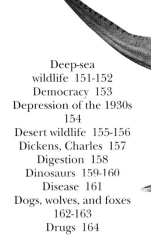

ABORIGINAL AUSTRALIANS TO ZOOS

HOW TO USE THE WEBSITE

1. Enter the website address
www.children.dkonline.com
2. Find the keyword at the top of the page above the entry heading.
3. Enter the keyword.
4. Click on the chosen link.
5. Go back to the book for your next chosen subject.
6. Enter a new keyword.

HAPPY SURFING!

ABORIGINAL AUSTRALIANS

THE FIRST INHABITANTS of Australia were nomadic (wandering) people who reached the continent from Southeast Asia about 40,000 years ago. When Europeans settled in Australia at the end of the 18th century, they called these native inhabitants "Aboriginals", meaning people who had lived there since the earliest times. Today there are about 455,000 Aboriginals in Australia. Most live in cities, but a few thousand still try to follow a traditional way of life. They travel through the bush, hunting with spears and boomerangs (throwing sticks) and searching for food such as plants, grubs, and insects. They have few possessions and make everything they need from natural materials. This way of life does not change or harm the fragile environment of the Australian outback (the interior). The well-being of the land, and its plants and animals are vital and sacred to the Aboriginal people.

ART
Aboriginal art is mostly about Dreamtime and is made as part of the ceremonies celebrating Dreamtime. Paintings of the people, spirits, and animals of Dreamtime cover sacred cliffs and rocks in tribal territories. The pictures are made in red and yellow ochre and white clay, and some are thousands of years old.

Private ceremonies and secret rituals are an important part of Aboriginal life. Through dancing, singing, and chanting, young Aboriginal people learn about Dreamtime.

Dancers, singers, and musicians paint their bodies with elaborate patterns.

The didjeridu, a wooden wind instrument, is used to play basic rhythms in Aboriginal music.

DREAMTIME

Aboriginal Australians believe that they have animal, plant, and human ancestors who created the world and everything in it. This process of creation is called Dreamtime. There are many songs and myths about Dreamtime, which generations of Aboriginal people have passed down to their children.

URBAN LIFE
The majority of Aboriginal Australians live in cities and towns. Some have benefitted from government education and aid programmes and have careers as teachers, doctors, and lawyers. Many, though, are poor and isolated from white society. They have lost touch with traditional Aboriginal tribal ways, and because they do not fit neatly into white Australian society, they cannot always share its benefits. However, there are now campaigns among urban Aboriginal people to revive interest in the tribal culture of their ancestors.

LAND CLAIMS
When British settlers arrived in Australia, they seized sacred sites and other land which belonged to Aboriginal people. With the help of Aboriginal lawyers, Aboriginal Australians campaigned to get the land back. In 1976, the Australian government agreed that Aboriginal people have rights to their tribal territories, and some land was returned.

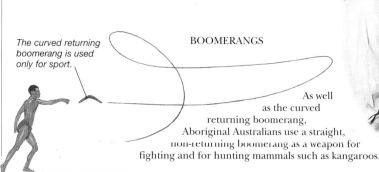

The curved returning boomerang is used only for sport.

BOOMERANGS

As well as the curved returning boomerang, Aboriginal Australians use a straight, non-returning boomerang as a weapon for fighting and for hunting mammals such as kangaroos.

Find out more
AUSTRALIA
AUSTRALIA, HISTORY OF
DANCE
MUSICAL INSTRUMENTS
MYTHS AND LEGENDS

AFRICA

FEW REGIONS OF THE WORLD are as varied as Africa. On this vast continent there are 53 independent nations and many times this number of peoples and ancient cultures. There are mountains, valleys, plains, and swamps on a scale not seen elsewhere. The northern coast is rich and fertile; below it lies the dry Sahara Desert. South of the Sahara, lush rainforest grows. Most of southern and eastern Africa is savanna, a form of dry plain dotted with trees and bushes. The nations of Africa are generally poor, though some, such as Nigeria, have rich natural resources. Many governments are unstable, and rebellions and civil wars are common. There are few large cities; most are near the coast. The rest of the continent is open countryside where people follow traditional lifestyles.

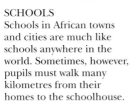

SCHOOLS
Schools in African towns and cities are much like schools anywhere in the world. Sometimes, however, pupils must walk many kilometres from their homes to the schoolhouse.

Africa is roughly triangular in shape. The Atlantic Ocean lies to the west and the Indian Ocean to the east. In the northwest only a few kilometres of sea separate the African continent from Europe.

The Tuareg peoples, who inhabit the Sahara, are pastoralists.

The Ashanti peoples of West Africa are mainly farmers.

The tall Masai of Kenya herd cattle on the open plains.

PEOPLE
In the African countryside many people live in tribal villages. Some, such as the Kikuyu of East Africa, are descended from tribes that have lived in the same place for many centuries. Others are recent immigrants from other parts of Africa or from other continents. Borders between countries take little account of these varied cultures. People of one culture may live in two different countries, and in one nation may be found more than a dozen different tribal groupings.

Few pygmies are taller than 1.25 m (4 ft). They live in the dense Congo rainforest.

The towers of mosques dominate Cairo's skyline.

The Bushmen roam the deserts of southern Africa and gather wild food from the harsh environment.

CAIRO
Cairo is the capital city of Egypt and the largest city in Africa, with a population of nearly 17 million. It sits on the River Nile near the head of the river's delta. The older part of the city contains narrow, winding streets. The new city has wider streets and many modern office buildings and flats. The people of Cairo are mostly Egyptian, although some come from all over North Africa, as well as from Europe and the Middle East.

KILIMANJARO
The tallest and most beautiful mountain in Africa is Kilimanjaro, in Tanzania. Its highest peak, which rises 5,895 m (19,340 ft), is an extinct volcano. Although the mountain is only a few kilometres from the equator, the top is always covered in snow. A footpath leads to the top, which can be reached in three days from the nearest road. Many people live on the lower slopes, where they farm tropical fruit.

SAHARA DESERT

The Sahara is the largest desert in the world and covers nearly one third of Africa. In recent years the desert has spread, destroying farmland and causing famine. In some areas irrigation has stopped the spread of the desert, but long-term irrigation can make the soil salty and infertile. Temperatures have been known to exceed 50°C (120°F) in this inhospitable environment.

In West Africa, drumming is a highly developed art. People once used drum beats to pass on messages.

MUSIC AND CULTURE

Africa has a rich and varied culture. North Africa shares the Islamic traditions of the Middle East, producing beautiful mosques and palaces. West African music has a strong rhythm, and there are many interesting dances from this region. The area is also home to a flourishing wood-carving industry. Eastern and southern Africa have become famous for beautiful beadwork and colourful festive costumes.

MEDICINE AND HEALING

When seeking a cure for sickness, some Africans consult Western-style doctors. Others consult a traditional healer (above). Healers are respected members of a community, with vast knowledge of local herbs and plants and the ways in which they can be used as medicines. To identify the source of an illness, the healer might contact good or evil spirits by going into a trance. Treatment may include animal sacrifice.

WAR AND FAMINE

Civil wars and famines are common in Africa. Many are caused by political disagreements, and some are the result of tribal conflicts. In Chad a civil war lasting many years was fought between the desert Tuaregs, backed by Libya, and the farmers of the wetter areas. In Rwanda and Burundi fighting between the Tutsi and Hutu tribes led to thousands of deaths. Other misery is caused by famine. Traditionally, most people grew enough food each year to last until the next harvest. However, African countries increasingly produce export crops and rely on imported food. If food distribution breaks down or drought ruins crops, thousands of people may starve.

RURAL LIFE

Although African cities have been growing fast, most Africans still live in the countryside. They grow their own food and only rarely have a surplus to sell or exchange for other goods. Many tribes have farmed the same land for generations, living in villages with all of their relatives. Sometimes the young men go to live in cities for a few years to earn money in mines or factories. Then they return to the village to marry and settle down. The types of crops grown vary widely. Yams, cassava, and bananas are produced in the lush tropical regions; farmers in drier areas concentrate on cattle and corn.

Road building in Nigeria

DEVELOPMENT

Poor infrastructure, including unreliable roads, railways, and electricity supplies, holds back the economic growth of many African nations. Most countries rely on loans from Western governments and international banks to pay for their development programmes.

Find out more

AFRICA, HISTORY OF
CENTRAL AFRICA
EAST AFRICA
SOUTH AFRICA
WEST AFRICA

POLITICAL AFRICA

Independent African states, with few exceptions, are territorially identical to the colonies they replaced. Until the 1960s, most of Africa was controlled by European countries as part of their overseas empires. By the late 1980s, nearly every country had gained its independence. In many cases, hasty attempts were made to set up European-style governments. Leaders often became dictators, or the army seized power. However, in recent years, there has been a shift towards multi-party democracy.

 ALGERIA
Area: 2,381,740 sq km
(919,590 sq miles)
Population: 34,178,000
Capital: Algiers

 ANGOLA
Area: 1,246,700 sq km
(481,551 sq miles)
Population: 12,799,000
Capital: Luanda

 BENIN
Area: 112,620 sq km
(43,480 sq miles)
Population: 8,791,000
Capital: Porto-Novo

 BOTSWANA
Area: 600,370 sq km
(231,804 sq miles)
Population: 1,991,000
Capital: Gaborone

 BURKINA
Area: 274,200 sq km
(105,870 sq miles)
Population: 15,746,000
Capital: Ouagadougou

 BURUNDI
Area: 27,830 sq km
(10,750 sq miles)
Population: 8,988,000
Capital: Bujumbura

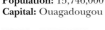 **CAMEROON**
Area: 475,440 sq km
(183,570 sq miles)
Population: 18,879,000
Capital: Yaoundé

 **CAPE VERDE**
Area: 4,033 sq km
(1,557 sq miles)
Population: 429,000
Capital: Praia

 CENTRAL AFRICAN REPUBLIC
Area: 622,984 sq km
(240,535 sq miles)
Population: 4,511,000
Capital: Bangui

 CHAD
Area: 1,284,000 sq km
(495,752 sq miles)
Population: 10,329,000
Capital: N'Djamena

 COMOROS
Area: 2,170 sq km
(838 sq miles)
Population: 752,000
Capital: Moroni

 CONGO
Area: 342,000 sq km
(132,040 sq miles)
Population: 4,013,000
Capital: Brazzaville

 DEMOCRATIC REPUBLIC OF THE CONGO
Area: 2,345,410 sq km
(905,563 sq miles)
Population: 68,693,000
Capital: Kinshasa

 DJIBOUTI
Area: 23,200 sq km
(8,958 sq miles)
Population: 516,000
Capital: Djibouti

 EGYPT
Area: 1,001,450 sq km
(386,660 sq miles)
Population: 83,083,000
Capital: Cairo

 EQUATORIAL GUINEA
Area: 28,050 sq km
(10,830 sq miles)
Population: 633,000
Capital: Malabo

 ERITREA
Area: 117,600 sq km
(45,406 sq miles)
Population: 5,647,000
Capital: Asmara

 ETHIOPIA
Area: 1,104,300 sq km
(426,373 sq miles)
Population: 85,237,000
Capital: Addis Ababa

 GABON
Area: 267,670 sq km
(103,347 sq miles)
Population: 1,515,000
Capital: Libreville

 GAMBIA
Area: 11,300 sq km
(4,363 sq miles)
Population: 1,783,000
Capital: Banjul

 GHANA
Area: 239,460 sq km
(92,456 sq miles)
Population: 23,832,000
Capital: Accra

 GUINEA
Area: 245,860 sq km
(94,926 sq miles)
Population: 10,058,000
Capital: Conakry

 GUINEA-BISSAU
Area: 36,120 sq km
(13,940 sq miles)
Population: 1,534,000
Capital: Bissau

 IVORY COAST
Area: 322,463 sq km
(124,503 sq miles)
Population: 20,617,000
Capital: Yamoussoukro

 KENYA
Area: 582,650 sq km
(224,962 sq miles)
Population: 39,003,000
Capital: Nairobi

 LESOTHO
Area: 30,350 sq km
(11,718 sq miles)
Population: 2,131,000
Capital: Maseru

 LIBERIA
Area: 111,370 sq km
(43,000 sq miles)
Population: 3,442,000
Capital: Monrovia

 LIBYA
Area: 1,759,540 sq km
(679,358 sq miles)
Population: 6,310,000
Capital: Tripoli

 MADAGASCAR
Area: 587,040 sq km
(226,660 sq miles)
Population: 20,654,000
Capital: Antananarivo

 MALAWI
Area: 118,480 sq km
(45,745 sq miles)
Population: 14,269,000
Capital: Lilongwe

 MALI
Area: 1,240,190 sq km
(478,837 sq miles)
Population: 12,667,000
Capital: Bamako

 MAURITANIA
Area: 1,030,700 sq km
(397,955 sq miles)
Population: 3,129,000
Capital: Nouakchott

 MAURITIUS
Area: 2,040 sq km
(7172 sq miles)
Population: 1,284,000
Capital: Port Louis

 MOROCCO
Area: 446,550 sq km
(172,414 sq miles)
Population: 34,859,000
Capital: Rabat

 MOZAMBIQUE
Area: 801,590 sq km
(309,493 sq miles)
Population: 21,669,278
Capital: Maputo

 NAMIBIA
Area: 824,290 sq km
(318,260 sq miles)
Population: 2,109,000
Capital: Windhoek

 NIGER
Area: 1,267,000 sq km
(489,188 sq miles)
Population: 15,306,000
Capital: Niamey

NIGERIA
Area: 923,770 sq km
(356,668 sq miles)
Population: 149,229,000
Capital: Abuja

RWANDA
Area: 26,340 sq km
(10,170 sq miles)
Population: 10,473,000
Capital: Kigali

 SÃO TOMÉ AND PRÍNCIPE
Area: 1,001 sq km
(386 sq miles)
Population: 213,000
Capital: São Tomé

 SENEGAL
Area: 196,720 sq km
(75,950 sq miles)
Population: 13,712,000
Capital: Dakar

 SEYCHELLES
Area: 455 sq km
(176 sq miles)
Population: 87,000
Capital: Victoria

 SIERRA LEONE
Area: 71,740 sq km
(27,699 sq miles)
Population: 6,440,000
Capital: Freetown

 SOMALIA
Area: 637,660 sq km
(246,200 sq miles)
Population: 9,832,000
Capital: Mogadishu

 SOUTH AFRICA
Area: 1,221,040 sq km
(471,443 sq miles)
Population: 49,052,000
Capital: Pretoria/Tshwane

 SUDAN
Area: 2,505,815 sq km
(967,493 sq miles)
Population: 41,088,000
Capital: Khartoum

 SWAZILAND
Area: 17,360 sq km
(6,703 sq miles)
Population: 1,124,000
Capital: Mbabane

 TANZANIA
Area: 945,090 sq km
(364,900 sq miles)
Population: 41,049,000
Capital: Dodoma

TOGO
Area: 56,790 sq km
(21,927 sq miles)
Population: 6,020,000
Capital: Lomé

TUNISIA
Area: 163,610 sq km
(63,170 sq miles)
Population: 10,486,000
Capital: Tunis

UGANDA
Area: 236,040 sq km
(91,136 sq miles)
Population: 32,370,000
Capital: Kampala

ZAMBIA
Area: 752,614 sq km
(290,586 sq miles)
Population: 11,863,000
Capital: Lusaka

 ZIMBABWE
Area: 390,580 sq km
(150,800 sq miles)
Population: 11,393,000
Capital: Harare

⚑	△	🏛	✪	●	•
Volcano	Mountain	Ancient monument	Capital city	Large city/ town	Small city/ town

STATISTICS

Area: 30,065,385 sq km (11,608,310 sq miles)
Population: 946,968,000
Number of independent countries: 53
Highest point: Kilimanjaro (Tanzania) 5,895 m (19,340 ft)
Longest river: Nile, 6,695 km (4,160 miles)
Largest lake: Lake Victoria: 69,484 sq km (26,828 sq miles)
Main occupation: Agriculture

MINING

Africans have been mining and processing minerals, including iron ore, copper, and gold, for more than two thousand years. Gold mined in the forest country of western Africa was carried across the Sahara by African traders and exported to Europe and Asia. During the colonial period mining was intensified. Today, South Africa, Zimbabwe, Zambia, and Democratic Republic of Congo possess heavily industrialized mining areas. These areas have yielded minerals such as gold, diamond, copper, and uranium.

Large-scale drilling equipment (above) is used in the gold mining industry.

Dogon dancers (right) from Mali perform a funeral dance.

MASKS AND DANCE

Masked dance is performed in many communities in west and central Africa and plays an important part in social events. Once inside the costume, the person takes on the character represented by the mask. Often parts of the body are exaggerated with padding or pieces of wood (left). The dance steps, songs, and sounds complete the costume and energetically represent both the spirit world and the world of humans.

CAPE VERDE

The independent republic of the Cape Verde islands lies 620 km (385 miles) off the coast of Senegal, in the Atlantic Ocean. The islands have a population of 429,000, but almost twice this number of Cape Verdeans live abroad.

HORN OF AFRICA

Because of its shape, the easternmost point of the African continent is called the Horn of Africa. It is one of the poorest regions on Earth, with few natural resources. Droughts and civil wars have killed thousands of people and made many more homeless.

SAO TOME AND PRINCIPE

The volcanic islands of São Tomé and Príncipe form a republic with a population of 213,000. São Tomé, the larger island, lies just north of the equator.

GAME PARKS AND CONSERVATION

The animal life of Africa is rich and varied. However in the last century, numerous animal and plant species have been lost forever. As the land has been turned into farms and industrial sites, many animals have been driven from their habitats. Their numbers have also been severely reduced by hunters. To protect animals from extermination, several African governments have set aside large game reserves where hunting is prohibited.

EUROPE

Madeira (to Portugal)
ALGIERS
RABAT
TUNIS
TUNISIA
TRIPOLI
Mediterranean Sea
Nile Delta
CAIRO
Giza 🏛
Thebes 🏛

MOROCCO
Canary Islands (to Spain)
LAÂYOUNE
Western Sahara (Occupied by Morocco)
Tropic of Cancer

ALGERIA
Atlas Mountains

LIBYA
EGYPT
Red Sea
Tropic of Cancer

Sahara
Ahaggar
Tibesti
Libyan Desert

ASIA

MAURITANIA
NOUAKCHOTT
MALI
Niger
NIGER
Lake Chad
CHAD
KHARTOUM
SUDAN
ERITREA
ASMARA

CAPE VERDE
PRAIA
SENEGAL
DAKAR
Sahel
Blue Nile
DJIBOUTI
Gulf of Aden

GAMBIA
BANJUL
BAMAKO
NIAMEY
OUAGADOUGOU
BURKINA
NIGERIA
ABUJA
NDJAMENA
White Nile
DJIBOUTI *Horn of Africa*

GUINEA-BISSAU
BISSAU
GUINEA
CONAKRY
FREETOWN
SIERRA LEONE
MONROVIA
LIBERIA
IVORY COAST
YAMOUSSOUKRO
GHANA
TOGO
BENIN
ACCRA
LOMÉ
PORTO-NOVO
Niger

ADDIS ABABA
ETHIOPIA

MALABO
CAMEROON
YAOUNDE
CENTRAL AFRICAN REPUBLIC
BANGUI
Ubangi
SOMALIA
MOGADISHU

Equator
EQUATORIAL GUINEA
SAO TOME & PRINCIPE
LIBREVILLE
GABON
Congo Basin
Congo
UGANDA
KAMPALA
Lake Turkana
Lake Victoria
KENYA
NAIROBI
Equator

SÃO TOMÉ
BRAZZAVILLE
KINSHASA
DEM REP CONGO
RWANDA
KIGALI
BURUNDI
BUJUMBURA
DODOMA
Kilimanjaro △ 5,895m

Cabinda (to Angola)
LUANDA
Lake Tanganyika
Zanzibar
TANZANIA

ANGOLA
Lake Nyasa
COMOROS
MORONI
MAYOTTE (to France)
Mamoudzou

ZAMBIA
LUSAKA
MALAWI
LILONGWE
Comoro Islands

Victoria Falls
HARARE
ZIMBABWE
MOZAMBIQUE
ANTANANARIVO
MADAGASCAR

NAMIBIA
WINDHOEK
BOTSWANA
Kalahari Desert
GABORONE
TSHWANE PRETORIA
MAPUTO
MBABANE
SWAZILAND

BLOEMFONTEIN
MASERU
LESOTHO
SOUTH AFRICA
CAPE TOWN
Cape of Good Hope
Tropic of Capricorn

ATLANTIC OCEAN

INDIAN OCEAN

Zambezi

SCALE BAR			
0	400	800	km
0		400	800 miles

HISTORY OF
AFRICA

FOR MUCH OF ITS HISTORY, Africa has been hidden from outsiders' eyes. The Sahara Desert cuts off communication from north to south for all but the hardiest traveller. The peoples of Africa have therefore developed largely by themselves. By about 2600 BCE, rich and powerful empires such as Ancient Egypt had arisen. The empires have disappeared, but they left behind buildings and other clues to their existence. Other African peoples left records of their history in songs that have been passed down from parent to child through countless generations. Europeans remained ignorant of this rich history until, during the 1400s, they explored the west coast. Soon they were shipping thousands of Africans to Europe and the Americas as slaves, a "trade" that destroyed many traditional societies. During the late 1800s, Europeans penetrated the interior of Africa and, within 20 years, had carved up the continent between them. Almost all of Africa remained under European control until the 1950s, when the colonies began to gain their independence. Today, the peoples of Africa are free of foreign control.

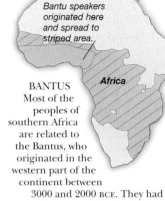

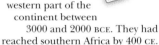

BANTUS Most of the peoples of southern Africa are related to the Bantus, who originated in the western part of the continent between 3000 and 2000 BCE. They had reached southern Africa by 400 CE.

Ivory traders

GREAT ZIMBABWE

The stone city of Great Zimbabwe was a major religious, political, and trading centre in southern Africa between the 11th and 14th centuries. It grew rich on the proceeds of herding cattle and mining gold, copper, and iron. The peoples of Great Zimbabwe exported their produce to the coastal port of Sofala in what is now Mozambique, and then up the coast of Africa to Arabia.

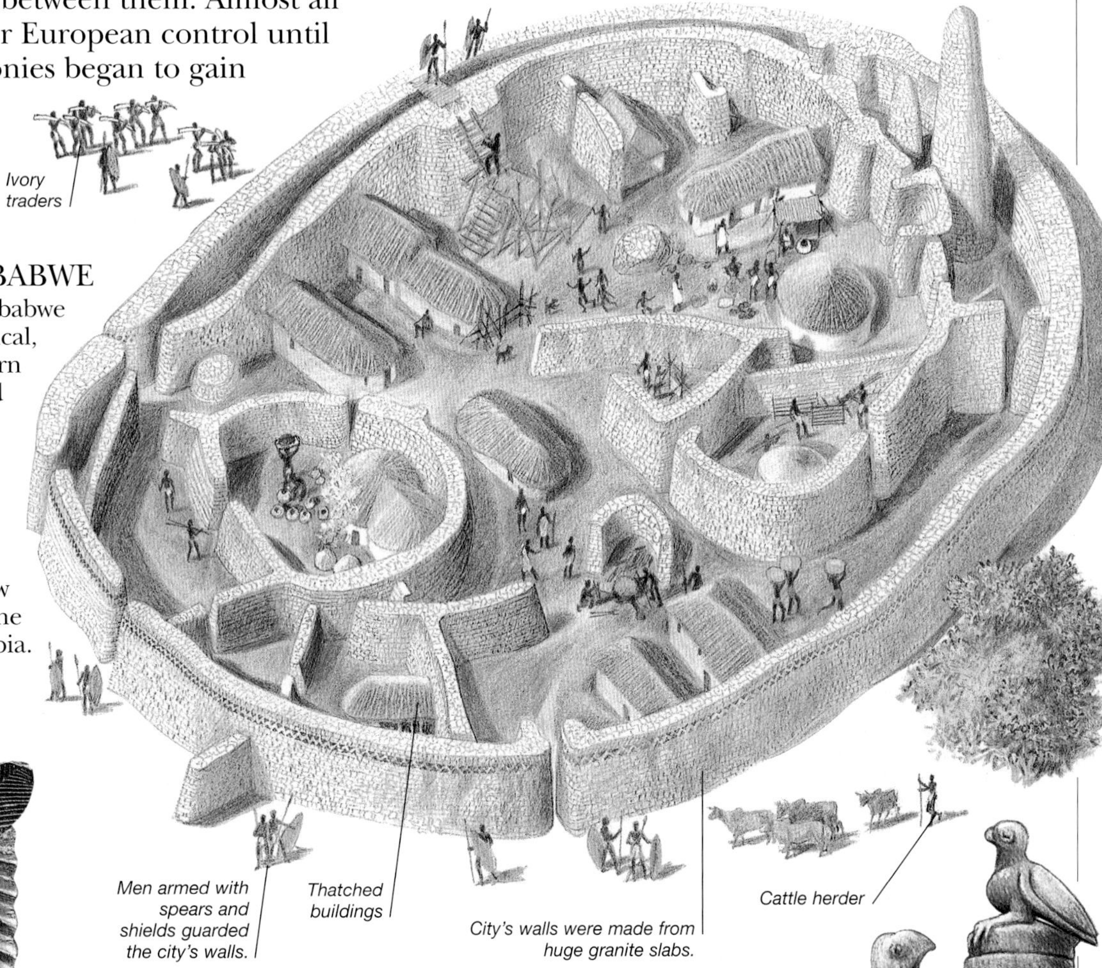

Men armed with spears and shields guarded the city's walls.

Thatched buildings

City's walls were made from huge granite slabs.

Cattle herder

Great enclosure at Great Zimbabwe

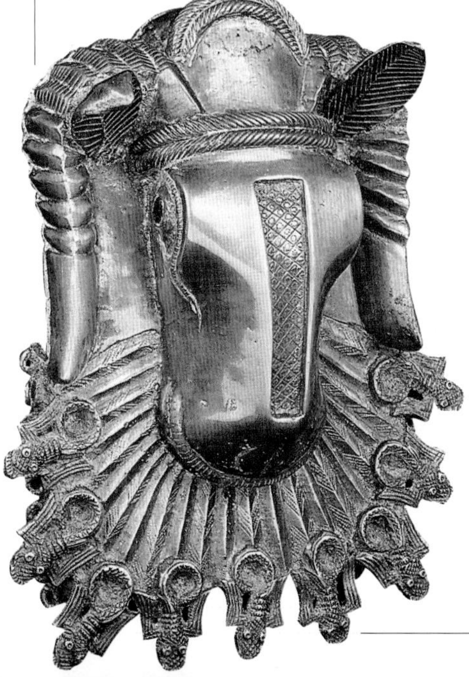

BENIN

The West African kingdom of Benin reached the height of its power between the 14th and 17th centuries. Its people traded ivory, pepper, palm oil, and slaves with the Portuguese. They also excelled in casting realistic figures in bronze. On the left is a Benin bronze mask.

SOAPSTONE BIRDS
Soapstone carvings of local birds on columns stood in an enclosure outside Great Zimbabwe. One of these birds has been the national symbol of Zimbabwe since the country gained its independence in 1980.

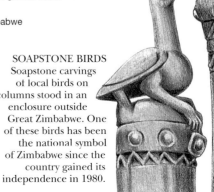

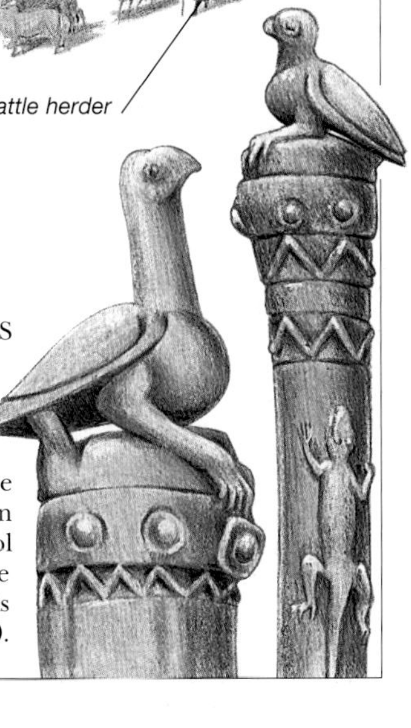

SCRAMBLE FOR AFRICA

Until the 1880s, European conquest in Africa was restricted to the coastal regions and the main river valleys. But European powers wanted overseas colonies (settlements). Throughout the 1880s and 1890s, European nations competed for land in Africa. By 1900, almost all of Africa was in European hands. The only independent states left were the ancient kingdom of Ethiopia in the east, and the free slave state of Liberia in the west. The cartoon (left) shows Germany as a bird "swooping" onto Africa.

ON THE SWOOP!

ZULU WARS
Some African peoples managed to resist the Europeans for a time. After 1838, the Zulus of southern Africa fought first the Boers (Dutch settlers) and then the British. In 1879, however, Britain finally defeated the Zulus. In 1887, Zululand became a British colony. Above is a picture of the British trying to break through Zulu lines.

INDEPENDENCE
The coming of independence to much of Africa after 1956 did not always bring peace or prosperity to the new nations. Many were weakened by famines and droughts or torn apart by civil wars. Few have managed to maintain civilian governments without periods of military dictatorships. In 1964 Malawi (formerly Nyasaland) became Africa's 35th independent state. Above is the celebration scene.

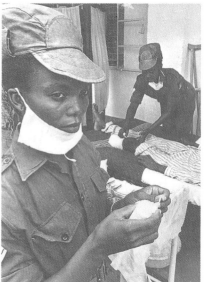

AFRICA
700-1200
Kingdom of Ghana in West Africa grows rich on cross-Saharan trade with the Arabs.

c. 800-1800 Kanem-Bornu kingdom.

1200s Trading cities flourish on east coast.

1235-1500 Kingdom of Mali.

1300-1600 Kingdom of Benin.

1300s Great Zimbabwe flourishes.

1350-1591 Kingdom of Songhai.

1500-1800s Europeans take Africans as slaves to America.

1838-79 Zulus fight against Boers and British.

1880s Europeans take almost total control of Africa.

1957-75 Most of Africa independent.

1990 Namibia independent.

APARTHEID

In 1948 the National Party came to power in South Africa. Years of segregation, known as apartheid, followed. This policy gave white people power but denied black people many rights, including the vote. In 1990 the African National Congress (ANC), a banned black nationalist movement led by Nelson Mandela, was legalized, and the apartheid laws began to be dismantled. In 1994, the first-ever free elections were held.

ORGANIZATION OF AFRICAN UNITY
Despite the many political differences that exist between the individual African states, they all share problems of poverty, poor health, and lack of schools. In 1963, the Organization of African Unity (OAU) was founded to co-ordinate policies to solve these problems. It was replaced in 2002 by the African Union (AU). Above are two members of the OAU medical unit treating civil war victims.

NELSON MANDELA
In 1994, Nelson Mandela (left), a leader of the ANC, became the President of South Africa.

Find out more
AFRICA
BENIN KINGDOM
EGYPT, ANCIENT
PREHISTORIC PEOPLES
SLAVERY

AIRCRAFT

LESS THAN 100 YEARS AGO, even the fastest ship took more than a week to cross the Atlantic Ocean. Today, most jet airliners (large passenger planes) can make this 4,800-km (3,000-mile) journey in less than seven hours. Aircraft are the fastest way to travel because they can soar straight over obstacles such as mountains and oceans. Powerful jet engines enable the fastest combat aircraft to reach speeds in excess of 2,400 km/h (1,500 mph) – more than twice as fast as sound. Even ordinary jet airliners fly at more than 850 km/h (530 mph). Modern aircraft are packed with advanced technology to help them fly safely and economically at great speed. Sophisticated electronic control and navigation systems keep the aeroplane on course. Computer-designed wings help cut fuel costs. And airframes (aircraft bodies) are made of metal alloys and plastic composites that are lightweight and strong.

JET AIRLINER
Like all jet airliners, the *Boeing 747-400* flies high above the clouds to avoid bad weather. Its airtight cabin is pressurized – supplied with air at a suitable pressure. This protects passengers and crew from the drop in air pressure and lack of oxygen at high altitudes.

The undercarriage (landing wheels) folds up inside the aeroplane during flight to reduce drag (air resistance).

The Boeing 747-400 airliner can carry 412 people and fly non-stop for more than 13,600 km (8,470 miles). Seats are arranged on two decks.

The aircraft's radar shows the crew the weather conditions up to 320 km (200 miles) ahead so that they can avoid storms.

FLIGHT DECK
The captain and crew control the aircraft from the flight deck. In the past, the flight deck of an aeroplane was a mass of dials and switches. New jet airliners are packed with electronics, and computer screens have replaced the dials. Other new features include computer-controlled autopilot systems that enable the plane to take off and land when bad weather obscures the pilot's vision.

FLYING AN AEROPLANE
Every aeroplane has three main controls: the throttle to control speed; rudder pedals for turning the plane's nose to the left or right (yawing); and a control column that tilts the aircraft to either side (rolling), or up and down (pitching). The pilot usually operates all three to guide the plane through the air.

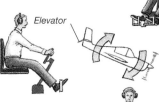
To roll, the pilot moves the control column to the left or right, which raises the ailerons on one wing and lowers them on the other.

Aileron

Elevator

To pitch up or down, the pilot pushes or pulls on the control column, raising or lowering the elevators on the tail wing.

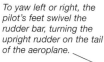
To yaw left or right, the pilot's feet swivel the rudder bar, turning the upright rudder on the tail of the aeroplane.

Rudder

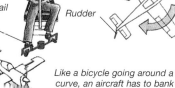
Like a bicycle going around a curve, an aircraft has to bank into a turn. To do this, the pilot uses the control column and the rudder pedals together so that the aircraft rolls and yaws at the same time.

OBSERVATION PLANES
Specially designed aircraft give a clear view of everything from traffic jams to diseased crops.

JET AIRCRAFT
Each year billions of people make long journeys in jet airliners and smaller business jets. These aircraft are powered by a type of jet engine called a turbofan. Turbofans are powerful and relatively quiet.

AEROPLANES
Aeroplanes are powered aircraft that have wings. The word aircraft describes all flying machines including helicopters, gliders, hang gliders, and aeroplanes. Most large airliners and combat aeroplanes have jet engines enabling them to fly fast and high. But jets are expensive and use a lot of fuel, so many smaller planes are driven by propeller, just like the first aeroplanes.

SEAPLANES
Aircraft are ideal for getting in and out of remote places. Seaplanes have floats instead of landing wheels to land and take off on water.

CONCORDE
This airliner, in service from 1976 to 2003, was supersonic, which means that it flew faster than sound. It cruised at more than twice the speed of sound, crossing the Atlantic Ocean in less than four hours.

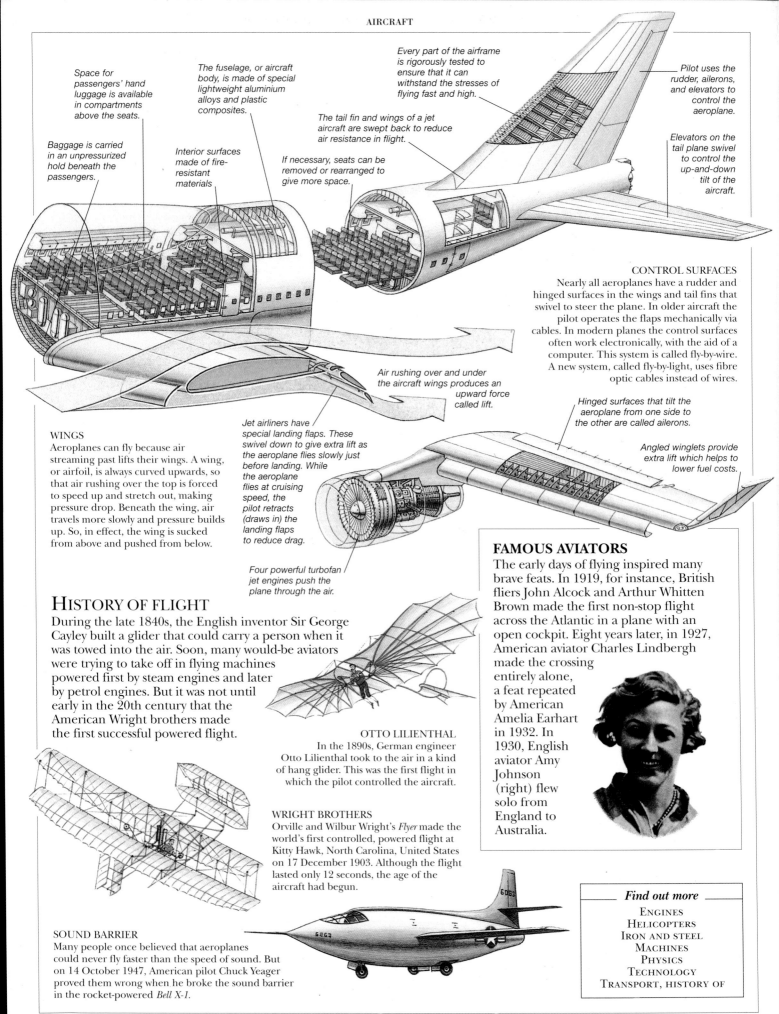

Space for passengers' hand luggage is available in compartments above the seats.

The fuselage, or aircraft body, is made of special lightweight aluminium alloys and plastic composites.

Every part of the airframe is rigorously tested to ensure that it can withstand the stresses of flying fast and high.

Pilot uses the rudder, ailerons, and elevators to control the aeroplane.

Baggage is carried in an unpressurized hold beneath the passengers.

Interior surfaces made of fire-resistant materials

The tail fin and wings of a jet aircraft are swept back to reduce air resistance in flight.

If necessary, seats can be removed or rearranged to give more space.

Elevators on the tail plane swivel to control the up-and-down tilt of the aircraft.

Air rushing over and under the aircraft wings produces an upward force called lift.

CONTROL SURFACES

Nearly all aeroplanes have a rudder and hinged surfaces in the wings and tail fins that swivel to steer the plane. In older aircraft the pilot operates the flaps mechanically via cables. In modern planes the control surfaces often work electronically, with the aid of a computer. This system is called fly-by-wire. A new system, called fly-by-light, uses fibre optic cables instead of wires.

Hinged surfaces that tilt the aeroplane from one side to the other are called ailerons.

Angled winglets provide extra lift which helps to lower fuel costs.

WINGS

Aeroplanes can fly because air streaming past lifts their wings. A wing, or airfoil, is always curved upwards, so that air rushing over the top is forced to speed up and stretch out, making pressure drop. Beneath the wing, air travels more slowly and pressure builds up. So, in effect, the wing is sucked from above and pushed from below.

Jet airliners have special landing flaps. These swivel down to give extra lift as the aeroplane flies slowly just before landing. While the aeroplane flies at cruising speed, the pilot retracts (draws in) the landing flaps to reduce drag.

Four powerful turbofan jet engines push the plane through the air.

HISTORY OF FLIGHT

During the late 1840s, the English inventor Sir George Cayley built a glider that could carry a person when it was towed into the air. Soon, many would-be aviators were trying to take off in flying machines powered first by steam engines and later by petrol engines. But it was not until early in the 20th century that the American Wright brothers made the first successful powered flight.

OTTO LILIENTHAL
In the 1890s, German engineer Otto Lilienthal took to the air in a kind of hang glider. This was the first flight in which the pilot controlled the aircraft.

WRIGHT BROTHERS
Orville and Wilbur Wright's *Flyer* made the world's first controlled, powered flight at Kitty Hawk, North Carolina, United States on 17 December 1903. Although the flight lasted only 12 seconds, the age of the aircraft had begun.

FAMOUS AVIATORS

The early days of flying inspired many brave feats. In 1919, for instance, British fliers John Alcock and Arthur Whitten Brown made the first non-stop flight across the Atlantic in a plane with an open cockpit. Eight years later, in 1927, American aviator Charles Lindbergh made the crossing entirely alone, a feat repeated by American Amelia Earhart in 1932. In 1930, English aviator Amy Johnson (right) flew solo from England to Australia.

SOUND BARRIER

Many people once believed that aeroplanes could never fly faster than the speed of sound. But on 14 October 1947, American pilot Chuck Yeager proved them wrong when he broke the sound barrier in the rocket-powered *Bell X-1*.

Find out more
ENGINES
HELICOPTERS
IRON AND STEEL
MACHINES
PHYSICS
TECHNOLOGY
TRANSPORT, HISTORY OF

ALEXANDER THE GREAT

BY 323 BCE ONE MAN HAD CONQUERED most of the known world and set up an empire that extended from Greece to India. The name of the general was Alexander, today known as Alexander the Great. He was the son of King Philip II, ruler of Macedonia, a small but powerful Greek kingdom. In 336 BCE Philip was murdered and Alexander became king, although he was only 20 years old. Alexander was an ambitious and brilliant general. In 334 he invaded the great Persian Empire ruled by Darius III. By a series of remarkable victories, Alexander then went on to conquer a vast empire running from Egypt in the west to India in the east. When Alexander died, aged only 33, he had led his armies at least 19,000 km (12,000 miles) and had encouraged the spread of Greek culture throughout the known world. After he died, his empire was divided. But he is still considered one of the greatest generals who ever lived.

ALEXANDER
As a young man Alexander (356-323 BCE) was brave and intelligent. He was taught by the Greek philosopher Aristotle, from whom he developed a lifelong interest in Greek culture.

PHALANX
The army that Alexander led into Persia (Iran) consisted mostly of infantry, or foot soldiers, armed with long spears. The infantry fought in a formation called a phalanx. The men were packed closely together with their spears pointing towards the enemy.

BUCEPHALUS
Alexander rode into battle on a beautiful horse called Bucephalus. According to legend, Bucephalus was completely wild and responded only to Alexander. When Bucephalus died, Alexander built a monument and town, called Bucephala, in honour of him. The city still exists in Pakistan today.

Map labels:
MACEDONIA
Granicus
Independent state of Sparta
Issus
Guagamela
BACTRIA
Susa
PERSIA
INDIA
Persepolis
Mediterranean Sea
Alexandria
Alexander the Great's empire, 334-323 BCE
EGYPT
Nile River
ARABIA
Dependent state of Cyrenaica

← Alexander's route
Independent region
Dependent region
Alexander's empire

ALEXANDRIA
In 332 BCE Alexander founded the city of Alexandria (named after himself) on the Mediterranean coast. It soon became a great port and a centre of Greek culture and learning, attracting poets and scientists from all over the world. Today, Alexandria is the second largest city in Egypt.

After Alexander's death, Ptolemy Soter, commander of Egypt, created a huge library at Alexandria. It was said to have contained more than 500,000 books; today only ruins remain.

BATTLES
Alexander fought many battles. Usually he had fewer men than his enemy, but he won because his men were well trained and equipped. At the Battle of Issus in 333 BCE Alexander, with 36,000 men, defeated Darius and his 110,000 troops. Two years later, with a force of 45,000 men, Alexander again overwhelmed Darius and his 100,000 soldiers at the Battle of Guagamela.

Find out more

EUROPE, HISTORY OF
GREECE, ANCIENT

ALFRED THE GREAT

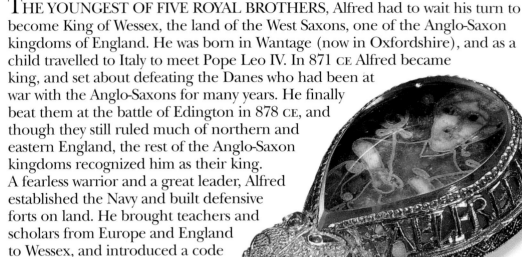

THE YOUNGEST OF FIVE ROYAL BROTHERS, Alfred had to wait his turn to become King of Wessex, the land of the West Saxons, one of the Anglo-Saxon kingdoms of England. He was born in Wantage (now in Oxfordshire), and as a child travelled to Italy to meet Pope Leo IV. In 871 CE Alfred became king, and set about defeating the Danes who had been at war with the Anglo-Saxons for many years. He finally beat them at the battle of Edington in 878 CE, and though they still ruled much of northern and eastern England, the rest of the Anglo-Saxon kingdoms recognized him as their king. A fearless warrior and a great leader, Alfred established the Navy and built defensive forts on land. He brought teachers and scholars from Europe and England to Wessex, and introduced a code of laws to improve government. Alfred's achievements were so important that he became known as "the Great".

849 CE Born.

853 CE Visits the Pope in Rome.

871 CE Becomes king of Wessex.

878 CE Defeats Danes at Battle of Edington.

886 CE Conquers London and fortifies it.

887–92 CE Establishes the Anglo-Saxon Chronicle.

897 CE Introduces the Navy to defend coast.

901 CE Dies in Winchester.

The Alfred Jewel, thought to contain a likeness of the king, was made in his lifetime.

BURNING CAKES

There are many stories about Alfred. One takes place during the war with the Danes. Alfred hid in a peasant's hut. The owner, who did not recognize the king, asked him to watch her cakes while she went out, but Alfred fell asleep, and the cakes burned.

Alfred lets the cakes burn.

DANELAW

From about 800 CE, Danish Vikings constantly attacked the Anglo-Saxon kingdoms, and took over much of the country. There were many battles. A few years after the Battle of Edington, Alfred forced the Danes to withdraw to the eastern part of England. This area was known as the Danelaw.

Anglo-Saxons

Danelaw

The Danes were confined to the eastern part of England.

THE NAVY

Alfred is often called "the father of the English Navy". When the Vikings began to attack his country, he ordered ships to be built that could outrun and outfight the Viking longships. By the 900s CE, fleets of these ships were stationed along the English coast and at ports, to guard against invasion.

Alfred's ships copied the design of Viking longships, but were wider and chunkier.

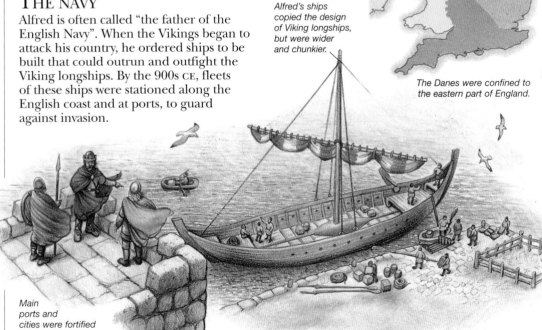

Main ports and cities were fortified against attack.

WINCHESTER
Alfred made his capital at Winchester, Hampshire, which the Anglo-Saxons called Winteceaster. The king fortified the town with thick walls. When he died on 26 October, 901 CE, Alfred was buried in Hyde Abbey. King Canute is also buried in Winchester.

Find out more
ANGLO-SAXONS
ENGLAND
VIKINGS

ALPHABETS

WHEN PEOPLE FIRST BEGAN TO WRITE, they did not use an alphabet. Instead, they drew small pictures to represent the objects they were writing about. This is called picture writing, and it was very slow because there was a different picture for every word. An alphabet does not contain pictures. Instead, it is a collection of letters or symbols which represent sounds. Each sound is just part of one word. Joining the letters together forms a whole word. The human voice can make about 35 different sounds in speech. So alphabets need at most 35 letters to write any word, and most alphabets manage with fewer. The Phoenicians, who lived about 3,000 years ago in the Middle Eastern country now called Syria, developed the first modern alphabet. The ancient Greeks adapted the Phoenician alphabet, and later the Romans improved it. The Roman alphabet is now used widely throughout the world.

Ancient Romans used certain letters for numbers. For example, C is 100.

abcdefghi
jklmnopqr
stuvwxyz

CAPITAL AND SMALL LETTERS
The first Roman alphabet had only capital letters. Small letters started to appear after the 8th century. In English, capital letters are used at the beginning of a sentence, and for the first letter of a name. Capital letters are also used when words are abbreviated, or shortened, to their first letters, such as UN for United Nations.

.,;?!éäêç

SYMBOLS AND ACCENTS
In addition to letters, writers use punctuation marks such as a full stop to show where a sentence ends. Some languages, such as French, also use accents – marks which show how to speak the word. The sloping acute accent over the *e* in *café* makes it sound like the *a* in *day*.

ROMAN ALPHABET

The alphabet used in English and other European languages is based on the Roman alphabet, which had 23 letters. This alphabet is also used in some Southeast Asian languages, such as Vietnamese and Indonesian.

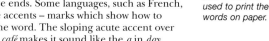

АБВГДЕЁЖЗИЙКЛМНОПРСТУФХЦЧШЩЪЬЫІЭЮЯ
Cyrillic (Russian)

ΑΒΓΔΕΖΗΘΙΚΛΜΝΞΟΠΡΣΤΥΦΧΨΩ
Greek

अ आ इ ई उ ऊ ए ऐ ओ औ ऋ क ख ग घ ङ च छ ज झ ञ ट ठ ड ढ ण त थ द ध न प फ ब भ म य र ल व श ष स ह क्ष त्र ज्ञ श्र
Hindi (India)

MODERN ALPHABETS
The Roman alphabet is only one of the world's alphabets. Many other languages use different symbols to represent similar sounds, and the words may be written and read quite differently from the Roman alphabet. Japanese readers start on the right side of the page and read to the left, or start at the top and read down the page.

In every alphabet, letters have a special order that does not change. Dictionaries, phone books, and many other books are arranged in alphabetical order so that it is easy to find a word or a name.

In traditional printing, raised lead letters are used to print the words on paper.

The Romans did not have the letter W. For J they used I, and for U they used V.

ROSETTA STONE
The ancient Egyptians used a system of picture writing called hieroglyphics. The meaning of this writing was forgotten 1,600 years ago, so nobody was able to read Egyptian documents until 1799 when some French soldiers made a remarkable discovery. Near Alexandria, Egypt, they found a stone with an inscription on it. The words were carved in hieroglyphics and in Greek. Using their knowledge of Greek, scholars were able to discover what the hieroglyphics meant.

CUNEIFORM
More than 5,000 years ago in Mesopotamia (now part of Iraq, Syria, Turkey, and Iran) a form of writing called cuneiform developed. It started off as picture writing, but later letters began to represent sounds. The Mesopotamians did not have paper; instead they wrote on damp clay using wedge-shaped pens. Cuneiform means "wedge-shaped".

CHINESE PICTOGRAMS
The earliest Chinese writing used pictograms (picture signs) standing for objects or ideas. Chinese writing still has no signs for sounds.

Bird   Horse   Tree   Sun

Find out more
BABYLONIANS
BRONZE AGE
EGYPT, ANCIENT
LANGUAGES
PHOENICIANS
WRITERS AND POETS

AMERICAN CIVIL WAR

ONLY 80 YEARS AFTER the states of America had united and won their independence from Great Britain, a bitter conflict threatened to destroy the Union. Between 1861 and 1865, civil war raged as the nation fought over several issues, one of which was slavery. Slavery was legal in the South but had been outlawed in the North. The immediate cause of the war was the election in November 1860 of Abraham Lincoln as president. Lincoln wanted to stop the spread of slavery, and he hoped it would die out in the South. The southern states wanted to continue with it, and one by one they left the Union to form their own alliance, called the Confederacy, with Jefferson Davis as president. Fighting broke out in April 1861. General Robert E. Lee, an able military leader, was the leading Confederate general. However, the Union army was larger, and the North had many industries which supplied the army, whereas the South's main business was agriculture. The war was brutal, and by the time the Confederacy was defeated in 1865, much of the South was devastated. The Union victory led to the abolition of slavery throughout the United States, but bitterness between North and South remained for many years.

Free states   Slave states   Territories

THE DIVIDED NATION
In 1860 the free states and slave states were divided as shown on the map above.

A MODERN WAR
The American Civil War was the first conflict in which railways and iron warships played an important part. It was also the first war to be widely photographed and reported in the world's newspapers.

THE END OF THE WAR
On 9 April 1865, Confederate general Robert E. Lee surrendered to Union general Ulysses S. Grant at Appomattox, Virginia, United States. More than 600,000 Americans were killed in the war, and many more were injured.

Union   Confederacy

TROOPS
Most of the American Civil War troops were infantrymen (foot soldiers). Three million people fought in the two opposing armies.

EVENTS IN CIVIL WAR

1860 Abraham Lincoln is elected president.

1860-1861 Eleven southern states leave the Union and join the Confederacy.

1861 Confederates attack Fort Sumter. Civil War begins.

1861 Confederate victory at Bull Run.

1862 Stalemate for months.

1862 Confederate victory at Fredericksburg.

1862 Naval battle between battleships *Monitor* and *Merrimack*.

1862 Battle of Shiloh, Tenn.

1863 Lincoln's Emancipation Proclamation proclaims freedom of slaves in Confederacy.

1863 Confederate victory at Chancellorsville.

1863 Confederate defeat at Gettysburg during invasion of the Union marks turning point in war.

1863 Confederate defeats at Vicksburg and Chattanooga.

1864 Union general W.T. Sherman captures Atlanta, Georgia, and begins "march to the sea".

1865 Confederate general Robert E. Lee surrenders to Union general Ulysses S. Grant; war ends.

1865 Slavery abolished in U.S.

Find out more
LINCOLN, ABRAHAM
SLAVERY
UNITED STATES OF AMERICA
UNITED STATES, HISTORY OF

AMERICAN REVOLUTION

EVERY YEAR ON 4 JULY, Americans celebrate the birth of their nation. Independence Day is a reminder of the moment when the 13 American colonies declared that they would no longer be ruled by Britain. The colonists did this because they had to pay British taxes, yet could not elect representatives to the British Parliament. The colonists had tried to make peace with Britain. At the First Continental Congress in 1774, representatives of each colony met to try and arrange fairer taxation. They failed, and fighting broke out between British soldiers and colonists at Lexington, Massachusetts, the following year. The colonists formed an army, led by George Washington. A second Congress again failed to make peace, and on 4 July 1776, the Americans declared their independence. France sent aid to the colonies which helped defeat the British. In 1781, the war ended. Britain recognized the independence of the United States two years later.

PAUL REVERE'S RIDE
On the night of 18 April 1775, silversmith Paul Revere took his now famous ride from Charlestown, Massachusetts, to warn the people that the British army was coming.

THE BATTLE OF LEXINGTON

British soldiers set out from Boston, Massachusetts, on 19 April 1775, to capture the military stores at Concord. On their way, the British met a group of armed Americans at Lexington. The fighting that followed was the first battle of the war.

BOSTON TEA PARTY

In 1773, the British government cut the tax on tea in Britain but kept the rate the same in America. The colonists had no legal way of objecting because they did not have a Member of Parliament in Britain. On the night of 16 December a group of colonists dressed as Native Americans boarded three tea ships in Boston harbour and threw all the tea into the water as a protest.

AMERICAN REVOLUTION

1767 Britain imposes high taxes on American colonies.

1773 Boston Tea Party protests unfair taxation.

1774-1775 Continental Congress against Britain.

1775 Battle of Lexington marks start of war.

1775 Battle of Bunker Hill won by British but strengthens American resistance.

1776 Declaration of Independence.

1777 Americans win Saratoga campaign.

1778 France supports American cause.

1781 General Cornwallis surrenders at Yorktown to Americans and French.

1783 Britain recognizes American independence in the Peace of Paris.

A NEW FLAG
The first flag of the new country of the United States consisted of 13 stripes and 13 stars, one for each of the original states.

Find out more
EXPLORERS
UNITED STATES, HISTORY OF
WASHINGTON, GEORGE

ANGLO-SAXONS

TRADITION HAS IT THAT AROUND 449 CE King Vortigern of Britain was finding it hard to fight off the invading Picts and Scots. So he invited the Saxons (a Germanic tribe) to come and help him. They quarrelled with the British and were later joined by other Germanic groups – the Angles and Jutes – who came together to form a single people (the Anglo-Saxons), and established a series of kingdoms. By 600 CE, they had driven out the native British and taken over most of the country. Eventually there were seven main kingdoms, and these in turn became three. These kingdoms were known as *Engla land*, or *Angle land*, which is where the name England comes from. Anglo-Saxon rule lasted about 500 years, until 1066. During that time, Anglo-Saxon kings fought many battles and made alliances with the Vikings and Danes. Christianity was brought to England. The greatest Anglo-Saxon king was Alfred.

ANGLO-SAXON OCCUPATION
By the end of the 9th century, Anglo-Saxon England was divided into Wessex, Mercia, and Northumbria.

Wooden building, with thatched roof

A minstrel entertains people in the mead hall.

ANGLO-SAXONS

c. 449 Angles, Saxons, and Jutes come to Britain.

597 Ethelbert, King of Kent, becomes a Christian.

802-39 King Egbert rules Wessex; unites Anglo-Saxon kingdoms.

830s Vikings invade.

871-899 Alfred reigns; beats Danes at Edington in 878.

978-1016 Ethelred II the Unready pays money to Vikings to keep the peace.

1016 Danish king Canute takes the English throne.

1042 Edward the Confessor becomes king.

1066 William of Normandy conquers England.

BATTLE OF MALDON

In 991 CE, the men of Essex, led by Brihtnoth, fought a battle at Maldon, Essex, against 5,000 Vikings, led by Olaf Tryggvason. The Vikings won. They became more powerful, and, by 1016, England had a Danish king. All we know about the battle comes from *The Battle of Maldon*, a poem from the 10th or 11th century.

Ash spear and shield

MEAD HALL

Daily life in an Anglo-Saxon village centred around the mead hall. This was a large building where people came to meet and feast. Travelling minstrels would sing or recite long story poems to entertain the people while they drank. The mead hall belonged to the local *eorl*, or lord.

CANUTE
In 1016, the Danes finally overthrew the Anglo-Saxons and took the English throne. The Danish prince Canute, or Cnut (994-1035 CE), became King of England. He was popular, ruled wisely, passed laws to restore order and kept up Anglo-Saxon customs. In 1018 he became King of Denmark, and in 1028 took over the Norwegian throne. For a short time England and Scandinavia formed an empire.

Canute

EDWARD THE CONFESSOR
A descendant of Alfred the Great, Edward the Confessor (1002-66), founded Westminster Abbey, and was made a saint in 1161. He was not a strong king, and allowed his Norman advisors to rule for him. Edward had no children, and after his death there was a squabble for the throne. William of Normandy claimed that Edward had promised it to him. Edward's brother-in-law, Harold, said the throne was rightly his. Harold was crowned in 1066.

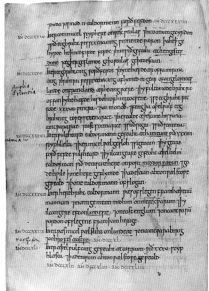

Anglo-Saxon Chronicle

BEOWULF

The most important piece of literature in the Anglo-Saxon language is *Beowulf* – a very long, epic (heroic) poem. It tells the story of the noble warrior Beowulf (his name means Bee Wolf) who fights the monster Grendel and Grendel's even more terrifying mother, who were threatening the people of the Danish King Hrothgar. It was written in the 700s CE, but the author is unknown.

Title page of *Beowulf*

ANGLO-SAXON CHRONICLE

Started by the Saxon King Alfred the Great, the Anglo-Saxon Chronicle was a kind of early newspaper. It recorded events in England, gave accounts of wars and battles, and included works translated from Latin. Alfred undertook many translations himself. The Chronicle continued until 1154, and is a very important source of information about the history and language of the Anglo-Saxon people.

Monks wrote in ink on specially prepared parchment.

MONKS
Books and manuscripts were produced by monks. They had to copy each book by hand, and so books were very precious. The monks worked in a special room in the monastery called a scriptorium. One monk prepared the parchment, a second copied in the words, and a third illustrated the manuscript (text). Books were written in Latin and Anglo-Saxon.

Illustrations and decorative initials added to the text

Coloured inks made from plants and minerals.

THE VENERABLE BEDE
Known as "The Father of English History", Bede, or Baeda (673?-735 CE) was a monk and teacher who lived and worked in a monastery in Jarrow, north-eastern England. He wrote many books on the Bible and scientific subjects. Bede's most famous work is *The Ecclesiastical History of the English Nation*, finished in 731 CE.

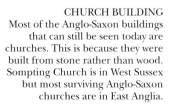

SUTTON HOO
In 1939, archaeologists unearthed buried treasure at Sutton Hoo in Suffolk, England. They found 11 burial mounds containing Anglo-Saxon coins, weapons, bowls, and ornaments dating from between 650 and 670 CE. The site was probably a memorial to a great king.

Iron helmet trimmed with bronze and silver

Sompting Church

CHURCH BUILDING
Most of the Anglo-Saxon buildings that can still be seen today are churches. This is because they were built from stone rather than wood. Sompting Church is in West Sussex but most surviving Anglo-Saxon churches are in East Anglia.

Find out more
ALFRED THE GREAT
ARCHAEOLOGY
NORMANS
UNITED KINGDOM, HISTORY OF
VIKINGS

ANIMALS

THE ANIMAL KINGDOM is one of the largest groups of living things; scientists believe that there are up to 30 million species. Animals range from tiny, simple creatures that look like blobs of jelly, to gigantic blue whales. The huge animal kingdom is divided into many groups. A lion, for example, belongs to the order Carnivora because it eats meat. It also belongs to the class of placental mammals. All mammals are vertebrates (animals with backbones) and belong to a group known as chordates. An animal is a living creature that feeds, moves, and breeds. During its life cycle, an animal is born, grows, matures, reproduces, and eventually dies. It ingests (takes in) food to build and develop its body. Food provides the animal with the energy to move around. Some types of animal do not move at all; the adult sponge, for example, spends its life anchored to a rock. All kinds of animals from dinosaurs to dodos have become extinct; many others, including elephants and tigers, may soon disappear if their habitat is destroyed and if they continue to be killed recklessly for their hides and bones.

FROG
Like all animals, the common green frog is aware of its surroundings and able to move, feed, and reproduce. Frogs belong to the class of animals called amphibians. All amphibians spend part of their lives in or near water.

INTERNAL SKELETONS
The animal world can be divided into vertebrate animals and invertebrate animals. Vertebrates have an internal skeleton with a vertebral column or backbone. In most cases, this is made of bone. Some sea-dwelling vertebrates, such as sharks, have a backbone made of tough, rubbery gristle called cartilage.

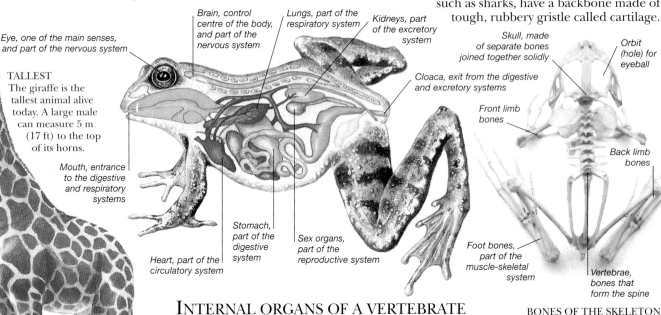

Eye, one of the main senses, and part of the nervous system

TALLEST
The giraffe is the tallest animal alive today. A large male can measure 5 m (17 ft) to the top of its horns.

Mouth, entrance to the digestive and respiratory systems

Brain, control centre of the body, and part of the nervous system

Lungs, part of the respiratory system

Kidneys, part of the excretory system

Cloaca, exit from the digestive and excretory systems

Heart, part of the circulatory system

Stomach, part of the digestive system

Sex organs, part of the reproductive system

Skull, made of separate bones joined together solidly

Orbit (hole) for eyeball

Front limb bones

Back limb bones

Foot bones, part of the muscle-skeletal system

Vertebrae, bones that form the spine

INTERNAL ORGANS OF A VERTEBRATE
Inside an animal, such as the frog above, are many different parts called organs. Organs are all shapes and sizes. Each one has a job to do. Several organs are grouped together to form a body system, such as the digestive system, the circulatory system, and the reproductive system. The nervous system and the hormonal system control and co-ordinate all the internal systems.

SMALLEST
The smallest organisms are single-celled creatures called protozoa – so tiny they can hardly be seen by the human eye. The tiniest mammals are the bumblebee bat and Savi's pygmy shrew. This pygmy shrew measures only 6 cm (2.3 in) including its tail.

BONES OF THE SKELETON
The skeletons of vertebrate animals are similar in design, but each differs in certain details through adaptation to the way the animal lives. A frog, for example, has long, strong back legs for leaping. All vertebrates have a skull that contains the brain and the main sense organs. Most vertebrates also have two pairs of limbs. Some bones, such as the skull bones, are fixed firmly together; others are linked by flexible joints, as in the limbs.

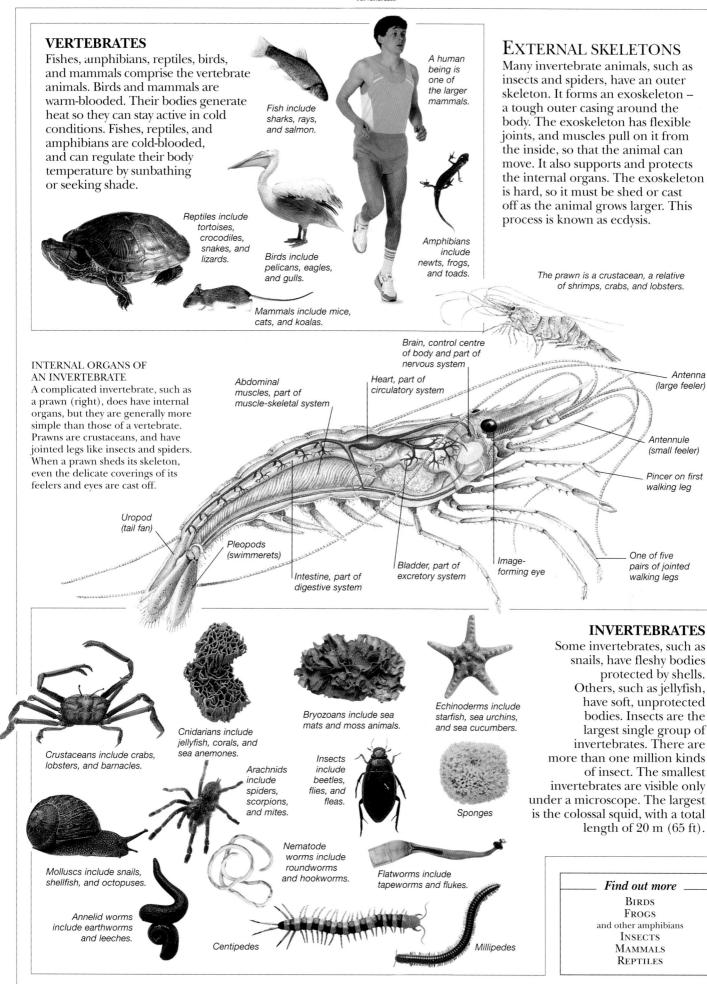

VERTEBRATES

Fishes, amphibians, reptiles, birds, and mammals comprise the vertebrate animals. Birds and mammals are warm-blooded. Their bodies generate heat so they can stay active in cold conditions. Fishes, reptiles, and amphibians are cold-blooded, and can regulate their body temperature by sunbathing or seeking shade.

Fish include sharks, rays, and salmon.

A human being is one of the larger mammals.

Reptiles include tortoises, crocodiles, snakes, and lizards.

Birds include pelicans, eagles, and gulls.

Amphibians include newts, frogs, and toads.

Mammals include mice, cats, and koalas.

EXTERNAL SKELETONS

Many invertebrate animals, such as insects and spiders, have an outer skeleton. It forms an exoskeleton – a tough outer casing around the body. The exoskeleton has flexible joints, and muscles pull on it from the inside, so that the animal can move. It also supports and protects the internal organs. The exoskeleton is hard, so it must be shed or cast off as the animal grows larger. This process is known as ecdysis.

The prawn is a crustacean, a relative of shrimps, crabs, and lobsters.

INTERNAL ORGANS OF AN INVERTEBRATE

A complicated invertebrate, such as a prawn (right), does have internal organs, but they are generally more simple than those of a vertebrate. Prawns are crustaceans, and have jointed legs like insects and spiders. When a prawn sheds its skeleton, even the delicate coverings of its feelers and eyes are cast off.

Brain, control centre of body and part of nervous system

Heart, part of circulatory system

Abdominal muscles, part of muscle-skeletal system

Antenna (large feeler)

Antennule (small feeler)

Pincer on first walking leg

Uropod (tail fan)

Pleopods (swimmerets)

Intestine, part of digestive system

Bladder, part of excretory system

Image-forming eye

One of five pairs of jointed walking legs

INVERTEBRATES

Some invertebrates, such as snails, have fleshy bodies protected by shells. Others, such as jellyfish, have soft, unprotected bodies. Insects are the largest single group of invertebrates. There are more than one million kinds of insect. The smallest invertebrates are visible only under a microscope. The largest is the colossal squid, with a total length of 20 m (65 ft).

Crustaceans include crabs, lobsters, and barnacles.

Cnidarians include jellyfish, corals, and sea anemones.

Bryozoans include sea mats and moss animals.

Echinoderms include starfish, sea urchins, and sea cucumbers.

Arachnids include spiders, scorpions, and mites.

Insects include beetles, flies, and fleas.

Sponges

Molluscs include snails, shellfish, and octopuses.

Nematode worms include roundworms and hookworms.

Flatworms include tapeworms and flukes.

Annelid worms include earthworms and leeches.

Centipedes

Millipedes

Find out more

BIRDS
FROGS
and other amphibians
INSECTS
MAMMALS
REPTILES

ANIMAL SENSES

ALL ANIMALS ARE AWARE of their surroundings. Touch, smell, taste, sight, and hearing are the five senses that animals and humans use to detect what is happening around them. Some animals, however, have a very different array of senses than humans. A dog's nose is so sensitive to odours that it "sees" the world as a pattern of scents and smells, in the same way that we see light and colour with our eyes. Many creatures, particularly fish, can determine where they are by picking up the tiny amounts of bio-electricity produced by other living things around them. A fish also detects vibrations in the water using a row of sense organs down each side of its body, called the lateral line.

An animal's senses, like its body shape, are a result of evolution and suit the animal's needs. Eyes would be of little use to a creature such as the cave fish, which lives in endless darkness. Instead, these creatures rely on other senses such as smell and touch. Some senses are extremely specialized. Long, feathery antennae enable a male emperor moth to "smell" the odour of a female moth 5 km (3 miles) away.

HUNTING SENSES
A shark can smell blood in the water hundreds of metres away. As this shark closes in for the attack, it makes use of its keen eyesight and electricity-sensing organs.

A clear lens at the front of the eye focuses rays of light into the back of the eye to produce a sharp image.

The otter's scenting organs can detect many scents in the air. These special organs lie inside the nose in the roof of the nasal cavity.

Lips detect sharp pieces of shell in food, then spit them out.

Sensitive forepaws manipulate food. The otter also uses a stone to crack open shellfish.

The skin and hair roots bear sensors that detect vibrations, light touch, heavy pressure, and heat and cold.

The otter hears by sensing vibrations when they strike its eardrums. To help the otter balance, tiny fluid-filled canals inside the ear work like miniature levels to register gravity.

Whiskers are sensitive to touch. They also respond to vibrations, so they are useful in murky water.

Claws and soles of feet are sensitive to touch.

OTTER

While the sea otter floats on its back in the water, eating a shellfish, its sense organs continuously send information about its surroundings to the brain. The organs include the eyes, ears, nose, tongue, whiskers, fur, skin, and balance sensors. Stretch receptors in the joints and muscles also convey information about the otter's body position. The smell of a poisoned shellfish or the ripples from a shark's fin instantly alert the otter to possible danger.

BLOODHOUND

Bloodhounds have been specially bred as tracker dogs. Their sense of smell may be as much as one million times sharper than a human's sense of smell. Bloodhounds can even detect the microscopic pieces of skin that are shed from a person's body.

The Bloodhound's sense of smell is so sharp that it can even pick up scent that is several days old.

Dog follows scent with nose very close to ground.

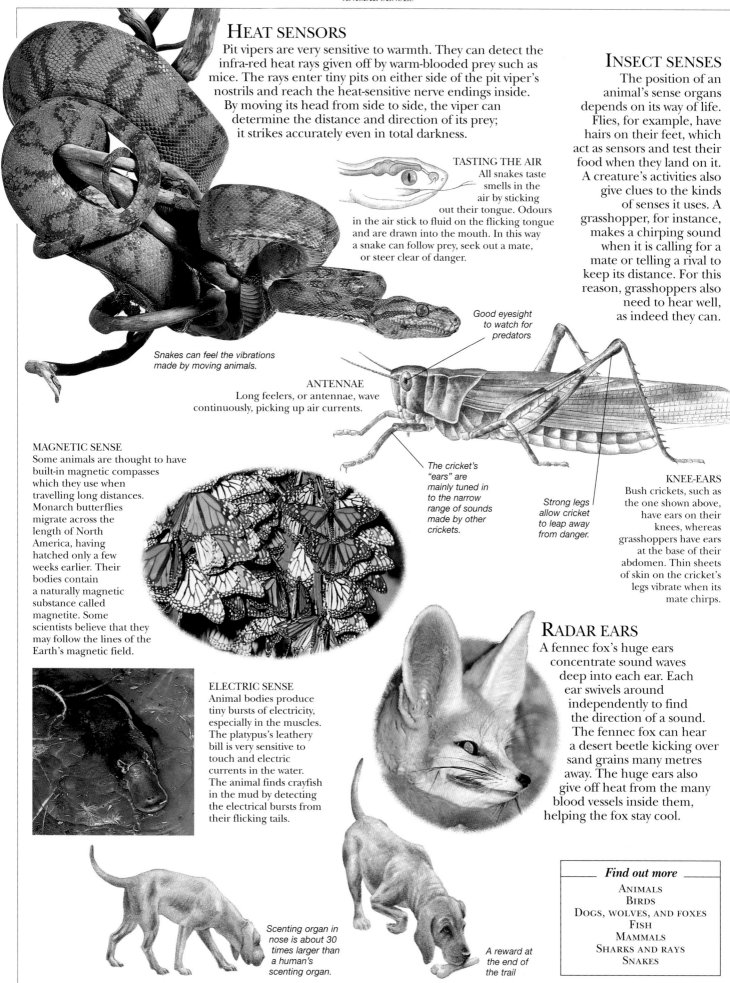

HEAT SENSORS

Pit vipers are very sensitive to warmth. They can detect the infra-red heat rays given off by warm-blooded prey such as mice. The rays enter tiny pits on either side of the pit viper's nostrils and reach the heat-sensitive nerve endings inside. By moving its head from side to side, the viper can determine the distance and direction of its prey; it strikes accurately even in total darkness.

TASTING THE AIR
All snakes taste smells in the air by sticking out their tongue. Odours in the air stick to fluid on the flicking tongue and are drawn into the mouth. In this way a snake can follow prey, seek out a mate, or steer clear of danger.

Snakes can feel the vibrations made by moving animals.

INSECT SENSES

The position of an animal's sense organs depends on its way of life. Flies, for example, have hairs on their feet, which act as sensors and test their food when they land on it. A creature's activities also give clues to the kinds of senses it uses. A grasshopper, for instance, makes a chirping sound when it is calling for a mate or telling a rival to keep its distance. For this reason, grasshoppers also need to hear well, as indeed they can.

Good eyesight to watch for predators

ANTENNAE
Long feelers, or antennae, wave continuously, picking up air currents.

The cricket's "ears" are mainly tuned in to the narrow range of sounds made by other crickets.

Strong legs allow cricket to leap away from danger.

KNEE-EARS
Bush crickets, such as the one shown above, have ears on their knees, whereas grasshoppers have ears at the base of their abdomen. Thin sheets of skin on the cricket's legs vibrate when its mate chirps.

MAGNETIC SENSE
Some animals are thought to have built-in magnetic compasses which they use when travelling long distances. Monarch butterflies migrate across the length of North America, having hatched only a few weeks earlier. Their bodies contain a naturally magnetic substance called magnetite. Some scientists believe that they may follow the lines of the Earth's magnetic field.

ELECTRIC SENSE
Animal bodies produce tiny bursts of electricity, especially in the muscles. The platypus's leathery bill is very sensitive to touch and electric currents in the water. The animal finds crayfish in the mud by detecting the electrical bursts from their flicking tails.

RADAR EARS
A fennec fox's huge ears concentrate sound waves deep into each ear. Each ear swivels around independently to find the direction of a sound. The fennec fox can hear a desert beetle kicking over sand grains many metres away. The huge ears also give off heat from the many blood vessels inside them, helping the fox stay cool.

Scenting organ in nose is about 30 times larger than a human's scenting organ.

A reward at the end of the trail

Find out more
ANIMALS
BIRDS
DOGS, WOLVES, AND FOXES
FISH
MAMMALS
SHARKS AND RAYS
SNAKES

ANTARCTICA

STRETCHING ACROSS AN AREA greater than the United States, the continent of Antarctica sits beneath a huge sheet of ice up to 2 km (1.2 miles) thick. Antarctica is centred on the South Pole and is surrounded by the ice-covered Southern Ocean. Powerful winds create a storm belt around the continent, bringing fog and severe blizzards. It is the coldest and windiest place on earth. Even during the short summers the temperature barely climbs above freezing, and the sea ice only partly melts. In winter, temperatures can plummet to -80°C (-112°F). Few animals and plants can survive on land, but the surrounding seas teem with fish and mammals. Due to its harsh climate, there are no permanent residents on Antarctica. The only people on the continent are tourists, and scientists and staff working in research stations. These few people have brought waste and pollution to the region. Other environmental concerns include overfishing, the depletion of the ozone layer above the region, and the effects of global warming, which has led to the melting of ice in some coastal areas.

Situated at the southernmost point of the world, Antarctica covers an area of about 14 million sq km (5.5 million sq miles). The nearest land masses are South America and New Zealand. The highest point is Vinson Massif, which rises to 4,897 m (16,067 ft).

Radio transmitters allow scientists to track the movements of penguins.

ANTARCTIC TEMPERATURES

2°C (28°F) Sea water freezes. On the Antarctic coast, summer temperatures are only a degree or so warmer than this.

-25°C (-13°F) Steel crystallizes and becomes brittle.

-40°C (-40°F) Synthetic rubber becomes brittle, and exposed flesh freezes rapidly.

-89°C (-128.6°F) Lowest temperature ever recorded, at Vostok Research Station, Antarctica, 1983.

SCIENTIFIC RESEARCH

There are 40 permanent, and as many as 100 temporary, research stations in Antarctica devoted to scientific projects for 15 different nations. Teams of scientists study the wildlife and monitor the ice for changes in the Earth's atmosphere. Antarctic-based research has resulted in a number of scientific breakthroughs, including the discovery of a hole in the ozone layer above the continent.

TOURISM

Cruise liners have been bringing tourists to the Antarctic region since the 1950s. In 1983, Chileans began to fly to King George Island where an 80-bed hotel has been built for holiday-makers. Antarctica receives several thousand tourists each year. Visitors come to see the dramatic landscape and unique wildlife, such as King penguins.

Platinum

Iron

Gold

MINERAL WEALTH

Antarctica has deposits of minerals, such as gold, copper, uranium, and nickel. However, extracting them may damage the fragile polar environment.

Find out more
CONTINENTS
GLACIERS AND ICECAPS
INUITS
POLAR WILDLIFE
RAIN AND SNOW

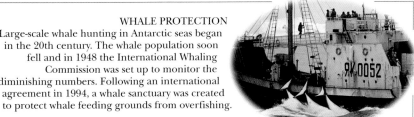

WHALE PROTECTION
Large-scale whale hunting in Antarctic seas began in the 20th century. The whale population soon fell and in 1948 the International Whaling Commission was set up to monitor the diminishing numbers. Following an international agreement in 1994, a whale sanctuary was created to protect whale feeding grounds from overfishing.

STATISTICS
Area: 14,000,000 sq km (5,405,430 sq miles)
Population: No permanent residents
Capital: None
Languages: English, Spanish, French, Norwegian, Chinese, Polish, Russian, German, Japanese
Religions: Not applicable
Currency: None
Main occupation: Scientific research
Main exports: None
Main imports: None

FOREIGN TERRITORIES
Various nations, including Australia, France, New Zealand, Norway, Argentina, Chile, and the UK claimed territory in Antarctica when it was first discovered in the 19th century. However, these claims have been suspended under the 1959 Antarctic Treaty which came into force in 1961. Under the treaty, the continent can be used only for peaceful purposes. Stations may be set up for scientific research but military bases are forbidden.

Map legend
Volcano | Mountain | Ancient monument | Capital city | Large city/ town | Small city/ town | Research Station

FROZEN SEAS
During the cold winter months, the seas surrounding Antarctica freeze, almost doubling the size of the continent.

ANTARCTIC ICE
Icebergs barricade more than 90 per cent of the Antarctic coastline. The continent contains over 80 per cent of the world's fresh water in the form of ice.

LAMBERT GLACIER
The Lambert Glacier is the world's largest series of glaciers. It is 80 km (50 miles) wide at the coast and reaches more than 300 km (186 miles) inland.

PETER I ISLAND
(to Norway)

TRANSANTARCTIC MOUNTAINS
The Transantarctic Mountains run across the continent, splitting it into Greater and Lesser Antarctica.

ROSS ICE SHELF
Ice shelves are permanent floating ice sheets that are attached to land and are constantly fed by glaciers. The Ross Ice Shelf is 183–914 m (600–3,000 ft) thick and about 966 km (600 miles) long.

Map labels
SOUTHERN OCEAN
Drake Passage
Scotia Sea
South Orkney Islands
South Shetland Islands
King George Island
Weddell Sea
Antarctic Peninsula
Palmer Land
Alexander Island
Bellingshausen Sea
Coats Land
Berkner Island
Ronne Ice Shelf
Queen Maud Land
Enderby Land
Kemp Land
Lambert Glacier
Cape Darnley
Mackenzie Bay
Prydz Bay
East ANTARCTICA
Princess Elizabeth Land
Davis Sea
Ellsworth Land
△ Vinson Massif 4897m
South Pole +
Amundsen-Scott (US)
West Antarctica
Transantarctic Mountains
Antarctica
South Geomagnetic + Pole
Vostok (Russian Federation)
Shackleton Ice Shelf
Amundsen Sea
Marie Byrd Land
△ Mount Sidley 4181m
Ross Ice Shelf
Roosevelt Island
Mount Erebus ▲ 3794m
Victoria Land
Wilkes Land
Cape Poinsett
Ross Sea
Limit of summer pack ice (December)
Cape Adare
Oates Land
George V Land
SOUTHERN OCEAN
Limit of winter pack ice (June)

N
W   E
S

SCALE BAR
0   500   1000   km
0   500   1000   miles

29

ANTS AND TERMITES

IMAGINE HOW MANY millions of ants and termites live on this planet. There are at least 9,500 different kinds of ants and 2,750 kinds of termites. These tiny creatures are among the most fascinating animals on Earth. Both ants and termites are social insects, living in large groups called colonies where each individual has a specific job to do. The queen (the main female) mates with a male, then spends her life laying eggs. The hordes of workers do such jobs as gathering food and rearing the young. Soldiers and guards protect the nest and the foraging workers. Ants eat a variety of food, including caterpillars, leaves, and fungi. Termites feed mostly on plant matter, and they are among nature's most valuable recyclers.

ANT HEAD
The Asian tree-living ant has simple jaws for feeding on soft insects. Other ants and termites have strong jaws for chewing wood and hard plant stems.

TERMITE MOUND

Many termites make small nests in dead trees or underground. A few kinds of termites build a mound which contains a termite city – a home for many millions of termites. In hot areas the mounds have tunnels and ventilation holes, and may be more than 6 m (20 ft) high. The mounds are often occupied for more than 50 years, and the thick walls help to keep out anteaters and other predators. The queen and king termites live in a royal chamber deep inside the mound.

Cooling chimney lets air in and out of the termite mound.

ANT HILL
Most of the passages of an ant hill are underground. Eggs, larvae (grubs), and pupae are kept in separate parts of the nest. Large-jawed sentries guard the entrances. A large ant nest may contain 100,000 ants.

Termite mound

Termite mound has many tunnels.

Front leg

Jaws

Antenna can bend like an elbow joint.

Eye

Middle leg

Thorax

Rear leg

Head

Claw

Ant squirts formic acid from rear of body in self-defence.

Abdomen

Worker ant

Fungus grows on the termites' dung (waste matter) inside the termite mound. These areas are called fungus gardens. Termites feed on the fungus.

Nursery for termite larvae

Queen lays 20,000 or more eggs daily in royal chamber.

Workers regurgitate (spit out) food for queen, king, and soldier termites. Courtier workers feed and clean queen and king.

Courtier workers

Queen termite

Soldier termite

King termite

Young female termite

WORKER ANT

All worker ants are female. Their long, claw-tipped legs allow them to run fast and climb well. Workers collect food, regurgitate it to feed the other ants, look after eggs and larvae, and clean the nest. They do not have wings, unlike the queen and male ants.

ARMY ANTS

A few ants, such as these army ants of South America, do not make permanent nests and are ever on the move. As the colony marches through the forests, they forage for insects, and sometimes even eat large animals alive.

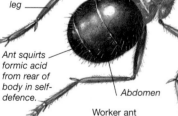

LEAF-CUTTING ANTS
Ants can lift objects that weigh more than they do. Leaf-cutting ants bite off pieces of leaves and carry them back to a huge underground nest. Here they chew the leaves and mix them with saliva to make a kind of compost. Fungus – the leaf-cutting ant's only food – grows on this compost.

TERMITES
The queen and male termites have wings. They take flight and mate, then the queen returns to the nest. The queen does not leave the nest again, and is cared for by the courtier workers. The main male, or king, is larger than the workers and remains with the queen.

Find out more
ANIMALS
ECOLOGY AND FOOD WEBS
INSECTS
SPIDERS AND SCORPIONS

ARCHAEOLOGY

FOR AN ARCHAEOLOGIST, brushing away the soil that hides a broken pot is like brushing away time. Every tiny fragment helps create a more complete picture of the past. Archaeology is the study of the remains of past human societies, but it is not the same as history. Historians use written records as their starting point, whereas archaeologists use objects. They excavate, or dig, in the ground or under water for bones, pots, and anything else created by our ancestors. They also look for seeds, field boundaries, and other signs of how long-dead people made use of the landscape. But archaeology is not just concerned with dead people and buried objects. It also helps us understand what may happen to our own society in the future. Archaeology has shown that human actions and changes in the climate or environment can destroy whole communities.

HEINRICH SCHLIEMANN
In 1870 the pioneer German archaeologist Heinrich Schliemann (1822-90) discovered the site of Troy in Turkey. He also set out basic rules for excavation, such as careful recordkeeping. He did not always follow his own rules. His impatient hunt for treasure sometimes destroyed the objects he was seeking.

A grid pattern divides the site into squares so that archaeologists can quickly record in which square they made each find.

In photographs of the site, the stripes painted on poles make it easy to judge the size of objects.

By sketching objects, archaeologists can sometimes record more detail than a camera can.

Small trowels allow archaeologists to remove soil carefully.

Archaeologists sieve the soil they remove to check for objects they may have overlooked.

A soft brush removes dry soil without damaging the object.

ANALYSIS

The position and location of the objects uncovered in a dig can provide important information. For this reason archaeologists measure, examine, record, and analyze everything they find, and preserve it if possible. Scientific methods such as radioactive dating enable archaeologists to find out the exact age of objects made thousands of years ago.

EXCAVATION

Archaeologists gather much of their information about the past by carrying out excavations, or digs. They decide where to dig by looking at aerial photographs, old pictures, maps, documents, or marks on the ground. Then they carefully remove layers of soil, often using trowels and other small tools. The archaeologists keep digging until they reach undisturbed soil with no trace of human occupation.

BRONZE AGE TOOLS
Archaeologists often find tools from ancient times. The axe and arrowhead shown above date from the Bronze Age and are estimated to have been used by humans between 3,000 and 8,000 years ago.

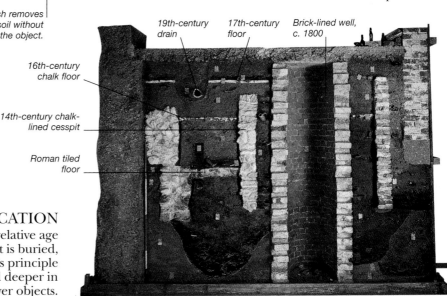

19th-century drain
17th-century floor
Brick-lined well, c. 1800
16th-century chalk floor
14th-century chalk-lined cesspit
Roman tiled floor

STRATIFICATION

Archaeologists on a dig determine the relative age of each object they find from where it is buried, using the principle of stratification. This principle says that older objects are usually buried deeper in the ground than newer objects.

TOLLUND MAN

In 1950, archaeologists in Denmark made a dramatic discovery. They found the remarkably well preserved body of a man in a peat bog called Tollund Mose. The man had been hanged and buried about 2,000 years ago. Most dead bodies soon rot underground, but the peat had tanned Tollund man so that his flesh was hard like a leather shoe. Many details remained, and scientists could even tell that his last meal had been a kind of porridge.

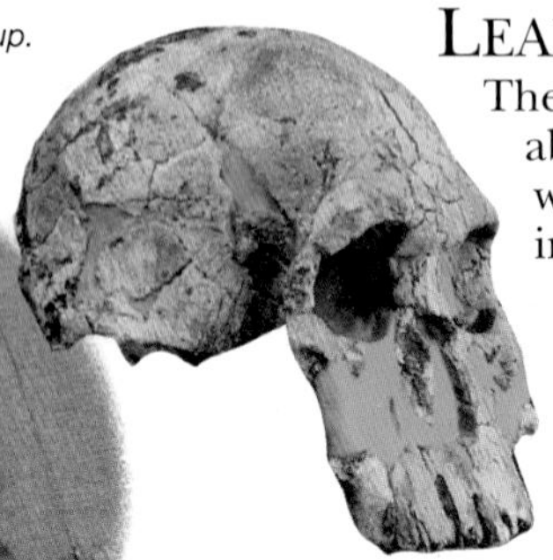

Richard Leakey measures and records every detail of the human remains that he digs up.

AERIAL PHOTOGRAPHY

Photography of the ground from aeroplanes began in the 1920s. It made archaeology easier because the high viewpoint reveals traces of buildings, roads, and fields that are invisible from the ground.

LEAKEY

The Leakey family has made major discoveries about the origins of human beings. Louis and his wife, Mary, began to work in the Olduvai Gorge in Tanzania (Africa) in the 1930s. There they showed that ancestors of human beings existed 1,750,000 years ago. Since the 1960s their son Richard has continued their research. We can now trace our ancestors back over more than six million years. Modern humans evolved around 200,000 years ago.

Among the objects found in the tomb of Tutankhamun was a pectoral, or brooch, in the shape of a scarab beetle.

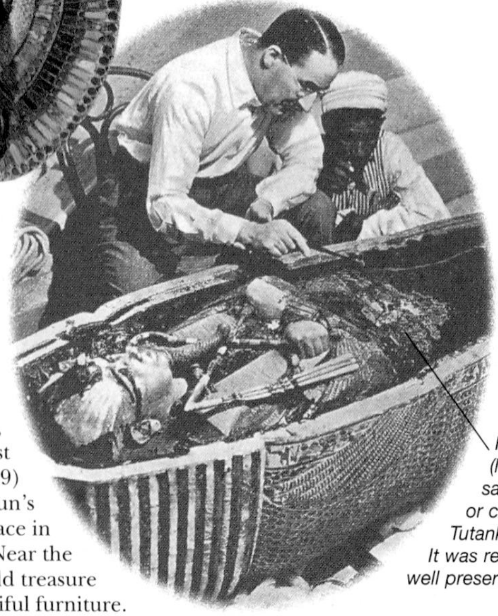

Archaeologists excavating the wreck of the Slava Rossi found Russian icons (religious paintings).

SHIPWRECKS

The development of lightweight diving equipment over the last 50 years has enabled archaeologists to excavate sites under water. They use many of the same methods that are used on land. Most underwater archaeologists look for shipwrecks, but they sometimes discover landscapes, buildings, and even towns of ancient civilizations.

TUTANKHAMUN

The discovery of the tomb of Tutankhamun was one of the most sensational events in the history of archaeology. Tutankhamun was a boy-king who ruled in Egypt 3,500 years ago. In 1922, the British archaeologist Howard Carter (1873-1939) found Tutankhamun's fabulously rich burial place in the Valley of the Kings. Near the boy-king's remains lay gold treasure and beautiful furniture.

Howard Carter (left) found the sarcophagus, or coffin, of Tutankhamun. It was remarkably well preserved.

Find out more
BRONZE AGE
EGYPT, ANCIENT
EVOLUTION
FOSSILS
GEOLOGY
IRON AGE
PREHISTORIC PEOPLES

ARCHITECTURE

MOST OF OUR BUILDINGS have been planned by architects. The word architect is Greek for "builder" or "craftsworker" and architects aim to design and construct buildings that are attractive, functional, and comfortable. Architecture means designing a building; it also refers to the building style. Styles of architecture have changed over the centuries and differ from culture to culture, so architecture can tell us a lot about people. The Ancient Greeks, for example, produced simple, balanced buildings that showed their disciplined approach to life. Architects are artists who create buildings. But unlike other artists, they must sell their ideas before they are able to produce their buildings.

Built around 200 BCE, this Indian stupa, or dome, was originally a mound covering a site sacred to Buddha or a relic of his.

In 447 BCE, the Greek architects Ictinus and Callicrates designed the Parthenon, a temple to the goddess Athena, in Athens, Greece. With its graceful columns, it is a perfect example of classical architecture.

CLASSICAL ARCHITECTURE

The Ancient Greeks and Romans developed a style that we call classical architecture. Most Greek buildings consisted of columns to support the roof. The types of columns varied according to the particular classical "order" (style) that was used. Everything was simple and perfectly even. The Romans, who came after the Greeks, developed the arch, dome, and vault.

Elegantly curving skyward in several tiers, pagodas were built as shrines to Buddha. On the right is the pagoda of Yakushi-ji Temple, Japan. Each element in the building's design originally had a religious meaning.

Milan Cathedral in Italy (right) is an example of late Gothic architecture.

GOTHIC ARCHITECTURE

With their multitudes of pointed arches, finely carved stonework, and intricate windows, Gothic buildings are the opposite of simple classical ones. The Gothic style of architecture began in western Europe in the 12th century. It was used mainly in building cathedrals and churches. Although most Gothic buildings were huge, their thin walls, pointed arches, and large areas of stained-glass windows made them seem light and delicate.

Following the client's brief, the architect presents a drawing (below) to the client to show how the finished building will look.

FRANK LLOYD WRIGHT

American architect Frank Lloyd Wright (1869-1959) influenced many other architects. He tried to blend buildings into their natural surroundings and create a feeling of space, with few walls, so that rooms could "flow" into one another. At Bear Run, Pennsylvania, he built Falling Water, a house over a waterfall.

ARCHITECTS

If you wanted to build a house, you would approach an architect, giving clear and precise details of what you required (a brief). An architect must know from a client what the building is to be used for, how many people will use it, and how much money is available. A good architect will make sure that the new design fits in with existing buildings around it, and is built from suitable material. The architect then presents drawings and plans to the client. When the plans are approved, work on the building can begin.

| Doric column | Ionic column | Corinthian column | Barrel vault | Groin vault | Rib vault | Dome |

EXTRAORDINARY ARCHITECTURE

Some architects design weird and wonderful buildings which really stand out from the rest. In 1965, a new town was built outside Paris, France, called Marne-la-Vallée. It has many extraordinary buildings, designed by various adventurous architects. The apartment complex, left, is like a monument that people can live in. Two circular buildings face each other across a central courtyard. It was designed by a Spaniard named Manolo Nunez-Yanowsky.

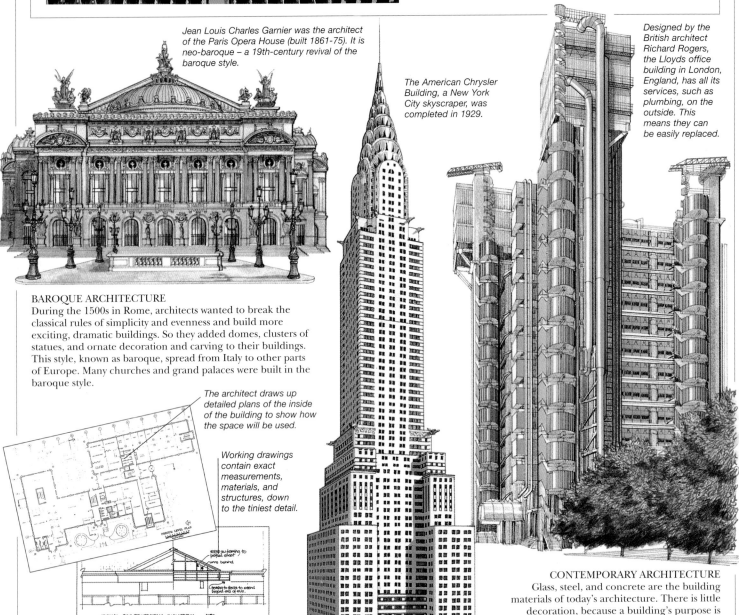

Jean Louis Charles Garnier was the architect of the Paris Opera House (built 1861-75). It is neo-baroque – a 19th-century revival of the baroque style.

The American Chrysler Building, a New York City skyscraper, was completed in 1929.

Designed by the British architect Richard Rogers, the Lloyds office building in London, England, has all its services, such as plumbing, on the outside. This means they can be easily replaced.

BAROQUE ARCHITECTURE

During the 1500s in Rome, architects wanted to break the classical rules of simplicity and evenness and build more exciting, dramatic buildings. So they added domes, clusters of statues, and ornate decoration and carving to their buildings. This style, known as baroque, spread from Italy to other parts of Europe. Many churches and grand palaces were built in the baroque style.

The architect draws up detailed plans of the inside of the building to show how the space will be used.

Working drawings contain exact measurements, materials, and structures, down to the tiniest detail.

TYPICAL BAY PROJECTION ELEVATION 1:50

The builder works from working drawings (above) when constructing the building.

CONTEMPORARY ARCHITECTURE

Glass, steel, and concrete are the building materials of today's architecture. There is little decoration, because a building's purpose is considered more important than its shape or form. The "international" style – glass and concrete suspended on a steel framework – is seen almost everywhere in the world.

Pediment

Gothic arch

Romanesque arch

Cornice

Find out more
CITIES
DAMS
INDUSTRIAL REVOLUTION
PLASTICS
RENAISSANCE

ARCTIC

THE SMALLEST OF THE world's oceans, the Arctic centres on the North Pole. Between the months of December and May, most of the Arctic Ocean is covered by polar sea ice, up to 30 m (98 ft) thick. The ocean is surrounded by the Arctic regions, where much of the ground is permanently frozen to depths of 460–600 m (1,500–2,000 ft). During the long, cold winters in the far north, much of the land is subject to periods of total darkness. This is because of the low angle of the Sun in relation to the ground. Beneath the rocks of the Arctic regions lie rich reserves of iron, nickel, copper, zinc, and oil. Severe weather conditions have made it hard to exploit these resources. But global warming is thinning the sea ice and opening up new areas of land. Arctic countries now want to claim areas of the sea bed.

The Arctic Ocean centres on the North Pole, the northern extremity of the Earth's axis. Three of the world's largest rivers, the Ob, Yenisey, and Lena, flow into the cold waters of the Arctic Ocean. The Arctic regions consist of Alaska, Canada, Greenland and northern Siberia.

ICE-BREAKING

Although half of the Arctic Ocean is covered by ice in winter, special ships called ice-breakers can still sail through the ice. During particularly harsh winters, ice can become so dense in harbours and ports that it freezes right down to the sea bed, marooning ships for months at a time. Ice-breakers are designed to crush the ice with their steel hulls, opening up a lane that other ships can pass through. The Russian atomic-powered *Arcticka* is the world's most powerful ice-breaker. It can cut through ice that is 2.1 m (7 ft) thick at 11 km/h (7 mph).

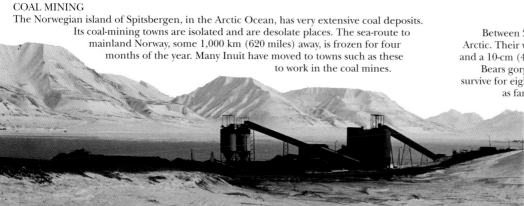

Teams of hardy husky dogs were traditionally used to pull sleds across the frozen ground.

ARCTIC SETTLERS

The Arctic is one of the world's most sparsely populated regions. Today, some 120,000 Inuit (Eskimo) peoples live in Greenland, Alaska, and Canada. Over the past 3,000 years they have adapted to their ice-bound conditions, hunting with kayaks (canoes) and harpoons, and existing on a diet of caribou, seal, whale meat, and fish. They lived in houses made of frozen snow (igloos) or semi-underground stone pit-houses. Today, snowmobiles (above) have replaced sleds, and rifles are used for hunting.

COAL MINING

The Norwegian island of Spitsbergen, in the Arctic Ocean, has very extensive coal deposits. Its coal-mining towns are isolated and are desolate places. The sea-route to mainland Norway, some 1,000 km (620 miles) away, is frozen for four months of the year. Many Inuit have moved to towns such as these to work in the coal mines.

POLAR BEARS

Between 25,000 and 40,000 polar bears roam the Arctic. Their white coats provide perfect camouflage, and a 10-cm (4-in) layer of body fat keeps them warm. Bears gorge on seals from April to July – they can survive for eight months without food. They can swim as far as 150 km (93 miles) in search of prey.

Find out more
GLACIERS AND ICECAPS
INUITS
OCEANS AND SEAS
OCEAN WILDLIFE
POLAR WILDLIFE

KEY

Volcano	Mountain	Ancient monument	Capital city	Large city/town	Small city/town

STATISTICS

GREENLAND
Area:
2,166,086 sq km
(836,330 sq miles)
Status: Self-governing
territory of Denmark
Claimed: 1380
Population: 57,600
Capital: Nuuk

JAN MAYEN
Area:
377 sq km (146 sq miles)
Status: Norwegian
dependency
Claimed: 1929
Population: None
Capital: None

SVALBARD
Area:
61,020 sq km
(23,560 sq miles)
Status: Norwegian
dependency
Claimed: 1920
Population: 2,200
Capital: Longyearbyen

Halibut

ARCTIC FISH
Large quantities of cod, haddock,
and halibut are found in the
Arctic Ocean. Arctic catches
are mainly processed in Greenland.

GREENLAND
Greenland, the world's largest
island, is a self-governing
territory of Denmark. The
interior of Greenland is covered
by an enormous ice-sheet, which
rises to a height of 3,000 m
(10,000 ft). The coastline is
deeply indented with fjords.

GIANT ICEBERGS
Icebergs are frozen lumps of freshwater ice
that have broken off a glacier. Most Arctic
icebergs have broken off the coastal
glaciers of Greenland, Baffin Island, and
Ellesmere Island. Each year, about 375
icebergs flow into the the North Atlantic
where they are extremely dangerous to
shipping. Icebergs can vary from the size
of a grand piano to a ten-storey building,
45 m (147 ft) high. They are moved by
winds and currents, and melt and break
up within two years of entering the ocean.

NORTHERN LIGHTS
The northern lights
(*aurora borealis*) occur
when highly charged
particles from the sun
collide with particles in
the Earth's atmosphere.
These glowing streaks
of light are brightest
at the North Pole.

ARCTIC TERN
The arctic tern (left)
breeds in the southern
Arctic and winters
in the Antarctic,
the longest annual
migration of any bird.

ARCTIC OCEAN
*The Arctic Ocean is
characterized by a wide
continental shelf and
deep basin around
the North Pole.*

PRUDHOE BAY
*Rich reserves of oil are
found in Alaska's Prudhoe
Bay. A 1,280-km
(795-mile) long
pipeline transports
oil from Prudhoe
Bay to the
ice-free port
of Valdez.*

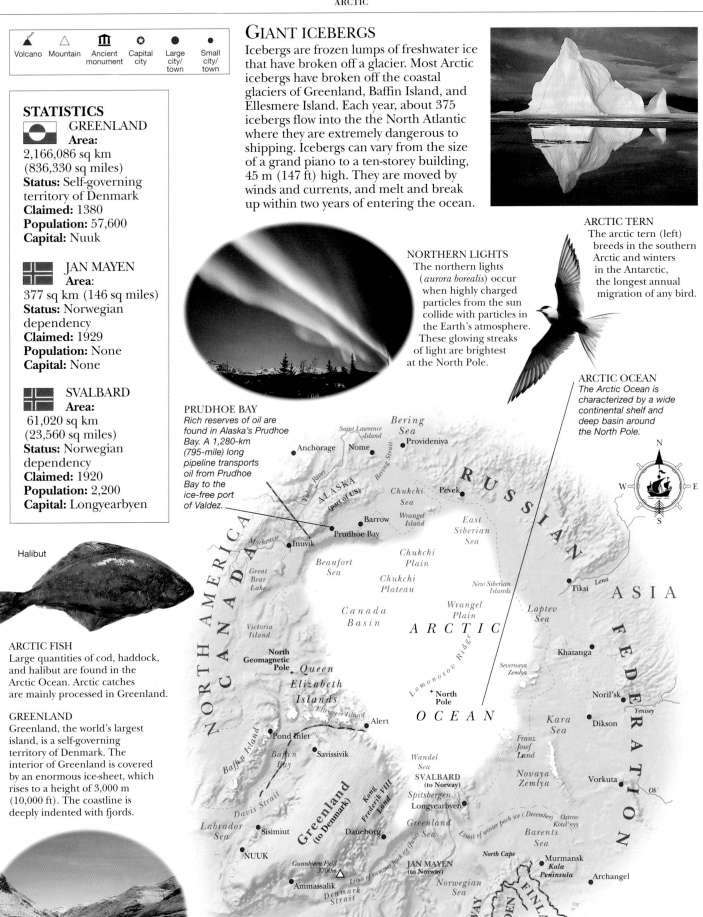

ARGENTINA

ARGENTINA CONSISTS OF THREE MAIN REGIONS. In the north lies the hot, humid lands of the Gran Chaco. In the centre, the temperate grasslands of the Pampas provide some of the world's best farming country. Argentina is a world leader in beef exports, and a major producer of wheat, maize, fruit, and vegetables. In the far south, the barren semi-desert of Patagonia is rich in reserves of coal, petroleum and natural gas. Argentina was settled by the Spanish in 1543. New European diseases, as well as conflict between the Spanish and Native Americans, considerably reduced Argentina's original population. In the 19th century, many immigrants from southern Europe, especially Spain and Italy, came to Argentina to work on farms and cattle ranches. Although Spanish is the official language today, many other languages are spoken, ranging from Welsh to Basque, reflecting the varied origins of Argentina's many settlers.

Argentina stretches for 3,460 km (2,150 miles) down the southeastern coast of South America. Its border in the west is defined by the Andes. To the south it straddles the Strait of Magellan.

GAUCHOS

These nomadic cowboys of the Argentine Pampas first appeared in the 18th century when they were hired to hunt escaped horses and cattle. Their standard equipment included a lasso, knife and *bolas* (iron balls on leather straps, thrown at the legs of the escaping animals). In the 19th century, they were hired by ranch-owners as skilled cattle-herders. Today, Argentine cow-herders keep their culture alive. They still wear the gaucho costume of a poncho (a woollen cape), high leather boots, and long, pleated trousers.

ARGENTINIAN WINE
European vines were introduced to Argentina by Spanish missionaries, and thrived in the temperate climate and fertile soils of the central regions. Argentina is the fourth-largest wine-producing country in the world – much of the wine is for sale in Argentina only.

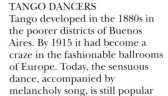

BUENOS AIRES

Argentina's capital, Buenos Aires, is one of the largest cities in South America. Situated on the Plate river estuary, it is also a major port and thriving industrial centre. It was founded by Spanish settlers in 1580, and some historic buildings survive. The city expanded in the 19th century when European immigrants flooded to Argentina. Its museums, library, opera house, and cafés all give the city a European flavour.

A street performance (below) of a tango in Buenos Aires. The South American version of the tango developed from a blend of rhythms brought to South America by African slaves, and rhythms from Spain.

TANGO DANCERS
Tango developed in the 1880s in the poorer districts of Buenos Aires. By 1915 it had become a craze in the fashionable ballrooms of Europe. Today, the sensuous dance, accompanied by melancholy song, is still popular on the streets of the city.

ANDES

This wall of mountains forms a natural border between Argentina and its western neighbour, Chile. In 1881, the two countries signed a treaty defining this boundary. In western Argentina, the extinct volcano, Cerra Aconcagua, reaches a height of 6,959 m (22,816 ft). It is the highest peak in the South American Andes.

Find out more
COAL
SOUTH AMERICA
SOUTH AMERICA, HISTORY OF

| Volcano | Mountain | Ancient monument | Capital city | Large city/town | Small city/town |

STATISTICS
Area: 2,766,890 sq km (1,068,296 sq miles)
Population: 40,914,000
Capital: Buenos Aires
Languages: Spanish, Italian, Amerindian languages
Religions: Roman Catholic, Jewish, Protestant
Currency: Argentine peso
Main occupation: Agriculture
Main exports: Beef, wheat, fruit, wine
Main imports: Designer clothing

TIERRA DEL FUEGO
This string of islands is separated from the South American mainland by the Strait of Magellan. They are divided between Argentina and Chile. The landscape, with its mountains, frozen lakes and glaciers, is bleak and windswept. It is also barren – only stunted trees and mosses grow there. Herds of sheep graze the land. Oil has been discovered in this remote area.

SCALE BAR

0   200   400   km

0   200   400   miles

BOLIVIA

PARAGUAY

BRAZIL

URUGUAY

Atacama Desert

Tropic of Capricorn

Gran Chaco

Pilcomayo

Bermejo

San Salvador de Jujuy

Salta

San Miguel de Tucumán

Santiago del Estero

Formosa

Resistencia

Corrientes

Posadas

Paraná

Uruguay

Cerro Ojos del Salado 6880m

La Rioja

Salado

Laguna Mar Chiquita

San Juan

Santa Fe

Córdoba

Paraná

Concordia

Rosario

Gualeguaychú

Cerro Aconcagua 6959m

Mendoza

Godoy Cruz

Salado

Río Cuarto

San Rafael

Junín

BUENOS AIRES

La Plata

River Plate

Pampas

Santa Rosa

Olavarría

Azul

Dolores

ARGENTINA

Tres Arroyos

Mar del Plata

Colorado

Bahía Blanca

Necochea

Zapala

Neuquén

Bahía Blanca

Río Negro

San Antonio Oeste

Viedma

Lago Nahuel Huapi

San Carlos de Bariloche

Gulf of San Matías

Península Valdés

Esquel

Chubut

Rawson

Chico

Patagonia

Sarmiento

Comodoro Rivadavia

Perito Moreno

Gulf of San Jorge

Caleta Olivia

Deseado

Golfo de Penas

Puerto Deseado

Chico

Santa Cruz

El Calafate

Bahía Grande

Río Gallegos

Strait of Magellan

Río Grande

Tierra del Fuego

Isla de los Estados

Cape Horn

Drake Passage

PACIFIC OCEAN

CHILE

Andes

ATLANTIC OCEAN

FALKLAND ISLANDS
Discovered by the British in 1592, the Falkland Islands are a self-governing British colony, 480 km (300 miles) off the coast of Argentina. The cool, windy islands are only suitable for grazing sheep, and meat and wool are their main resource. In 1982, Argentina claimed the Falklands as their territory, and invaded the islands. They surrendered after 10 weeks, but British troops still protect the islands.

FALKLAND ISLANDS (to UK)

West Falkland

East Falkland

ARMOUR

ANCIENT WARRIORS quickly realized that they would survive in battle if they could protect themselves against their enemies. So they made armour – special clothing which was tough enough to stop weapons from injuring the wearer. Prehistoric armour was simple. It was made of leather but was strong enough to provide protection against crude spears and swords. As weapons became sharper, armour too had to improve. A thousand years ago the Roman Empire employed many armourers who made excellent metal armour. But after the fall of Rome in the 5th century, blacksmiths began to make armour and its quality fell. In the 14th century, specially trained armourers invented plate armour to withstand lances, arrows, and swords. But even the thickest armour cannot stop a bullet, so armour became less useful when guns were invented. Today no one uses traditional armour, but people in combat still wear protective clothing made out of modern plastics and tough metals.

ANIMAL ARMOUR
Soldiers have used animals in warfare, such as dogs for attack and horses for riding into battle. Armour protected these animals when they fought. The most elaborate animal armour was the elephant armour of 17th-century India.

Arrows bounced off the curves of the helmet. Knights often wore mail or padding beneath the helmet.

The breastplate was flared so that enemy sword strokes bounced off.

The vambrace was a cylindrical piece to protect the upper arm.

The cowter protected the elbow, but allowed it to move freely.

The gauntlet was made up of many small pieces so that the hand could move freely.

The cuisse protected only the front of the leg.

Poleyns had to bend easily when the knight rode a horse.

Greaves were among the earliest pieces of body armour to be made of sheet metal.

SUIT OF ARMOUR
Late 15th-century armour provided a knight with a protective metal shell. The armour was very strong, and cleverly jointed so that the knight could move easily. However, the metal suit weighed up to 30 kg (70 lb), so that running, for example, was virtually impossible.

HELMETS
A single heavy blow to the head can kill a person, so helmets, or armoured hats, were among the first pieces of armour to be made. They are still widely used today. Different shapes gave protection against different types of weapon.

Bronze Age helmets protected against swords more than 3,000 years ago.

Pikemen of the 16th century

Twelfth-century helm

Modern helmets give protection against shrapnel (metal fragments from bombs).

BULLETPROOF VEST
Modern police and security forces sometimes wear bulletproof vests to protect themselves from attack by criminals and terrorists. The vests are made of many layers of tough materials such as nylon and are capable of stopping a bullet.

CHAIN MAIL
Chain mail was easier and cheaper for a blacksmith to make than a complicated suit of plate armour. Mail was very common between the 6th and 13th centuries. It was made of a large number of interlocking rings of steel. It allowed the wearer to move easily, but did not give good protection against heavy swords and axes.

Find out more
ALEXANDER THE GREAT
KNIGHTS AND HERALDRY
MEDIEVAL EUROPE
ROMAN EMPIRE
VIKINGS

ASIA

The Ural Mountains form the border between the continents of Asia and Europe. Asia is separated from Africa by the Red Sea. The Bering Strait, only 88 km (55 miles) wide, marks the gap between Asia and North America. Australia lies to the southeast.

THE LARGEST OF THE SEVEN CONTINENTS, Asia occupies one-third of the world's total land area. Much of the continent is uninhabited. The inhospitable north is a cold land of tundra. Parched deserts and towering mountains take up large areas of the central region. Yet Asia is the home of well over half of the world's population, most of whom live around the outer rim. China alone has more than 1,300 million people, and India has more than 1,000 million. Altogether, Asia contains 48 nations, and many times this number of peoples, languages, and cultures. It has five main zones. In the north is the Russian Federation. Part of this is in Europe, but the vast eastern region, from the Ural Mountains to the Pacific Ocean, is in Asia. The Pacific coast, which includes China, Korea, and Japan, is known as the Far East. To the south of this lie the warmer, more humid countries of Southeast Asia. India and Pakistan are the principal countries of the Indian subcontinent in south Asia. One of the world's first civilizations began here, in the Indus Valley. Bordered by the Mediterranean and Arabian seas, the Middle East lies to the west where Europe, Asia, and Africa meet.

MIDDLE EAST

The hot, dry lands of the Middle East occupy the southwest corner of Asia. Almost the entire Arabian peninsula, between the Red Sea and The Gulf, is desert. To the north, in Iraq and Syria, lie the fertile valleys of the rivers Tigris and Euphrates. Most of the people of the Middle East are Arabs, and speak Arabic.

The Arabs of the Middle East drank coffee long before it reached other countries.

Siberian scientists looking for minerals in north Asia have to work in subzero temperatures, and the cold can freeze their breath.

SIBERIA

The northern coast of Asia is fringed by the Arctic Ocean. The sea here is frozen for most of the year. A layer of the land, called permafrost, is also always frozen. This area is part of the vast region of the Russian Federation called Siberia. Despite the cold, Russian people live and work in Siberia because the region is rich in timber, coal, oil, and natural gas.

ANCIENT TRADE ROUTES

Even 2,000 years ago, there was trade between the Far East and Europe. Traders carried silk, spices, gems, and pottery. They followed overland routes across India and Pakistan, past the Karakoram mountains (above). These trade routes were known as the Silk Road; they are still used today.

TROPICAL RAIN FORESTS

The warm, damp climate of much of Southeast Asia provides the perfect conditions for tropical rain forests, which thrive in countries such as Burma (Myanmar) and Malaysia. The forests are the habitat for a huge variety of wildlife, and are home to tribes of people whose way of life has not changed for centuries. But because many of the forest trees are beautiful hardwoods, the logging industry is now cutting down the forests at an alarming rate to harvest the valuable timber.

Sunlight breaks through the dense foliage of the rain forest only where rivers have cut trails through the trees.

PROSPERITY

Some Asian countries, such as Japan and Singapore, are among the world's most prosperous nations. The discovery of oil in a number of other countries, such as Saudi Arabia in the Middle East, and Brunei in Southeast Asia, has made them very wealthy.

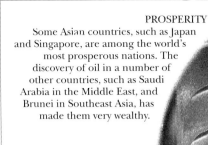

Brunei's vast oil wealth has enabled the sultan (ruler) to build a magnificent new palace. It is called Istana Nurul Iman, and is only open to the public at the end of the Islamic fasting month of Ramadan.

"Floating markets" are a common sight on the busy waterways of the Far East.

Vanilla vines grow well in the warm climate of Indonesia, and women harvest the pods by hand.

FAR EAST

East Asia is often called the Far East. In the 19th century, European traders and travellers used this name to distinguish east Asia from the Middle East. The Far East includes China, Japan, and Korea.

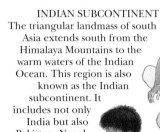

KOREA

The Korean peninsula juts out from northern China towards Japan. The two Korean nations were at war between 1950 and 1953. They have lived in constant mistrust of each other since the war ended, but are now trying to mend the divisions between them. South Korea has a booming economy and is heavily supported by the United States. North Korea is Communist and poorer. The climate favours rice growing, with warm summers and icy winters.

Construction work is a common sight in South Korea, as new offices and factories are built for the country's expanding industries.

SOUTHEAST ASIA

Many different people live in the warm, tropical southeastern corner of Asia. There are ten independent countries in the region. Some of them – Burma (Myanmar), Laos, Thailand, Cambodia (or Kampuchea), and Vietnam – are on the mainland attached to the rest of Asia. Further south lie Brunei, Malaysia, and the tiny island nation of Singapore. Indonesia stretches across the foot of the region. It is a scattered nation of more than 13,500 islands. The islands of the Philippines are to the east. Although some of these countries are very poor, Southeast Asia as a whole has one of the most rapidly developing economies in the world.

Hundreds of different languages are spoken in the Indian sub-continent, but Indian schools teach pupils to read and write Hindi, which is the country's official language.

INDIAN SUBCONTINENT

The triangular landmass of south Asia extends south from the Himalaya Mountains to the warm waters of the Indian Ocean. This region is also known as the Indian subcontinent. It includes not only India but also Pakistan, Nepal, Bangladesh, and Bhutan. At the very southern tip of India lies the island nation of Sri Lanka.

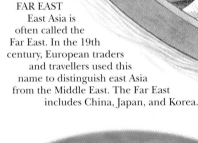

The port of Shanghai lies at the mouth of the River Yangtze.

RIVER YANGTZE

The Yangtze (or Chang Jiang), the world's third-longest river, flows 6,380 km (3,964 miles) through the middle of China, from its source in Tibet to the sea at Shanghai. In 1997, the first stage was completed on the Three Gorges Dam, China's largest construction project since the building of the Great Wall.

Find out more

CHINA
INDIA
JAPAN
RELIGIONS
RUSSIAN FEDERATION
SOUTHEAST ASIA

ASIA

Asia is the world's largest continent. It is a region of contrasts: both in its landscape, and peoples. The break up of the Soviet Union produced five new central Asian republics. The countries in the south are mainly Muslim, but are divided by religious differences and conflicts.

 AFGHANISTAN
Area: 647,500 sq km (250,001 sq miles)
Population: 33,610,000
Capital: Kābul

 ARMENIA
Area: 29,800 sq km (11,506 sq miles)
Population: 2,967,000
Capital: Yerevan

 AZERBAIJAN
Area: 86,600 sq km (33,436 sq miles)
Population: 8,239,000
Capital: Baku

 BAHRAIN
Area: 665 sq km (257 sq miles)
Population: 728,000
Capital: Manama

 BANGLADESH
Area: 143,998 sq km (55,598 sq miles)
Population: 156,051,000
Capital: Dhaka

 BHUTAN
Area: 47,000 sq km (18,147 sq miles)
Population: 691,000
Capital: Thimphu

 BRUNEI
Area: 5,770 sq km (2,228 sq miles)
Population: 389,000
Capital: Bandar Seri Begawan

 BURMA
Area: 678,500 sq km (261,970 sq miles)
Population: 48,138,000
Capital: Rangoon

 CAMBODIA
Area: 181,040 sq km (69,000 sq miles)
Population: 14,494,000
Capital: Phnom Penh

 CHINA
Area: 9,396,960 sq km (3,628,166 sq miles)
Population: 1,338,613,000
Capital: Beijing

 CYPRUS
Area: 9,251 sq km (3,572 sq miles)
Population: 797,000
Capital: Nicosia

 EAST TIMOR
Area: 15,007 sq km (5,794 sq miles)
Population: 1,132,000
Capital: Dili

 GEORGIA
Area: 69,700 sq km (26,911 sq miles)
Population: 4,616,000
Capital: Tbilisi

 INDIA
Area: 3,287,590 sq km (1,269,338 sq miles)
Population: 1,166,079,000
Capital: New Delhi

 INDONESIA
Area: 1,904,570 sq km (735,555 sq miles)
Population: 240,272,000
Capital: Jakarta

 IRAN
Area: 1,648,000 sq km (636,293 sq miles)
Population: 66,429,000
Capital: Tehran

 IRAQ
Area: 437,072 sq km (168,754 sq miles)
Population: 28,946,000
Capital: Baghdad

 ISRAEL
Area: 20,700 sq km (7,992 sq miles)
Population: 7,234,000
Capital: Jerusalem

 JAPAN
Area: 377,800 sq km (145,869 sq miles)
Population: 127,079,000
Capital: Tokyo

 JORDAN
Area: 92,300 sq km (35,637 sq miles)
Population: 6,343,000
Capital: Amman

 KAZAKHSTAN
Area: 2,717,300 sq km (1,049,150 sq miles)
Population: 15,400,000
Capital: Astana

 NORTH KOREA
Area: 120,540 sq km (46,540 sq miles)
Population: 22,665,000
Capital: Pyongyang

 SOUTH KOREA
Area: 98,480 sq km (38,023 sq miles)
Population: 48,510,000
Capital: Seoul

 KUWAIT
Area: 17,820 sq km (6,880 sq miles)
Population: 2,691,000
Capital: Kuwait City

 KYRGYZSTAN
Area: 198,500 sq km (76,640 sq miles)
Population: 5,432,000
Capital: Bishkek

 LAOS
Area: 236,800 sq km (91,428 sq miles)
Population: 6,835,000
Capital: Vientiane

 LEBANON
Area: 10,400 sq km (4,015 sq miles)
Population: 4,017,000
Capital: Beirut

 MALAYSIA
Area: 329,750 sq km (127,317 sq miles)
Population: 25,716,000
Capital: Kuala Lumpur

 MALDIVES
Area: 300 sq km (116 sq miles)
Population: 396,000
Capital: Male'

 MONGOLIA
Area: 1,565,000 sq km (604,247 sq miles)
Population: 3,041,000
Capital: Ulan Bator

 NEPAL
Area: 147,181 sq km (56,827 sq miles)
Population: 28,563,000
Capital: Kathmandu

 OMAN
Area: 212,460 sq km (82,030 sq miles)
Population: 3,418,000
Capital: Muscat

 PAKISTAN
Area: 796,100 sq km (307,374 sq miles)
Population: 176,243,000
Capital: Islamabad

 PHILIPPINES
Area: 300,000 sq km (115,831 sq miles)
Population: 97,977,000
Capital: Manila

 QATAR
Area: 11,586 sq km (4,473 sq miles)
Population: 833,000
Capital: Doha

RUSSIAN FED.
Area: 17,075,400 sq km (6,592,800 sq miles)
Population: 140,041,000
Capital: Moscow

 SINGAPORE
Area: 697 sq km (239 sq miles)
Population: 4,658,000
Capital: Singapore City

 SRI LANKA
Area: 65,610 sq km (25,332 sq miles)
Population: 21,325,000
Capital: Colombo

 SYRIA
Area: 185,180 sq km (71,500 sq miles)
Population: 20,178,000
Capital: Damascus

TAIWAN
Area: 36,179 sq km (13,969 sq miles)
Population: 22,974,000
Capital: Taipei

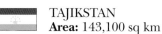 **TAJIKISTAN**
Area: 143,100 sq km (55,251 sq miles)
Population: 7,349,000
Capital: Dushanbe

 **THAILAND**
Area: 514,000 sq km (198,457 sq miles)
Population: 65,905,000
Capital: Bangkok

TURKEY
Area: 780,580 sq km (301,384 sq miles)
Population: 76,806,000
Capital: Ankara

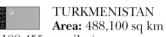 **TURKMENISTAN**
Area: 488,100 sq km (188,455 sq miles)
Population: 4,885,000
Capital: Ashgabat

U. A. E.
Area: 83,600 sq km (32,278 sq miles)
Population: 4,798,000
Capital: Abu Dhabi

 UZBEKISTAN
Area: 447,400 sq km (172,741 sq miles)
Population: 27,606,000
Capital: Tashkent

 VIETNAM
Area: 329,560 sq km (127,243 sq miles)
Population: 86,968,000
Capital: Hanoi

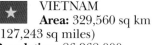 **YEMEN**
Area: 527,970 sq km (203,849 sq miles)
Population: 23,823,000
Capital: Sana

Volcano	Mountain	Ancient monument	Capital city	Large city/town	Small city/town

STATISTICS
Area: 46,519,416 sq km
(17,961,247 sq miles)
Population:
3,152,429,000
Highest point: Mount
Everest (Nepal)
8,850 m (29,029 ft)
Longest river: Yangtze
(China) 6,380 km
(3,964 miles)
Largest lake: Caspian
Sea 371,000 sq km
(143,205 sq miles)

SCALE BAR

0	500	1000	km
0	500	1000	miles

MOUNT EVEREST
The Himalayan mountain range runs along the China-Nepal border southeast from the Pamir mountains. It is a group of rugged peaks and valleys, sometimes described as the "roof of the world". The highest point in the Himalayas is Mount Everest (right) – the world's highest mountain.

URAL MOUNTAINS
The Ural Mountains form a natural border between Asia and Europe.

KURILE ISLANDS
The Kurile Islands are part of the Russian Federation, but Japan claims the southernmost islands in this chain as part of its own territory.

ARCTIC OCEAN

PACIFIC OCEAN

INDIAN OCEAN

EUROPE

AFRICA

AUSTRALIA

Bering Sea
East Siberian Sea
Laptev Sea
Kara Sea
Central Siberian Plateau
West Siberian Plain
Sea of Okhotsk
Kamchatka
Kurile Islands
Sakhalin

RUSSIAN FEDERATION

Lchashen
Black Sea
Mediterranean Sea
ANKARA
TURKEY
GEORGIA TBILISI
CYPRUS **ARMENIA** YEREVAN **AZERB.**
NICOSIA
LEBANON BEIRUT **SYRIA** DAMASCUS BAKU
JERUSALEM AMMAN
ISRAEL
JORDAN **IRAQ** BAGHDAD
Ur KUWAIT
TEHRAN
SAUDI MANAMA **BAHRAIN**
RIYADH **QATAR** DOHA
ARABIA ABU DHABI
U.A.E.
Arabian Peninsula
OMAN MUSCAT
Gulf of Oman
SANA
YEMEN
Gulf of Aden
Socotra (to Yemen)
Red Sea
Arabian Sea

ASTANA
KAZAKHSTAN
Aral Sea
Lake Balkhash
Syr Darya
UZBEKISTAN TASHKENT
BISHKEK **KYRGYZSTAN**
TURKMENISTAN
ASGABAT Amu Darya
DUSHANBE **TAJIKISTAN**
IRAN
KABUL
AFGHANISTAN
ISLAMABAD
Tarim He
Kunlun Mountains
PAKISTAN
NEW DELHI
Indus
NEPAL KATHMANDU
THIMPHU **BHUTAN**
Mount Everest 8850m
DHAKA
Narmada Ganges
Brahmaputra
BANGLADESH
INDIA
Godavari
Krishna

ULAN BATOR
MONGOLIA
Altai Mountains
Gobi
Inner Mongolia
Yellow River
BEIJING
CHINA
Plateau of Tibet
Himalayas
Salween
Mekong
Yangtze
Xi jiang

Sea of Japan (East Sea)
JAPAN
NORTH KOREA TOKYO
PYONGYANG
Honshu
SEOUL
SOUTH KOREA
Yellow Sea
East China Sea
Anyang
TAIPEI
TAIWAN
Ryukyu Islands
Tropic of Cancer
Philippine Sea

HANOI
BURMA NAY PYI TAW
Irrawaddy
LAOS
VIENTIANE
VIETNAM
Hainan Dao
MANILA
Luzon
THAILAND
BANGKOK
CAMBODIA
PHNOM PENH
Mekong
South China Sea
PHILIPPINES
Mindanao
Equator

Bay of Bengal
Andaman Islands (to India)
Andaman Sea
Gulf of Thailand
Nicobar Islands (to India)
SRI LANKA
COLOMBO

BANDAR SERI BEGAWAN
MALAYSIA **BRUNEI**
KUALA LUMPUR
PUTRAJAYA
SINGAPORE
Sumatra
Borneo
Celebes
INDONESIA
Moluccas
New Guinea
Papua (Irian Jaya)
Java Sea
JAKARTA Java
Flores Sea Flores
EAST TIMOR DILI
Timor
Timor Sea

Tropic of Cancer

SEOUL
Modern office blocks crowd together in Seoul, the capital city of South Korea, but a few ancient buildings still survive. The South Gate (below) was built at the end of the 14th century as part of a wall that once surrounded the city. Today, Seoul is spreading far beyond its original boundaries as rapid industrial growth creates a need for more offices, factories, and homes.

EAST TIMOR
In 1975 Indonesia invaded the Portuguese colony of East Timor, the eastern part of the island of Timor. The following year the region was made a province of Indonesia. In a UN-monitored referendum in 1999, voters rejected Indonesian rule and in 2002 East Timor became an independent state.

JAVA
Rice terraces (right) provide the staple food for Indonesia. These fields are on the island of Java, which has only seven per cent of Indonesia's land area but is the home of some 60 per cent of the country's people.

HISTORY OF
ASIA

THE VAST CONTINENT OF ASIA is home to the oldest civilizations and religions in the world. Because Asia contains many virtually impassable deserts and mountain ranges, individual countries developed separately from each other. However, links between these countries sprang up as merchants travelled along the Silk Road, Indian kings invaded neighbouring countries, Buddhist monks crossed the Himalayas, and Arab traders sailed across the Indian Ocean. As a result, the great Hindu, Buddhist, and Islamic religions spread across the continent. For much of the last 500 years, Europe controlled large parts of Asia, but since 1945 Asian countries have gained their independence. Many of them are now world-class economies.

EARLY CIVILIZATIONS

Asia's extreme land forms, such as the towering peaks of the Himalayas, which separate India from China, meant that early Asian cultures had little contact with each other, or the rest of the world. As a result, the first great Asian civilizations, such as the Indus Valley civilization in the Indian subcontinent, and the Shang Dynasty in China, developed very different and distinct cultures.

Bactrian (two-humped) camel pottery made in China.

HINDUISM

Hinduism began in the ancient civilizations of the Indus Valley, in India, around 2500 BCE. Over the centuries, the religion spread across India to Sri Lanka and the islands of Southeast Asia. Hinduism is the oldest religion in the world still practised today, and provides a thread linking together all of India's history.

ARAB TRADERS

Arab merchants were great travellers and adventurers, crossing deserts and oceans in search of new markets in which to buy and sell their goods. On their journeys, they converted local people to their Islamic religion, founded by Muhammad in Arabia in the early 600s. As a result, Islam spread across Asia as far as the southeastern islands.

SILK ROAD

The Silk Road was an important trading route that stretched across Asia from Loyang, China's capital, in the east to the Mediterranean Sea in the west. It was called the Silk Road because of the Chinese silk that was traded along its length. The road was not continuous, but was made up of a series of well-marked routes connecting major towns. Here merchants bought and sold their goods, creating a link between Asia and Europe.

Buddhist monks shave their heads and wear saffron-coloured robes.

BUDDHIST MONKS

Siddhartha Gautama, the founder of Buddhism, was born in India c. 563 BCE. By his death c. 483 BCE, his teaching had spread throughout India. From about 100 CE, Buddhist monks took Buddhism across the Himalayas to China, and along the Silk Road into central Asia. Today, most of the world's Buddhists live in Asia.

MONGOLS

The Mongols were fierce warriors who lived as nomads on the steppes, or grasslands, of central Asia. In the 1200s they created an empire that stretched from China into eastern Europe. Their power declined in the 1300s, but in 1369 one of their leaders, Tamerlane the Great, became ruler of central Asia. He built many fine mosques in his capital, Samarkand.

EUROPEAN DOMINATION

In 1498, Portuguese explorer Vasco da Gama sailed to India around the southern tip of Africa. He was the first European to reach Asia by sea. Other Europeans followed, and over the next 400 years, Europeans dominated much of Asia, first as traders and merchants, then as conquerors and colonizers. Only Persia (present-day Iran), Afghanistan, Thailand, and Japan remained free from European control.

Portuguese colonial house in Macau

WORLD WAR II

During World War II (1939-45), the Japanese invaded China and much of Southeast Asia in order to create an empire. Some welcomed the Japanese invaders, because they threw out the European colonial masters and gave the people a greater degree of independence. After Japan's defeat in 1945, Britain, France, the Netherlands, and the USA returned to take control of their former colonies.

COMMUNIST ASIA

In 1949, the Communist Party finally gained power in China after years of civil war. Communists also took control in North Korea, Mongolia, North Vietnam, Cambodia, and Laos. The Communist governments of these countries improved people's living standards, but failed to match the economic success of Japan and other Asian countries.

The Red Guard, followers of Chinese Communist leader Mao Zedong

Chinese students bearing a portrait of Mao Zedong (1893-1976)

Chinese demonstrate their revolutionary fervour in 1967

ASIA

c. 2,500 BCE Hinduism is founded in India.

c. 563-c. 483 BCE Life of Buddha.

500s BCE The Silk Road is established.

250 BCE Buddhism spreads to Sri Lanka and Southeast Asia.

100 CE Monks take Buddhism to China and into central Asia.

850-1200 Chola kings of India take Hinduism to Sri Lanka and into Southeast Asia.

1279 Mongol Empire under Kublai Khan reaches greatest extent.

1369 Tamerlane the Great creates a new Mongol Empire in the city of Samarkand.

1498 Vasco da Gama sails to India.

1600 British merchants establish an East India Company in order to trade with India.

1619 Dutch begin to control the East Indies.

1757 British take over Bengal and expand their rule in India.

1850s French begin to control Southeast Asia.

1937 Japanese troops invade China.

1941-45 World War II rages in eastern Asia and the Pacific.

1947-48 British rule in India comes to an end.

1949 Indonesia becomes independent.

1999 Portuguese hand Macau back to China.

INDEPENDENCE

Following World War II, the European countries began to grant their Asian colonies independence. India became independent from Britain in 1947-48, and Indonesia gained its independence from the Netherlands in 1949. The last colony – the Portuguese territory of Macau – was handed back to China in 1999.

TIGER ECONOMIES

Japan and other countries began rebuilding their economies after World War II. They concentrated on heavy industries such as car manufacturing and shipbuilding, and on hi-tech industries such as computing and electronics. Today Japan is the world's second biggest economy, while Taiwan, South Korea, Singapore, and China have become industrial powerhouses.

Find out more
ASIA
CHINA
COMMUNISM
INDIA
JAPAN
WORLD WAR II

ASSYRIANS

ABOUT 3,000 YEARS AGO, a mighty empire rose to power in the Middle East where Iraq is today. This was the Assyrian Empire. It lasted for more than 300 years and spread all over the surrounding area from the River Nile to Mesopotamia. Under King Shalmaneser I (1273-1244 BCE) the Assyrians conquered Babylon and many other independent states, and eventually united the region into one empire. With an enormous army, armoured horses, fast two-wheeled chariots, and huge battering rams, the Assyrians were highly skilled, successful fighters, ruthless in battle. The Assyrian Empire grew quickly with a series of warlike kings, including Ashurbanipal II and Sennacherib. Great wealth and excellent trading links enabled the Assyrians to rebuild the cities of Nimrud and Nineveh (which became the capital), and to create a new city at Khorsabad. Assyria was a rich, well-organized society, but by the 7th century B.C. the empire had grown too large to protect itself well. In about 612 BCE, the Babylonian and Mede peoples destroyed Nineveh, and the Assyrian Empire collapsed.

WARRIORS
The Assyrians were famed and feared for their strength in battle and for torturing their victims. They developed the chariot and fought with swords, shields, slings, and bows.

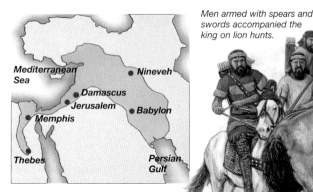

ASSYRIAN EMPIRE
In the 7th century BCE the Assyrian Empire reached its greatest extent. It stretched down to the Persian Gulf in the south and the Mediterranean coast in the west, and included Babylon.

Men armed with spears and swords accompanied the king on lion hunts.

LION HUNT
Hunting and killing lions was a favourite pastime of the Assyrian kings. Lions represented the wild strength of nature. It was considered a noble challenge to seek them out and kill them, although captive lions were also hunted. Only the king was allowed to kill a lion.

ROYAL LIFE
Stone reliefs tell us much about the lives of the Assyrian royalty. This relief sculpture shows King Ashurbanipal II (669-621 BCE) drinking wine in his garden with his queen. It looks like a quiet, domestic scene, but on another section of this sculpture there is a head hanging from a tree. It is the head of Teumann, the king of the Elamites, whose defeat the king and queen are celebrating.

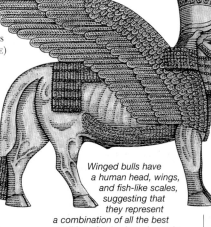

Winged bulls have a human head, wings, and fish-like scales, suggesting that they represent a combination of all the best qualities of animals and people.

WINGED BULLS
Massive stone sculptures (right) of winged bulls were placed on each side of important doors and gateways.

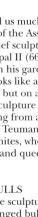 

Assyrian slaves had to drag the massive sculptures to the palace.

Find out more
BABYLONIANS
MIDDLE EAST

ASTRONAUTS
AND SPACE TRAVEL

The astronaut wears a special undergarment with tubes that water flows through, keeping the astronaut's body cool.

The different parts of the suit, such as the gloves and helmet, are locked in position.

Pressure helmet

Visor

Cap

Communications headset

Water inlet and outlet

ON 12 APRIL 1961, the world watched in wonder as Yuri Gagarin of Russia blasted off from Earth aboard a huge rocket and entered space. He was the first cosmonaut, the Russian word for astronaut, a person trained to work in space. Eight years later, Neil Armstrong walked on the Moon and became the first human being to step onto another world away from our planet. Since then, a few hundred other astronauts, both men and women, have voyaged into space. Astronauts have jobs to do during their missions. They help with the construction of the International Space Station and perform scientific experiments under the weightless conditions of space. Today, astronauts are preparing for the next major landmarks in space exploration – to go back to the Moon and then perhaps to Mars.

Communications input socket

There is no air in space to carry sound waves, so astronauts communicate by radio.

Main tanks provide oxygen for the astronaut to breathe.

Wrist clamp

Reserve oxygen tanks provide emergency oxygen supply.

Oxygen inlets and outlets

Urine transfer collection

Extra vehicular glove

Control panel allows the astronaut to adjust the temperature and oxygen flow in the suit.

Battery provides power for spacesuit systems.

Integrated thermal micrometeoroid garment

Strap-on fastener

Urine-collection device worn by the astronaut is like a big nappy.

Layers of different plastics make the suit strong yet flexible.

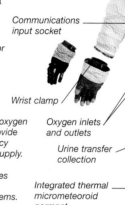

Lunar overshoe

Cosmonaut Salizhan S. Shapirov installing navigation and communication equipment outside the International Space Station.

SPACESUIT

Space is a perilous place for a human being. There is no air to breathe, and without a spacesuit for protection, an astronaut would explode. This is because the human body is built to function under the constant pressure of the Earth's atmosphere, which is not present in space.

WEIGHTLESSNESS

We have weight because of the pull of the Earth's gravity. In space, gravity holds the astronauts and their spacecraft in orbit around the Earth. But there is no force holding the astronauts to their spaceship, so they float around inside it. This is called weightlessness.

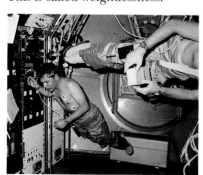

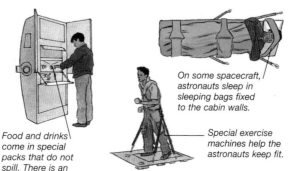

On some spacecraft, astronauts sleep in sleeping bags fixed to the cabin walls.

Food and drinks come in special packs that do not spill. There is an oven to heat food.

Special exercise machines help the astronauts keep fit.

TRAINING
People have to undergo long training programmes to become astronauts. They also must be very fit. These cosmonauts are practising working under weightless conditions using a life-size model of a *Salyut* spacecraft inside a huge water tank.

LIVING IN SPACE
While on board a spacecraft, astronauts consume the same kind of food and drink as they do on Earth. There is usually no bath or shower; astronauts wash with damp pieces of cloth instead. Regular exercise is essential, because living in weightless conditions can weaken bones and muscles.

Find out more
GRAVITY
ROCKETS AND MISSILES
SOVIET UNION, HISTORY OF
SPACE FLIGHT

ASTRONOMY

THERE ARE AMAZING SIGHTS to be seen in the heavens – other worlds different from our own, great glowing clouds of gas where stars are born and immense explosions in which stars end their lives. Astronomers are scientists who study all the objects in the universe, such as planets, moons, comets, stars, and galaxies. Astronomy is an ancient science. The early Arabs and Greeks looked up to the sky and tried to understand the moons, stars, and planets. However, most of these objects were too distant for early astronomers to see in any detail. It was only after the invention of the telescope in the 17th century that people really began to learn about the universe. Today, astronomy makes use of a vast array of equipment to explore space. Astronomers use ground-based telescopes of many kinds, launch spacecraft that visit the other planets in the solar system, and send up satellites to study the universe from high above the Earth's surface.

OBSERVATORY
Astronomers study space from observatories (above) that are often at the top of a mountain where there is a clear view of the sky. This photograph took several hours to make. The stars trace circles because the rotation of the Earth makes them appear to move across the sky.

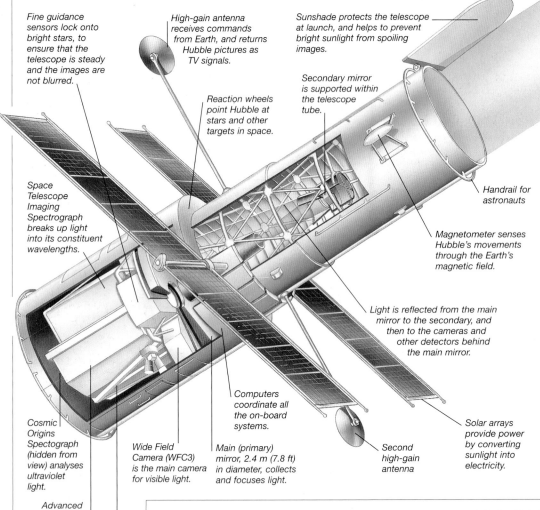

Fine guidance sensors lock onto bright stars, to ensure that the telescope is steady and the images are not blurred.

High-gain antenna receives commands from Earth, and returns Hubble pictures as TV signals.

Sunshade protects the telescope at launch, and helps to prevent bright sunlight from spoiling images.

Reaction wheels point Hubble at stars and other targets in space.

Secondary mirror is supported within the telescope tube.

Space Telescope Imaging Spectrograph breaks up light into its constituent wavelengths.

Handrail for astronauts

Magnetometer senses Hubble's movements through the Earth's magnetic field.

Light is reflected from the main mirror to the secondary, and then to the cameras and other detectors behind the main mirror.

Cosmic Origins Spectograph (hidden from view) analyses ultraviolet light.

Computers coordinate all the on-board systems.

Wide Field Camera (WFC3) is the main camera for visible light.

Main (primary) mirror, 2.4 m (7.8 ft) in diameter, collects and focuses light.

Second high-gain antenna

Solar arrays provide power by converting sunlight into electricity.

Advanced Camera for Surveys is very sensitive, but has a more restricted view than the WF/PC.

Near-Infrared Camera and Multi-Object Spectrometer contains three infrared detectors.

SPACE TELESCOPE
The optical telescope is one of the main tools of an astronomer. Most astronomical optical, infrared, and ultraviolet telescopes focus light from distant stars using a large curved mirror instead of lenses. This is because it is not possible to construct a lens big enough, and even if it were, a lens would produce distorted images. Launched in 1990, the Hubble Space Telescope is an optical telescope that orbits high above the Earth in order to avoid the blurring effect produced by the Earth's atmosphere.

RECEIVING DATA ON EARTH
All signals to and from the Hubble Space Telescope pass through NASA's Goddard Space Flight Center, Maryland, USA. Here, engineers constantly monitor the spacecraft's health. Hubble astronomers work at the Space Telescope Science Institute, and control the telescope's observing schedule. Astronomers from far-off countries use Hubble through remote control. An astronomer (right) receives a Hubble image of the Tarantula nebula (a group of stars).

EXPLORING THE UNIVERSE

Stars and other objects in the universe produce streams of tiny particles and many kinds of waves, such as radio waves. Except for light, these waves and particles are all invisible, but astronomers can study them to provide information about the universe. The atmosphere blocks many of the rays, so detectors are mounted on satellites that orbit above the Earth's atmosphere.

INFRARED RAYS

Objects in space can also send out infrared (heat) rays. Satellites and ground-based telescopes pick up these rays. They can reveal the centres of galaxies, and gas clouds called nebulae (right), where stars are forming.

X-RAYS

Special satellites carry detectors that pick up x-rays. These satellites have discovered black holes, which give out x-rays as they suck in gases from nearby stars. This is an x-ray image of a supernova, which is an exploding star.

GAMMA RAYS

Some satellites detect gamma rays, which are waves of very high energy. Gamma rays come from many objects, including pulsars, which are the remains of exploded stars. This is a gamma ray map of our own galaxy.

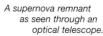

ULTRAVIOLET RAYS

Stars that are much hotter than our Sun give out far more ultraviolet radiation than visible light. This ultraviolet image of a spiral galaxy was taken from a space observatory to help astronomers understand when and where new stars have formed.

VISIBLE LIGHT

Telescopes on the ground and on satellites detect the light rays that come from planets, comets, stars, and galaxies. The Earth's atmosphere distorts light rays, making pictures slightly fuzzy. However, new computer-controlled telescopes are able to reduce this distortion.

RADAR SIGNALS

Astronomers produce radar maps of planets and moons by bouncing radio waves off their surfaces. The radar map of Venus (left) was recorded by the *Pioneer Venus* spacecraft of the United States. The map is colour-coded to represent plains and mountains on the planet's surface.

Radio image of a quasar. A quasar is a kind of powerful galaxy with a very bright centre.

RADIO WAVES

Many bodies produce their own radio waves, which are picked up by the large dishes of radio telescopes. Objects called pulsars, quasars, and radio galaxies were discovered in this way.

A supernova remnant as seen through an optical telescope.

An array of sensitive light detectors pick up flashes of light produced when neutrinos enter the tank.

NEUTRINOS

Tiny particles called neutrinos come from stars. Most neutrinos pass right through the Earth, but special detectors lying deep underground can detect a few of them. By studying neutrinos, astronomers can find out about the Sun and exploding stars.

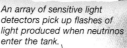

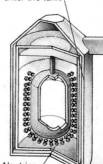

Neutrino detectors consist of large tanks of water, in which flashes of light occur as the neutrinos pass through.

SKYWATCHERS OF THE PAST

In the third century BCE, the Greek scientist Aristarchus suggested that the Earth and planets move around the Sun. The telescope, first used to observe the heavens by Italian scientist Galileo, proved this to be true and led to many other discoveries. In the 1920s, the astronomer Edwin Hubble found that stars exist in huge groups called galaxies and that the universe is expanding in size.

The ancient observatory at Jaipur, India, contains stone structures that astronomers built to measure the positions of the Sun, Moon, planets, and stars.

Find out more

BLACK HOLES
MOON
PLANETS
SATELLITES
SPACE FLIGHT
STARS
SUN
TELESCOPES
UNIVERSE

ATLANTIC OCEAN

THE UNDERWATER LANDSCAPE of the Atlantic is dominated by the mid-Atlantic ridge, the world's longest mountain chain. Some of the ridge's peaks rise above sea level as volcanic islands, such as Iceland and the Azores. The deepest part of the Atlantic, the Puerto Rico Trench, plunges to 9,200 m (30,185 ft) below sea level. The Atlantic Ocean is rich in oil and natural gas. In recent years, offshore oil reserves have been exploited in the Gulf of Mexico, the Niger Delta and the North Sea. Sand, gravel and shell deposits are also mined by the USA and UK for use in the construction industry. The Atlantic is the most productive and heavily utilized fishing ground in the world, providing millions of tonnes a year. The Atlantic Ocean has been crossed by shipping routes for many centuries. It is still heavily used for sea-borne trade, especially the bulk transport of raw materials, such as oil, grain, and iron, to industrial centres.

SUBTROPICAL SCILLIES
The Gulf Stream is a warm ocean current that flows up the east coast of North America, and then across to western Europe, driven by north-easterly trade winds. These winds carry moisture and warmth from the ocean to the land. In England's Scilly Islands, subtropical plants flourish in winter because of the impact of the current.

The Atlantic Ocean is bounded by the Americas in the west, and by Europe and Africa in the east. Along the mid-Atlantic ridge, a long submarine mountain chain, high volcanic peaks pierce the water's surface as islands.

ATLANTIC TOURISM

The volcanic islands which have emerged along the ocean's mid-Atlantic ridge, especially the Canaries, Azores and Madeira, are major tourist attractions. The fertile black soil of the Canaries is ideal for the cultivation of bananas, tomatoes, sugar cane and tobacco. The mild sub-tropical climate attracts winter visitors from Europe.

A trawler braves the rough seas of the Atlantic. Its crew are fishing for lobster.

SUBMARINE ACTIVITY
During the Cold War, from the 1950s to the 1980s, the Atlantic Ocean was patrolled by both the US and Russian navies. Since the 1990s, US and Russian scientists are sharing advances in submarine technology – developed for defence purposes – to survey, map, and analyze the unexplored world beneath the Atlantic.

ATLANTIC FISHING

The Atlantic Ocean, a productive fishing ground for centuries, contains over half the world's total stock of fish. In the North, cod, haddock, mackerel, and lobster are the main catch, while the South Atlantic catch is dominated by hake, tuna, and pilchard. Freezer trawlers, that can catch and process a tonne or more of fish in just an hour, are in danger of over-fishing the Atlantic. Countries claim exclusive rights to zones extending 370 km (200 nautical miles) from their coastlines to conserve fish stocks.

NAVIGATION
Compasses are vital in cross-ocean navigation. The compass needle points to magnetic north, in the Canadian Arctic.

ICELANDIC HEATING
Iceland was formed by volcanic action along a fault line in the Earth's crust, 65 million years ago. Iceland still has over 100 volcanoes, many still active. The vast natural heat reserves beneath Iceland's icy surface, are being harnessed to provide hot water and heating for much of the population.

Plumes of steam rise from a geothermal power station (left). Iceland has the most solfataras (volcanic vents) and hot springs in the world. The intense heat deep underground creates bubbling hot springs and mud pools.

Find out more

OCEANS AND SEAS
SHIPS AND BOATS
SUBMARINES
VOLCANOES
WIND

OVERSEAS TERRITORIES AND DEPENDENCIES

 ASCENSION
Area: 90 sq km
(35 sq miles)
Status: British dependent
territory of St Helena
Claimed: 1673
Population: 1,200
Capital: Jamestown
(St Helena)

 BERMUDA
Area: 53 sq km
(20.5 sq miles)
Status: British Crown colony
Claimed: 1612
Population: 68,000
Capital: Hamilton

BOUVET ISLAND
Area: 49 sq km
(19 sq miles)
Status: Norwegian
dependency
Claimed: 1928
Population: None
Capital: None

 FAEROE ISLANDS
Area: 1,399 sq km
(540 sq miles)
Status: Self-governing
territory of Denmark
Claimed: 1380
Population: 48,000
Capital: Tórshavn

 FALKLAND ISLANDS
Area: 12,173 sq km
(4,699 sq miles)
Status: British
dependent colony
Claimed: 1832
Population: 3,100
Capital: Stanley

 SAINT HELENA
Area: 122 sq km
(47 sq miles)
Status: British
dependent territory
Claimed: 1673
Population: 7,600
Capital: Jamestown

 TRISTAN DA CUNHA
Area: 98 sq km
(38 sq miles)
Status: British dependent
territory of St Helena
Claimed: 1612
Population: 300
Capital: Jamestown
(St Helena)

SOUTH GEORGIA & THE SOUTH SANDWICH ISLANDS

Area: 3,903 sq km
(1,507 sq miles)
Status: British dependent
territory
Claimed: 1775
Population: No permanent
residents
Capital: None

Volcano Mountain Ancient monument Capital city Large city/town Small city/town

ATLANTIC YACHT RACING
Cross-ocean racing began in 1866,
with a race from Connecticut, USA,
to Cowes in the Isle of Wight, which
took 13 days. Single-handed ocean
races became popular in the 1960s.

BERMUDA TRIANGLE
The Bermuda Triangle lies between
Bermuda, Florida, and Puerto Rico.
Many ships, submarines, and
aeroplanes have disappeared
in its waters. In 1872 a deserted
sailing ship, the *Mary Celeste*,
was found drifting across
the Atlantic – its ten
crew members were
never located.

SCALE BAR
0   1000   2000   km
0   1000   2000   miles

INDEPENDENT STATES

 CAPE VERDE
Area: 4,030 sq km
(1,556 sq miles)
Population: 429,000
Capital: Praia

 ICELAND
Area: 103,000 sq km
(39,770 sq miles)
Population: 307,000
Capital: Reykjavík

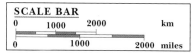

ATMOSPHERE

There is no definite upper limit to the atmosphere. The final layer before outer space is called the exosphere; it contains hardly any air at all.

A layer of very thin air called the thermosphere extends from about 80 to 480 km (50 to 300 miles) above the ground. It contains the ionosphere – layers of electrically charged particles, from which radio waves can be bounced around the world.

The mesosphere extends from 50 to 80 km (30 to 50 miles) above the Earth. If meteors fall into this layer, they burn up, causing shooting stars.

Under the mesosphere lies the stratosphere. It extends from 11 to 50 km (7 to 30 miles) up. The stratosphere is a calm region. Airliners fly here to avoid the winds and weather lower down.

Although it is the narrowest layer, the troposphere contains most of the gas in the atmosphere. It reaches about 11 km (7 miles) above the ground, but this varies around the globe and from season to season. Most weather occurs in the troposphere.

WITHOUT THE ATMOSPHERE, it would be impossible to live on Earth. The atmosphere forms a layer, like a blanket around the Earth, protecting us from dangerous rays from the Sun and from the cold of outer space. It contains the air that we breathe, together with water vapour and tiny pieces of dust. Air contains the gases oxygen, carbon dioxide, and nitrogen, which are necessary for life; water vapour forms the clouds that bring rain. The atmosphere is held by the pull of the Earth's gravity and spreads out to about 2,000 km (1,250 miles) above the Earth. Three quarters of the air in the atmosphere lies beneath 10,700 m (35,000 ft) because the air gets thinner higher up. The air at the top of Mount Everest is only one third as thick as it is at sea level. That is why mountain climbers carry an air supply and why high-flying aircraft are sealed and have air pumped into them.

LAYERS OF THE ATMOSPHERE

The Earth's atmosphere is divided into several layers. The main layers, from the bottom upwards, are called the troposphere, the stratosphere, the mesosphere, the thermosphere, and the exosphere.

OZONE LAYER

Within the stratosphere, there is a thin layer of the gas ozone. Ozone is a form of oxygen that absorbs ultraviolet rays from the sun. Without the ozone layer, these rays would reach the ground and kill all living creatures. Pollution and the use of certain chemicals are destroying the ozone layer.

Compared to the size of the Earth, the atmosphere forms a very narrow band – approximately equivalent to the skin around an orange.

OTHER ATMOSPHERES

Other planets' atmospheres are very different from Earth's. Neptune (above) is surrounded by a thick layer of hydrogen and helium. A small amount of methane gas in this atmosphere makes Neptune look blue.

SKY AND SUNSET

When light travels through the atmosphere, it hits gas molecules and tiny particles such as pollen and dust. This causes the light to scatter, or bounce off, in all directions. Some colours are scattered more than others.

BLUE SKY
The atmosphere scatters mainly blue light; this is why the sky looks blue. The other colours of light are scattered much less than blue so that they come to Earth directly. This causes the area of sky around the Sun to look yellow.

SUNSET AND SUNRISE
At sunset and sunrise, when the Sun is below the horizon, the light travels through much more of the atmosphere before we see it. The blue light is scattered so much that it is absorbed, or soaked up, by the atmosphere. Only red light reaches us, so the sky looks red.

Find out more
CLIMATES
OXYGEN
PLANETS
SUN
WEATHER

ATOMS AND MOLECULES

LOOK AROUND YOU. There are countless millions of different substances, from metals and plastics to people and plants. All of these are made from about 100 different kinds of "building blocks" joined together in different ways. These building blocks are tiny particles called atoms. Atoms are so small that even the tiniest speck of dust contains more than a million billion atoms. Some substances, such as iron, are made of just one kind of atom; other substances, such as water, contain molecules – atoms joined together in groups. Such molecules may be very simple or very complex. Each water molecule contains two hydrogen atoms and one oxygen atom; plastics are made of molecules which often contain millions of atoms. An atom itelf is made up of a dense centre called a nucleus. Particles that carry electricity, called electrons, move around the nucleus. Scientists have discovered how to split the nucleus, releasing enormous energy which is used in nuclear power stations and nuclear bombs.

A drop of water contains about 1,000 million billion molecules.

A molecule of water contains three atoms – two hydrogen atoms and one oxygen atom.

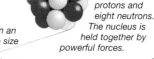

Protons and neutrons are made up of quarks.

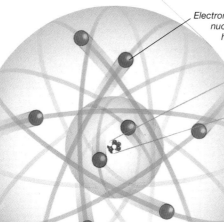

Electrons whiz around the nucleus. An atom of oxygen has eight electrons.

There is a lot of empty space in an atom. If the nucleus were the size of a tennis ball, the nearest electron would be 1 km (about half a mile) away.

The nucleus of an oxygen atom has eight protons and eight neutrons. The nucleus is held together by powerful forces.

PROTONS AND NEUTRONS

The nucleus of an atom contains particles called protons and neutrons. These contain even smaller particles called quarks. Protons carry electricity. However, they carry a different kind of electricity from electrons. They have a "positive charge", whereas electrons have a "negative charge". Neutrons have no electric charge.

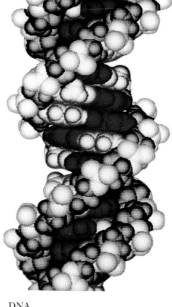

DNA
All plants and animals contain molecules of DNA (deoxyribonucleic acid). DNA carries the blueprint for life: coded information in DNA molecules determines the characteristics of each living thing and its offspring. A DNA molecule consists of millions of atoms arranged in a twisted spiral shape.

DISCOVERING THE ATOM

About 2,400 years ago, the Greek philosopher Democritus believed that everything was made up of tiny particles. It was not until 1808 that English scientist John Dalton proved that atoms exist. Around 1909, New Zealand scientist Ernest Rutherford (below) discovered the nucleus.

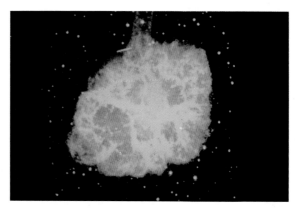

IMMORTAL ATOMS

The particles that make up atoms never disappear but are constantly journeying through the universe as part of different substances. All these particles originated with the formation of the universe around 13,700 million years ago. The atoms that make everything on Earth were formed from these particles in stars, which then exploded like the crab nebula (above).

Find out more
CHEMISTRY
OXYGEN
PHYSICS
PLASTICS
REPRODUCTION

AUSTRALIA

LOCATED BETWEEN THE INDIAN AND PACIFIC OCEANS, Australia is a continent, and the sixth largest country in the world. It is a land of varied landscapes, including tropical rainforests, vast deserts, snow-capped mountains, rolling tracts of pastoral land, and magnificent beaches. The country boasts a great number of natural features, the most famous of which are the Great Barrier Reef and Uluru (Ayers Rock). Australians have an outdoor lifestyle and enjoy a high standard of living. Almost 90 per cent of the country's 21.2 million people live in the fertile strip of land on the east and southeast coast. Many of them live in Melbourne and Sydney, Australia's two largest cities, and in the nation's capital, Canberra. Today few people live in the dry Australian interior known as the Outback. The original inhabitants of Australia, the Aborigines, learned to survive in the harsh conditions there. However, only a small number of the 517,000 Aboriginal population live a traditional life in the Outback today. Other Australians are descendants of settlers from Britain, continental Europe and Southeast Asia.

Australia lies southeast of Asia, with the Pacific Ocean to the east and the Indian Ocean to the west. It is the only country that is also a continent. Together with several nearby islands, Australia covers a total area of 7.61 million sq km (2.94 million sq miles).

SURFING

Surfing is a favourite Australian sport. Surfing carnivals are held regularly in many towns. Polynesian people invented the sport hundreds of years ago; recently it has expanded to include windsurfing, trick surfing, and long-distance surfing. Surfers often travel vast distances to reach a beach with the best waves of the day.

At a surfing carnival lifeguards give demonstrations of lifesaving. Surfing competitions are hotly contested and often draw many spectators.

During the celebrations of Australia's 200th anniversary, ocean-going sailing ships gathered in Sydney's famous harbour.

BEACH CULTURE

The majority of Australians live in towns and cities along the coast. Therefore the beach is the most popular venue for leisure pursuits. Australia's climate is ideal for beach activities such as surfing, swimming, sailing and beach volleyball. Mild winter temperatures mean that these sports can be enjoyed all year round.

SYDNEY

Sydney is the oldest and largest city in Australia. Sydney was founded in 1788 as a British prison colony with about 1,000 prisoners and their guards; today it is home to more than 4 million people. The city stands around Port Jackson, a huge natural bay spanned by Sydney Harbour Bridge. Sydney is a busy industrial centre and tourist resort.

FILMMAKING

The Australian film industry produces a number of important films each year. Some, such as *Picnic at Hanging Rock* (1975), which tells of the mysterious disappearance of a group of Australian schoolgirls, have received international acclaim.

Australia's currency is the Australian dollar. On one side the coins feature a portrait of the Queen of England, who is the head of state.

TASMANIA

The island of Tasmania lies off the southeast coast of Australia and is a state in itself, with a population of nearly half a million. The island has a cooler, damper climate than the rest of the country and is famous for its fruit, vegetables, and sheep. Tin, silver, and other products are mined. Much of western Tasmania is unpopulated and covered in dense forest where native wildlife, such as the Tasmanian devil, below, survive in large numbers.

GREAT DIVIDING RANGE

Running along the eastern coast of the continent from Cape York to Ballarat is a 3,700 km (2,300 mile) mountain chain called the Great Dividing Range. The tallest mountain is Kosciuszko, at 2,228 m (7,310 ft). Other peaks are much lower. The mountains divide the fertile coastal plains from the dry interior. The steep hills were once a major barrier to travel; even today only a few roads and railways cross from east to west.

The Three Sisters formation in New South Wales belongs to the Great Dividing Range.

Outback ranchers ride motorbikes or horses to round up cattle and sheep.

OUTBACK

Very few people live in Australia's interior, called the Outback. However, sheep and cattle are farmed on the dry land. Some ranches, called stations, cover hundreds of square kilometres. Because of the great distances, Outback Australians live isolated lives and communicate by radio.

STRIP MINING

Australia has huge mineral wealth, and mining is an important industry. The country produces one third of the world's uranium, which is essential for nuclear power. In recent years iron ore has been excavated in large strip mines where giant digging machines remove entire hills.

Ancient rock and bark paintings show that Aboriginal culture flourished nearly 40,000 years before European settlers arrived.

ULURU (AYERS ROCK)

One of the most impressive natural sights in Australia is Uluru (formerly known as Ayers Rock). This huge mass of sandstone stands in the middle of a wide, flat desert and is 335 m (1,142 ft) high. Although it lies hundreds of kilometres from the nearest town, Uluru is a major tourist attraction with its own hotel. The rock is particularly beautiful at sunset, when it seems to change colour.

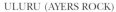

PERTH

Founded in 1829, Perth (below) is the state capital of Western Australia and its financial and commercial heart. Most Australian people live in cities, and the population of Perth reflects the European ancestry of a large percentage of today's Australians.

CANBERRA

Canberra, the capital city of Australia, is situated in the Australian Capital Territory (A.C.T.), an area of 2,360 sq km (911 sq miles) completely surrounded by the state of New South Wales. The capital was designed as a city of parks and gardens by American landscape architect, Walter Burley Griffin. Construction of the city began in 1913. Canberra is a political and educational centre rather than a commercial or industrial town.

Hay Street mall (left) is a pedestrian shopping precinct located in Perth's central business district.

ADELAIDE

Adelaide (right) is the capital and chief port of South Australia. A well-planned city, it was designed in a grid pattern by Colonel William Light, the first surveyor-general of South Australia. The city is bordered by 6.9 sq km (2.7 sq miles) of parkland, and was named after Queen Adelaide, wife of King William IV of England.

MELBOURNE

The capital city of Victoria and the second largest city in Australia, Melbourne (below) displays a dramatic mixture of old and new. Melbourne was founded in 1835 by an Australian farmer, John Batman. Nearly 20 years later, gold was discovered in Victoria and Melbourne's population climbed sharply. Today, Melbourne is a leading seaport, and the commercial and industrial centre of Victoria.

BRISBANE

The state capital of Queensland and its largest city, Brisbane (right) is a bustling seaport lying above the mouth of the Brisbane river at Moreton Bay. In this way, it is similar to Australia's other state capitals, all of which were founded near rivers close to ocean harbours. Like other state capitals, Brisbane too is the commercial centre of its state, with its main business district situated near the waterfront.

St Paul's Cathedral stands proudly amid modern architecture in Melbourne. The building was designed by William Butterfield in the 1880s in a Gothic style.

Find out more

ABORIGINAL AUSTRALIANS
ARCHITECTURE
AUSTRALIA, HISTORY OF
CITIES
FARMING

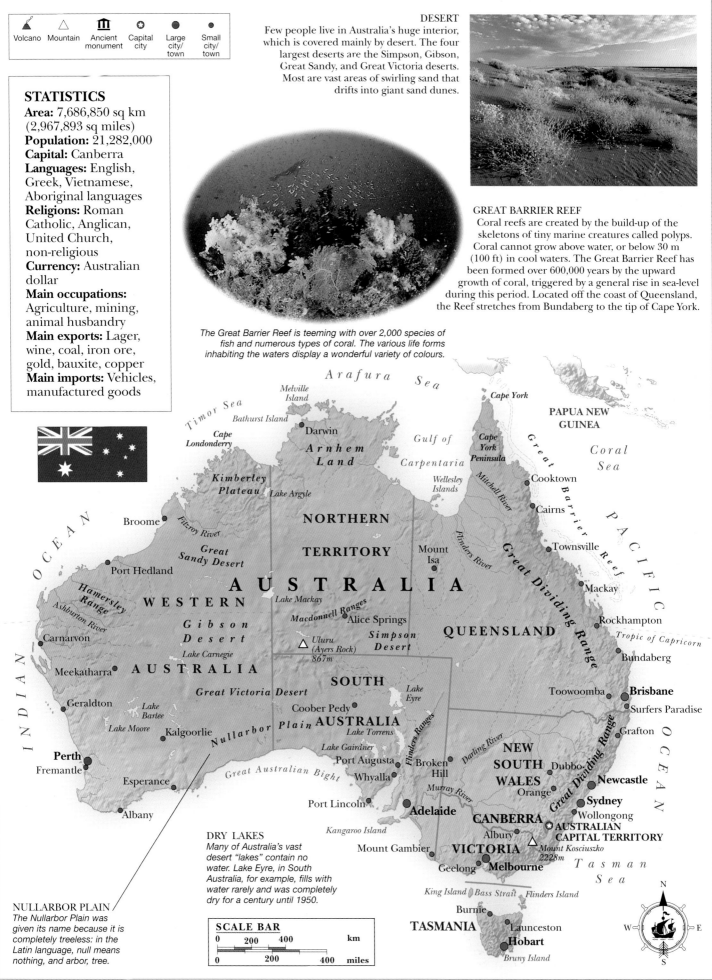

| Volcano | Mountain | Ancient monument | Capital city | Large city/town | Small city/town |

STATISTICS
Area: 7,686,850 sq km (2,967,893 sq miles)
Population: 21,282,000
Capital: Canberra
Languages: English, Greek, Vietnamese, Aboriginal languages
Religions: Roman Catholic, Anglican, United Church, non-religious
Currency: Australian dollar
Main occupations: Agriculture, mining, animal husbandry
Main exports: Lager, wine, coal, iron ore, gold, bauxite, copper
Main imports: Vehicles, manufactured goods

DESERT
Few people live in Australia's huge interior, which is covered mainly by desert. The four largest deserts are the Simpson, Gibson, Great Sandy, and Great Victoria deserts. Most are vast areas of swirling sand that drifts into giant sand dunes.

GREAT BARRIER REEF
Coral reefs are created by the build-up of the skeletons of tiny marine creatures called polyps. Coral cannot grow above water, or below 30 m (100 ft) in cool waters. The Great Barrier Reef has been formed over 600,000 years by the upward growth of coral, triggered by a general rise in sea-level during this period. Located off the coast of Queensland, the Reef stretches from Bundaberg to the tip of Cape York.

The Great Barrier Reef is teeming with over 2,000 species of fish and numerous types of coral. The various life forms inhabiting the waters display a wonderful variety of colours.

NULLARBOR PLAIN
The Nullarbor Plain was given its name because it is completely treeless: in the Latin language, null means nothing, and arbor, tree.

DRY LAKES
Many of Australia's vast desert "lakes" contain no water. Lake Eyre, in South Australia, for example, fills with water rarely and was completely dry for a century until 1950.

SCALE BAR

| 0 | 200 | 400 | km |
| 0 | 200 | 400 | miles |

HISTORY OF
AUSTRALIA

c. 40,000 BCE First Aborigines arrive in Australia from Asia.

1770 Captain Cook sails into Botany Bay and claims Australia for Britain.

1788 British convicts arrive.

1901 Australia becomes an independent dominion within the British Empire.

1915 Australian troops fight at Gallipoli in World War I.

1945-65 Australia pays fares for poor Europeans to settle in Australia.

AS RECENTLY AS 1600, the only people who knew about Australia were the Aboriginal peoples who had lived there for more than 40,000 years. The rest of the world had no idea that the continent existed. In 1606, the Dutch explorer William Jansz landed in northern Australia. Although he did not know it, he was the first European to see the country. Further exploration of the coastline by Dutch and British explorers revealed that Australia was an island. In 1770, the British captain James Cook claimed the east coast of Australia for Britain and named it New South Wales. The British sent convicts to their new colony, forming the basis of Sydney, today the country's largest city. Throughout the 19th century, the population of Australia grew as more convicts arrived, followed by free immigrants. For many of them life was tough, but the British colony grew richer when gold was discovered in 1851. Farming also became established. In 1901, Australia became an independent commonwealth, although it remained close to Britain for many years and Australian troops fought in both world wars on the side of Britain. More recently, Australia has branched away from Britain and set up links with other countries.

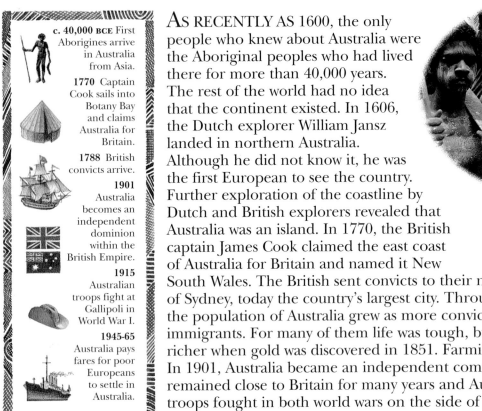

ABORIGINES
The first Aboriginal peoples probably arrived in Australia from the islands of Southeast Asia about 40,000 years ago. In 1770, there were about 300,000 Aborigines in Australia.

Convict ships in the bay

Chopping wood to make timber huts

The convicts carried supplies onto the shore.

At first, the convicts (prisoners) were miserable and hungry.

The first British settlement in Australia was at Port Jackson in Sydney Harbour, next to the location of the present-day Sydney Opera House.

BOTANY BAY
In 1770, the English explorer James Cook dropped anchor in Botany Bay, south of what is now the city of Sydney. In 1788, the first 750 British settlers arrived in Australia. These people were convicts – guarded by 250 soldiers – who had been transported abroad to relieve the overcrowded British prisons. They lived in a prison camp set up on the shores of Sydney Harbour. The colonists came close to starvation, but gradually their lives improved. The tents they lived in were replaced by brick and timber huts, and eventually the colony began to prosper. In 1868, the transportation of convicts ended, leaving more than 160,000 convicts living in Australia.

EXPLORATION

The first explorers of Australia mapped out the coastline but left the interior largely untouched. In 1606, the Dutch navigator William Jansz briefly visited northeastern Australia. Between 1829 and 1830, the English explorer Charles Sturt explored the rivers in the south but failed to find the inland sea that many people assumed existed in the centre of Australia. Between 1839 and 1840, Edward Eyre, from England, discovered the vast, dry salt lakes in South Australia before walking along its southern coast. In 1860 and 1861, the Irishman Robert O'Hara Burke and Englishman William Wills became the first people to cross Australia from south to north. In 1862 John McDouall Stuart succeeded in crossing the continent from South Australia and returning alive.

Burke and Wills
Sturt
Eyre
Cook
Jansz

Alice Springs
Perth
Brisbane
Sydney
Adelaide
Melbourne

Map showing the routes of the different explorers of Australia

BURKE AND WILLS

In 1860 and 1861, Burke and Wills succeeded in crossing Australia from south to north. However, they both died of starvation on the return journey south.

GOLD RUSH

Gold was discovered in 1851 in New South Wales and Victoria. Thousands of prospectors rushed from all over the world, including China, to make their fortunes in Australia. The national population rose from 400,000 in 1850 to 1,100,000 by 1860. Conditions were tough for the gold miners, and in 1854 a group of miners at Eureka Stockade at Ballarat, near Melbourne, refused to pay the licence fee required to mine for gold. The government sent in troops; 24 miners and six soldiers were killed in the battle that followed.

The Aborigines were amazed to see the crowds of white people landing in their territory.

OVERCOMING ABORIGINES

During the 19th century, the European settlers disrupted the Aboriginal way of life. Many Aboriginal languages and customs died out as their land was taken. Children were taken away from their parents to be educated in the European way. As a result, the Aborigine population fell from 300,000 in 1770 to about 60,000 by 1900.

IMMIGRATION

In 1880, there were only two million people on the vast Australian continent. A century later, almost 15 million people lived there. Most had come to Australia from Britain, Italy, and Greece. In a deliberate attempt to boost the population after 1945, the Australian government offered to pay part of the passage for poor Europeans. About two million people took advantage of the scheme, which ended in 1965, with one million coming from Britain alone. Asians and other non-white peoples were denied entry until the 1960s. Many children travelled on their own. The group of immigrants (left) are on their way to a farm school in Western Australia from Waterloo Station, London, England.

URANIUM MINING

Australia is rich in minerals, like uranium, the raw material used to fuel nuclear power stations and produce nuclear bombs. Although uranium mining increased dramatically during the 1970s, many Australians opposed it because of the dangers of radiation from uranium. In addition, many of the uranium deposits lie within Aboriginal tribal lands. Protests have therefore regularly occurred to prevent the exploitation of this dangerous mineral.

Find out more

ABORIGINAL AUSTRALIANS
AUSTRALIA
COOK, JAMES
EMIGRATION AND IMMIGRATION
NUCLEAR ENERGY

AUSTRIA

| Volcano | Mountain | Ancient monument | Capital city | Large city/ town | Small city/ town |

Austria is a landlocked country, located at the heart of Europe. To the west it is Alpine. The northeast is the fertile valley of the Danube.

AUSTRIA OCCUPIES a strategic position at the heart of Europe. Both the River Danube and the Alpine passes in the west have been vital trade routes for many centuries, linking south and east Europe with the north and west. Until 1918, Austria was part of the Habsburg Empire, which dominated much of Central Europe. Today, it is a wealthy, industrialized economy. In the northeast, the fertile plains that surround the Danube provide rich farming country, and potatoes, beet and cereals are grown there. In the west, the magnificent mountain scenery of the Alps attracts millions of visitors. Austria is rich in mineral resources, especially iron. It uses hydroelectric power, generated by fast mountain streams, to provide power for its steel and manufacturing industries.

STATISTICS
Area: 83,850 sq km (32,375 sq miles)
Population: 8,210,000
Capital: Vienna
Languages: German, Croat, Slovene
Religions: Roman Catholic, Protestant, Muslim, Jewish
Currency: Euro

AUSTRIAN COFFEE
Coffee was introduced to Vienna by the Turks in the 17th century. Coffee, accompanied by pastries or chocolate cakes, is a famous Viennese speciality.

MOZART
The composer Wolfgang Amadeus Mozart (1756-91) was born in Salzburg and spent his childhood there. His remarkable early talent and the continuing popularity of his music draw many visitors to the city. This miniature comes from the Mozart Museum in Salzburg.

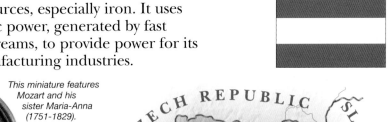

This miniature features Mozart and his sister Maria-Anna (1751-1829).

The Schönbrunn Palace, the summer residence of the Habsburgs

SCALE BAR
0   50   100   km
0   50   100 miles

VIENNA
The Habsburg family ruled Austria for several centuries, and Vienna was the capital of their empire. Vienna stands on the River Danube, and is a gateway between East and West Europe. The city is most famous for its magnificent 17th-century architecture. Today, it is a major centre of trade and industry.

THE TIROL
The Alpine district of western Austria is known as the Tirol. The region has a very strong identity and folk culture, and historically it was an important link between Germany and Italy. Salt, copper mining, and dairy farming are important to the economy of the Tirol. Tourists are drawn by its spectacular beauty, especially in winter when skiing is a major attraction.

Find out more
COMPOSERS
EUROPE
EUROPE, HISTORY OF

AZTECS

MORE THAN SEVEN HUNDRED YEARS AGO a civilization was born in what is now Mexico. The Aztecs, founders of this civilization, were the last native American rulers of Mexico. They were a wandering tribe who arrived in the Mexican valley during the 13th century. The Olmecs and Toltecs had already established civilizations in this area, and influenced the Aztecs. Over the next 200 years the Aztecs set up a mighty empire of some 12 million people. The Aztecs believed that the world would come to an end unless they sacrificed people to their sun god, Huitzilopochtli. They built pyramids and temples where they sacrificed prisoners from the cities they had conquered. In 1519 Spanish conquistadors (adventurers) arrived in Mexico and defeated the Aztecs. Moctezuma II, last of the Aztec emperors, was killed by his own people, and the Aztec empire collapsed.

Victim being sacrificed on top of the temple.

Preaching priest

Aztec pyramid with temple at top

The bodies of sacrificed victims were thrown to the ground.

Causeway

Temple precinct at Tenochtitlán

TENOCHTITLÁN

The Aztec capital, called Tenochtitlán, was a "floating city", built in Lake Texcoco, on one natural and many artificial islands. To reach the mainland, the Aztecs built causeways (raised roads) and canals between the islands. Today Mexico City stands on the site.

HUMAN SACRIFICES
Aztec priests used knives with stone blades to kill up to 1,000 people each week, offering the hearts to their sun god, Huitzilopochtli.

AZTEC ARTISTS
The Aztecs made beautiful jewellery using gold, turquoise, pearls, shells, and feathers. They also used other valuable stones, such as obsidian and jade.

Ceremonial jade mask

TRIBUTES
The Aztecs became very rich by collecting tributes (payments) from conquered tribes. Cloth, maize (a type of corn), pottery, and luxury goods were brought to Tenochtitlán from the conquered cities by porters, and exchanged in four huge markets. Officials made lists of all the tributes in picture writing. The Aztecs declared war on any tribe that refused to pay tribute.

Find out more
CONQUISTADORS
SOUTH AMERICA
SOUTH AMERICA, HISTORY OF

BABYLONIANS

ONE OF THE FIRST CIVILIZATIONS developed about 6,000 years ago in the Middle East, between the Tigris and Euphrates rivers. This region was known as Mesopotamia, meaning "land between rivers". The land was fertile, and farming methods were highly refined. The people were among the first to develop a system of writing, use the wheel, and build cities. One of these cities was Babylon, founded before 2500 BCE. It became the capital city of Babylonia (now part of Iraq). Babylon was an important trading centre. It was also a religious centre and the site of many splendid temples. Its people were strong and prosperous under the great king Hammurabi, who united the different areas into one empire. Babylon became even more magnificent later, under King Nebuchadnezzar II. In 538 BCE, the Persian king Cyrus the Great conquered Babylon; Alexander the Great conquered it again in 331 BCE. The city was then ruled by the Parthians and the Persian Sassanid dynasty until the 7th century CE, but by then had lost its importance and fallen into ruins.

CYLINDER SEAL
The Babylonians wrote using cylinder seals. These seals were often made of semiprecious stone and were very delicately carved. To sign or stamp a document, a person rolled a cylinder seal over damp clay. This seal shows clearly the god Shamash, the goddess Ishtar (with wings), and the god, Ea.

Ziggurat

Ishtar Gate was named after the goddess Ishtar. The gate has been reconstructed and today it stands in the Berlin Museum, Germany.

BABYLONIAN EMPIRE
Babylon was one of several important cities in Mesopotamia. For about 2,000 years, its fortunes rose and fell. At its height, under King Hammurabi, and later King Nebuchadnezzar II, the Babylonian empire controlled the entire southern area of Mesopotamia.

BABYLON
The city of Babylon was rebuilt many times before its final destruction. It reached the height of its glory in about 600 BCE. It was an impressive city, with massive walls and elaborate religious buildings, including a pyramid-like ziggurat. Babylon also had a fabulous Hanging Garden – one of the Seven Wonders of the Ancient World.

RUINS OF BABYLON
About 90 km (55 miles) south of Baghdad, Iraq, lie the ruins of ancient Babylon. Although the ruins are sparse, it is still possible to see where the palaces and ziggurat once stood. During the 19th century, archeologists excavated the site. Today, various parts of the ancient city wall have been rebuilt, as shown above.

HAMMURABI
Under King Hammurabi (1792-1750 BCE), Babylon gained control of a large part of Mesopotamia. Hammurabi is famous for the laws he introduced, which are carved on a stela, or pillar, of stone. The stone shows a portrait of Hammurabi standing before Shamash, the god of justice. Beneath this are the laws of Babylon, carved in cuneiform (wedge-shaped) writing. They deal with all aspects of life and show that Babylon was a sophisticated civilization.

NEBUCHADNEZZAR
Nebuchadnezzar II (605-562 BCE) was one of the most famous kings of Babylonia. Among other conquests, he captured Jerusalem and forced thousands of its people into exile in Babylonian territory. This story is told in the Bible, in the Book of Daniel. Nebuchadnezzar is said to have gone mad at the end of his reign, as shown in this picture of Nebuchadnezzar by the English artist William Blake (1757-1827).

Find out more
ALPHABETS
ASSYRIANS
PHOENICIANS
WONDERS
of the ancient world

BALTIC STATES
AND BELARUS

THE THREE BALTIC STATES – Lithuania, Latvia, and Estonia – were once Soviet republics. They were the first republics to declare their independence from the Soviet Union in 1991. Traditionally all three countries, with their fertile land and high rainfall, depended on agriculture and rearing dairy cattle. The Soviets, however, encouraged the growth of heavy industry and manufacturing, turning these small republics into industrial nations. When the republics became independent, they had to deal with price rises, food shortages, and pollution. Despite these problems they are beginning to forge links with east and west Europe, and new industries are being developed. Land-locked Belarus was also part of the Soviet Union. Its capital, Minsk, was founded in about 1060. Most of its historic buildings were destroyed during World War II.

The Baltic Republics occupy a small stretch of Baltic coast, flanked to the east by Russia, and to the west by Poland and the Russian enclave of Kaliningrad. Belarus lies along the southern border. The Baltic Sea provides an outlet to the North Sea.

ESTONIAN NATIONALITY
During the Soviet era, many Russians were settled in the Baltic States. This led to tensions with the Baltic peoples, who tried hard to maintain their own national identity. In Estonia, two-thirds of the population is Estonian. Their language is Finno-Ugric, related to both Finnish and Hungarian.

 BELARUS
Area: 207,600 sq km (80,154 sq miles)
Population: 9,649,000
Capital: Minsk
Languages: Belorussian, Russian

ESTONIA
Area: 45,125 sq km (17,423 sq miles)
Population: 1,300,000
Capital: Tallinn
Languages: Estonian, Russian

LATVIA
Area: 64,589 sq km (24,938 sq miles)
Population: 2,232,000
Capital: Riga
Languages: Latvian, Russian

LITHUANIA
Area: 65,200 sq km (25,174 sq miles)
Population: 3,555,000
Capital: Vilnius
Languages: Lithuanian, Russian

RIGA
The capital of Latvia lies on the west of the Dvina River, 15 km (9 miles) upstream from the Baltic Sea. The city was founded in 1201, and became an important Baltic trading centre. Surviving medieval buildings, such as the castle and cathedral, reflect its prosperity. However, much of this historic legacy was destroyed during the German occupation in World War II (1941-44). It is now a major industrial centre and port, although it is ice-bound between December and April.

THE BALTIC COAST
All the Baltic states face the Baltic Sea. In winter, the Baltic Sea is frozen, but in summer Baltic resorts attract tourists. Industrial pollution is damaging this coastline.

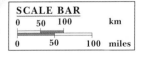

SCALE BAR
0 50 100 km
0 50 100 miles

Find out more
EUROPE, HISTORY OF
OCEANS AND SEAS
SOVIET UNION, HISTORY OF

Volcano | Mountain | Ancient monument | Capital city | Large city/town | Small city/town

BARBARIANS

BY THE FOURTH CENTURY CE, the once great Roman Empire was in decline. A great threat came from tribal groups living outside the boundaries of the empire. The Romans had mixed feelings about these tribes. They thought they were uncivilized because they did not live in cities, but often recruited their warriors to serve in the Roman army. Today we often call these tribes barbarians. But in fact they were superb metalworkers, farmers, and great warriors, with well-organized laws and customs. Around 370 CE hordes of one particular tribe, the Huns, moved from central Asia. Other tribes were pushed westwards and some of those nearest the empire asked the Romans for shelter. But in 406 hordes of Alans, Vandals, and Sueves swept into Gaul (modern France); in 410 the Goths, under Alaric, attacked and captured Rome, and even more barbarians entered the Roman Empire. In 452 the Huns, led by Attila, attacked northern Italy. Many areas of the empire were now conquered by barbarian tribes, who set up their own kingdoms.

ATTILA THE HUN
The nomadic Huns were jointly ruled by Attila (434-453) and his brother Bleda. In 452, after killing Bleda, Attila invaded Italy.

SACK OF ROME
In 410 Alaric, king of the Visigoths, captured and looted the great city of Rome which had been unconquered for 800 years. The sacking of Rome shocked the civilized world, but the empire itself did not collapse until 476.

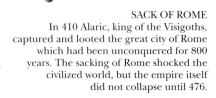

BARBARIAN INVASIONS
By 500 CE, barbarian tribes had overrun the Western Roman Empire. They divided their territory into separate kingdoms. With time, the invaders adopted some Roman ways, laws, and some Latin words. This map shows the routes of the barbarian invasions in the fifth century.

CRAFTWORK

Each barbarian tribe had its own culture, laws, and customs. Even before the year 500 many barbarians had lived inside the Roman Empire, and many eventually became Christians. The barbarians were not just warriors. Their metalwork and jewellery were particularly beautiful.

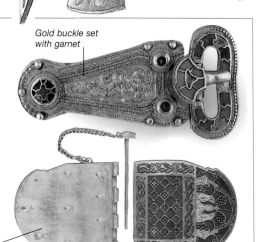

Gold buckle set with garnet

This gold and enamelled fibula was used to fasten a barbarian man's cloak.

> ### *Find out more*
> CHARLEMAGNE
> EUROPE, HISTORY OF
> ROMAN EMPIRE
> VIKINGS

BATS

WHEN MOST OTHER CREATURES return to their homes for the night, bats take to the air. Bats are the only mammals capable of flight. They are night-time creatures with leather-like wings that enable them to swoop and glide through the darkness catching moths and other airborne insects. Although most bats are insectivorous (insect eaters), some feed on fruit, nectar, pollen, fish, small mammals, and reptiles. Bats usually give birth to one or two young each year. The young are left in a nursery roost, clustered together for warmth, while the mothers fly off to feed. There are about 1,100 different kinds of bats, including red bats, brown bats, and dog-faced bats. They make up one quarter of all mammal species, yet few people have ever seen one. Today, many kinds of bats are becoming rare as their roosts are destroyed and their feeding areas are taken over for farming and building. In Britain, all bats and their roosts are protected by law.

VAMPIRE BAT
The vampire bat of South America bites mammals and birds to feed on their blood, but it does not usually attack humans.

Bats sleep upside down in a nesting place called a roost.

Bat's wings are supported during flight by long, thin arm and finger bones. When resting, the bat hangs in its roost by its clawed back feet.

FISHING BAT
The South American fishing bat has long legs and sharp claws for catching fish. It uses echolocation to detect ripples on the water's surface, then flies low with its feet dangling in the water. When the bat hooks a fish, its legs pull the slippery prey up to its mouth, where sharp teeth hold the fish securely.

HORSESHOE BAT
There are 77 different kinds of horseshoe bats. Their name comes from the fleshy, curved flaps on their noses, which help with echolocation. The greater European horseshoe bat has a wingspan of more than 30 cm (12 in).

At the top of each wing is a claw which the bat uses to cling onto rocks as it clambers about in the caves where it lives.

FRUIT BAT
The fruit bat is the largest bat; some measure almost 2 m (7 ft) from one wing tip to the other. It is also called the flying fox because it has a fox-like face. Fruit bats roost in trees or caves and fly out at dawn and dusk to feed on fruit, flowers, and leaves. Fruit bats are found in Africa, southern Asia, and Australia. In areas where they live in large numbers, fruit bats cause great damage by eating farm crops.

ECHOLOCATION
Bats find their way in the dark by making squeaks and clicks, which are so high-pitched that most humans cannot hear them. This is called echolocation. The sounds made by the bat bounce off a nearby object such as a tree or a moth. The bat can detect the returning echoes with its large, forward-pointing ears, and in a split second it has worked out the size, distance, and direction of the object.

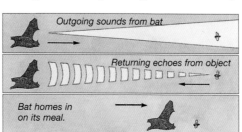

Outgoing sounds from bat

Returning echoes from object

Bat homes in on its meal.

Find out more
ANIMALS
ANIMAL SENSES
FLIGHT, ANIMAL
MAMMALS
WHALES AND DOLPHINS

BEARS AND PANDAS

Small ears
Large head
Small eyes with poor eyesight
Short muzzle
Keen sense of smell

Huge, powerful paws

ALTHOUGH BEARS are often portrayed as cuddly, they are among the most dangerous of all creatures. There are seven kinds of bears. The largest is the polar bear. It stands nearly 3 m (10 ft) tall and weighs more than half a tonne. The smallest bear is the sun bear from Southeast Asia, which measures about 1.2 m (4 ft) from head to tail. Other bears include the grizzly and the sloth bear. Bears are heavily built mammals, which eat both flesh and plants. Giant pandas, which eat mostly bamboo shoots, are also bears. The giant panda is a large black and white creature that weighs about 135 kg (300 lb). Today they are very rare. The red panda, which is much smaller, is more closely related to the raccoon. Bears and the giant panda have poor eyesight, so they find their food mainly by smell.

DANCING BEAR
Bears have sometimes been taken from their natural habitats and trained to entertain people, but this cruel practice is now banned in most countries.

BLACK BEAR

There are two kinds of black bear – one from North America and the other from Southeast Asia. Not all American black bears are completely black. Some are dark brown or reddish brown. Black bears are skilful tree climbers and run fast – up to 40 km/h (25 mph). American black bears inhabit the forests of North America, and many live in national parks.

PAWS
A bear's paws are large, broad, and powerful, with tough, thick claws. Pandas have unusual paws. A modified wristbone acts like a thumb, allowing the panda to grasp bamboo shoots (above).

GIANT PANDA

The giant panda is also called the panda bear. Giant pandas live in central and western China and eat mostly bamboo shoots. There are only a few hundred giant pandas left in the wild, and they have become a worldwide symbol of conservation.

GRIZZLY BEAR

The huge grizzly bear has no enemies apart from humans. Grizzly bears live in North America, Europe, and Asia. The grizzly is also called the brown bear. A female grizzly bear gives birth to two or three cubs in a winter den. Grizzly bears eat almost anything, including spring shoots, autumn fruits, animal flesh, and honey taken from bees' nests.

RACCOON
There are 14 kinds of raccoon; all are found in the Americas. They are fast, agile creatures related to bears. Raccoons are active mainly at night, when they feed on fish, nuts, rubbish dumps, farm crops, and livestock.

In autumn, grizzly bears scoop up salmon that have swum upriver to spawn (lay their eggs).

Find out more
ANIMALS
ANIMAL SENSES
CONSERVATION
and endangered species
MAMMALS
POLAR WILDLIFE

BEES AND WASPS

Beekeepers used to destroy the hive and the bees to harvest honey from straw hives, or skeps.

HONEYBEES, BUMBLEBEES, and common wasps are a familiar sight to many of us, but there are thousands more, such as carpenter bees, stingless bees, mud wasps, and potter wasps. Bees and wasps first existed millions of years ago and live in almost every part of the world. These insects fly well, and the movement of their powerful wings makes the buzzing sound. Many bees and wasps are solitary, living in a nest in the ground or in a hollow plant stem. Some, such as bumblebees and honeybees, live in large groups, or colonies, in trees, roofs, and rock crevices. In a bumblebee colony the queen resembles her workers and shares many of their jobs. In a honeybee colony, however, the queen does not share these jobs and spends most of her life laying eggs. A honeybee colony may contain 50,000 bees.

Honey is a food that bees produce and store inside the hive. The bees feed on honey through winter.

Queen honeybee lays 1,500 eggs every day during summer.

Eggs hatch into larvae after a few days. The larvae become pupae, then adult bees.

Workers gather food, care for young, and clean and protect the hive.

Drone (male) mates with queen bee, then dies.

BEEHIVE
Beekeepers provide hives where the honeybees raise their young and store their food of honey. Inside the hive are rows of wax combs full of eggs, growing larvae (grubs) and pupae, the queen with her drones (males) and workers, and cells of stored pollen and honey. In a hive there may be about 40,000 worker bees, a few hundred drones, and one queen.

PARASITIC WASPS
These wasps paralyze spiders and insects, then lay eggs on their victim. These eggs hatch into larvae that eat the animal alive.

Wasp eggs develop into larvae inside the nest.

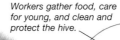

WASP'S NEST
After the winter hibernation, the queen wasp builds a papery nest. The queen scrapes up and chews wood, mixes it with saliva to make a pulp, then builds the nest with the pulp. The queen wasp lays eggs in hexagonal (six-sided) cells inside the papery nest, then catches and chews up insects to feed to the growing larvae. The larvae develop into worker adults who continue to enlarge and reinforce the nest. The males and the new queen are produced later in the season. A big nest may house 5,000 workers. They fly out to feed on plant sap, fruit, and nectar.

Shaft of wasp's sting

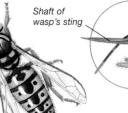

COMMON WASP
Yellow and black markings warn other animals of the wasp's venomous sting. Some wasps use the sting as a defence against predators and to kill or subdue prey. Bees sting only if they are provoked.

Only female wasps (the queen and workers) sting.

BEE DANCE
When a honeybee finds a good source of food, it informs other bees in the hive by "dancing" in a figure of eight pattern. The bee dance shows the other bees where the source of nectar or pollen is in relation to the position of the sun.

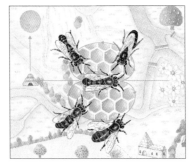

Find out more
ANIMALS
FLOWERS AND HERBS
INSECTS

BEETLES

WHIRLIGIG BEETLES, CLICK BEETLES, and deathwatch beetles belong to the largest group of animals in the world. Of all the animals known to science, one in three belongs to the group of insects called beetles. Many beetles can fly, and have hard, often colourful wing cases. These wing cases are modified forewings. They fold over the insect's back when the beetle is not in flight, and protect the wings beneath. During flight, the front wing cases are usually raised to allow the main wings to beat. Some beetles are active predators; the long-legged tiger beetle, for example, hunts down and eats smaller insects. Others, such as the Colorado beetle, eat only plant material. A few beetles are a nuisance to humans; Colorado beetles destroy potato crops, and elm bark beetles spread Dutch elm disease, destroying thousands of elm trees. But many kinds of beetles help to recycle dead leaves, dead animals, and other plant and animal material. Beetles are among only a few creatures that can break down dead wood.

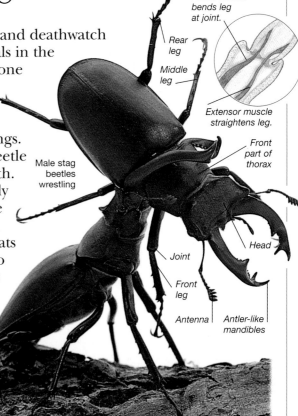

Flexor muscle bends leg at joint.

Rear leg

Middle leg

Extensor muscle straightens leg.

Male stag beetles wrestling

Front part of thorax

Head

Joint

Front leg

Antenna

Antler-like mandibles

GLOW-WORM
The glow-worm is a beetle. It has organs on the underside of its tail, which produce a pale green glowing or flashing light. The light is used by the female to attract a mate or, in some species, a meal.

Tiger beetle

Wasp beetle

Two-lined collops beetle

Weevil

DUNG BEETLE
Dung beetles are so named because they feed on, and lay eggs in, animal droppings. The larvae (grubs) hatch and feed on the droppings before developing into pupae (chrysalises). Some dung beetles shape a lump of dung into a ball and roll it into their burrow before laying eggs in it.

Some dung beetles are also called scarab beetles. The Ancient Egyptians believed they were sacred.

STAG BEETLE
Stag beetles take their name from their antler-like mandibles (jaws). Enlarged mandibles are found only on the male, and are so heavy that the beetle cannot give a strong bite. The huge mandibles are mainly for show, as when males threaten and wrestle with each other in order to mate with a female.

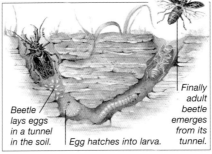

Beetle lays eggs in a tunnel in the soil.

Egg hatches into larva.

Finally adult beetle emerges from its tunnel.

LADYBIRD
The bright colours of ladybirds warn predators not to attack them because they taste bad. Many ladybirds feed on greenfly and other aphids that damage garden plants. This makes ladybirds popular insects with humans.

COCKCHAFER BEETLE
The cockchafer beetle is a slow, awkward flier. It is attracted to light and often crashes into windows. The larvae, called white grubs, live in soil where they eat the roots of grasses and other plants. Adult cockchafer beetles are sometimes called May bugs or June bugs.

LIFE CYCLE OF A WOOD-BORING BEETLE
A beetle starts life as an egg, then hatches into a larva (grub). The larvae of some beetles, such as the longhorn, eat wood and make tunnels in wooden furniture. During its life inside the wood, a larva changes into a pupa, then into an adult. As it leaves the wood, the adult woodborer beetle makes an exit hole. Old furniture sometimes contains hundreds of these tiny holes, which are nicknamed woodworm.

Find out more
ANIMALS
FLIGHT, ANIMAL
INSECTS
MOUNTAIN WILDLIFE

BENIN KINGDOM

THE KINGDOM OF BENIN lay in the Niger River delta area of what is now southern Nigeria. Benin began as a city-state in the 11th century, and by about 1450, was a wealthy kingdom that continued to flourish for another 300 years. Two peoples, the Binis and Yoruba, made up the kingdom, which was ruled by powerful kings called obas. The wealth of the kingdom came from trade, either across the Sahara with other African peoples or on the coast with Europeans. The centre of the kingdom was Benin City. It contained a huge royal palace, where the obas lived. The people of Benin were skilled craftworkers, who produced wonderful carvings and brasses. The Portuguese arrived in the region in the 15th century, and in 1897, the British conquered the kingdom, and made it part of colonial Nigeria.

Sahara Desert

Benin

BENIN
Benin Kingdom was situated in West Africa on the site of present-day Benin City, which is named after the kingdom.

Ceremonial sword

Benin anklet

OBAS
The obas were immensely wealthy and controlled trade. One of the most important obas was Ewuare the Great (reigned 1440-80), who made Benin City powerful. Obas ruled through ministers, to whom they delegated some authority. The people of Benin revered the obas as gods, and made sacrifices to them.

This wide-bladed sword was designed for ornamentation rather than use in combat.

An oba, or great king, flanked by two of his courtiers

A brass plaque that decorated the wooden pillars supporting the oba's palace.

BENIN CITY
Dutch traveller Olfert Dapper described Benin City in 1668 as large and prosperous, surrounded by a high earth wall. It contained many fine buildings including the obas' palace. There were also special areas for craftspeople.

BENIN KINGDOM

1000s Benin City is founded.

1450 Benin at its most powerful.

1486 First Portuguese explorer visits Benin.

1500s English, Dutch, and French merchants start trading.

1680s Benin resumes slave trade.

1668 Olfert Dapper writes a history of Benin.

1897 British capture Benin City and burn it.

BENIN BRONZES
The kingdom of Benin was famous for its "bronzes", most of which were actually brass castings. The "bronzes", some of which were large and striking heads, represented obas and other dignitaries. Craftworkers also made likenesses of European traders who came to the region. Other Benin art included ivory carvings and plaques. These and other artefacts were made by guilds of craftspeople, who lived in special areas in Benin City called wards.

TRADE AND SLAVERY
For hundreds of years, Benin traded with African kingdoms to the north. From about 1480, the Portuguese began buying slaves, cloth, pepper, and ivory from Benin. The obas stopped trading slaves in 1550, but in the 1600s they again began selling slaves to the Europeans.

Find out more
AFRICA
AFRICA, HISTORY OF
SLAVERY

BIG BANG

NEARLY FOURTEEN BILLION YEARS AGO, the universe exploded out of virtually nothing. The first scientist to propose this astonishing theory, now known as the Big Bang, was George Lemaître (1894-1966). His idea was supported by the work of Edwin Hubble (1889-1953), which showed that the universe is expanding. If this is so, the entire cosmos must have originated from a single point of explosion. But what was that single point? Scientists call it a "singularity" – a tiny, infinitely dense dot that once contained all the matter of the universe. Such a thing is impossible to imagine, and even astronomers do not really understand it. Yet within a few minutes of the Big Bang, the single point would have been converted into an immense, expanding cloud of gas. Over millions of years this became the galaxies, stars, and planets of the universe.

FRED HOYLE
It was astronomer Fred Hoyle (1915-2001) who suggested the term "Big Bang", as a joke. He believed the universe had no beginning and no end.

The Big Bang, 13.7 billion years ago

Galaxies started to form 500 million years after the Big Bang.

Stars formed in spinning clouds of dust and gas.

The solar system formed, 4.6 billion years ago.

First life forms appeared on Earth, 3.8 billion years ago.

RED SHIFT
The light from some stars looks redder than it should. This is due to the Doppler Effect, and shows that these stars are moving away from us. Distant galaxies also look redder but because the whole of space is expanding their lightwaves are stretched when they reach us. This is called red shift.

Stretched wave, light redder

Star

The Earth

Wavelength and colour unchanged

Star

Compressed waves, light bluer

Star

If a star is moving away, its light waves are stretched out and shift towards the red end of the spectrum.

If a star is staying in the same position relative to Earth, then the wavelengths of light emitted remain unchanged.

If a star is moving towards the Earth, light waves are compressed and shift to the blue end of the spectrum.

As the ambulance moves away, the siren's sound waves stretch, increasing their wavelength and lowering their pitch.

DOPPLER EFFECT
Christian Doppler (1803-53) showed that sound waves are compressed if the source is moving towards your ear, and stretched if it is moving away. This alters the pitch of the sound you hear. The same principle applies to light waves arriving from distant stars.

The sound waves of an ambulance siren are compressed as it comes nearer, reducing their wavelength and raising their pitch.

CHAIN OF EVENTS
Scientists believe that the universe was created in an explosive event called the Big Bang. At the instant of creation, matter was concentrated in an infinitely small, dense dot called a singularity. This then began to expand and cool, allowing the conversion of energy into particles. After thousands of years, these particles joined to make atoms of hydrogen and helium that would eventually form galaxies and stars.

Find out more
ASTRONOMY
PHYSICS
STARS
UNIVERSE

BIOLOGY

THE NATURAL WORLD is full of marvels and mysteries: the beautiful colours of a flower, the magnificent display of a peacock, the magic of new life when a child is born. Biology is the science of all living things, from the tiniest microscopic organisms (living things) to the largest whales in the sea; it is the study of all plants and animals and their environments, or surroundings. Biologists study how living things grow, feed, and move, how they reproduce, and how they evolve (change) over long periods of time. Biology covers an enormous range of topics and deals with millions of species (kinds) of organisms. Because of this, biology is divided into different specialized branches such as anatomy, which deals with the structure of living things, and physiology, which is concerned with the way animals and plants function. Biology is important in other sciences and professions that deal with living things, such as agriculture, forestry, and medicine.

BOTANY
The study of plants and flowers is called botany. It is one of the two main branches of biology.

Stamen of flower

Cross-section of stamen

Botanists study the structure of plants and how they reproduce.

ZOOLOGY
Zoology, the other main branch of biology, is the scientific study of animals.

Clump of a frog's newly laid eggs, called frogspawn

Zoologists study the life and growth of animals.

LABORATORY
A biologist works in a specially equipped room called a laboratory. Biologists use a variety of techniques to study animals and plants. They may dissect (cut up) specimens, or use powerful microscopes to probe into the structure of tiny microscopic organisms, such as cells and bacteria.

EVERYDAY BIOLOGY
There are biological processes going on all around us. For example, bread dough rises when it is left in a warm place. This is because live yeast in the dough gives off gas that make the dough expand, a process called fermentation.

Once the bread is cooked, it is full of little holes made by the gas bubbles.

Carbon dioxide gas makes the dough rise.

Yeast is made up of single-celled living organisms. Yeast cells obtain their energy from the dough mixture and give off carbon dioxide gas in the process.

HISTORY OF BIOLOGY
The Greek philosopher Aristotle was one of the first biologists. He studied birds and animals in about 350 BCE. During the 17th century, the English scientist Robert Hooke discovered living cells through the newly invented microscope. In 1953, English scientist Francis Crick and American scientist James Watson discovered the structure of dioxyribose nucleic acid (DNA), the chemical that controls all cells and life patterns.

Francis Crick (left) and James Watson

Tiger pierid butterfly of Central and South America

Hairstreak butterfly of South America

TAXONOMY
Biologists classify living organisms into different groups so they can understand the relationships between them. This is called taxonomy. For instance, butterflies and moths belong to the same taxonomic group, called Lepidoptera.

HUMAN BIOLOGY
Human biology is concerned with all the different systems of the human body. These include the digestive system, the circulatory system, the respiratory (breathing) system, the reproductive system, the nervous system, and the muscular and skeletal systems.

Find out more
CHEMISTRY
DARWIN, CHARLES
EVOLUTION
GENETICS
HUMAN BODY
PLANTS
REPRODUCTION

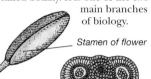

BIRDS

IN THE ENTIRE ANIMAL WORLD, birds are the only living creatures with feathers. They are also warm-blooded, like mammals. There are about 9,000 different kinds of birds, living in all parts of the world. They include exotic, colourful birds such as parrots, garden birds such as robins and thrushes, water birds such as ducks, sea birds such as puffins and penguins, and many more. Most birds are well adapted for flying and have large, powerful chest muscles to allow them to flap their wings. Their bones are light, with tiny honeycombed holes to keep them lightweight, which assists them during flight. Feathers are light too. They protect the bird's body and keep it warm. Wing feathers fit together to form a smooth, airtight surface for gliding. Tail feathers provide balance and help the bird steer in midair. A few birds, however, cannot fly. Flightless or nearly flightless birds include ostriches, penguins, and the rare kakapo, a kind of parrot from New Zealand. Birds do not have teeth, which would be too heavy; instead they have a strong, light bill, or beak. Most birds, particularly eagles and other birds of prey, have good eyesight and hearing. Their sense of smell, however, is poor.

Outer feathers produce lift for flight.

Short, strong beak for cracking open seeds.

Brightly coloured plumage attracts a female in the breeding season.

PLUMAGE

A bird's feathers are called its plumage. Some birds, such as the wren and the sparrow, have brown plumage for camouflage. Other birds have plumage with dazzling colours and patterns. It is usually the males that have bright plumage, to help them attract a mate during the breeding season. The distinctive colouring also helps the members of a flock keep together.

Male chaffinch in flight

Long tail feathers act as a rudder, to help with steering during flight.

Skeleton of a pigeon

Humerus (upper arm bone)

Skull

Radius and ulna (forearm bones)

Spine (backbone)

Mandibles (beak)

Keel on breast bone

Ribs

Sternum (breast bone)

Femur (thigh bone)

Pelvis (hip bone)

Pygostyle (tail bone)

Tibia (shin bone)

Tarsus (ankle bone)

Internal system of a starling

Beak (bill)

Lungs

Gullet

Kidney

Crop

Heart

Liver

Gizzard

Intestine

Cloaca

THE BIGGEST AND SMALLEST BIRDS
The tiny bee hummingbird is one of the world's smallest birds. It measures about 5 cm (2 in) from beak to tail, and is so light that 17 bee hummingbirds would weigh only 28 gm (1 oz). The ostrich, which is more than 2.5 m (8 ft) tall, is the world's largest bird, but it cannot fly at all.

This ostrich head looks huge in comparison to a tiny bee hummingbird.

A bee hummingbird is so small that it can fit in the palm of your hand.

BIRD BONES

Most of the bones in a bird's skeleton are hollow, to save body weight. Wings are controlled by powerful muscles attached to the keel, which is a ridge along the edge of the breastbone.

INSIDE A BIRD

Most of a bird's body is taken up by the muscles, heart, lungs, and digestive system. Birds have two stomachs, as in the starling shown here. The first stomach, the crop, stores food; the second, the gizzard, grinds the food to a pulp.

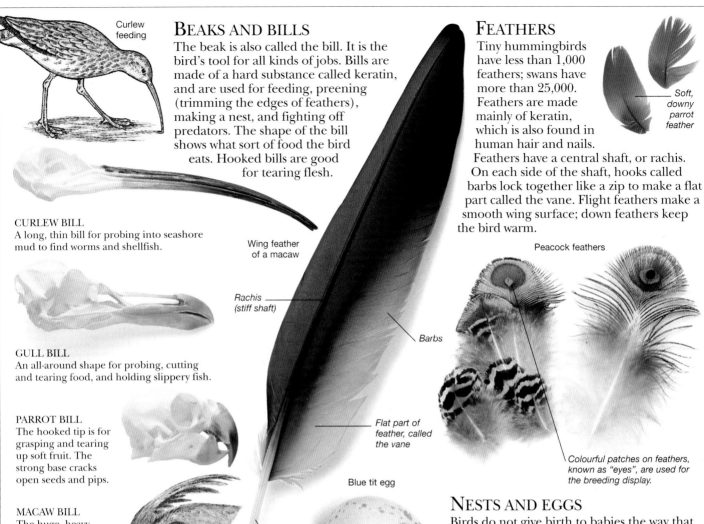

BEAKS AND BILLS

The beak is also called the bill. It is the bird's tool for all kinds of jobs. Bills are made of a hard substance called keratin, and are used for feeding, preening (trimming the edges of feathers), making a nest, and fighting off predators. The shape of the bill shows what sort of food the bird eats. Hooked bills are good for tearing flesh.

Curlew feeding

CURLEW BILL
A long, thin bill for probing into seashore mud to find worms and shellfish.

GULL BILL
An all-around shape for probing, cutting and tearing food, and holding slippery fish.

PARROT BILL
The hooked tip is for grasping and tearing up soft fruit. The strong base cracks open seeds and pips.

MACAW BILL
The huge, heavy macaw's bill breaks up nuts and seeds. Many macaws and other parrots are becoming rare because the tropical rain forests in which they live are being destroyed.

Wing feather of a macaw

Rachis (stiff shaft)

Barbs

Flat part of feather, called the vane

Quill or base of feather, embedded in skin

Blue tit egg

Hard, chalky eggshell

Baby bird

Food store of yolk

FEATHERS

Tiny hummingbirds have less than 1,000 feathers; swans have more than 25,000. Feathers are made mainly of keratin, which is also found in human hair and nails.

Feathers have a central shaft, or rachis. On each side of the shaft, hooks called barbs lock together like a zip to make a flat part called the vane. Flight feathers make a smooth wing surface; down feathers keep the bird warm.

Soft, downy parrot feather

Peacock feathers

Colourful patches on feathers, known as "eyes", are used for the breeding display.

NESTS AND EGGS

Birds do not give birth to babies the way that mammals do. Instead, they lay eggs with hard shells, then sit on them to keep them warm. The baby bird develops inside the shell, nourished by the yolk. After a few weeks the bird pecks its way out of the shell. Some birds, such as flamingos, build big nests for their eggs. Others, such as guillemots, do not make nests, but lay eggs on a cliff edge. Some cuckoos lay eggs in another bird's nest and abandon them, leaving the owner of the nest to raise the young.

BIRD BEHAVIOUR
During the day, birds are busy looking after their young, communicating with other birds, eating, and preening. Bird behaviour such as migrating in winter or pecking at food is instinctive, so it does not have to be learned. Some birds, such as the tawny frogmouth of Australia, feed at night, but during the day the frogmouth sits very still, looking like a tree stump.

BREEDING DISPLAY
During the breeding season, the male blue bird of paradise hangs upside down in a tree, showing off his feathers to attract a female. The males of some kinds of birds, such as the grouse, fight over a patch of ground called a lek. Without a territory, no females will come to mate.

Blue bird of paradise

Day-old blue tit nestlings

NESTLINGS
Most newly hatched birds are helpless, for they have no feathers and cannot see. They stay in the nest to be fed and protected by one or both parents until their feathers grow. A parent bird may make dozens of trips back to the nest each day, bringing food for the chicks.

Eyelids still joined together

Find out more
ANIMALS
ANIMAL SENSES
ECOLOGY AND FOOD WEBS
FARM ANIMALS
FLIGHT, ANIMAL
LAKE AND RIVER WILDLIFE
SEASHORE WILDLIFE
ZOOS

BLACK DEATH

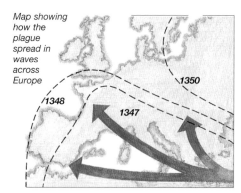

Map showing how the plague spread in waves across Europe

1350

1348

1347

THE MEDITERRANEAN ISLAND OF SICILY was a terrifying place in 1347. Everywhere people were dying of a mysterious disease. Those who caught it usually had violent stomach cramps and boils under their arms. Dark patches covered their bodies, and death followed within three days. The disease became known as the Black Death because of the dark patches; today we know it was bubonic plague. It spread into Italy and France. By the end of 1348 millions had died – about one third of the population of Europe. There was panic as the Black Death advanced. People avoided each other, fearful that they might catch the plague. Many townspeople fled into the countryside carrying the disease with them. There was a shortage of food because there were fewer people to farm the land. Fields were filled with rotting animal bodies.

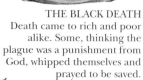

SPREAD OF PLAGUE
The Black Death began in Asia. It spread through Turkey, then arrived on ships at Sicily in October 1347, and reached Britain near the end of 1348. The plague reappeared every few years until the early 18th century; outbreaks were even reported in the early 19th century.

15th-century illumination

THE BLACK DEATH
Death came to rich and poor alike. Some, thinking the plague was a punishment from God, whipped themselves and prayed to be saved.

Large plague grave where victims were buried

CROSS OF DEATH
Crosses were painted on the doors of plague-ridden houses. Criminals and volunteers put the dead bodies on carts and buried them in large graves.

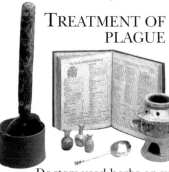

BUBONIC PLAGUE

Fleas living on black rats carried the bubonic plague. The fleas passed on the disease when they bit people. A more infectious form of the plague – pneumonic plague – was spread by coughing.

TREATMENT OF PLAGUE

Doctors used herbs or cut open people's veins to let out "bad" blood. But these methods failed. Many people refused to go near sufferers, even sick members of their own family.

PEASANTS REVOLT
The Black Death killed so many people that there was a shortage of workers. The survivors demanded higher wages and organized revolts in France and England against high taxes and strict, out-of-date laws.

Find out more
DISEASE
MEDIEVAL EUROPE
PEASANTS REVOLT

BLACK HOLES

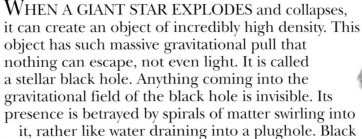

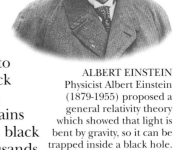

WHEN A GIANT STAR EXPLODES and collapses, it can create an object of incredibly high density. This object has such massive gravitational pull that nothing can escape, not even light. It is called a stellar black hole. Anything coming into the gravitational field of the black hole is invisible. Its presence is betrayed by spirals of matter swirling into it, rather like water draining into a plughole. Black holes may also develop at the centre of galaxies from clouds of gas, rather than from the remains of giant stars. These are called supermassive black holes and can have up to hundreds of thousands of times the mass of our Sun. The gravitational force is so immense that thousands of stars may be dragged into the vortex. As they become squeezed together on the edge of the funnel, they form a whirlpool concentration of gas, dust, and smashed stars that flares with brilliant light.

ALBERT EINSTEIN
Physicist Albert Einstein (1879-1955) proposed a general relativity theory which showed that light is bent by gravity, so it can be trapped inside a black hole.

Inside a large star, nuclear fusion converts hydrogen into helium. As it runs low on hydrogen, the star expands into a "red giant".

The star finally dies in an explosion that is called a supernova.

SUPERNOVA REMNANT
The cloud of debris and gas created by a supernova is called a supernova remnant. At the centre sits the black hole. When the mass of the original star is not enough to create a black hole, the result may be a pulsar neutron star. This spins rapidly, emitting beams of light.

STAR CYCLE
Astronomers believe that many massive stars end as black holes. As it uses up the last of its fuel, a large star expands to become an even bigger "supergiant" star. Eventually it explodes as a supernova. The centre then collapses to become a neutron star, or a black hole.

If enough debris falls back on to the stellar core it can become a black hole.

GRAVITATIONAL WELL
If the gravity of empty space is like a flat plane, then a black hole's gravity is like a funnel-shaped well. Any object that strays within the area of the dent will probably spiral towards the middle. Eventually, it swirls down the "gravitational well", into a region from which even light cannot escape.

An object is drawn by gravity towards the black hole.

Once the object has plunged into the vortex there is no escape.

Eventually it becomes part of the mass of the black hole.

Gas drawn from nearby blue supergiant star

The accretion disc swirling into the black hole

ACCRETION DISC
Matter spiralling into a black hole is known as an accretion disc. It may contain stars and planets as well as debris and gases. You can't see black holes but the material falling into them causes them to give out enormous amounts of radiation.

Find out more
ASTRONOMY
EINSTEIN, ALBERT
GRAVITY
STARS

BRAIN AND NERVES

THE BRAIN AND OTHER PARTS of the nervous system – the spinal cord and nerves – are made from billions of interconnected nerve cells called neurons that transmit millions of high-speed nerve signals, or impulses, every second. When signals reach the brain, it processes them and sends out instructions to the body. The spinal cord that runs from the brain down the back, relays signals between spinal nerves and the brain, and also controls many reflexes. Cable-like nerves contain bundles of neurons: sensory neurons carry signals from receptors in the skin and sense organs to the spinal cord and brain, enabling us to sense and respond to our surroundings; motor neurons carry signals from the brain and spinal cord to muscles, telling them to move the body in a smooth, co-ordinated fashion.

SLEEP
When we sleep, the body rests but the brain is still working, controlling our breathing and heartbeat. We remember some of our night thoughts as dreams.

CEREBRAL HEMISPHERES
The largest parts of the brain are the two folded cerebral hemispheres. Our thoughts are based in these hemispheres. The outer layer of the brain is called the cerebral cortex. It is rich in nerve cell bodies. The inner layer is called the white matter. It consists mainly of nerve fibres. If the two hemispheres were spread out, they would cover an area the size of a pillowcase.

Skull

White matter

Meninges are membranes which surround and cushion the brain within the skull.

Hypothalamus has overall control of the internal organs and is linked to the pituitary gland and hormonal system.

Pituitary gland

Cerebellum processes and coordinates signals going out to muscles from hemispheres.

Spinal cord

Brain stem

Area associated with touch

Area involved with consciousness, creativity, and personality

Area that controls the muscles which make body movements

Area that controls vision

Area that controls hearing, smell, and taste

Area associated with coordination and balance

Area that controls breathing and blood pressure

Nerve fibre (axon)

Neuron cell body

Cerebral cortex

White matter

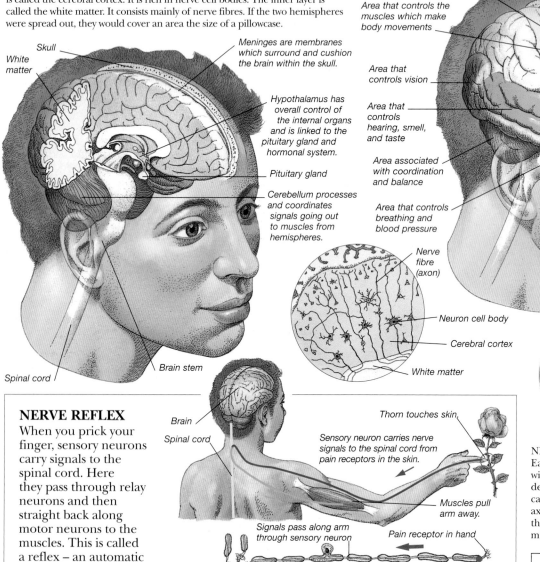

NERVE REFLEX
When you prick your finger, sensory neurons carry signals to the spinal cord. Here they pass through relay neurons and then straight back along motor neurons to the muscles. This is called a reflex – an automatic reaction that we make without thinking.

Brain

Spinal cord

Thorn touches skin.

Sensory neuron carries nerve signals to the spinal cord from pain receptors in the skin.

Muscles pull arm away.

Signals pass along arm through sensory neuron

Pain receptor in hand

Relay neuron in spinal cord

Motor neuron carries signals to muscles in upper arm.

NERVE CELLS
Each neuron has a main cell body with fine spidery connections called dendrites, and a long, wirelike fibre called the axon. The dendrites and axon connect the neuron to thousands of other neurons, creating millions of pathways for nerve signals.

Find out more
HEART AND BLOOD
HUMAN BODY
MUSCLES AND MOVEMENT

BRAZIL

Brazil borders every country in South America, except Chile and Ecuador. Its Atlantic border is 7,400 km (4,600 miles) long.

BRAZIL, THE LARGEST COUNTRY in South America, is a land of contrasts. To the south, it is dominated by the rolling grasslands of the Brazilian highlands, while arid deserts lie to the northeast. Three-fifths of Brazil's total land area is covered by the world's largest rain forest, which forms the drainage basin of the Amazon, the world's second-longest river. Increasingly, the rain forest is being cleared for agriculture, cattle ranching, mining, and the timber industry as Brazil's rapidly growing population places more pressure on the land. Rural poverty drives many people to overcrowded cities. São Paulo, the fastest growing city on the continent, is a major industrial centre. Brazil was colonized in the 16th century by the Portuguese, who imported African slaves to work on sugar plantations. Today, Brazil is the largest Roman Catholic nation in the world, and has a vibrant mix of Indian, Portuguese, and African cultures.

SHANTY TOWNS

For many people living in rural poverty, cities seem to offer a chance of employment and a better life. Yet a severe lack of housing in Brazil's major cities has led to the growth of *favelas*. These shanty towns, built of wood and corrugated iron, sprawl over land which is unfit for other development.

RIO CARNIVAL
Every year, just before Lent, Rio de Janeiro is transformed by a five-day carnival. Huge parades snake their way through the city. Brightly dressed singers, musicians, and dancers fill the streets with colour, spectacle, and the sound of *samba* music.

About 22 per cent of the world's coffee comes from Brazil. It is grown in the warm fertile soils of central and southern Brazil.

RIO DE JANEIRO
Rio de Janeiro is located on the Atlantic coast, and sprawls across bays, islands, and the foothills of the coastal mountains. It is dominated by the distinctive shape of Sugarloaf Mountain and the monumental statue of Christ the Redeemer. Founded by the Portuguese in 1565, it was capital of Brazil from 1763 to 1960. Today, this rapidly growing city is a major international port, and a commercial, manufacturing and cultural centre. It is also famous for its beaches, annual carnival, and exciting nightlife.

GOLD RUSH
Brazil's mineral wealth ranges from iron and tin to gold and precious stones, such as diamonds and topaz. Since the 1980s, thousands of miners have flooded to the Serra Pelada region, burrowing into the hillside with their bare hands in search of gold.

Carnival party-goers compete with each other for the prize for the most outrageous costume and best-decorated float.

Swarms of gold prospectors, known as garimpeiros, cover this Brazilian hillside. They chip away rock with pick axes, hoping they might find their fortune in gold.

AMAZONIAN RAIN FOREST

The largest surviving area of rain forest in the world is in the Amazon river basin. It is the most biologically diverse habitat in the world and supports millions of species of plants and animals. Scientists estimate that more than 2,000 species can live in just one rain forest tree. The annual average temperature is 26°C (79°F), while annual rainfall can be as high as 2,000 mm (80 in). Rain forest soils are easily washed away when trees and plants are removed. As more and more land is cleared for farming and timber, the rain forest is lost forever.

Brazil nuts

When rain forests are cleared in equatorial regions, heavy rainfall erodes the soil, leaving a green desert. Crops cannot grow in these conditions and many animals lose their natural habitat.

Tropical hardwoods are a valued resource and large logging companies are responsible for much of the loss of rain forest habitat. When landless peasants settle in the Amazonian rainforest, they clear the forest and farm the land until it degenerates to scrub, or is sold to cattle ranchers.

FOREST RESOURCES

The Amazonian rain forest is rich in many resources, from plants with medicinal properties and rubber trees which produce latex, to brazil nuts. Brazil nuts (left) can be eaten or crushed to make oil. They are exported worldwide.

AMAZONIAN INDIANS

It is estimated that some 260,000 native Brazilians still live in the rain forest. These peoples, also known as the Amazonian Indians, live a traditional way of life. They survive by hunting, fishing, and clearing small patches of forest for farming corn and manioc. Many Indian groups have been wiped out by disease or by land-hungry miners, settlers, and loggers. Today, most live in protected areas.

In Manaus (right) during the dry season, trucks reverse down to the edge of the Amazon to receive cargo.

WATER HIGHWAY

The mighty Amazon river has the greatest volume of water of any river in the world. It is navigable along its entire 6,400-km (4,000-mile) length. It is a major transport artery, carrying 10 per cent of all Brazilian cargo. The river teems with barges, passenger ships, and patrol boats. River ports, such as Manaus and Belém, are important commercial centres.

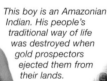

This boy is an Amazonian Indian. His people's traditional way of life was destroyed when gold prospectors ejected them from their lands.

MANAUS

Manaus was a rich city in the 19th century, its wealth based on the rubber industry. Today, it is a centre for the cattle-ranching, mining, and timber industries of Amazonia. It is also an important cultural centre in this remote region, and is famous for its domed opera house. With a population of one million, Manaus is a magnet for the rural poor who continue to settle there.

Find out more

FOOTBALL AND RUGBY
FOREST WILDLIFE
RIVERS
SOUTH AMERICA
SOUTH AMERICA, HISTORY OF

Legend

Volcano	Mountain	Ancient monument	Capital city	Large city/town	Small city/town

STATISTICS

Area: 8,514,877 sq km
(3,287,612 sq miles)
Population: 198,739,000
Capital: Brasília
Languages: Portuguese,
German, Italian, Spanish,
Polish, Japanese,
Amerindian languages
Religions: Roman
Catholic, Protestant,
Afro-American Spiritist
Currency: Real
Main occupations: Saw
milling, manufacturing,
coffee and sugar farming
Main exports: Coffee, soya
beans, sugar, orange juice,
steel, cars, computers
Main imports: Gasoline

IGUACU FALLS

These horseshoe-shaped falls lie on the
Argentine-Brazilian border, where the
Iguaçu river plunges and divides into
some 275 waterfalls, ranging in height
from 60–82 m (200–269 ft). Many of the
individual falls are broken by protruding
rocks, deflecting water and spray to
create a wall of rainbows. At the bottom
of the falls, a curtain of mist rises 150 m
(500 ft) into the air.
This spectacular
region is protected
by the Iguaçu
National Park.

SOCCER
Soccer is a
popular sport in
Brazil. It is followed by
many people, and is even
played on the streets.

*Brazilian soccer
star, Rivaldo.*

MIGRATION
*Northeastern Brazil is
dominated by vast cattle
ranches. Prolonged drought
has driven millions
of farmers
to the cities
of the south.*

BRASILIA
In 1960, the Brazilian
capital began to move to the
purpose-built city of Brasília. It was
thought that this move would kickstart
the development of the sparsely-inhabited interior.
Built to a cross-shaped plan, Brasília's wide boulevards
and large, open plazas are lined with striking federal and
civic buildings, and modern sculptures.

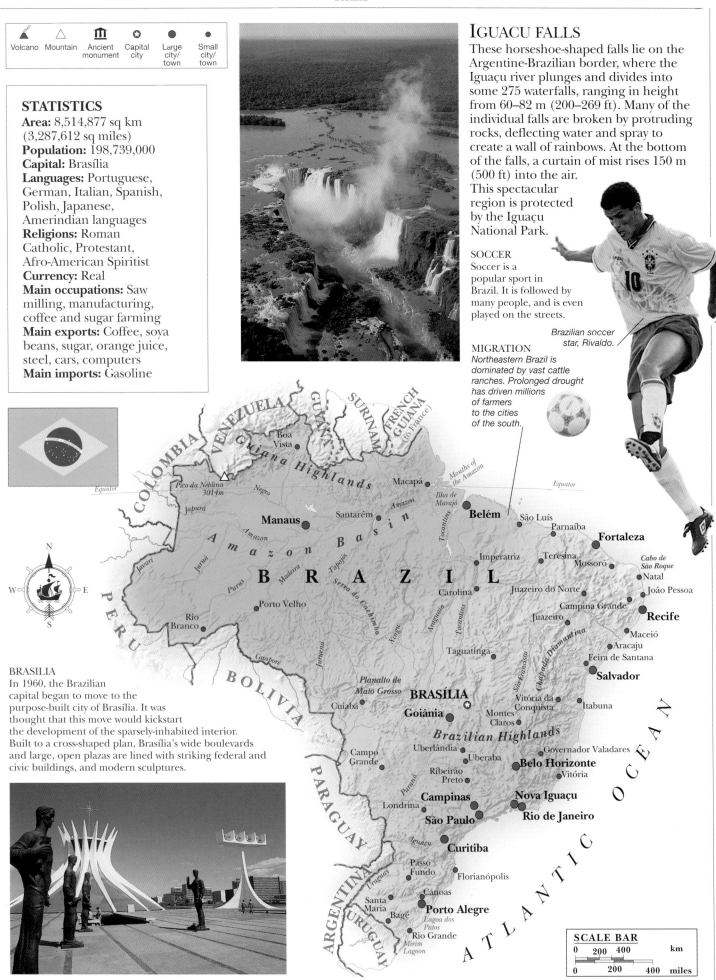

SCALE BAR

0	200	400	km
0	200	400	miles

BRIDGES

TRAVEL ON LAND is easier, safer, and more direct with bridges. Motor vehicles and trains can speed over lakes, rivers, and deep valleys. Bridges raise busy roads over others so that the roads do not meet. Major roads and railways enter cities on long bridges sometimes called viaducts. Footbridges allow people to cross roads, rivers, and railways safely.

The first bridges were made by placing tree trunks across rivers, and laying flat stones on rocks in shallow streams. Later, people made rope bridges by weaving plants together, and built stone bridges with strong arches. Similar kinds of bridges are built today with concrete and other strong, modern materials instead of natural materials. Steel beams and cables are used as supports. The world's longest bridge crosses Lake Pontchartrain in the United States. It is almost 39 km (24 miles) long. Land cannot be seen from its centre.

SUSPENSION BRIDGE
A pair of long steel cables fixed to high towers suspends the roadway. Suspension bridges can span the longest distances because they are lightweight.

ARCH BRIDGE
A curved arch firmly fixed to the banks supports the bridge. Arches are very strong structures.

CANTILEVER BRIDGE
Each half of the bridge is balanced on a support in the river. Where the two halves meet, there may be a short central span.

CABLE-STAYED BRIDGE
Sets of straight steel cables attached to towers hold up the bridge from above.

BASCULE BRIDGE
Sections of the bridge tilt like a drawbridge, allowing ships into port.

BEAM BRIDGE
Several columns in the river-bed or the ground support the bridge from beneath. Sometimes the bridge is made of a hollow girder through which cars and trains can run.

BUILDING A SUSPENSION BRIDGE

The supports and ends of the bridge are built first, firmly fixed in the ground or the riverbed and banks. The deck of the bridge carrying the road or railway is then built out from the ends and supports, or lifted onto them.

SUSPENDING THE CABLES
The towers of a suspension bridge are built first. Steel ropes are then placed over the towers. A machine moves along the ropes, spinning long lengths of wire into strong steel cables.

KINDS OF BRIDGES

There are various ways of building bridges to span rivers and other barriers. Most bridges rest on solid supports. Pontoon bridges, which are found on some lakes, float on the surface of the water.

RAISING THE DECK
Long lengths of cable, called hangers, are fixed to the suspending cables. The deck of the bridge is made in sections elsewhere. The sections are taken to the bridge, lifted into position, and attached to the hangers.

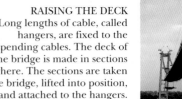

THE LONGEST SPANS
The Akashi-Kaikyo Bridge in Japan, has the longest single span of any bridge. The central span is 1,991 m (6,532 ft) long. The bridge was completed in 1997. The Humber Bridge, England, (left) has the fifth longest single span, at 1,410 m (4,626 ft).

TACOMA BRIDGE DISASTER
The Tacoma Narrows Bridge in Washington, United States, failed in 1940. The wind made the bridge twist back and forth until the deck gave way. Nobody was hurt.

AQUEDUCTS
Bridges that carry water are called aqueducts. The aqueduct may be part of a canal, or it may bring a water supply to a town or city. The Romans built many aqueducts with high stone arches, several of which survive today.

Find out more
ARCHITECTURE
PORTS AND WATERWAYS

ANCIENT
BRITAIN

THE TERM ANCIENT BRITAIN describes the period
of British history from about 3500 BCE until the Romans
invaded in 43 CE Prehistoric people had lived in Britain for
many thousands of years before this, but evidence shows that
real changes began during the Neolithic, or New Stone Age,
when early people in Britain, like those elsewhere, learned to
make pottery, and to grow their own food by farming. They
were also the first people in Britain to leave behind large-scale
monuments, which they built with simple stone tools. They, and the
people of the Bronze and Iron Ages, who included the Celts, are
known as Ancient Britons. They lived in a harsh environment, but
developed stunning art, and became skilled warriors.

SKARA BRAE
Britain's best-preserved prehistoric village is
Skara Brae, Orkney. Skara Brae dates back to
the Stone Age, around 5,000 years ago. There
were very few trees on Orkney, so the people
built their houses out of stone. They even used
stone to make the furniture – including beds
and cupboards – which still survives.

STONEHENGE
Europe's greatest prehistoric
monument is Stonehenge, a
massive stone circle used for
religious ceremonies, which
stands on Salisbury Plain,
England. Stonehenge was
built in stages between
2950 and 2500 BCE. Its
gigantic stones are called
sarsens. These came from
about 30 km (18.6 miles)
away. No one knows how
the Ancient Britons moved
them to Stonehenge.

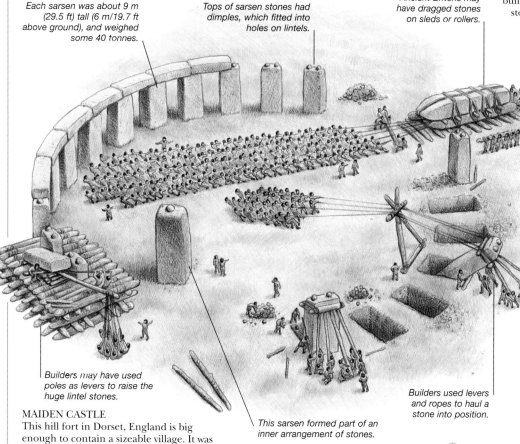

Each sarsen was about 9 m
(29.5 ft) tall (6 m/19.7 ft
above ground), and weighed
some 40 tonnes.

Tops of sarsen stones had
dimples, which fitted into
holes on lintels.

Ancient Britons may
have dragged stones
on sleds or rollers.

Builders may have used
poles as levers to raise the
huge lintel stones.

This sarsen formed part of an
inner arrangement of stones.

Builders used levers
and ropes to haul a
stone into position.

Mold cape

METALWORKING
Britain's metalworkers became
highly skilled. In about 2500 BCE,
they found out how to use copper
and gold. Soon after, they were
working in bronze, and discovered
iron c. 800 BCE. They continued to
use gold, making beautiful objects
such this finely worked cape which
was buried in a warrior's grave at
Mold, North Wales.

MAIDEN CASTLE
This hill fort in Dorset, England is big
enough to contain a sizeable village. It was
built in the 6th century BCE, and enlarged
some 200 years later. Its Iron Age inhabitants
protected themselves with huge ditches,
throwing up the earth to make ridges.

WOAD
Ancient Britons
decorated their
bodies with a blue dye
made from the woad
plant. They made the
dye by mixing up a paste
of woad leaves and water,
and rolling this into a ball.
When the ball dried, the paste
on the inside turned blue. The
Ancient Britons probably wore the
dye to make themselves look
fearsome in battle.

Woad leaves provide a
rich blue dye.

Woad plant

Find out more
BRONZE AGE
CELTS
ROMAN EMPIRE
STONE AGE
UNITED KINGDOM, HISTORY OF

BRITISH EMPIRE

Surrounding fence kept out enemies and any dangerous wildlife.

THE LARGEST EMPIRE THE WORLD has ever seen – the British Empire – began in the 1600s as merchants set up trading colonies on the east coast of America. More colonies were established in the Caribbean, India, and, after 1770, Australia, Oceania, and Africa. By 1920, the British Empire had reached its greatest extent. It grew through military conquest and the need for British industry to acquire raw materials. A vast civil service held it together. But such a large empire was too big to last, and by the end of the 20th century almost every colony had received its independence.

JAMESTOWN

In 1607, Britain set up its first permanent overseas colony at Jamestown, Virginia, on the east coast of North America. The settlement was named after King James I, and consisted of log cabins surrounded by a protective wooden fence.

Settlers built cabins of wood from local forest.

Women looked after the animals and helped to harvest the crops.

CAPTURING CANADA

In the early 1600s, the French established colonies along the St Lawrence River in Canada. The British set up the Hudson's Bay Company in 1670 to trade furs and other goods with Inuits from the north of Canada. This caused tension between the British and French in the region. In 1759, the British army, under General Wolfe, captured Quebec, the capital of French Canada. The British defeated the French army, and took control of the whole of Canada.

THE RAJ

In 1600, English merchants set up the East India Company. It soon controlled large parts of India. Following the Indian Mutiny of 1857, the British government took over. By 1886, Britain controlled the whole Indian subcontinent. For the Victorians, India was the "jewel in the crown", and British rule was known as the "Raj" after the Hindu word meaning "reign".

THE INDIAN MUTINY

In 1857, a mutiny broke out among Indian troops, who feared they might be converted to Christianity, and suspected their gun cartridges were greased with pig fat (offensive to Muslims), or cow fat (offensive to Hindus). The British put down the mutiny, and took steps to reform the Indian government and army.

IMPERIAL TRADE

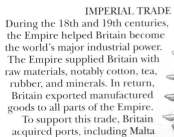

During the 18th and 19th centuries, the Empire helped Britain become the world's major industrial power. The Empire supplied Britain with raw materials, notably cotton, tea, rubber, and minerals. In return, Britain exported manufactured goods to all parts of the Empire. To support this trade, Britain acquired ports, including Malta and the Falkland Islands.

AUSTRALIA

The first colonists in Australia were British convicts sent out from 1788 to serve their sentences. Later arrivals included Irish people fleeing famine, and others seeking a new life in the wide open spaces of Australia. The discovery of gold in 1851 caused a rush of prospectors, leading to great social and economic change. In 1901, the six separate colonies in Australia were joined together as a single country.

IMPERIAL DREAM

Thousands of British men and a few women went to serve abroad. Some, such as Cecil Rhodes (1853-1902), made their fortunes in the empire, and believed British rule was the most advanced form of government the world had seen. Rhodes did much to enlarge the empire in Africa. He dreamed of a railway from Cairo to Cape Town passing entirely through British territory.

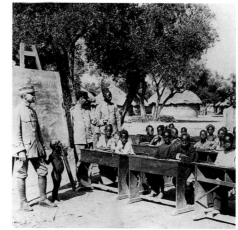

MISSIONARIES

As the empire expanded, British Christian missionaries set out to convert the local people. They set up schools and hospitals, and did much to bind the different parts of the empire together through Christianity and the British way of life. One of the most famous missionaries was Scotsman David Livingstone. In 1841 he arrived in Cape Town; by the time of his death in 1873, he had explored most of Africa.

WORLD WAR I

In 1914, war broke out between Britain and Germany. World War I involved 2.8 million troops from all over the empire. Indian troops fought on the Western Front. Australian and New Zealand (ANZAC) troops fought at Gallipoli, and African forces overran German colonies in Africa.

Britain and its overseas possessions

EXTENT OF EMPIRE

The British Empire reached its greatest extent in the years after the end of World War I in 1918, when former German and Turkish possessions were added to it. King George V (1865-1936) of Britain ruled over an empire that contained 410 million people – one in five of the world's population. It spread over 29,500,000 sq km (11,400,000 sq miles), and touched every continent.

DECOLONIZATION

The first countries to gain independence were the white dominions of Canada (1867), Australia (1901), and New Zealand (1907). Non-white countries followed. The Indian subcontinent became independent in 1947-48; Ghana and Malaya left the empire in 1957. Decolonization (withdrawal from the empire) continued through the 20th century, sometimes violently. By 2009, Britain governed 14 overseas territories, mostly small islands.

COMMONWEALTH

In 1931, more than 50 newly independent British colonies joined what is known as the British Commonwealth. The British queen, Elizabeth II, is its head, even though most members are republics or have their own monarchs. Commonwealth leaders meet once every two years to discuss matters such as trade.

THE BRITISH EMPIRE

1497 John Cabot claims Newfoundland for England.

1600 East India Company established.

1607 Jamestown founded.

1620s Caribbean island colonies established.

1763 Britain gains Canada under Treaty of Paris.

1783 Britain loses US colonies.

1788-1867 British convicts are transported to Australia to serve their sentences there.

1814 Britain acquires its first African colony in the Cape.

1867 Canada becomes the first dominion in the British Empire.

1876 Queen Victoria is created Empress of India.

1886 Britain takes control of India.

1901-10 Australia, New Zealand, and South Africa become British dominions.

1920s Empire at its greatest extent.

1931 Statute of Westminster recognizes full independence of the dominions.

1947 India and Pakistan become independent.

1997 Britain returns Hong Kong to China.

Find out more

EMIGRATION AND IMMIGRATION
UNITED KINGDOM
UNITED KINGDOM, HISTORY OF
VICTORIA, QUEEN
WORLD WAR I

BRONZE AGE

MESOPOTAMIA
One of the earliest Bronze Age civilizations began in Mesopotamia, a plain lying between the Tigris and Euphrates rivers. Its fertile land was farmed by the Sumerians, Assyrians, and Akkadians.

THE BRONZE AGE refers to a period of time during which the predominant metal employed by a culture was bronze. It usually succeeds the Stone Age and the Copper Age and is followed by the Iron Age. The Bronze Age spans c. 3500 to 1000 BCE, but its onset occurred at different times in different parts of the world. During this period, civilizations sprang up in Egypt, Mesopotamia, the Hwang Ho Valley in China, on the Aegean Islands of the Mediterranean, and in the Indus Valley. People learnt to grow crops and domesticate animals, so they no longer needed to move to find food. This allowed communities more time to learn how to use metals. Bronze was formed by melting copper and tin together and was found to be harder and longer lasting than other metals. It was used to make weapons and ornaments, sometimes by pouring hot molten bronze into moulds, for example to make metal pins, or by being heated and beaten into shape. Metalworkers also used gold and copper for luxury items such as jewellery.

BRONZE AGE

3500 BCE Beginning of the Bronze Age in the Middle East. First cities built in Mesopotamia, and people begin to use bronze.

3250 BCE First picture writing develops in Mesopotamia.

3000 BCE The wheel appears in Mesopotamia, and the plough is first used in China.

2800 BCE Rise of Bronze Age culture of the Indus Valley, an agriculturally based civilization in India.

2650 BCE Start of great pyramid building era in parts of Egypt.

2500 BCE Use of bronze spreads across Europe. First stage of Stonehenge built in England.

2100 BCE Sumerian city of Ur reaches the height of its power.

c. 1600 BCE Bronze Age begins in China. Manufacture of magnificent bronze ceremonial vessels.

c. 1200 BCE Rise of the Assyrian empire.

1000 BCE Iron begins to replace bronze as the main metal used.

AEGEAN CIVILIZATIONS

The rise of the Aegean civilizations coincided with the start of bronzeworking in the region. Several important cultures arose during the Aegean Bronze Age (c. 3000 to 1100 BCE): chiefly the Cycladic, Minoan, and Mycenaean cultures. People became highly skilled in architecture, painting, and other crafts. Metalworkers used bronze to make weapons, such as this Mycenaean dagger blade (right) and tools for everyday use such as axes, adzes, and tweezers. People were often buried with a variety of valuable bronze weapons, household utensils, or ornaments. The Aegean people produced bronze objects in great quantity.

THE MYCENAEANS
The city of Mycenae was ruled by the legendary king Agamemnon, and when this gold funeral mask (shown right) was found, it was believed to have belonged to him. Mycenae was famous for its grand palace, walled fortress, and the beehive-shaped tombs where kings were buried. The Mycenaeans were wealthy and powerful, and dominated the Aegean region from 1450 BCE onwards.

SHANG DYNASTY
The Bronze Age coincided with the rise of the Shang dynasty (c. 1600 to 1046 BCE), which was located in the Hwang Ho Valley in China. Its Bronze Age lasted from 1500 to 1000 BCE. Shang techniques for metalworking and writing spread throughout the area. Most bronze vessels (such as the ritual water vessel shown below) were made for use in religious ceremonies. Bronze was also used to make weapons and chariot fittings for soldiers of the great Shang armies.

WRITING AND THE WHEEL

The earliest form of writing, called cuneiform, emerged during the Bronze Age. It was invented by the Sumerians, who also made the first wheels. Wheels were used on wagons and war chariots, and to make pottery. The chariot shown left is from the city of Ur and is being pulled into battle by wild asses.

Find out more
ASSYRIANS
BABYLONIANS
CELTS
GREECE, ANCIENT
PREHISTORIC PEOPLES
SUMERIANS

BUDDHISM

ONE OF THE WORLD'S great religions, Buddhism, began in India about 2,500 years ago. It grew and spread, and today there are more than 350 million Buddhists, mainly in Asia. All Buddhists follow the teachings of Buddha, a name which means "Enlightened One". Buddha himself was born in about 563 BCE. He was originally called Siddhartha Gautama, and was a wealthy prince who became horrified at the suffering in the world. He left his wealth and family, and began to meditate (think deeply). After three years he achieved enlightenment, or complete understanding, became a monk, and travelled extensively to pass his ideas on to others.

Buddhists believe that everyone is reborn after their old body has died. The quality of their new life depends on their karma. Karma is the total of all the good and bad deeds they did in the life they have just left. Buddhists aim to achieve absolute peace – a state they call nirvana. Buddha taught that nirvana could be achieved by following the Eightfold Path: rightness of views, intention, speech, action, livelihood, concentration, mindfulness, and effort.

GOLDEN PAGODA
Buddhist temples usually contain relics of Buddha such as robes or a sandal. Some, such as the Golden Pavilion in Kyoto, Japan, are magnificent buildings inlaid with gold and decorated with diamonds.

BUDDHAS
Although they vary greatly in size, images of the Buddha all look similar. They represent Buddha sitting on a lotus flower. In the home a small Buddha forms part of a shrine. The image reminds followers of the goodness of Buddha and helps them meditate and pray.

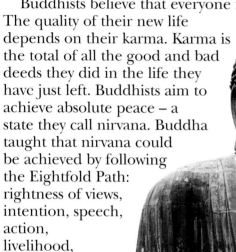

Buddhists burn incense at the shrine and leave offerings of flowers.

FESTIVALS
Bodhi Day – the day Gautama became the Buddha.

Parinirvana – passing of the Buddha into nirvana.

Wesak or Vesakha Puja – a three-day festival to celebrate the main events of Buddha's life.

Dharmachakra Day – when Buddha gave his first sermon.

WHEEL OF LIFE
Buddhists share with Hindus a belief in the Wheel of Life, also called the Wheel of the Law. This is the continuous cycle of birth and rebirth that traps people who have not yet achieved nirvana. The spokes of the wheel remind the Buddhist of the Eightfold Path.

MONKS
Buddhist monks give up most possessions. They keep only their saffron yellow robes, a belt, a needle, a razor, a water strainer, and a bowl to receive alms (gifts). Monks spend their time praying, teaching, and meditating. Each day they go out to collect food. In some Buddhist countries, boys spend a short time at a monastery as part of their schooling.

___
Find out more
ASIA
CHINA
HINDUISM
JAPAN
RELIGIONS
___

BUTTERFLIES AND MOTHS

AS BRILLIANT IN COLOUR as many exotic flowers, butterflies are among the most beautiful of all creatures. Butterflies are more familiar to us than moths because they are active by day, whereas moths are active mainly by night. However, there are more than 160,000 different kinds of moths compared to about 18,000 kinds of butterflies. Together these creatures make up the insect group called Lepidoptera. Moths and butterflies have a life cycle in four stages – egg, caterpillar (larva), pupa (chrysalis), and imago (adult). The change in form from caterpillar to butterfly is called metamorphosis. All butterflies and moths are plant eaters and live wherever plants grow, except in extremely cold regions. Some, such as red admiral butterflies, hibernate (sleep) during winter. Others, such as bogong moths, migrate long distances to find food. A few butterflies and moths are pests to humans. Cabbage white caterpillars devour garden vegetables, and clothes moth caterpillars eat the natural fibres in clothing.

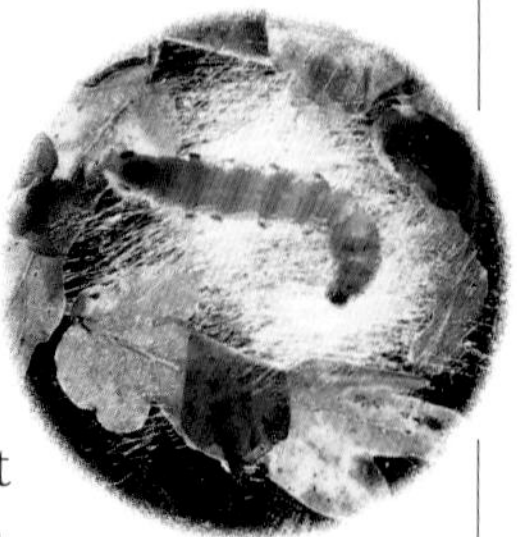

Wings and body are covered with scales.

Butterflies often have slim, non-furry bodies.

Most butterflies have thin antennae with clubbed ends.

Forewing

Hind wing

MORPHO BUTTERFLY

Butterflies, particularly those living in tropical regions, are often more brightly coloured than moths. The blue morpho shown above is found in South America.

SILKWORM

The silkworm is the caterpillar of a moth. It spins a cocoon of silky thread around its body, then changes into a pupa inside the cocoon. People produce silk thread from silkworm cocoons.

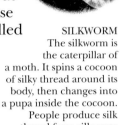

Swallowtail butterfly

MOTH

Moths usually fly at night. Their wings are often but not always dull in colour. When the moth is at rest, it holds its wings to the side of its body. A moth's body is usually plump and hairy, and the antennae are feathery or fernlike. This *brahmaeid* moth from Southeast Asia has fernlike antennae.

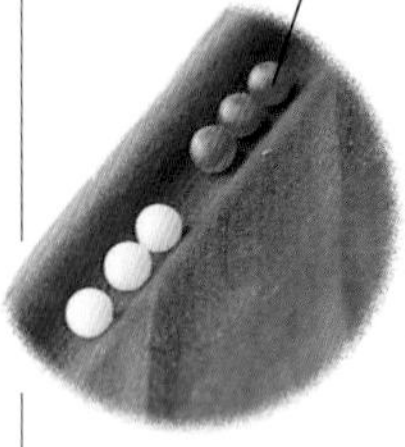

The owl butterfly lays its eggs in batches. The eggs become darker as the time for hatching approaches. Their actual size is only about 1 mm (1/20th inch).

Egg

Caterpillar cuts open egg with its strong jaws and emerges from egg head first.

Hairy head waves around as the pink-striped body struggles to escape from the shell.

EGG TO CATERPILLAR

After mating, a female moth lays eggs on or near a suitable source of food for the caterpillars to eat when they hatch. The eggs of some kinds of moths hatch only when the weather becomes warmer after a cold spell. This usually means that spring has arrived; the plants are beginning to grow again, and they provide food for the hungry caterpillars.

Legs

Caterpillar eats the eggshell, which contains important nutrients.

FEEDING

Each type of caterpillar feeds on a certain kind of vegetation. It spends almost all its time eating; as a result caterpillars can cause great damage to plants and farm crops. Caterpillars stop eating only to moult, or discard their skin when it has become too tight. The caterpillar expands in size before the new skin hardens.

Not all moths are dull in colour – many are beautiful, including the moths shown here.

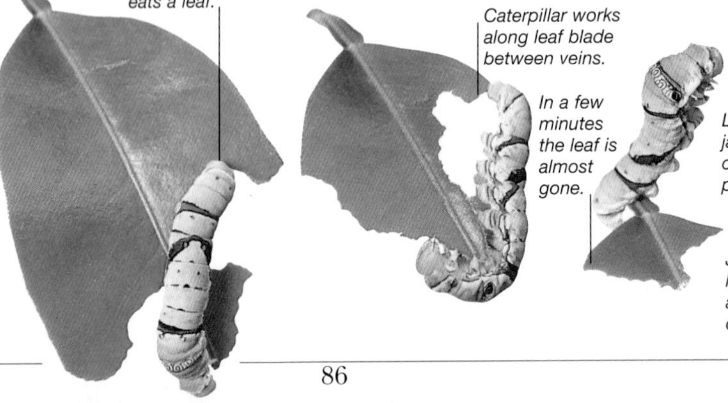

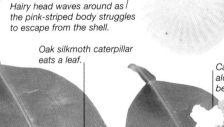

Oak silkmoth caterpillar eats a leaf.

Caterpillar works along leaf blade between veins.

In a few minutes the leaf is almost gone.

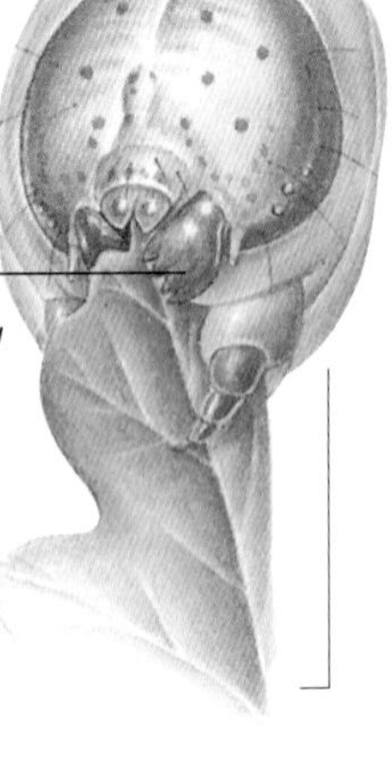

Large, powerful jaws rapidly snip off and chew small pieces of food.

Jaws are hardened with a substance called chitin.

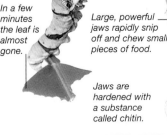

Caterpillar is attached to twig by silken thread.

Caterpillar spins silk girdle around its body, then skin of caterpillar begins to split.

Silk girdle is finished. The pupa is starting to form inside.

New skin of pupa

Spinnerets produce silken thread.

Caterpillar of the citrus swallowtail butterfly attaches its body to a twig and prepares to change into a pupa (chrysalis).

Empty skin and legs of caterpillar

CATERPILLAR TO CHRYSALIS

Before its final moult, a caterpillar stops feeding and may change colour. It finds a safe place to pupate (change into a pupa, or chrysalis). It anchors itself to a stem with silk thread from spinnerets at its rear end. Many moth caterpillars spin a silken cocoon around themselves for protection. Leafroller caterpillars curl leaves around their bodies and, using their mandibles (mouthparts), stitch them together with silk.

PUPA TO BUTTERFLY

The pupa stage is often called the resting stage. But inside its hard skin the creature is undergoing an amazing transformation, controlled by its chemical hormones. After several weeks, the skin of the pupa splits and the adult butterfly or moth emerges. Its damp, crumpled wings soon spread and dry.

SCALES

Tiny overlapping scales cover the wings of moths and butterflies. The colours and arrangement of the scales create the beautiful pattern of the whole wing.

With folded wings, the Indian leaf butterfly looks just like a dead leaf.

Adult blue morpho butterfly with wings closed

CAMOUFLAGE

Seen alone, a butterfly or moth may look so colourful that it would easily be noticed. But in many species the wing colours and patterns are designed to blend in with the natural surroundings. The shape of the wing may also closely resemble a natural object such as a leaf or a fruit.

Resting pupa of blue morpho butterfly disguised as a leaf

Butterfly begins to emerge.

Blood pumps into wing veins to expand them. Wings gradually dry and harden.

Indian leaf butterfly with wings open

The Taenaris macrops butterfly from New Guinea feeds on ripe bananas.

When the wings are open, the eyespots flash like the eyes of a predator.

CONSERVATION

Hundreds of species of moths and butterflies are in danger of extinction. They are threatened because the areas where they live are cleared for farms and homes. Butterflies and moths are also killed and sold to collectors because of their great beauty.

Spanish moon moth is now a protected species.

Queen Alexandra's birdwing butterfly is in danger because the forests where it lives are being cut down.

Large blue butterflies were extinct in Britain, but have now been reintroduced.

EYESPOTS

The eyespots on a butterfly's wings look like the eyes of a predator such as the owl above.

Find out more
ANIMALS
CAMOUFLAGE, ANIMAL
FLIGHT, ANIMAL
INSECTS

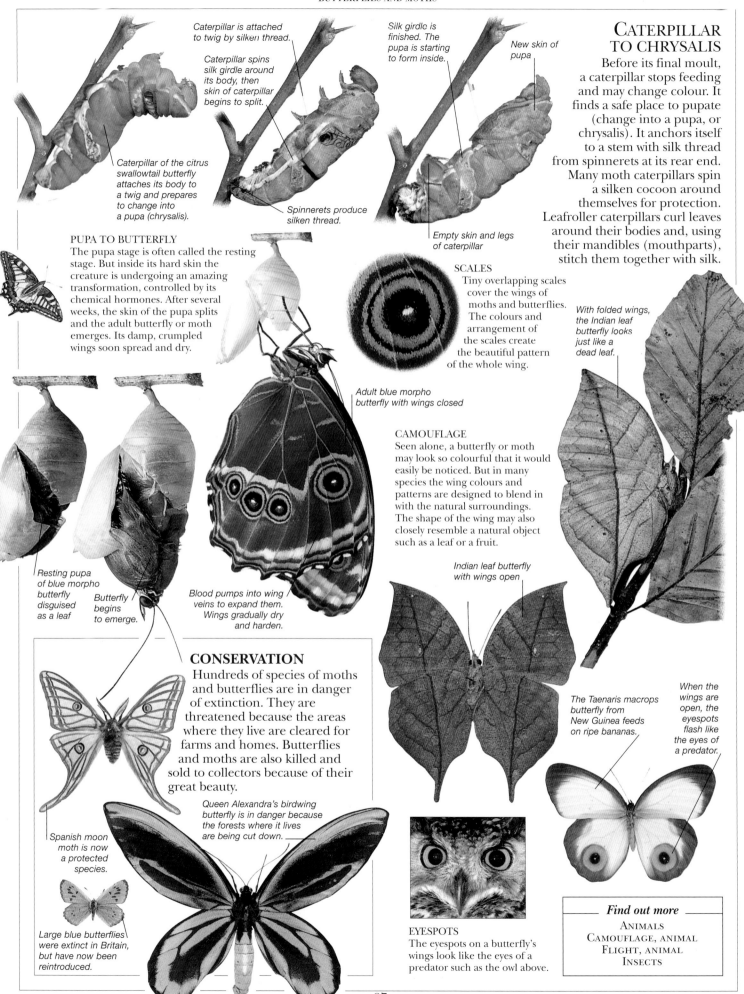

LORD
BYRON

Childe Harold and Ianthe

IN MARCH 1812 a young English poet said, "I woke one morning and found myself famous". His name was George Gordon, Lord Byron, and the first two parts of his long poem *Childe Harold's Pilgrimage* had just been published. The poem describes the life of a young man who is adventurous, an outsider from society. Characters like this became known as "Byronic heroes", and readers were fascinated by their exciting stories. Like his heroes, Lord Byron was an adventurer, too. He travelled widely, and published a number of long poems, such as *Don Juan, The Corsair,* and *The Vision of Judgement.* These were full of action, but also poked fun at the society of the time. Byron's works made him one of the best-known writers in Europe. He was part of the Romantic movement in literature, which regarded imagination and feelings as important.

CHILDE HAROLD
Like Byron himself, the character of Childe Harold travelled all over Europe, commenting on everything he saw – scenery, people he met, and his own feelings. Readers liked the fact that the poem was a mixture of adventure story and travel guide.

1788 Born in London.

1798 Inherits title, Sixth Baron Byron.

1807 Publishes first book, *Hours of Idleness;* it is attacked by the *Edinburgh Review.*

1809 Byron responds with the satire *English Bards and Scotch Reviewers.*

1812 *Childe Harold's Pilgrimage* (cantos 1 and 2).

1816 Leaves England for Europe; travels widely.

1819 Publishes the first two cantos (parts) of *Don Juan.*

1821 Writes several plays and the satire *The Vision of Judgement.*

1824 Dies at Missolonghi in Greece.

SCANDAL
The British public liked Byron's poems, but people were scandalized by his lavish lifestyle, his love affairs, and his satires on politicians and the nobility. In 1816 Byron and his wife separated, and British society turned against him. He was forced to leave the country, and never returned.

Lord Byron

NEWSTEAD ABBEY
Byron inherited the Gordon family home, Newstead Abbey, in Nottinghamshire. The house had once been a monastery and was in a poor state of repair. Byron spent little time there. The poet built up huge debts as a result of his lifestyle, and sold Newstead to raise money.

Newstead Abbey

TRAVELS
Byron travelled throughout Europe, going to far-flung places such as Spain, Albania, and the eastern Mediterranean. Few British people visited those countries at that time. He lived for several years in Italy, but loved Greece most of all. Byron used his knowledge of continental Europe in his poems, and his work has always been as popular in Europe as in his native Britain.

Greek soldiers under siege.

WAR IN GREECE
During Byron's lifetime, Greece was ruled by Turkey, but the Greeks wanted independence. In 1821 the Greeks revolted. Three years later, Byron went to join the freedom fighters. He gave a lot of money to the rebels and set up his own brigade of fighters. But in 1824, Byron was struck down by a fever at the town of Missolonghi, and died before he had a chance to join the fighting.

Find out more
LITERATURE
THEATRE
WRITERS AND POETS

BYZANTINE EMPIRE

IN 330 CE THE ROMAN EMPEROR CONSTANTINE built a new city on the site of the old Greek town of Byzantium. It was called Constantinople (now Istanbul) after him, and it became the capital of the eastern part of the Roman Empire. As the western provinces of the Empire were overrun by the Germanic tribespeople, the eastern half remained prosperous, and Constantinople became the main political centre of the Roman Empire. When the Western Empire collapsed in the late 5th century, the Eastern Empire (which became known as the Byzantine Empire) survived and even expanded. Christianity became the state religion, and Constantinople became a Christian centre. Artists and scholars from all over Europe and the Middle East came there to study. Under Emperor Justinian I, the Byzantine Empire regained much of the territory of the old Roman Empire. Trade, art, and architecture thrived. But the empire suffered many attacks. By 642 Muslim Arabs had overrun Byzantine territories in North Africa and the Middle East. Gradually the empire lost its lands in Asia Minor (Turkey) and southeast Europe. In 1453 the Ottomans captured Constantinople, and the Byzantine Empire ended.

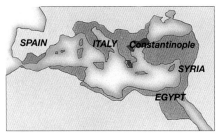

BYZANTINE EMPIRE
In 565 CE, the Byzantine Empire stretched from Spain in the west to Syria in the east. By 1350, the empire had shrunk to a fragment of its former area.

Central dome measures 31 m (100 ft) across.

HAGIA SOPHIA
Justinian I (483-565) built Hagia Sophia (Church of Holy Wisdom) in the centre of Constantinople. It was the largest Christian church in the Eastern world and was intended to provide a spiritual centre for the Byzantine Empire. After 1453, the church became a mosque (Muslim house of worship). Today the Hagia Sophia is a museum.

Marble floors

BYZANTINE EMPIRE

395 Roman Empire splits into East and West, with Constantinople as the capital of the Eastern Empire.

476 The Western Roman Empire collapses.

527-65 During the reign of Justinian I, the Byzantine Empire reconquers much of the old Roman Empire.

635-42 Byzantine Empire loses control of the Middle East and North Africa to the Arabs.

1071 Byzantine Empire loses Asia Minor to the Turks. Calls in help from Europe.

1354 Ottoman Turks gain a foothold in Europe and begin to encircle Constantinople.

1453 Constantinople falls to the Ottoman Turks; the Byzantine Empire comes to an end.

CONSTANTINE THE GREAT
In 314, Constantine the Great (288-337) became Roman emperor. At that time Christianity was forbidden, but in about 312, Constantine himself had been converted, some say by the sight of a cross in the sky. Christianity became the official religion of the Byzantine Empire, and within a century the traditional pagan temples were largely abandoned.

SIEGE OF CONSTANTINOPLE
By the year 1453, the Ottoman Turks had overrun the entire Byzantine Empire and reached the gates of Constantinople. Under the leadership of Sultan Mehmet, the Ottomans besieged the city and captured it after two months. The Christian inhabitants of Constantinople were allowed to remain in the city, which became the capital of the Muslim Ottoman empire.

Find out more
CHRISTIANITY
OTTOMAN EMPIRE
ROMAN EMPIRE

JULIUS
CAESAR

IN 49 BCE A BRILLIANT MILITARY COMMANDER and politician named Julius Caesar became head of the Roman Republic. Caesar made himself popular with people by paying for magnificent public games in Rome. After holding various public offices, including that of consul, he was given command of an army and extended the boundaries of the Roman Republic by conquering Gaul (modern France, Belgium, and Switzerland). He also invaded Britain twice. The senate, a group of elected representatives who ruled Rome, feared he might make himself king, so they ordered Caesar to surrender his army, but instead he marched towards Rome. Pompey the Great, Caesar's son-in-law, headed the senate's troops. In 48 BCE Pompey was murdered; and in 45 BCE Caesar was elected dictator. But a year later he was violently assassinated.

100 BCE Born in Rome.
65 BCE Elected public games organizer.
62 BCE Elected praetor, a law official.
60 BCE Forms First Triumvirate.
59 BCE Elected consul.
58 BCE Begins Gaul campaign.
55 BCE Invades Britain.
49 BCE Fights civil war. Becomes dictator.
48 BCE Defeats Pompey.
46 BCE Defeats Pompey's supporters.
45 BCE Made dictator for life.
44 BCE Assassinated.

As Caesar wondered whether or not to cross the River Rubicon, legend has it that a vision of a larger-than-life man appeared, playing a trumpet, luring him across the river. Caesar took it to be a sign from the gods, and gave the order for his troops to proceed.

Each army unit, or legion, carried its own standard, shaped like an eagle.

TRIUMVIRATE

In 60 BCE Caesar, wanting to be elected consul, allied his fortunes with Pompey (above) and Crassus, another leading politician, to form a three-man group (a triumvirate), which was the most powerful political group in Rome.

CROSSING THE RUBICON

Caesar's victories in Gaul made him very popular with many Romans. However, others feared and distrusted him. In 49 BCE the senate ordered him to give up his army. Caesar refused and crossed the River Rubicon to invade Italy and begin the civil war.

CAESAR'S DEATH

Many politicians in Rome thought that Caesar had too much power. Led by Marcus Brutus and Gaius Cassius, a number of Pompey's supporters plotted against Caesar and decided to kill him. On 15 March (the Ides of March), 44 BCE, the plotters attacked Caesar in the senate and stabbed him to death. Civil war raged after his death; finally, his adopted son Octavian emerged as victor, and the Roman Empire was born.

LAUREL CROWN
Victorious Roman military commanders often wore laurel wreaths to symbolize their power. Later, emperors would wear a crown of gold olive leaves after a great victory.

Find out more
EUROPE, HISTORY OF
ROMAN EMPIRE

CAMERAS

ALTHOUGH THE FIRST PHOTOGRAPH was taken only about 180 years ago, cameras are much, much older. Hundreds of years ago, the Chinese found that light entering a dark room through a pinhole would project a fuzzy image of the world outside onto the opposite wall. Many years later, in 1500 in Europe, a room like this was called a camera obscura, which is Latin for "darkened room". In the 17th century some artists drew sketches with the aid of a camera obscura which had a lens instead of a pinhole to make the image sharper and brighter. The discovery of chemicals that darkened when exposed to light finally made it possible to fix the image permanently – on paper, on glass plates, or on film. Today, digital cameras use light-sensitive electronic sensors instead of film. Sophisticated electronic technology in most cameras ensures that each picture gets the right amount of light (autoexposure) and is perfectly sharp (autofocus). But all cameras still work on the same basic principle as the camera obscura of old.

Screen allows users to check pictures instantly.

Removable memory card stores images.

Autofocus system ensures sharp image.

Filter used to enhance image and protect lens.

Sensor is made of millions of pixels. Each measures brightness and colour of one tiny part of the image.

Light travels from subject to lens.

Circuit processes output from sensor into digital form, so it can be viewed, deleted, or stored.

SINGLE-LENS REFLEX CAMERA
The single-lens reflex (SLR) camera (above) may use either film or a digital sensor. It is popular with photographers for its versatility, and because the viewfinder shows exactly the same view that the camera will record. The lens can be interchanged with others to give a wide view or to magnify the subject.

KINDS OF CAMERAS

There are many different types of cameras, including film, digital, compact, single-lens reflex, disposable, instant-picture, and large-format cameras. However, film usage has dropped so dramatically that many manufacturers have stopped making it. Today, tiny digital cameras are also built into most mobile phone handsets.

DIGITAL CAMERA
A digital camera captures images electronically rather than on standard film and stores them on removable memory cards. Images can then be transferred to a computer and printed out or sent over the Internet.

Photos stored on the camera's memory card can be viewed on the LCD (liquid crystal display).

DIGITAL PHOTO PRINTERS
Some digital cameras can be connected directly to printers in order to print out photos, and many printers have slots for memory cards to be inserted. This makes transferring images to a computer unnecessary.

POLAROID CAMERA
The Polaroid "instant-picture" camera took just 90 seconds to process a picture. Today, however, they have been replaced by instant digital techniques, like portable printers.

MOVIE CAMERAS
The movement we see in the cinema is an illusion. A movie (cinema) film is really a series of still pictures projected on to the screen in such quick succession that they seem to merge into one another. If the subject is in a slightly different place in each picture it looks as if it is moving. Most movie cameras take 24 pictures, or frames, every second, on a very long strip of film wound steadily through the camera. The film stops while each picture is taken, then advances quickly, ready for the next picture.

LARGE-FORMAT CAMERA
In early cameras, the lens was focused by moving a bellows – a concertina-like cloth tunnel – in and out. Many photographers still use large-format bellows cameras for high-quality studio work.

Find out more
FILMS
LIGHT
PHOTOGRAPHY
TELESCOPES
TELEVISION

ANIMAL
CAMOUFLAGE

A BUTTERFLY that looks like a flower, a bird that resembles a log, a fish that seems as lifeless as a stone – many animals and plants survive by blending in with their surroundings. This is called camouflage. Camouflage includes colour, shape, and patterning. For example, it is difficult to spy a newborn deer among the trees because of its pale brown colour and speckled coat. A dead-leaf mantis is also difficult to see because of its leaf shape, and a chameleon can change its colour to match the colour of its surroundings. Camouflage helps animals hide from predators. It also helps predators such as tigers and leopards ambush their prey without being seen. Some animals such as rabbits camouflage themselves by staying absolutely still when in danger so their movements do not give them away.

Chameleon quickly changes colour to brown when it moves onto a leafless branch.

Chameleon matches the green colouring of its leafy branch.

ARCTIC HARE

The Arctic hare is brown in summer to match its surroundings of soil and shrubs. In autumn it sheds its fur and grows a new white coat, for camouflage in the winter snow. The Arctic fox preys on the Arctic hare. In winter the Arctic fox also has a white coat for camouflage.

CHAMELEON

The chameleon is famous for changing its colour and pattern to match its surroundings. Its colour alters when cells in the skin change size, moving their grains of colour nearer the surface or deeper into the skin. When the Jackson's chameleon shown here was taken off its branch, its colour changed from green and yellow to mottled brown. But it took the chameleon about five minutes to do so.

TIGER STRIPES

The tiger is camouflaged by its stripes, which match the light and dark patterns of sunlit grasses. The tiger hunts mainly by ambush, creeping stealthily towards its prey in the undergrowth, then charging over the last few metres.

STICK INSECT

The spindly stick insect is very difficult to recognize among twigs and branches because of its shape and colour. It can fold its thin legs alongside its body and look even more like a twig. When danger threatens, it stays absolutely still – like a stick.

Find out more

ANIMALS
ANIMAL SENSES
BIRDS
FISH
INSECTS
LIONS, TIGERS,
and other big cats

CANADA

THE SECOND LARGEST COUNTRY in the world is also one of the emptiest. Much of Canada is virtually uninhabited The northern part of the country is very cold and covered with snow and ice for much of the year. Few people live among the high Rocky Mountains in the west. Even in the huge wheat-growing plains in the centre there are few people. The majority of Canada's 33.5 million inhabitants live in the southeast, close to the border with the United States. Most Canadians speak English, but for some, particularly those in the province of Québec, French is the first language. This is because they are descendants of the French who settled in Canada in the 16th century. The languages of the native North American and Inuit inhabitants are rarely heard today. Much of Canada's trade is with its neighbour, the United States. However, Canada has close links with many European, Asian, and African nations.

Canada occupies the northern half of North America, stretching from the Pacific to the Atlantic oceans. Part of the country lies within the Arctic Circle. At 6,416 km (3,987 miles) the Canadian-US border is the world's longest continuous frontier between two nations.

TORONTO

More than five million people live in the city of Toronto. It is Canada's business centre and capital of the province of Ontario. Toronto has many skyscrapers, including the 553 m (1,815 ft) high Canadian National Tower.

Maple syrup is obtained by cutting into the maple tree and directing the flow of its sap into a collecting vessel.

SPORTS AND LEISURE

Winter sports such as skiing, skating, and ice hockey are popular in Canada because winters are long and there is plenty of snow and ice. Modern ice hockey was invented in Canada in the 1870s and is now played nearly everywhere in the world. During the summer, sailing, canoeing, and field hockey are also popular.

Ice hockey is the Canadian national sport. The country produces some of the best players in the world.

ROCKY MOUNTAINS

Western Canada is dominated by the Rocky Mountains, which stretch from the United States border in the south to Alaska in the north. The mountains are covered in trees and are a haven for bears and other wildlife.

LAW AND ORDER

The nickname of the Royal Canadian Mounted Police – the national police force – is the Mounties. They boast that they "always get their man".

NATURAL RESOURCES

Canada is rich in minerals such as zinc and iron ore and has huge reserves of oil, coal, and natural gas. Just off Canada's east coast lies the Grand Banks, one of the world's richest fishing areas. Waters within 320 km (200 miles) of Canada's coastline are reserved for Canadian fishermen only. The vast forests that grow across the country are a major source of timber. The country's exports are mainly sent south to the United States; the two countries have formed a free-trade zone with Mexico, which means that most exports or imports among them are not taxed.

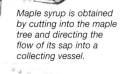

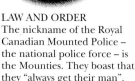

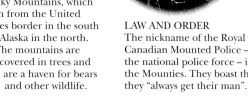

PROVINCES showing date of joining the Confederation of Canada

 ALBERTA 1905
Area: 661,190 sq km
(255,286 sq miles)
Population: 3,632,000
Capital: Edmonton

 BRITISH COLUMBIA 1871
Area: 947,800 sq km
(365,946 sq miles)
Population: 4,420,000
Capital: Victoria

 MANITOBA 1870
Area: 649,950 sq km
(250,946 sq miles)
Population: 1,214,000
Capital: Winnipeg

 NEW BRUNSWICK 1867
Area: 73,440 sq km
(28,355 sq miles)
Population: 749,000
Capital: Fredericton

 NEWFOUNDLAND AND LABRADOR 1949
Area: 404,720 sq km
(156,649 sq miles)
Population: 509,000
Capital: St. John's

 NOVA SCOTIA 1867
Area: 55,490 sq km
(21,425 sq miles)
Population: 940,000
Capital: Halifax

 ONTARIO 1867
Area: 1,068,630 sq km
(412,298 sq miles)
Population: 12,987,000
Capital: Toronto

 PRINCE EDWARD ISLAND 1873
Area: 5,660 sq km
(2,185 sq miles)
Population: 140,000
Capital: Charlottetown

 QUÉBEC 1867
Area: 1,540,680 sq km
(594,857 sq miles)
Population: 7,783,000
Capital: Québec City

 SASKATCHEWAN 1905
Area: 652,330 sq km
(251,865 sq miles)
Population: 1,024,000
Capital: Regina

TERRITORIES showing date of joining the Confederation of Canada

 NORTHWEST TERRITORIES 1870
Area: 1,346,106 sq km
(519,734 sq miles)
Population: 43,000
Capital: Yellowknife

 NUNAVUT 1999
Area: 2,093,190 sq km
(808,185 sq miles)
Population: 32,000
Capital: Iqaluit

 YUKON TERRITORY 1898
Area: 483,450 sq km
(186,660 sq miles)
Population: 33,000
Capital: Whitehorse

In Québec, winding streets connect the Lower Town sector on the waterfront and Upper Town on Cape Diamond, a bluff rising 91 m (300 ft) above the St. Lawrence.

QUÉBEC

Québec City (above) is the oldest city in Canada and the capital of the province of Québec. The French style of its buildings reminds the visitor that many of the city's first colonists came from France. Québec City was founded in 1608 by the French explorer Samuel de Champlain, and Québec itself remained a French colony until the British took it over in 1759. Today Québec is the centre of French Canadian culture. French is still the official language, and most of the population is Roman Catholic.

The Québecois, the people of Québec, see themselves as different from other Canadians, and over the years many of them have campaigned for independence.

This observation deck has a 360-degree view of Vancouver. It is perched on top of Harbour Centre Tower.

VANCOUVER
Vancouver is Canada's leading Pacific port. Situated in southwestern British Columbia, Vancouver overlooks the Strait of Georgia and is surrounded by mountains. The city's many landmarks date from the 1880s and span architectural styles from Renaissance and Art Deco to Modern and Post Modern.

YUKON TERRITORY

Few people live in the Yukon Territory in northwestern Canada but the region is rich in silver, zinc, lead, and gold. During the 1890s it was the site of the Klondike gold rush. Prospectors and adventurers who came to the Yukon hoping to strike gold founded Whitehorse, which became the territorial capital in 1952. Winters in the Yukon are long and cold, but in summer the weather becomes warm, with temperatures reaching 16°C (60°F). This allows the growth of many kinds of vegetation, which take on a rich variety of colours in the autumn. Moose, caribou, beavers, and bears are common in the Yukon.

Find out more

CANADA, HISTORY OF
INUITS
MOUNTAINS
NATIVE AMERICANS
SPORTS

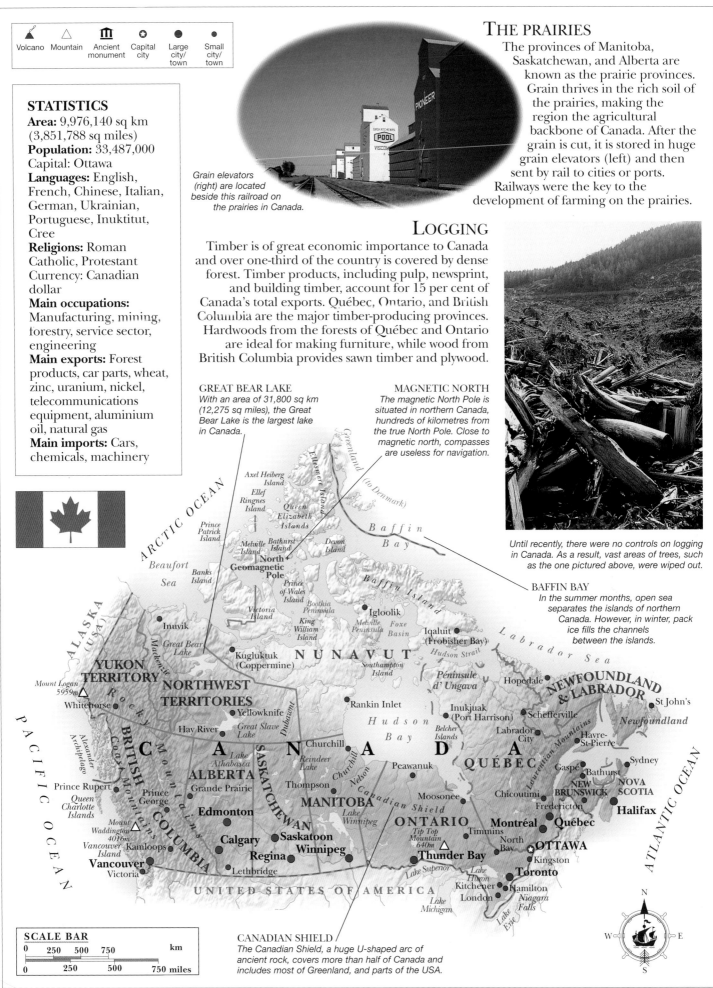

Volcano | Mountain | Ancient monument | Capital city | Large city/town | Small city/town

STATISTICS
Area: 9,976,140 sq km (3,851,788 sq miles)
Population: 33,487,000
Capital: Ottawa
Languages: English, French, Chinese, Italian, German, Ukrainian, Portuguese, Inuktitut, Cree
Religions: Roman Catholic, Protestant
Currency: Canadian dollar
Main occupations: Manufacturing, mining, forestry, service sector, engineering
Main exports: Forest products, car parts, wheat, zinc, uranium, nickel, telecommunications equipment, aluminium oil, natural gas
Main imports: Cars, chemicals, machinery

THE PRAIRIES
The provinces of Manitoba, Saskatchewan, and Alberta are known as the prairie provinces. Grain thrives in the rich soil of the prairies, making the region the agricultural backbone of Canada. After the grain is cut, it is stored in huge grain elevators (left) and then sent by rail to cities or ports. Railways were the key to the development of farming on the prairies.

Grain elevators (right) are located beside this railroad on the prairies in Canada.

LOGGING
Timber is of great economic importance to Canada and over one-third of the country is covered by dense forest. Timber products, including pulp, newsprint, and building timber, account for 15 per cent of Canada's total exports. Québec, Ontario, and British Columbia are the major timber-producing provinces. Hardwoods from the forests of Québec and Ontario are ideal for making furniture, while wood from British Columbia provides sawn timber and plywood.

GREAT BEAR LAKE
With an area of 31,800 sq km (12,275 sq miles), the Great Bear Lake is the largest lake in Canada.

MAGNETIC NORTH
The magnetic North Pole is situated in northern Canada, hundreds of kilometres from the true North Pole. Close to magnetic north, compasses are useless for navigation.

Until recently, there were no controls on logging in Canada. As a result, vast areas of trees, such as the one pictured above, were wiped out.

BAFFIN BAY
In the summer months, open sea separates the islands of northern Canada. However, in winter, pack ice fills the channels between the islands.

CANADIAN SHIELD
The Canadian Shield, a huge U-shaped arc of ancient rock, covers more than half of Canada and includes most of Greenland, and parts of the USA.

SCALE BAR
0 250 500 750 km
0 250 500 750 miles

Canada's most popular emblem is the leaf of the local tree, the red maple.

HISTORY OF
CANADA

ABOUT TWENTY-FIVE THOUSAND YEARS AGO Canada's first people walked across the land that then existed between Siberia and Alaska. The first Europeans (Vikings) reached the Canadian coast about 1,000 years ago, but they did not establish lasting settlements. The original Native American inhabitants of the country lost control when British and French settlers began to establish trading posts for fur during the 17th century. Britain and France fought each other for the land, and in 1759 Britain won control of the whole country. A century later, Canada became independent of British rule but remained a British dominion (territory). After World War II, Canada became very prosperous and developed a close business relationship with the United States. During the 1970s French Canadians demanded more power and threatened to make the province of Québec independent. However, Canada is still united.

CANADA

c. 25,000 BCE First people come to Canada.

c. 1005 CE Vikings land in Newfoundland.

1497 John Cabot explores Newfoundland.

1534 Jacques Cartier sails St. Lawrence River.

1605 First European settlement established by French at Port Royal.

1670 Hudson's Bay Company receives royal charter from English king to trade in Canada.

1689-1763 Frequent wars between French, British, and Native Americans.

1759 Britain captures Québec from French.

1778 James Cook, the English explorer, claims west coast for Britain.

1867 Dominion of Canada established.

1885 Canadian Pacific Railway links the coasts.

1891-1914 More than three million people arrive from Europe.

1949 Newfoundland joins the dominion.

1999 Nunavut is the last province created.

Native Americans were the first inhabitants of Canada.

Snowshoes

Wood cabin

European traders exchanged goods with Native Americans who trapped wild animals for their furs.

Traders travelled by canoe to trading posts. Transport by canoe also opened the way to missionaries and explorers in Canada.

HUDSON'S BAY COMPANY

Both the British and French set up companies in the 17th century to trade in valuable Canadian furs. These companies grew wealthy and powerful and acted like independent governments. The British Hudson's Bay Company ruled much of northern Canada until 1869 when its lands were made part of the Dominion of Canada.

PIERRE TRUDEAU
Since the 1960s Canada has become increasingly independent of Britain. A new flag was adopted in 1965 and two years later a world fair – Expo '67 – was held to show off Canadian skills in the centenary year of independence. In 1968 Pierre Trudeau (right) was elected as prime minister. A great intellectual, he was a strong supporter of a unified Canada.

CABOT AND CARTIER

The Italian explorer John Cabot, sailing for England, was the first European, after the Vikings, to visit Canada when he sailed along the coast of Newfoundland in 1497. The French explorer Jacques Cartier sailed up the mouth of the St. Lawrence River in 1534. Following these two voyages, both Britain and France laid claim to Canada.

John Cabot

Yukon Territory

Northwest Territories

Nunavut

British Columbia

Alberta

Saskatchewan

Manitoba

Ontario (formerly Upper Canada)

CANADA IN 1867

Québec (formerly Lower Canada)

Newfoundland and Labrador

Prince Edward I.

Nova Scotia

New Brunswick

DOMINION
In 1867, the four British colonies of Nova Scotia, New Brunswick, and Upper and Lower Canada formed the self-governing Dominion of Canada. Six more colonies joined after 1867. Newfoundland joined in 1949 and Nunavut was created in 1999.

Find out more
CANADA
COOK, JAMES
INUITS
NATIVE AMERICANS
VIKINGS

CARIBBEAN

STRUNG OUT LIKE a rope of pearls, there is a long row of tropical islands curving for more than 3,200 km (2,000 miles) between Mexico and Venezuela. Together they are usually called the Caribbean islands, sometimes the West Indies. Some are tiny, uninhabited rocks or coral reefs; others are much larger islands with thriving populations. On Martinique for instance, about 400,000 people live around the wooded slopes of several volcanoes which tower hundreds of metres above the sea. There are 13 countries and 12 other territories in the Caribbean. Cuba, with a population of more than 13 million people, is the biggest nation. Although each country has its own distinctive culture, many have connections with other countries. These links are left over from the 18th and 19th centuries, when the whole region was colonized by European kingdoms. The ruling nations brought African slaves to the Caribbean to harvest sugar cane. Today, descendants of these slaves make up a large proportion of the population.

The Caribbean Sea is about 1,943,000 sq km (750,193 sq miles) in area. It is enclosed on three sides by Central America, South America, and the Caribbean Islands.

Brian Lara (right) plays cricket for the West Indies. With 400 runs, he holds the world record for the highest test match score.

TOURISM
The Caribbean islands are very beautiful, with lush trees, colourful birds, long sandy beaches, and months of sunshine. The region attracts tourists from all over the world. This has created many new jobs, particularly in the towns. Tourism is now the main source of income for several islands.

CRICKET
Cricket is a reminder of the Caribbean's colonial past. It is played, and passionately supported, in many of the former British colonies. For international test matches, the Caribbean islands join forces and compete as the West Indies. The West Indies were victorious in the cricket World Cup in 1975 and 1979.

AGRICULTURE
More than half the people of the Caribbean earn a living from agriculture. Many work for a landowner, producing crops such as sugar and coffee. They may also rent or own a small plot of land. On this land they grow food to feed their families or to sell in local markets.

BASTILLE DAY
The islands of Guadeloupe and Martinique are part of France and the people have strong links with this country. They speak the French language, use French currency for money, fly the French flag, and celebrate French holidays such as Bastille Day. Other Caribbean islands have close political and financial links with Britain, the Netherlands, or the United States.

ARCHITECTURE
Brilliant colours enhance the traditional shapes of Caribbean architecture. Similarly, Caribbean music, literature, art, and food are a unique mixture of European and African culture.

Find out more
CENTRAL AMERICA
COLUMBUS, CHRISTOPHER
CRICKET
SLAVERY

⚒	△	🏛	✪	●	•
Volcano	Mountain	Ancient monument	Capital city	Large city/ town	Small city/ town

 ANGUILLA
Area: 102 sq km
(39 sq miles)
Status: British dependent territory
Claimed: 1650
Population: 14,400
Capital: The Valley

ANTIGUA AND BARBUDA
Area: 442 sq km (170 sq miles)
Population: 85,600
Capital: St. John's

ARUBA
Area: 193 sq km
(75 sq miles)
Status: Dutch autonomous region
Claimed: 1643
Population: 103,000
Capital: Oranjestad

BAHAMAS
Area: 13,935 sq km
(5,380 sq miles)
Population: 309,100
Capital: Nassau

BARBADOS
Area: 431 sq km
(166 sq miles)
Population: 284,600
Capital: Bridgetown

 CAYMAN ISLANDS
Area: 259 sq km (100 sq miles)
Status: British dependent territory
Claimed: 1670
Population: 49,000
Capital: George Town

CUBA
Area: 114,524 sq km
(44,218 sq miles)
Population: 11,452,000
Capital: Havana

 DOMINICA
Area: 751 sq km
(290 sq miles)
Population: 72,600
Capital: Roseau

 DOMINICAN REPUBLIC
Area: 48,442 sq km
(18,704 sq miles)
Population: 9,650,000
Capital: Santo Domingo

 GRENADA
Area: 344 sq km
(133 sq miles)
Population: 90,700
Capital: Saint George's

 GUADELOUPE
Area: 1,779 sq km
(687 sq miles)
Status: French overseas department
Claimed: 1635
Population: 440,000
Capital: Basse-Terre

 HAITI
Area: 27,750 sq km
(10,714 sq miles)
Population: 8,300,000
Capital: Port-au-Prince

 JAMAICA
Area: 10,991 sq km
(4,244 sq miles)
Population: 2,700,000
Capital: Kingston

 MARTINIQUE
Area: 1,101 sq km
(425 sq miles)
Status: French overseas department
Claimed: 1635
Population: 393,000
Capital: Fort-de-France

 MONTSERRAT
Area: 101 sq km
(38 sq miles)
Status: British dependent territory
Claimed: 1632
Population: 9,000
Capital: Plymouth

 NETHERLANDS ANTILLES
Area: 960 sq km (371 sq miles)
Status: Dutch autonomous region
Claimed: 1816
Population: 221,000
Capital: Willemstad

 PUERTO RICO
Area: 8,897 sq km
(3,435 sq miles)
Status: US commonwealth territory
Claimed: 1898
Population: 3,971,000
Capital: San Juan

 ST. KITTS AND NEVIS
Area: 261 sq km
(101 sq miles)
Population: 40,100
Capital: Basseterre

 ST. LUCIA
Area: 616 sq km
(238 sq miles)
Population: 160,300
Capital: Castries

 ST. VINCENT AND THE GRENADINES
Area: 388 sq km (150 sq miles)
Population: 104,600
Capital: Kingstown

 TRINIDAD AND TOBAGO
Area: 5,128 sq km (1,980 sq miles)
Population: 1,230,000
Capital: Port-of-Spain

 TURKS AND CAICOS ISLANDS
Area: 430 sq km (166 sq miles)
Status: British dependent territory
Claimed: 1766
Population: 22,900
Capital: Cockburn Town

VIRGIN ISLANDS
Area: 352 sq km
(136 sq miles)
Status: US unincorporated territory
Claimed: 1917
Population: 109,800
Capital: Charlotte Amalie

VIRGIN ISLANDS, BRITISH
Area: 153 sq km (59 sq miles)
Status: British dependent territory
Claimed: 1672
Population: 24,400
Capital: Road Town

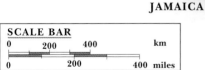

SCALE BAR

| 0 | 200 | 400 | km |
| 0 | 200 | 400 | miles |

ISLAND GROUPS
The larger islands of the Caribbean between Cuba and Puerto Rico are often called the Greater Antilles, to distinguish them from the Lesser Antilles to the east. The small islands from the Virgin Islands to Dominica are sometimes called the Leeward Islands; and the islands to the south (Martinique to Grenada), the Windward Islands.

98

CARS

IF YOU COULD line up all the world's cars end to end, they would form a traffic jam stretching all the way to the moon; and the line is getting longer, because a new car is made every second. Most cars are family cars, used for trips to school, work, and shops, to see friends and take holidays. But there are also a number of special-purpose cars, including taxis, sports cars, and police patrol cars.

Petrol or diesel engines power modern cars, just as they did the first cars of the 19th century. But the cars of today are very different from cars even 30 years ago. The latest cars have low, sleek shapes that are attractive and also reduce drag, or air resistance. Other features include powerful brakes for stopping quickly and electronic engine control systems that allow cars to travel faster and use less fuel.

HOW A CAR WORKS

In most cars, the engine is at the front and drives the back or front wheels (or all four wheels) through a series of shafts and gears. There are usually four or five different gears; they alter the speed at which the engine turns the wheels. In low gear, the wheels turn slowly and produce extra force for starting and climbing hills. In high gear, the wheels turn fast for travelling at speed.

A car radiator is full of water. A pump keeps water flowing around the engine to keep it cool. As the car moves forward, cold air rushes through the radiator, cooling the water before its next circuit around the engine.

The steering wheel turns the steering gear via a long shaft.

Tread, or grooves on the tyres, improve traction (grip) in the rain.

This car has a manual gearbox, which means the driver uses the gear lever to change gear. In some cars, gear changes are automatic.

Turning the steering wheel inside the car turns a system of gears that point the front wheels towards the left or right.

Suspension springs and shock absorbers soften a bumpy ride for the passengers and keep the wheels firmly on the ground as the car travels over uneven surfaces.

Pressing on the brake pedal pushes a special liquid down tubes, which in turn push on pistons at each wheel. These pistons squeeze the brake pads against steel discs or drums attached to the wheels, slowing down the wheels and stopping the car.

ANTI-POLLUTION DEVICE
Waste gases from the engine of a car are highly toxic (poisonous). To keep them under control some cars have special filters, called catalytic converters, fitted to the exhaust system. These filters remove poisonous gases.

TYPES OF CARS

Cars have numerous uses, and there are many different kinds of cars available to suit almost any task. Most family cars combine a large interior with speed and fuel economy. However, for other, more specialized vehicles, speed, luxury, or power may be the most important design feature.

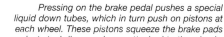

SPORTS CAR
With its large engine, sleek design, and usually seating for only two people, a sports car is designed purely for speed. Some can travel at about 300 km/h (200 mph).

CRASH PROTECTION
The driver and passengers are cocooned in a strong steel cage to protect them in a crash. But the rest of the car is designed to crumple easily and absorb some of the impact. Wearing seat belts can protect car passengers from injury in a crash.

LUXURY CAR
Large, carefully crafted cars such as the world-famous Rolls-Royce are among the most beautiful and expensive automobiles in the world.

OFF-ROAD VEHICLE
Rugged vehicles built specially for driving across country have powerful engines, four-wheel drive, and heavy ridged tyres for extra grip.

HISTORY OF THE CAR

People laughed at the first rickety "horseless carriages" of the 1880s. But rapid technical progress soon made it clear that cars were here to stay. In 1903, cars could already reach speeds of more than 110 km/h (70 mph). But they were expensive and often broke down. Since then cars have become steadily cheaper and more reliable. Now they are everyday transport for millions of people throughout the world.

NICOLAS CUGNOT

The first road vehicles were powered by steam. In 1769, Nicolas Cugnot, a French soldier, built a steam carriage for dragging cannon. It travelled about 5 km/h (3 mph) and had to stop about every 10 minutes to build up steam.

DAIMLER AND BENZ

In the 1880s, German engineers Karl Benz and Gottlieb Daimler worked independently to produce the first petrol engine. In 1885, Karl Benz built his flimsy motorized tricycle (left), the first petrol-powered car.

PANHARD AND LEVASSOR

In the 1890s, two Frenchmen, René Panhard and Emile Levassor, built the first car with the engine in the front, the arrangement found in most cars to this day.

The production line for the Ford Model T

FORD MODEL T

Early cars were handmade and cost so much money that only the rich could afford them. In 1908, Henry Ford opened a factory to produce large numbers of the Model T (above). This was the first car cheap enough to be purchased by more people.

Rear airfoil

Wide tyres, called slicks, are smooth to minimize rolling resistance, but wide to give a good grip on the track.

The lightweight body is carefully shaped to keep drag to a minimum.

Powerful disc brakes can slow the car from 300 km/h to 65 km/h (200 mph to 40 mph) in less than three seconds.

The frame is made of ultra-light carbon-fibre composites.

A computer continually adjusts the suspension to make sure the wheels do not bounce up from the track.

Aerofoils at the front and back work like upside-down aeroplane wings. Air rushing over them pushes the car firmly onto the track, which improves traction.

NEW DESIGNS

Prototypes (test models) of new cars are packed with electronics and computers that can do anything from parking the car automatically to steering the car automatically. Many parts of these cars are made of plastics and other new materials; some new engine designs contain ceramic components instead of metal ones.

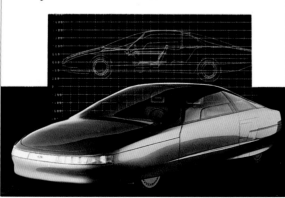

RACING CAR

Grand Prix racing cars are designed for speed alone, so they are built very differently from road cars. They have big, powerful eight-cylinder engines made of special light materials. This allows them to reach top speeds of up to 400 km/h (250 mph). Their ultra-low shape allows them to slice through the air easily so they can travel as fast as possible. Indeed, the driver has to lie almost flat to fit in.

Find out more

ENGINES
PHYSICS
PLASTICS
POLLUTION
TECHNOLOGY
TRANSPORT, HISTORY OF
WHEELS

CASTLES

THE MASSIVE WALLS AND TOWERS of a castle were designed to make it impossible for enemy soldiers to destroy it. Inside was a whole world in miniature – lords and ladies, government officials, soldiers, servants, animals, gardens, treasure stores, and dungeons where prisoners could be tortured. The best site for a castle was on a hill surrounded by water. If there were no natural features, the builders made an artificial hill or dug a deep ditch and filled it with water to make a moat. A well-built castle with a good military commander in charge could withstand an enemy siege for many months. Most castles were built between the 9th century and the 16th century, when many countries were almost constantly at war. Early castles were small and made of wood; the later stone buildings housed town-sized populations; many are still standing today. The invention of gunpowder at the end of the 13th century made castles hard to defend. As times grew more peaceful, kings and lords moved into comfortable country houses.

LOOPHOLES
Archers fired through loopholes – narrow slits in the walls which were wider on the inside to make aiming easier. The inner walls were often higher than the outer walls, so archers could fire at the attackers over the heads of their own soldiers.

Siege engines had to be tall enough for attackers to fire down on castle soldiers.

Sandbags protected the attacking archers.

Towers which stuck out from the walls gave archers a clear view of the attackers trying to climb the walls.

Even if the attackers built a bridge across a moat, they could be stopped by boiling water or hot sand dropped on them from above.

DEFENDING A CASTLE

During a siege, attackers tried to climb over the walls, smash them down with siege engines, or starve out the inhabitants. The defenders used archers with bows and arrows to keep attackers away from the walls. If the archers failed, soldiers pushed the attackers' scaling ladders away with poles and poured tubs full of boiling water or hot sand onto the enemy below. Deep moats or solid rock foundations stopped the attackers from digging under the walls. In peacetime, the knights and soldiers of the castle trained for war by jousting and playing war games in elaborate tournaments.

Attackers used a battering ram to break down drawbridge.

Deep moats surrounded castle walls.

101

HOW CASTLES DEVELOPED

International wars, especially the Crusades in the Middle East, led to bigger armies, more powerful weapons, and stronger, more sophisticated defences. These wars speeded up castle building.

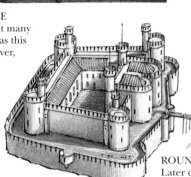

NORMAN CASTLE
The Normans built many stone castles such as this one (above) at Dover, England, between the 11th and 13th centuries.

Motte

Bailey

MOTTE AND BAILEY
Early castles were built as a motte (hill) and bailey (court). They were made of wood and burned easily.

"Fairy tale" turret

SPANISH CASTLE
Some castles, such as the Alcázar in Segovia, Spain, became magnificent royal palaces.

ROUND TOWERS
Later castles had round towers. Rocks bounced off the curved surface and did less damage.

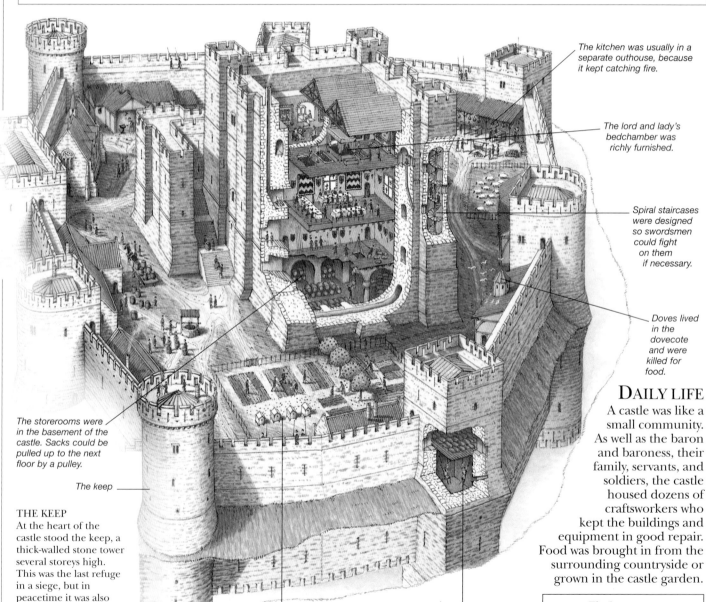

The kitchen was usually in a separate outhouse, because it kept catching fire.

The lord and lady's bedchamber was richly furnished.

Spiral staircases were designed so swordsmen could fight on them if necessary.

Doves lived in the dovecote and were killed for food.

The storerooms were in the basement of the castle. Sacks could be pulled up to the next floor by a pulley.

The keep

THE KEEP

At the heart of the castle stood the keep, a thick-walled stone tower several storeys high. This was the last refuge in a siege, but in peacetime it was also home to the lord's family and followers.
The entrance to the keep was always on the first floor, through the guardroom. Above this was a great hall for feasting, and sometimes sleeping. The lord's own rooms were on the top floor.

Bees were kept to provide honey, and herbs were grown for medicinal purposes.

Prisoners were kept in chains in the dungeons.

DAILY LIFE

A castle was like a small community. As well as the baron and baroness, their family, servants, and soldiers, the castle housed dozens of craftsworkers who kept the buildings and equipment in good repair. Food was brought in from the surrounding countryside or grown in the castle garden.

Find out more
CRUSADES
KNIGHTS AND HERALDRY
MEDIEVAL EUROPE
NORMANS

CATS

WHEN YOU WATCH a cat stalking a bird, it is easy to see how cats are related to lions and tigers. All cats are excellent hunters. They have acute senses and sharp teeth and claws, and they are strong and agile. Cats do most of their hunting at night, and have evolved excellent eyesight in dim conditions. Even a domestic cat, or house cat, could survive in the wild by catching mice, small birds, insects, and other creatures. Many exotic pedigree (purebred) cats, however, might not be able to live for long in the wild, since most are used to a pampered lifestyle indoors.

The ancestor of our domestic cats is a wild tabby-coloured cat – the African wild cat – that has existed for about one million years. This small wild cat spread through Africa, Asia, and Europe, until it was gradually tamed by people in Africa, where it helped protect food stores from rats and mice. Since then, domestic cats have been bred by people into many different types, from striped tabbies and Persian longhairs to the tailless Manx cat. Three thousand years ago, domestic cats were a common sight in Egypt, where they were held in great esteem. Today there are more than 500 million domestic cats around the world.

WILD CATS
The wild cat looks similar to the domestic tabby cat, but it has a heavier build and a larger head. Wild cats have black stripes on their legs and tail.

AGILITY
Cats have exceptional balance and often climb trees, walls, and fences when they are hunting or exploring. Cats also have extremely quick reflexes in case of a fall. As a cat drops, the balance organs inside its ears tell it at once which way is up. The cat rights its head, followed by its body, then lands safely on all four paws.

Long flexible tail helps cat balance on narrow ledges.

BLACK CATS
For thousands of years, black cats have been associated with magic and witchcraft. They are still believed by some people to bring both good and bad luck.

Cat suddenly falls.

Head twists around first.

Large ears can pick up faint sounds.

Pupils open wide in dim light to let in more light.

Pupils are narrow in bright light to let in less light.

Body follows head around.

EYES
In dim conditions, a cat's pupils open wide to let the maximum amount of light into the eye. The tapetum lucidum, a mirror-like layer inside the eye, reflects the light at the back of the eye. This is why a cat's eyes shine in the dark.

Touch-sensitive whiskers for feeling in the dark

Legs stretch out for landing.

DOMESTIC CAT

There are around 75 official breeds of domestic cat, and many more unofficial breeds. Cat experts are continually creating new varieties by selective breeding. The Bombay cat (left) is a new breed which was developed in the United States in the 1970s. It was bred by mating a Burmese with an American Black Shorthair. Although the Bombay has very short, dense hair, it still shows all the main features of a typical cat.

Claws retracted in sheaths to keep them sharp

KITTENS

Young cats are called kittens. They spend hours chasing their tails, springing on each other, and having mock fights. Their play has a serious purpose. It helps them develop hunting skills, quick reactions, and strength and suppleness for those times when they have to fend for themselves.

SLEEPING

The average cat sleeps 16 hours each day, usually in short intervals called cat naps. A cat's body is designed for quick bursts of action, with much rest between.

GROOMING

Cats are famous for their cleanliness. Every day they spend at least an hour washing their fur with saliva and licking it with their rough-surfaced tongues. This makes the fur smooth and glossy. It also helps keep body heat in, removes pests, and stimulates the skin's blood flow.

BEHAVIOUR

Domestic cats resemble their wild ancestors in several ways. Although most domestic cats do not have to catch their own food, they show many signs of hunting behaviour such as being particularly active at dawn and dusk, and stalking and pouncing on pretend prey. Much of this behaviour is instinctive, or inborn, and does not have to be learned. A cat that is brought up away from all other cats still behaves in this way.

HUNTING

A cat's sensitive nose easily picks up the scent of a mouse. As the cat nears its victim, its eyes and ears also come into use. After stalking up silently and slowly, the cat leaps forward with bared claws and grabs the prey, often biting it on the back of the head to break its neck.

LEAPING

Long, supple legs, with strong muscles and flexible joints, give cats great jumping ability. A cat usually looks before it leaps, moving its head from side to side so that it can judge the distance accurately. If the jump is too big, the cat may try to find another route.

During lactation (milk-feeding), the kittens suck milk from teats on their mother's abdomen.

The mother cat guards her young until they are able to fend for themselves.

HAIRLESS CAT

The sphynx breed of cat was developed in the 1960s from a kitten that was born without fur. The sphynx has bare skin except for a few fine, dark, downy hairs on its face, paws, and tail tip. It is unlikely that a hairless cat such as this one could survive in the wild for long.

BREEDING

Female cats, or queens, are pregnant for about nine weeks. They give birth to between one and 10 kittens, but two to five kittens is average. A family of young kittens is called a litter. Newborn kittens are helpless. Their eyes are closed for the first week or more, and they do not begin to crawl for about two weeks. They feed on their mother's milk at first. After about eight weeks they gradually stop taking milk and begin to eat solid foods. This process is called weaning. About four weeks later, the mother cat is ready to mate again.

Ancient Egyptians kept domestic cats to guard grain stores. Cats became so celebrated that some were worshipped as gods, and statues such as the one shown here were made.

Find out more

ANIMAL SENSES
ANIMALS
EGYPT, ANCIENT
LIONS, TIGERS, and other big cats
MAMMALS

CAUCASUS REPUBLICS

THESE RUGGED AND MOUNTAINOUS republics lie between the flat steppelands of the Russian Federation and the high plateaux of Southwest Asia. All three countries were once part of the Soviet Union, and gained their independence in 1991. The region is rich in natural resources, with many contrasting climates and landscapes. Georgia's western borders on the Black Sea coast are lush and green with a warm, humid climate, while much of Armenia is semi-desert and high plateau. Farming is important for all three countries; crops include apricots, peaches, cereals, citrus fruits, grapes and tea. The mountains are rich in mineral resources, such as iron, copper and lead, while the Caspian Sea has plentiful oil. There are over 50 ethnic groups living in the Caucasus, each retaining their own language and culture. Since independence, there have been growing ethnic and religious tensions.

Georgia, Azerbaijan, and Armenia are sandwiched between the high mountains of the Greater and Lesser Caucasus. The Black Sea borders the west of the region, while the landlocked Caspian lies to the east. Beyond the Caucasus Mountains to the north lies the Russian Federation.

CAUCASUS
The Caucasus in the north of the region form a high mountain barrier isolating it from the Russian Federation. Many peaks in the Caucasus rise to more than 4,600 m (15,000 ft).

OIL RIGS
In 1900, Azerbaijan was one of the world's main oil producers, supplying the entire Soviet Union. Caspian Sea oil resources are still being exploited, although lack of investment in rigs has reduced the potential output. Oil is piped from Baku, the centre of the industry, to Iran, Russia, Kazakhstan, and Turkmenistan.

BLACK SEA
The Black Sea is an inland sea between Asia and Europe. It is connected to the Mediterranean Sea by the Bosporus, the Sea of Marmara and the Dardanelles.

YEREVAN
Yerevan, the capital of Armenia, is located on the Razdan river, 23 km (14 miles) from the Turkish frontier. The city has long been a commercial centre, and today its markets are packed with traders selling fruit, vegetables, and rugs woven locally from silk and wool. During the Soviet era, the city expanded rapidly, its growth encouraged by the building of hydro-electric plants on the Razdan, which powered chemicals and engineering industries.

⚲ Volcano	△ Mountain	⛫ Ancient monument
✪ Capital city	● Large city/ town	• Small city/ town

SCALE BAR
0   50   km
0   50   miles

ARMENIA
Area: 29,000 sq km (11,505 sq miles)
Population: 2,967,000
Capital: Yerevan

AZERBAIJAN
Area: 86,600 sq km (33,436 sq miles)
Population: 8,239,000
Capital: Baku

GEORGIA
Area: 69,700 sq km (26,911 sq miles)
Population: 4,616,000
Capital: Tblisi

Find out more
ASIA
ASIA, HISTORY OF
MOUNTAINS
OIL
SOVIET UNION, HISTORY OF

CAVES

BENEATH THE SURFACE of the Earth lies a secret world. Caves run through the rock, opening out into huge chambers decorated with slender stone columns. Underground rivers wind through deep passages, and waterfalls crash down on hidden lakes. Caves such as these are many thousands of years old; they were formed as water slowly dissolved limestone rocks. But not all caves are underground. Sea cliffs contain caves that have been eroded by the waves. Caves also develop inside glaciers and within the solidified lava around volcanoes.

Caves are damp, dark places. Some are only large enough to contain one person; others, such as the network of caves in Mammoth Cave National Park, United States, stretch for hundreds of kilometres. One of the world's deepest caves, in France, lies almost 1.5 km (1 mile) below the ground. Prehistoric peoples used caves for shelter. Caves at Lascaux, France, contain wall paintings and ancient tools that are perhaps 20,000 years old. A few cave dwellers still live today in parts of Africa and Asia.

Stalactites and stalagmites take thousands of years to grow.

STALACTITES
Slender stalactites often hang from a cave roof. Drops of water seeping down from above dissolve a white mineral called calcite from the rock. As the water dries, small amounts of calcite are left behind. These build up to form stalactites. This process is usually very slow; stalactites grow only about 2.5 cm (1 in) in 500 years.

Water drop falls from tip of stalactite.

STALAGMITES
Water dripping from the roof or from a stalactite falls to the cave floor, leaving layers of calcite on the floor. In this way a pillar called a stalagmite slowly builds upwards.

HOW CAVES FORM
Large cave systems lie beneath the ground in regions made of limestone rock. For thousands of years, rainwater, which is naturally acidic, dissolved away the limestone. Small cracks formed, slowly widening to create deep holes, which became underground caves and rivers as water continued to erode the rock.

A stalactite and stalagmite may grow and meet to form a column from floor to roof.

Ridges and grooves in the limestone surface

Water seeps through rock joints; rock develops cracks which widen into potholes.

Step-like rock formations

Stream emerges over waterfall.

Craggy limestone cliffs

Sinkhole – point at which a stream plunges underground

Sparse vegetation

Steep channel carved by stream.

Ground water fills a previously dry cavern to the level of the water table, which can rise and fall over time.

Underground lake

Later passage eroded by stream.

Stream emerges via cave mouth and flows along the valley bottom.

Potholers marvel at the fascinating rock formations around an underground lake at the mouth of a cave in France.

POTHOLING
The sport of exploring caves is called potholing. Clambering about in caves is a dirty and often wet pastime, so potholers wear tough clothing. Other important equipment includes nylon ropes, a helmet with a light, and ladders made of steel cables. Potholers work in teams and may stay in a cave for several days. Potholing can be dangerous; rain can cause flooding, and potholers can be trapped by sudden rockfalls.

Find out more
BATS
GEOLOGY
PREHISTORIC PEOPLES
ROCKS AND MINERALS
VOLCANOES

CELTS

BOUDICCA
In 61 CE, Boudicca (or Boadicea), queen of the Iceni, a Celtic tribe in Britain, led a massive revolt against oppression by the Romans. The Britons, however, were no match for the well-organized Romans, and the revolt was suppressed.

TWO THOUSAND YEARS AGO, much of western Europe was inhabited by a fierce, proud, artistic people known as the Celts. They were skilled warriors, farmers, and metalworkers. For several hundred years their art and culture dominated northwest Europe. All Celts shared a similar way of life, but they were not a single group of people. They included many different tribes such as the Atrebates of southern Britain and the Parisii of northern France. Most Celts lived in villages or hill forts, some of which developed into small towns. But the Celts never formed a unified nation. Between 300 BCE and 100 CE they were absorbed into the Roman Empire. Today Celtic-speaking people can still be found in parts of Britain, Ireland, and France.

Livestock were kept for food and dairy produce.

Huts were covered in clay and thatch to protect them from bad weather.

Woven wooden frame of hut

The Celts wove their own cloth on looms.

THE HOME
Celtic families lived together in one large hut. Some huts were made of stone; others of wattle and daub – wood-framed huts covered in clay to make a hard wall. Thatch was often used to keep the rain out. An iron cauldron hung over a fire for cooking meat or boiling water. Bread was cooked in a domed clay oven. Members of the family wove cloth, worked as farmers, or made pots.

DRUIDS
Druids, a very important group in Celtic society, were priests who led religious ceremonies, acted as judges and advisers, and were responsible for teaching the sons of chiefs. Druidism involved the worship of many gods. Oak trees and mistletoe were also sacred to Druids.

METALWORKING
The Celts worked with many different metals including iron, bronze, copper, gold, and silver. Farm tools, weapons, shields, chariots, and helmets were made from metal, and many were beautifully decorated with distinctive plants and animals, as shown on the border around this page.

The spread of Celtic occupation in Europe

Early Celts

6th-5th centuries BCE   4th century BCE

CELTIC LANDS
The earliest Celts lived in central Europe, in what is now southern Germany. By about 500 BCE Celts had spread out to cover much of Europe, from Ireland to the Black Sea.

Find out more
BRITAIN, ANCIENT
IRON AGE

CENTRAL AFRICA

The Equator runs through the countries of Central Africa, exercising a strong influence on both climate and vegetation. The extreme north of the region borders the arid Sahara Desert. The south is dominated by the Congo River basin and equatorial rain forest.

MUCH OF CENTRAL AFRICA is covered by dense rain forest, drained by the Congo River which flows in a sweeping arc for 4,666 km (2,900 miles). Most of the countries in this region were once French colonies. Their fortunes have varied since independence in the 1960s. The Democratic Republic of Congo has rich mineral deposits and fertile land, but civil wars and conflict with Rwanda (1996-97) have kept it poor. Chad has also suffered from civil wars while the Central African Republic is one of the world's poorest countries, the victim of an unstable government. To the west, Gabon, Cameroon, and Congo have profited from oil and timber, and are comparatively stable. Everywhere, most people support themselves by farming. In the humid tropical lowlands, diseases such as malaria are widespread, and infant mortality is high.

FULANI
The Fulani are nomads who spread across West Africa and into Chad, Guinea, and Cameroon during the 11th century. From the 14th century, they converted to Islam, spreading the faith through persuasion and conquest. Some Fulani are still cattle-herding pastoralists, while others have adopted settled agriculture, or live in towns.

TIMBER INDUSTRY
The equatorial rain forests of Central Africa are a major source of hardwoods, such as mahogany, ebony, and teak. Timber is an important export for several countries, especially Gabon and Cameroon. However, the timber industry poses a severe threat to the rain forests, which take many years to recover. In addition, most timber companies are foreign-owned, and take profits out of the countries.

Controlled fires, as pictured above, "burn off" rain forest in Cameroon, clearing land for agriculture and industry.

Established in 1925, Virunga National Park (right) is Africa's oldest national park. It is also a World Heritage site.

OIL WEALTH
The Congo, Gabon, and Cameroon have all discovered extensive offshore oil reserves in the Atlantic Ocean. Exports of oil are vital economically, as they can earn these countries foreign currency. In the Congo, oil accounts for 85 per cent of the country's exports. This over-dependence on oil can be disastrous when world oil prices fluctuate. Oil is also Gabon's main export, and profits from oil have been ploughed back into its health service, one of the best in Africa.

VIRUNGA NATIONAL PARK
Virunga National Park is located in the northeast corner of the Democratic Republic of Congo, and was created in 1925. It is dominated by the Virunga Mountains, a range of both dormant and active volcanoes which extend into Rwanda and Uganda. The mountains are cloaked with cloud forests, and are a famous refuge for gorillas, an endangered species. Lake Edward occupies much of the centre of the park, and the open countryside surrounding it is populated by herds of elephants and okapi.

LIBREVILLE
Gabon's capital, Libreville ("free town"), was founded by freed slaves in 1849. It lies on a string of hills which enclose a port. The modern European-style centre is ringed by traditional African villages.

> ### Find out more
> AFRICA
> AFRICA, HISTORY OF
> FOREST WILDLIFE
> SLAVERY

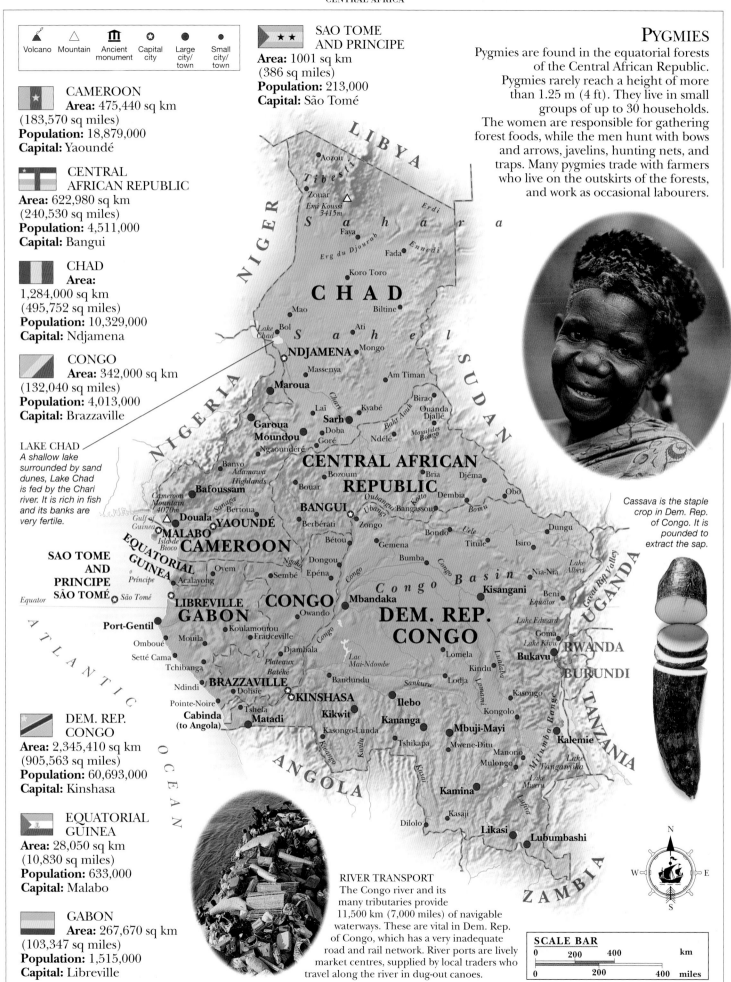

Volcano   Mountain   Ancient monument   Capital city   Large city/town   Small city/town

CAMEROON
Area: 475,440 sq km (183,570 sq miles)
Population: 18,879,000
Capital: Yaoundé

CENTRAL AFRICAN REPUBLIC
Area: 622,980 sq km (240,530 sq miles)
Population: 4,511,000
Capital: Bangui

CHAD
Area: 1,284,000 sq km (495,752 sq miles)
Population: 10,329,000
Capital: Ndjamena

CONGO
Area: 342,000 sq km (132,040 sq miles)
Population: 4,013,000
Capital: Brazzaville

LAKE CHAD
A shallow lake surrounded by sand dunes, Lake Chad is fed by the Chari river. It is rich in fish and its banks are very fertile.

SAO TOME AND PRINCIPE

DEM. REP. CONGO
Area: 2,345,410 sq km (905,563 sq miles)
Population: 60,693,000
Capital: Kinshasa

EQUATORIAL GUINEA
Area: 28,050 sq km (10,830 sq miles)
Population: 633,000
Capital: Malabo

GABON
Area: 267,670 sq km (103,347 sq miles)
Population: 1,515,000
Capital: Libreville

SAO TOME AND PRINCIPE
Area: 1001 sq km (386 sq miles)
Population: 213,000
Capital: São Tomé

PYGMIES
Pygmies are found in the equatorial forests of the Central African Republic. Pygmies rarely reach a height of more than 1.25 m (4 ft). They live in small groups of up to 30 households. The women are responsible for gathering forest foods, while the men hunt with bows and arrows, javelins, hunting nets, and traps. Many pygmies trade with farmers who live on the outskirts of the forests, and work as occasional labourers.

Cassava is the staple crop in Dem. Rep. of Congo. It is pounded to extract the sap.

RIVER TRANSPORT
The Congo river and its many tributaries provide 11,500 km (7,000 miles) of navigable waterways. These are vital in Dem. Rep. of Congo, which has a very inadequate road and rail network. River ports are lively market centres, supplied by local traders who travel along the river in dug-out canoes.

SCALE BAR
0   200   400   km
0   200   400   miles

CENTRAL AMERICA

LIKE LINKS IN A CHAIN, the seven Central American countries seem to tie together the continents of North and South America. The climate is hot and steamy; trees, plants, and jungle animals thrive around the marshy coasts and on the high mountains. More than 2,500 years ago Native Americans made Central America their home. Some of the people who live there today are direct descendants of these early inhabitants. Many are *mestizos*: people with both Native American and European ancestors. European people first came to Central America in about 1500, and the Spanish empire ruled the area for more than three centuries. By 1823, many of the countries had gained independence, but this did not bring peace and prosperity to their people. Most Central Americans are still very poor and have no land. There are too few jobs and not enough food. Governments in the region have been unable to solve these problems, and wars and revolutions are common.

Central America forms an isthmus, or narrow land bridge, from Mexico in the north to Colombia in the south.

There are many active volcanoes in Central America. The largest is Tajumulco in Guatemala.

The soil in the valleys is very fertile.

Jungle covers the eastern coastal plain and many mountains.

MAYAS

Between 250 and 900 CE Native American people called Mayas lived in Central America, where they created a vast empire. They built great cities at Palenque and Tikal (in present-day Mexico and Guatemala) and constructed huge stone temples and palaces in the shape of pyramids. To feed the people in the cities, the Mayas became skilled at cultivating food. They used ingenious farming methods to grow plentiful crops on the small areas of suitable land.

PEOPLE
More than 42 million people live in Central America, mostly in the countryside and in small towns. The biggest city is Guatemala City, which has a population of over 2 million. Most people speak either Spanish or one of the local Native American languages. In Belize, many people speak English. Many Central Americans are Christians, and the Roman Catholic Church is an important influence in everyday life and culture.

EDUCATION
Civil wars and other armed conflicts have disrupted normal life in Central America. One result is that many people are illiterate. However, in Nicaragua there is a major campaign to teach people to read.

Bananas grown in Honduras are eaten all over the world.

Nicaragua was an important cotton producer until civil war disrupted farming.

In Panama sugar is extracted from sugar cane, which grows rapidly in the hot, humid climate.

Belize processes grapefruit and exports juice.

Coffee is Guatemala's most important export.

INDUSTRY

Agriculture is the major industry in Central America; many of the countries depend on one main crop for their income. Both Belize and El Salvador also make textiles and light industrial products. Guatemala produces oil for export.

Find out more

AZTECS
CARIBBEAN
CONQUISTADORS
MEXICO

Volcano | Mountain | Ancient monument | Capital city | Large city/town | Small city/town

STATISTICS
Area: 523,160 sq km (201,993 sq miles)
Population: 42,068,000
Number of independent countries: 7

PANAMA CANAL
The Panama Canal is a great international waterway connecting the Atlantic and Pacific Oceans. It is more than 80 km (50 miles) long and up to 150 m (500 ft) wide, with a minimum depth of 12 m (39 ft). Over 13,000 ships from all over the world pass through the canal's locks each year. Most of their cargo travels to and from the United States.

PACIFIC COASTAL STRIP
Half the population of Central America lives on the western slopes, which are higher and drier than the lowlands that border the Caribbean coast. Most people in the west work as farmers, producing coffee, bananas, sugar cane, and cotton.

MEXICO

BELIZE
San Ignacio
Flores
Belize City
BELMOPAN

GUATEMALA
Volcán Tacaná 4093m
Puerto Barrios
Cobán
Huehuetenango
Quezaltenango
Zacapa
GUATEMALA CITY
Escuintla
Santa Ana
Santa Rosa de Copán
Puerto Cortés
San Pedro Sula
La Ceiba
Bay Islands
Gulf of Honduras

HONDURAS
Comayagua
Juticalpa
TEGUCIGALPA
San Miguel
Choluteca
Laguna de Caratasca

SAN SALVADOR
EL SALVADOR
Gulf of Fonseca

NICARAGUA
Jinotega
Estelí
Matagalpa
Chinandega
León
Lake Managua
MANAGUA
Juigalpa
Rivas
Volcán Concepción 1610m
Bluefields
Corn Islands
Golfo de Papagayo
Liberia
San Juan

Patuca
Coco
Wawa
Mosquito Coast
Cayos Miskitos

Caribbean Sea

PACIFIC OCEAN

Volcán Barva 2906m
Puntarenas
Alajuela
Limón
Península de Nicoya
SAN JOSÉ
Cartago
COSTA RICA
Cordillera de Talamanca
Volcán Barú 3475m
David
Santiago
Chitré
Península de Osa
Chiriquí Gulf
Península de Azuero
Mosquito Gulf
Colón
Lake Gatún
PANAMA
Panama Canal
PANAMA CITY
Pearl Islands
Gulf of Panama
Gulf of Darien

COLOMBIA

SCALE BAR
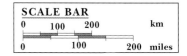
0   100   200   km
0   100   200   miles

BELIZE
Area: 22,960 sq km (8,865 sq miles)
Population: 308,000
Capital: Belmopan
Currency: Belizean dollar

COSTA RICA
Area: 51,100 sq km (19,730 sq miles)
Population: 4,254,000
Capital: San José
Currency: Colón

HONDURAS
Area: 112,090 sq km (43,278 sq miles)
Population: 7,793,000
Capital: Tegucigalpa
Currency: Lempira

EL SALVADOR
Area: 21,040 sq km (8,124 sq miles)
Population: 7,185,000
Capital: San Salvador
Currency: US dollar

NICARAGUA
Area: 130,000 sq km (50,193 sq miles)
Population: 5,891,000
Capital: Managua
Currency: Córdoba

GUATEMALA
Area: 108,890 sq km (42,043 sq miles)
Population: 13,277,000
Capital: Guatemala City
Currency: Quetzal

PANAMA
Area: 77,080 sq km (29,761 sq miles)
Population: 3,360,000
Capital: Panama City
Currency: Balboa

COSTA RICA
More than half of Costa Rica's people live on a broad, fertile plateau surrounded by volcanic ranges (above). Small farms dot the area; coffee, corn, rice, and sugar are grown on the hillsides. Unlike other Central American countries, Costa Rica enjoys political stability.

CENTRAL ASIA

A LANDSCAPE OF HIGH MOUNTAINS, fertile valleys, and extensive deserts, Central Asia was once peopled by nomads, who roamed the land with their animal herds, searching for new pastures. The Silk Road, a trade route from China to Europe, once passed through the region, and a number of towns were founded along it. From 1922 to 1991 most of the region was part of the Soviet Union. During this period traditional ways of life began to disappear, and new technology made the land more productive. Today, the independent states of the region use mountain streams to generate electricity, and divert water to irrigate the arid land. A large range of crops – vegetables, wheat, fruit, and tobacco – are grown. Cotton is a major crop, and is exported by Uzbekistan. Afghanistan, to the south, has been plagued by warfare. Its economy is in a state of collapse due to the conflict.

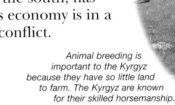

In the east and south, the Central Asian mountains form a barrier between Central Asia, and China and Pakistan. To the west lies Iran and the eastern shores of the Caspian Sea. To the north lie the flat steppelands of Kazakhstan.

SAMARQAND
One of the oldest cities in Central Asia, Samarqand was situated on the ancient Silk Road from China to Europe. Some of its finest buildings date to the 13th and 14th centuries, when Samarqand was the centre of an Islamic empire. The monuments of the Registan Square (below) are decorated with mosaics, marble, and gold.

Animal breeding is important to the Kyrgyz because they have so little land to farm. The Kyrgyz are known for their skilled horsemanship.

Samarqand is still a major trading centre, exporting silk and cotton, fruit, vegetables, and tobacco.

KYRGYZ NOMADS
Mainly from Kyrgyzstan, the Kyrgyz are a nomadic people, who traditionally live on the high plateaux by herding sheep, goats, yak, horses, and camels. They lived in *yurts*, felt-covered frame tents. During the Soviet era many Kyrgyz were forced to settle on large collective farms.

ARAL SEA

CARPETS
Woollen carpets from Turkmenistan and Uzbekistan have distinctive geometrical designs. They are made by hand-knotting the wool. They are used as saddle-cloths, wall-hangings, and prayer mats.

In Uzbekistan, cotton-farmers are diverting the flow of the Amu Darya to water their fields. The inland Aral Sea, also fed by the river, is drying up. More than half the sea's water has been lost since 1960 and its salinity has increased fourfold. The sea is too salty for fish, and fishing ports are now surrounded by grounded ships and barren land. Fertilizers have poisoned drinking water, leading to health problems.

COTTON HARVEST
Uzbekistan is one of the world's largest cotton-cultivators. Cotton is also grown elsewhere in Central Asia, which is the most northerly of the great cotton regions of the world. Uzbekistan makes and exports machinery used to harvest and process the cotton. The gathering of the white, fluffy cotton is highly mechanized.

Find out more
ASIA
DAMS
ISLAM
OCEANS AND SEAS
SOVIET UNION, HISTORY OF

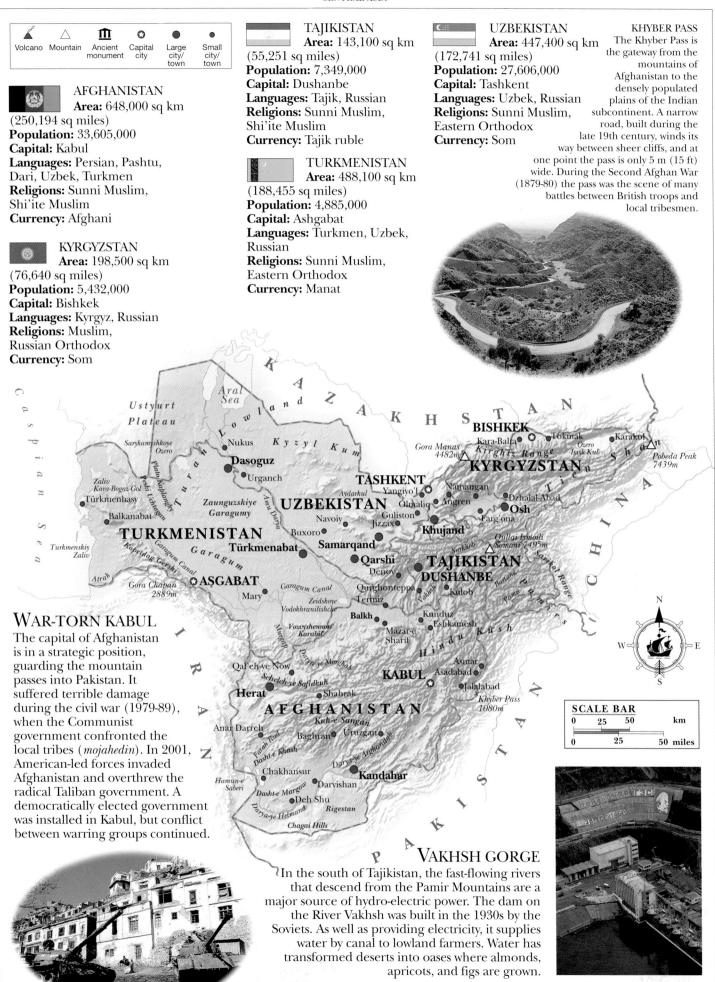

Volcano | Mountain | Ancient monument | Capital city | Large city/town | Small city/town

AFGHANISTAN
Area: 648,000 sq km (250,194 sq miles)
Population: 33,605,000
Capital: Kabul
Languages: Persian, Pashtu, Dari, Uzbek, Turkmen
Religions: Sunni Muslim, Shi'ite Muslim
Currency: Afghani

KYRGYZSTAN
Area: 198,500 sq km (76,640 sq miles)
Population: 5,432,000
Capital: Bishkek
Languages: Kyrgyz, Russian
Religions: Muslim, Russian Orthodox
Currency: Som

TAJIKISTAN
Area: 143,100 sq km (55,251 sq miles)
Population: 7,349,000
Capital: Dushanbe
Languages: Tajik, Russian
Religions: Sunni Muslim, Shi'ite Muslim
Currency: Tajik ruble

TURKMENISTAN
Area: 488,100 sq km (188,455 sq miles)
Population: 4,885,000
Capital: Ashgabat
Languages: Turkmen, Uzbek, Russian
Religions: Sunni Muslim, Eastern Orthodox
Currency: Manat

UZBEKISTAN
Area: 447,400 sq km (172,741 sq miles)
Population: 27,606,000
Capital: Tashkent
Languages: Uzbek, Russian
Religions: Sunni Muslim, Eastern Orthodox
Currency: Som

KHYBER PASS
The Khyber Pass is the gateway from the mountains of Afghanistan to the densely populated plains of the Indian subcontinent. A narrow road, built during the late 19th century, winds its way between sheer cliffs, and at one point the pass is only 5 m (15 ft) wide. During the Second Afghan War (1879-80) the pass was the scene of many battles between British troops and local tribesmen.

WAR-TORN KABUL
The capital of Afghanistan is in a strategic position, guarding the mountain passes into Pakistan. It suffered terrible damage during the civil war (1979-89), when the Communist government confronted the local tribes (*mojahedin*). In 2001, American-led forces invaded Afghanistan and overthrew the radical Taliban government. A democratically elected government was installed in Kabul, but conflict between warring groups continued.

VAKHSH GORGE
In the south of Tajikistan, the fast-flowing rivers that descend from the Pamir Mountains are a major source of hydro-electric power. The dam on the River Vakhsh was built in the 1930s by the Soviets. As well as providing electricity, it supplies water by canal to lowland farmers. Water has transformed deserts into oases where almonds, apricots, and figs are grown.

SCALE BAR
0   25   50   km
0   25   50 miles

CHARLEMAGNE

TWELVE CENTURIES AGO one man ruled most of western Europe. Charlemagne could hardly read or write, yet he built up a vast empire. Charlemagne was a Frank, one of the peoples who had invaded the Roman Empire when it collapsed in the 5th century, and who then settled in northern France. When he became king in 768 CE, his territory was small, and threatened by its French neighbours. Charlemagne soon overcame them all and then invaded northern Italy. He was a great warrior. He fought the people of Hungary, and the Saxons in Germany. He also invaded Spain and stopped the Muslims living there from threatening the rest of Europe. Charlemagne's aim was not just to rule more countries; he wanted to convert the inhabitants to Christianity. To achieve this goal he became ruthless with those who opposed him. However, he was not an especially cruel ruler. He reformed the countries he conquered, and, perhaps because he was not an educated man, he encouraged learning and set up many schools. The Pope, who was head of the Christian Church, rewarded Charlemagne by crowning him Emperor of the Romans in 800, for Charlemagne's European empire was the first to be formed since the fall of Rome. When he died 14 years later, Charlemagne was the most powerful ruler in Europe.

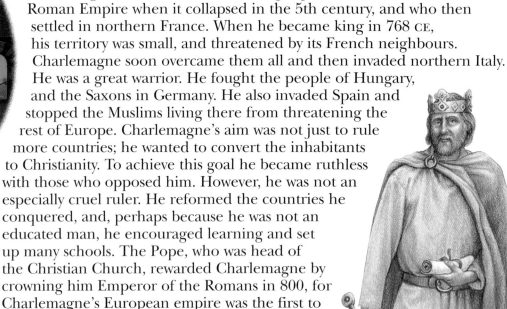

THRONE
Charlemagne was a very powerful ruler, but his marble throne was plain and undecorated. The throne was a copy of the one described in the Bible from which King Solomon ruled his kingdom of Israel. Charlemagne built a chapel in his palace to house his throne. The chapel survives today as part of Aachen Cathedral, in Germany.

WHAT HE LOOKED LIKE
There are few known portraits of Charlemagne, but those that remain show a tall, bearded, blond-haired man.

This coin dates from Charlemagne's period of rule.

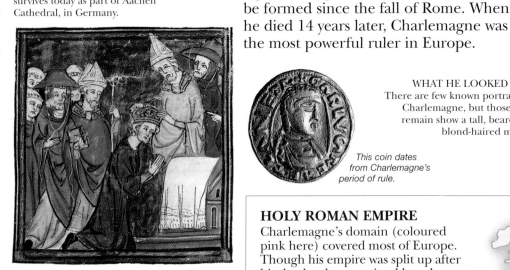

CORONATION
Pope Leo III crowned Charlemagne Emperor of the Romans on Christmas Day in 800, at St. Peter's Basilica in Rome. Charlemagne became the first man for three centuries to hold the title Roman Emperor. It carried great prestige, though in practice gave him no additional powers.

HOLY ROMAN EMPIRE
Charlemagne's domain (coloured pink here) covered most of Europe. Though his empire was split up after his death, what remained later became known as the Holy Roman Empire (coloured green). The last emperor, Francis II, resigned the title in 1806. Some say he abolished the empire to stop Napoleon Bonaparte, emperor of France, from taking the title. Others say Napoleon ended it because he didn't want a rival emperor in Europe.

Holy Roman Empire

Charlemagne's empire

Part of both empires

ROYAL TOMB
Scenes from Charlemagne's life cover his tomb in Aachen Cathedral. One panel shows his armies besieging the town of Pamplona in Spain. The tomb is richly decorated with gold, and set with precious stones.

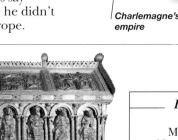

Find out more
BARBARIANS
MEDIEVAL EUROPE
NAPOLEON BONAPARTE

CHEMISTRY

HAVE YOU EVER WONDERED why cooking changes raw, tough food into a tasty meal? Cooking is just one example of a chemical reaction that converts raw materials into new substances. Chemists use chemical reactions to make plastics, medicines, dyes, and many other materials that are important in everyday life. They also study what substances are made of and how they can be combined to make new materials. Chemicals are the raw materials used by a chemist. More than 4 million different chemicals have been made by chemists; there are about 35,000 chemicals in common use. These chemicals can be made by combining simple substances, called elements, into more complicated substances called compounds. Early chemists considered four elements – fire, water, air, and earth. Today, we know there are 92 that occur in nature, and a few others that can be made in laboratories. The most common element in the universe is hydrogen, which is the main component of stars.

APPARATUS
Chemists use special flasks and jars to mix chemicals, together with equipment that is electronic and automated.

CHEMICAL REACTIONS

When different substances combine together to form new materials, a chemical reaction occurs. Some reactions need heat to start them off; others produce heat as the reaction proceeds.

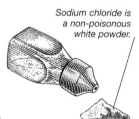

Sodium is a soft, silvery metal.
Chlorine is a poisonous yellow-green gas.
Sodium chloride is a non-poisonous white powder.

Chemists use a shorthand to describe chemicals. H_2O is the symbol for water and shows that each water molecule contains two hydrogen atoms (H) and one oxygen atom (O).

ELEMENTS AND COMPOUNDS
Elements are substances which are made of a single kind of atom. When different elements combine, their atoms join to produce a new substance, which is called a compound. For example, common salt is a compound called sodium chloride. It is made by combining the element sodium and the element chlorine. When the two elements combine, they form a compound which is entirely different from either of the elements used to produce it.

HISTORY OF CHEMISTRY
The Egyptians were the first chemists. The word chemistry comes from *Chem*, the name for Ancient Egypt. Modern chemistry began around 1790 when a Frenchman, Antoine Lavoisier, explained how chemical reactions work. In 1808, an English scientist, John Dalton, showed that substances were made from atoms. By 1871, a Russian teacher, Dimitri Mendeleyev, had produced the periodic table, which classifies elements according to their properties and is the cornerstone of chemistry.

ALCHEMY
Early chemistry, called alchemy, was a mixture of magic and guesswork. From about A.D. 300, alchemists tried to make gold from lead, mercury, and other cheap metals. They also tried to find an elixir, or preparation, to prolong life. Although the alchemists did not succeed in these aims, they found ways of separating substances and making them pure. They also discovered many new substances.

Find out more
ATOMS AND MOLECULES
EGYPT, ANCIENT
HEAT
PHYSICS
SCIENCE, HISTORY OF

CHINA

TO DESCRIBE CHINA you need to use enormous numbers. The country is vast, covering more than 9.3 million sq km (3.6 million sq miles). China's written history stretches back 3,500 years – longer than any other nation's. 1,338 million people live there, and one-fifth of the world's population is Chinese. In such a large country, there are many variations, including four major language families. The land, too, is tremendously varied. The east and southeast, where most people live, is green and fertile. Other parts of the country are barren deserts of sand and rock. Organizing and feeding the huge and varied Chinese population is a mammoth task. Since 1949 China has been ruled by a Communist government that has tried to provide adequate food, education, and health care to every part of the nation. During the late 1970s, Communist party moderates embraced economic reforms that lifted government controls and encouraged private enterprise. Consequently, China became the world's third-largest economy in the mid 1990s. China's human rights record, however, is still criticized because of political oppression at home and in Tibet.

China is the fourth-largest country in the world. It is situated in eastern Asia. The Russian Federation and Mongolia lie to its north, and Southeast Asia and the Indian subcontinent to its south and west. The East China Sea is to its east.

TRANSPORTATION
The bicycle is a common method of transport in China, although private cars are becoming more common.

Tiananmen Square, Beijing

Chinese farmers make use of every suitable piece of land, carving steps or terraces in the hillsides to grow rice and other crops.

Rice is grown in flooded fields called paddies.

BEIJING
The capital city of China is Beijing, formerly Peking. Modern Beijing spreads out around the older central area. To the north and west are houses and Beijing University. The industrial area is to the east of the centre. At the heart lies Tiananmen (Gate of Heavenly Peace) Square. Here parades and celebrations take place on national holidays. In 1989, the government forcibly disbanded a pro-democracy student demonstration here, killing thousands.

AGRICULTURE AND LAND USE
Most Chinese people are crowded together in just 15 per cent of the total land area, mainly in river valleys in the east. Three in ten live in huge cities; the rest live in the countryside. There they grow rice and wheat and raise pigs and other livestock. Much of the rest of the country is mountainous and wild. The Takla Makan Desert in the west is dry and cold, and few people live there.

NEW YEAR
China's most important festival is the celebration of New Year. Each year is named after an animal and people celebrate with colourful processions. Tangerines with leaves are the lucky fruits of the New Year. Odd numbers are unlucky so people always give presents of tangerines in pairs.

FAMILY LIFE
The family is the most important institution in Chinese life. Children respect their parents and look after them in their old age. China's population is growing, and the government now rewards parents who limit their families to just one child. This policy works well in the cities, but in farming communities, people need large families to labour in the fields.

116

HAN CHINESE

China has a large number of ethnic groups. The Han Chinese people make up about 90 per cent of the total population. Their ancestors may have come east from Turkestan, which is now partly in western China and partly in Central Asia and Afghanistan. However, it is possible that Han Chinese people descended from Mongolian tribes who moved south.

PANDAS

The giant panda lives only in the mountainous forests of southwestern China. It feeds almost exclusively off bamboo. The woody grass is low in nutrients, so pandas must eat about 38kg (84 lb) of it every day to survive. The panda is classified as an endangered species, and fewer than 1,600 remain in the wild today. They live in areas of forest set aside as nature reserves by the Chinese government.

LHASA

Monasteries in Lhasa, capital of Tibet, are reminders that the city was once the centre of Lamaism (Tibetan Buddhism). The religion is an important part of Tibetan life, and at one time one-sixth of all Tibetan men were monks. The head of the religion, the Dalai Lama, was also the ruler of the country. However, in 1950 Communist China invaded Tibet, and has ruled the region ever since.

INDUSTRIAL TAIWAN

Boasting a highly educated and ambitious workforce, Taiwan is one of Asia's wealthiest economies. The country produces about 10 per cent of the world's computers, and is the world's leading television producer. It also specializes in shoe-manufacturing. Taiwan's mineral industry is not a significant earner as mineral resources are relatively modest.

SHANGHAI

The largest city in China, Shanghai (right), is one of the world's biggest seaports. For centuries China was closed to the west, but in 1842 the Treaty of Nanking, between China and Britain, opened the port to western trade. Since then Shanghai has been the leading commercial and industrial centre in China. Today, about half of China's foreign business passes through the city.

The spectacular Potala Palace (left), in Lhasa, was built in the 17th century.

To Western eyes in the Middle Ages, the Chinese junk (left) seemed an ungainly figure. However, the junk is still widely used today, thus proving its seaworthiness.

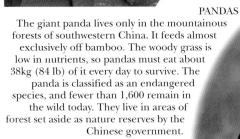

JUNK

The junk is an ocean-going sailing vessel of ancient unknown origin. By the Middle Ages, Chinese junks had sailed to the waters of Indonesia and India. The junk carries up to five sails consisting of panels of linen or matting flattened by bamboo strips. Each sail can be spread or closed at a pull, like a venetian blind. A massive rudder, which steers the boat, takes the place of a keel or a centreboard, and keeps the boat from tipping over or drifting with the wind. The hull is partitioned by solid bulkheads, which add greatly to the boat's strength.

Most Chinese people work in agriculture. However, over 10 per cent of China's 750 million-strong workforce is employed in industries such as textiles (left) and electronics.

MEDICINE

Medicine in China is a mixture of East and West. Modern surgical and drug techniques are borrowed from Europe and the United States. However, doctors still use traditional cures that have been popular for thousands of years, including herbs and other natural remedies. To relieve pain, Chinese doctors sometimes use acupuncture, a technique in which fine needles are inserted into specially-chosen parts of the body. "Barefoot doctors", or locally-trained healers, keep people healthy in the countryside with natural remedies.

Acupuncture charts show the positions of meridians, or lines of energy, where the acupuncturist inserts needles.

A Chinese apothecary, or chemist, makes use of a wide range of natural plant and animal cures.

INDUSTRY

Chinese factories have been modernized since 1949, but in comparison with the factories of Japan or the United States, some are still old-fashioned. However, China's economy has grown rapidly since the 1980s. It has set up industries in partnership with foreign companies and encouraged private enterprise. By 2009, it was the world's largest economy after the United States and Japan.

The Chinese eat with chopsticks. They hold both sticks in one hand, and pinch the tips together to pick up food.

Buddhist monks in Tibet, southwest China, spend much time studying and writing.

FOOD

Rice is one of the main ingredients of Chinese food, as are noodles and many vegetables. Dried foods, soya beans, fish, and meat are also used in Chinese cooking, which varies considerably in the different regions of China.

CHINESE LANGUAGE

Mandarin, the main language of China, is spoken in all but the southeast coastal areas. Within each language there are many dialects, or regional variations. Although each vocabulary is different, all the variations are written in the same script.

The Beijing Opera performs traditional and new works, mainly with political themes.

Chinese writing consists of thousands of symbols, each one representing a different word or idea.

HONG KONG AND MACAO

At midnight on 29-30 July, 1997, Hong Kong (above) returned to Chinese sovereignty after it had been a British colony for 157 years. Two years later, Hong Kong's neighbour, Macao, ceased to be a Portuguese colony. It officially came under Chinese rule at midnight on 19-20 December, 1999.

CULTURE

China has a rich and ancient culture: paintings found in some Chinese tombs are more than 6,000 years old. Today, artistic traditions continue in the form of folk dancing and music; films, opera, and theatre are all very popular. Artists are encouraged to produce works that depict the achievements of the Chinese people.

Find out more

ASIA
ASIA, HISTORY OF
COMMUNISM
MAO ZEDONG
MONGOL EMPIRE

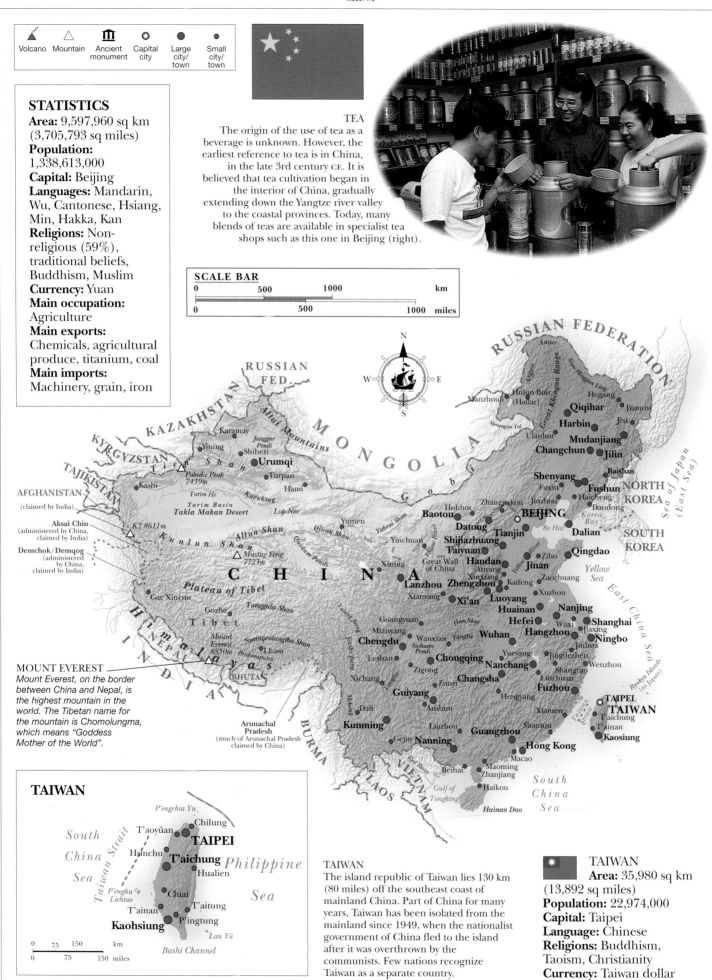

STATISTICS
Area: 9,597,960 sq km (3,705,793 sq miles)
Population: 1,338,613,000
Capital: Beijing
Languages: Mandarin, Wu, Cantonese, Hsiang, Min, Hakka, Kan
Religions: Non-religious (59%), traditional beliefs, Buddhism, Muslim
Currency: Yuan
Main occupation: Agriculture
Main exports: Chemicals, agricultural produce, titanium, coal
Main imports: Machinery, grain, iron

Legend
- Volcano
- Mountain
- Ancient monument
- Capital city
- Large city/town
- Small city/town

TEA
The origin of the use of tea as a beverage is unknown. However, the earliest reference to tea is in China, in the late 3rd century CE. It is believed that tea cultivation began in the interior of China, gradually extending down the Yangtze river valley to the coastal provinces. Today, many blends of teas are available in specialist tea shops such as this one in Beijing (right).

SCALE BAR
0 — 500 — 1000 km
0 — 500 — 1000 miles

MOUNT EVEREST
Mount Everest, on the border between China and Nepal, is the highest mountain in the world. The Tibetan name for the mountain is Chomolungma, which means "Goddess Mother of the World".

Aksai Chin (administered by China, claimed by India)
Demchok/Demqog (administered by China, claimed by India)
Arunachal Pradesh (much of Arunachal Pradesh claimed by China)
AFGHANISTAN (claimed by India)

TAIWAN
The island republic of Taiwan lies 130 km (80 miles) off the southeast coast of mainland China. Part of China for many years, Taiwan has been isolated from the mainland since 1949, when the nationalist government of China fled to the island after it was overthrown by the communists. Few nations recognize Taiwan as a separate country.

TAIWAN
Area: 35,980 sq km (13,892 sq miles)
Population: 22,974,000
Capital: Taipei
Language: Chinese
Religions: Buddhism, Taoism, Christianity
Currency: Taiwan dollar

119

CHRISTIANITY

FROM VERY HUMBLE ORIGINS, Christianity has grown to be the largest of all world religions. Christians are the followers of Jesus Christ, a Jew who lived almost 2,000 years ago in the land that is now Israel. Jesus was a religious teacher, but Christians believe that he was also the Son of God and that he came into the world to save people from sin, or doing wrong. Jesus was killed by his enemies, but his disciples (group of followers) taught that he rose from the dead and rejoined his father in heaven, a basic Christian belief called the Resurrection. After Jesus' death, his followers began to spread his teaching. Christianity grew, although it was banned in the Roman Empire and all the lands around the Mediterranean Sea, and many early Christians died for their beliefs. Today, more than 2 billion people throughout the world practise Christianity.

There are different divisions within Christianity; the three most prominent are Protestantism, the Roman Catholic Church, and the Eastern Orthodox Church. Each has its own way of worshipping. But despite their differences, all Christian groups share a belief in the teachings of Jesus Christ. Most Christians worship by meeting in groups called congregations. They pray together and sing hymns (sacred songs).

Church windows tell Bible stories in pictures made from stained glass.

In New Testament stories Jesus compares God to a good shepherd, caring for his "flock" of believers.

BIBLE

The Bible is sacred to both Christians and Jews, who believe it contains the word of God. It consists of two parts – the Old and New Testaments. Both Jews and Christians accept the Old Testament, but only Christians accept the New Testament. The New Testament includes the gospels, or teachings of Christ, as told by his followers – Matthew, Mark, Luke, and John. Christians try to follow the central message of the New Testament, which is to love God and their fellow humans and to forgive their enemies.

COMMUNION

Before he died, Jesus shared a simple meal of bread and wine with his closest followers. He asked them to remember him in this special way. Today the ceremony of Holy Communion, in which worshippers receive bread and wine, is a reminder of Christ's Last Supper and helps Christians feel closer to God. Roman Catholic and Eastern Orthodox churches celebrate communion daily in the form of Mass.

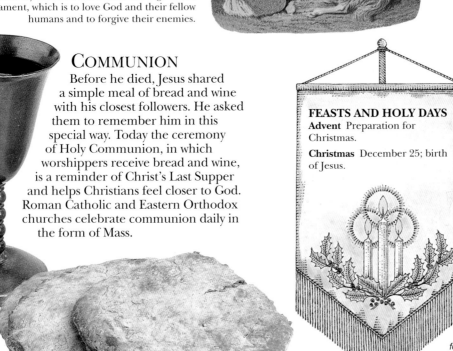

FEASTS AND HOLY DAYS

Advent Preparation for Christmas.

Christmas December 25; birth of Jesus.

The birth of Jesus is remembered at Christmas. This feast is popular with many non-Christians as well, who enjoy the atmosphere of festive goodwill.

Palm Sunday Jesus enters Jerusalem, Sunday before Easter.

Good Friday Jesus' death, the Friday before Easter Sunday.

Easter Sunday late March or April; celebrates Jesus' Resurrection (coming back to life).

Easter is the most important feast in the Christian calendar. It celebrates the rising of Jesus from the dead three days after his crucifixion.

ROMAN CATHOLICISM

Roman Catholics make up the largest Christian group. They believe that the Pope, the head of the Catholic Church, is God's representative on Earth. His authority on religious matters should always be obeyed. The Pope lives in a tiny independent state in Rome called Vatican City. The Roman Catholic Church is spread worldwide and is the main religion of many countries, including Spain, Ireland, Colombia, and Brazil. Catholics try to attend Mass on Sundays and to regularly confess their sins to a priest. They pray to God and have special regard for Mary, the mother of Jesus. They also pray to the Christian saints, deeply religious people, some of whom died for their faith.

ROSARY
Catholics use a rosary – a symbolic string of beads – to help them pray. They say a prayer for each bead in the chain.

ORTHODOX CHURCH
At first, there was only one Church. In 1054 CE, however, the Christian Church divided. The Pope in Rome and the Patriarch, head of the church of Constantinople (now Istanbul, Turkey), disagreed about the leadership of the Christian world. As a result, the Church in Rome (Catholic) and the Eastern Church (Orthodox) separated. Roman Catholics and members of Eastern Orthodox churches such as those of Russia and Greece share many beliefs. However, Orthodox Christians do not accept the authority of the Pope. Many Christians in eastern Europe and western Asia belong to Orthodox churches. In their churches religious portraits called icons are considered sacred.

BAPTISM

Adults and children enter the Christian church through baptism, a ceremony in which they are sprinkled with water or immersed in it. Baptism washes away a person's sins. Children are often named, or christened, at their baptism. Parents promise to raise them as good Christians. In some countries baptism takes place outdoors in lakes or rivers. Jesus was baptized in the Jordan River in the Middle East.

Most of the Christians who worship in the United States are members of Protestant churches.

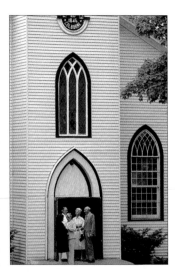

PROTESTANTISM
In the early 16th century, some Christians felt that the Roman Catholic Church was no longer correctly following the teachings of Christ. Martin Luther, a German monk, led the protests. Others who agreed with him broke away and formed protest groups in a movement that became known as the Reformation. Today, most Christians who are not members of the Roman Catholic or Orthodox churches are called Protestants. Some Protestant churches, called Evangelical churches, are among the fastest growing Christian groups in the world. They have mainly Afro-Caribbean congregations.

MOTHER TERESA
Christians believe it is their duty to help relieve the suffering of the poor and sick. Mother Teresa founded the Missionaries of Charity for the homeless and dying in India. She became famous for her work among lepers. In 1979, she was awarded the Nobel Peace Prize. She died in 1997.

Mother Teresa was born in Albania in 1910, but became an Indian citizen. All the nuns in her missions wear a flowing Indian dress called a sari.

___ **Find out more** ___

ITALY
JESUS CHRIST
REFORMATION
RELIGIONS

SIR WINSTON CHURCHILL

IN 1940, BRITAIN badly needed a strong leader. The country was at war with Germany and faced the danger of invasion. Winston Churchill's appointment as prime minister provided the leadership that the British people wanted. He went on to guide the country through the worst war the world had ever experienced. In his underground headquarters he formed the plans which helped to win the war. Churchill's wartime glory came at a surprising time. He was 65 and had held no important government post for many years. He had been almost alone in urging a strong army and navy to oppose the German threat. Working people remembered how he helped crush the general strike of 1926 and cut their wages. But when victory came in World War II, all of this was forgotten, and everyone cheered Churchill as one of the greatest politicians of the age.

1874 Born at Blenheim Palace, Oxfordshire, England.

1893 Enters the Royal Military College at Sandhurst.

1899 Taken prisoner during Boer War in South Africa, but escapes.

1900 Elected Member of Parliament.

1908-15 Holds cabinet posts.

1919 Appointed secretary of state for war.

1940-45 As prime minister, leads Britain in World War II.

1951-55 Prime minister.

1965 Dies.

YOUNG WINSTON
As a young soldier and newspaper reporter in India and Africa, Churchill had many adventures. He became world famous when he escaped from a Boer prison in 1899.

BRITISH BULLDOG
Churchill's famous British determination was often portrayed in cartoons and posters. This 1942 American poster shows him as a bulldog.

WARTIME PRIME MINISTER
As wartime leader, Churchill travelled the country visiting bombed cities and raising people's spirits. His simple "V for Victory" sign seemed to sum up British determination to win the war. His most important work took place behind the scenes, where he directed the British war effort. He met the leaders of the then Soviet Union and the United States to draw up plans for fighting the war and for the postwar peace settlement. Above he is seen giving the "V" sign to American sailors.

PAINTING
Churchill was an enthusiastic amateur painter. He also wrote many books about history. These hobbies kept him busy after 1945 when he lost his post as prime minister in a disastrous election. He did not return to power until 1951.

BROADCASTS
During World War II, Churchill made many radio broadcasts, which inspired the nation. Churchill always explained the situation clearly and listed the dreadful problems which lay ahead, yet he left no doubt that the enemy would eventually be defeated.

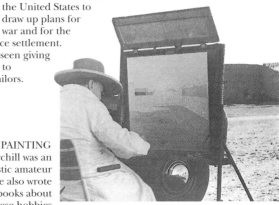

Find out more
UNITED KINGDOM, HISTORY OF
WORLD WAR I
WORLD WAR II

CITIES

MORE THAN HALF OF ALL the world's people live in cities. The world's largest city, Tokyo, Japan, has a population of more than 36 million. But not all cities are vast, because the word city can mean different things. In many places, a city is any large town. In Europe, it is usually a town with a cathedral. And in some places, like the United States, "city" is the name given to an urban area with definite boundaries.

City people need many services: water, power, sanitation, transport, schools, and shops are all essential. Providing these services requires a lot of organization. Badly run cities are unpleasant and unhealthy, with problems such as poor housing, traffic congestion, and pollution. The first cities developed as trading centres in Asia and the Middle East about 7,000 years ago. Rich cities, such as Alexandria in Egypt, became the centres of government and power. Like today's cities, they had markets, banks, hotels, factories, and places of entertainment.

CAPITAL CITIES
The most important town of any country is called the capital. It is usually the place where the government is based, but it may not be the biggest city in the country. Some capital cities, such as Brasilia, have been specially built in modern times.

Brasilia was built to replace Rio de Janeiro as the capital of Brazil.

Factories require a lot of space, so they are built in the outer parts of cities. They need easy access to roads and railways so they can send their goods to other parts of the country.

The city centre usually contains the most stylish shops. Shopping precincts are built close to residential areas on the outskirts of town.

Land is expensive in the city centre, so office developments grow upwards rather than outwards.

Cities must have a good public transport system, with flyovers or underground railways, to avoid traffic jams.

Quiet parks and other recreation areas provide a restful break from the busy city streets.

MODERN CITY
The oldest part of the city often forms the centre. Further out are the industrial zones and the areas where people live, all connected by a network of roads.

PLANNING
Many cities grow up around their historical centres with no overall plan. However, some cities, such as Washington, D.C., have been carefully planned from the start. Streets and squares, transport, sewers, business centres, and sports facilities are all carefully mapped out before any building starts.

Swiss-French architect Le Corbusier (1887-1965) planned Washington D.C. for three million people.

The city streets follow a grid pattern.

Some families live in homes close to the city centre. More live a few kilometres from the centre in less crowded areas called suburbs.

Find out more
ARCHITECTURE
INDUSTRIAL REVOLUTION
TECHNOLOGY

CLIMATES

SOME PARTS OF THE WORLD, such as the tropical rain forests of South America, are hot and damp throughout the year. Other regions, such as the Arctic, have long, freezing winters. Conditions such as these are known as the climate of an area. Climate is not the same as weather. Weather can change within minutes; climate describes a region's weather conditions over a long period of time. Every region has its own climate. This depends on how near it is to the equator, which governs how much heat it gets from the Sun. Landscape also influences climate; high mountain regions, such as the Himalayas, are cooler than nearby low-lying places. The ocean can prevent a coastal region from getting very hot or very cold, while the weather in the centre of a continent is more extreme. The climate of a region affects landscape and life – clothing, crops, and housing. But climate can change. Today, climatologists, people who study climates, believe that the world's climate is gradually warming up.

THE FREEZING ANTARCTIC
Only hardy creatures, such as penguins, can survive amid the ice and snow of the Antarctic.

The cool forest climate exists only in the northern half of the world.

The treeless landscape of the polar regions is called the tundra.

POLAR CLIMATE
It is cold all year, and ice and snow always cover the ground. No crops grow, and the few people who live there hunt animals for food.

In temperate climates, trees shed their leaves in winter.

TROPICAL CLIMATE
It is hot all year round in tropical regions, and torrents of rain fall often every afternoon. Rain forest covers much of the land. In regions where wet and dry seasons occur, tropical grasslands grow.

The Sahara is the largest desert in the world.

WORLD CLIMATES
The different climates of the world run in broad zones around the Earth on either side of the equator. They range from hot and rainy climates at the equator to cold climates at the poles. There are five main climatic zones, each of which is shown on this map by a different colour.

DESERT CLIMATE
In the dry, barren deserts, cold, clear nights usually follow burning-hot days. However, high mountain deserts may have cold, dry winters.

TEMPERATE CLIMATE
Warm summers and cool winters feature in warm temperate climates. Rain may fall all year, or the summer can be dry and sunny, as in Mediterranean regions.

COOL FOREST CLIMATE
Summers are cool and short, and winters are long and cold. Pines and other conifers grow in huge forests which cover much of the land.

Away from the equator, the Sun's rays are spread over a wide area.

SUN AND CLIMATE
The Sun's rays warm the equator directly from above, making the tropics hot. Away from the equator, the Sun's rays are less direct, making climates cooler.

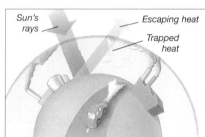

Sun's rays *Escaping heat* *Trapped heat*

GREENHOUSE EFFECT
The atmosphere works like a greenhouse, trapping the Sun's heat and warming the Earth. Pollution in the air traps more heat, making the Earth warmer. Unless pollution is reduced, the Earth's climate could be upset.

CLIMATIC CHANGES
Great climatic changes, such as ice ages, come and go during thousands of years. But severe changes in climate can also occur suddenly or within a few years. Dust from volcanic eruptions can obscure the Sun, making a climate cooler. Changes in winds can cause rainfall to shift from a region, bringing drought. Human activities, such as pollution, also affect climate greatly.

SAHARA DESERT
The Tuareg nomads are one of the few peoples that live in the punishing climate of the Sahara Desert, coping with the searing heat of the day and the freezing temperatures at night.

Find out more
ATMOSPHERE
EARTH
GLACIERS AND ICECAPS
WEATHER
WIND

CLOCKS AND WATCHES

HAVE YOU EVER COUNTED how many times you look at a clock in one day? Time rules everyday life. To catch a bus, get to school, or meet a friend, you need to be on time. Clocks and watches make this possible. Clocks are timekeeping devices too large to be carried; watches are portable. Some tell the time with hands moving around a dial; others with numbers. All clocks and watches use a controlling device, such as a pendulum, that steadily keeps the time.

Early people relied on the passing of days, nights, and seasons to indicate time. Later, they used other methods, such as sundials, water clocks, and candles with marks on them.

Mechanical timepieces were developed between the 15th and 17th centuries with the invention of clockwork and the pendulum. Springs or falling weights moved gearwheels to drive the clocks. These clocks had hands and a dial, and could be made small enough to allow the invention of the watch. Today, many clocks and watches are electronic and rely on the regular vibrations of a quartz crystal to keep time accurately.

SUNDIAL
The Sun's shadow moves slowly around a dial marked off in hours. As the shadow moves, it indicates the time. The sundial, which was invented about 5,000 years ago in Egypt, was one of the earliest methods of measuring time.

WATER CLOCK
Water flows in and out of bowls so that changing levels of water, or a moving float, indicate the passing time. This Chinese water clock dates back to the 14th century.

ASTRONOMICAL CLOCK
This beautiful clock in Prague, Czech Republic, not only shows the hours and minutes but also the signs of the zodiac and the phases of the moon.

Anchor

Ends of anchor engage teeth of escape wheel.

Escape wheel moves with each swing of the pendulum and turns the second hand. Other wheels (not shown) turn hour and minute hands.

Weight pulls cord, driving main wheel that turns other wheels.

Main wheel

Swinging pendulum rocks anchor.

PENDULUM CLOCK

In the 1580s the Italian scientist Galileo noticed that each swing of a suspended weight, or pendulum, takes a fixed time. He suggested that this regular movement could be used to control a clock. But it was another 70 years before the first pendulum clock was built.

MECHANICAL WATCHES
Mechanical watches are controlled by the oscillations of a wheel linked to a spring. The first watch was invented in Germany in about 1500.

This 19th-century fob watch was worn on the end of a small chain.

Watch unit and strap

Cover and display window

LCD (liquid crystal display)

Microchip

Quartz crystal

Battery

DIGITAL WATCH

A battery powers a digital watch, and a tiny quartz crystal regulates its speed. Electricity from the battery makes the crystal vibrate thousands of times each second. The microchip uses these regular vibrations to make the numbers on the display change every second, so the watch shows the time very precisely.

ATOMIC CLOCK

If it were to run for more than one million years, this atomic clock would be less than one second off! The atomic clock is the most accurate of all clocks. It is controlled by vibrating atoms and is used in science to measure intervals of time with extraordinary accuracy.

Find out more
ELECTRONICS
ROCKS AND MINERALS
TIME

COAL

PEOPLE HAVE used coal for cooking and heating for thousands of years. During the 19th century, coal was the world's most important fuel. It powered the steam engines that made the Industrial Revolution possible. Today, coal is still used in vast amounts. Most coal is burned at power stations to produce electricity, and burning coal meets much of the world's energy needs. Coal is also an essential raw material for making many products, the most important of which are iron and steel. Coal is often called a fossil fuel because it is formed from the fossilized remains of plants that are millions of years old. Sometimes a piece of coal bears the imprint of a prehistoric plant or insect. The Earth contains reserves of coal which, with careful use, may last for hundreds of years. But many people are concerned that coal burning adds to global pollution.

A lump of anthracite, a type of hard black coal

FORMATION OF COAL

1 PREHISTORIC SWAMP
Coal began to form in swamps as long ago as 300 million years. Dying trees and other plants fell into the water, and their remains became covered in mud.

2 PEAT
The plant remains slowly dried out under the mud, forming layers of peat, a fuel that can be dug from the ground.

3 LIGNITE
Layers of peat became buried. Heat and pressure turned the peat into lignite, or brown coal. Lignite is dug from shallow pits called strip mines.

4 BLACK COAL
Intense heat and pressure turned deeper layers of peat into a soft black coal called bituminous coal, and anthracite.

MINING

Mine shafts are dug down to seams (layers) of coal far below the surface. Miners dig a network of tunnels to remove coal from the seams. In addition to coal, many other useful minerals, such as copper, are mined. The deepest mine is a gold mine in South Africa nearly 4 km (2.5 miles) deep.

Pumps circulate fresh air through the mine.

Skip (shuttle car) lifts coal to surface.

Air shaft

Railway takes miners to the coal faces.

Miners' cage carries miners up and down mine.

Miners use cutting machine to dig out coal at coal face.

Miners have lamps on their helmets which light up everything in front of them in the dark depths of a mine.

Conveyor belts take coal to shaft.

Supports hold roof and sides of tunnels in place.

COAL MINERS

For centuries, miners had to cut coal by hand. Now there are drills and computer-controlled cutting machines to help them.

USES OF COAL

A few steam-powered trains still burn coal, and some homes have open fires or coal-fired heating systems. The main use for coal is in the production of electricity. Heating coal without air produces coke, which is used to make steel, and coal gas, which may be burned as a fuel. Another product is coal-tar pitch, which is used in making roads. Coal is also treated to make chemicals which are used to produce drugs, plastics, dyes, and many other products.

A large coal-fired power station in Berlin, Germany

Find out more
ELECTRICITY
INDUSTRIAL REVOLUTION
IRON AND STEEL
OIL
PREHISTORIC LIFE
TRAINS

COLD WAR

POTSDAM

In 1945, British Prime Minister Winston Churchill, US President Harry Truman, and Premier Joseph Stalin of the Soviet Union (left to right) met at Potsdam, Germany, to decide the future of the Western world. But serious disagreements arose because Stalin was not prepared to release the countries of Eastern Europe from Communist control. This greatly worried the Western leaders.

WHEN WORLD WAR II ENDED in 1945, Europe was in ruins. The United States, and what was then the Soviet Union, had emerged as the world's two most powerful countries or "superpowers". By 1949, two new power blocs of countries had formed. The Eastern bloc, led by the Soviet Union, was Communist; the Western bloc, headed by the United States, was Capitalist. Over the next 40 years the two superpowers opposed each other in what became known as the Cold War. Each bloc attempted to become the most powerful by building up stocks of weapons. The Cold War was a time of great tension but during the late 1980s the rivalry eased. Both sides began to disarm, and in 1991 the Soviet Union broke up, bringing the Cold War to an end.

THE IRON CURTAIN

As soon as World War II ended, Stalin shut the borders of Eastern Europe. Winston Churchill declared that "an iron curtain has descended across the continent" of Europe. The Communists seized control of the countries behind the imaginary Iron Curtain. These countries became Soviet satellites – nations controlled by the Soviet Union. Yugoslavia broke away in 1948; Albania also rejected Soviet control in 1960.

Soviet Union
East Germany
West Germany
Czechoslovakia
Albania

BERLIN AIRLIFT
In 1945, Britain, France, the United States, and the Soviet Union divided Berlin between them. In 1948, Stalin blocked all traffic to West Berlin. But in the Berlin airlift, the Western allies flew in supplies, and Stalin lifted the blockade.

NATO
In 1949, the United States and several European countries formed the North Atlantic Treaty Organization (NATO). A military organization, its aim was to prevent a Soviet invasion of Europe. In response to this the Soviet Union formed an alliance of Communist states called the Warsaw Pact.

The NATO symbol

KOREAN WAR
In 1950, Communist North Korea, equipped with Soviet weapons, invaded South Korea. The United States led a United Nations force to drive the Communists out. When the United Nations troops invaded North Korea, China sent soldiers to fight them. It was the first time the United States had fought a "hot war" against Communism.

INF TREATY
From the 1960s onwards, relations between the two superpowers improved. In 1987, US President Ronald Reagan and Soviet General Secretary Mikhail Gorbachev signed the Soviet-American Intermediate-Range Nuclear Forces (INF) Treaty. The INF treaty cut down on the number of nuclear weapons and was a major breakthrough in the Cold War.

Find out more
COMMUNISM
RUSSIAN FEDERATION
SOVIET UNION, HISTORY OF
UNITED NATIONS
VIETNAM WAR
WORLD WAR II

COLOMBIA

Volcano	Mountain	Ancient monument	Capital city	Large city/ town	Small city/ town

COLOMBIA IS DOMINATED by the Andes in the west, and the upper reaches of the mighty Amazon in the east. Much of the land is sparsely populated and not suitable for agriculture. The rainforests of the east are rich in wildlife, containing over 1,500 species of birds, numerous monkeys, and endangered felines such as jaguars and ocelots. In the lowlands to the west of the Andes, the subtropical climate provides ideal conditions for growing both coffee, Colombia's main crop, and coca, the basis of Colombia's illegal drugs trade. Originally populated by many native tribes, Colombia was settled by the Spanish in 1525. Colombia became independent in 1819, but has had a history of civil wars and conflict, most recently as a result of the drugs trade.

Colombia lies in the far north of the South American continent, and borders both the Caribbean Sea and the Pacific Ocean.

EMERALDS
Most of the world's emeralds are found in Colombia, and some of the finest examples are found near the capital, Bogotá.

STATISTICS
Area:
1,138,910 sq km (439,733 sq miles)
Population: 45,644,000
Capital: Bogotá
Languages: Spanish, Amerindian languages, English Creole
Religions: Roman Catholic
Currency: Colombian peso
Main occupations: Agriculture, mining, coffee manufacturing
Main exports: Coffee, coal, cocaine, gold, platinum, silver, emeralds

Guambiano Indians

AMERINDIANS
The original American Indian population of Colombia intermarried with Spanish colonists. Today, half of Colombia's population is *mestizo*, which means of mixed European and Indian descent. Yet some 400 Indian tribes survive, speaking more than 180 languages. These Guambiano Indians live on reservations, where they make a living from growing maize, wheat, and potatoes, and selling their craft goods to tourists.

Map labels
Caribbean Sea
Ríohacha
Santa Marta
Barranquilla
Cartagena
Gulf of Darien
Sincelejo
PANAMA
Montería
Cúcuta
Barrancabermeja
Bello
Medellín
Bucaramanga
Itagüí
Sogamoso
VENEZUELA
Llanos
Manizales
Tunja
Meta
Armenia
BOGOTÁ
Tuluá
Villavicencio
PACIFIC OCEAN
Buenaventura
Magdalena
Cali
COLOMBIA
Guaviare
Popayán
San José del Guaviare
Pasto
Florencia
Vaupés
Mitú
BRAZIL
Equator
ECUADOR
Caquetá
Putumayo
PERU
N W E S

COFFEE
Colombia's main export is coffee, grown on tropical evergreen shrubs which require both high temperatures and high rainfall. Its berry-like fruits are processed to extract the seeds, which are then dried in the sunlight. Further processing frees the seeds from their coverings, and the beans are ready for export. Drying the beans by hand is very hard work, and increasingly machines are being used.

SCALE BAR
0	400	800	km
0	400	800	miles

Find out more
FOREST WILDLIFE
SOUTH AMERICA
SOUTH AMERICA, HISTORY OF

COLOUR

A WORLD WITHOUT COLOUR would be a dull place. It would also be difficult to live in. Imagine how hard it would be to tell if traffic lights meant stop or go if there were no red or green. Nature has colour signals too: the bright colours of a tree frog warn other animals that it is poisonous, and the beautiful colours of a flower attract bees to its nectar. Not every creature sees colours in the same way; some animals, such as guinea pigs and squirrels, are colour blind and cannot distinguish between different colours at all. Colour is really the way our eyes interpret different kinds of light. Light is made up of tiny, invisible waves, and each wave has a particular size or wavelength. Each coloured light is composed of different wavelengths, which our eyes are able to detect. White light, such as light from the Sun, is actually a combination of light of all the colours of the rainbow.

PRISM
A triangular chunk of glass, called a prism, separates all the colours in white light. When light goes through a prism, it is refracted, or bent, because glass slows it down. But every colour goes through at a different speed, and is bent to a different degree. So the colours spread out when they leave the prism.

Indigo

Violet

Blue

Green

Yellow

Orange

Red

SPECTRUM
When a prism splits white light into colours, they always come out in the same order, with red at one end and violet at the other. This is called the spectrum. When sunlight is refracted by raindrops, a rainbow is produced which contains all the colours of the spectrum.

Mixing any two primary colours produces secondary colours.

MIXING COLOURS
Red, green, and blue are called the primary colours of light. This is because you can mix red, green, and blue light in different proportions to make any colour in the spectrum. In printing there is a different set of primary colours: cyan (green-blue), magenta (blue-red), and yellow. These too can be mixed to give any colour except white.

PAINT PRIMARIES
Red, yellow and blue are the primary colours of paints. Mixing them together in the correct amounts gives black.

LIGHT PRIMARIES
When the three primary colours of light are mixed together in the correct proportions they make white. During rock concerts and theatre performances, lighting technicians produce a wide range of colours on the stage by mixing different coloured spotlights.

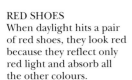

COLOURED OBJECTS
Objects look coloured because of the way they reflect the light that hits them. When white light falls on any surface, some colours are absorbed, or taken in, and some bounce off. When we look at the surface, we see only the colours that bounce off. It is this coloured light that produces the colour we perceive the object to be.

RED SHOES
When daylight hits a pair of red shoes, they look red because they reflect only red light and absorb all the other colours.

BLACK SHOES?
In blue light, red shoes look black because all the blue light is absorbed, and no light is reflected.

Find out more
CAMOUFLAGE, ANIMAL
EYES
LIGHT
PAINTING
RAIN AND SNOW

CHRISTOPHER
COLUMBUS

IN 1492 THREE SMALL SAILING SHIPS named the *Niña*, the *Pinta*, and the *Santa Maria* left Spain on a daring voyage. Their aim was to find a new sea route to Asia in search of spices and gold. In command was Christopher Columbus, an Italian sailor from Genoa. Unlike other explorers of the time, who were sailing east, Columbus believed that if he sailed west he would reach India and its luxuries within a few months. The Spanish were eager to profit from trade with India and the rest of Asia, and Columbus persuaded Queen Isabella of Spain to pay for his expedition. He set sail on 3 August and two months later sighted land which he believed was Asia. In fact, Columbus had arrived in the Caribbean Islands. He did not realize what he had found, but his journey paved the way for later European settlement in the Americas.

North America

South America

Landed on San Salvador 12 October 1492.

Cuba

Hispaniola

Began homeward voyage 16 January 1493.

THE FIRST VOYAGE
Columbus's voyage to the Caribbean lasted four months. He made three more voyages, reaching Central America on his final voyage.

PTOLEMY'S WORLD MAP
The map used by Columbus had been produced by the ancient Greek mapmaker Ptolemy in the 2nd century. The world it showed did not include the continents of North and South America, Australia, or the Pacific.

EXPLORING THE CARIBBEAN

When Columbus arrived in the Caribbean he was welcomed by the Carib and Arawak people. Native Americans became known as Indians because the early explorers thought they were in India.

Captain's cabin held navigation equipment and a chest to store treasure captured on the voyage.

THE CREW
The *Santa Maria* carried a crew of 40. The main risk of a long voyage was running out of food and fresh water.

Food and other supplies were stored here.

Bowsprit was a spar, or horizontal mast, supporting triangular sails.

THE *SANTA MARIA*
Columbus's flagship was a slow, clumsy, wooden cargo ship, no larger than a modern fishing trawler. The ship relied on wind power, and conditions on board were cramped and difficult.

Spare canvas for mending sails.

Off-duty sailors slept wherever there was space.

Find out more

CARIBBEAN
CONQUISTADORS
EXPLORERS

COMETS AND METEORS

ON A CLEAR NIGHT you may see several shooting stars in the space of an hour. A shooting star, or meteor, looks like a streak of light which suddenly darts across the sky and disappears. A meteor occurs when a piece of dust from space, called a meteoroid, burns up as it enters the Earth's atmosphere. As the meteor plummets to Earth at a speed of about 240,000 km/h (150,000 mph), friction with the air produces intense heat which leaves a bright glow in the sky. Meteors usually burn up about 90 km (56 miles) from the Earth's surface.

Many meteoroids are fragments from comets which orbit the Sun. A comet appears as a faint, fuzzy point of light that moves across the night sky for weeks or months. As it nears the Sun, the comet grows a "tail". Then it swings past the Sun and travels away, becoming smaller and fainter. Comets often reappear at regular intervals (every few years) as they travel past Earth on their orbits.

COMET TAIL
As a comet approaches Earth, the heat of the Sun turns the ice into gas. The gas escapes, along with dust, and forms one or more tails (the gas and dust form separate tails). The tails always point away from the Sun. They get shorter as the comet moves away from the Sun.

Dust tail can be up to about 1 million km (600,000 miles) long. It shines white because the particles of dust reflect sunlight.

Gas tail can be up to 100 million km (62 million miles) long. The gas tail has a bluish glow. This is because the heat of the Sun makes the gas molecules emit blue-coloured light.

The size of a comet's nucleus can range from a few hundred metres across to more than 10 kms (about 6 miles) across.

The solar wind – a blast of charged particles that stream from the Sun – blows the comet's gas tail away from the Sun. When the comet approaches the Sun, its tails follow. The tails lead when the comet moves away from the Sun.

COMETS
A comet consists of a central core, or nucleus, of dust and ice; a cloud of gas and dust around the nucleus, called the coma; and one or more tails. Astronomers have observed hundreds of comets and believe that about one billion (10^{12}) other comets orbit the Sun unseen, far beyond the most distant planet.

In 2004, the Stardust spacecraft flew past comet Wild 2, sending back many pictures including this enhanced, composite image.

HALLEY'S COMET
The English astronomer Edmund Halley (1656-1742) was the first to realize that some comets appear regularly. In 1705 he showed that the comet now called Halley's Comet returns past the Earth every 75 or 76 years.

Chinese astronomers probably observed Halley's Comet more than 2,200 years ago. The comet also appears in the 11th-century Bayeux tapestry, which shows the Norman Conquest of England.

METEORS
There are two ways in which meteors occur: individually and in showers. This spectacular meteor shower (left) occurred in 1833. Similar impressive displays occur every 33 years during November. At this time the Earth passes through a swarm of meteors, called the Leonids, that spread out along the orbit of a comet.

METEORITES
Huge lumps of rock called meteorites pass through the Earth's atmosphere without burning up completely. About 25,000 years ago, a meteorite that weighed about 900,000 tonnes (more than 890,000 tons) caused a crater in Arizona, United States (above), 1,200 m (4,000 ft) across. Some scientists believe that the impact of a huge meteorite about 65 million years ago may have destroyed many animal species.

COMMUNISM

AFTER 1917, A NEW WORD came into popular use – Communism. For it was then that Russia set up the world's first Communist government. By 1950, nearly one-third of the world's population lived under Communist rule. The word communism comes from the Latin word *communis,* meaning " belonging to all". More than 2,000 years ago, the Greek writer, Plato, put forward the earliest ideas that resembled Communism in his book *The Republic.* Much later, Vladimir Lenin (1870-1924), the Russian revolutionary developed modern Communism from the writings of the German philosopher Karl Marx. Unlike Capitalists, who believe in private ownership, Communists believe that the state should own a country's wealth and industry, and wealth should be shared according to need. In Communist countries, the Communist party controls every aspect of daily life.

During the 20th century, Communism was a major political force. But people in Communist countries resented economic hardship and their lack of freedom. From the late 1980s, various countries, including the former Soviet Union, rejected Communist rule.

CHAINS AROUND THE WORLD
"The workers have nothing to lose . . . but their chains. They have a world to gain," wrote Marx in his *Communist Manifesto.* On this magazine cover, a worker strikes down "chains" that bind the world.

KARL MARX

Communism is based on the ideas of Karl Marx (1818-83). His major work, *Das Kapital,* became the Communist "bible". He believed that all history is a struggle between the rich rulers and the poor workers, and that the workers will eventually overthrow their rulers in a revolution. Marx died in exile in London, England.

SPREAD OF COMMUNISM
After 1917, Communism spread from Russia to many other countries elsewhere in the world (shown in red above). In Eastern Europe and North Korea, Communist governments were installed by the Soviet army. In China and Southeast Asia, local armed Communist groups took power after fighting long wars.

CAPITALISM	COMMUNISM
Owner Worker	Worker Worker
Under Capitalism, a few companies own the factories. Workers are paid wages but do not always share the profits.	Under Communism, the factories are owned by the state. The state sets wage levels for workers, and uses profits for other investments.

CHINA
In 1949, China became a Communist state under Mao Zedong (1893-1976). China has the largest Communist party in the world, with 70 million members. Since the 1970s China's rulers have gradually abandoned Communist economic policies, encouraging private enterprise to create economic growth. But the party has kept a tight grip on power. It encourages people to take part in group sports, such as tai chi (left).

FIDEL CASTRO
In 1959, Fidel Castro (left), a Cuban lawyer, led a revolution against Cuba's dictator, President Batista. Castro became head of government, and Cuba became a Communist state. Castro seized all American property and promised freedom to the Cuban people. In the 1960s, Castro encouraged and supported Communist movements throughout Central and South America.

Find out more
COLD WAR
DEMOCRACY
MAO ZEDONG
RUSSIAN REVOLUTION
SOUTH AMERICA, HISTORY OF
SOVIET UNION, HISTORY OF

COMPOSERS

AN AUTHOR CREATING A STORY has a choice of more than a hundred thousand words made up from the 26 letters of the alphabet. With only the 12 notes of the chromatic scale – the notes on the piano from any C to the next C above – a composer can make an infinite variety of music of many different styles. These can include jazz, folk, popular, or what is known as classical music.

Composers learn their craft through writing exercises in harmony and counterpoint. Harmony is placing the main tune on the top line with chords (three or more notes sounding together) in support; counterpoint is placing the principal theme in any position with other tunes weaving around it. Composers also discover what instruments can or cannot do, what they sound like, and how to explore their capabilities. The best way to learn all this is to study the music of many composers. Great composers move audiences to tears of joy or sadness with their talent for expressing emotion through music.

In the 15th century beautiful coloured pictures decorated the margins of composers' works.

PURCELL
English composer Henry Purcell (1659-95) sang in the king's chapel in London (above) when he was a boy. At the age of 20 he became the organist at Westminster Abbey, London. He composed beautiful chamber music and dramatic operas such as *Dido and Aeneas*.

Each member of the orchestra uses a line of the score showing only the music for his or her individual instrument.

HOW COMPOSERS WORK

Most composers begin by either inventing themes or melodies that are developed for one or more instruments, or by setting words for one or more voices. Sometimes, as with operas and choral works, both voices and instruments are used. Blending them together so that all are heard clearly is a skilled job. The music is written out in a score. As a symphony can last up to an hour, or an opera up to three hours, composing can be seen to be hard work.

Composers of orchestral music write a complete score, which includes the instrumental parts played by every section of the orchestra.

Many composers like to write music sitting at the piano, so that they can play the tunes as they work on them.

BAROQUE MUSIC

The music of the 17th and early 18th centuries was called Baroque, after the elaborate architectural styles popular in the same period. It is complex music in which the instruments weave their melodies in and out like threads in a rich, colourful tapestry.

BACH

The greatest of the Baroque composers was Johann Sebastian Bach (1685-1750) of Germany. The *Brandenburg Concertos*, which he completed in 1721, are among his best-known works.

HANDEL
George Frideric Handel (1685-1759) was born in Germany and moved to England in 1712. He composed music for the English royal family and wrote many famous choral works.

Handel wrote one of his most famous pieces of music to accompany a royal fireworks display in 1749.

CLASSICAL ERA

Serious music is often called classical to distinguish it from popular music. However, for musicians, classical music is the music composed in the late 18th and early 19th centuries. Classical composers extended the harmony and forms of the Baroque era. The symphony developed in this period. Joseph Haydn (1732-1809) composed 104 symphonies.

MOZART

Wolfgang Amadeus Mozart (1756-91) of Austria was a talented composer and performer by the age of five. He went on to write chamber music, symphonies, and concertos, as well as great operas such as *The Magic Flute*.

Mozart performed all over Europe when he was only six.

BEETHOVEN

The German composer Ludwig van Beethoven (1770-1827; above) was completely deaf for the last 10 years of his life but continued to compose some of the greatest music in the world. His late works moved towards the Romantic movement.

ROMANTIC MOVEMENT

From about 1820 composers began to experiment with new harmonies and forms, achieving a much wider emotional range. For composers such as Tchaikovsky, formal rules were less important than creating drama, painting pictures in sound, or telling stories.

TCHAIKOVSKY

The Russian composer Peter Ilyich Tchaikovsky (1840-93) was unhappy in his personal life, which brought great emotional depth to his music. He wrote many well-known ballets and symphonies, including the famous *1812 Overture*.

Stravinsky's ballet The Firebird caused a sensation at its first performance in Paris in 1910.

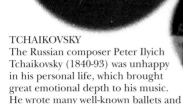

Playing a tune on an electric piano adds the notes to the score on the screen.

COMPUTER COMPOSITION

Computers can help composers to write music. The composer can use an electronic instrument to enter the melodies into the computer, where they can be stored, altered, and printed out.

MODERN MUSIC

In the 20th century there were great changes in serious music. Russian-born composer Igor Stravinsky (1882-1971) experimented with new harmonies, creating sounds that his audiences sometimes found difficult to understand. Composers such as the German Karlheinz Stockhausen (b. 1928) challenged listeners' ideas about music. In *Zyklus*, for example, Stockhausen tells the percussionist to start on any page of the score and play to the end before starting again at the beginning.

COMPOSERS

800s Composers begin to write down their music. At the same time, monks develop a form of chant, called plainsong, for singing church services.

1300-1600 Composers of the late Medieval and Renaissance period start to develop harmony by combining different voices together, producing a richer sound called polyphony.

1597 Jacopo Peri (1561-1633) of Italy composes *Dafne*, the first opera.

1600s Baroque music begins, and composers gradually make their music more complicated and elaborate.

1750-1820 The rise of classical music introduces simpler, popular tunes that more people could enjoy.

1817-23 Beethoven composes the *Choral symphony*, the first symphony to use a choir.

1820s The romantic era begins, and composers start to look for new ways to make their music appeal to the listeners' emotions.

1850s Composers in eastern and northern Europe begin to write nationalistic music, based on traditional songs and stories from their countries.

1865 Richard Wagner's (1813-83) opera *Tristan and Isolde* points the way towards Modern music.

1888 Russian nationalist composer Nikolai Rimsky-Korsakov composes his *Scheherazade*, based on the *Thousand and One Nights*.

1900s The modern era in music begins. Composers of the impressionist movement write music that creates atmosphere, movement, and colour in sound.

1905 French impressionist composer Claude Debussy (1862-1918) writes *La Mer* (The Sea).

1924 George Gershwin composes *Rhapsody in Blue* for jazz orchestra and piano.

1959 German composer Karlheinz Stockhausen (born 1928) writes *Zyklus* for one percussion player.

Find out more

DANCE
MUSIC
MUSICAL INSTRUMENTS
RENAISSANCE
TECHNOLOGY

COMPUTERS

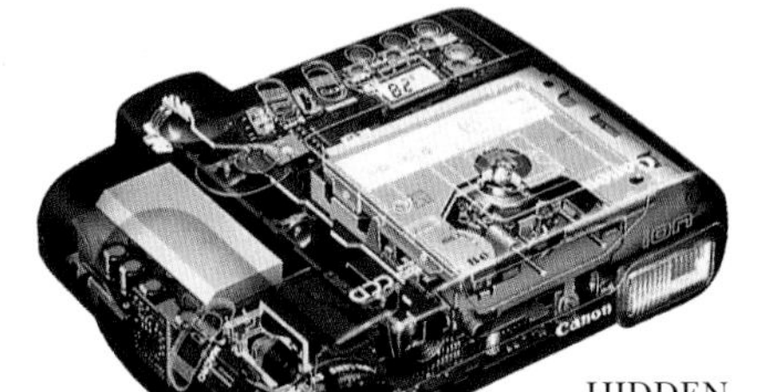

ACCURATE WEATHER FORECASTING, safe air travel, reliable medical technology – in today's world we take these things for granted, but they would be impossible without computers. Although a computer cannot "think" for itself like a person, it works like an electronic brain, doing tasks and interpreting data (information) very quickly. The computer in an air-traffic control system, for instance, can keep track of hundreds of aircraft at the same time and indicates which routes they should follow to avoid collisions. A personal computer can be used for a variety of tasks from word processing to searching the Internet and sending email. A computer consists of thousands of tiny electronic circuits. Before a computer can work, it must be given a set of instructions, called a program (or software), which tells the mechanical and electronic components inside the computer how to carry out a particular job. Additional components, such as a memory card or an internal modem, can be slotted into the computer as required.

HIDDEN COMPUTERS
People usually think of computers as having a screen and a keyboard, but this is not always the case. Many devices, such as washing machines, cars, and cameras, contain tiny computers that are specially programmed to control their function.

PERSONAL COMPUTERS
Many homes, schools, and offices use personal computers – small computers designed for use by one person. A personal computer, such as the laptop shown here, consists of four basic units: a keyboard, to type in information; a memory, to store information and programs; a processing unit, to carry out the instructions contained in the program; and a monitor, for displaying the results of the computer's work.

DATA STORAGE
The hard disc, shown below, is where all the computer's programs and data are stored permanently. Electronic memory chips, however, store data being used by the working computer. This data disappears when the power is switched off.

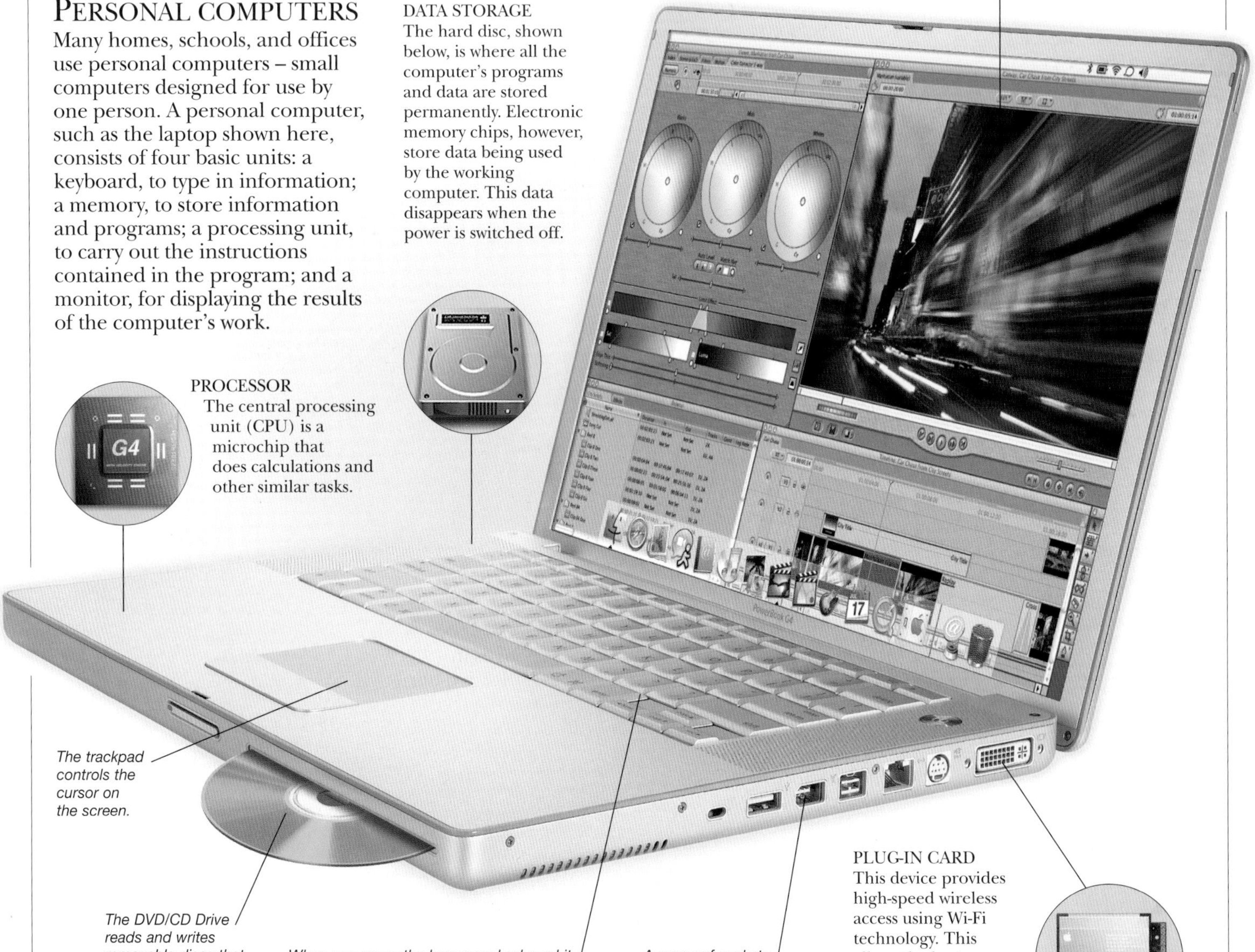

PROCESSOR
The central processing unit (CPU) is a microchip that does calculations and other similar tasks.

The monitor displays data.

The trackpad controls the cursor on the screen.

The DVD/CD Drive reads and writes removable discs that can store millions of pages of data.

When you press the keys on a keyboard it feeds information into the computer. Letters or numbers appear on screen, or the computer performs a function.

A range of sockets provides connections to external drives. Printers, MP3 players, and flash discs can be plugged into various ports.

PLUG-IN CARD
This device provides high-speed wireless access using Wi-Fi technology. This allows the laptop to connect to the Internet without plugging a cable into a telephone socket.

HOW COMPUTERS WORK

A computer converts everything it handles, such as letters of the alphabet, into numbers. The numbers are stored in the computer in the form of electronic signals in which "on" stands for 1 and "off" stands for 0. All numbers, letters, and pictures are represented by sequences of 1s and 0s. This is called binary code. The computer does all its different tasks, such as inserting a word into a sentence, by doing rapid calculations with these numbers. Once it has finished its job, the computer changes the numbers into words and pictures that we can understand.

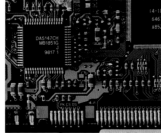

All computers contain a set of microchips (left). Inside a microchip are millions of tiny electronic parts that store and process electronic signals.

SOFTWARE

The programs that make a computer perform different tasks are called software. A computer can perform many different jobs simply by using different software programs, from computer games and word processing packages to painting programs and scientific applications that do complex calculations.

HARDWARE

Computer machinery is called hardware. There are many different kinds of hardware: personal computers, small portable computers, and large mainframe computers on which many people can work simultaneously. Hardware also includes components such as monitors, printers, and other computer equipment (below).

Processor, memory, and hard drive are inside tower unit.

DVD/CD Drive reads and writes data onto discs.

Monitor displays information. Speakers are built in to the computer.

USB connectors enable memory sticks, cameras, and other hardware to connect to the computer.

Keyboard

Mouse

Printer produces paper copy of images or data from computer.

Scanner built into printer can turn images from photos or books into data usable by the computer.

HISTORY OF COMPUTERS

In 1834, English inventor Charles Babbage designed the first programmable mechanical computer. However, he could not make the machine as it was too complex for the technology of his day. The first electronic computer, ENIAC, was built in the US in 1946. During the 1980s, transistors and microchips enabled computers to become smaller and more powerful. Easy-to-use software programs such as those developed by Microsoft (below) encouraged the spread of computers in people's homes. In the 1990s, web browsers opened the Internet to private individuals.

In 1975, American Bill Gates (1955-) founded the Microsoft company. By the late 1990s, Microsoft was supplying more than half the world's software.

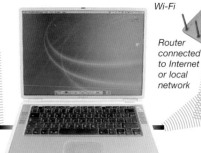

Bluetooth

Mobile phone

Wi-Fi

Router connected to Internet or local network

NEW TECHNOLOGY

Computers are becoming increasingly portable and versatile. Wireless or "Wi-Fi" technology means they can connect to the Internet via radio signals, and the similar "Bluetooth" enables them to communicate without cables over short distances with pocket computers, mobile phones, and even printers, keyboards, and mice.

Using wireless connections, a laptop computer can be used to send e-mails or surf the Internet from almost anywhere.

Handheld or "pocket" computers can send and receive e-mails, be used as mobile phones, and let you work on files from your desktop computer.

Find out more

ELECTRONICS
MACHINES
MATHEMATICS
ROBOTS
TECHNOLOGY

CONQUISTADORS

AT THE BEGINNING OF THE 16TH CENTURY the first Spanish adventurers followed Christopher Columbus to the Caribbean and South and Central America. These conquistadors (the Spanish word for conquerors) were soldiers hungry for gold, silver, and land. They took priests with them, sent by the Catholic Church to convert the Native Americans. The two most famous conquistadors were Hernando Cortés (1485-1547), who conquered the Aztecs of Mexico, and Francisco Pizarro (1470-1541), who conquered the Incas of Peru. Although the conquistadors took only small numbers of soldiers along, they were successful partly because they had brought guns, horses, and steel weapons. But what also came with the conquistadors were European diseases such as smallpox and measles, against which the Native Americans had no resistance. These diseases wiped out more than 70 million Native Americans and destroyed their civilizations. By seizing the land, the conquistadors prepared the way for a huge Spanish empire in the Americas that was to last until the 19th century.

EL DORADO
The first conquistadors heard legends of a golden kingdom ruled by "El Dorado", the golden man. They kept searching for this amazing place but never found it. Most of the beautiful goldwork they took to Europe was melted down and reused.

HERNANDO CORTES
In 1519, Cortés set out from Cuba to conquer Mexico, against the governor Velázquez's wishes. Velázquez believed that Cortés was too ambitious. From an early age Cortés had sought adventure and wealth. Eventually his wish was fulfilled and he controlled the whole of Mexico.

Hernando Cortés

Moctezuma

MOCTEZUMA MEETS CORTES
When the Aztec emperor Moctezuma met Cortés in Tenochtitlán, he believed that Cortés was the pale-skinned, bearded god Quetzalcoatl, who was prophesied to return from the east. He welcomed Cortés with gifts and a ceremony. But Cortés captured him and took over the Aztec empire.

NEW SPAIN
The Spanish quickly settled in the conquered areas and created the empire of New Spain. The wealth from its silver mines and ranches became the envy of Europe.

■ Aztecs
■ Incas

NATIVE AMERICANS
After conquest, the Native Americans were treated cruelly and forced to work for the Spanish. Many slaved in the gold mines. It was not long before their old way of life disappeared forever.

FRANCISCO PIZARRO
In 1532, Pizarro marched into Peru with 200 soldiers. He seized the Inca emperor, Atahualpa, ransomed him for a roomful of gold, then had him killed. The leaderless Inca empire crumbled.

Find out more
AZTECS
COLUMBUS, CHRISTOPHER
EXPLORERS
INCAS
MAYA
SOUTH AMERICA, HISTORY OF

CONSERVATION
AND ENDANGERED SPECIES

ANIMALS AND PLANTS ARE DYING OUT at a greater rate today than ever before. Living things have become extinct throughout the Earth's history – often due to dramatic changes in the climate – but today, humans are posing a greater threat. Thousands of animals and plants are endangered (in danger of extinction) because we cut down forests and drain wetlands to farm or build on the land where they live. We change the environment so much that animals and plants cannot survive. This is called habitat loss. Another great threat is hunting. People hunt animals for their fur, hide, horns, and meat, and sometimes simply because they consider animals a nuisance. Pollution is yet another serious threat, damaging many oceans, rivers, and forests. Conservation is the management and protection of wildlife and its habitats. It includes sheltering and trying to save wild animals and plants from destruction by humans. People are more aware of these threats to wildlife than ever before, and there are conservation organizations in many parts of the world. They work to protect endangered creatures by setting aside areas in the wild where animals and plants can live in safety.

GREENPEACE
International organizations such as Greenpeace work in various ways to save endangered polar wildlife, particularly whales and seals. Here, a Greenpeace worker is spraying a seal pup with harmless red dye so that seal hunters will not want to kill the pup for its beautiful fur.

PYGMY HOG
There may be only about 100 pygmy hogs left on Earth following the destruction of their grassland home in the Himalayan foothills of Assam, India.

SIAMESE CROCODILE
Many crocodiles and alligators have been killed for their skins, to be made into leather bags, shoes, and belts. Today, about 20 members of the crocodile family are in danger of extinction, including the Siamese crocodile and the Orinoco crocodile.

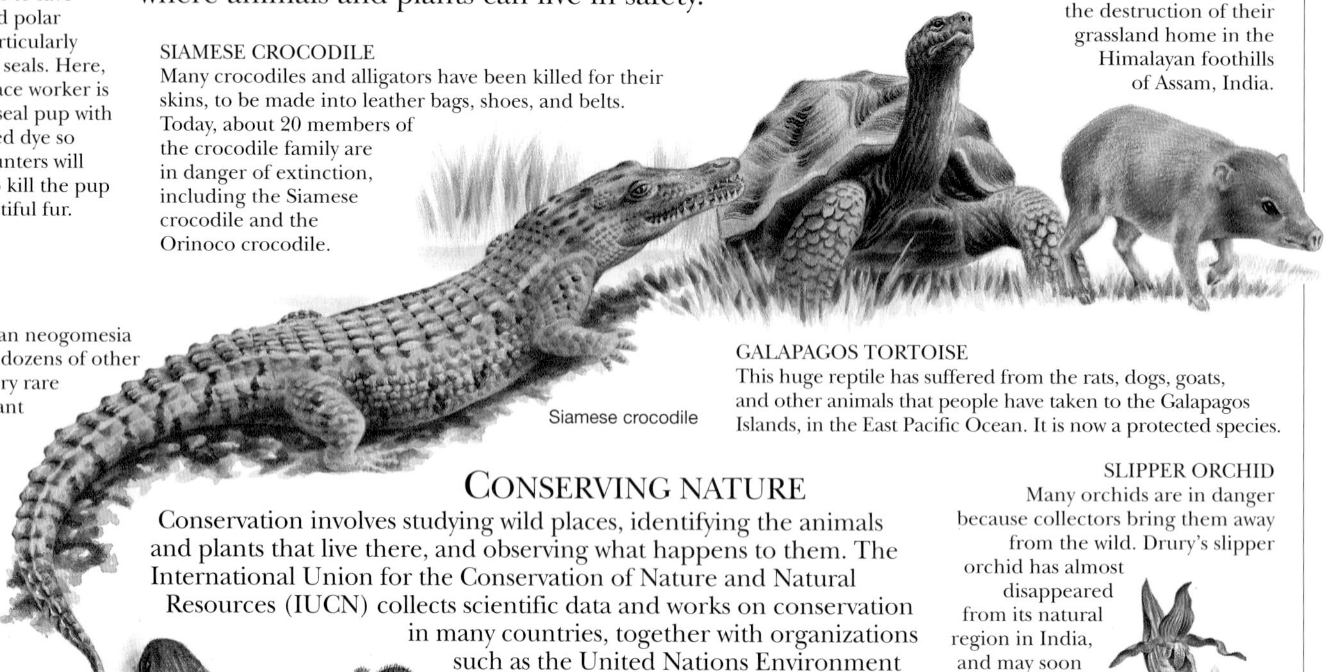

Siamese crocodile

CACTUS
The Mexican neogomesia cactus and dozens of other cacti are very rare because plant collectors have taken them from the wild.

Neogomesia cactus

GALAPAGOS TORTOISE
This huge reptile has suffered from the rats, dogs, goats, and other animals that people have taken to the Galapagos Islands, in the East Pacific Ocean. It is now a protected species.

SLIPPER ORCHID
Many orchids are in danger because collectors bring them away from the wild. Drury's slipper orchid has almost disappeared from its natural region in India, and may soon be extinct.

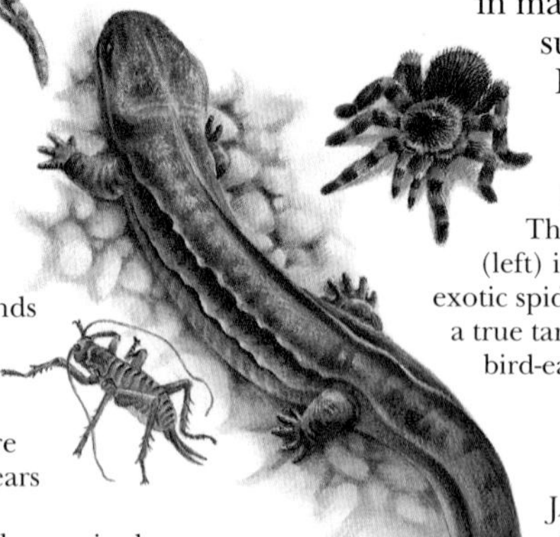

CONSERVING NATURE

Conservation involves studying wild places, identifying the animals and plants that live there, and observing what happens to them. The International Union for the Conservation of Nature and Natural Resources (IUCN) collects scientific data and works on conservation in many countries, together with organizations such as the United Nations Environment Programme (UNEP).

RED-KNEED TARANTULA
The red-kneed tarantula from Mexico (left) is rare because many people keep exotic spiders as pets. This tarantula is not a true tarantula but a member of the bird-eating spider group.

GREY BAT
Many kinds of bats are threatened because of the loss of their forest homes to farmland, and because of the increasing use of insecticides on the food they eat. The American grey bat shown right is endangered.

GIANT WETA CRICKET
There are many kinds of weta crickets in New Zealand. Fossils have been found that are more than 180 million years old. Today, several species of weta cricket are in danger of extinction, including the giant weta cricket shown here.

JAPANESE GIANT SALAMANDER
The Japanese giant salamander, shown left, is the world's largest amphibian, growing to more than 1.5 m (5 ft) long. Today it is protected, and is very rare to find.

AFRICAN VIOLET
The African violet is a well-known houseplant, but it has almost disappeared from its natural habitat – tropical mountain forests in Tanzania, Africa.

SPADEFOOT TOAD
There are many kinds of spadefoot toad. The Italian spadefoot toad shown here is particularly endangered.

MONK SEAL
Nature reserves have been set up for the Mediterranean monk seal so that it is not disturbed by tourists on the coasts where it breeds.

GOLDEN LION TAMARIN
Clearing forests for timber and farmland endangers the lives of many monkeys. Many tamarins and marmosets have been killed in South America, because people mistakenly believed that they spread the diseases malaria and yellow fever.

VICTORIA'S BIRDWING BUTTERFLY
The Victoria's birdwing butterfly was first collected by scientists in 1855, when they shot it with guns. Today this butterfly and many other kinds of butterflies are endangered because collectors kill them.

DODO
The dodo was a flightless bird that lived on islands in the Indian Ocean. All dodos were extinct by about 1800.

JACKASS PENGUIN
This flightless sea bird is also called the black-footed penguin. Its numbers have decreased in South Africa because of water pollution and because fishing boats catch the fish the penguin eats.

SUMATRAN RHINOCEROS
Rhinoceroses are in great danger of extinction, but poachers (illegal hunters) still kill them and sell their horns. The horns are carved into dagger handles or powdered into traditional Chinese medicine. There are only a few hundred Sumatran rhinoceroses left, in Sumatra and mainland Southeast Asia.

CAPTIVE BREEDING
One way to help an endangered species recover its numbers is by breeding it in captivity. Experts capture a few animals from the wild, raise them carefully, and encourage them to breed in captivity. Later, they release, or reintroduce, the offspring into a suitable area. The notornis is a flightless bird that scientists believed to be extinct until it was rediscovered in 1948. Eggs from its nests are hatched in an incubator, and the chicks are kept warm with tiny electric blankets. They are fed by someone wearing a puppet-like glove that resembles the parent bird.

HABITAT LOSS
Tropical rain forests are being destroyed at an alarming rate. Trees are burned or sold for timber, and the land is farmed or used for roads and buildings. Scientists believe that many rain forests contain kinds of animals and plants that we have never seen. For every plant or creature that is threatened or extinct, there may be 100 that we do not know about.

Notornis

CONTROLLING TRADE
Some animals and plants are taken from the wild for their skins and other products. Elephants are killed for their ivory tusks. Colourful flowers are made into pulp to make dyes. The Convention on International Trade in Endangered Species (CITES) has lists of hundreds of species, or kinds, of plants and animals. Selling or exporting these animals or their products without a special licence is illegal. All whales, dolphins, and porpoises are on this list; so are all monkeys, apes, and lemurs.

SNAKE SKIN
The brightly coloured objects shown above were once the skins of snakes and lizards. The skins are dyed different colours, then made into all sorts of leather goods, including bags and shoes.

SNOW LEOPARD
The snow leopard lives high in the mountains of the Himalayas and Central Asia. In winter its fur becomes thicker to keep out the bitter cold. In the past, the snow leopard's winter coat was much prized by fur traders. Today, the snow leopard and many other big cats are protected by the CITES agreement, but they are still hunted illegally in some remote areas.

Find out more
ANIMALS
ECOLOGY AND FOOD WEBS
FOREST WILDLIFE
NATIONAL PARKS
PLANTS
POLLUTION

CONTINENTS

ALMOST A THIRD OF THE SURFACE of the Earth is land. There are seven vast pieces of land, called continents, which make up most of this area. The rest consists of islands which are much smaller land masses completely surrounded by water. The seven continents are crowded into almost one half of the globe; the huge Pacific Ocean occupies most of the other half. The largest continent is Asia, which has an area of more than 44 million sq km (17 million sq miles).

Most scientists now agree that, about 200 million years ago, the continents were joined together in one huge land mass. Over millions of years they drifted around and changed shape, and they are still moving today. The continents lie on vast pieces of solid rock, called plates, which collide and move against one another. These movements cause volcanoes and earthquakes, push up mountains, and create huge trenches in the Earth's crust.

3 THE WORLD TODAY
The Americas have moved away from the other continents and joined together, and India has joined Asia. Australia and Antarctica have drifted apart.

Europe
Asia
North America
Africa
South America
Australia
Antarctica

The continents are made of many smaller pieces of land which have been pushed together.

1 PANGAEA
The continents were joined in one supercontinent, called Pangaea, which began to break apart about 200 million years ago.

Asia
North America
Europe
India
Australia
North America
PANGAEA
South America
Antarctica
Africa

Asia
North America
Laurasia
Africa
Europe
India
South America
Gondwanaland
Australia
Antarctica

2 BREAK-UP
About 135 million years ago, Pangaea split up into two areas – Gondwanaland and Laurasia.

CONTINENTAL DRIFT

A glance at the globe shows that the eastern sides of North and South America and the western sides of Europe and Africa follow a similar line. In 1912, Alfred Wegener, a German meteorologist, suggested that the continents once fitted together like pieces of a jigsaw. This huge piece of land then broke up, and the continents drifted apart.

PLATE TECTONICS

The continents and oceans lie on top of several huge plates of rock about 100 km (60 miles) deep. These plates float on the hot, semi-molten rock in the mantle underneath. Heat from the Earth's interior makes the plates move, carrying the continents with them. Mountains and undersea ridges, deep trenches, and huge valleys form at the edges of the plates as they move and collide.

Pacific Ocean
Trench
South America
Atlantic Ocean
Mountains and volcanoes
American plate
Undersea ridge
Nazca plate
Africa
Molten rock from Nazca plate forces its way up, forming volcanoes along edge of continent.
Indian Ocean
Nazca plate moves under South American plate, forming trench in ocean floor.
Hot rock rises from below, pushing the American and African plates apart and forming an undersea ridge.
Mantle
African plate
Indian plate

MOVING PLATES

The plates move about 2.5 cm (1 in) every year – about as fast as your fingernails grow. The Atlantic Ocean is widening at this speed as the Americas drift apart from Europe and Africa.

SAN ANDREAS FAULT
The San Andreas fault in the United States is at the border between two plates. They slide against one another, causing severe earthquakes.

Find out more
EARTH
EARTHQUAKES
GEOLOGY
MOUNTAINS
OCEANS AND SEAS
VOLCANOES

JAMES
COOK

IN THE LATE SUMMER OF 1768, a small sailing ship left Plymouth, England, on an expedition to the Pacific Ocean. In charge of the ship was Lieutenant James Cook, who was to become one of the greatest explorers the world has ever known. Cook was an outstanding navigator. He was also a fine captain. He insisted that his sailors eat sauerkraut (pickled cabbage) and fresh fruit, and so became the first captain to save his crew from scurvy, a disease caused by lack of vitamin C. The voyage lasted three years. On his return to England, Cook was sent on two more voyages: one to the Antarctic, the other to the Arctic. On these voyages he became the first European to visit a number of Pacific islands, sailed further south than any other European, and added many lands, including Australia and New Zealand, to the British Empire.

1728 Born in Yorkshire, England.

1746 Signs on as ship's boy on the coal ship *Freelove*.

1759 Charts St. Lawrence River in Canada.

1772-75 Voyage to discover "southern continent", a land that scientists thought must exist. Circles Antarctica.

1775 Promoted to captain.

1776-79 Voyage to discover a northwest passage around North America.

1779 Killed in Sandwich Islands (Hawaii).

ENDEAVOUR

Cook's ship, the *Endeavour*, was originally a coal ship. Cook chose this ship because it was sturdy, spacious, and easy to handle. On the *Endeavour* voyage, Cook added many new territories to the British Empire.

The Endeavour was 32 m (106 ft) long, weighed 368 tonnes and carried 112 sailors and five scientists.

Cook purified the air in the ship once a week by burning vinegar and gunpowder.

Cook stocked up with fresh fruit at every landing.

KEEPING RECORDS
Cook made many maps, took regular measurements, and recorded every event of the voyages in minute detail. The scientists on board collected botanical specimens from the lands they visited. In an age before cameras, artists on board made drawings of all the people, plants, and wildlife they saw to show to people at home. They collected so many specimens in one bay in Australia that they named it Botany Bay. It later became a dreaded prison colony.

Sydney Parkinson was the ship's artist on board the Endeavour. *He drew this plant,* Banksia serrata,1, *in around 1760.*

FIRST VOYAGE
The British Royal Navy sent Cook on his first voyage to observe the planet Venus passing between the Earth and the Sun. He also had secret orders from the government to sail into uncharted regions to prove the existence of a southern continent, which they wanted to add to their empire. He did not succeed, but in the attempt he became the first European to visit New Zealand and the east coast of Australia.

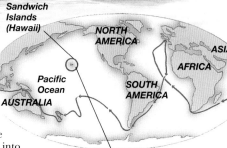

Sandwich Islands (Hawaii)

NORTH AMERICA

ASIA

AFRICA

Pacific Ocean

SOUTH AMERICA

AUSTRALIA

Islanders killed Captain Cook here on 14 February 1779.

Find out more
AUSTRALIA, HISTORY OF
EXPLORERS
NEW ZEALAND, HISTORY OF

CORALS
ANEMONES, AND JELLYFISH

Tentacles trail more than 15 m (50 ft) from a man-of-war.

Sea wasp

IN THE WARM, TROPICAL SEAS surrounding coral islands are some of the most fascinating sea creatures. Despite being so different in appearance, corals, jellyfish, and anemones belong to the same family. The fabulous corals that make up coral reefs are created by little animals called polyps, which look like miniature sea anemones. Every polyp builds a cup-shaped skeleton around itself, and as the polyps grow and die, their skeletons mass together to create a coral reef. Unlike coral-building polyps, jellyfish can move around freely, trailing their long tentacles below their soft bodies as they swim. Some jellyfish float on the surface and are pushed along with the current. Anemones anchor themselves to rocks, where they wait for fish to swim through their tentacles.

Carijoa coral

JELLYFISH
The sea wasp jellyfish uses its tentacles to sting fish. Tentacles contain venom which is painful to humans and can cause death.

Clown fish

CLOWN FISH
These fish live in harmony with sea anemones. The thick, slimy mucus on their bodies keeps them safe from the stinging cells. Clown fish keep anemones clean by feeding on particles of food among their waving tentacles.

MAN-OF-WAR
The Portuguese man-of-war is not one jellyfish. It is a floating colony of hundreds of jellyfish-like creatures known as polyps. Some polyps form the float, which drifts on the water; others bear stinging tentacles for paralyzing prey; still others digest the prey and pass the nutrients through the body.

Stinging cell body

Whip thrown out

Stinging tip

Stinging tip

Coiled whip

Trigger

STINGING CELLS
Each jellyfish tentacle is armed with deadly weapons. If a fish touches a tentacle, stinging cells containing tiny coiled-up threads are triggered into action. They shoot out a hollow whip like a harpoon, injecting paralyzing poison into the prey.

CORAL SHAPES
The shape of a coral depends on the arrangement and growing pattern of the tiny polyps that build it. Corals can be dazzling in colour and extraordinary in shape, resembling all sorts of objects. This Carijoa coral looks like a branching tree.

Common sea anemone

Anemone slowly engulfing a trapped fish.

ANEMONE
As a fish stops struggling, the anemone's tentacles shorten and pull it into the mouth, through to the stomach chamber in the "body" of the anemone. Any undigested remains pass out the same way.

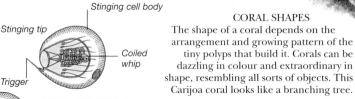

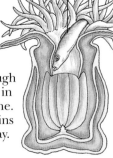

HOW CORAL REEFS ARE FORMED

Corals grow in shallow water around an island.

Coral reef builds up as island sinks.

Island disappears, leaving an atoll.

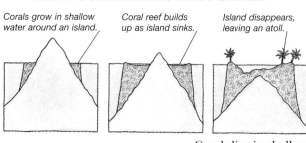

Corals live in shallow water around an island where bright sunlight makes them grow. As movements in the Earth's surface make the island sink, corals form a reef. Finally the island disappears, leaving a ring of reefs called an atoll.

HYDRA
The tiny hydra is a freshwater polyp that lives in ponds. It may be green, brown, or grey in colour. Hydras feed on other tiny water creatures which they catch with their tentacles. Each tentacle has stinging cells that contain poison to paralyze the prey. Hydras reproduce by growing "buds" on their "stalk". The buds break off to form new hydras. This is a form of asexual reproduction.

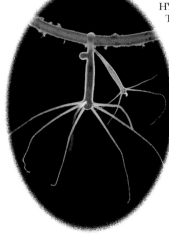

Find out more

ANIMALS
DEEP-SEA WILDLIFE
OCEAN WILDLIFE

CRABS
AND OTHER CRUSTACEANS

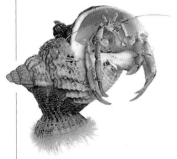

THOUSANDS OF DIFFERENT kinds of crabs scuttle over our sandy shores and skulk in rock pools. They range from tiny parasitic crabs living inside mussels to the giant Japanese spider crab, whose legs can be more than 3 m (10 ft) long. Crabs breathe underwater using gills, but some can also survive out of water for a long time. All crabs are protected by strong, hard shells like a suit of armour on the outside of their bodies. Crabs, along with lobsters and crayfish, belong to the animal group called crustaceans. Their bodies are divided into sections, with jointed limbs and two pairs of antennae on the head. A crab begins life as an egg, which develops into a larva, then into an adult crab. Each time the crab reaches another growing stage, it sheds the outer layer of its shell, revealing a new layer beneath.

HERMIT CRAB
The hermit crab often makes its home in the empty shell of a whelk, which protects it from predators such as gulls.

EDIBLE CRAB
The so-called edible crab is only one of many kinds of crustaceans that are caught, cooked, and eaten by people around the world.

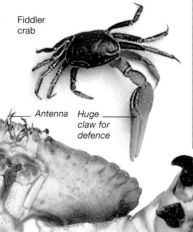

Fiddler crab

Eye on stalk

Antenna

Huge claw for defence

Carapace (shell)

Eight walking legs

LOBSTER
The lobster scavenges on the seabed for dead fish and other animal remains. One claw has blunt knobs for crushing; the other has sharp "teeth" for cutting. The biggest lobsters are 60 cm (2 ft) long and can live as long as humans – up to 70 years.

Antenna

Crushing claw

Carapace over front part of body

Four pairs of walking limbs

Eye on stalk

Six segments on abdomen

Telson (tailpiece)

SHRIMPS AND PRAWNS
These little sea creatures are good scavengers. During the day they dig into the sand and hide. At night they emerge to hunt for food using their long feelers. When in danger, prawns and shrimps escape by scooting backwards with a flick of their tail fan.

Long antenna (feeler)

Shrimp

Tail fan

Feeding claw

Tail fan

Prawn

Feeding claw

Long antenna (feeler)

BARNACLES
These sea crustaceans have no heads. Their long, feathery legs beat the water, collecting tiny food particles. Acorn barnacles live in volcano-shaped shells cemented on to rocks. Goose barnacles attach themselves to driftwood by their stalks.

Goose barnacles

Acorn barnacles

WHERE CRUSTACEANS LIVE
Some crustaceans such as the yabby (a freshwater shrimp) and the water flea live in rivers and lakes. A few crustaceans live on land. The woodlouse, for example, can be found under dead leaves and in damp woodland areas.

Woodlouse

Water flea

Yabby

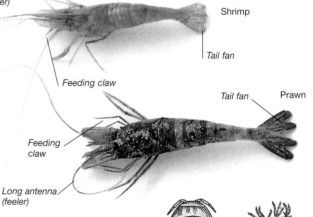

Find out more
ANIMALS
OCEAN WILDLIFE
SEASHORE WILDLIFE

CRICKET

PLAYED WITH A BAT AND BALL, cricket is a popular team game. The object is to score the highest number of runs by hitting the ball and running the length of the pitch to the far wicket as many times as possible, before fielders from the other team reach the wicket with the ball. The game is played by two teams of 11 players, each team taking it in turns to bat or field. Batting sessions, called "innings", end when 10 of the 11 players are out. Batters are out if the ball hits the wicket – or if the ball would hit the wicket were the batter's leg not in the way (leg before wicket). A batter is also out if a fielder catches the ball or runs the batter out (reaches the wicket with the ball). Two umpires on the field (and sometimes a third off-field umpire) judge whether the batter is in or out. Invented by the English, cricket is now played worldwide by men and women. Top teams include England, Australia, and India.

Ball is hit with full face of bat.

Good footwork

The BAT and BALL

HISTORY OF CRICKET
Cricket began in England, probably in the 1500s, with club-like bats and a two-stump wicket. From the 1800s it developed into today's game.

BATTING

The bowler delivers the ball to the striking batter, who can either guard the wicket with defensive strokes, or play attacking strokes to hit the ball and score runs. Batters do not always have to run: four runs are scored automatically if the ball reaches the boundary, and six if it goes over the boundary without bouncing.

EQUIPMENT

To avoid injury, batters and wicketkeepers wear protective gear. Leg pads and gloves must be worn, and many players also wear helmets. Clothing is traditionally white, but in some competitions players wear coloured clothes. Cricket bats are made of willow, which does not split.

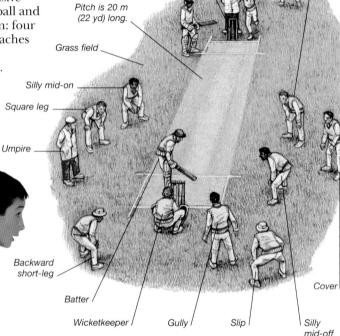

Wicket *Umpire* *Bowler* *Mid-off*
Non-striking batter *Cover point*
Pitch is 20 m (22 yd) long.
Grass field
Silly mid-on
Square leg
Umpire
Backward short-leg
Batter
Wicketkeeper *Gully* *Slip* *Silly mid-off*
Cover

Leg pad

BOWLING

Each bowler delivers one "over" (six balls) before another bowler takes a turn. Fast bowlers use speed to get batters out. Medium bowlers are not as fast, but they make the ball swerve in the air. Spin bowlers hold the ball in different ways to make it turn when it bounces.

PITCH

The captain of the fielding side places his or her fielders in good positions to prevent runs and to catch the ball when possible. The wicketkeeper and slip are there to catch the batter out if he or she misses the ball. Other fielders stand further away on the boundary. One umpire stands at the bowler's end and another stands at square leg.

Cricket ball showing cork and twine core and red leather casing

Bat *Batting glove*

Find out more
HEALTH AND FITNESS
OLYMPIC GAMES
SPORTS

CROCODILES AND ALLIGATORS

LYING LOW IN THE WATER looking like an old log, but ready to snap up almost any animal, the crocodile seems like a survivor from the pre-historic age, and it is. One hundred million years ago, crocodiles were prowling through the swamps with the dinosaurs. Crocodiles and alligators belong to the reptile group called crocodilians. This group includes 14 kinds of crocodiles, eight kinds of alligators (six of which are commonly called caimans), and one kind of gharial. Crocodilians are carnivorous (meat-eating) reptiles; they lurk in rivers, lakes, and swamps, grabbing whatever prey they can. Crocodiles and alligators eat fish and frogs whole. They drag larger prey, such as deer, under the water and drown it. To remove chunks of flesh, they grip the animal in their jaws and spin rapidly.

Nile crocodiles measure up to 6 m (20 ft) long and weigh more than 1 tonne.

Female carries the young in her mouth.

CROCODILE
The fourth tooth on each side of the crocodile's lower jaw is visible when the mouth is closed.

ALLIGATOR
Unlike crocodiles, no lower teeth are visible when the alligator's mouth is closed.

CAIMAN
The caiman has a broad mouth for eating a variety of prey.

GHARIAL
The gharial has a long, slender mouth with sharp teeth for catching fish.

NILE CROCODILE
The Nile crocodile is found in many watery parts of Africa. Like most reptiles, the female lays eggs, which she looks after until they hatch. The newly hatched young listen for their mother's footsteps and call to her. She gently gathers them into her mouth in batches and carries them to the safety of the water.

YOUNG
After about three months, the young crocodiles hatch out of the eggs. The mother guards them closely because they are in danger of becoming food for large lizards and foxes.

CROCODILE SMILE
Crocodiles often bask in the sun with their mouths wide open. Blood vessels inside the mouth absorb the sun's warmth. This raises the animal's body temperature and gives the crocodile the energy to hunt for its prey in the evening.

ALLIGATOR
There are two kinds of true alligators – the Chinese and the American alligators. Today, the Chinese alligator is in great danger of extinction – only a few hundred survive. The American alligator lives in rivers and swamps across the southeastern United States, where it eats fish, water birds, and anything else it can catch. In more populated areas, the American alligator also grabs unwary farm animals.

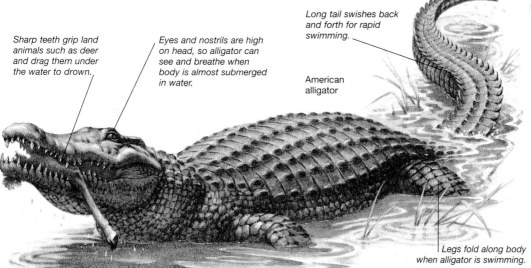

Sharp teeth grip land animals such as deer and drag them under the water to drown.

Eyes and nostrils are high on head, so alligator can see and breathe when body is almost submerged in water.

Long tail swishes back and forth for rapid swimming.

American alligator

Legs fold along body when alligator is swimming.

> **Find out more**
> ANIMALS
> LIZARDS
> PREHISTORIC LIFE

OLIVER CROMWELL

ONE OF THE PEOPLE WHO SIGNED King Charles I's death warrant in January 1649 was Oliver Cromwell. A Puritan member of parliament, he had been a prominent parliamentary leader in the English Civil War (1642-49) against the king and his Royalist supporters. Following the king's execution, the monarchy was abolished and a new constitution declared England a republican "Commonwealth". Cromwell headed its Council of State. In 1653 he was made Lord Protector, which gave him the power to decide how to rule the country. However, he faced many difficulties in leading the new Commonwealth, as people held very different political and religious views. Cromwell governed England until his death in 1658, and in 1660, Charles ll was offered the throne, signalling the end of the Commonwealth.

1599 Born in Huntingdon.

1628 Becomes MP for Huntingdon.

1629 Becomes a Puritan (strict Protestant).

1641 Uprising in Ireland.

1642 Civil War begins.

1644-45 Cromwell leads the cavalry to defeat Royalists at Marston Moor and Naseby.

1649 The Commonwealth is declared.

1649-50 Cromwell's army crushes Irish Royalists.

1650-51 Scottish Royalists are defeated at the battles of Dunbar and Worcester.

1653 Made Lord Protector.

1657 Refuses the Crown.

1658 Dies – buried in state.

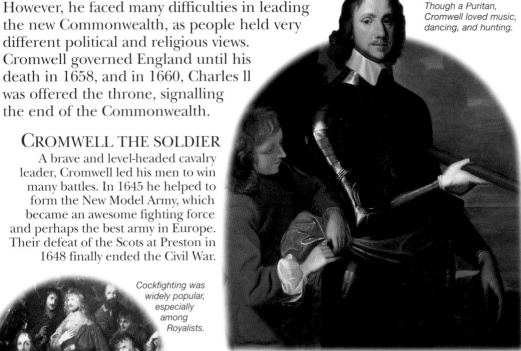

Though a Puritan, Cromwell loved music, dancing, and hunting.

CROMWELL THE SOLDIER

A brave and level-headed cavalry leader, Cromwell led his men to win many battles. In 1645 he helped to form the New Model Army, which became an awesome fighting force and perhaps the best army in Europe. Their defeat of the Scots at Preston in 1648 finally ended the Civil War.

THE COMMONWEALTH

The new government tried to create a just and godly "Commonwealth". It banned popular pleasures including Sunday sports, bear-baiting, and cockfighting. Christmas and May Day celebrations were also forbidden. Theatres were closed, but soon reopened.

Cockfighting was widely popular, especially among Royalists.

TROUBLE IN IRELAND

From the 16th century onwards, English Protestants moved into Ireland and dispossessed people of their land. The Irish rebelled against Charles I's rule and he tried to suppress them. In 1649 Cromwell went to Ireland to put down a Royalist uprising. There were terrible massacres at Drogheda and Wexford.

Cromwell's coat of arms

THE LORD PROTECTOR

In 1653 Cromwell was made Lord Protector for Life, to govern with a Council of State and a single-chamber parliament. Later he was asked to take the Crown, but he refused. However, he lived regally and his son Richard succeeded him.

RELIGIOUS TOLERANCE

Cromwell thought that people should be free to worship God in the way they believed to be right. Religious freedom and tolerance were guaranteed, though not to Catholics and Quakers. In practice, most people enjoyed tolerance.

Find out more

ENGLISH CIVIL WAR
STUARTS
UNITED KINGDOM, HISTORY OF

CRUSADES

NINE CENTURIES AGO the Pope appealed to Christians to recapture the holy city of Jerusalem from the Turkish Muslims who had seized it. Thousands of European Christians – knights, princes, pilgrims, and peasants – responded to the call and set out on a long warring pilgrimage, called a crusade, from western Europe to Palestine (now Israel). Four years later, after battles, starvation, and disease, the surviving crusaders captured the city of Jerusalem. The crusaders set up a Christian kingdom on the shores of Palestine that lasted nearly a century. But in 1187, Saladin recaptured Jerusalem. At least seven more crusades set out. None were successful, but relations between Christians and Muslim worlds were long poisoned by the memory of the Crusades.

THE CHILDREN'S CRUSADE
In 1212, a tragic crusade occurred when thousands of Christian children set off on foot from Europe to Jerusalem. Most starved to death, or were sold into slavery.

Richard I sailed from London.

Philip of France set off from Vezelay.

• **Vezelay**

• **Regensburg**

Verona •

The Third Crusade made Richard I popular in his own time and earned him the nickname "the Lionheart".

Constantinople •

Krak des Chevaliers was the strongest crusader castle.

Crusader ship

• **Acre**

THE THIRD CRUSADE
King Richard I of England (ruled 1189-99) took part in the Third Crusade with the king of France and the Holy Roman Emperor. King Richard I captured the port of Acre, but was caught and held for ransom on his return journey. Ultimately, they failed to take Jerusalem on this crusade, but did make a truce with Saladin allowing Christian pilgrims to enter the city.

ACRE BESIEGED
Huge wooden siege towers helped the crusaders attack the city of Acre. The defenders threw spears, hot sand, and boiling water on them.

SULTAN SALADIN
Leader of the Muslim forces, Saladin (1137-93) was a great commander. As sultan of Egypt and Syria, he made Egypt one of the most powerful regions in the Middle East.

JOURNEY TO JERUSALEM
The journey from Europe to the Holy Land was long and dangerous, and many of the crusaders died on the way. Those who went back to Europe from Palestine took silks and spices with them, as well as Islamic learning such as mathematics and astronomy.

THE CRUSADES

1096 First Crusade (also known as the People's Crusade) sets off. Many peasants die on the way, though knights survive.

1097 Crusaders arrive in Constantinople (now Istanbul).

1098 French and Norman armies capture Antioch.

1099 Crusaders capture Jerusalem. Divide coastal land into four kingdoms.

1147-49 Second Crusade attacks Muslims in Spain, Portugal, and Asia Minor.

1187 Saladin conquers Jerusalem and most of Palestine.

1189 Third Crusade sets off led by the kings of England and France and Frederick I, the Holy Roman Emperor. Frederick dies on the way.

1191-92 Crusaders capture Acre but return to Europe.

1202-04 Fourth Crusade sets off. Crusaders capture Constantinople and steal treasure.

1217 Fifth Crusade sets off. Crusaders capture Damietta, Egypt, but return it and make a truce.

1228-29 Sixth Crusade. Emperor Frederick II makes a 10-year truce.

1248-54 Seventh Crusade. Louis IX of France captures Damietta but is forced to return it.

1270 Eighth Crusade. Louis IX dies. This final crusade returns to Europe.

Find out more
CHRISTIANITY
ISLAM

DAMS

EVERY DAY, FACTORIES and homes use up huge amounts of water. For example, an oil refinery uses 10 times as much water as the petrol it makes. Dams help to provide us with much of the water we need by trapping water from flowing rivers. Building a dam across a river creates a huge lake, called a reservoir, behind the dam. Reservoirs also provide water to irrigate large areas of farmland. A dam can store the water that falls in rainy seasons so that there is water during dry periods. By storing water in this way, dams also prevent floods. Flood barriers can stop the sea from surging up a river and bursting its banks. Some provide electricity as well as water. They contain hydroelectric power stations powered by water from their reservoirs.

Lake Mead

Lift shaft inside dam goes down to hydroelectric power station.

Water from the reservoir enters the intake towers.

Roadway along top of dam

Arched, concrete dam wall

Water flows down pipes to hydroelectric power station.

Pipes carry excess water to the Colorado River so that the dam does not break or overflow.

Hoover dam

Dam shown with water removed from one side.

Tunnel that was excavated to divert river while dam was built.

Water flows down to Colorado River.

Hydroelectric power station

Overflow water

CONCRETE DAMS

There are two main types of concrete dam: arch dams and gravity dams. Arch dams (either single-arch or multiple-arch) are tall, curved shells of concrete as little as 3 m (10 ft) thick. Because their arched shape makes them very strong, they do not burst. Large gravity dams are also made of concrete. Their vast weight keeps them from giving way.

HOOVER DAM
The Hoover Dam in the United States, one of the world's highest concrete dams, is 221 m (726 ft) high. It is an arch dam that spans the River Colorado, supplying water for irrigation and electricity to California, Arizona, and Nevada. Lake Mead, the reservoir formed by the dam, is 185 km (115 miles) long.

EMBANKMENT DAMS

The biggest dams are embankment dams, made by piling up a huge barrier of earth and rock. A core of clay or concrete in the centre keeps water from seeping through the dam. The side is covered with stones to protect it from the water. The world's highest dam is the Rogun Dam in Tajikistan, an embankment dam 335 m (1,099 ft) high.

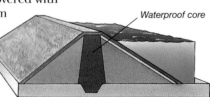

Waterproof core

FLOOD BARRIERS
Movable dams, called flood barriers, are built on rivers to control flooding. Built in 1982, this barrier across the River Thames in England protects London from flooding by North Sea gales. Large, curved gates rise if the river gets too high.

THE EFFECTS OF DAMS
The reservoir that forms in the valley behind a dam floods the land, often damaging the environment. For example, the Aswan High Dam in Egypt was built to control the flooding of the River Nile, but changing the river's flow has destroyed the fertility of the surrounding land.

A dam prevents fish, such as salmon, from swimming up and down a river. Some dams have a fish ladder, a pipe, or pools through which fish can swim past the dam.

Find out more
ELECTRICITY
FARMING
LAKES
RIVERS
WATER

DANCE

WHEN PEOPLE HEAR MUSIC, they often tap their feet and clap their hands. Dancing is a natural activity, and there are many different styles, ranging from the hectic breakdance to the graceful, elegant waltz. However, all forms of dance share the same rhythmic movements that people have enjoyed since time began. Prehistoric cave paintings show people moving in a lively way. They kept time by clapping and stamping. Later, dancers began to move in patterns with more formal steps, and dancing in couples or in groups at balls or dances became a part of social life. In many countries special costumes are part of folk-dancing traditions.

RITUAL DANCE
In religious rituals, dance is a way of thanking the gods or asking for their help. These Native Americans are performing a fertility dance. It is important that the steps are always danced in the same order.

Square dancers often dress up in cowboy or cowgirl style.

This modern jazz dancer combines the grace and elegance of traditional ballet with soft, fluid poses that more closely express personal feelings. The swirling movements of her dress complement and enhance her performance.

SQUARE DANCING
Square dancing is very sociable. Four couples form a square and change partners in a sequence of moves. A caller shouts out instructions such as "Swing your partner to the right". This traditional North American dance has many variations.

MODERN DANCE
Most traditional dances have a prearranged series of steps and movements, but modern dance forms encourage dancers to move more freely. Contemporary dance emerged at the beginning of the 20th century. US dancer Isadora Duncan was one of the first performers to move away from orthodox ballet and develop her own style. Jazz dance emerged in the 1920s and has been central to modern dance.

Love – putting on a ring

Marriage – tying the love knot around the bride's neck

Modern dancers often devise their own steps and perform barefoot.

There are six styles of Indian classical dance. These styles usually involve miming out stories from ancient mythology.

MIME
Mime mixes dance and acting to create a language without words which can be understood by people from many cultures. The dancer shown here is from India, but mime is also part of other Eastern and Western dance styles.

ROCK AND ROLL
The emergence of rock and roll music in the 1950s led to the first mass form of modern dance. The music had a strong beat and lyrics that young people could relate to. Rock and roll steps were wild and daring, and were very different to conservative social dancing.

DANCE AND WORSHIP
In India, almost all performing arts are linked to religion. *Bharatanatyam* is a classical dance style from Tamil Nadu, southern India. It is linked to ancient temple dances. Performers paint their hands and feet with red dye. In ancient times, the dancers came from special families and were known as *devadasis*.

Find out more

FILMS
INDIA
THEATRE

CHARLES
DARWIN

ON 27 DECEMBER 1831, HMS *Beagle* sailed from Plymouth, England to survey the east and west coasts of South America. On board was the ship's naturalist, Charles Darwin. The ship sailed beyond the Americas to the Pacific Ocean, where Darwin made many scientific discoveries, especially on the Galapagos and Keeling Islands. As a schoolboy, Darwin had often been in trouble with his headmaster for spending time on chemistry experiments and collecting specimens instead of studying Greek and Latin. But his boyhood interest in the natural world led him to make startling discoveries about life on Earth and the development of the planet. When he returned from sea in 1836, he married, settled in London, and wrote up the notes of his discoveries. These formed the basis of his famous theory of evolution.

1809 Born in Shrewsbury, Shropshire, England.

1825-27 Studies medicine at Edinburgh University.

1827 Studies divinity at Cambridge, but spends more time on biology, zoology, and geology.

1831-36 HMS *Beagle* voyage.

1858 Evolutionary theory first explained to the world.

1859 Publishes *On the Origin of Species* – it is a best-seller.

1882 Dies; buried at Westminster Abbey, London.

The *Beagle*

Darwin made careful notes of everything he observed.

Galapagos finch

Galapagos tortoise

VOYAGE OF THE *BEAGLE*

On the five-year voyage, HMS *Beagle* made many stops, during which Darwin studied plant and animal life, and land formation. On the outward-bound journey, the ship sailed to the Canaries, across the Atlantic (where Darwin realized that the Cape Verde islands had been made by volcanoes erupting under the sea), along South America's east coast, round Cape Horn, and up the west coast, where he witnessed an earthquake.

PACIFIC OCEAN

Galapagos Islands

NORTH PACIFIC OCEAN

SOUTH ATLANTIC OCEAN

Darwin studied the wildlife in the isolated Galapagos Islands.

The ship returned via New Zealand, New South Wales, and the Keeling Islands.

CORAL
On the Keeling Islands, Darwin studied coral reefs, whose structure was not understood at the time. He thought they were formed by coral building up on the sea floor while the floor itself was gently subsiding. Modern deep-sea drillings have since proved that Darwin was right.

THE ORIGIN OF SPECIES
As a result of his study of wildlife on the Galapagos Islands, Darwin began to believe that species (types of plants and animals) were not fixed forever, but that they evolved (changed) to suit their environment. In 1859, he published *On the Origin of Species*, a book in which he set out his evolutionary theory, suggesting that humans evolved from apes.

ALFRED WALLACE
Welsh naturalist Alfred Wallace (1823-1913) carried out studies that led him to agree with Darwin's theories. He travelled to the Amazon and to Malaysia, where he began to think that nature encouraged the survival of the fittest. He sent Darwin an article, and friends encouraged them both to publish their views. On 1 July 1858, members of the scientific Linnaean Society heard papers by both men.

Find out more
CORALS, ANEMONES
and jellyfish
EVOLUTION
FOSSILS
GEOLOGY

DEEP-SEA WILDLIFE

THE DEPTHS OF THE SEA form the largest wildlife habitat on Earth. In waters below about 1,000 m (3,000 ft) no plants can grow because there is no sunlight. Yet here, in the vast blackness, many extraordinary creatures live. These animals are found nowhere else. They have adapted to survive where the water pressure is up to 1,000 times that at the surface. Some deep-sea fish feed on the bodies and remains of plants and animals that sink down from the water above. Some other fish have enormous mouths and long, back-curved teeth for grabbing and swallowing anything that swims by. These fish have huge stomachs which stretch to hold prey that is even bigger than themselves. On the deep-sea floor, sea anemones, worms, sea cucumbers, brittlestars, crabs, prawns, and other shellfish sieve the mud searching for tiny particles of food. Many kinds of deep-sea squid, shrimps, and jellyfish are also found here.

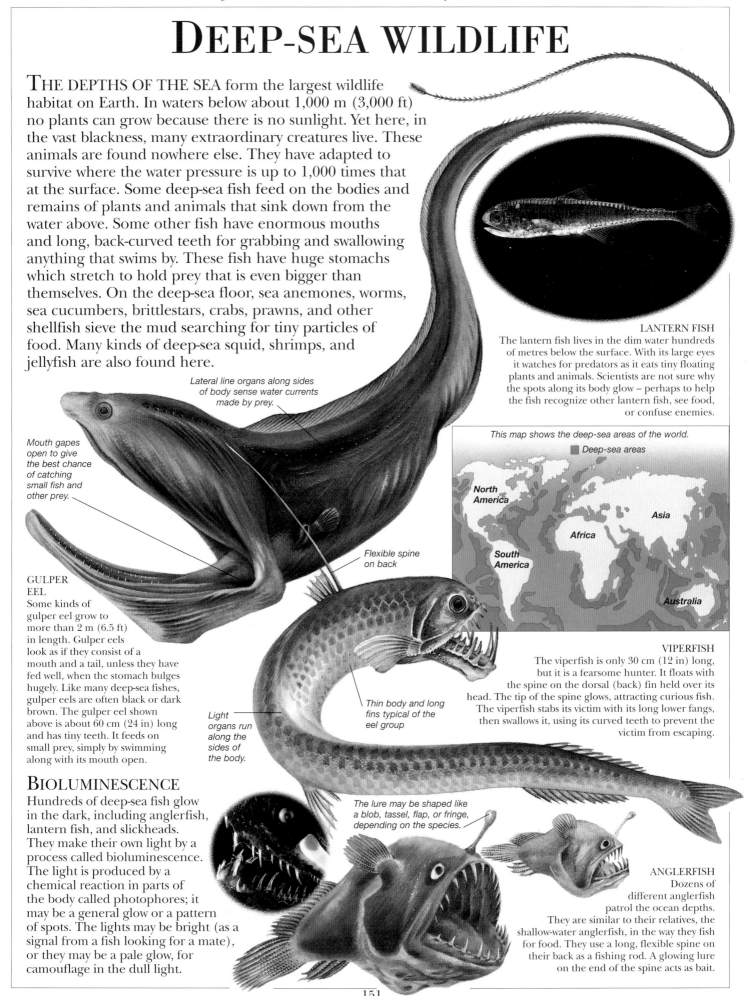

LANTERN FISH
The lantern fish lives in the dim water hundreds of metres below the surface. With its large eyes it watches for predators as it eats tiny floating plants and animals. Scientists are not sure why the spots along its body glow – perhaps to help the fish recognize other lantern fish, see food, or confuse enemies.

Lateral line organs along sides of body sense water currents made by prey.

Mouth gapes open to give the best chance of catching small fish and other prey.

This map shows the deep-sea areas of the world.
■ *Deep-sea areas*

North America
South America
Africa
Asia
Australia

Flexible spine on back

GULPER EEL
Some kinds of gulper eel grow to more than 2 m (6.5 ft) in length. Gulper eels look as if they consist of a mouth and a tail, unless they have fed well, when the stomach bulges hugely. Like many deep-sea fishes, gulper eels are often black or dark brown. The gulper eel shown above is about 60 cm (24 in) long and has tiny teeth. It feeds on small prey, simply by swimming along with its mouth open.

Light organs run along the sides of the body.

Thin body and long fins typical of the eel group

VIPERFISH
The viperfish is only 30 cm (12 in) long, but it is a fearsome hunter. It floats with the spine on the dorsal (back) fin held over its head. The tip of the spine glows, attracting curious fish. The viperfish stabs its victim with its long lower fangs, then swallows it, using its curved teeth to prevent the victim from escaping.

BIOLUMINESCENCE

Hundreds of deep-sea fish glow in the dark, including anglerfish, lantern fish, and slickheads. They make their own light by a process called bioluminescence. The light is produced by a chemical reaction in parts of the body called photophores; it may be a general glow or a pattern of spots. The lights may be bright (as a signal from a fish looking for a mate), or they may be a pale glow, for camouflage in the dull light.

The lure may be shaped like a blob, tassel, flap, or fringe, depending on the species.

ANGLERFISH
Dozens of different anglerfish patrol the ocean depths. They are similar to their relatives, the shallow-water anglerfish, in the way they fish for food. They use a long, flexible spine on their back as a fishing rod. A glowing lure on the end of the spine acts as bait.

CONSERVATION

Unlike other wildlife areas, such as the rain forests, the deep sea is not in great danger from habitat loss or pollution. However, harmful polluting chemicals have been found at great depths. Fishing boats have also overfished many shallow seas and are now fishing in deeper waters. Deep-sea fish such as these orange roughie fish (right) may soon be in danger because of overfishing.

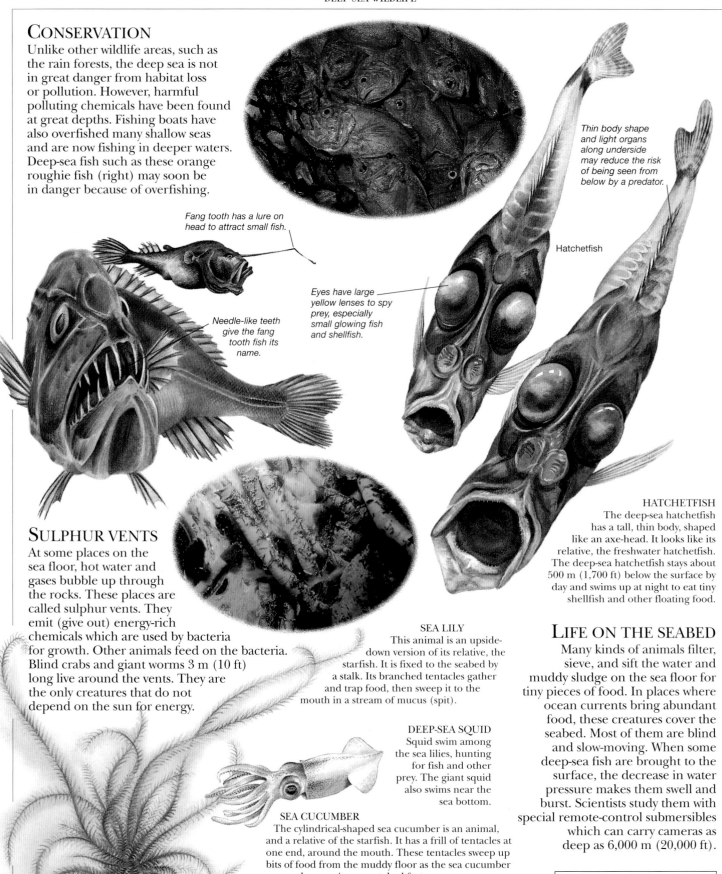

Fang tooth has a lure on head to attract small fish.

Needle-like teeth give the fang tooth fish its name.

Eyes have large yellow lenses to spy prey, especially small glowing fish and shellfish.

Thin body shape and light organs along underside may reduce the risk of being seen from below by a predator.

Hatchetfish

HATCHETFISH

The deep-sea hatchetfish has a tall, thin body, shaped like an axe-head. It looks like its relative, the freshwater hatchetfish. The deep-sea hatchetfish stays about 500 m (1,700 ft) below the surface by day and swims up at night to eat tiny shellfish and other floating food.

SULPHUR VENTS

At some places on the sea floor, hot water and gases bubble up through the rocks. These places are called sulphur vents. They emit (give out) energy-rich chemicals which are used by bacteria for growth. Other animals feed on the bacteria. Blind crabs and giant worms 3 m (10 ft) long live around the vents. They are the only creatures that do not depend on the sun for energy.

SEA LILY

This animal is an upside-down version of its relative, the starfish. It is fixed to the seabed by a stalk. Its branched tentacles gather and trap food, then sweep it to the mouth in a stream of mucus (spit).

DEEP-SEA SQUID

Squid swim among the sea lilies, hunting for fish and other prey. The giant squid also swims near the sea bottom.

SEA CUCUMBER

The cylindrical-shaped sea cucumber is an animal, and a relative of the starfish. It has a frill of tentacles at one end, around the mouth. These tentacles sweep up bits of food from the muddy floor as the sea cucumber moves along on its many tubed feet.

Sea cucumber

Sea lily

LIFE ON THE SEABED

Many kinds of animals filter, sieve, and sift the water and muddy sludge on the sea floor for tiny pieces of food. In places where ocean currents bring abundant food, these creatures cover the seabed. Most of them are blind and slow-moving. When some deep-sea fish are brought to the surface, the decrease in water pressure makes them swell and burst. Scientists study them with special remote-control submersibles which can carry cameras as deep as 6,000 m (20,000 ft).

Find out more

ANIMALS
ATMOSPHERE
FISH
OCEAN WILDLIFE
OCTOPUSES AND SQUID
SEASHORE WILDLIFE

DEMOCRACY

THE WORD DEMOCRACY COMES FROM the ancient Greek words *demos*, which means "people", and *kratia*, which means "power". Democracy means "rule by the people". Within a democracy, all adults have the right to play a part in the government of their country. In most democracies, all persons over the age of 18 can elect a member of parliament to represent them in the national government; and a councillor – their representative in local government. Occasionally they vote about an issue in a referendum. Twenty-five hundred years ago the people of Athens, Greece, practised a form of democracy. Men met in one place to decide on laws for their community. Today, most democracy is representative. Because there are usually too many people in a country to be involved in making every decision, the people elect representatives to make decisions on their behalf.

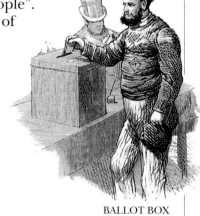

BALLOT BOX
When people vote in an election, they mark their votes on a piece of paper which they then drop into a ballot box. Their vote is secret, because no one can tell who marked each piece of paper. Today, electronic voting booths are replacing ballot boxes.

A French journal shows political parties campaigning for votes in the United States, 1908.

REPRESENTATIVE DEMOCRACY
Representative democracy means that citizens vote for certain people to represent them. People form political parties and citizens vote for their favoured party in elections. The different parties compete with each other for votes in election campaigns. Getting the right to vote (suffrage) has been a dedicated struggle for both men and women. Today, adult men and women in most countries can vote.

Indians queue to cast their vote at polling booths around the country.

MAJORITY RULE
Democracy means government by the people, but one group of people might want to do one thing and another group something completely different. In that case, the view of the majority (the larger group of people) rules. This could lead to the views of the minority being ignored, so many democratic countries and organizations have a constitution (a set of rules) that safeguards the rights of individuals and minorities. A few countries still do not have a democracy and are ruled by just one person, usually called a "dictator".

Pro-democracy demonstrators in former Czechoslovakia light candles at a vigil.

Minority vote

Majority vote

VOTING
India is the biggest representative democracy in the world: more than 600 million people are able to vote. In the general election of 2004, close to 400 million people went to the polling stations to vote for their representatives in the national parliament. When so many people vote, it can take several days for all the votes to be counted.

EASTERN EUROPE
From 1989, people in Communist Eastern Europe demanded democratic governments. They felt they did not have enough say in how their countries were run. In 1990, what was then Czechoslovakia became the first of many Eastern European Communist countries to declare themselves a real democracy.

Find out more
COMMUNISM
GOVERNMENTS AND POLITICS
GREECE, ANCIENT
LAW

DEPRESSION
OF THE 1930s

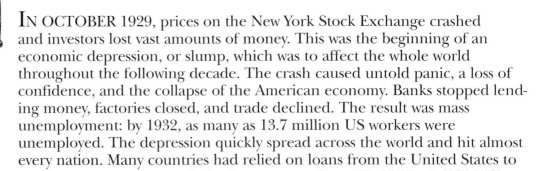

1929 :	1930 :	1931 :	1932 :
1 billion	800 million	600 million	400 million

IN OCTOBER 1929, prices on the New York Stock Exchange crashed and investors lost vast amounts of money. This was the beginning of an economic depression, or slump, which was to affect the whole world throughout the following decade. The crash caused untold panic, a loss of confidence, and the collapse of the American economy. Banks stopped lending money, factories closed, and trade declined. The result was mass unemployment: by 1932, as many as 13.7 million US workers were unemployed. The depression quickly spread across the world and hit almost every nation. Many countries had relied on loans from the United States to help them recover from World War I (1914-18). Now these loans stopped. Businesses collapsed, and millions of people were thrown out of work. Unemployment caused misery and poverty.

Disillusioned and frightened people turned to extreme right-wing political parties, such as the National Socialist German Workers' (Nazi) Party in Germany. The build-up to World War II ended the Depression, because increased production of arms created jobs.

DUST BOWL
During the 1930s, a terrible drought turned the soil of the American Midwest into dust. High winds blew clouds of dust over fields and farms, which hid the sunlight. The region became known as the Dust Bowl. Many ruined farmers were forced to trek across the country to find work in the orchards and farms of California, United States.

TENNESSEE VALLEY AUTHORITY
When Franklin D. Roosevelt became US President in 1933, he set up many programmes to improve the economy. The Tennessee Valley Authority was given money to employ people to build massive dams and hydroelectric power stations in southeastern United States.

Amount of sales on the New York Stock Exchange 1929-32.

WALL STREET CRASH
On 24 October 1929, known as "Black Thursday", the boom years that had followed World War I came to an end. To get richer, people had been investing a lot of money in the New York Stock Exchange. When it crashed, people wildly tried to sell their shares. In two months, share values had declined by one third. Many people lost all their savings, and thousands of companies collapsed.

JARROW MARCH
In Britain, mass unemployment led to "hunger marches". In 1936, some 200 out-of-work and hungry men marched 480 km (300 miles) from Jarrow, in the northeast of England, to the capital, London, in order to draw people's attention to their plight.

___ *Find out more* ___
MONEY
ROOSEVELT, FRANKLIN DELANO
WORLD WAR I
WORLD WAR II

DESERT WILDLIFE

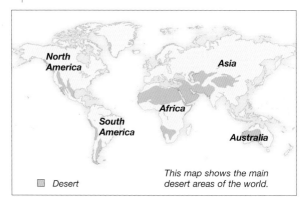

This map shows the main desert areas of the world.

☐ Desert

THE VAST, DRY EXPANSE OF A DESERT may look uninhabited, but all kinds of plants and animals survive in these sandy regions – including insects, reptiles, mammals, and fish. Deserts are the driest places on Earth; some have less than 10 cm (4 in) of rainfall each year. Desert animals have adapted to the lack of water in various ways. Camels, for example, can survive for a long time without drinking. Other animals find enough water in the plants and insects they eat, so they never have to drink at all. Plants such as baobab trees have deep-growing roots to search for water underground.

Other problems for desert wildlife are the extremes of temperature and the lack of shelter. Some deserts are scorching hot; others are freezing cold. Desert mammals have thick fur to keep out heat as well as cold. Many find shelter from the sun and icy winds by digging burrows. In hot deserts, animals stay in their burrows by day and hunt at night when the temperature is lower.

MONGOOSE
These adaptable mammals hunt by day for all kinds of small animals, including bees, spiders, scorpions, mice, and snakes. A mongoose has extremely quick reactions, so it can easily dodge an enemy such as a snake. The mongoose then leaps onto the snake and kills it with one bite.

TAWNY EAGLE
The tawny eagle survives well in desert conditions. Its incredible eyesight enables it to spot a rabbit or lizard thousands of metres away. When it sees prey, the tawny eagle dives at great speed and grabs the victim in its powerful talons.

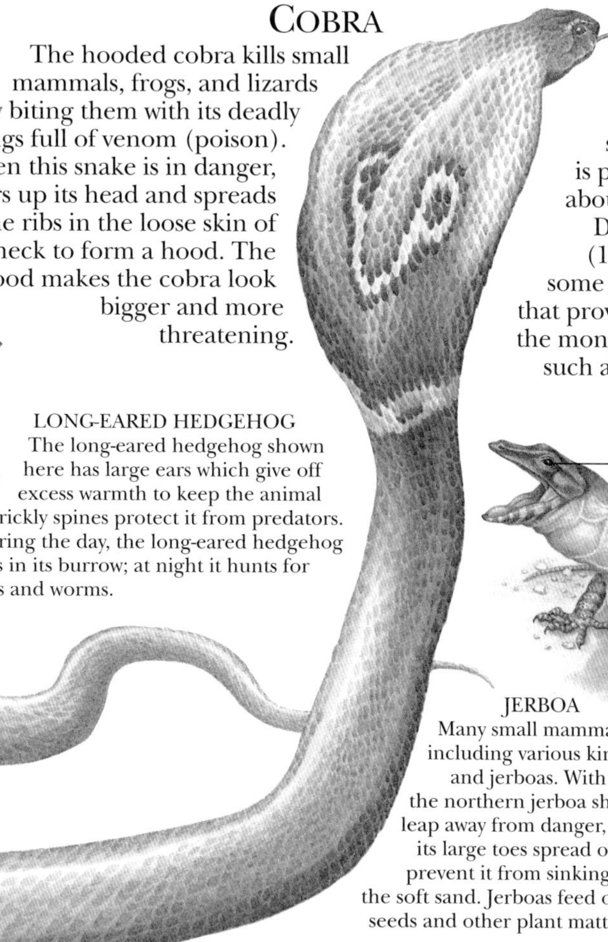

COBRA
The hooded cobra kills small mammals, frogs, and lizards by biting them with its deadly fangs full of venom (poison). When this snake is in danger, it rears up its head and spreads out the ribs in the loose skin of its neck to form a hood. The hood makes the cobra look bigger and more threatening.

COLD DESERTS
It is often bitterly cold at night and during the winter in deserts such as the Gobi Desert in Asia. This is partly because the Gobi is very high – about 1,000 m (3,500 ft) above sea level. Day temperatures rise as high as 50°C (122°F), then fall to -40°C (-40°F). For some creatures, a burrow is the only place that provides warmth. Some animals, such as the mongoose, dig their own burrow; others, such as snakes, take over an empty burrow or kill and eat the occupier.

LONG-EARED HEDGEHOG
The long-eared hedgehog shown here has large ears which give off excess warmth to keep the animal cool. Prickly spines protect it from predators. During the day, the long-eared hedgehog stays in its burrow; at night it hunts for insects and worms.

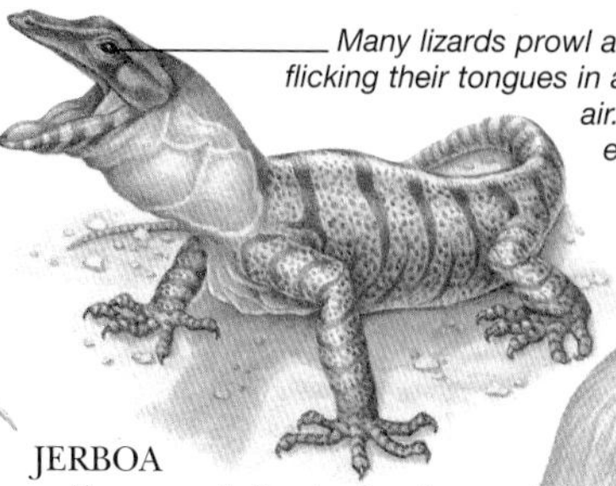

Long-eared hedgehog

Many lizards prowl across the dry sand, flicking their tongues in and out to taste the air. This monitor lizard eats eggs belonging to birds and other reptiles.

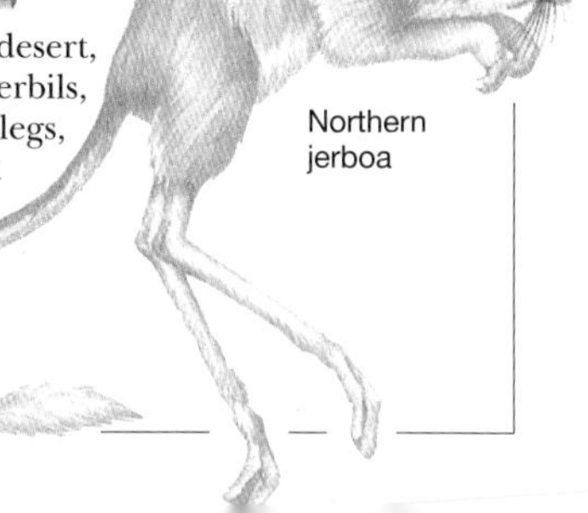

JERBOA
Many small mammals live in the desert, including various kinds of mice, gerbils, and jerboas. With its long back legs, the northern jerboa shown here can leap away from danger, keeping its large toes spread out to prevent it from sinking in the soft sand. Jerboas feed on seeds and other plant matter.

Northern jerboa

CONSERVATION

Desert wildlife is vulnerable due to habitat loss and over hunting. Irrigation has led to some desert areas being turned into farm land for growing cereals, fruit, and other crops, and this destroys the delicate balance between the natural plant life and the animals that live on them.

DORCAS GAZELLE

Dorcas gazelles are found across northern Africa, the Middle East, and India. They are an endangered species because they are being forced out of their natural habitat by farm animals and crops.

Dorcas gazelle

DATE PALM

The date palm tree has many different uses. The nourishing date fruit is food for people and animals, the stringy bark and wood are made into matting and ropes, and the leaves are fashioned into roofs and sunshades.

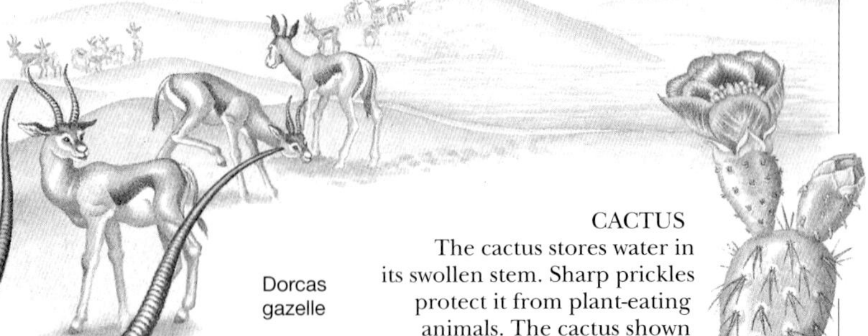

CACTUS

The cactus stores water in its swollen stem. Sharp prickles protect it from plant-eating animals. The cactus shown here is called the prickly pear cactus. The fruit is edible.

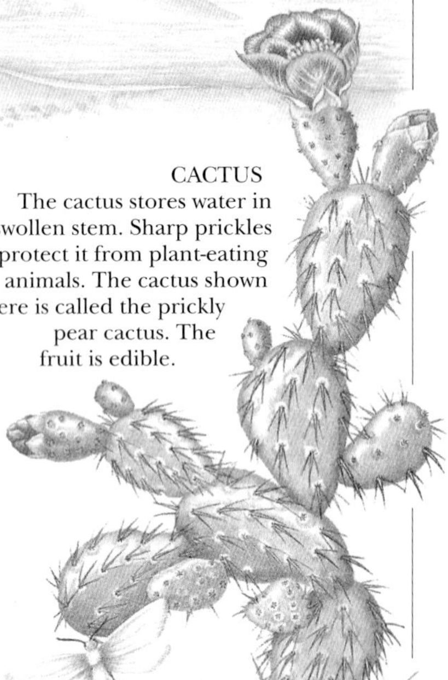

HOT DESERTS

The Sahara in Africa is the world's largest and hottest desert. At midday in the Sahara, the scorching sand is so hot that it can burn through skin in seconds. The temperature in the shade soars to more than 55°C (130°F). Few animals are active. Yet as the sun sets and the air and sand cool, many creatures emerge from under rocks and out of burrows. Dew falls at night, providing the plants and animals with much-needed moisture.

ROADRUNNER

The roadrunner can fly, but it usually races along the ground and runs into the undergrowth if it is disturbed. Roadrunners live in deserts and dry, open country in North America, feeding on all kinds of small animals, including grasshoppers and snakes, eggs, and certain fruits.

SIDEWINDER

A row of S-shaped marks in the sand at daybreak is a sign that a sidewinder snake passed during the night, probably on the trail of a mouse or a rat. This snake's wavelike way of moving means that only two small parts of its body touch the ground at any time, giving a better grip on the shifting sand.

ADDAX

This large grazing antelope from the Sahara never drinks – it obtains enough water from its food. Like other sandy desert dwellers, the addax's feet splay out widely to spread the animal's weight and keep it from sinking in the sand. The addax's horns have spiral ridges. The horns are used for defence and in contests for control of the herd.

NAKED MOLE RAT

This hairless rat is virtually blind and lives in underground tunnels in groups called colonies. The colonies are organized in a similar way to an ant's nest, with one queen who gives birth to all the young. Naked mole rats feed only on tubers which they find in the soil.

YUCCA MOTH AND YUCCA PLANT

The yucca is a desert lily. It has pale, scented flowers which attract the tiny female yucca moth. The moth climbs into the flower and gathers pollen, then flies to another yucca. Here the yucca moth lays its egg in the flower's ovary (egg-bearing part), and transfers pollen. As the yucca's fruit ripens, the moth caterpillar feeds on it. The yucca moth and the yucca flower could not exist without each other.

PINK FAIRY ARMADILLO

Measuring only 15 cm (6 in) long, the pink fairy armadillo lives in the deserts of South America. It leaves its tunnel at nightfall to dig up ants, worms, and other food.

Find out more

ANIMALS
ANIMAL SENSES
BUTTERFLIES AND MOTHS
CAMOUFLAGE, ANIMAL
INSECTS
REPTILES
SNAKES

CHARLES DICKENS

IN 1836, A YOUNG ENGLISH JOURNALIST published his first novel. The book was called *Pickwick Papers*, and its unknown writer, Charles Dickens, quickly became famous. Pickwick was followed by many other novels, and made Dickens one of the best-loved of English writers. His books appealed to children and adults alike. They dealt with all levels of society, and included scenes of both touching emotion and hilarious comedy. As a journalist, Dickens was also good at tackling the important social problems of the time. In all his books, he brought to life poverty, bad schools, injustice, crime, and the poor working conditions in England's factories. His sympathy for the deprived, together with his entertaining stories, mean that his books are still very popular today. Many are made into films and television series.

1812 Born in Portsmouth, England.

1824 Goes to work in blacking warehouse.

1836-37 *Pickwick Papers* appears, first in instalments, then as a complete book.

1837-38 *Oliver Twist.*

1838-39 *Nicholas Nickleby.*

1852-53 *Bleak House.*

1855-57 *Little Dorrit.*

1860-61 *Great Expectations.*

1867-68 Reading tour in United States.

1870 Dies.

BLACKING FACTORY
When Dickens was 12 years old, his father was put in prison for debt. Charles had to go to work for a company that sold blacking – black polish that people used on shoes and iron fireplaces. He never forgot the poor conditions in the blacking factory, and his memories helped to make his descriptions of poverty both realistic and moving.

GREAT EXPECTATIONS
One of Dickens's most popular books, *Great Expectations* tells the story of Pip, a young boy who grows up expecting to become rich. In the end he learns to accept poverty and his poor friends.

DICKENS THE WRITER
In the 19th century, novels often came out in instalments, and this was the way Dickens usually worked. He liked to end episodes on a cliff-hanger, or dramatic scene, which kept his readers interested. Dickens edited a series of weekly magazines, including *Household Words*, in which his books appeared. He also wrote articles about current issues.

OLIVER TWIST
This much-loved novel tells the story of the orphan Oliver, who is brought up in a workhouse. In its most famous scene, he angers the workhouse staff by asking for more food. The novel has been adapted for film and television, and was made into a musical.

Dickens enjoyed performing, and played all the characters in public readings of his works.

PUBLIC READINGS
Towards the end of his life, Dickens gave a series of public readings. He adapted his books specially for performing, and went on a series of reading tours, including one to the United States. The tours were hugely successful, but exhausted Dickens and made him ill.

Find out more
LITERATURE
VICTORIANS
WRITERS AND POETS

DIGESTION

HUMANS NEED FOOD TO SUPPLY ENERGY and to grow and repair itself. Food contains water and five vital nutrients – proteins, carbohydrates, fats, vitamins, and minerals. For food to be useful, the body has to break it down, or digest it, and to release simple, usable nutrients. The digestive system consists of a long tube called the alimentary canal which runs from the mouth to the anus. Each part does a particular job. The stomach is like a bag where chewed food is mixed with acids and digestive juices. The small intestine pushes the food along by a squeezing action called peristalsis. The tiny particles of digested food pass easily through the walls of the small intestine and into the bloodstream, to be used by the body. The large intestine digests and absorbs water from the food and turns the waste products into semi-solid lumps called faeces.

DIGESTION

Digestion begins in the mouth, as teeth crush the food. Watery saliva moistens the food and makes it easy to chew and swallow. The muscular walls of the stomach churn food into a soup-like liquid that is released in spurts into the small intestine. This is where most digestion takes place and where simple nutrients are absorbed through the lining of the small intestine into the bloodstream.

VILLI
Each fold of the lining of the small intestine has thousands of microscopic finger-shaped projections called villi. The villi allow the small intestine to absorb more nutrients.

Teeth chew, crunch, and grind food into a pulp.

Tongue tastes different flavours.

Salivary glands produce a watery liquid to mix with food and help with swallowing.

Oesophagus pushes swallowed food down through the chest, behind the windpipe and heart, into the stomach.

Liver

Stomach is where muscles crush food into a pulp and mix it with digestive juices.

Small intestine absorbs digested food into the body.

Large intestine absorbs water from undigested pieces of food.

Rectum is the last part of the large intestine.

STOMACH
This bag is lined with a thick layer of slimy mucus. Tiny glands in the lining produce strong digestive juices, which contain substances such as enzymes and acids.

EATING FOOD
When you swallow food, it enters your throat. A flap called the epiglottis folds over the entrance to the windpipe so that food goes into the oesophagus and not into the trachea, where it could cause choking.

LIVER
The liver is the body's "chemical factory". It receives digested nutrients, such as glucose (sugar), from the small intestine, and either stores them, converts them, or dispatches them to another part of the body.

SMALL INTESTINE
The small intestine is coiled into the lower part of the body. It is very long, measuring about 6 m (20 ft) in length. Its lining has many folds and ridges, so that it can absorb nutrients efficiently.

Pancreas produces digestive juices.

LARGE INTESTINE
The large intestine is much shorter than the small intestine, but three times as wide, measuring up to 7 cm (2.5 in) in width.

Anus is where waste products leave the body as faeces.

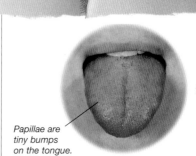

TONGUE
The surface of the muscular tongue is covered by tiny bumps called papillae. Some house taste buds that detect five basic tastes in foods: sweet, salty, sour, bitter, and umami (a savoury taste). Before tastes can be detected by taste buds, they have to dissolve in saliva.

Papillae are tiny bumps on the tongue.

ENZYMES
Digestive juices contain proteins called enzymes, which break down food into simple substances the body can absorb.

Find out more

HEALTH AND FITNESS
HUMAN BODY
LUNGS AND BREATHING
MUSCLES AND MOVEMENT

DINOSAURS

WE HAVE KNOWN ABOUT DINOSAURS for only 150 years or so, but these great creatures roamed the Earth for 160 million years – long before humans appeared. Scientists first learned about dinosaurs in the 1820s, when they discovered the fossilized bones of unknown creatures. Today, these fossils show us where dinosaurs lived, what they looked like, and what they ate. Dinosaurs were reptiles and lived on land. Their name means "terrible lizard", and like lizards, many of them had tough, scaly skin. There were hundreds of different kinds of dinosaurs, divided into two main groups. The Ornithischians (bird-hipped dinosaurs), such as *Protoceratops*, had hipbones similar to birds; the Saurischians (lizard-hipped dinosaurs), such as *Diplodocus*, had hipbones similar to lizards. Not all dinosaurs were giants – *Compsognathus* was the size of a chicken and *Heterodontosaurus* was the size of a large dog. Some dinosaurs, such as *Tyrannosaurus rex*, were carnivores (meat eaters); others, such as *Stegosaurus*, were herbivores (plant eaters). About 65 million years ago, dinosaurs and the swimming and flying reptiles that lived at the same time died out. The reason for this is still uncertain.

REPTILES
Dinosaurs were reptiles, like crocodiles, alligators, and the lizard shown above. Like other reptiles, dinosaurs had scaly skin, and laid eggs. Unlike lizards and other reptiles, dinosaurs had long legs, so they could move faster on land.

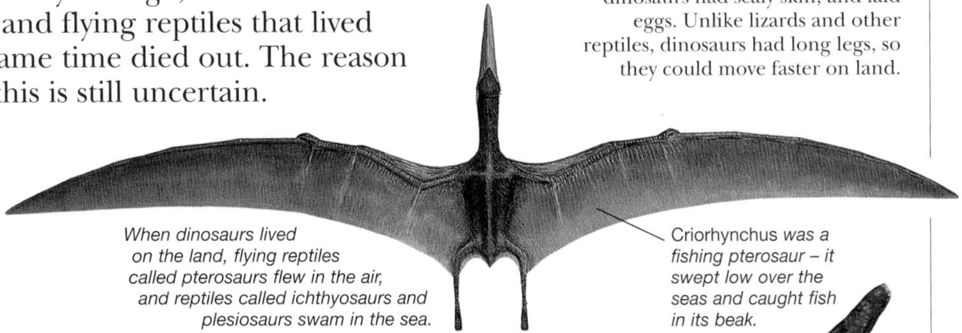

When dinosaurs lived on the land, flying reptiles called pterosaurs flew in the air, and reptiles called ichthyosaurs and plesiosaurs swam in the sea.

Criorhynchus was a fishing pterosaur – it swept low over the seas and caught fish in its beak.

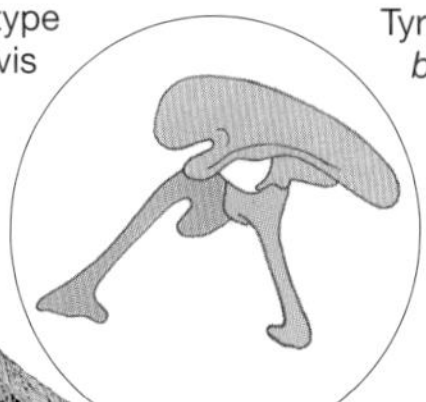

A lizard-type pelvis

Tyrannosaurus rex belonged to the group of lizard-hipped dinosaurs called Saurischians.

Tyrannosaurus had tiny hands which did not reach its mouth. We do not know what the hands were used for.

Carnivorous dinosaurs often had large, strong claws for grabbing their prey. The claw shown here belonged to Baryonyx, which is nicknamed "Claws".

TYRANNOSAURUS REX

The gigantic *Tyrannosaurus* was one of the largest carnivorous (meat-eating) dinosaurs. Scientists first discovered its fossils in North America. *Tyrannosaurus* measured 14 m (46 ft) in length and stood almost 6 m (20 ft) high. Its massive teeth were more than 15 cm (6 in) long. *Tyrannosaurus* weighed almost 7 tonnes (7 tons), so it was probably too heavy to run and hunt other dinosaurs. *Tyrannosaurus* fed on small creatures and dead dinosaurs.

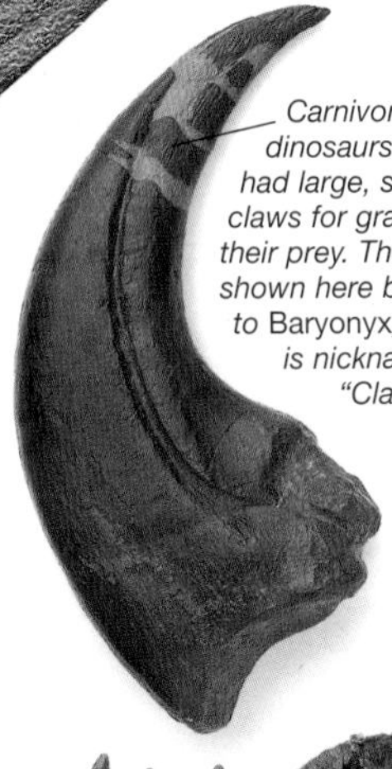

GORGOSAURUS
Carnivorous dinosaurs, such as the *Gorgosaurus*, had huge teeth and powerful jaw muscles for a strong bite. Not all dinosaur teeth were this large, however; some were as small as human teeth.

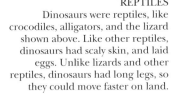

Jaw bone of a *Gorgosaurus*

DIPLODOCUS

The largest dinosaurs, including *Diplodocus*, belonged to the group of plant eaters called sauropods. At 27 m (88 ft) in length, *Diplodocus* was one of the longest dinosaurs. Its long, thin tail made up most of its length. With its slim body, it probably weighed only about 9 tonnes (9 tons).

Protoceratops was about 2 m (6 ft) long. It probably snipped at plants with its beak-like mouth.

Diplodocus was a herbivore; all its teeth were at the front of its mouth for nibbling at tough leaves.

PROTOCERATOPS

Scientists discovered fossils of *Protoceratops* in the Gobi Desert, Mongolia, in the 1920s. The bones of adults and young were found, together with fossilized eggs. About 80 million years ago, this area was a nesting site for many families of *Protoceratops*.

BREEDING

The fossils of *Protoceratops* show that the female scooped out a shallow hole in the sand and laid the eggs in a circular pattern. Scientists found many nests near each other, which shows that these dinosaurs bred in colonies, or groups, in the same way as some birds do today.

TYPES OF DINOSAURS

Dinosaurs varied greatly in size and shape, and they did not all live at the same time. Some lived 200 million years ago; others lived 70 million years ago. This chart gives the sizes of some dinosaurs in comparison to the size of a 10-year-old child.

m.y.a. = million years ago

Coelophysis
210 m.y.a.

Diplodocus
140 m.y.a.

Iguanodon
120 m.y.a.

Ornithosuchus
210 m.y.a.

Triceratops
65 m.y.a.

Protoceratops
80 m.y.a.

Comp-
sognathus
140 m.y.a.

Baryonyx
120 m.y.a.

Euplocephalus
75 m.y.a.

Tyrannosaurus
70 m.y.a.

Scientists have been able to reconstruct some dinosaur species, such as this Tuojiangosaurus.

THE END OF THE DINOSAURS

There are many ideas about the end of the dinosaurs. Some people believe they died out because a giant meteorite crashed into the Earth, throwing up a dust cloud and blotting out the sun. Without sunlight, the plants and the dinosaurs that fed on them could not survive.

BARYONYX

In 1983, the fossilized claw and bones of a dinosaur were found in Surrey, England. This dinosaur is named *Baryonyx*. Fossilized scales of fish were found in this dinosaur's stomach, so it was probably a fish eater and may have used its claws to catch fish.

IGUANODON

Iguanodon was a herbivore. As an adult it was about 10 m (33 ft) long, with small hooves on its hands and feet. Some scientists believe that *Iguanodon* lived in herds because, in some areas of Europe, they have found many fossilized skeletons of *Iguanodon* together in one place.

Iguanodon had versatile hands – the three middle fingers acted like hooves, the little finger could grasp food, and the spiked thumb was a fearsome weapon.

Iguanodon belonged to the bird-hipped group of dinosaurs called Ornithischians.

Heavy tail balanced the rest of Iguanodon's body.

A bird-type pelvis

Find out more

EVOLUTION
FOSSILS
PREHISTORIC LIFE
PREHISTORIC PEOPLES

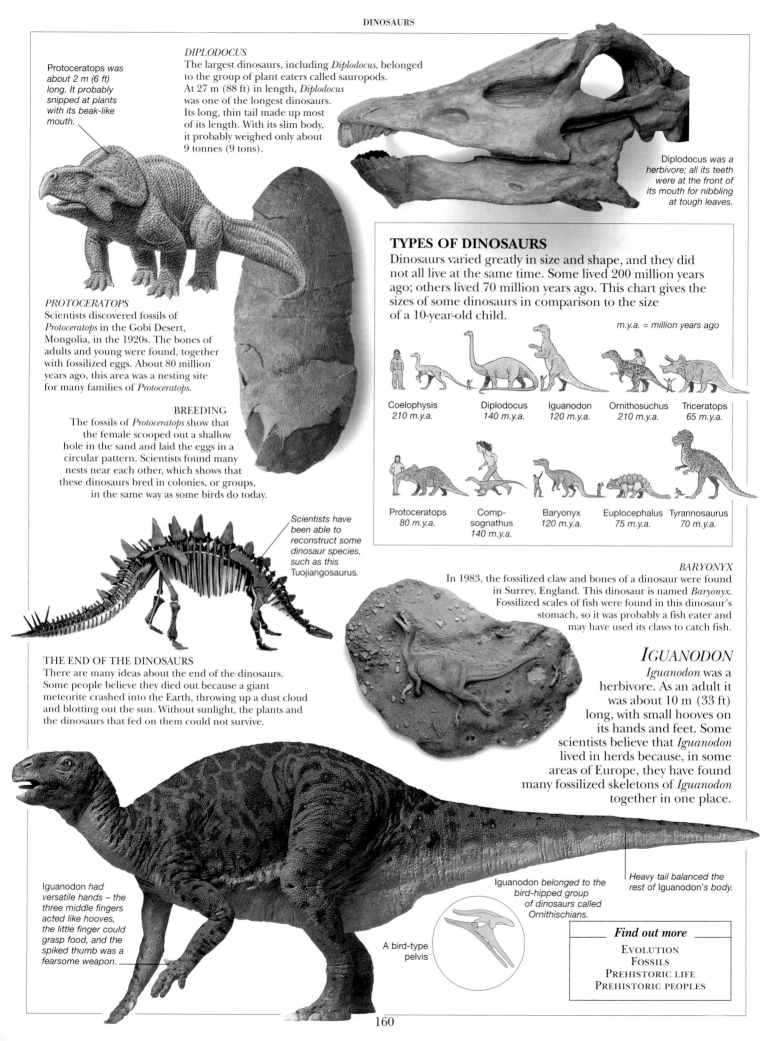

DISEASE

EVERYONE EXPERIENCES DISEASE at some point in their lifetime. Diseases happen when part, or parts, of the body stop working normally. They may be relatively harmless or quite serious. There are thousands of diseases that can strike almost any part of the body. They range from measles and the common cold to heart disease and emotional disorders, like depression. Some diseases are chronic (last for a long time), such as arthritis that makes the joints swell painfully. Other diseases, which are called acute, occur in short, sharp attacks and include flu (influenza). There are many different causes of disease. Harmful micro-organisms (microscopic living things) can invade the body and cause infectious diseases. Poor living conditions can also cause disease. Some diseases are present from birth; others may be passed from parent to child. The reasons for some diseases such as cancers are unclear. Scientists are constantly working to understand the causes of diseases and find possible cures.

ENVIRONMENTAL DISEASE

Living conditions affect people's health. Nuclear radiation in the atmosphere can cause cancer; pollution of the air from chemicals such as lead can affect health, particularly that of children; and swimming in water that is polluted with sewage can cause serious infections such as hepatitis, typhoid, and cholera.

Covering a sneeze can help prevent the flu virus from spreading.

There are several different types of bacteria (below). Each consists of a single living cell. Some bacteria cause disease in humans and animals, but most are harmless.

Causes boils

Causes typhoid

Causes sore throat

Viruses are smaller than a living cell. Viruses cause disease when they enter healthy cells in order to reproduce. The flu virus (above) is spread from person to person by coughing and sneezing.

BACTERIA AND VIRUSES

Infectious diseases are caused by micro-organisms, especially bacteria and viruses, that invade the body. They are the only diseases that can spread from person to person. Typhoid and cholera are examples of diseases caused by bacteria; chickenpox and measles are caused by viruses.

Heart disease is often caused by blockage of blood vessels in the heart. It has been linked to a rich, fatty diet and smoking.

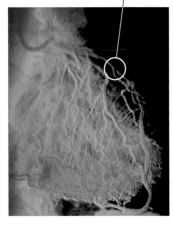

AIDS

Our body's defence system, the immune system, helps us fight disease. In the 1980s a new condition called AIDS (acquired immunodeficiency syndrome) started to spread. It is caused by HIV, a virus that stops the immune system working properly so that the body can no longer defend itself. It can result in death.

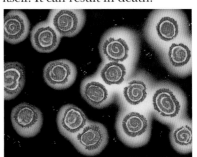

HIV viruses seen under the microscope.

HEREDITARY AND CONGENITAL DISEASES

Parents can pass on certain diseases, called hereditary diseases, to their children. Sickle cell anaemia is a hereditary blood disease. Hereditary diseases do not usually affect all the children in a family, and may appear late in life. Diseases present from birth such as spina bifida, a defect of the spinal cord and nervous system, are called congenital diseases.

Hereditary diseases are passed from parents to children in their genes.

NUTRITIONAL DISEASES

In parts of the world, particularly Africa and Asia, many people do not have enough to eat. Lack of food can cause many disorders, including anaemia, rickets, and scurvy. In places such as Europe and North America, many people eat too much. Overeating can also cause disorders, including obesity (fatness), diabetes, and heart disease.

EPIDEMICS

When a disease affects many people at the same time, it is called an epidemic. Epidemics of AIDS and of malaria, a disease carried by mosquitoes, affect many parts of Africa. AIDS epidemics are also affecting industrialized countries. In Western countries, too, so many people suffer from heart disease and cancer that these diseases are sometimes described as epidemic.

Find out more

DRUGS
GENETICS
HEALTH AND FITNESS
MEDICINE
MEDICINE, HISTORY OF
MICROSCOPIC LIFE
SCIENCE

DOGS
WOLVES, AND FOXES

WHEN A PET DOG BARKS at a stranger, or walks around in a circle before settling down to sleep, it is behaving in the same way that its wild wolf cousins did thousands of years ago. The dog family is made up of about 36 different species, one of which is the domestic dog. There are more than 300 breeds of domestic dog, from labradors to Yorkshire terriers. Others types of dog include the Asian dhole, the African wild dog, many kinds of foxes, and three species of jackals. These fast-running hunters are built for chasing prey; their elongated skulls are thought to be adaptations for seizing prey on the run. Many wild dogs, such as wolves and dingos, live in extended family groups called packs. Each pack has a leader, to whom all the other animals in the pack submit. A domestic dog sees its owner as a pack leader and is willing to obey that person's commands.

EARLY DOGS
The domestic dog is one of the 36 species of the dog family. As this early cave painting shows, it existed as long ago as the Stone Age.

Extremely sensitive nose for tracking animals and people

Reasonable eyesight in daylight; night vision weak.

GREY WOLF
This wolf is believed to be the ancestor of our domestic dogs. It is the largest member of the dog family, measuring at least 2 m (6 ft) in length, including its tail. Where food is readily available, wolves may form a pack consisting of up to 20 wolves. When food is difficult to find, a large pack of wolves splits up into smaller groups of about seven animals.

Good hearing, with ears that turn to locate the source of a sound

Dogs have four claws on each paw. The tough toe pads help them grip well when they run.

Long, strong legs for fast, sustained running

GERMAN SHEPHERD
This dog has a long muzzle and large ears, and still resembles its wolf ancestors. It is a strong, agile, extremely intelligent breed of dog – popular both as a working dog and as a pet.

Tail is used to give social signals, such as wagging when happy.

Fur coat keeps animal warm and dry.

Meat-eating teeth, with large, pointed canines for seizing and tearing at prey

DOMESTIC DOGS
Dogs have lived in harmony with humans for more than 10,000 years. It is quite possible that over thousands of years, humans have caught and tamed several members of the dog family, at first to help with hunting, herding, and guarding, and, much later, to keep as pets. Today, 210 breeds of domestic dogs are recognized in Britain, and more than 160 in the United States.

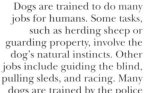

WORKING DOGS
Dogs are trained to do many jobs for humans. Some tasks, such as herding sheep or guarding property, involve the dog's natural instincts. Other jobs include guiding the blind, pulling sleds, and racing. Many dogs are trained by the police and the army to find people who are trapped or in hiding.

RED FOX

Few animals are as adaptable as the red fox, which lives in almost every country north of the equator. Red foxes eat almost anything, including insects and fish. The fox springs up and pounces on its prey like a cat. This creature's legendary cunning helps it survive in suburban gardens and city dumps. In towns and cities, it feeds on scraps from dustbins and rubbish heaps.

Crossbreeds are domestic dogs that are not pedigree – such as the three dogs shown here.

COYOTE

The North American coyote is closely related to wolves, jackals, and domestic dogs. Like most dogs, the female is pregnant for nine weeks before giving birth to about five puppies. The puppies feed on their mother's milk for up to seven weeks. After the first four weeks they also eat food regurgitated, or brought up, by their parents. Coyotes were thought to live alone, but we now know that some form small packs.

A female coyote usually has one litter of puppies each year.

PANTING
When a dog becomes hot, it cannot lose heat from its skin because it does not have sweat glands on its body. Instead, the dog opens its mouth and pants to give off heat from its mouth and tongue.

YORKSHIRE TERRIER
This small dog measures only 18 cm (7 in) in height. It is an agile runner, originally bred for catching rats.

MANED WOLF
The maned wolf is being bred in zoos and parks in an attempt to save it from extinction.

TOY DOGS
Dog breeders have created dogs of all sizes and shapes by mating dogs with unusual features, such as short legs or small ears. The smallest breeds, known as toy dogs, have become quite different from their distant ancestors, the wolves. A chihuahua, one of the smallest recognized breeds, can weigh less than 1 kg (2 lbs).

CRAB-EATING FOX
The crab-eating fox, also called the common zorro, is from South America. It eats many kinds of food, including crabs, as it forages along the coast. Other common zorros live far inland in woods and grassland and have never even see a crab.

CONSERVATION
The long-legged, maned wolf from South America is one of many members of the dog family that are officially listed as in danger of extinction. Many wolves and foxes, including the grey wolf, have been hunted not only for their beautiful fur, but also because they sometimes attack farm animals. One of the greatest threats to the dog family is the loss of the natural areas where they live, which are now used for farmland, houses, and factories.

PUPPIES
Young dogs, such as the labrador puppy shown here, spend much of their time in play – tumbling, jumping, and biting and shaking things. These games help the young dog develop hunting skills for adult life.

Find out more
ANIMALS
ANIMAL SENSES
CATS
CONSERVATION
and endangered species
FARM ANIMALS
MAMMALS
MOUNTAIN WILDLIFE

DRUGS

IF YOU ARE ILL, the doctor might give you a drug. Drugs, or medicines, are substances used in the treatment of illnesses. They can relieve the symptoms (effects) of a disease, ease pain, and prevent or cure illnesses. Drugs are also used to treat a wide range of emotional disorders such as depression. There are thousands of different kinds of drugs in use today. Each drug has a specific function and often acts on a single part of the body, such as the stomach. There are many sources of drugs. They may be natural or synthetic (artificial). Medicinal plants and herbs yield natural drugs which have been in use for thousands of years. Scientists search constantly for new drugs and often make them from chemicals. In many cases, the discovery of a drug has eased suffering and saved many lives. Antibiotics such as penicillin, for example, cure infections that would have been fatal 50 years ago.

Drugs can be dangerous. Today, many containers are made with specially designed tops that are difficult for children to remove.

Some drugs, such as antihistamines for treating allergies (sensitivity to certain substances), work more quickly if they are injected directly into the bloodstream through a needle and syringe.

The body can absorb creams and ointments through the skin. Medicinal creams are often used to treat skin disorders.

Some drugs, particularly those for small children, are dissolved in a sweet-tasting syrup. Special spoons that hold a fixed amount of liquid ensure that the patient receives the correct dose. Medicines can also be given by oral syringe.

ORAL MEDICINES
Many drugs are taken orally (by mouth). The drug passes through the digestive system and into the bloodstream, which carries the drug to the relevant part of the body.

Some powdered drugs dissolve in water, which helps them enter the bloodstream more rapidly than if they are taken as pills.

Tablets containing drugs are made with a smooth shape so that they are easy to swallow.

Tablets and capsules contain carefully measured amounts of drugs. When they are swallowed, the drugs slowly filter into the bloodstream via the digestive system. Some tablets have a coating which dissolves slowly, releasing the drug at a controlled rate.

TYPES OF DRUG

Different drugs have different uses. They range from antibiotics (for treating infections) to painkillers, such as aspirin. Anaesthetics are used to put patients to sleep before surgery. There are different ways of taking drugs. They can be swallowed, injected, put on the skin, used in a spray, or inhaled.

DRUG ADDICTION

Many drugs, including some of those recommended by doctors, are addictive. This means that the user becomes dependent on them. Drug addiction can lead to illness and death. The use of many dangerous drugs such as heroin, LSD, and cocaine is illegal. However, other addictive drugs, such as alcohol and nicotine (in cigarettes), are not controlled by law.

SOURCES OF DRUGS

In the past, all drugs used in treating illnesses came from natural sources, particularly herbs and plants. Today, most drugs are made from chemicals, and some are made by genetic engineering, a method in which the cells in bacteria or yeasts are altered to produce drugs.

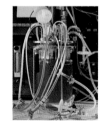
Some drugs, such as insulin (for treating diabetes), are made in human form using engineered bacteria.

The heart drug digitalis originally came from a flower called the foxglove.

Aspirin is made from chemicals like those found originally in willow tree bark.

The antibiotic penicillin first came from a mould called penicillium.

Find out more

CHEMISTRY
DISEASE
FLOWERS AND HERBS
HEALTH AND FITNESS
MEDICINE
MEDICINE, HISTORY OF

EARS

THE EARS ARE THE ORGANS of hearing and balance. They collect sound vibrations from the air and turn them into messages called nerve signals which are passed to the brain. Each ear has three main parts – the outer ear, the middle ear, and the inner ear. The outer ear includes the part you can see. It consists of the ear flap, or auricle, and the ear canal. The middle ear consists of the eardrum and three tiny bones called the ossicles. These three bones send sounds from the eardrum to the inner ear. The main part of the inner ear is the snail-shaped cochlea, which is full of fluid. The cochlea changes vibrations into nerve signals. The inner ear also makes sure that the body keeps its balance. Although we can hear many different sounds, we cannot hear as wide a range as most animals. Also, unlike rabbits and horses, we cannot swivel our ears towards the direction of a sound – we have to turn our heads.

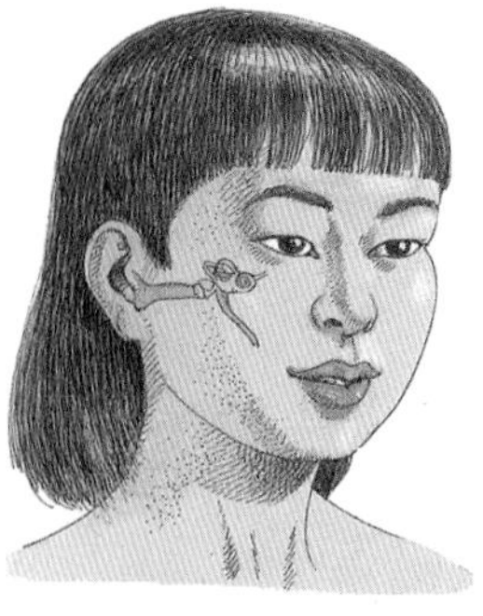

INSIDE THE EAR
The ear canal is slightly curved. It measures about 2.5 cm (1 in) in length. The delicate parts of the middle and inner ear lie well protected deep inside the skull bone, just behind and below the level of the eye.

Cochlea

Inner ear

Hair cells

Inside the cochlea

Semicircular canals

Fluid in cochlea

Bones of middle ear

Stapes (stirrup)

Malleus (hammer)

Inner ear

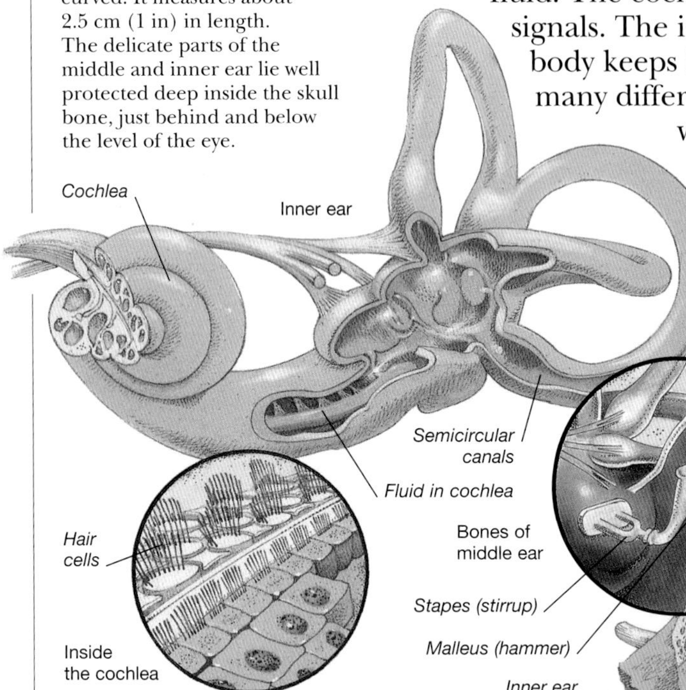

MIDDLE EAR BONES
The middle ear bones (ossicles) are called the malleus (hammer), incus (anvil), and the stapes (stirrup).

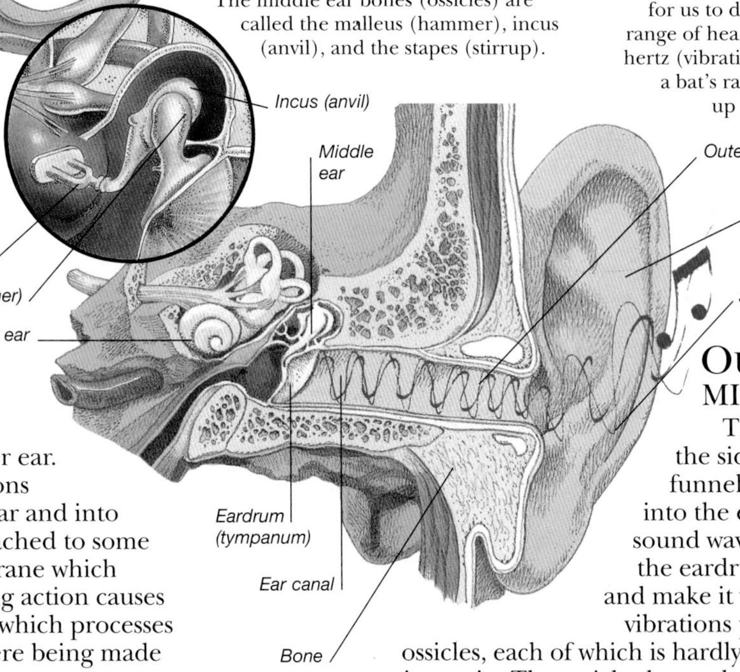

Incus (anvil)

Middle ear

Outer ear canal

Ear flap (auricle)

Soundwaves

Eardrum (tympanum)

Ear canal

Bone

INNER EAR

The stirrup bone presses like a piston on a thin, flexible membrane called the oval window that covers the entrance to the inner ear. Movements of the oval window send vibrations passing through the fluid inside the inner ear and into the cochlea. The vibrations bend 'hairs' attached to some of the 20,000 hair cells that rest on a membrane which runs the length of the cochlea. That bending action causes those hair cells to send signals to the brain, which processes the signals and identifies the sounds that were being made so that they can be heard.

OUTER AND MIDDLE EAR

The ear flap on the side of the head funnels sound waves into the ear canal. The sound waves bounce off the eardrum at the end and make it vibrate. These vibrations pass along the ossicles, each of which is hardly bigger than a rice grain. The ossicles have a lever-like action that makes the vibrations louder.

Ultrasonic sound is above the human range of hearing.

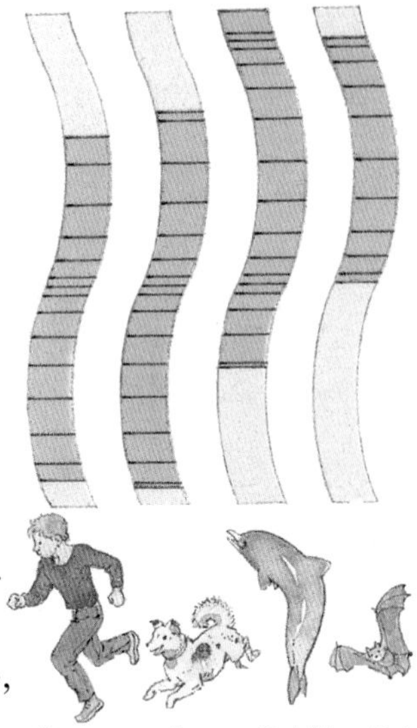

Human   Dog   Dolphin   Bat

RANGE OF HEARING
Humans can hear sounds that vary from a low growl to a piercing scream. Many animals, including dogs, can hear sounds which are far too high-pitched for us to detect. A human's range of hearing is 30–20,000 hertz (vibrations per second); a bat's range of hearing is up to 100,000 hertz.

ANIMAL HEARING
Creatures such as fish and squid have sense organs to detect vibrations in the water. Fish have a lateral line – a narrow groove along each side of the body. Hair cells in the lateral line senses the sound or movement of nearby animals. The catfish, shown here, has whiskers called barbels to smell and feel for prey in murky river bottoms.

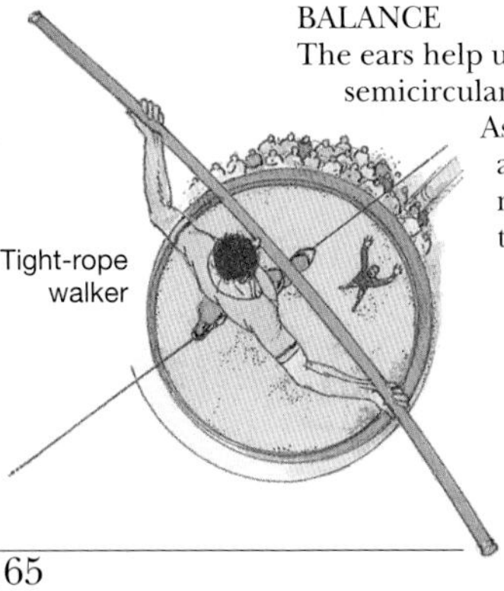

BALANCE
The ears help us keep our balance. The three semicircular canals inside the ear contain fluid. As you move your head, the fluid flows around. Tiny hair cells sense this movement and produce nerve signals to tell the brain which way "up" you are.

Tight-rope walker

Find out more
HUMAN BODY
SKELETONS
SOUND

EARTH

A LARGE BALL OF ROCK spinning through space is our home in the universe. This is the Earth, one of eight major planets that circle around the Sun. The Earth is the only place we know of that supports life. It has liquid water and a protective atmosphere, both of which are essential for life. And of all the planets in the solar system, the Earth is at just the right distance from the Sun to be neither too hot nor too cold. Land makes up less than a third of the surface of the Earth; more than two thirds is the water in the oceans. The Earth's interior consists of layers of rock that surround a core made of iron and nickel.

The processes that support life on Earth are in a natural balance. However, many people are worried that pollution, human over-population, and misuse of resources may destroy this balance and make the Earth unsafe for plants and animals.

EARTH IN SPACE
When astronauts first saw the Earth from space, they were enthralled by the beauty of our blue planet. This picture shows the Earth over the Moon's horizon.

ATMOSPHERE
A layer of air called the atmosphere surrounds the Earth. It is roughly 2,000 km (1,250 miles) deep and contains mainly the gases nitrogen and oxygen. The atmosphere shields the Earth from harmful ultraviolet rays coming from the Sun and prevents the Earth from becoming too hot or too cold.

Clouds containing tiny drops of water float low in the atmosphere, carrying water from the seas and land which falls as rain.

Atmosphere

OCEANS
The oceans are large water-filled hollows in the Earth's crust. Their average depth is 3.5 km (2.2 miles).

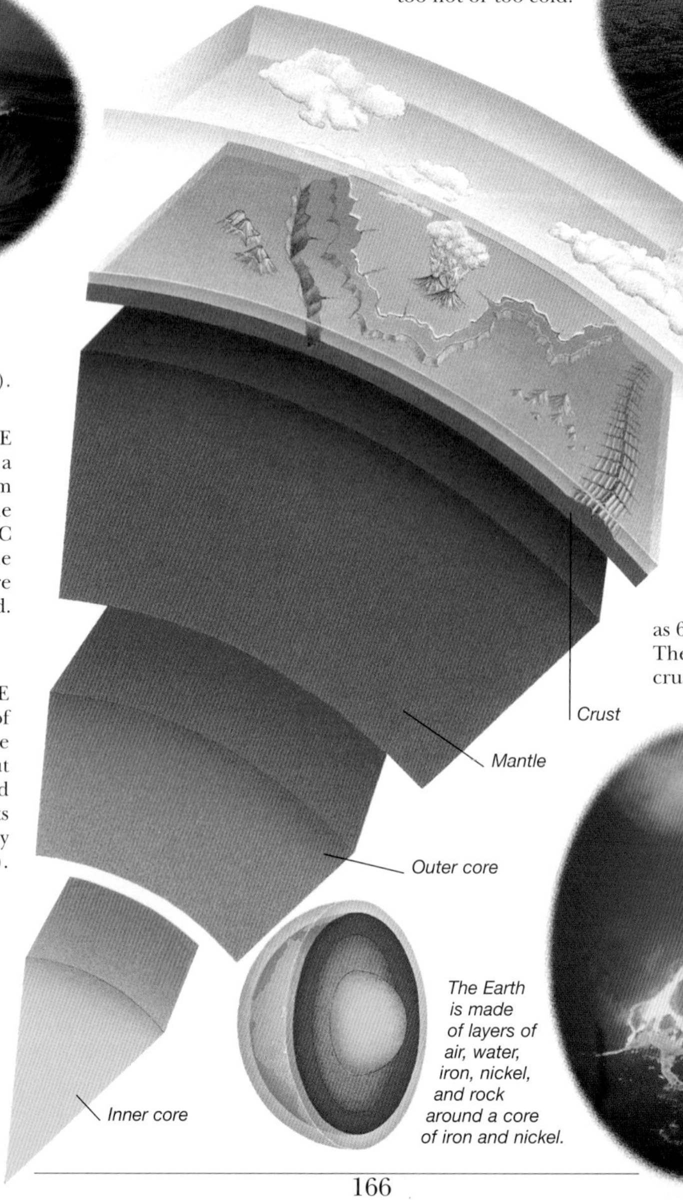

MANTLE
Under the crust is the mantle, a layer of rock about 2,900 km (1,800 miles) thick. The temperature rises to 3,700°C (6,700°F) at the base of the mantle, but high pressure there keeps the rock solid.

OUTER CORE
The core of the Earth consists of two layers – the outer core and the inner core. The outer core is about 2,000 km (1,240 miles) thick and is made of liquid iron. Its temperature is approximately 2,200°C (4,000°F).

INNER CORE
A ball of solid iron and nickel about 2,740 km (1,712 miles) across lies at the center of the Earth. The temperature at the centre is about 4,500°C (8,100°F).

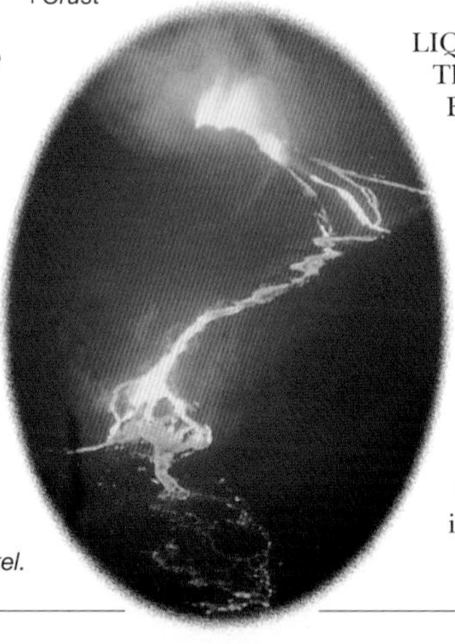

CRUST
The top layer of rock at the surface of the Earth is called the crust. It is up to 70 km (44 miles) deep beneath the continents, but as little as 6 km (4 miles) deep under the oceans. The temperature at the bottom of the crust is about 1,050°C (1,900°F).

Crust

Mantle

Outer core

Inner core

The Earth is made of layers of air, water, iron, nickel, and rock around a core of iron and nickel.

LIQUID ROCK
The interior of the Earth is very hot, heated by radioactive decay of the rocks inside the Earth. The temperature is so high that some rock inside the Earth is molten. This liquid rock rises to the surface at volcanoes, where it is called lava.

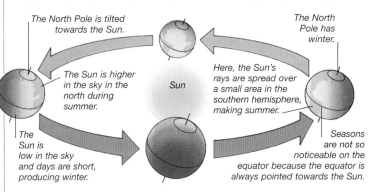

The North Pole is tilted towards the Sun.

The North Pole has winter.

The Sun is higher in the sky in the north during summer.

Sun

Here, the Sun's rays are spread over a small area in the southern hemisphere, making summer.

The Sun is low in the sky and days are short, producing winter.

Seasons are not so noticeable on the equator because the equator is always pointed towards the Sun.

SEASONS

Seasons change as the Earth moves around the Sun. The Earth's axis is not at right angles to its orbit but tilted over by 23.5°. This makes the Poles point toward or away from the Sun at different times of the year.

EARTH FACTS		
Diameter at equator	12,756 km	(7,926 miles)
Diameter at poles	12,714 km	(7,900 miles)
Circumference at equator	40,075 km	(24,901 miles)
Land area	29.2% of Earth's surface	
Ocean area	70.8% of Earth's surface	
Mass	6,000 billion billion tonnes	(5,900 billion billion tons)
Time for one spin	23 hours	56 minutes 4 seconds
Time to orbit Sun	365 days 6 hours	9 minutes 9 seconds
Distance from Sun	150 million km	(93 million miles)

The Earth spins around its axis, which passes through the North and South Poles. It also orbits the Sun at the same time.

1 A large clump inside a cloud of gas and dust contracted (shrank) to form the Sun about 4,4540 million years ago. A disk of gas and dust formed around the young Sun. Small particles stuck together and grew into chunks of rock and ice. Chunks came together to form planets.

2 The Earth may have taken about 100 million years to grow into a ball of rock. The new planet became hot as the rock particles crashed into one another. The surface was molten, and the young Earth glowed red-hot.

FORMATION OF THE EARTH

Scientists have calculated that the Earth is nearly 4,600 million years old. Some Moon rocks and meteorites (pieces of rock that fall to Earth from space) are the same age, which suggests that the whole solar system formed at the same time. The Sun, Earth, and the other planets were formed from a huge cloud of gas and dust in space.

3 Radioactivity in the rocks caused more heat, and the whole planet melted. Molten iron then sank to the centre of the Earth to form its core. Lighter rocks floated above the iron, and about 4,500 million years ago the surface cooled to form the crust. Volcanoes erupted and poured out gases, which formed the atmosphere, and water vapour, which condensed (changed into liquid) to fill the world's oceans.

GEOTHERMAL ENERGY

The heat from the interior of the Earth provides a source of safe, clean energy called geothermal energy. Hot rocks lie close to the surface in Iceland, Italy, and other parts of the world. The rocks heat underground water and often make it boil into steam. Wells dug down to these rocks bring up the steam and hot water, which are used to generate electricity and heat buildings.

Water that filled the oceans may have also come from comets that collided with the young Earth.

THEORIES OF THE EARTH

People once believed that the Earth was flat. About 2,500 years ago, the Greeks found out that the Earth is round. Aristarchus, a Greek scientist, suggested in about 260 BCE that the Earth moves around the Sun. It was not until 1543 that Polish astronomer Nicolaus Copernicus (1473-1543; right) reasserted this idea. New theories are still evolving. For instance, one idea called the Gaia theory suggests that the whole planet behaves as a living organism.

4 Tiny living things began to grow at least 3,500 million years ago. Some produced oxygen, which began to build up in the atmosphere about 2,300 million years ago. The continents broke up and slowly moved into their present-day positions. They are still moving slowly today, a process called continental drift.

Find out more
ATMOSPHERE
CLIMATES
CONTINENTS
GEOLOGY
OCEANS AND SEAS
RADIOACTIVITY
ROCKS AND MINERALS
UNIVERSE

EARTHQUAKES

INSTANT CHAOS
Destruction can be so swift and sudden that people have no time to escape. Falling masonry crushes cars and blocks roads.

ONCE EVERY 30 SECONDS, somewhere in the world, the Earth shakes slightly. These earth tremors are strong enough to be felt, but cause no damage. However, every few months a major earthquake occurs. The land shakes so violently that roads break up, forming huge cracks, and buildings and bridges collapse, causing many deaths. Earthquakes are caused by the movements of huge plates of rock in the Earth's crust. They occur in places that lie on the boundaries where these plates meet, such as the San Andreas fault which runs 435 km (270 miles) through central California. In some cases, scientists can tell in advance that an earthquake is likely to occur. In 1974, for example, scientists predicted an earthquake in China, saving thousands of lives. But earthquake prediction is not always accurate. In 1989, a major earthquake struck San Francisco, United States, without warning, killing 67 people.

The rocks suddenly slip along the fault; a movement of a few metres is enough to cause a severe earthquake.

FAULT
A deep crack, or fault, marks the boundary of two plates.

The place within the Earth where an earthquake occurs is the focus.

The earthquake is usually strongest at the epicentre, the point on the Earth's surface directly above the focus.

CAUSES OF EARTHQUAKES

The Earth's crust consists of several vast plates of solid rock. These plates move very slowly and sometimes slide past each other. Most severe earthquakes occur where the plates meet. Sometimes the edges of the plates grip each other and cannot move, so pressure builds up. Suddenly the plates slip and lurch past each other, making the land shake violently.

Rocks grip along the fault.

RICHTER SCALE
The severity of an earthquake is measured on the Richter scale, which runs from 0 to 9. An earthquake reaching 8 on the scale can flatten a city. The Richter scale measures the movement of the ground, rather than the damage an earthquake causes, which varies from place to place.

An earthquake in the Indian Ocean on December 26, 2004, caused tsunamis that devastated the coasts of parts of South East Asia, India, and Africa. It was one of the worst natural disasters of recent times.

TSUNAMIS
Earthquakes that occur on the sea floor often produce a wave called a tsunami, which races towards the shore. The wave is not very high mid-ocean, but it begins to rise as it nears the coast, sometimes growing to about 75 m (250 ft) high. The tsunami smashes onto the shore, destroying buildings and carrying boats far inland. Tsunamis, which are often wrongly called tidal waves, are also caused by volcanic eruptions.

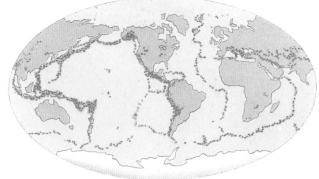

EARTHQUAKE BELTS
Earthquakes occur only in certain parts of the world. This map shows the world's earthquake belts, which also extend through the oceans. Most severe earthquakes happen near boundaries between plates in the Earth's crust, so the belts follow the edges of the plates.

SEISMOLOGY
Sensitive equipment can pick up vibrations far from an earthquake. This is because the sudden slip of rocks produces shock waves which move through the Earth. The study of earthquakes and the shock waves they cause is called seismology.

Find out more
CONTINENTS
EARTH
GEOLOGY
VOLCANOES

EAST AFRICA

EAST AFRICA IS A REGION of physical contrasts, ranging from the semi-desert of the north to the fertile highlands of Ethiopia and Kenya, and from the coastal lowlands to the forest-covered mountains of the west. Most people live off the land. Coffee, tea, and tobacco are grown as cash crops, while nomadic groups herd cattle in the savannah grassland which dominates much of the region. Four of the world's poorest countries – Ethiopia, Eritrea, Somalia, and Djibouti – lie along the Horn of Africa. Their traditional livelihoods of farming, herding, and fishing have been disrupted by drought, famine, and civil war between ethnic groups. Kenya, with its fertile land and warm, moist climate is by contrast, comparatively stable, its income boosted by wildlife tourists. Ethnic conflict has brought chaos to Sudan, Rwanda, and Burundi, while Uganda is slowly recovering from civil war.

East Africa straddles the Horn of Africa, and is bordered by both the Red Sea and the Indian Ocean. It is dominated by the Great Rift Valley and, in the north, the upper reaches of the River Nile. Desert in the north gives way to savannah grasslands in much of the region.

DINKA

The Dinka (above) are a nomadic people who live in the highlands of Sudan. They move their herds of cattle around according to the seasons, taking them to graze the savannah grasslands in spring, when the rivers flood and the land is fertile. Cattle are of supreme importance to the Dinka. They form part of a bride's wealth, and are offered as compensation, or payment, for marriage. Young men are presented with a special ox, and their adult name is inspired by the shape and colour of the animal.

TEA CULTIVATION
The highlands of Ethiopia and Kenya are major tea-producing areas. The flavour of tea grown slowly in cool air at altitudes of 1,000-2,000 m (3,000-7,000 ft) is considered the finest. The leaves are dried, rolled, and blown with hot air, which ferments them, producing a rich black colour and strong flavour.

Tea bushes are regularly clipped to stimulate the growth of tender young shoots and new leaves. They are harvested by hand.

MOGADISHU
The capital of Somalia was one of the earliest Arab trading settlements in eastern Africa, dating to the 10th century. The city is dominated by a major port, and is a mixture of historic Islamic buildings and modern architecture. Civil war in the 1980s and 1990s has, however, destroyed much of the city.

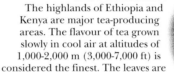

The various styles of architecture in Mogadishu (right) reflect the city's history.

LALIBELA
The kings of Ethiopia converted to Christianity in the 4th century, but it was not until the 12th century that Christianity held sway over most of the population. King Lalibela built 11 remarkable churches, which were carved out of rock below ground level. They are still major pilgrimage centres for Ethiopian Christians today.

KAMPALA

Since 1962, Kampala has been the capital of independent Uganda. It is located in the southern part of the country, on the hills overlooking Lake Victoria. It is an export centre for coffee, cotton, tea, sugar, and tobacco. Locally produced foods, such as cassava, millet, and sweet potatoes, are sold at lively street markets. Kampala has rainfall on nearly every day of the year, and violent thunderstorms 242 days a year.

THE GREAT RIFT VALLEY

Stretching from Syria in Asia to Mozambique, the Rift Valley is a huge gash in the Earth's surface, formed where Africa and the Arabian peninsula are gradually moving apart. The Great Rift Valley, which began to form some 30 million years ago, is 6,400 km (4,000 miles) long, and up to 64 km (40 miles) wide. In Kenya and Tanzania, the valley is marked by deep fjord-like lakes. Elsewhere, volcanic peaks have erupted and wide plateaux, such as the Athi Plains in Kenya, have formed where lava has seeped through the Earth's surface.

MASAI

The Masai people herd cattle in the grasslands of Kenya and Tanzania. The young men paint their bodies with ochre and have elaborate plaited hairstyles. Masai warriors wear beaded jewellery. Each man may take several wives, and is responsible for his own herd of cattle, which are driven to pasture far from the village during the dry season. Mothers pass on cattle to their sons. The staple diet of the Masai is cow's milk, supplemented by maize.

The Masai keep their cattle for milk. They also drink blood drawn from the veins of living cows.

Tooled leather sandals from Uganda

Diseases such as cholera thrive in crowded refugee camps like the one pictured here.

A herd of elephants wander the savannah in Kenya in search of water. A number of lions monitor the elephants waiting to kill any weak animal.

WILDLIFE

The Great Plains of East Africa contain some of the world's most spectacular wildlife. In Kenya, ten per cent of all the land has been absorbed into more than 40 national parks. Tourists go on wildlife safaris to Kenya (below) to see herds of lions, antelopes, leopards, and elephants. Poaching animals, especially elephants for ivory, remains a major problem, and national parks are closely guarded by game wardens.

GORILLAS

The forested mountains of Rwanda and Uganda are the last remaining refuge for gorillas, the world's rarest ape. Gorillas have long been targeted by poachers, hunters and collectors. The Albert National Park was established in 1925 for their protection, but civil war in the 1960s disrupted the gorilla population, while much of their forest habitat was cleared for agriculture, further reducing numbers.

Since the 1980s, national parks have been carefully guarded, and limited educational and tourist programmes put in place. Gorilla numbers in Rwanda have risen, but recent conflict now threatens their survival.

REFUGEE CAMP

Many of the boundaries in central east Africa date back to colonial times and cut across ethnic borders. In Rwanda, the majority Hutus rebelled against the ruling Tutsis with terrible consequences. The country descended into violent chaos, and many people were forced to flee to refugee camps in Tanzania. There has also been conflict between Hutus and Tutsis in neighbouring Burundi.

Find out more

AFRICA
ELEPHANTS
GRASSLAND WILDLIFE
LIONS, TIGERS,
and other big cats

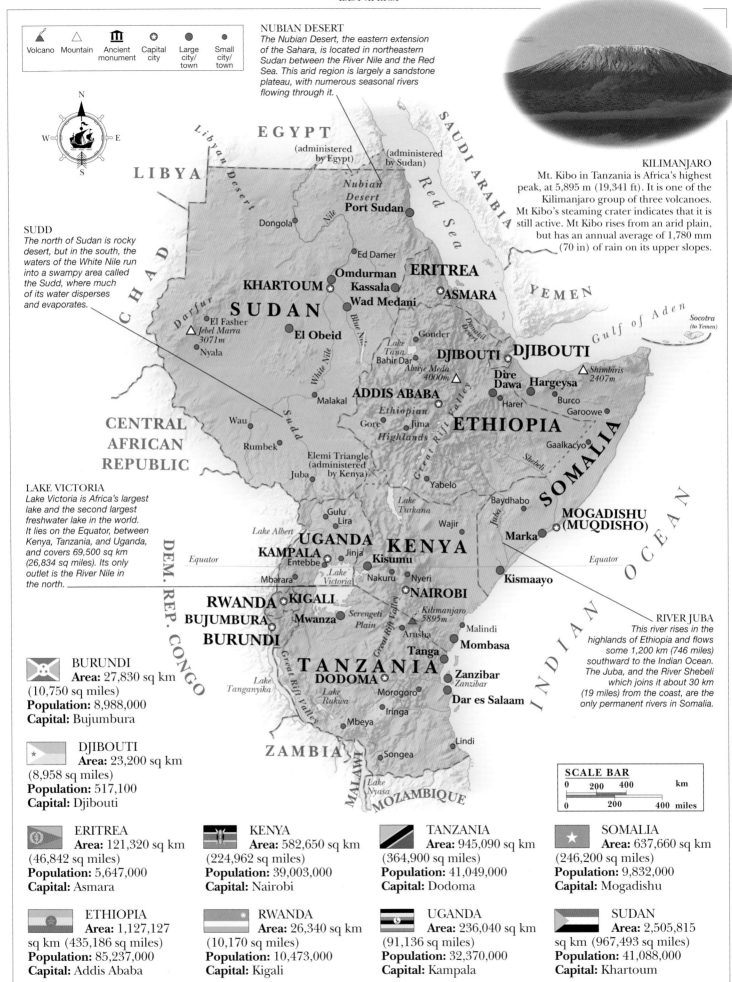

Volcano | **Mountain** | **Ancient monument** | **Capital city** | **Large city/town** | **Small city/town**

NUBIAN DESERT
The Nubian Desert, the eastern extension of the Sahara, is located in northeastern Sudan between the River Nile and the Red Sea. This arid region is largely a sandstone plateau, with numerous seasonal rivers flowing through it.

KILIMANJARO
Mt. Kibo in Tanzania is Africa's highest peak, at 5,895 m (19,341 ft). It is one of the Kilimanjaro group of three volcanoes. Mt Kibo's steaming crater indicates that it is still active. Mt Kibo rises from an arid plain, but has an annual average of 1,780 mm (70 in) of rain on its upper slopes.

SUDD
The north of Sudan is rocky desert, but in the south, the waters of the White Nile run into a swampy area called the Sudd, where much of its water disperses and evaporates.

LAKE VICTORIA
Lake Victoria is Africa's largest lake and the second largest freshwater lake in the world. It lies on the Equator, between Kenya, Tanzania, and Uganda, and covers 69,500 sq km (26,834 sq miles). Its only outlet is the River Nile in the north.

RIVER JUBA
This river rises in the highlands of Ethiopia and flows some 1,200 km (746 miles) southward to the Indian Ocean. The Juba, and the River Shebeli which joins it about 30 km (19 miles) from the coast, are the only permanent rivers in Somalia.

BURUNDI
Area: 27,830 sq km (10,750 sq miles)
Population: 8,988,000
Capital: Bujumbura

DJIBOUTI
Area: 23,200 sq km (8,958 sq miles)
Population: 517,100
Capital: Djibouti

ERITREA
Area: 121,320 sq km (46,842 sq miles)
Population: 5,647,000
Capital: Asmara

ETHIOPIA
Area: 1,127,127 sq km (435,186 sq miles)
Population: 85,237,000
Capital: Addis Ababa

KENYA
Area: 582,650 sq km (224,962 sq miles)
Population: 39,003,000
Capital: Nairobi

RWANDA
Area: 26,340 sq km (10,170 sq miles)
Population: 10,473,000
Capital: Kigali

TANZANIA
Area: 945,090 sq km (364,900 sq miles)
Population: 41,049,000
Capital: Dodoma

UGANDA
Area: 236,040 sq km (91,136 sq miles)
Population: 32,370,000
Capital: Kampala

SOMALIA
Area: 637,660 sq km (246,200 sq miles)
Population: 9,832,000
Capital: Mogadishu

SUDAN
Area: 2,505,815 sq km (967,493 sq miles)
Population: 41,088,000
Capital: Khartoum

SCALE BAR
0 200 400 km
0 200 400 miles

ECOLOGY AND FOOD WEBS

WE CAN LOOK AT NATURE in the same way that we look at a complicated machine, to see how all the parts fit together. Every living thing has its place in nature, and ecology is the study of how things live in relation to their surroundings. It is a relatively new science and is of great importance today. It helps us understand how plants and animals depend on each other and their surroundings in order to survive. Ecology also helps us work towards saving animals and plants from extinction and solving the problems caused by pollution. Plants and animals can be divided into different groups, depending on their ecological function. Plants capture the Sun's light energy and use it to produce new growth, so they are called producers; animals consume (eat) plants and other animals, so they are called consumers. All the plants and animals that live in one area and feed off each other make up a community. The relationships between the plants and animals in a community is called a food web; energy passes through the community via these food webs.

ECOSYSTEM

A community and its surroundings, including the soil, air, climate, and the other communities around it, make up an ecosystem. The Earth can be seen as one giant ecosystem spinning through space. It recycles its raw materials, such as leaves and other plant matter, and is powered by energy from the Sun.

The European kingfisher has little to fear. Its brightly coloured plumage warns predators that it is foul-tasting. The kingfisher is well named – it is extremely skilful at fishing.

FOOD CHAINS AND FOOD WEBS

A plant uses the Sun's energy to grow. A herbivore (plant eater) eats the plant. A carnivore (meat eater) or an omnivore (plant and meat eater) then eats the herbivore. This series of events is called a food chain.

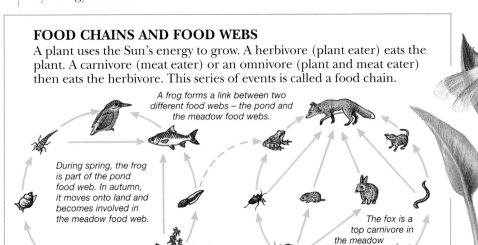

A frog forms a link between two different food webs – the pond and the meadow food webs.

During spring, the frog is part of the pond food web. In autumn, it moves onto land and becomes involved in the meadow food web.

Pond food web

Meadow food web

The fox is a top carnivore in the meadow food chain.

CARNIVORE
The adult frog is carnivorous; it catches flies and other small creatures.

OMNIVORE
Many small fish are omnivores, feeding on whatever they can find – from water weeds to tiny animals such as tadpoles.

Plants form the beginning of the food chain in a pond, as they do on land.

DETRITIVORE
Certain types of worms and snails are called detritivores because they eat detritus, or rotting matter, at the bottom of a pond or river. They help recycle the materials and energy in dead and dying plants and animals.

HERBIVORE
As a young tadpole, the frog is a herbivore, eating water weeds.

KINGFISHER
Some carnivores are called top carnivores because they have almost no predators. Their usual fate is to die of sickness, injury, or old age, at which time they become food for scavengers. The European kingfisher shown here eats a wide variety of food, including small fish such as minnows and sticklebacks, water snails and beetles, dragonfly larvae, tadpoles, and small frogs. The kingfisher is therefore at the top of a complex food web.

HABITAT

A habitat is a place where a certain animal or plant usually lives. There are several characteristic habitats, such as oak forests, mangrove swamps, and chalk cliffs. A habitat often has one or a few main plants, such as the pampas grass which grows in the grassland habitats of South America. Certain characteristic animals feed on these plants. Some animals live in only one or two habitats; the desman, for example, is a type of muskrat found only in fast-running mountain streams. Other animals, such as red foxes and brown rats, are able to survive in many different habitats. The coral reef shown here is one of the Earth's richest habitats in terms of species, but the water is poor in nutrients.

BIOME

A biome is a huge habitat, such as a tropical rain forest or a desert. The deserts of Africa, central Asia, and North America each have distinct kinds of plants and animals, but their ecology is similar. Each of these large habitats, or biomes, has a big cat as a top predator – the caracal (a kind of lynx) in Africa, the puma in North America, and Pallas's cat in central Asia. The major types of plants that grow in a biome are determined by its climate. Areas near the equator with very high rainfall become tropical rain forests, and in cold regions near the Arctic and Antarctic, only tundra plants can survive.

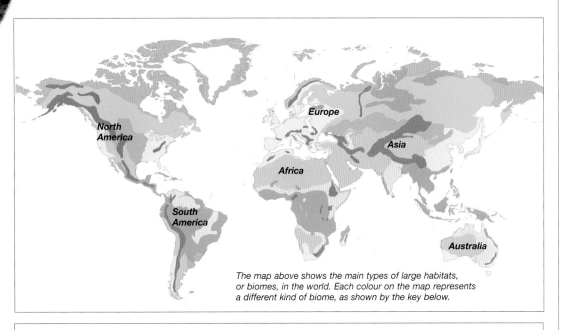

The map above shows the main types of large habitats, or biomes, in the world. Each colour on the map represents a different kind of biome, as shown by the key below.

○ Desert   ○ Wetland   ○ Savannah   ● Tropical rain forest   ○ Temperate grassland

○ Temperate forest   ○ Coniferous forest   ○ Tundra   ● Mountains

PESTICIDES

Farmers and gardeners use pesticides to kill insects that are pests on vegetable and cereal crops. In 1972, the insecticide called DDT was banned in the United States because it caused great damage to wildlife. When DDT is sprayed on crops, some of it is eaten by herbivores such as mice and squirrels. The insecticide builds up inside the animal's body. A bird of prey such as a hawk eats the animal, and the DDT becomes concentrated (builds up) in the bird's body. The DDT causes the bird to make very thin or deformed eggshells, which break and kill the developing chicks inside. Since DDT was banned, the number of falcons has slowly risen.

Today, falcons and other birds of prey are rare. Many have died as a result of the pesticides used by farmers to kill insects on farm crops.

Find out more

ANIMALS
BIRDS
CONSERVATION
and endangered species
DESERT WILDLIFE
LAKE AND RIVER WILDLIFE
PLANTS
POLLUTION

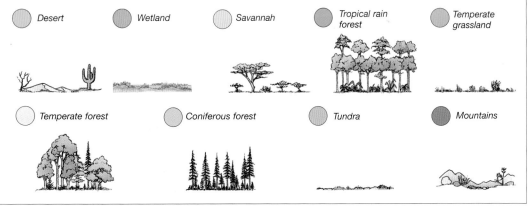

ANCIENT EGYPT

THE RICH, FERTILE SOIL of the Nile Valley gave birth to Egypt, a civilization that began over 5,000 years ago and lasted more than 3,000 years. The River Nile made the black soil around it productive, and the civilization of Egypt grew wealthy. For much of its history Egypt was stable. Its pharaohs ruled with the help of officials called viziers who collected taxes and acted as judges. The Egyptians worshipped many gods and believed that when they died they went to the next world. Pharaohs built elaborate tombs for themselves; the best known are the magnificent pyramids. The Egyptians also made great advances in medicine. Gradually, however, the civilization broke down, leaving it open to foreign invasion. In 30 BCE the Romans finally conquered the empire.

PHARAOHS

The rulers of Ancient Egypt were called pharaohs, meaning "Great House". They were thought to be divine and had absolute power: all the land in Egypt belonged to them. People believed the pharaohs were the sons of Ra, the Sun god. Above is a famous pharaoh, Tutankhamun, who died when he was only 18.

The internal layout of the Great Pyramid

Grand Gallery

King's Chamber

Entrance

Escape shaft

Queen's Chamber

PYRAMIDS

The Egyptians believed in an eternal life after death in a "perfect" version of Egypt. After their bodies had been preserved by embalming, pharaohs were buried in pyramid tombs. The earliest pyramids had steps. People believed the dead king's spirit climbed the steps to join the Sun god at the top. Later, the pyramids were built with smooth slanted sides. However, people could rob the pyramid tombs easily, so later pharaohs were buried in unmarked tombs in the Valley of the Kings and guarded day and night.

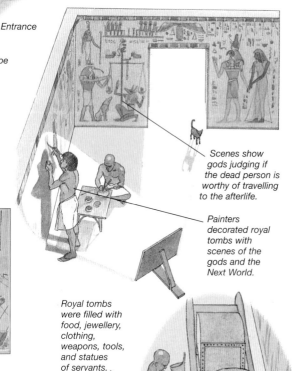

Scenes show gods judging if the dead person is worthy of travelling to the afterlife.

Painters decorated royal tombs with scenes of the gods and the Next World.

Royal tombs were filled with food, jewellery, clothing, weapons, tools, and statues of servants.

Painting of the time shows cattle being transported across the River Nile in special wide boats.

TRANSPORT AND TRADE

The quickest way to travel in Egypt was by water. Barges carried goods along the Nile, and Egyptian traders travelled to ports around the eastern Mediterranean and the Red Sea in wooden reed ships. Using a system called bartering, they exchanged gold, grain, and papyrus sheets for silver, iron, horses, cedar wood, and ivory.

Inside a tomb

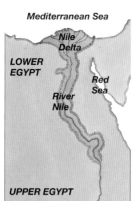

Mediterranean Sea

Nile Delta

LOWER EGYPT

Red Sea

River Nile

UPPER EGYPT

Desert

RIVER NILE

Each year, the River Nile burst its banks and spread water and fertile silt over the land. This "inundation" of the Nile Valley made the land fertile for about 10 km (6 miles) on either side of the river. The Egyptians planned their agricultural system around this, farming the land by storing the floodwaters. The desert on either side provided a natural defensive barrier and a rich source of minerals and stone.

Water was drawn from ponds or lagoons with a shadoof.

People carried water to the land on their backs.

FARMING AND FISHING

Most Egyptians were farmers who worked for priests, wealthy landowners, or the pharaoh. They were paid in crops. They watered the lands with floodwaters trapped in lagoons or with water-lifting machines called shadoofs. Crops grown included emmer for bread, barley for beer, beans, onions, dates, melons, and cucumbers. People also fished from the Nile.

Seed was scattered by hand, then trodden in by animals and watered.

The Egyptians used wooden ploughs drawn by oxen.

The Egyptians fished from papyrus reed boats using baskets, nets, spears, and lines with hooks.

The royal name of Tutankhamun

NEFERTITI

Nefertiti was the wife of the pharaoh Ikhnaton, who ruled from 1367 to 1355 BCE. She had great influence over her husband's policies. Usually, however, the only women who held important titles were priestesses.

MEDICINE AND MAGIC

Egyptian doctors were the first to study the body scientifically. They also carried out some effective dentistry. However, many "cures" were based on magic.

HIEROGLYPHICS

The Egyptians developed picture writing, or hieroglyphics, around 3000 BCE. At first each object was shown exactly by its picture, or pictograph. Gradually the pictures came to stand for sounds. Groups of "sound hieroglyphs", or phonograms, were used to spell words.

Scarab beetles were sacred to the Egyptians, who used them as charms to ward off illness.

Headrest amulet

Relief of the time showing Ancient Egyptian medical tools.

ANCIENT EGYPT

c. 10,000-5000 BCE First villages on the banks of the Nile. Slow growth of the two kingdoms of Upper and Lower Egypt.

c. 2630 BCE First step pyramid built at Saqqara.

c. 2575 BCE During Old Kingdom period, bronze replaces copper. Pyramids built at Giza. Dead bodies are embalmed.

c. 2134 BCE Old Kingdom ends with power struggles.

c. 2040 BCE Middle Kingdom begins. Nobles from Thebes reunite the country. Nubia conquered.

c. 1640 BCE Middle Kingdom ends.

1550 BCE New Kingdom begins. Permanent army.

1400 BCE Egypt reaches height of its power.

1070 BCE Egyptian power begins to decline.

332 BCE Alexander the Great conquers Egypt.

51 BCE Cleopatra rules.

30 BCE Egypt becomes a Roman province.

MUMMIES

The Egyptians thought that if they preserved their bodies after death, they would "live" forever. So they made "mummies" – corpses that did not decay. Embalmers removed the liver, lungs, and brain from the dead body, leaving the heart inside. They then coated the body with saltlike natron crystals to preserve it, and finally wrapped the whole package in bandages.

An idealized portrait of the dead person was painted on the coffin.

The internal organs were wrapped in linen and placed in canopic jars.

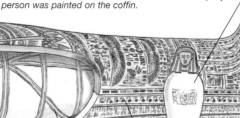

Linen protected the body.

Coffin was richly decorated with hieroglyphs of spells to help the dead person in the afterlife.

Find out more

AFRICA, HISTORY OF
ALPHABETS
ARCHAEOLOGY
CATS

ALBERT
EINSTEIN

PHYSICIST ALBERT EINSTEIN was one of the greatest scientific thinkers of all time. His theories, or ideas, on matter, space, and time revolutionized our understanding of the universe, and have formed the basis for much of modern physics. He is probably best known for his work on relativity, first published in 1905, which astounded the scientific community. In this, Einstein showed that distance and time are relative, not fixed. The faster anything travels, the slower time seems to pass. His work on relativity led to other revolutionary ideas on energy and mass, and in 1921 he was awarded the Nobel Prize. From 1933 he lived in the United States. A scientific genius, he was also a pacifist, and deeply religious.

1879 Born in Ulm, Germany.

1900 Graduates in maths and physics, Switzerland.

1902-09 Works in Patent Office, Switzerland.

1905 Publishes Special Theory of Relativity.

1916 Publishes General Theory of Relativity.

1921 Awarded Nobel Prize for Physics.

1933 Emigrates to USA.

1955 Dies Princetown, USA.

THE YOUNG EINSTEIN
Einstein was born in Germany, and, as a small boy, was very curious about things around him. When he was 15, the family moved to Switzerland, where Einstein was educated. By the time he graduated, he was already pondering the nature of light. He worked in a Patent Office and at the age of 26, wrote his first paper on relativity.

Albert Einstein working in his study in the United States.

Someone in a descending lift drops a ball. The ball appears to travel further to someone watching from outside than it does to the person inside the lift, over the same amount of time. Is the ball going faster?

A visual puzzle helps to demonstrate the theory of relativity.

Different relative viewpoints can alter our perceptions.

Einstein was famous for his untidiness.

RELATIVITY
The concept of relativity is very difficult to grasp. One of the central ideas is "time dilation", time seeming to slow down when things are moving in relation to an observer who is still. This effect increases at very high speeds approaching the speed of light. This increase is not easy to show, because we cannot notice it at the slow speeds we experience. Nothing can travel faster than light, which always travels at the same speed.

ATOMIC ENERGY
Einstein produced the famous equation $E = mc^2$, where energy (E) = mass (m) multiplied by the square of the speed of light (c). It showed that an immense amount of energy could be released by splitting the nucleus of an atom. This contributed to the development of the atom bomb. From 1946, Einstein was opposed to atomic weapons.

SCIENTIST
Einstein developed his revolutionary theories by devising what he called "thought experiments". For example, he wondered what the world would look like if he rode on a beam of light. Such simple questions often had surprising answers, which Einstein confirmed with complex mathematics. At the time, many people did not believe Einstein's theories, but later research has proved him correct.

Find out more
ATOMS AND MOLECULES
SCIENCE, HISTORY OF
TIME

ELECTRICITY

A FLASH OF LIGHTNING that leaps through the sky during a thunderstorm is one of the most visible signs of electricity. At almost all other times, electricity is invisible but hard at work for us. Electricity is a form of energy. It consists of electrons – tiny particles that come from atoms. Each electron carries a tiny electric charge which is an amount of electricity. When you switch on a light, about one billion billion electrons move through the bulb every second. Cables hidden in walls and ceilings carry electricity around houses and factories, providing energy at the flick of a switch. Electricity also provides portable power. Batteries produce electricity from chemicals, and solar cells provide electricity from the energy in sunlight. Lamps, motors, and dozens of other machines use electricity as their source of power. Electricity also provides signals which make telephones, radios, televisions, and computers work.

Electricity flows into homes through cables that run either underground or above street level on poles.

Some power stations generate electricity by burning coal and oil. Other stations are powered by nuclear energy.

A transformer boosts the voltage (force) of the electricity to many thousands of volts.

Tall pylons support long cables that carry the electricity safely above the ground to all parts of an area.

Another transformer reduces the voltage of the electricity to levels suitable for domestic appliances.

CURRENT ELECTRICITY

Electricity comes in two forms: electricity that flows, and static electricity, which does not move. Flowing electricity is called current electricity. Billions of electrons flow along a wire to give an electric current. The electricity moves from a source such as a battery or power station to a machine. It then returns to the source along another wire. The flow of electric current is measured in amperes (A).

CONDUCTORS AND INSULATORS

Electricity flows only through materials called conductors. These include copper and many other metals. Conductors can carry electricity because their own electrons are free to move. Other substances, called insulators, do not allow electricity to flow through them. This is because their electrons are held tightly inside their atoms.

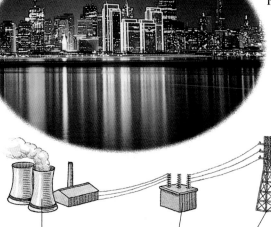

Electrons flow through copper conductor.

Most plastics are insulators.

Batteries produce direct current, which flows one way around a circuit.

Battery pushes electric current around the circuit.

Power stations produce alternating current, which flows first in one direction and then the other.

Wires connect battery and bulb to form a circuit.

Bulb in bulb holder

SUPERCONDUCTORS

Ordinarily conductors, while letting most electricity flow through them, also resist it to some extent. So a measure of electricity is lost. However, some materials lose their resistance when very cold. They become superconductors.

A superconductor can produce a strong magnetic field which makes a small magnet hover above it.

ELECTRIC CIRCUITS

Electric current needs a continuous loop of wire to flow around. This is called a circuit. If the circuit is broken, the electricity can no longer flow.

STATIC ELECTRICITY

There are two types of electric charge, positive (+) and negative (–). Objects usually contain equal numbers of both charges so they cancel each other out. Rubbing a piece of amber (dried gum or resin from trees) against wool or fur makes it pick up extra electrons, which carry a negative charge. This charge is called static electricity. It produces an electric force which makes light objects, such as hair and feathers, cling to the amber.

GENERATOR

Generators produce electricity from the energy of movement. A coil of wire moves between the poles of a magnet. This produces an electric current in the coil. Small, simple generators that power bicycle lamps are called dynamos. Large generators in power stations produce huge amounts of electricity for homes and factories.

Basic generator

Coil of wire

Magnetic field produced by magnet.

A simple generator (above) contains a coil of wire that spins between the poles of a magnet. A current flows in the coil when it moves through the magnetic field.

Instead of a simple magnet, there is a set of electromagnets – coils that use electricity to produce a strong magnetic field.

Electromagnets spin inside another set of coils. This produces electricity in the outer set of coils.

A shaft connected to the turbine (a set of vanes) drives the generator.

In a hydroelectric power station, water falling from a dam spins a turbine.

ELECTRICITY FROM CHEMICALS

Chemical energy from food changes into movement in your muscles. Chemical energy can also change into electrical energy. This is how a battery works. Chemicals react together inside a battery and produce an electric current. When there are no fresh chemicals left, the current stops. Fuel cells also produce electricity from chemicals in the form of gases.

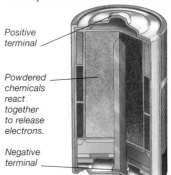

ELECTRIC EEL

The rivers of South America are the home of the electric eel. This eel has special organs in its long body that work like batteries to produce electricity. With a powerful electric shock, the electric eel can stun its prey.

Positive terminal

Powdered chemicals react together to release electrons.

Negative terminal

BATTERY

Connecting a battery in a circuit makes the chemicals inside react to produce an electric current. The battery provides a force that pushes electrons around the circuit. The energy provided by this force is measured in units called volts.

Inside the battery, the electrons flow from the positive terminal and back to the negative terminal.

Shaft of motor

The magnetic force pushes on the coil and makes it spin around.

Gears connect motor to wheels of car.

Coil of wire

Electric current flows from battery into coil, producing a magnetic field.

Magnet produces magnetic field.

ELECTRIC MOTOR

Many machines are powered by an electric motor, which contains a coil of wire placed between the poles of a magnet. The electric current fed to the motor flows through the coil, producing a magnetic field. The magnet pushes on the coil and makes it spin around and drive the shaft of the motor.

ELECTRIC SHOCKS

Living things make use of electricity. Weak electric signals pass along the nerves to and from the brain. These signals operate the muscles, maintain the heartbeat, and control the way in which the body works. A strong electric current can give an electric shock that damages the human body and may even cause death. *Never* play with the main electricity supply because of the danger of electric shock.

DISCOVERY

About 2,500 years ago, the Ancient Greeks found that rubbing amber (a yellow solid) produces a charge of static electricity. The Greek for amber is *elektron*, which is how electricity got its name. Around 1750, American scientist Benjamin Franklin (left) discovered that lightning is electricity and explained what electric charges are. At the end of the 18th century, Italian scientists Luigi Galvani and Alessandro Volta produced the first electric battery.

Benjamin Franklin (1706-90) studied the electrical nature of lightning by flying a kite during a thunderstorm.

A bird sitting on an electric cable does not get an electric shock. The electricity does not pass into its body because the bird is touching only one wire and does not complete an electric circuit.

Find out more

ATOMS AND MOLECULES
ELECTRONICS
ENERGY
FISH
MAGNETISM

ELECTRONICS

The semiconductor silicon comes from sand, which is a compound of silicon and oxygen.

A diode is made from the junction between pieces of n- and p-type semiconductors.

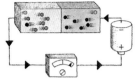

A diode allows current to flow through it in only one direction. The current is carried by the flow of holes and electrons.

If a battery is connected the other way around, holes and electrons cannot cross the junctions so current cannot flow.

SEMICONDUCTORS
Most electronic components are made of materials such as silicon, which are called semiconductors. Semiconductors control the flow of current because they contain a variable number of charge carriers (particles that carry electricity). In n-type semiconductors, the charge carriers are negatively charged electrons; in p-type semiconductors, the charge carriers are positively charged "holes" – regions where electrons are absent.

ELECTRICITY is a source of power that drives machines and provides heat and light. Electricity is also used to produce signals that carry information and control devices. Using electricity in this way is called electronics. We are surrounded by thousands of electronic machines, including computers, MP3 players, telephones, and televisions. All these machines contain circuits through which electric currents flow. Tiny electronic components in the circuits control the flow of the current to produce signals. For instance, a varying current may represent sound in a telephone line, or a number in a computer. The most important electronic component is the transistor. A small radio receiver may contain a dozen transistors; a computer contains millions of transistors inside microchips.

CIRCUIT BOARD
An electronic device such as a telephone contains an electronic circuit consisting of several components joined together on a circuit board. Every circuit is designed for a particular task. The circuit in a radio, for instance, picks up and amplifies (boosts) radio waves so they can be converted into sound.

Capacitor stores electric charge. In a radio circuit, capacitors help tune the circuit so that it picks up different radio frequencies.

Resistor reduces the amount of current flowing in the circuit.

Diode allows current to pass in only one direction.

Transistor boosts the strength of electrical signals.

Variable resistor allows the flow of current to be varied.

Wires are used to connect some components.

Microchip in plastic casing

Metal tracks on the underside of the board connect components.

CONTROLLING CURRENT
Electronic circuits do several basic jobs. They may amplify current; they may produce an oscillating current – one that rapidly changes direction, essential for generating radio waves; or they may switch current on and off.

Oscillation: Some circuits convert a steady one-way current (direct current, or DC) into a varying alternating current (AC).

Amplification: An amplifier circuit generates a strong AC current that is an accurate copy of a weaker AC current.

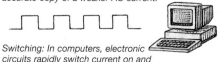

Switching: In computers, electronic circuits rapidly switch current on and off in a code that represents data.

MICROCHIPS
Microchips, or silicon chips, contain circuits consisting of millions of microscopic components. These circuits are squeezed onto the surface of a semiconductor less than 25 mm (1 in) square.

TRANSISTOR
Transistors lie at the heart of most electronic machines. They boost current and voltage in amplifier circuits, store information in computers, and perform many other tasks. Physicists William Shockley, John Bardeen, and Walter Brattain invented the transistor in 1947.

Find out more
COMPUTERS
ELECTRICITY
RADIO
TECHNOLOGY
TELEVISION

ELEPHANTS

GREAT TUSKS, huge ears, and a strong trunk make the elephant one of the most magnificent creatu res on Earth. Elephants are the largest living land mammals and have a long fossil history. They are extremely strong and highly intelligent, and have been trained to work for humans for thousands of years. There are three kinds of elephants – African Savannah, Forest, and Asian (Indian). African elephants are slightly bigger than Asian elephants, with much larger ears. A large male measures more than 3 m (10 ft) high at the shoulder and weighs more than 5.4 tonnes (5.3 tons). The elephant's trunk reaches to the ground and high into the trees to find food. It is also used for drinking, smelling, greeting other members of the herd, and as a snorkel in deep water.

WOOLLY MAMMOTH
The prehistoric mammoth became extinct about 10,000 years ago. Frozen remains of mammoths have been found in Alaska and Siberia.

Head and jaws are huge, with wide, ridged teeth for chewing plant matter.

Huge ears help to cool elephant by allowing heat to escape.

Ears are used to threaten other animals.

TRUNK
The trunk is formed from the nose and the long upper lip. It is extremely sensitive to touch and smell. The elephant uses its trunk to grasp leaves, fruits, and shoots, and place them in its mouth. In order to drink, the elephant must squirt water into its mouth because it cannot drink through its trunk.

Two nostrils at tip of the trunk

When bathing, the elephant sucks water into its trunk, then squirts it over the body.

Tusks are massive upper incisor teeth, made of ivory (dentine). They can split bark from trees and gouge roots from the ground.

Wide, flat, soft-soled feet leave hardly any tracks.

ASIAN ELEPHANT
There are probably fewer than 50,000 Asian elephants left in the wild, in remote forests of India, China, and Southeast Asia. Female or cow elephants are quite easy to tame between the ages of about 10 and 20 years. They are caught and kept in captivity, and used for clearing forests and towing logs. Asian elephants are also dressed and decorated for ceremonies and processions.

AFRICAN ELEPHANTS
In the late 1970s there were about 1.3 million elephants in Africa. Today there are half that number. Poachers kill them for their ivory, and farms are built on the land where they live. In reserves, however, where elephants are protected, their numbers have increased. Here, they are culled (killed in a controlled way) to prevent them from damaging the countryside. Today elephants are on the official list of endangered species, and the trade in elephants and ivory is controlled by international agreement.

A six-year-old male African elephant

BREEDING
A newborn elephant calf weighs 100-120 kg (220-260 lb) at birth. It sucks milk from the teats between its mother's front legs until it is about four years old. A young elephant stays with its mother for the first 10 years of its life. By the age of six it weighs about one tonne, and at about 15 years of age it is ready to breed.

Find out more
ANIMALS
CONSERVATION
and endangered species
FOREST WILDLIFE
MAMMALS

ELIZABETH I

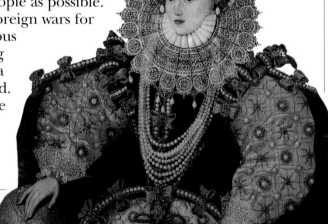

MORE THAN 400 YEARS AGO, one woman brought 45 years of peace and prosperity to England through her determination and wisdom. Queen Elizabeth I began her life as a neglected princess, whose mother had been executed by her father. She was ignored and imprisoned as a girl, but upon the death of her half sister, Queen Mary, Elizabeth became a strong and popular queen. She tried to end years of religious conflict between Catholics and Protestants by insisting that the Church of England should be only moderately Protestant, so that it included as many people as possible. Elizabeth avoided expensive foreign wars for many years. Her most dangerous conflict was with Philip II, king of Spain, who sent the Armada (fleet of ships) against England. The queen's court was a centre for poets, musicians, and writers. Her reign is often called England's Golden Age.

1533 Born, the daughter of Henry VIII and Anne Boleyn.

1536 Mother is executed for treason.

1554 Imprisoned in the Tower of London.

1558 Becomes queen.

1559 Establishes Protestant Church of England by the Act of Supremacy.

1587 Orders execution of Mary, Queen of Scots.

1588 Faces the Armada.

1603 Dies.

SIR WALTER RALEIGH
One of Elizabeth's favourite courtiers was Sir Walter Raleigh (1552-1618). In 1584 she knighted him, and later made Raleigh her Captain of the Guard. He made several voyages across the Atlantic, set up an English colony in Virginia, and brought tobacco and potatoes from the Americas to Europe.

ELIZABETHAN AGE
Elizabeth was the first monarch to give her name to an age. During her reign the arts of music, poetry, and drama flourished. Despite foreign threats and religious unrest at home, she won the loyalty and admiration of her subjects.

SPANISH ARMADA
In July 1588 Philip II, king of Spain, launched his Armada of nearly 150 ships to invade England and restore the Catholic religion. Sir Francis Drake (1540-96) sailed in command of a large group of warships to oppose the Armada. Aided by stormy weather, the English defeated the great fleet.

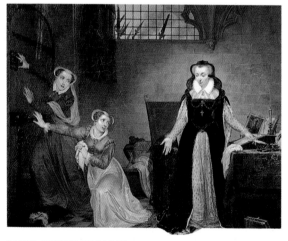

MARY, QUEEN OF SCOTS
Mary was Elizabeth's Catholic cousin and heir. Forced to abdicate her own throne in Scotland, she fled to England to seek Elizabeth's protection. Mary became involved in Catholic plots against Elizabeth, who reluctantly ordered her execution.

Find out more
HENRY VIII
STUARTS
TUDORS
UNITED KINGDOM, HISTORY OF

EMIGRATION AND IMMIGRATION

WHEN YOU EMIGRATE, YOU LEAVE the country of your birth and settle elsewhere to live and work. When you arrive in a new country, you become an immigrant. Since the 17th century, many British people have left to start new lives elsewhere, in North America, Australia, New Zealand, or African and Asian countries that were once part of the British Empire. In the same way, people from all over the world have arrived to settle in Britain. Some came from countries of the Empire, and later the Commonwealth, to work, because they held British passports. After Britain joined the European Union, large numbers of Europeans came to work in Britain. Other immigrants – refugees of war or religious or political persecution – come to Britain to seek asylum (safety).

EAST END OF LONDON
Many immigrants to Britain first landed at London's docks and so settled in the nearby East End. Huguenots (French Protestants) fleeing persecution in the 1680s and Jews escaping massacres in Russia and Eastern Europe in the 1880s both settled there. Synagogues show where the Jewish communities were. More recently, people from Bengal and Bangladesh have come to the area.

EMPIRE WINDRUSH
During World War II (1939-45), many islanders from the British West Indies fought in the British armed services. Their islands were poor, and, after the war, some decided to move to Britain in search of jobs. In June 1948, the first group arrived on a boat, the *Empire Windrush*. More followed, and a West Indian community was established.

IMMIGRATION CONTROL
When immigrants arrive at a port or airport they must fill in forms to apply for permission to stay. Britain has always had some form of restriction on immigration, although people from the Empire were allowed in. In 1962, the law was changed so that black Commonwealth citizens could only enter if they had a job to come to. Since then, the law has been tightened many times, making it harder to enter the country.

Some of the first 510 Jamaicans to sail to Britain in search of work arrive at Tilbury Docks.

EMIGRATION
For at least 400 years, more people left Britain than have arrived. In 1620, a group known as the Pilgrim Fathers left for North America because of religious persecution, while many more left because of poverty. Today, there are thousands of people in Canada, Australia, and elsewhere who can trace their families back to Britain.

EMIGRATION AND IMMIGRATION

1620 Pilgrims leave for New World.

1685 Huguenots flee France.

1880s Jews flee Eastern Europe.

1905 Aliens Act restricts entry of foreigners to Britain.

1948 *Empire Windrush* brings 510 Jamaicans to Britain.

1962 Commonwealth Immigration Act restricts immigration from Commonwealth.

1971 Immigration Act allows entry to those with British-born parents or grandparents.

2000s Increasing numbers of asylum seekers come to Britain.

RACE RELATIONS
Racism is the belief that people of one culture or skin colour are superior to others. Many people who have settled in Britain have faced hostility and sometimes violence as a result of racism. In response, governments have made race discrimination illegal and have promoted equal opportunities for all Britons, black and white.

Orphaned boys taken to Australia in the 1920s by Dr. Barnado's children's charity.

Find out more
BRITISH EMPIRE
GOVERNMENT AND POLITICS
UNITED KINGDOM, HISTORY OF

ENERGY

THE MOVEMENT OF A CAR, the sound of a trumpet, the light from a candle – all these things occur because of energy. Energy is the ability to make things happen. For example, when you throw a stone you give it energy of movement which shows itself when the stone smashes glass. All life on Earth depends on energy, almost all of which comes from the Sun. The Sun's energy makes plants grow, which provides the food that animals eat; the energy from food is stored in an animal's muscles, ready to be converted into movement. Although energy is not an object that you can see or touch, you can think of it as something that either flows from place to place, or is stored. For instance, energy is stored by water high at the top of a waterfall. As soon as the water starts to fall, the stored energy changes into moving energy which flows to the bottom of the waterfall.

WORK, ENERGY, AND POWER
When a force moves an object, energy is transferred, or passed, to the object or its surroundings. This transfer of energy is called work. The amount of work done depends on the size of the force and how far it moves. For instance, this weightlifter does a lot of work lifting a heavy weight through a large distance. Power is the rate of doing work. The weightlifter produces more power the faster he lifts the weight.

POTENTIAL ENERGY
Energy can be stored as potential energy until it turns into another form such as movement. Examples include water in a raised reservoir waiting to flow through turbines, chemical energy in a battery waiting to drive an electric current, and a coiled spring waiting to be released.

KINETIC ENERGY
An object such as an aeroplane needs energy to make it move. Moving energy is called kinetic energy. When the plane stops, it loses kinetic energy. This often appears as heat – for instance, in the plane's brakes.

TYPES OF ENERGY
Energy takes many forms, and it can change from one form into another. For example, power stations turn the chemical energy stored in coal or oil into heat energy which boils water. Turbines change the heat energy of the steam into electrical energy which flows to homes and factories.

Heat energy, such as the warmth of the Sun, is carried by invisible waves called infrared or heat radiation.

Light is one form of energy that travels in waves. Others include X-rays and radio waves.

Sound waves are vibrations of the air, so they carry kinetic energy.

Some power stations produce electricity from nuclear energy, which comes from the nuclei (centres) of atoms.

Electrical devices turn the energy of electric currents into many other forms of energy, including heat, light, and movement.

A battery runs out when all its stored energy has been converted into heat in the wires, and heat and light in the bulb.

Oil and coal contain stored chemical energy which changes into heat and light when these fuels are burned.

ENERGY CYCLE
Energy cannot be created or destroyed; it can only change from one form into another. The only exception might seem to be when matter changes into energy in a nuclear reactor. However, the rule still applies because matter and energy are really the same and one can be converted into the other.

ENERGY RESOURCES
The Earth's population uses a huge amount of energy. Most of this energy comes from coal, oil, gas, and the nuclear fuel uranium. However, these fuels are being used up and cannot be replaced. Today, scientists are experimenting with energy sources, called renewable resources, that will not run out. These include the Sun, wind, waves, and tides.

Rows of solar panels for producing electricity

Find out more
ELECTRICITY
HEAT
LIGHT
NUCLEAR ENERGY
SOUND
SUN
WATER
WIND

ENGINES

FOUR-STROKE ENGINE
Most car engines are four-stroke engines, which means that each piston makes a set of four movements.

WHEN PREHISTORIC PEOPLE discovered fire, they also found a way of obtaining energy; because burning releases heat and light. About one million years later, the steam engine was invented, and for the first time people could harness that energy and turn it into movement. Today, there are many different kinds of engines which drive the world's transport and industry. All engines serve one function – to use the energy stored in a fuel such as oil or coal, and change it into motion to drive machines. Before engines were invented, tasks such as building and lifting depended on the strength of people and their animals. Today, engines can produce enough power to lift the heaviest weights and drive the largest machines. The most powerful engine is the rocket engine; it can blast a spacecraft away from the pull of the Earth's gravity and out into space.

Piston 4 rises and pushes waste gases out through exhaust valve.

Piston 2 rises and compresses (squeezes) fuel-air mixture.

Piston 3 is pushed down by expanding gases when the mixture explodes.

Spark plug produces electrical spark that ignites fuel-air mixture.

Valves open and close to admit and expel the fuel-air mixture.

Piston 1 moves down and sucks fuel-air mixture in through inlet valve.

The piston moves up and down inside the cylinder.

Most engines have between four and eight cylinders. These work in sequence to produce continuous movement.

Crankshaft changes the up-and-down movement of the pistons into circular movement, which drives the wheels.

INTERNAL-COMBUSTION ENGINE
The engine that powers almost all the world's cars is the internal-combustion engine. It uses the power of gases created by exploding fuel to produce movement. A mixture of air and tiny droplets of petrol enters the engine's cylinders, each of which contains a piston. An electrical spark ignites (sets alight) the fuel mixture, producing gases which thrust each piston down.

ELECTRIC MOTORS
Petrol and diesel engines produce waste gases that pollute the air and contribute to the greenhouse effect (which causes the Earth's temperature to rise). Electric motors are clean, quiet, and produce no pollution. Several car manufacturers are developing cars powered by electric motors. Hybrid cars such as the Toyota Prius (below) use a combination of electric and petrol or gas power to provide good performance with low pollution.

DIESEL ENGINE
Many trains and lorries have powerful diesel engines, which are internal-combustion engines that burn diesel fuel instead of petrol. The engine works in the same way as a petrol-fuelled engine, but does not have spark plugs. Instead, each cylinder has an injector that squirts diesel fuel into the cylinder. The piston compresses the air, making it very hot. The hot air is all it needs to make the diesel fuel explode.

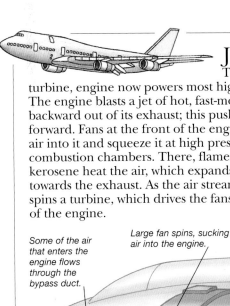

JET ENGINE

The jet, or gas turbine, engine now powers most high-speed aircraft. The engine blasts a jet of hot, fast-moving air backward out of its exhaust; this pushes the engine forward. Fans at the front of the engine spin and suck air into it and squeeze it at high pressure into several combustion chambers. There, flames of burning kerosene heat the air, which expands and rushes towards the exhaust. As the air streams out, it spins a turbine, which drives the fans at the front of the engine.

FRANK WHITTLE
In 1928, English pilot and engineer Frank Whittle (born1907) suggested the idea of the jet engine. Whittle's engine powered an experimental aircraft for the first time in 1941. However, the first jet-powered flight was made during the 1930s in Germany, where engineer Hans von Ohain had developed his own jet engine.

Burning kerosene fuel inside the combustion chambers heats the air and makes it expand violently.

Some of the air that enters the engine flows through the bypass duct.

Large fan spins, sucking air into the engine.

Hot air and exhaust gases rush out of the engine, spinning the turbine as they go.

Fast-spinning fans called compressors increase the pressure of the air and push it into the combustion chambers.

TURBOFAN ENGINE

A turbofan engine is a very efficient kind of gas turbine engine. Some of the air flows through a bypass duct around the main part of the engine. This increases the amount of air flowing through the engine, giving it more thrust. The duct also helps make the engine quieter.

JAMES WATT
The first engine was a simple steam engine invented by the Greek scientist Hero in the 1st century CE, but it was little more than a toy. In 1712, the British engineer Thomas Newcomen built the first real engine. It was a huge steam engine used to pump water out of mines. In 1769, another British engineer, James Watt (left), greatly improved the steam engine. The unit of power, the watt, is named after him.

STEAM ENGINE
The steam engine was developed during the 18th century and greatly changed people's lives. It led to the development of industry and transport. People left the land to work in the new factories which contained steam-powered machines, and steam railways allowed people to travel further and faster than ever before.

Boiler burns wood or coal, producing heat.

Hot air and smoke pass through pipes that run through the water tank. The heat turns the water into steam.

Steam and smoke escape through a valve and pour out of the smokestack.

Steam passes through a pipe to a cylinder. The steam pushes a piston back and forth inside the cylinder.

The movement of the piston drives the wheels of the train.

Find out more
AIRCRAFT
CARS
ELECTRICITY
ROCKETS AND MISSILES
TRAINS
TRANSPORT, HISTORY OF

ENGLAND

ST. GEORGE'S FLAG
The red cross of St. George of England is the national flag.

MORE THAN EIGHTY PER CENT of the population of the United Kingdom, around 50 million people, live in England. The country has always been the largest, wealthiest, and most crowded region of Great Britain. The Industrial Revolution began in England in the late 1700s, causing a huge shift from agriculture to industry, and the emergence of industrial centres, such as Birmingham and Manchester. In the 19th and early 20th centuries, England was a major power as the centre of the British Empire. Today, England's manufacturing has declined but the country remains a centre for scientific research. Tourism based on England's heritage and traditions is also a major industry, employing thousands of people.

England stretches from Land's End in Cornwall, upwards to the border of Scotland. It covers 130,360 sq km (50,332 sq miles). It is divided into counties.

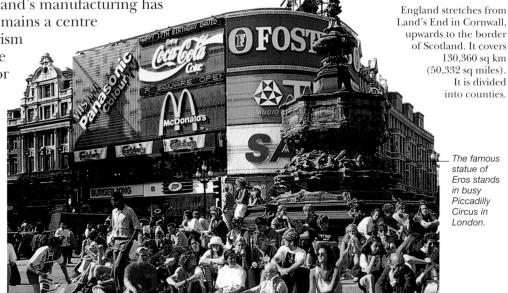

The famous statue of Eros stands in busy Piccadilly Circus in London.

LONDON

London is England's capital, and a leading international centre for finance, business, theatre, art, and music. One of the biggest cities in Europe, London is a popular destination for millions of tourists every year. The city was founded by the Romans on the banks of the River Thames in 43 CE.

RURAL ENGLAND
England is only a small country, but from the Yorkshire Moors in the north to the spectacular South Downs, it contains varied and beautiful countryside. Urbanization (the growth of towns) has destroyed much of England's rural areas. Preserving what remains has become an important issue.

THE ENGLISH LANGUAGE
Because the British Empire was so vast, English is spoken worldwide. More than 300 million people speak English as a first language, and it is the second or third language for another 600 million. It is the global language for air traffic control and science.

ARCHITECTURE
Most English people live in towns and cities, many of which are very crowded. Home ownership is valued, and town houses vary from from small terraced houses to apartment blocks. The most popular town houses include semi-detached houses, with their own gardens.

ENGLISH BREAKFAST
Traditional English cooking is variable, and not always liked by the people outside England. One popular speciality is the English breakfast with fried bread, eggs, bacon, sausages, tomatoes, and black pudding.

Find out more
INDUSTRIAL REVOLUTION
UNITED KINGDOM
UNITED KINGDOM, HISTORY OF

ENGLISH CIVIL WAR

IN 1649 CHARLES I, king of England, was put on trial for treason and executed. His death marked the climax of the English Civil War, also called the English Revolution, a fierce struggle between king and Parliament (the law-making assembly) over the issue of who should govern England. The struggle had begun many years before. Charles I believed that kings were appointed by God and should rule alone; Parliament believed that it should have greater power. When the king called upon Parliament for funds to fight the Scots, it refused to co-operate, and in 1642 civil war broke out. England was divided into two factions – the Royalists (also called Cavaliers), who supported Charles, and the Parliamentarians (also called Roundheads), who supported Parliament. Charles was a poor leader, and the Roundheads had the support of the navy and were led by two great generals – Lord Fairfax and Oliver Cromwell. By 1649 Cromwell had defeated Charles and declared England a republic. Despite various reforms, Cromwell's rule was unpopular. In 1660 the army asked Charles's son, Charles II, to take the throne and the monarchy was restored.

CHARLES I
King Charles I (reigned 1625-49) was the only English monarch to be executed. He ignored the Parliament, and ruled alone from 1629 to 1640. After a disagreement with the Parliament in 1642, Charles raised an army and began the civil war which ended his reign. The picture above depicts the scene of his execution.

Parliamentary (New Model) army

Royalist cavalry

Royalist officers wore wide-brimmed hats.

Pikeman

BATTLE OF NASEBY
At the Battle of Naseby in 1645 the heavily armed and well-organized pikemen and musketeers of Cromwell's "New Model Army" crushed the Royalists.

OLIVER CROMWELL
The English Republic (1649-60) was organized and ruled mainly by Lord Protector Oliver Cromwell (1599-1658). Cromwell was an honest, moderate man and a brilliant army leader. But his attempts to enforce religious purity upon England made him unpopular with many.

RUMP PARLIAMENT
At the end of the English Civil War, all that was left of King Charles's parliament was a "rump" parliament, whose members refused to leave. In 1653 Cromwell, determined to get rid of any remnant of the king, dismissed Parliament. He pointed at the mace, the speaker's symbol of office, and laughingly called it a bauble (left).

DIGGERS
During the turbulent years new political groups emerged. Some, such as the Diggers, were very radical. They believed that ordinary people should have a say in government and wanted to end private property.

Find out more
CROMWELL, OLIVER
UNITED KINGDOM
UNITED KINGDOM, HISTORY OF

EUROPE

COMPARED TO ITS mighty eastern neighbour, Asia, Europe is a tiny continent. But the culture of Europe has extended far beyond its boundaries. Europe has a long history of wealth, industry, trading, and empire building. Much of its prosperity comes from its green and fertile land, which is watered by numerous rivers and plenty of rain. Yet the climate varies considerably across the continent. The countries of southern Europe border the Mediterranean Sea. Holiday-makers visit the coast of this enclosed sea to enjoy its long, hot summers. The far north, by contrast, reaches up into the icy Arctic Circle. There are also a number of high mountain ranges within Europe, including the Alps and the Pyrenees. The ethnic composition of Europe's 725 million people is as varied as the landscape. The continent is culturally diverse with a rich history. The Nordic people of the north have blond hair, fair skin, and blue eyes, while many Europeans in the south have darker skin and dark, curly hair.

EURO
The European Union made a major move towards monetary union when the Euro was introduced as a single European currency. Eleven EU countries, including Germany and France, formally adopted the currency in 1999, and the Euro replaced the national currencies of 12 countries at the start of 2002 (Greece joining in with the original 11). Other EU countries, such as Britain and Denmark, kept their national currencies.

Europe lies to the north of the Mediterranean Sea and overlooks the northern part of the Atlantic Ocean. It includes the surrounding islands, such as the British Isles and Iceland. The Ural Mountains in the Russian Federation mark the long eastern frontier with Asia.

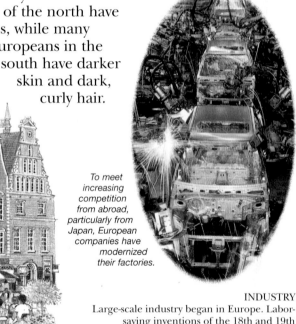

To meet increasing competition from abroad, particularly from Japan, European companies have modernized their factories.

INDUSTRY
Large-scale industry began in Europe. Labor-saving inventions of the 18th and 19th centuries enabled workers in European factories to manufacture goods cheaply and in large numbers. The Industrial Revolution soon spread to other parts of the world, including the United States, India, and Japan. Manufacturing industries still play a vital role in most European countries.

Old European buildings may look picturesque, but the architecture is more than decorative. The mellow brick and stone provide essential protection against the cool, damp weather.

Austrian composer Johann Strauss Jr. (1825-99) named his famous waltz tune The Blue Danube after the river.

DANUBE RIVER
Europe's second-longest river is the Danube. The Danube flows from the Black Forest in Germany to the Black Sea and passes through nine European countries: Germany, Austria, Slovakia, Hungary, Croatia, Serbia, Romania, Bulgaria, and Ukraine.

CITIES
Most European cities pre-date those in Australia and America. Many are of ancient origin and have grown gradually over several centuries. As a result, they differ enormously in design and layout to their modern counterparts abroad. Originally designed to cope with small volumes of traffic, Europe's cities are composed of an irregular mixture of narrow winding streets, and wider boulevards. Modern cities, designed with current modes of transport in mind, are carefully planned and tend to follow a more uniform grid pattern.

TRADE

Europeans have always been great traders. Between the 15th and 18th centuries, the countries of Europe were the most powerful in the world. They took their trade to all corners of the globe, and their settlers ruled parts of the Americas, Africa, India, Southeast Asia, and Australia. Almost all of these regions are now independent, but many still retain traces of European culture.

European trade and money formed the basis of the world's banking system.

The people paint the houses white to reflect the heat of the sun.

SCANDINAVIA

A great hook-shaped peninsula encloses most of the Baltic Sea in northern Europe and extends into the Arctic Ocean. Sweden and Norway occupy this peninsula. Together with Denmark to the south, they make up Scandinavia. Finland, to the east of the Baltic, and the large island of Iceland in the North Atlantic, are often also included in the group.

In the warm climate of the Mediterranean region olives, oranges, lemons, sunflowers, melons, tomatoes, and aubergines grow well.

Goats and sheep are more common than cattle, which require richer pasture.

MEDITERRANEAN

Ten European countries border the Mediterranean Sea: Spain, France, Monaco, Italy, Slovenia, Croatia, Bosnia and Herzegovina, Montenegro, Albania, and Greece. A small part of Turkey is also in Europe. The Mediterranean people have traditionally lived by farming (above), but many of these countries now have thriving industries. Though the climate around the Mediterranean is much warmer than that of northern Europe, winters can still be quite chilly.

ART AND CULTURE

Europe has its own traditions of art and culture which are quite distinct from those of other parts of the world. Oil painting, classical music, and ballet had their origins in Europe. The traditions of European theatre, music, literature, painting, and sculpture all began in ancient times.

Tallinn (left), Estonia's capital city, is a major Baltic port.

BALTIC STATES

Lithuania, Latvia, and Estonia, low-lying agricultural countries on the eastern coast of the Baltic Sea, are together called the Baltic States. They were formed in 1918 and remained independent until 1940 when they were occupied by the Soviet Union. In 1991, Lithuania became one of the first of the former Soviet republics to achieve independence, followed a few months later by Estonia and Latvia.

Find out more

FRANCE
GERMANY
ITALY
RUSSIAN FEDERATION
SCANDINAVIA
SPAIN
UNITED KINGDOM

STATISTICS

Area: 10,498,000 sq km
(4,053,309 sq miles)
Population: 727,247,000
Highest point: El' brus,
Caucasus Mountains
(European Russia)
5,642 m (18,511 ft)
Longest river: Volga
(European Russia)
3,688 m (2,290 miles)
Largest lake: Ladoga
(European Russia)
18,300 sq km
(7,100 sq miles)
Main occupations:
Agriculture,
manufacturing, industry
Main exports:
Machinery and transport
equipment
Main imports: Oil and
other raw materials

EUROPEAN UNION
In 1957, five European
countries agreed to
form the European
Economic Community (EEC).
In December 1991, the Maastricht
Treaty created the European Union
(EU). The EU flag (above) has
12 yellow stars on a blue background.
The Union now has 27 members.

ALBANIA
Area: 28,750 sq km
(11,100 sq miles)
Population: 3,639,000
Capital: Tirana

ANDORRA
Area: 468 sq km
(181 sq miles)
Population: 84,000
Capital: Andorra la Vella

AUSTRIA
Area: 83,850 sq km
(32,375 sq miles)
Population: 8,210,000
Capital: Vienna

BELGIUM
Area: 33,100 sq km
(12,780 sq miles)
Population: 10,414,000
Capital: Brussels

BELARUS
Area: 207,600 sq km
(80,154 sq miles)
Population: 9,649,000
Capital: Minsk

BOSNIA AND HERZEGOVINA
Area: 51,130 sq km (19,741 sq miles)
Population: 4,613,000
Capital: Sarajevo

BULGARIA
Area: 110,910 sq km
(42,822 sq miles)
Population: 7,205,000
Capital: Sofia

CROATIA
Area: 56,540 sq km
(21,830 sq miles)
Population: 4,489,000
Capital: Zagreb

CZECH REPUBLIC
Area: 78,370 sq km
(30,260 sq miles)
Population: 10,212,000
Capital: Prague

DENMARK
Area: 43,069 sq km
(16,629 sq miles)
Population: 5,501,000
Capital: Copenhagen

ESTONIA
Area: 45,125 sq km
(17,423 sq miles)
Population: 1,300,000
Capital: Tallinn

FINLAND
Area: 338,130 sq km
(130,552 sq miles)
Population: 5,250,000
Capital: Helsinki

FRANCE
Area: 551,500 sq km
(212,930 sq miles)
Population: 62,151,000
Capital: Paris

GERMANY
Area: 356,910 sq km
(137,800 sq miles)
Population: 82,330,000
Capital: Berlin

GREECE
Area: 131,990 sq km
(50,521 sq miles)
Population: 10,737,000
Capital: Athens

HUNGARY
Area: 93,030 sq km
(35,919 sq miles)
Population: 9,906,000
Capital: Budapest

ICELAND
Area: 103,000 sq km
(39,770 sq miles)
Population: 307,000
Capital: Reykjavik

IRELAND
Area: 70,280 sq km
(27,155 sq miles)
Population: 4,203,000
Capital: Dublin

ITALY
Area: 301,270 sq km
(116,320 sq miles)
Population: 58,126,000
Capital: Rome

KOSOVO
Area: 10,887 sq km
(4,203 sq miles)
Population: 2,217,000
Capital: Pristina

LATVIA
Area: 64,589 sq km
(24,938 sq miles)
Population: 2,232,000
Capital: Riga

LIECHTENSTEIN
Area: 160 sq km
(62 sq miles)
Population: 35,000
Capital: Vaduz

LITHUANIA
Area: 65,200 sq km
(25,174 sq miles)
Population: 3,555,000
Capital: Vilnius

LUXEMBOURG
Area: 2,586 sq km
(998 sq miles)
Population: 492,000
Capital: Luxembourg

MACEDONIA
Area: 25,715 sq km
(9,929 sq miles)
Population: 2,020,000
Capital: Skopje

MALTA
Area: 320 sq km
(124 sq miles)
Population: 405,000
Capital: Valletta

MOLDOVA
Area: 33,700 sq km
(13,000 sq miles)
Population: 4,321,000
Capital: Chisinau

MONACO
Area: 1.95 sq km
(0.75 sq miles)
Population: 33,000
Capital: Monaco

MONTENEGRO
Area: 14,026 sq km
(5,416 sq miles)
Population: 672,000
Capital: Podgorica

NETHERLANDS
Area: 37,330 sq km
(14,410 sq miles)
Population: 16,716,000
Capital: Amsterdam, The Hague

NORWAY
Area: 323,900 sq km
(125,060 sq miles)
Population: 4,661,000
Capital: Oslo

POLAND
Area: 312,680 sq km
(120,720 sq miles)
Population: 38,483,000
Capital: Warsaw

PORTUGAL
Area: 92,390 sq km
(35,670 sq miles)
Population: 10,708,000
Capital: Lisbon

ROMANIA
Area: 237,500 sq km
(88,934 sq miles)
Population: 22,215,000
Capital: Bucharest

RUSSIAN FED.
Area: 17,075,400 sq km
(5,592,800 sq miles)
Population: 140,041,000
Capital: Moscow

SAN MARINO
Area: 61 sq km
(24 sq miles)
Population: 30,300
Capital: San Marino

SERBIA
Area: 77,474 sq km
(29,913 sq miles)
Population: 7,379,000
Capital: Belgrade

SLOVAKIA
Area: 49,500 sq km
(19,100 sq miles)
Population: 5,463,000
Capital: Bratislava

SLOVENIA
Area: 20,250 sq km
(7,820 sq miles)
Population: 2,006,000
Capital: Ljubljana

SPAIN
Area: 504,780 sq km
(194,900 sq miles)
Population: 40,525,000
Capital: Madrid

SWEDEN
Area: 449,960 sq km
(173,730 sq miles)
Population: 9,060,000
Capital: Stockholm

SWITZERLAND
Area: 41,290 sq km
(15,940 sq miles)
Population: 7,604,000
Capital: Bern

UKRAINE
Area: 603,700 sq km
(223,090 sq miles)
Population: 45,700,000
Capital: Kiev

UNITED KINGDOM
Area: 244,880 sq km
(94,550 sq miles)
Population: 61,113,000
Capital: London

VATICAN CITY
Area: 0.44 sq km
(0.17 sq miles)
Population: 900
Capital: Vatican City

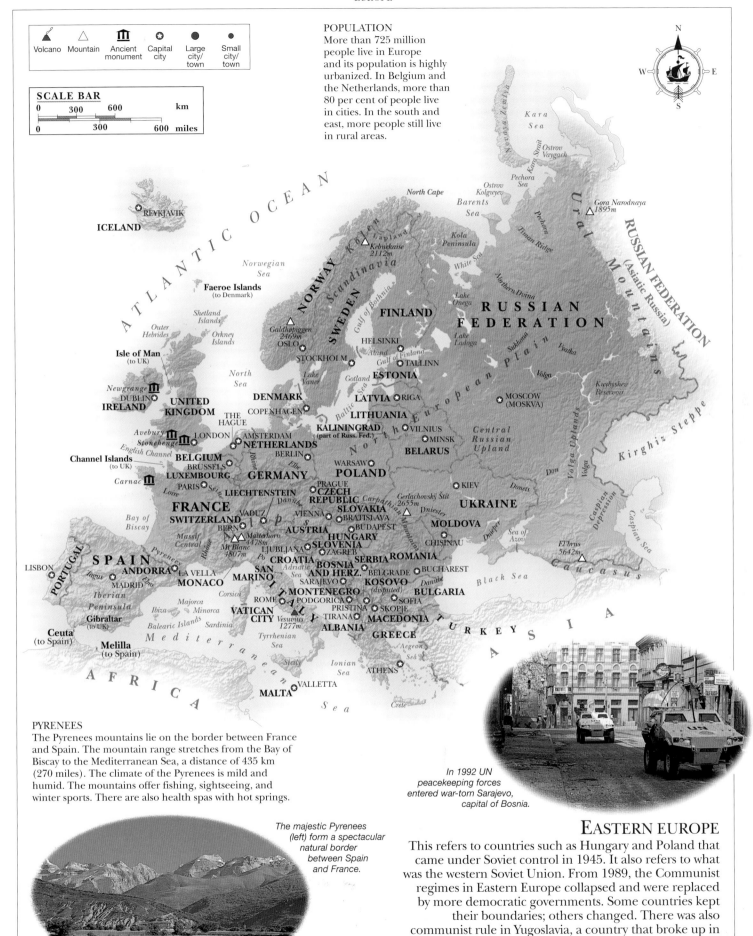

POPULATION
More than 725 million people live in Europe and its population is highly urbanized. In Belgium and the Netherlands, more than 80 per cent of people live in cities. In the south and east, more people still live in rural areas.

Volcano · Mountain · Ancient monument · Capital city · Large city/town · Small city/town

SCALE BAR

0 — 300 — 600 km

0 — 300 — 600 miles

PYRENEES
The Pyrenees mountains lie on the border between France and Spain. The mountain range stretches from the Bay of Biscay to the Mediterranean Sea, a distance of 435 km (270 miles). The climate of the Pyrenees is mild and humid. The mountains offer fishing, sightseeing, and winter sports. There are also health spas with hot springs.

The majestic Pyrenees (left) form a spectacular natural border between Spain and France.

In 1992 UN peacekeeping forces entered war-torn Sarajevo, capital of Bosnia.

EASTERN EUROPE
This refers to countries such as Hungary and Poland that came under Soviet control in 1945. It also refers to what was the western Soviet Union. From 1989, the Communist regimes in Eastern Europe collapsed and were replaced by more democratic governments. Some countries kept their boundaries; others changed. There was also communist rule in Yugoslavia, a country that broke up in the early 1990s. After much bitter fighting, the nations of Bosnia and Herzegovina, Croatia, Kosovo, Macedonia, Montenegro, Serbia, and Slovenia, were formed.

EUROPEAN UNION

JEAN MONNET
French economist Jean Monnet (1888-1979) helped to set up the European Coal and Steel Community, and was its first president. He told the French government that this would prevent another war with Germany.

IN THE 75 YEARS BETWEEN 1870-1945, France and Germany fought each other three times. After the end of World War II in 1945, they decided to live together as friends, not enemies, by combining their industrial strength. Four other countries joined them, and by 1951 the European Steel and Coal Community was created. Seven years later, the six countries signed the Treaty of Rome to set up the European Economic Community. Since then, the Community has grown into a European Union (EU) of 27 countries, including Britain and Ireland. The EU has a huge impact on daily life in Europe, from the price of food to the colour of passports. Many Europeans, however, resist the idea of the EU becoming a "superstate" with its own army and constitution.

THE FLAG
The flag of the European Union was first used in 1955 and consists of 12 five-pointed stars on a blue background.

Countries of Europe which do not form part of the EU.

A meeting of the European Parliament in Strasbourg.

MEPs sit in a semi-circle.

EUROPEAN PARLIAMENT

Every five years, the voters of Europe elect 785 Members of the European Parliament (MEPs) to represent them in Strasbourg, France. MEPs have the power to approve or throw out the Commission (the EU government), reject the annual budget, and question the Commission on its policies. The European Parliament is not as powerful as a national parliament, but it plays an important part in deciding how the European Union will develop.

EU MEMBERSHIP
The original members of the EU were France, Germany, Netherlands, Belgium, Luxembourg, and Italy. Britain, Ireland, and Denmark joined in 1973, Spain and Portugal in 1981, Greece in 1986, and Finland, Sweden, and Austria in 1995. Cyprus, Czech Republic, Estonia, Hungary, Latvia, Lithuania, Malta, Poland, Slovakia, and Slovenia joined in 2004. Bulgaria and Romania became members in 2007.

Original members

Current members

Common passport allows holder to travel freely in the EU.

WHAT THE EU DOES
The EU looks after farming, fishing, economic, industrial, and cultural affairs. It helps the poorer parts of Europe by building roads, and paying for education and training projects. Everybody in the EU holds a common European passport.

The EU helps farmers to produce and sell food.

EUROPEAN UNION

1951 France, Germany, Italy, and the Benelux countries set up European Coal and Steel Community.

1957 ECSC members sign Treaty of Rome to set up European Economic Community (EEC) and Euratom, the atomic energy authority.

1967 ECSC, EEC, and Euratom merge to form the European Community.

1979 European Monetary System begins operation.

1993 Moves towards closer union result in the European Union (EU).

2004 Ten more countries join the EU.

2007 The EU expands to 27 countries when two more join.

Euro coins

EUROPEAN MONETARY UNION

EU countries first linked their currencies together in 1979. In 1999, 11 member countries joined the euro, or single currency. Euro bank notes and coins came into use in those countries in 2002, replacing national currencies such as the French franc and German mark. There are currently 16 members of the Eurozone, after Slovakia joined in 2009.

Find out more
EUROPE
EUROPE, HISTORY OF
TRADE AND INDUSTRY

HISTORY OF
EUROPE

EUROPE IS THE SECOND SMALLEST continent, but it has played an important part in world history. The Ancient Greek and Roman empires stretched into North Africa and the Middle East, and their art, thinking, and science are still influential today. More than a thousand years later, Portuguese and Spanish explorers sailed to new continents, and even around the world. This marked the start of a period of European dominance of world affairs that lasted 400 years. Throughout its long history, however, Europe's countries have rarely been at peace, and in the 20th century, quarrels between European nations led to two world wars. Since 1945, with the rise of the United States as a world superpower, Europe's global political influence is less, but it remains culturally important.

PREHISTORIC EUROPE
The first Europeans were primitive hunters who moved around in search of food and shelter. By about 5000 BCE, Europeans were growing crops, and domesticating animals. They settled in villages, and in northern Europe, they built large burial mounds for their dead.

GREECE AND ROME
In about 900 BCE, the Greeks set up powerful city states, such as Athens. Their merchants traded around the coast of the Mediterranean Sea, founding colonies from Spain to the Black Sea. Rome was founded in 753 BCE, and by 117 CE the Roman Empire controlled most of Europe, northern Africa, and the Middle East.

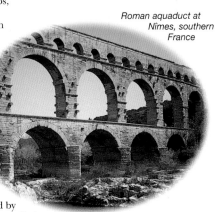

Roman aquaduct at Nîmes, southern France

Rose window, Chartres Cathedral

CHRISTIANITY
In the 300s, Christianity became the major religion in the Roman Empire. Gradually, over the next 700 years, it spread throughout Europe. The leaders of the Christian Church, such as the pope in Rome, were very powerful. It unified the continent, and dominated all aspects of daily life, including education.

MEDIEVAL TRADE
Trade prospered in medieval Europe. In the 13th century, a group of towns around the Baltic and North Sea formed the Hanseatic League, trading from ports such as Lübeck and Bruges, and monopolising trade until the 1600s. Cloth, spices, and gold were sold at great trade fairs.

Portuguese caravel

EUROPEAN DOMINATION
In mid-1400s, the Portuguese set out to explore the coast of Africa in a new, fast ship – the caravel. They set up trading stations, and were followed by other European explorers and traders, who moved outward from Europe to all parts of the globe. Europeans soon came to dominate world trade, setting up colonies in the Americas, Asia, and Africa, and building vast empires.

THE ENLIGHTENMENT

In the 18th century, European thinkers began to reject old beliefs based on religion and superstition, and developed new ideas based on reason and science. An intellectual revolution, called the Enlightenment, broke out across Europe. New ideas about government led to the French and American revolutions. Religious toleration increased, and economics, philosophy, and science prospered.

WORLD WARS

In the 1900s, conflicts between European powers caused two devastating World Wars. World War I (1914-18) weakened Europe, but war broke out again in 1939. At its end in 1945, cities were in ruins, thousands were homeless, and two new "superpowers" – the USA and the Soviet Union – had emerged.

Kemal Ataturk (1881–1939), "Father of the Turks"

Russian tanks in the streets of Budapest, Hungary in 1956.

Intellectuals gather to discuss new ideas in science.

BREAK-UP OF EMPIRES

After World War I, the multinational empires of Germany, Austro-Hungary, Ottoman Turkey, and Russia broke up as the different nationalities within them created independent countries, such as Czechoslovakia and Poland. Kemal Ataturk abolished the old Islamic government of the Ottoman Empire, and created the non-religious country of Turkey.

COMMUNIST EUROPE

By 1945, Europe was effectively divided into Communist countries, dominated by the former Soviet Union, and non-communist nations influenced by the United States. Germany was split into two nations. Life was often harsh in Communist countries, and civil liberties were restricted. Revolts broke out in East Germany (1953), Hungary (1956), and Czechoslovakia (1968), but Russian troops put them down.

THE COLLAPSE OF COMMUNISM

By the late 1980s, Communism was losing its hold, and the Soviet Union (USSR) withdrew its support from Eastern Europe. In 1989, East Germans demonstrated for union with West Germany, and pulled down the wall that divided their capital city, Berlin. Germany was reunited the following year. Popular protests then overthrew Communist governments throughout Eastern Europe.

HISTORY OF EUROPE

5000 BCE Stone Age peoples begin to settle in villages.

900 Greek city states founded.

753 Rome founded.

117 CE Roman Empire at its height.

313 Christianity is tolerated throughout Roman Empire.

1000s Christianity spreads throughout Europe.

c. 1241 Hanseatic League established between Hamburg and Lübeck merchants.

1492 Columbus crosses Atlantic; leads to European dominance in the Americas.

1498 European explorers reach India.

1517 Reformation leads to emergence of Protestantism.

1700s Age of Enlightenment.

1800s European empires control most of Africa and Asia.

1914-18 World War I devastates Europe.

1939-45 World War II leads to division of Europe into Communist and non-communist sectors.

1957 Treaty of Rome sets up European Economic Community (EEC).

1989 Fall of Berlin Wall leads to end of Communism in Eastern Europe.

1991 USSR divided into 15 separate countries.

1991-99 Wars in the Balkans as Yugoslavia breaks up.

YUGOSLAVIA

In the 1990s, Yugoslavia fell apart as Serbia, the largest and most powerful province, tried to take control. Slovenia, Croatia, and Bosnia and Herzegovina all declared independence, leading to terrible atrocities on all sides. Serbia pursued "ethnic cleansing" – killing or expelling all non-Serbs, notably in Bosnia and Kosovo. War between Serbia and NATO – a military alliance of Western Europe and the USA – led to an uneasy peace in 1999.

Find out more
EUROPEAN UNION
MEDIEVAL EUROPE
WORLD WAR I
WORLD WAR II

EVOLUTION

AROUND 150 YEARS AGO, an English naturalist named Charles Darwin shocked the world when he wrote a book suggesting that humans were related to apes. Today Darwin's idea still forms the basis of what we call the theory of evolution. The word evolution means unfolding, and it is used to describe the way that all living things evolve, or change with time. There are three main parts to the theory. The first is called variation. All living things vary in size, shape, colour, and strength. No two animals or plants are exactly the same. The second part of the theory is that these variations affect whether or not a living thing can survive and breed. Certain features, such as colour, may mean that one animal or plant has a better chance of surviving than another. Some animals and plants have features that suit their surroundings. In other words, they are better adapted, and these useful features are called adaptations. The third part of the theory is inheritance. The adaptations that help a living thing to survive, such as its colour or shape, may be passed on to its offspring. If the offspring inherit the adaptations, they too will have a better chance of survival. Gradually, over many generations, the better-adapted plants and animals flourish, and those that are less well adapted die out. Many people believe that this process of evolution has led to the millions of different species that inhabit the Earth today.

NATURAL SELECTION
Charles Darwin wrote a book called *On the Origin of Species*, published in 1859, which explained his theory of evolution. Many people laughed at Darwin's idea that humans were related to animals. Above is a cartoon of the time, picturing Darwin as a monkey.

African elephant of today

Evolution of the elephant

Moenitherium *lived about 38 million years ago.*

Woolly mammoth *lived about two million years ago.*

Platybelodon *lived from 12 to 7 million years ago.*

Trilophodon *lived from 26 to three million years ago.*

EVIDENCE FROM THE PAST

Fossils, the remains of animals and plants preserved in rocks, provide evidence for evolution. They show how animals and plants have gradually changed through time. For example, each of the elephants shown above lived for a certain amount of time, as we know by the age of their fossilized bones. Scientists cannot be certain that the first type of elephant gradually evolved into the next, but it is unlikely that each elephant appeared, completely separate from the others. It is far more likely that these elephants were related. As we find more fossils, the relationships between various kinds of animals and plants become clearer.

EVIDENCE FROM THE PRESENT
Animals and plants alive today also provide evidence for evolution. In Hawaii, there are several kinds of honeycreepers that look similar. It is unlikely that this is by chance. More likely, these different honeycreeper birds all evolved from one kind of honeycreeper. This first honeycreeper flew to the islands five million years ago. Since that time, natural selection has produced several similar, but separate, species.

There are 28 species of honeycreepers on the Hawaiian Islands. Scientists believe they evolved from one species of bird.

Akiapolaau searches for insects with upper bill.

Kiwi beak and tubular tongue are suited to sipping nectar.

Maui parrotbill uses lower bill for chiselling into wood for insects.

Apapane has useful all-round beak.

Kona finch has strong bill for crushing seeds.

Original species of honeycreeper

Kauai akialoa has long beak for probing for insects.

195

HOW EVOLUTION OCCURS

Imagine some green frogs, living and breeding in green surroundings. Most of the young inherit the green colouring of their parents. They are well camouflaged and predators do not notice them in the grass. Their green colour is an adaptation which helps them to survive. A few of the young have different colours, because of variation. Predators can see them in the grass and these frogs are soon eaten – this is natural selection at work. Then the environment slowly changes to yellow as the grass dies. Now the green frogs show up on the sand, and predators eat them. Gradually, the following generations of frogs change from mainly green to mainly yellow. A new species has evolved.

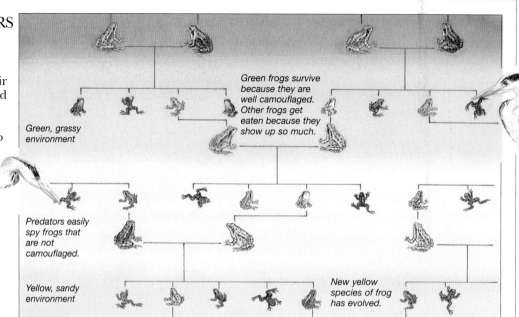

Green, grassy environment

Green frogs survive because they are well camouflaged. Other frogs get eaten because they show up so much.

Predators easily spy frogs that are not camouflaged.

Yellow, sandy environment

New yellow species of frog has evolved.

CHANGING ENVIRONMENTS

As the environment changes, living things evolve. About 200 years ago in Britain, peppered moths had mostly light-coloured wings that matched the light-coloured tree trunks where they rested, so birds could not see them easily. During the Industrial Revolution, smoke from factory chimneys made the tree trunks darker in some areas. Light-coloured moths became easier to see. Gradually, more dark-coloured moths evolved, which were better camouflaged on the dark tree trunks.

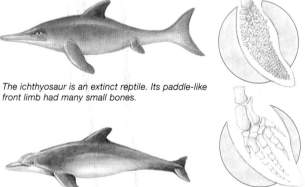

The ichthyosaur is an extinct reptile. Its paddle-like front limb had many small bones.

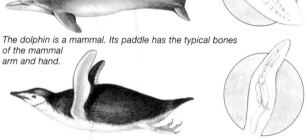

The dolphin is a mammal. Its paddle has the typical bones of the mammal arm and hand.

The penguin is a bird that cannot fly. It has the typical bird's wing bones in its paddle.

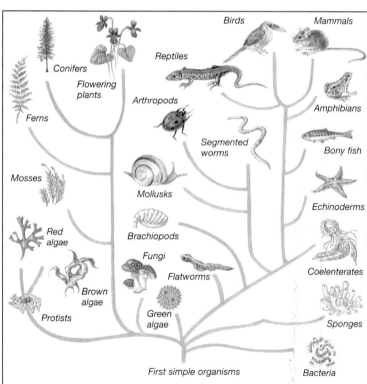

Conifers

Flowering plants

Ferns

Mosses

Red algae

Brown algae

Protists

Birds

Mammals

Reptiles

Arthropods

Amphibians

Segmented worms

Bony fish

Mollusks

Brachiopods

Fungi

Echinoderms

Flatworms

Green algae

Coelenterates

Sponges

First simple organisms

Bacteria

EVOLUTIONARY TREE

Scientists believe that all living things are related and that they have evolved from the same ancestors over millions of years. This chart is called an evolutionary tree. It has lines between the main groups of animals and plants alive today, showing which ones are most closely related.

CONVERGENT EVOLUTION

Evolution sometimes makes different animals and plants look similar. This is called convergent evolution. It means that different animals or plants that live in the same environment, such as the sea, gradually take on the same adaptations, such as body shape. All the animals shown above have evolved, or developed, the same streamlined body form, because this is the best shape for moving speedily through water.

Find out more

ANIMALS
DARWIN, CHARLES
DINOSAURS
FOSSILS
GEOLOGY
PREHISTORIC LIFE
PREHISTORIC PEOPLES

EXPLORERS

TODAY, PEOPLE ARE AWARE of the remotest corners of the world. But hundreds of years ago, many did not know that countries apart from their own even existed. In the 6th century, the Irish Saint Brendan is said to have sailed across the Atlantic in search of a land promised to saints. But it was not until the early 15th century that strong seaworthy ships were developed and Europeans such as Christopher Columbus were able to explore in earnest. Turkish Muslims had been controlling the overland trade route between Europe and the Indies (the Far East – now East Asia) since the 11th century. They charged such high prices for Eastern goods that European merchants became eager to find a direct sea route to the Far East which would bypass the Turks. The sailors who searched for these routes found the Americas and other lands previously unknown to Europeans. Of course, people already lived in most of these "newly discovered" lands, and the results of these explorations were often disastrous. All too often, the new arrivals exploited and enslaved the native peoples, destroying their cultures.

VIKINGS
The Vikings came from Norway, Sweden, and Denmark. Looking for new lands in which to settle, they sailed to Iceland, Greenland, and North America in their long ships, navigating by the sun and the stars.

EARLY IDEAS
The first explorers had few maps. Early ideas about the shape of the world were hopelessly inaccurate. Many scholars thought the world was flat and that those who went too far might fall off the edge. Some believed that the world was supported by a tortoise (above).

PERILS OF THE SEA
Early sailors faced many natural dangers such as storms, reefs, icebergs, and fog. The sea was an alien territory, and rumours and legends spoke of huge sea monsters which swam in unknown waters. These stories were probably based on sightings of whales and other marine creatures. They were exaggerated by returning sailors telling tall tales of their adventures. Writers and artists added more gruesome details to these descriptions and so the myths grew.

PACIFIC ISLANDS
Europeans exploring the Pacific Ocean in the 1500s were amazed to find that prehistoric peoples had found the Pacific Islands before them. In about 3,000 BCE, the original Polynesians moved from southeast Asia to the islands in the western Pacific, sailing in fragile canoes. By 1000 CE, they had settled on hundreds of other islands.

Maori ancestors leaving for New Zealand

DISCOVERIES
Explorers took gold, treasure, and exciting new vegetables from the Americas to Europe; they also carried silks, jewels, and spices from the East. People in Europe were eager to obtain these and wanted more. This led to a great increase in trade with both East and West.

Silk from China

Potatoes from North America

Tomatoes and chillies from the Americas

Spices from South Asia

Chocolate was made from cacao beans from the Americas.

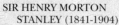

INQUISITIVE EUROPEANS

Once Europeans had an idea of the correct shape of the world, they set out to explore it more thoroughly. Some were driven by curiosity, some by greed, and some by a desire to convert the peoples who lived in faraway places to Christianity. All faced hardships and dangers.

SIR HENRY MORTON STANLEY (1841-1904)

Welshman Henry Stanley worked for a New York newspaper. He led an expedition into Africa to find the missing Scottish explorer David Livingstone. When he found him, he uttered the famous words "Dr. Livingstone, I presume?" Stanley later explored much of central Africa around Lake Victoria.

MARY KINGSLEY (1862-1900)

A fearless and determined Englishwoman, Mary Kingsley travelled in West Africa, trading and making scientific studies. On her travels, she was entertained by cannibals. She was one of the first to demand fair treatment for the people of Africa by their colonial rulers.

AMERIGO VESPUCCI (1454-1512)

The first European to explore the Brazilian coast, Italian-born Amerigo Vespucci gave his name to America. He was in charge of a school of navigation in Seville, Spain. Vespucci believed in a southwestern route to the Indies around South America.

FERDINAND MAGELLAN (1480-1521)

Leader of the first European expedition to sail around the world, Portuguese explorer Magellan proved that there was a southwestern route to the Indies through the Pacific.

VASCO DA GAMA (1469-1524)

Despite bad weather and hardships on the voyage, Portuguese-born Vasco da Gama reached the East African coast and proved that there was a southeastern route to India. He was the first European to sail around the southern tip of Africa.

Marco Polo's journey from Italy to China lasted more than 24 years.

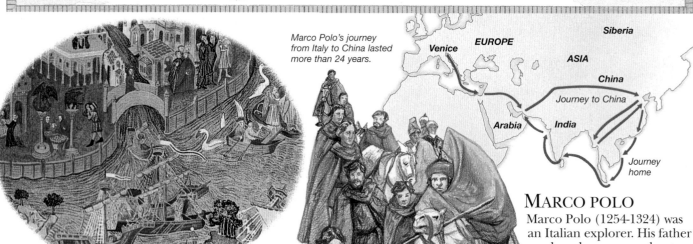

Marco Polo leaving Venice

WONDERS OF CHINA

On his travels, Marco Polo became a favourite of Kublai Khan, the Mongol ruler. Marco later published a detailed account of his journey and the wonders he had seen. Few believed the account and it was years before Europeans realized that he had experienced a great civilization – the empire of China.

MARCO POLO

Marco Polo (1254-1324) was an Italian explorer. His father and uncle were merchants from Venice, Europe's greatest trading centre. They took the 17-year-old Marco with them on a journey from Italy to China.

Find out more

COLUMBUS, CHRISTOPHER
CONQUISTADORS
COOK, JAMES
PIRATES

EYES

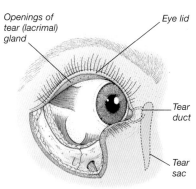

EAGLE SIGHT
A golden eagle has extremely powerful eyesight. It can see rabbits and other prey from a distance of more than 1 km (half a mile).

AS YOU READ THIS PAGE, you are using the two organs of sight – the eyes. Our eyes enable us to learn a great deal about the world around us. Each eyeball measures about 25 mm (1 in) across and sits in the front of the skull in the eye socket, or orbit. The eyes can swivel around in their sockets so that you can see things above, below, and to the side. Each eye has an adjustable lens and sees a slightly different view of the same scene. The eyes work together, controlled by the brain. This is called binocular vision. The lens of each eye allows rays of light to enter from the outside and project a picture onto the retina – the inner lining of the eye. The retina converts the light into nerve signals which travel along optic nerves to the brain, where images are formed.

Openings of tear (lacrimal) gland

Eye lid

Tear duct

Tear sac

EYE SOCKETS
The eyelid and eyelashes protect the front of the eye. When you blink, the eyelids sweep moisture over the eyeball, keeping it clean. The moisture is produced in the tear glands above the eyes. These glands also produce tears when you cry. Tiny holes drain fluid through tear ducts into the tear sac, which empties inside the nose.

OUTER EYE
Light rays enter the curved front of the eye called the cornea, where they are partly focused. They pass through the pupil, which enlarges in dim conditions to let in more light and shrinks in bright conditions to protect the inside of the eye from too much light. The rays are then focused onto the retina by the lens.

Choroid, containing nourishing blood vessels

Muscles anchored at back of eye socket move the eye.

Cornea is like a transparent window in the front of the eyeball. The cornea partly focuses light rays.

Retina, bearing light-sensitive cells

Sclera – tough outer covering

Sclera

Pupil is a hole within the iris.

Iris makes pupil larger or smaller.

Conjunctiva – thin covering layer

Lens fine-focuses light rays.

Aqueous fluid

Fovea

EYEBALL
Three pairs of muscles turn the eyeball to look up, down, and from side to side and rotate it. Pads of fat cushion the eye and the optic nerve, which is stretched and pulled by eye movements.

Optic nerve to brain

Blind spot, containing no light-sensitive cells, where optic nerve leaves eye

INNER EYE
Inside the eye is the retina, which contains about 120 million rod cells, mainly around the sides, and seven million cone cells, mainly in the fovea. The image on the retina is upside down, but the brain turns it the right way up as it processes nerve signals from the eye.

Eye muscles

Vitreous fluid

RODS AND CONES
The retina contains millions of light-sensitive cells called rods and cones. The rods work best in dim light, while cones are sensitive to different colours. Rods and cones produce nerve signals when light falls on them.

CLEAR AND DEFECTIVE VISION
Clear vision depends on the lens bending light rays to the correct angle so that the rays form a sharp picture on the retina. In long-sighted people, the eyeball is too short and nearby objects appear blurry. In short-sighted people, the eyeball is too long, making distant objects out of focus. Glasses and artificial lenses, such as contact lenses, help the eye's own lens to focus the rays correctly, thus correcting defective vision.

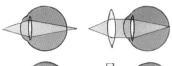

LONGSIGHTEDNESS
Rays are focused behind the retina. A convex lens corrects the focus.

SHORTSIGHTEDNESS
Rays are focused in front of retina. A concave lens corrects the focus.

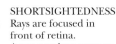

Find out more

CAMERAS
COLOUR
EARS
HUMAN BODY
LIGHT

FARM ANIMALS

Female sheep are called ewes, males are rams, and the young are called lambs.

Merino sheep have the best quality wool. The ancestor of today's Merino sheep is the Spanish Merino – a breed of sheep that is about 1,000 years old.

The Suffolk is an English breed that was first developed about 100 years ago.

Meat from adult sheep is called mutton.

Female chickens are called hens. Males, like the one shown here, are usually more colourful. They are called cocks, cockerels, or roosters.

HAMBURGERS, sausages, butter, and cheese are produced from animals that we keep on farms. Many other foods, including eggs, bacon, and yoghurt, also come from farm animals. Farm animals include pigs, cows, sheep, rabbits, goats, and chickens. People keep these animals for their meat, milk, fur, and skins. We use the skins, or hides, of cows, pigs, and sheep to make shoes, and the wool of sheep, goats, and rabbits to make clothes. People have been keeping animals on farms for at least 9,000 years. Many are kept in small enclosed areas called pens, others in fields, and still others in cages. The first farm animals were wild creatures that people captured and domesticated, or tamed. Today's chickens are descended from tropical forest birds of southeast Asia. Through the ages, farmers have bred (mated) the healthiest, most docile animals with the best milk, meat, or wool production, to produce the breeds that we know today.

The female pig is called a gilt before she has any young, and a sow once she has young. Male pigs are called boars.

AMERICAN HAMPSHIRE PIG
The American Hampshire pig has little fat on its body, so the pork and bacon from this pig are lean (that is, they have little fat).

The Rhode Island red is named after the state of Rhode Island in the United States. It is a good egg layer and is well known for its meat.

Chicks are sold for meat when they are about eight weeks old and weigh about 2 kg (4.5 lb).

POULTRY

Many people keep chickens as a source of meat and eggs. These chickens scratch around in farmyards and fields, eating seeds, worms, insects, and scraps. They lay their eggs in a small chicken coop or any other secluded place. This is called free-range rearing – the chickens are able to wander freely. Most chickens are raised indoors, under controlled conditions.

PLYMOUTH ROCK
There are about 7,000 million chickens around the world, and about 500 breeds. The Leghorn is the most common egg-laying hen. The Plymouth rock shown here is a fast-growing chicken that produces tasty meat in a short time.

SHEEP
Wool comes from sheep, goats, rabbits, camels, alpacas, and vicunas. Young sheep, or lambs, produce the softest, finest wool. The largest flocks of sheep are in Australia, where there are about 140 million sheep. The sheep we farm for wool are sheared for their fleeces (coats) once a year. An expert shearer with electric clippers can shear one sheep every 40 seconds. The wool is washed and combed, then stretched and twisted into yarn for woollen fabric. Here, a woman in Nepal, Asia, is spinning wool by hand to make into carpets and rugs.

INTENSIVE REARING

Some farm animals such as pigs and chickens are kept under controlled conditions in huge hangar-like buildings. Chickens are raised by the thousands in this way, for their meat or their eggs. These chickens sit in wire cages and cannot run around freely or scratch for their food. The food, temperature, and light in the building are controlled so that each chicken lays up to 300 eggs each year. Pigs are kept in pig units like the one shown here. They are fed an exact mixture of nutrients that makes them put on the most weight in the least time. Some kinds of pigs gain more than 0.7 kg (1.5 lb) in weight each day. A pig may be sold for pork when it is only three months old.

PIG

There are about 400 million pigs in Asia, and another 400 million scattered around the rest of the world. Some pigs are allowed to roam freely to feed on roots, worms, and household scraps; others are kept inside buildings (see above). There are more than 80 breeds of pigs, and some of the largest weigh more than 200 kg (450 lb). Almost every part of a pig can be eaten, including the trotters, or feet. Pork is the name for fresh pig meat; cured or preserved pig meat is called bacon or ham.

ZEBU

Cattle are the most numerous of farm animals, with 200 million in India and about 1,000 million in the rest of the world. They were first used to pull carts. Today some cattle are bred for their meat (beef breeds), others for their milk (dairy breeds), and some for both (dual-purpose breeds). There are about 200 breeds of cattle. The zebu cattle shown here have a hump at the shoulders, and a long, narrow face. They were originally from India and are suited to hot climates. Zebu are also used to pull ploughs.

TURKEY

Today's most common breed of turkey is the White Holland, which was developed from the bronze turkey, shown here. Turkeys came originally from North America. When Europeans first travelled to North America in the 16th century, they domesticated (tamed) turkeys and took some back to Europe.

Every year on 25 December, millions of turkeys are eaten in celebration of Christmas.

Male turkeys, or toms, are often twice the weight of the female hens. Young turkeys are called poults.

In many parts of the world, people keep goats for their milk, which is made into cheese and yoghurt.

DUCKS AND GEESE

Waterfowl such as ducks and geese are kept mainly for their meat, especially in Southeast Asia. They also provide fluffy down (underfeathers) for stuffing mattresses, quilts, and clothing. Geese are good guards in the farmyard, as they hiss at strangers. The most common egg-laying waterfowl are Indian runner ducks, khaki campbell ducks, and Emden and Chinese geese.

The Toulouse goose, from France, looks like its wild ancestor, the greylag goose. Adult birds weigh more than 13 kg (28 lb).

The Indian runner duck is kept in large flocks and can move swiftly on its long legs.

GOAT

The goat was one of the first animals to be domesticated. Goats feed on thorny bushes, spiky grasses, and woody stems, and they can leap up easily into the branches of small trees to eat the leaves. Almost 500 million goats are kept worldwide, often in dry and mountainous regions. They are used for their milk, meat, skins, and wool. The main dairy breed is the Anglo-Nubian, which produces up to 660 litres (1,200 pints) of milk each year.

Find out more

ANIMAL SENSES
BIRDS
FARMING
FARMING, HISTORY OF
GRASSLAND WILDLIFE
HORSES, ZEBRAS, AND ASSES
MOUNTAIN WILDLIFE

FARMING

To STOCK THE FOOD SHELVES of supermarkets in the world, farmers make nature and technology work in harmony. They use machinery to plough and reap great fields of wheat; they fertilize and irrigate greenhouses full of vegetables and orchards of fruit; and they rear animals indoors to fatten them quickly. Through this intensive agriculture, Western farmers feed up to ten people from land that once fed one. However, not all the world's farmers can be so productive. Those who have plots on hilly land cannot use machines. Instead they graze a few animals or cultivate the land with inefficient hand tools. Farmers in dry climates must be content with lower yields or choose less productive crops that will tolerate dry soil. And farmers who cannot afford machines and fertilizers are forced to use slower farming methods that have not changed for centuries.

SUBSISTENCE FARMING

In some developing countries, most farming families grow only sufficient food for themselves. This is called subsistence farming. In a good year it provides enough food for all. But a drought or an increase in the population may lead to famine and starvation.

Superwheat

CROPS

Almost all crops that are grown today are the descendants of wild plants. However, special breeding has created varieties that give high harvests. Grain crops such as wheat have especially benefitted. Modern varieties have much larger grains than traditional species. However, this new "superwheat" is not as resistant to disease as other varieties and must be grown carefully.

Ordinary wheat

Ploughing

Planting seeds

Harvesting

Spraying

FARM MACHINERY

Modern grain farming requires special machinery at different times of the year. In spring a plough breaks the soil into furrows for planting. A seed drill puts a measured amount of seed into the prepared soil and covers the seed so that birds do not eat it. A sprayer covers crops with pesticides to kill harmful diseases and pests. Finally a combine harvester cuts the crop and prepares it for storage.

A baler rolls up the straw – the cut stalks of wheat left after the grain has been harvested – and ties it into tight round bundles called bales.

ORGANIC FARMING

Some farmers in Western countries prefer to grow crops and raise animals in a natural or organic way. They do not use artificial pesticides or fertilizers. Organic food is more expensive. Some people believe it is safer and healthier to eat, but not all scientific evidence supports this view.

Organic farmers use natural fertilizers such as seaweed or animal dung to make the soil more productive.

In intensive chicken houses conveyor belts carry food to the hens in the crowded cages, and take away the eggs.

INTENSIVE FARMING

The purpose of intensive farming is to increase the production of crops and animals, and to cut food prices. Food animals such as chickens and pigs are kept indoors in tiny, overcrowded pens. Many people feel this is unnatural and cruel, and prefer to eat only "free-range" animals – animals that have been allowed to move freely in the farm.

Find out more

FARM ANIMALS
FARMING, HISTORY OF

HISTORY OF
FARMING

EARLY FARMING
The first farmers domesticated (tamed) wild animals and kept them in herds to provide meat, milk, hides, and wool. Some people became nomadic herders rather than farmers; they moved their animals continuously in search of new pasture. The picture shown here was painted in a cave in the Sahara Desert in Africa about 8,000 years ago, at a time when the desert was grassland.

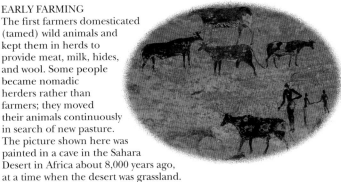

GROWING CROPS and breeding animals for food are among the most important steps ever taken by humankind. Before farming began, people fed themselves by gathering berries and other plant matter and hunting wild animals. People were nomadic – they had to move around to find food. About 12,000 years ago in the Middle East, people discovered they could grow cereal crops, such as wheat. These people were the first farmers. With the start of farming, people began to settle permanently in one place. Villages grew into towns and cities. Farmers produced enough food to support the population, so some people were free to do other jobs such as weaving, and making pottery and tools. Since everyone depended on farming for their food, however, many people died of starvation when the crops failed because of bad weather. Over the centuries people have tried many different ways of producing better crops. In the agricultural revolution of the 1700s, new scientific methods helped overcome the problem of crop failure. Today, farming is a huge international industry.

CROP GROWING
In about 10,000 BCE, farmers in the Middle East began to plant crops to provide food. Cereals, such as wheat, barley, millet, and corn, were the main crops. In the Far East, people first grew rice in about 6,000 BCE.

The huge Berkshire pig was first bred for meat in the 18th century.

IRRIGATION
Farmers need a good supply of water for their crops. In China and other Far Eastern countries, where rice is the main crop, water flows along channels on the terraced hillsides to make the paddies for growing rice.

MEDIEVAL FARMING
In the 11th century the hard horse collar came to Europe from China. It allowed horses, rather than oxen, to pull ploughs. By the 13th century, European farms consisted of open fields and each peasant farmer had a piece of land. Later, much of the land was enclosed with ditches or hedges.

Seed drill

AGRICULTURAL REVOLUTION
During the 18th century, new methods of agricultural production were developed and breeds of livestock were improved, such as the huge Berkshire pig (above). The invention of new machines, such as the seed drill, allowed farmers to produce more crops.

MECHANIZATION
During the 19th century, the development of steam power and, in the 20th century, the combustion engine changed agriculture forever. Tractors replaced horses as the main source of power, and railroads and refrigerated ships meant that food could be transported all over the world.

Steam tractor

Find out more
ENGINES
FARM ANIMALS
FARMING

FILMS

IN A PARIS café in December 1895, people sat down to watch the world's first motion picture. It was shown by two French brothers, Louis and Auguste Lumière, and though it consisted only of a few short, simple scenes, films have been popular ever since. The first films were silent, with titles on the screen to explain the story. A pianist accompanied the film with the right type of music – for example, fast and furious music during a chase scene. The United States took the lead in making films. Soon the public began to select its favourite actors and actresses, and the first film stars were created, such as Rudolph Valentino. In 1927, the first full-length "talkie" – film with sound – was shown, and from then on the public would settle for nothing less. Technical improvements continued. In the United States, Metro-Goldwyn-Mayer and a few other powerful studios made 95 per cent of the films. During the 1950s, television captured people's attention and the film industry went into decline. In recent years films have become popular again. Russia, Germany, France, and Japan have produced films that have influenced filmmaking throughout the world, and there are many national film industries.

CHARLIE CHAPLIN
The British actor Charles Chaplin (1889-1977) created a movie character that touched the hearts of millions: a silent little tramp with a funny walk.

HOLLYWOOD
Southern California, United States, had the ideal climate and scenery for making films. Between 1907 and 1913 a Los Angeles district called Hollywood became the centre of the American film industry. Not all stars were human: King Kong (above) was an animated model.

The senior electrician on the film set is called the gaffer.

Teams of expert makeup artists and dressers prepare an actress or actor for a day's shoot.

A continuity worker makes sure that scenes shot out of order match each other. He or she notes the details of each shot, to ensure that there are no mistakes when the scenes are put in order.

Sound technicians follow the actors with microphones suspended from long poles (booms).

Lighting experts operate huge lamps, to ensure that the light looks as natural as possible in a film. Lighting is needed on location as well as in the studio.

The producer chooses the script, finds financial backing, picks the director and the technical teams, oversees the filming, and organizes publicity.

The art director designs the sets and chooses suitable locations for filming away from the studio.

The cinematographer leads a team which also includes the camera operator and camera assistants, who help with focusing, load magazines, and operate the clapper board. Workers called grips move the camera down tracks or rails for the camera to run along smoothly.

The director guides the actors' performances, the action, and the camera angles, and gives the film its style and character.

FILM SET

Set builders make film sets – from city streets to tropical jungles – inside huge buildings like aircraft hangars, or outdoors on studio grounds. Hundreds of people are involved in getting things ready for the first filming of the day. When all is satisfactory, a red warning light goes on, the studio is told to stand by for a take (an attempt at a scene), sound and cameras roll, and the director shouts "Action!"

Acting on the big screen is very different from the theatre. In close-ups, every movement can be seen, and actors have to play their part with subtle facial expressions. They must also be able to act the story out of sequence.

Stuntmen and stuntwomen take the place of actors in dangerous action. They risk their lives performing stunts, such as falling from a great height, crashing a car, or leaping from a moving train.

SPECIAL EFFECTS

Special effects have created a vast new fantasy world in films. In a technique known as back projection, first used as early as 1913, the cinematographer projected a previously filmed background onto a screen from behind. Actors or models were then filmed in front of the screen, giving the impression that they were actually at that location. Glass screens painted with realistic backgrounds, studio sets wired up with controlled explosions, special smoke and wind machines, and stop-frame animation of models were all used to help bring make-believe scenes to life. As recently as the 1970s, life-like models were still being filmed in a studio to produce gruesome horror effects, such as the shark in *Jaws*, and convincing space battles, such as those in *Star Wars*. Today, almost all of these effects are created digitally using powerful computers.

The actors are filmed against a background of solid blue or green colour.

"BULLET-TIME" SLOW MOTION EFFECT

Each small hole in the scene above conceals a still camera taking a picture of the scene from a different angle. The series of shots is put together in sequence on computer, along with thousands of extra "in-between" frames created in software. The effect is of the camera moving around the action in extreme slow motion.

The actors are superimposed on a new background, and the wires supporting them are erased.

On computer, the coloured background is easily removed using a software filter – sometimes called "Chromakey".

SPIELBERG

Directors often become "stars" in their own right. Director Steven Spielberg was born in 1946. He shot his first film when he was 12 and won a contract with Universal Studios, Hollywood, after leaving college. He became the most successful American director of the 1970s, 1980s, and 1990s with blockbusters such as *Jaws* (1975) and *Jurassic Park* (1993), and Oscar winners such as *Schindler's List* (1993).

DIGITAL TRICKERY

Digital video editing software allows moviemakers to insert actors into almost any environment imaginable. Actors are filmed in front of a green or blue "matte" background, which is later replaced with a new scene – one either filmed elsewhere or created on computer. Real people can also be combined with computer-generated characters and models, as in *Harry Potter*, and whole armies can be created that have an "artificial life" entirely of their own, as in *Lord of the Rings*.

EDITING

The film editor sees that all the shots are in the right order, and that the film lasts the right amount of time. But editing is more complex than that. A good editor can improve the film by cutting out sequences that slow down the action or inserting close-up shots to make a scene more dramatic. Editing is a highly skilled process. In the past it involved physically cutting and taping together pieces of film, though now it is usually done digitally. Director and film editor work together for hours to get the right combination of shots in each scene.

DUBBING

The sound editor is responsible for assembling the soundtrack for the film. This consists of dozens of separate tracks, including all the dialogue, music, sound effects, and background sound. After editing, these sounds have to be balanced against each other and blended in a process called dubbing. Technicians known as mixers watch the film and operate controls on a sound console to get perfect timing and balance of sounds.

FILMS

1895 First public film show held in Paris.

1905 In the United States the first nickelodeon film theatre opens.

1907 Hollywood founded.

1927 *The Jazz Singer* (USA) is the first full-length film with sound.

1929 First Academy Awards.

1928 American cartoonist Walt Disney (1901-66) launches his most popular cartoon character, Mickey Mouse, in the film *Steamboat Willie*.

1935 First full-spectrum Technicolor feature, *Becky Sharp*, is released.

1953 First CinemaScope (wide screen) movie, *The Robe*, released.

1995 *Toy Story*, first completely computer-animated feature film, released.

2003 *Lord of the Rings* trilogy is the first film to win an award for Best Digital Acting Performance.

Find out more

CAMERAS
MUSIC
TELEVISION
THEATRE

FIRE OF LONDON

IN 1666, THE WORST FIRE IN LONDON'S HISTORY raged for five days. It destroyed most of the business part of the city, wiped out 13,200 houses, 87 churches, including St Paul's Cathedral, and dozens of important halls and public buildings. Surprisingly, only nine people were killed. King Charles II and his brother the Duke of York took charge of fighting the fire. They stopped it from spreading further by blowing up houses in its path. Thousands of people were made homeless and had to camp in fields outside the city. However, the fire did destroy the rats that spread the terrible bubonic plague and the unhealthy buildings where the disease thrived. After the fire, the architect Sir Christopher Wren suggested a new layout for the city, but it was rejected by business men. Wren was also responsible for rebuilding St Paul's and more than 50 other churches. Diarist Samuel Pepys left a vivid account of the fire.

A plague doctor

THE GREAT PLAGUE
In 1664-65, bubonic plague, the Black Death, swept through London, killing nearly 70,000 people. Doctors wore leather clothing, gloves, and bird-like masks to protect themselves. The beaks were stuffed with medicinal herbs to prevent the doctors catching the plague.

SAMUEL PEPYS
Pepys (1633-1703) was a civil servant at the Admiralty, and worked hard to make sure that England had a powerful navy. He is famous for his diary, which contains accounts of the Great Plague and the Great Fire. Pepys took the news of the fire to King Charles II, who acted quickly to fight it.

Old St Paul's Cathedral had been on the site since 1087.

Many people took to boats on the river to escape the flames.

Fire burned houses at the northern side of London Bridge.

HOW IT STARTED
The fire began very early on 2 September 1666, in Farriner's baker's shop in Pudding Lane. In those days most of the houses in London were built of wood, and were huddled close together in narrow streets. This allowed the fire to spread quickly. The warehouses on the banks of the River Thames were full of oil, tar, and corn. They too were wooden, and flames soon engulfed them. A Frenchman, Robert Hubert, later confessed to starting the fire. He was hanged.

A flaming urn, made of gilt bronze, tops the Monument.

THE MONUMENT
The government decided to build a memorial to remember the fire. Called the Monument, it was finished in 1677. It is nearly 62 m (203 ft) high, and stands the same distance west of the place where the fire started. It is the world's tallest free-standing stone column. People can climb the 311 steps to a viewing gallery.

The Monument

The River Thames was a barrier that helped stop the spread of fire.

Houses and buildings on the south side of the river escaped fire.

OLD ST PAUL'S
Old St Paul's was the fourth cathedral built on the site. Fire and Viking invaders destroyed the others. By 1664, the cathedral was in a very bad state, and repairs had begun in 1666, supervised by Sir Christopher Wren (1632-1723). When the fire destroyed the old building, Wren designed a new one.

Old St. Paul's Cathedral

Find out more
ARCHITECTURE
BLACK DEATH
STUARTS

FISH

FEATURES OF A FISH

The cod has all the features of a typical fish – a streamlined body for speed, a powerful tail, and fins for balance and steering. The lateral line along the body is a row of sense organs. These organs detect movements made by other creatures in the water.

Eye

Lateral line

Mouth

First dorsal fin

Operculum (gill cover)

Pectoral fin

Pelvic fin

Vent

GILLS

All fish can obtain oxygen by absorbing it from the water through gills – blood-rich structures on each side of the head.

First anal fin

Second anal fin

Caudal fin (tail)

FOR ALMOST 530 MILLION YEARS, fish have swum in the oceans. The first fishes had no scales, fins, or jaws, unlike those we know today. The range of fish that live in our rivers, lakes, and seas is enormous – from the great whale shark to the tiny pygmy goby. In between are thousands of other fish, such as swordfish, sardines, parrotfish, and the comically rounded puffer fish. Some live in freshwater; others in saltwater. Some skitter just below the surface; others dart about in the depths. Despite their wide variety, most fish have a streamlined shape, ideally suited to a watery environment. A covering of scales and slimy mucus protects fish from parasites and helps them slip rapidly through the water. Fish propel themselves along by their tail, and steer and manoeuvre with their fins. Among the thousands of kinds of fish are some extraordinary exceptions. Lampreys have no jaws, mudskippers can skip across mud flats, and catfish can crawl and have no scales at all.

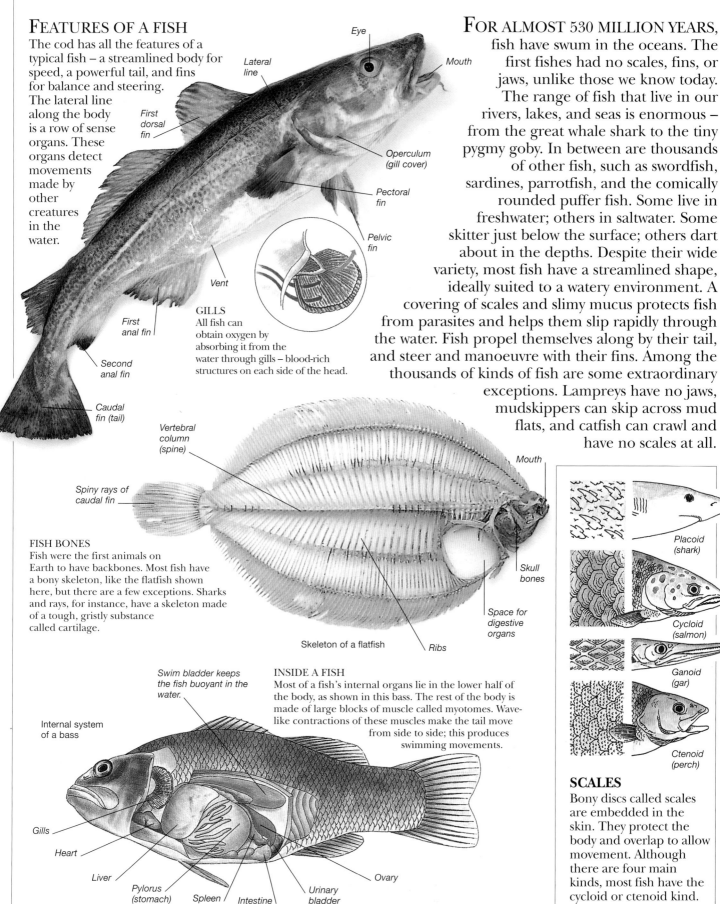

Vertebral column (spine)

Spiny rays of caudal fin

Mouth

Skull bones

FISH BONES

Fish were the first animals on Earth to have backbones. Most fish have a bony skeleton, like the flatfish shown here, but there are a few exceptions. Sharks and rays, for instance, have a skeleton made of a tough, gristly substance called cartilage.

Skeleton of a flatfish

Ribs

Space for digestive organs

Swim bladder keeps the fish buoyant in the water.

Internal system of a bass

INSIDE A FISH

Most of a fish's internal organs lie in the lower half of the body, as shown in this bass. The rest of the body is made of large blocks of muscle called myotomes. Wave-like contractions of these muscles make the tail move from side to side; this produces swimming movements.

Gills

Heart

Liver

Pylorus (stomach)

Spleen

Intestine

Urinary bladder

Ovary

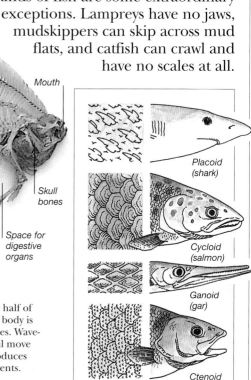

Placoid (shark)

Cycloid (salmon)

Ganoid (gar)

Ctenoid (perch)

SCALES

Bony discs called scales are embedded in the skin. They protect the body and overlap to allow movement. Although there are four main kinds, most fish have the cycloid or ctenoid kind.

STRANGELY SHAPED FISH

Each kind of fish is suited to its own way of life. The long nose of the butterfly fish has a mouth at its tip and so can pick up food from rock crevices. Flying fish use their enlarged fins as "wings" for gliding as they leap out of the water. The bright colours on a lionfish warn other creatures of the deadly poison in its fin spines.

Lionfish

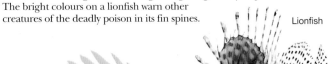

Flying fish

Long-nosed butterfly fish

SCHOOL OF FISH

Small fish often live in large groups called schools, or shoals, twisting and turning together as they search for food. A predator is sometimes so confused by their numbers and quick, darting movements that it cannot single out a fish to attack.

School of sea goldfish on a Red Sea coral reef

FEEDING

Fast predatory fish such as barracudas have long, slim, streamlined bodies and sharp teeth. Slower swimmers usually have more rounded bodies. Despite its shape, the parrotfish is an agile swimmer. It slips through cracks in the rock in search of food.

Parrotfish eating algae on a coral reef

Sea horses

SEA HORSE

Sea horse eggs are deposited by the female into the male's front pouch, where they develop for about four weeks. When the eggs hatch, the young sea horses emerge from the pouch.

Sea horses use their tails to cling to seaweed.

BREEDING

Most fish reproduce by depositing their eggs and sperm in the water, then leave the fertilized eggs to develop into fish. Some fish, such as sticklebacks and bowfins, look after the eggs and the young (called fry) once they have hatched. Other fish, such as some types of sharks, give birth to fully formed young fish after the eggs have developed in the mother's body.

MOUTHBREEDERS

Some cichlid fish, found in African lakes, keep their eggs safe inside their mouths. When the young hatch they swim out, then return to the parent's mouth for safety.

Cichlid fish and young

EUROPEAN EELS

Adult eels lay eggs in the Sargasso Sea. The eggs hatch into larvae which swim north for the next three years. Upon reaching Europe they change into elvers and swim up streams. There, they grow into yellow eels, then adults.

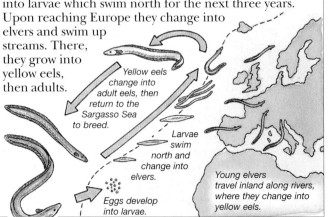

Yellow eels change into adult eels, then return to the Sargasso Sea to breed.

Larvae swim north and change into elvers.

Eggs develop into larvae.

Young elvers travel inland along rivers, where they change into yellow eels.

Royal gramma fish

TROPICAL OCEAN FISH

Fish, especially those from tropical waters, are among the brightest of all animals. Their dazzling colours and lively patterns have many different purposes. They help fish hide from predators among the coral, warn neighbouring fish to keep out of their territory, show other creatures that they are poisonous, or advertise for a mate.

Find out more

ANIMALS
DEEP-SEA WILDLIFE
MIGRATION, ANIMAL
OCEAN WILDLIFE
SEASHORE WILDLIFE

FISHING INDUSTRY

THE WORLD'S RIVERS, seas, and oceans provide one of the most important of all foods. Fish are a rich source of protein and other vital nutrients. It is possible to catch a few fish using just a hook on the end of a piece of string. But to feed large numbers of people, a huge industry exists to catch millions of fish. Japanese fishing boats, for instance, catch more than 16,700 tonnes (16,400 tons) of fish each day. Fishing fleets use different methods to catch these vast numbers of fish, such as nets, traps, and hooks. Some nets are several miles long and can catch more than 100 million fish in one haul. Baskets, boxes, and other traps are left in the sea for shellfish, such as crabs, lobsters, and crayfish. Hooks are arranged in a longline – a single line carrying hundreds of hooks – that is attached to a fishing boat and can trap huge numbers of fish at one time.

WHALING
For two centuries whaling has been a major industry and has made some species of whale almost extinct. As whales come to the surface to breathe, whale hunters shoot them with harpoons – huge explosive arrows fired from guns.

Drift nets are up to 100 km (60 miles) long. They catch fish very effectively, but may also harm other marine life.

FISHING GROUNDS
Fishing boats catch most fish near the coast in the seas above the continental shelf (shown in the dark blue on the map). This shelf is an extension of the continents covered by shallow sea water. Deep-water currents rich in nutrients rise onto the shelf and create good feeding grounds for fish.

At night lights attract fish into the dip nets.

The purse seiner tows its net in a huge circle to enclose the fish.

SEA FISHING
Seines are nets that hang down from the surface. Drawing the net into a circle around a school, or group, of fish forms a huge bag which encloses the catch. Gill nets are long curtains of net which trap fish by the gills. Some gill nets float on the surface as drift nets; others are fixed to the sea bottom with anchors. A trawl is a large net bag towed behind a boat. Dip nets are hung over the side of the fishing boat on a frame. Lifting the frame catches the fish.

Weights keep the mouth of the trawl net open.

FREEZING FISH
Once a fish is dead, its flesh quickly rots. Freezing, canning, drying, smoking, and pickling all slow the decay and preserve the fish. Freezing is the best method. Large fishing boats have freezing plants on board to preserve the catch – the harvest of fish – before returning to port.

FISH FARMS
Not all fish are caught in the wild. Some fish, such as carp, salmon, trout, and shellfish, can be bred in controlled conditions on fish farms. In the United States, fish farmers raise catfish for food. Fish farmers build pens in lakes, ponds, or estuaries (river mouths). They hatch fish from eggs, then keep the fish until they are big enough to sell.

Find out more
FARMING
FISH
OCEANS AND SEAS
OCEAN WILDLIFE

FLIES AND MOSQUITOES

Housefly can walk upside down.

SOME OF THE SMALLEST creatures in the world are the most dangerous to humans. Flies and mosquitoes carry some of the world's most serious diseases. With their habit of sucking blood and scavenging on rubbish, many of these insects spread cholera, malaria, and yellow fever. There are about 120,000 kinds of fly, including bluebottles, horseflies, fruit flies, tiny gnats, and almost invisible midges. We call many small, winged insects flies, but the only true flies are those with two functional wings; they belong to the insect group *Diptera*. All flies lay eggs. The eggs hatch into larvae called grubs or maggots. The maggots feed and grow into pupae or chrysalises, from which the adult flies finally emerge. Despite their unpopularity with humans, flies play a vital role in nature. They pollinate flowers and recycle nutrients as they scavenge, and they are a source of food for many larger animals.

Housefly has excellent eyesight and sponge-like mouthparts.

Eggs

Larva (maggot)

The bluebottle, or blowfly, lays thousands of eggs in dustbins and on meat. Within just a few weeks these eggs produce thousands more flies.

Housefly feeding on rotting meat

Compound eye

Antenna

Tiny hairs and hooks on feet enable fly to walk on the ceiling.

Wing

MOSQUITO

The mosquito has needle-shaped mouthparts that pierce the skin to suck the blood of humans, horses, and other animals. If a female *Anopheles* mosquito bites a person with malaria, it takes in blood infected with the microscopic organisms that cause this disease. When the mosquito goes on to bite another victim, the organisms pass into that person's blood, and so the disease spreads. The map below shows those parts of the world where malaria is most severe.

FLIES AND DISEASE

Houseflies, bluebottles, and similar flies feed on and lay their eggs in rotting matter, including rubbish and excrement. Their mouthparts and feet pick up bacteria, or germs, which rub off when they settle on our food, dishes, and kitchen equipment. The illnesses which spread in this way range from minor stomach upsets to deadly infections such as typhoid.

North America

Asia

Africa

South America

Australia

Areas where malaria occurs

Malaria is one of the most serious and widespread diseases. It kills about one million people each year.

Hoverfly's wing tips make a figure-of-eight pattern with each wing beat.

HOVERFLY

The hoverfly is one of the most expert fliers. It can hover perfectly still, even in a wind, then dart straight up, down, sideways, or backwards. Tiny ball-and-stick structures behind the wings, called halteres, rotate rapidly and act as stabilizers during flight.

LIFE CYCLE OF A DRONE FLY
The drone fly is a kind of hoverfly. It resembles a bee in appearance and makes a low droning sound in flight. After mating, the female lays her eggs near a puddle, a polluted pond, or other stagnant (non-moving) water. The larvae, known as rat-tailed maggots, live in the water, breathing through the long tail which acts like a snorkel. The rat-tailed maggots wriggle onto drier soil before pupating. When the adults emerge from the pupal cases, they fly off to feed on pollen and nectar from flowers.

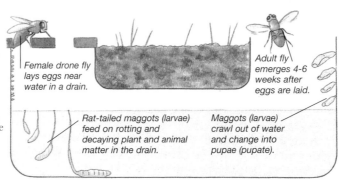

Female drone fly lays eggs near water in a drain.

Adult fly emerges 4-6 weeks after eggs are laid.

Rat-tailed maggots (larvae) feed on rotting and decaying plant and animal matter in the drain.

Maggots (larvae) crawl out of water and change into pupae (pupate).

Find out more
ANIMALS
DISEASE
FLIGHT, ANIMAL
INSECTS

ANIMAL
FLIGHT

BIRDS, BATS, AND INSECTS are the only animals that truly fly. Other animals, such as flying squirrels, flying fish, and flying lizards, swoop or glide but cannot climb upwards into the air under their own power. Life in the air has several advantages for flying animals – some birds, such as hawks, can hunt their prey in midair; other birds can quickly escape from their predators. Birds are also able to migrate very long distances to find more suitable feeding and breeding areas in a cold season – the Arctic tern, for example, migrates about 18,000 km (11,000 miles) from the North Pole to the South Pole every year. Another bird, the swift, spends much of its life in the air, landing only to nest. A swift eats and drinks on the wing for nine months of the year. Birds, bats, and insects are also able to find food on land quickly and efficiently – a hummingbird hovers to gather nectar, a fruit bat flies into a tree to feed on fruit, and a dragonfly swoops over a pond to catch small flies. All flying animals from bees to buzzards need plenty of food to provide them with the energy to take to the air. Animals first began to fly about 300 million years ago, when Earth's prehistoric coal swamps were becoming overcrowded with all kinds of creatures. Through evolution, special features began to develop, such as a flap of skin on the body for gliding. In order to fly, an animal needs a lightweight body and strong muscles with which to flap its wings. Birds have hollow bones to save weight when they are in flight, so that a huge bird such as the golden eagle weighs less than 4 kg (9 lb).

ARCHAEOPTERYX
One of the first birds known to have existed is called *Archaeopteryx*. Fossil remains date back 150 million years. *Archaeopteryx* could glide and fly through the air.

Elastic fibres allow the wings to shrink so the bat can fold them neatly.

SOOTY TERN
The sooty tern lives on the wing for up to 10 years. It returns to the ground only to breed.

WINGS
The wings of a flying animal are light so that they can be flapped easily. They are broad and flat, to push the air downwards and give lift. Wings must also be flexible for control in the air. An insect's wings are made of a thin membrane stiffened by tube-like veins. A bird's wings have bones and muscles at the front; feathers form the rest of the surface. A bat's wings consist of a thin layer of muscles and tough fibres sandwiched between two layers of skin that are supported by bones.

Main bones in the wing

Skin stretches between the forearm and finger bones.

Powerful wing-flapping pectoral muscles are in the bat's chest.

Bat

Feathers near the wing root shape the wing smoothly into the body.

Flight feathers are light and stiff, with strong shafts and large, smooth vanes.

Covert feathers are at the front of the wing. They are small and packed closely together, to give a smooth edge.

Wing of a kestrel

Primary flight feathers help to reduce turbulence.

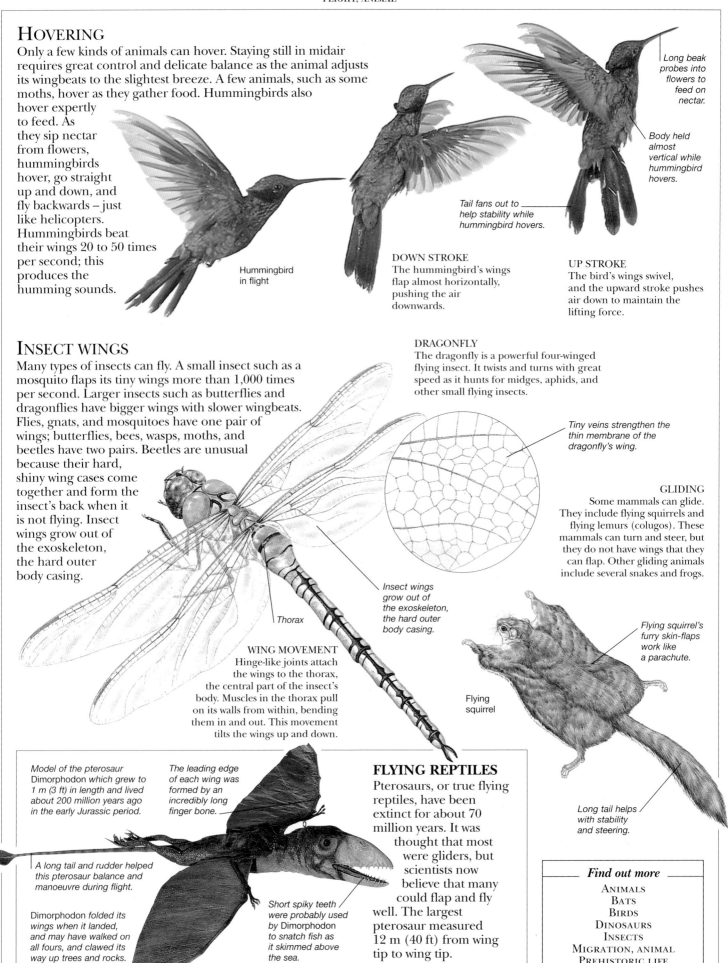

HOVERING

Only a few kinds of animals can hover. Staying still in midair requires great control and delicate balance as the animal adjusts its wingbeats to the slightest breeze. A few animals, such as some moths, hover as they gather food. Hummingbirds also hover expertly to feed. As they sip nectar from flowers, hummingbirds hover, go straight up and down, and fly backwards – just like helicopters. Hummingbirds beat their wings 20 to 50 times per second; this produces the humming sounds.

Long beak probes into flowers to feed on nectar.

Body held almost vertical while hummingbird hovers.

Tail fans out to help stability while hummingbird hovers.

Hummingbird in flight

DOWN STROKE
The hummingbird's wings flap almost horizontally, pushing the air downwards.

UP STROKE
The bird's wings swivel, and the upward stroke pushes air down to maintain the lifting force.

INSECT WINGS

Many types of insects can fly. A small insect such as a mosquito flaps its tiny wings more than 1,000 times per second. Larger insects such as butterflies and dragonflies have bigger wings with slower wingbeats. Flies, gnats, and mosquitoes have one pair of wings; butterflies, bees, wasps, moths, and beetles have two pairs. Beetles are unusual because their hard, shiny wing cases come together and form the insect's back when it is not flying. Insect wings grow out of the exoskeleton, the hard outer body casing.

DRAGONFLY
The dragonfly is a powerful four-winged flying insect. It twists and turns with great speed as it hunts for midges, aphids, and other small flying insects.

Tiny veins strengthen the thin membrane of the dragonfly's wing.

Thorax

Insect wings grow out of the exoskeleton, the hard outer body casing.

WING MOVEMENT
Hinge-like joints attach the wings to the thorax, the central part of the insect's body. Muscles in the thorax pull on its walls from within, bending them in and out. This movement tilts the wings up and down.

GLIDING
Some mammals can glide. They include flying squirrels and flying lemurs (colugos). These mammals can turn and steer, but they do not have wings that they can flap. Other gliding animals include several snakes and frogs.

Flying squirrel's furry skin-flaps work like a parachute.

Flying squirrel

Long tail helps with stability and steering.

Model of the pterosaur Dimorphodon which grew to 1 m (3 ft) in length and lived about 200 million years ago in the early Jurassic period.

The leading edge of each wing was formed by an incredibly long finger bone.

A long tail and rudder helped this pterosaur balance and manoeuvre during flight.

Dimorphodon folded its wings when it landed, and may have walked on all fours, and clawed its way up trees and rocks.

Short spiky teeth were probably used by Dimorphodon to snatch fish as it skimmed above the sea.

FLYING REPTILES

Pterosaurs, or true flying reptiles, have been extinct for about 70 million years. It was thought that most were gliders, but scientists now believe that many could flap and fly well. The largest pterosaur measured 12 m (40 ft) from wing tip to wing tip.

FLOWERS AND HERBS

Stamen (male parts)

Stigma receives pollen

Style

Anther with pollen

Petals are brightly coloured to attract insects in search of nectar.

Ovary contains ovules (seeds).

Filament

Sepals protect inner parts of flower.

The flower head contains the reproductive parts of the plant – as shown by this pink lily flower.

THE EXQUISITE BEAUTY, colour, and perfume of flowers have inspired artists and poets for centuries. Flowers are among the most brightly coloured of all living things. They include sun-loving desert marigolds, hardy poppies in the snowy Arctic, tropical orchids, and cultivated garden roses, as well as some tiny inconspicuous flowers. Without the thousands of different flowers and herbs that grow on the Earth, bees could not make honey, butterflies and hummingbirds would have no food, we would have no flowerbeds, and perfume would have no fragrance. For most of us, the word "flower" describes any flowering plant that is particularly colourful or pretty. To the botanist, who studies plants, however, a flower refers strictly to the reproductive part of a plant – its bloom or blossom. The word "herb" is an everyday name we give to smaller, less colourful flowering plants whose leaves and blossoms have a strong, pleasant scent and taste.

FLOWER STRUCTURE

Sepals are usually green and scaly, and protect the flower in its bud. They often drop off once the flower has blossomed. Petals may be large and colourful to attract bees and butterflies. The male cells lie in the pollen grains, contained in the anthers. The female cells are inside the ovary, below the stigma and style.

HERBS

Plants known as herbs usually have green, juicy stems, unlike trees and shrubs, which have hard, woody stems. Some herbs and other flowering plants are described as annuals because they grow, flower, produce seeds, and die all in one year. Others are known as biennials because their life cycle takes two years; perennials live for an indefinite number of years.

Thyme is a fragrant addition to meats, as a garnish, and for mouth, throat, and chest illnesses.

HERB GARDEN
Tending the herb garden was once an important part of daily life because people relied on natural products which they grew themselves. Herbs are used to add flavour to food, scent the air, help us relax, and treat illnesses. Many of our modern medicines contain herbs; peppermint, for example, is used in many anti-indigestion pills. Herbal oils, known as essential oils, are extracted from herbs and used in the production of perfume and bath oils.

Basil is popular in Mediterranean cooking and is also used as an insect repellent.

Parsley is a garnish, an ingredient in sauces, and a treatment for urinary illness.

Sage flavours many dishes, from pork to poultry, and is used to treat sore throats and colds.

Rosemary is a companion to lamb dishes, and brewed in tea for headaches and upset stomachs.

Bay adds flavour to casseroles and stocks.

Oregano (wild marjoram) is used for meat, stuffing, and pizza, and to aid digestion.

Tarragon is often used in French cooking.

Mint is used to make tea and mint jelly; it also clears a stuffy nose and eases indigestion.

POLLINATION

To produce a seed, the male cell in a pollen grain must fertilize a female cell in the ovule. For this to happen the pollen must travel from its anther to the female stigma. In some flowers, the pollen is small and light, with wings, and is blown from one flower to another by the wind.

Wild dog rose

Cultivated tea rose

BEES AND FLOWERS

Bees help pollination. As a bee feeds on nectar and pollen, more pollen inside the flower sticks to the bee's legs and body and is carried by the bee to the next flower, where it pollinates the female parts.

NECTAR

Butterflies, moths, bats, and birds feed on the sweet, energy-rich nectar inside each flower. Bees convert nectar into honey in the beehive.

HORTICULTURE

From the beginnings of civilization, people have cultivated flowers for their scent and colour. Today's garden roses have been bred from wild ancestors so that they have larger, more numerous, and more colourful petals, sweeter scents, and a longer flowering time. The art of gardening is called horticulture.

BIRD-OF-PARADISE FLOWER

The bird-of-paradise plant comes originally from riverbanks in southern Africa and is now grown in many parks and gardens. Each plant has brilliant orange flowers which form a shape that looks like the head and beak of a bird of paradise. The bird-of-paradise flowers rise one after the other from a long, stiff, green-pink casing.

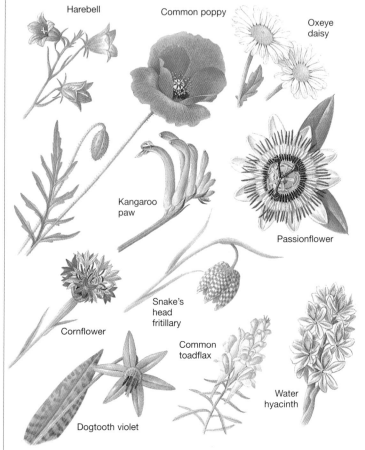

Harebell

Common poppy

Oxeye daisy

Kangaroo paw

Passionflower

Cornflower

Snake's head fritillary

Common toadflax

Water hyacinth

Dogtooth violet

PERFUME

A flower's smell attracts butterflies, bees, and people too. Lily of the valley and rose are used in the manufacture of perfumes and soaps.

Lily of the valley flowers have a sweet scent. Their leaves are scented too.

WILD FLOWERS AND CONSERVATION

Many wild flowers are in danger of extinction. Marshes are drained, and forests are felled for farmland and buildings, so the flowers that grow there are destroyed. Rare and beautiful blooms are at risk because they are dug up illegally by plant collectors. To save rare flowers, the places where they grow must be protected. As forests are cut down, thousands of flowers are disappearing even before they are known to science.

Find out more

BEES AND WASPS
CONSERVATION
and endangered species
FRUITS AND SEEDS
PLANTS

FOOTBALL AND RUGBY

AT PACKED STADIUMS in almost every country, football and rugby fans cheer the skills of their favourite players. Association football (soccer) is the most popular spectator sport in the world, and more people play it than any other team sport. More than 200 countries play soccer at international level. Other forms of football are popular, but less widespread. Soccer is played with a round ball, but rugby football and American football is played with an oval ball. American football is the top US spectator sport, with professional and college-level games drawing huge crowds. Some European countries have taken up American football, and Canadians play a similar sport. Rugby players compete mainly in Britain, France, Australia, Italy, New Zealand, and South Africa. Other types of football include rugby league, Gaelic football, played in Ireland, and Australian Rules football.

A player dives for the ball in American football

ANCIENT FOOTBALL
Mob football was the ancestor of modern football. It was a violent game played in England, with few rules, and was banned in the 14th century. It was not until late in the 19th century that the modern form of the game was played.

AMERICAN FOOTBALL
In American football, players score points by crossing the ball over their opponents' goal line for a touchdown (six points), or kicking it between the goalposts for a field goal (three points). Each team has 11 players, selected from a squad of up to 45.

SOCCER
In soccer, the most popular form of football, two teams of 11 aim to send the ball into the opposing goal with their feet or head. Only one team player, the goalkeeper, is allowed to touch the ball with his or her hands.

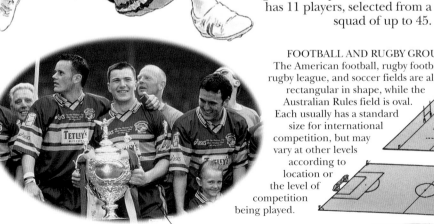

COMPETITION SOCCER
The best known soccer tournament is the FIFA World Cup, held every four years. Other prestigious football competitions generate similar interest – in particular, the European Championship.

The Leeds Rhinos celebrate winning a national cup challenge.

FOOTBALL AND RUGBY GROUNDS
The American football, rugby football, rugby league, and soccer fields are all rectangular in shape, while the Australian Rules field is oval. Each usually has a standard size for international competition, but may vary at other levels according to location or the level of competition being played.

American football
The American football field has lines across its width every 4.5 m (5 yards).

Rugby football and rugby league
The rugby field has H-shaped goal posts.

Soccer
The goalposts support a crossbar, and have a net at the back to catch the ball once a goal is scored.

Australian Rules
Goals kicked between the inner posts on an Australian Rules field score the most points.

Nou Camp, the home stadium of the Barcelona football team.

STADIUMS
Important football and rugby games take place in stadiums. In recent years, stadiums have changed a lot. Fans used to stand on terraces, but these have now been replaced by seats, and stadiums have better facilities, access for disabled supporters, and restaurants. Some stadiums have roofs that can be pulled across.

RULES OF THE GAME
Each type of rugby and football has different rules. A football game is ruled by a referee and two referee's assistants (linesmen). In rugby, the referee is supported by two touch judges. The referee has a whistle and the assistants and touch judges have flags to signal when a rule has been broken. A yellow card is shown as a warning; a red card means the player is sent off.

Red and yellow cards

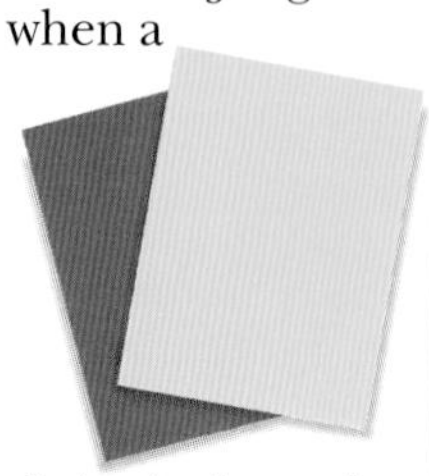

RUGBY
In 1823, schoolboy William Webb Ellis invented rugby when he picked up a football during a game and ran with it. Today, there are two forms of the game: Rugby Union, played between two teams of 15, and Rugby League, played between two teams of 13. Players run with the ball, kick it, or use their hands, but must always pass backwards.

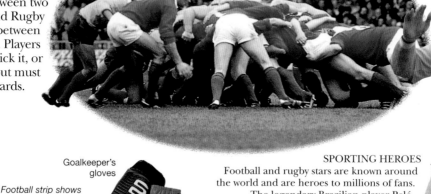
Rugby Union players form a scrum, each team trying to gain possession of the ball.

Goalkeeper's gloves

Football strip shows which team the player is on.

SPORTING HEROES
Football and rugby stars are known around the world and are heroes to millions of fans. The legendary Brazilian player Pelé (b. 1940), considered the best footballer ever, was the star of four World Cup competitions. Australian Rugby Union player David Campese (b.1962) won 101 international caps in a 14-year career.

David Campese

Rugby boot

Shin pads

Gum shield

Edson Arantes do Nascimento, better known to the world as Pelé.

Football

MINERVA SUPREME

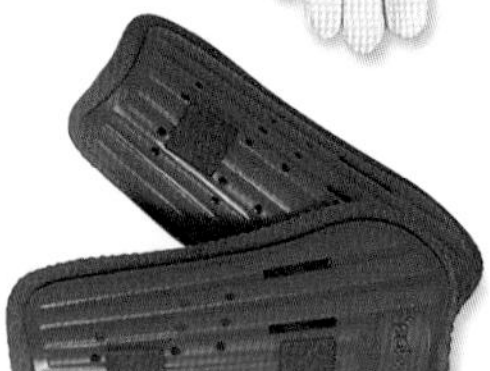

Rugby ball

Shin pads under socks protect from injury.

Players may wear trainers to practise.

EQUIPMENT
All you need to play a basic game of football or rugby is a ball, but modern equipment incorporates high-tech materials to help and protect players. Boots have studs to stop players slipping. Gloves with palm grips help football goalkeepers to catch the ball. Rugby balls have a non-slip covering to prevent players from dropping them during passing.

Find out more
OLYMPIC GAMES
SPORTS
WALES

FORCE AND MOTION

WHAT IS IT THAT MAKES objects move? Why does a boat float? How does a magnet work? Left to itself, any object would remain still, but when it is pushed or pulled, it begins to move. Something that pushes or pulls is called a force. Forces often produce motion, or movement. For example, an engine produces a force that pushes a car forward. There are several different kinds of forces. A magnet produces a magnetic force which pulls pieces of iron towards it, and a rubber band produces an elastic force when you stretch it. Liquids produce forces too. A boat floats because of the force of water pushing upwards on the hull. And a drop of water holds together because of a force called surface tension which makes all liquids seem as though they have an elastic skin around them. From the smallest particle inside an atom to the largest galaxy, the whole universe is held together by powerful forces. One of these forces is gravity, which holds us onto the surface of the Earth.

CHANGING DIRECTION

When you move in a circle, on a fairground ride for example, a constant force is needed to change the direction of your motion. This force acts towards the centre of the circle. On the ride shown above, the force comes from the tension in the ropes that support the seats.

ACCELERATION

The action of a force produces motion, making an object accelerate (speed up). For example, the force produced by the engine makes a ship accelerate. The stronger the force, the greater the acceleration.

INERTIA

It takes a strong force to start a heavier (more massive) object moving. In the same way, a strong force is needed to make it slow down and stop. This reluctance to start or stop moving is called inertia. The heavier the object, the greater its inertia.

Water and air resist motion, producing a force called drag. A small boat accelerates easily and soon reaches its cruising speed. But, drag increases as speed increases. When drag force balances the driving force of the engines, speed stays constant.

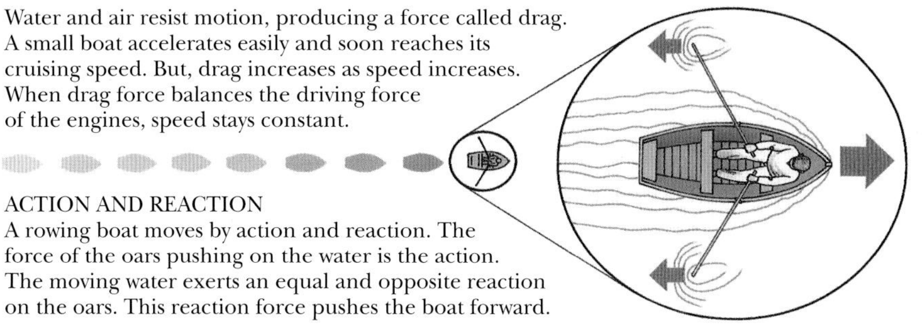

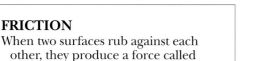

ACTION AND REACTION

A rowing boat moves by action and reaction. The force of the oars pushing on the water is the action. The moving water exerts an equal and opposite reaction on the oars. This reaction force pushes the boat forward.

NEWTON'S LAWS OF MOTION

In 1687, the English scientist Isaac Newton (1642-1727) published his three laws of motion. The first law explains that an object stays at rest or moves at a constant speed unless a force pushes or pulls it. The second law explains how force overcomes inertia and causes acceleration. The third law explains that when a force (or action) pushes one way, an equal force (or reaction) always pushes in the opposite direction.

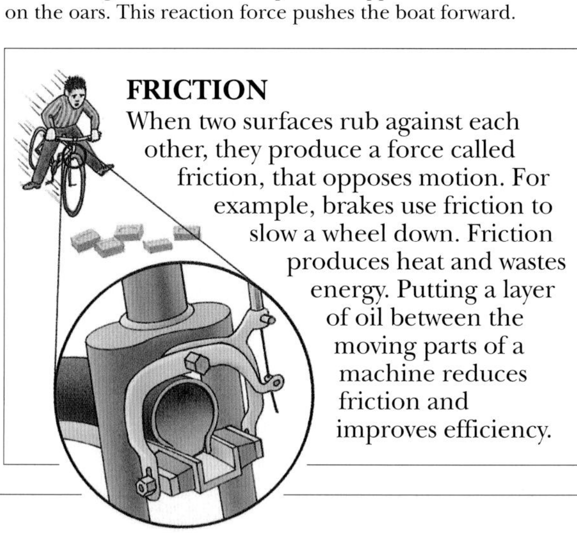

In an arch bridge, the piers (ends of the bridge) support the weight of the arch.

FRICTION

When two surfaces rub against each other, they produce a force called friction, that opposes motion. For example, brakes use friction to slow a wheel down. Friction produces heat and wastes energy. Putting a layer of oil between the moving parts of a machine reduces friction and improves efficiency.

STATIC FORCES

When two teams in a tug-of-war pull equally hard on the rope, neither team moves. This is because the forces produced by the teams balance exactly. Forces that balance and produce no movement are called static forces. A bridge stays up because of the balance of static forces. Its weight pushing down is balanced by parts of the structure pushing up.

Find out more

ATOMS AND MOLECULES
BRIDGES
GRAVITY
MAGNETISM
PHYSICS

FOREST WILDLIFE

This map shows the main forest areas of the world.

North America
Europe
Asia
Africa
South America
Australia

☐ Temperate forest
☐ Coniferous forest
☐ Tropical forest

TREES ARE THE MOST IMPORTANT plants in a forest. They provide all kinds of animals, including monkeys, squirrels, and parrots, with food, homes, and escape routes from predators. The most common tree in any kind of forest often gives the forest its name, from the pine forests in the cold north, to the steamy teak forests in the tropical regions.

A temperate forest consists of different layers of vegetation. The forest floor is covered with leaf litter. Here, parts of trees and other plants rot into the soil, helped by the millipedes, worms, and other small creatures that feed on them. The next layer of the forest is called the herb layer. It consists of small flowers and ferns that grow wherever enough sunlight filters through the trees. Bushes, shrubs, and young trees make up the under-storey of the forest. Next is a layer of tall tree trunks, laced with trailing vines and creepers. The uppermost part of the forest is called the canopy. Leaves grow in the sunlight; insects, birds, and bats pollinate the flowers; and fruit ripens to feed a host of creatures.

LONG-EARED OWL
The long-eared owl swoops silently among the trees at twilight and during the night. These owls roost by day in a tree, and their mottled brown plumage provides good camouflage. The tufts on the feathers on this owl's head look like long ears – hence the name.

WOLVERINE
The wolverine of northern forests is an exceptionally strong animal for its size. It tackles animal prey much larger than itself and also eats carrion (dead animals), fruit, and berries. The wolverine is nicknamed the "glutton" because of its large appetite.

CONIFEROUS FORESTS
Pines and firs make up coniferous forests. These trees are evergreen – they keep their leaves all year, providing shelter for animals. The leaves are very tough, and only a few animals can eat and digest them. A few types of conifer, such as the larches, lose their leaves in autumn.

BROAD-LEAVED FORESTS
The trees in a broad-leaved forest are called deciduous trees because their leaves drop off in the autumn, to be replaced by new leaves the next year. These trees blossom in the spring, which is the main animal breeding time. The new shoots provide food for animals. In the autumn, animals feed on the fruit, nuts, and berries of these trees, so they can survive the winter.

Ferns, such as bracken, grow quickly and rapidly cover clearings. Bracken is common on every continent except Antarctica. It spreads by sending out branching underground stems.

Bluebells are one of the spring woodland flowers. Some bluebells have pink flowers; others have white ones.

Wood anemone

ROE DEER
The roe deer's reddish brown coat blends in well with the bracken where it lives. It lives alone for most of the year, feeding at twilight on the buds, shoots, and leaves of trees and shrubs.

Several heavy-bodied, strong-legged birds live in the forest, including pheasants such as the blue peacock shown here. These birds can fly but they often avoid danger by running into the dense forest undergrowth.

CONSERVATION
As the forests are cut down or burned, animals lose their homes. Tree-living creatures such as this American uakari monkey are most at risk. These monkeys depend on the flowers and fruit from the large old trees in rain forests. Worldwide conservation organizations are trying to stop the destruction of the rain forests in order to save monkeys and thousands of other creatures.

TANAGER
The paradise tanager is a noisy, active bird that lives high up in the rain forest canopy. Paradise tanagers keep their bright plumage all year and flutter from tree to tree in search of insects and ripe fruit.

TROPICAL FORESTS
In tropical forests, the climate is much the same all year round. High temperatures and heavy rainfall make tropical rain forests some of the richest places for wildlife. There are many more species of trees than in any other kind of forest, and thousands more kinds of animals.

SLOTH
Few animals move more slowly than the sloths of Central and South America. They hang from branches with their curved claws and eat leaves. Tiny green simple plants called algae grow on their coats, and this helps camouflage the sloths among the trees.

PARROT
The male and female eclectus parrots shown here are so differently coloured that for many years people believed they were two different species of birds. These parrots live in the forests of New Guinea and Australia. Like all parrots, they have huge bills for cracking seeds.

TOUCANET
With its large, light bill, the toucanet is an excellent berry picker. Its bright colours help it advertise for a mate in the breeding season. There are 42 kinds of toucanets, and they are all found in tropical South America. Toucanets nest in tree holes and eat birds' eggs and nestlings, fruit, insects, frogs, and lizards.

Several kinds of frogs, lizards, snakes, and squirrels have evolved, or developed, ways of gliding through the air from a high branch to escape from predators or to reach food. The gliding snake flattens its ribs as it leaps, to make a streamlined ribbon shape.

Atlas moth resting on a bromeliad flower

POISON ARROW FROG
It is so damp in rain forests that frogs spend their lives in the trees and do not need to find water elsewhere. Frogs lay their eggs, or spawn, in pools of rain which collect on leaves, fungi, and in flowers such as bromeliads, which grow on trees. Poison Arrow frogs live in the rain forests of South America. Their bright colours warn predators of the deadly poison in their skin.

ATLAS MOTH
The atlas moth is one of the largest moths in the world, with a wingspan of 30 cm (12 in). Today, atlas moths are rare. In the past, people killed thousands of them simply for their butterfly collections.

LEMUR
There are 19 different kinds of lemur. These mammals are related to monkeys, and they live in trees in Madagascar, an island off the east coast of Africa. Mouse lemurs weigh only 60 gm (2 oz).

Ground ginger is a spice made from the root of the ginger plant, which came originally from the forests of Asia.

Leaf roller ants curl up leaves on the forest floor and join the edges into a tube to make a nesting site.

Find out more
ANIMALS
BIRDS
BUTTERFLIES AND MOTHS
CONSERVATION
and endangered species
FROGS AND OTHER AMPHIBIANS

FOSSILS

THE FIRST PLANTS, the earliest animals, the beginnings of human life – we know about prehistoric times because of fossils. Preserved or mineralised for thousands or even millions of years, fossils may comprise, for example, parts of animals, moulds, footprints, and burrows. By studying fossils, we can learn what ancient creatures and plants looked like and how they lived. Most fossils are of plants and animals that lived in water. When the living plant or animal died, its soft parts rotted away, leaving the hard pieces such as bones or leaf veins. Gradually, layers of mud piled up and squeezed the remains of the plant or animal at great pressure. Slowly the mud, bones, and other remains fossilized, or turned to rock, in the place where they lay underground. Over many thousands of years, the movements of the Earth twisted and buckled the rocks, lifting the fossils closer to the surface of the soil. Sun, rain, and wind wore away the rocks and exposed the fossil.

Fossil collecting is a hobby that anyone can enjoy. You can find fossils in rocks, on beaches, and in quarries.

AMMONITE
Some of the most common fossils are the shells of sea creatures called ammonites. Ammonites were related to squid and octopuses. They were very widespread about 250 million years ago. The smallest ammonites measured less than 2 cm (1 in) across; the largest measured about 2.5 m (8 ft) across. Ammonites died out with the dinosaurs about 65 million years ago.

Fossil of a fish called Sparnodus – an ancestor of the sea bream

Fin on back for steering and stability

Backbone

Long jaws and short, sharp teeth

Large eye socket

Powerful two-lobed tail

Ribs

Front paddle for steering

Rear paddles

TYPES OF FOSSILS

When rock-forming minerals slowly replace the original parts of a dead creature or plant, they make a mineralized fossil. Sometimes the parts of a creature or plant rot away after being buried, leaving a hole in the rock; this is called a mould fossil. If the hole fills up with rock minerals, it becomes a cast fossil. The fossilized signs of animals, such as footprints, droppings, and tracks, are called trace fossils.

Mineralized fossil of a poplar leaf, 25 million years old

Cast fossil of a creature called a trilobite, which lived in the sea

ICHTHYOSAUR

Sometimes the outline of an animal's skin is preserved as well as its bones. This happened to the ichthyosaur shown above – a sea reptile from about 150 million years ago. The ichthyosaur looked like a dolphin, so it probably led a life similar to that of dolphins. The outline of this fossil shows a fin on the back and a two-lobed tail. The dozens of sharp teeth in the long jaws tell us that this animal grabbed fish and other slippery prey.

The word fossil *literally means "dug up". People who study fossils are called palaeontologists.*

Find out more
DINOSAURS
EVOLUTION
PREHISTORIC LIFE
ROCKS AND MINERALS

FRANCE

THE LARGEST COUNTRY in western Europe is France – a land of green, open spaces dotted with picturesque towns and small cities. Its many fine old country palaces, or châteaux, are reminders of France's long history. But it is a modern nation too, with flourishing industries. France is also one of the leading countries in the European Union (EU), the organization that promotes political and economic union between the member states. Northern France has cool, wet weather. The south, with its Mediterranean coast, is drier and warmer. Rolling hills rise from the coasts and valleys, providing good farmland. The rugged hills of the Massif Central occupy the middle of the country. The mountains of the Pyrenees and the Alps line the southwest and eastern borders. France also includes the Mediterranean island of Corsica, and some islands thousands of kilometres away in the Pacific Ocean and the Caribbean Sea. A democratically elected government and president rule France from Paris.

France shares its long eastern border with Italy, Switzerland, Germany, Luxembourg, and Belgium. Spain is to the south. The south of France lies on the Mediterranean Sea coast, and the Atlantic Ocean is to the west.

Workers on small, family-run estates may still pick grapes by hand. Many people spend their holidays grapepicking, but it is hard work.

Even the smaller winemakers now use some modern equipment, such as stainless-steel fermentation vats.

WINEMAKING

France produces about a fifth of the world's wine. Many famous wines are named after French regions, such as Champagne and Bordeaux. Most French wine comes from co-operatives – local groups of farms that share wine-producing and bottling facilities. Some wine, however, is still made on the small estates attached to the old châteaux. The grapes are picked in the early autumn. Pressing the grapes extracts the juice, which then ferments (reacts with yeast) in large vats to produce the alcohol and the delicious taste of the wine. Only when this process is complete can the wine be bottled.

The Louvre, in Paris, is one of the world's most famous art galleries. The glass pyramid was added in 1989.

MARSEILLES

France's biggest seaport is Marseilles, on the Mediterranean coast. The warm climate of southern France makes possible the lively, outdoor lifestyle of the city. There is a long history of trade with the rest of the Mediterranean. Marseilles has a large Arab population, mainly from North Africa.

PARIS

People have lived on the river Seine where Paris now stands since ancient times. Paris is the capital of France. France has a population of more than 62 million; one fifth live in and around Paris. It is one of Europe's great cities, with wide, tree-lined streets called boulevards, and many famous monuments and museums. The city of today was largely replanned and rebuilt during the 19th century.

EIFFEL TOWER

Built to impress visitors to the Paris Exhibition of 1889, the Eiffel Tower was originally meant to be a temporary structure. It was designed by the French engineer Alexandre-Gustave Eiffel. Eiffel was internationally famous for his bridge and aqueduct designs. The tower is built of steel girders weighing 7,000 tonnes (7,700 US tons), and 2.5 million rivets hold it together. It reaches a height of 322 m (1,050 ft) and up until the erection of the Empire State Building in New York in 1931, it was the tallest building in the world. Visitors can reach its various levels by lift or by climbing hundreds of steps.

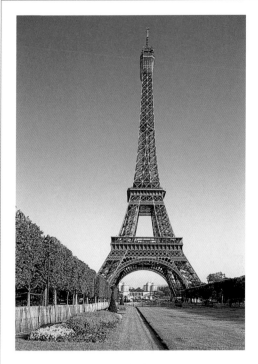

When it was first built in the 19th century, the Eiffel Tower was fiercely criticized. It has now become the symbol of Paris and a much loved feature of the city.

MONACO

A tiny country on the Côte d'Azur, Monaco lies in southeastern France. The heart of the country is the sophisticated city of Monte Carlo, famous for its casinos and motor racing Grand Prix. Monaco is an independent principality, ruled for much of its history by the Grimaldi family (above). Only a small part of the population is originally from Monaco; more than half the people are citizens of France. They are drawn by the lenient tax laws and high standard of living, and earn more per capita than any other country in the world.

Normandy is a region of lowland, gentle hills, and farmland, and is especially known for its hedgerows.

NORMANDY

The region of Normandy lies between Paris and the English Channel. Normandy is a farming area, known throughout France for its dairy products and its apples. By grazing their cattle in the orchards, many local farmers get double use from the land. They sell the apples as dessert fruit, or turn them into cider and a delicious apple brandy called calvados. Cream from the Normandy cattle makes some of France's most famous cheeses, including Brie and Camembert.

LOIRE RIVER

The valley of the Loire river is famous for its beautiful castles, called châteaux, such as this one at Gien. Kings, nobles, or wealthy landowners built the châteaux as their homes. They often chose a site on high ground and surrounded the château with a moat, which made it easy to defend the château from attackers. The Loire valley is also an important wine-producing area.

TGV design has evolved over the years. This train has a sharp aerodynamic nose to increase its speed.

TRANSPORT

The French are not only pioneers of aviation – they co-built Concorde – they also lead the world in high-speed train technology. With speeds of up to 300 km/h (185 mph) the French TGV (Trains à Grande Vitesse) is the world's fastest train. The first TGV line, from Paris to Lyon, was opened in 1983. TGV lines have since been built to Belgium, Italy, and Spain. The Channel Tunnel links France to the United Kingdom.

FRENCH CUISINE

French cooks are considered among the best in the world. There are numerous good restaurants, even in quite small towns, and the quality of ordinary daily food is very high. Food specialists who take great pride in their work produce outstanding cooked meats, pastries, and bread, including the famous stick-shaped baguette. French cheeses, such as Camembert, are eaten all over the world.

A patisserie specializes in sweet, delicious pastries, and produces a wide range for its customers every day.

TOUR DE FRANCE

Cycling is an enormously popular pastime in France. The world's most famous cycling race is the Tour de France (Tour of France), which takes place every summer. The route follows public roads, covering about 3,500 km (2,200 miles), primarily in France and Belgium, but briefly in four other countries. The race takes place over 26 days, and the world's best cyclists take part.

The town square is the traditional spot for games such as boules or petanque, French versions of bowling.

In fine weather, café owners put tables and chairs out on the pavements so their customers can eat and drink in the open air.

The extract of scented flowers, such as lavender, is a major ingredient in perfume.

COUNTRY TOWNS

Much of France consists of open country where most working people earn a living from farming. One in every five French people lives and works in the countryside. The farming communities spread out around small market towns, which provide markets, banks, restaurants, and shops and supermarkets. Each town contains a *mairie*, the offices of the local government administration. The *mairie* often overlooks the central square, where people meet to talk and perhaps enjoy a game of *boules*.

CHARTRES

France is a mainly Roman Catholic country. There are churches in every village, and cathedrals in the cities. The cathedral of Chartres, in northern France, was completed in 1260. It is famous not only for its fine architecture but also for its magnificent stained-glass windows. There are 176 windows, covering a total area of 2,600 sq m (28,000 sq ft), the equivalent of 10 tennis courts.

PERFUME AND FASHION

Two of France's best-known industries are the manufacture of perfume and haute couture, or high fashion. Many of the most famous and most expensive brands of perfume are French. French designers dominated fashion for most of the last century. The Paris collections, shown in the spring of each year, are the most important of the international fashion shows and are attended by designers from all over the world. They set the trends which the rest of the world will follow.

The 176 luminous stained-glass windows of Chartres Cathedral (right) attest to the talents of Chartres craftsmen.

> ### Find out more
>
> EUROPE
> EUROPE, HISTORY OF
> FRENCH REVOLUTION
> NAPOLEON BONAPARTE
> NORMANS

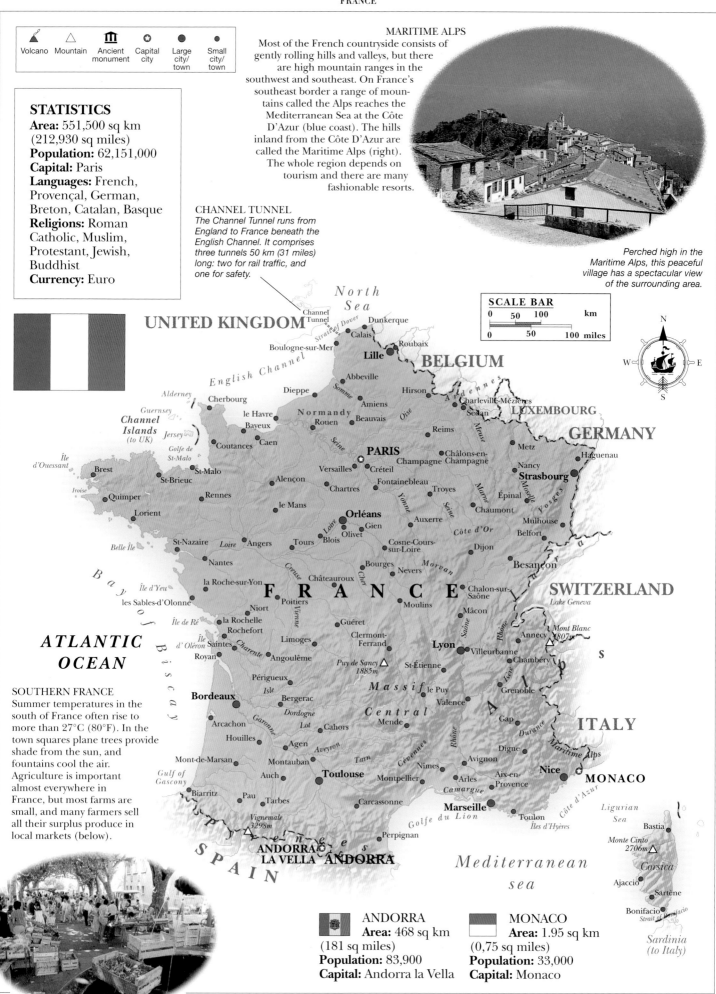

Volcano △ Mountain 🏛 Ancient monument ✧ Capital city ● Large city/town • Small city/town

STATISTICS
Area: 551,500 sq km (212,930 sq miles)
Population: 62,151,000
Capital: Paris
Languages: French, Provençal, German, Breton, Catalan, Basque
Religions: Roman Catholic, Muslim, Protestant, Jewish, Buddhist
Currency: Euro

MARITIME ALPS
Most of the French countryside consists of gently rolling hills and valleys, but there are high mountain ranges in the southwest and southeast. On France's southeast border a range of mountains called the Alps reaches the Mediterranean Sea at the Côte D'Azur (blue coast). The hills inland from the Côte D'Azur are called the Maritime Alps (right). The whole region depends on tourism and there are many fashionable resorts.

Perched high in the Maritime Alps, this peaceful village has a spectacular view of the surrounding area.

CHANNEL TUNNEL
The Channel Tunnel runs from England to France beneath the English Channel. It comprises three tunnels 50 km (31 miles) long: two for rail traffic, and one for safety.

SCALE BAR
0   50   100   km
0   50   100 miles

SOUTHERN FRANCE
Summer temperatures in the south of France often rise to more than 27°C (80°F). In the town squares plane trees provide shade from the sun, and fountains cool the air. Agriculture is important almost everywhere in France, but most farms are small, and many farmers sell all their surplus produce in local markets (below).

North Sea
UNITED KINGDOM
BELGIUM
LUXEMBOURG
GERMANY
SWITZERLAND
ITALY
MONACO
SPAIN
ANDORRA

English Channel
Strait of Dover
Channel Islands (to UK)
Alderney
Guernsey
Jersey
Île d'Ouessant
Iroise
Belle Île
ATLANTIC OCEAN
Bay of Biscay
Golfe de St-Malo
Île d'Yeu
Île de Ré
Île d'Oléron
Gulf of Gascony

Channel Tunnel
Dunkerque
Calais
Roubaix
Boulogne-sur-Mer
Lille
Abbeville
Dieppe
Cherbourg
le Havre
Bayeux
Caen
Coutances
St-Malo
St-Brieuc
Brest
Quimper
Lorient
Rennes
le Mans
Angers
St-Nazaire
Nantes
la Roche-sur-Yon
les Sables-d'Olonne
Niort
la Rochelle
Rochefort
Saintes
Royan
Bordeaux
Arcachon
Houilles
Mont-de-Marsan
Biarritz
Pau
Tarbes
Auch
Montauban
Toulouse
Normandy
Rouen
Amiens
Beauvais
Hirson
Charleville-Mézières
Sedan
Reims
Metz
Haguenau
Nancy
Strasbourg
Épinal
Chaumont
Mulhouse
Belfort
Châlons-en-Champagne
Champagne
PARIS
Versailles
Créteil
Fontainebleau
Troyes
Chartres
Alençon
Orléans
Olivet
Gien
Auxerre
Dijon
Côte d'Or
Besançon
Tours
Blois
Châteauroux
Bourges
Nevers
Morvan
Moulins
Chalon-sur-Saône
Lake Geneva
Mâcon
Annecy
Mont Blanc 4807m
Chambéry
Lyon
Villeurbanne
St-Étienne
Grenoble
Gap
Digne
Guéret
Clermont-Ferrand
Limoges
Angoulême
Périgueux
Bergerac
Cahors
Agen
Mende
le Puy
Valence
Avignon
Nîmes
Arles
Aix-en-Provence
Nice
MONACO
Digne
Poitiers
Châteauroux
Puy de Sancy 1885m
Massif Central
Cévennes
Vignemale 3298m
ANDORRA LA VELLA ANDORRA
Perpignan
Montpellier
Marseille
Toulon
Golfe du Lion
Îles d'Hyères
Carcassonne
Camargue
Côte d'Azur
Maritime Alps
Ligurian Sea
Bastia
Monte Cinto 2706m
Corsica
Ajaccio
Sartène
Bonifacio
Strait of Bonifacio
Sardinia (to Italy)
Mediterranean sea

Rivers/labels: Somme, Oise, Seine, Meuse, Moselle, Marne, Yonne, Vosges, Loire, Creuse, Vienne, Cher, Saône, Rhône, Isère, Charente, Isle, Dordogne, Lot, Garonne, Aveyron, Tarn, Durance, **FRANCE**

ANDORRA
Area: 468 sq km (181 sq miles)
Population: 83,900
Capital: Andorra la Vella

MONACO
Area: 1.95 sq km (0,75 sq miles)
Population: 33,000
Capital: Monaco

FRENCH REVOLUTION

THE EXECUTION OF LOUIS XVI
"Because the country must live, Louis must die." With those words, the king of France was killed on the guillotine on 21 January 1793.

"LIBERTY! EQUALITY! FRATERNITY!" This slogan echoed through France in 1789 as the hungry French people united to overthrow the rich noblemen who ruled the country. The Revolution put ordinary people in control of France and gave hope to oppressed people all over the world. The Revolution started when the bankrupt king Louis XVI summoned the French parliament for the first time since 1614. Instead of helping him raise taxes, they siezed power. In Paris, a crowd stormed the Bastille prison, the symbol of royal authority. The king had to support the Revolution, but in 1792 France became a republic, and Louis was executed. Counterrevolution broke out in parts of France in 1793, which led to a Reign of Terror that undid many of the benefits of the revolution. In 1799 a military takeover put Napoleon in power and ended the Revolution.

THE REVOLUTION

May 1789 Estates General (parliament) meets at Versailles.

July 1789 Paris crowd storms Bastille prison.

Aug 1789 Declaration of the Rights of Man.

June 1790 Nobility is abolished.

June 1791 Louis XVI tries to flee from Paris.

Aug 1792 King Louis imprisoned.

Sept 1792 Monarchy abolished and France becomes a republic.

Mar 1793 Counter-revolution in Vendée region.

Sept 1793 Start of Reign of Terror.

July 1794 Terror ends when Robespierre is overthrown.

Nov 1795 A new republic, the Directory, takes power.

Nov 1799 Napoleon Bonaparte overthrows Directory and assumes power.

MAXIMILIEN ROBESPIERRE
When 35-year-old lawyer Robespierre came to power in 1793, he took severe measures to safeguard the Revolution. He presided over the Reign of Terror but was himself executed in 1794.

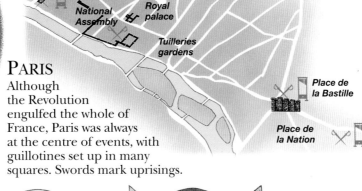

Place de Louis XV

National Assembly

Royal palace

Tuilleries gardens

Place de la Bastille

Place de la Nation

PARIS
Although the Revolution engulfed the whole of France, Paris was always at the centre of events, with guillotines set up in many squares. Swords mark uprisings.

The red bonnet worn by the revolutionaries, and the republican tricolor flag

MARIANNE
The new revolutionary calendar started from the day the king was overthrown. Marianne – a symbolic but imaginary revolutionary woman shown here on a stamp – illustrated the first month.

SANS-CULOTTES
The well-dressed aristocrats sneered at the revolutionaries and called them sans-culottes, or people without trousers. The revolutionaries adopted this name as their own. Their simple clothes came to symbolize the new way of life in revolutionary France.

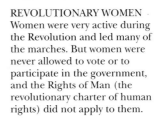

REVOLUTIONARY WOMEN
Women were very active during the Revolution and led many of the marches. But women were never allowed to vote or to participate in the government, and the Rights of Man (the revolutionary charter of human rights) did not apply to them.

Find out more
EUROPE, HISTORY OF
FRANCE
NAPOLEON BONAPARTE

FROGS AND OTHER AMPHIBIANS

AMPHIBIANS ARE A GROUP of creatures that are able to live both on land and in the water. The group includes frogs, toads, salamanders, newts, and caecilians. Amphibians have existed for millions of years and are found everywhere but Antarctica and Greenland. Frogs are the most widespread amphibians, surviving in deserts, rain forests, and mountainous regions. The limbless caecilian is found only in tropical areas. Caecilians burrow in the earth and swim by wriggling like eels. Frogs, by contrast, can swim, hop, and climb trees using their long back legs. Most amphibians breed in water, where they lay eggs that develop into larvae (tadpoles). During the larval stage, amphibians breathe through gills; as adults they develop lungs for breathing on land. Several kinds of frogs and salamanders are brightly coloured, and some have glands in the skin that produce toxins (poisons) to ward off predators.

Frogs rely on their eyes to watch for prey. They also use their eyes to judge distances when they are leaping.

Front legs act as shock absorbers when the frog lands.

Frog's toes are sticky.

AMPHIBIANS

Some amphibians lay spawn (eggs) in water; others lay eggs out of water, on leaves, or in holes underground. The frog spawn you see in a pond hatches into limbless tadpoles. As the tadpoles grow in the water, they develop limbs. They gradually change into frogs and climb onto the land. This process is called metamorphosis.

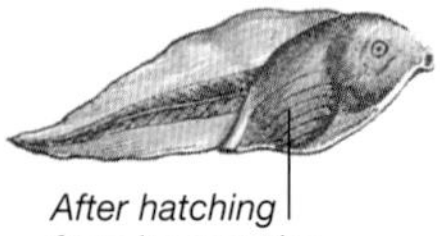

After hatching from its egg, the tadpole starts to swim, breathing through gills.

About 16 weeks after hatching, the young frog leaves the water.

Tail becomes smaller and eventually disappears.

Limbs form, and internal lungs develop. Tadpole begins to gulp air from the surface of the water.

RED-EYED TREE FROG

Tree frogs often have longer, leaner bodies than frogs that live mainly in water. A frog's long back legs can kick powerfully for swimming and leaping away from predators. The red-eyed tree frog shown above has sticky discs on its toes that give a good grip on leaves and bark. Today, red-eyed tree frogs are in danger of extinction.

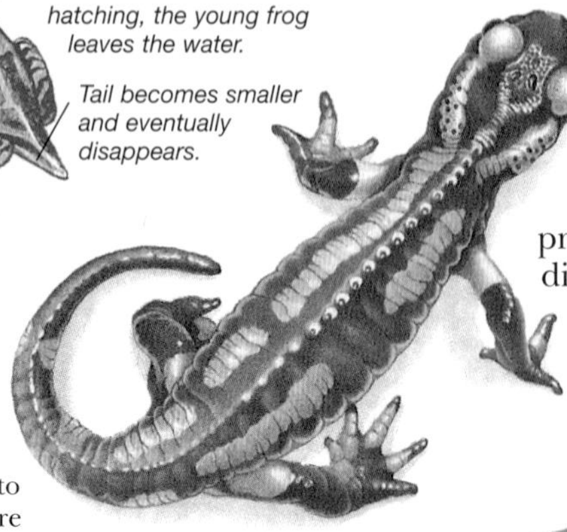

Mandarin newt

SALAMANDER

After the tadpole stage, the fire salamander crawls up onto land and lives among leaves in moist woodland areas. The females return to the water to give birth to 10 to 15 live young. The fire salamander is so called because it hides in logs and is sometimes seen emerging from a log fire.

Fire salamander

CANE TOAD

The cane or marine toad shown here originated in Central and South America. During the 1930s it was brought to Australia to eat the beetles that were pests in sugar cane plantations. Today the cane toad itself is regarded as a pest.

Cane toad grows up to 23 cm (9 in) in body length.

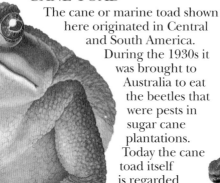

NEWT

Salamanders and their relatives, the newts, resemble lizards in shape. In the breeding season newts often become brighter in colour, and may be red, yellow, or orange, such as the mandarin newt shown here. These colours warn predators that the glands in the skin produce horrible-tasting or poisonous fluids.

Asian leaf frog

Tomato frog

Find out more

ANIMALS
CAMOUFLAGE, ANIMAL
CONSERVATION
and endangered species

FRUITS AND SEEDS

ALL FLOWERING PLANTS, from tiny duckweeds to mighty oaks, develop from seeds. Each seed contains an embryo (a young plant) plus a store of food for the embryo's growth. A fruit is the seed container; it protects the developing seeds until they are dispersed by animals, the wind, water, or the plant itself. Fruits include lemons, melons, cherries, and tomatoes. The hard little stones or pips inside are the seeds. Many fruits, such as oranges and blackcurrants, are an important source of food. They contain large amounts of vitamin C, necessary for good health. People have cultivated fruits for centuries; today, fruit growers produce millions of tonnes of fruit every year. Strangely enough, some foods that we call vegetables, such as cucumber, are in fact fruits, bursting with tiny seeds. So too are spices such as whole chillis and peppercorns. Yet rhubarb, which is often cooked as a fruit, is really the pink stem of a leaf.

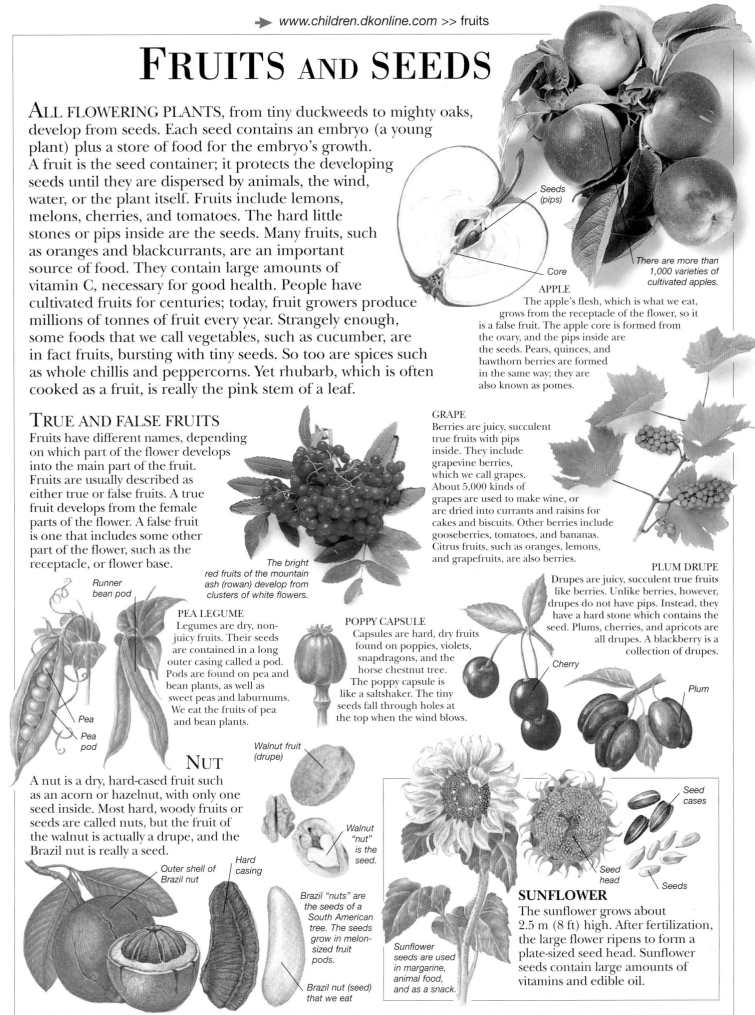

Seeds (pips)

Core

There are more than 1,000 varieties of cultivated apples.

APPLE
The apple's flesh, which is what we eat, grows from the receptacle of the flower, so it is a false fruit. The apple core is formed from the ovary, and the pips inside are the seeds. Pears, quinces, and hawthorn berries are formed in the same way; they are also known as pomes.

TRUE AND FALSE FRUITS
Fruits have different names, depending on which part of the flower develops into the main part of the fruit. Fruits are usually described as either true or false fruits. A true fruit develops from the female parts of the flower. A false fruit is one that includes some other part of the flower, such as the receptacle, or flower base.

The bright red fruits of the mountain ash (rowan) develop from clusters of white flowers.

GRAPE
Berries are juicy, succulent true fruits with pips inside. They include grapevine berries, which we call grapes. About 5,000 kinds of grapes are used to make wine, or are dried into currants and raisins for cakes and biscuits. Other berries include gooseberries, tomatoes, and bananas. Citrus fruits, such as oranges, lemons, and grapefruits, are also berries.

PLUM DRUPE
Drupes are juicy, succulent true fruits like berries. Unlike berries, however, drupes do not have pips. Instead, they have a hard stone which contains the seed. Plums, cherries, and apricots are all drupes. A blackberry is a collection of drupes.

Cherry

Plum

Runner bean pod

Pea

Pea pod

PEA LEGUME
Legumes are dry, non-juicy fruits. Their seeds are contained in a long outer casing called a pod. Pods are found on pea and bean plants, as well as sweet peas and laburnums. We eat the fruits of pea and bean plants.

POPPY CAPSULE
Capsules are hard, dry fruits found on poppies, violets, snapdragons, and the horse chestnut tree. The poppy capsule is like a saltshaker. The tiny seeds fall through holes at the top when the wind blows.

Walnut fruit (drupe)

Walnut "nut" is the seed.

NUT
A nut is a dry, hard-cased fruit such as an acorn or hazelnut, with only one seed inside. Most hard, woody fruits or seeds are called nuts, but the fruit of the walnut is actually a drupe, and the Brazil nut is really a seed.

Outer shell of Brazil nut

Hard casing

Brazil "nuts" are the seeds of a South American tree. The seeds grow in melon-sized fruit pods.

Brazil nut (seed) that we eat

Seed cases

Seed head

Seeds

Sunflower seeds are used in margarine, animal food, and as a snack.

SUNFLOWER
The sunflower grows about 2.5 m (8 ft) high. After fertilization, the large flower ripens to form a plate-sized seed head. Sunflower seeds contain large amounts of vitamins and edible oil.

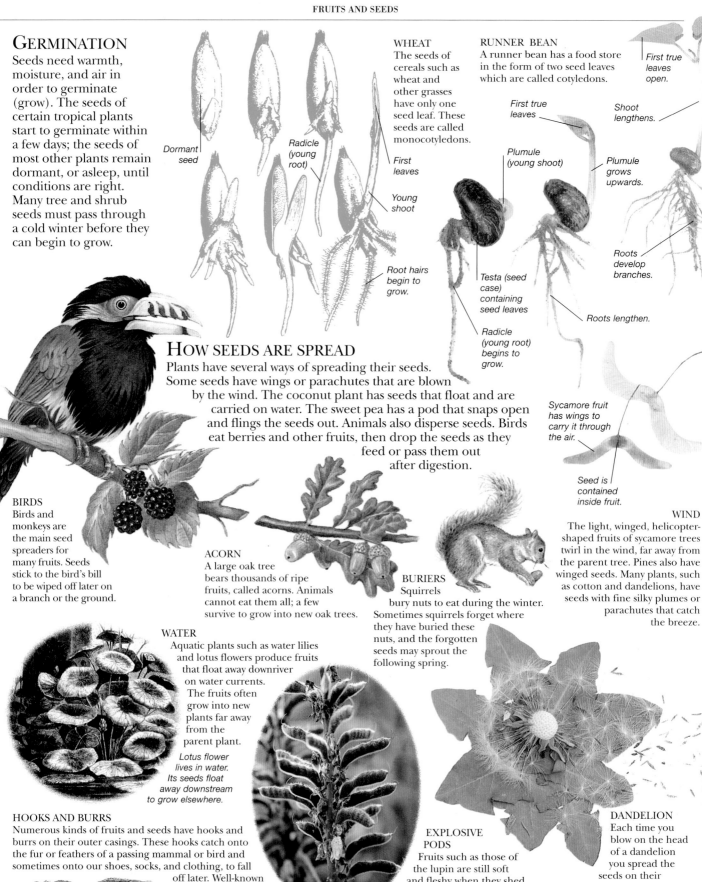

GERMINATION

Seeds need warmth, moisture, and air in order to germinate (grow). The seeds of certain tropical plants start to germinate within a few days; the seeds of most other plants remain dormant, or asleep, until conditions are right. Many tree and shrub seeds must pass through a cold winter before they can begin to grow.

Dormant seed

Radicle (young root)

First leaves

Young shoot

Root hairs begin to grow.

WHEAT
The seeds of cereals such as wheat and other grasses have only one seed leaf. These seeds are called monocotyledons.

RUNNER BEAN
A runner bean has a food store in the form of two seed leaves which are called cotyledons.

First true leaves open.

First true leaves

Plumule (young shoot)

Shoot lengthens.

Plumule grows upwards.

Testa (seed case) containing seed leaves

Radicle (young root) begins to grow.

Roots develop branches.

Roots lengthen.

HOW SEEDS ARE SPREAD

Plants have several ways of spreading their seeds. Some seeds have wings or parachutes that are blown by the wind. The coconut plant has seeds that float and are carried on water. The sweet pea has a pod that snaps open and flings the seeds out. Animals also disperse seeds. Birds eat berries and other fruits, then drop the seeds as they feed or pass them out after digestion.

Sycamore fruit has wings to carry it through the air.

Seed is contained inside fruit.

BIRDS
Birds and monkeys are the main seed spreaders for many fruits. Seeds stick to the bird's bill to be wiped off later on a branch or the ground.

ACORN
A large oak tree bears thousands of ripe fruits, called acorns. Animals cannot eat them all; a few survive to grow into new oak trees.

BURIERS
Squirrels bury nuts to eat during the winter. Sometimes squirrels forget where they have buried these nuts, and the forgotten seeds may sprout the following spring.

WIND
The light, winged, helicopter-shaped fruits of sycamore trees twirl in the wind, far away from the parent tree. Pines also have winged seeds. Many plants, such as cotton and dandelions, have seeds with fine silky plumes or parachutes that catch the breeze.

WATER
Aquatic plants such as water lilies and lotus flowers produce fruits that float away downriver on water currents. The fruits often grow into new plants far away from the parent plant.

Lotus flower lives in water. Its seeds float away downstream to grow elsewhere.

HOOKS AND BURRS
Numerous kinds of fruits and seeds have hooks and burrs on their outer casings. These hooks catch onto the fur or feathers of a passing mammal or bird and sometimes onto our shoes, socks, and clothing, to fall off later. Well-known hooked fruits are burdock, cleavers, agrimony, and South African grapple fruit.

In autumn, the badger picks up many seeds on its fur as it pushes through undergrowth. The seeds eventually drop off and grow into new plants.

EXPLOSIVE PODS
Fruits such as those of the lupin are still soft and fleshy when they shed their seeds. When they are fully ripe, the casing suddenly splits open, and the seeds pop out with explosive force.

DANDELION
Each time you blow on the head of a dandelion you spread the seeds on their feathery parachutes.

Find out more
BIRDS
FLOWERS AND HERBS
PLANTS
TREES

GAS

BURNING GAS TO MAKE HEAT is a quick and easy way to warm the home and to cook. Gas is also used in industry, both for heat and as a raw material. Most of the gas we use for fuel is natural gas. It is extracted from deposits buried deep underground or under the seabed. Gas for burning can also be made by processing coal to produce coal gas. These fuel gases are not the only kinds of gas: there are many others with different uses. For instance, the air we breathe is made up of several gases mixed together.

FORMATION OF NATURAL GAS

The natural gas we use today is millions of years old. It was formed from the remains of prehistoric plants that lived on land and in the sea. New gas deposits are still being created.

1 In the sea, tiny plants sink, and a layer of dead plants builds up on the seabed. The sea plants are buried in mud.

GAS DELIVERY

Natural gas is piped to homes for use in cookers and heaters. Gas stored in metal bottles supplies homes that are not connected to the pipeline.

2 On land too, mud covers dead plants and trees. Slowly the mud hardens into rock. More layers of rock form above and press down on the plants, burying them deeper and heating them up.

3 The pressure and heat slowly change the sea plants into oil and then into gas. Land plants turn first to coal before becoming oil and gas. A layer of rock now traps the gas in a deep deposit. Earth movements may have raised the rocks containing the gas above sea level, so that the gas now lies under the land.

Huge drills on a production platform sink wells to reach gas deposits, which lie as deep as 6 km (4 miles) below the seabed.

6 Gas flows from terminals to large tanks, where it may be frozen and stored as a liquid. The gas can also be stored in huge underground caverns. Pumps push gas along pipes to the places where it is needed.

4 Gas flows up the well to the production platform, and a pipeline takes it to a terminal on land. Gas from inland wells flows straight to the terminal.

GAS FOR INDUSTRY

Not all gas is used in the home. Many power stations burn gas to generate electricity. In dry places, such as deserts, the heat from burning gas is used to process sea water in order to produce salt-free drinking water. Gas is also used as a fuel in factories producing all kinds of things, from roasted peanuts to cars. Chemicals made from gas are vital ingredients in the manufacture of plastics, fertilizers, paints, synthetic fibre, and many other products.

5 Raw gas has to be cleaned and dried before it can be used. The gas terminal removes impurities and water.

Gas storage tank

Gas deposit

Oil deposit

A gas layer often forms above a layer of oil.

The pressure of the gas helps force the oil up wells to the production platform.

USEFUL GASES

Gas wells produce several different sorts of gas. Methane is the main component, but other fuel gases, called propane and butane, also come from gas deposits. The gas terminal stores these gases in metal cylinders for use in houses where the gas pipe does not reach. Gas deposits are also a source of helium. Helium is used to fill balloons because it is very light and does not burn. Air is another source of useful gases. Carbon dioxide, the gas that makes the bubbles in fizzy drinks, comes from air. Air also contains a little neon gas. Some advertising signs are glass tubes filled with neon. The gas glows when electricity passes through it.

Neon sign

Helium gas balloons

Find out more
COAL
HEAT
OIL
OXYGEN
SCIENCE

GENETICS

THE SCIENCE OF GENETICS has officially existed ever since the word "gene" was coined in 1909 by the Danish botanist Wilhelm Johannsen (1857-1927). He invented the term to describe the "particles" of inheritance that pass characteristics from one generation of plant or animal to the next. The field of genetics developed over the course of the 20th century, and produced important discoveries about how genes work. Scientists showed that genes are sections of the long molecules of deoxyribonucleic acid (DNA) that are connected together to form chromosomes. Genes contain the instructions by which plant and animal cells are built. Genes are passed from both parents to their children through sexual reproduction. By this process, called heredity, inheritable characteristics are passed from one generation to the next.

Each "rung" is a pair of chemicals called bases.

DNA

Deoxyribonucleic acid is the full name of DNA. It is the molecule that holds the coded instructions within genes. Its structure is a double helix, with chemical bonds that attach one side of the helix to the other, rather like the rungs on a ladder. Each "rung" is made up of a pair of chemicals selected from a choice of four chemicals, so the way in which genetic information is coded is actually very simple.

The sides of the "ladder" are made up of phosphate and sugar molecules.

The DNA molecule looks something like a twisted ladder in this model. In real life it is a chain of tens of thousands of atoms.

HEREDITY

When a plant or animal is created, it inherits a combination of genetic information from both of its parents. Heredity is the passing of characteristics from parents to children. It means that a baby inherits certain features from each of its parents, but it also ensures that each baby is usually different from its brothers and sisters.

Blue eye

Some of the features controlled by genes can be easily seen. The genes in this girl's cells make her eyes blue, her hair straight, and her skin fair.

Albino hamster has white fur and red eyes.

Hamster with normal colouring

MUTATION
When new DNA is being created, sometimes a mistake can occur during the copying process. These mistakes are called mutations, and they may appear as a defect or a new characteristic. If a mutation turns out to be useful, it may become common in future generations.

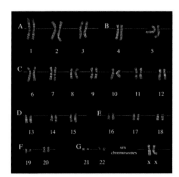

Children resemble their parents but are not identical to them.

Wavy hair

GENES
Each chromosome consists of a long molecule of DNA. Normally the molecule is unravelled, but it coils up to give the chromosome its characteristic shape (right) when a cells divides. Each gene is a short section of the chromosome that contains the instructions needed to make a particular protein. This is just one of the large group of chemicals that control the features, such as eye colour. Humans have around 23,000 genes.

The genes in this boy's cells make his eyes brown, his hair wavy, and his skin dark.

The sex chromosomes determine whether a cell is male or female. Males contain an XY pair, while females contain an XX pair.

CHROMOSOMES
The nucleus of a living cell contains a number of pairs of chromosomes. They are rather like filing cabinets that store all of the genetic information of the plant or animal. Chromosomes are arranged in pairs that carry identical or different forms of the same genes.

X chromosome

MENDEL

Gregor Mendel (1822-84), Austrian scientist, discovered the laws of heredity through experiments with pea plants. In 1866, he showed that features in a plant, such as the production of a smooth or a wrinkled pea, are determined by the genetic information given to the plant by its parents. He called this information "particles", some 43 years before the word "gene" was invented by the Danish scientist Wilhelm Johannsen (1857-1927).

Gregor Mendel was an ordained priest and combined this with his work as a scientist.

PATTERNS OF INHERITANCE

Different forms of the same gene are called alleles, and they can be dominant or recessive. Dominant alleles always show up, even if the information they carry comes from only one parent. Recessive means that a certain feature might not be seen in a plant or animal even though it is carrying the right alleles. Recessiveness is sometimes linked to gender.

Male cat carrying tortoiseshell allele ♂

Female tortoiseshell cat ♀

The cats produce male and female kittens. Only females can be tortoiseshell.

♂   ♂   ♀   ♀

The second kitten, who carries two tortoiseshell alleles, does not have a tortoiseshell coat because he is male.

Only one kitten is tortoiseshell like her mother, because she carries two alleles and is female.

TWINS

If a fertilized human embryo splits in two it will develop into identical twins. Each twin shares the same genetic information. In fact, they are not entirely identical because each foetus develops in a slightly different way after the original split. Therefore identical twins can appear to be remarkably similar yet have quite different personalities. Non-identical twins develop from two separate embryos.

Identical twins are of the same sex because they come from a single embryo.

The world's media took a great interest in Dolly, the first large mammal to be cloned.

CLONING DOLLY

Clones are one or more identical organisms that share identical genes but unlike twins are not produced by natural reproduction. For many years, scientists have been interested in cloning identical copies of animals and plants. In 1996, scientists successfully cloned a sheep, known as Dolly. The experiment led to a worldwide debate about the ethics of cloning.

GM FOODS

The plants and animals that produce GM (genetically modified) foods have had their genes changed by scientists. In theory, genetic modification is just a way of speeding up the process of selection by breeding, which is already done in the natural way. There is much to be learnt before we can be sure that genetic modification is a safe thing to do.

GENETICS

1859 Darwin publishes his theory of evolution.

1866 Mendel establishes laws of inheritance.

1869 Friedrich Miescher isolates 'nuclein', later called DNA.

1905 X and Y sex chromosomes discovered.

1910 Thomas Morgan confirms chromosome theory of heredity.

1927 Genetic mutation in fruit flies created using X-rays.

1941 Proved that one gene produces one protein.

1944 Shown that DNA controls heredity.

1953 Watson and Crick discover the structure of DNA.

1966 Genetic code cracked.

1984 Discovery of DNA fingerprinting.

2003 Human genome project to identify genes, is completed.

Find out more

ATOMS AND MOLECULES
RADIOACTIVITY
REPRODUCTION

GEOLOGY

OUR EARTH CHANGES all the time. Mountains rise and wear away. Continents move, causing oceans to widen and narrow. These changes are slow. It would take a million years to notice much difference. Other changes, such as when an earthquake shakes the land or a volcano erupts, are sudden. Geology is the study of how the Earth changes, how it was formed, and the rocks that it is made of.

Clues to the Earth's history are hidden in its rocks. Geologists survey (map out) the land and dig down to the rocks in the Earth's crust. The age and nature of the rocks and fossils (evidence of prehistoric plants and animals) help geologists understand the workings of the Earth. Geologists also help discover valuable deposits of coal, oil, and other useful minerals. They study the land before a large structure such as a dam is built, to make sure that the land can support the great weight. Geologists also warn people about possible disasters. Using special instruments, they detect the movement of rocks and try to predict volcanic eruptions and earthquakes.

GEOLOGISTS AT WORK
Rocks at the Earth's surface reveal their past to the expert eyes of geologists. For example, huge cracks in layers of rock show that powerful forces once squeezed the rocks.

SATELLITE MAPPING
Satellites circle the Earth and send back photographs of the surface from space. The pictures show features of the land in great detail and help geologists identify the rocks. Satellites have also measured the size and shape of the Earth.

Studying the rocks in the ocean floor can reveal the slow movements of the Earth's crust.

AERIAL SURVEYS
Aeroplanes carry special cameras that produce three-dimensional views of the land below, and instruments that measure the strength of the Earth's magnetism and gravity.

SEISMIC TESTS
Special trucks strike the ground with huge hammers, producing shock waves, called seismic waves, which bounce off the layers of rock below. Computers use these waves to draw pictures of the layers of rock within the Earth.

SANDSTONE
The top and youngest layer of rock is sandstone. It sometimes forms from desert sands. The criss-cross pattern shows how the wind blew sand to form the rock.

SHALE
A layer of shale rock shows that the land must have been beneath shallow water. Mud from a nearby river built up and compacted, forming shale.

BASALT
Lava from a volcano formed this layer of basalt. The land rose from the sea, and a volcano erupted nearby to cover the rock below with lava.

LIMESTONE
The lowest and oldest layer contains fossils of tiny creatures, showing that 100 million years ago, during the time of the dinosaurs, the region was under the sea.

ROCK SAMPLE
The layers of rock in this sample (above) come from deep underground.

DRILLING
Rigs bore shafts as deep as 3,000 m (10,000 ft) below the ground and bring up samples of the rock layers beneath.

RADIOACTIVE DATING
Rocks contain substances which decay over millions of years, giving off tiny amounts of nuclear radiation. By a process called radioactive dating, which measures this radioactivity, geologists can find out how old the rocks are.

THE HISTORY OF GEOLOGY

The Ancient Greeks and Hindus were the first peoples to study and date the rocks of the Earth. During the late 18th century, the Scottish scientist James Hutton became the first European geologist to realize that the Earth is millions of years old and that it changes constantly. But his ideas were not accepted until after his death. In 1912, Alfred Wegener, a German meteorologist, proposed that the continents move. But it was more than 50 years before his idea was found to be true.

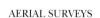

In 1795 James Hutton founded the modern science of geology with his book The Theory of the Earth.

EXAMINING THE EARTH

The Earth's crust is made of layer upon layer of different kinds of rock which have been laid down over millions of years. The topmost layers usually formed most recently and the lowest layers are the oldest. By uncovering these layers of rock, geologists can trace back the history of the Earth.

GERMANY

GERMANY OCCUPIES A CENTRAL position in northern Europe, and its 83.3 million people play a central role in the economy, way of life, and traditions of Europe. Germany is an old country, and its borders have changed often over the centuries. For much of the second half of the 20th century, Germany consisted of two separate nations: West Germany (the Federal Republic of Germany) and East Germany (the German Democratic Republic). In 1990 they became one nation and the Berlin Wall was removed. Germany is a rich and fertile land, and its farms are among the world's most productive. The landscape rises gently from the sandy coasts and islands on the North Sea and Baltic Sea. Flat plains dominate the northern part of the country, and in the south there are forests and the soaring Alps. The region's cool, rainy weather helps agriculture. Farms produce livestock and dairy products, cereals, potatoes, sugar beet, fruits, and vegetables. Most people, however, live in and around the towns where Germany's energetic industries are based.

Germany lies at the heart of Europe. From the flat plains of the north to the snow-capped peaks of the Bavarian Alps, the landscape is varied.

Sausage sellers specialize in various kinds of wurst and often sell their wares from tiny stalls or vans.

Beer gardens attached to bars and pubs are popular in warm weather.

The Brandenburg Gate stands on the line that once divided East and West Berlin.

WURST AND BEER
Germany produces some excellent wine and is also famous for its beer. Germans often drink beer with the traditional snack of a sausage (or wurst) and a bread roll, accompanied by a large dollop of mild mustard. There are numerous kinds of wurst, and every region has its speciality. Frankfurters, a type of wurst, originally came from Frankfurt.

BERLIN
Reinstated as the capital of all Germany in 1990, Berlin grew up on the banks of the River Spree. Canals also link Berlin to the Elbe and Oder rivers. Berlin was devastated in World War II. In 1949 the city was split between the two states of East and West Germany. For many years a wall separated the people in the eastern and western sectors, and the two parts of the city still look very different. New buildings have made western Berlin look like any other modern European city. Eastern Berlin still suffers poor infrastructure and buildings.

Leitz camera factory

INDUSTRY
There is a wide range of industries in Germany that produce electrical goods, computers, tools, textiles, and medicines. Coal mines in the central Ruhr region produce large quantities of brown coal, or lignite, to fuel the factories. Western Germany is famous for high-quality precision goods, such as BMW cars and Leitz cameras.

BAVARIA

Covering the entire southeastern part of the country, Bavaria is the largest state in Germany. Most of the region is cloaked by forests and farms. In the south, the Bavarian Alps form a natural border with Austria. Bavaria is a magnet to tourists, who come to see its fairy-tale palaces (left) and spectacular scenery. The region's traditional costume is *lederhosen* (leather shorts), braces, and a cap for men, and *dirndlkleider* (a full-length dress with puffed sleeves) for women.

The enchanting, grey granite Schloss Neuschwanstein is hidden away in the Bavarian Alps.

DÜRER

Born in Nuremberg, Albrecht Dürer (1471-1528), is famous for his paintings and engravings. He produced his first self-portrait at the age of 13, and painted himself at intervals throughout his life. He produced this self-portrait (above) when he was 26. At the age of 15 Dürer was apprenticed to Michael Wolgemut, Nuremberg's chief painter and book illustrator. He was inspired by the painters of the Italian Renaissance and resolved to depict people and things in realistic detail. In 1512, Dürer became court painter to the Emperor Maximilian, and gained international fame.

SEMPER OPERA HOUSE

The architect Gottfried Semper (1803-79) built his first opera house, the Royal Theatre, on Theaterplatz square in Dresden, in the years 1838-1841. Almost 30 years later it burnt to the ground and the opera was forced to move to temporary premises. Public pressure persuaded Semper to create a second opera house between 1871 and 1878. The new building (right) followed the style of the Italian High Renaissance. Following its destruction during an air raid in the Second World War, it was rebuilt in its original form between 1977 and 1985. Its exquisite acoustics and opulent interior decoration make it a model for opera houses throughout the world.

DRESDEN

The city of Dresden in eastern Germany was once the capital of a historic German state called Saxony. Although there are still some beautiful buildings in Dresden, including the former royal palace (below), most of the city's fine architecture was destroyed by Allied bombing in World War II (1939-45). Dresden has now been completely rebuilt, and many of the buildings restored.

Dresden was once admired as the "Florence on the Elbe".

BROTHERS GRIMM

Jakob (1785-1863) and Wilhelm (1786-1859) Grimm were born in Hanau, near Frankfurt. Devoted to each other, the brothers went to the same school and university, and lived together until Wilhelm's death. The Grimm brothers are famous for their collections of German folktales, which include the well-known tales of *Cinderella, Hänsel and Gretel, Rapunzel, Snow White and the Seven Dwarfs, Sleeping Beauty* and *Little Red Riding Hood*. The brothers did not create these stories themselves, but gathered them together from the accounts of country folk, and old books. Most of the stories date back hundreds of years.

Snow White and the Seven Dwarfs

RIVER RHINE

The Rhine is the longest river in Germany. It begins in Switzerland and later forms the German border with France. Then it cuts through the western part of Germany towards the Netherlands and the sea. Large river barges can sail up the Rhine as far as Basle, Switzerland. Vineyards on the steep banks of the southern part of the river produce much of Germany's famous white wine.

The buildings in parts of Bonn have a modern architectural style.

BONN

Between 1949 and 1990, Bonn was the capital of West Germany. Bonn, an ancient city, stands on the River Rhine on the site of a Roman camp. It is an old university town with many beautiful buildings in traditional German style. Bonn was the birthplace of composer Ludwig van Beethoven (1770-1827).

SPORTING ACHIEVEMENT

Germany has produced some excellent sports people over the last few decades. Sporting stars include Boris Becker, Steffi Graf, and Michael Stich in tennis, Michael Schumacher in motor racing, and Katja Seizinger in skiing. The German government encourages sports, mainly because it promotes good health. Prizewinning athletes also bring great honour to their country.

The joining of East and West Germany brought together some of the world's finest athletes. When the two countries were rivals, East German competitors were aided by excellent sports facilities, and special privileges gave them time to train. They won many more events than West German counterparts.

RUHR VALLEY

Much of Germany's heavy industry is concentrated in the valley of the Ruhr river. Huge coal seams provide the valley with a rich source of power, and factories in the region produce iron, steel, and chemicals. The Ruhr Valley is Germany's most densely populated area.

Wild boar still roam in the larger forests and are hunted for their meat.

FORESTS

Great forests cover many of the hills and mountains of the central and southern regions of Germany. These forests are prized for their beauty and for their valuable timber, which is used widely in industry. The most famous forests include the Thüringer Wald, the forests of the Harz Mountains in central Germany, and the Schwarzwald, or Black Forest, in southwest Germany.

OBERAMMERGAU

Once every 10 years an extraordinary event takes place in this small town in the Bavarian Alps in southern Germany. The inhabitants of Oberammergau get together to perform a passion play, which tells the story of Christ's crucifixion. The villagers first performed the play in 1634 in an effort to stop the plague. They have maintained the custom ever since. It is now a major tourist attraction, and thousands of visitors from Germany and abroad attend.

Find out more

EUROPE
EUROPE, HISTORY OF

Volcano △ **Mountain** 🏛 **Ancient monument** ✪ **Capital city** ● **Large city/town** ● **Small city/town**

STATISTICS

Area: 356,910 sq km (137,800 sq miles)
Population: 83,330,000
Capital: Berlin
Languages: German
Religions: Protestant, Roman Catholic, Muslim
Currency: Euro
Main occupations: Engineering, manufacturing
Main exports: Cars, heavy engineering, electronics, chemicals
Main imports: Energy sources, raw materials

CARS
Germany is Europe's largest vehicle producer, specializing in high-quality cars. American and Japanese car companies are based here, attracted by the skilled workforce.

HAMBURG
Located on the Elbe river, Hamburg is the second largest city in Germany and its economic centre. The city is also the country's busiest port.

RIVER RHINE
The Rhine is Germany's main waterway. It is an important transport route to and from northern ports. It meanders across 1,320 km (820 miles) from its source in Switzerland to the North Sea.

GERMAN BORDERS
Germany is positioned in the very centre of Europe, and has land borders with no less than nine countries. It is not surprising, then, that it is Europe's biggest trading nation. All kinds of raw materials flow into Germany across its borders, for the nation has few natural resources. Manufactured goods cross Germany's borders in the opposite direction. Of all Germany's borders, that with France is the busiest: nearly ten per cent of all German trade is with France.

GERMANY

DENMARK

North Sea
Baltic Sea

North Frisian Islands

Helgoland
East Frisian Islands

Kiel
Fehmarn
Lübeck
Rügen
Pomeranian Bay
Rostock
Schwerin
Neubrandenburg
Oderhaff

Bremerhaven
Hamburg
Müritz

NETHERLANDS
Oldenburg
Bremen
Elbe
Oder
Eberswalde-Finow

Ems
Weser
Aller
Havel
BERLIN

Osnabrück
Hanover (Hannover)
Wolfsburg
Potsdam
Frankfurt an der Oder

Münster
Lene
Magdeburg
Elbe
Spree

Harz
Saale
Cottbus

Essen
Dortmund
Halle
Leipzig

BELGIUM
Duisburg
Ruhr
Kassel
Dresden

Düsseldorf
Cologne (Köln)
Erfurt
Jena
Chemnitz

Aachen
Thüringer Wald
Werra

Bonn
Rheinisches Schiefergebirge
Fulda
Erzgebirge
Fichtelberg 1214m

LUXEMBOURG
Mosel
Koblenz
CZECH REPUBLIC

Frankfurt am Main
Main
Mainz
Rhine (Rhein)
Würzburg

Heidelberg
Nuremberg (Nürnberg)
Bohemian Forest
Grosser Arber 1456m

FRANCE
Neckar
Heilbronn
Regensburg
Danube (Donau)

Stuttgart

Schwäbische Alb
Danube (Donau)
Ulm
Augsburg
Lech
Inn

Freiburg im Breisgau
Black Forest
Munich (München)

Konstanz
Oberammergau
Bavarian Alps
Zugspitze 2962m

Lake Constance

SWITZERLAND
LIECHTENSTEIN
AUSTRIA

POLAND

SCALE BAR
0   50   100   km
0   50   100 miles

GLACIERS
AND ICECAPS

SNOW FALLING on the world's tallest mountain peaks never melts. The temperature rarely rises above freezing, and fresh falls of snow press down on those below, turning them to ice. A thick cover of ice, called an icecap or ice sheet, builds up, or snow collects in hollows. Ice flows down from the hollows in rivers of ice called glaciers. They move very slowly, usually less than 1 m (3.3 ft) a day, down towards the lower slopes. There it is usually warmer, and the glaciers melt.

However, in the Arctic and the Antarctic, ice and snow remain throughout the year, though in recent times, large areas of ice have been melting because of global warming. Ice sheets covered much of North America and Europe during the last Ice Age over the last million years. When the weather became warmer, about 10,000 years ago, the ice sheets retreated. Ice sheets now exist only in Greenland and Antarctica.

GLACIERS
Glaciers often join together, just as small rivers meet to form bigger rivers. The ice may be more than 1 km (0.5 mile) deep.

ICECAP
Icecaps cover vast areas. When the thickness of the ice reaches about 60 m (200 ft) its enormous weight sets it moving.

VALLEY GLACIER
The ice fills a valley, moving faster at the centre than at the sides of the glacier. Cracks called crevasses open in the surface.

MORAINE
The glacier acts like a huge conveyor belt, carrying broken rocks, called moraines, down from the mountaintop. The moving ice also plucks stones and boulders from the base and sides of the valley. This material is carried along within the glacier, and is called englacial moraine.

CIRQUES
The hollow where the ice collects to start the glacier is called a cirque or corrie.

SHAPING THE LANDSCAPE
Glaciers slowly grind away even the hardest rock and reveal a changed landscape when they retreat. Deep valleys and lakes, together with rivers and waterfalls, now exist where there were none before.

Waterfall

A river flows down the centre of the valley.

Deep U-shaped valley carved out by the glacier

Lake formed behind moraines

Streams of water form as the glacier melts.

FROZEN MAMMOTHS
In the Russian Federation, ice and frozen soil have preserved huge hairy elephants, called mammoths, just as if they were in a deep freeze. The last mammoths lived in North America, Europe, and Asia during the Ice Age.

Rocks in the melting ice build up a wall called a terminal moraine.

FJORDS
The sea rose at the end of the Ice Age, drowning valleys formed by glaciers. These deep, steep-sided inlets are called fjords. The coast of Norway has many fjords.

ICEBERGS
Huge pieces of floating ice are called icebergs. Nine tenths of the ice floats below the water, so icebergs are a danger to ships. In 1912 the ocean liner *Titanic* sank after colliding with an iceberg.

ICE AGE
A deep ice sheet covered about a third of the world's land during the last Ice Age. Ice extended as far south as St. Louis, Missouri, and London. There had been ice ages before the last one, and there could be more in the future.

Find out more
ANTARCTICA
ARCTIC
MOUNTAINS
POLAR WILDLIFE
RAIN AND SNOW

GLASS AND CERAMICS

STICKY CLAY AND DRY SAND are more familiar on the end of a spade than on the dinner table. Yet these are the basic ingredients in the manufacture of the pottery plates we eat from, and the jars and bottles in which we buy preserved food and drink. Glass and ceramic materials share some useful qualities: they resist the flow of heat and electricity, and they have a hard, non-reactive surface. But they are different in other ways: light passes through glass but not ceramics, and ceramics stay strong when they are heated. In their most basic forms glass and ceramic objects are brittle, but special additives and manufacturing methods make both materials much tougher.

Glass and ceramics are ancient materials. The Egyptians made decorative glass beads more than 5,000 years ago, and pottery is even older.

Spark plug for car engine

CERAMICS
Damp clay is easy to mould into pottery and tiles; heat sets the shape permanently. Ceramics resist heat and electricity, so they are ideal for insulating objects that get hot, such as spark plugs.

STAINED GLASS
Strips of lead hold together the many pieces of coloured glass in the stained glass windows that decorate homes, churches, and temples.

GLASS
Containers of clear glass protect their contents and display them to good advantage. Lenses are specially shaped pieces of glass that bend and concentrate light. But not all glass is functional; some glassware is simply decorative.

Glass bottle for holding medicines

Glass bottle for holding ink

Ornate glassware jug made in the 1930s

Magnifying glass which is a large convex lens.

Pottery mug

Ceramic tile

ENAMEL
Enamel is a glass-like layer on metal and other objects that protects them from damage and corrosion. Coloured enamel gives ornaments a beautiful appearance.

MAKING GLASS

Sand   Limestone   Soda ash   Recycled glass

Heating sand, limestone, and soda ash in a furnace together with recycled glass produces molten glass.

The molten glass is poured onto a pool of molten tin, which makes the glass spread into a flat sheet suitable for windows.

The glass sets and hardens on the cooler tin.

FIBREGLASS
Strengthening plastic with fibres of glass produces a material called fibreglass or glass-reinforced plastic, which is tough enough to be used for car bodies.

A lump of hot, soft glass is placed in a bottle-shaped mould.

Blowing air into the mould makes the glass inflate into a bubble, which expands to form the bottle.

The glass then cools and sets hard.

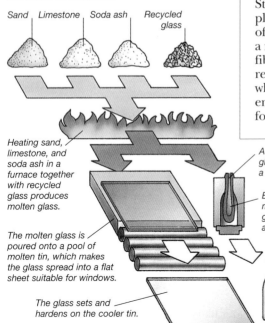

HEAT RESISTANCE
Ceramics can withstand very high temperatures. Ceramic tiles keep the astronauts cool even when the space shuttle glows red from the intense heat of re-entry.

GLASS BLOWING
The breath of the glass blower inflates soft glass on the end of a tube into a bubble. Skilful shaping makes the bubble into fine glassware as it cools.

Find out more
HEAT
LIGHT
PLASTICS
SCIENCE

GOVERNMENT AND POLITICS

PLATO
More than 2,000 years ago the Greek philosopher Plato wrote the first book about governments and how they rule people – what we today call politics. His book, *The Republic*, set out ideas for how a perfect state might be governed.

THE ADMINISTRATION OF A COUNTRY'S affairs is undertaken by a government whose policies direct decision making. Governments have many roles: they decide how money raised through taxes will be divided among the different public services, such as health, education, welfare, and defence. They also maintain the police for the safety of society and the armed forces for the defence of the nation. As a result of differing cultural and political traditions, government and policies vary from country to country. There are, however, three main types of government: republican, monarchical, and dictatorial. Most countries are republics, with people voting in an election to choose their government and head of state. In a monarchy, the head of the royal family is the head of state. Countries in which a single ruler has seized absolute power – often through a military takeover – are known as dictatorships.

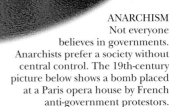

MONARCHY
In a monarchy a king or queen rules the country. Few modern monarchs have real political power, but four centuries ago, European monarchs made the laws and collected taxes.

PARLIAMENT

Many Western nations are democracies – they hold elections, in which the people vote for, or select, the next government from a range of political parties. Some countries, such as Britain and the Netherlands, have a parliamentary democracy. Elected politicians from different parties sit in parliament with the government and discuss the best way to run the country.

The government is usually from the political party with the greatest number of votes in the election, and the leader of this party becomes leader of the government and the country.

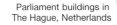
Parliament buildings in The Hague, Netherlands

Thabo Mvuyelwa Mbeki is sworn in as president of the Republic of South Africa in 1999.

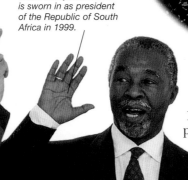

PRESIDENCY

In a republic, such as South Africa, the people vote for their head of state. In this case, the president holds real political power, and is responsible for the administration of the country and for its foreign policy. In France, power is divided between the president and the prime minister. In some countries, such as India, the president is more of a symbolic figurehead, who takes on a ceremonial role, rather like that of some monarchs.

ANARCHISM
Not everyone believes in governments. Anarchists prefer a society without central control. The 19th-century picture below shows a bomb placed at a Paris opera house by French anti-government protestors.

239

HOUSE OF LORDS

The House of Lords has some powers to amend or reject government legislation. It used to contain only hereditary peers, that is men who inherited titles such as earl from their fathers, as well as bishops and law lords. Many people thought this system undemocratic, so, in 1999, all but 92 hereditary peers were removed, leaving only peers chosen for life.

WESTMINSTER

The two Houses of Parliament – the House of Commons and the House of Lords – together with The Crown make up the Westminster government. Laws are proposed in either the Commons or the Lords, but all three must give assent to a bill (a proposed law) before it becomes an Act of Parliament, or law.

BRITISH MONARCHY

The monarchy once had great power but now plays a ceremonial role. The monarch has the right to be consulted about government policy, can chose a new prime minister, and can call a general election, although in practice she or he only acts on the advice of the prime minister.

GOVERNMENT

The government runs the country. It proposes new laws to parliament, and takes decisions on every aspect of our daily lives. The British government consists of 20 or so ministers who sit in the Cabinet, plus another 90 or so junior ministers. The head is the prime minister, who always sits in the House of Commons and is usually the leader of the largest political party. Other ministers can sit in the Commons or the Lords.

Elizabeth II, current monarch of the UK

CIVIL SERVICE

The civil service is the bureaucracy, or administrative machine, that carries out the instructions of the government once a law is passed. Civil servants collect taxes and duties, distribute benefits, and run the many government departments.

Government industrial chemists at work

THE SPEAKER

The Speaker of the House of Commons controls debates and keeps order in the Commons. She or he is a member of parliament (MP) and is elected at the start of each new session, once a year. Once elected, the speaker becomes neutral and may not cast a vote.

John Bercow MP, Speaker of the House of Commons from 2009

No. 10 Downing Street, the prime minister's official residence

POLITICAL PARTIES

Political parties are organizations formed to represent particular views in government or local councils. Britain has three main parties: the Labour, Conservative, and Liberal Democrat Parties. Since 1945, the government has always been either Labour or Conservative. Nationalist parties support independence for their own areas. Politicians who do not belong to a political party are called independents.

VOTING SYSTEMS

Most British elections are held under the first-past-the-post system, in which the person who gains the biggest number of votes wins. Other elections are based on proportional representation. In this system, seats are shared out according to the number of votes cast for each candidate or party.

Local governments are led by a mayor who wears a chain of office.

PRESSURE GROUPS

People form pressure groups to obtain action or change in a particular cause. Some groups, such as the environmental organization Greenpeace, campaign on a range of issues, often taking direct action such as confronting whaling ships. Others are concerned with local causes, such as stopping a hospital closure, or individual cases, such as freeing a wrongly convicted person in jail. Pressure groups can be very effective in achieving their demands or getting politicians to change their minds.

Inside of the new Scottish Parliament building

LOCAL GOVERNMENT

Every British city and town has its own city or district council. In rural areas, county and district councils share power. Local government looks after education, housing, social services, the environment, and public health, and carries out national government's orders.

DEVOLUTION

Until recently, parliament in London was the only law-making body in the country. In 1999, parliament agreed to devolve (hand down) power to parliaments in Scotland and Wales, giving them limited powers to make their own laws. Northern Ireland was also given a devolved assembly, in 1998, but it was not until 2007 that the local parties could agree to work together.

BRITISH GOVERNMENT

1265 Representatives from each county and town summoned to parliament, the first time "commoners" attend.

1300s Commons and Lords become separate Houses of Parliament.

1376 First speaker elected.

1642 English Civil War between King and parliament.

1688 Glorious Revolution: monarch cannot pass laws without parliament's consent.

1707 English and Scottish parliaments united.

1832 Property-owning men gain vote.

1835 Town councils set up.

1853 Modern civil service begins.

1867 Working-class men in towns gain the vote.

1872 Secret voting introduced to stop bribery of voters.

1911 Payment for MPs.

1911 Power of House of Lords reduced; House of Commons is supreme.

1918 Women aged 30 gain the vote.

1928 Every adult aged 21 has the vote.

1958 Life Peers first sit in the House of Lords.

1969 Voting age reduced to 18.

1999 Scottish parliament and Welsh Assembly meet for the first time.

1999 House of Lords reformed, only 92 hereditary peers remain.

CITIZENSHIP

Many people know little about the government and politics of Britain because they did not learn much about them at school. In 2002, a new subject, citizenship, became part of the national curriculum. Every child learns how the government works and how they can influence and take part in decisions through voting in elections.

Former prime minister Tony Blair and the children of the future.

Find out more

DEMOCRACY

ENGLISH CIVIL WAR

LAW

GRASSLAND WILDLIFE

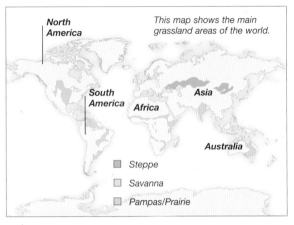

This map shows the main grassland areas of the world.

Steppe
Savanna
Pampas/Prairie

GRASSLAND AREAS
The main grassland areas in the world are the Asian steppes, African savannas and grasslands, North American prairies, and South American pampas, which blend into tropical Amazonian savanna. There are also tropical grasslands in parts of India and across Australia.

VAST AREAS OF AFRICA, the Americas, Asia, and Australia consist of grasslands – areas too dry for forests but not too dry for grasses. Grasses themselves are flowering plants that can grow again quickly after animals eat them. Grasses also recover quickly if fire sweeps across the plains in the hot, dry season. The fire burns only the upper parts of the grass, so the roots and stems are not damaged. Grasslands provide a home for many different animals; each survives by feeding on a different part of the grass plants. Zebras, for example, eat the coarse, older grass, while wildebeest (gnu) graze on new shoots. Thomson's gazelles nibble close to the ground. Grasshoppers, ants, and termites shelter among the grass stems and roots; these insects, in turn, are food for larger animals such as ant-eaters and armadillos. The lack of trees in grassland areas means that small animals and certain birds have to dig burrows for shelter and for breeding. Each type of grassland has bur-rowing rodents; prairie dogs and pocket gophers live in North America, susliks in Asia, ground squirrels in Africa, and vizcachas and tuco-tucos in South America.

Thistles grow in grassy areas throughout the world. Their prickles protect them against grazing animals. The flowers are often purple, and form fluffy white seed heads.

SOUTH AMERICAN PAMPAS
The largest mammals on the South American pampas are the pampas deer, guanaco, and rodents such as the viscacha, which burrows for shelter and safety. A fast-running bird called the rhea also lives on the South American pampas, feeding on grasses and other plants.

VISCACHA
The viscacha is related to the guinea pig. A male viscacha weighs about 8 kg (17 lb), almost twice the size of the female. Viscachas dig a system of burrows with their front feet and pile up sticks and stones near the various entrances. They eat mainly plant leaves and stems.

BURROWING OWL
The burrowing owl lives on the South American pampas. It often makes its nest in an empty burrow taken over from a viscacha. Burrowing owls eat grasshoppers, insects, small mammals, birds, lizards, and snakes.

GIANT ANTEATER
With large claws on its second and third fingers, the giant anteater can easily rip a hole in an ants' nest or a termite mound as it searches for food. The giant anteater uses its long, sticky tongue to lick up the ants and termites. Its tongue measures about 60 cm (24 in) in length.

Tail protects anteater's body as it sleeps in a shallow hole, listening for predators such as pumas.

PAMPAS GRASS
The white, fluffy seed heads of pampas grass are a familiar sight in parks and gardens. Wild pampas grass covers huge areas of Argentina, in South America. Pampas leaves have tiny teeth, like miniature saws, that easily cut human skin.

JACKAL

Golden jackals eat whatever they can find on the African savanna, including fruits, small mammals, eggs, birds, and the carcasses (dead bodies) of larger animals such as zebras.

Jackals sometimes hunt in groups, pursuing small grazing animals such as these Thomson's gazelles.

The crested porcupine lives on the African savanna.

SAVANNA

The huge grassland areas of eastern and southern Africa are called savannas. These areas are home to the world's largest herds of grazing animals, including zebra, wildebeest, and hartebeest. Many large grazers wander from one area to the next, following the rains to find fresh pasture. Acacia and baobab trees dot the landscape, providing shade for resting lions, ambush cover for leopards, and sleeping places for baboons.

THOMSON'S GAZELLE

These swift-moving mammals live on the grassy plains of Africa in herds of up to 30 animals. They all have horns, but those of the male are larger than those of the female. Thomson's gazelles are often the prey of other grassland animals, such as the cheetah and the jackal.

CONSERVATION

Many grassland areas are now used as farmland, and the natural wildlife is being squeezed into smaller areas. As a result, these areas become overgrazed and barren. Grassland animals are also threatened by human hunters. In the past the Asian saiga antelope was killed for its horns. Today it is protected by law, but it is still seriously endangered with only 50,000 left in the wild.

A newborn saiga antelope is fluffy and has no horns.

CRESTED PORCUPINE

The crested porcupine has sharp spines on its back for protection. It warns enemies to stay away by rattling the hollow quills on its tail. If an intruder ignores these warnings, the porcupine runs backwards into the enemy, and the quills come away and stick into the intruder's flesh.

Wild peonies are found in many grassy habitats around the world. Many garden peony plants came originally from the hardy wild peonies that grow in grassland areas.

GRASS SNAKE

The grass snake lives on riverbanks and in marshes, mainly in Europe and Asia. Grass snakes are good swimmers.

STEPPE

The vast plains of Asia are called steppes. In the western part of Asia the rainfall is more than 25 cm (10 in) each year, and grasses and other plants grow well. Towards the eastern part of Asia there is less than 6 cm (2.5 in) of rainfall yearly, and the grasses fade away into the harsh Gobi Desert. Saiga antelopes, red deer, and roe deer graze on the rolling plains.

PALLAS'S CAT

This long-furred cat lives in mountains, high steppes, and open country across central Asia. At night it hunts for hares, birds, and mice.

Total body length of about 60 cm (24 in)

Strong, agile, stout body with short legs

Soft, thick fur to keep out the cold winds

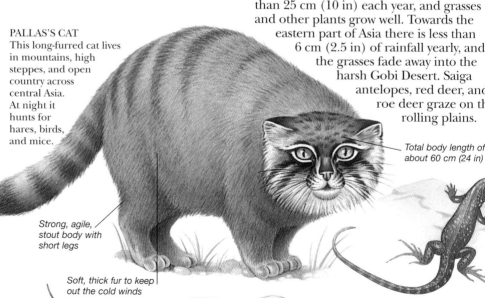

BROOK'S GECKO

Sharp claws and sticky toe pads enable the gecko to climb well over smooth rocks, along crevices, and in cracks. The Brook's gecko is active at night, catching insects, and hides by day under rocks or in an empty termite or ant nest.

PALLAS'S SANDGROUSE

The mottled plumage (feathers) of Pallas's sandgrouse gives it excellent camouflage among the brownish grasses and stones of the Asian steppe. It needs little water and can survive on very dry, tough seeds and other plant parts.

Find out more

HORSES, ASSES, AND ZEBRAS
LIONS, TIGERS, and other big cats
LIZARDS
REPTILES

GRAVITY

FALLING

Earth's gravity makes falling objects accelerate (speed up). Their speed does not depend on how heavy they are: a light object falls as fast as a heavy object unless air slows it down. The Italian scientist Galileo Galilei (1564-1642) noticed this about 400 years ago.

A heavy rock weighs much more than an egg of the same size. However, both objects fall at the same rate and hit the ground at the same time.

THE EARTH MOVES around the sun, travelling about 50 times faster than a rifle bullet. A strong force holds the Earth in this orbit. This is the force of gravity; without it, the Earth would shoot off into space like a stone from a catapult. Everything possesses gravity; it is a force that attracts all objects to each other. However, the strength of the force depends on how much mass is in an object, so gravity is only strong in huge objects such as planets. Although you cannot feel it, the force of gravity is also pulling on you. The Earth's gravity holds you to the surface of the Earth, no matter where you are. This is because gravity always pulls towards the centre of the Earth. Sometimes you can see or feel the effects of gravity. For example, the effort you feel when you climb up a flight of stairs is because you are fighting against the force of gravity.

When you drop a ball, it falls because gravity is pulling it towards the centre of the Earth.

Gravity pulls all objects down towards the centre of the Earth.

MASS AND WEIGHT

An object's mass is the amount of material it contains. Mass stays the same wherever the object is in the universe. The weight of an object is the force of gravity pulling on it. Weight can change. Because the moon is smaller than the Earth, its gravity is weaker, about one sixth as strong as Earth's. Therefore, an astronaut on the moon weighs only one sixth of her weight on Earth, but her mass remains the same.

MOON AND EARTH

Gravity keeps the moon moving in its orbit around the Earth. The moon's gravity has effects on the Earth, too. When the moon is directly over the sea, its gravity pulls the sea water towards it, which produces a high tide; low tide follows when the Earth rotates away again.

Objects fall in the opposite direction on the other side of the Earth.

The force of gravity gets weaker as you go further from the centre of the Earth. On top of a high mountain, gravity is slightly weaker than at sea level; so objects weigh fractionally less.

EARTH'S GRAVITY

People on the opposite side of the Earth are upside down in relation to you. But they do not fall off into space. They are held on to the surface of the Earth just as you are. This is because the force of gravity pulls everything towards the centre of the Earth. Down is always the direction of the Earth's centre.

ISAAC NEWTON

British scientist Isaac Newton (1642-1727) was the first person to understand the force of gravity. In 1666, after watching an apple fall to the ground, he wondered whether the force of gravity that makes things fall also holds the moon in its orbit around the Earth. This was a daring idea, and it took Newton many years to prove it to be true. He declared his law of gravity to be a universal law – a law that is true throughout the universe.

CENTRE OF GRAVITY

It is best to carry a large, unwieldy object such as a ladder by holding it above its centre. The weight of the ladder balances at the centre, which is called its centre of gravity or centre of mass. An object with a large or heavy base has a low centre of gravity. This stops it from falling over easily.

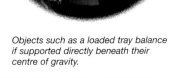

Objects such as a loaded tray balance if supported directly beneath their centre of gravity.

Find out more
ASTRONAUTS
PHYSICS
PLANETS
SCIENCE, HISTORY OF
UNIVERSE
WEIGHTS AND MEASURES

GREECE

| Volcano | Mountain | Ancient monument | Capital city | Large city/town | Small city/town |

Lying at the eastern end of the Mediterranean, Greece is surrounded by the Mediterranean, Aegean, and Ionian Seas. It consists of a mainland, the Peloponnese peninsula, and over 2,000 islands.

STATISTICS
Area: 131,990 sq km (50,961 sq miles)
Population: 10,737,000
Capital: Athens
Languages: Greek, Turkish, Macedonian, Albanian
Religions: Greek Orthodox, Muslim
Currency: Euro

GREECE IS A LAND of wild mountains, remote valleys, and scattered islands. Most people make their living by farming; olives can grow on the dry hillsides, hardy sheep and goats thrive in the rugged landscape. Greece is the world's third largest producer of olive oil, and also exports citrus fruits, grapes, and tomatoes. With one of the largest merchant fleets in the world, Greece is a seafaring nation – people and goods travel by boat. In recent years, tourism has transformed the Greek economy. Millions of visitors are attracted to Greece by its landscape, and by its rich history as the birthplace of democracy in the 5th century BCE.

THE GREEK ISLANDS
The Greek mainland is surrounded by many islands. Ships and ferries unite these scattered communities. In summer, the islands, with their warm climate, fishing villages, and beautiful beaches, are major tourist centres, attracting over nine million visitors. In winter, the small islands are deserted by summer residents, who return to the mainland.

ORTHODOX PRIESTS
The Eastern Orthodox Church was founded in Constantinople (Istanbul) in the 4th century CE. The Greek Orthodox Church became independent in 1850 and is the official religion of Greece, with more than 10 million faithful. Distinctively dressed priests are a common sight.

ATHENS
The ancient city of Athens, the cultural centre of Greece in the 5th century BCE, is generally believed to be the birthplace of western civilization. The fortified acropolis (above) rises 100 m (328 ft) above the city. It is crowned by the Parthenon temple, dedicated to the city's patron goddess Athena, and built in 432 BCE. Today, this busy modern city is a major commercial, shipping and tourist centre, and seat of the Greek government.

OCTOPUS
Octopuses are a Greek delicacy, but are becoming scarce due to overfishing in the Mediterranean.

SCALE BAR
0   50   100   km
0   50   100   miles

Find out more
ARCHAEOLOGY
CHRISTIANITY
DEMOCRACY
GREECE, ANCIENT

ANCIENT
GREECE

MANY WESTERN WORDS, monuments, ideas, and sources of entertainment have their roots in the world of Ancient Greece. About 2,500 years ago, the Greeks set up a society that became the most influential in the world. Greek architects designed a style of building that is copied to this day. Greek thinkers asked searching questions about life that are still discussed. Modern theatre is founded on the Ancient Greek plays that were performed under the skies thousands of years ago. And the Greeks set up the world's first democracy (government by the people) in Athens. However, only free men born in Athens were actually allowed to have a say in government. Ancient Greek society went through many phases, with a "golden age" between around 600 and 300 BCE. Arts and culture flourished at that time. The Macedonians, under Philip of Macedon, finally conquered the civilization, but it continued under Philip's son Alexander, who spread Greek culture and thinking throughout the Middle East and North Africa.

TEMPLE OF HERA
The Greeks built temples to worship their many gods. This temple at Paestum, Italy, was built to honour the goddess Hera, who was the protector of women and marriage.

PERICLES
As leader of Athens, Pericles (c.494-429 BCE) carried out a programme to beautify the city. This included the building of the Parthenon, a temple to the goddess Athena.

There were many busy markets in Athens, where people came to buy and sell their goods.

ATHENS
During the golden age, the Greek world consisted of independent, self-governing cities, known as city-states. With its own superb port at Piraeus, Athens was the most important city-state. It became the centre of Greek civilization and culture, attracting many famous playwrights and thinkers, such as Socrates. Athens practised the system of *demokratia* (democracy). People gathered together in the agora (marketplace) to shop and talk. The acropolis (high city) towered above Athens.

SPARTA

Spartan hoplites

The second major city-state of Greece, Sparta, revolved around warfare. Spartans led tough, disciplined lives. Each male Spartan began military training at the age of seven and remained a soldier until 60. Women kept very fit by running and wrestling. The fierce Spartan hoplites (foot soldiers) were feared throughout the Greek world.

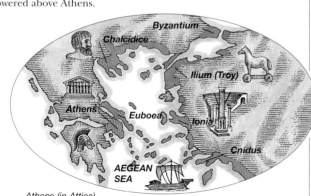

Athens (in Attica) and dependent states (shown in pink), c. 450 BCE

GREEK WORLD
The Greek world consisted of many city-states and their colonies, spread throughout the Mediterranean region.

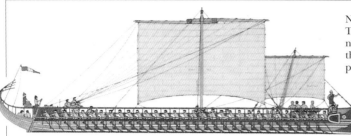

NAVY
The Athenians possessed a powerful navy, consisting of a fleet of more than 200 triremes – warships powered by a square sail and rowed by 170 men seated in three ranks. The battle tactic involved rowing furiously and ramming the enemy's ship. In 480 BCE, during wars against the Persians, the Athenian navy crushed the Persian fleet at the sea battle of Salamis.

Modern reconstruction of a Greek trireme

ANCIENT GREECE

1500 BCE Minoan civilization (on island of Crete) at its height.

c. 1400 Mycenaean civilization, centred in great palaces on the Greek mainland, dominates Greece.

c. 1250 Probable date of the Trojan Wars between Mycenaeans and the city of Troy.

c. 1000 Establishment of the first city-states in mainland Greece.

776 First Olympic Games held at Olympia, Greece.

750s First Greek colonies founded.

c. 505 Democracy is established in Athens.

400s Golden age of Greek theatre.

490-479 Persian Wars; Greek states unite to defeat Persians.

490 Greeks defeat Persians at Marathon.

480 Greeks destroy the Persian fleet at the Battle of Salamis.

479 Final defeat of Persians at Plataea.

461-429 Pericles rules in Athens; Parthenon built.

431-404 Peloponnesian War between Athens and Sparta leads to Spartan domination of Greece.

359 Philip becomes king of Macedonia.

338 Philip of Macedonia conquers Greece.

336-323 Alexander the Great, son of Philip, sets up Greek empire in Middle East.

The main actors performed on the proskenion *(stage).*

All the actors were men, even those playing women's roles. They wore painted masks to hide their faces.

The audience bought stone tokens, which were like tickets, and sat in a semi-circle of tiered seats set into the hillside.

The chorus commented on the action of the play in song and dance.

The circular space in front of the stage was called the orchestra.

GREEK THEATRE

Drama was born in Athens. It began as singing and acting as part of a religious festival to honour the god Dionysus. The audience watched a series of plays; at the end of the festival, prizes were given for the best play and best actor. From these beginnings, playwrights such as Sophocles and Aristophanes started to write tragedies and comedies. Tragedies involved dreadful suffering; comedies featured slapstick humour and rude jokes.

THINKERS
Great thinkers from Athens dominated Greek learning and culture during the 5th and 4th centuries BCE. Socrates (469-399 BCE; above) was one of the most famous. He discussed the meaning and conduct of life. He also questioned people cleverly, often proving that their ideas were wrong. Socrates wrote no books himself, but one of his followers, Plato (427-347 BCE), made him the subject of many of his books.

VASE PAINTING
Painted scenes on Greek pottery give us clear clues about daily life in Ancient Greece. The paintings often show a touching scene, such as a warrior bidding his family farewell as he goes off to war. They also show the many gods that the Greeks worshipped.

Amphora (vase) from Attica shows Zeus, king of the gods, at the birth of Athena, his daughter.

Find out more
ALEXANDER THE GREAT
ARCHITECTURE
DEMOCRACY
GREECE
OLYMPIC GAMES
THEATRE

GUNPOWDER PLOT

IN THE LATE 1500s AND EARLY 1600s, Roman Catholics in England, urged on by the Catholic rulers of Spain, constantly schemed to replace England's Protestant rulers with Catholics. In 1605, a small group of Catholics hatched a plot to blow up James I and his government when the king opened a new session of parliament. The so-called Gunpowder Plot was due to take place on 5 November, but it failed because one of the conspirators warned his brother-in-law, Lord Mounteagle, not to attend parliament on that day. Mounteagle warned the government, and the cellars under parliament were searched. There, the king's soldiers found a young conspirator, Guy Fawkes, with 20 barrels of gunpowder. He was arrested, tortured, tried, and executed. The other plotters fled, but were later caught and were also executed.

RELIGIOUS INTOLERANCE
Anti-Catholic feeling was common in England and Scotland. Protestants distrusted Roman Catholics because they feared the political power of the pope. After the plot, fear of Catholics intensifed, and the conspirators were executed.

Bates — Robert Winter — Christopher Wright — John Wright — Thomas Percy — Guy Fawkes — Robert Catesby — Thomas Winter

JAMES I
The first of the Stuart monarchs, James I was a staunch Protestant. He came to the throne in 1603, after the death of Elizabeth I. During Elizabeth's reign, Catholics had been persecuted. Mass was forbidden and Catholics could not hold high office. There were many Catholic plots. James I also distrusted Catholics. He angered them by refusing to reverse anti-Catholic laws.

THE CONSPIRACY
The leader of the Gunpowder Plot was Robert Catesby (1573-1605), a wealthy Roman Catholic. He recruited 12 other conspirators, including Guy Fawkes, who was chosen to light the fuse and blow up the Houses of Parliament. The conspirators hoped that their actions would encourage a rebellion, which would lead to England becoming a Catholic nation. Thomas Tresham, one of the conspirators, gave the plot away.

The House of Lords as the Queen formally opens parliament

STATE OPENING
Today, the British monarch still opens each session of parliament. There is a formal opening ceremony, at which the Queen reads out the government's programme for the year. It is the only day on which the Queen wears her crown, the symbol of her authority.

BONFIRE NIGHT
On 5 November 1605, supporters of the king celebrated the failure of the Gunpowder Plot by lighting bonfires. Ever since then, every year on 5 November, people in Britain remember the Gunpowder Plot. They build bonfires and let off fireworks. Children make dummy "guys" and ask people for a "penny for the guy". In some towns elaborate bonfire processions still take place.

Models of Guy Fawkes are still burned on Bonfire Night.

Find out more
ELIZABETH I
GOVERNMENT AND POLITICS
HENRY VIII
STUARTS

HABSBURGS

FAMILY CREST
The crest of the Habsburg family was the black double-headed eagle. It appeared on all their flags and banners.

DURING THE 900s a family named Habsburg owned some land in France and Switzerland. From this they rose to dominate European history for more than 1,000 years. The name Habsburg comes from one of the family's first castles, the Habichtsburg, in Switzerland. Through a series of wars, inheritances, and careful marriages, the family acquired more and more land. By the 1500s it owned most of southern and central Europe and much land in the Americas. The Habsburg possessions became so big that in 1556 the Habsburg emperor, Charles V, split the land between members of his family. Philip II governed one half from Madrid, Spain, while Ferdinand of Austria governed the other half from Vienna, Austria. The Spanish Habsburgs died out in 1700, but the Austrian Habsburgs continued to expand their empire. In the 19th century, however, their power began to weaken because the empire contained so many different peoples. When it collapsed after World War I (1914-18), four new nations emerged: Austria, Czechoslovakia, Hungary, and Yugoslavia.

CHARLES V
Under Charles V, who reigned as Holy Roman Emperor from 1519 to 1556, the Habsburgs reached the height of their power. Charles V ruled a vast empire shown in pink on the map above.

Joseph II

JOSEPH II
From the time of Rudolf I onwards, the Habsburg family extended its power throughout Europe. Joseph II, son of Maria Theresa, was appalled by the living conditions of his poorer subjects. He began reforms that included freeing serfs and abolishing privileges.

HABSBURGS

1273 Rudolf I becomes the Holy Roman Emperor.

1282 Albert I becomes first Habsburg ruler of Austria.

1438 Albert II becomes Holy Roman Emperor.

1519 Charles V becomes Holy Roman Emperor.

1526 Ferdinand, brother of Charles, acquires Bohemia.

1556 Charles V splits Habsburg lands in half.

1700 Charles II, last Spanish Habsburg monarch, dies.

1740-1780 Maria Theresa increases Habsburg power in Europe.

1781 Joseph II, son of Maria Theresa, introduces major reforms and frees serfs.

1867 Austrian empire is split between two monarchs: Austrian and Hungarian.

1918 Charles I, last Habsburg emperor, gives up throne.

MARIA THERESA
In 1740, Maria Theresa came to the Austrian throne. She was only 23 and her empire was bankrupt. Over the next 40 years, she pulled Austria back from poverty and restored Habsburg power in Europe.

AUSTRIA
Under Maria Theresa, Austria became the leading artistic centre of Europe. Austria was home to the composers Franz Joseph Haydn and Wolfgang Amadeus Mozart. Artists and architects came from all over Europe to work on great palaces such as the Schönbrunn in Vienna (above).

Find out more
AUSTRIA
CHARLEMAGNE
EUROPE, HISTORY OF
FRANCE
SWITZERLAND

HEALTH AND FITNESS

Regular, vigorous exercise helps prevent heart disease.

Better hygiene and a more balanced diet could eliminate much ill health in developed nations.

ARE YOU HEALTHY? Before answering, think about what you understand by "health". It doesn't just mean freedom from disease. Health is a measure of how sound and vigorous both your body and mind are. A truly healthy person has a sense of physical and mental well-being. Our health is precious and easily damaged. But there is much we can do to maintain it. Eating well, exercising, and getting enough sleep all help keep us healthy. Standards of health and health hazards are different from place to place. In some parts of the world many people have serious health problems because they are poor, hungry, and without clean drinking water. In other places stress at work, lack of exercise, and too much food bring their own health problems, such as heart disease. People also damage their health through the use of alcohol, tobacco, and dangerous drugs.

KEEPING HEALTHY

Food plays a large part in health. A healthy diet includes fresh fruit and vegetables, meat, fish, bread, eggs, and milk, but not too many fatty, salty, or sugary foods. Exercise keeps the heart strong and prevents us from gaining too much weight.

IMMUNIZATION

Good health includes preventing disease. Immunization, sometimes called inoculation or vaccination, involves injecting the body with a vaccine. This is a tiny dose of the infecting agent of the disease, which has been specially treated to render it safe. The vaccination provides immunity, or protection, against the disease. It is now possible to immunize against diphtheria, polio, tetanus, measles, mumps, rubella, tuberculosis, meningitis, and lots of others. Immunization has completely eliminated one disease, that is smallpox.

A doctor or nurse usually gives immunizations by injection.

Observing a child at play can help the pysychiatrist to make an assessment.

MENTAL HEALTH

A healthy mind is just as important as a healthy body. Stress, drug abuse, physical disease, and family problems such as divorce can all damage mental health. Specialist doctors who treat mental health problems are called psychiatrists. Other sources of help include drug therapy, counselling, and self-help groups.

HEALTH CHECKUPS

Through routine medical checkups, doctors can detect health problems such as cancer at the early stages, when treatment is most effective. Checkups can also reveal hereditary health problems – diseases that pass from parents to children.

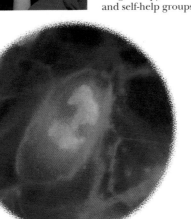

To reveal cancer cells on a microscope slide, technicians stain the tissue sample with coloured dyes.

PUBLIC HEALTH

Dirty conditions and lack of hygiene can affect health. If not controlled, insanitary conditions can spread throughout cities and affect large populations. The Great Plague of London in 1665 was caused by poor hygiene. During the 1840s, pioneers of public health in Europe worked to introduce clean water supplies and good sewage systems. Institutions such as the World Health Organization, have been set up to monitor public health internationally.

EXERCISE ROUTINES

Regular exercise improves blood circulation, makes the heart and lungs work well, keeps muscles strong and toned, and keeps joints supple. It is good for the brain as well as the body, and makes us feel happy and alert. With all exercise routines, you need to do a warm-up sequence before you start and a cool-down sequence at the end, to prevent strain on muscles.

CYCLING

Cycling is an enjoyable way to exercise as it takes place in the fresh air and can easily be fitted into your daily routine, if you cycle to school, for example. Cycling can be as vigorous or as gentle as you like, builds stamina, strengthens leg muscles, and improves the oxygen flow to heart and brain. As it is not a weight-bearing activity, it can be done safely by all age groups.

Always wear a safety helmet.

Keep your bicycle oiled and serviced.

Use the ball of the foot on the pedals.

HEALTHY EATING

Food is the fuel that gives us energy day after day. It also provides us with all the materials our bodies need for growing and for repairing themselves, and the vitamins we need to maintain strong and healthy immune systems that fight off illness. One third of our daily diet should be fresh fruit and vegetables.

Globe artichokes are good for the liver.

Fennel helps the kidneys to function well.

Courgettes are rich in folic acid and potassium.

Avocado pears contain the vitamins E and B6, and the mineral potassium.

Garlic improves blood circulation.

Red peppers are an excellent source of vitamin A.

Onions help lower fat levels in blood.

Stretching exercises keep you supple.

FITNESS AND FUN

Make sure you choose an exercise that you enjoy doing. The more fun you have, the more you will exercise and the healthier you will feel. There are many types of exercise to choose from that are both fun and can improve strength, stamina, and mobility. Trampolining, football, tennis, badminton, all types of dancing, gymnastics, swimming, running, or athletics are all good choices.

POSTURE

Good posture is part of being fit and well. Standing up straight, but relaxed, with your weight balanced on both feet encourages good circulation and prevents back strain. Sitting in a slumped position strains your back, shoulders, neck, and chest, and inhibits your breathing.

Strain on neck and back.

Pressure on the chest prevents proper breathing.

Keep knees slightly bent.

MENTAL FITNESS

It is important to keep your brain fit, as well as your body. A healthy diet, regular sleep, and plenty of exercise to make sure that the blood delivers nutrients and oxygen to the brain will keep your brain in good physical condition. Doing crosswords and puzzles, and playing board games that make you think, such as chess, are enjoyable ways to stay mentally alert.

Stand comfortably straight, not rigidly.

Find out more
DIGESTION
HEART AND BLOOD
SPORTS

HEART AND BLOOD

OUR BODIES CONTAIN about 4.5 litres (8 pints) of blood. Throughout life the heart, an organ inside the chest, pumps blood to every part of the body, keeping us alive. The heart is such a powerful pump that it takes only about a minute for each blood cell to travel all the way around the body and back to the heart. Travelling along tubes called blood vessels, blood carries oxygen and nourishment from digested food to every part of the body. Blood also carries away harmful waste products such as carbon dioxide. Blood consists of red and white blood cells, platelets, and a watery liquid called plasma. A drop of blood the size of a pinhead contains millions of red cells and thousands of white cells. About once every second the muscular walls of the heart contract, squeezing blood out of the heart and into blood vessels called arteries. The arteries divide many times until they form a network of tiny blood vessels called capillaries. The capillaries gradually join up again to form veins, which carry the blood back to the heart.

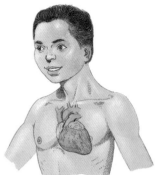

HUMAN HEART
The heart is protected by the rib cage. An adult's heart is the size of a clenched fist and weighs about 300 g (9 oz).

ARTERIES
These blood vessels carry blood away from the heart to the body. Arteries have thick walls that can resist high blood pressure produced when the heart beats. The coronary arteries deliver oxygen-rich blood to the walls of the heart itself.

CAPILLARIES
The tiny blood vessels that carry blood between the smallest arteries (arterioles) and the smallest veins (venules) are called capillaries. Capillaries allow oxygen and nutrients to pass through their walls to all the body cells.

INSIDE THE HEART
The heart consists of two pumps, left and right, that work together. Each side has two chambers, an upper atrium and lower ventricle. Oxygen-poor blood from the body enters the right atrium through two big veins, the superior and posterior venae cavae. Blood passes into the right ventricle, which pumps it to the lungs to pick up along the pulmonary arteries – the only arteries to carry oxygen-rich blood. From there it passes to the left ventricle, which pumps it along the aorta and its branches to all parts of the body to deliver its oxygen before returning to the right atrium. Valves inside the heart ensure that blood flows in one direction only.

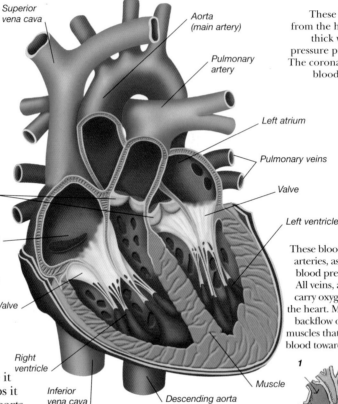

Superior vena cava
Aorta (main artery)
Pulmonary artery
Left atrium
Pulmonary veins
Valve
Valves
Right atrium
Left ventricle
Valve
Right ventricle
Inferior vena cava
Descending aorta
Muscle

VEINS
These blood vessels have thinner walls than arteries, as they are not subject to the high blood pressure created by each heartbeat. All veins, apart from the pulmonary veins, carry oxygen-poor blood from the body to the heart. Many have valves that prevent the backflow of blood from the heart. Skeletal muscles that surround veins help to squeeze blood towards the heart when they contract.

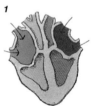 

1 Blood enters atria (upper chambers).
2 Blood flows through to ventricles (lower chambers).

BLOOD CELLS
There are three types of blood cells. Red blood cells carry oxygen from the lungs to the rest of the body. White blood cells protect the body against illness and fight infection. Platelets, which are actually small cell fragments, help the blood to clot. All blood cells are produced in the bone marrow inside the bones.

White cell

Red cell   Platelets

HOW BLOOD CLOTS
When you cut yourself and blood flows out of the wound, platelets in the blood stick together and a fine meshwork of fibres forms. This meshwork traps more blood cells and forms a clot to seal the wound.

HEARTBEAT
On average, an adult's heart beats 60 to 70 times each minute. This rises to more than 150 beats after strenuous activity. Each heartbeat has three phases. During diastole (1) blood fills the two atria. They contract during atrial systole (2) to push blood into the ventricles that contract together during venticular systole (3) to pump blood into the arteries.

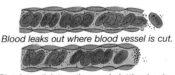

Blood leaks out where blood vessel is cut.

Platelets stick together, and clotting begins.

Tiny meshwork of platelets begins to form.

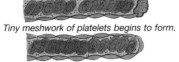

Blood clot forms, sealing the cut.

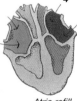

3 Ventricles contract to pump blood into arteries.
4 Atria refill with blood.

Find out more

BRAIN AND NERVES
HUMAN BODY
LUNGS AND BREATHING
MUSCLES AND MOVEMENT

HEAT

STAND IN THE SUNSHINE: you feel warm. Go for a fast run: you will get hot. The warmth of sunshine comes from heat generated in the centre of the Sun. Your body also produces heat all the time, and this heat keeps you alive. Heat is important to us in many ways. The Sun's heat causes the weather, making winds blow and rain fall. The Earth's interior contains great heat, which causes volcanoes to erupt and earthquakes to shake the ground. Engines in cars, aircraft, and other forms of transport use the heat from burning fuel to produce movement. Power stations change heat into electricity which comes to our homes. Heat is a form of energy.

White-hot steel

Everything, even the coldest object, contains heat – a cold object simply has less heat than a hot object. All things are made of tiny particles called molecules. Heat energy comes from the vibrating movement of molecules. Hot objects have fast-moving molecules; molecules in colder objects move more slowly.

SOLIDS, LIQUIDS, AND GASES
A substance can be a solid, a liquid, or a gas, depending on how hot it is. Changing the temperature changes the substance from one state to another. For instance, liquid water becomes a solid – ice – when it is cold and a gas – steam – when it is hot.

A process called convection spreads heat through gases and liquids. For example, hot air above a heater rises. Cold air flows in to take its place, becomes hot, and rises. In this way, a circular current of air moves around a room, carrying heat with it.

A gas, such as steam, has molecules that move about freely so that the gas spreads out to fill its container.

A liquid, such as water, has molecules that are close together. The molecules can move around more easily than in a solid, so a liquid can flow.

A solid, such as the ice on this window pane, has rows of molecules that vibrate back and forth. The molecules are locked together, so solids are often hard and cannot be squashed.

Warm rising air

Convection heater

BOILING POINT
At a temperature called the boiling point, a liquid changes into a gas. Below the boiling point the gas changes back to a liquid again. The boiling point of water is 100°C (212°F).

MELTING POINT
Heating a solid makes it melt into liquid. This happens only at a certain temperature, which is called the melting point. Below this temperature, the liquid freezes to a solid again. The melting point of ice is 0°C (32°F).

Cool incoming air

All objects give out heat rays that travel through air and space. The heating element of an oven cooks food with heat rays. The transmission (movement) of heat by heat rays is called radiation. It is not the same as nuclear radiation.

Heat travels through solid objects by a process called conduction. Metal conducts heat well. For instance, a metal spoon in a cup of coffee gets hot quickly. Other substances, such as wood and plastic, do not conduct heat well. They are called insulators and are used to make items such as saucepan handles.

A liquid slowly changes into a gas at a temperature lower than its boiling point. This is called evaporation. The steam from this hot cup of coffee is evaporated water.

HEAT ENERGY
Heat is just one of many forms of energy. Sources of heat change one type of energy into heat energy. A burning fire, for example, changes chemical energy in its fuel into heat energy. Electric heaters change electrical energy into heat.

The digestive system of an animal or a person changes chemical energy from food into heat energy inside the body.

INFRA-RED RAYS
Heat rays are also called infra-red rays. They are invisible rays very similar to red light rays, which is why the rays are called infra-red. All objects give out these rays, and hot objects produce stronger infra-red rays than cold objects. Some electric heaters have curved reflectors that send heat rays forward just as a mirror reflects light rays.

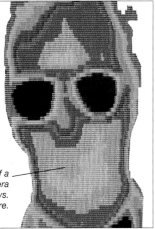

This is a thermogram (heat picture) of a person's face. It was taken by a special camera that uses infra-red rays instead of light rays. The hottest parts are yellow in the picture.

253

TEMPERATURE

Temperature is a measure of how hot an object is. A hot object has a higher temperature than a cold object. When objects are extremely cold, they have negative temperatures: a minus sign indicates how many degrees the temperature is below zero on the temperature scale.

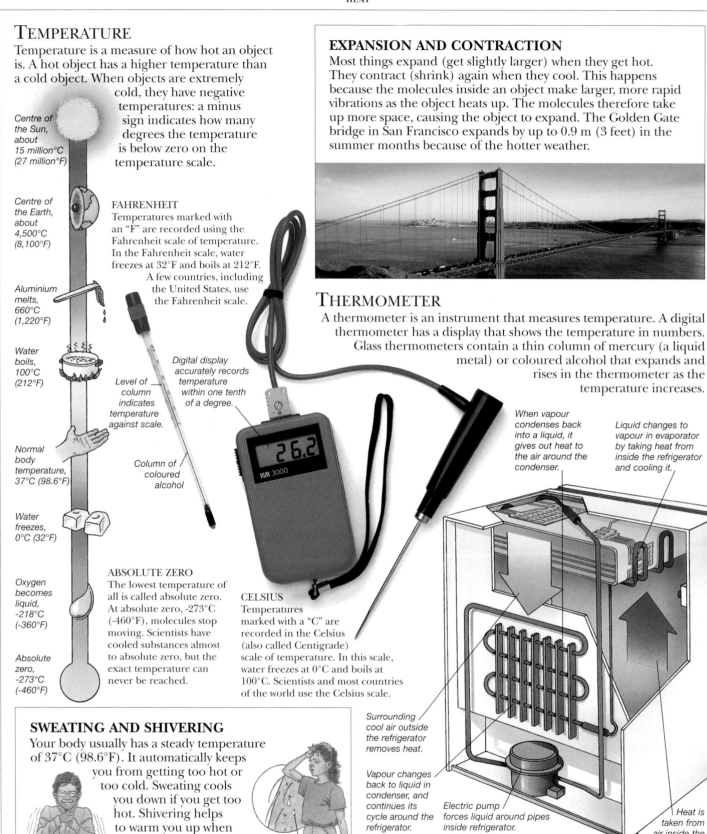

Centre of the Sun, about 15 million°C (27 million°F)

Centre of the Earth, about 4,500°C (8,100°F)

Aluminium melts, 660°C (1,220°F)

Water boils, 100°C (212°F)

Normal body temperature, 37°C (98.6°F)

Water freezes, 0°C (32°F)

Oxygen becomes liquid, -218°C (-360°F)

Absolute zero, -273°C (-460°F)

FAHRENHEIT

Temperatures marked with an "F" are recorded using the Fahrenheit scale of temperature. In the Fahrenheit scale, water freezes at 32°F and boils at 212°F. A few countries, including the United States, use the Fahrenheit scale.

Digital display accurately records temperature within one tenth of a degree.

Level of column indicates temperature against scale.

Column of coloured alcohol

ABSOLUTE ZERO

The lowest temperature of all is called absolute zero. At absolute zero, -273°C (-460°F), molecules stop moving. Scientists have cooled substances almost to absolute zero, but the exact temperature can never be reached.

CELSIUS

Temperatures marked with a "C" are recorded in the Celsius (also called Centigrade) scale of temperature. In this scale, water freezes at 0°C and boils at 100°C. Scientists and most countries of the world use the Celsius scale.

EXPANSION AND CONTRACTION

Most things expand (get slightly larger) when they get hot. They contract (shrink) again when they cool. This happens because the molecules inside an object make larger, more rapid vibrations as the object heats up. The molecules therefore take up more space, causing the object to expand. The Golden Gate bridge in San Francisco expands by up to 0.9 m (3 feet) in the summer months because of the hotter weather.

THERMOMETER

A thermometer is an instrument that measures temperature. A digital thermometer has a display that shows the temperature in numbers. Glass thermometers contain a thin column of mercury (a liquid metal) or coloured alcohol that expands and rises in the thermometer as the temperature increases.

When vapour condenses back into a liquid, it gives out heat to the air around the condenser.

Liquid changes to vapour in evaporator by taking heat from inside the refrigerator and cooling it.

Surrounding cool air outside the refrigerator removes heat.

Vapour changes back to liquid in condenser, and continues its cycle around the refrigerator.

Electric pump forces liquid around pipes inside refrigerator.

Heat is taken from air inside the refrigerator.

REFRIGERATOR

When liquids evaporate (change into a gas), they take heat from their surroundings. In a refrigerator, a liquid circulates, going through a cycle of evaporation and condensation (changing back into a liquid again). As the liquid evaporates, it takes heat from the food in the refrigerator.

SWEATING AND SHIVERING

Your body usually has a steady temperature of 37°C (98.6°F). It automatically keeps you from getting too hot or too cold. Sweating cools you down if you get too hot. Shivering helps to warm you up when you get too cold. Hairs on your skin stand up when your body gets cold and help to trap a layer of air around the skin, which stops heat loss.

Shivering makes muscles move and produce heat.

Drops of sweat evaporate, which cools the skin.

Find out more

ATOMS AND MOLECULES
EARTH
ENGINES
SCIENCE
STARS
SUN
VOLCANOES

HELICOPTERS

OF ALL FLYING machines, the helicopter is the most versatile. It can fly forwards, backwards, or sideways. It can go straight up and down, and even hover in the air without moving. Because helicopters can take off vertically, they do not need to use airport runways and can fly almost anywhere. They can rescue people from mountains, fly to oil rigs out at sea, and even land on the roofs of skyscrapers. Helicopters come in many shapes and sizes. Some are designed to carry only one person; others are powerful enough to lift a truck. All helicopters have one or two large rotors. The rotor blades are shaped like long, thin wings. When they spin around, they lift the helicopter up and drive it through the air.

Gas turbine engine (one of three)

Rotor blades, made of ultra-strong plastics

Cockpit with automatic flight control system

ALL-PURPOSE HELICOPTER

The Agusta Westland AW101 can transport 30 passengers or troops, carry 16 stretcher patients as an air ambulance, or lift a load of more than 5.1 tonnes. It flies at 280 km/h (170 mph).

Radar dome contains radar antenna.

Mission control console, equipped with radar screens and computers

Tail plane and fins keep the helicopter stable as it flies.

Tail rotor turns the helicopter's nose to the left or right and stops the helicopter from spinning around.

Helicopter body, made of light metal alloys and strong plastics

Wheels fold into pods on sides of helicopter.

Crewman lowered down to life raft

Life raft contains survivors from shipwreck.

TAKING OFF
The rotor blades produce a lifting force which supports the helicopter.

The "collective pitch" stick adjusts the rotors so the helicopter can go up, hover, or go down.

Another control, the cyclic pitch stick, makes the main rotor tilt so that it can pull the helicopter in any direction – backwards, forwards, or sideways.

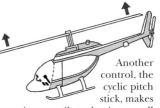

The tail rotor keeps the helicopter from spinning around. Pedals control the tail rotor so the helicopter can be turned to face any direction.

DEVELOPMENT

The Italian artist and scientist Leonardo da Vinci sketched a simple helicopter about 500 years ago, but it was never built. It was not until 1907 that a helicopter carried a person. It was built by a French mechanic named Paul Cornu.

Igor Sikorsky, a Russian-American, built the VS-300 in 1939. It was the first single-rotor helicopter, and it set the style for machines to come.

TWIN-ROTOR HELICOPTER

Large helicopters, such as this Boeing Chinook, may be twin-rotor machines. They have two main rotors that spin in opposite directions, and no tail rotor. The twin-rotor Boeing CH-47 Chinook (pictured) is widely used around the world for transporting troops and equipment.

Main rotor

Main rotor

Find out more
AIRCRAFT
PHYSICS
PLASTICS
TRANSPORT, HISTORY OF

HENRY VIII

THE SON OF HENRY VII, Henry VIII was the second of the Tudor monarchs, and probably the most famous king of England. Strong-willed, pleasure-loving, unpredictable, and obstinate, he inspired both admiration and fear. Henry wanted England to be a great power in Renaissance Europe, and used the money his father had amassed to establish Britain as a great naval force and to fight wars all over Europe. Resenting the power of the pope, who would not grant him a divorce from his first wife, Henry passed the Act of Supremacy in 1534. This set up the Church of England as a separate institution to the Catholic Church, and made the monarch its supreme head. Henry married six times, trying to produce a male heir.

1491 Born at Greenwich.

1509 Becomes king and marries Catherine of Aragon.

1533 Marries Anne Boleyn.

1536-39 Suppresses the monasteries.

1536 Anne Boleyn beheaded. Henry marries Jane Seymour.

1537 Son Edward born. Queen Jane dies.

1540 Henry marries Anne of Cleves; the marriage is annulled. Then marries Catherine Howard.

1542 Catherine is executed for treason.

1543 Henry marries Catherine Parr.

1547 Dies; buried at Whitehall.

Henry VIII enjoyed music, dance, games, sport, and hunting.

WAR AND PEACE

Henry sought glory through war with France. He strengthened the navy and had many powerful new ships built. At the Battle of the Spurs (1513), he led his army to victory, then in 1520 he organized a peace treaty between France and England at the ceremony of the Field of the Cloth of Gold. In 1544 he again made war with France. England captured Boulogne and France agreed to pay the king the sum of 2,000,000 crowns.

THOMAS CRANMER

Thomas Cranmer

Henry had many advisors. Those who disagreed with him were usually executed, but Thomas Cranmer (1489-1556), who supported Henry's marriage to Anne Boleyn, was made Archbishop of Canterbury in 1533.

THE SIX WIVES

Henry's first wife was Catherine of Aragon, mother of Mary I. Because no male heir was born, the king divorced Catherine and married Anne Boleyn, mother of Elizabeth I. For this, he was excommunicated by the pope. After Anne, Henry had four more wives: Jane Seymour, mother of King Edward VI; Anne of Cleves; Catherine Howard; and Catherine Parr, who outlived the king.

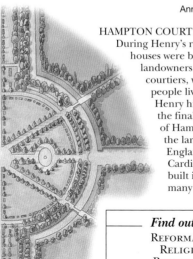

Anne Boleyn

THE ENGLISH REFORMATION

In 1534, Henry abolished the authority of the pope in England and founded the Church of England. This was the beginning of the English Reformation. Monasteries were closed and the king acquired their wealth and lands. The buildings fell into ruin or were destroyed.

Kirkstall Abbey, Yorkshire, destroyed in the Reformation.

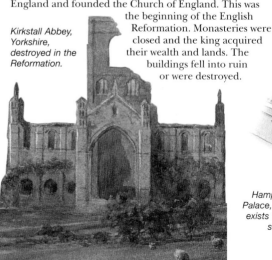

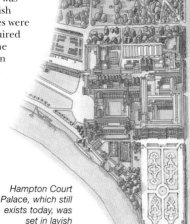

Hampton Court Palace, which still exists today, was set in lavish gardens.

HAMPTON COURT

During Henry's reign, great houses were built by rich landowners and the king's courtiers, while many people lived in poverty. Henry himself oversaw the final building stages of Hampton Court, the largest house in England, begun by Cardinal Wolsey and built in brick, like many Tudor houses.

Find out more

REFORMATION
RELIGIONS
RENAISSANCE
TUDORS

HIBERNATION

MANY WARM-BLOODED ANIMALS need extra energy in order to stay warm in the cold winter months, but the source of that energy – food – is scarce in winter. Some animals survive winter by migrating to a warmer place; others, such as bats and hedgehogs, hibernate in a safe and unexposed place such as a nest, burrow, or cave. In true hibernation, the body processes slow down almost to a standstill – the heartbeat occurs only every now and then, and the animal takes only a few breaths per minute. The body temperature falls to only a few degrees above the outside temperature – as low as 0°C (32°F) in a hamster. If the outside temperature drops below zero, chemical reactions in the animal's body switch on to keep it from freezing to death. A hibernating animal feasts on extra food in the autumn so it can build up reserves of fat in its body and survive the winter months without food.

Senses such as hearing and sight are inactive during hibernation.

Dormouse curls up into a ball shape to reduce heat loss from its body.

Dormouse builds nest on or near ground, using stems, moss, and leaves.

Furry tail wraps around face for protection and insulation.

Up to half of body weight is lost during hibernation.

DORMOUSE

One of the best-known hibernators is the dormouse. In autumn it feeds eagerly to build up stores of body fat, then settles into a winter nest among tree roots or in dense undergrowth. Its heart slows to only one beat every few minutes, and its breathing slows down. Its body temperature also drops to a few degrees above the surroundings.

BLACK BEAR

The winter sleep of bears, skunks, and chipmunks is not as deep as the true hibernation of bats and mice. The American black bear's heartbeat slows but the body temperature drops by only a few degrees. This means that the bear can rouse itself from its sleep quite rapidly during a spell of slightly warmer weather. Although it wakes up, the bear does not eat and continues to live off its body fat until the spring. Some female bears give birth during the winter months.

TORPOR

To save energy, some small, warm-blooded animals such as bats and hummingbirds allow their bodies to cool and their heartbeat and breathing to slow down for part of the day or night. This is called torpor. Large animals such as bears do not become torpid because they would need too much energy to warm up again afterwards. Bats often huddle together as they hang upside down to prevent too much heat loss. When the cold season comes, bats fly to a special cave or tree called a hibernaculum, where they begin true hibernation.

AESTIVATION

Many desert animals sleep during the hot, dry season to survive the intense heat. This is called aestivation – the opposite of hibernation. Desert creatures which aestivate include lizards, frogs, insects, and snails. Before aestivation begins, snails seal their shell openings with a film of mucus that hardens in the heat.

Snails cluster on grass stems to aestivate, away from predators on the ground.

Find out more

ANIMALS
BATS
BEARS AND PANDAS
MIGRATION, ANIMAL
SNAILS AND SLUGS

HINDUISM

MORE THAN 5,000 YEARS ago Hinduism, one of the world's oldest religions, began in India. Hinduism has no single founder but grew gradually from early beliefs. Today there are many different Hindu groups or sects. They may worship the same Hindu gods, but they do not all share the same religious beliefs. Nevertheless, most Hindus believe that people have a soul which does not die with them. Instead the soul moves out from a dying body and enters the new one being born. People who live good lives are reincarnated, or born again, in a higher state. Bad deeds can lead to rebirth as animal or an insect. It is possible to escape from the cycle of death and rebirth through Karma, that is, good deeds that bring an individual to the state of Moksha (liberation). Hindus are born into castes, or groups, which give them their rank in society. Rules restrict how people of different castes may mix and marry. Today, there are over 900 million Hindus in the world. They live mainly in India and East Africa.

HINDU FESTIVALS

Holi Two-day festival in spring.

Janmashtami August/September; festival to mark the birth of Lord Krishna.

Durga puja September/October; nine-day festival, offering prayers to Durga, the goddess of universal energy.

Diwali Festival of lights.

Temple festivals are held once a year.

GODS

There are three primary gods – Vishnu, Brahma, and Shiva – created by the energy of the universe. For the purpose of worship, however, a Hindu may choose any one of the gods as his deity. Vishnu, the preserver, appears in ten different incarnations (forms). Two of the most popular are Rama and Krishna. Stories of the gods and their battles against evil are told in ancient Indian scriptures (writings) such as the Mahabharata.

More gentle than the fierce Shiva, Vishnu comes to restore order and peace to the world.

The four heads of Brahma, the creator, looking in all four directions, show that he has knowledge of all things.

Shiva, the destroyer, rules over the death and life of everything in the world. It is thought that when Shiva dances, he destroys old, worn out life.

MARRIAGE

Family life and marriage are very important to Hindus. Parents are often involved in their children's choice of partner. Women are required to be dutiful and obedient to their fathers and husbands. A wedding ceremony is accompanied by music and feasting. The bride and groom exchange colourful garlands of flowers and make solemn promises to each other before a priest.

TEMPLES

In southern and central India there are large temples that contain ornate carvings and statues of the many Hindu gods. Priests look after the temples. They bathe the statues every day, and decorate them with ornaments. Visitors come to pray and bring offerings of flowers and food. After the food has been blessed, it is shared by the worshippers or given to the poor.

Find out more

EAST AFRICA
INDIA AND SUBCONTINENT
RELIGIONS

HOLOCAUST

IN 1933, ADOLF HITLER'S NAZI PARTY came to power in Germany. The Nazis were deeply anti-Semitic (prejudiced against Jews) and began to attack German Jews. At first they rounded up Jews and sent them to labour or concentration camps, together with other people the Nazis did not like, such as gypsies, homosexuals, communists, and others. Jews in German-occupied Europe were forced into ghettos (closed-off areas of a city) or shot. In 1942, the Nazis decided to kill all European Jews in an act of genocide (the deliberate extermination of an entire people). No-one knows how many were murdered in death camps such as Auschwitz and Treblinka, but more than six million Jews lost their lives before the end of World War II. This terrible event in human history is called the Holocaust.

YELLOW STAR
After 1941, Jews over the age of six in German-occupied Europe had to sew a yellow star, the Star of David, onto their clothes. This made it easier to identify them. Jews also wore yellow stars in the camps.

Oscar Schindler

GHETTOS

In Warsaw and other East European cities occupied by the Germans after 1939, Jews were herded into ghettos. These ghettos were isolated from the rest of the city and their inhabitants denied proper food or medical care. In 1943, the Germans attacked the Warsaw ghetto in order to kill everyone inside. The Jews fought back, but by 1945 only about 100 of the original 500,000 inhabitants were still alive.

RESISTANCE
Many Jews resisted the Nazis, by attacking German forces and supplies. Both the Hungarian and Italian governments, although German allies, refused to hand over their Jews, while the Swedish diplomat Raoul Wallenberg helped many Jews escape to Sweden in 1944. Most famously, German businessman Oscar Schindler saved about 1,200 Jews from death, by giving them essential war work in his munitions factory.

THE "FINAL SOLUTION"

After the invasion of Poland in 1939 and Russia in 1941, the number of Jews under German rule increased. At a conference at Wannsee, Berlin in 1942, the Nazis decided on what they called the "Final Solution": to kill all Jews in specially built extermination camps. These included Auschwitz and Treblinka in Poland, and Belsen, Dachau, and Buchenwald in Germany.

Gates to Auschwitz

COMMEMORATION
After the war, the United Nations tried to repay the Jews for their suffering by creating a Jewish homeland – Israel – in Palestine in 1948. Holocaust museums have been opened in Berlin and elsewhere. Many countries have an official Holocaust commemoration day on 27 January – the anniversary of the liberation of Auschwitz, the first camp to be freed.

THE HOLOCAUST

1933 Hitler's Nazi Party takes power in Germany.

1935 Nuremberg Laws forbid marriage between Jews and non-Jews.

1937 Jewish businesses confiscated.

1938 The Night of Broken Glass (9-10 November); synagogues, shops and homes destroyed.

1942 "Final Solution" begins.

1943 Jews in the Warsaw ghetto wiped out.

1945 Concentration camps liberated.

1948 Israel founded.

ANNE FRANK
In order to escape the Nazis, many European Jews went into hiding. Thirteen-year-old Anne Frank and her family hid for two years in the back attic of a house in Amsterdam, Holland. In 1944, they were betrayed and sent to a concentration camp, where Anne died of typhus in 1945, aged 16. While in hiding, Anne kept a diary of daily events and her hopes for the future. Published in 1947, her diary was translated into more than 50 languages.

Jewish Museum, Berlin

Find out more
ISRAEL
JUDAISM
WORLD WAR II

HORSES
ZEBRAS, AND ASSES

FOR THREE THOUSAND YEARS before trains and cars were invented, horses were a fast, efficient method of transport. These swift, graceful creatures are easy for humans to train. Today there are more than 75 million domestic (tame) horses, and they are divided into more than 100 different breeds. Horses, asses, and zebras belong to the equid family, a group that includes donkeys and mules. Equids are long-legged mammals with hoofed feet, flowing tails, and a mane on the upper part of the neck. They can run or gallop with great speed. A keen sense of smell, good eyesight, and sharp hearing mean that they are always alert and ready to flee from danger. Horses, asses, and zebras are grazing animals that feed almost entirely on grasses, which they crop with their sharp front teeth.

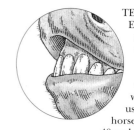

TEETH
Experts can tell the age of a horse by the number, angle, and size of its teeth, and the way the teeth have worn down with use. Most adult horses have between 40 and 42 teeth.

UNICORN
The unicorn is an imaginary horselike creature. It often appears in legends and folktales as a symbol of purity.

Poll · Forelock · Large ears can swivel to detect which direction a sound comes from. · Eyes are on the side of the head for good all-round vision. · Mane covers upper neck. · Withers · Back · Flank · Croup · Dock · Muzzle · Long jaws and strong cheek muscles for chewing grass · Neck · Chest · Elbow · Horse uses long, coarse hairs of tail as a fly-whisk and as a social signal. · Knee · Heel · Frog · Sole · Horseshoe · Cannon · Bones · Fetlock · Pastern · Hoof

THE FIRST HORSES
Hyracotherium, one of the first equids, lived in woodland areas more than 50 million years ago. It was only 60 cm (2 ft) high. Through evolution, horses gradually became larger and began to live in more open grassland areas.

Today's domestic horse · Hyracotherium

HOOVES
Horses walk on the tips of their toes. On each foot is a strong, hard hoof: the core is made of bone and the outer coating is keratin. There is a pad on the sole of the hoof called the frog. The frog acts like a shock absorber when the horse runs. People also put metal horseshoes on a horse's hooves to protect them on hard roads and rough ground.

ADULTS AND YOUNG
An adult male horse is called a stallion; an adult female is a mare. Young males are called colts; young females are fillies.

HORSES AND HUMANS
Domestic horses are trained to do many jobs, from pulling carts to carrying soldiers into battle. Many sports and leisure activities involve horses, such as show jumping, polo, rodeo, flat racing, and steeplechasing. Champion horses are worth millions of pounds, and the first prize at a famous horse race may be thousands of pounds.

In some countries horses and mules are still used instead of cars. They are also used on farms to till fields, fertilize the crops, and pull produce to market.

260

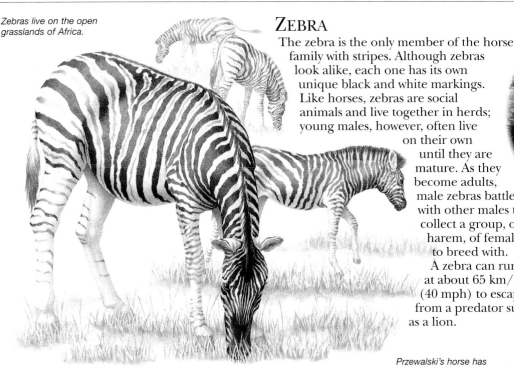

Zebras live on the open grasslands of Africa.

ZEBRA

The zebra is the only member of the horse family with stripes. Although zebras look alike, each one has its own unique black and white markings. Like horses, zebras are social animals and live together in herds; young males, however, often live on their own until they are mature. As they become adults, male zebras battle with other males to collect a group, or harem, of females to breed with. A zebra can run at about 65 km/h (40 mph) to escape from a predator such as a lion.

DONKEY

A donkey is a domesticated ass. Donkeys, together with horses and asses, have been hauling loads for people for thousands of years. They are often called beasts of burden. Another beast of burden, the mule, is the offspring of a female horse and a male donkey.

ASS

There are two kinds of wild ass – the African ass and the Asian ass. The African ass lives in dry, rocky areas of North Africa; the Asian ass is found in Asia. Asses need very little water and survive in the wild by eating tough, spiky grasses. Like other members of the horse family, the female ass has one young at a time, called a foal. The foal can walk a few minutes after birth.

A wild ass and a smaller domesticated ass

Przewalski's horse has a stiff upright mane.

PRZEWALSKI'S HORSE

Also called the Asian horse or "wild horse", Przewalski's horse is closely related to the domestic horse. Herds of these horses once lived on the high plains of Mongolia, in northern Asia. Today there are only a few hundred left in zoos and wildlife parks. Although introduced back into the wild, they must be kept away from domestic horses to avoid cross breeding.

GALLOPING

Horses move at a walk, trot, canter, or gallop, in increasing order of speed. When a horse gallops, all its hooves are off the ground for a split second during each stride. The fastest race horses can gallop at more than 65 km/h (40 mph) over a short distance.

All four hooves lift off the ground in mid-gallop.

Light horses are best equipped for racing.

HOW WE MEASURE HORSES

Horses can be measured in hands from the ground to the withers (the highest point of the shoulder). One hand equals 10 cm (4 in). Shire horses are the largest and Shetland ponies are among the smallest horses.

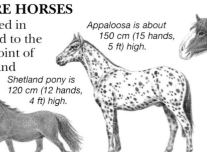

Shire horse may be more than 180 cm (18 hands, 6 ft) at the shoulders and weigh more than 1,135 kg (2,500 lb).

Appaloosa is about 150 cm (15 hands, 5 ft) high.

Shetland pony is 120 cm (12 hands, 4 ft) high.

TYPES OF HORSES

There are three main kinds of horses – draught horses such as Shires; light horses such as Arabian horses; and ponies such as Shetland ponies. Draught horses pull ploughs, and light horses take part in races.

Find out more

ANIMALS
MAMMALS
MOUNTAIN WILDLIFE
TRANSPORT, HISTORY OF

HUMAN BODY

FROM THE MOMENT we are born to the moment we die, our bodies do not stop working for a second. The human body is a complex collection of more than 100,000 million living units called cells. There are more than 200 different types of cells, including nerve cells or neurons, muscle cells, fat cells, epidermal cells, blood cells, and gland cells that release secretions, such as hormones and enzymes. Each type of cell in the body does a particular job. Cells that do similar jobs are grouped together to form tissues, such as muscle tissue and nerve tissue. Tissues, in turn, are grouped together to form organs, which are separate structures within the body. The lungs, heart, liver, and kidneys are some of the main organs. Linked organs work together as systems, and each system carries out one or more major functions. For example, the heart, blood vessels, and blood form the circulatory system, which carries oxygen and nutrients around the body and carries away waste products. All the different systems work together, under the control of the brain, to produce a living, walking, talking human body.

THE BODY'S ABILITIES
The human body is capable of amazing feats of balance and co-ordination. Many animals can run faster or jump higher, but our bodies are very adaptable. An extremely complex brain controls the body and gives us the intelligence to use our physical abilities to the best advantage.

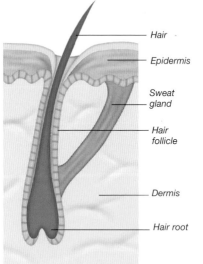

Hair
Epidermis
Sweat gland
Hair follicle
Dermis
Hair root

SKIN
The body is covered by skin. Skin is flexible and helps protect the body. It keeps water and harmful bacteria out, and keeps body fluids in. Skin is also wear-resistant because it continually renews itself. The base of the upper layer, or epidermis, divides constantly to make new cells. The new cells move upwards as if on a conveyor belt, to replace cells that are worn out.

CELL
Every second, millions of cells die and millions more replace them. An average cell measures about 0.025 mm (one thousandth of an inch) across, but there are many different kinds of cells in the body, each adapted for a certain job. Nerve cells are long and thin. Like wires, nerve cells conduct (carry) electrical nerve signals. Red blood cells are doughnut-shaped and contain chemicals that carry oxygen around the body. Epithelial cells on body surfaces, such as the lining of the mouth, are broad and flat and fit together like paving stones.

Skin cell
Red blood cell
Nerve cell
Bone cell
Muscle cell
Fat cell

NERVOUS SYSTEM
The brain and the nerves make up the nervous system. Nerves extend from the brain and spinal cord to all body parts, carrying signals in the form of tiny electrical impulses. The signals bring information from the sense organs to the brain and take instructions from the brain to the muscles. The brain controls many processes automatically, such as breathing, heartbeat, and digestion, without our having to think about them.

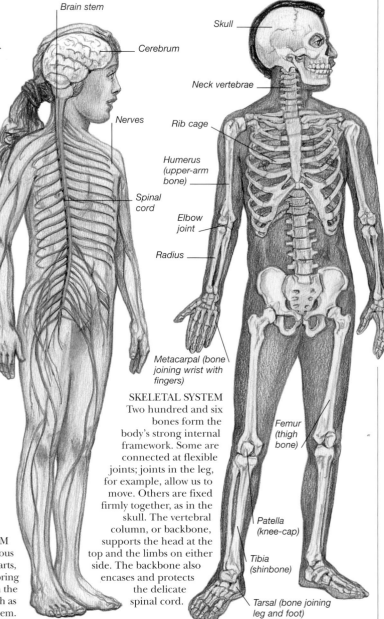

Brain stem
Cerebrum
Nerves
Spinal cord

Skull
Neck vertebrae
Rib cage
Humerus (upper-arm bone)
Elbow joint
Radius
Metacarpal (bone joining wrist with fingers)

SKELETAL SYSTEM
Two hundred and six bones form the body's strong internal framework. Some are connected at flexible joints; joints in the leg, for example, allow us to move. Others are fixed firmly together, as in the skull. The vertebral column, or backbone, supports the head at the top and the limbs on either side. The backbone also encases and protects the delicate spinal cord.

Femur (thigh bone)
Patella (knee-cap)
Tibia (shinbone)
Tarsal (bone joining leg and foot)

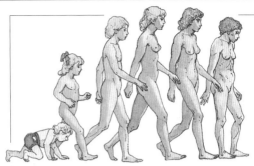

There are several stages of development in everyone's lifetime – from birth through childhood, adolescence, and adulthood, to old age.

GROWTH AND DEVELOPMENT

As the human body grows, it develops many skills. Babies learn to smile, sit up, crawl, walk, and talk. Learning continues at school. On average, the peak of physical abilities is reached at about 18 to 25 years of age. Later, more changes occur with age. The skin becomes wrinkled and less elastic, the joints are less flexible, bones become more brittle, muscles are less powerful, and there is some loss of height and greying of hair.

In many older people, decrease in physical strength is offset by the wisdom and knowledge gained from a lifetime of experience.

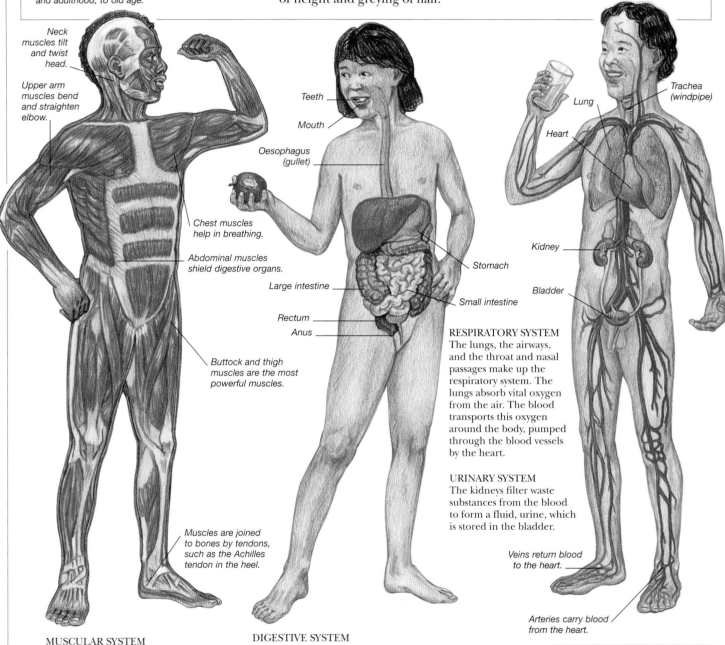

Neck muscles tilt and twist head.

Upper arm muscles bend and straighten elbow.

Chest muscles help in breathing.

Abdominal muscles shield digestive organs.

Buttock and thigh muscles are the most powerful muscles.

Muscles are joined to bones by tendons, such as the Achilles tendon in the heel.

Teeth

Mouth

Oesophagus (gullet)

Stomach

Large intestine

Small intestine

Rectum

Anus

Trachea (windpipe)

Lung

Heart

Kidney

Bladder

Veins return blood to the heart.

Arteries carry blood from the heart.

RESPIRATORY SYSTEM
The lungs, the airways, and the throat and nasal passages make up the respiratory system. The lungs absorb vital oxygen from the air. The blood transports this oxygen around the body, pumped through the blood vessels by the heart.

URINARY SYSTEM
The kidneys filter waste substances from the blood to form a fluid, urine, which is stored in the bladder.

MUSCULAR SYSTEM
There are about 650 muscles in the body. Some, such as the arm muscles, can be controlled at will, to pull on the bones of the skeleton and move the body. Others, such as the muscles of the heart and intestine, work automatically.

DIGESTIVE SYSTEM
The mouth, oesophagus, stomach, and intestines are part of the digestive system. These organs work together to break down food into particles that are small enough to pass through the lining of the intestine and into the blood. The mouth and teeth chop and chew food, and the stomach churns it with powerful digestive chemicals. The liver is the main organ for converting absorbed nutrients into forms more suitable for use by the various organs. The large intestine deals with wastes and leftover food.

Find out more
BRAIN AND NERVES
EARS
EYES
HEART AND BLOOD
LUNGS AND BREATHING
REPRODUCTION
SKELETONS
TEETH

HUMAN RIGHTS

MOST OF US BELIEVE that we have the right to be treated fairly and equally within society, regardless of our race, sex, religion, or social group. This equal treatment includes the right to vote, to work, and to be educated. When these rights are protected by law, they are called legal or human rights. In some countries, they are spelled out in the constitution. However, through history, many groups, including African-Americans, black South Africans, Native Americans, and women, have not been considered equal to others, and have had few, if any, civil or human rights. This kind of targetted mistreatment is called discrimination. In the 20th century, many different groups, including blacks, homosexuals, women, and people with disabilities, fought long and sometimes bitter campaigns to achieve their rights and obtain equal treatment within society.

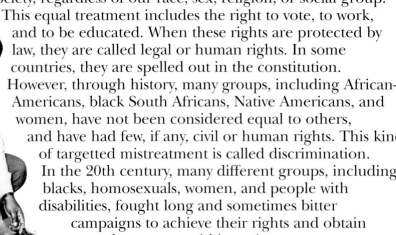

MOHANDAS GANDHI
Human rights activists – those who fight for civil rights – use peaceful methods. They unite and mobilize people. In 1915, Mohandas Gandhi (1869-1948) began to lead the struggle against British rule in India. Using non-violent civil disobedience, Gandhi's fasts and marches helped lead to India's independence from British rule in 1947.

NELSON MANDELA
In 1948, the South African government introduced apartheid, under which the black majority had no civil rights. The African National Congress (ANC), headed by Nelson Mandela (b.1918), led a long fight against apartheid. It was finally repealed in 1991.

AFRICAN-AMERICAN RIGHTS

Until slavery was abolished in 1865, African-Americans were treated as property in the southern states. Following abolition, southern states introduced laws which segregated (separated) races, and made African-Americans second-class citizens. Under the leadership of Martin Luther King, Jr. (1929-68), a civil rights movement emerged. It used non-violent methods, such as sit-ins (see left), where African-Americans peacefully occupied segregated public places. Finally Congress passed the Civil Rights Act in 1964 and the Voting Rights Act in 1965. These laws outlawed discrimination on the grounds of race, colour, or religion in schooling, voting, and employment.

AMNESTY INTERNATIONAL

A worldwide human rights organization, Amnesty International was founded in 1961 following a legal appeal by a British lawyer, Peter Benenson, after he read about two Portuguese students who were imprisoned for raising their glasses in a toast to freedom. Amnesty works to obtain prompt and fair trials for all prisoners, to end torture and executions, and to secure the release of people imprisoned solely for their political or religious beliefs and who have not used or advocated violence. The organization has more than 2.2 million members and has its headquarters in London. In 1977, Amnesty International was awarded the Nobel Peace Prize for its work.

AMERICAN INDIAN MOVEMENT
Since the 1960s, Native Americans have become more forceful in demanding equal rights. In 1968, the American Indian Movement (AIM) formed to fight for civil rights and improved conditions on reservations. A militant organization, AIM conducted a number of high-profile protests. In 1973, they occupied Wounded Knee in South Dakota, the site of a massacre of Sioux people in 1890. Federal marshals surrounded the protestors, and a siege began in which two AIM members were killed. Since then, some Native Americans have won land rights, but discrimination still continues today.

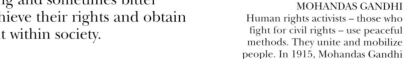

> **Find out more**
> AFRICA, HISTORY OF
> KING, MARTIN LUTHER
> LAW
> MANDELA, NELSON
> NATIVE AMERICANS
> SLAVERY
> TUBMAN, HARRIET

HUNDRED YEARS WAR

IN 1337, THE ENGLISH KING EDWARD III, whose mother was French, landed in Normandy, laid claim to the French crown, and began what historians call the Hundred Years War. To the people who fought it, it was more like a series of small wars separated by truces. It lasted through the reigns of five English and five French kings. Edward III failed to gain the French crown, and died in 1377. His heir, Richard II, took little interest in the war, but Henry V, who came to the throne in 1413, wanted to fight for the French crown and started the conflict again. Before 1420, the English won most of the battles, including Crécy (1346), Poitiers (1356), and Agincourt (1415), but by 1453, France had taken back all England's French lands, except Calais, which England lost in 1558.

ENGLAND AND FRANCE
Through royal marriages, the English already held large areas in the north and west of France. By the Treaty of Troyes in 1420, it was agreed that Henry V of England would become French king after the death of Charles VI of France.

English troops kept the sun behind them so that it shone directly into the eyes of the French soldiers.

French troops had to attack uphill.

Welsh and English archers fired faster than French cross-bow men.

French cavalry bogged down in the mud.

BATTLE OF CRÉCY
On 26 August 1346, Edward III's 8,000 troops were trapped at Crécy, but clever tactics and the skill of the English archers defeated a French army of 20,000. Edward's 16-year-old son, known as the Black Prince because of the black armour he wore, commanded his own troops in the battle.

HENRY V AND AGINCOURT
On 25 October 1415, Henry V (1387-1422) led his troops into battle at Agincourt. An English army of only 13,000 archers, pikemen, and cavalry defeated a French force of 50,000. Shakespeare described this English victory in *Henry V*.

ENGLISH LONGBOW
The longbow was normally made from yew, and the arrows were ash. In the 14th and 15th centuries, all English men were required by law to practise archery after church on Sundays, to be ready for war.

Archers practise with their longbows.

HUNDRED YEARS WAR

1338 Edward III of England claims French crown.

1346 Battle of Crécy.

1347 English capture Calais.

1356 Battle of Poitiers.

1415 Henry V declares war on Charles VI of France.

1415 Siege of Harfleur.

1415 Battle of Agincourt.

1419 English capture Normandy.

1420 Treaty of Troyes. Henry V marries King of France's daughter and claims French throne.

1428-29 Siege of Orléans.

1430 Joan of Arc taken.

1450 French reconquer Normandy.

1453 Battle of Castillon.

1453 Fall of Bordeaux ends war.

Find out more
ARMOUR
CASTLES
JOAN OF ARC
KNIGHTS AND HERALDRY
UNITED KINGDOM, HISTORY OF

INCAS

IN THE 12TH CENTURY, a tribe of Native Americans moved down from the Andes mountains in South America to settle in the fertile Cuzco valley. By the end of the 15th century they had conquered a huge territory of 1,140,000 sq km (440,000 sq miles) containing more than 10 million people. The Incas won this land with their powerful army and then controlled it with a remarkable system of communications. Inca engineers built a network of paved roads that crisscrossed the empire. Relays of imperial messengers ran along these roads (there were no horses or wheeled vehicles), travelling 250 km (150 miles) a day as they took messages to and from the capital city of Cuzco. At the head of the empire was the chief Inca, who was worshipped as a god and held absolute power over all his subjects. But in 1525 the chief Inca, Huayna Capac, died, and civil war broke out between two rivals for his throne. In 1532 a small force of Spanish soldiers arrived in the country and found it in disarray. They quickly overwhelmed the Incan army, and by 1533 the Inca empire was almost completely under Spanish rule.

South America

Inca empire

INCA EMPIRE
In 1525, at its height, the Inca empire stretched for more than 3,200 km (2,000 miles) along the Pacific coast of South America, ruling over much of present-day Ecuador, Peru, Bolivia, and Chile.

MACHU PICCHU
Covering an area of 13 sq km (5 sq miles), the fortress city of Machu Picchu was built on a series of terraces carved into the side of a mountain more than 2,280 m (7,500 ft) above sea level.

Llamas have been used as pack animals for 4,000 years.

An Inca woman weaving an elaborately designed piece of cloth.

QUIPU
The Incas did not read or write. Instead, they used quipus – lengths of knotted string – to record every aspect of their daily life. Historic events, laws, gold reserves, population statistics, and other items of information were all stored accurately in this way.

The colour of string, number of knots, and length of string on the quipu all meant different things.

The Incas were expert goldsmiths and often placed gold figurines (right) in their graves. Much of the Incan gold was melted down by Spanish invaders.

WEAVING
The Incas wove lengths of beautiful, colourful cloth with elaborate patterns. The wool they used came from the mountain animals – llamas, alpacas, and vicunas – that the Incas kept on their farms. Many of their designs depicted jaguars and pumas.

TERRACE FARMING
The Incas were expert at farming every available piece of fertile land in their mountainous empire. They built terraces along the steep hillsides and watered them with mountain streams so that crops could be grown and animals kept to feed all the people who lived in the cities.

Find out more
CONQUISTADORS
FARMING
SOUTH AMERICA
SOUTH AMERICA, HISTORY OF

INDIA
AND SUBCONTINENT

A TRAVELLER IN INDIA would need to speak more than 1,000 languages to understand conversations in every part of the country. Hindi and English are the two official languages, and 14 other languages are spoken nationwide. Many people, however, speak a local language of their own. The majority of Indians are Hindu in religion, but there are many Muslims, Sikhs, Christians, and Buddhists. Geographically, the country is very varied too. The north is mountainous, and in the centre the River Ganges waters a rich plain of productive farmland. In the south a hot and fertile coastal region surrounds a dry inland plateau. With a population of more than 1,000 million, India is the second most populated country in the world (China is the first). About 70 per cent of the people live in small, often very poor villages, and work on the land. The rest live in big cities where some work in modern factories and offices. Recent advances in farming have made the land more productive, and after many years of famine, India can now feed itself.

PRINTING BLOCKS
Traditional wooden printing blocks are still used in the production of colourful textiles.

India, Pakistan, Nepal, Bhutan, Bangladesh, and Sri Lanka occupy the Indian Subcontinent. China is to the north, and to the east lie the jungles of Southeast Asia. The Indian Ocean washes the southern shores; the mountains and deserts of Iran and Afghanistan enclose the Subcontinent on the west.

TEA

In 1824, tea plants were discovered in the hills along the frontier between Burma and the Indian state of Assam. The British first introduced tea culture to India in 1836 and Sri Lanka in 1867, and today most of the world's tea comes from the Indian Subcontinent. The low tea bushes grow well on the sheltered, well-drained foothills of the Himalayas. Only the leaves near the tip of the plant are picked; they are then dried, rolled, and heated to produce the final product. Tea also grows in southern India and Sri Lanka.

Picking tea is laborious and often painful work. Most tea pickers are women. They spend long days picking the crop by hand.

TEXTILES
The production of textiles, carpets, and clothing is one of the major industries in India. Millions of people work at spinning, weaving, and finishing a wide range of cotton and other goods, often printed with designs that have been in use for centuries. Many of these products are exported. There are large factories, but some people also work in their own homes.

KARAKORAM MOUNTAINS
A high mountain range separates the Indian Subcontinent from China to the north. Most of the range is part of the Himalayas. At its western end, the Himalayas continue as the Karakoram range, which forms Pakistan's northern border. Few people have their homes in these mountainous regions. Nevertheless, the mountains have a great influence on people living thousands of kilometres away. Most of the rivers that irrigate the fertile plains of the Indian Subcontinent begin in the Himalayas.

MODERN INDIA
India is one of the most industrial countries in Asia, with a wide range of engineering, electronic, and manufacturing industries. Its railway system is one of the world's biggest. However, traditional costumes and ways of life coexist with modern industries.

PAKISTAN

Pakistan was formed in 1947, when the end of British rule in India led to the creation of two separate states; the predominantly Hindu India, and the predominantly Muslim Pakistan. Pakistan originally included what is now Bangladesh, then known as East Pakistan. Bangladesh became independent in 1971 after a revolt against rule from West Pakistan (present-day Pakistan). India and Pakistan are in bitter conflict over the area at Pakistan's northeastern border known as Kashmir; both India and Pakistan consider the region to be a part of their country. In the 2000s, Pakistan has also faced problems with militants in the North-West Province, as the conflict in Afghanistan spilled over the border.

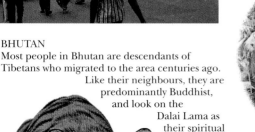

Expansion of Mumbai is confined by its island location, therefore the city has one of the highest population densities in the world.

SHERPAS
The Sherpa people (right) of Nepal are famed for their mountaineering skills. They often act as guides for trekkers and tourists on expeditions in the Nepalese Himalayas.

MUMBAI

One of India's largest cities is Mumbai, which has a population of more than 10 million. The city is the capital of the western state of Maharashtra, and is a major port for western commerce. Mumbai is built on an island, and has a superb natural harbour to the east. Cotton is grown nearby, and Mumbai is the largest cotton textile centre in the country. In 2008, Mumbai suffered a terrorist attack in which more than 200 people died.

KERALA
The state of Kerala in southwest India borders the Arabian Sea. The eastern part of the state is hilly, but much of the land area is a flat plain. Kerala is one of the most densely-populated states in India. Fishing is important for the local economy. Near the coast, the people of Kerala grow crops of cashew nuts, coconuts, and rice, and there are tea, rubber, coffee, and pepper plantations to the east. Although the government has encouraged modern farming techniques, traditional methods of agriculture and transport are common, such as the canoe in the picture (left). Forestry is also important in Kerala. In the mountains there are forests of teak, ebony, and rosewood, as well as a wide variety of wildlife.

BHUTAN
Most people in Bhutan are descendants of Tibetans who migrated to the area centuries ago. Like their neighbours, they are predominantly Buddhist, and look on the Dalai Lama as their spiritual leader. The dense forests and high mountains that cover the country are home to many animals native to the Indian Subcontinent, such as tigers (left), monkeys, and elephants. In an effort to protect Bhutan's culture and natural environment the government of Bhutan does not allow many tourists to enter the country.

INDIAN PEOPLE

India has one of the most diverse populations in the world. Throughout history, one group after another has settled in India, each bringing its own culture, customs, and languages. The groups often intermarried, but not all aspects of society became mixed and diluted: many groups clung to their traditions. For instance, there is no one Indian language, and people in different parts of the country often have their own unique local language.

BOLLYWOOD

The Indian film industry produces even more films than Hollywood, in the United States. About 800 full-length feature films are shot each year, mainly in Mumbai, nicknamed "Bollywood". Chennai (Madras) is also a centre of the film industry.

A still from a film by Indian film director, Satyajit Ray. His work is shown and admired worldwide.

MUSIC

Traditional Indian music is very complex, with a wide range of rhythms. Melodies are based on ragas – a fixed series of notes the performer must play as a basis for improvising or making up the tune. In the 1980s, bhangra, a new music combining traditional Indian music from the province of Punjab with western rock music, became popular among young people.

The Taj Mahal is built of the finest white marble and is a supreme example of Islamic architecture.

SACRED WATERS

From its source in the Himalayas, the Ganges river (below) flows eastward across India, then turns south. The river's 2,510-km (1,560-mile) course takes it through Bangladesh to reach the sea in the Bay of Bengal. Hindus consider the river to be sacred. They believe that bathing in its waters washes away sins, and cures illness. Indians rely on the waters of the Ganges for the irrigation of agricultural land.

Cows are sacred to Hindus in India and must not be harmed.

DANCE

Traditional Indian dances have a variety of forms and rhythms. They differ according to region, occupation, and caste.

DELHI

The ancient city of Delhi lies on the hot plains of northern India. In 1638 it became the capital city of the Indian Mogul empire. When the British took control of India in the 1800s, they moved the capital to Kolkata (Calcutta), in the east of the country. In 1912, the British began to build a new city in the outskirts of Delhi from where they could govern their vast Indian empire. New Delhi has been the nation's capital since India gained independence in 1947.

TAJ MAHAL

The Taj Mahal (left), at Agra in northern India, was built in 1631 by Shah Jahan, the Mogul emperor of India. It was constructed as a tomb and memorial for his beloved wife, Mumtaz Mahal. She was the mother of 14 children. The Taj Mahal is built of white marble and inlaid with semi-precious stones.

Find out more

ASIA
ASIA, HISTORY OF
BUDDHISM
DANCE
FILM
HINDUISM

Legend:
- ⚒ Volcano
- △ Mountain
- 🏛 Ancient monument
- ✪ Capital city
- ● Large city/town
- • Small city/town

STATISTICS

Area: 3,287,590 sq km (1,269,338 sq miles)
Population: 1,166,079,000
Capital: New Delhi
Languages: Hindi, English Urdu, Bengali, Marathi, Telugu, Tamil, Bihari, Gujarata, Kanarese
Religions: Hindu, Muslim, Christian, Sikh, Buddhist
Currency: Rupee
Main occupations: Agriculture, industry
Main exports: Rice, iron ore, cut diamonds, coal
Main imports: Petroleum, coal, steel

AMRITSAR

The city of Amritsar is in Punjab in northwest India. It is the most important religious centre for the Sikhs, who live mainly in northern India. The town surrounds a sacred pool, and on a small island in the pool stands the Golden Temple (above). In 1984 Sikhs fighting for an independent Sikh state in the area occupied the temple, and the government sent in troops to remove them.

SCALE BAR

| 0 | 250 | 500 | km |
| 0 | 250 | 500 | miles |

NATURAL BORDER

A massive, towering wall of snow-capped mountains stretches in an arc between the Indian Subcontinent and the rest of continental Asia.

BANGLADESH
Area: 143,998 sq km (55,598 sq miles)
Population: 156,051,000
Capital: Dhaka

BHUTAN
Area: 47,000 sq km (18,147 sq miles)
Population: 691,000
Capital: Thimphu

NEPAL
Area: 147,000 sq km (56,757 sq miles)
Population: 28,563,000
Capital: Kathmandu

PAKISTAN
Area: 803,940 sq km (310,403 sq miles)
Population: 172,243,000
Capital: Islamabad

SRI LANKA
Area: 65,610 sq km (25,332 sq miles)
Population: 21,325,000
Capital: Colombo

BANGLADESH

Bangladesh lies on the Ganges delta, where the Ganges, Brahmaputra and Meghna rivers split up into dozens of smaller rivers before flowing into the Bay of Bengal. The area is prone to monsoons, which are a type of tropical storm, and floods are very common throughout most of the country. Most people live in wooden houses raised on stilts above the flood level, to avoid their homes being washed away in severe monsoons.

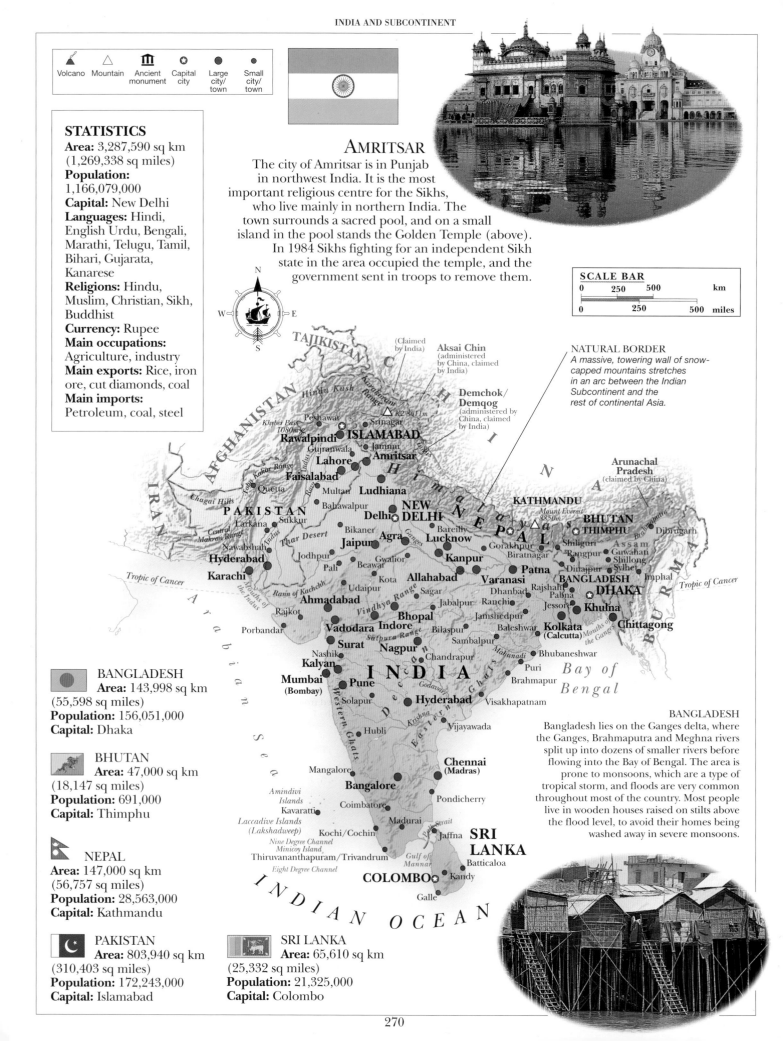

Map labels:

TAJIKISTAN · CHINA · AFGHANISTAN · IRAN · PAKISTAN · INDIA · NEPAL · BHUTAN · BANGLADESH · BURMA · SRI LANKA

Aksai Chin (Claimed by India) (administered by China, claimed by India)
Demchok/Demqog (administered by China, claimed by India)
Arunachal Pradesh (claimed by China)

Hindu Kush · Karakoram Range · K2 8611m · Mount Everest 8850m · Himalayas · Vindhya Range · Satpura Range · Western Ghats · Eastern Ghats · Deccan · Thar Desert · Chagai Hills · Central Makran Range · Toba Kakar Range · Sulaiman Range · Rann of Kachchh · Mouths of the Indus · Mouths of the Ganges

Khyber Pass 1080m · Peshawar · Srinagar · Jammu · ISLAMABAD · Rawalpindi · Gujranwala · Amritsar · Lahore · Faisalabad · Quetta · Multan · Ludhiana · Bahawalpur · Larkana · Sukkur · NEW DELHI · Delhi · Bikaner · KATHMANDU · BHUTAN · THIMPHU · Bareilly · Dibrugarh · Nawabshah · Jaipur · Agra · Lucknow · Gorakhpur · Shiliguri · Rangpur · Guwahati · Assam · Shillong · Jodhpur · Beawar · Kanpur · Biratnagar · Dinajpur · Sylhet · Imphal · Hyderabad · Pali · Gwalior · Patna · BANGLADESH · Karachi · Kota · Allahabad · Varanasi · Rajshahi · Pabna · DHAKA · Udaipur · Sagar · Dhanbad · Jessore · Khulna · Ahmadabad · Jabalpur · Ranchi · Kolkata (Calcutta) · Chittagong · Rajkot · Bhopal · Bilaspur · Jamshedpur · Baleshwar · Porbandar · Vadodara · Indore · Sambalpur · Surat · Nagpur · Chandrapur · Mahanadi · Bhubaneshwar · Nashik · Kalyan · Puri · Mumbai (Bombay) · Pune · Hyderabad · Brahmapur · Solapur · Visakhapatnam · Hubli · Vijayawada · Mangalore · Chennai (Madras) · Bangalore · Pondicherry · Amindivi Islands · Kavaratti · Coimbatore · Laccadive Islands (Lakshadweep) · Madurai · Kochi/Cochin · Nine Degree Channel · Minicoy Island · Jaffna · SRI LANKA · Thiruvananthapuram/Trivandrum · Gulf of Mannar · Batticaloa · Eight Degree Channel · COLOMBO · Kandy · Galle

Rivers: Indus · Ravi · Chenab · Sutlej · Ganges · Brahmaputra · Godavari · Krishna

Tropic of Cancer · Arabian Sea · Bay of Bengal · INDIAN OCEAN · Gulf of Mannar · Strait

INDIAN OCEAN

MORE THAN 1,000 MILLION PEOPLE live in the countries that fringe the Indian Ocean, and on some of the 5,000 islands that are scattered across its surface. The world's third-largest ocean provides a major link between Europe and Asia. The monsoon winds, which bring heavy rainfall to many of the countries surrounding the ocean, also have an impact on the currents, which reverse direction completely between March and August. Early navigators used the winds and currents to carry them from Arabia to southern India and Indonesia, bringing Islamic religion and culture with them. Malays and Indonesians took the journey westwards, settling in Madagascar. Most of the islands of the Indian Ocean are small and uninhabited. However, many tourists are drawn to their beautiful palm-fringed beaches, and in some places tourism is beginning to supplement traditional ways of life based on fishing and farming.

The Indian Ocean is bounded by Africa to the west, India and Australia to the east, and Asia to the north. In the south, it merges with the Antarctic Ocean. In the north, the Suez Canal gives access, via the Red Sea, to the Mediterranean.

MONSOON
The lands around the Indian Ocean are dependent on monsoon rainfall. Monsoons are seasonal winds, blowing from the southwest in summer and northeast in winter, that bring torrential downpours. Very heavy monsoon rains swell rivers, causing disastrous flooding often accompanied by diseases such as cholera. The Bay of Bengal is especially vulnerable to flooding.

SEYCHELLES
The island republic of the Seychelles consists of 40 scattered mountainous islands. These are surrounded by over 70 coral islands, which are low-lying and sparsely populated. The main islands are outstandingly beautiful; their hillsides blanketed with tropical vegetation, fringed by silvery-white beaches. Temperatures are constant throughout the year, reaching a daytime high of 30° C (86° F). The Seychelles attract year-round visitors from the northern hemisphere.

STILT FISHERMEN
There are less areas of shallow seas, where fish breed, in the Indian Ocean than in the Pacific or the Atlantic. Large-scale fishing, using trawlers and factory ships, has therefore not developed in the region. Most fishing takes place on a local basis, near island coastlines. Tuna is the most valuable catch. In Sri Lanka, fishermen – precariously perched on stilts – use poles and lines to catch their fish.

MADAGASCAN VILLAGE
Most Madagascans are descended from Malays and Indonesians, who crossed the Indian Ocean in the 7th century CE. These villagers come from the southeastern coast. The east coast is densely populated and poor. Most of Madagascar's ruling class come from the central plateau.

MADAGASCAR
The world's fourth-largest island lies off Africa's eastern coast. Most of the population is concentrated in the narrow strip of fertile land along the east coast, which has a humid, tropical climate. Farming dominates the economy. Rice and cassava are the main crops, while coffee and vanilla are grown for export. Poultry, sheep, pigs, and goats are all kept on a small scale. The government's attempts to modernize livestock farming have not been successful.

Find out more
AFRICA
ASIA
CORALS
OCEANS AND SEAS
SOUTHEAST ASIA

CHRISTMAS ISLAND

Area: 134.6 sq km
(52 sq miles)
Status: Australian external
territory
Claimed: 1958
Population: 1,400
Capital: Flying Fish Cove

COMOROS

Area: 2,170 sq km
(838 sq miles)
Population: 752,000
Capital: Moroni
Languages: Arabic,
Comoran, French
Religions: Muslim,
Roman Catholic
Currency: Comoros franc

MADAGASCAR

Area: 587,040 sq km
(226,660 sq miles)
Population: 20,654,000
Capital: Antananarivo
Languages: Malagasy,
French
Religions: Traditional
beliefs, Christian, Muslim
Currency: Malagasy franc

MALDIVES

Area: 300 sq km
(116 sq miles)
Population: 396,000
Capital: Male'
Languages: Dhivehi
(Maldavian)
Religions: Sunni Muslim
Currency: Rufiyaa

MAURITIUS

Area: 2,040 sq km
(788 sq miles)
Population: 1,284,000
Capital: Port Louis
Languages: English, French,
French Creole
Religions: Hindu, Roman
Catholic
Currency: Mauritian rupee

REUNION

Area: 2,517 sq km
(972 sq miles)
Status: French overseas
department
Claimed: 1649
Population: 802,000
Capital: Saint-Denis

SEYCHELLES

Area: 455 sq km
(176 sq miles)
Population: 87,476
Capital: Victoria
Languages: English, French,
French Creole
Religions: Roman Catholic
Currency: Seychelles rupee

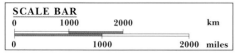

Volcano | Mountain | Ancient monument | Capital city | Large city/town | Small city/town

SCALE BAR

0 — 1000 — 2000 — km

0 — 1000 — 2000 — miles

ARAB DHOW

Dhows are Arab trading boats made of teak or coconut planks, sewn together with twine. They are lateen-rigged, which means that they have one, or sometimes two, triangular sails. Dhows are fast and manoeuvrable. They were a vital tool in the Arab exploration of the Indian Ocean from the 8th century CE. Using the monsoon winds, Arab merchants soon gained control of Indian Ocean trade and spread Islam as far as Indonesia.

THE MALDIVES

The Maldives consist of 1,800 low-lying coral islands, which form the crowns of ancient submerged volcanoes. None of the islands are higher than 1.8 m (6 ft), and all but 20 have fewer than 1,000 inhabitants. Rising sea levels, caused by global warming, threaten to submerge the islands.

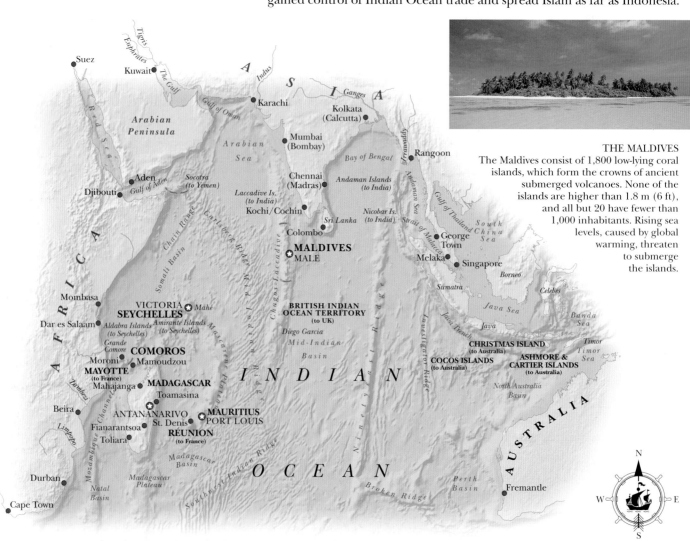

INDUSTRIAL REVOLUTION

THE WORLD WE LIVE IN TODAY, with its factories and huge cities, began less than 300 years ago in Britain, then spread to Europe and the United States. Beginning in about 1760, great changes took place that altered people's lives and methods of work forever, changes that are known today as the Industrial Revolution. Machines powered by water and, later, steam were invented to produce cloth and other goods more quickly. It took many workers to run these big machines, so poor people moved from the country into the new industrial towns to be near the factories. There were more jobs and higher wages in the cities, but life was often miserable. Although the Factory Act in 1833 banned young children in Britain from working in factories, there were no laws to control how long people worked each day, or to make sure the machines were safe.

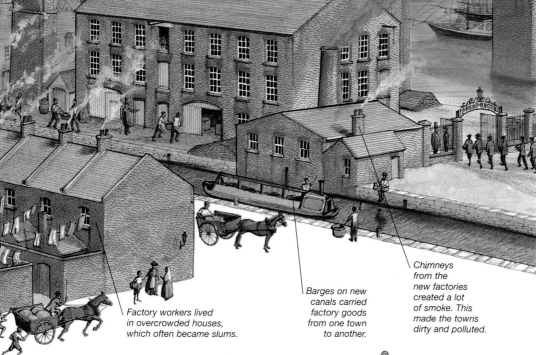

Factory workers lived in overcrowded houses, which often became slums.

Barges on new canals carried factory goods from one town to another.

Chimneys from the new factories created a lot of smoke. This made the towns dirty and polluted.

FACTORY OWNERS
Robert Owen (1771-1858) was a generous British factory owner who tried to improve working conditions. Many other owners grew rich by demanding long hours of work for low wages.

NEW TOWNS
Factory towns were built as fast and as cheaply as possible. Large families were crowded into tiny houses, and the water supply was often polluted. Diseases spread rapidly, and many people died young.

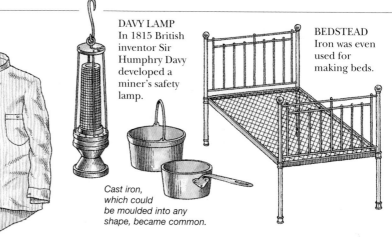

NEW TECHNOLOGY
Stronger metals were needed to make machines, so cast iron and steel were developed. Steam to drive the new engines was made by burning coal to boil water. Coal mines were driven deep into the ground. Cotton cloth was the first product to be made completely by machine. The new goods were produced in large numbers so they were cheap to buy.

Cotton replaced wool as the main material for making clothes.

DAVY LAMP
In 1815 British inventor Sir Humphry Davy developed a miner's safety lamp.

Cast iron, which could be moulded into any shape, became common.

BEDSTEAD
Iron was even used for making beds.

1708 Englishman Abraham Darby invents coke-smelting of iron.

1733 John Kay, England, develops "flying shuttle", which mechanizes weaving.

1760 Start of Industrial Revolution, Britain.

1765 James Hargreaves, England, invents "spinning jenny". It increases output of spun cotton. Scotsman James Watt develops steam engine, which is used to drive machinery in cotton industry.

1769 Richard Arkwright's water frame used to spin strong thread. Speeds up production; early beginning of Factory Age, England.

1779 English weaver Samuel Crompton develops spinning "mule", which spins many threads at once.

1784 Henry Cort, England, develops puddling furnace and rolling mill. Produces high quality iron.

1789 First steam-powered spinning loom, England. Speeds up textile production.

1793 Eli Whitney's cotton gin mechanizes cotton production, United States.

1804 Englishman Richard Trevithick builds first railway locomotive.

1825 First public railway from Stockton to Darlington, England.

1828 Development of hot-blast smelting furnace, England.

1842 Mines Act, Britain, bans women and children from working underground.

1851 Great Exhibition, London, displays new industrial products and techniques.

1855 Bessemer converter developed in England. Changes pig iron into steel.

1870 Industrialization established in Britain, Germany, and United States.

MILLS
The first factories were water-driven cotton mills which produced cloth. They were noisy, dangerous places to work in. Mill owners employed many women and children because they could pay them lower wages than men.

STEAM HAMMER
Unlike humans, steam-powered machines could work tirelessly, turning out vast quantities of goods. This steam hammer, invented in 1839, could hammer iron forgings with tremendous power and great accuracy.

The Clifton suspension bridge, Avon

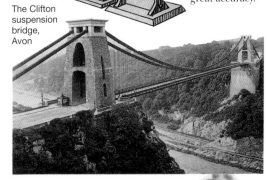

BRUNEL
Isambard Kingdom Brunel (1806-59) was probably the greatest engineer of the Industrial Revolution. His most famous bridge was the Clifton suspension bridge across the Avon Gorge. He also designed and built the Great Western Railway and the *Great Britain*, which was the first large steamship with an iron hull and a screw propeller.

CO-OPS AND UNIONS
Working people fought to improve their conditions. Some set up labour unions to fight for shorter hours and better pay. Others created co-op stores to provide wholesome food at reasonable prices. These stores later grew into a co-operative movement.

Find out more
FARMING
FARMING, HISTORY OF
SCIENCE
SCIENCE, HISTORY OF
TRADE AND INDUSTRY
VICTORIANS

INDUS VALLEY CIVILIZATION

ABOUT 4,500 YEARS AGO, one of the greatest ancient civilizations developed along the banks of the Indus River in the western Punjab. The Indus Valley people occupied a huge area, bigger than Ancient Egypt and Sumer together. Many of them lived in villages, farming the valley's fertile soil. But the civilization centered on the two large cities, Harappa and Mohenjo-daro. These cities were carefully planned, with streets running in straight lines, similar to a modern American town. With their courtyard houses and walled citadels, they were the most impressive cities of their time. But floods often damaged the walls, and the buildings needed repairing regularly. It was probably a combination of water damage and poor harvests that led to the decline of the civilization. After 1600 BCE the Indus Valley civilization came to an end.

INDUS VALLEY
The Indus River flows through eastern Pakistan. The Indus people lived in a broad strip of land on either side of the river.

SEAL
Indus merchants carried small seals such as this, which they probably used as stamps to sign documents or mark goods. Each seal has a picture of an animal, together with a few characters in the Indus Valley's unique script. No scholar has been able to decipher this writing.

Citadel area contained large buildings, such as the great bath and granary, protected by a strong wall.

Most houses had two stories and a central courtyard.

Straight main streets show that city was carefully planned.

MOHENJO-DARO
Flat-roofed, mud-brick houses lined the straight streets of Mohenjo-daro. Each house had several rooms, with small windows to keep out the hot sun. A courtyard provided a shaded space for working. Most houses also had a bathroom, with a toilet that drained out into sewers beneath the streets. The city also contained a great bathhouse, which may have been used for religious purposes. Historians think that Mohenjo-daro and Harappa each had about 40,000 inhabitants.

INDUS GODS
Many houses in Mohenjo-daro and Harappa contained small pottery statues of a female figure with a head-dress and jewellery. She was probably a mother goddess. Indus Valley people may have worshipped her at home, hoping that she would bring them good harvests, and a plentiful food supply.

WHEELED TOYS
The children of the Indus Valley played with pottery toys such as this wheeled ox-cart. It is probably a model of similar, full-size carts that were used to take corn to the city's great granary. Archaeologists have also found dice, marbles, and small wheeled animals.

Find out more
ASIA, HISTORY OF
CITIES
RELIGIONS
WHEELS

INFORMATION TECHNOLOGY

THE TERM "INFORMATION TECHNOLOGY", or IT for short, is used to describe technologies that handle, store, process, and transmit, or pass on, information. When people talk about IT, they usually mean the use of computers to store and pass on information, but radio, television, telephones, fax machines, and DVDs are also examples of information technology. Information technology in some form has existed since humans developed pictures and writing, while later inventions such as printing made information more widely available. But modern information technology is based on electronics; vast amounts of information, including pictures and sounds, can be stored as electric signals and transmitted anywhere in the world. Information technology is used in every part of our lives from schools and hospitals, to shopping. Its impact has been enormous, making the world truly a "global village".

An early dial telephone

Camera

EARLY IT
The telephone and the camera were the information technology tools of the 19th century. They had a great impact on society. With the telephone, people could talk to each other all around the world. Using the camera, they could make a record of their lives and families.

USING INFORMATION TECHNOLOGY

To use information technology, you need access to hardware and software. Hardware means the actual machinery, namely computers. Software refers to the programs or applications inside the computer, which actually run it. Programs range from word processing to multimedia and games. They are constantly being updated.

Touching this icon produces information as a piece of sound.

This icon takes the user to other similar pages of information.

MULTIMEDIA
Most computers take Digital Versatile Discs (DVDs), which can give information in multimedia form – words, pictures, and sounds. Multimedia programs are a good way to learn, because they give information in an interesting way and allow you to see how things work. Using the computer mouse, you can move from one bit of information to another.

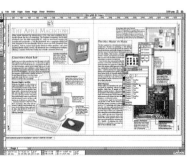

DESKTOP PUBLISHING
Software programs known as desktop publishing (DTP) enable words and pictures to be moved around on screen. DTP is used in publishing, but it also means people can write and design fan magazines, posters, and newsletters in their own homes.

SPREADSHEETS
Some computers contain software programs called spreadsheets. A spreadsheet program stores figures or other information that needs to be shown in the form of tables or charts. The program can do calcuations, such as adding up, or working out percentages. Spreadsheets have many uses, including working out accounts or progress charts.

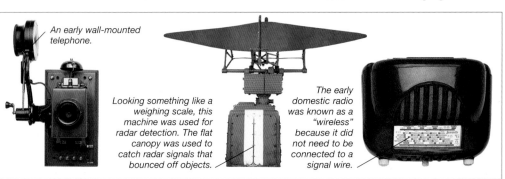

EARLY ELECTRONICS
The use of electronics in information technology has a long history. Materials and designs used for early technology may look dated, but the early inventions served the same purpose as today's modern examples.

An early wall-mounted telephone.

Looking something like a weighing scale, this machine was used for radar detection. The flat canopy was used to catch radar signals that bounced off objects.

The early domestic radio was known as a "wireless" because it did not need to be connected to a signal wire.

OFFICE COMMUNICATION

In the early 20th century, a new kind of work place came into being – the office. Early offices contained manual typewriters and telephones. These were followed by machines powered by electricity, such as electric typewriters and photocopiers. Today, the modern office is totally computerized, and relies completely on information technology, from computers and e-mail to fax machines and picture scanners.

TRANSPORT

Information technology is important in transport, and is used to control airplanes, large ships, and even some cars. The cockpit of an aircraft in particular has become very sophisticated. The information supplied by the technology to the pilots is so accurate that pilots do not need to look out of the aircraft to fly safely, but can rely on the technology.

On-line shoppers can browse through pictures of items for sale displayed in virtual shops.

HOSPITALS

Information technology is very useful in hospitals, and medicine generally, and it is now possible to diagnose and treat many illnesses without physically looking inside the body. Scanning devices enable a doctor to monitor the development of an unborn baby on screen, checking on progress and identifying any problems at an early stage.

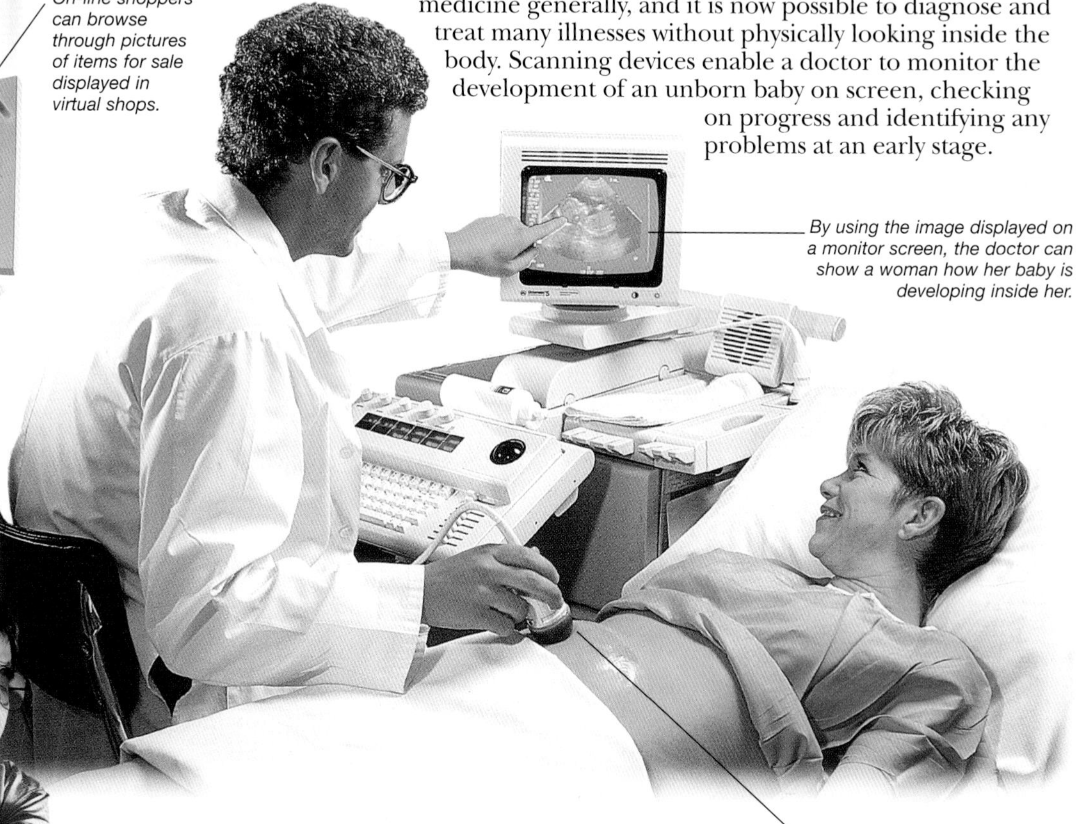

By using the image displayed on a monitor screen, the doctor can show a woman how her baby is developing inside her.

ON-LINE SHOPPING

E-commerce – buying and selling over the Internet – developed in the 1990s, and now many people shop on-line. To do so, you must pay with a debit or credit card. Fraud is a risk, but special programs keep credit card numbers safe.

The scanning device is held in the doctor's hand and moved over the woman's stomach, where it collects information that is shown on screen.

DISABILITY

Information technology has brought major advantages for people with disability. This is because the technology can be designed to make the most of each person's physical abilities. For example, word-activated processors are available for blind people, who can both receive and send sound messages. People with physical disabilities can communicate via e-mail, or access information through the Internet, without leaving home.

Find out more

COMPUTERS
ELECTRONICS
INTERNET
TECHNOLOGY

INSECTS

THE EARTH IS CRAWLING with insects; in fact, they make up the largest group of animals. There are at least one million different species, including beetles, butterflies, ants, and bees. Insects first appeared on Earth more than 500 million years ago and are found in almost every kind of habitat, from cold mountains to tropical rain forests. Although all insects have six legs and a body covered by a hard exoskeleton (outer skeleton), they vary enormously in size and shape. The goliath beetle weighs more than 100 g (3.5 oz); the tiny fairyfly is almost invisible to the human eye. Some insects cause problems for humans. Flies spread disease, and weevils and locusts eat farm crops. Parasites such as ticks and lice live and feed on farm animals and sometimes on humans, too. But insects are a vital part of nature. They pollinate flowers and other crops and are an important source of food for many birds, bats, and reptiles. Certain insects are also very useful to humans – without bees, for example, there would be no honey.

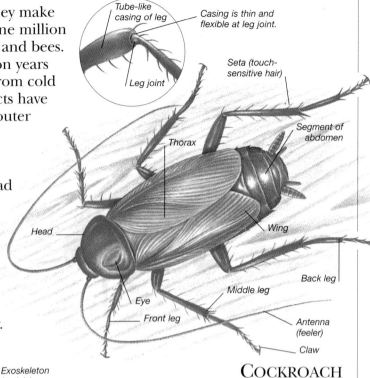

Tube-like casing of leg
Casing is thin and flexible at leg joint.
Leg joint
Seta (touch-sensitive hair)
Thorax
Segment of abdomen
Head
Wing
Eye
Middle leg
Back leg
Front leg
Antenna (feeler)
Claw

COCKROACH

A typical insect such as the common cockroach above has a body in three main parts. At the front is the head, which encloses the brain and bears the antennae, mouthparts, and eyes. In the middle is the thorax, where the six legs join. At the rear is the abdomen, which contains the digestive, reproductive, and sex organs. The hard, outer skeleton is made mainly of a substance called chitin.

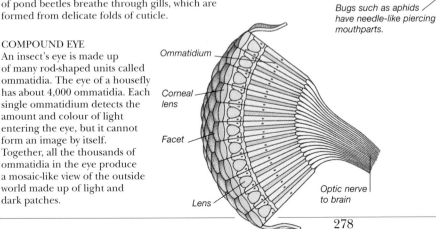

Antenna
Brain
Heart
Crop
Midgut
Malpighian tubules (kidneys) help to control water balance.
Exoskeleton (cuticle)
Rectum
Eye
Mouthparts
Main nerves
Hindgut
Spiracle
Trachea
Sex organs
Anus
Leg joint

INSIDE AN INSECT
The tough exoskeleton, or cuticle, surrounds and protects the soft internal organs. An insect breathes through tiny air tubes called tracheae, which form a network inside its body. The tubes open at holes called spiracles in the cuticle. Water-dwelling insects such as the grubs of pond beetles breathe through gills, which are formed from delicate folds of cuticle.

COMPOUND EYE
An insect's eye is made up of many rod-shaped units called ommatidia. The eye of a housefly has about 4,000 ommatidia. Each single ommatidium detects the amount and colour of light entering the eye, but it cannot form an image by itself. Together, all the thousands of ommatidia in the eye produce a mosaic-like view of the outside world made up of light and dark patches.

Ommatidium
Corneal lens
Facet
Lens
Optic nerve to brain

Bugs such as aphids have needle-like piercing mouthparts.
Housefly sucks up liquid food through its padded, sponge-like mouthparts.
Butterfly's tubular mouthparts work like a drinking straw.

FEEDING

Insects feed on almost anything – wood, blood, nectar, paper, shoe polish, seaweed, and other insects. The mouthparts of most insects, however, are specialized for eating a particular kind of food. Some mouthparts are adapted to bite, others to pierce, suck, sponge, scrape, and probe. The mouthparts have four main structures. The mandibles are hard jaws that bite and chew; the maxillae are secondary jaws; the labrum and labium are the upper and lower lips.

COURTSHIP

Some insects, such as the praying mantises shown here, have complicated courtship behaviour. After mating, the female mantis often grasps and eats the male mantis; the nutrients in the body of the male help the eggs to develop.

Indian beetle has antler-like antennae.

Weevil has elbow-jointed antennae.

ANTENNAE
Sense organs called antennae detect smells and vibrations in the air and in solid objects. Often, the male has larger, more branched antennae than the female. These help detect the scent that she releases into the air at mating time. Near the antennae there are often several tiny single-lens eyes called ocelli.

The praying mantis is the only insect that can turn its head to look directly behind.

METAMORPHOSIS

Most insects hatch from eggs. Some insects, such as the butterfly, hatch into a larva or caterpillar, which feeds voraciously and moults (sheds its skin) several times. It then forms a chrysalis and pupates, finally emerging as a mature adult butterfly. These great changes in form are known as complete metamorphosis. Other insects, such as grasshoppers, hatch into nymphs, which look like small versions of the parent but without proper wings. They moult in order to grow and finally become adult after the final moult when they have wings. This is called incomplete metamorphosis.

Female damselfly lays eggs on stem of reed.

Emerging nymph climbs up reed stem.

Adult emerges from nymph skin.

Young nymph (larva)

Older nymph (larva) develops wings.

LIFE CYCLE
A damselfly begins life as an egg in a pond or a stream. It passes through ten or more moults, taking up to two years altogether, before changing into an adult.

TYPES OF INSECTS

There are about 20 main groups of insects. Beetles and weevils form the largest single group of insects, which contains more than 350,000 species known to entomologists (scientists who study insects). Most insects have wings at some stage during their life cycle; bristletails, silverfish, and firebrats do not. Fleas are also wingless; their wings have disappeared during the course of evolution.

Cockroaches (*Blattodea*)

Flies, mosquitoes, gnats (*Diptera*)

Earwigs (*Dermaptera*)

Mantises (*Mantodea*)

Fleas (*Siphonaptera*)

Dragonflies and damselflies (*Odonata*)

Bugs such as greenfly, shieldbugs, cicadas, and water striders (*Hemiptera*)

Grasshoppers, crickets, locusts (*Orthoptera*)

Bees, wasps, ants, ichneumons (*Hymenoptera*)

Termites (*Isoptera*)

Silverfish and bristletails (*Thysanura*)

Lice (*Psocoptera, Phthiraptera*)

Lacewings and antlions (*Neuroptera*)

Stick and leaf insects (*Phasmatodea*)

Thrips (*Thysanoptera*)

Scorpionflies (*Mecoptera*)

Stoneflies (*Plecoptera*)

Weevils and beetles (*Coleoptera*)

Butterflies and moths (*Lepidoptera*)

FLEA

A flea can leap more than 30 cm (12 in) up into the air, which is similar to a person jumping 245 m (800 ft), or a 70-storey building, or St. Paul's Cathedral in London, England.

Legs kick down for extra acceleration.

Like other insects, fleas have powerful muscles, and the elastic springiness of the cuticle helps the legs to rebound quickly during movement.

St. Paul's Cathedral

Find out more
ANIMALS
ANTS AND TERMITES
BEETLES
BUTTERFLIES AND MOTHS
FLIES AND MOSQUITOES
FLIGHT, ANIMAL

INTERNET

THE INTERNET IS A WAY for computers around the world to swap information. It started as a US military research project in 1969, but was opened to the public in 1988. At first, the Internet just carried email and simple data files. In the early 1990s the invention of the World Wide Web brought the Internet to the world's attention. It gave anyone an easy way to access information across the Internet. Today, words, pictures, music, videos, and any other type of data can be passed across the Internet almost instantly. This has changed the way we live and it is estimated that more than a quarter of the world's population now has Internet access.

This diagram is a representation of a tiny section of the Internet. Each small straight line is a connection between two computers.

A page from the Dorling Kindersley website.

HOW THE INTERNET WORKS

Computers can exchange information with nearby computers over connections called networks. The Internet (short for Inter-network) connects together separate networks, enabling computers all over the world to swap data. To send a data file, such as an MP3 music file, to a particular computer, the file is broken into chunks that are passed between these computers until they reach their destination. Computers usually swap data through wires as electrical signals, or fibre optic cables as pulses of light.

WORLD WIDE WEB
The World Wide Web (WWW, or "web") is a standard way of making information available over the Internet. When a user accesses information on the web, their computer requests data files, called web pages, from other computers on the Internet, called servers. On the user's computer, a program called a web browser displays the words and pictures from the web page on the screen. Web pages include links that, when clicked, access related pages. Search engines are programs that help users find useful pages. The user chooses words to search for – called search terms – and a special server creates a clickable list of relevant pages.

This transmitter/receiver is knowns as a "dongle" and connects a computer to the Internet using a mobile phone network.

Many mobile phones can now connect to the Internet. This Blackberry enables users to email while on the move.

CONNECTING TO THE INTERNET
A device called a modem, shown below, is required to translate messages into electronic data that can be sent from one computer to another and displayed on screen. To use the Internet from home, the user normally connects to a computer at an Internet Service Provider (ISP), a company that offers Internet connections for a small fee. A telephone network is used to connect to an ISP. For people on the move, mobile devices can connect to the Internet without using any wires by using a radio link, such as a mobile phone network.

A modem is used to connect a computer to the Internet via a telephone line.

USES FOR THE INTERNET
The ability to find information via the World Wide Web is just one of many uses for the Internet. Text messages can be swapped between messenger programs enabling real-time chat. Music and video can be compressed into manageable amounts of data so radio and television can be sent over the Internet. Video-phone calls, as shown, are also increasingly popular. Exchanging computer game data allows players across the the world to compete with one another.

Find out more

COMPUTERS
INFORMATION TECHNOLOGY
TELEPHONES
SATELLITES

INUITS

THE FROZEN ARCTIC was one of the last regions of the world to be inhabited by humans. The Inuit (Eskimo) people, who originally came from Asia, settled in the Arctic about 4,000 years ago. A Native American tribe named them *Eskimo*, which means "eaters of raw meat"; but the newcomers called themselves *Inuit*, which simply means "real men". Inuits were nomadic. They moved about in family groups, hunting animals such as seals and caribou. Inuit families survived the bitter cold of winter by digging shelters into the ground. They made roofs for the shelters from driftwood or whalebone, with a covering of turf. For clothes, they used double layers of caribou or polar bear fur. Today, most Inuits live in small settlements or towns, but they are proud of their culture. They preserve it in language, art, and song, and hunting is still an essential part of Inuit life.

Polar Inuits

North Alaskan Inuits

West Greenland Inuits

GREENLAND

ALASKA

CANADA

Pacific Inuits

Caribou Inuits

Today, Inuits hunt on snowmobiles instead of sledges.

A hunting trip takes many days, and supplies are carried by snowmobile.

INUIT COMMUNITIES
Inuits live in Siberia in the Russian Federation, in Alaska, Canada, and Greenland. There are many different groups, each named after the area in which they live. The Polar Inuits of Greenland live the furthest north of all the world's peoples.

To catch a seal, the Inuit cuts a hole in the sea ice. When the seal comes up to the hole to breathe, the Inuit shoots it.

HUNTING
Inuits hunt for food to eat, and furs to sell. They do not hunt animals for sport. They respect foxes, caribou, seal, walrus, and other Arctic wildlife, and their hunting does not threaten the long-term survival of these animal species. Hunting takes patience and skill, and some Inuits travel 5,000 km (3,000 miles) a year on hunting trips. When they are hunting away from home in winter, they build temporary shelters, called igloos, from blocks of snow.

Inuits eat raw and cooked seal meat.

Inuit artists use their skills to decorate everyday tools, such as this arrow straightener.

INUIT ART
During the long winter months there is little daylight in the Arctic, so the hours of hunting are limited. In the past, skilled Inuit carvers used the time to work wood, bone, soapstone (soft rock), and walrus tusks. They created beautiful statues of animals, people, and especially favoured hunting scenes. Today, museums and collectors eagerly seek good Inuit carvings.

INUIT LIFE
There are about 35,000 Inuits in North America. Most live in wooden houses equipped like a typical North American home. Some Inuits are still full-time hunters; most others work in many different businesses and industries.

A team of 10 to 15 husky dogs pull the traditional Inuit sledge. With an expert driver at the reins, a dog team can travel 80 km (50 miles) in a day.

Find out more
ANTARCTICA
ARCTIC
CANADA
CANADA, HISTORY OF
POLAR WILDLIFE

IRAN

Volcano | Mountain | Ancient monument | Capital city | Large city/ town | Small city/ town

Iran lies at the heart of Asia, bordered by the Caspian Sea in the north, and The Gulf and Gulf of Oman to the south. The Elburz Mountains and Zagros Mountains enclose the central plateau, a land of barren, rocky deserts.

A LAND OF RUGGED MOUNTAINS and harsh deserts, Iran was ruled for many centuries by the shah, or king. In the 1979 revolution, the shah was overthrown and Iran became an Islamic republic, ruled according to strict Islamic laws. Between 1980 and 1988, border disputes led to a devastating war between Iran and its western neighbour, Iraq. The cost of the prolonged war strained the economy. Although Iran has very substantial oil reserves, it has very few other industries. Eggs from sturgeon caught in the Caspian Sea are used to make caviar, an expensive delicacy, which is exported. Fine, hand-made carpets are also an important source of income for villagers, who grow wheat, barley, and rice and herd sheep. Iran's strict Islamic laws have discouraged tourists, although the country has a great wealth of historic buildings and magnificent mosques.

STATISTICS
Area: 1,648,000 sq km (636,293 sq miles)
Population: 66,429,000
Capital: Tehran
Languages: Farsi (Persian), Azerbaijani, Gilaki, Mazenderani, Kurdish, Baluchi, Arabic, Turkmen
Religions: Shi'ite Muslim, Sunni Muslim
Currency: Iranian rial

CARPET-WEAVERS
Iran's famous carpets are made by hand-knotting the wool, which is coloured with a range of vegetable dyes. Many of the patterns used are hundreds of years old, and were created for the opulent carpets used in the royal palaces and mosques. Each region prides itself on its carpets, specializing in unique designs and colour combinations.

CASPIAN SEA
The Caspian is a salt lake that lies between Europe and Asia. It sits 28m (92 ft) below sea level.

THE KURDS

The Kurds are an ethnically and linguistically distinctive group, who live in Iran, Iraq, and Turkey. They were once sheep- and goat-herding nomads in the Iranian highlands, although in recent years they have turned to farming and village life. There are about 25 million Kurds, the largest group of stateless people in the world. In Iran, they are pressured to become part of mainstream society, and they are severely discriminated against in Turkey.

ARMENIA
AZERBAIJAN
TURKEY
Caspian Sea
TURKMENISTAN
Khvoy
Tabriz
Ardabil
Maragheh
Rasht
Lake Urmia
Saqqez
Zanjan
Elburz Mountains
Qazvin
Amol
Sari
Gorgan
Bojnurd
Koppeh Dagh
Shahrud
Mashhad
Sabzevar
Qolleh-ye Damavand 5671m
Semnan
TEHRAN
Sanandaj
Hamadan
Qom
Dasht-e Kavir
IRAQ
Kermanshah
Arak
Kashan
IRAN
Birjand
Khorramabad
Isfahan
Dezful
Karun
Shahr-e Kord
Zagros Mountains
Iranian Plateau
Dasht-e Lut
AFGHANISTAN
Tigris
Yazd
Daryacheh-ye Sistan
Ahvaz
Anar
Khorramshahr
Abadan
Kerman
Kazerun
Bam
Zahedan
Shiraz
Sirjan
Mirjaveh
KUWAIT
Bushire
Rud-e Mand
PAKISTAN
The Gulf
Kangan
Hamun-e Jaz Murian
Gavbandi
Bandar-e 'Abbas
Strait of Hormuz
Makran Coast
Gulf of Oman
Arabian Sea

N
W
E
S

MASHHAD

Most Iranians belong to the minority Shi'ah branch of Islam, and Mashhad is their main shrine, the place where the Shi'ah leader Riza (770–819) was martyred. Iran has a religious government that imposes severe restrictions on the people. Women must wear the chador, a dress covering all but the face and hands, and behaviour is closely monitored.

SCALE BAR
0 100 200 300 km
0 100 200 300 miles

Find out more
ASIA
EARTHQUAKES
ISLAM
PERSIANS, ANCIENT

IRELAND

OFF THE NORTHWEST COAST of Europe lies one of the most beautiful islands in the world. For centuries, writers and singers have praised the lush countryside and wild mountains of Ireland. Despite its beauty, Ireland is not a rich country and has few natural resources. It has no coal, no iron ore or vast reserves of oil. Nevertheless, Ireland's influence has been far-reaching, for the country is rich in its people and their distinctive Gaelic culture. Few corners of the world lack an Irish community whose members keep alive the memory and customs of their homeland. In 1973, Ireland (Eire) joined the European Economic Community (now the European Union). Until then, its powerful neighbour and former ruler, the United Kingdom, had always dominated the country's economy. As a member of the Union, Eire has become more prosperous and economically independent of the United Kingdom. New high-tech industries are replacing traditional agriculture and textiles as the main sources of employment.

Ireland is the smaller of the two main British Isles. The other – Britain – is to the east, and the Atlantic Ocean is to the west. Ireland is divided into Ireland (Eire), which is independent, and the province of Northern Ireland, which is part of the United Kingdom.

Blocks of peat – carbon-rich soil consisting of decomposed plant life – are dug up from the marshy countryside and left to dry before being used as fuel.

DUBLIN
The capital city of Ireland is Dublin. It lies on the Liffey river not far from the Irish Sea. The Vikings founded Dublin in the 9th century, and the city has many historic buildings and beautiful town squares.

COUNTRYSIDE
Wet west winds blow across Ireland from the Atlantic Ocean, soaking parts of the country with more than 200 cm (80 in) of rain each year. This makes the farmland very productive; about 16 per cent of the people work in farming and food processing industries.

GEOGRAPHY
Mountains to the south, west, and north surround Ireland's large, central plain. The plain is marshy in places, and there are many lakes, called loughs. Lough Neagh (right) in Northern Ireland, the biggest lake in the British Isles, is famous for its wildfowl and salmon.

The Ha'penny Bridge, which spans the Liffey river, is accepted as the symbol of Dublin. Opened in 1816, its name comes from the fee once charged to use it.

MUSIC
Ireland has a strong musical tradition. Irish rock and classical artists are well known internationally. The Corrs, U2, and Boyzone are all very successful Irish bands. Traditional Irish music and dancing is also very important to Ireland's cultural heritage.

Pipes, fiddles, and banjos are all used in traditional Irish music.

INDUSTRY
Once renowned for its traditional industries of glass, lace, and linen, Ireland now also produces medicine, electronics, and other modern goods. Many people work in the tourism industry.

Find out more

CELTS
EUROPE
TRADE AND INDUSTRY
UNITED KINGDOM
UNITED KINGDOM, HISTORY OF
VIKINGS

STATISTICS

Area: 70,280 sq km
(27,155 sq miles)
Population: 4,203,000
Capital: Dublin
Languages: English,
Irish Gaelic
Religions: Roman
Catholic, Anglican,
Jewish, non-religious
Currency: Euro
Main occupations:
Manufacturing,
agriculture, food
processing
Main exports: Cattle,
beef, dairy products
Main imports: Textiles,
machinery, vehicles

HURLING

An outdoor stick-and-ball game,
somewhat akin to field hockey, hurling
is an ancient Gaelic sport. References
to the game can be found in the oldest
Irish manuscripts dating from the
13th century BCE, and many heroes of
ancient tales were expert hurlers.
The stick used is called a hurley –
camán in Gaelic. The 18th century
was the golden age of hurling, but
between 1790 and 1800 the landed
gentry withdrew support of the game.
The potato famine of 1845-47
further impeded its development.
Hurling enjoyed a revival with the
foundation of the Gaelic Games
Association in 1884.

GLENDALOUGH

The vale of Glendalough in the Wicklow
Mountains is famous for its association
with Saint Kevin, a hermit who founded
a monastery there in the 6th century CE.
Saint Kevin, who is said to have performed
many miracles, was believed to be
120 years old when he died in 618.

SCALE BAR

| 0 | 25 | 50 | km |

| 0 | 25 | 50 | miles |

SLIEVE LEAGUE

*The cliffs of Donegal are
some of the highest in
Europe. Rising vertically to
its 670 m (2,197 ft) summit,
Slieve League has been cut
away by sea erosion.*

SHANNON RIVER

The longest river in the British Isles,
the Shannon, is about 380 km
(240 miles) long. It rises in
northwest Ireland, and flows into
the sea just west of Limerick. As it
winds its way down the country, the
river passes through numerous lakes,
the largest of which is Lough Derg.

Map key: Volcano, Mountain, Ancient monument, Capital city, Large city/town, Small city/town

Malin Head
Lough Foyle
Aran Island
NORTHERN IRELAND (to United Kingdom)
Slieve League
Donegal
Donegal Bay
Upper Lough Erne
Sligo Bay
Sligo
Ballina
Lough Conn
Cavan
Achill Island
Castlebar
Carrick on Shannon
Lough Gowna
Dundalk
Dundalk Bay
Clew Bay
Shannon
Longford
Drogheda
Lough Mask
Tuam
Lough Ree
Irish
Lough Corrib
Athlone
Boyne
Lucan
DUBLIN
Galway
Suck
Liffey
Dún Laoghaire
Galway Bay
Shannon
Newbridge
Sea
Aran Islands
IRELAND
Lugnaquillia 926m
Ennis
Lough Derg
Portlaoise
Wicklow Mountains
Wicklow Head
Carlow
Glendalough
Limerick
Kilkenny
Slaney
Tipperary
Clonmel
Wexford
Galtymore Mountain 919m
Galty Mountains
Barrow
Carnsore Point
Tralee
Blackwater
Waterford
St George's Channel
Dingle Bay
Carrauntoohil 1038m
Killarney
Lee
Macgillycuddy's Reeks
Cork
St George's
Caha Mountains
Celtic Sea
Bantry Bay
Fastnet Rock
ATLANTIC OCEAN

284

IRON AGE

IN SEVERAL EARLY LANGUAGES the word for iron meant "metal from the sky". This was probably because the first iron used to make tools and weapons came from meteorites which fell to Earth from space. Ironworking probably began in the Middle East some 6,000 years ago. At first, people hammered iron while it was cold. Later they learned how to smelt iron – heat the iron ore so they could extract the iron and work with it properly. Unlike bronze, which early people also used, iron did not melt. Instead it was reduced to a spongy mass which people hammered and reheated until it was the right shape. Special furnaces were needed to reach the right temperature. The Hittites, who lived in what is now Turkey, were the first people we know of who traded in iron. But it was not until around 1000 BCE that knowledge of smelting spread and the Iron Age truly began. In western Europe, the Celts were one of the first peoples to make and use iron.

IRON AGE

4000 BCE First iron objects, made from meteoric iron, appear in the Middle East.

c. 1500 BCE People in the Middle East find out how to extract (smelt) iron from iron ore and how to work it by heating and hammering (wrought iron). The Hittites dominate the trade.

1000 BCE Iron Age begins in the Middle East and Greece. Iron-working also develops in India.

c. 800 BCE Use of iron spreads across Europe. Celts become expert workers in iron.

c. 400 BCE Chinese discover how to make cast-iron objects by melting iron ore and pouring it into moulds.

1760 CE Industrial revolution leads to a renewed use of iron. Also leads to great advances in ironworking techniques.

This razor is around 2,500 years old and would have been as sharp as a modern razor.

HILL FORT
The Celts fortified hill tops with ditches and ramparts. These forts were places of refuge in wartime; they were also administrative and trading centres, and enclosures for livestock.

Iron horseshoe

IRONWORKING

Early furnaces were shallow stone hearths which people filled with iron ore and charcoal. Bellows helped raise the temperature to about 1,200°C (2,192°F), hot enough to make the iron workable. The Celts used deeper furnaces in which the iron collected at the bottom and impurities, called slag, gathered at the top.

Hammering the iron into shape

Heating iron ore in a furnace

Spring

Iron pin

Brooch made of glass discs

TOOLS
People made useful tools from iron such as a saw with a serrated edge (far left) and tongs (left); the tongs were used to hold metal while beating it into shape.

WEAPONS
Iron weapons were greatly superior to bronze ones. They had much sharper edges and, thus, were more effective. This dagger has a handle shaped like a human figure.

CLOTHING
The Celts loved decoration. Celtic clothes were woollen, often with checked patterns. Richer men and women wore heavy twisted neckbands called torcs in gold or bronze, and cloaks fastened with ornate brooches.

Find out more
BRONZE AGE
CELTS
INDUSTRIAL REVOLUTION
IRON AND STEEL

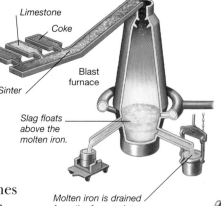

IRON AND STEEL

HUGE STRUCTURES such as oil tankers and bridges, and tiny objects such as nuts and bolts are made from steel. The world produces more than one billion tonnes (984 million tons) of steel every year; it is the most widely used of all metals. Steel is made from iron, one of the most common metals in the Earth's crust, and carbon, which comes from coal. Iron has many uses, which include making car engine parts and magnets. Our bodies need iron to work properly. A healthy diet must include foods such as green vegetables, which contain iron. Pieces of iron fall to Earth in meteorites from space. But most iron comes from iron ore in rock. Heating the ore with coke (from coal) produces iron. The Hittites of Turkey perfected iron smelting about 1500 BCE. This was the beginning of the Iron Age, during which iron gained widespread use for making weapons and tools.

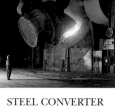

Iron and steel were once used to make weapons and armour, such as this 16th-century helmet.

Iron ore, Limestone, Coke, Sinter, Blast furnace

Slag floats above the molten iron.

Molten iron is drained from the furnace into large ladles.

Oxygen is blown through pipe onto surface of pig iron.

After blowing with oxygen, the converter tilts to discharge molten steel.

Molten steel from converter

Continuous casting

The molten steel may be cast into large blocks called ingots.

RAW MATERIALS
Iron-making starts with iron ore, coke (a form of carbon from coal), and limestone. They are mixed and treated to make lumps called sinter.

BLAST FURNACE
The ingredients enter the top of the blast furnace and move down inside. A blast of very hot air flows up the furnace. The heat produces molten iron from the ore and coke. Limestone removes impurities which form a layer called slag.

MAKING IRON AND STEEL
Making metals by heating their ores is called smelting. Huge factories smelt iron ore by heating it with coke to produce iron, which is rich in carbon. Removing most of the carbon produces steel. Steels of different quality are made by adding metals, such as nickel.

Casting uses molten steel from the converter.

Forging

Rolling

CONTINUOUS CASTING
Molten steel from the converter sets as it cools and is held in shape by rollers. The long slab is then cut up into lengths and rolled into steel products.

STEEL CONVERTER
Molten iron from the blast furnace is poured into a steel converter where hot air or oxygen is blown over it. The heat burns up most of the carbon from the iron, leaving molten steel. Steel from old cars and other waste can be recycled by adding it to the converter.

RUST
Iron and steel objects get rusty when they are left outside in damp conditions. Moist air causes rust. It changes iron into iron oxide, a red-brown compound of iron and oxygen. Rusting weakens the metal so that it crumbles away.

SHAPING STEEL
Passing a hot slab between rollers presses the soft steel into plates or sheets. A forge presses the steel into more complex shapes. Casting uses a mould, in which molten steel cools and sets into shape.

USES OF STEEL
Different kinds of steel are made by varying the amount of carbon and other metals in it. Low-carbon steel goes into car bodies; stronger medium-carbon steel is used for making ships and steel beams that support structures. High-carbon steel is very strong but difficult to shape, and is used for springs and rails that get much wear. Steel containing tungsten metal resists heat and is used in jet engines.

STAINLESS STEEL
Adding the metals chromium and nickel produces stainless steel, which does not rust. Cutlery and saucepans are often made of stainless steel. This metal is also used to make equipment that must be kept very clean in places such as hospitals and dairies.

Find out more
COAL
INDUSTRIAL REVOLUTION
IRON AGE
METALS

ISLAM

IN THE 7TH CENTURY, the prophet Muhammad founded a religion in Arabia that was to become a powerful force in the world. The religion came to be known as Islam and its followers are called Muslims (or Moslems). Muslims believe that many prophets or teachers have been sent by God, including Moses and Jesus Christ, but Muhammad was the last of them. Like Christians and Jews, Muslims believe in one God, Allah. Islam means "submission to the will of God", and Muslims commit themselves to absolute obedience to Allah. Islamic life is based on a set of rules called the five pillars of Islam. Muslims believe that by following these rules, they will reach heaven. There is also a strict code of social behaviour, and alcohol and gambling are forbidden. Some Muslim women wear clothes that cover their bodies completely. Today there are more than 1,300 million Muslims living mainly in the Middle East, Asia, and Africa. Islam is a rapidly growing faith. Its popularity has been increased by Islamic fundamentalists – extremely religious people who call for a return to strict, traditional Islamic values.

KORAN
The sacred book of Islam is the Koran. Muslims believe the Koran is the direct word of God as revealed to his messenger, Muhammad.

ISLAMIC FESTIVALS
Day of Hijrah First day of Islamic year.

Ramadan Month-long fast.

Eid ul-Fitr Feast to mark the end of Ramadan.

Lailat ul-Qadr Revelation of Koran to Muhammad.

Meelad ul-Nabi Muhammad's birthday.

Lailut ul-Isra Death of Muhammad.

MOSQUES
The Muslim place of worship is the mosque. Before entering, Muslims remove their shoes and wash. The faithful kneel to pray, with their heads touching the floor. At prayer time Muslims face the mihrab, an empty recess which faces the direction of Mecca. Although they must attend the mosque on Fridays, at other times Muslims pray wherever they are.

MINARETS
Five times a day muezzins, or criers, stand at the top of tall towers called minarets to call fellow Muslims to prayer.

BLUE MOSQUE
The first mosques were very simple, but some later buildings such as the Blue Mosque at Istanbul, Turkey (right), are magnificent examples of Islamic art. Islam forbids realistic images of humans or other living things, so the tiled walls are decorated with intricate designs and beautiful calligraphy.

Before kneeling in prayer in the mosque, Muslims wash their faces, hands, and feet.

MUHAMMAD
The shahada is the Islamic declaration of faith. "None is to be worshipped save Allah: Muhammad is his prophet."

MECCA
The birthplace of Muhammad is Mecca, Saudi Arabia, and every Muslim tries to visit the holy city at least once in a lifetime. The Kaaba, the sacred shrine, is the central point of this pilgrimage. Inside the Kaaba is a black stone which dates from ancient times.

Muslim pilgrims must walk seven times around the Kaaba.

Find out more
CRUSADES
MIDDLE EAST
MUHAMMAD
RELIGIONS

ISRAEL

Volcano	Mountain	Ancient monument	Capital city	Large city/ town	Small city/ town

Israel lies at the eastern end of the Mediterranean Sea. Lebanon lies to the north, Syria and Jordan to the east, and Egypt to the southwest.

THE MODERN STATE OF ISRAEL has existed only since 1948. It was created on the sites where there had been Jewish settlements in earlier times. Jews from all over the world flocked to the new state, especially the survivors of Nazi anti-semitism. They revived the ancient language of Hebrew as the national language of Israel. But there have been many problems. The region had previously been the land of Palestine, and many Arab Palestinians had to leave when the country became Israel. However, others have remained, and today they make up about 15 per cent of Israel's 7.2 million population. Israel has also fought wars with neighbouring Arab countries to secure its borders. It still occupies some territory gained in these wars, causing continual Palestinian unrest. Israel is now a wealthy country. The Israelis have developed many modern industries and converted large areas of desert into farmland.

STATISTICS

Area: 20,700 sq km (7,992 sq miles)
Population: 7,234,000
Capital: Jerusalem
Languages: Hebrew, Arabic, Yiddish, German, Russian, Polish, Romanian, Persian
Religions: Jewish, Muslim, Christian, Druze
Currency: New Israeli shekel
Main occupations: Agriculture, manufacturing, finance
Main exports: Potash, bromine, salt, wine, citrus fruits
Main imports: fuels

WAILING WALL
Israel occupies much of the "Holy Land" described in the Bible. The land is sacred, not only to Jews but also to Christians and Muslims. The Wailing Wall in Jerusalem is the most sacred Jewish monument. It is all that remains of a temple built by King Herod 2,000 years ago. Visitors gave the wall its name when they heard the sad sound of devout Jews mourning the destruction of the temple.

TEL AVIV-YAFO

The main commercial and industrial centre of Israel is Tel Aviv-Yafo, the country's second largest city. It was once two separate towns, but Tel Aviv grew rapidly and absorbed its neighbour, the ancient port of Yafo.

DEAD SEA
The world's saltiest sea, the Dead Sea, is also the lowest area of water on Earth; it is 400 m (1,312 ft) below the level of the Mediterranean Sea. The River Jordan flows into this hot, barren place. The water evaporates in the heat of the sun, but the salt in the water is left behind. Over the centuries the salt has become very concentrated.

Visitors to Dead Sea resorts bathe in mud because they believe it is good for their skin.

Tel Aviv's centre symbolizes the modern, prosperous face of Israel.

SCALE BAR

| 0 | 25 | 50 | km |

| 0 | 25 | 50 miles |

Find out more
CHRISTIANITY
CRUSADES
ISLAM
JUDAISM
MIDDLE EAST

ITALY

Many Italian farmhouses are old and picturesque; the machinery is usually modern.

SHAPED LIKE A BOOT, complete with heel and toe, Italy juts out far into the Mediterranean Sea from southern Europe. Between the country's east and west coasts rise the Apennine Mountains, which divide Italy into two along its length. Northern Italy is green and fertile, stretching from the snow-capped Alps to the middle of the country. It includes farmlands in the great flat valley of the Po River, and large industrial towns such as Turin and Milan. Factories in the north produce cars, textiles, clothes, and electrical goods. These products have helped make Italy one of the most prosperous countries in Europe. Southern Italy, by contrast, is dry and rocky. There is less farming and industry, and the people are poorer. Sicily and Sardinia, the two largest islands of the Mediterranean, are also part of Italy.

Rome, the capital, lies at the centre of the nation. It is the home of Italy's democratic government and also the Vatican, the headquarters of the Roman Catholic Church.

Italy is in southern Europe and forms part of the northern coast of the Mediterranean Sea. It shares borders with France, Switzerland, Austria, and Slovenia.

AGRICULTURE
Italian farmers use modern machinery to grow food for Italy's 58.1 million people, and for exporting. Italy is famous for its olives and olive oil, tomatoes, wine, pasta, cheese, fruit, and meat products, such as salami and ham. Italy also grows large quantities of grain, particularly wheat, as well as rice, potatoes, and sunflowers, which are used to make cooking oil. Almost one-third of Italians live in rural areas, many in old farmhouses.

ROME
A walk through Rome is like a walk through history. Since the city was first built, more than 2,500 years ago, each new generation has added something. Today, modern city life goes on around Ancient Roman arenas, 15th-century churches, and 17th-century palaces. Like many of Italy's historic towns, Rome attracts thousands of tourists every year.

PASTA
There are at least 200 shapes of pasta, including ravioli, spaghetti, and macaroni. Pasta is a type of dough made from durum wheat flour, which is rich in gluten, a kind of protein. Served with a tasty sauce, it is Italy's favourite dish. Marco Polo is said to have brought the recipe for pasta from China to Italy.

VENICE
Venice is one of the world's oldest cultural and tourist cities. From the late medieval period, it became Europe's greatest seaport, serving as the continent's commercial and cultural link to Asia. Like several other Italian towns, Venice boasts many magnificent buildings from the past. Its ornate marbled and frescoed palaces, towers, and domes attract thousands of tourists every year. The city was built on about 120 small islands, in a lagoon which remains permanently flooded. A causeway over 4 km (2.5 miles) long connects Venice with mainland Italy. Cars are not allowed in the old city, and people travel by boat on more than 170 canals. The traditional boat, called a gondola (above), is still a common form of transport.

Ferrari makes one of the leading Grand Prix racing cars.

CARS
The Italian motor industry produces some of Europe's finest cars. Manufacturers such as Alfa Romeo, Ferrari, and Lamborghini have always had a reputation for speed and stylish design.

The fairytale fortress of Rocca Tower, perched high on a rocky outcrop, overlooks San Marino.

The Doric Temple (right) in the Valley of the Temples, Sicily, was built during the period 460-450 BCE.

SAN MARINO

San Marino is the third-smallest independent state in Europe, after Monaco and the Vatican City. It is about 14 km (9 miles) long and 8 km (5 miles) wide, and is situated mostly on the slopes of Monte Titano on the Adriatic coast. Tourism provides a great source of income to the country, as do the frequent issues of its own postage stamps. The Sammarinese, as the inhabitants of San Marino are called, are ruled by two capitani reggenti ("captains regent") who are elected every six months. San Marino has had a treaty of friendship with Italy since 1862.

SICILY

Sicily is the largest island in the Mediterranean Sea. It belongs to Italy, from which it is separated by the Strait of Messina. The island's highest point is Mount Etna, an active volcano which reaches a height of 3,332 m (10,930 ft). Farming and tourism are the primary sources of income. Increasing numbers of tourists are attracted by the island's beautiful beaches and ancient ruins.

VATICAN CITY

Vatican City is a walled city in Rome, and the headquarters of the Roman Catholic Church. It is the official residence of the Pope, and the smallest independent state in the world, with an area of 0.44 sq km (0.17 sq miles). The Vatican has its own flag, national anthem, stamps, and coins, as well as a newspaper and radio station. St. Peter's Basilica, which overlooks a grand piazza (left), dominates the city.

St. Peter's Basilica, Vatican City, Rome, is the world's largest Christian church. Shaped like a cross, it is nearly 210 m (700 ft) long and extends to about 137 m (450 ft) at its widest point.

ROMAN CATHOLICS

More than half of all Christians are Roman Catholics. They follow the leadership of the Pope in the Vatican and, together with other Christians, believe in three beings in one God: the Creator and Father; Jesus Christ as God become man; and the Holy Spirit. More than 80 per cent of Italians are Roman Catholic.

Mary, the virgin mother of Christ, is regarded by Roman Catholics as the highest of all human beings.

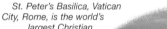

SARDINIA

Sardinia is an island 175 km (109 miles) off mainland Italy, in the Mediterranean Sea. It is a self-governing political region of Italy with its own president and elected regional assembly. The central Italian government, however, controls education, justice, communications such as railways and postal services, defence, and national taxation.

This is the southernmost reach of the Gennargentu Mountains, Sardinia.

MALTA

Malta is a small country in the Mediterranean Sea just south of Sicily. Since ancient times, it has been a vital naval base because of its position on trade routes to the East. Romans, Arabs, French, Turks, Spanish, and British have all colonized or fought over the island. Malta finally gained independence from Britain in 1964, joining the EU in 2004. Tourism is a major source of the country's income.

Find out more

EUROPE
EUROPE, HISTORY OF
RENAISSANCE
ROMAN EMPIRE

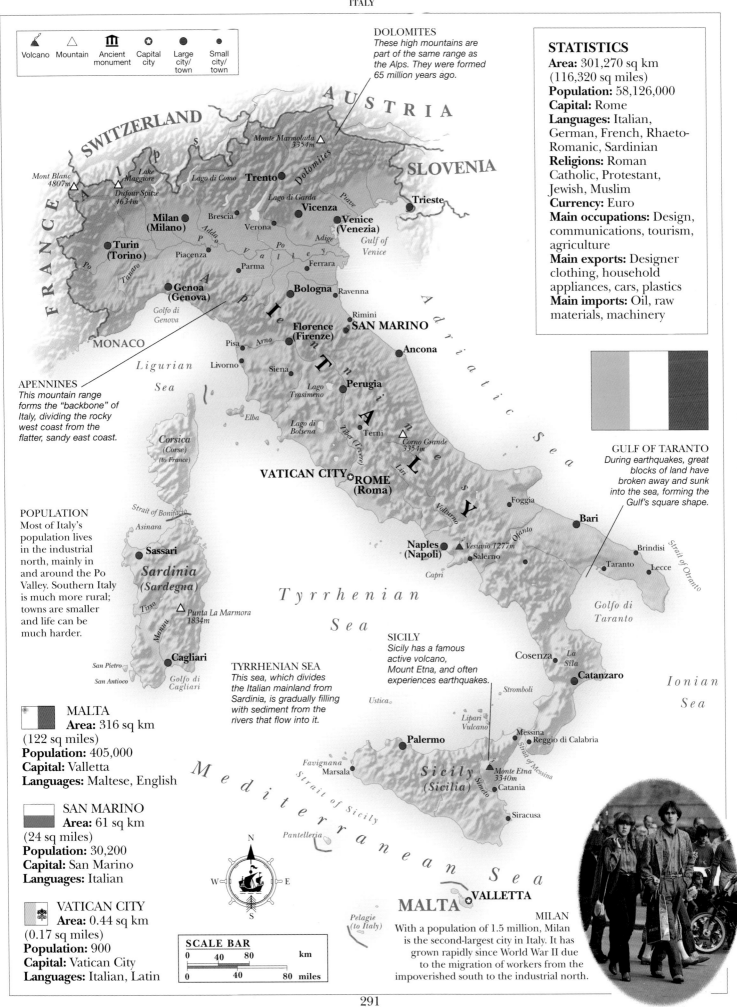

Volcano △ Mountain 🏛 Ancient monument ✦ Capital city ● Large city/town • Small city/town

DOLOMITES
These high mountains are part of the same range as the Alps. They were formed 65 million years ago.

STATISTICS
Area: 301,270 sq km (116,320 sq miles)
Population: 58,126,000
Capital: Rome
Languages: Italian, German, French, Rhaeto-Romanic, Sardinian
Religions: Roman Catholic, Protestant, Jewish, Muslim
Currency: Euro
Main occupations: Design, communications, tourism, agriculture
Main exports: Designer clothing, household appliances, cars, plastics
Main imports: Oil, raw materials, machinery

SWITZERLAND
AUSTRIA
SLOVENIA
FRANCE
MONACO

Mont Blanc 4807m △
Dufour Spitze 4634m △
Monte Marmolada 3354m △
Lake Maggiore
Lago di Como
Trento
Lago di Garda
Piave
Trieste
Milan (Milano)
Brescia
Vicenza
Verona
Venice (Venezia)
Adige
Gulf of Venice
Turin (Torino)
Piacenza
Po
Parma
Adda
Tanaro
Po
Ferrara
Genoa (Genova)
Golfo di Genova
Bologna
Ravenna
Rimini
SAN MARINO
Adriatic Sea
Florence (Firenze)
Pisa
Arno
Ancona
Livorno
Siena
Lago Trasimeno
Perugia
Ligurian Sea
Elba
Lago di Bolsena
Tiber (Tevere)
Terni
Corno Grande 3354m △
Corsica (Corse) (to France)
VATICAN CITY
ROME (Roma)
Liri
Foggia
Strait of Bonifacio
Asinara
Volturno
Bari
Brindisi
Naples (Napoli)
Vesuvio 1277m △
Salerno
Ofanto
Strait of Otranto
Sassari
Capri
Taranto
Lecce
Sardinia (Sardegna)
Tirso
Punta La Marmora 1834m △
Golfo di Taranto
Tyrrhenian Sea
Cosenza
La Sila
Catanzaro
Ionian Sea
San Pietro
San Antioco
Cagliari
Golfo di Cagliari
Stromboli
Messina
Reggio di Calabria
Ustica
Strait of Messina
Lipari Vulcano
Favignana
Marsala
Palermo
Sicily (Sicilia)
Monte Etna 3340m △
Catania
Simeto
Siracusa
Pantelleria
Mediterranean Sea
Pelagie (to Italy)

APENNINES
This mountain range forms the "backbone" of Italy, dividing the rocky west coast from the flatter, sandy east coast.

GULF OF TARANTO
During earthquakes, great blocks of land have broken away and sunk into the sea, forming the Gulf's square shape.

POPULATION
Most of Italy's population lives in the industrial north, mainly in and around the Po Valley. Southern Italy is much more rural; towns are smaller and life can be much harder.

TYRRHENIAN SEA
This sea, which divides the Italian mainland from Sardinia, is gradually filling with sediment from the rivers that flow into it.

SICILY
Sicily has a famous active volcano, Mount Etna, and often experiences earthquakes.

MALTA
Area: 316 sq km (122 sq miles)
Population: 405,000
Capital: Valletta
Languages: Maltese, English

SAN MARINO
Area: 61 sq km (24 sq miles)
Population: 30,200
Capital: San Marino
Languages: Italian

VATICAN CITY
Area: 0.44 sq km (0.17 sq miles)
Population: 900
Capital: Vatican City
Languages: Italian, Latin

MALTA ✦ **VALLETTA**

N
W — E
S

SCALE BAR
0   40   80   km
0   40   80   miles

MILAN
With a population of 1.5 million, Milan is the second-largest city in Italy. It has grown rapidly since World War II due to the migration of workers from the impoverished south to the industrial north.

JAPAN

THE TOPS OF A SUBMERGED mountain chain form the islands of Japan. About three-quarters of the country is too steep to farm or build on. Japan has a population of 127 million, most of whom live in valleys and on the narrow coastal plain. Japan is a leading industrial nation, but its success is fairly recent: until 1853 the country was closed to foreigners and the government refused to import modern machines. More recently, Japanese companies have been very successful in exporting their own goods, so Japan sells more than it buys and has become very wealthy. Western influence is strong, but the Japanese are very proud of their traditional culture and religion. They continue to practise old customs while developing more modern technology. Most people follow both the Buddhist and Shinto religions. The head of state is an emperor, but the government is democratic. In the past the country was ruled by noblemen and samurai, professional soldiers who had a strict code of honour. Although the samurai have long been disbanded, their code still influences everyday life.

BONSAI
Japanese bonsai trees are pruned so that they do not grow more than a few centimetres high.

Japan is located in the Pacific Ocean, off the east coast of Asia. North and South Korea are to the west, and the Russian Federation to the north. There are four main islands, covering almost 370,000 sq km (144 sq miles).

TOKYO

The largest city in Japan is the capital, Tokyo. About 35 million people live in the city and suburbs, and the whole area is extremely overcrowded. Fumes from cars and industry are a major problem, but effective measures are being taken to reduce pollution.

INDUSTRY
Although Japan has few raw materials such as metal ores or coal, Japanese industry is among the most successful in the world. The country's main resource is its workforce. Japanese workers are very loyal to their companies, and workers take their holidays together, exercise together, and sing the company song daily. Managers are equally devoted to the company and pride themselves on their cooperation with the workers. New technology and techniques are introduced quickly and help boost prosperity.

SUSHI
Traditional Japanese food consists mainly of fish and rice. Often the fish is eaten raw or lightly cooked in dishes called sushi.

SUMO WRESTLING
The national sport of Japan is sumo wrestling. It attracts large crowds and is shown on television. The two contestants try to push each other out of a small ring. Success depends on strength and weight, so sumo wrestlers go to schools where they train and follow a special diet. Successful wrestlers may become extremely rich and famous. The sport is traditional and follows an elaborate pattern controlled by officials in decorative costume.

BULLET TRAIN
Japan has more than 25,000 km (16,000 miles) of railway. The most famous train is the Shinkansen, or bullet train, which runs from Tokyo to Fukuoka. The train covers the 1,176 km (731 miles) in less than six hours at an average speed of 195 km/h (122 mph) per hour.

Mount Fuji, a 3,776 m (12,388 ft) tall volcano is sacred to the Japanese.

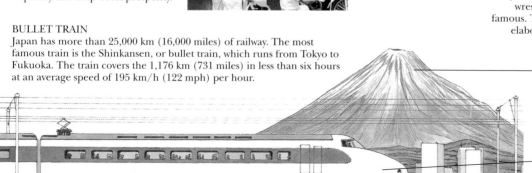

Japanese people travel more by train than travellers in any other country.

RICE CAKES
Rice cakes called *chimaki* are traditionally eaten throughout Japan. The rice cakes are cone-shaped and wrapped in a bamboo leaf. A similar snack, called *sasadango*, is also eaten in some areas of northern Japan.

VEHICLE INDUSTRY

Japanese vehicle manufacturers became world leaders in the 1980s thanks to their stylish designs, new technology and efficient production methods. Today, motor vehicles are the country's biggest export. Japanese vehicle manufacturers have also opened a number of factories in Europe and the USA.

KYUSHU

The southernmost island of Japan, Kyushu, is mountainous; the highest point is a volcano, Mount Aso. Kyushu is the most densely populated of the Japanese islands, and is linked to Honshu island by a railway tunnel under the Shimonoseki Strait.

SAKE
Sake is a Japanese alcoholic beverage made from fermented rice. It is the national beverage, and is served with special ceremony. Before being served, it is warmed in a small earthenware or porcelain bottle (right) called a *tokkuri*.

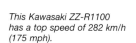

This Kawasaki ZZ-R1100 has a top speed of 282 km/h (175 mph).

ZEN GARDEN

Rock gardens, designed to represent the universe in miniature, are found in Zen Buddhist monasteries in Japan. These gardens are not literal representations of a landscape, but they give the impression of water and land. Sand or gravel symbolizes water, while rocks represent land. The Zen garden has no plants, trees or water, only raked gravel or sand, and rock groupings. These "dry gardens" were introduced by Buddhist monks in the 1300s.

KITES
Carp kites are flown on the fifth day of May to celebrate *Kodomono-hi* or children's day. The carp is a strong robust fish, renowned for its energy and determination, as it must swim upstream against the current, often jumping high out of the water. The carp therefore provides a good example to Japanese boys in particular, who must overcome obstacles and be successful. A group of carp kites represent a family and the largest kite symbolizes the father.

Zen Buddhists believe that performing simple tasks such as raking pebbles in a Zen garden can bring enlightenment to the mind.

OSAKA
Japan's third-largest city is Osaka, on the south coast of the island of Honshu. Osaka is a major industrial centre, with steel, chemical, and electrical industries. It is also one of the oldest cities in Japan, and has many Buddhist and Shinto temples. Osaka is the site of an impressive castle built in the 16th century by the shogun (warlord) Toyomoti Hideyoshi, who once ruled Japan. In 1970 Osaka was the host city for the World's Fair.

Find out more

ASIA
DEMOCRACY
EARTHQUAKES
ROBOTS
TECHNOLOGY

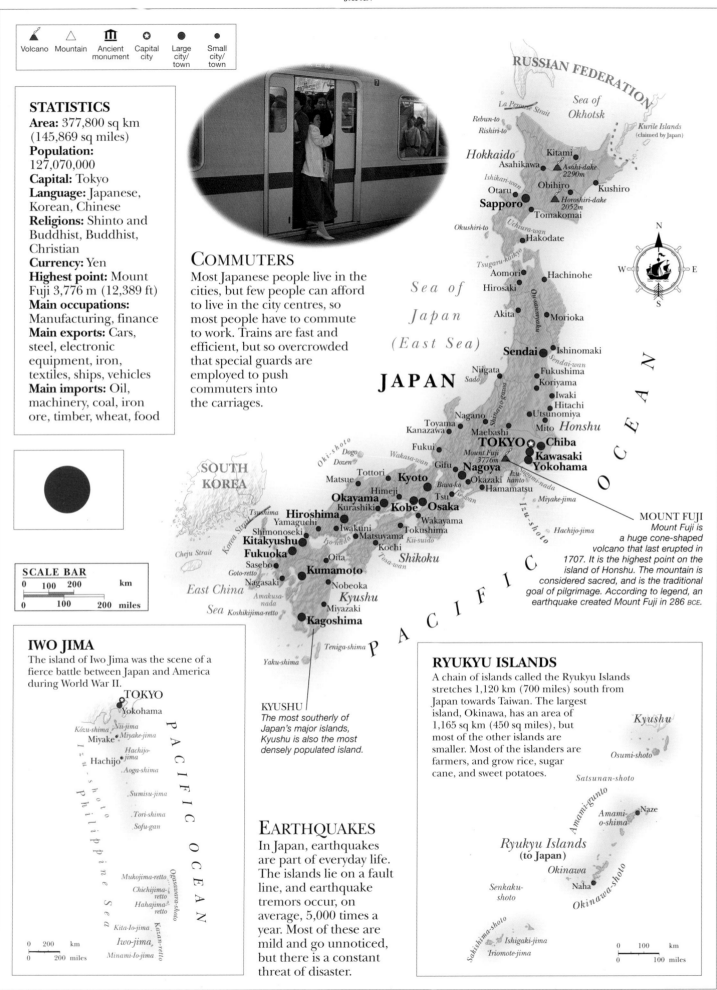

Legend

▲	Volcano
△	Mountain
🏛	Ancient monument
✪	Capital city
●	Large city/town
•	Small city/town

STATISTICS

Area: 377,800 sq km (145,869 sq miles)

Population: 127,070,000

Capital: Tokyo

Language: Japanese, Korean, Chinese

Religions: Shinto and Buddhist, Buddhist, Christian

Currency: Yen

Highest point: Mount Fuji 3,776 m (12,389 ft)

Main occupations: Manufacturing, finance

Main exports: Cars, steel, electronic equipment, iron, textiles, ships, vehicles

Main imports: Oil, machinery, coal, iron ore, timber, wheat, food

SCALE BAR

0 100 200 km

0 100 200 miles

COMMUTERS

Most Japanese people live in the cities, but few people can afford to live in the city centres, so most people have to commute to work. Trains are fast and efficient, but so overcrowded that special guards are employed to push commuters into the carriages.

MOUNT FUJI

Mount Fuji is a huge cone-shaped volcano that last erupted in 1707. It is the highest point on the island of Honshu. The mountain is considered sacred, and is the traditional goal of pilgrimage. According to legend, an earthquake created Mount Fuji in 286 BCE.

IWO JIMA

The island of Iwo Jima was the scene of a fierce battle between Japan and America during World War II.

0 200 km

0 200 miles

KYUSHU

The most southerly of Japan's major islands, Kyushu is also the most densely populated island.

EARTHQUAKES

In Japan, earthquakes are part of everyday life. The islands lie on a fault line, and earthquake tremors occur, on average, 5,000 times a year. Most of these are mild and go unnoticed, but there is a constant threat of disaster.

RYUKYU ISLANDS

A chain of islands called the Ryukyu Islands stretches 1,120 km (700 miles) south from Japan towards Taiwan. The largest island, Okinawa, has an area of 1,165 sq km (450 sq miles), but most of the other islands are smaller. Most of the islanders are farmers, and grow rice, sugar cane, and sweet potatoes.

0 100 km

0 100 miles

JESUS CHRIST

ONE OF THE WORLD'S MAJOR RELIGIONS – Christianity – was inspired by a man named Jesus Christ. We know about Jesus from the New Testament gospels, which were written by Matthew, Mark, Luke, and John. The gospels declare that Jesus was a Jew born in Bethlehem, in the Roman province of Judea, and was believed to be the Son of God. At the age of 30 he began to travel around Palestine (then under Roman rule) preaching a new message. He told stories called parables to explain his ideas. The gospels also describe miracles – amazing things he did such as raising the dead. However, some people thought his ideas might cause rebellion against Roman rule. He was arrested, tried, and sentenced to death. Christians believe that Jesus then rose from the dead. The Christian church was founded on the belief, and soon his ideas swept across the Roman Empire.

NATIVITY
The birth of Jesus, which took place in a stable in Bethlehem, is called the Nativity. Every year, on 25 December, Christians celebrate Jesus' birthday.

WHERE JESUS LIVED
Jesus spent his childhood in Nazareth. He preached mainly in Judea and Galilee.

Sidon
Tyre
Galilee
Nazareth
Tiberias
Caesarea
Samaria
Jericho
Judea
Jerusalem
Bethlehem
Dead Sea
Gaza

Jesus' travels around the Holy Land

SERMON ON THE MOUNT
Jesus taught that God was a kind, loving father, and that people should not fight back when attacked but should "turn the other cheek". He stressed the importance of love. His Sermon on the Mount contained new ideas describing how ordinary people who were humble, gentle, and poor would go to heaven. He also taught his followers a special prayer – the Lord's Prayer.

RESURRECTION
According to the Bible, three days after Jesus' death, the tomb in which his body had been placed was found empty. The gospels of Matthew, Mark, Luke, and John tell how he appeared to his disciples and, after 40 days of teaching them, rose to heaven.

LAST SUPPER
Near the end of his life Jesus shared a last supper with his 12 disciples. Using bread and wine as symbols of his body and blood, Jesus told them to remember him by this feast. To this day, the last supper is re-enacted during communion, when Christians take wine and wafers of bread as part of church services.

CRUCIFIXION
Jesus was accused of treason against Rome and tried by the Roman governor, Pontius Pilate. He was sentenced to be crucified – nailed to a cross on a hill called Calvary, outside Jerusalem. After his death his body was sealed in a tomb.

Find out more
CHRISTIANITY
RELIGIONS

JOAN OF ARC

IN THE EARLY 15TH CENTURY the French finally defeated the English, who had ruled much of their country. The warrior who led them into battle was a woman who has since become one of the best-loved heroines of French history. Joan of Arc was born into a farming family in 1412. She could not read or write, but she was inspired and stubborn, and could debate with educated people. As a young girl, Joan heard "voices" of saints and angels. The voices told her that she must restore the rightful king to the throne of France. Joan convinced the heir to the throne (the Dauphin) – who later became King Charles VII – to support her. In 1429, when only 17, she led the French army to victory at Orléans. Joan led her country's troops in other successful battles, but in 1430 she was caught by a powerful group of French people from Burgundy. They sold her to the English, who imprisoned her and put her on trial as a heretic – a person who does not believe in the official teachings of the Church. Joan was found guilty, and on 30 May, 1431, she was executed in Rouen by being burned at the stake. After her death the English were driven out of France, and Joan's reputation as a heroine flourished. Legends about Joan became widespread, and in 1920 she was made a saint.

The banner flown by Joan in battle

MEETING THE DAUPHIN
This contemporary tapestry shows Joan's arrival at the Château of Chinon in February 1429, in the company of six armed men. She is greeted by the Dauphin Charles, who wears a golden crown – a token of his claim to the disputed French throne.

THE MAID OF ORLEANS
Joan of Arc was a brave fighter who wore a suit of armour like a man. She was deeply religious, and prayed for guidance before going into battle. She was known as the "Maid of Orléans" because she led the French army to victory at Orléans.

JOAN'S HELMET
Joan may have worn this helmet in battle against the English. There is a hole in the side made by an arrow or a crossbow bolt.

Joan leads the French troops into battle at Orléans.

CROSS OF LORRAINE
During World War II (1939-45), France was occupied by Germany, partly under German military control and partly under a pro-German French government. The fighters of the French Resistance movement adopted the cross of Lorraine, originally Joan of Arc's symbol, because they shared her aim – to rid their country of foreign domination.

THE FEARLESS LEADER
Joan demonstrated that previous French defeat had resulted from military error and that, with better tactics, victories were possible. At first the troops were reluctant to follow Joan, but they soon realized that they won when obeying her commands. Joan's first victory was the lifting of the English siege of Orléans in 1429, which swelled the troops' confidence in their young leader. The Orléans victory was followed by similar success at Jargeau, Meung, Beaugency, and Patay. Her thrilling run came to an end when she was captured at Compiègne on 24 May, 1430.

___ *Find out more* ___
FRANCE
HUNDRED YEARS WAR

JUDAISM

THE HISTORY OF THE JEWISH PEOPLE and of their religion, Judaism, are closely linked. All Jews believe in one God who, more than 4,000 years ago, made a special agreement with their ancestor, Abraham. They were to become God's chosen people. In return they promised to obey his laws, and worship no other gods. Jews believe that a Messiah, God's messenger, will one day come to transform the world into a better place and to restore the ancient Jewish kingdom that was destroyed in the 6th century BCE. Judaism aims for a just and peaceful life for all people on earth. Jewish scriptures explain that to achieve this aim, correct behaviour is very important. Orthodox Jews – those who interpret the scriptures very strictly – obey many rules about their day-to-day activities, including how to dress and what to eat. For example, they do not eat pork or shellfish. Many Jews, however, are not orthodox and apply the rules less strictly. For all Jews, Hebrew is the language of worship. It is also the national language of Israel, the Jewish homeland. However, Jews live and work all over the world, speaking many different languages. Their strong family life and the laws which guide them unite them wherever they live.

JEWISH FESTIVALS

Yom Kippur (Day of Atonement) Tenth day of New Year; holiest of festivals, with 24 hours of fasting.

Purim (Feast of Lots) Early spring festival.

Passover (Pesach) Eight-day spring festival.

Shavuot (Feast of Weeks) Harvest festival in early summer.

Rosh Hashanah (New Year) Early autumn festival.

Sukkoth (Feast of Tabernacles) Nine-day autumn festival.

Hanukkah (Festival of Lights) Eight-day winter festival.

Jews light candles in a menorah, or branched candlestick, during Hanukkah.

Jewish men wear a skull cap called a yarmulke or kipa.

TALMUD

Jewish religious leaders are called rabbis. They are responsible for teaching and explaining the laws of Judaism. They study two holy books: the Talmud (right), and the Torah which is kept as a scroll. The Talmud contains instructions for following a Jewish way of life and understanding Jewish laws.

During prayers Jewish men wear a tallith, or prayer shawl, over their shoulders.

The Talmud contains instructions for following the Jewish way of life.

SYNAGOGUE

Jews worship in the synagogue. Prayer, study, and special family occasions such as weddings and bar and bat mitzvahs (the celebrations of children becoming adult Jews) take place here. A *minyan* (quorum of 10 males) is required to formally recite Kaddish (memorial prayers) and read from the Torah.

TORAH

The first five books of the Hebrew Bible – the Torah (left) – contain the laws of Judaism and the early history of the Jewish people. Other sections of the Hebrew Bible contain the psalms, the words of the prophets, and other holy writings. For Jews, the Torah is the most important of books.

Find out more

ISRAEL
MIDDLE EAST
RELIGIONS

JOHN F. KENNEDY

AN ASSASSIN'S BULLET abruptly ended the promise that John Fitzgerald Kennedy brought to the US presidency. His family name meant politics in their hometown of Boston. Kennedy graduated from Harvard University, then served in the US Navy. After the war, Kennedy launched his political career, serving first in the House of Representatives, then in the Senate. In 1956, he began a long campaign for the presidency, which ended with his winning by a small margin in 1960. He brought youth and vigour to the White House, and his wife Jackie became a fashion icon.

1917 Born in Brookline, Massachusetts, USA.

1940 Graduates from Harvard University.

1941-45 Serves in US Navy during World War II.

1946 Wins election to US House of Representatives.

1952 Elected to US Senate.

1953 Marries Jacqueline Bouvier.

1960 Elected 35th President of the US.

1961 Berlin Wall divides East and West Berlin.

1962 Presides over the Cuban missile crisis.

1963 Assassinated in Dallas, Texas.

THE KENNEDY DYNASTY

Kennedy was born into America's most glamorous and famous political dynasty. His grandfather was a state senator in Massachusetts, and his father served as ambassador to Great Britain. His mother's father was mayor of Boston and a US congressman. Three of the nine Kennedy children developed political careers: John; Robert, who became attorney general during his brother's presidency, then served as a US senator for New York until his own assassination in 1968; and Edward (known as Ted), who has represented Massachusetts in the Senate since 1962.

In his time, President Kennedy was the youngest man elected as president of the United States, and the first Roman Catholic to hold the office.

Cartoon of Cuban leader Fidel Castro

CUBAN MISSILE CRISIS

When satellites revealed Soviet missiles in Cuba within striking distance of several US cities, Kennedy ordered a naval blockade. For 13 days, the world was on the brink of war, until the missiles were withdrawn.

KENNEDY'S ASSASSINATION

In 1963, Kennedy and his wife, campaigning in Texas, rode an open-top car through Dallas. Shots rang out and Kennedy slumped down. He died half an hour later. Police arrested Lee Harvey Oswald, who denied the shooting. Two days later, as Oswald was taken to jail, he was killed by a lone gunman in front of a nationwide television audience.

WARTIME HERO

Kennedy served in the US Navy during World War II. After saving his crew in an encounter with a Japanese destroyer near the Solomon Islands, he was awarded a medal for bravery.

John Kennedy was also awarded the Purple Heart, a medal given to those wounded in action.

A NEW BEGINNING

Kennedy campaigned for president with the promise of a new frontier for Americans. Although many voters worried about his lack of experience, Kennedy defeated Richard Nixon. In his inaugural address, Kennedy urged Americans to, "Ask not what your country can do for you – ask what you can do for your country." During Kennedy's short time in office, the US had its first manned space flights, the civil rights movement brought equality closer for African Americans, and the testing of atomic bombs was outlawed.

Find out more

COLD WAR
GOVERNMENT AND POLITICS
WORLD WAR II

MARTIN LUTHER
KING

IN 1963 A BAPTIST MINISTER from Alabama, United States, led 250,000 people in a march on Washington, D.C., and delivered a moving and powerful speech. He was Martin Luther King, Jr., and his mission in life was to achieve equality and freedom for black Americans through peaceful means. Under his leadership the civil rights movement won many victories against segregation laws; laws that prevented blacks from voting, separated blacks from whites in schools and other places, and gave white people better opportunities and more freedom. Martin Luther King encouraged people to practise non-violent protest: demonstrations, "sit-ins", and peaceful disobedience of the segregation laws. King went to jail several times and faced constant threats of violence and death, but he continued to work for civil rights. Some white people hated him because he wanted to win more rights for black people, and some black people disliked him because he refused to use more extreme and violent methods. King was assassinated in 1968, but his dream of a country without racial discrimination lives on today. In 1986, the United States began to observe a national holiday in his name.

1929 Born, Atlanta, USA.

1954 Baptist minister.

1955 Philosophy Doctorate.

1955-56 Leads Montgomery bus boycott.

1957 Southern Christian Leadership Conference.

1961 Freedom Rides to support desegregation.

1963 March on Washington, D.C.

1964 Nobel Peace Prize.

1965 Selma-Montgomery march.

1968 Assassinated.

PUBLIC SPEAKER

Martin Luther King's words inspired millions of Americans, black and white. At the August 1963 march on Washington, King made a speech that has since become famous. He said: "I have a dream that one day this nation will rise up and live out the true meaning of its creed: We hold these truths to be self-evident; that all men are created equal."

CIVIL RIGHTS MOVEMENT

Black Americans remained second-class citizens throughout the southern states in the first half of the 20th century. They were not allowed to vote, and restrictions were placed on where they could sit in buses and restaurants. During the late 1950s, a movement arose which demanded equal rights for all Americans. Martin Luther King and others organized non-violent protests designed to force changes in the law. In 1964-65, racial discrimination was finally outlawed throughout the United States.

BUS BOYCOTT

In December 1955, Rosa Parks, a black seamstress who worked in an Alabama department store, was arrested for refusing to give up a bus seat reserved for white people. For one year, Martin Luther King and his friends persuaded people to boycott (refuse to use) every bus in Montgomery, Alabama, until the segregation of the bus seats was declared illegal.

Find out more

AMERICAN CIVIL WAR
HUMAN RIGHTS
SLAVERY
UNITED STATES OF AMERICA
UNITED STATES, HISTORY OF

KNIGHTS AND HERALDRY

A THOUSAND YEARS AGO men who fought in battle on horseback were called knights. At first they were just powerful warriors who terrified the enemy's foot soldiers. But by the 13th century the knights of western Europe had an important role in society. They fought in the armies of the king or queen in return for land. Knights also protected the peasants who lived and worked on the land, and in exchange the peasants gave the knights their service and produce. Heraldry developed as a way of identifying knights in battle. Armour completely covered the knights' faces and bodies, and they all looked alike. Thus, each knight chose "arms" – a unique coloured pattern or picture which everyone could recognize. He displayed his arms on a linen tunic worn over his armour. This was his "coat of arms". The chosen pattern remained in the knight's family and was passed on from father to son.

Argent a mullet azure

Vert a lily or

Ermine a cross crosslet gules

Azure a dolphin argent

Sable a bee or

A fall from horseback meant defeat, and often injured the knight.

The knight's symbol, or device, was painted or sewn onto all his equipment.

TOURNAMENTS AND JOUSTING

Tournaments began in France in the middle of the 11th century as peacetime training exercises for knights. They soon developed into major events with elaborate rules. Teams of knights fought fierce mock battles over great areas of land, and the losing side paid a ransom or handed over valuable possessions. During the 13th century, tournaments became better organized and took place in a single field. Only two knights jousted at a time, or fought with blunt weapons. Later, tilting replaced jousting and the knights used lances to knock their rivals to the ground.

Gules a lion rampant or

Or a chief indented purpure

CHIVALRY

The period between the 11th and 14th centuries is often known as the "age of chivalry". Knights of the time were supposed to follow a special code of chivalry – a system of rules about honour, obedience to God and the king, and protecting the weak. In reality, many knights forgot the code. They honoured only people of noble birth and stole from the poor and weak.

In English legend, Saint George was a chivalrous knight who rescued a maiden from a dangerous dragon.

Argent a talbot statant sable

Azure a fess erminois

Gules a lymphad argent

Azure an owl argent

Vair a chevron sable

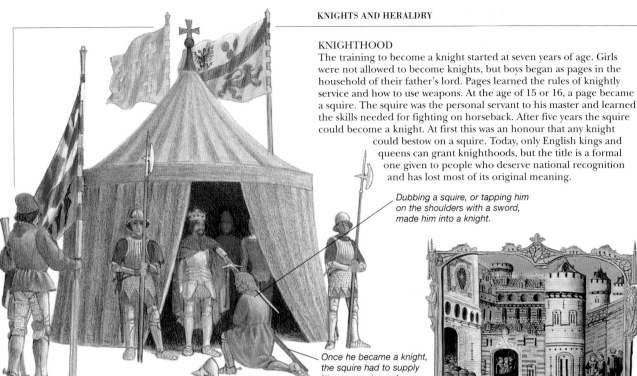

KNIGHTHOOD

The training to become a knight started at seven years of age. Girls were not allowed to become knights, but boys began as pages in the household of their father's lord. Pages learned the rules of knightly service and how to use weapons. At the age of 15 or 16, a page became a squire. The squire was the personal servant to his master and learned the skills needed for fighting on horseback. After five years the squire could become a knight. At first this was an honour that any knight could bestow on a squire. Today, only English kings and queens can grant knighthoods, but the title is a formal one given to people who deserve national recognition and has lost most of its original meaning.

Dubbing a squire, or tapping him on the shoulders with a sword, made him into a knight.

Once he became a knight, the squire had to supply his own equipment.

Argent a thistle proper

Or a lion passant gules

Gyronny argent and gules

Argent an eagle displayed sable

Sable a cross engrailed or

Gules a rod of Aesculapius or

Azure a harpy or

Vert a unicorn rampant argent

THE KNIGHTS OF THE ROUND TABLE

King Arthur and his knights are said to have held their court at a round table in the ancient capital of Camelot. If it really did exist, Camelot was probably built in the west of Britain some fifteen centuries ago. According to legend, Arthur led his band of Celtic knights in battle against Saxon invaders. The knights of Camelot became heroes and had many adventures.

Caerleon Castle, Wales, possible site of Camelot

KNIGHTS HOSPITALLERS

Knights from northwest Europe fought in the Crusades – a series of religious wars between Christians and Muslims that took place in the Middle East during the 11th, 12th, and 13th centuries. The warriors formed powerful alliances, one of which was the Knights Hospitallers. This group originally looked after a hospital for pilgrims to the Holy Land.

NAMING SHIELDS

The blazon, or description, below each shield names the field and charge and gives their colours and other details in a language based on medieval French.

The charge is a dragon vert (green). He is sitting "sejant" – with forepaws on the ground.

KEY TO BLAZONS	
Argent	Silver
Azure	Blue
Gules	Red
Or	Gold
Purpure	Purple
Sable	Black
Vert	Green

The field on this shield is or (gold).

Or a dragon sejant vert

SHIELDS

Each knight displayed his arms on a shield. The shield had two parts: the field, or surface, painted in a plain colour or a pattern; and the charge, which displayed a symbol, such as an animal or bird. The arms appeared everywhere on the knight's equipment. Sometimes the area above the shield design might show an image of a helmet with a crest, silk wreath, and mantling (a cloth for protection from the sun). The knight's motto, or slogan, could also be added below the shield. The full combination of designs was called a heraldic achievement (a herald was an expert in arms).

Gules a barrel palewise or

Argent a rose gules

Vert a garb or

Sable a boar's head erased or

Find out more

ARMOUR
CASTLES
CHRISTIANITY
CRUSADES
MEDIEVAL EUROPE

KOREA

Volcano	Mountain	Ancient monument	Capital city	Large city/ town	Small city/ town

THE KOREAN PENINSULA has a long history of invasion and occupation by its two powerful neighbours, China and Japan. In 1948, it was divided into Communist North and pro-American South, and the invasion of the South by the North led to the Korean War (1950-53). The war devastated both countries, but their subsequent histories have been very different. South Korea, once a rural society, became a major industrial power, and one of the world's leading ship-builders and car manufacturers. It also became a centre of high technology and electronics. The economy of the North, an isolated and repressive Communist regime, is a marked contrast. Heavy industry has created severe pollution and nationwide electricity blackouts are common. Floods and droughts have wrecked harvests and many people have suffered great hardship.

NORTH KOREA

Area: 120,540 sq km (46,540 sq miles)
Population: 22,665,000
Capital: Pyongyang
Languages: Korean, Chinese
Religions: Non-religious, traditional beliefs, Ch'ondogyo, Buddhist
Currency: North Korean Won

The Korean peninsula is bordered by China and, in the far northeast, Russia. On the west it is bordered by the Yellow Sea and, in the east, by the Sea of Japan. The peninsula is divided, along the 38th parallel, into North and South Korea.

NORTH KOREA

The independent Communist republic of North Korea invaded the South in 1950, leading to the Korean War (1950-53). The border that now divides the two countries is the most militarized in the world. North Korea now has one of the world's largest military organizations, a huge army and an advanced arms industry. Its military might is regularly displayed at regimented parades.

GINSENG
Korea is a major exporter of the valuable ginseng root, believed to improve health, and promote long life and vigour.

SOUTH KOREA

Area: 99,020 sq km (38,232 sq miles)
Population: 48,508,000
Capital: Seoul
Languages: Korean, Chinese
Religions: Mahayana Buddhist, Protestant, Roman Catholic, Confucianism
Currency: Won

SEOUL
Seoul was the capital of Korea from 1394 to 1948, when it became capital of South Korea. It is a fast-expanding city of over 10 million people. The orderly, rectangular street patterns of the centre give way to sprawling suburbs on the low surrounding hills. Seoul is a major commercial and manufacturing centre, with many small-scale textile factories. It is congested with traffic, and pollution is becoming a major problem.

Map labels

RUSS. FED.

CHINA

Paektu-san 2750m
Tumen
Najin
Ch'ongjin
Hyesan
Kanggye
Hamgyong-sanmaek
Kimch'aek
Ch'osan
Yalu
Huich'on
Sinp'o
Nangnim-sanmaek
Hamhung
Sinuiju
Chongju
Taedong-gang
Sunch'on
Wonsan

NORTH KOREA

East Korea Bay
Sea of Japan (East Sea)

Sinmi-do
Korea Bay
PYONGYANG
Namp'o
Sariwon
Kosong
(North and South Korea have been divided by a ceasefire agreement since 1953)
Changyon
Sokch'o
Haeju
Ch'unch'on
Ongjin
T'aebaek-sanmaek
Kangnung
Paengnyong-do
SEOUL (SOUL)
Tonghae
Inch'on
Suwon
Yellow Sea
Ch'onan
Ch'ungju
Sangju
Andong
Taejon
Kimch'on
P'ohang
Kunsan
Taegu
SOUTH KOREA
Namwon
Masan
Ulsan
Kwangju
Pusan
Sunch'on
Koje-do
Mokp'o
Namhae-do
Tsushima
Chin-do
Kogum-do
Ko-saki
JAPAN
Korea Strait
Cheju Strait
Cheju
East China Sea
Cheju-do

SCALE BAR
0 50 km
0 50 miles

N
W E
S

Find out more
ASIA
ASIA, HISTORY OF
CHINA
COMMUNISM
JAPAN

LAKE AND RIVER WILDLIFE

THE WATER IN LAKES and rivers is teeming with all kinds of life. Grasses, reeds, and other plants grow along the water's edge, providing food and shelter for insects, nesting birds, and mammals such as water voles and muskrats. In rivers, the fast-flowing water sweeps away plants, but in lakes, tiny floating plants are food for small creatures such as water fleas and shrimps, which are in turn eaten by bigger fish. Larger floating waterweeds provide shade for basking fish. Fallen leaves, animal droppings, and rotting plant matter form a rich mud at the bottom of rivers and lakes, where worms, snails, and other small organisms live. Today, many lakes and rivers are suffering from serious pollution. Industrial chemicals, farm fertilizers, untreated sewage, and a host of other damaging substances discharged into lakes and rivers have upset or destroyed the natural wildlife balance.

FRESH WATER
The water in lakes and rivers is called fresh water. Although it makes up only about 0.03 per cent (that is, 1 part in 3000) of all the water on Earth, fresh water is home to thousands of different plants and animals.

Pickerell weed grows at the water's edge of lakes and rivers.

MUSKRAT
The muskrat is a rodent that usually eats water plants but also feeds on small animals such as fish, frogs, and freshwater shellfish.

Muskrat swims powerfully with its webbed back feet and uses its long, hairless tail as a rudder for steering.

RUDDY DUCK
The ruddy duck is found in open waters in many parts of Europe. It has a stiff, upward-pointing tail and dives in search of plants, small water insects, larvae, and worms.

GIANT OTTER
The largest member of the otter family lives in South America. The giant otter grows to more than 1.5 m (5 ft) long including its tail. It hunts catfish, piranha, and other fish. Unlike other otters, the giant otter prefers to stay in streams and pools and is not often seen on land. Today, this otter is very rare and is on the official list of endangered species.

PIKE
The northern pike is a large, fearsome predator with a huge mouth and sharp teeth for seizing many kinds of fish, as well as frogs, water birds, and small mammals. Pike live in lakes and slow-moving rivers; the biggest pike grow to more than 1 m (3 ft) long.

FALSE MAP TURTLE
One of the many water creatures that suffer from pollution of rivers and lakes is the false map turtle from North America, shown here. The harmful chemical waste that we pour into the water has also reduced this turtle's food of snails and shellfish.

RIVER PLANTS
The speed of the water in a river has a great effect on the wildlife. In a fast river the water sweeps the river bed clean of sand and mud, leaving only pebbles. Nothing can grow in the middle of a river, and the river bank consists mainly of plants such as willows that hang over the water. In a slow river, sand and mud can settle, and plants such as irises take root more easily.

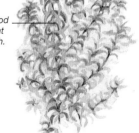

Pond weed is food for many different lake and river fish.

CRAYFISH
The crayfish, found in rivers, is a freshwater relative of sea-living lobsters. It is active mainly at night and walks along the river bed on its four pairs of legs, eating a wide range of food, from plant matter to worms, shellfish, and small fish.

Cattail grows to 2.5 m (8 ft) high.

LAKE WILDLIFE

Trees such as willows and alders line the edge of many lakes; rushes, tussock sedges, reeds, and other marshy plants grow closer to the water. Plants such as water lilies and water horsetails grow in the shallow water and stick up above the surface. Each type of plant is food for a different assortment of animals.

HERON

Many kinds of herons visit lakes and rivers all over the world. Herons wade slowly in shallow water, at times standing perfectly still for several minutes, then suddenly striking at a frog or a fish with their long, spear-shaped bills.

WILLOW
The willow tree thrives in the damp soil of river banks and the shores of lakes. Its long, penetrating roots help strengthen the bank.

MOORHEN
During the breeding season the male and female moorhen build a nest among the vegetation at the water's edge, and the female lays up to 11 eggs. The moorhen's long, splayed toes enable it to walk on floating leaves on rivers, lakes, and marshes. These birds eat pond weeds, fruit, and sometimes insects.

Dragonflies are a familiar sight around lakes and rivers during the summer months.

WATER LILIES
There are about 200 kinds of water lilies. Their leaves and flowers float on the surface of the water, and their long stems stretch down about 2 m (6 ft) to the roots embedded in the mud below.

WATER BOATMAN
This aquatic insect uses its paddle-like legs to row across the surface of the water. The back swimmer, a similar creature, swims upside down, often near the surface.

WATER SNAKE
Many snakes can swim; the water snake is an expert swimmer. It glides across the lake with hardly a ripple. Water snakes prey on small mammals, frogs, fish, and small water birds and their eggs and nestlings.

Diving beetles breathe by trapping air under the hard wing cases that cover the body.

MIRROR CARP
Carp are fish that live in slow-flowing rivers and weed-filled lakes. Mirror carp are so named because their bodies are covered with large, shiny, mirror-like scales. Mirror carp search the river bottom for small plants, shellfish, and worms.

Insect larvae, fish fry (young), and other small creatures shelter among the plants along the water's edge.

DIVING BEETLE
The diving beetle is a fierce predator. It hunts tadpoles, small fish, aquatic worms, and insects.

CONSERVATION
The axolotl shown here is a kind of Mexican salamander. It cannot survive on land and is found only in lakes such as Lake Xochimilco, Mexico. Like many other lake and river creatures, the axolotl is threatened by pollution. Thousands of lakes in the world are now lifeless, because of the damaging substances that flow into them. Today, many lakes and rivers are being turned into nature reserves in order to protect the birds, fish, mammals, and other wildlife they contain.

Axolotl means "water beast".

Find out more
ANIMAL SENSES
BIRDS
FISH
FROGS AND OTHER AMPHIBIANS
SNAKES

LAKES

WATER FROM RIVERS, MOUNTAIN SPRINGS, and rain fills hollows in the ground and forms lakes, which are areas of water surrounded by land. Lakes also form in depressions dug out of the ground by glaciers, or in holes in limestone rocks. Some lakes are artificial: reservoirs are lakes made by building dams across rivers. Several landlocked seas such as the Caspian Sea and the Dead Sea are really lakes. The Caspian Sea, which lies between Europe and Asia, is the world's biggest lake. Its surface covers an area almost as large as Japan.

Lakes sustain a wealth of plant and animal life and are often surrounded by fertile land. Freshwater lakes provide water for towns and cities, and recreation areas for swimming, sailing, and water-skiing. Large lakes, such as the Great Lakes in North America, are used to transport goods in ships. However, lakes do not last forever. Silt and plants can fill up a lake over a period of years and turn it into a swamp.

SALTY LAKES
Salt collects in lakes that have no outlet, such as the Dead Sea between Israel and Jordan. The water is so salty that people can float in it without swimming.

VOLCANIC LAKES
Rainwater fills the volcanic crater at the summit of Mount Mazama, Oregon, United States, to form Crater Lake. It is 589 m (1,932 ft) deep, making it the deepest lake in the United States.

KINDS OF LAKES

Lakes form in hollows dug by glaciers during the Ice Age, and in places where glaciers have left barriers of rock across valleys. Water dissolves huge holes in limestone regions, which often fill with rainwater to create lakes. Lakes can also form in volcanic craters.

FRESHWATER LAKES
The water in freshwater lakes is not salty like the sea, because the lakes are constantly fed and drained by rivers. The largest group of freshwater lakes are the Great Lakes in the United States and Canada. Lake Superior (left) is the largest of the Great Lakes.

Plants grow on the damp, fertile soil.

SWAMPS AND MARSHES

The Everglades is a large region of swamps in the United States. Swamps, or marshes, can form at the edge of a lake where the ground is soaked with water or covered with shallow water. They also form on land where water cannot drain away.

THE LIFE OF A LAKE

Lakes are not permanent features of the landscape. They may come and go as their water supply rises and falls. Lakes can slowly fill with soil and stones washed down from the land above the lake. The outlet river may deepen and drain the lake.

River flows into lake.

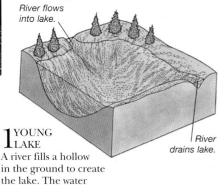

1 YOUNG LAKE
A river fills a hollow in the ground to create the lake. The water flows through the lake, running out into another river.

River drains lake.

2 SHRINKING LAKE
The river carries soil, which falls to the bottom as it enters the lake. A layer of soil builds up along the edge of the lake.

Soil and mud build up at sides and bottom of lake.

3 DYING LAKE
The soil layers extend into the lake. Plants grow and the layers become land. This continues until the lake vanishes.

Find out more

DAMS
GLACIERS AND ICECAPS
LAKE AND RIVER WILDLIFE
MARSH AND SWAMP WILDLIFE
RIVERS
WATER

LANGUAGES

OUR ABILITY TO TALK is one of the skills that makes humans different from the rest of the animal world. Although some animals communicate with gestures, such as mating displays, human speech is much more highly developed. In English, for example, most people use a vocabulary (a list of words) of about 5,000 words in talking, and 10,000 in writing. A language is a way of organizing spoken sounds to express ideas. Human language developed over thousands of years, and people in different countries use different languages. Some languages share words with the languages of nearby countries. For instance, book is *libro* in both Italian and Spanish, and *livre* in French; in English we get the word library from the same source. There are now some 5,000 different languages and many dialects – local versions of major languages.

TOWER OF BABEL
At the beginning of this Bible story, everyone spoke the same language. But when people tried to build a tower to reach heaven, God became angry. He made many languages so people could not understand and help one another.

English is now spoken worldwide by more than a billion people, many as a second or third language.

More than a half of China's 1.3 billion population speak Mandarin Chinese.

France once ruled many countries in West Africa, and people there still speak French as well as their local languages.

There are at least 845 languages in India. Hindi and English are the official languages.

Some people have no difficulty in learning foreign languages and can speak several fluently; the record is about 28.

There are about 700 languages in Papua New Guinea.

LATIN
For many centuries, educated people of many nationalities spoke Latin as well as their native, or first, language. Throughout Europe, scholars, governments, and the Christian Church used Latin.

COMMON LANGUAGES

A map of national languages shows how European nations have spread around the world: for example, English settlers took their language to the United States, Canada, Australia, and New Zealand. Spain conquered much of South America, and Spanish is still spoken there. But many people using these languages also have their own local language, which is part of their native culture.

- Mandarin Chinese
- English
- Russian
- Spanish
- French
- Portuguese
- Arabic
- Other

SIGN LANGUAGE

Human speech and hearing make language possible. People who have difficulty speaking or hearing cannot use a spoken language. Instead, they communicate using hand signals. There are signs and gestures for all the common words, and signs for individual letters.

S P E A K

Find out more
ALPHABETS
FILM
WRITERS AND POETS

LAW

EVERY SOCIETY HAS its own set of laws to safeguard the rights of its citizens and to balance individual freedom against the needs of the people in general. On the simplest level, there are laws to protect citizens from attack or robbery as they walk along the street. These and other similar rules are called criminal laws. However, the law does much more than provide simple protection. It also settles arguments between individuals. For example, if you believe that you have bought damaged goods, and the person who sold them disagrees, the law must decide who is right. The branch of law that deals with arguments such as these is called civil law. The law is very complex because it must meet the different needs and expectations of society's millions of members. It includes not only civil and criminal branches, but also other smaller divisions, such as family law, which settles arguments when people divorce. Understanding the law takes a long time; lawyers, who apply and interpret the law, study for many years. Most lawyers specialize in just one area of the law.

JUDGES
The judge helps the jury understand the laws relating to the trial, and passes sentence (decides the punishment) if there is a guilty verdict.

Witness answers questions

Jury of 12 people

Defence lawyer addresses the jury.

Defence tries to convince the jury that the prisoner is not guilty.

Prosecution tries to prove guilt.

FAIR AND JUST LAW
A statue representing justice wears a blindfold to show that the law does not favour any one person. However, not all law is good law, for governments can make laws that remove freedoms as well as ones that safeguard them. The scales show that justice weighs opposing evidence in the same way that a balance weighs goods. The sword represents punishment.

DEATH PENALTY
In past centuries a serious crime was punishable by death and, until the mid-19th century, hangings were public. Some countries still apply the death penalty, and in Europe people were executed for murder up to the mid-20th century.

JURY TRIAL
A person accused of a serious crime has the right to a trial by jury, a group of men and women (usually 12) chosen at random from the community. A prosecuting lawyer tries to convince the jury that the defendant – the accused person – is guilty. A defence lawyer sets out to prove the defendant's innocence. Witnesses tell the court what they know about the crime. The jury listens to the facts, or evidence, and decides whether the prosecution has proved guilt.

WORLD LAW
International problems call for worldwide co-operation. Air disasters, for example, may involve companies and individuals from many countries. Lawyers must agree on ways of establishing liability (blame) and compensating people for loss. Many countries share extradition treaties, so that criminals such as terrorists can be sent home for trial if they are caught elsewhere.

Passengers from many countries

Aeroplane made in the United States.

Accident happens over Spain.

ALTERNATIVES TO PRISON
Electronic tags locked to the ankles of criminals keep them at home and out of trouble. A box placed next to the offender's telephone monitors the range of the tag. If the wearer of the tag moves too far away, the box dials up a police central computer and sounds the alarm.

Offenders learn useful skills by following a schedule of duties such as working in the kitchen.

PRISON AND PUNISHMENT
People found guilty of serious crimes usually go to prison. This is to deter them from criminal activity in future and to protect others from danger for the term of their sentence. Prisons also aim to reform offenders – for example by teaching skills to improve their employment prospects on release.

TRIAL BY ORDEAL
In medieval England, justice was often barbaric. People accused of a crime had to prove they were innocent by undergoing an ordeal. They chose between a challenge, such as carrying a red-hot stone, or fighting their accuser. If they survived the ordeal, they were believed to be innocent.

COURTS
The Old Bailey, in London, houses the Central Criminal Court. There are many types of law court. In England and Wales these include crown and magistrate's courts, which handle criminal cases, and county courts for civil or non-criminal cases. The Scottish system differs, and includes district and sheriff courts.

Law Lords and clerks entering the High Court

BARRISTER AND SOLICITOR
There are two types of lawyer in Britain: barristers and solicitors. Barristers are trained to argue cases in court. Solicitors prepare cases that barristers present, and do legal work outside the courtroom.

The Law Courts, London

NON-CRIMINAL LAW
Most lawyers spend time dealing with non-criminal law, also known as civil law. This is concerned with rights and duties between citizens. It includes contract law, which is concerned with trade and other agreements between people, property law, and matters such as wills and divorce.

ADVERSARIAL SYSTEM
The British legal system is known as adversarial, because there are two sides, who argue to convince a jury that they are right. The side that brings a case to court is known as the prosecution, and the side that defends a charge in court is known as the defence. In civil cases, the prosecution is often known as "the plaintiff".

LAWS
In Britain, parliament makes laws. The courts then follow the law, but lawyers can appeal through the court system to try and change the law if it is unfair. The final decision is made by the Law Lords who sit in the House of Lords. British law is based on common law, which dates back to the Anglo-Saxons. Court decisions are based on precedent – previous decisions made on similar court cases.

Find out more
ANGLO-SAXONS
GOVERNMENT AND POLITICS
MEDIEVAL EUROPE

LEONARDO DA VINCI

A HIGHLY TALENTED ARTIST and scientist, Leonardo da Vinci was years ahead of his time. He was one of the greatest figures in the movement called the Renaissance, the revival of art and learning that began in Italy in the 15th century. Today, many people remember Leonardo for painting some of the most famous pictures of his time, but he achieved a great deal more than this. He designed castles and weaponry, invented machines, studied physics and mathematics, and made accurate scientific drawings of plants, animals, and the human body. He was probably one of the world's greatest all-round geniuses.

1452 Born near the village of Vinci, in Italy.

1466 Moves to Florence; works in studio of the artist Verrochio.

1482 Works as architect, engineer, and painter in Milan, in northern Italy.

1503 Begins *Mona Lisa*.

1503 Designs famous flying machine.

1513 Makes pioneering study of lenses and optics.

1515 Studies anatomy.

1516 Dies in France.

MONA LISA
Leonardo's best-known portrait is of Mona Lisa, the wife of a rich Florentine. The painting is famous for Mona Lisa's haunting smile, and for the softly blended colours, an effect known as *sfumato*. The painting is in the Louvre gallery in Paris.

MACHINERY

Leonardo's notebooks are crammed with designs for ingenious machines. Some of these devices, such as a pump, an armoured car, and a machine for grinding lenses, could actually have been built and used. Others, like his famous "ornithopter" flying machine with its flapping wings, would never have worked, but they were still ahead of their time.

RENAISSANCE MAN

In Leonardo's time, it was still possible for a person to become skilled in many different branches of learning – such a person was called a "Renaissance man". Leonardo produced new ideas in practically every area he studied. He wrote down many of these ideas in a series of beautifully illustrated notebooks.

ARCHITECTURE
Buildings and town planning fascinated Leonardo. He designed an "ideal city" which was never built. The streets of the city were arranged in a grid pattern, like a modern American town. He also designed bathhouses, together with drainage networks and systems for rubbish collecting, which were unknown at the time.

Tank design

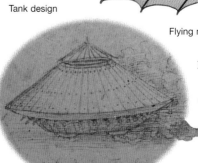

Flying machine

ANATOMY
In the 16th century, people knew little about anatomy (the study of the human body and how it works). Leonardo was one of the first to dissect, or cut up, dead bodies and draw them, sketching every muscle and bone in detail. If his drawings had been published, they would have proved helpful to doctors and other scientists.

Find out more
HELICOPTERS
PAINTING
RENAISSANCE

LEWIS AND CLARK

IN 1803, U.S. PRESIDENT Thomas Jefferson sent Meriwether Lewis and William Clark to lead an expedition to explore the wild and largely unknown lands west of Missouri to the Pacific Ocean. Their instructions were to explore and chart the region, to make contact with Native Americans, and to find out if there was a water link between the Atlantic and Pacific oceans. Lewis and Clark were not experienced explorers, but they successfully led a band of about 40 men, travelling by boat, horse, and foot, some hazardous 13,000 km (8,000 miles) to the Pacific and back. They returned home as heroes with important exciting new information about the region, which later encouraged U.S. expansion westward.

MERIWETHER LEWIS
Lewis (1774-1809) was private secretary to President Jefferson. Co-leader of the expedition, he served as the party's naturalist, collecting animal and plant specimens.

SACAJAWEA
Lewis and Clark encountered many Native Americans on their journey. None was as important as Sacajawea (1786-1812), also known as "Bird Woman". She joined the expedition in 1805 and guided the explorers over mountain trails. Her presence encouraged friendly relations with the Native Americans.

WILLIAM CLARK
Clark (1770-1838) was a lieutenant in the army. He resigned in 1796 but rejoined the army in 1803 to go westward with Lewis. Although untrained, he mapped accurate routes for the expedition and assembled records of the journey for publication.

ROUTE OF THE EXPEDITION

The expedition left St. Louis on 14 May 1804, travelling along the Missouri River by boat. In November the explorers reached what is now North Dakota, where they spent the winter with native Mandans. In April 1805, they continued up the Missouri. Leaving the river they struggled on a perilous journey over the Rocky Mountains, then paddled up the Columbia River, finally reaching the Pacific in November. They spent the winter on the Pacific coast, before retracing their steps, arriving back in St. Louis on 23 September 1806.

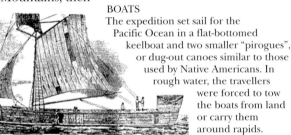

BOATS
The expedition set sail for the Pacific Ocean in a flat-bottomed keelboat and two smaller "pirogues", or dug-out canoes similar to those used by Native Americans. In rough water, the travellers were forced to tow the boats from land or carry them around rapids.

WILDLIFE
The expedition returned with valuable samples of animals, plants, rocks, and minerals. Lewis became particularly interested in grizzly bears, one of which tried to attack him. He reported a large number of grizzlies, which pleased President Jefferson, who was eager to develop the fur trade in the United States.

Grizzly bear

Early settlers travelled across North America in a covered wagon.

WESTWARD EXPANSION

Lewis and Clark's expedition proved there was no direct water link between the Atlantic and Pacific oceans. However, Lewis and Clark's information about the diversity and richness of the lands attracted hundreds of traders and settlers to the West. From the 1840s, increasing numbers made their way on the long journey westward in covered wagons, or prairie schooners.

Find out more

BEARS AND PANDAS
MOUNTAIN WILDLIFE
NATIVE AMERICANS
UNITED STATES OF AMERICA
UNITED STATES, HISTORY OF

LIGHT

WITHOUT LIGHT, life on Earth would be impossible. Sunlight provides the energy to make plants grow and keep all living things alive. Light itself is a form of energy which travels as tiny packets of electromagnetic energy called photons. When photons enter our eyes they stimulate special light-sensitive cells so that we can see. Other forms of energy which travel as electromagnetic waves include radio waves, x-rays, and microwaves in microwave ovens. Just as there is a spectrum of colours in light, there is also an electromagnetic spectrum. In fact, light waves are also a type of electromagnetic wave, and the colours in light form a small part of the electromagnetic spectrum. Light waves and all other electromagnetic waves travel at 300,000 km (186,000 miles) per second, which is so fast that they could circle the world almost eight times in a second. Nothing in the universe can travel faster than light.

FLUORESCENT LIGHT

Most modern light bulbs are fluorescent tubes like this one. When an electric current is passed through the gas in the tube, gas atoms emit invisible, ultraviolet light. The ultraviolet light strikes phosphors – chemicals in the tube's lining – and makes them glow with a brilliant white light.

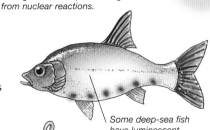

Electrical contact is made when the bulb terminal is screwed into the socket.

The electronics hidden inside the white plastic base control the light.

Inside a glass tube, an electric current flows through a gas (mercury vapour) making it emit invisible ultra-violet (UV) light.

A chemical coating inside the bulb converts the UV light into visible white light.

The explosion of gunpowder inside a firework produces a burst of coloured light.

Nuclear reactions inside the centre of the Sun produce intense heat and light. All stars produce light from nuclear reactions.

BRIGHTNESS OF LIGHT

The further you are from a light, the less bright it will seem. This is because light spreads out in all directions from its source. So when you are far away, the light is spread over a wide area. Many stars, for instance, are much brighter than our Sun, but their light is spread out over so vast an area that by the time it reaches us, the stars do not even seem as bright as a candle.

Some deep-sea fish have luminescent stripes and spots along their bodies that give out light.

Searchlights give out very intense light, often produced by an electric spark between two pieces of carbon.

SOURCES OF LIGHT

Many different objects give off light. The Sun, traditional electric light bulbs, and fireworks are incandescent, which means they glow because they are hot. But not all lights are hot. Chemicals, not heat, produce the glowing spots on the bodies of some deep-sea fish. All cool lights, including fluorescent lights, are called luminescent.

Shine a torch on a wall and watch the pool of light grow larger and dimmer as you move the torch further away.

A candle is a wide source of light, so it produces a fuzzy shadow.

Candles and lanterns give out light.

When things burn they give out light as well as heat.

LIGHT AND SHADOW

Light travels in straight lines, so, in most cases, it cannot go around obstacles in its path. When light rays hit a solid object, some bounce back and some are absorbed by the object, warming it up a little. The area behind receives no light rays and is left in shadow.

Current flowing through metal filament makes it glow white hot.

INCANDESCENT LIGHT BULB

In the middle of an incandescent electric light bulb is a tiny spiral of tungsten wire called the filament. When an electric current is sent through the filament, it warms up so much that it glows white hot. It is the brightly glowing filament that produces light.

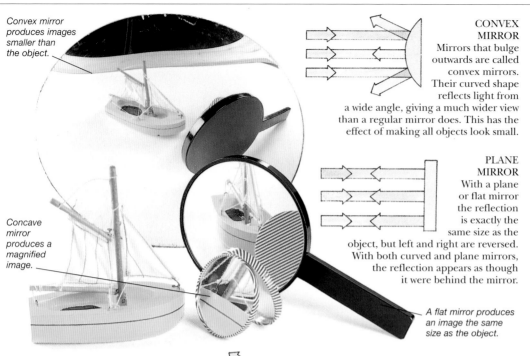

Convex mirror produces images smaller than the object.

Concave mirror produces a magnified image.

CONVEX MIRROR

Mirrors that bulge outwards are called convex mirrors. Their curved shape reflects light from a wide angle, giving a much wider view than a regular mirror does. This has the effect of making all objects look small.

PLANE MIRROR

With a plane or flat mirror the reflection is exactly the same size as the object, but left and right are reversed. With both curved and plane mirrors, the reflection appears as though it were behind the mirror.

A flat mirror produces an image the same size as the object.

MIRRORS

Light passes easily through transparent substances such as glass and water, but not through opaque objects such as paper. Most opaque objects have a rough surface which scatters light in all directions. However, a mirror has a smooth surface, so it reflects light in a regular way. When you look at your face in a mirror, the light bounces straight back, producing a sharp image. Most mirrors are made of glass; your face is reflected from a shiny metal coating at the back of the mirror, not from the glass.

CONCAVE MIRROR

A concave mirror, which is curved inwards, forms two kinds of image. If the object is close to the mirror, the reflection is larger than the real thing. If the object is far away, the image formed is small and upside down.

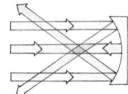

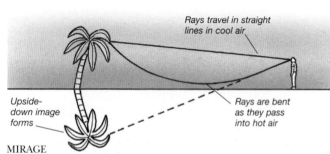

Rays travel in straight lines in cool air

Upside-down image forms

Rays are bent as they pass into hot air

MIRAGE

In the hot desert, weary travellers are often fooled by the sight of an oasis. The oasis appears on the horizon, only to vanish as the travellers hurry towards it. What they have seen is an illusion called a mirage. In the example above, light rays travelling from the palm tree are bent upwards by the warm air. The observer's eyes interpret the light as having travelled in a straight line so he sees a watery reflection of the tree on the ground.

FIBRE OPTICS

Fibre optic cables are channels that carry light. They are flexible so they can carry light around corners. The fibres are long, thin filaments of glass; the light bounces back and forth along the inner surface of the glass. Fibre optics are valuable for seeing into awkward places. Doctors can use fibre optic endoscopes to see inside a patient's body without opening the body up.

LENSES AND REFRACTION

Glasses, cameras, telescopes, and microscopes use lenses to create particular kinds of images. The lenses in a telescope, for example, produce a magnified view of a distant object. All lenses work on the principle that although light always travels in straight lines, it travels slower through glass than through air. If a light ray strikes glass at an angle, one side of the ray will hit the glass just before the other and will slow down earlier. The effect is to bend the light ray slightly, just as a car pulls to one side if it has a puncture. This bending of light is called refraction.

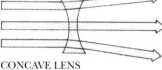

CONCAVE LENS

A concave lens is thicker at the edges than in the centre, so it spreads light rays out. If you look through a concave lens, everything appears smaller.

Focus

CONVEX LENS

Convex lenses bring light rays together. At the focus, where light rays from a distant object meet, they form an image of the object which can be seen on a screen.

Magnifying glasses are convex lenses.

Light refracts when it passes through water, because the water slows it down. This makes objects look as though they are bent.

ABRAHAM LINCOLN

ONE OF THE MOST FAMOUS PRESIDENTS in history is Abraham Lincoln. But when he was elected in 1860, less than half the country supported him, and he remained very unpopular with many people for the entire five years of his presidency. Lincoln did not approve of slavery, and many landowners in the southern United States still kept slaves. As a result of his election, 11 southern states left the Union and declared themselves an independent Confederacy, or alliance. Civil war then broke out between the Union and the Confederacy. Lincoln was a capable war leader. He struggled to keep the remaining states united behind his leadership. Many people in his own government opposed him. But in 1865 he led the Union states to victory. Afterwards, Lincoln tried to repair the damage done by the war and bring together the two opposing sides.

LINCOLN'S BIRTHPLACE
This log cabin in Kentucky, United States, is a replica of the birthplace of Abraham Lincoln. The poverty of Lincoln's childhood influenced his political ideas.

1809 Born in Kentucky.

1831 Moves to New Salem, Illinois, where he worked as a storekeeper, surveyor, and postmaster while studying law.

1834 Elected to state legislature.

1836 Qualifies as a lawyer.

1842 Marries Mary Todd.

1846 Elected to Congress.

1855, 1859 Runs unsuccessfully for Senate.

1860 Elected president.

1861 Mobilizes 75,000 volunteers to put down the southern rebellion.

1863 Issues Emancipation Proclamation.

1864 Re-elected president.

1865 Assassinated.

GETTYSBURG ADDRESS
Abraham Lincoln was famous for his speeches. In 1863, he attended the dedication of a national cemetery on the site of the Civil War battlefield in Gettysburg, Pennsylvania. He made a speech known as the Gettysburg Address. He hoped that "these dead shall not have died in vain".

THE DEATH OF LINCOLN
On 14 April 1865, Abraham Lincoln was watching a play at Ford's Theatre in Washington, D.C. John Wilkes Booth, an actor who supported the southern states in the Civil War, crept quietly into the president's box and shot him. The president died of his wounds the next day.

ABOLITION
The move to abolish slavery in the United States grew under Lincoln. Led by white middle-class Northerners, many freed slaves joined the abolition movement. Some, such as Andrew Scott (right), fought in the Union army during the Civil War. Slaves fled from South to North (and freedom) via the Underground Railroad – a secret escape route. Harriet Tubman, a famous pioneer of the railroad, helped 300 slaves to escape in this way.

MOUNT RUSHMORE
The faces of four American presidents – George Washington, Thomas Jefferson, Theodore Roosevelt, and Abraham Lincoln – are carved out of rock on the side of Mount Rushmore in the Black Hills of South Dakota, United States.

Find out more
AMERICAN CIVIL WAR
SLAVERY
TUBMAN, HARRIET
UNITED STATES OF AMERICA
UNITED STATES, HISTORY OF

LIONS
TIGERS, AND OTHER BIG CATS

FEW CREATURES ARE HELD in such awe as lions, tigers, cheetahs, and leopards, which we often call the big cats. These agile predators have strong, razor-sharp teeth and claws, muscular bodies, and excellent senses. Their beautiful striped and spotted fur breaks up their outline and camouflages them, allowing them to ambush unwary zebras, giraffes, and other prey. There are seven kinds of big cats. The tiger is the largest. A fully grown tiger may measure more than 3 m (10 ft) from nose to tail; a fully grown lion is almost as big.

The first large cats lived 45 million years ago. Many, including the lion, cheetah, and leopard, still inhabit parts of Africa. Snow leopards and lions dwell in the mountains and forests of Asia. Jaguars are the largest of the big cats in North and South America. They are equally at home swimming in lakes or climbing trees.

CUBS
Like all young big cats, tiger cubs have pale markings when they are born. After a few months, the pale stripes change to black and orange.

HUNTING PREY
Lions live mainly on savannas (grassy plains) and scrubland, and the females do most of the hunting. This picture shows two adult lionesses charging at a young gazelle, separating it from the rest of the herd.

LION PRIDE
Lions are the only big cats that live in groups, called prides, which may be up to 30 strong. The pride roams over an area of 100 sq km (40 sq miles) or more, depending on the abundance of prey in the area. The large male lions protect the pride's territory against other prides. The lions also defend the females against other males.

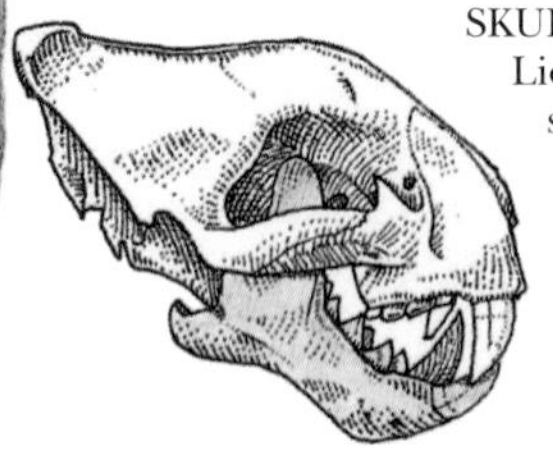

SKULL AND TEETH
Lions and other big cats have short, strong skulls with powerful jaws. Their spear-like canine teeth are used to grab hold of the victim's flesh. The large molar teeth cut flesh and gristle as the jaw opens and closes.

Lion has a thick, shaggy mane.

Large, strong canine teeth for tearing prey

Large feet and sharp claws

The dominant male is the strongest member of the pride. It can measure 2.5 m (8 ft) in length, and 1 m (3 ft) high at the shoulder.

CARNIVORES
Lions, tigers, and other big cats are true carnivores (flesh eaters). Lions usually eat large prey such as antelopes and zebras. One giraffe is often enough to feed a whole pride of lions.

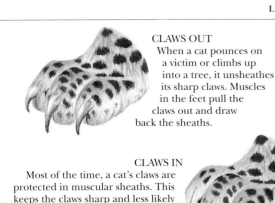

CLAWS OUT
When a cat pounces on a victim or climbs up into a tree, it unsheathes its sharp claws. Muscles in the feet pull the claws out and draw back the sheaths.

CLAWS IN
Most of the time, a cat's claws are protected in muscular sheaths. This keeps the claws sharp and less likely to break. The claws are extended when the cat cleans its feet.

LEOPARD
The leopard weighs about 60 kg (130 lb), and its body measures about 1.5 m (5 ft). Leopards are adaptable creatures. They can survive in hot tropical forests or on cold mountainsides. They may also live close to towns and villages.

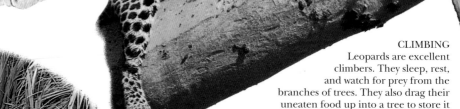

CLIMBING
Leopards are excellent climbers. They sleep, rest, and watch for prey from the branches of trees. They also drag their uneaten food up into a tree to store it and to keep it away from scavengers.

PANTHER
The black panther (right) is a leopard or a jaguar with dark colouring. In daylight, its spots show black in its dark grey-brown fur.

JAGUAR
The jaguar (below) stalks its prey in the same way as the tiger. Jaguars eat a variety of other creatures, including tapirs, fish, frogs, rodents, sloths, and small caimans (South American crocodiles).

ROARING
Only the big cats can roar, and they do so loudly, although the jaguar and snow leopard roar only rarely. The roar is a way of expressing anger, and warns other creatures to keep away.

TIGER
Unlike most cats, the tiger does not mind water. A tiger sometimes pulls its dead prey near the water's edge, because it needs to take frequent drinks during a meal. Tigers stalk their prey through dense undergrowth, then bound over the last 15 m (50 ft) or so, taking their victim by surprise. On average, a tiger consumes about 18 kg (40 lb) of meat a day.

CHEETAH
No animal can outrun a cheetah over a short distance. Cheetahs can speed along at about 100 km/h (60 mph) – as fast as a car. Unlike other cats, the cheetah's claws are always extended, because it has no sheaths to withdraw them into. This gives the cheetah extra grip as it starts its run. If a stalking cheetah is detected before it gets within about 180 m (600 ft) of its prey, it does not make the final dash.

Asia

Africa

☐ Lions

Asia

🐾 Tigers

Asia

Africa

⬛ Cheetahs

Asia

Africa

☐ Leopards

CONSERVATION
Leopards and other big cats have been overhunted for their fur and because they attack livestock and, very rarely, people. The trade in big cats and fur products is now banned by an international agreement. The maps show the main areas of the world where these big cats still live.

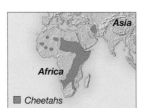

Cheetah

Find out more
ANIMALS
ANIMAL SENSES
CAMOUFLAGE, ANIMAL
CATS
CONSERVATION
and endangered species
MAMMALS
ZOOS

LITERATURE

LITERATURE INCLUDES PLAYS, poems, novels, and short stories. It is writing that carries strong and lasting value through offering the reader important insights into the nature of human emotions. For example, the English playwright William Shakespeare (1564-1616) often based his plays on old or well-known stories, and because Shakespeare was a very skilled writer and had a great understanding of human nature, his plays still excite audiences of all nationalities hundreds of years after they were written. Literature can be powerful, as it can express the writer's thoughts, ideals, and beliefs. Authors, or writers, have often used literature to protest injustice in the world, make a social criticism, and influence the opinions of peoples or governments. For instance, in *The Grapes of Wrath*, American novelist John Steinbeck (1902-68) drew public attention to the suffering of homeless farmers fleeing from Oklahoma to California during the Great Depression of the 1930s.

GULLIVER'S TRAVELS

English author Jonathan Swift (1667-1745) wrote *Gulliver's Travels* in 1726. Although he did not write the book for children, the first two parts have long been popular with young people.

When the people of Lilliput find Gulliver sleeping in their land, they tie him down on the ground so that he cannot move.

PLOT

The collection of events that occur in a work of literature is called the plot. *Gulliver's Travels* tells the story of Lemuel Gulliver, a ship's surgeon. In the first part, Gulliver is shipwrecked in an imaginary land called Lilliput, where the people are only a few centimetres tall. In the second tale, he meets the giants of Brobdingnag. In the third story, Gulliver visits various strange lands. Finally he is marooned among the Houyhnhnms – a race of horses that are wiser and more intelligent than their repulsive human servants, the Yahoos. Rejected by the Houyhnhnms, Gulliver returns to England, where he is no longer able to tolerate the company of other humans.

The arrogant and petty-minded Lilliputians represent the ruling class of 18th-century England.

Gulliver is visited by a Lilliputian noble.

CHARACTERS

An essential part of most literature is the writer's description of the characters – the people who take part in the plot. A writer portrays a character's personality by describing how they react to events in the story. For example, Swift shows that Gulliver is a kindhearted man by describing how he entertains the tiny Lilliputian people: "I would sometimes lie down, and let five or six of them dance on my Hand. And at last the Boys and Girls would venture to come and play at Hide and Seek in my Hair."

THEME

Writers use their plots and characters to explore key themes such as love, death, morality, and social or political issues. *Gulliver's Travels* seems just an adventure story, but the underlying theme is 18th-century England, where the Lilliputians and other nationalities represent different types of people with their good and bad qualities.

ORAL LITERATURE

Long before writing was invented, storytelling, or oral literature, was used to pass on myths and history. The heroine of a traditional Arabic story called *The Thousand and One Nights* is a storyteller named Scheherazade (right). Her cruel husband vows to kill her in the morning, but she charms him with a tale and so delays her death. Each night she tells another story and lives for one more day. After many stories her husband changes his mind and spares Scheherazade's life.

This copy of the Book of Kings *is written in Arabic script.*

EPICS AND SAGAS

Epics and sagas tell of legendary heroes and their deeds. An epic tells the story as a long poem, while a saga is written in prose. The national Persian epic, the *Book of Kings (Shah-nameh)* by Firdausi (c.935-1020), is 1,000 years old, and tells the story of Persian kings and their battles against monsters in mythical times. Other great epics include Homer's *Iliad* and *Odyssey*; Virgil's *Aeneid*; *Beowulf*, a 10th-century epic written in Old English; and John Milton's *Paradise Lost* and *Paradise Regained*.

BIOGRAPHY

A biography is a book that describes a person's life. In an autobiography the author writes of his or her own life. US writer Mark Twain (right) was portrayed in J. Kaplan's biography *Mr. Clemens and Mark Twain* (the title refers to Twain's real name, Samuel Langhorne Clemens).

POETRY

Poetry uses devices, such as rhythm and rhyme, to focus attention on the words. Rhythm is the use of sound patterns, such as repeated accents or beats, to make a line flow. One of the world's greatest poets was the American Walt Whitman (1810-92), whose poems express a great love of his country and its people. His collection of poems *Leaves of Grass* (1855) is considered one of his best works.

NOVELS

A novel is a long fictional (invented) story, written in prose. This form of writing only began in the early 17th century, and has had a dramatic rise in popularity because there are novels to suit all tastes. Some offer insights into everyday life, and some tell of fantastic adventures that keep you turning the pages. American author Louisa May Alcott wrote *Little Women* (1868-69), which tells the story of four sisters and their lives. This remains one of the best-loved children's books ever written. Many successful modern authors are now rewarded with high incomes from sales of their books, as well as from cinema films based on their novels.

Louisa May Alcott

DRAMA

Literature that is written to be performed by actors is called drama. Different countries have their own forms of drama. There is little scenery in Japanese Noh drama (below), which was first performed in the 14th century. The all-male actors use dance, mime, and masks for each performance, which can last for several hours. Noh drama is influenced by the religious beliefs of Buddhism and Shintoism.

Noh actors perform a programme of five plays, based on classical literature, romances, or poetry, accompanied by a chorus with an orchestra of drums and flute.

STORIES

Most stories describe a single incident or events that take place over a short period of time. There are children's stories about every subject ranging from adventures to ghosts. One of the best-known story writers was the Danish author Hans Christian Andersen (1805-75), who wrote tales such as *The Emperor's New Clothes* and *The Ugly Duckling*.

A Hans Christian Andersen story, The Princess and the Pea, *tells how a single pea beneath a heap of mattresses keeps a princess awake all night.*

Find out more

ALPHABETS
FILM
THEATRE
WRITERS AND POETS

LIZARDS

THE LARGEST GROUP of reptiles is the lizard family, with about 3,400 species. Lizards live in almost every habitat except the open sea and the far north. The huge Komodo dragon is the largest, and tiny geckos are the smallest – some are less than 2 cm (1 in) long. A typical lizard such as the iguana has a slim body, a long tail, legs that splay out sideways, and five-toed feet. There are many variations, however; skinks are often extremely long, with short legs. They seem to move effortlessly through loose soil with a wriggling motion. Snake-lizards are even more snake-like, with no front legs and small, paddle-shaped back legs. Several kinds of lizards, including the slow-worm, have lost their limbs during the course of evolution. Like other reptiles, most female lizards lay eggs, which they bury in the soil or hide under rocks until the young hatch.

Lizards can hear through their ear openings.

Green iguana

Long tail for balance

Typical scaly skin like other reptiles, such as snakes and crocodiles

Outstretched claws give extra balance.

CRESTED WATER DRAGON

This lizard is found in Asia and lives mainly in trees that grow close to water. Like most lizards, the water dragon is able to swim. Unlike most other lizards, however, which move on all four legs, the crested water dragon runs on two legs if it is threatened, which gives it more speed on land.

LIZARD TAILS

In the same way that a starfish regrows its arms, a lizard can regrow its tail. When a predator such as a bird or cat grabs a lizard by its tail, the lizard sheds the tail in order to escape. The vertebrae (backbones) along the tail have cracks in them, so the tail breaks off easily. The broken-off part of the tail often twitches for a few minutes, confusing the enemy while the lizard runs away. The tail grows back to its original length in about eight months.

Loose skin around neck looks like a huge collar.

The more the frilled lizard opens its mouth, the more the frill expands.

Tail waves around to frighten enemy.

Tree skink has lost the end of its tail.

Tail has regrown fully within a few months.

Tokay gecko

FRILLED LIZARD

The Australian frilled lizard has a flap of loose skin around its neck which folds flat along the body. The lizard raises the frill to make itself look bigger in order to scare away a predator. It also waves its tail and head around to alarm its enemy, then scuttles away.

TOKAY GECKO

The pads on the feet of the tokay gecko are covered with about one million microscopic hair-like structures which help the gecko grip on to surfaces. The rubber soles of plimsolls and walking boots look like the soles of the gecko's feet.

318

TEGU LIZARD
The young tegu lizard shown left is found in tropical areas of South America. It feeds mostly on young birds and mammals, and also eats other lizards. Like most lizards, the tegu has a tough, scaly skin, a forked tongue, five claws on its feet, and movable eyelids.

Five claws on feet

Forked tongue

Male anole lizard inflates its red throat sac.

ANOLE LIZARD
Anole lizards belong to the iguana family of lizards. There are many different kinds, found in tropical areas of Central and South America. Anole lizards are territorial (they guard their territory). The males inflate their red-coloured throat sacs, which they display to each other as a sign of aggression. Anole lizards are sometimes called American chameleons.

KOMODO DRAGON
The Komodo dragon is the largest lizard – up to 3 m (10 ft) long. It scavenges on dead animals and also catches deer, pigs, and wild boars. Komodo dragons are only found on a few of the Lesser Sunda Islands, Indonesia.

Komodo dragon lizards feasting on the carcass (dead body) of a deer

GILA MONSTER
Only three lizards have a poisonous bite – the Gila monster, the Mexican beaded lizard, and the Komodo dragon. The Gila monster, shown here, is found in dry, scrubby areas. It hides in a burrow by day and emerges at night to eat small animals such as mice, and the eggs of birds and other reptiles.

Gila monster feeding on newborn mice

THORNY DEVIL
The extraordinary looking thorny devil is also called the moloch. Spines protect its body from nose to tail. Thorny lizards live in dry parts of Australia, where they forage for ants. When the young molochs hatch from their eggs, they look like tiny, spiny versions of their parents.

GREEN GECKO
Many lizards are coloured to blend in with their surroundings. Tree- climbing lizards such as this green gecko are often bright green to match the leaves; desert-dwelling lizards are sand-coloured or brown. Many kinds of chameleons can change their colour according to their surroundings.

IGUANA
Like all lizards, iguanas depend on heat from the environment to keep their bodies warm and active. They spend much of the day basking in the sun, absorbing its warmth to prepare for activity. At night they become slow and sluggish as their body temperature falls. The Galapagos marine iguanas shown here dive to more than 11 m (35 ft) deep into the sea in search of seaweed.

After each dive, Galapagos marine iguanas sunbathe on the rocks to warm up again.

Slowworms grow to about 50 cm (20 in) in length.

SLOWWORM
The slowworm is not really a worm, but a lizard. It is not slow either; when disturbed, slowworms can wriggle away rapidly to safety. Slowworms are found in fields and scrubland in Europe, northern Africa, and southwest Asia. They feed on slugs, spiders, and insects. Unlike most lizards, slowworms give birth to fully formed young.

Find out more
CAMOUFLAGE, ANIMAL
DESERT WILDLIFE
REPTILES
SNAKES

LOW COUNTRIES

SMALL AND DENSELY populated, the Low Countries are highly developed industrial nations with thriving economies. Nearly one-third of the Netherlands lies below sea level. Over the last four centuries, Dutch engineers have reclaimed land by pushing back the North Sea with a network of barriers, or dykes. In northern Belgium, the land is also flat and low-lying, although to the south it rises towards the forested uplands of the Ardennes. Belgium only became independent in the 19th century. It is divided by language; Dutch (Flemish) is spoken in the north, while French is spoken in the south. Farming is important throughout the region. The fertile land and cool, rainy climate is ideally suited to dairy and arable farming. Major industries produce iron and steel, natural gas, clothing, textiles and electrical goods. The tiny country of Luxembourg has the highest living standards in Europe, and is known as a major banking centre.

The Low Countries lie in northwest Europe, with Germany to the east and France to the south. To the west, lies the North Sea.

BULB FIELDS
The Dutch have been famous for their flower bulbs since the 16th century, when tulips first arrived in Europe from the Middle East. In spring, fields of spring flowers are a spectacular sight. Fresh cut flowers are flown all over the world.

AMSTERDAM

A city of 90 islands, connected by 1,000 bridges, Amsterdam is linked by canal to the North Sea. The city became important in the Middle Ages, and many of the churches, towers, and gabled merchants' houses of the old city still stand. In the 17th century, Amsterdam was the financial capital of the world. Since 1945, new suburbs have been built on polders (reclaimed land), tripling the size of the city.

LUXEMBOURG
The capital of Luxembourg stands on a sandstone plateau, cut into deep ravines by the Alzette river. The Old Town centres on the Grand Ducal Palace (1572), the cathedral and the Town Hall. Luxembourg is a thriving industrial and banking centre.

LAND RECLAMATION
Over the centuries, low-lying land has been reclaimed from the sea. Engineers built dykes to enclose areas of shallow water, which were then drained. From the 14th century, windmills were used to drain water and pump it into canals. On the windswept lowlands, windpower was very effective, although it has now been replaced by steam and electric pumps. However, storms and high tides are still a major threat to the people of the Netherlands.

Porters carry trays of cheese at the amous market in Alkmaar.

CHEESE

Much of the cheese produced in the Netherlands is made from the milk of cows, which graze on areas of reclaimed land. The country's most famous cheeses are Gouda and Edam, with its rind of red wax.

Windmills tap the energy of the wind by means of sails mounted on a rotating shaft.

Find out more
EUROPE
EUROPEAN UNION
FLOWERS AND HERBS
PORTS AND WATERWAYS
WORLD WAR I

Volcano · Mountain · Ancient monument · Capital city · Large city/town · Small city/town

BELGIUM
Area: 33,100 sq km (17,780 sq miles)
Population: 10,414,000
Capital: Brussels
Languages: Flemish, French, German, Dutch
Religions: Roman Catholic, Muslim
Currency: Euro

LUXEMBOURG
Area: 2,586 sq km (998 sq miles)
Population: 492,000
Capital: Luxembourg
Languages: Letzeburgish, German, French
Religions: Roman Catholic, Protestant, Greek Orthodox, Jewish
Currency: Euro

NETHERLANDS
Area: 37,330 sq km (14,410 sq miles)
Population: 16,716,000
Capital: Amsterdam, The Hague ('s-Gravenhage)
Languages: Dutch, Frisian
Religions: Roman Catholic, Protestant, Muslim
Currency: Euro

EU HEADQUARTERS
In 1957, all three countries were founding members of the European Economic Community (EEC). Brussels is now the administrative headquarters of the European Union (EU), while Luxembourg is the headquarters of the European Investment Bank and the Court of Justice.

BELGIAN BEER
Belgium is famous for its beer, produced in many local breweries, and exported worldwide. Another important export is fine Belgian chocolate; Belgium is the world's third-largest exporter.

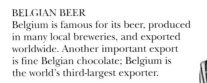

SCALE BAR
0 · 50 · 100 km
0 · 50 · 100 miles

BRUSSELS
Brussels, the capital of Belgium, is an international economic and financial centre. The city expanded rapidly in the 19th century, and became the centre of Belgium's growing steel, chemical, and textile industries. The Grand Place (above) is the heart of the Old Town. Brussels is now a major financial centre, with its own Stock Exchange.

WAR CEMETERY
The Flanders region of southwest Belgium is imprinted with memories of World War I. One of the costliest battles of the four-year war was Passchendaele in 1917, where an estimated 800,000 Allied and German troops were killed. Vast war cemeteries, such as Tyne Cot near Ieper (left), attract many visitors.

LUNGS AND BREATHING

WE NEED OXYGEN TO LIVE, and we get oxygen by breathing air. When we breathe in, air is sucked through the nose or mouth, down the windpipe, and into the lungs, two powerful organs in the chest. The lungs absorb as much oxygen from the air as possible. The oxygen travels in the blood from the lungs to every part of the body. Our bodies use oxygen to release energy from sugars obtained from the food we eat. This also releases harmful carbon dioxide, which is breathed out of the body by the lungs. The whole process is called respiration. The lungs, together with the airways, throat, and nasal passages, form the respiratory system. Each lung is surrounded by two thin coverings or membranes called pleurae. The lungs themselves contain air tubes, blood vessels, and millions of tiny air sacs called alveoli. If you spread these air sacs out flat, they would cover the area of a tennis court.

HOW WE MAKE SOUNDS
We use the air flowing in and out of our lungs to make sounds. We speak, shout, laugh, and cry by making air flow over two small leathery flaps called the vocal cords. These are in the larynx (voice box), in the lower part of the throat. Muscles in the throat stretch the flaps tighter to change from low notes to high notes.

BREATHING

Lungs empty of air as you breathe out.

Diaphragm relaxes and rises.

Diaphragm contracts and flattens.

Lungs fill with air as you breathe in.

BREATHING OUT
When you breathe out, the diaphragm and chest muscles relax. The lungs are spongy and elastic, so they spring back to their smaller size after they have been stretched. This blows air back out of the lungs.

BREATHING IN
When you breathe in, the diaphragm contracts (becomes flatter) and pulls down the base of the lungs. Muscles between the ribs contract to swing the ribs up and out. These actions stretch and enlarge the lungs, so that air is sucked in.

Air flows in through the nose and mouth, down the throat, along the trachea (windpipe), and into the lungs.

Pharynx (throat)

Larynx (voice box) at top of trachea

Trachea (windpipe)

Trachea divides into two main bronchi.

Lung

The rib cage is flexible, so the lungs can expand and shrink when we breathe.

Bronchiole

Bronchi continue to branch and divide.

Diaphragm is a dome-shaped sheet of muscle

Alveolus

Capillary blood vessels

Air space inside alveolus

The alveoli are grouped together like bunches of grapes. Tiny tubes called bronchioles bring fresh oxygen-containing air to the alveoli.

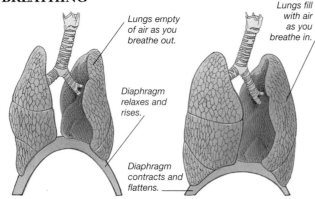

LUNGFISH
Most animals that live on land have lungs. Many water animals, however, including most fish, breathe using feathery flaps called gills. Oxygen in the water passes through the thin gill coverings to the blood inside the fish's body. The lungfish shown here is an unusual animal because it has lungs and gills, so it can breathe in both ways and can survive out of water for a long time.

ALVEOLUS
Each alveolus is surrounded by a network of very fine blood vessels called capillaries. Oxygen passes from the air space inside the alveolus, through the lining, and into the blood. Carbon dioxide passes in the opposite way.

Find out more
BRAIN AND NERVES
HEART AND BLOOD
HUMAN BODY
MUSCLES AND MOVEMENT
OXYGEN
SKELETONS

MACHINES

INCLINED PLANE

Simple machines reduce the effort needed to move or lift an object, but the object has to travel a greater distance. The simplest machine is the ramp, or inclined plane. You need less force to push an object with a downwards load up an inclined plane than you need to lift it straight up. This is because the object moves a greater distance along the plane. The gentler the slope, the further you have to push, but the easier it is.

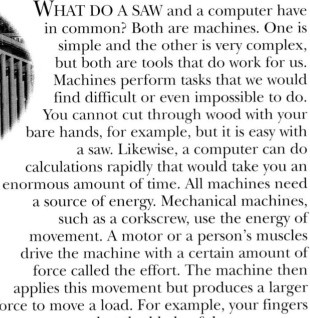

WHAT DO A SAW and a computer have in common? Both are machines. One is simple and the other is very complex, but both are tools that do work for us. Machines perform tasks that we would find difficult or even impossible to do. You cannot cut through wood with your bare hands, for example, but it is easy with a saw. Likewise, a computer can do calculations rapidly that would take you an enormous amount of time. All machines need a source of energy. Mechanical machines, such as a corkscrew, use the energy of movement. A motor or a person's muscles drive the machine with a certain amount of force called the effort. The machine then applies this movement but produces a larger force to move a load. For example, your fingers operate a can opener, but the blade of the can opener moves with much more force than that produced by your fingers. Many hand-powered machines help us perform tasks for which we do not have enough strength. They use devices known as simple machines. These include levers, gears, pulleys, and screws.

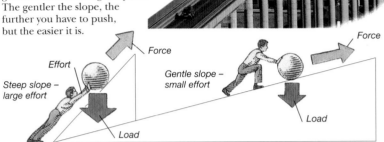

Force

Effort

Steep slope – large effort

Load

Gentle slope – small effort

Force

Load

SCREW

A screw moves forward a shorter distance than it turns. It therefore moves forward with a much greater force than the effort needed to turn it. The screw bites into the wood with great force and is held strongly.

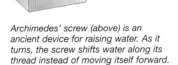

Archimedes' screw (above) is an ancient device for raising water. As it turns, the screw shifts water along its thread instead of moving itself forward.

The screw makes use of the principle of the inclined plane.

The thread of the screw is like a slope wrapped around a cylinder.

PLOUGH

The plough has a cutting blade that bites into the soil and a V-shaped blade that turns the soil over.

PERPETUAL MOTION

Many inventors have tried to build a machine that, once started, would never stop. It would run on its own without any source of energy. However, such a perpetual motion machine is impossible. This is because all machines lose some energy as they work. Without a constant source of energy, a machine always slows down and stops.

In this machine, the motion of the balls was supposed to keep the wheel turning.

WEDGE

The wedge is a form of inclined plane. Instead of moving a load along a slope, the wedge is a slope that pushes a load aside or upward as it moves forward. The wedge pushes with greater force than the effort needed to move the wedge. Sharp blades are thin wedges that make cutting an easy task.

Effort

Axe is a kind of wedge

Force

Force

PULLEYS

Lifting a heavy load is easy with a pulley system. It contains a set of wheels fixed to a support. A rope goes around grooves in the wheels. Pulling the rope raises the lower wheel and the load. A pulley system allows you to lift a heavy load with little effort, but you must pull the rope a large distance to raise the load by a small amount.

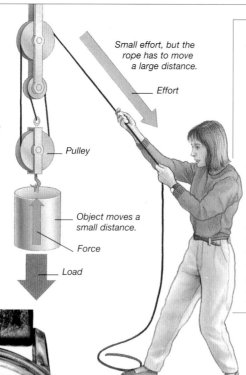

Small effort, but the rope has to move a large distance.

Effort

Pulley

Object moves a small distance.

Force

Load

AUTOMATIC MACHINES

Many machines do not need to be operated by people. These are automatic machines. They contain mechanisms or computers to control themselves. These machines may simply perform a set task whenever it is required; automatic doors, for example, open as people arrive. Other machines are able to check their own work and change the way they operate to follow instructions. One example is an aircraft autopilot, which guides the plane through the skies.

Traffic lights are machines that control traffic automatically.

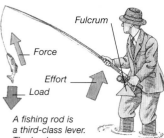

Fulcrum

A pair of scissors consists of two levers hinged together.

Force

Load

GEARS

Gears are intermeshing toothed wheels. They can increase force or speed depending on the relative size of the wheels and their number of teeth. A gearwheel driven by a smaller wheel turns less quickly than the smaller wheel but with greater force. A wheel driven by a larger wheel turns faster but with less force.

Mechanical clocks and watches contain gears that turn the hands at different speeds.

LEVER

A long stick propped up on a small object (a fulcrum) helps you move a heavy load. The stick is a simple machine called a lever. Pushing down on the end furthest from the fulcrum raises the other end with greater force, helping you move the load. Other kinds of levers can increase either the force applied to, or the distance moved by, a load.

Effort

Fulcrum

There are three types of lever. A crowbar is called a first-class lever. The fulcrum is between the load and the effort, which is the force that you apply.

Force

Fulcrum

Load

Effort

A wheelbarrow is a second-class lever. The load lies between the fulcrum and the effort.

Fulcrum

Force

Effort

Load

A fishing rod is a third-class lever. The load moves a greater distance than the effort, but with less force. The effort pushes between the load and the fulcrum.

WHEEL AND AXLE

Several machines use the principle of the wheel and axle. One example is the winch, in which a handle (the wheel) turns a shaft (the axle) that raises a load. The handle moves a greater distance than the load rises. The winch therefore lifts the load with a greater force than the effort needed to turn the handle.

Effort

Force

Load

STEERING WHEEL
The steering wheel on a car is an example of the wheel and axle. The shaft turns with greater force than the effort needed to turn the steering wheel.

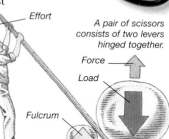

Find out more

COMPUTER
ENGINES
INDUSTRIAL REVOLUTION
ROBOTS
TECHNOLOGY

MAGNA CARTA

IN 1215, KING JOHN OF ENGLAND signed a document known as Magna Carta, or Great Charter. The document, which was complicated, set out rules and conditions for ruling the country, and was a major event in the history of English government. Magna Carta resulted from disagreements between King John and his barons. The barons wanted to be more involved in the government of England, while John wanted to keep power for himself, and angered them by imposing heavy taxes. Some barons rebelled, and drew up a list of demands that John was forced to accept, and which became Magna Carta. The charter mainly concerned the rights of barons, but it did promise justice to all. It is seen as a step towards making the monarchy answerable to the law.

THE CHARTER
The original charter was on parchment and carried King John's seal. There were 63 clauses, setting out the duties of the king and subjects. The king's right to tax the barons was limited, and the rights of the Church were guaranteed. Four copies of Magna Carta survive today.

King John agreeing to Magna Carta.

KING JOHN
The youngest son of Henry II, King John (reigned 1199-1216) was weakened by wars with France and quarrels with the pope and the English Church.

SEALING THE CHARTER

King John had agreed to grant the barons all their demands. In the last month of negotiations, Archbishop Langton persuaded the barons to include some clauses that benefited the king's subjects. On 15 June 1215, John set his Great Seal on a draft version of the charter, called the Articles of the Barons. A final version was ready by 19 June. Twenty-five barons were appointed to see that it was carried out. Magna Carta was reissued several times. In the 1640s, during the English Civil War, it was used to criticise King Charles I.

RUNNYMEDE

It was at Runnymede, a meadow beside the River Thames, that King John met the barons and agreed to sign Magna Carta. The site, chosen because it was midway between the king's residence, Windsor Castle, and the barons' assembly point in the town of Staines, has been preserved as an open space ever since. The memorial commemorating the charter was presented in 1957 by the American Bar Association.

STEPHEN LANGTON
Churchman Stephen Langton (1165-1228) was a close friend of Pope Innocent III. The pope made Langton a cardinal in 1206 and, two years later, helped him to be elected as Archbishop of Canterbury, an appointment which King John opposed. Langton supported the barons against the king and helped them to persuade the king to agree to the charter. Langton wrote a large part of the text of Magna Carta.

Find out more

ENGLISH CIVIL WAR
HUMAN RIGHTS
UNITED KINGDOM, HISTORY OF

MAGNETISM

ORIGIN OF MAGNETISM
Iron contains millions of tiny magnets called magnetic domains. Normally, all the domains point in different directions so their magnetism cancels out. In a magnet, the domains point the same way so that their magnetism combines.

MAGNETIC FIELD
The area around a magnet in which its magnetic force works is called its magnetic field. For instance, a paper clip is pulled towards the magnet (right) when it is placed within the magnetic field of the magnet.

All magnets attract iron and steel objects but not plastic or wooden ones.

THE FORCE of magnetism is invisible, yet you can see its power when a magnet drags a piece of metal towards it. A material that attracts certain metals such as iron is called a magnet. Materials that are attracted by a magnet are called magnetic. Every magnet has two poles – places at which magnetic objects cluster. The Earth itself is a huge magnet; its magnetic poles are close to the geographical North and South Poles. One pole of a magnet is attracted to the Earth's northern magnetic pole and is called the magnet's north pole; the other is attracted to the south and is called the magnet's south pole. Materials that retain their magnetism all the time are called permanent magnets. An electric current flowing in a coil of wire produces a magnet called an electromagnet that can be switched on and off. Electromagnets are used in electric motors, loudspeakers, and many other devices.

LODESTONE
Magnetite is an iron ore that often possesses magnetism. It was once commonly called lodestone, which means "guiding stone", because early navigators used it as a compass.

MAGNETIC POLES

The north pole of one magnet and the south pole of another magnet attract each other.

A magnetic pole, such as a south pole, repels (pushes away) another pole of the same kind.

ELECTROMAGNETS
An electromagnet is a coil of wire. An electric current within the coil creates a magnetic field. The field can be made stronger by winding the wire around a piece of iron. Turning off the current switches off the magnetic field. Some cranes use an electromagnet instead of a hook.

The geographical North and South Poles lie on the Earth's axis, which is the line around which the Earth spins.

The pattern of lines shows the Earth's magnetic field. The field is strongest where the lines are closest together.

The magnetic north and south poles lie a small distance away from geographical North and South.

GEOMAGNETISM
The Earth produces a magnetic field which makes it seem as though it has a huge "bar" magnet inside it. Electric currents flowing within the Earth's liquid iron core cause the Earth's magnetism, which is called geomagnetism.

COMPASS
The needle inside a magnetic compass is a thin, light magnet, balanced so that it swings freely. The needle's north pole points towards the Earth's magnetic north pole, which is very close to the geographical North. People use magnetic compasses to navigate at sea and on land.

> *Find out more*
> EARTH
> ELECTRICITY
> NAVIGATION
> SCIENCE

326

MAMMALS

THE ANIMAL GROUP CALLED MAMMALS includes the heaviest, tallest, and fastest animals on land – the elephant, the giraffe, and the cheetah. Mice, whales, rhinoceroses, bats, and humans are also mammals. Like birds, mammals are warm-blooded (endothermic), but three features set them apart from all other creatures. All mammals are covered in fur or hair, all feed their young on milk, and all have a unique type of jaw. The jawbone helps us to identify the fossilized bones of prehistoric mammals that lived on Earth millions of years ago. Mammals are also members of the group known as vertebrates because they all have vertebrae (backbones). Today there are more than 5,000 kinds of mammals, including carnivores (flesh eaters) such as tigers; herbivores (plant eaters) such as rabbits; and omnivores (flesh and plant eaters) such as bears. Cattle, sheep, goats, and most other farm animals are mammals, and many pets are mammals too, including cats, dogs, and guinea pigs. Mammals live nearly everywhere. They are found on land, in the sea, and in the sky, from the coldest Arctic to the most searing heat of the desert.

A mammal's body is covered in fur.

MARSUPIAL YOUNG
Marsupials are very tiny when they are born. At birth, a kangaroo is less than 2.5 cm (1 in) long. It crawls through its mother's fur into a pocket-like pouch on the abdomen, where it attaches itself to her teat and suckles milk.

A kangaroo's large tail is so strong that it can act as a prop for the kangaroo to lean on.

Young male joey

PLACENTAL MAMMALS
Most mammals, including monkeys, cats, and dogs, are called placental mammals because the young develop inside the mother's womb, or uterus, and are fed by means of the placenta. The placenta is a specialized organ embedded in the wall of the womb. It carries nutrients and other essential materials from the mother's blood to the baby's blood. These nutrients help the young to grow and develop. After the young are born, the placenta comes out of the uterus as afterbirth.

POUCHED MAMMALS
Kangaroos, opossums, wallabies, koalas, wombats, and bandicoots are all known as pouched mammals or marsupials. These animals carry their young in their pouches until the young are able to fend for themselves. Once it has left the pouch, the joey (young kangaroo) returns to the pouch to suck milk. Marsupials are found in Australia and New Guinea, South America, and North America. A few marsupials, such as the shrew opossum of South America, do not have pouches.

MONOTREME MAMMALS
Five kinds of mammals lay eggs. They are called monotreme mammals, and include the platypus and the four types of echidna (spiny ant-eater). All are found in Australasia. After about 10 days, the young hatch out of the eggs, then feed on their mother's milk.

PRIMATES
Monkeys, apes, and humans belong to a group called primates. Primates are able to grasp with their hands. Most primates have thumbs and big toes, with flat fingernails rather than claws. Members of the primate group range in size from the mouse lemur, which weighs only 60 g (2 oz), to the gorilla, which weighs up to 275 kg (610 lb).

SPINY ANTEATER
The short-beaked spiny ant-eater, or echidna, lays a single egg in a temporary pouch on its abdomen. The young echidna hatches, then sucks milk from mammary glands on its mother's abdomen.

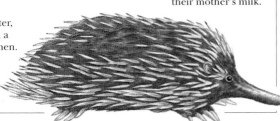

MAMMAL GROUPS

There are about 27 main groups of mammals, some of which are shown below. Rodents make up half of all mammals; bats account for a quarter. There are only three kinds of elephant, and the aardvark is in a group of its own.

Humans

Elephants

Cats, dogs, and other carnivores

Camels, horses, and other hoofed mammals

Aardvarks

Anteaters, armadillos, and other toothless mammals

Bats and flying foxes

Monkeys, apes, and other primates

Sea cows and dugongs

Seals, sea lions, and walruses

Whales, dolphins, and porpoises

Hares, rabbits, and pikas

Hedgehogs, moles, and other insectivores

Squirrels, rats, mice, and other rodents

Tree shrews

Most puppies feed on their mother's milk for two or three months. A mother shrew suckles her young for four weeks; a mother whale feeds her youngster for six months or more.

MAMMAL MILK

Mammals are the only creatures that feed their young with milk. When the female is about to give birth, she starts to produce milk in mammary glands on the chest or abdomen. When the young are born, they suck the milk from the mother's teats. Mother's milk is an ideal food for the young – warm and nourishing, and full of special substances which protect the young from disease. As the babies grow larger and stronger, they take less milk and begin to eat solid foods. This process is called weaning.

Rhinoceros

The gestation usually lasts for 15 months; one young is born.

GESTATION

The time between mating and birth, when the young develop in the mother's womb, is called the gestation or pregnancy period. In general, large mammals have longer pregnancies and fewer young than small mammals.

Rabbit

Gestation usually lasts for 30 days; as many as eight young are born in a litter.

Dirty fur harbours pests and also lets heat escape, so many mammals spend time cleaning or grooming their fur.

HAIR AND FUR

Fur or hair protects the mammal's skin from injury and the sun's rays. It also keeps heat in and moisture out. The colours and patterns of the fur provide camouflage. Water-dwelling mammals such as beavers have special oily, waterproof fur. The porcupine's spines are modified hairs and the rhinoceros's horn is made from a hair-like fibrous substance.

ARMADILLO

Some mammals, such as armadillos and pangolins, have reptile-like scales instead of fur. The scales, or scutes, of an armadillo are made of a type of horn and bone that grows from the skin. Hairs grow between the scutes and also cover the animal's soft-skinned underbelly.

BODY TEMPERATURE

Mammals and birds are called warm-blooded animals because they can maintain a high body temperature even in cold conditions. Mammals do, however, need plenty of food to provide the energy for warmth. The heat to warm a mammal is produced by chemical reactions in the body, particularly in the muscles.

Huskies are able to stay warm in deep snow because of their thick fur.

Find out more
ANIMALS
ANIMAL SENSES
ELEPHANTS
FARM ANIMALS
FLIGHT, ANIMAL
HIBERNATION
PREHISTORIC LIFE

NELSON MANDELA

1918 Born in Mvezo, Transkei.

1942 Gained law degree; practises in Johannesburg.

1952 Becomes deputy national president of the ANC.

1962 Imprisoned as a leader of the ANC.

1964 Sentenced to life imprisonment and sent to Robben Island (until 1985).

1990 Released from prison.

1993 Wins Nobel Peace Prize.

1994 Elected first black president of South Africa.

1999 Steps down as president.

IN FEBRUARY 1990 the 72-year-old Nelson Mandela walked into freedom after spending more than 27 years in prison. He had spent his life opposing the white-led South African government, which practised the policy of apartheid, or separate development of the races. Within four years Mandela led his party, the African National Congress (ANC), to victory in the general election and became the first-ever black president of a multiracial, democratic South Africa. By the time he retired in 1999 he was one of the most famous and deeply-loved political leaders in the world.

AFRICAN NATIONAL CONGRESS

In 1912, the African National Congress was formed to protect the interests of the black population of South Africa. It tried to achieve a multiracial, democratic country through peaceful means, but the South African government thought it was revolutionary, and banned it in 1961. From 1952, Mandela was a senior member of the organization. He became its leader in 1991.

ROBBEN ISLAND
Nelson Mandela spent 18 of his 27 years in prison on Robben Island, a high-security prison off the coast of Cape Town. He broke rocks in the quarry, and studied with other ANC prisoners. Now the prison is closed, and people visit Mandela's cell.

TRUTH AND RECONCILIATION
In order to heal the wounds left by apartheid, Mandela set up the Truth and Reconciliation Commission. Nobel Peace Prize winner, Archbishop Desmond Tutu, ran the Commission. It examined the events of the apartheid era, and tried to reconcile (bring together) former enemies.

FREE NELSON MANDELA
People campaigned worldwide to free Mandela from prison. They boycotted (refused to buy) South African goods, such as fruit and wine, and demonstrated against the South African government. In 1988, a huge rock concert was held at London's Wembley Stadium to mark Mandela's 70th birthday.

WINNIE MANDELA
In 1961, Mandela married Winnie Mdikizela (b. 1934). She campaigned for his release, but her political activities were controversial. They divorced in 1996.

PRESIDENT

The first multiracial elections in South Africa were held in 1994. Mandela led the ANC to a huge victory, and became president. He worked to obtain peace, and unite all the peoples of his troubled country. When famous people – including the Prince of Wales and the Spice Girls – came to see him, he always wore one of his distinctive shirts.

Find out more
AFRICA, HISTORY OF
HUMAN RIGHTS
SOUTH AFRICA

MAO ZEDONG

1893 Born in Shaoshan, Hunan province.

1921 Founding member of Chinese Communist Party.

1928 Establishes Chinese Soviet (Communist) Republic in Jianxi province.

1934-35 Leads The Long March.

1945-49 Leads Communists in fight to overthrow Nationalist government.

1958 Great Leap Forward

1966-69 Cultural Revolution

1976 Dies.

ONE MAN TRANSFORMED CHINA from a backward peasant society into one of the most powerful nations in the world. That man was Mao Zedong. Mao was born to a peasant family, and as a young man he travelled widely, observing the conditions of the poor. He became interested in Communism as a way to improve people's lives and, in 1921, helped set up the Chinese Communist Party. There followed a long period of struggle between the Communists, led by Mao, and the Nationalist Party (who believed in strong national government), led by Chiang Kai-shek. The struggle ended in a civil war. In October 1949, the Communist Party was victorious and took power in China. Mao proclaimed China a People's Republic. Under his leadership, the Communists put everything under state control. Mao's face became a familiar sight. Since his death in 1976, many people have criticized Mao for causing the deaths of millions during his rule.

Route of the March

The Long March

LONG MARCH

In October 1934, Mao led his Communist supporters from their stronghold, Juichin, in Jianxi province to Yenan in Shensi province in northwest China. Jianxi was under attack from Chiang Kai-shek. More than 100,000 people marched for more than a year, covering 9,700 km (6,000 miles). Only 8,000 marchers survived the ordeal.

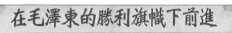

在毛澤東的勝利旗幟下前進

CULTURAL REVOLUTION

After the failure of the Great Leap Forward, Mao lost influence inside the Communist Party. In 1966, he launched the Cultural Revolution, a campaign to regain power and get rid of foreign influences. For three years, China was in turmoil as every aspect of society was criticized by the Red Guards, followers of Mao. They armed themselves with the *Little Red Book*, which contained Mao's thoughts.

PERSONALITY CULT

Mao Zedong encouraged a cult of his personality to unite the country. His round face with the familiar mole on the chin adorned every public building in China. He was praised as the father and leader of his nation, and huge rallies were held at which he addressed his followers.

GREAT LEAP FORWARD

In 1958 Mao launched a plan to improve the Chinese economy. The Great Leap Forward, as it was called, set up huge agricultural communes and encouraged the growth of small, labour-intensive industries. However, the policy failed and led to millions of deaths through famine.

Find out more

CHINA
COMMUNISM

MARSH AND SWAMP WILDLIFE

THE SALT AND FRESHWATER habitats of swamps and marshland are called wetlands. Marsh and swamp wildlife includes crocodiles, frogs, birds, fish, and countless plants. At different times of the year the water level of marshes and swamps rises and falls. In summer the land dries up, and in winter it floods. Wetlands are usually unsuitable for large mammals – except the African swamps where hippopotamuses live. Smaller mammals such as muskrats live in North American swamps, and the European marshes are home to many birds. The main plant life consists of reeds, rushes, saw grass, and cattail. Large trees are found only in the tropical mangroves, where the trees form dense thickets. Willows and other waterside trees grow in the higher, drier ground around the marsh.

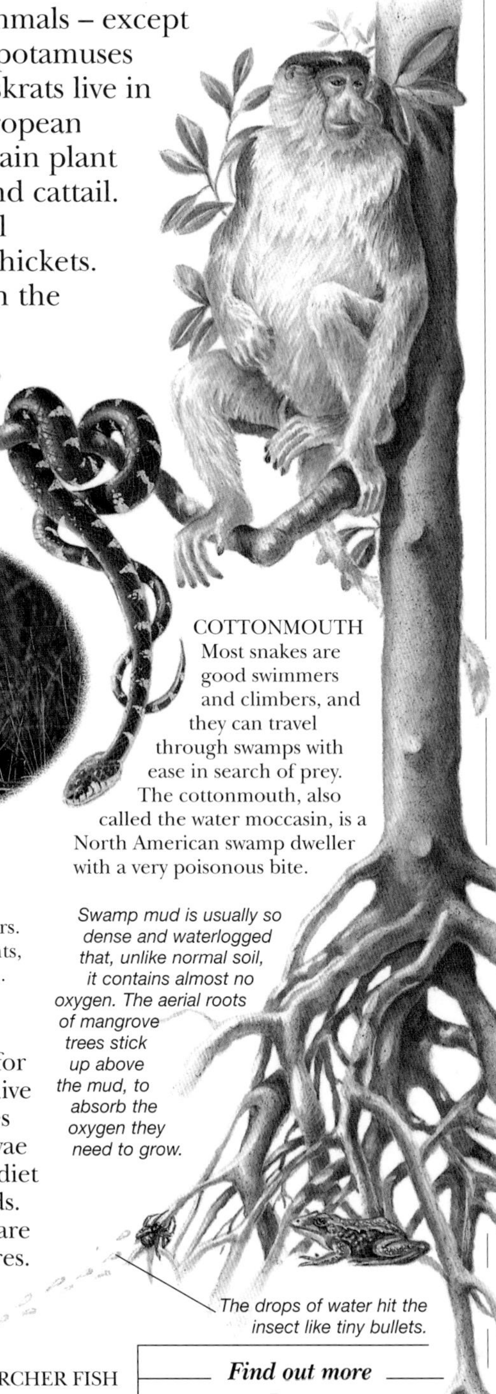

PROBOSCIS MONKEY
This large-nosed monkey lives among the mangrove trees of river and coastal swamps. The proboscis monkey is a good swimmer. Proboscis monkeys eat leaves, flowers, and fruit.

CONSERVATION
Farming and industry threaten many swamplands, but some animals, such as the marsh harriers shown here, are protected. They live in the Coto Doñana National Park in Spain – one of Europe's most important wetlands.

PELICAN
Most of these fish-eating birds build their nests in remote marshland areas. Some species breed on the ground, some in trees. Others, such as spot-billed and Dalmatian pelicans, are very rare, because of destruction of their nesting sites.

Front fins help the mudskipper walk on mud and grip roots.

COTTONMOUTH
Most snakes are good swimmers and climbers, and they can travel through swamps with ease in search of prey. The cottonmouth, also called the water moccasin, is a North American swamp dweller with a very poisonous bite.

SWAMP RABBIT
This large rabbit from North America can swim well and dives to escape from predators. Swamp rabbits eat water plants, grasses, and other vegetation.

Swamp mud is usually so dense and waterlogged that, unlike normal soil, it contains almost no oxygen. The aerial roots of mangrove trees stick up above the mud, to absorb the oxygen they need to grow.

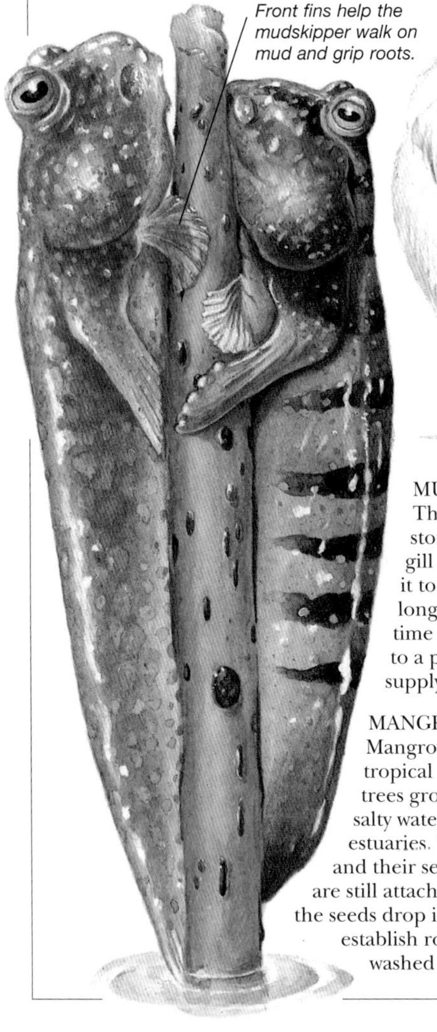

MUDSKIPPER
This unusual fish has a store of water in its large gill chambers which allows it to live out of water for long periods. From time to time it skitters over the mud to a pool to take in a new supply of water.

MARSHLAND
Marshes are nursery areas for many insects whose larvae live in water, such as dragonflies and mosquitoes. Insect larvae and worms form the main diet of many fish and water birds. Frogs, toads, and tadpoles are also eaten by larger creatures.

MANGROVE SWAMPS
Mangroves are trees that grow in muddy tropical swamps. Some kinds of mangrove trees grow in fresh water; others tolerate salty water and grow on the coast or in river estuaries. Their roots and trunks trap mud, and their seeds begin to grow while they are still attached to the parent tree. When the seeds drop into the mud, they quickly establish roots so they are not washed away.

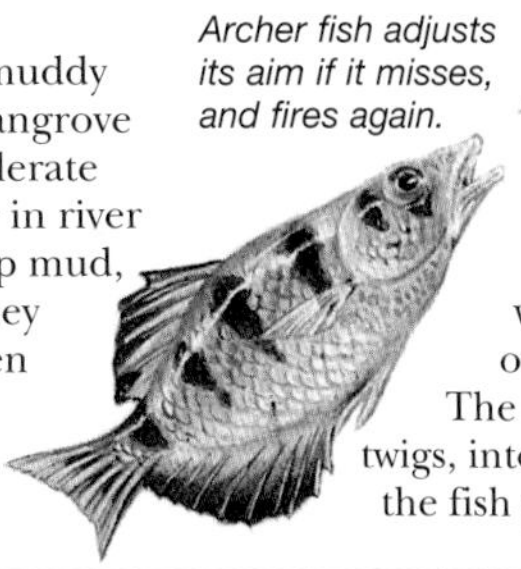

Archer fish adjusts its aim if it misses, and fires again.

ARCHER FISH
The archer fish spits drops of water at insects on over-hanging twigs. The insects fall off the twigs, into the water, where the fish gulps them down.

The drops of water hit the insect like tiny bullets.

Find out more
BIRDS
FISH
FROGS AND OTHER AMPHIBIANS
MONKEYS AND APES
SEASHORE WILDLIFE
SNAKES

MATHEMATICS

PROBABILITY THEORY
Probability theory is the analysis of chance. For instance, if you repeatedly roll two dice, you can use probability theory to work out how often you can expect a certain number to come up.

SENDING A SPACECRAFT to a distant planet is like trying to throw a stone at an invisible moving target. Space scientists do not use trial and error; instead they use the science of mathematics to direct the spacecraft precisely to its target. Mathematics is the study of number, shape, and quantity. There are several different branches of mathematics, and they are valuable both in science and in everyday life. For instance, arithmetic consists of addition, subtraction, multiplication, and division of numbers; it helps you work out the change when you buy something. Geometry is the study of shape and angle; it is useful in carpentry, architecture, and many other fields. Algebra is a kind of mathematical language in which problems can be solved using symbols in place of varying or unknown numbers. Branches of mathematics that relate to practical problems are called applied mathematics. However, some mathematicians study pure mathematics – numerical problems which have no known practical use.

SYMMETRY

A symmetrical object is made up of alike parts. Many symmetrical patterns and shapes occur in nature. A starfish exhibits bilateral symmetry, since it looks the same when reflected in a line drawn along the length of one of its arms. This line is called an axis. The starfish also displays rotational symmetry, as it looks the same when rotated around its central point.

INFINITY

Pure mathematicians study the fundamental ideas of numbers and shapes. One such idea is the concept of infinity, which means "never-ending". The pattern shown above is called a fractal. It is produced by a computer according to a strict formula (rule). You can enlarge any part of the pattern again and again, but you will still get a pattern that is just as intricate. The pattern is infinitely complex.

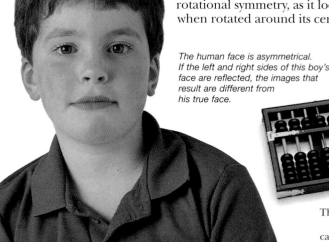

The human face is asymmetrical. If the left and right sides of this boy's face are reflected, the images that result are different from his true face.

EUCLID

The ancient Greek mathematician Euclid (c. 330-275 BCE) was the first to formulate theories on the nature of shapes and angles. His book *Elements* outlined the principles of geometry, and it was a standard textbook for centuries. Euclid found many practical uses for geometry, such as in optical science.

ABACUS
The abacus, or counting frame, is an ancient calculating device which comes from China. It consists of rows of beads that represent units of tens, hundreds, and thousands. The abacus is worked by moving the beads along the rows. People in Asian countries still use the abacus as a rapid tool for adding, subtracting, multiplying, and dividing.

PARTS OF A CIRCLE
A circle is a shape in which every point on its circumference, or outside margin, is the same distance from the centre. The diameter is the line that exactly bisects a circle, passing through the centre. The distance from the centre to the circumference is the radius. The slice of circle between two radii is a sector, and the part of the circumference that bounds a sector is an arc.

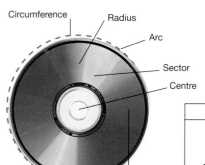

Circumference — Radius — Arc — Sector — Centre — Diameter

Find out more
COMPUTERS
NUMBERS
SCIENCE, HISTORY OF
WEIGHTS AND MEASURES

MAYA

DEEP IN THE TROPICAL FORESTS of Mexico, the Mayan people created one of the most amazing ancient civilizations, which reached its height between 250 and 900 CE. The Maya built cities with huge stone temples. Each city was the centre of a separate kingdom, with a king who was treated like a god. The Maya were great scholars who developed systems of mathematics and astronomy. They even created their own writing system and used it to carve inscriptions about their history on stone plaques that they set up in their cities. Despite their sophistication, the Maya had only the simplest technology. They used stone tools, and did not know about the wheel. By the 1500s the Spanish had conquered the region.

MAYAN CIVILIZATION
The Maya came from the Yucatan Peninsula and the highlands to the south, in what is now eastern Mexico. They also built cities in parts of modern Guatemala and Honduras.

FLINT CARVING
Craftworkers made their tools out of stones such as flint or obsidian (a black, naturally occurring glass). They could work these materials to make a sharp edge. The Maya became highly skilled at this type of stoneworking, and made intricate carvings in strange shapes to show off their skill. Many were made to place in graves or as offerings to the gods.

Outer shell of stone concealed earth base and royal tomb.

Temple contains historic inscriptions.

Priests used the main staircase.

PALENQUE
The Temple of the Inscriptions at Palenque was a famous Mayan pyramid. Deep inside the base was a secret chamber containing the tomb of a local king, Pacal, who died in about 684 CE. In the temple on top of the pyramid were stone tablets carved with glyphs that recorded the history of the local kings up to Pacal's reign. Its ruins still exist today.

People taking part in ceremonies could stand on the main stepped levels.

Stone ring acted as "goal".

Players used their elbows to hit the ball.

GLYPHS
Mayan writing was made up of a series of signs, which archaeologists call glyphs. Many of the glyphs were simplified pictures of the objects they stood for. Some represented sounds, which were used to build up words. Others were symbols that stood for different numbers. The Maya used glyphs to record their calendar, and to write inscriptions about their history.

Glyph describing a Mayan noble woman called Lady Xoc

Pot shaped like a jaguar

BLOOD SACRIFICE
Some Mayan communities believed that their gods would be pleased if people were killed in their honour. They also saw sacrificial blood as food for the gods. In some places a pot shaped like a jaguar, a beast sacred to the Maya, was used to collect the blood.

BALL GAME
Many cities had a ball court where people played a game with a rubber ball. Players wore padded clothing, and were only allowed to touch the ball with their hips, arms, or elbows. The aim was to get the ball through a small stone ring at the side of the court. Players who lost were sometimes put to death.

Find out more
BRONZE AGE
CENTRAL AMERICA
WHEELS

MEDICINE

TWO HUNDRED AND FIFTY YEARS AGO, people lived on average for just 35 years. Today, in the industrialized parts of the world, the average lifespan has increased to more than 70 years. Better food and hygiene have helped, but one of the main reasons for this change is the advances made in medicine. Medicine is the branch of science concerned with the prevention, diagnosis (identification), and treatment of disease and damage to the human body. Medical scientists are constantly searching for new ways of treating diseases. Treatments include drugs, radiation therapy, and surgery. Preventive measures, such as vaccinations against infections, are becoming an increasingly important part of modern medicine.

DIAGNOSIS
A doctor's first step with a sick patient is to diagnose the illness. This can be done in various ways – by asking the patient about his or her symptoms (physical feelings), by making a physical examination of the ill person, and by carrying out medical tests if necessary.

SURGERY
Medical treatments may include drugs or surgery. Surgery is the branch of medicine that involves operating, or cutting into the body, to treat the cause of an illness. Today surgery is so advanced that surgeons can sometimes repair or replace organs such as the kidneys and the heart.

BRANCHES OF MEDICINE
Medicine is a huge subject and nobody can hope to know it all. Thus doctors, nurses, and other medical workers often become expert in a single area of medicine, a process which can take years and years of study.

Neurology is concerned with disorders of the brain and nerves.

Ophthalmology is the treatment of disorders of the eyes.

Orthopaedics is the care of the spine, bones, joints, and muscles.

Psychiatry is the study of mental health problems.

Cutting into the body to cure illness is called surgery.

Dermatology is concerned with the skin and skin diseases.

Paediatrics is the medical care of children.

RECOVERY
Recovery from an illness or an operation may take only a few hours or as long as several weeks. Much depends on the severity of the illness and the impact the treatment has on the body.

MEDICAL TECHNOLOGY
Modern medicine makes use of a wide range of technology. Latest developments include body scanners which use a strong magnetic field or ultrasound (very high-frequency sound waves) to produce an image of the interior of the human body. Such equipment has revolutionized medicine.

Doctors use MRI scanners to check patients for tumours or damage to the brain.

Rue is prescribed for some digestive disorders.

Catmint is a cold cure that was first used by prehistoric people.

Mint is used for settling a stomach upset.

HOLISTIC MEDICINE
The word *holistic* means "of the whole". The principle of holistic medicine is to treat the whole person – body and mind – rather than just the affected part. Holistic therapies (treatments) include acupuncture (stimulating the nerves by inserting needles into the skin) and aromatherapy (treatment using oils containing fragrant plant extracts).

Find out more
DISEASE
DRUGS
HEALTH AND FITNESS
HUMAN BODY
MEDICINE, HISTORY OF
MUSCLES AND MOVEMENT
TECHNOLOGY

HISTORY OF
MEDICINE

TREPANNING
Ten thousand years ago, the first
doctors tried to cure an ill person
by cutting a hole in his or her skull.
Healers believed that the hole in the
head released evil spirits that caused
pain. This was known as trepanning.

SINCE THE EARLIEST TIMES, people have looked for ways of curing
their illnesses. Early people believed that disease was a punishment from
the gods. They also believed that priests and magicians could heal them.
In Ancient Greece, people visited temples when they were ill and
sacrificed animals to Asclepius, the Greek god of healing. They also drank
and bathed in medicinal waters and followed strict diets in the hope of
being cured. During the fifth century BCE the Greek doctor Hippocrates
declared that it was nature, not magic, that caused and cured disease.
Hippocrates was famed as "the father of medicine", and he and his
followers wrote many medical books. The spirit of enquiry, which was part
of the Renaissance (a cultural movement in 14th-century Europe),
encouraged experiments that put European medicine on a firm scientific
basis. Many people began to question the traditional ideas about
medicine. Scientists such as Vesalius (1514-1564) began to study the
bodies of dead people to learn more about disease and how to treat
it. Since then, there have been many more discoveries in medicine,
and the battle against disease continues.

HUMOURS
The Greek physician Galen (c. 130-200 CE)
introduced the idea that the body contained four
fluids called humours – blood, phlegm, yellow
bile, and black bile. He believed that a person's
mood depended on which of these four fluids
ruled the body, and that if the fluids were not
balanced, illness
would result.

HERBALISM

For thousands of years, people have used herbs and plants in
healing. Herbalists wrote lists of herbs and their uses. Monks were
also famed for their knowledge of herbs. The first pharmacists,
called apothecaries, used herbs to make potions, or medicines.
But in Europe during the Renaissance many herbalists were
accused of being witches. Many people are now turning to herbs
as a natural way of treating illnesses.

WILLIAM HARVEY
In 1628, an English doctor
named William Harvey
(1578-1657) discovered
that blood constantly
circulates around the
body. He described how
blood is pumped by the
heart into the arteries
and returns to the heart
in the veins. He showed
that valves in the veins stop the blood
from flowing backwards. At first, Harvey
was scorned for contradicting old ideas,
but later he became physician to Charles I,
king of England.

*Harvey drew detailed diagrams to
explain his theory of circulation.*

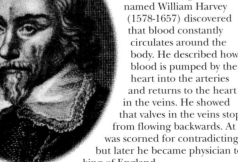

335

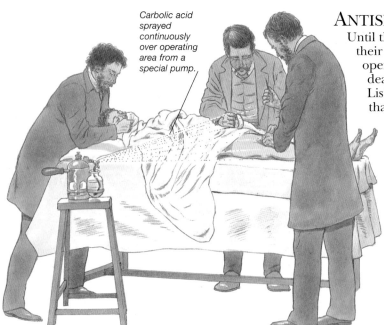

Carbolic acid sprayed continuously over operating area from a special pump.

ANTISEPTICS

Until the late 19th century, surgeons did not wash their hands or their medical instruments before operating on a patient. Many patients died from deadly infections following an operation. Joseph Lister (1827-1912), an English surgeon, guessed that infection with bacteria might be the cause of these deaths. In 1865, Lister developed an antiseptic spray called carbolic acid. This spray could destroy bacteria in the operating room, so there was a dramatic drop in the number of deaths following operations.

Leeches are parasites that attach themselves to a host. They secrete a substance that stops blood clotting while they feed on it.

BLOOD-LETTING

Doctors once believed that too much blood in the body was the cause of disease. They removed the excess blood by blood-letting. Doctors either cut open a vein to let the blood out, or they applied bloodsucking creatures called leeches to the body. The leech attached itself to the patient with its sucker, made a wound, then sucked out blood. The exact spot for blood-letting depended on what was wrong with the patient.

ALEXANDER FLEMING

Bacteria cause many of the illnesses that affect humans, so for years scientists tried to find a substance that would kill bacteria but would not harm human tissue. The Scottish bacteriologist Alexander Fleming (1881-1955) was the first person to identify an antibacterial substance. Fleming carried out his research in a laboratory at St. Mary's Hospital, London. In 1928, Fleming noticed that a mould that had accidentally developed on a dish of bacteria culture caused the bacteria to die. In 1941, the researchers Howard Florey and Ernst Chain purified the mould, *Penicillium*, to produce penicillin, the world's first antibiotic. Penicillin is widely used in the treatment of many diseases, including meningitis and pneumonia. Fleming shared the 1945 Nobel Prize for medicine with Florey and Chain.

HISTORY OF MEDICINE

c. 8000 BCE Early healers practise trepanning.

400s BCE Hippocrates, a Greek, begins scientific medicine.

1543 Vesalius publishes first scientific study of human body.

1615 Santorio, an Italian doctor, designs mouth thermometer.

1683 Anton van Leeuwenhoek, a Dutch scientist, discovers bacteria.

1796 Edward Jenner gives first smallpox vaccination.

1816 Rene Laennec, a French doctor, invents stethoscope.

1842 American surgeon, Horace Long, operates using general anaesthetic.

1895 Wilhelm Roentgen, a German physicist, discovers x-rays, which enable doctors to see inside the human body.

1898 Polish-born Marie Curie and her husband, Pierre Curie of France, discover the chemical element radium to treat cancer.

1928 Scottish bacteriologist, Alexander Fleming, discovers penicillin.

MEDICAL PIONEERS

Through the centuries many people have shaped modern medicine. The Flemish doctor Vesalius produced accurate drawings of the human body; Dutchman Anton van Leeuwenhoek (1632-1723) first discovered microbes, now called bacteria; and the English doctor Edward Jenner (1749-1823) discovered vaccinations – a way of preventing certain diseases by injection.

LOUIS PASTEUR
Frenchman Louis Pasteur (1822-1895) showed that bacteria caused disease. He invented pasteurization – the heating of milk and beer to destroy harmful bacteria.

SIGMUND FREUD
The Austrian doctor Sigmund Freud (1856-1939; below) was interested in finding out how the mind works. He treated patients with mental disorders by listening to them talk about their dreams and thoughts. This treatment was called psychoanalysis. In 1900, Freud published *The Interpretation of Dreams*, which explained his method.

Find out more
DRUGS
EGYPT, ANCIENT
GREECE, ANCIENT
MEDICINE

MEDIEVAL EUROPE

LORDS AND LADIES feasting in castle banquet halls, peasants working on the land, knights in armour – all these are associated with a time in European history known as the medieval period or the Middle Ages. This was a time of great change in western Europe between the 5th and 15th centuries. During the 5th century the Roman Empire fell, to be replaced by smaller kingdoms set up by invading Germanic tribes in Western Europe. Trade collapsed, and people had to make their living from the land. Gradually, powerful landowners or lords emerged and the feudal system developed. The early medieval period of Europe is sometimes called the Dark Age because the learning of Ancient Greece and Rome almost disappeared. But the Christian Church gave leadership to the people. Trade gradually improved. By about the 13th century the Middle Ages had reached their height. Feudalism governed society, and monasteries (where monks lived) were the centres of learning. The medieval times came to an end in the 15th century when the Renaissance swept through Europe.

FAIRS
Great fairs were held every year in towns, such as Winchester, England, which were on important trade routes. Merchants travelled from all over Europe to sell their goods at these fairs.

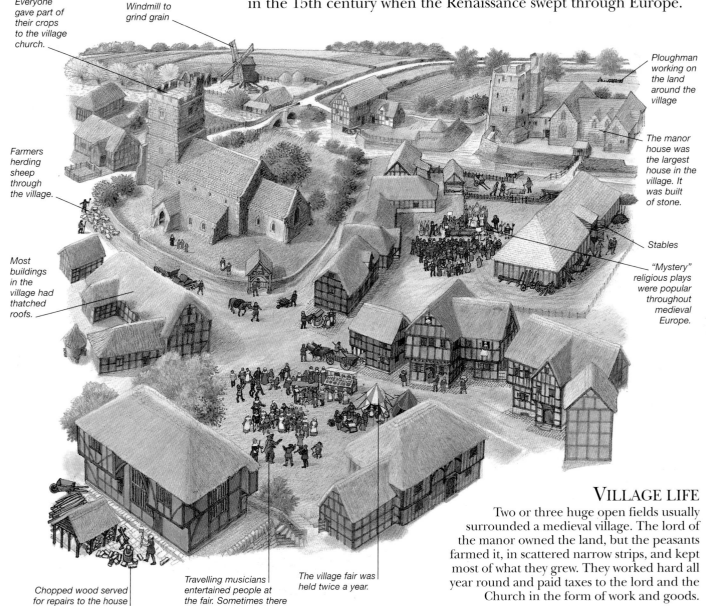

Everyone gave part of their crops to the village church.

Windmill to grind grain

Ploughman working on the land around the village

Farmers herding sheep through the village.

The manor house was the largest house in the village. It was built of stone.

Most buildings in the village had thatched roofs.

Stables

"Mystery" religious plays were popular throughout medieval Europe.

Chopped wood served for repairs to the house and to make fire.

Travelling musicians entertained people at the fair. Sometimes there were dancing bears.

The village fair was held twice a year.

VILLAGE LIFE
Two or three huge open fields usually surrounded a medieval village. The lord of the manor owned the land, but the peasants farmed it, in scattered narrow strips, and kept most of what they grew. They worked hard all year round and paid taxes to the lord and the Church in the form of work and goods.

Shoemakers

TOWN SCENE

Trade increased in the later medieval period, making merchants wealthy and powerful. Towns became important trading centres with a new class of craftspeople. The craftspeople created organizations called guilds to control the prices and quality of their goods.

People bought fabric to make their own clothing.

The poultry trader sold geese.

FEUDALISM

Kings gave their vassals – powerful nobles – tracts of land called fiefs. In return for this land the vassals fought for the king when required. The vassals divided their land into manors (estates), which they gave to lesser nobles and knights. In return, the knights and lesser nobles worked for the lord of the manor, and had to fight for him when called on.

14th-century manuscript (right) shows feudal structure, with the king at the top.

Hunting (above) was a popular sport for upper-class medieval women.

A French medieval woman, Christine de Pisan (left), earned her living as a writer.

WOMEN

Peasant women worked very hard all their lives. They brought up their children, spun wool and wove clothing, and helped with all the farmwork. Upper-class women also led busy lives. They often ran the family estates while their husbands were away travelling around their lands, fighting against neighbouring lords, or on a Crusade to the Holy Land. Women also nursed the sick and provided education for children in their charge.

MEDIEVAL EUROPE

400 CE Roman empire begins to decline.

450 German tribes – Angles, Jutes, and Saxons – settle in Britain.

480s Franks set up kingdom in Gaul (now France).

800 Charlemagne, king of the Franks, unites western Europe.

900-1000s Europe is divided into feudal estates; there is widespread poverty and disease in the region.

1066 Normans conquer England.

1000s-1200s High Middle Ages: trade improves, population grows, towns develop, and learning flourishes.

c. 1100 First universities are founded.

1215 Magna Carta: English barons win power and rights from King John.

1300-1500 Late Middle Ages.

c. 1320 Renaissance, a rebirth of arts and learning, begins in Italy.

1337 Hundred Years' War begins between England and France.

1348 Black Death, a killing plague, reaches Europe. Eventually, it wipes out one third of the population of Europe.

1378-1417 Great Schism: Catholic Europe is divided in support of two different popes, Urban VI and Clement VII.

1454 Johannes Gutenberg, a German, develops movable type. Printing begins in Europe.

Find out more

BLACK DEATH
EUROPE, HISTORY OF
KNIGHTS AND HERALDRY
MAGNA CARTA
RENAISSANCE
ROMAN EMPIRE

METALS

IMAGINE A WORLD WITHOUT METALS. There would be no cars or aeroplanes, and skyscrapers would fall down without the metal frames that support them. Metals have countless uses because they possess a unique combination of qualities. They are very strong and easy to shape, so they can be used to make all kinds of objects from ships to bottle tops. All metals conduct electricity. Some are ideal for wires and electrical equipment. Metals also carry heat, so they make good cooking pots. These qualities can be improved by mixing two or more metals to make alloys. Most metallic objects are made of alloys rather than pure metals. There are more than 80 kinds of pure metals, though some are very rare. Aluminium and iron are the most common metals. A few metals, such as gold, occur in the ground as pure metals; the rest are found as ores in rock. Metals can also be obtained by recycling old cars and tins. This reduces waste and costs less than processing metal ores.

Gold watch

Copper wire

Mercury thermometer

Silver-plated frame

PURE METALS

The rarity and lustre of gold and silver have been prized for centuries. Other pure metals have special uses. Electrical wires are made of copper, which conducts electricity well. Mercury, a liquid metal, is used in thermometers.

Aeroplane fuselage made of aluminium alloys

BOEING 737-400

ALUMINIUM

The most common metal in the Earth's crust is aluminium. The metal comes from an ore called bauxite, which contains alumina, a compound of aluminium and oxygen. Aluminium is light, conducts electricity and heat, and resists corrosion. These qualities mean the metal and its alloys can be used in many things, including aircraft and bicycles, window frames, paints, saucepans, and electricity supply cables.

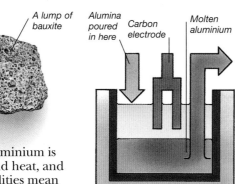

A lump of bauxite

Alumina poured in here

Carbon electrode

Molten aluminium

ELECTROLYSIS Passing an electric current through alumina separates it into aluminium and oxygen. This process is called electrolysis.

Thin, flexible aluminium foil is useful for cooking and storing food because it is nonreactive and can stand high temperatures.

ALLOYS

Most metal objects are made of steel or other alloys. This is because alloys are often stronger or easier to process than pure metals. Copper and tin are weak and pliable, but when mixed together they make a strong alloy called bronze. Brass is a tough alloy of copper and zinc that resists corrosion. Alloys of aluminium are light and strong and are used to make aircraft.

METAL FATIGUE

Metals sometimes fail even though they may be very tough and strong. Corrosion weakens some metals, as in the case of rusty steel. Repeated bending can cause metal parts to break, an effect called metal fatigue.

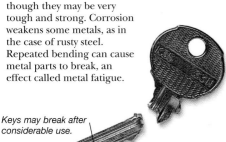

Keys may break after considerable use.

METALWORKING

There are many ways of shaping metal. Casting is one method of making objects such as metal statues. Hot, molten metal is poured into a mould where it sets and hardens into the required shape. Metal can also be pressed, hammered, or cut into shape.

WELDING

Metal parts can be joined by welding. Welders apply heat, from a gas flame or an electric spark, to the edges of two pieces of metal. The heat causes the edges to melt so that they can be joined together.

Find out more

BRONZE AGE
IRON AGE
IRON AND STEEL
ROCKS AND MINERALS
SCIENCE

MEXICO

THE WEALTH OF MEXICO has traditionally come from the land. Precious metals lie buried in the mountains and rich crops grow in the valleys. Oil flows from wells on the coast. The Mexican people began to exploit these advantages centuries ago. Farming supported most of the people, and from the country's mines came silver to make beautiful jewellery. The mineral wealth of the country attracted invading European soldiers in the 16th century, and Spain ruled Mexico for three centuries. A revolt against Spanish rule gave the Mexican people independence in 1821. The discovery of oil early in the 20th century brought new wealth to Mexico. The government invested this in new factories, and in social services to relieve hunger and improve health and education. In 1994, the North American Free Trade Agreement (NAFTA) reduced trade barriers between Mexico, Canada, and the United States, promising long-term economic benefits. However, the border between Mexico and the US has been strengthened as a result of US concern over the many illegal crossings made each year.

Mexico is part of the continent of North America and lies between the United States to its north and Central America to its south.

José Guadalupe Posada (1852–1913) drew humorous illustrations, many of which supported the Mexican revolution.

POLITICS AND REVOLUTION

Mexico was a Spanish colony from 1521 to 1821, when it became an independent republic. After a long period of political unrest, there was a revolution in 1910, in which half a million people died. From 1929, the Institutional Revolutionary party governed Mexico, but in 2000 it lost the presidential election for the first time. Mexico is now a fully functioning democracy.

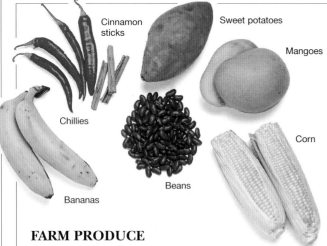

Cinnamon sticks

Sweet potatoes

Mangoes

Chillies

Beans

Corn

Bananas

FARM PRODUCE

Only one-seventh of the population of Mexico works on the land, growing staple or food crops. Increasingly, however, farmers are growing coffee, cotton, sugar, and tomatoes for export. These cash crops take vital land away from the crops that the Mexican people themselves need for food. Most of the farmers are members of co-operatives, pooling their limited resources to help one another.

MEXICO CITY

More than 19 million people live in and around Mexico City, the capital of Mexico, making it one of the most populated cities in the world. The city lies 1.6 km (1 mile) above sea level in a natural basin surrounded by mountains. These mountains trap the pollution from the city's industries. As a result, Mexico City is one of the world's most unhealthy cities, with an inadequate water supply, a lack of housing, and the constant threat of earthquakes adding to its many problems.

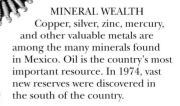

Mexican artisans are skilled at making fine jewellery from the precious metals found in their country.

MINERAL WEALTH

Copper, silver, zinc, mercury, and other valuable metals are among the many minerals found in Mexico. Oil is the country's most important resource. In 1974, vast new reserves were discovered in the south of the country.

Find out more

CONQUISTADORS
NORTH AMERICA
VOLCANOES

Volcano	Mountain	Ancient monument	Capital city	Large city/ town	Small city/ town

STATISTICS
Area: 1,958,200 sq km (756,061 sq miles)
Population: 111,212,000
Capital: Mexico City
Languages: Spanish, Nahuatl, Maya, Zapotec, Mixtec, Otomi, Totonac, Tzotzil, Tzeltal
Religions: Roman Catholic, Protestant
Currency: Mexican peso
Main occupations: Subsistence farming, manufacturing, oil production
Main exports: Oil, cotton, machinery, coffee
Main imports: Machinery, vehicles, chemicals

SIERRA MADRE
The main mountain system of Mexico, the Sierra Madre, runs 2,400 km (1,500 miles) southeast from the border with the United States. There are three ranges, in the east, south, and west, and they enclose Mexico's central plateau. Mexico's third highest mountain, Volcán Iztaccihuatl (right), is in the Sierra Madre del Sur, the southern range. The mountain has three separate summits, and its name means "White Woman" in the Aztec language, because the peaks resemble a woman wearing a hood.

The tallest peak of Volcán Iztaccihuatl rises to 5,268 m (17,274 ft).

POPULATION
Most of northern Mexico is sparsely populated due to the hot, dry climate and lack of cultivable farmland. As people have migrated from the countryside in search of work, the cities have grown dramatically; almost 75 per cent of Mexicans now live in urban areas. Mexico city is home to almost a quarter of the population and is one of the world's largest cities. Rapid, unplanned growth has led to poor sanitation and water supplies.

GUANAJUATO
Spanish prospectors searching for gold founded Guanajuato (below) in 1554. The town is the capital of Guanajuato state in the mountains of central Mexico and rises more than 2,050 m (6,726 ft) above sea level. It is built in a ravine and has steep, winding streets.

RIO GRANDE
The Rio Grande flows from Colorado in the United States and forms much of Mexico's northern border. It crosses a vast arid region on its way to the Gulf of Mexico.

BAJA CALIFORNIA
Baja California is also called Lower California. The peninsula is in Mexico, and is not part of the US state with which it shares a name.

MEXICAN FABRICS
Mexican people have been expert weavers since ancient times. They produce brightly coloured fabrics with bold, geometric designs, such as the striped skirt worn by the girl on the left. Today most Mexican fabrics are mass-produced in large factories.

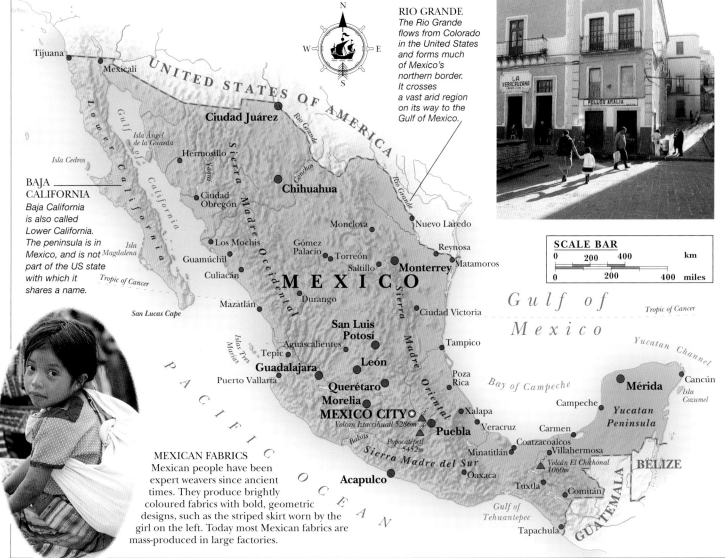

SCALE BAR
0   200   400   km
0   200   400 miles

MICROSCOPES

WITHIN ALL OBJECTS there is a hidden world, much too tiny for us to see. With the invention of the microscope in the 16th century, scientists were able to peer into this world and unravel some of the great mysteries of science. They discovered that animals and plants are made of millions of tiny cells, and later were able to identify the minute organisms called bacteria that cause disease. Early microscopes consisted of a single magnifying lens; today's microscopes have several lenses and can be used to see very tiny objects. Electron microscopes are even more powerful. Instead of light they use a beam of electrons – tiny particles which are normally part of atoms – to magnify objects many millions of times. Scientists use electron microscopes to study the smallest of living cells and to delve into the structure of materials such as plastics and metals.

Observer looks through eyepiece.

Objective lenses of different power can be swung into position when needed.

The objective lens produces an image which the eyepiece magnifies (makes larger).

The object being studied rests on a glass slide.

Condenser lenses concentrate a beam of light onto the object.

A strong beam of light strikes a mirror under the microscope. The beam shines onto the object from below.

Optical microscopes can reveal living cells such as these cells which come from a human cheek. They are magnified more than 200 times.

OPTICAL MICROSCOPE

The optical, or light, microscope has two main lenses: the objective and the eyepiece. High-quality microscopes contain several additional lenses which help to give a clear, bright image. Different objectives can be fitted which give a range of magnification from about 10 times to 1,500 times normal size.

INVENTING THE MICROSCOPE

EN L'AN 2000

Although the Romans used magnifying lenses about 2,000 years ago, the first true microscope appeared around 1590, built by Dutch spectacles makers Hans and Zacharias Janssen. In 1663, English scientist Robert Hooke studied insects and plants with a microscope. He found that cork was made up of tiny cells, a discovery of great scientific importance. Microscopes aroused great interest in microscopic life, as this old etching shows.

ELECTRON MICROSCOPES
Objects must be cut into thin slices in order to see them with a microscope. However, a scanning electron microscope can magnify a whole object such as this ant (right), which is about 15 times normal size.

With a scanning electron microscope the image appears on a monitor screen.

IMAGING ATOMS
Special electron microscopes can show individual atoms, which are so small that a line of 0.5 million atoms would only span the width of a human hair. This piece of silicon (above) is magnified 45 million times, revealing its atoms.

Find out more
ATOMS AND MOLECULES
BIOLOGY
MICROSCOPIC LIFE

MICROSCOPIC LIFE

ALL AROUND US there are living things that we cannot see because they are too small. They float in the air, they swim in puddles and oceans, and they coat rocks, soil, plants, and animals. Microscopic life includes bacteria and viruses; single-celled organisms, called protoctists; and single-celled plants, called algae. It also includes the microscopic stages in the lives of larger plants and animals, such as the tiny pollen grains of flowers and the spores of mushrooms. From bacteria to algae, all are so small that we can see them only through a microscope. Viruses, which are the smallest and simplest of all living things, must be magnified one million times before we can see them. Microscopic life has a crucial role to play. Plankton consists of millions of algae and protozoa, and is an important food for water creatures. Bacteria in soil help to recycle nutrients. Some microscopic life, such as bacteria, can cause disease.

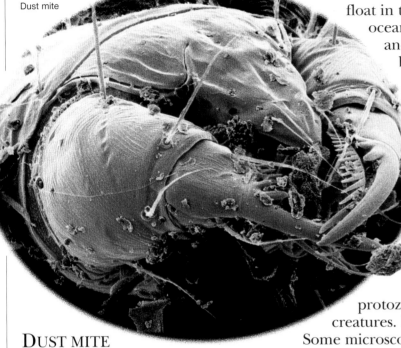

Dust mite

DUST MITE

This microscopic animal can be found in everyone's home. It lives among dust, fluff, cat fur, and bits of dirt. Dust mites eat the dead skin you shed every day.

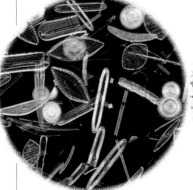

DIATOM

Microscopic plants called diatoms live in lakes, rivers, and oceans. There are thousands of different kinds of diatoms, providing food for many insects and water creatures. Diatoms live and grow by using sunlight and the nutrients in the water. Around their bodies are strong shell-like walls made of silica – the same material found in sand grains.

POLLEN

Microscopic grains of pollen grow on the male part of a plant, called the stamen. Each kind of plant has a different type of pollen grain with its own pattern and shape.

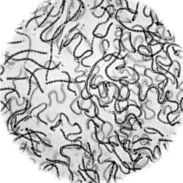

ALGAE

The slimy scum that you see on the surface of a stagnant pond is blue-green algae. These algae are not true plants. They are more closely related to bacteria. Blue-green algae were among the first forms of life to appear on Earth more than 2,000 million years ago.

Hollyhock pollen grain

Passionflower pollen grain

AMOEBA

The amoeba is a single-celled organism. It lives in ponds and puddles. We need to magnify an amoeba at least one thousand times before we can see it. The amoeba moves by stretching out a part of its body known as a pseudopod, or "false foot". The rest of the body then flows into the pseudopod. Amoebas feed by engulfing prey such as bacteria with their pseudopods; then the whole body flows over the prey.

Amoeba divides in half, forming two daughter cells.

Food is stored in a small bag called the food vacuole.

Pseudopod (false foot)

Nucleus – control centre of amoeba

Cell membrane, the skin around the cell

HOW AN AMOEBA REPRODUCES

To reproduce, the amoeba divides into two. This is called fission. First the nucleus splits in two, then the rest of the body divides in half to form two separate amoebas. These are called daughter cells.

Find out more

DISEASE
HUMAN BODY
MICROSCOPES
OCEAN WILDLIFE

MIDDLE EAST

The Middle East consists of 15 independent countries. They sit at the crossroads of three great continents – to the northwest lies Europe, to the southwest is Africa, to the north and east are the Caucasus and Central Asian republics, all part of Asia.

LESS THAN 100 YEARS AGO, many of the inhabitants of the Middle East were Bedouins – desert-dwelling nomads who lived in tents and led their animals in search of food. The rest of the population lived in small towns and villages and made a living as farmers or craftsworkers. Almost everyone was poor and uneducated. Today, the lives of their children and grandchildren have been transformed by the discovery of oil. Many people have grown rich from the new industries and services related to oil production and refining. In some countries, notably Kuwait and Bahrain, there is free education and medical care for everyone. Oil transformed the international importance of the Middle East as well. The region had little influence in world affairs. Now it controls one quarter of the world's oil production, and decisions made in the Middle East affect the economies of Europe, America, and Asia. But despite this massive change, traditional customs have not been completely abandoned, and the religion of Islam continues to dominate daily life throughout the Middle East, as it has done for more than 1,300 years.

WATERWAYS

Rising in the mountains of Turkey, the Tigris and Euphrates rivers irrigate the almost rainless land of the Middle East as they flow in parallel to the Persian Gulf. The fertility of the Euphates-Tigris Delta, known as Mesopotamia in ancient times, gave rise to the world's first cities.

MODERNIZATION
The discovery of oil brought great wealth and rapid industrial and social change to the Middle East. But governments in the region recognize that the oil will eventually run out. So they have spent some of the money they earned from selling oil in encouraging and modernizing local industry and business. Many Middle East countries have also invested in property and businesses in other nations throughout the world.

At a banking school in the Middle East, students learn the skills that will help them modernize business in their country.

The areas of desert bordering the Euphrates and Tigris rivers are swamps and marshlands. Here, small boats replace the camel as the most common means of transport.

LANDSCAPE AND CLIMATE

Most of the Middle East consists of hot, dry, rocky deserts. A crescent of fertile land stretches west from the Tigris and Euphrates rivers through northern Iraq and Syria and then south into Lebanon and Israel. Turkey and Iran are mountainous, as are the southern parts of the Arabian peninsula. In the southeast of Saudi Arabia lies the Rub' al Khali, a vast, uninhabited sandy desert known as the Empty Quarter.

Camels are well adapted to the harsh conditions of the Middle East, and are still a popular form of transport.

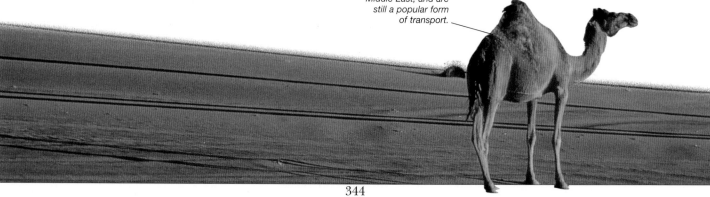

SUEZ CANAL

More than 160 km (100 miles) in length, the Suez Canal links the Mediterranean Sea and the Red Sea. The canal took ten years to build, and when completed in 1869, it cut more than 11,000 km (7,000 miles) from the distance that sailing ships travelled to reach the Far East. Today, nearly 50 ships pass through the canal each day. The Suez Canal is an important trade route and has often been at the centre of conflict in the Middle East. The waterway has been closed by war and political disagreements several times, most recently by the Arab-Israeli Six Day War of 1967.

The Suez Canal is not wide enough for ships travelling in opposite directions to pass each other. Vessels must travel in convoy (above), passing only at by-passes, where stretches of the canal have been doubled.

Splendid architecture, financed by revenue from oil, can be found in Abu Dhabi (below).

DUBAI

The city-state of Dubai on the Gulf has a modern centre, but on the outskirts it merges into the surrounding desert. Rainfall on the Arabian Peninsula where Dubai stands averages less than 100 mm (4 in) a year, and in most places the only natural water comes from underground springs. Desalination plants turn salt water from the Gulf into a supply of drinking water for the city.

Dubai, part of the federation of United Arab Emirates, is generally flat with large areas covered by dunes and barren rock.

ABU DHABI

The rulers of many Middle East states invested income from sales of oil to improve the living conditions of their people and develop the economies of their nations. In the 1960s the city of Abu Dhabi was just a fishing village on the Gulf. Today it is the capital city of the Abu Dhabi sheikdom in the United Arab Emirates, complete with an international airport and high-rise downtown area. Abu Dhabi's revenues from oil royalties give it one of the world's highest per capita incomes.

UNITED ARAB EMIRATES

Like many Middle East nations, the United Arab Emirates has no democratic government. Instead, the country is ruled by a group of wealthy emirs (kings) who have absolute power over their people. Each emir controls his individual emirate, or kingdom, but they meet in the Federal Supreme Council of Rulers to make decisions that affect the whole country. Today, oil provides most of the country's wealth, but shipping has traditionally been important, and there are major ports at Abu Dhabi, Dubai, and Sharjah.

The port at Sharjah is built to accommodate the most modern container ships.

Muslim guerrillas fight in the streets of Lebanon.

MIDDLE EAST WARS

Bitter wars have caused much suffering and death in the Middle East. Israel and its Arab neighbours have fought four wars over the last 60 years. Iran and Iraq were constantly at war throughout the 1980s, and Lebanon was devastated by a civil war. In 1991 UN forces defeated Iraq after the Iraqis invaded Kuwait. In 2003 American and British forces invaded Iraq and overthrew the dictator Saddam Hussein.

A statue of the former Iraqi dictator Saddam Hussein is toppled in a square in central Baghdad after the 2003 invasion.

Find out more
DESERT WILDLIFE
IRAN
ISLAM
ISRAEL
OIL

BAHRAIN
Area: 680 sq km (263 sq miles)
Population: 728,000
Capital: Manama

Volcano | Mountain | Ancient monument | Capital city | Large city/town | Small city/town

CYPRUS
Area: 9,251 sq km (3,572 sq miles)
Population: 797,000
Capital: Nicosia

SYRIA
Area: 185,180 sq km (71,500 sq miles)
Population: 20,178,000
Capital: Damascus

IRAN
Area: 1,648,000 sq km (636,293 sq miles)
Population: 66,429,000
Capital: Tehran

TURKEY
Area: 769,630 sq km (297,154 sq miles)
Population: 76,805,000
Capital: Ankara

OIL INDUSTRY
Deposits of oil and natural gas were first discovered in the Gulf in the early 1900s. Today, more than half the world's oil reserves are located in the Gulf. The oil industry has made several of the countries very rich, particularly Saudi Arabia, Iran, Iraq, United Arab Emirates, Bahrain, and Kuwait.

IRAQ
Area: 438,320 sq km (169,235 sq miles)
Population: 28,426,000
Capital: Baghdad

ISRAEL
Area: 20,700 sq km (7,992 sq miles)
Population: 7,234,000
Capital: Jerusalem

JORDAN
Area: 89,210 sq km (34,440 sq miles)
Population: 6,342,000
Capital: Amman

KUWAIT
Area: 17,820 sq km (6,880 sq miles)
Population: 2,691,000
Capital: Kuwait

LEBANON
Area: 10,400 sq km (4,015 sq miles)
Population: 4,017,000
Capital: Beirut

OMAN
Area: 212,460 sq km (82,030 sq miles)
Population: 3,418,000
Capital: Muscat

QATAR
Area: 11,000 sq km (4,247 sq miles)
Population: 833,000
Capital: Doha

SAUDI ARABIA
Area: 2,149,690 sq km (829,995 sq miles)
Population: 28,687,000
Capital: Riyadh

The roofs of buildings in Bahrain extend across pavements, providing shade from the scorching sun.

BAHRAIN
The island of Bahrain is little more than 50 km (30 miles) long. Oil wells and refineries provide employment for many people, but tourism is important, too; in 1986 a causeway was opened, linking Bahrain to Saudi Arabia. Since then, many visitors from neighbouring Gulf States with strict Islamic laws have visited Bahrain to enjoy its liberal lifestyle.

UNITED ARAB EMIRATES
Area: 83,600 sq km (32,278 sq miles)
Population: 4,798,000
Capital: Abu Dhabi

YEMEN
Area: 527,970 sq km (203,849 sq miles)
Population: 23,823,000
Capital: Sana

SCALE BAR
0 | 200 | 400 | km
0 | 200 | 400 | miles

ANIMAL
MIGRATION

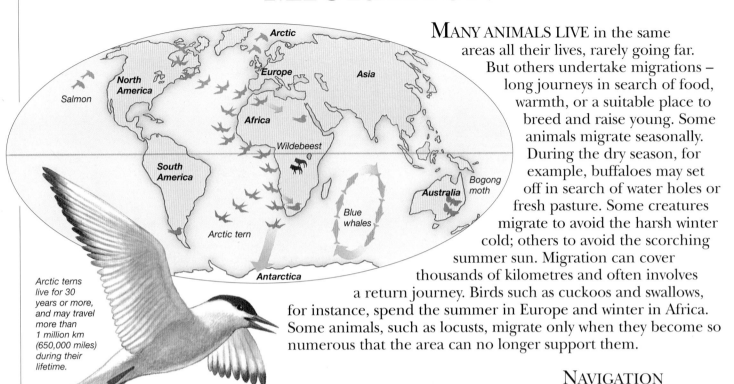

MANY ANIMALS LIVE in the same areas all their lives, rarely going far. But others undertake migrations – long journeys in search of food, warmth, or a suitable place to breed and raise young. Some animals migrate seasonally. During the dry season, for example, buffaloes may set off in search of water holes or fresh pasture. Some creatures migrate to avoid the harsh winter cold; others to avoid the scorching summer sun. Migration can cover thousands of kilometres and often involves a return journey. Birds such as cuckoos and swallows, for instance, spend the summer in Europe and winter in Africa. Some animals, such as locusts, migrate only when they become so numerous that the area can no longer support them.

Arctic terns live for 30 years or more, and may travel more than 1 million km (650,000 miles) during their lifetime.

ARCTIC TERN
The longest migration in the world is made by the Arctic tern. This champion migrator travels from the top of the globe to the bottom each year and back again. Arctic terns spend the summer in the Arctic, where they rear their young and feed on insects, fish, and shellfish. After the short summer they fly south, and some reach the Antarctic. The direct journey is 15,000 km (9,000 miles), yet many terns go even farther, flying east across the North Atlantic, then west across the South Atlantic. After another summer near the South Pole, they migrate north again.

Wildebeest wander north to find fresh pasture.

Serengeti National Park in Africa

Female wildebeest usually remain in familiar groups, which vary in number up to several hundred animals.

NAVIGATION
Some animals seem to navigate, or find their way, by following the position of the Sun, Moon, or stars. Others may have a built-in compass that senses the Earth's magnetic field or the electric field of ocean currents. Scientists are not sure how animals know where to migrate, especially young animals that have never made the journey before.

WILDEBEEST
During the dry season in Africa, huge herds of gnus (also called wildebeest) set out in search of fresh grassland and water. Sometimes they travel more than 1,500 km (1,000 miles) before they reach a suitable place.

SALMON
Salmon hatch from eggs in rivers and streams, then swim to the ocean, where they spend most of their lives. As adults they migrate thousands of kilometres back to the river where they were born, to breed. They are so sensitive to the chemicals in the stream where they hatch that they can find their way back to the same spot even after a few years. Salmon are powerful swimmers, and leap out of the water as they fight their way upstream.

Spring: Adult bogong moths migrate to mountain regions above 1,200 m (4,000 ft).

Summer: Adults gather in mountain caves and among rocks to rest during the hot, dry season.

BOGONG MOTH
Some animals migrate in summer rather than winter. During the hot, dry summer in southeast Australia, bogong moths sleep in cool caves and rock crevices high in the mountains. This type of hibernation is called aestivation. In autumn the moths fly down over the lowlands. Some keep flying when they reach the coast, and perish at sea.

Autumn: Adult moths wake and fly down to the lowlands to lay eggs.

Find out more
ANIMALS
BIRDS
BUTTERFLIES AND MOTHS
FISH
HIBERNATION

MONEY

THE NEXT TIME YOU ARE about to buy something, look at your money. Coins and notes are just discs of metal and sheets of paper, yet the shop accepts them as payment for useful, valuable goods. Money is a token which people trade for goods of an agreed value, and strange objects have been used for money throughout the world. Tibetans once used blocks of dried tea! It does not really matter what you use as money, provided everyone can reach an agreement about what it is worth. Many early coins were made from precious metals, such as gold and silver, but in 11th-century China, paper bank notes, or bills, first appeared. Unlike gold, bank notes had no real value. However, the bank that issued them promised to exchange them for gold. English bank notes still have the same promise printed on them. The United States government stopped exchanging bills for gold in 1971.

MINT

A government-controlled factory called a mint produces coins. Each coin is stamped with a special design, including its value, and often the year of manufacture. This stamping process is known as "minting".

Some Native Americans used wampum belts made of clamshell beads for money.

The first Chinese coins were made of bronze in the shape of tools, such as the head of a hoe.

The weight of a coin made of precious metal indicates its value.

A strip of plastic or metal thread is embedded in the paper.

Specially made paper includes a watermark, which is visible only when the note is held up to the light.

The loops and whirls are machine-engraved and extremely difficult to copy.

PROOF NO. 398 2/5

BANK NOTES

Governments issue bank notes and guarantee their value. It is a crime for anyone else to copy and print bank notes. The crime is called forgery, or counterfeiting, and bank notes have complicated designs to make copying difficult. Thomas De La Rue & Company is one of the world's most successful bank note printers. Their specimen note includes various security features which make their notes very difficult to copy.

COINS

People from ancient Lydia (now Turkey) were the first to make coins, about 2,700 years ago. Their coins were made from electrum, a mixture of gold and silver. Today, coins are used only for small denominations (sums of money). Paper money is used for larger sums, because notes are more difficult to forge than coins.

The metal of a modern coin is almost worthless, so the value of the coin is stamped on it.

BANKS

Most people deposit, or store, their money in a bank. Banks keep this money safe in a vault or lend it to their other customers. The bank has an account, or record, of how much each of its customers has deposited. Banks pay out notes and coins when their customers need money to make purchases. People with bank accounts can also buy things by writing cheques – notes which the bank promises to exchange for cash.

The built-in computer chip contains your personal bank details.

The raised letters include your name, card number, and card expiry date.

CREDIT CARDS

A credit card is a piece of plastic that can be used in place of money. In many countries, credit cards have a built-in computer chip containing information that can be read by a machine when the card is used. The credit card company pays for the goods, and you pay the credit card company a month or so later.

Find out more

PLASTICS
ROCKS AND MINERALS
TECHNOLOGY
TRADE AND INDUSTRY

MONGOL EMPIRE

IN THE LATE 1100s a masterful chieftain united a group of wandering tribes into a powerful army. He was called Genghis Khan; the tribes were the Mongols. All were toughened by a harsh life spent herding on the treeless plains of northeastern Asia. Determined to train the best army of his time, Genghis built up a formidable cavalry force. Using their traditional composite bows and new weapons such as gunpowder, they were invincible. In 1211, the Mongols invaded China, then swept through Asia. They moved at incredible speed, concentrating their forces at critical moments. All their military operations were planned to the smallest detail. Looting and burning as they came, they struck terror into the hearts of their enemies. In 1227, Genghis Khan died, leaving a huge empire to his four sons, who extended it through Asia Minor into Europe. However, the empire broke apart as rival khans (Mongol kings) battled for control.

GENGHIS KHAN
Temüjin (1162-1227) was the son of a tribal chief. His father was murdered when Temüjin was still a child, and when he grew up he defeated his enemies, united all other tribes under his control, and took the title Genghis Khan, "prince of all that lies between the oceans". He aimed to conquer the world.

Armour-piercing arrow

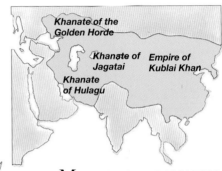

Khanate of the Golden Horde
Khanate of Jagatai
Empire of Kublai Khan
Khanate of Hulagu

MONGOL KHANATES
After Genghis's death, the Mongol Empire divided into four khanates, or states, with different rulers. Kublai, grandson of Genghis, ruled the eastern khanate. The smaller western empires, although briefly united in the 1300s by Tamerlane the Great, gradually disintegrated.

Cavalry controlled horses with their feet to leave their hands free for fighting.

Horses in battle gear

COMPOSITE BOW
Mongols made their deadly bows out of wood, horn, and sinew, which gave the bows incredible power. The Mongols were superb archers, able to string, aim, and fire at full gallop. They developed armour-piercing arrows, whistling arrows for signalling, and even arrows tipped with grenades.

Strung bow

Unstrung bow

MONGOL EMPIRE
1206 Temüjin unites all the tribes of Mongolia.
1219 Mongols invade Persia.
1223 Mongols invade Russia.
1237 Batu, grandson of Genghis Khan, invades north Russia.
1240 Batu invades Poland and Hungary.
1260 Mamelukes, Egyptian warriors, defeat Mongols.
1279 Kublai Khan defeats China.
1370 Tamerlane the Great conquers the western khanates.

YURTS
Tribes wandered the Mongolian steppes following their herds of sheep, goats, cattle, and horses. They lived in circular tents called yurts, which they took with them when they moved. The women drove wagons which held the yurts; the men hunted, looked after the herds, and traded for grain and metal. Mongols of today still live in yurts.

Find out more
ARMOUR
ASIA, HISTORY OF
EXPLORERS

MONKEYS AND APES

AMONG THE MOST INTELLIGENT creatures on Earth are the apes – chimpanzees, gorillas, gibbons, and orang-utans. They have large brains, long arms, fingers, and toes, and their bodies are covered in hair. In body shape and intelligence these creatures resemble humans. Apes and humans both belong to the larger group known as primates. Closely related to apes are monkeys, a larger group of animals that includes baboons, macaques, colubuses, and marmosets. Monkeys and apes have a similar body plan, although monkeys tend to be smaller. A pygmy marmoset weighs only 150 g (5 oz), whereas a huge male "silverback" gorilla weighs as much as 180 kg (400 lb). Both monkeys and apes have a rounded face, small ears, and large eyes which face forward. They use their front limbs like arms, and their hands can grasp strongly and manipulate delicately. Most monkeys have tails, which they use as a counterbalance as they swing through trees. In some monkeys the tail is strong and prehensile (grasping); apes, however, have no tails. Apes and monkeys feed on a variety of foods, including fruit, leaves, insects, and birds' eggs.

ORANG-UTAN

The richly coloured orang-utan is found in the forests of Borneo and Sumatra in southeast Asia. Orang-utans spend most of their time high up in the trees searching for fruit, shoots, leaves, and insects. They live alone, except where there is plenty of food.

Prehensile hand can grasp.

Arms are very long in relation to the body.

Shaggy coat of reddish-brown hair

GORILLA

Measuring up to 2 m (6 ft) in height, gorillas are the largest apes. Gorillas are slow, gentle creatures – unless disturbed – and they spend their time resting and eating leaves, stems, and shoots. Gorillas live in small family groups that travel slowly through the forest, eating some but not all of the food in one place before moving on to another area.

Today, orang-utans are in danger of extinction because their forest homes are being cleared for timber and farmland.

BREEDING
A gorilla group contains between five and 10 animals. There is one large male, several females, and their young of various ages. The young are born singly; a female gives birth about every four years.

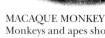

PRIMATES
All monkeys and apes belong to the mammal group called primates. Other primates include bush babies, pottos, tarsiers, and humans. Today, many primates, including gibbons and the other apes, are on the official list of endangered species.

MACAQUE MONKEY
Monkeys and apes show behaviour that we describe as "intelligent". These creatures communicate well, have good memories, and are able to solve problems. A famous example is the Japanese macaque monkey, which discovered that by washing its food in water it could get rid of the dirt and sand on it. Other members of the troop saw what the monkey was doing and copied it.

GIBBON

A gibbon's muscular arms and hands are so long that the knuckles touch the ground even when the gibbon stands upright. Gibbons live in family groups of a male, a female, and two to four young. There are 14 kinds of gibbon; the largest is the siamang, which weighs about 10 kg (22 lb). The siamang is so heavy that it cannot swing out to the tips of thin branches as other gibbons can.

The acrobatic gibbon swings through the trees of southeast Asia and rarely comes down to the ground.

Gibbons feed mainly on fruit and young leaves.

Young chimpanzees spend much of their time playing with objects and chasing each other. This helps prepare the chimp to find food and fight off enemies in adult life.

Most monkeys and apes depend on trees for shelter and food, particularly in the rain forests.

COMMUNICATION

Many monkeys communicate by sounds. The howler monkey of South America produces extremely loud howling noises using its specialized larynx (voice box). These sounds warn other howler troops to stay out of the group's territory. The leading male howler is usually the main shouter and can be heard nearly 3 km (2 miles) away.

CONSERVATION

The forests where monkeys and apes live are being cut down at a great speed. Newly planted trees are soon removed for timber, so they do not provide homes for the local wildlife. Dozens of different kinds of monkeys are at risk. Among them is the woolly spider monkey of Brazil. Some non-profit organizations have taken up their cause. Their three-point programme works through rescue and rehabilitation, conservation education, and research.

CHIMPANZEE

Chimpanzees are the animals which remind us most of ourselves – because of their facial expressions and the way they play games, make tools, and solve puzzles. Chimpanzees live in groups which sometimes fight with neighbouring groups. Their main foods are fruit, leaves, seeds, flowers, insects, and sometimes larger creatures such as monkeys and deer. Chimpanzees live deep in the forests and open grassland of Africa. Pygmy chimps or bonobos are found only in the thick forests of the Democratic Republic of Congo (Zaire).

BABOON

The African baboon can climb but usually walks or gallops on all fours. Baboons are easy to study because they live in open country, and scientists have learned much about their social life. Baboons live in troops. Each troop is based around senior females and their offspring. Growing males tend to live alone while they are maturing. When a male becomes an adult he joins a troop, but has to battle with other males to establish his rank. The troop protects itself against predators such as lions and against other baboon troops that stray into its territory.

Find out more

ANIMALS
ANIMAL SENSES
CONSERVATION
and endangered species
FOREST WILDLIFE
MAMMALS

MOON

Lava once flowed from the Moon's interior, following huge meteorite impacts more than 4,000 million years ago. The lava solidified into smooth-floored plains called seas, or maria.

Craters were formed by meteorite impacts. A few are a result of volcanic activity within the Moon.

OUR NEAREST NEIGHBOUR in space is the Moon. It orbits, or circles, the Earth keeping the same face pointed towards us. The Moon is a hostile place. It has no atmosphere to keep the temperature fairly even, as Earth does. Instead, temperatures range from a scorching 115°C (240°F) during the Moon's day to an icy -160°C (-260°F) at night. There is no water, so no plants or animals can live there. Great plains stretch over the Moon's surface, dotted with huge mountains and scarred by numerous craters. The Moon does not produce light of its own. We see the Moon because it acts like a huge mirror, reflecting light from the Sun. The Moon is a natural satellite – something that orbits around a planet or a star. There are many moons circling the other planets in the solar system.

BIRTH OF THE MOON
There have been many theories to explain the formation of the Moon. Scientists have suggested that the Moon may be a piece of the Earth that broke away millions of years ago. Today, however, most astronomers believe that the Moon was formed when an asteroid the size of Mars struck the Earth about 4.5 billion years ago.

The gravitational attraction of the Moon causes tides to rise and fall in the Earth's oceans.

1 New moon (moon invisible)

3 Half moon (first quarter)

5 Full moon

7 Half moon (last quarter)

2 Crescent moon

4 Gibbous moon (waxing)

6 Gibbous moon (waning)

8 Old moon

Moon seen from here

PHASES OF THE MOON
As the Moon orbits the Earth, different shapes, or phases, appear, depending on the amount of the sunlit side of the Moon that is visible from Earth.

LUNA 3
Until 1959, the far side of the Moon had never been seen. In October of that year, the Russian space probe *Luna 3* (right) sent back the first photographs of this part of the Moon.

OTHER MOONS
Our solar system contains more than 150 known moons. Nearly all circle the giant outer planets and are made of ice mixed with rock. The largest planet, Jupiter, has at least 63 moons, three of them larger than our own moon. One, Io (seen alongside Jupiter, left), is alive with active volcanoes. Another, Ganymede, is the largest satellite in the solar system. Some of Saturn's moons are very small and orbit in the outer sections of the planet's rings.

Armstrong's crew member, Edwin Aldrin, stands by the lunar module.

LUNAR LANDINGS
In 1966, the Russian *Luna 9* spacecraft made the first controlled landing on the Moon. It was only three years later, in July 1969, that American astronaut Neil Armstrong climbed down from the *Apollo 11* lunar module to become the first person on the Moon.

MOON FACTS

Distance from Earth	384,401 km (238,855 miles)
Diameter at equator	3,477.8 km (2,160.5 miles)
Time for each orbit	27 days, 7 hours, 43 minutes
Time between full moons	29 days, 12 hours, 43 minutes
Gravity at surface	1/6 of Earth's surface gravity
Brightness	1/425,000 brightness of Sun

Find out more
ASTRONOMY
EARTH
OCEANS AND SEAS
PLANETS
SPACE FLIGHT

WILLIAM MORRIS

THE 19TH-CENTURY CRAFTSMAN and thinker William Morris first trained as an architect, but became a painter, furniture maker, wallpaper and fabric designer, writer, lecturer, printer, poet, and political activist. Morris believed that everyday objects should be beautiful as well as useful, and that they should be made by craftspeople, not on a factory production line. He was also a socialist who believed that everybody had the right to art, education, and freedom in their lives. His interest in medieval art led him to associate with the Pre-Raphaelite Brotherhood, a group of young artists who wanted to return to the way people had painted before the Renaissance. Many people still find Morris's political ideas inspiring. A number of his designs for fabrics are still popular.

1834 Born in Walthamstow, England.

1853-56 Joins Pre-Raphaelite Brotherhood.

1861 Founds a company of fine-art workmen.

1869-70 Writes *The Earthly Paradise.*

1877 Founds the Society for the Protection of Ancient Buildings.

1891 Sets up the Kelmscott Press.

1896 Dies at Kelmscott in Oxfordshire.

KELMSCOTT PRESS
Morris set up the Kelmscott Press in 1891, at Hammersmith, London to print his own books. He designed three styles of type for them.

Morris's wife Jane Burden was the model for his only surviving oil painting, Queen Guenevere.

THE RED HOUSE
In 1859 architect Philip Webb (1831-1915) designed a house at Bexley Heath, Kent, for Morris and his new wife. It was built in red brick in an informal style, and furnished and decorated by Morris and his friends.

Wallpaper

Tapestry

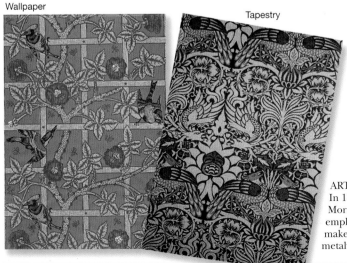

CRAFTSMAN AND SOCIALIST
Morris believed that the industrial revolution was taking away the dignity of people's labour. He formed a national group, the Socialist League, and lectured widely on the need for change. His views on art and handicraft went together with his thoughts about the nature of a good and just society.

ARTS AND CRAFTS
In 1861 Morris founded a company, Morris, Marshall, Faulkner & Co., that employed artist-craftsmen to design and make wallpaper, furniture, stained glass, metalwork, tapestries, and carpets.

Find out more
PAINTERS
PAINTING
RENAISSANCE

MOSSES, LIVERWORTS
AND FERNS

MISTY TROPICAL RAIN FORESTS and moist, shady woodlands shelter some of the simplest land plants. These are mosses and liverworts, also seen on logs, stone walls, and garden lawns. They are quite different to other plants. They have no true root systems, flowers, or seeds. Instead, mosses and liverworts have tiny rootlets that absorb only a small amount of water from the soil, and short-stemmed leaves that take in moisture from the air. There are 11 different types of non-flowering plants.

Ferns are also flowerless. They are an ancient group of plants that have grown on Earth for more than 300 million years. Unlike mosses and liverworts, ferns do have true roots, with tubes inside their stems that carry water to the leaves. The giant tree ferns are the largest of all ferns. They grow up to 20 m (65 ft) high and look like palm trees. The smallest ferns in tropical rain forests are tiny, with leaflike fronds less than 1 cm (0.5 in) long. Ferns grow in most kinds of soil, but not in hot desert sand.

Carpet of moss covers wet bark on log.

HORSETAILS
Horsetails are fern-like plants with no flowers. About 300 million years ago, forests of giant horsetails grew up to 46 m (150 ft) high. Their remains have turned into coal.

HOW MOSS REPRODUCES
The leafy moss plant has male and female organs. The fertilized spores grow in the brown spore-containing capsules, which are held above the leaves on long stalks.

FERN
A new fern frond gradually unfurls. When it is mature, brown dots called sori appear on the frond. These sori contain spores. The spores grow into tiny heart-shaped plants, which bear male and female organs.

Tip of frond uncurls.

Polypody fern fronds stay green all winter.

Sori are on the underside of fern frond.

Fern

Curled-up frond of polypody fern

MOISTURE-LOVING PLANTS
Mosses and liverworts grow beside streams and rivers because they need the moisture from the water. They do not have roots to absorb water from the soil and pass it to their leaves. Instead, their leaves take in moisture from the air.

Liverwort

Bracken spreads into a pasture, reducing the grazing area.

BRACKEN
Bracken is found on every continent except Antarctica. It has far-reaching roots and underground stems, and spreads quickly across grassland and woodland. Bracken is a nuisance to many farmers and gardeners because it is very difficult to remove once it has become established.

LIVERWORT
The liverwort grows close to the ground, from which it soaks up moisture. Some liverworts, mosses, and ferns grow on trees and other plants, which they cling to for support.

Liverworts take their name from their shape, which looks like the human liver.

BOG MOSS
Sphagnum moss is one of the few plants found in wet, marshy areas. It grows very well in swamps, forming wet, spongy hummocks. As the sphagnum dies, it rots slowly, and over many centuries turns into mossy peat below the surface.

Find out more
FOREST WILDLIFE
MARSH
and swamp wildlife
PLANTS
SOIL

MOUNTAINS

CONTINENTS COLLIDE and grind against one another, while hot, molten rock bubbles beneath the Earth's surface. These powerful forces thrust up mountains reaching as high as 8 km (5 miles). Many mountains are still growing, and those that formed long ago are slowly wearing away. Some mountains are volcanoes, made of layers of solidified lava which build up as the volcano erupts. There are mountains under the oceans and on other planets. The highest known mountain is on Mars; it is three times as high as Mount Everest.

The Earth has two vast mountain ranges. The Rocky Mountains and Andes run through North and South America; the mighty Himalayas, Alps, and Atlas Mountains stretch across Asia, Europe, and North Africa. These mountains are "young": they formed during the last 50 million years. Other ranges, such as the Urals in Russia, are much older and lower. The forces of erosion have worn them down since they were first formed more than 200 million years ago.

High on the mountaintop it is so cold that plants cannot grow. There is only snow and bare rock.

MOUNT EVEREST
The world's highest mountain is Mount Everest, on the border of China and Nepal. It rises to 8,850 m (29,035 ft). Above are Edmund Hillary of New Zealand (left) and Tenzing Norgay of Nepal who first climbed Everest in 1953.

MOUNTAIN CLIMBING
Mountain climbing requires special equipment, such as ropes to prevent falls, and crampons – steel spikes fixed to mountaineers' boots which grip ice.

Higher still, only plants that are adapted to the cold are able to grow.

Forests of pine trees grow higher up the mountain where it is colder.

AVALANCHE
Snow and ice can suddenly crash down a steep mountainside. This is called an avalanche, and it often occurs in spring as the snow melts.

MOUNTAIN ZONES
A high mountain has several zones, or regions, containing different kinds of plants. Forests cover the mountain's lower reaches. Further up is a zone of small, low-lying plants. Snow covers the summit, which is bare of plant life. Zones occur because the air becomes colder higher up the mountain.

Forests of broad-leaved trees and a wide range of other vegetation grow at the base of the mountain.

Squeezing action pushes up blocks of rock.

Formation of block mountains

Block wears away over many years to produce a mountain.

FAULTING AND FOLDING

As the continents move, they squeeze layers of rock. These movements produce huge cracks, or faults, and push up blocks of rock which form block mountains. The movements also make the Earth's surface buckle, forming fold mountains. Dome mountains appear when molten granite pushes the rock above it into a huge hump.

Formation of fold mountains

As layers of rock are squeezed, they form zigzag folds.

The rocks then crack and wear away at the top of the curve, forming jagged mountains.

EROSION
Ice, wind, and running water break up rock, slowly wearing it away over millions of years. This process of erosion carves out deep valleys and creates high peaks. Continuing erosion wears away the peaks, so that the mountains become lower and more rounded.

Find out more
CONTINENTS
GLACIERS AND ICECAPS
MOUNTAIN WILDLIFE
OCEANS AND SEAS
VOLCANOES

MOUNTAIN WILDLIFE

LAMMERGEIER
The lammergeier is one of the biggest vultures. It has a wingspan of about 3 m (10 ft) and soars over the high mountain peaks of Africa, Asia, and Europe. This bird of prey feeds mostly on carrion (bodies of dead animals).

THE MOUNTAIN RANGES of the world are home to all kinds of wildlife – from tiny beetles to huge bears. The lower slopes are often covered with lush vegetation and are rich in animal life. Higher up the mountain the temperature is lower, and there is less wildlife. Mammals living here have thick fur to survive the cold. In places too steep for most creatures to climb, sure-footed goats and chamois leap with ease over the rocks. Near the top of the mountain the wind is so strong that only powerful birds such as condors can fly. In some windy areas the insects have lost their wings during the course of evolution; wings would be useless to them. Spiders and wingless insects live higher up the mountain than any other creature. As you climb higher the temperature drops by 3.6°C (6.5°F) for every 300 m (1,000 ft) of height. Above about 2,400 m (8,000 ft) small shrubs grow, bent and twisted by the icy winds. Higher up still, only mosses and lichens grow, and at the very top there is permanent snow and ice.

CONSERVATION
Wildlife parks protect mountain animals such as the bobcat shown here. In the past people hunted the bobcat for its fur; today this cat is an endangered species.

This map shows the main mountain ranges of the world.

North America
Europe
Asia
Africa
South America
Australia

▮ Mountains

The mountain goat is a North American relative of the European chamois. Its body is more thickset and sturdy, and it is three times the weight of a chamois. The mountain goat moves slowly and deliberately through deep snow.

CHAMOIS
A rubbery hoof pad allows the chamois to grip stony surfaces with ease as it leaps nimbly among rocks in search of grasses, herbs, and flowers. Chamois live in groups of up to 30 females and young. The males live alone except in the breeding season.

MOUNTAIN PLANTS
High up where trees do not grow, alpine flowers bloom in the short summer. The word *alpine* means above the tree line. The leaves of most alpine flowers grow low and flat so they are protected from the bitter winds. These flowers are pollinated mainly by flies, butterflies, and other insects that have survived the winter as eggs or as adults under the snow.

The trumpet gentian is named for its deep trumpet of petals. It grows in stony places and in damp, short turf at heights of 3,000 m (10,000 ft), in the Alps, Pyrenees, and Apennines of Europe.

Today the edelweiss is a protected plant in many areas.

SPECTACLED BEAR
The only bear in South America is the spectacled bear, so-named because of the markings around its eyes. It lives in the Andes Mountains and is found in warm, moist forests and mountains at heights of 3,500 m (11,500 ft). Spectacled bears eat a wide range of foods, including leaves, fruits, insects, eggs, small deer, and other mammals.

The alpine longhorn beetle shown here suns itself on mountain flowers and feeds on their pollen.

ROCK HYRAX
The small, furry, stoutly built hyrax of Africa is the closest living relative of the elephant – the largest animal on land. Rock hyraxes live at heights of up to 4,000 m (13,300 ft) in rocky places such as Mount Kenya.

Hyraxes eat mainly grasses.

___ *Find out more* ___
ANIMALS
BEARS AND PANDAS
BIRDS
CONSERVATION
and endangered species
LIONS, TIGERS,
and other big cats
MOUNTAINS

MUHAMMAD

PROPHET OF ISLAM
Muslims believe that Angel Gabriel told Muhammad that he had been chosen by God to be a prophet, in the same way as Moses and Abraham before him.

DURING THE 600s, one man founded what was to become one of the world's great religions. His name was Muhammad, and the religion was Islam. Muhammad came from Mecca in southwestern Arabia (now Saudi Arabia), and was born into one of the city's Arab clans around 570 CE. Orphaned at an early age, he became a merchant and married Khadija, a wealthy widow, with whom he had three daughters. At the time, the Arab people worshipped many gods and prayed to idols and spirits. Muhammad came to believe that there was only one God, named Allah, and that he had been chosen to be Allah's prophet. Muhammad's family and friends were the first to share his beliefs, but his views angered the people of Mecca and he was forced to flee to Medina, a city north of Mecca. There he proclaimed the principles of Islam and won many converts. After a holy war, Muhammad led his followers to conquer Mecca in 630. Missionaries spread the message of Islam far and wide, and by the time of Muhammad's death in 632, Arabia was an Islamic state.

HEGIRA

People came to Mecca to worship and trade at the Kaaba, a huge shrine that contained hundreds of idols. Muhammad was persecuted when he spoke out against the worship of idols. In 622, he fled with a few of his followers to Medina. Their journey is called the Hegira (meaning "flight" or "migration"). Today, the Kaaba is a holy shrine for Muslims (followers of Islam). It is surrounded by a great mosque (Muslim prayer hall) and visited by thousands of pilgrims each year.

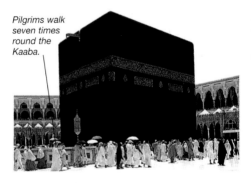

Pilgrims walk seven times round the Kaaba.

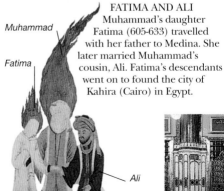

Muhammad

Fatima

Ali

FATIMA AND ALI
Muhammad's daughter Fatima (605-633) travelled with her father to Medina. She later married Muhammad's cousin, Ali. Fatima's descendants went on to found the city of Kahira (Cairo) in Egypt.

MUHAMMAD'S TEACHINGS
Muhammad did not claim to be divine. He believed that he was the last of the prophets and that he had received messages from God, which he had to pass onto others. He taught that there is only one God, that people should be obedient to God's will, and that all people were equal. He also preached against the selfishness of the rich, the unjust treatment of women, slaves, and poor people, and cruelty to animals. In 632, knowing that his life was coming to an end, he led a farewell pilgrimage to Mecca. There he delivered a famous sermon on the most important principles of Islam.

DEATH OF MUHAMMAD
After the farewell pilgrimage, Muhammad went back to Medina, but died within a few days of his return. His tomb lies in the Prophet's Mosque at Medina. After his death, his followers wrote down his teachings in the Qur'an (Koran), the holy book of Islam.

MOUNT HIRA
At age 40, Muhammad began to meditate in a cave on Mount Hira, north of Mecca. Here he had a vision in which the Angel Gabriel spoke the words of God to him and told him that he was to preach that people should believe in only one God – Allah. The teachings of Allah were revealed to Muhammad in a series of visions throughout his life.

MUHAMMAD

c. 570 CE Born in Mecca.

595 Marries Khadija, a wealthy widow.

610 Has a vision of the Angel Gabriel telling him to proclaim a new faith, Islam.

613 Begins preaching to the people of Mecca.

622 Leaves Mecca and travels to Medina.

624 Meccan army defeated at Battle of Badr by much smaller Muslim force.

630 Conquers Mecca.

632 Dies in Medina.

Find out more
ISLAM
RELIGIONS

MUSCLES AND MOVEMENT

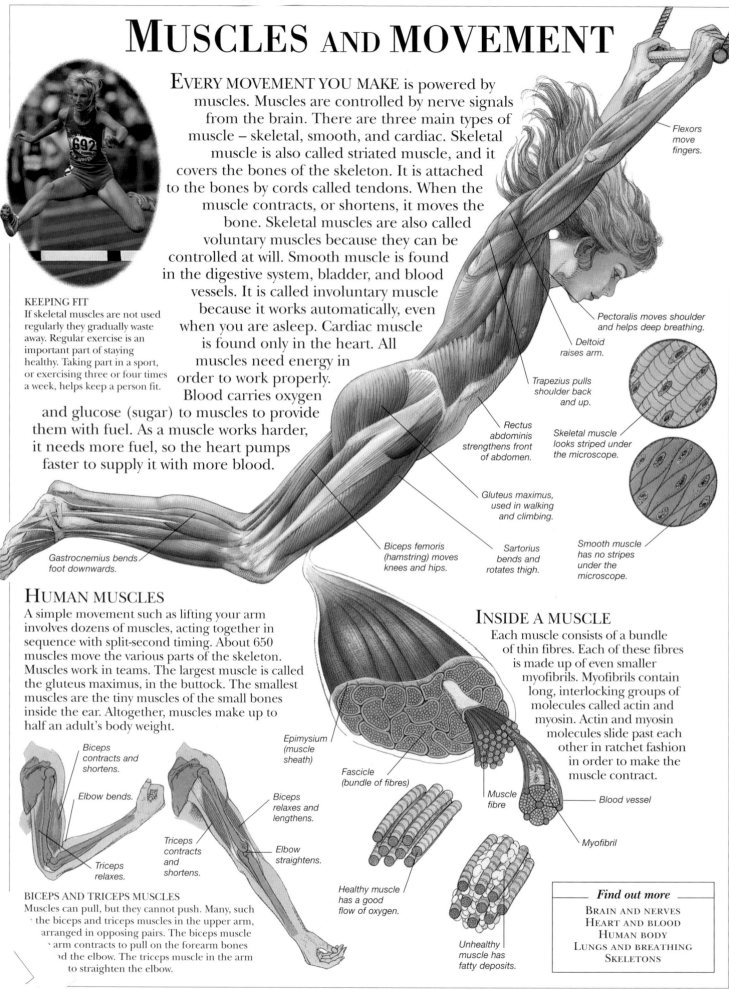

EVERY MOVEMENT YOU MAKE is powered by muscles. Muscles are controlled by nerve signals from the brain. There are three main types of muscle – skeletal, smooth, and cardiac. Skeletal muscle is also called striated muscle, and it covers the bones of the skeleton. It is attached to the bones by cords called tendons. When the muscle contracts, or shortens, it moves the bone. Skeletal muscles are also called voluntary muscles because they can be controlled at will. Smooth muscle is found in the digestive system, bladder, and blood vessels. It is called involuntary muscle because it works automatically, even when you are asleep. Cardiac muscle is found only in the heart. All muscles need energy in order to work properly. Blood carries oxygen and glucose (sugar) to muscles to provide them with fuel. As a muscle works harder, it needs more fuel, so the heart pumps faster to supply it with more blood.

KEEPING FIT
If skeletal muscles are not used regularly they gradually waste away. Regular exercise is an important part of staying healthy. Taking part in a sport, or exercising three or four times a week, helps keep a person fit.

Flexors move fingers.

Pectoralis moves shoulder and helps deep breathing.

Deltoid raises arm.

Trapezius pulls shoulder back and up.

Rectus abdominis strengthens front of abdomen.

Skeletal muscle looks striped under the microscope.

Gluteus maximus, used in walking and climbing.

Smooth muscle has no stripes under the microscope.

Gastrocnemius bends foot downwards.

Biceps femoris (hamstring) moves knees and hips.

Sartorius bends and rotates thigh.

HUMAN MUSCLES
A simple movement such as lifting your arm involves dozens of muscles, acting together in sequence with split-second timing. About 650 muscles move the various parts of the skeleton. Muscles work in teams. The largest muscle is called the gluteus maximus, in the buttock. The smallest muscles are the tiny muscles of the small bones inside the ear. Altogether, muscles make up to half an adult's body weight.

Biceps contracts and shortens.

Elbow bends.

Triceps relaxes.

Triceps contracts and shortens.

Biceps relaxes and lengthens.

Elbow straightens.

BICEPS AND TRICEPS MUSCLES
Muscles can pull, but they cannot push. Many, such the biceps and triceps muscles in the upper arm, arranged in opposing pairs. The biceps muscle arm contracts to pull on the forearm bones d the elbow. The triceps muscle in the arm to straighten the elbow.

INSIDE A MUSCLE
Each muscle consists of a bundle of thin fibres. Each of these fibres is made up of even smaller myofibrils. Myofibrils contain long, interlocking groups of molecules called actin and myosin. Actin and myosin molecules slide past each other in ratchet fashion in order to make the muscle contract.

Epimysium (muscle sheath)

Fascicle (bundle of fibres)

Muscle fibre

Blood vessel

Myofibril

Healthy muscle has a good flow of oxygen.

Unhealthy muscle has fatty deposits.

Find out more

BRAIN AND NERVES
HEART AND BLOOD
HUMAN BODY
LUNGS AND BREATHING
SKELETONS

MUSHROOMS
TOADSTOOLS, AND OTHER FUNGI

BRIGHTLY COLOURED TOADSTOOLS, delicate mushrooms, and the furry green mould on a rotting piece of bread all belong to a unique group of organisms called fungi. Fungi are neither plants nor animals. They are the great decomposers of the natural world. Fungi feed by releasing chemicals called enzymes which rot away whatever they are feeding on. The dissolved nutrients and minerals are absorbed and recycled by the fungi. Many kinds of fungi grow in damp woodlands and lush, grassy meadows, especially during autumn. There is no scientific difference between mushrooms and toadstools, but toadstools are often more colourful, and some are extremely poisonous. The part of a mushroom that we eat is called the cap. It contains spores – minute cells which grow into new mushrooms when they are released from the cap. Some harmful fungi cause diseases on plants and ringworm in humans. Yeast is a fungus used to make bread dough rise. Another fungus is used to make the antibiotic drug penicillin.

Champignon mushrooms grow in a ring in meadows and in gardens. Many people used to believe these were magic fairy rings.

MOULD
The decaying parts of plants and animals are rotted away by pinmould, which grows on damp bread, and is the blue mould growing on this peach.

BEEFSTEAK FUNGUS
This fungus grows on trees. It is called the beefsteak bracket because it looks like a piece of undercooked steak.

EDIBLE FUNGI
Many mushrooms and other fungi are edible; some are not only delicious but also are a good source of minerals and fibre. Cultivated mushrooms are farmed in dark, damp sheds on beds of peat. Collecting wild fungi to eat can be very dangerous. Some deadly poisonous fungi look just like edible mushrooms.

Ring where rim of cap was attached to stalk

Cap

Gills inside cap

Stalk

Young cap

Spores are released from between the gills of mature caps.

OYSTER MUSHROOM
The oyster mushroom is common on beech trees; its cap looks like the shell of an oyster. Oyster mushrooms are tasty and keep well when they are dried.

DUTCH ELM DISEASE
Dead and dying elm trees are a familiar sight in Europe and North America. A deadly fungus carried on the bodies of elm bark beetles, which live on elm trees, has killed millions of trees. The fungus grows through the bark, blocking the water-carrying tubes inside the trunk.

FIELD MUSHROOM
During the autumn, field mushrooms spring up overnight in damp pastures and meadows.

CHANTERELLE
The funnel-shaped cap of the chanterelle mushroom is yellow and smells like an apricot. It is found in oak, beech, and birch woods. It grows slowly, preserves well, and is much prized by chefs.

GIANT PUFFBALL
When the giant puffball ripens, its top breaks open, and clouds of tiny spores puff out with the slightest breeze or the smallest splattering of rain.

MOREL
Prized for its flavour, the morel's cap is crisscrossed with patterned ridgework.

POISONOUS FUNGI
People die every year from eating poisonous fungi. Some of these are brightly coloured toadstools which are easily recognized. Others, such as the destroying angel, look harmless, but cause death rapidly if they are eaten.

Death cup

The bright red fly agaric toadstool is poisonous. Small amounts can cause unconsciousness.

The harmless-looking death cup is one of the most poisonous fungi. Less than 28 g (1 oz) can kill a person in only a few hours.

Fly agaric

Find out more
DRUGS
FOOD
FOREST WILDLIFE
PLANTS
SOIL

MUSIC

MUSICIANS MAKE MUSIC by carefully organizing sounds into a regular, pleasing pattern to entertain listeners. Notes are the starting point for all music. A note is a regular vibration of the air which musicians create with musical instruments or with their voices. The more rapid the vibration, the higher the pitch of the note – the higher it sounds to a listener. Certain notes sound better together than others. Most music uses these notes, organized into a scale. A scale is a series of notes that increase gradually and regularly in pitch. Musicians usually play or sing notes at fixed time intervals. We call this regular pattern of notes the rhythm or meter of the music. A melody or tune is a combination of the rhythm, the notes the musician plays, and their order. The melody is the overall pattern that we hear and remember – and whistle or hum days or perhaps weeks later.

Ancient musicians of Ur in Sumer (now southern Iraq) played lyres, flutes, pipes, and percussion instruments.

THE FIRST MUSIC
The chanting of prehistoric people was probably the earliest music. The oldest surviving musical instruments are mammoth bones from northern Eurasia; musicians may have banged them together or blown them to make notes about 35,000 years ago.

The key signature shows which key the music is in. A key is a series of related notes.

A curved tie line joining two identical notes means they must be played as one unbroken note.

The clef shows the pitch at which to play the music. This is the treble clef.

The shape of each note tells the musician how long to play it. This is a quarter note.

The speed of the music is often written in Italian. Allegro means "quickly".

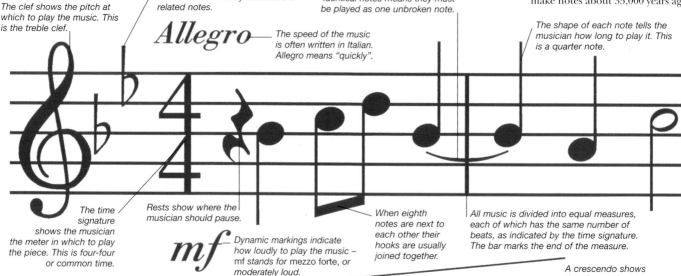

The time signature shows the musician the meter in which to play the piece. This is four-four or common time.

Rests show where the musician should pause.

When eighth notes are next to each other their hooks are usually joined together.

All music is divided into equal measures, each of which has the same number of beats, as indicated by the time signature. The bar marks the end of the measure.

Dynamic markings indicate how loudly to play the music – mf stands for mezzo forte, or moderately loud.

A crescendo shows that the music gets gradually louder.

The position of the notes on or between the five horizontal staff lines indicates their pitch. Musicians use letters of the alphabet as names for each of the eight notes in an octave.

c d e f g a b c

NOTATION

Composers need a way of writing down the music they create. Musical notation is a code of symbols and signs that records every aspect of the music. In the 9th century, monks began to use musical notation to help them remember the tunes of holy songs. The system in use today had developed fully by about 1200 CE.

JAZZ

The essential ingredient of jazz is improvisation – the musicians make up some or all of the music as they play it. Black musicians created the very first jazz music at the beginning of the 20th century in New Orleans, U.S.A. Jazz is a mixture of blues, religious gospel, and European music.

Charlie "Bird" Parker (1920-55) popularized a new form of jazz, called "bebop", in the 1940s.

CHAMBER MUSIC
Classical – rather than pop – music for small groups of instruments is called chamber music. Chamber music was so called because it began as music for enjoyment in chambers, or rooms, in the home. Composers wrote different types of music for theatres or churches. Today, performances of chamber music often take place in concert halls.

TRADITIONAL MUSIC

In much traditional music the composer is unknown, and the music itself may not be written down. Performers are often non-professional musicians who learn the tunes "by ear" – by listening to each other play – so they do not need a written score. Musicians sometimes make small changes as they play, so there are often many slightly different versions of the same traditional melody.

Cheerleaders keep time with marching music and encourage spectators to join in songs and chants.

Buddhist monks blow large horns as part of their religious ceremonies.

RELIGIOUS MUSIC

Music has always played an important part in religion. In religious ceremonies, music inspires people to think about their God or gods. It accompanies religious songs and sacred dances. Composers also choose religious themes for music that is not part of worship: *Messiah* by the German composer George Frideric Handel (1685-1759) sets part of the Bible to music.

MILITARY AND MARCHING MUSIC

Music with a strong, steady beat helps soldiers march in step. Today, military bands are not the only ones to play marching music. American high schools and football teams often have their own marching bands, which entertain the crowds at halftime and on special occasions.

ROCK MUSIC

During the 1950s a new form of popular music was heard for the first time. Rock and roll songs had a powerful beat and words that young people could relate to. This form of music began in the United States, where it grew from traditional rhythm and blues played by black musicians. Over the years it has influenced many other musical forms.

American-born singer Elvis Presley (1935-77) sold millions of rock and roll records and starred in 33 movies.

CLASSICAL MUSIC

Classical music has become increasingly popular in recent years, partly thanks to the efforts of young musicians such as violinist Vanessa Mae. Mae started writing her own music at age nine, and by age 18 had made several records and performed in classical concerts all over the world. She has also mixed classical with modern by combining the sounds of acoustic and electric violins.

Find out more
COMPOSERS
FILMS
MUSICAL INSTRUMENTS
SOUND
THEATRE

MUSICAL INSTRUMENTS

THE POUNDING BEAT of an electric guitar might seem far removed from the delicate trill of a classical violin, yet these two instruments make their different sounds in a similar way. Both use a stretched string to create the vibrations we hear as music. The guitar and the violin evolved in a similar manner, but they actually belong to different families of musical instruments. String instruments such as the violin make their notes when the musician plucks the strings or draws a stretched bow – a bundle of horsehair – across them. Electric instruments, such as the electric guitar, produce weak vibrations that must be amplified for the audience to hear the music. There are five other groups: woodwind, percussion, brass, keyboard, and electronic. This short list includes a huge variety: some instruments, such as the hollow wooden flute, are very simple; others, such as the synthesizer, are highly complex.

CONCH HORNS
Conch sea shells made fine trumpets in ancient times – as they still do in modern Peru.

STRING INSTRUMENTS
Vibrating strings stretched across these instruments make the musical note: the finer the string and the shorter its length, the higher the note. The size of the instrument also affects its sound. The small violin, for example, produces higher sounds than the large double bass. Musicians pluck the strings of guitars, harps, and lutes, and usually use a bow to play the violin, viola, cello, and double bass.

Playing the violin

CELLO
The four cello strings make a rich, mellow sound.

VIOLIN
To play the violin the musician holds it under the chin.

WOODWIND INSTRUMENTS
Blowing into a woodwind instrument makes the air inside vibrate; this produces the musical notes. Covering the holes in the tube with fingers or keys changes the length of the vibrating air, producing different notes. The instruments with the shortest tubes, such as the piccolo, make the highest notes. Other woodwind instruments are the bassoon, English horn, saxophone, clarinet, oboe, and flute.

FLUTE
To play a side-blown flute such as this one, you blow across the tube.

Upper joint

Keys

Body joint

Keys

Head joint

Lip plate

Blowhole

Bell joint

Reed

OBOE
The mouthpiece of an oboe is a double reed (a piece of thin wood). The instrument makes a clear, sad sound.

Tip

Reed

OBOE REED
Most professional oboe players make their own reeds by binding two pieces of split cane to a tube called a staple.

Staple

A flautist playing a side-blown concert flute

Playing the oboe

A wood frame pulls horsehair tight across the bow. Sliding the bow across the strings makes them vibrate.

BRASS

Some of the most exciting sounds in music come from brass instruments. This group includes the French horn, trumpet, bugle, cornet, trombone, and tuba. The instruments are long tubes of brass or other metal curved around for easier handling. Sounds produced by the musician's lips on the mouthpiece vibrate down the tube. Pressing the valves opens more of the tube, making the pitch of the note lower. The trumpet has a long history. When the Egyptians buried King Tutankhamun more than 3,000 years ago, they placed a trumpet in his tomb.

Playing the horn

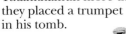

THE CORNET

Musicians in military and brass bands often play the cornet, which is descended from the horns that were blown to announce the arrival of a mailcoach. The cornet is one of the smallest brass instruments, with a tube about 1.5 m (4.5 ft) long.

Cornet player

FRENCH HORN

Uncurled, this horn is 5 m (16 ft) long. It developed from an 18th-century hunting horn and makes a rich, warm sound. The Austrian composer Wolfgang Amadeus Mozart created four pieces of music for the French horn.

KEYBOARDS

Hammers strike strings in the piano when the pianist presses a key. Pedals keep the note sounding when the key is released.

PERCUSSION

Bells, gongs, and drums are percussion instruments and there are many more, because all over the world people find different objects, such as beads and seeds, that make a noise when beaten or shaken. Some percussion instruments, such as the xylophone and timpani, are tuned to play definite notes.

SNARE DRUM

The wire spring on the bottom skin of the snare drum vibrates when the player strikes the top skin.

Bass strings

Treble strings

Tuning pins

Sounding board

Iron frame

Pedals

Keyboard

Dampers

Hammers

TRADITIONAL INSTRUMENTS

Musicians in symphony orchestras play only a few of the world's vast range of musical instruments. Many more are used in the traditional or folk music of individual countries. Some of these instruments developed unique shapes in different parts of the world, as musicians explored the music-making potential of local materials. However, some are remarkably similar: the bagpipes are played in Europe, Asia, and Africa.

A flute player from Thailand

ELECTRONIC INSTRUMENTS

These instruments can produce an exciting array of sounds, by either simulating existing instruments or synthesizing completely new sounds. The musician can feed sounds into the memory of the instrument and then play them back together to simulate a whole orchestra.

Find out more

COMPOSERS
FILM
MUSIC
SOUND

MYTHS AND LEGENDS

BEFORE THERE WERE ANY BOOKS, storytelling was an important way of passing on knowledge and beliefs from one generation to the next. Often, the stories took the form of myths which explained mysteries of nature, such as the origins of thunder. Ancient peoples told stories about gods and goddesses, and about human heroes with special powers. These myths became part of art and literature. Some legends may have had a basis on real people and events. To make a better tale, parents exaggerated the details as they repeated the legends to their children. Every country has its own legends. Paul Bunyan, the hero of stories told by North American lumberjacks, supposedly carved out the Grand Canyon by dragging his pick behind him. Sometimes, legendary monsters were created, such as the werewolf which appears in stories from many cultures.

THE TROJAN HORSE LEGEND
Greek soldiers conquered the besieged city of Troy by hiding in a huge wooden horse. When the Trojans took the horse inside the city walls, the Greeks emerged and conquered Troy.

SUN GODS

The same myths can be found in widely different cultures thousands of kilometres apart. This is because natural things such as the rain, the sea, and the moon are common to everyone. Many peoples worshipped sun gods: Surya in India and Apollo in Ancient Greece were both believed to ride across the sky in chariots of flame.

The Indian sun god, Surya – as painted on a doorway in Jaipur, India

The Egyptian sun god, Ra

WILLIAM TELL
A famous Swiss legend describes how William Tell insulted his country's hated Austrian rulers. His punishment was to shoot an apple balanced on his son's head. He succeeded, and later led a revolt against Austrian rule.

CREATION MYTHS

Most peoples used myths to explain how the world may have begun. This Native American myth was told by members of the Kwakiutl tribe.

A raven, flying over water, could find nowhere to land. He decided to create the world by dropping small pebbles to make islands.

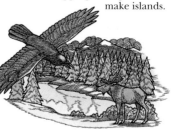

Then he created trees and grass. Beasts lived in the forest, birds flew in the air above, and the sea was filled with fish.

After many failed attempts, the raven succeeded in making the first man and woman out of clay and wood. At last, his world was complete.

GODS AND GODDESSES

The ancient Greeks worshipped many gods and goddesses. The goddess Athena took part in battles and loved bravery. Athens, the capital of Greece, is named after her. Quetzalcoatl appears in Mexican mythology as one of the greatest Aztec gods. As god of air, Quetzalcoatl created the winds that blew away the rain.

Athena, the Greek goddess of bravery

Quetzalcoatl, the Mexican god of air

___ *Find out more* ___
GREECE, ANCIENT
LITERATURE
RELIGIONS

NAPOLEON BONAPARTE

15 August 1769 Born on the island of Corsica.

1779-85 Military school

1799 Becomes ruler of France.

1804 Crowned Emperor.

1812 Defeated in Russia.

1814 Exiled to island of Elba in the Mediterranean.

1815 Returns to France; defeated at Waterloo.

5 May 1821 Dies in exile on the island of St. Helena.

IN A LAVISH CEREMONY IN 1804, Napoleon Bonaparte crowned himself Emperor of the French. He was an unlikely figure to lead his country, and spoke French with a thick Corsican accent. Yet he was one of the most brilliant military leaders in history. Napoleon first caught the public eye in 1793, when he commanded an attack against the British fleet occupying the French port of Toulon. In 1795 he crushed a revolt in Paris and soon led the French armies to victory in Italy. By 1799, Napoleon was strong enough to take power with the help of the army. He made himself First Consul and restored the power of the French government after the chaos left by the French Revolution. He introduced many social reforms, laying the foundations of the French legal, educational, and financial systems. Napoleon was a military genius who went on to control Europe from the English Channel to the Russian border. But he suffered a humiliating defeat in Russia, and when the British and Prussians beat him at the Battle of Waterloo in 1815, Napoleon was sent out of France into exile on a British island in the South Atlantic. He died six years later.

NAPOLEONIC EMPIRE

At the height of his power in 1812, Napoleon ruled Europe from the Baltic to the south of Rome, and his relations ruled Spain, Italy, and parts of Germany. The rest of Germany, Switzerland, and Poland were also under French control, and Denmark, Austria, and Prussia were allies. Only Portugal, Britain, Sweden, and Russia were independent.

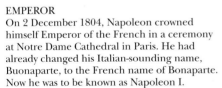

EMPEROR
On 2 December 1804, Napoleon crowned himself Emperor of the French in a ceremony at Notre Dame Cathedral in Paris. He had already changed his Italian-sounding name, Buonaparte, to the French name of Bonaparte. Now he was to be known as Napoleon I.

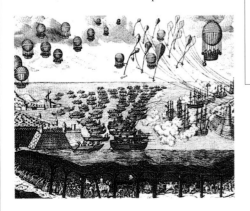

1812 AND THE RETREAT FROM MOSCOW

Napoleon invaded Russia in June 1812 with a force of more than 500,000 men. The Russians retreated, drawing the French army deeper into the country. Napoleon captured the capital, Moscow, but was forced to retreat because he could not supply his army. The harsh Russian winter killed many troops as they returned to France.

INVASION OF ENGLAND
In 1805 Napoleon assembled an army of 140,000 soldiers by the English Channel and drew up plans to invade England which he called "a nation of shopkeepers". These plans included crossing the Channel by ship and balloon, and digging a tunnel under the sea. The invasion was cancelled when the British admiral Nelson defeated the French fleet at the Battle of Trafalgar.

Find out more
EUROPE, HISTORY OF
FRANCE
FRENCH REVOLUTION

NATIONAL PARKS

THE NATIONAL PARKS contain some of the most stunning landscapes in England, Scotland, and Wales. National parks are protected zones, specially set up by an Act of Parliament of 1949, to conserve and protect areas of natural beauty. Much of the land in national parks is privately owned, but the act says that the public must be able to visit and enjoy them. Each park has a staff of wardens, who work with farmers and residents to preserve the area. Northern Ireland does not have national parks, but it has scenic conservation areas. There are eight national parks in England, three in Wales, and two in Scotland.

WILDLIFE
Animals, birds, and flowers, sometimes rare varieties, flourish in the national parks because the parks and their wildlife are strictly protected.

LEISURE IN THE PARKS
The national parks are like a massive playground for the people of Britain. Walkers and climbers, birdwatchers and sightseers make around 100 million visits to the national parks each year. Most come for just a day, and picnic sites are popular. Park rangers and volunteers maintain the national parks, and provide information for the millions of visitors.

Walkers in
Exmoor National Park

OUTSTANDING NATURAL BEAUTY

Some of the most beautiful countryside in Britain is inside the national parks. The wilderness of Dartmoor, the peaks of Snowdonia, and the slopes of the Lake District are all within national parks. To protect the appearance of the parks, strict rules control what can be built within their boundaries. Development is limited, and must not spoil views or be out of place.

LOCATION OF PARKS
Ten national parks were set up under the 1949 Act. The first four were created in 1951, and the others before the end of the 1950s. The Broads were not included then, but are today considered to be a national park. Three new national parks have been created in recent years: Loch Lomond and the Trossachs in 2002, the Cairngorms in 2003, and the New Forest in 2005. The South Downs is planned to become a national park in 2011.

Young people watch a warden build a dead hedge fence.

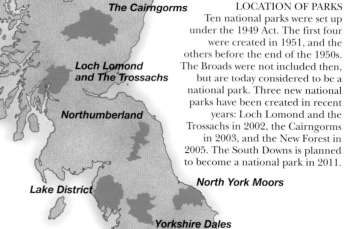

The Cairngorms

Loch Lomond and The Trossachs

Northumberland

Lake District

North York Moors

Yorkshire Dales

Peak District

Snowdonia

Norfolk Broads

Pembrokeshire Coast

Brecon Beacons

Exmoor

South Downs

New Forest

Dartmoor

CONSERVATION
An important aim of the national parks is to conserve the landscape, and maintain it, particularly given the numbers of visitors. Staff use environmentally friendly materials and, sometimes, traditional craft-based techniques to carry out repairs, such as mending fencing and building dry-stone walls.

> *Find out more*
> ENGLAND
> SCOTLAND
> WALES

NATIVE AMERICANS

THE FIRST PEOPLE to live in North America arrived from Asia more than 20,000 years ago. They wandered over the Bering Strait, which was a land bridge at the time and now separates Asia and North America, following animals they were hunting. Gradually these early people settled into different tribes. Over the centuries the tribes developed organized societies. During the 1500s, Europeans arrived in North America for the first time. They thought they were in the "Indies", or Asia, so they called the native Americans "Indians", a misleading name. The Europeans wanted land and threatened the existence of native North Americans. The natives fought many wars with the new settlers. During the 1800s, the tribes resisted when the United States government tried to make them leave their homelands. After a bitter struggle the native Americans were moved onto reservations – areas of land set aside for them – where many still live today.

Smoke flap open for ventilation

Straight poles are bound together at the top to form a cone shape.

Bison hide was used to make the tepee cover.

WOMEN
Women played an important part in the life of a tribe. They provided the food, made the clothes, and raised the children. The women of the Hopi Indians of the Southwest also owned the houses and organized the village.

Lodge pins made from bone held the hides together.

Paintings that told a story decorated the hides.

Door flap

TEPEES
The Sioux and other tribes on the Great Plains lived in tepees. Tepees were made of bison hides stretched over a wooden frame and were easy to put up. Flaps at the top of the tepee could be opened to allow smoke from the fire to escape.

A fire was lit inside the tepee for cooking and warmth.

GERONIMO
One of the most successful native chiefs in leading resistance to the "white man" was Geronimo (1829-1909), of the Chiricahua Apache Indians. Geronimo led raids across the southwestern states and into Mexico. In 1886, he was captured and exiled to Florida. Later he was released and became a national celebrity.

SIGN LANGUAGE
Each tribe of the natives spoke its own language. But people from different tribes were able to communicate with each other using a special sign language they all understood.

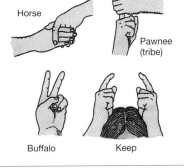

Horse

Pawnee (tribe)

Buffalo

Keep

TRIBES
The native peoples of North America belonged to numerous tribes. Most of them hunted, fished, and farmed. Among the best known tribes are the Cheyenne, Comanche, and Sioux, who lived on the Great Plains; the Apache, Navajo, and Pueblo, who lived in the Southwest; and the Iroquois, Huron, and Cherokee, who lived in the East.

SIOUX

The Sioux lived on the Great Plains. They hunted bison on horseback, using the skins for clothing and tepees, the meat for food, and the bones and horns for tools. The Sioux were noted for their bravery and fighting skills, and fought a long series of battles with European settlers and gold miners who took over their territory in the 1880s. In 1876, the Sioux defeated the US cavalry at the now famous Battle of the Little Bighorn in Montana. Eventually the Sioux were driven onto reservations.

PUEBLOS

The Pueblos were a peaceful tribe that lived in the southwest. They farmed vegetables for food and were skilled craftsworkers, weaving brightly-coloured cloth from home-spun cotton and making pots. Their multi-storeyed houses were built of stone or adobe (sun-dried clay bricks) and were occupied by several families. Today, many Pueblos live on reservations in Arizona and New Mexico.

CANOES

Northern tribes who lived by rivers and lakes, such as the Penobscot and Malecite, built canoes from the bark of birch trees. These strong, fast canoes were light enough to be carried overland when they could not be paddled.

Bark hull   *Paddles*

WEAPONS

Natives used bows and arrows, knives, and clubs as weapons. Many also carried tomahawks. During the 16th century, they got rifles from European traders.

Bow made of wood

Quiver used for holding arrows

Bow case holds the bow when not in use.

Tomahawks were axes with stone or iron heads. It was the Europeans who first made a combined axe blade and tobacco pipe.

CRAFTSWORK

Many natives were skilled craftsworkers. They produced beautifully decorated clothes and head-dresses. This pair of men's moccasins, from the Blackfeet tribe of western Canada, are made of stitched leather decorated with leather thongs and embroidered with coloured beads.

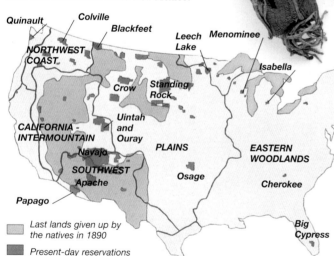

MODERN RESERVATIONS

The 1.5 million natives in the United States live on reservations that they govern themselves. The Navajo reservation, for example, covers over 6 million hectares in Arizona, New Mexico, and Utah. Recently, several tribes, such as the Pacific Northwest Coast Indians, have protested successfully and regained lost land.

Quinault **Colville**
Blackfeet
NORTHWEST COAST
Leech Lake **Menominee**
Isabella
Crow **Standing Rock**
Uintah and Ouray
CALIFORNIA - INTERMOUNTAIN
Navajo **PLAINS**
SOUTHWEST **EASTERN WOODLANDS**
Apache **Osage**
Papago **Cherokee**
Big Cypress

☐ Last lands given up by the natives in 1890
■ Present-day reservations

TRIBAL LANDS

Before the Europeans arrived, the natives occupied most of what later became the United States. The tribes were roughly grouped into six geographical regions. European settlement gradually forced the natives to the west and southwest, so that by 1890 they were living on a few scattered reservations.

Find out more

AZTECS
CANADA, HISTORY OF
INCAS
NORTH AMERICA
UNITED STATES OF AMERICA
UNITED STATES, HISTORY OF

NAVIGATION

EVEN IN A CITY with signs and street names to help you, it is easy to get lost. But imagine you were out in the open country or sailing in a boat without a map. How would you find your way? The earliest sailors faced this problem as they made their voyages of discovery. The answer was to watch the Sun by day and the stars by night. Because the Sun always rises in the east and sets in the west, sailors could work out which direction they were travelling in. The position of stars in the sky also gave them their direction: Polaris, the North Star, for instance, is almost in line with the Earth's North Pole. Navigation is the process of working out where you are and in what direction you are travelling. This can be on land, at sea, or in the air. Today, navigators have many aids to help them find their way. There are detailed maps of almost every part of the world, and electronic systems which use radar and satellites can fix the position of an aircraft or ship to within a few metres. Such advances in navigation make even the longest journey easy and safe.

MAP AND COMPASS
Marks on a map show paths, hills, and other features. A magnetic compass shows which way to point a map so that it represents the landscape. The Chinese first used magnetic compasses about 1,000 years ago; about 2300 BCE, the first map was drawn in Babylon.

NAVIGATION SYSTEMS

Today, ships and aircraft routinely travel around the world without any danger of becoming lost. They are equipped with electronic systems that use radio beacons on land and navigation satellites in space. These systems calculate the location of a ship or aircraft and the direction in which it is travelling with great precision.

SEXTANT
For more than 250 years, navigators have used a device called a sextant. A sextant gives a measurement of the angle between two objects, such as the horizon and the Sun. From this angle, it is possible to work out the latitude of a ship or aircraft.

Radar warns a navigator of nearby objects such as other boats or aircraft. A radar scanner sends out a beam of radio waves as it rotates, and receives the echoes bouncing back from any object within range.

For safety, a boat or aircraft travelling at night carries a red light on the port side (left) and a green light on the starboard side (right). This tells others the direction it is travelling in.

Boats and aeroplanes use signals beamed from navigation satellites, such as those of the Global Positioning System (GPS), to guide them anywhere in the world.

A radio receiver on board a boat compares the times that signals arrive from land-based radio beacons and uses this information to calculate the boat's position. This system is called radio direction finding.

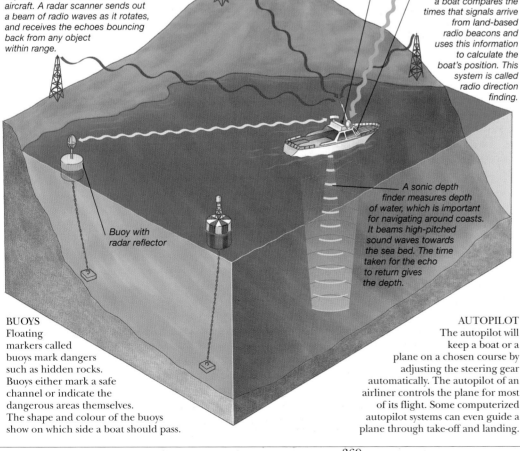

Buoy with radar reflector

A sonic depth finder measures depth of water, which is important for navigating around coasts. It beams high-pitched sound waves towards the sea bed. The time taken for the echo to return gives the depth.

LIGHTHOUSE
Coastal waters can be dangerous because of rocks or tides. Lighthouses send out a bright beam of light to warn ships. The interval at which the light flashes identifies the lighthouse and so helps navigators find their position.

BUOYS
Floating markers called buoys mark dangers such as hidden rocks. Buoys either mark a safe channel or indicate the dangerous areas themselves. The shape and colour of the buoys show on which side a boat should pass.

AUTOPILOT
The autopilot will keep a boat or a plane on a chosen course by adjusting the steering gear automatically. The autopilot of an airliner controls the plane for most of its flight. Some computerized autopilot systems can even guide a plane through take-off and landing.

Find out more
AIRCRAFT
MAGNETISM
OCEANS AND SEAS
PORTS AND WATERWAYS
SATELLITES
SHIPS AND BOATS

NESTS AND BURROWS

MOST ANIMALS need shelter and a place to bring up their young. A nest in a tree or a burrow underground protects an animal against predators and extremes of temperature. Many creatures, including birds and squirrels, build nests. Some creatures weave complicated nests. The harvest mouse makes a ball-shaped nest among corn stalks, where it rests and sleeps. Other animals, including birds, build a nest only during the breeding season, in which they lay eggs or give birth to live young. They line the nest with moss, grass, fur, or feathers to keep it warm and dry. Rabbits and foxes dig burrows, or tunnels, in the ground; a desert tortoise digs a burrow in which to hide from the midday sun. Some burrows are shallow; others, such as rabbit warrens, are deep, with escape routes, dead ends, and a separate burrow for the breeding nest.

Nesting boxes and dovecotes encourage many birds to breed in the same place each year.

Natural building materials from the surrounding area, such as lichens, help camouflage the nest.

Nest has a soft, thick lining of moss, hair, and feathers to keep eggs warm.

Wagtail weaves twigs and stems together to strengthen the nest.

NESTS
Many birds spend weeks making a nest in a sheltered place. Each kind of bird has its favourite materials, such as twigs, grass, or fur. Each also chooses a particular place to make the nest, such as a tree or a spot on the ground. A pied wagtail, for example, often builds its nest around farm buildings and uses twigs, straw, leaves, and moss, with a lining of hair and feathers. A grey wagtail builds its nest beside fast-flowing water and uses grasses and moss, with a lining of hair.

Flamingo nests are cone-shaped and made of mud.

FLAMINGO
Many animals, such as these African flamingos, nest in large groups called colonies. When a predator approaches, flamingos make such a noise that few predators dare to enter the colony. In a flamingo colony there is safety in numbers.

TRAP-DOOR SPIDER
The trap-door spider digs a small burrow in loose soil and hides in it. Using silk that it produces from its body, the spider glues particles of soil together to make a neatly fitting, well-disguised door. As an insect or other prey passes by, the spider flips open the door and grabs the victim.

Young platypuses stay in the breeding nest in a burrow underground and suckle milk from their mother for up to four months.

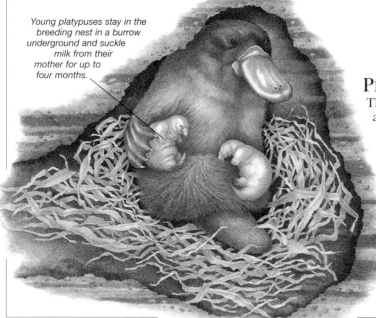

PLATYPUS BURROW
The Australian platypus digs a complex breeding burrow up to 20 m (66 ft) long in the riverbank. Here, the female lays eggs and raises the young when they hatch. Each time the platypus enters or leaves the burrow to feed, it digs its way out and rebuilds the series of doors made of mud along the tunnel to protect its young from intruders.

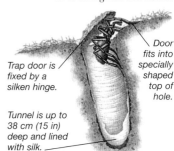

Trap door is fixed by a silken hinge.

Door fits into specially shaped top of hole.

Tunnel is up to 38 cm (15 in) deep and lined with silk.

Find out more
ANIMALS
ANTS AND TERMITES
BEES AND WASPS
BIRDS
SPIDERS AND SCORPIONS

NEW ZEALAND

THE ISLAND NATION of New Zealand is a fascinating mixture of cultures and peoples. Maori people were the original inhabitants of the country, which they call Aotearoa, and they still live there, together with the descendants of the early British settlers and immigrants from other European and Asian countries. Only 4.2 million people live in New Zealand, and there are few large towns. The people are young – more than half of them are less than 35 years old – and the number of births per 1,000 of population is among the highest of all developed nations. A former British colony, New Zealand became fully independent in 1947. It is a leading Pacific nation and has strong links with many of the small islands in the region, such as Niue. The landscape of New Zealand is varied. There are towering mountains, glaciers, volcanoes, lakes, hot springs, sandy beaches, rolling hills, and plains.

New Zealand lies in the Pacific Ocean, east of Australia. There are two large islands – the North Island and the South Island – and many smaller ones, making a total area of 268,670 sq km (103,733 sq miles).

KIWI
New Zealand lies far from other land masses, and as a result its wildlife has developed in an unusual way. The kiwi, which cannot fly, is the most famous of all New Zealand creatures. There are several other species of flightless birds.

WELLINGTON
The capital of New Zealand is Wellington, which stands at the southern tip of the North Island. The city lies around a large natural harbour and is a busy port. Older wooden buildings stand close to recent structures built in a more modern style.

Sheep shearers work very quickly: some can clip a lamb in under a minute.

MAORI CULTURE
The Maoris, a Polynesian people, arrived in New Zealand around 950 CE. from islands in the Pacific. Today their descendants keep alive the rich culture of wood carving, weaving, and music and dance, which they brought with them.

FARMING
New Zealand has a warm, moist climate which is ideal for many types of farming. Sheep and cattle ranching are the biggest businesses. There are two cattle and 13 sheep for every human in New Zealand. The country exports more dairy produce and lamb than any other nation and is the second largest exporter of wool. Over the past 15 years production of other crops, such as kiwi fruit, oranges, and lemons, has increased. Newly built fishing boats have helped New Zealand's fleet increase its catch, and today the country is a major seafood exporter.

SOUTH ISLAND
Although the South Island is the largest New Zealand island, it has fewer inhabitants than the North Island. The western side of the island is covered by the Southern Alps, a region of mountains and glaciers, parts of which have not been explored. The rest of the island consists of farmland, grazing land for sheep and cattle, and a few ports and coastal cities.

Find out more
BRITISH EMPIRE
FOOTBALL AND RUGBY
MOUNTAINS
NEW ZEALAND, HISTORY OF
PACIFIC OCEAN

STATISTICS

Area: 268,680 sq km
(103,730 sq miles)
Population: 4,213,000
Capital: Wellington
Languages:
English, Maori
Religions: Anglican,
Presbyterian,
Roman Catholic,
Methodist,
non-religious
Currency:
New Zealand dollar
Main occupations:
Agriculture
Main exports: Butter,
wool, lamb, fruit,
vegetables, fish, cork,
wood, textiles
Main imports:
Manufactured goods,
iron, steel

Map legend

Volcano · Mountain · Ancient monument · Capital city · Large city/town · Small city/town

SCALE BAR
0   50   100   km
0   50   100 miles

SOUTHERN ALPS
On the west coast of the South Island the Southern Alps nearly reach the shore of the Tasman Sea. The terrain is mountainous and steep, with only a few passes between the east and west coasts.

Sutherland
Falls, 580 m
(1,904 ft)

AUCKLAND
The city of Auckland stands at a point where the North Island narrows to a strip less than 1.5 km (1 mile) wide. The Pacific lies to the east, and the Tasman Sea to the west, so Auckland has two harbour areas and is New Zealand's chief port. Auckland is important as a distribution centre, particularly for New Zealand's vital dairy industry, and high-rise buildings tower over the city's business centre. Auckland has a mixed population: a third of the people who live in the city are Polynesian.

Map labels

Three Kings Islands
Cape Reinga · North Cape
Great Exhibition Bay
Paihia
North Island
Ruawai
Great Barrier Island
Auckland
Whitianga
Tasman Sea
Hamilton
Bay of Plenty
East Cape
Rotorua
Raukumara Range
North Taranaki Bight
Lake Taupo
Taupo
New Plymouth
Gisborne
Cape Egmont · Mount Taranaki 2518m · Mount Ruapehu 2797m
Hawke Bay
South Taranaki Bight
Wanganui
Hastings
Palmerston North
Cape Farewell
D'Urville Island
Masterton
Tasman Bay
Karamea Bight
Nelson · Picton
Cape Foulwind
Cook Strait
WELLINGTON
Cape Campbell · Cape Palliser
Westport
NEW ZEALAND
Clarence
Greymouth
Kaikoura
South Island
Fox Glacier
Southern Alps
Pegasus Bay
Milford Sound
Mt Cook 3744m
Christchurch
Canterbury Plains
Ashburton
Lake Wakatipu
Canterbury Bight
Waitaki
Timaru
Lake Te Anau
Queenstown
Te Anau
Fiordland
Clutha
Otago Peninsula
Waiau
Dunedin
PACIFIC OCEAN
Invercargill
Foveaux Strait
Stewart Island
South West Cape

Compass
N · E · S · W

RUGBY
Rugby is New Zealand's favourite sport. The national team, the All Blacks, are world famous. They are named after their black shirt and shorts. The All Blacks perform the *haka*, a Maori dance, before each international game. Rugby was introduced to New Zealand by Charles John Monro, a New Zealander educated in England. The first game was played by Nelson College and Nelson Football Club in 1870.

Aged 19, Jonah Lomu (right) became the youngest ever All Black team member. He was voted player of the tournament at the 1995 World Cup.

MOUNT TARANAKI
The peak of Mount Taranaki in the southwest of the North Island is 2,517 m (8,260 ft) high, so the volcano is visible from many kilometres away. Taranaki is now extinct, but Ruapehu and Ngauruhoe, in the centre of the island, are occasionally active.

HISTORY OF
NEW ZEALAND

ABOUT 1,000 YEARS AGO, a group of people ventured ashore on a string of islands in the South Pacific. These people were the Maoris, and they had travelled in canoes across the Pacific Ocean from the distant islands of Polynesia to a land they called Aotearoa. For about 700 years, the Maoris lived on the islands undisturbed. In 1642, the Dutch Explorer Abel Tasman visited the islands, and named them New Zealand, after a province in the Netherlands. Soon, American, Australian, and European sealers and whalers were exploiting the rich coastal waters, and in 1840, the British founded the first European settlement. The Maoris fought protest wars until 1870, when they lost control of their lands. As a British colony, New Zealand grew wealthy by exporting its agricultural produce. In 1907, New Zealand became independent. More recently, New Zealand has formed several alliances with its neighbours in the South Pacific to keep the region free from nuclear weapons.

NEW ZEALAND

c. 950 CE First Maoris arrive.

1642 Dutch navigator Abel Tasman visits islands.

1769-77 British explorer Captain James Cook visits islands four times.

1814 British missionaries arrive.

1840 British settlement established in Wellington. Treaty of Waitangi.

1843-70 Land wars between Maoris and British settlers.

1852 Britain grants New Zealand self-government.

1863 Gold Rush draws many immigrants from Europe.

1893 Women get to vote.

1898 State pensions given.

1907 New Zealand becomes an independent dominion in the British Empire.

1914-18, 1939-45 Troops fight with Britain in two world wars.

1960s Troops fight with Americans in the Vietnam War.

1985 New Zealand joins its Pacific neighbours in declaring the region a nuclear-free zone.

MAORIS

Long before the Europeans arrived in New Zealand, the Maoris had established a thriving agricultural community. They grew sweet potatoes and caught fish and fowl. They wore colourful clothes woven from flax. They lived in houses made of rushes and wood. Today, more than 500,000 Maoris still exist, most of whom live in the North Island.

Traditional Maori cloak made out of feathers

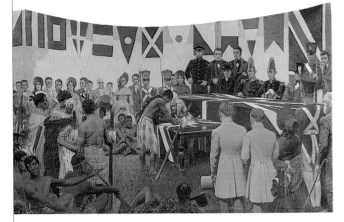

TREATY OF WAITANGI
In 1840, the Maoris granted sovereignty, or ownership, of their country to Britain. In return, Britain promised protection of their rights and property. New Zealand then became a colony of the British Empire.

INDEPENDENCE
In 1852, Britain granted new Zealand self-government. The country gave pensions to workers and was the first in the world to give women the right to vote. In 1907, New Zealand gained full independence, but ties with Britain remained strong. The British monarch, Queen Elizabeth II, seen here with Prince Philip in a traditional Maori cloak, is the nation's head of state.

Protestors try to interrupt the path of a nuclear submarine.

NUCLEAR-FREE ZONE
In 1983, anti-nuclear protesters blockaded the USS *Phoenix* nuclear submarine in Auckland harbour. In 1985, New Zealand signed the treaty of Rarotonga, which declared the South Pacific region to be a nuclear-free zone. When France continued to carry out nuclear tests in Mururoa Atoll, in the South Pacific Ocean, these were fiercely opposed by other Pacific countries.

Find out more
BRITISH EMPIRE
COOK, JAMES
NEW ZEALAND

FLORENCE
NIGHTINGALE

THE FOUNDER OF MODERN nursing, Florence Nightingale was a remarkable woman. She reformed nursing practice, and revolutionized healthcare. Florence Nightingale came from a wealthy family, and received a good education. Her parents were horrified when she said she wanted to be a nurse. Nursing in the 19th century was dirty and dangerous, and nurses tended to be poor, uneducated women. However, she was a determined woman, and, in 1853, began work supervising a women's hospital in London. The following year, she went to the Crimean War, where she completely reorganized the military hospital at Scutari, Turkey, reducing death rates dramatically. She returned to England as a heroine, and worked for nursing reforms until her death.

1820 Born in Florence, Italy.

1853 Supervises women's hospital, London.

1854 Goes to Crimea to nurse soldiers.

1856 Returns to England.

1859 Publishes *Notes on Nursing.*

1860 Sets up world's first training school for nurses, in London.

1907 Becomes first woman to receive Order of Merit.

1910 Dies, aged 90.

THE LAMP
Florence Nightingale was nicknamed "The Lady with the Lamp" because she carried a lamp through the wards.

Florence Nightingale walked through the wards, checking that soldiers were comfortable and free of pain.

SCUTARI

When Florence Nightingale arrived at the military hospital in Scutari, she found appalling conditions. Rats and lice infested the hospital, medical supplies were almost non-existent, and wounded soldiers were effectively left to die of neglect. With her team of workers and money raised by the British public, Nightingale washed and painted wards, cleared drains, set up laundries, bought in supplies, and introduced strict nursing discipline. Male army doctors resented her, but death rates dropped from 40 to 2 per cent.

Florence Nightingale in the Military Hospital at Scutari, Turkey

MARY SEACOLE
Born in Jamaica, Mary Seacole (1805-81) gained nursing experience during fever epidemics. In 1854, she volunteered to nurse in the British army, but was refused, probably because she was black. Undaunted, she went to the Crimea, where she nursed the wounded on the battlefield.

NURSING REFORMS
After 1856, Florence Nightingale campaigned for nursing reforms. In 1857, as a result of her efforts, an Army Medical School was set up. The British public subscribed £45,000 to her Nightingale Fund, which she used to found the world's first modern training school for nurses at St. Thomas' Hospital, London. She personally drew up the curriculum.

YOUNG FLORENCE
From an early age, Florence Nightingale wanted activity and challenge. But, as a young middle-class woman, she was supposed to play the piano and entertain, rather than work. In her diary, she wrote of her boredom. Finally, when she was 30, she began her career, spending time with the nursing Sisters of St. Vincent in Alexandria, Egypt.

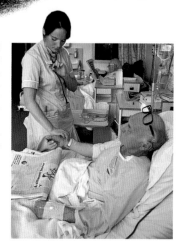

___ *Find out more* ___
MEDICINE, HISTORY OF
VICTORIANS
WOMEN'S RIGHTS

NORMANS

BAYEUX TAPESTRY
Dating to the 11th century, the Bayeux tapestry was produced to record the Norman Conquest of England. It shows scenes of battle, and can be seen today at Bayeux, in France.

TODAY, SOLID STONE CASTLES in England, Sicily, and France stand as reminders of the Normans, warriors from northern France, who transformed Europe during the 11th and 12th centuries. The Normans were descendants of the Norsemen, or Vikings, and were formidable fighters. They settled in northern France during the early 900s in an area now known as Normandy. The Normans were not only warriors but also skilled administrators. Their dukes created a complex and efficient society, dividing their kingdom into areas called fiefs. A knight controlled each fief. The Normans reached their height of power under William, Duke of Normandy, who led the conquest of England in 1066. They quickly transformed England into a Norman kingdom, building castles to defend their conquests, as well as churches, monasteries, and cathedrals. By the mid-12th century, the Saxons and Normans had begun to merge into one nation, ruled by the Plantagenet dynasty. In 1204 the king of France conquered Normandy and took it over.

WILLIAM THE CONQUEROR
William, Duke of Normandy (c. 1028-87), was a brilliant, but ruthless general and administrator. He led the Norman invasion of England and, after defeating the Saxon king, Harold II, was crowned king of England.

DOMESDAY BOOK
In 1085, King William I ordered a complete survey of England. Known as the Domesday Book, it contained thorough details of people, goods, animals, and lands for almost the whole country.

Map labels:
Sovereign states
SCOTLAND
IRELAND
Conquered territory
Unconquered territory
WALES
ENGLAND
BRITTANY
Paris
AQUITAINE

EMPIRE
At the height of Norman power, Henry II (reigned 1154-89) ruled England and much of France, and a separate group of Normans had conquered southern Italy and Sicily.

ARCHITECTURE
The Normans were skilled architects. They built strong castles to guard their conquests, such as the Tower of London, which stands to this day. They also built churches, cathedrals, and monasteries. Norman churches have intricately carved arches over the doors and windows, and massive walls and pillars.

Find out more
ARCHITECTURE
BRITAIN, ANCIENT
CASTLES
UNITED KINGDOM, HISTORY OF
VIKINGS

NORTH AFRICA

The North African coast occupies the southern shores of the Mediterranean, where the climate is mild and the land fertile. The Atlas Mountains and the rolling hills of Algeria and Tunisia lie between the coast and the sand seas and barren rocks of the Sahara.

THE COUNTRIES OF NORTH AFRICA have suffered many invasions, from the Romans to the French and British. But the conquest by the armies of Islam in the 7th century was to have a major impact on the region, giving it a shared religion, language, and sense of identity. Much of North Africa is dominated by the largest desert on Earth, the Sahara. It is sparsely populated by dwindling numbers of nomads. Most people live along the fertile coastal strip on the banks of the Nile. Cities increasingly attract migrants from the country – Cairo is the fastest-growing city in the Islamic world with a population of over 15 million. In Algeria and Libya, the desert has revealed hidden riches – vast reserves of oil are fuelling modernization programmes. Many tourists visit Morocco, Tunisia, and Egypt, attracted by ancient ruins, medieval cities, and baking hot beaches.

KAIROUAN
When Islamic Arabs conquered North Africa in the 7th century, they founded many cities that are still important today. The walled city of Kairouan, in Tunisia, is a sacred shrine for Muslims in Africa. The Great Mosque was built in the 9th century. Its imposing marble courtyard, where the people pray, is surrounded by columns.

People who live in the desert regions of Africa, such as these Berber men (left), wear loose clothes to keep cool, and veils to protect themselves from the wind-blown sands of the desert.

BERBERS
The Berbers are the original people of Northwest Africa. They were converted to Islam in the 8th century. Arab invaders drove them into the Atlas Mountains where many still live in remote villages. In the Sahara, Berber live a nomadic life herding camels, sheep, and goats.

NILE AGRICULTURE
The River Nile floods every summer, carrying rich mud from the highlands of Ethiopia and Sudan to the arid deserts of Egypt. It was this annual miracle that provided the foundations of Ancient Egyptian civilization. Today, nearly 99 per cent of the Egyptian population live along the green and fertile land on the banks of the Nile. Egypt is a leading producer of dates, melons, and cotton. Most Egyptian farmers use centuries-old methods; donkeys and asses are still used to pull heavy loads and carry water.

LEPTIS MAGNA
The Roman ruins at Leptis Magna, Libya (right) are the finest in Africa. The city dates to the 5th century BCE. It became part of the Roman Empire and was abandoned after the Arab conquest in 643 CE.

ALGIERS
The capital of Algeria forms a vast amphitheatre of dazzling white buildings on the Mediterranean coast. The old Muslim quarter of the city sprawls across the hills, a maze of winding streets and high-walled houses. The French colonial quarter, with its public squares and tree-lined avenues, is found near the harbour. The French captured the city, an unruly centre of Mediterranean piracy, in 1830. They left in 1962.

Find out more
AFRICA
AFRICA, HISTORY OF
DESERT WILDLIFE
ISLAM

Volcano	Mountain	Ancient monument	Capital city	Large city/town	Small city/town

 ALGERIA
Area: 2,381,740 sq km
(919,590 sq miles)
Population: 34,178,000
Capital: Algiers

MOROCCO
Area: 698,670 sq km
(269,757 sq miles)
Population: 34,859,000
Capital: Rabat

EGYPT
Area: 1,001,450 sq km
(386,660 sq miles)
Population: 83,083,000
Capital: Cairo

TUNISIA
Area: 163,610 sq km
(63,170 sq miles)
Population: 10,486,000
Capital: Tunis

LIBYA
Area: 1,759,540 sq km
(679,358 sq miles)
Population: 6,310,000
Capital: Tripoli

WESTERN SAHARA
Area: 266,000 sq km
(102,703 sq miles)
Population: 405,000
Capital: Laayoune
Status: disputed territory
occupied by Morocco

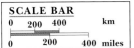

SCALE BAR
0   200   400   km
0   200   400   miles

ATLAS MOUNTAINS

The Atlas Mountains are a group of ranges, running roughly parallel to the Mediterranean coast. They stretch 2,410 km (1,500 miles) from southeast Morocco to northeast Tunisia. The High Atlas Mountains rise to 4,165 m (13,655 ft) at the summit of Jbel Toubkal. Mountain reservoirs provide water for lowland farmers and many tourists visit the Middle Atlas range for winter sports.

RIVER NILE
The Nile is the world's longest river. It flows 6,695 km (4,158 miles) to the Mediterranean Sea.

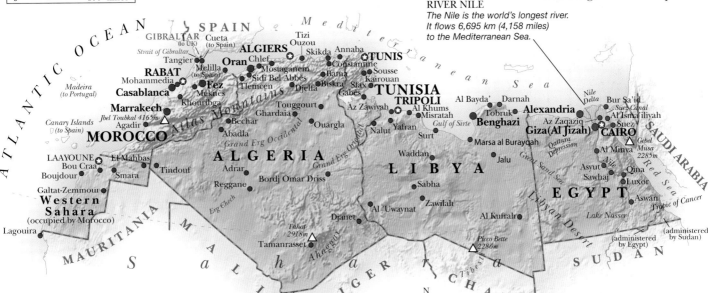

OILFIELDS

The oil reserves of Libya were discovered in the 1950s. Profits from oil were invested in industry and agriculture. New roads, railways, schools, and hospitals were also built. In the 2000s, oil accounted for 96 per cent of Libyan exports. The government has been trying to improve industrial and agricultural outputs in order to reduce this over-dependence on oil.

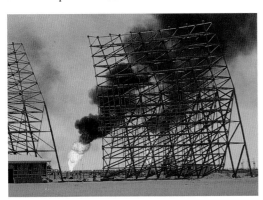

WEAVING
Morocco is famous for its colourful, hand-knotted carpets. Berbers weave carpets, tent hangings, and even produce embroidered boots (left).

SOUK

The souk (market) is the commercial heart of North African towns. Each trade is located in a particular street. Smelly trades, such as tanning leather, are always located as far away from the mosque as possible.

NORTH AMERICA

The North American continent stretches from the Arctic Circle to the Tropics and is flanked by the Atlantic, Pacific, and Arctic Oceans. The five Great Lakes of North America form the largest area of fresh water in the world.

THE NORTH AMERICAN continent is a region of great contrasts. Impressive mountain chains – the Appalachians and Rockies – run down its east and west coasts, enclosing a vast, and mostly flat, landscape, criss-crossed by mighty rivers such as the Mississippi and Missouri. The north is blanketed with coniferous forests. The central Great Plains are grasslands, once grazed by huge herds of buffalo. In the north the Arctic region is permanently frozen, while in the south arid deserts and rocky canyons bake in year-round sunshine. Tropical forests cover southern Mexico, and in the southeastern USA, semi-tropical wetlands harbour many endangered species. Native Americans are descendants of the peoples who first settled the continent over 25,000 years ago. They were displaced by European colonists who explored and settled on the continent from the 16th century. Successive waves of immigrants, first from Europe, and then from the rest of the world, continued to settle in North America, drawn by its wealth of natural resources, its fertile prairies, and its vibrant cities – home to most of its population.

THE BIG FREEZE
Severe winter weather is common in the centre of the continent, especially around the Great Lakes, which often freeze over in winter. Chicago, on Lake Michigan, is prone to severe snowstorms, which can cut off the city. In 1998, a freak icestorm in the Canadian Great Lakes region froze power lines, blacking out the area for several days.

ROCKIES
The Rocky Mountains form the backbone of the American continent, separating the great plains of the east from the high plateaux and basins of the west. Stretching from the Canadian Arctic to New Mexico, they are highest in Colorado, where some 254 mountains are over 4,000 m (13,000 ft). The highest point, Mt Elbert, is 4,312 m (14,149 ft).

TUNDRA IN ALASKA
Tundra is a Finnish word meaning "treeless heights". It describes the landscape of Alaska (above), where the only vegetation is lichens, mosses, turf and low-lying shrubs. The average temperature is below freezing and in winter it can plummet to -32°C (-89.6°F). These low temperatures leave a layer of permanently frozen soil which can reach depths of 1,525 m (5,000 ft).

AUTUMN IN NEW ENGLAND
The climate of North America ranges from the hot rainforests of Yucatán to the frozen Arctic. The eastern coast of the USA has four distinct seasons. The colours of autumnal leaves, especially the bright red of the maple, is a famous sight which attracts many tourists.

GRAND CANYON
Canyons are dramatic, deep rock formations created by the eroding flow of a river. The most famous is the Grand Canyon in Arizona, formed by the Colorado River. It is 350 km (220 miles) long, and plunges to depths of 1,820 m (5,970 ft). The processes of erosion started about 5-6 million years ago. Some of the rocks at the base are 2 billion years old – the oldest rocks known in the USA.

Moose live in the subarctic forests. They have huge antlers, long legs and fleshy muzzles.

Limestone, sandstone, shale and granite are eroded at different speeds, giving the Grand Canyon its distinctive layered colours.

Manatees grow to an average length of 3 m (10 ft). These huge, gentle creatures are found in Florida's shallow coastal waters.

FLORIDA EVERGLADE

The Everglades (left) is a vast area of semi-tropical marshland which stretches across the southwestern part of Florida. A series of low islands, called "hammocks", are home to a great variety of trees, ranging from tropical hardwoods, such as mahogany, to bay trees, eucalyptus and mangroves. Over 400 species of bird are found in the Everglades, and other animals such as alligators, tree frogs, and otters thrive in the swampy conditions. The Everglades' unique ecosystem is supported by a cycle of dry winters and wet summers.

MISSISSIPPI

At 6,020 km (3,740 miles) long, the Mississippi is the main river artery of the USA and one of the busiest commercial waterways in the world. It rises in northern Minnesota, flowing south and receives the waters of the Missouri and Ohio rivers in its middle reaches. It drains into the Gulf of Mexico, where it forms a delta which is moving the shoreline out to sea at a rate of nearly 10 km (6 miles) every 100 years.

This bison's thick hair and beard accentuate its size.

This satellite image (above) shows the Mississippi and Missouri rivers converging at St Louis during flooding in 1993.

A barn and yellow canola crop on the Great Plains just east of Washington

GREAT PLAINS

The Great Plains, which stretch across the centre of North America, were once areas of grassland (prairie) grazed by huge herds of buffalo (bison). Over-hunting wiped out the buffaloes and, as the frontier of pioneer settlement moved further west throughout the 19th century, the Plains were settled by farmers. Today, this is one of the most intensively farmed regions in the world, a vast producer of both maize and wheat.

BISON

The so-called American buffalo that used to roam the Great Plains of North America is actually a bison. A fully grown bison stands 2 m (6.6 ft) high and weighs more than 900 kgs (1,985 lbs). Traditionally the bison provided food and clothing for the Native Americans living on the Plains. Up until the 18th century, the bison population flourished as the Native American method of hunting had little effect on numbers. It was not until the "white man" arrived with rifles that the herds were dramatically reduced. During construction of the railways in the 19th century, whole herds were shot to feed the rail workers. Today, only 40,000-50,000 bison remain. Most live in reserves, protected by American law.

URBAN LIFE

Much of the North American continent, such as the drier south and west, is sparsley populated, but there are great concentrations of population and industry in urban areas – especially in the temperate regions along the coasts and the shores of the Great Lakes. New York City (right) lies at the centre of a vast conurbation of cities, which stretches from Boston to Washington D.C. Accessible to both the Atlantic Ocean and the Hudson River, New York City developed as a major port. Today, it is the USA's main financial, commercial, and cultural centre. Toronto is the largest urban area in Canada. It is an important commercial, financial, and industrial centre. The city and its surrounding area produce more than half of Canada's manufactured goods.

BALD EAGLE

The bald eagle, the only eagle native to North America, has been the US national bird since 1782. It has a wingspan of 2 m (7 ft), and is found mainly along the coasts. It is a protected species in the USA.

NATIVE AMERICANS

The first people to settle North America crossed into the continent from Asia more than 25,000 years ago. As they settled, they adapted to many different climatic conditions, resources, and terrain. Today, after centuries of conflict with European settlers, many Native Americans now live on Government reservations. The Navajo are the largest tribe in the USA. Most of them live in a large reservation in the Southwest. The tribe is famous for weaving and silverwork and many of their hand-made artefacts are sold to tourists.

OIL RIG

The USA has an abundance of natural resources, including oil, coal, and minerals. Oil was found along the coast of East Texas in 1901. After Alaska, Texas is the USA's main oil-producing state. Oil is transported to refineries on the Gulf Coast by pipeline, tanker, and train. Houston is the capital of the oil business, although it is also the centre of high-tech industries and home to the space shuttle programme.

NATURAL HAZARDS

A chain of volcanoes stretches from the US-Mexican border to the southern end of South America. Popocatapetl, one of Mexico's many dormant volcanoes, is 5,452 m (17,888 ft) high, with a crater 152 m (500 ft) deep. Central Mexico is also vulnerable to earthquakes, which often hit the country's most heavily populated regions. In 1985, an earthquake in Mexico City killed some 9,500 people.

El Castillo, the temple-pyramid at Chichén-Itzá is 22m (73ft) high. It stands in the main plaza of the city.

Joshua trees grow in the higher and cooler parts of California's desert.

DESERT

The barren deserts of the Southwest are harsh and arid places, swept by fierce wind eddies and baked by searing heat. Only the hardiest animals, such as snakes, lizards, and reptiles, can survive these conditions. Spiny-leaved Joshua trees thrive in the desert, and can live for up to 1,000 years.

Rugged formations of pink and grey rocks and boulders form a stark desert vista.

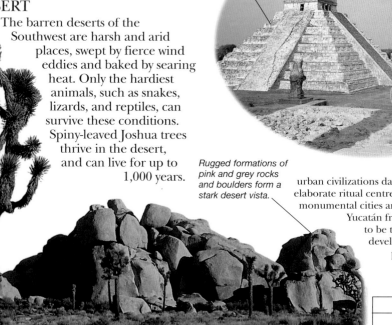

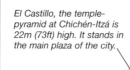

CHICHEN-ITZA

The history of Mexico's urban civilizations dates back to c. 1150 BCE, and the elaborate ritual centres of the Olmec. The Maya built monumental cities and temples in the jungles of the Yucatán from c. 200 CE. They are thought to be the first American civilization to develop a writing system. The Mayan pyramid-temple at Chichén Itzá dates to the 12th century CE.

Find out more

CANADA
MEXICO
NATIVE AMERICANS
UNITED STATES OF AMERICA

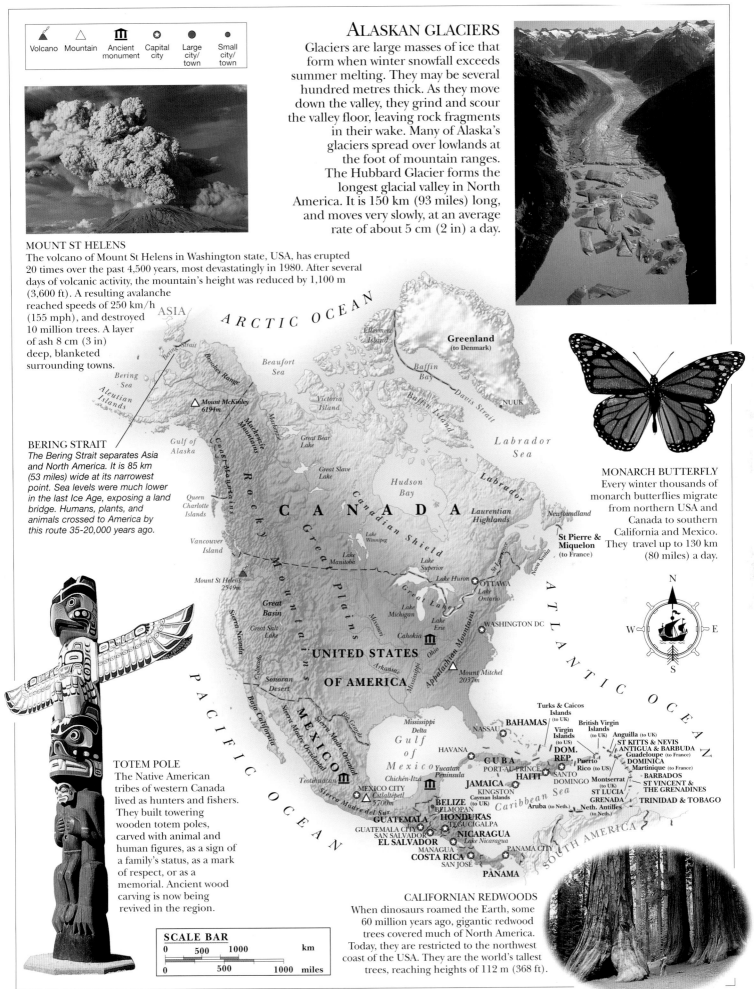

| Volcano | Mountain | Ancient monument | Capital city | Large city/ town | Small city/ town |

ALASKAN GLACIERS

Glaciers are large masses of ice that form when winter snowfall exceeds summer melting. They may be several hundred metres thick. As they move down the valley, they grind and scour the valley floor, leaving rock fragments in their wake. Many of Alaska's glaciers spread over lowlands at the foot of mountain ranges. The Hubbard Glacier forms the longest glacial valley in North America. It is 150 km (93 miles) long, and moves very slowly, at an average rate of about 5 cm (2 in) a day.

MOUNT ST HELENS

The volcano of Mount St Helens in Washington state, USA, has erupted 20 times over the past 4,500 years, most devastatingly in 1980. After several days of volcanic activity, the mountain's height was reduced by 1,100 m (3,600 ft). A resulting avalanche reached speeds of 250 km/h (155 mph), and destroyed 10 million trees. A layer of ash 8 cm (3 in) deep, blanketed surrounding towns.

BERING STRAIT

The Bering Strait separates Asia and North America. It is 85 km (53 miles) wide at its narrowest point. Sea levels were much lower in the last Ice Age, exposing a land bridge. Humans, plants, and animals crossed to America by this route 35-20,000 years ago.

MONARCH BUTTERFLY

Every winter thousands of monarch butterflies migrate from northern USA and Canada to southern California and Mexico. They travel up to 130 km (80 miles) a day.

TOTEM POLE

The Native American tribes of western Canada lived as hunters and fishers. They built towering wooden totem poles, carved with animal and human figures, as a sign of a family's status, as a mark of respect, or as a memorial. Ancient wood carving is now being revived in the region.

CALIFORNIAN REDWOODS

When dinosaurs roamed the Earth, some 60 million years ago, gigantic redwood trees covered much of North America. Today, they are restricted to the northwest coast of the USA. They are the world's tallest trees, reaching heights of 112 m (368 ft).

SCALE BAR

| 0 | 500 | 1000 | km |
| 0 | 500 | 1000 | miles |

Map labels: ASIA, ARCTIC OCEAN, Ellesmere Island, Greenland (to Denmark), Bering Strait, Beaufort Sea, Baffin Bay, Baffin Island, Davis Strait, NUUK, Bering Sea, Brooks Range, Mount McKinley 6194m, Victoria Island, Aleutian Islands, Mackenzie Mountains, Mackenzie, Gulf of Alaska, Great Bear Lake, Hudson Bay, Labrador Sea, Coast Mountains, Great Slave Lake, Labrador, Queen Charlotte Islands, CANADA, Canadian Shield, Laurentian Highlands, Newfoundland, St Pierre & Miquelon (to France), Vancouver Island, Rocky Mountains, Lake Winnipeg, Lake Manitoba, Lake Superior, Nova Scotia, St Lawrence, Great Plains, Lake Huron, OTTAWA, Lake Ontario, Mount St Helens 2549m, Great Basin, Sierra Nevada, Great Salt Lake, Lake Michigan, Lake Erie, Great Lakes, WASHINGTON DC, Missouri, Cahokia, Ohio, ATLANTIC OCEAN, UNITED STATES OF AMERICA, Colorado, Arkansas, Mississippi, Appalachian Mountains, Mount Mitchel 2037m, Sonoran Desert, Baja California, Sierra Madre Occidental, Rio Grande, Sierra Madre Oriental, Mississippi Delta, Gulf of Mexico, Turks & Caicos Islands (to UK), NASSAU, BAHAMAS, Virgin Islands (to US), British Virgin Islands (to UK), Anguilla (to UK), ST KITTS & NEVIS, ANTIGUA & BARBUDA, Guadeloupe (to France), DOMINICA, Martinique (to France), HAVANA, CUBA, PORT-AU-PRINCE, DOM. REP., Puerto Rico (to US), MEXICO, Teotihuacan, Yucatan Peninsula, Chichén-Itzá, MEXICO CITY, Citlaltépetl 5700m, Sierra Madre del Sur, BELIZE, BELMOPAN, Cayman Islands (to UK), JAMAICA, KINGSTON, HAITI, SANTO DOMINGO, Montserrat (to UK), BARBADOS, ST VINCENT & THE GRENADINES, ST LUCIA, GRENADA, TRINIDAD & TOBAGO, Aruba (to Neth.), Neth. Antilles (to Neth.), Caribbean Sea, GUATEMALA, GUATEMALA CITY, HONDURAS, TEGUCIGALPA, SAN SALVADOR, EL SALVADOR, NICARAGUA, Lake Nicaragua, MANAGUA, COSTA RICA, SAN JOSÉ, PANAMA CITY, PANAMA, SOUTH AMERICA, PACIFIC OCEAN, N, S, E, W

NORTHERN IRELAND

LYING JUST ACROSS THE IRISH SEA from Scotland, Northern Ireland is part of the United Kingdom. It covers an area of 14,121 sq km (5,452 sq miles), and has a population of just over 1.7 million people, split between a Protestant majority and a slightly smaller number of Roman Catholics. Also known as Ulster, Northern Ireland consists of the six counties of Antrim, Londonderry, Tyrone, Fermanagh, Armagh and Down. Remaining part of the United Kingdom when southern Ireland split away in 1920, Northern Ireland has had a troubled history, dominated by religious and political conflict. Since the late 1990s, peace initiatives have been taking place. In 1998, Catholics and Protestants agreed to share power in a self-governing assembly, but it has proved difficult to make this arrangement work.

Northern Ireland occupies the northeastern part of Ireland. It is bordered by the Republic of Ireland to the south and west, with the Irish Sea to the east.

BELFAST

Belfast is the biggest city in Northern Ireland, and capital of the province. Sitting on the northeast coast, Belfast is a major UK port and manufacturing centre, which was once world famous for its engineering works and shipyards. The *Titanic*, for instance, was built in Belfast. Political troubles have divided the city in recent years.

GIANT'S CAUSEWAY
A major landmark, the Giant's Causeway lies off the coast of County Antrim on the north coast. The thousands of rocks that make up the Causeway are shaped like hexagons, or eight-sided columns. They were created when lava from underground volcanoes cooled in the sea some 60 million years ago. Its name comes from a legend that giants built a causeway to Scotland so they could cross the Irish Sea.

LINEN
The textile industry is one of Northern Ireland's chief industries. Linen-making is traditional. Woven from flax, linen from Northern Ireland is among the finest in the world. Farming and engineering are also important to the economy.

MUSIC
There is a long tradition of music-making in Northern Ireland, and many famous musicians have been born there. Music varies from the pipe and drum bands of the Orange Order, through to traditional Gaelic music and more modern pop music.

The famous singer Van Morrison grew up in Northern Ireland.

PEOPLE
Many of Belfast's children have grown up surrounded by violence, caused by the long-running conflict between Protestants and Roman Catholics. Most Protestants wish to remain part of the United Kingdom, although some favour self-government. Many Roman Catholics would like to unite with the Republic of Ireland in the south.

ORANGE ORDER
The Orange Order (supporter, left), a society to support Protestantism, was founded in 1795. It was named after William of Orange, who became the first Protestant king of Britain.

Find out more

IRELAND
UNITED KINGDOM
UNITED KINGDOM, HISTORY OF

NUCLEAR ENERGY

THE ATOMS THAT MAKE UP everything in the universe are the source of a huge amount of energy called nuclear energy. Nuclear energy produces the searing heat and light of the Sun, the deadly explosions of nuclear weapons, and vast amounts of electricity in nuclear power stations. Nuclear energy is based on the fact that matter and energy are different forms of the same thing, and one can be converted into the other. In a nuclear reaction, a tiny amount of matter changes into an enormous amount of energy. The nuclear reaction occurs in the nuclei (centres) of atoms. This can happen in two ways: when the nucleus of a heavy atom splits, in a process called fission, and when two lightweight nuclei join together, in a process called fusion. In nuclear weapons, fission or fusion occurs in a split second. By contrast, nuclear power stations produce electricity from fission reactions that work at a controlled rate.

Experimental nuclear fusion reactor near Oxford, England

Hydrogen nucleus with extra neutron

Neutron

Hydrogen nucleus with two extra neutrons

Helium nucleus

NUCLEAR FUSION

Scientists are trying to build reactors that use nuclear fusion, a process which produces less dangerous waste than nuclear fission (below). Nuclear fusion occurs when hydrogen atoms smash together and join to form heavier atoms of helium. However, nuclear fusion is extremely difficult to achieve. Hydrogen atoms must be held by a magnetic field and heated to a temperature higher than that in the Sun's centre for fusion to occur.

Neutron hits nucleus of uranium atom.

Fission occurs, releasing energy and neutrons.

NUCLEAR FISSION

Nuclear power stations produce energy from the fission of atoms of uranium within uranium oxide pellets. The impact of a particle called a neutron makes an atom of uranium split, releasing heat energy and two or three neutrons. The neutrons strike other uranium atoms and make them divide. Soon, many atoms split, producing a huge amount of energy.

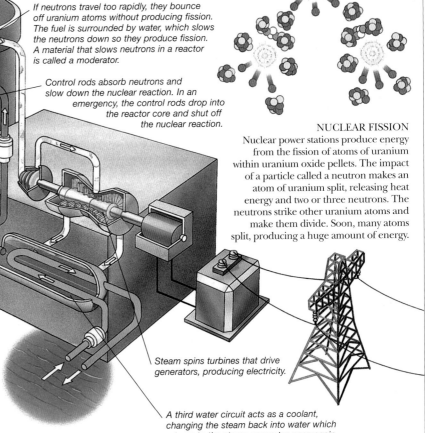

Reactor core contains pellets of uranium dioxide fuel held in fuel rods. Two thimble-sized pellets would produce enough electricity for a person for one year.

Pump for high-pressure water system

If neutrons travel too rapidly, they bounce off uranium atoms without producing fission. The fuel is surrounded by water, which slows the neutrons down so they produce fission. A material that slows neutrons in a reactor is called a moderator.

Control rods absorb neutrons and slow down the nuclear reaction. In an emergency, the control rods drop into the reactor core and shut off the nuclear reaction.

The high-pressure water flows through pipes in a steam generator which transfers its heat to a separate water system. The water in this second system boils to form steam.

Water is pumped around the reactor core at high pressure in a sealed circuit. The nuclear reactions heat the water to more than 300°C (570°F), but the high pressure keeps it from turning into steam.

Steam spins turbines that drive generators, producing electricity.

A third water circuit acts as a coolant, changing the steam back into water which returns to the steam generator once again.

Pressurized water reactor (PWR)

Protective clothing worn when handling nuclear waste

NUCLEAR RADIATION

Some waste from nuclear power stations is radioactive – it produces deadly nuclear radiation consisting of tiny particles or invisible waves that can damage living cells. Some radioactive waste may last for thousands of years, so it is buried underground in sealed containers. Many people are concerned about the dangers of nuclear waste and are demanding an end to nuclear energy production.

NUCLEAR POWER STATION

A fission reaction becomes continuous only if there is a certain amount of fuel present, called the critical mass. In a nuclear reactor, rods contain uranium fuel. The fuel rods are placed close together to provide the critical mass that starts the reaction.

NUMBERS

WHEN WE WANT TO KNOW how many things we have, or measure how large something is, we use numbers. Numbers are symbols that describe an amount. There are only ten number symbols: 0, 1, 2, 3, 4, 5, 6, 7, 8, and 9, but they can be put together in many different ways to make other numbers of any size. As well as counting and measuring, numbers can also be used to work out time and distances, or to put things in order. The skill of working with numbers is called arithmetic. Early humans probably used their fingers and thumbs to count. Because we have ten digits – eight fingers and two thumbs – we developed a system of counting that was based on tens. This is called the decimal system, after the Latin word for ten. Numbers are just as important as words for passing on information. They can be written down, so that other people can read and use them.

FRACTIONS
Sometimes the number 1 has to be divided into portions. Parts of a whole number are called fractions.

COUNTING
When people needed to count higher than ten, they used objects such as pebbles to represent multiples of ten. So, five pebbles and three fingers stood for the number 53. Making calculations with pebbles led to the invention of the abacus, and later the slide rule, and calculator.

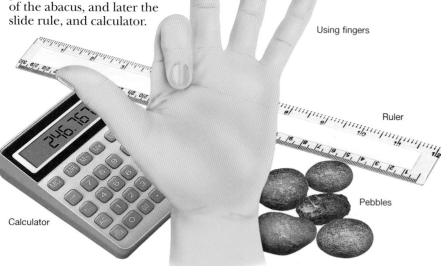

Calculator

Using fingers

Ruler

Pebbles

Cardinal numbers

A fraction, two-thirds

A decimal fraction, ten and sixty-five hundredths

NUMBERS IN HISTORY
People have invented many different ways of representing numbers with symbols. The modern decimal system has now been taken up all over the world, but older systems are still used in a few places. Even the Ancient Roman system is used sometimes, especially on clock faces.

The Babylonians invented a number system based on ten about 3,500 years ago, but the symbols took a long time to write down.

I II III IV V VI VII VIII IX X

The Ancient Roman number system goes back to about 500 BCE. It is an awkward system, but it is still sometimes used today.

In about 200 BCE the Hindus used a number system based on ten. About 1,400 years ago they modified it to include zero.

o 1 2 3 4 6 ^ 8 9 10

By the 15th century, Hindu-Arabic numbers had replaced Roman numerals as the most popular number system.

0 1 2 3 4 5 6 7 8 9 10

Today, most countries use a modern version of the Hindu-Arabic number system, because it makes calculations easy.

Cricket scoreboard

USING NUMBERS
If you look around, you will see how numbers are used in everyday life. For example, scoreboards, speed limits, distances, prices, TV channels, and the time of day are all shown using numbers. Page numbers in the index of this book show where to find the topics that interest you. Money is also divided into units to make it simple to understand.

TYPES OF NUMBER
Whole numbers that stand for quantities, such as 1, 2, or 3, are called cardinal numbers. Numbers that put things in order, such as 1st, 2nd, or 3rd, are known as ordinal numbers. In a fraction, the number below the line shows how many parts the whole is divided into; the number above shows how many of those parts are being described.

Find out more
ALPHABETS
COMPUTERS
MATHEMATICS
SCIENCE

OCEANS AND SEAS

YOUR FEET MAY BE RESTING firmly on the ground, but more than two thirds of our planet is covered with water. Oceans and seas make up 71 per cent of the Earth's surface. They influence the climate, supply us with food, power, and valuable minerals, and provide a home for a fascinating range of plant and animal life.

The oceans and seas began millions of years ago when the Earth cooled from its original molten state. Water vapour escaped from inside the Earth in volcanic eruptions, cooled, and fell as rain. It filled vast hollows and basins surrounding rocky land masses. These gradually moved around to form the continents and oceans as they exist today. As rivers formed on the land and flowed into the seas, they dissolved minerals from the rocks, making the oceans and seas salty.

OCEAN HUNTERS
Fishing boats sail the oceans and seas to bring us the fish and other sea creatures that we eat. The best fishing grounds are in shallow seas, where the water teems with fish. But catches must be controlled; otherwise the numbers of fish will fall as the fish fail to breed.

SPRING TIDES
High, spring tides occur when the Earth, Sun, and Moon are in line.

Sun
Rise in water level
Moon
Earth

TIDES

Twice a day the level of the seas rises and falls. These changes in level are called tides. They are caused mainly by the pull of the Moon's gravity on the Earth. When the Moon lies directly over the ocean, its gravity pulls the water towards it. Water also rises on the opposite side of the Earth, because the Earth itself is pulled towards the Moon.

THE WORLD'S OCEANS AND SEAS
Oceans are vast bodies of water, usually separating the continents. The Pacific Ocean, which is the largest and deepest, lies between America and Asia and covers more than a third of the globe. The others, in order of size, are the Atlantic, Indian, Southern, and Arctic oceans. The Arctic Ocean lies between the land masses around the North Pole and is largely covered by ice. Seas, bays, and gulfs are smaller bodies of water that lie between arms of land, or between islands and land masses. Some, such as the Caspian and Dead seas, are entirely surrounded by land and are really not seas but large lakes.

Pacific Ocean

Indian Ocean

North Pacific Ocean

Southern Ocean

The Southern Ocean surrounds Antarctica. It includes all the waters between 60 degrees South latitude and the continent of Antarctica.

Indian Ocean

Atlantic Ocean

The Arctic Ocean is an ice-covered ocean at the North Pole.

OCEAN CURRENTS

The water in the oceans is constantly moving in great circular streams, or currents, which can flow about as fast as you walk. Winds blow the surface layer of the oceans to form these currents, which carry warm or cold water along the shores of continents, greatly affecting the weather there. Sometimes, currents flow deep below the surface, moving in the opposite direction to surface currents. For example, surface currents carry warm water away from the equator, while currents deep beneath the sea bring cold water back to the equator. Most seas have strong currents. But the waters of the Sargasso Sea, which lies in the North Atlantic Ocean, are almost still, causing the sea to become choked with seaweed.

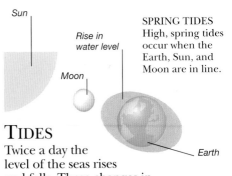

THE *KON TIKI* EXPEDITION
Early peoples may have used the currents to travel across oceans. In 1947 the *Kon Tiki* expedition, led by Norwegian explorer Thor Heyerdahl, tested this theory by sailing a light wooden raft from Peru to the Polynesian Islands.

GULF STREAM
Water heated by the Sun flows out from the Gulf of Mexico. This warm current crosses the Atlantic Ocean and flows around the shores of western Europe. There the winter weather is mild, while places on the other side of the ocean away from the current are freezing cold.

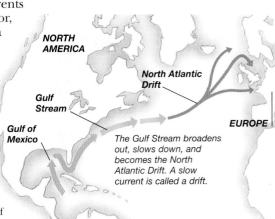

NORTH AMERICA
North Atlantic Drift
Gulf Stream
Gulf of Mexico
EUROPE
The Gulf Stream broadens out, slows down, and becomes the North Atlantic Drift. A slow current is called a drift.

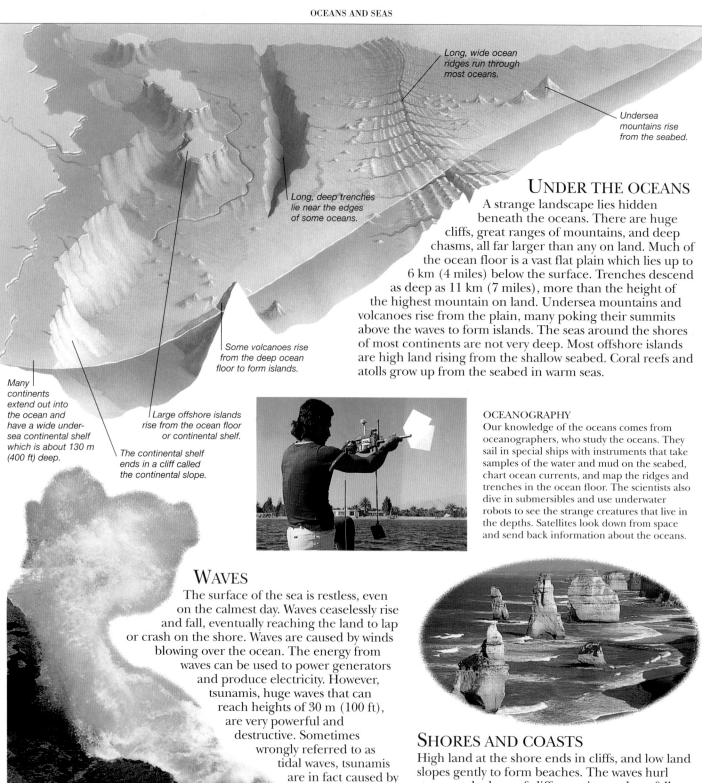

Long, wide ocean ridges run through most oceans.

Undersea mountains rise from the seabed.

Long, deep trenches lie near the edges of some oceans.

Some volcanoes rise from the deep ocean floor to form islands.

Many continents extend out into the ocean and have a wide undersea continental shelf which is about 130 m (400 ft) deep.

Large offshore islands rise from the ocean floor or continental shelf.

The continental shelf ends in a cliff called the continental slope.

UNDER THE OCEANS

A strange landscape lies hidden beneath the oceans. There are huge cliffs, great ranges of mountains, and deep chasms, all far larger than any on land. Much of the ocean floor is a vast flat plain which lies up to 6 km (4 miles) below the surface. Trenches descend as deep as 11 km (7 miles), more than the height of the highest mountain on land. Undersea mountains and volcanoes rise from the plain, many poking their summits above the waves to form islands. The seas around the shores of most continents are not very deep. Most offshore islands are high land rising from the shallow seabed. Coral reefs and atolls grow up from the seabed in warm seas.

OCEANOGRAPHY
Our knowledge of the oceans comes from oceanographers, who study the oceans. They sail in special ships with instruments that take samples of the water and mud on the seabed, chart ocean currents, and map the ridges and trenches in the ocean floor. The scientists also dive in submersibles and use underwater robots to see the strange creatures that live in the depths. Satellites look down from space and send back information about the oceans.

WAVES
The surface of the sea is restless, even on the calmest day. Waves ceaselessly rise and fall, eventually reaching the land to lap or crash on the shore. Waves are caused by winds blowing over the ocean. The energy from waves can be used to power generators and produce electricity. However, tsunamis, huge waves that can reach heights of 30 m (100 ft), are very powerful and destructive. Sometimes wrongly referred to as tidal waves, tsunamis are in fact caused by earthquakes and volcanic eruptions.

SHORES AND COASTS
High land at the shore ends in cliffs, and low land slopes gently to form beaches. The waves hurl stones at the base of cliffs, causing rocks to fall and form coasts with bays and headlands. Strange rock formations and caves may result. The waves batter the rocks and break them up into pebbles and then into sand. Beaches form at the base of cliffs, and the sea also sweeps pebbles and sand along the shore to form beaches elsewhere.

Water reaches base of circle in trough of wave.

Water reaches top of circle in crest of wave.

Crest topples over to break on shore.

HOW WAVES MOVE
The water in a wave does not move forwards. It moves in a circle, so the water only goes up and down as a wave passes. The approaching shore holds back the base of the wave, making the top of the wave move faster to break on the shore.

Find out more

CONTINENTS
DEEP-SEA WILDLIFE
EARTHQUAKES
FISHING INDUSTRY
INDIAN OCEAN
OCEAN WILDLIFE
SEASHORE WILDLIFE

OCEAN WILDLIFE

LIFE BEGAN IN THE OCEANS millions of years ago. Today, oceans cover 71 per cent of the planet's surface and provide homes for countless fish, octopuses, seals, sharks, and jellyfish. Ocean wildlife is at its richest in the warm shallow waters of coral reefs, where dazzlingly colourful angelfish and butterfly fish live. In deeper waters, whales, dolphins, and porpoises are found. Most plants and animals live close to the water's surface. Sunlight filters through the surface, allowing microscopic organisms such as diatoms to flourish. An intricate web of small animals feeds on these tiny organisms; larger sea creatures eat the smaller ones, and so on, up the food chain to the large predators such as sharks. Today, many marine plants and animals are threatened; we dump chemical wastes in the oceans, fertilizers flow into the oceans from rivers, and we catch so many fish that fish-eating sea mammals such as seals and dolphins have to compete with us for their food.

Seabirds

PLANKTON
Billions of tiny organisms float in sea water. Together they are called plankton, from the Greek word *planktos*, meaning "wanderer". Plankton are food for many fish and other sea creatures.

COELACANTH
The coelacanth is a survivor from prehistoric times, although scientists first discovered it in 1938. The coelacanth lives around the Comoro Islands, off southeast Africa, and in the eastern Indian Ocean, in water 70–400 m (230–1,300 ft) deep. Adult coelacanths measure about 1.7 m (5.5 ft) in length. Today this fish is threatened because of fish collectors and souvenir hunters.

Common squid

Finback whale

FINBACK WHALE
The finback whale is the second largest living animal (the blue whale is the largest) and is found from the Poles to the tropics. Finbacks grow to about 25 m (85 ft) in length and weigh 73 tonnes (71 tons). They feed by straining shrimplike creatures called krill from the water, using fringes of baleen hanging from the upper jaws.

OPEN OCEAN
Many animals in the open sea are streamlined (sleek in shape) so that they can swim away quickly from predators and chase after prey. There are fish of all shapes and sizes in the open ocean, as well as enormous schools of jellyfish, and mammals such as seals. Sea birds such as albatrosses, petrels, and shearwaters feed at the surface.

SAND TIGER
Sharks are the most aggressive hunters in the ocean. The ferocious sand tiger shark hunts even before it is born, when it is still in its mother's womb. There are 10–15 embryo sharks in the womb, and as they develop, they eat each other until there are only one or two left. The survivors are born fully formed, then swim away to begin their fish-eating lives, growing to 3.5 m (12 ft) in length.

SARDINE
Pacific sardines are related to herrings. Other members of the herring family are the sprat and the shad. All of them are hunted by bigger ocean dwellers such as seals.

HERRING
There were once vast shoals of herring in the oceans; they were an easy catch for fishing boats, and people valued them for their tasty flesh. Today, herring is much less common because people have overfished the oceans. Herring feed on plankton.

SWORDFISH
This spear-nosed hunter is one of the fastest fish in the sea; it can swim in bursts at speeds of 95 km/h (60 mph). The swordfish resembles the marlin and sailfish, and weighs up to 675 kg (1,500 lb). Swordfish injure their prey with sideways slashes of the sword, and then devour them.

Swordfish

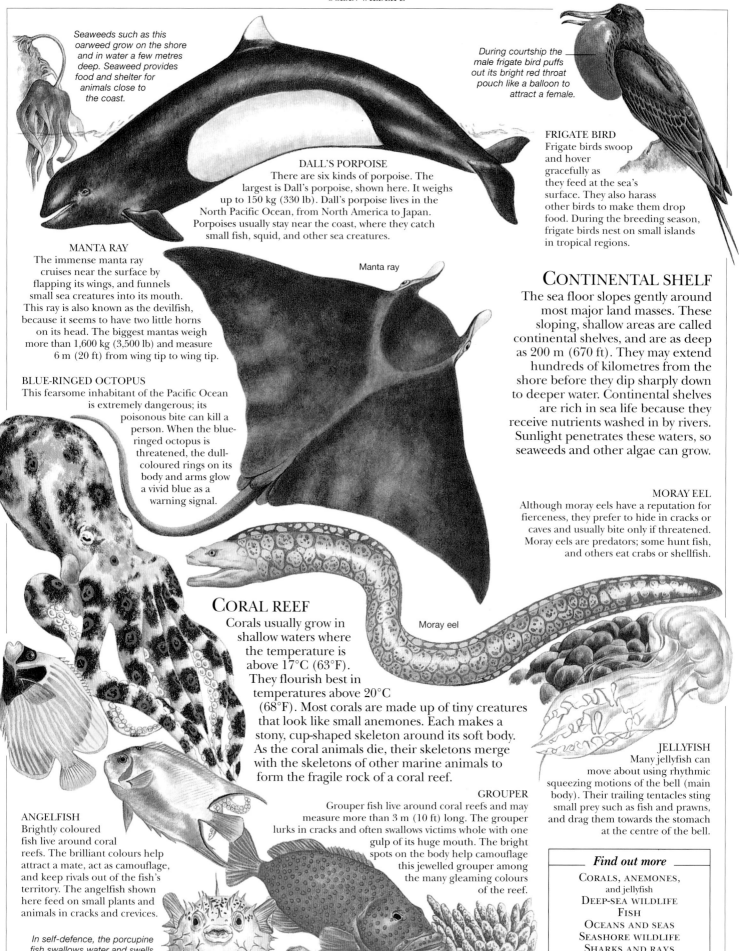

Seaweeds such as this oarweed grow on the shore and in water a few metres deep. Seaweed provides food and shelter for animals close to the coast.

During courtship the male frigate bird puffs out its bright red throat pouch like a balloon to attract a female.

DALL'S PORPOISE
There are six kinds of porpoise. The largest is Dall's porpoise, shown here. It weighs up to 150 kg (330 lb). Dall's porpoise lives in the North Pacific Ocean, from North America to Japan. Porpoises usually stay near the coast, where they catch small fish, squid, and other sea creatures.

Manta ray

FRIGATE BIRD
Frigate birds swoop and hover gracefully as they feed at the sea's surface. They also harass other birds to make them drop food. During the breeding season, frigate birds nest on small islands in tropical regions.

MANTA RAY
The immense manta ray cruises near the surface by flapping its wings, and funnels small sea creatures into its mouth. This ray is also known as the devilfish, because it seems to have two little horns on its head. The biggest mantas weigh more than 1,600 kg (3,500 lb) and measure 6 m (20 ft) from wing tip to wing tip.

BLUE-RINGED OCTOPUS
This fearsome inhabitant of the Pacific Ocean is extremely dangerous; its poisonous bite can kill a person. When the blue-ringed octopus is threatened, the dull-coloured rings on its body and arms glow a vivid blue as a warning signal.

CONTINENTAL SHELF
The sea floor slopes gently around most major land masses. These sloping, shallow areas are called continental shelves, and are as deep as 200 m (670 ft). They may extend hundreds of kilometres from the shore before they dip sharply down to deeper water. Continental shelves are rich in sea life because they receive nutrients washed in by rivers. Sunlight penetrates these waters, so seaweeds and other algae can grow.

MORAY EEL
Although moray eels have a reputation for fierceness, they prefer to hide in cracks or caves and usually bite only if threatened. Moray eels are predators; some hunt fish, and others eat crabs or shellfish.

Moray eel

CORAL REEF
Corals usually grow in shallow waters where the temperature is above 17°C (63°F). They flourish best in temperatures above 20°C (68°F). Most corals are made up of tiny creatures that look like small anemones. Each makes a stony, cup-shaped skeleton around its soft body. As the coral animals die, their skeletons merge with the skeletons of other marine animals to form the fragile rock of a coral reef.

JELLYFISH
Many jellyfish can move about using rhythmic squeezing motions of the bell (main body). Their trailing tentacles sting small prey such as fish and prawns, and drag them towards the stomach at the centre of the bell.

GROUPER
Grouper fish live around coral reefs and may measure more than 3 m (10 ft) long. The grouper lurks in cracks and often swallows victims whole with one gulp of its huge mouth. The bright spots on the body help camouflage this jewelled grouper among the many gleaming colours of the reef.

ANGELFISH
Brightly coloured fish live around coral reefs. The brilliant colours help attract a mate, act as camouflage, and keep rivals out of the fish's territory. The angelfish shown here feed on small plants and animals in cracks and crevices.

In self-defence, the porcupine fish swallows water and swells into a ball shape with its spines poking outwards.

Find out more
CORALS, ANEMONES, and jellyfish
DEEP-SEA WILDLIFE
FISH
OCEANS AND SEAS
SEASHORE WILDLIFE
SHARKS AND RAYS
WHALES AND DOLPHINS

OCTOPUSES AND SQUID

SEA CREATURES SUCH AS THE OCTOPUS and squid have always held a strange fascination for humans. With their powerful tentacles and strange shape, they were once thought of as sea monsters. Octopuses and squid are clever, active creatures, the biggest and most intelligent of all the invertebrates (animals without backbones). They have sharp eyesight, a large brain, fast reactions, and the ability to remember. Octopuses, squid, and their relatives the cuttlefish, are molluscs, related to shelled animals with soft bodies such as snails and clams. Unlike snails and clams, octopuses, squid, and cuttlefish have no outer shells, though squid have a very thin shell called a pen inside the body. The white oval cuttlebones of cuttlefish are often seen washed up on beaches. An octopus has eight "arms" covered with suckers, which it uses for moving around. Squid and cuttlefish have eight short "arms" and two long tentacles, which curl and uncurl. They use their arms as rudders for swimming and their tentacles for catching prey.

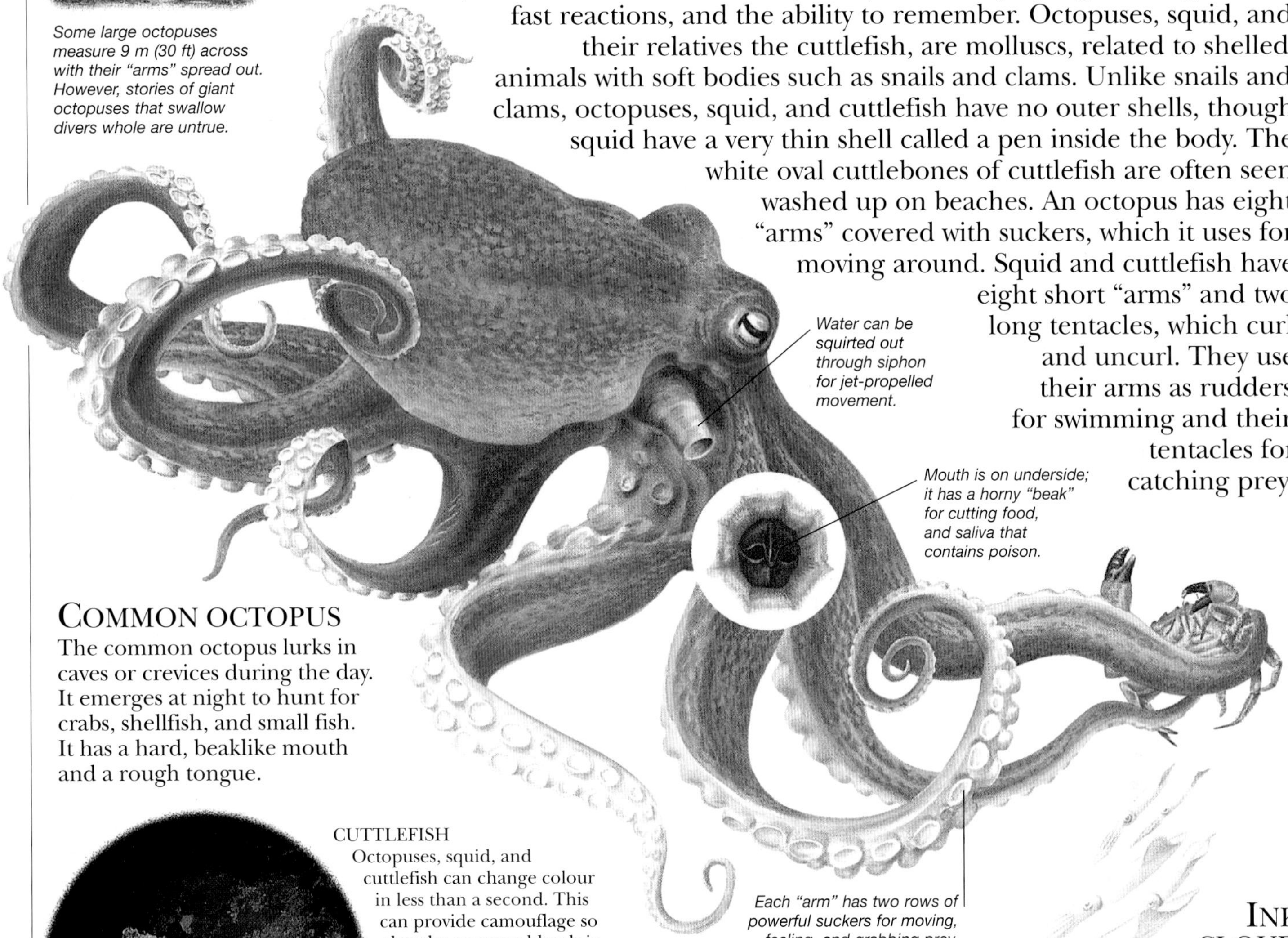

Some large octopuses measure 9 m (30 ft) across with their "arms" spread out. However, stories of giant octopuses that swallow divers whole are untrue.

Water can be squirted out through siphon for jet-propelled movement.

Mouth is on underside; it has a horny "beak" for cutting food, and saliva that contains poison.

COMMON OCTOPUS

The common octopus lurks in caves or crevices during the day. It emerges at night to hunt for crabs, shellfish, and small fish. It has a hard, beaklike mouth and a rough tongue.

CUTTLEFISH

Octopuses, squid, and cuttlefish can change colour in less than a second. This can provide camouflage so that the creature blends in with its surroundings. The dappled red colouring of the cuttlefish shown here is a good disguise among the coral. Change of colour may also indicate a change of mood – a male cuttlefish turns black with rage when it is angry.

Each "arm" has two rows of powerful suckers for moving, feeling, and grabbing prey.

INK CLOUD

Octopuses and squid have an ink gland attached to their digestive system. To confuse an enemy, they squirt ink out of the siphon and cannot be seen behind the dark, watery screen. This ink was once used by artists and is called sepia, which is also the scientific name for cuttlefish.

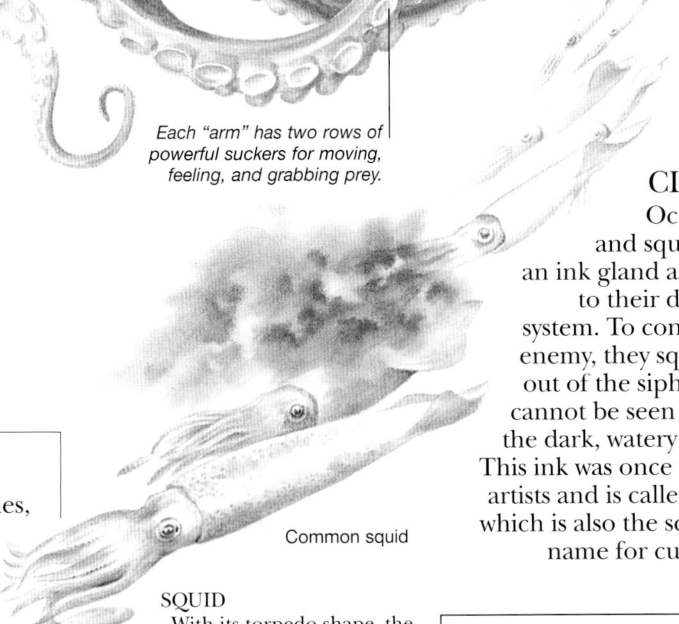

Common squid

GIANT SQUID

Measuring 20 m (60 ft) in length including its tentacles, the giant squid is the world's largest invertebrate. It is an important source of food for sperm whales.

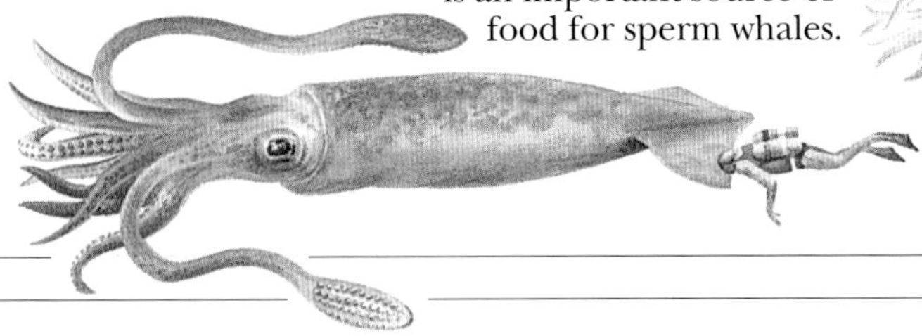

SQUID

With its torpedo shape, the common squid is an especially fast swimmer. Powerful muscles inside the body squirt water rapidly through the siphon, pushing the creature along through the water.

Find out more
ANIMALS
DEEP-SEA WILDLIFE
OCEAN WILDLIFE

OIL

WITHOUT OIL, modern life would grind to a halt. Oil is needed to make the fuels that drive cars, lorries, diesel trains, ships, and aircraft. Power stations burn oil to produce much of the world's electricity, and many homes use oil-burning boilers for heating. Oil is also very important because it is needed to make plastics, textiles, and other useful products. Oil is a dark, thick liquid which lies deep underground and beneath the sea bed. Oil wells are bored to obtain oil, which is also called crude oil or petroleum. Crude oil contains a mixture of chemicals and many different types of oil. Lubricating oil is made from crude oil. It helps machine parts slide easily so that the machine works well.

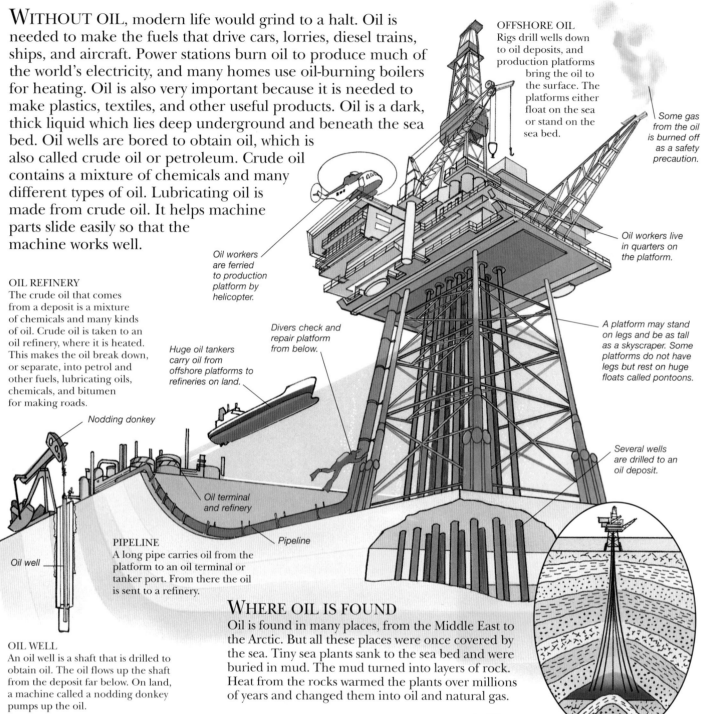

OFFSHORE OIL
Rigs drill wells down to oil deposits, and production platforms bring the oil to the surface. The platforms either float on the sea or stand on the sea bed.

Some gas from the oil is burned off as a safety precaution.

Oil workers are ferried to production platform by helicopter.

Oil workers live in quarters on the platform.

Divers check and repair platform from below.

Huge oil tankers carry oil from offshore platforms to refineries on land.

A platform may stand on legs and be as tall as a skyscraper. Some platforms do not have legs but rest on huge floats called pontoons.

Several wells are drilled to an oil deposit.

Nodding donkey

Oil terminal and refinery

Pipeline

OIL REFINERY
The crude oil that comes from a deposit is a mixture of chemicals and many kinds of oil. Crude oil is taken to an oil refinery, where it is heated. This makes the oil break down, or separate, into petrol and other fuels, lubricating oils, chemicals, and bitumen for making roads.

PIPELINE
A long pipe carries oil from the platform to an oil terminal or tanker port. From there the oil is sent to a refinery.

Oil well

OIL WELL
An oil well is a shaft that is drilled to obtain oil. The oil flows up the shaft from the deposit far below. On land, a machine called a nodding donkey pumps up the oil.

WHERE OIL IS FOUND
Oil is found in many places, from the Middle East to the Arctic. But all these places were once covered by the sea. Tiny sea plants sank to the sea bed and were buried in mud. The mud turned into layers of rock. Heat from the rocks warmed the plants over millions of years and changed them into oil and natural gas.

VEGETABLE OILS
Plants and vegetables, such as olives, corn, and sunflowers, provide valuable oils. Olive oil is made by crushing ripe olives; sunflower oil comes from sunflower seeds. These oils are used in cooking, and sunflower oil is used to make margarine. Factories treat plant and vegetable oils to make soaps and paints; vegetable oil can also be used as fuels, such as biodiesel.

Olive oil

Olives

CHEMICALS FROM OIL
An oil refinery produces many chemicals from crude oil, which are called petro-chemicals. Factories use these chemicals to make plastics, textiles, and other products. Polythene, for example, is made from a gas that comes from oil. Chemicals from oil are also used to make drugs, fertilizers, detergents, and dyes and paints in all colours.

PETROL
Petrol is one of the most important of all oil products. Diesel fuel is another kind of motor fuel made from oil.

Find out more
COAL
GAS
GEOLOGY
PLASTICS
ROCKS AND MINERALS

OLYMPIC GAMES

EVERY TWO YEARS, the world's best athletes compete in the Summer or Winter Olympics. More than 10,000 athletes from around 200 nations take part in the Summer Olympics, in more than 25 sports. The Winter Games are smaller, with 2,000 athletes from about 80 countries competing in seven sports.

The inspiration for today's Olympics came from Ancient Greek games of more than 2,000 years ago. The modern Olympics began in Athens, Greece, in 1896. Individual excellence and team achievement are the theme of the Olympic Games, and not competition between nations. The International Olympic Committee (IOC) chooses a city, not a country, to host the games. No one country "wins" the games, and there is no prize money. Instead, individuals and teams compete for gold (first place), silver (second), and bronze (third) medals – as well as for the glory of taking part.

Five interlocking rings make up the Olympic symbol.

The opening ceremony for the Olympics is a spectacular occasion.

Ski jumping, shown here, is one of the most exciting events in the Winter Olympics.

ANCIENT GAMES
The ancient Olympics began as a religious festival. At first they consisted of just one race, but at their height the games lasted five days and included sports such as wrestling and chariot racing. Only men could compete in, or watch the ancient Olympics. Women held their own games in honour of the goddess Hera.

OLYMPIC FLAME
The Olympic Games open with a spectacular ceremony. The most important part is the lighting of the Olympic Flame with a burning torch. Teams of runners carry the torch from Olympia, in Greece, site of the ancient games, to the stadium where the games are to be held. This ceremony dates back to 1928, when Baron Pierre de Coubertin, founder of the modern Olympics, urged the athletes to "keep alive the flame of the revived Olympic spirit".

POLITICS AND THE GAMES
The huge international audience for the Olympics ensures that any political protests, or terrorist acts that may occur, gain maximum publicity. In 1968, winning athletes raised clenched fists to show that they supported a campaign to give black people more power. Four years later, an act of terrorism caused the deaths of 11 Israeli athletes at Munich, Germany.

The black power salute

WINTER OLYMPICS
A separate Winter Games takes place every four years, midway between two Summer Olympics. It includes ice and snow sports such as skating and skiing.

The Games include a variety of team and individual sports. New ones are added, and old ones are sometimes dropped.

Running   Cycling

Weightlifting   Gymnastics

> **Find out more**
> DANCE
> FOOTBALL AND RUGBY
> GREECE, ANCIENT
> HEALTH AND FITNESS
> SPORTS

OTTOMAN EMPIRE

DURING THE LATE 13TH CENTURY, a group of nomadic Turkish tribes settled in Anatolia, in modern Turkey. They were led by Osman, their first sultan, or ruler. He gave his name to the Ottoman Empire – one of the greatest empires in the world. The empire expanded through war and alliance with neighbours. By 1566, it had spread along the Mediterranean Sea across the Middle East to the Persian Gulf. The Ottomans owed their success to their military skill. Their armies included many Christian recruits organised into groups of highly trained foot soldiers called Janissaries. The empire grew wealthy on the trade it controlled throughout the Middle East. Art and architecture flourished within its borders. Discontent with Ottoman rule, and widespread famine eventually weakened the empire, and it declined during the 19th century before it finally collapsed in 1918. The country of Turkey emerged out of its ruins.

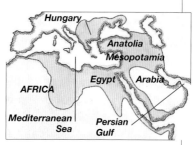

Ottoman Empire at its greatest extent

SULEIMAN THE MAGNIFICENT
The greatest of all Ottoman sultans was Suleiman I (1494-1566), known as Suleiman the Magnificent. During his reign the Ottoman Empire reached the height of its power. A patron of the arts, Suleiman reformed the educational and legal systems.

Janissaries could be recognised by their elaborate headdresses.

Public letter writers wrote letters for people.

THE OTTOMANS

Although the Ottomans were Muslims, they allowed Christians and Jews to practise their own religions and tolerated the many different peoples who lived within their empire. The sultans lived in great luxury and wealth and encouraged the arts and learning. Ottoman women had to live in a separate section of the household called a harem.

OTTOMAN EMPIRE

1281-1324 Osman founds Ottoman Empire.

1333 Ottomans capture Gallipoli, Turkey, giving them a foothold in Europe.

1453 Ottomans capture city of Constantinople (now Istanbul), the capital of the Byzantine Empire; the city becomes the capital of the new empire.

1566 Ottoman Empire reaches its greatest extent.

1571 Christian navy destroys Turkish fleet at Lepanto.

1697-1878 Russia slowly expels the Turks from the lands around the Black Sea.

1878-1913 Turks expelled from most of their European possessions.

1914-18 Ottoman Empire fights with Germany and Austria in World War I.

1918 Troops of several allied nations including Britain and Greece occupy the Ottoman Empire.

1922 Last sultan is overthrown. Turkey is declared a republic.

BATTLE OF LEPANTO
To stop the growth of Ottoman power, Pope Pius V formed a Christian league that included Spain, Venice, Genoa, and Naples. In 1571 the Christian forces defeated the Turks at the Battle of Lepanto, off the coast of Greece. The defeat was a very serious setback to the Ottoman Empire and ended Turkish naval power in the Mediterranean Sea.

SICK MAN OF EUROPE
During the 19th century, the Ottoman Empire lost its grip on its European possessions and was in danger of falling apart. The empire became known as the "Sick Man of Europe".

A CONSULTATION ABOUT THE STATE OF TURKEY.

A 19th-century cartoon mocks the declining state of the Ottoman Empire.

Find out more
BYZANTINE EMPIRE
ISLAM

OXYGEN

WE CANNOT SEE, SMELL, or taste oxygen, yet without oxygen, none of us could survive longer than a few minutes. It is fortunate, then, that oxygen is the most common substance on Earth. Oxygen is a gas. Mixed with other gases, it makes up about one fifth of the air we breathe. Most of the oxygen in the world, though, does not float free as a gas. Instead, the oxygen is bound up in combination with other substances – in a solid or liquid form. This is because oxygen is chemically reactive: it readily combines with other substances, often giving off energy in the process. Burning is an example of oxygen at work. When a piece of timber burns, oxygen is combining with the wood and giving off heat. Oxygen is also found in water, combined with atoms of another gas, hydrogen. Oxygen can be extracted from water by passing an electric current through it. The electricity breaks the water into its parts (the gases oxygen and hydrogen), and oxygen bubbles off.

RESPIRATION

Our bodies need oxygen to release the energy consumed when we use our muscles. The oxygen we breathe in is used to "burn" the food we eat, producing energy. This process is called respiration. Blood carries the oxygen from the lungs, which extract it from the air, to the muscles where it is needed.

BURNING

Nothing can burn without oxygen. In outer space there is no air or oxygen, so it would be impossible to light a fire. The rocket motors used to launch spacecraft need oxygen to burn the rocket fuel and propel the craft upwards. Spacecraft therefore carry their own supply of pure oxygen which mixes with the fuel in the rocket motor. When anything burns in pure oxygen, it produces a very hot flame. In welding machines a fuel gas is burned with pure oxygen, producing a flame hot enough to melt metals.

OXYGEN CYCLE

Breathing air or burning fuel removes oxygen from the atmosphere and gives off carbon dioxide. Plants do the reverse. During the day, they produce energy for growth by the process of photosynthesis. The green parts of the plant take in sunlight, water, and carbon dioxide to make new cells, and give off oxygen. So oxygen continually passes into and out of the air. This is called the oxygen cycle.

People and animals breathe in oxygen.

Green plants absorb carbon dioxide breathed out by living creatures.

Mountain climbers, astronauts, and undersea divers carry a supply of oxygen to breathe. A special valve releases the oxygen at the correct pressure for breathing.

OXYGEN IN WATER

Sea water contains dissolved oxygen. Fish use this oxygen to breathe. Water flows over their gills, which extract the oxygen. Unlike other fish, some sharks can breathe only when moving in the water. To avoid suffocating, they must swim constantly, even when asleep.

Find out more

CHEMISTRY
HUMAN BODY
LUNGS AND BREATHING
PLANTS
SCIENCE

PACIFIC OCEAN

ON A MAP OF THE PACIFIC OCEAN, the sunny, tropical Pacific islands look like tiny grains of sand scattered on the sea. The first adventurous settlers of these islands sailed from Southeast Asia. They spread gradually across the region, travelling over the vast expanses of ocean in their light wooden sailing boats. Today the islands are divided into three main groups: Micronesia to the north, Melanesia to the south, and Polynesia to the east. There are twelve independent countries in the Pacific, including Fiji, Tonga, and Nauru, one of the world's smallest nations. Europeans first arrived in the Pacific in the 16th century, and a number of islands maintain strong links with Europe. New Caledonia, for instance, is French. Many Pacific islanders lead lives that have barely changed for centuries, but there are a number of important modern industries, including large-scale fishing and mining, as well as tourism.

There are some 25,000 Pacific islands, but only a few thousand are inhabited. They stretch across the central part of the Pacific Ocean, straddling the equator and occupying an area larger than the whole of Asia. To the west and southwest lie Southeast Asia, Australia, and New Zealand; North and South America are to the east.

Wooden sailing boats called outriggers have a main hull and floats on either side, like a catamaran.

ISLAND LIFE
Many Pacific islands are very small. They are the tops of submerged mountains. Coral reefs protect them from the Pacific waves. On the remoter islands, people live much as their ancestors did. Their simple houses have thatched roofs made of palm fronds. Families keep pigs and chickens and grow fruit and vegetables. They use traditional boats for fishing and for trade between the islands.

Those taking part in the spectacular traditional dances of Papua New Guinea wear costumes decorated with feathers and beads.

United States military bases cover virtually all of some Pacific Islands, mainly in Micronesia.

EASTER ISLAND
Tiny, remote Easter Island is one of the furthest east of the Pacific islands. A Dutch admiral gave the island its name when he landed there on Easter Day in 1722. More than 1,000 years ago the islanders' Polynesian ancestors carved mysterious stone statues, which still dot the dry, barren landscape.

There are more than 600 of these huge heads on Easter Island, some over 20 m (65 ft) tall.

PAPUA NEW GUINEA
New Guinea, one of the world's largest islands, is part of Melanesia. Half of it belongs to Indonesia and is called Irian Jaya. The other half is a mountainous independent country called Papua New Guinea. Its thick tropical forests are the home of many remote tribes who have little contact with the outside world.

WAKE ISLAND
The United States controls a number of Pacific islands, including Wake Island (above) and Midway, which was the scene of a major battle in World War II. The islands of Hawaii form one of the 50 states of the United States.

Find out more
OCEANS AND SEAS
WORLD WAR II

Volcano	Mountain	Ancient monument	Capital city	Large city/town	Small city/town

STATISTICS

Area: 790,225 sq km (305,106 sq miles)
Population: 8,490,000
Number of independent countries: 12
Languages: English, local languages and dialects
Religions: Protestant, Roman Catholic, Hindu
Highest point: Mount Wilhelm (Papua New Guinea) 4,509 m (14,793 ft)
Main occupations: Agriculture, fishing

NEW CALEDONIA

The Isle of Pines (above) is one of the smallest inhabited islands in the New Caledonia group. Like many of the Pacific Islands, New Caledonia is governed by a larger, more powerful country. France rules New Caledonia, and French aid provides one-third of the country's income. Most of the rest comes from the export of nickel – the islands have 40 per cent of the world's reserves of the metal.

FIJI
Area: 18,270 sq km (7,054 sq miles)
Population: 945,000
Capital: Suva
Currency: Fiji dollar

KIRIBATI
Area: 710 sq km (274 sq miles)
Population: 113,000
Capital: Bairiki
Currency: Australian dollar

MARSHALL ISLANDS
Area: 181 sq km (70 sq miles)
Population: 65,000
Capital: Delap District
Currency: U.S. dollar

MICRONESIA
Area: 2,900 sq km (1,120 sq miles)
Population: 107,000
Capital: Palikir
Currency: U.S. dollar

NAURU
Area: 21.2 sq km (8.2 sq miles)
Population: 14,000
Government Centre: Yaren
Currency: Australian dollar

PAPUA NEW GUINEA
Area: 462,840 sq km (178,700 sq miles)
Population: 6,057,000
Capital: Port Moresby
Currency: Kina

PALAU
Area: 497 sq km (192 sq miles)
Population: 21,000
Capital: Koror
Currency: U.S. dollar

SAMOA
Area: 2,840 sq km (1,027 sq miles)
Population: 220,000
Capital: Apia
Currency: Tala

SOLOMON ISLANDS
Area: 289,000 sq km (111,583 sq miles)
Population: 596,000
Capital: Honiara
Currency: Solomon Islands dollar

TONGA
Area: 750 sq km (290 sq miles)
Population: 121,000
Capital: Nuku'alofa
Currency: Tongan pa'anga

TUVALU
Area: 26 sq km (10 sq miles)
Population: 12,000
Capital: Fongafale
Currency: Australian dollar

VANUATU
Area: 12,190 sq km (4,706 sq miles)
Population: 219,000
Capital: Port-Villa
Currency: Vatu

SCALE BAR

| 0 | 1000 | 2000 | km |
| 0 | 1000 | 2000 | miles |

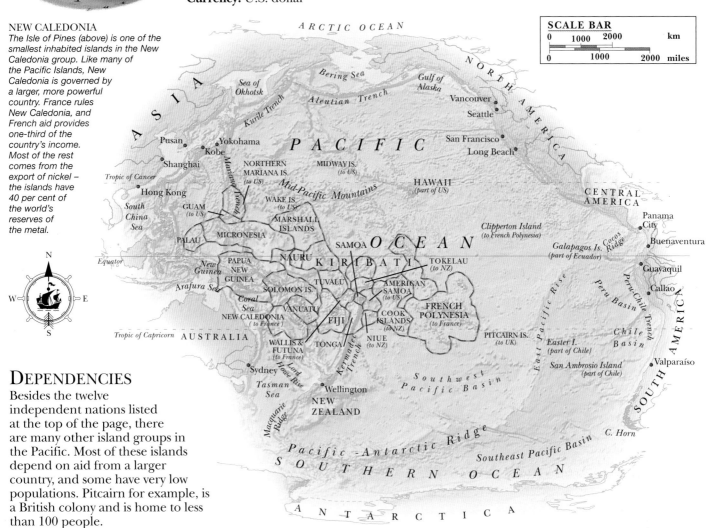

DEPENDENCIES

Besides the twelve independent nations listed at the top of the page, there are many other island groups in the Pacific. Most of these islands depend on aid from a larger country, and some have very low populations. Pitcairn for example, is a British colony and is home to less than 100 people.

PAINTERS

ARTISTS USE PAINT in the same way that writers use words to convey ideas on paper. Painters capture the likeness of a face or a flower, but they can do much more than just paint a realistic image. Painters work skilfully with colour, texture, and shape to create all kinds of eye-catching images of the world as they see it. Many cultures throughout history has produced its own great painters, from Giotto in the 14th century to Picasso in the 20th century. There have been many different groups, or movements, in painting, such as classicism, cubism, and pop art. Painters change the way we see the world. Rembrandt's portrait paintings, for example, are powerful studies from real life, whereas Salvador Dali's strange surrealist (dreamlike) landscapes are drawn from his imagination. Painters use all kinds of paint to create a picture – thick blobs of oil colour daubed onto a canvas with a palette knife; delicate brushstrokes of water-colour on a sheet of paper. Some painters dab paint on with sponges, rags, even their fingers; others flick paint onto a surface. Whatever the medium (materials) used, each great painter has his or her own distinctive style.

EARLY PAINTERS
The artists of ancient Egypt decorated the walls of tombs with scenes of gods and goddesses and of hunting and feasting. The Minoan people of early Greece painted their houses and palaces with pictures of dancers, birds, and flowers. Roman artists painted gods and goddesses and scenes from classical mythology.

MEDIEVAL PAINTERS
Up until the 14th century, Western artists painted mostly Christian subjects – the life of Christ and the saints. Painters used rich colours and thin layers of gold to make these religious paintings. These early artists used different methods of painting people from later Western painters, but although the paintings may look flat to us, they are no less powerful. Artists worked on wood panels for altarpieces and painted directly on church walls.

People in medieval paintings sometimes look stiff and expressionless, like the figures in this 11th-century picture (left) of an emperor, a saint, and an angel.

The Sistine Chapel ceiling, painted by Michelangelo.

RENAISSANCE
One of the greatest periods in European painting was the Renaissance, which reached its height in Italy in the late 15th and early 16th centuries. During the Renaissance, painters developed more realistic styles of painting. They studied perspective and the human body, painted more realistic landscapes, and developed portrait painting.

MICHELANGELO
Michelangelo Buonarroti (1475-1564) is one of the best-known Italian Renaissance painters. Much of his work was for Pope Julius II, who commissioned him to paint the ceiling of the Sistine Chapel in the Vatican, in Rome, between 1508 and 1512.

Michelangelo had difficulty in reaching certain parts of the ceiling in the Sistine Chapel, so he built a scaffold and sometimes lay on his back to paint.

GIOTTO
The Italian artist Giotto (c.1266-1337) painted at the beginning of the Renaissance. He brought a new sense of naturalness to paintings. The painting shown above is called *The Flight into Egypt*. It shows Mary and Jesus on a donkey being led by Joseph.

REMBRANDT

Most people know the Dutch artist Rembrandt Harmenszoon van Rijn (1606-69) only by his first name. He is well known for his portraits which are full of expression. The painting shown here is one of many self-portraits.

ROMANTIC MOVEMENT

During the late 18th and early 19th centuries, painters such as the French artist Eugène Delacroix (1798-1863) began a new style of painting, which became known as the Romantic Movement. The romantics used bright colour and a free handling of paint to create their dramatic pictures. The English painter J.M.W. Turner (1775-1851) painted landscapes and seascapes flooded with light and colour.

EASTERN PAINTERS

While European art was developing, Eastern artists were evolving their own styles of painting. The Chinese observed nature accurately and painted exquisite pictures with simple brushstrokes in ink on silk and paper. Some Japanese artists, such as Hokusai (1760-1849), made beautiful prints.

This painting is by the modern Japanese painter Kaii Higashiyama (born 1918); it is called Flowery Glow.

PICASSO

Many people believe that the Spanish painter Pablo Picasso (1881-1973) was the most creative and influential artist of the 20th century. From a very young age, Picasso was extremely skilful at drawing and painting. His restless personality led him to paint in many different styles. One style was his "blue period" of painting, when he concentrated on blue as the main colour for his pictures. In 1907, Picasso painted a picture called *Les Demoiselles D'Avignon*, which shocked many people – it was a painting of human figures represented by angular and distorted shapes. This led to a style of painting called cubism.

This is a detail from the painting by the French artist Fragonard (1732-1806) called The Swing.

This photograph shows Picasso with a painting of his children, Claude and Paloma. He is on his way to show this painting at an exhibition of his work.

The Poppy Field, *by Claude Monet*

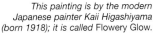

MONET

Claude Monet (1840-1926) was the leader of the impressionists. He painted many pictures of the flowers in his garden at Giverny and in the French countryside, including the picture above right, called *The Poppy Field*. Seen close up, the picture consists of many brushstrokes of different colours, but from a distance the dabs of colour come together to form a field of red flowers.

IMPRESSIONISM

At an exhibition in Paris in 1874 a painting by the French artist Claude Monet caused an uproar. Art critics and the public were used to seeing realistic objects in pictures, but Monet and his fellow artists, known as impressionists, painted in dabs of colour to create the effect of light and shade. Other great artists of the impressionist movement were Camille Pissarro, Pierre Auguste Renoir, Edgar Degas, Mary Cassatt, and Alfred Sisley.

HOCKNEY

David Hockney (born 1937) is a well-known British painter. He is famous for his pictures of California, especially paintings of swimming pools such as this one, called *A Bigger Splash*. Hockney works with many different materials, including photographs and colour photocopies.

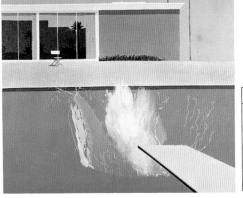

MODERN PAINTERS

Since the beginning of the 20th century, painters have experimented with different ways of creating pictures. Picasso and Georges Braque stuck fabric, sand, and newsprint on to canvases to make collages. Piet Mondrian painted in straight lines and right angles. Action painting was developed by the American artist Jackson Pollock, who splashed paint onto huge canvases on his studio floor.

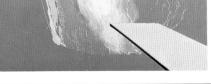

Find out more
ARCHITECTURE
COLOUR
LEONARDO DA VINCI
MORRIS, WILLIAM
PAINTING
RENAISSANCE

PAINTING

SINCE PREHISTORIC PEOPLE first applied natural pigments to cave walls, artists have painted to express themselves. Paintings can be important historical documents, providing clues as to how people dressed at the time of the painting and what their customs and interests were. Training is not necessary in order to paint, but it can help in learning basic techniques. A painting can be done with oil paints, watercolours, or as a fresco – that is, painting onto wet plaster. The type of paint depends on what the powdered pigment or colour is mixed with to allow it to be brushed onto the painting. Oil paints use a vegetable oil such as linseed or poppy oil. Before oil paints were developed in the 15th century, artists made tempera paintings in which the pigments were mixed with an emulsion such as egg yolk. Artists may paint onto almost any surface: from rock and wood to fabric, paper, metal, plastics – even skin. They may also choose any subject, such as a still life or something abstract like random shapes.

CAVE PAINTING
Eighteen thousand years ago, people used burned bones and wood, and different-coloured earth mixed with water or animal fat, to paint scenes on cave walls. South African bushmen produced this cave painting. It shows men hunting an eland, a type of deer.

OIL PAINTING

Oil paint has the advantage of drying slowly. This gives the artist time to change things on the painting while the paint is still wet, and makes it easier to blend colours and tones or even scrape off the paint where it is not working successfully. Oil paint can be applied thickly or thinly. It is flexible enough to be built up in layers to produce a particular effect. The paint is applied to a canvas (a piece of fabric stretched onto a frame) with brushes, a painting knife, or the fingers.

Palette

Thumb hole allows artist to hold palette with one hand while painting with the other.

Linseed oil is a popular binder for oil paint.

Turpentine for thinning paint

The best brushes for oil painting are made from hog's hair or sable. Some brushes are made of synthetic fibres.

Pigments for making oil paints may come from natural sources such as berries, bark, roots, and earth, or from petroleum and metals.

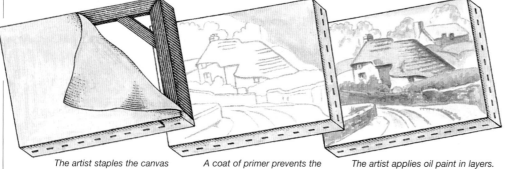

The artist staples the canvas to a wooden frame. This makes the canvas taut.

A coat of primer prevents the canvas from absorbing the paint; then an outline is done.

The artist applies oil paint in layers. When dry, the painting will be coated with varnish to protect it against dirt.

PREPARING FOR OIL PAINTING
Linen or cotton canvas is a popular surface or "support" for oil painting. Before beginning, the canvas must be specially prepared (left). Once it is ready, the painter can begin to apply layers of paint. Some artists draw outlines in charcoal or pencil on the canvas first; others put the paint straight on. Oil paint can be thinned down with turpentine to produce an effect rather like a watercolour.

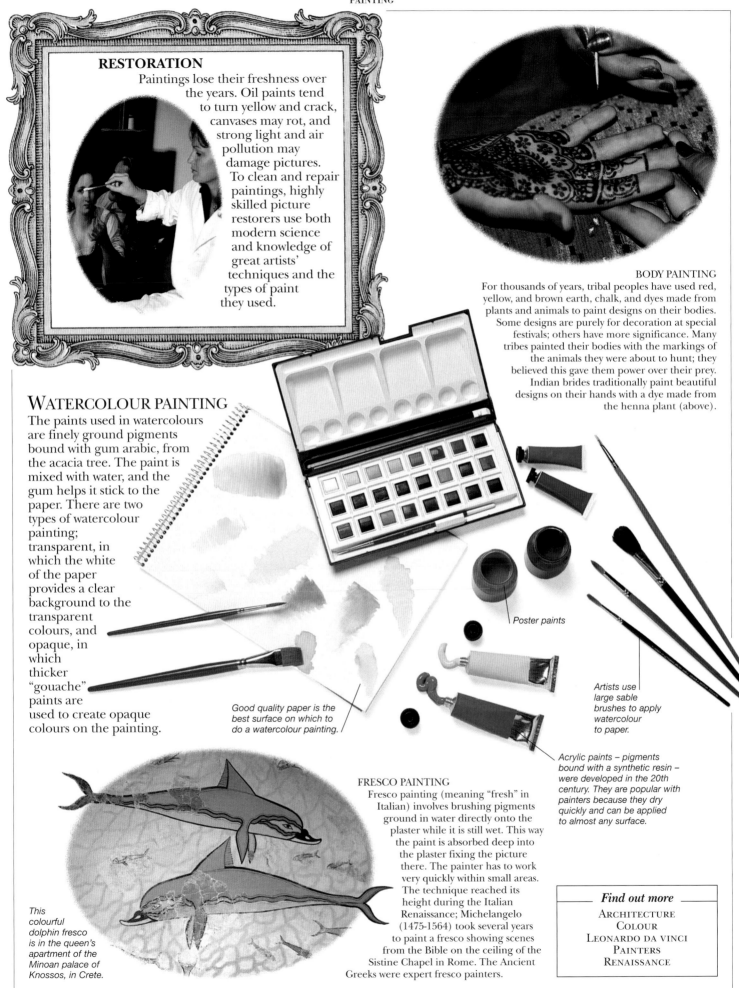

RESTORATION

Paintings lose their freshness over the years. Oil paints tend to turn yellow and crack, canvases may rot, and strong light and air pollution may damage pictures. To clean and repair paintings, highly skilled picture restorers use both modern science and knowledge of great artists' techniques and the types of paint they used.

BODY PAINTING

For thousands of years, tribal peoples have used red, yellow, and brown earth, chalk, and dyes made from plants and animals to paint designs on their bodies. Some designs are purely for decoration at special festivals; others have more significance. Many tribes painted their bodies with the markings of the animals they were about to hunt; they believed this gave them power over their prey. Indian brides traditionally paint beautiful designs on their hands with a dye made from the henna plant (above).

WATERCOLOUR PAINTING

The paints used in watercolours are finely ground pigments bound with gum arabic, from the acacia tree. The paint is mixed with water, and the gum helps it stick to the paper. There are two types of watercolour painting; transparent, in which the white of the paper provides a clear background to the transparent colours, and opaque, in which thicker "gouache" paints are used to create opaque colours on the painting.

Poster paints

Good quality paper is the best surface on which to do a watercolour painting.

Artists use large sable brushes to apply watercolour to paper.

Acrylic paints – pigments bound with a synthetic resin – were developed in the 20th century. They are popular with painters because they dry quickly and can be applied to almost any surface.

FRESCO PAINTING

Fresco painting (meaning "fresh" in Italian) involves brushing pigments ground in water directly onto the plaster while it is still wet. This way the paint is absorbed deep into the plaster fixing the picture there. The painter has to work very quickly within small areas. The technique reached its height during the Italian Renaissance; Michelangelo (1475-1564) took several years to paint a fresco showing scenes from the Bible on the ceiling of the Sistine Chapel in Rome. The Ancient Greeks were expert fresco painters.

This colourful dolphin fresco is in the queen's apartment of the Minoan palace of Knossos, in Crete.

Find out more

ARCHITECTURE
COLOUR
LEONARDO DA VINCI
PAINTERS
RENAISSANCE

PANKHURST FAMILY

IN THE YEARS LEADING UP TO WORLD WAR I, the cry of "votes for women" was front-page news. Thousands of long-skirted women marched, demonstrated, and fought for their right to vote. Three fearless women inspired them: Emmeline Pankhurst and her daughters, Christabel and Sylvia. They were not the first to demand votes for women, but they used completely new methods. In 1903 they founded the Women's Social and Political Union (WSPU). At a time when women were supposed to live quiet, respectable lives, the Pankhursts declared war on Parliament for refusing the vote to women, fought with police, and even went to prison for their cause.

1858 Emmeline born.

1880 Christabel born.

1882 Sylvia born.

1903 WSPU founded, Manchester.

1905 Christabel arrested for the first time.

1911 WSPU attacks on property.

1912 Christabel flees to Paris.

1928 Emmeline dies.

1958 Christabel dies.

1960 Sylvia dies.

Women carried placards demanding the vote.

WSPU members demonstrated outside the Houses of Parliament.

Emmeline Pankhurst

Police treated protesters brutally.

EMMELINE AND CHRISTABEL
Both women, shown here in prison clothes, were forceful personalities and brilliant organizers. Christabel (right) trained as a lawyer, but because she was a woman was not allowed to practise. Emmeline, her mother, was an inspiring speaker.

WSPU
The Pankhursts founded the Women's Social and Political Union (WSPU). Its aim was to get the vote "by any means". The WSPU used daring tactics and thousands of women joined in the fight. Emmeline inspired them; Christabel led them like an army commander. They heckled politicians, attacked property, and hundreds were arrested.

SYLVIA PANKHURST
A dedicated campaigner, Sylvia went to prison 13 times. She was a talented artist, and designed WSPU banners and badges. She worked with poor women in London's East End, and fell out with Emmeline and Christabel because she believed the WSPU was too middle class.

CASTING THE FIRST VOTE
In 1914, World War I began, and the WSPU split. Emmeline and Christabel supported the war effort; Sylvia opposed it. After the war, in 1918, women finally won their right to vote, largely thanks to the Pankhursts. Christabel stood for Parliament, but did not win a seat.

PUBLICITY
The Pankhursts publicised their cause brilliantly. They adopted three distinctive colours: green (for hope); purple (for dignity); and white (for purity). WSPU members carried these colours at all times, as sashes, badges, or banners, so people recognized them immediately. Today, these are still the colours of the women's movement.

VOTES FOR WOMEN

WSPU badge designed by Sylvia Pankhurst

Find out more
GOVERNMENT AND POLITICS
HUMAN RIGHTS
WOMEN'S RIGHTS
WORLD WAR I

PEASANTS REVOLT

IN JUNE 1381, A MAJOR UPRISING occurred in England when angry peasants marched on London in protest against an unfair poll tax and harsh working conditions. Known as the Peasants' Revolt, it was the most important uprising by ordinary people in English history. The leaders were Wat Tyler, Jack Straw, and John Ball, a former priest. They led 100,000 men from Kent and Essex to London burning buildings and looting along the way. They also murdered the Archbishop of Canterbury, and some government ministers. Richard II, the 14-year-old king, met the peasants at Smithfield and agreed to abolish serfdom and the poll tax. Most peasants dispersed, but Tyler was killed. After the revolt, Richard failed to keep his promises, but such a heavy poll tax was not imposed again, and serfdom gradually disappeared.

WAT TYLER AND JACK STRAW
Wat Tyler led the Kentish rebels. Jack Straw, a thresher, led a group who set fire to buildings, including the palace of John of Gaunt, the king's uncle.

MORE REVOLTS
Rebellions broke out in St Albans, Hertfordshire, Bury St. Edmonds, Suffolk, Cambridgeshire, Huntingdonshire, Norfolk, and Sussex. Most of the outbreaks were fairly short-lived. The violence frightened the government and after the revolt Jack Straw and John Ball were executed.

POLL TAX
Poll means "head", and the poll tax was levied on every person over the age of 14. In 1377, parliament imposed a poll tax of one groat to meet the costs of the Hundred Years War. In 1380, it was raised to one shilling (5p) per head, a huge amount then. This sparked off the revolts.

Gold noble

Groat

Peasants and Richard II at Smithfield, London

Wat Tyler falls from his horse and is killed.

RICHARD II
Grandson of Edward III, Richard II (1367–1400) became king in 1377, aged 10. He used courage and daring to suppress the Peasants' Revolt. He was deposed by Henry IV in 1400 and was either murdered or died of starvation.

Agricultural tools of the 1300s

Scythe

Sickle

WEAPONS
The peasants had few real weapons they could use in a revolt. Instead they took with them the tools of their trade – pitchforks, scythes, billhooks, and sickles – all of which could cause ugly wounds. As the revolt progressed, many peasants looted swords and daggers.

Pitchfork

SERFDOM
Farming was hard in the 1300s. Many peasants were serfs, or villeins, who effectively belonged to the lords of the manor, and were forced to pay heavy dues. However, after the Black Death (1347-50), which killed thousands, surviving peasants were able to demand higher wages and better working conditions.

Find out more
BLACK DEATH
FARMING, HISTORY OF
HUNDRED YEARS WAR
MEDIEVAL EUROPE
UNITED KINGDOM, HISTORY OF

ANCIENT
PERSIANS

MORE THAN 3,000 YEARS AGO, the present-day country of Iran was home to various tribes, including the Medes and the Persians. For many years, the Medes ruled the area, but in 550 BCE Cyrus, the Persian king of a small state called Ashan, conquered the Medes and set out to create a vast kingdom. Within 30 years Persia had become the most powerful nation in the world, and the Persian Empire covered all of Mesopotamia, Anatolia (Turkey), the eastern Mediterranean, and what are now Pakistan and Afghanistan. For more than 200 years the Persian Empire was the greatest the world had ever seen. The Persians were skilled warriors, horse riders, and craft workers. They were also highly organized. Under Darius I, also called Darius the Great, the empire was divided into provinces called satrapies. A network of roads linked the provinces and enabled people to trade easily. Darius introduced a postal system and a single currency to unify the empire. The empire flourished until the Greek leader Alexander the Great conquered Persia in 331 BCE.

CYRUS THE GREAT
Cyrus (ruled 550-529 BCE) founded the Persian Empire. During his reign many different peoples, including Babylonians, Egyptians, Greeks, and Syrians, lived in the Persian Empire.

People bringing gifts to the royal palace

Reliefs show people arriving for a festival on New Year's Day

PERSEPOLIS

In about 520 BCE Darius I began to build the city of Persepolis. Building continued in the reign of Xerxes I (486-465 BCE). Persepolis was the site of many beautiful buildings, including the royal palace. The city was used only once a year at New Year, when the peoples of the empire brought tributes (gifts) to the king.

Remains of Persepolis include statues such as the carved head of this horse in the Central Palace.

ZOROASTRIANISM
The Persian people followed the teachings of a prophet named Zoroaster, who lived from about 628 to 551 BCE. Zoroastrianism was the main religion in Persia until the country became Muslim in the 7th century CE.

Zoroastrian priests carried a mace with a bull's head as a symbol of the priests' religious battle against evil.

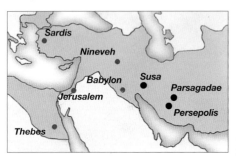

PERSIAN EMPIRE
At its height, the Persian Empire stretched from the borders of India to the River Nile in Egypt. Susa was the administrative capital of the empire, Persepolis was the royal capital, and the two cities were linked by a 2,700-km- (1678-mile-) long Royal Road.

Sardis
Nineveh
Babylon
Susa
Parsagadae
Jerusalem
Persepolis
Thebes

PERSEPOLIS TODAY
When Alexander the Great invaded the Persian Empire, he burned Persepolis to the ground. But the ruins of the city, including the royal palace, can still be seen today in southern Iran.

ANCIENT PERSIANS

550 BCE Cyrus the Great defeats the Medes peoples and forms the Persian Empire.

538 BCE Cyrus conquers the Babylonian Empire.

529 BCE Cyrus dies.

525 BCE Persians conquer Egypt.

521-486 BCE Reign of Darius the Great.

510 BCE Persians invade southeast Europe and central Asia.

499-449 BCE Persian Wars between Persian Empire and Greek states, because Persian kings felt threatened by the democracy of Greece.

490 BCE Greeks defeat Persians at the Battle of Marathon.

480 BCE Greek navy defeats Persians at the Battle of Salamis.

334 BCE Alexander the Great invades Persia.

331 BCE Alexander defeats Persians at the Battle of Gaugamela. Persian Empire collapses.

Find out more

ALEXANDER THE GREAT
ASSYRIANS
BABYLONIANS
GREECE, ANCIENT
MIDDLE EAST

PHOENICIANS

A TINY GROUP OF CITIES perched along the coast of the Mediterranean produced the most famous sailors and traders of the ancient world. These seafaring people were called the Phoenicians. The cities of Phoenicia were linked by the sea, and they traded in many goods, including purple dyes, glass, and ivory. From 1200 to 350 BCE the Phoenicians controlled trade throughout the Mediterranean. They spread their trading links to many points around the coast. Their most famous trading post was Carthage on the north coast of Africa. During its history, Phoenicia was conquered by several foreign empires, including the Assyrians, Babylonians, and Persians. These foreign rulers usually allowed the Phoenicians to continue trading. But in 332 BCE Alexander the Great conquered Phoenicia, and Greek people came to live there. The Greeks brought their own culture with them, and the Phoenician culture faded away.

Phoenicians made purple dye from the liquid produced by crushing murex seashells.

Sardinia · Sicily · Byblos · Gades · Black Sea · Rhodes · Tingis · Malta · Carthage · Cyprus · Sidon · Tyre · Mediterranean Sea

PHOENICIA
Phoenicia lay on the coast of the eastern Mediterranean roughly where Lebanon is today. The Phoenicians spread throughout the Mediterranean, to Carthage, Rhodes, Cyprus, Sicily, Malta, Sardinia, Gades (Cadiz), and Tingis (Tangier).

When arriving at a new place to trade, the Phoenicians would lay their goods out on the beach and let the local people come and look at what they had brought.

Sculptures show that Phoenician men wore distinctive conical hats.

Phoenicians traded in a vast array of goods from the Mediterranean, including metals, farm animals, wheat, cloth, jewellery, and gemstones.

Phoenician glassware, such as this glass jar, was a luxury in the ancient world.

PHOENICIAN SHIPS
The Phoenicians' ships were famous all over the Mediterranean, and were the main reason for the Phoenicians' success as traders. The ships had oarsmen, sails, and heavy keels, which enabled them to sail in any direction.

DYEING
The Phoenicians were the only people who knew how to produce a vivid purple dye from murex shells. The dye was considered to be exceptionally beautiful but it was also very expensive. Only high government officials, for example, could wear purple dyed cloth in the Roman Empire.

PHOENICIAN GLASSWARE
Ancient Egyptians made glass many years before the Phoenicians did, but Egyptian glass was cloudy, whereas Phoenician glass was clear. The Phoenicians were able to make clear glass because their sand contained large amounts of quartz.

BYBLOS
The Phoenician port of Byblos was famous for its trade in papyrus – a kind of paper made in Egypt by pressing together strands of papyrus reeds. The Greeks called papyrus *biblos* after the port of Byblos. A number of our words concerned with books, such as Bible, and bibliography (a list of books), come from *biblos*.

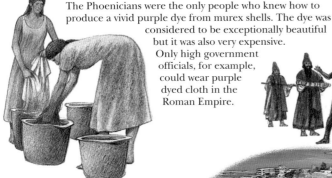

The papyrus reed grows in the warm, damp conditions of the River Nile in Egypt.

Find out more
ALEXANDER the great
ALPHABETS
ASSYRIANS
BABYLONIANS
GREECE, ANCIENT
PERSIANS, ANCIENT
SUMERIANS

PHOTOGRAPHY

A 19th-century photographer tries to hold a baby's attention while he struggles to operate his bulky camera.

MORE THAN TWO HUNDRED million times a day, a camera shutter clicks somewhere in the world to take a photograph. There are family snapshots capturing happy memories, dramatic news pictures, advertising and fashion shots, pictures of the planet beamed back from satellites in space, and much more. The uses of photography are numerous, and new applications are being found all the time. The first photographs were made by coating sheets of polished metal with light-sensitive chemicals, but the image appeared in dull, silvery grey and could only be seen from certain angles. During the 19th century, new processes were invented for spreading the chemicals onto a glass plate or onto a film of cellulose (a kind of plastic). Eventually, photographs could be made in either black-and-white or full colour. Film is still in use today, although it is fast being replaced by digital photography. Digital cameras use a light-sensitive chip, instead of film, and store pictures as digital image files that can be transferred to a computer. There, they can be altered before being printed or sent anywhere in the world via the Internet.

HIGH-SPEED PHOTOGRAPHY
With the use of special cameras and lights, high-speed photography can reveal movement too fast for the eye to see. A brief burst of light from an electronic flash, lasting less than one millionth of a second, freezes objects moving at hundreds of kilometres per hour.

Flash "freezes" the explosion as the bullet enters the apple.

HISTORY OF PHOTOGRAPHY

A Frenchman named Joseph Niépce took the first photograph in 1826. The exposure took eight hours to make, and the picture was fuzzy and dark. In 1837, another Frenchman, Louis Daguerre, discovered how to make sharp photographs in a few minutes. Just two years later an English scientist, William Fox Talbot, invented the process that is still used for developing films today. In the early days, cameras were bulky, and for each picture photographers had to carry a separate glass plate. Then, in 1888, American George Eastman invented the Kodak camera. It was small and light and came loaded with a roll of film rather than plates. Taking a picture became so easy that anyone could try it.

People in early portraits often look uncomfortable and stiff because they had to keep still for several minutes.

ALL-ROUND VIEW
Photography can create strange and dramatic views of familiar objects. Extreme "fisheye" lenses with angles of view as wide as 180 degrees can produce highly distorted images of the world.

A special macro lens is needed to focus at distances as close as this.

Circular fisheye shot of the view from the top of the Great Pyramid of Khufu in Egypt

The Kodak Box Brownie was so simple that Eastman claimed even a child could use it.

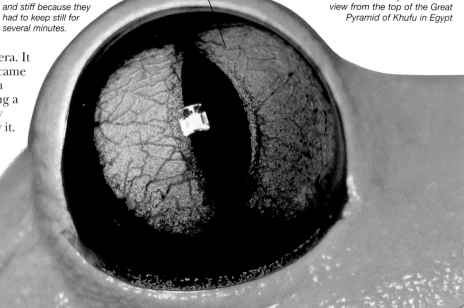

CLOSE-UP PHOTOGRAPHY
Macro, or close-up, photography magnifies tiny details barely visible to the naked eye, such as the beautiful gold-coloured eye of a leaf frog (right).

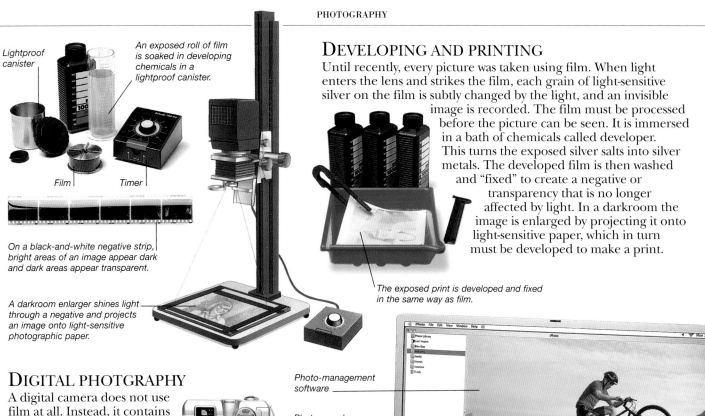

Lightproof canister

An exposed roll of film is soaked in developing chemicals in a lightproof canister.

Film

Timer

On a black-and-white negative strip, bright areas of an image appear dark and dark areas appear transparent.

A darkroom enlarger shines light through a negative and projects an image onto light-sensitive photographic paper.

DEVELOPING AND PRINTING

Until recently, every picture was taken using film. When light enters the lens and strikes the film, each grain of light-sensitive silver on the film is subtly changed by the light, and an invisible image is recorded. The film must be processed before the picture can be seen. It is immersed in a bath of chemicals called developer. This turns the exposed silver salts into silver metals. The developed film is then washed and "fixed" to create a negative or transparency that is no longer affected by light. In a darkroom the image is enlarged by projecting it onto light-sensitive paper, which in turn must be developed to make a print.

The exposed print is developed and fixed in the same way as film.

DIGITAL PHOTGRAPHY

A digital camera does not use film at all. Instead, it contains a light-sensitive image sensor – a chip made up of millions of tiny silicon photo diodes, each of which records the brightness and colour of the light falling on it when the picture is taken. The picture information is translated into digital data and stored on the camera's memory card from where it can be printed or downloaded to a computer.

Photo-management software

Photos can be viewed immediately on the camera's LCD (liquid crystal display) screen.

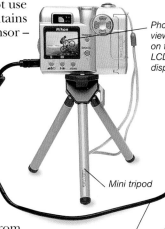

Mini tripod

Connection cable

Laptop computer

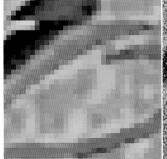

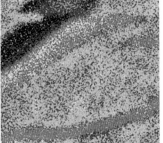

A digital image enlarged until it becomes "pixellated"

Film grain magnified until it becomes visible

DIGITAL AND FILM IN CLOSE-UP

Both digital and film images are made up of minute blocks of colour, so small that they are normally invisible to the naked eye. However, it is possible to see individual pixels when a digital photograph is enlarged on screen and to see separate grains when film or a photographic print is viewed under a microscope or magnifying glass.

CAMERA PHONES

Most new mobile phones have built-in digital cameras, capable of taking photographs and recording short video clips. Both pictures and movies can be sent immediately to other mobile phones, the Internet, or transferred wirelessly to TVs, computers, and printers. As image quality improves, many people choose to use a single device to combine the functions of phone, email, palmtop, camera, video camcorder, and music player.

Find out more
CAMERAS
COLOUR
FILMS
LIGHT
TELEVISION

PHYSICS

THE SCIENCE OF PHYSICS used to be called natural philosophy, which means thinking about and investigating the natural world. Physicists seek to understand and explain the universe from the largest, most distant galaxy to the tiniest invisible particle. Great physicists have wrestled with fundamental questions such as what is it that holds us to the Earth, what is time, and what is inside an atom. Physicists work with theory and experiment. They conduct experiments and then think of a theory, or idea, that explains the results. Then they try new experiments to test their theory. Some theories have become so good at explaining nature that many people refer to them as the laws of physics. For example, one such law states that nothing can travel faster than the speed of light. The German-born physicist Albert Einstein (1879-1955) proposed this in 1905 as part of his revolutionary theory of relativity.

ASTROPHYSICS
Astronomers use physics to find out about the origins and interiors of the Sun and stars. This branch of physics is called astrophysics.

BRANCHES OF PHYSICS
Physics is the science of energy and matter (the materials of which everything is made). There are several branches of physics. They cover a range of subjects from atoms to space.

OPTICS AND THERMAL PHYSICS
Heat and light are important forms of energy: the Sun sends out light and heat that make life possible on Earth. The physics of light is called optics; the branch of physics concerned with heat is called thermal physics.

STATICS
Statics is the branch of physics concerned with calculating and understanding forces that support buildings and bridges.

Satellites transmit radio waves for long-distance communication.

Laws of mechanics are put to use to design and run a car.

MECHANICS
The study of force and movement is a branch of physics known as mechanics.

Coal is burned to produce electricity.

ELECTRICITY
One of the most useful forms of energy is electricity. Physicists study the nature of electricity and find ways of using it in electrical appliances, microchips, and computers.

Accelerator speeds up atomic particles and forces them to collide.

ELECTROMAGNETISM
Physicists have discovered a group of mostly invisible rays called electromagnetic waves. Electromagnetism is the physics of the relationship between magnetism and electric currents.

KINETIC THEORY
Physicists use the idea of molecules to explain the way solids, liquids, and gases behave. This branch of physics is called kinetic theory.

MAGNETISM
Physicists study magnets and the forces that magnets produce. This includes the Earth's magnetism, which comes from the movements of the molten metal core at the centre of the Earth.

Sound waves reflected from the ocean floor bring back information about deep-sea structures.

QUANTUM MECHANICS
Energy can only exist in tiny packets called quanta. This idea is very important in the study of atoms, and it has given rise to a branch of physics called quantum mechanics.

ACOUSTICS
The science of sound is called acoustics. Physicists can use sound to study the interior of the Earth and the oceans.

NUCLEAR PHYSICS
Physicists are constantly searching for a greater understanding of the particles that make up the nucleus (centre) of an atom. This branch of physics is called nuclear physics.

Atomic particles crash into each other to release vast amounts of energy.

GEOPHYSICS
The interior of the Earth is hidden from us, but physicists have discovered that there is great heat and pressure beneath the Earth's crust, which sometimes erupts in volcanoes. Geophysics is the branch of physics concerned with the Earth.

LANDMARKS IN PHYSICS

200s BCE Greek scientist Archimedes explains floating and the way levers work.

1687 English physicist Isaac Newton puts forward the laws of motion and gravity.

1900 German physicist Max Planck introduces quantum theory.

1905 German physicist Albert Einstein publishes his theory of relativity.

1938 German physicists Fritz Strassmann and Otto Hahn split the atom.

English physicist Stephen Hawking (born 1942) developed new theories about the nature of matter, black holes in space, and the origin of the universe that have opened doors to new possibilities in physics.

Find out more
EINSTEIN, ALBERT
ELECTRICITY
FORCE AND MOTION
GRAVITY
HEAT
LIGHT
MAGNETISM
SCIENCE
SOUND

PILGRIMS

ON A BLUSTERY SEPTEMBER DAY in 1620, a small ship set sail from the port of Plymouth, England, bound for North America. The 102 settlers on board hoped that in the New World they could worship freely in their own way, which they had not been able to do in England. Because of their Puritan faith, and because they started one of the colonies that would later grow into the United States, the group became known as the Pilgrims. The Pilgrims landed in what is now Massachusetts and established a settlement called Plymouth. The first winter was hard. The settlers had little food, and it was difficult to farm and fish. But with help from the local Native Americans, the settlement eventually prospered. The Pilgrims replaced their wooden homes with more secure dwellings and started trading furs with the Native Americans. More groups of Puritans came to join the original settlers; together they created one of the first successful European settlements in North America.

16 September 1620 Mayflower sets sail from Plymouth.

19 November Cape Cod is sighted.

Cape Cod Bay

21 November Mayflower anchors in Provincetown harbour.

26 December Plymouth colony founded, Massachusetts.

MAYFLOWER
The Pilgrims sailed to North America in a two-masted ship, the *Mayflower*. The ship was about 30 m (90 ft) long and was built to carry wine and other cargo.

EARLY SETTLEMENT
The first settlements in Plymouth were built of wood from the local forests. The chimneys were made of sticks held together with clay, and the roofs were waterproofed with bark.

Splitting logs to make planks

Food had to be cooked in the open.

Every member of the family had to work hard to build a house and plant crops for food.

GOVERNMENT
The early Plymouth settlers elected their own government which met annually to make laws and levy taxes.

PURITANISM
The Puritan religion stressed hard work and obedience and disapproved of frivolity and idleness.

The Pilgrims held prayer meetings outside until they built churches.

PURITANS
The people known as the Puritans wished to purify the Church of England of its pomp and ritual. They dressed in simple clothes and tried to live in accordance with the Bible.

THANKSGIVING
In the autumn of 1621, the Pilgrims celebrated their first successful harvest. They invited the local Native Americans to join them in a feast of thanksgiving. Thanksgiving, which became a national holiday in 1863, is celebrated in the United States on the fourth Thursday in November.

Find out more
EXPLORERS
NORTH AMERICA
RELIGIONS
UNITED STATES, HISTORY OF

PIRATES

IN TALES ABOUT PIRATES, shady figures row through the moonlight to bury treasure on tropical islands. The reality of a pirate's life, though, was very different from the storybook version. Most pirates were simply criminals who robbed ships at sea and often murdered the crews. Pirates first appeared when trading ships began to cross the Mediterranean about 4,000 years ago. They have flourished ever since in every ocean of the world, but were particularly active from 1500 to 1800. Some pirates, such as Blackbeard, cruised the Caribbean Sea, which was also called the Spanish Main. Others, such as Captain Kidd, attacked ships in the Indian Ocean. Sometimes countries at war encouraged piracy, but only against enemy shipping. They called the pirate ships privateers and gave them letters of marque – official licences to plunder enemy ships. Pirates still exist in the waters off Somalia. They hijack ships, take them into their own ports, and demand ransoms for the ships' owners.

TREASURE MAPS
Buried pirate treasure, marked with an X on a map, is largely the invention of adventure writers. Most of the time pirates attacked lightly armed merchant ships, stealing food and weapons.

PIRATE SHIPS

Traditional pirate vessels were generally small, fast, and manoeuvrable. They floated high in the water so they could escape into shallow creeks and inlets if pursued. They were armed with as many cannons as possible. Some cannons were heavy guns which fired large metal balls; others were lighter swivel guns which fired lead shot.

ANNE BONNY
Anne Bonny was born in Ireland. She fell in love with the pirate "Calico Jack" Rackham and sailed with him. On a captured ship she met another woman pirate, Mary Read. The women pirates were arrested in 1720 but escaped the gallows, as they were both expecting babies.

BLACKBEARD
One of the most terrible pirates was Edward Teach. His nickname was Blackbeard, and his favourite drink was rum and gunpowder. In battle he carried six pistols and wore burning matches twisted into his hair. He died on a British warship in 1718.

SPANISH DOLLAR
The pirate's currency was a Spanish gold dollar worth eight reales (called *real de a ocho*). The pirate term "pieces of eight" comes from the habit of cutting these into eight pieces, each worth one real.

> *Find out more*
> SHIPS AND BOATS

PLANETS

EARTH IS ONE of eight major planets moving around the Sun. Planets are large balls of rock, metal, gases, and liquids orbiting a star. In our solar system, all the planets travel in the same direction around the Sun, each revolving in an elliptical (oval) orbit. Through a telescope, the planets appear as discs of light moving slowly across the night sky. They do not, however, produce light themselves, but reflect light from the Sun. All the planets except Mercury are surrounded by a layer of gas called an atmosphere. The four smaller planets, such as Earth, have a rocky surface, but the four giant planets are mostly gas and liquid. The giant planets are each surrounded by rings. There is a huge difference in temperature between the planets nearest to the Sun and those farthest away. Mercury is hotter than an oven by day, while Neptune is about 200°C (392°F) below freezing. As far as we know, Earth is the only planet that supports life. However, the Sun is one of millions of stars, and planets have already been discovered orbiting hundreds of them. Another planet somewhere might support life.

THE SUN
The Sun is a star – a vast ball of hot gas, far larger than any of the planets.

MARS
Mars is a small, dry planet with a red, rocky surface. It is cold – about -23°C (-9°F) – and has two polar caps of ice and frozen gas. Mars has two tiny moons named Phobos and Deimos.

Mars
Earth
Venus
The Moon

MERCURY
Mercury is so close to the Sun that it has no atmosphere or oceans. It has a rocky surface that rises to a temperature of about 350°C (662°F).

VENUS
Thick clouds cover the whole surface of Venus. They trap the Sun's heat, making Venus the hottest planet in the solar system. The surface temperature of Venus is about 480°C (896°F).

EARTH
The Earth has an atmosphere of air and oceans filled with water. The Earth's average temperature is 22°C (72°F). A source of energy and liquid water are essential for life on the planet. If the Earth were hotter, the water would evaporate; if it were colder, the water would freeze.

JUPITER
Jupiter is the largest planet in the solar system. It has no solid surface as it is made up of a mixture of liquids and gases, with belts of swirling gas forming an atmosphere around it. It is a cold planet, surrounded by a ring of dust, and orbited by more than 60 moons.

ASTEROIDS

Thousands of tiny bodies called asteroids orbit the Sun, mainly travelling in a belt between Mars and Jupiter. Dating from the earliest days of the solar system, most asteroids are lumps of rock and metal just a few kilometres in diameter. Jupiter's gravitational pull can send asteroids into erratic orbits, causing them to collide with planets and other asteroids. Many objects made of ice and rock are also known to exist in the Kuiper Belt, an area in the solar system beyond the orbit of Neptune.

PLANET PICTURES

Space technology has shown us what the other planets in the solar system look like and what they are made of; it has also established that these other planets are unlikely to support life. The images shown right and at the foot of the next page were taken from a variety of spacecraft.

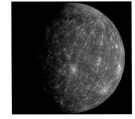

The heavily cratered surface of Mercury is revealed in this photograph taken by the Messenger spacecraft.

Photograph taken by the Pioneer-Venus probe shows thick yellowish clouds covering the surface of Venus.

Picture of the Earth taken by the Meteosat weather satellite. Colours have been enhanced using a computer.

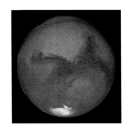

This snapshot of Mars was created from a series of images taken by NASA's Hubble Space Telescope.

SATURN'S RINGS

Jupiter, Saturn, Uranus, and Neptune are all surrounded by rings. Saturn's rings are the most spectacular, visible from the Earth through binoculars. They consist of millions of lumps of ice mixed with fragments of rock. Astronomers are not sure how the rings formed. They may have formed at the same time as the planet, or may represent the remains of a large, icy moon that broke apart.

NEPTUNE

Neptune (below) has a striking blue atmosphere made up of hydrogen, helium, and methane gases, surrounding a rocky core about as large as the Earth. Neptune has five rings and 13 known moons.

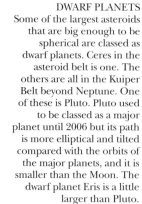

DWARF PLANETS

Some of the largest asteroids that are big enough to be spherical are classed as dwarf planets. Ceres in the asteroid belt is one. The others are all in the Kuiper Belt beyond Neptune. One of these is Pluto. Pluto used to be classed as a major planet until 2006 but its path is more elliptical and tilted compared with the orbits of the major planets, and it is smaller than the Moon. The dwarf planet Eris is a little larger than Pluto.

URANUS

Uranus (left) has a solid core of metal surrounded by ice and gases. Its blue-green atmosphere is made of gases, including methane, hydrogen, and helium. Uranus is extremely cold – about -214°C (-353°F). It has 13 rings and 27 moons.

SATURN

Saturn (left) is huge, almost as big as Jupiter. Dense storm clouds circle the planet, giving it a banded appearance. It has a solid core of rock and ice, surrounded by hydrogen in liquid and gas form. The planet spins so fast – the rotation takes only 10 hours – that its poles are noticeably flattened and its equator bulges outward. Saturn has more than 60 moons.

SOLAR SYSTEM

The solar system consists of the Sun, planets, moons, asteroids, and comets. It formed about 4.5 billion years ago from a huge cloud of gas and dust. The Sun's force of gravity holds all the planets in their orbits. The planets are grouped in two bands. The inner band consists of Mercury, Venus, Earth, and Mars; in the outer band are Jupiter, Saturn, Uranus, and Neptune.

Neptune
Jupiter
Sun
Uranus
Saturn
Mars
Venus
Earth
Mercury

VOYAGER SPACECRAFT

We have incredible pictures of the planets and their moons because space probes have flown to all of the planets except Pluto. *Voyager 2* was one of the most successful interplanetary spacecraft. It travelled for over a decade photographing the planets, and in 1990, made its way out of the solar system. *Voyager 2* made use of the gravity of the planets to give it an extra push on its long journey – a similar effect to stepping off a merry-go-round while it is moving.

Voyager 1 *picture of Jupiter showing the Great Red Spot which is thought to be a huge storm.*

Image taken by Voyager 1 *showing Saturn and its rings, which are thought to consist of a mixture of ice and rock.*

Voyager 2 *image of Uranus. Its atmosphere looks blue because the methane gas it contains cuts out red light.*

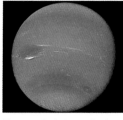

Voyager 2 *photograph of Neptune. The two dark blurs are enormous storms in Neptune's atmosphere.*

Find out more

ASTRONOMY
GRAVITY
MOON
SUN
UNIVERSE

PLANTS

LIFE ON EARTH could not exist without plants. Humans and animals need plants for food and oxygen. The cereal you eat for breakfast, the orange juice you drink, even the jeans you wear, are all derived from plants. Trees provide us with wood for fuel, furniture, and tools. In almost every country, flowers and vegetables are grown by the millions for food and pleasure. Scientists use plants to make drugs such as digitalis (from foxglove) and morphine (from poppies). Plants range from tiny mosses to gigantic coniferous trees so tall you cannot see their tops. What they all have in common is their unique ability to capture and use the Sun's light as an energy source. This process is called photosynthesis, and it powers all plant life and growth. About 400,000 plants are already known to us, from rare exotic flowers to common garden vegetables. Even more plants await discovery, especially in tropical regions. Today, however, more than 25,000 different trees, flowers, and other plants are in danger of extinction due to the destruction of their natural habitats.

FLOWERS
The flowers of a plant contain both male and female reproductive parts, the pollen and ovule cells. If pollinated the ovule develops into a seed.

STEM
Sturdy stem supports leaves and flowers and carries water and food to leaves and fruit.

LEAVES
Green leaves capture light energy from the Sun by the process known as photosynthesis.

Inside a leaf

Upper epidermis

Air spaces

Leaf vein

Palisade cell containing chloroplasts

Mesophyll cell

Guard cells

Stoma

Seed is inside fruit (bean pod).

FRUIT
The fruit contain seeds which eventually grow into new plants. The large fruit on this plant are called beans.

STRUCTURE OF A PLANT
During its lifetime, a typical flowering plant such as this runner bean grows a stem, roots, shoots, leaves, flowers, and fruit. Trees, which are huge plants, have a trunk – a stiff, woody stem full of fibres.

Carbon dioxide is taken in from air through tiny holes called stoma.

Light energy from Sun

Oxygen is given off into the air through stoma.

Water is taken in from soil through roots.

PHOTOSYNTHESIS
In order to grow, plants use energy from sunlight. This process is called photo-synthesis. A green substance called chlorophyll is contained in the cells of a plant's leaves. Chlorophyll captures energy in the light waves from the Sun, then carries out chemical reactions in which carbon dioxide gas from the air is combined with water from the soil. This process creates sugars and other substances which the plant uses for energy and growth.

Xylem (water-carrying tube)

Cortex

Phloem (sap-carrying tube)

Root hair

Root cap

Inside a root

ROOTS
From the soil, the roots take in water and minerals which pass to the leaves and fruit through tiny tubes in the stem. Roots also anchor the plant firmly in the ground.

REPRODUCTION
Most plants reproduce sexually. Pollen fertilizes the ovules in the ovaries, which ripen into fruit that contains seeds. Other plants, such as the potato, reproduce asexually. They grow by tubers which develop into new plants that look like the parent plant.

HOW A STRAWBERRY PLANT REPRODUCES
The parent strawberry plant sends out runners along the ground. Buds and roots develop on these runners and grow into new strawberry plants. This is a form of asexual reproduction, also called vegetative propagation.

Flower

Parent strawberry plant

Runner

New strawberry plant

MAIN GROUPS OF PLANTS

The plant kingdom is made up of many different groups. These groups are divided into flowering and non-flowering plants, as shown here.

Seaweed is an alga that grows in sea water and attaches itself to rocks.

Moss grows on logs and walls and in moist, shady woodland areas.

Liverworts are small non-flowering plants related to mosses.

Lichen is now classified as a fungi. It has no true leaves, stems, or roots.

Horsetails were among the earliest plants on Earth.

Microscopic plants are so small that we can see them only through a microscope.

Club mosses are among the first plants to develop with true stems.

Coniferous trees include fir trees and pine trees. They are also called evergreen trees.

Ferns grow in all parts of the world. Some are as large as trees; others are tiny and look like moss.

Weeds are unwanted flowering plants that include dandelions, nettles, and buttercups.

Fruit trees provide many kinds of fruit, including apples, lemons, and bananas. All are rich in vitamins.

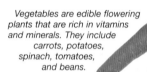

Vegetables are edible flowering plants that are rich in vitamins and minerals. They include carrots, potatoes, spinach, tomatoes, and beans.

True flowering plants include roses, tulips, and other garden plants.

Bushes are woody plants that are smaller than trees. They usually have one main stem.

Herbs have scented leaves. They include basil and oregano.

Grasses include lawn grass and cereals such as wheat, rice, barley, and corn.

Deciduous trees are also called broadleaved trees. They lose their leaves each autumn.

Shrubs are woody plants with more than one main branch growing from the ground.

WEEDS

A weed is simply a plant growing where it is troublesome to humans. Most weeds grow fast, come into flower quickly, then spread their seeds. Some weeds, such as the convolvulus shown above, have pale, delicate flowers; others are colourful, such as the dandelions and buttercups that grow on lawns.

FOOD FROM PLANTS

We grow plants for food on farms and in gardens, too. Food plants include cereals such as rice, fruit such as oranges, and vegetables such as carrots. Spices such as cinnamon are parts of plants and are used for flavouring. Some plant parts cannot be eaten because they are bitter, sour, or poisonous. Potatoes are an important food crop, but we eat only the tuber that grows underground. The fruit and leaves of the potato plant, which grow above ground, are poisonous.

CHOCOLATE

Inside every large fruit, or pod, of the tropical cacao tree are about 40 cacao beans. These beans are roasted, shelled, then ground into a paste. The cacao paste is mixed with sugar at a high temperature to make chocolate.

THE BIGGEST FLOWER

The giant rafflesia is a parasitic plant. It has no leaves and draws its food from the liana creepers it lives on. It has the world's largest flower, at 1 m (3 ft) across. Because of its smell, it is also called the stinking giant.

MISTLETOE

This plant "steals" its food and energy by growing and feeding on trees. It grows high up in the branches, and its roots grow into the bark and absorb the tree's nutrients.

CARNIVOROUS PLANTS

Some plants obtain extra food from animals. One plant, commonly called the Venus's-flytrap, usually grows in swamps, where the soil is poor. Flesh-eating or carnivorous plants trap and digest insects and other small creatures.

When a small creature touches sensitive hairs on the leaves of the Venus's-flytrap, the leaves snap shut with one of the fastest movements in the plant world.

The flytrap shuts in one fiftieth of a second, when trigger hairs at the base of each leaf are moved.

Venus's-flytrap flower

Find out more

FLOWERS AND HERBS
FRUITS AND SEEDS
MICROSCOPIC LIFE
MOSSES,
liverworts, and ferns
SOIL
TREES

PLASTICS

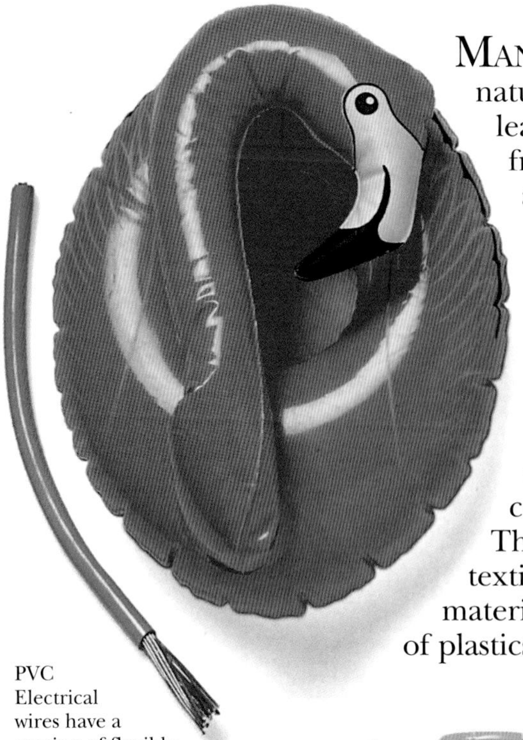

MANY MATERIALS that we use are natural materials, such as cotton, wool, leather, wood, and metal. They come from plants or animals, or they are dug from the ground. Plastics can be used in place of natural materials, and they are used to make clothes, parts for cars, and many other products. Plastics are synthetic materials, which means that they are made from chemicals in factories. The chemicals come mainly from oil, but also from natural gas and coal. An important quality of plastics is that they are easy to shape. They can be used to make objects of all kinds as well as fibres for textiles. Extra-strong glues, long-lasting paints, and lightweight materials that are stronger than metal – all of these products are made of plastics with special qualities. None can be made with natural materials.

BAKELITE
Bakelite was invented in 1909 by the American chemist Leo Baekeland. It was the first plastic to be made from synthetic chemicals.

PVC
Electrical wires have a coating of flexible PVC (polyvinyl chloride), which is also used to make inflatable toys.

KINDS OF PLASTICS
There are thousands of different plastics. Some of the most common types are shown here.

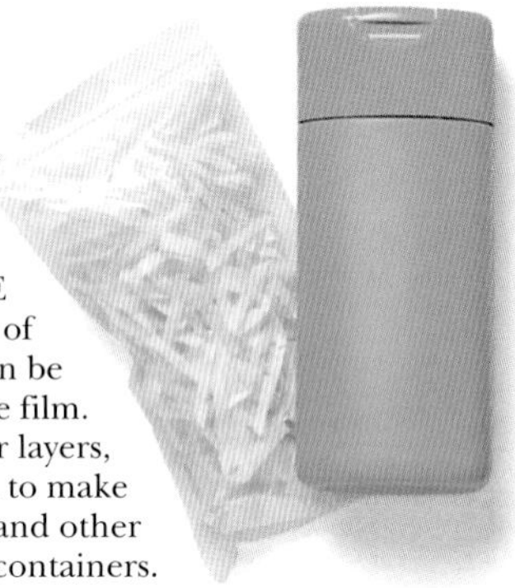

POLYTHENE
Plastic bags are often made of polythene, a plastic that can be made into a tough, flexible film. When produced in thicker layers, polythene is also used to make bottles, bowls, and other household containers.

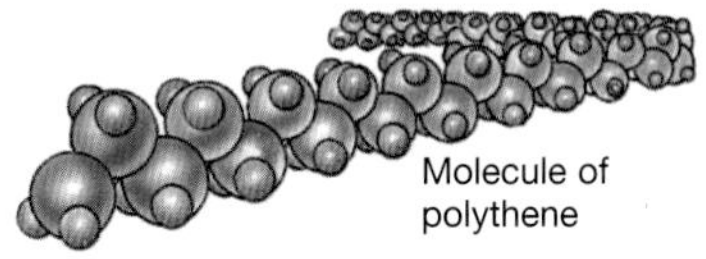

NYLON
Fibres of nylon, a strong but flexible plastic, are used to make ropes and hard-wearing fabrics. Solid nylon is used to make gearwheels and other hardware.

Molecule of polythene

POLYMERS
Plastics are polymers, which are substances with molecules composed of long chains of atoms. This is why the names of plastics often begin with poly, which means "many". Long molecules give plastics their special qualities, such as flexibility and strength.

POLYSTYRENE
Packaging made from polystyrene is light and rigid. Tough plastics often contain polystyrene.

BEECH STARSHIP 1
In aircraft, composites can be used to replace many metal parts. This aircraft is made almost entirely of composites which are highly resistant to corrosion and cracking.

POLYCARBONATE
Goggles need to be clear and strong, two qualities of polycarbonate plastic. Other uses include car lights and crash helmets.

COMPOSITES
Strong fibres are put into tough plastics to create materials called composites, (right) which are very strong yet light and easily shaped. Thin fibres of glass, carbon, or Kevlar (a strong plastic) are used.

Carbon-fibre sheet
Layer of epoxy (plastic adhesive)
Honeycomb of tough plastic
Epoxy layer
Carbon-fibre sheet

Find out more
ATOMS AND MOLECULES
CHEMISTRY
COAL
MACHINES
OIL
TECHNOLOGY

POLAR WILDLIFE

THE NORTH AND SOUTH POLES are the coldest places on Earth. But despite freezing temperatures, icy water, and biting winds, many different plants and animals live near the Poles and are found nowhere else in the world. All survive because they have adapted to the harsh conditions. Plants in these regions are low-growing, to protect them from the cold wind, and they complete their life cycle during the few short weeks of summer. Polar animals, too, have adapted to the cold conditions; some have thick fur or feathers; others have a layer of fatty blubber to conserve body warmth. The biggest animals, the great whales, roam the waters of Antarctica, near the South Pole, and the largest bear, the polar bear, lives in the Arctic, near the North Pole. Many other warm-blooded animals, including wolves, foxes, reindeer, hares, and lemmings, also live here. Polar animals are often white in colour for camouflage on the ice. The cold seas are also teeming with life, particularly in summer. Around Antarctica, ocean currents bring up nutrients from the deep sea to feed the plankton, which in turn feeds animals such as krill.

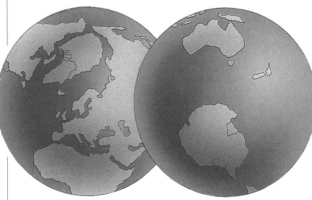

NORTH POLE
In the central Arctic Ocean at the top of the globe, there are vast areas of drifting ice several metres thick.

SOUTH POLE
At the bottom of the globe, the continent of Antarctica is almost completely covered by a massive sheet of ice.

ARCTIC SKUA
The skua snatches food from other birds such as gulls and puffins. It pesters them in midair until they drop their catch of fish.

NARWHAL
The narwhal belongs to the whale family. It hunts in small groups among pack ice searching for cod, flatfish, shrimps, and squid. Narwhals have only two teeth. In the male, the left tooth usually develops into a tusk, which can measure up to 2.5 m (8 ft) long.

POLAR BEAR CUBS
Young polar bears are born in winter in a den made by their mother under the snow. The cubs stay in the den for four months, feeding on their mother's milk, then begin to learn how to hunt. The cubs leave their mother at about two years old.

BEARDED SEAL
Bearded seals live all around the Arctic region, mainly in shallow water. They eat shellfish on the seabed, as well as crabs and sea cucumbers. In the breeding season, male bearded seals make eerie noises under water. The female seals give birth to pups on ice floes in the spring.

HOODED SEAL
In summer, hooded seals migrate north to the waters around Greenland. They hunt deep-water fishes such as halibut and redfish, as well as squid. They spend the winter further south, off northeastern North America, resting on ice floes and rarely coming onto land.

The male hooded seal inflates the hood – a sac of loose skin on its nose – to scare off other males.

POLAR BEAR

The huge polar bear is covered in thick, water-repelling fur, except for its footpads and the tip of its nose. Polar bears have an excellent sense of smell for locating prey, and they can bound across the ice at great speed. An adult polar bear weighs about half a tonne. It is so strong that a single blow of its paw can kill a person.

Claws are very sharp for gripping prey.

Polar bears eat seals, fish, birds, and small mammals. They also scavenge on the carcasses (dead bodies) of whales.

CONSERVATION

Today, polar bears and whales are protected from hunting by law. But many polar animals are still threatened by oil spills, overfishing, and global warming melting the ice. Fishing boats catch huge quantities of fish, which affects the numbers of animals that depend on fish for food.

KRILL

The shrimp-like creatures shown left are called krill. They are the main food for baleen (whalebone) whales, such as the blue whale, which scoop up thousands of krill from the ocean every day.

PENGUINS

There are 17 different kinds of penguins; all live in the southern hemisphere. Penguins cannot fly, but they are expert swimmers and divers. They can speed along in the water after fish and squid using their flipper-shaped wings.

EMPEROR PENGUIN

The emperor penguin has a bright orange bib around its neck. To escape the leopard seal, it dives out of the water with great speed. It breeds in the coldest place on Earth – on Antarctic ice where the average temperature is -20°C (-4°F). After the female has laid an egg, the male penguin keeps it warm between his feet and belly for about 60 days. The newborn chicks stay warm by standing on their parents' feet.

ICE FISH

The blood of most fish freezes solid at about – 35°C (-32°F), and the waters in the polar regions sometimes drop even lower. The ice fish, also called the crocodile fish, has special chemicals in its blood to stop it from freezing.

LEOPARD SEAL

The four main kinds of seals around Antarctica are the leopard, crabeater, Ross, and Weddell seals. The leopard seal measures up to 3 m (10 ft) in length. It patrols the pack ice and island coasts hunting for penguins and other seals, especially crabeater seals.

There is little life on the continent of Antarctica itself, apart from a few mosses, lichens, and tiny creatures such as mites.

TUNDRA

The lands on the edge of the Arctic Ocean are bleak and treeless. This region is called the tundra. The brief summer in the Arctic allows small plants such as sedges, cushion-shaped saxifrages, heathers, mosses, and lichens to grow. These plants provide food for many insects and the grazing caribou. Birds such as snow geese breed along the shores and migrate south in autumn.

MUSK OX

The musk ox is a type of goat. It is the only large mammal that can survive winter on the tundra. The musk ox's thickset body has dense underfur and a thick, shaggy outer coat of tough hairs. Musk oxen stand together in a herd for warmth and as protection against predators such as wolves.

SNOW GOOSE

About 100 kinds of birds migrate to the tundra to breed in spring. Snow geese arrive two weeks before there are any plants to eat, but they have a store of body fat which allows them to make a nest and lay eggs before they eat. Later they feed the chicks on the newly growing grasses.

Dwarf willows are among the world's smallest shrubs. They grow low and spread sideways to stay out of the icy winds.

ARCTIC SAXIFRAGE

The cushion shapes of tundra flowers such as saxifrage and crowberry help prevent the plants from freezing. These plants also provide shelter for the tiny creatures living inside them.

Find out more

ANTARCTICA
ARCTIC
BEARS AND PANDAS
FISH
OCEANS AND SEAS
SEASHORE WILDLIFE
WHALES AND DOLPHINS

POLLUTION

OIL ON BEACHES, vehicle exhaust fumes, litter, and other waste products are called pollutants, because they pollute (dirty) our environment. Pollutants can affect our health and harm animals and plants. We pollute our surroundings with all kinds of chemical waste from factories and power stations. These substances are the unwanted results of modern living. Pollution itself is not new – a hundred years ago factories sent out great clouds of poisonous smoke. Today, there are many more factories and many more pollutants. Pollution has spread to the land, air, and water of every corner on Earth, even to Antarctica and Mount Everest. Scientists are worried that the gases released by factories and vehicles are even changing the atmosphere and causing the surface temperature of the planet to heat up. We can reduce pollution by recycling waste and using biodegradable materials that eventually break down in the soil.

ACCIDENTAL POLLUTION
As well as everyday pollution, there is also accidental pollution – for example, when a ship leaks oil and creates a huge oil slick in the ocean. This kind of pollution causes damage to the environment and kills millions of fish and sea birds, like the oil-covered birds shown above.

ATMOSPHERIC POLLUTION
Ozone is a kind of oxygen present in the atmosphere. It forms a protective layer that blocks out the Sun's ultraviolet radiation, which can cause skin cancer in humans. Chemicals called CFCs (chlorofluorocarbons) destroy the ozone.

GLOBAL WARMING
Burning fossil fuels releases carbon gases into the atmosphere. They act like the panes of glass in a greenhouse, trapping the heat. Many scientists now believe that the Earth is becoming too warm. If the Earth becomes just a few degrees warmer, sea levels will rise, drowning low-lying coastal cities.

Many factories release pollutants as a by-product.

ACID RAIN
Vehicle exhausts produce fumes that contain nitrogen oxides. The coal we burn in power stations produces sulphur dioxide. When these two substances mix with water in the air, they turn into acids, then fall as acid rain. Acid rain damages trees, eats into buildings, and kills wildlife in rivers. Today, it is possible to reduce the amount of sulphur dioxide given off by power stations, but the process is expensive.

Farmers spray crops with fertilizers to help them grow, and pesticides to control pests and weeds, but these chemicals harm the other kinds of wildlife that live and feed on the crops.

RECYCLING
If we save the glass, metal, plastics, and paper that we use every day, they can be recycled and used again. This helps preserve the Earth's natural resources. Recycling cuts down litter, reduces air and water pollution, and can save energy. Many towns have "bottle banks" to collect glass for recycling.

Ships leak oil into the sea, which is harmful to sea creatures.

TRAFFIC POLLUTION
Lorry, car, and bus exhausts belch out lead (which can damage the nervous system), carbon monoxide, carbon dioxide, and nitrogen oxides, which cause acid rain and the smog called photochemical smog. Some of these harmful substances are reduced by special catalytic converters attached to vehicle exhausts.

Every day we drop litter on the ground – sweet wrappers, paper bags, empty tin cans, bottles, and cigarette packets. Litter is ugly, unhygienic, and a fire risk, and it can kill animals that eat it.

WASTE DUMPING
In many parts of the world people bury toxic (poisonous) chemicals and other dangerous waste products. These substances leak into the soil and water, killing wildlife. We treat the seas as waste dumps, and the North Sea is now seriously polluted. For the wildlife in the seas to survive, we must produce less harmful waste products.

HOLES IN THE OZONE LAYER
In the late 1970s, scientists detected "holes" in the ozone layer above the South and North Poles. Probably caused by air pollutants, such as CFCs and methane, the "holes" seemed to be growing larger. In 1987, more than 30 countries signed an agreement called the Montreal Protocol, which has sharply reduced the production of CFCs worldwide.

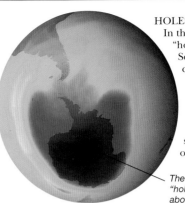

The dark patch is the "hole" in the ozone layer above the Antarctic.

An aerosol is a mixture of product and propellant.

The can is pressurized by the propellant gas.

HOUSEHOLD POLLUTION
Some of the polluting gases that were destroying the ozone layer came from household devices. The most damaging were chlorofluorocarbons (CFCs), used as propellants in aerosol cans and inside the cooling systems of refrigerators. Today, in the move to reduce pollution, less harmful gases have replaced CFCs.

CLEANING UP
Neutralizing chemicals can be used to clean up pollution. Spilt oil, for example, can be countered with detergents. But unfortunately these chemicals can do just as much damage as the original spill. Sometimes the only way to clean up is to physically remove the pollutant. Sadly the damage is often already done, although it may not be very obvious.

Where possible, mechanical scoops remove spilt oil sludge.

Special V-shaped paddles are used to push the oil sludge into heaps.

OIL BARRIER
Crude oil is a particularly harmful chemical pollutant. However, because oil floats on water, an oil slick created by a spillage from a wrecked tanker can be contained by barriers. The oil must then be dispersed or collected quickly because, if it is left, it will eventually thicken and sink. Also, oil barriers cannot withstand storms.

ENERGY SAVING
Much of the pollution that we produce is the result of burning fossil fuels in power plants and motor vehicles. Generators and engines can be made more efficient so that they use less fuel. Individuals too can save energy and reduce pollution by making use of energy-efficient light bulbs and other appliances in the home, and by using cars less.

Energy-saving lamps reduce pollution, but just switching off lights helps even more.

RAIN FORESTS
Since 1945, more than half of the world's rain forests have been destroyed. They are cut down for timber or burnt to clear space for farmland. Burning produces carbon dioxide, contributing to global warming. Scientists are increasingly concerned about the impact of this on the environment.

Find out more
ATMOSPHERE
CLIMATES
CONSERVATION
and endangered species
ENERGY

PORTS AND WATERWAYS

SHIPS LOAD AND UNLOAD their cargoes at ports, or harbours – sheltered places on coasts or rivers with cranes and warehouses to handle ships, passengers, and goods. Road and rail connections link the ports with inland areas. The earliest ports were simply landing places at river mouths. Here ships were safe from storms, and workers on board could unload cargo into smaller boats for transport upriver. Building walls against the riverbanks created wharfs to make loading easier. In the 18th and 19th centuries, port authorities added docks – deep, artificial pools – leading off the rivers. Ships and boats use waterways to sail to inland towns or as shortcuts from one sea to another. Waterways can be natural rivers, or artificial rivers called canals. One of the world's largest waterway systems, based on the Mississippi River, links the Great Lakes with the Gulf of Mexico. It includes 24,000 km (15,000 miles) of waterways.

Navigation lights guide ships safely into the port.

Because oil burns easily, oil tankers use special terminals to unload their cargo.

Huge tanks at the terminal store the oil until it is needed.

Ships and boats unload at wharfs.

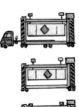

LOADING AND UNLOADING

Ships carry nearly two thirds of all goods in containers, but many items do not fit neatly inside them. Cranes lift these individual large pieces of cargo on and off the ships. Loose cargo such as grain is sucked up by huge pumps and carried ashore through pipes. Vehicles drive onto special ships known as "ro-ros": roll-on, roll-off ferries.

CONTAINERS

A special wheeled crane handles containers. It lifts them off the ship and can either stack them nearby or lower them onto the back of a truck. Cranes, ships, and trucks around the world have the same size fittings so that they can move containers easily between different countries.

DOCKS

Huge gates at the entrance to the docks maintain the water level inside. The warehouses and cranes of the old-style docks are disappearing today as more ships carry goods in containers – large steel boxes of standard size that are easy to stack and move.

LOCKS

To raise or lower ships from one water level to another, canals and harbours have locks. If a ship is going to a lower water level, the lock fills with water and the ship sails in. Closing the upper gates and letting out the water gradually lowers the ship to the level of the water outside the lower gates.

PANAMA CANAL

Ships travelling around the South American coast from the Caribbean Sea to the Pacific Ocean must sail nearly 10,000 km (6,000 miles). So the United States built a huge canal through Panama in Central America where the Pacific and the Caribbean are just 82 km (51 miles) apart. The canal opened in 1914.

SINGAPORE

At the centre of the sea routes of southern Asia lies Singapore, one of the busiest ports in the world. Its large, modern docks handle goods from all over the world. Many large ships from Europe and the Americas unload their cargoes here into smaller vessels for distribution to nearby countries.

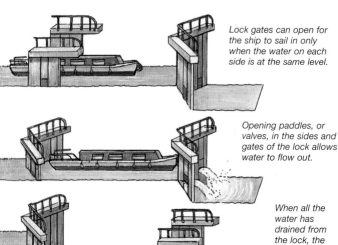

Lock gates can open for the ship to sail in only when the water on each side is at the same level.

Opening paddles, or valves, in the sides and gates of the lock allows water to flow out.

When all the water has drained from the lock, the gates open and the ship can continue on its way.

Find out more

NAVIGATION
SHIPS AND BOATS
TRADE AND INDUSTRY

PORTUGAL

PORTUGAL'S LONG ATLANTIC coast has shaped its destiny as a seafaring nation. It is a land with few natural resources, and its economy has traditionally been based on fishing and farming. The grapes that grow on the moist, fertile slopes of the Douro river produce fine wines and port, while olives, cork trees, and tinned fish are also major exports. Today, Portugal is becoming more industrialized, and its textile industry is expanding. Although it has a good internal road network, its transport links to its eastern neighbour, Spain, are poor, and most heavy goods are still moved by ship. Tourism, especially to the mild south coast, is increasingly important.

On the southwestern side of the Iberian peninsula, which it shares with Spain, Portugal is the westernmost country in mainland Europe. It also includes the Azores and Madeira, two self-governing island groups in the Atlantic Ocean.

ALGARVE

The fertile coastal lowlands in the south of Portugal are densely inhabited. Inland, the mainly agricultural economy is based on corn, figs, olives, almonds, and grapes. Many fishing villages line the coast. In recent years, these quiet backwaters have been transformed by tourism (above). Some traditional villages have been completely swallowed up by tourist development. Tourists come for mild winters, fine scenery and some of the best golf courses in Europe.

VINEYARDS
Vineyards blanket the terraced hills that line the valley of the Douro river (left). The grapes harvested here are used to make Portugal's distinctive wines and famous fortified wine, which is named "port" after Porto, a major town on the Douro estuary. Grapes are transported down the river by barge to the towns of Porto and Villa Nova da Gaia, where the wine is blended and matured in casks and bottles and shipped all over the world. The island of Madeira is also famous for its wine, which is heated over a period of six months by a combination of hot water pipes and the rays of the sun. It is then fortified with brandy, which helps to give Madeira wine a richer flavour.

Port is a sweet dessert wine, made by adding brandy to the fermenting grapes.

LISBON

Portugal's capital and main port lies on the banks of the Tagus river, 13 km (8 miles) from the coast. Baixa, the historic city centre (below), lies on the north bank. In 1755, most of the city was destroyed by an earthquake and completely rebuilt. Today, it is the bustling commercial heart of the city. Lisbon's manufacturing centre, dominated by large cement and steel works, lies on the south bank.

CORK CULTIVATION

Portugal is the world's leading producer of cork, made from the bark of the cork oak tree. Trees are first stripped of cork at 15 to 20 years old, and then every 10 years thereafter. Cork is used to make stoppers for bottles and jars.

FESTIVALS
Portugal is a Roman Catholic country; many villages hold an annual festival to mark a particular saint's day or religious holiday. Colourful parades march through the streets, accompanied by the Portuguese guitar (a type of mandolin), and the entire village comes together for a lavish meal, with music and dancing. Plaintive folk songs (*fados*) are famous throughout Portugal.

Find out more
EUROPE
EUROPE, HISTORY OF

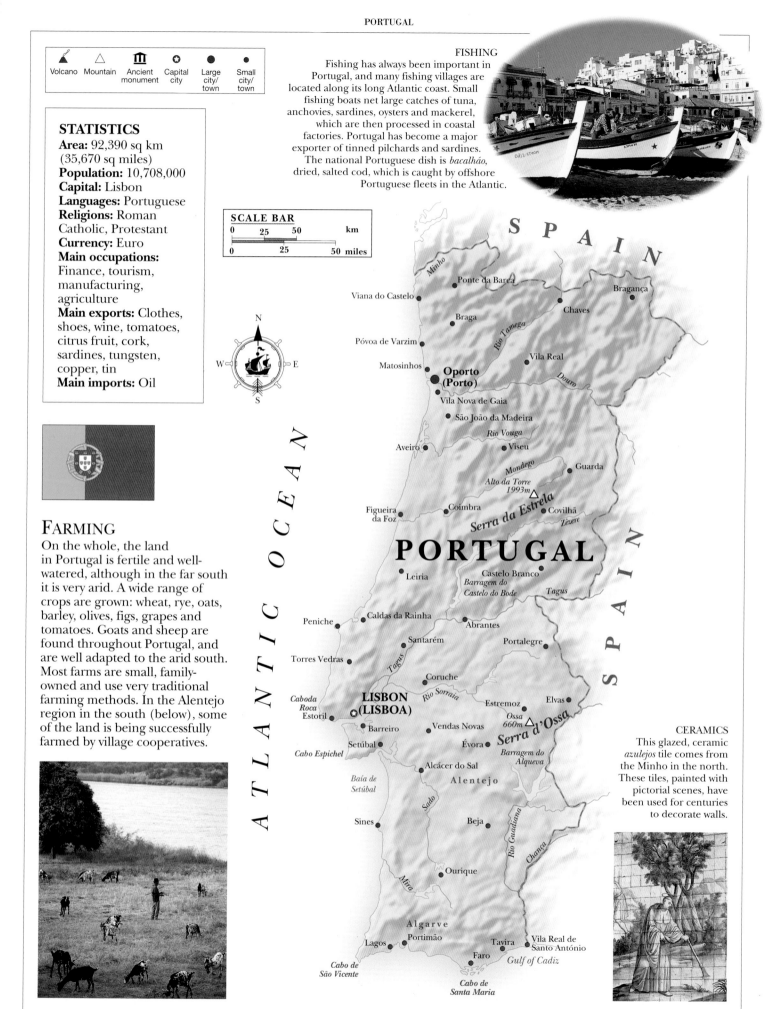

STATISTICS

Area: 92,390 sq km
(35,670 sq miles)
Population: 10,708,000
Capital: Lisbon
Languages: Portuguese
Religions: Roman
Catholic, Protestant
Currency: Euro
Main occupations:
Finance, tourism,
manufacturing,
agriculture
Main exports: Clothes,
shoes, wine, tomatoes,
citrus fruit, cork,
sardines, tungsten,
copper, tin
Main imports: Oil

Volcano Mountain Ancient monument Capital city Large city/town Small city/town

FISHING

Fishing has always been important in
Portugal, and many fishing villages are
located along its long Atlantic coast. Small
fishing boats net large catches of tuna,
anchovies, sardines, oysters and mackerel,
which are then processed in coastal
factories. Portugal has become a major
exporter of tinned pilchards and sardines.
The national Portuguese dish is *bacalháo*,
dried, salted cod, which is caught by offshore
Portuguese fleets in the Atlantic.

SCALE BAR
km
0   25   50
0   25   50 miles

FARMING

On the whole, the land
in Portugal is fertile and well-
watered, although in the far south
it is very arid. A wide range of
crops are grown: wheat, rye, oats,
barley, olives, figs, grapes and
tomatoes. Goats and sheep are
found throughout Portugal, and
are well adapted to the arid south.
Most farms are small, family-
owned and use very traditional
farming methods. In the Alentejo
region in the south (below), some
of the land is being successfully
farmed by village cooperatives.

CERAMICS

This glazed, ceramic
azulejos tile comes from
the Minho in the north.
These tiles, painted with
pictorial scenes, have
been used for centuries
to decorate walls.

PREHISTORIC LIFE

WHEN PLANET EARTH FORMED more than 4,600 million years ago, there was no life. Torrential storms raged, lightning bolts flashed, volcanoes poured out poisonous gases, and there was no atmosphere to protect the Earth from the sun's radiation. Slowly, warm shallow seas formed. In these seas the first forms of life appeared, protected by the water. We call these early beginnings "prehistory" because they happened before written history. Fossils – the preserved remains of plants and animals – provide the only records of prehistoric life. We know from fossils more than 2,000 million years old that some of the earliest forms of life were bacteria. Gradually, plants called blue-green algae evolved, or developed. These produced oxygen – the gas that plants and animals need for life. Oxygen was released into the air from the sea and formed a protective blanket of ozone in the atmosphere. The ozone screened out the sun's radiation, and living things began to invade the land and take to the air. Millions of kinds of animals and plants have existed since the first signs of life – some, such as insects, have thrived; others, such as the dinosaurs, have died out as the Earth's environment has changed.

2,000 MILLION YEARS AGO
The earliest forms of life were bacteria and blue-green algae. The algae grew in rings or short columns called stromatolites, which are fossilized in rocks. Today, stromatolites still form in shallow tropical seas.

Some of the earliest remains of the life on Earth are fossils called stromatolites.

600 MILLION YEARS AGO
Rare fossils of soft-bodied creatures show us that many different animals had evolved by this time. They included the first kinds of jellyfish, corals, sea pens, and worms.

Sea pens existed 600 million years ago.

Trilobites were common 450 million years ago. They are ancient relatives of crabs.

450 MILLION YEARS AGO
Fossils from this time are much more common, because animals had developed hard shells that preserved well. They include trilobites, nautiloids, sea urchins, and giant eurypterids, or sea scorpions, more than 2.5 m (8 ft) long.

One of the first fishes, about 390 million years old

390 MILLION YEARS AGO
Fish were the first creatures with backbones. They evolved quickly into many different kinds. Gradually, they developed jaws and fins. The first small land plants, such as mosses, appeared on the swampy shores.

Cooksonia was one of the first land plants to appear on Earth.

HOW WE KNOW THE AGE OF FOSSILS

Stages	Million years ago (mya)
Quaternary period	1.8–today
Tertiary period	65–1.8
Jurassic and Cretaceous periods	195.5–65
Triassic period	252–199.5
Carboniferous and Permian periods	354–252
Devonian period	418–354
Ordovician and Silurian periods	490–418
Cambrian period	543–490
Pre-cambrian period	4,560–543

Scientists called palaeontologists find out how old a fossil is from the age of the rocks around it. This is called relative dating. They also measure the amounts of radioactive chemicals in the rocks and fossils to find out when they formed. This is called absolute dating.

Prehistoric time is divided into different stages, called eras, which are further divided into periods. Each of these stages lasted for many millions of years. If you dig deep down into the Earth's surface, you can find fossils of animals and plants that lived during the different periods.

350 MILLION YEARS AGO
As plants became established on land, they were soon followed by the first land animals, such as millipedes and insects. Woody trees that looked like conifers stood more than 30 m (100 ft) high. Sharks and many other fish swam in the seas.

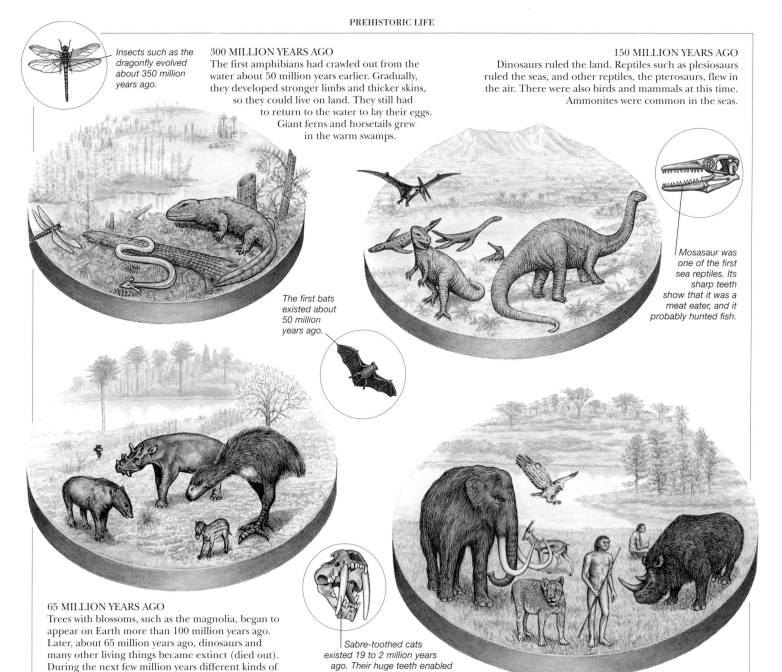

Insects such as the dragonfly evolved about 350 million years ago.

300 MILLION YEARS AGO
The first amphibians had crawled out from the water about 50 million years earlier. Gradually, they developed stronger limbs and thicker skins, so they could live on land. They still had to return to the water to lay their eggs. Giant ferns and horsetails grew in the warm swamps.

150 MILLION YEARS AGO
Dinosaurs ruled the land. Reptiles such as plesiosaurs ruled the seas, and other reptiles, the pterosaurs, flew in the air. There were also birds and mammals at this time. Ammonites were common in the seas.

Mosasaur was one of the first sea reptiles. Its sharp teeth show that it was a meat eater, and it probably hunted fish.

The first bats existed about 50 million years ago.

65 MILLION YEARS AGO
Trees with blossoms, such as the magnolia, began to appear on Earth more than 100 million years ago. Later, about 65 million years ago, dinosaurs and many other living things became extinct (died out). During the next few million years different kinds of mammals and birds became more common.

Sabre-toothed cats existed 19 to 2 million years ago. Their huge teeth enabled them to attack and kill large prey.

EXTINCTION

There is concern over the fact that many animals and plants are in danger of dying out, or becoming extinct. But ever since life began, animals and plants have died out, to be replaced by others. This process is part of nature. As the conditions on Earth change, some living things cannot adapt; they eventually become extinct. Scientists believe that 99 per cent of all the different plants and animals that ever lived have died out naturally. In prehistoric times there were mass extinctions when hundreds of different things died out together. These extinctions were often due to dramatic changes in climate. About 225 million years ago, 90 per cent of all the living things in the sea died out. Today, animals and plants are dying out more quickly because humans damage and destroy the areas where they live.

STEGOSAURUS
This dinosaur lived about 150 million years ago in North America. It became extinct about 140 million years ago.

NEANDERTHAL PEOPLE
These people lived from about 120,000–35,000 years ago. They were smaller than humans, and are now thought not to be ancestral to them. It is debated, however, whether they interbred with humans.

GREAT ICE AGE

About 2 million years ago, several ice ages gripped the Earth, with warmer stretches between. Humans evolved – probably in Africa – and spread around the world. In the north, they hunted woolly mammoths, woolly rhinos, and sabre-toothed cats. About 18,000 years ago, ice sheets covered much of northern Europe, northern Britain, and North America.

Find out more
COAL
DINOSAURS
EVOLUTION
FOSSILS
PREHISTORIC PEOPLES

PREHISTORIC PEOPLES

COMPARED WITH the rest of life on Earth, human beings arrived quite recently, after the dinosaur age and the age of mammals. The whole story of human evolution is incomplete, because many parts of the fossil record have never been found. Human-like mammals first emerged from the ape family about five million years ago in central Africa. They came down from the trees and began to walk on two legs. Hominins, or early humans, were more apelike than human and lived in the open. Over millions of years they learned to walk upright and developed bigger brains. These large brains helped them to develop language and the ability to work together. Hominins lived in groups and shared work and food, wandering through the countryside gathering fruits, roots, nuts, berries, and seeds, and hunting animals. Standing upright left their hands free to make tools and weapons, shelters and fire. They lived in caves and in shelters made from branches and stones. These early humans spread slowly over the rest of the world and soon rose to dominate life on Earth.

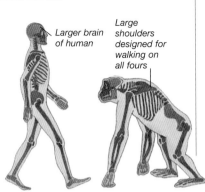

Larger brain of human

Large shoulders designed for walking on all fours

HUMAN OR APE?
Humans have smaller jaws and larger brains than apes. The human hand has a longer thumb; apes have longer fingers. The human pelvis and thigh allow upright motion, giving the spine an S-shaped curve. Human legs are longer than arms; apes have the reverse. Unlike apes, humans cannot use their big toes as extra thumbs; the foot has adapted to walking and can no longer grasp.

WISDOM TOOTH
Early people needed wisdom teeth in order to eat roots and berries. Today, we no longer need wisdom teeth, and many people do not even develop them.

Lucy's remains were found at Hadar.

Lucy gathered fruit to eat.

Fossil remains of the earliest hominins have all been found in East Africa.

Homo habilis

Simple stone tool

Simple clothing

Homo erectus

Homo erectus made more advanced tools, such as this spear.

Sophisticated carving

Sewn leather clothing

Neanderthal man

Modern people wear shoes.

Rough woven cloth

Modern people wear shoes.

LUCY
In 1974, archaeologists discovered a complete fossil hominin skeleton in Ethiopia, northeastern Africa. She was nicknamed Lucy, after the Beatles' song *Lucy in the Sky with Diamonds.* Lucy was 3 million years old. Although nearly human, she was probably not one of our direct ancestors.

When alive, Lucy was about the same height as a 10-year-old girl, and weighed 27 kg (60 lb).

FROM HOMININS TO HUMANS

About 2.3 million years ago hominins called *Homo habilis* (meaning "handy man") shaped crude stone tools and built rough shelters. Other, more advanced hominins, called *Homo erectus*, moved out of Africa into Europe and Asia. They lived in camps, made use of fire, and probably had a language. After the Ice Age, Neanderthals lived in Europe. Neanderthals looked much like people today, wore clothes, made flint tools and fire, and buried their dead. They vanished about 30,000 years ago and were replaced by "modern people", who invented farming about 9,000 years ago and began to settle down in communities. Shortly after, the first civilizations began.

MODERN PEOPLE
When humans learned to domesticate animals and grow crops, they stopped wandering and settled down on farms. Thus towns began to develop.

> *Find out more*
> ARCHAEOLOGY
> BRONZE AGE
> EVOLUTION
> PREHISTORIC LIFE
> STONE AGE

RADIO

EARLY RADIO WAS often called "the wireless" because radio uses invisible waves instead of wires to carry messages from one place to another. Today, radio waves are an important means of communicating sounds, pictures, and data all over the world. Within the circuits of a radio transmitter, rapidly varying electric currents generate radio waves of different lengths that travel to a radio receiver. Radio waves are a type of electromagnetic (EM) wave, similar to light and x-rays. Like these waves, radio waves travel at the speed of light, 300,000 km (186,000 miles) per second, nearly one million times the speed of sound waves. Radio waves can travel through the air, solid materials, or even empty space, but are sent most efficiently by putting the transmitting antenna on high ground like a hill.

MORSE CODE
Early radio signals consisted of beeps, made by tapping a key. Operators tapped out a message using a series of short and long beeps called Morse code, invented by Samuel Morse (1791-1872) in 1837.

RADIO STUDIO
A microphone converts sound waves from the announcer's voice into electrical signals, which are then transmitted as radio waves.

RADIO FREQUENCIES
Radio waves consist of rapidly oscillating (varying) electric and magnetic fields. The rate of oscillation is called the frequency of the wave, measured in hertz (Hz). One Hz equals one oscillation per second; one kilohertz (kHz) equals 1,000 hertz. Bands of certain frequencies are used to transmit different kinds of information.

Long waves (30-300 kHz) can travel 1,000 km (about 600 miles). They are used for national broadcasts and to send information to ships.

A transmitter receives radio programmes by cable from the studio. The transmitter antenna beams radio waves that spread out like ripples in water.

Communications satellites pick up and rebroadcast radio programmes using super-high-frequency waves with frequencies of more than 3 million kHz.

Television programmes are carried on UHF (ultra-high-frequency) radio waves (300,000-3,000,000 kHz).

Dish sends and receives radio waves

VHF (very-high-frequency) radio waves (30,000-300,000 kHz) move in straight lines so they cannot travel over the horizon. Police, fire brigade, and citizens' band radios use VHF waves for short-range communications.

Many radio stations transmit programmes on the medium-wave band. These medium-frequency (300-3,000 kHz) channels are restricted to within a few hundred kilometres.

International radio stations and amateur radio enthusiasts use short-wave radio signals. Short waves (3,000-30,000 kHz) can travel great distances. They bounce around the world, reflected off the Earth's surface and a layer of the atmosphere called the ionosphere.

RADIO RECEIVER
When radio waves reach the antenna of a radio, they produce tiny varying electric currents in the antenna. As the tuner knob is turned, an electronic circuit selects a single frequency from these currents corresponding to a radio channel. The signal is then converted into sound waves. Modern digital radios,, as above, receive signals coded using a computer code. This gives better sound quality and access to more stations.

PIONEERS OF RADIO
In 1864, Scottish physicist James Clerk Maxwell developed the theory of electromagnetic waves, which are the basis of radio. In 1888, Heinrich Hertz, a German physicist, discovered radio waves. Italian Guglielmo Marconi (1874-1937, right) created the first radio system in 1895, and in 1901 he transmitted radio signals across the Atlantic.

Find out more

ASTRONOMY
NAVIGATION
SOUND
TELEPHONES
TELEVISION

RADIOACTIVITY

SOME ELEMENTS GIVE out invisible particles called radiation. Substances that produce radioactivity are described as radioactive. Radioactivity comes out of the central part (the nucleus) of atoms of a radioactive substance, and carries away energy from inside atoms. This energy can be both useful and harmful; it can be used to generate electricity, or to create enormous explosions. A radioactive substance, such as uranium, is made up of big, unstable atoms. Some of the particles that form the atoms break off and are radiated as alpha particles or beta particles, or as gamma rays. Eventually atoms reach a stable state – stop decaying – and the substance is no longer radioactive. This process can take millions of years.

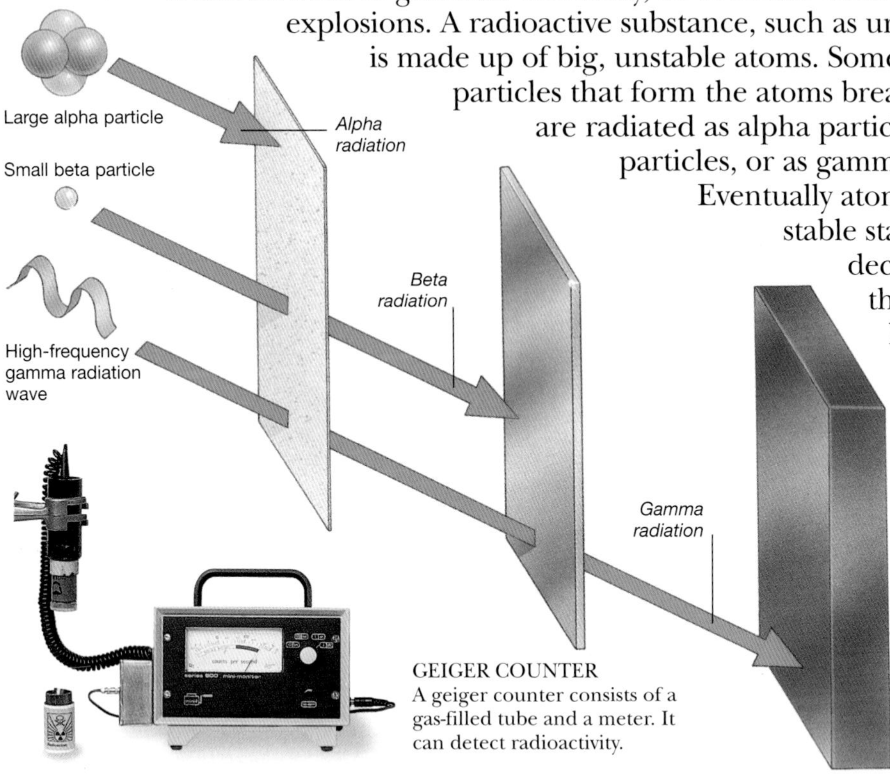

MARIE CURIE
Polish-born scientist Marie Curie (1867-1934), and her husband, Pierre, won the 1903 Nobel physics prize for discovering radioactivity. She did not know it was harmful, and died from radiation poisoning.

Large alpha particle

Small beta particle

High-frequency gamma radiation wave

Alpha radiation

Beta radiation

Gamma radiation

GEIGER COUNTER
A geiger counter consists of a gas-filled tube and a meter. It can detect radioactivity.

TYPES OF RADIOACTIVITY
Radioactive substances give off three types of radiation: alpha, beta, and gamma. Alpha particles are larger than those of beta radiation, so cannot penetrate as far. Gamma radiation is a very high frequency wave and can pass through most materials. Only direct collisions with atoms can stop it. Shields to protect people from gamma radiation are made from dense material, such as lead.

SOURCES OF RADIOACTIVITY

Earth's rocks are naturally radioactive as they contain radioactive substances from when our planet formed.

In this laboratory experiment, a radioactive substance emits radiation through a small hole in its lead casing.

The explosion of a nuclear weapon produces both electromagnetic (light) and radioactive radiation, with devastating effect.

In a nuclear power station, the heat produced by radioactivity is used to make steam and drive an electricity generator.

Radon is a naturally occurring radioactive gas that seeps out of the ground in some parts of the world, such as these hot springs.

DEEP-SPACE NUCLEAR GENERATORS
Spacecraft that visit regions of the solar system far from the Sun can't use solar panels to generate power because they don't get enough sunlight. Instead, these probes often take along a small block of radioactive plutonium, which generates heat that is converted into useful electricity. The New Horizons probe, shown here before launch, carries its plutonium well protected inside the black cylinder seen on the left.

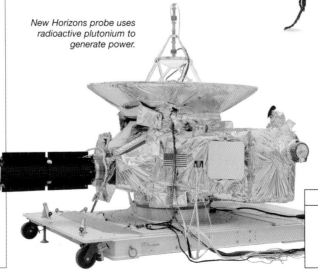
New Horizons probe uses radioactive plutonium to generate power.

Radiation damage has caused this rare mutation of yellow eyes.

Mutant house fly

GENE MUTATION
Alpha and beta particles, x-rays, and gamma rays produced by radioactivity can damage living things, because they alter the DNA of genes. This can result in life-threatening diseases such as cancer. It can also lead to mutations, or changes, in the next generation.

Find out more
ATOMS AND MOLECULES
GENETICS
NUCLEAR ENERGY
X-RAYS

RAIN AND SNOW

THE WATER THAT FALLS from the sky as rain or snow is taking part in a continuous cycle. It begins when the water on the Earth's surface evaporates, or dries out, and enters the air as invisible water vapour. Rising air carries the vapour into the sky. The air cools as it rises, and the water vapour turns into tiny water droplets. These droplets are so small that they float in the air, and a cloud forms. A rain cloud contains millions of water droplets which merge together to form larger drops. When these drops become too large and heavy to float, they fall to the ground as rain and the cycle starts all over again. If the air is very cold, the water in the cloud freezes and forms snowflakes or hailstones. However, rainfall and snowfall are not equal all over the world. Deserts have hardly any rain at all; tropical regions can have so much rain that there are severe floods, while in the polar regions snow falls instead of rain.

LIFE-GIVING RAIN
Rain is vital to life on Earth. Plants need water to grow, providing food for us and other animals. Rain also fills the rivers and lakes which provide our water supply.

WATER CYCLE
Water enters the air from lakes, rivers, seas, and oceans through the process of evaporation. In addition, plants, animals, and people give out water vapour into the atmosphere. The vapour stays in the air for an average time of 10 days and then falls as rain or snow. It joins the sea, rivers, and underground watercourses, and the cycle begins once more.

Trees and other plants release water vapour into the air from their leaves.

Cloud begins to form from water vapour in the atmosphere.

Water joins rivers and streams and flows down to the sea.

Water droplets fall from a cloud especially over high ground where the air is cooler. The general name for rain, snow, sleet, hail, mist, and dew is precipitation.

Wind and the sun's heat cause water to evaporate from the oceans and other large areas of water.

Water seeps underground through a layer of porous, or permeable, rock and flows down to the sea.

RAINBOW
If the sun shines on a shower of rain, you may see a rainbow if you are looking towards the rain and the sun is behind you. The raindrops in the shower reflect the sun's light back to you. As the sunlight passes through the raindrops, it splits up into a circular band of colours. You see the top part of this circle as a rainbow.

SNOW AND HAIL
In cold weather, the water in a cloud freezes and forms ice crystals. These crystals stick together and fall as snowflakes. The snow may melt slightly as it falls, producing sleet. In some clouds, strong air currents can toss frozen raindrops up and down. Each time they rise and fall, the frozen drops collect more ice crystals and water, and frozen layers build up like the skin around an onion. Eventually they become so heavy that they fall to the ground as hailstones.

ICE CRYSTAL
A microscope reveals that snowflakes are made of tiny six-sided ice crystals. No two crystals are exactly the same.

Find out more
COLOUR
RIVERS
STORMS
WATER
WEATHER
WIND

REFORMATION

ON 31 OCTOBER 1517, German monk Martin Luther pinned a list of 95 theses, or complaints, on a church door in Wittenberg, Saxony. This sparked off a movement known as the Reformation because its followers demanded the reform of the Catholic Church, then the most powerful force in Europe. Many, like Luther, believed it was corrupt, and attacked its wealth and the sale of indulgences (pardons for sins). In 1521, Luther was expelled from the Church. He set up his own church which became known as Protestant because its followers "protested" against what they felt were the errors of the Catholic Church. Protestantism spread through Europe. Then, in a movement called the Counter-Reformation, the Catholic Church began to reform itself. The Counter-Reformation led to religious persecution and bitter civil wars.

MARTIN LUTHER
Martin Luther (1483-1546) inspired the Reformation. He attacked the sale of indulgences and said that no amount of money paid to the clergy could pardon an individual for his sins. Only through faith could people be saved.

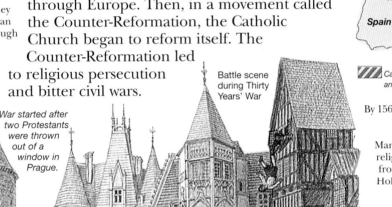

Battle scene during Thirty Years' War

War started after two Protestants were thrown out of a window in Prague.

England
Germany
France
Spain
Italy

///// Catholic and Protestant   ▓ Protestant   ☐ Catholic

PROTESTANTISM
By 1560, Europe had two main religions – Roman Catholic and Protestant. Protestantism began in Germany. Many German rulers adopted the new religion so that they could break away from the control of the Pope and the Holy Roman Emperor (the "political" Catholic ruler).

INQUISITION
In 1231, the Pope set up the Inquisition – a special organization that searched out and punished heretics (those who did not conform to the Catholic faith). Inquisitors arrested, tortured, and executed alleged heretics and witches (above). During the Reformation, 300 years later, the Inquisition tried to crush the new Protestant churches, but failed.

THIRTY YEARS' WAR
The Thirty Years' War lasted from 1618 to 1648. It began as a religious struggle between Catholics and Protestants in Germany. Then it grew into a war between the Habsburg rulers of the Holy Roman Empire and the kings of France for possession of land. In 1648, the Catholic side acknowledged it could not extinguish Protestantism.

COUNCIL OF TRENT
The Counter-Reformation began when Catholic leaders met at the Council of Trent in 1545. The council established the main principles of Catholicism and set up places for training priests and missionaries. During this time the Jesuits, an important teaching order founded in 1534, became popular.

Find out more

EUROPE
EUROPE, HISTORY OF
HABSBURGS
RELIGIONS
UNITED KINGDOM, HISTORY OF

RELIGIONS

PEOPLE HAVE ALWAYS SEARCHED for answers to life's mysteries and unexpected events. This questioning may have led to the growth of religions, to give meaning to life and death. Most religious people believe in a god or several gods. Gods are thought of as supreme beings who created the world or who control what happens in it. Religions may be highly organized, and teach people how to live, with a set of beliefs and rituals to follow. There may be special places in which to worship, and a spiritual leader for guidance. Some religions believe there is a spirit or a god in every object, from animals to rocks. Many believe in a life after death. Other religions have less formal rules, and people follow beliefs in their own way. The world's six major organized religions are Christianity, Judaism, Islam, Hinduism, Buddhism, and Sikhism.

MOTHER GODDESSES
Pregnant female figures mostly found in domestic locations may have been worshipped as a symbol of the making of new life.

RELIGION AND ART
Many people use art, architecture, and sculpture to convey their religious ideas, and to show the important icons of their religion. This Christian sculpture of the Virgin Mary holding Jesus shows her crowned as the Queen of Heaven.

GODS
Many religions worship either a single God, or several gods. There may be myths or stories associated with the god, which demonstrate an important lesson. Ganesha (right) is the Hindu god of wisdom. According to legend, his father accidentally cut off his head and in desperation replaced it with that of an elephant.

WORSHIP AND PRAYER
Each religion has its own system of worship and prayer. Worship shows reverence towards a god or deity, in a public ceremony or service. It often takes place in a special building, such as a mosque or church. Prayers can be spoken or thought during worship or in private, and are a thanksgiving or request to a god or holy object. The girl above prays during the Buddhist Festival of Hungry Ghosts in Singapore.

JERUSALEM
Jerusalem is sacred to three religions. Jews pray at the Wailing Wall, the ruins of a temple destroyed in 70 CE. The Dome of the Rock mosque is holy to Muslims as the place where Prophet Muhammad rose to heaven. The Church of the Holy Sepulchre is built on the site of the crucifixion and burial of Jesus Christ.

DEATH AND HEAVEN
Many faiths believe that the human body is a temporary container for the soul. After death the soul may be reborn in another body or go to heaven as a reward for good deeds on earth. Most religions have special rituals or funerals to honour and remember the dead, such as the Day of the Dead in Mexico (above). Candles are lit to help dead relatives find their way to the land of the living.

SACRED TEXTS
Many religions have texts which teach and guide. Muslims read the Qur'an, Christianity is based on the Bible, Buddhists follow the Dharma, and the Talmud (above) is central to Judaism.

JUDAISM

The religion of the Jewish people, Judaism, began over 4,000 years ago. Jews worship one God. They believe that God has made the Jews his chosen people. The Jewish festival of Passover, held in the spring, commemorates the time when the Jews left their exile in Egypt to return to Israel.

Plate with Passover meal

HINDUISM

The Hindu religion developed in India thousands of years ago. Hindus have many gods, but they are all part of one great power, called Brahman. Hindus believe that when we die, we are reborn as a person, animal, or plant. The better our deeds in one life, the better our rebirth. The Hindu festival of Diwali celebrates the victory of good over evil.

Candles are lit at the festival of Diwali.

Buddhist monks have few possessions, and devote their lives to explaining the Buddha's teachings.

BUDDHISM

Followers of the great Indian teacher, the Buddha, are known as Buddhists. Like Hindus, they believe in rebirth after death. By trying to follow a lifestyle of correct behaviour, meditation, and wisdom, they hope to break out of the cycle of death and rebirth to reach a state of purity known as enlightenment.

CHRISTIANITY

Christians believe that Jesus of Nazareth was the son of God. He lived in the Roman province of Palestine and was crucified. Christians believe that Jesus's life, death, and resurrection free believers from their state of sin. Easter, which celebrates the resurrection of Jesus, is the most important Christian festival. Eggs are given to symbolize the coming of new life.

Easter egg

ISLAM

Followers of Islam are called Muslims. Their faith was first revealed to the prophet Muhammad in the 7th century. Muslims believe in one God. They promise to pray five times a day, fast during the month of Ramadan, give alms to the poor, and make the pilgrimage to the holy city of Mecca at least once in their lives.

When they pray, Muslims face the direction of Mecca.

Sikh boy wearing turban

SIKHISM

The spiritual leader Guru Nanak founded Sikhism in northern India in the 16th century. Sikhs follow the ten Gurus who revealed the truth about God, and stress the importance of serving the community, as well as worship. Male (and some female) Sikhs wear the turban to show their faith and their membership of the Sikh community.

Find out more
BUDDHISM
CHRISTIANITY
HINDUISM
ISLAM
JUDAISM

RENAISSANCE

ITALY IN THE 15TH CENTURY was an exciting place. It was here that educated people began to develop new ideas about the world around them and rediscovered the arts and learning of Ancient Greece and Rome. For a period of about 200 years that became known as the Renaissance (rebirth) people made great advances in education, technology, and the arts. Helped by the invention of printing, the Renaissance gradually spread from Italy to the rest of Europe. Although the Renaissance mainly affected the wealthy, it had a huge impact on the way that everybody lived and perceived the world around them. The Renaissance produced great artists such as Michelangelo and Raphael. It also produced a new way of thinking called humanism, as scholars and thinkers such as Erasmus began to challenge the authority of the Roman Catholic Church. Humanism gave human beings more importance. It meant that artists such as Leonardo da Vinci began to produce realistic images instead of symbolic scenes. Scientists challenged old ideas about the nature of the universe, and conducted pioneering experiments.

COPERNICUS
By observing the movement of planets and stars, astronomers such as Nicolaus Copernicus (1473-1543) began to challenge ideas about the solar system which had been accepted since the time of the Ancient Greeks. Copernicus was first to suggest that the Earth revolves every 24 hours and that it travels around the Sun once a year. Many people did not accept his findings until many years later.

TECHNOLOGY
Renaissance scientists invented or developed new scientific instruments to help them in their work. The armillary sphere, a skeleton sphere with the Earth in the centre, was used to measure the position of the stars. Galileo invented the useful proportional compass, which could be set at any angle.

Armillary sphere

Proportional compass

Galileo at work

GALILEO
Galileo Galilei (1564-1642) was an Italian astronomer and physicist. He disproved many of the Ancient Greek thinker Aristotle's theories, including the theory that heavy objects fall faster than light ones. He perfected a refracting telescope and observed that the Earth and all the planets of the solar system revolve around the Sun.

RENAISSANCE MUSIC

When the first music was printed in Italy in the late 15th century, new musical styles began to spread throughout Europe. Non-religious music became more common, showing the influence of the humanist approach to life which characterized the Renaissance period. Music became more harmonious and melodic than before. William Byrd (1543-1623), left, was the first Englishman to have his music printed in England. He was a well known organist, first at Lincoln Cathedral, and then later at the Queen Elizabeth I Chapel Royal in London. He was also a composer with more than 470 works to his name, making him one of the masters of European Renaissance music.

ERASMUS
Desiderius Erasmus (1466-1536), a Dutch priest, wanted to reform the Roman Catholic Church. He criticized the superstitions of the clergy, and published studies of the Old and New Testaments, giving a better understanding of the Bible. A leading humanist, he questioned the authority of the Church – a shocking idea at the time.

BOTTICELLI

The paintings of Sandro Botticelli (1444-1510) show many of the features typical of Renaissance art: clear lines, even composition, and an emphasis on human activity. Renaissance artists painted realistic, mythological, and Biblical subjects. Most tried to make their paintings as realistic as possible by using perspective to give scenes an appearance of depth. Above is the Botticelli painting *Venus and Mars*.

MEDICIS

The Medicis were a great banking family who ruled Florence for more than 300 years. They became very powerful. Many of them, particularly Lorenzo "the Magnificent" (1449-92), encouraged artists such as Michelangelo, and helped them financially.

MICHELANGELO

Michelangelo (1475-1564) was a very skilled Italian artist and sculptor. His marble statue of David (left) is one of the finest examples of Renaissance sculpture. People admired the statue's youthful strength and beauty, which demonstrated the new realistic style of art.

Dome rises more than 120 m (400 ft) from the floor of the church.

Begun in 1505, the building took 150 years to complete.

ST. PETER'S

Situated in Vatican City, Rome, Italy, St. Peter's Church has a rich history. Ten different architects worked on its construction. Michelangelo designed the dome. The Italian architect Bernini (1598-1680) designed the inside of the church and the majestic piazza outside the church. St. Peter's houses many fabulous works of art, and marble and detailed mosaics decorate the walls.

SCULPTURE

Renaissance sculptors made great use of marble, copying the style of Ancient Roman statues. A new understanding of anatomy inspired sculptors to carve nude figures, with accurate depictions of muscles and joints. Some sculptors even dissected corpses to discover how the human body works.

ARCHITECTURE

Renaissance architecture was modelled on classical Roman building styles. Architects featured high domed roofs, vaulted ceilings, decorative columns, and rounded arches in their buildings. One of the most influential architects was Andrea Palladio (1508-80). The classical designs used by Palladio for his many villas and palaces were widely copied by later architects.

RENAISSANCE

1420-36 Architect Filippo Brunelleschi develops the system of perspective.

1430-35 Donatello's sculpture of David is the first large nude statue since the Roman Empire.

1480-85 Sandro Botticelli paints *The Birth of Venus.*

1497 Leonardo da Vinci paints *The Last Supper.*

1501 Petrucci publishes first printed music in Venice.

1501-04 Michelangelo sculpts *David.*

1502 Leonardo paints the *Mona Lisa.*

1505 Architect Donato Bramante begins the new St. Peter's in Rome. Completed in 1655.

1508 Artist Raphael begins to decorate the Pope's apartments in the Vatican.

1508-12 Michelangelo decorates the Sistine chapel.

1509 Erasmus writes *In Praise of Folly*, criticizing the Church.

c.1510 Renaissance art in Venice reaches its peak with artists such as Titian, Veronese, and Tintoretto.

1513 Death of Pope Julius II.

1532 Niccolo Machiavelli's book *The Prince* is published, suggesting how a ruler should govern a state.

1543 Astronomer Copernicus claims that the Earth and the other planets move around the sun.

1564 Death of Michelangelo.

1565 Architect Palladio begins to build the Villa Rotunda in Venice.

1593 Galileo develops the thermometer.

1608 Galileo develops the telescope.

Find out more
ARCHITECTURE
ASTRONOMY
LEONARDO DA VINCI
PAINTERS
PAINTING

REPRODUCTION

FOR LIFE TO CONTINUE on Earth, humans and other animals must produce young. The process of creating new life is called reproduction. Human beings reproduce in much the same way as other mammals. From birth, a woman has many tiny pinhead-sized ova (egg cells) in two organs inside the abdomen called ovaries. From puberty onwards, one of these egg cells is released each month as part of the menstrual cycle. Throughout life, a man produces small tadpole-shaped cells called sperm in sex organs called the testes. During sexual intercourse, sperm cells leave the man's body and enter the woman's body, swimming towards her ovaries. If a sperm meets a ripe egg cell, the two join together. This is called fertilization. The egg cell can only be fertilized for about 24 hours after ovulation. Once fertilized, the egg travels to the uterus to continue its development. During the following nine months the tiny egg develops into a fully formed baby, ready to be born.

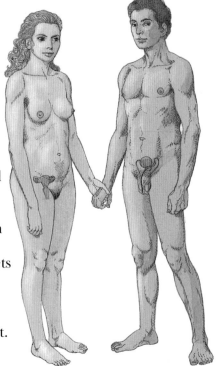

FOETUS
A developing baby, or foetus, lives inside the uterus, cushioned from bumps, bright lights, and noise by a surrounding fluid called the amniotic fluid. However, the baby can hear the regular thump of the mother's heartbeat and the gurgling of food in her intestines.

SEX ORGANS
The main female sex organs, the ovaries, are inside the abdomen. The main male organs, the testes and penis, hang outside the abdomen. Other differences between males and females, such as the woman's breasts, are called secondary sexual characteristics.

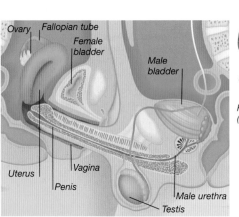

Ovary
Fallopian tube
Female bladder
Male bladder
Uterus
Vagina
Penis
Male urethra
Testis

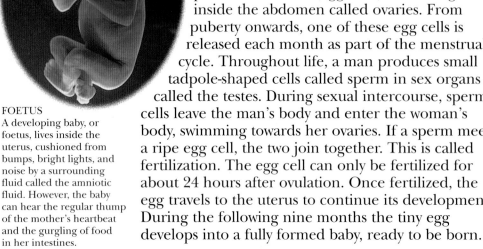

Ovary
Fallopian tube (oviduct)
Uterus (womb)
Vagina

FEMALE SEX ORGANS
About 300,000 eggs are stored in each ovary. During one menstrual cycle, an egg ripens and leaves the ovary, moving into the Fallopian tube, or oviduct. If it is not fertilized by a sperm, it reaches the uterus, dies and breaks down, then leaves the body during the process called menstruation.

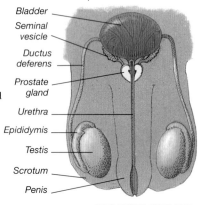

Bladder
Seminal vesicle
Ductus deferens
Prostate gland
Urethra
Epididymis
Testis
Scrotum
Penis

MALE SEX ORGANS
Each testis makes more than 250 million sperm cells every day. The cells are stored in the testis itself and in a long, winding tube called the epididymis. If they are not released, they break down and are reabsorbed into the bloodstream.

SEXUAL INTERCOURSE

During sexual intercourse, the man's penis becomes stiff enough to insert into the woman's vagina, which also enlarges. After a while muscular contractions squeeze sperm cells from the man's testes out of the penis and into the vagina, in a fluid called semen. This process is called ejaculation. The sperm cells swim through the uterus, propelled by their tails, and travel along the Fallopian tube. Sometimes, one of these sperm cells reaches the egg cell and fertilizes it, resulting in pregnancy.

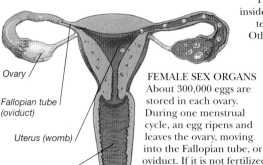

Sperm cells cluster around egg cell in Fallopian tube.

Only one sperm penetrates egg to fertilize it.

Barrier around dividing cells keeps out other sperm cells.

Fertilized egg divides into two cells within 36 hours, four within 48 hours, then eight, and so on.

Embryo enters uterus about four days after fertilization as a solid ball of 32 cells.

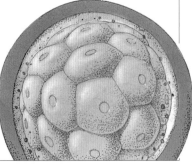

FERTILIZATION
An egg cell begins to divide and develop into a baby only when it is joined by a sperm cell. After intercourse, hundreds of sperm cells may reach the egg, but only one breaks through the outer layer. Once this occurs, genetic material in the sperm – the instructions needed to make a new human – joins the genetic material inside the egg. The coming together of sperm and egg and their genes is called fertilization.

PREGNANCY

About one week after fertilization, the now hollow ball of cells embeds itself in the blood-rich lining of the uterus where it absorbs nutrients. The cells continue to divide and change, forming the first body tissues such as blood vessels and nerves. Gradually the ball of cells folds and twists into the basic body shape of the baby. Meanwhile, other cells form the placenta, a saucer-shaped organ, in the lining of the uterus. The placenta is fed with blood from the mother, and oxygen and nutrients pass to the baby through the umbilical cord. This lifeline consists of three blood vessels; the largest vein carries nutrients and oxygen-rich blood to the baby, and the smaller ones carry waste and blood low in oxygen back to the placenta.

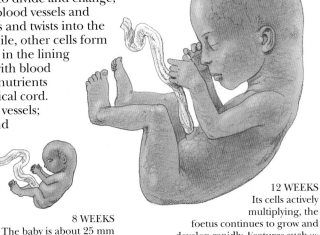

5 WEEKS
The developing baby is now about 10 mm (½ in) long. It has a recognizable head, back, and heart, and the beginnings of a mouth and eyes. The limbs are forming as small buds. At this stage, the developing baby is called an embryo.

8 WEEKS
The baby is about 25 mm (1 in) long, and all the major parts of the body have formed – even the fingers and toes. The developing baby is now called a foetus.

12 WEEKS
Its cells actively multiplying, the foetus continues to grow and develop rapidly. Features such as fingernails, toenails, and eyelids are now visible. The baby is about 13 cm (5 in) long. There are still 28 weeks to go before it is born.

PUBERTY

Babies and children have sex organs, but they are not able to release egg or sperm cells. At puberty, which generally starts when people are between 10 and 15 years old, chemicals called sex hormones are released into the bloodstream from hormonal glands. These sex hormones cause the sex organs to mature (become fully developed). Other changes occur at this time too, particularly a spurt in growth.

In a boy, the testes produce a sex hormone called testosterone. This makes hair grow on the face and body. It also makes the voice deeper, encourages muscle development, and sets off production of sperm.

In a girl, the ovaries produce progesterone and oestrogen, which cause the breasts to develop and fatty tissue to form, giving the body a more rounded shape. From puberty onwards, a woman's body also undergoes a monthly process called the menstrual cycle, as shown below. Changing levels of hormones thicken the uterus lining and enrich it with blood, which will nourish a fertilized egg if it implants.

BIRTH

Birth is the process that ends pregnancy and pushes a baby out of the uterus, usually after 38-40 weeks of pregnancy. When the baby has reached full term (left), it is about 50 cm (20 in) long. Labour is triggered by the hormone oxytocin and by changes in the level of other hormones in the mother's blood. During labour the cervix widens to allow birth to take place, and powerful contractions in the uterus push the baby out through the vagina, usually head first. If a baby is born feet first it is called a breech birth. The baby then takes its first breaths and the umbilical cord is cut. The placenta is expelled from the uterus a few minutes later as afterbirth.

PREMATURE BABIES
If a baby is born before the 37th week of pregnancy it is called premature and may have difficulty breathing. The baby is placed in an incubator and monitored very carefully until it is strong enough to breathe for itself.

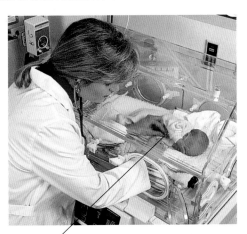

A doctor checks the heartbeat of a premature baby in its incubator.

1st week	2nd week	3rd week	4th week
Lining of uterus breaks down and passes out of the vagina during menstruation or a period.	*Lining starts to thicken again in preparation for next egg. Next egg begins to ripen in ovary.*	*Ripe egg is released from ovary. Egg can be fertilized for up to 24 hours in Fallopian tube.*	*Egg reaches uterus and implants if fertilized, or breaks down if not fertilized.*

Find out more
ANIMALS
HUMAN BODY

REPTILES

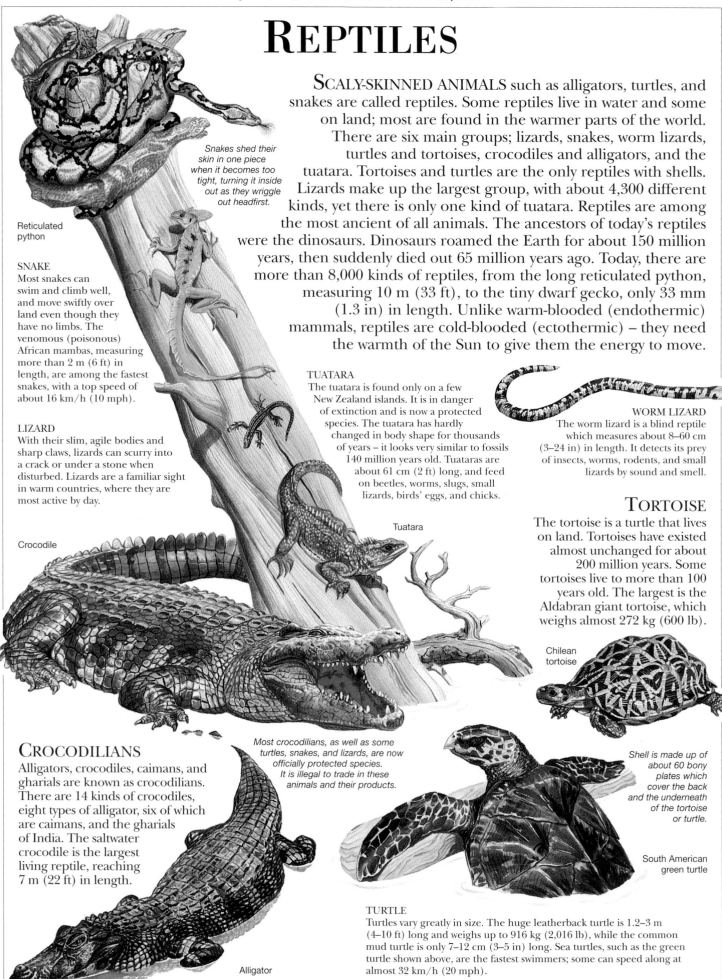

SCALY-SKINNED ANIMALS such as alligators, turtles, and snakes are called reptiles. Some reptiles live in water and some on land; most are found in the warmer parts of the world. There are six main groups; lizards, snakes, worm lizards, turtles and tortoises, crocodiles and alligators, and the tuatara. Tortoises and turtles are the only reptiles with shells. Lizards make up the largest group, with about 4,300 different kinds, yet there is only one kind of tuatara. Reptiles are among the most ancient of all animals. The ancestors of today's reptiles were the dinosaurs. Dinosaurs roamed the Earth for about 150 million years, then suddenly died out 65 million years ago. Today, there are more than 8,000 kinds of reptiles, from the long reticulated python, measuring 10 m (33 ft), to the tiny dwarf gecko, only 33 mm (1.3 in) in length. Unlike warm-blooded (endothermic) mammals, reptiles are cold-blooded (ectothermic) – they need the warmth of the Sun to give them the energy to move.

Snakes shed their skin in one piece when it becomes too tight, turning it inside out as they wriggle out headfirst.

Reticulated python

SNAKE
Most snakes can swim and climb well, and move swiftly over land even though they have no limbs. The venomous (poisonous) African mambas, measuring more than 2 m (6 ft) in length, are among the fastest snakes, with a top speed of about 16 km/h (10 mph).

LIZARD
With their slim, agile bodies and sharp claws, lizards can scurry into a crack or under a stone when disturbed. Lizards are a familiar sight in warm countries, where they are most active by day.

Crocodile

TUATARA
The tuatara is found only on a few New Zealand islands. It is in danger of extinction and is now a protected species. The tuatara has hardly changed in body shape for thousands of years – it looks very similar to fossils 140 million years old. Tuataras are about 61 cm (2 ft) long, and feed on beetles, worms, slugs, small lizards, birds' eggs, and chicks.

Tuatara

WORM LIZARD
The worm lizard is a blind reptile which measures about 8–60 cm (3–24 in) in length. It detects its prey of insects, worms, rodents, and small lizards by sound and smell.

TORTOISE
The tortoise is a turtle that lives on land. Tortoises have existed almost unchanged for about 200 million years. Some tortoises live to more than 100 years old. The largest is the Aldabran giant tortoise, which weighs almost 272 kg (600 lb).

Chilean tortoise

CROCODILIANS
Alligators, crocodiles, caimans, and gharials are known as crocodilians. There are 14 kinds of crocodiles, eight types of alligator, six of which are caimans, and the gharials of India. The saltwater crocodile is the largest living reptile, reaching 7 m (22 ft) in length.

Most crocodilians, as well as some turtles, snakes, and lizards, are now officially protected species. It is illegal to trade in these animals and their products.

Shell is made up of about 60 bony plates which cover the back and the underneath of the tortoise or turtle.

South American green turtle

Alligator

TURTLE
Turtles vary greatly in size. The huge leatherback turtle is 1.2–3 m (4–10 ft) long and weighs up to 916 kg (2,016 lb), while the common mud turtle is only 7–12 cm (3–5 in) long. Sea turtles, such as the green turtle shown above, are the fastest swimmers; some can speed along at almost 32 km/h (20 mph).

BREEDING

Most reptiles lay eggs, from which the young hatch. Snake and lizard eggs usually have a leathery, flexible shell.The eggs of crocodiles and tortoises are hard and rigid, and the temperature at which the eggs are incubated determines the sex of the hatchling. The loggerhead turtle, shown here, digs a deep hole in the beach sand and lays its eggs under the cover of darkness. The eggs take several weeks to hatch and are at risk from foxes and monitor lizards, which dig them up and eat them. After hatching, the young turtles have to avoid sea birds and crabs as they scuttle down to the sea.

The female loggerhead turtle swims ashore and crawls up the beach at night to lay eggs.

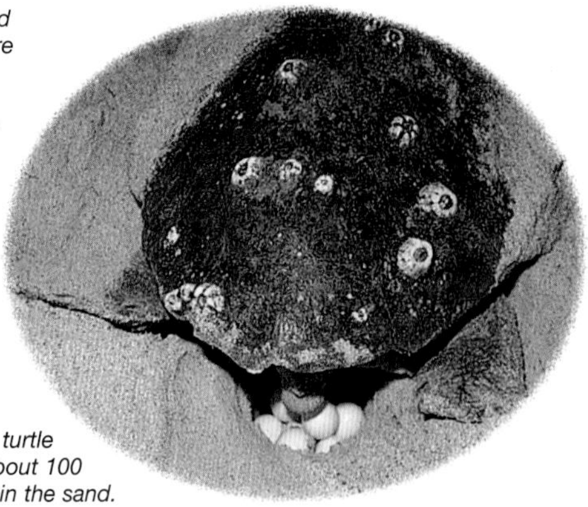

The female turtle lays about 100 eggs in the sand.

SCALES

A reptile's scaly skin provides good protection against predators and stops the animal from drying out. The arrangement of the scales helps scientists identify species. Some reptiles, such as chameleons, have special cells in the skin. These cells make the coloured pigments inside the skin expand or contract. This is how the chameleon changes its colour, for camouflage.

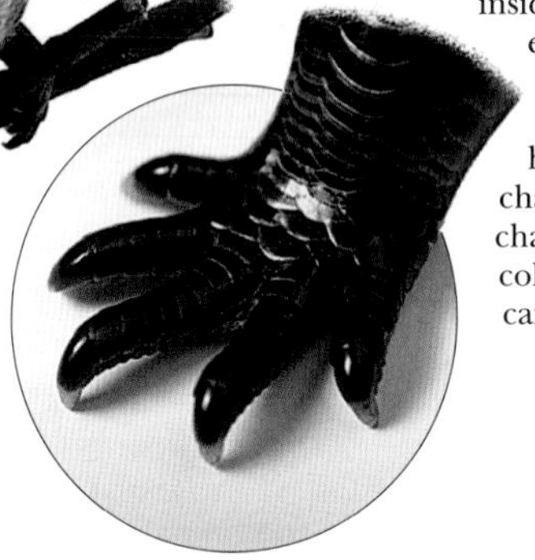

BLUE-TONGUED SKINK

The reptiles tongue has several uses. Lizards and snakes use it to detect their surroundings. The tongue flicks out to pick up chemicals in the air and carries them back to Jacobson's organs, special sensory organs in the roof of the mouth. When in danger, the Australian blue-tongued skink opens its mouth wide, thrusts out its bright blue tongue, hisses, and puffs up its body to frighten away a predator.

WALL GECKO

Wall geckos have tiny, sticky pads on their toes, which enable them to run up smooth glass windows and upside-down across the ceiling.

Some geckos are smaller than the human palm.

TEMPERATURE REGULATION

We often describe reptiles as cold-blooded, but this is not strictly true. Reptiles cannot generate body heat internally, in the way that mammals do, but they can control their body temperature by their behaviour. Reptiles bask in the Sun to absorb warmth, then hide in the shade when they become too hot.

At dawn the lizard sunbathes with the length of its body facing the Sun to absorb maximum heat.

During the hot midday Sun the lizard stays in the shade to avoid overheating.

At dusk the lizard basks with its head facing the Sun to keep up its body temperature.

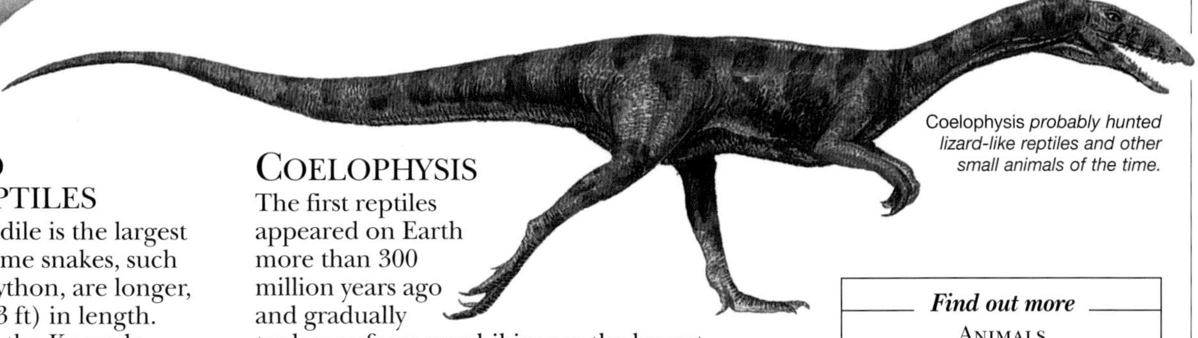

LARGEST AND SMALLEST REPTILES

The saltwater crocodile is the largest reptile, although some snakes, such as the reticulated python, are longer, growing to 10 m (33 ft) in length. The largest lizard is the Komodo dragon, a type of monitor lizard. The smallest of all reptiles are some kinds of geckos, only about a centimetre long when fully grown.

COELOPHYSIS

The first reptiles appeared on Earth more than 300 million years ago and gradually took over from amphibians as the largest animals on land. Dinosaurs, such as the *Coelophysis* shown here, were early reptiles that evolved about 200–220 million years ago. *Coelophysis* was about the size of an adult human.

Coelophysis probably hunted lizard-like reptiles and other small animals of the time.

Find out more

ANIMALS
CROCODILES AND ALLIGATORS
DINOSAURS
LIZARDS
SNAKES

RIVERS

Rain feeds the river system.

WATER RUNS DOWN from high ground, cutting out a channel in the rock as it moves. This flowing water forms a river, which can be fed by a melting glacier, an overflowing lake, or a mountain spring. Rivers shape the landscape as they flow: the water sweeps away soil and eventually creates deep valleys in the land. One of the world's deepest valleys, cut by the River Kali Gandak through the Himalayas, is 5.5 km (3.4 miles) deep. Rivers also flow deep underground, slowly wearing away limestone rocks to form caves.

Rivers are important for transport and as a source of water, which is why most big cities lie on rivers. The longest rivers are the River Nile in Africa, which is 6,670 km (4,145 miles) long, and the River Amazon in South America, which is 6,448 km (4,007 miles) long.

TRIBUTARIES
The streams and rivers that flow into a big river are called its tributaries.

WATERFALL
The river plunges over a shelf of hard rock to form a waterfall.

RIVER SYSTEM

Small rivers and streams feed a large river with water. A river system consists of the whole group of rivers and streams. A watershed, or high ridge, separates one river system from another. Streams flow in opposite directions on either side of a watershed.

GORGE
The waterfall slowly wears away the rock, cutting a deep gorge.

RAPIDS
Fast, swirling currents form where water flows down a steep slope. These parts of the river are called rapids.

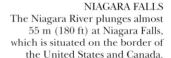

NIAGARA FALLS
The Niagara River plunges almost 55 m (180 ft) at Niagara Falls, which is situated on the border of the United States and Canada.

RIVER VALLEY
The river carries along stones and mud, which grind against the river-bed and sides, deepening and widening the V-shaped valley.

Weathering on the valley sides breaks up soft rock and soil. This material falls into the river and is carried away by the current.

OXBOW LAKE
The river cuts through the neck of a loop by wearing away the bank. Material is deposited at the ends of the loop, eventually forming a lake.

FLOODS
Rivers can overflow with heavy rain, or when water surges up from the sea. Flooding is severe in low-lying places, such as parts of Brazil in South America, which are often hit by tropical storms. Destruction of surrounding forests may be increasing the flow of water, making floods worse.

FLOOD PLAIN
Further down the river, the valley flattens out. This area, called the flood plain, is sometimes submerged during floods. The river runs through the plain in loops called meanders.

Some rivers do not form deltas, but flow into the sea through a single wide channel called an estuary.

USES OF RIVERS

Great rivers that flow across whole countries carry boats that take goods from place to place. Some rivers have dams which build up huge stores of water in reservoirs. This water is used to supply towns and cities, irrigate crops, and generate electricity in hydroelectric power stations. Rivers are also a source of fish, but many rivers are now polluted by farms and factories.

DELTA
The river sometimes fans out into separate streams as it reaches the sea. The streams dump mud which forms an area of flat land called a delta.

RIVER RHINE
The River Rhine is an important trade route. Barges carry goods between towns in northern Europe.

Find out more
DAMS
GLACIERS AND ICECAPS
LAKE AND RIVER WILDLIFE
LAKES
RAIN AND SNOW
WATER

ROBOTS

WHEN PEOPLE THINK OF ROBOTS, they often imagine the metal monsters of science fiction movies. However, most robots at work today look nothing like this. A robot is a computer-controlled machine that carries out mechanical tasks. The Czech playwright Karel Capek invented the word *robot*, which comes from a Czech word meaning "forced labour". Indeed, robots do jobs that would be dangerous or boring for people to do. Many factories have robots that consist of a single arm that is fixed in one spot. The robot simply repeats a task that it has been instructed to perform, such as spray-painting car parts. Today, engineers are developing much more sophisticated robots. These robots can move around, and their electronic detectors enable them to sense their surroundings. They also have "intelligence", which means that they can respond to what they see and hear and make decisions for themselves. Intelligent robots are designed to act as guards and firemen, and may travel into space to study distant worlds.

SCIENCE FICTION ROBOTS
The robots of science fiction, such as C3-P0 from the film *Star Wars*, are often anthropoid (human-like). In reality, anthropoid robots are rare. However, Japanese engineers have built experimental robots with two legs.

ROBOT ARM
Sophisticated robots work in factories, assembling, spraying, and welding components (parts). A skilled welder or painter will have programmed the robot by leading it (or a similar robot) through the task. Some robots can understand simple spoken instructions too. Robots often have sensors such as laser vision systems which help the robots to find and work on complex parts.

Held too tightly – loosen grip.

Brain sends nerve signals to muscles in the hand, adjusting the strength of the grip so the egg is neither dropped nor squashed.

Held too loosely – tighten grip.

Touch sensors in your hand detect how hard you are pressing on the egg.

FEEDBACK
When you pick up an egg, your senses begin sending signals to your brain. From this information, your brain automatically adjusts the movement of your hand and the pressure of your fingers. This adjustment is called feedback. Advanced robots control their actions by feedback from electronic detectors such as lasers, television cameras, and touch sensors.

SPACE ROBOT
In January 2004, two unmanned exploration rovers, *Spirit* (right) and *Opportunity*, touched down on Mars. They photographed the planet and analysed samples of rock. Robot space probes such as these are designed to obey instructions from controllers on Earth, but decide for themselves how to carry out the orders.

Space probes need to be able to work independently because radio instructions could take minutes or even hours to travel from Earth.

REMOTE CONTROL
Mobile robots do dangerous jobs such as repairing and dismantling nuclear reactors and detonating concealed bombs. These robots are remotely controlled – a human operator controls the general actions of the robot from a safe distance, and onboard computers control detailed movements.

This bomb disposal robot runs on tracks so that it can climb into awkward places. It carries cameras to send back pictures to the operator, and a gun for detonating the bomb.

Find out more

COMPUTERS
SCIENCE
TECHNOLOGY

437

ROCKETS AND MISSILES

THE INVENTION OF THE ROCKET ENGINE was a landmark in history. Not only did it give humans a tool with which to explore space, but it also produced the missile, a weapon of terrible destructive power. A rocket engine is the most powerful of all engines. It has the power to push a spacecraft along at more than 40,000 km/h (25,000 mph), the speed necessary for it to break free from Earth's gravity. In a rocket engine, fuel burns to produce gases that rush out of the nozzle at the back, thrusting the rocket forward. However, unlike other engines, rockets do not need to use oxygen from the air to burn their fuel. Instead they carry their own supply of oxygen, usually in the form of a liquid, so that they can operate in space where there is no air. There is one major difference between a missile and a space rocket: missiles carry an explosive warhead instead of a satellite or human cargo.

A few seconds after takeoff, booster fuel is expended.

Third stage fires for about 12 minutes, carrying its satellite payload into orbit about 320 km (200 miles) above the Earth's surface.

First stage propels rocket for about three minutes, by which time rocket is more than 50 km (30 miles) above the Earth.

Once first stage has run out of fuel, it falls away and second stage takes over, burning for about two minutes.

ROCKET STAGES
Most space rockets are made up of several stages, or segments, each with its own rocket engines and propellant, or fuel. By detaching the stages as they are used, the rocket can reach higher speeds because its weight is kept to a minimum. There are two main types of rocket propellant: solid and liquid. Solid fuel burns rapidly and cannot be controlled once ignited. But rockets powered by liquid propellant can be controlled by opening and closing valves that adjust the flow of fuel into the engine.

NUCLEAR MISSILES
Deadly nuclear warheads and precise navigational systems make nuclear missiles the most dangerous weapons in the history of warfare. A single warhead has the power to destroy a large city and cause millions of deaths. Nuclear missiles can be launched from submarines, aircraft, trucks, and hidden underground launch sites.

ARIANE ROCKET

Vehicle equipment bay contains satellite that is being carried into orbit.

Guidance systems keep rocket on the correct course.

Third stage with one liquid-propellant rocket

Tank containing oxidizer, a liquid that contains oxygen

Tank containing highly inflammable liquid fuel

Pumps push fuel and oxidizer to the nozzle, where they burn and produce a violent rush of hot gases that push the rocket upwards.

Second stage with one liquid-propellant rocket

Two solid-propellant and two liquid-propellant strap-on booster rockets give space rocket an extra push in the first part of its flight.

First stage with four liquid-propellant rocket engines

TYPES OF MISSILES
Huge intercontinental ballistic missiles (ICBMs) blast up into space and come down on their targets thousands of kilometres away. However, not all rocket-powered missiles travel into space; many have replaced guns for short-range attacks on tanks, ships, and aircraft. Many of these missiles home in on their targets automatically.

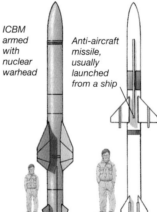

ICBM armed with nuclear warhead

Anti-aircraft missile, usually launched from a ship

Size of rockets compared to a child 1.2 m (4 ft) tall

Radar-guided anti-ship missile. It can be launched from the air, from land, or from a warship.

Anti-tank missile, guided to target by remote control

DEVELOPMENT OF ROCKETS
In the 13th century, the Chinese used a simple type of rocket powered by gunpowder to scare enemy horses. Six hundred years later, Englishman Sir William Congreve developed a gunpowder rocket that the English forces used during the Napoleonic Wars. During World War II (1939-45), German scientist Wernher von Braun invented the first successful long-range rocket, the V-2, the forerunner of the ICBM.

Early Chinese rockets

Find out more
ASTRONAUTS and space travel
COLD WAR
NUCLEAR ENERGY
SPACE FLIGHT
SUBMARINES
TECHNOLOGY
WORLD WAR II

ROCKS AND MINERALS

WE LIVE ON THE SURFACE of a huge ball of rock, the Earth. The landscape everywhere is made up of rocks. Most are covered by soil, trees, or grass. Others, such as Uluru (Ayers Rock) in Australia, a massive lump of sandstone 348 m (1,142 ft) high, rise from the ground and are visible. The oldest rocks on Earth are about 4,000 million years old. Other rocks are much more recent, and new rocks are forming all the time. All rocks contain substances called minerals. Marble consists mainly of calcite, for example, and granite contains the minerals mica, quartz, and feldspar.

Rocks form in different ways: from molten rock within the Earth, from the fossils of animals and plants, and by the action of heat and pressure on ancient rocks inside the Earth. But no rocks, however hard, last forever on the Earth's surface. They are slowly eroded, or worn away, by the action of wind, rain, and other weather conditions.

HOW ROCKS FORM

All rocks started out as clouds of dust in space. The dust particles came together and formed the rocks that make up the planets, moons, and meteorites. There are now three main kinds of rocks on the Earth's surface: igneous, sedimentary, and metamorphic rocks. Each kind of rock forms in a different way.

GIANT'S CAUSEWAY
The steps of this unusual rock formation in Northern Ireland are made of columns of basalt, rock which developed when lava from a volcano cooled and set. The rock cracked into columns as it cooled.

Mud and pebbles are buried and squashed together, producing a hard sedimentary rock called conglomerate.

SEDIMENTARY ROCKS
Ice, wind, and running water wear away rocks into pebbles and small particles called sediment. Layers of sediment containing sand, clay, and animal skeletons are buried and squeezed so that they slowly change into hard rocks called sedimentary rocks.

Limestone contains the remains of shellfish. Chalk, another kind of limestone, is made of the skeletons of sea animals.

Bubbles of gas trapped in the lava created holes in this piece of rock.

When lava from a volcano cools on the Earth's surface, it forms basalt.

IGNEOUS ROCKS
Deep underground the heat is so intense that some rock is molten (melted). When it cools, this molten rock, or magma, sets hard to produce an igneous rock. This may happen underground, or the magma may rise to the surface as lava and solidify.

Lava flows from a volcano and solidifies, forming basalt, an igneous rock.

Sedimentary rocks, such as conglomerate, form on the beach at the mouth of a river.

River carries sediment from the land to the sea.

Red-hot magma heats surrounding limestone, turning it into marble.

Hot magma solidifies, forming granite, an igneous rock.

Shale forms from clay at the river bed.

Clay forms shale, a sedimentary rock that crumbles easily. This rock is slate, the metamorphic rock which forms from shale.

METAMORPHIC ROCKS
Heat and pressure deep underground bake and squeeze sedimentary and igneous rocks. The minerals within the rocks change, often becoming harder. In this way they form new rocks called metamorphic rocks. After millions of years, the top rocks are worn away and metamorphic rocks appear on the surface.

When magma slowly cools deep underground, it often forms granite, a hard rock which is used as a building material.

Heating and compressing limestone turns it into marble, a hard metamorphic rock.

MINERALS

An impressive rock collection will feature rocks that contain beautiful mineral crystals. Minerals are the different substances of which rocks are made. For example, limestone and marble contain the white mineral calcite. Minerals include precious stones such as diamonds, and ores – minerals that contain metals such as iron and aluminium. Almost all metals are produced by mining and quarrying ores, and then treating the ores to extract their metals.

DESERT ROSE
The mineral gypsum forms petal-shaped crystals in deserts and dry regions. This happens as water dries up, leaving mineral deposits behind. The crystals often look like flowers, so they are called desert roses or gypsum flowers.

TURQUOISE
Jewellers cut beautiful gemstones and ornaments from turquoise, a blue-green mineral that often runs in a thin vein through other rocks.

HALITE
Table salt comes from the mineral halite. Halite forms where sea water dries at the shore. Underground deposits of halite are the remains of ancient salt lakes. Pure salt has no colour, but impurities in halite give it a pink colour.

SULPHUR
Yellow crystals form when molten sulphur cools. Large underground deposits in places such as the United States provide sulphur for making rubber and chemicals.

CRYSTALS

Minerals often form crystals – solids which grow in regular shapes with flat sides. Light sparkles from crystals because they are often transparent and have smooth, shiny surfaces. Each mineral forms crystals with particular shapes, such as columns and cubes. Crystals grow from molten minerals or minerals that are dissolved in liquids, such as water.

Hexagonal crystals form in six-sided columns.

Cubic crystals form in four-sided columns.

GALENA
Glistening grey crystals of galena stick out from a piece of white limestone. Galena forms cubic crystals. It is the main ore in which lead is found, and it often appears as a vein in limestone. Lead is combined with sulphur in galena. Smelting the ore by heating it in a furnace removes the sulphur and leaves lead metal.

Some minerals, such as solecite, form needle-shaped crystals.

Crystals form in columns, such as in this piece of the mineral beryl.

QUARTZ
Quartz is one of the most common minerals. Electronic clocks and watches contain small cut pieces of quartz that control time-keeping with great accuracy.

USES OF ROCK

Rocks in one form or another surround us in towns, cities, and the countryside. Hard rocks such as granite, sandstone, and limestone provide good building materials for houses and walls, and roads contain fragments of crushed rock. Soft rocks have uses too. Heating clay or shale with crushed limestone produces cement for making concrete and laying bricks. Bricks themselves are made by baking clay in moulds.

The first tools were made of stone. Early people broke pieces of rocks and stone to make sharp cutting implements such as axes.

Sculptors work rocks, stones, and pure minerals to make statues and ornaments.

Find out more
ATOMS AND MOLECULES
CLOCKS AND WATCHES
COMETS AND METEORS
FOSSILS
GEOLOGY
SCIENCE
VOLCANOES

ROMAN EMPIRE

TWO THOUSAND YEARS AGO a single government and way of life united most of western Europe, the Middle East, and the north coast of Africa. The Roman Empire was based on good organization and centralized control. Towns in different countries were planned in exactly the same way. A network of stone-paved roads (parts of which remain today) connected every area to Rome. The reign of the first emperor, Augustus, began a long period of stability known as the Pax Romana, or Roman Peace, which lasted for about 200 years. Strong border defences manned by the Roman army protected the empire, while a skilled civil service governed it. Trade flourished and the people were united. The empire reached the height of its power in about 200 CE and then began to decline slowly. It was divided into two parts in 395. In 476, barbarian tribes conquered Rome, putting an end to the Western Empire. The Eastern Empire (based in Constantinople, now called Istanbul, Turkey) continued until 1453.

GRAFFITI
The Romans were fond of making fun of each other. This caricature was found on a wall in Pompeii. It is a mockery of a leading local citizen – probably a noble, judging from his laurel wreath.

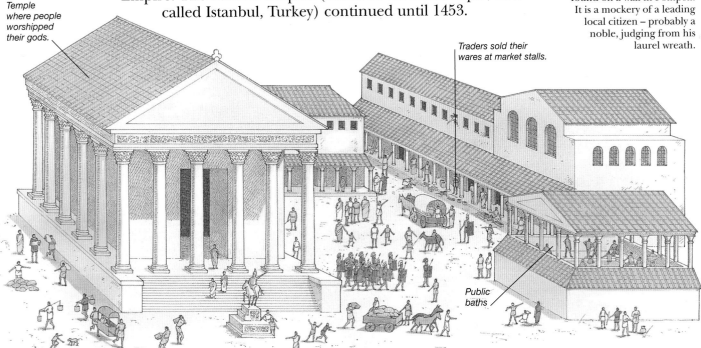

Temple where people worshipped their gods.

Traders sold their wares at market stalls.

Public baths

CITY LIFE

Roman cities were carefully planned with straight streets, running water, and sewers. The forum, or central market-place, was surrounded by shops, law courts, and the town hall. The rich, always Roman citizens, lived in fine villas; the poor lived in apartment-style buildings. There were many temples. Most of the hard work was done by slaves, who had none of the rights granted to citizens, such as access to the baths.

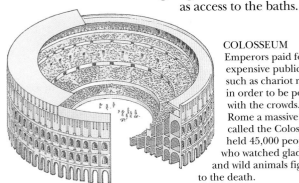

COLOSSEUM
Emperors paid for expensive public games, such as chariot racing, in order to be popular with the crowds. In Rome a massive theatre called the Colosseum held 45,000 people, who watched gladiators and wild animals fight to the death.

ROMAN BATHS
The Romans loved bathing. They scraped off the dirt, rubbed oil into their skin, relaxed in steam rooms, swam in warm pools, and plunged into icy water.

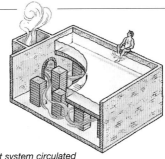

The hypocaust system circulated hot air under the floors and through the walls to heat houses and baths.

People rubbed oil, which they carried in oil flasks, on their bodies.

Bathers scraped the sweat and dirt off their bodies with strigils.

Commanding officers often wore crests on their helmets so that their men could recognize them in battle.

ROMAN ARMY

The power of the empire depended on the might of its professional armies, or legions. Soldiers belonging to a legion (about 5,000 men) were called legionaries. They were highly trained and well equipped with spears, shields, and short swords. They built roads and forts to defend their conquests. Upon retirement, veteran soldiers were often given land in colonies throughout the empire.

ROMAN EMPIRE

c.753 BCE First settlement built.

509 BCE Last king of Rome driven out of city. Republic established.

275 BCE Italy conquered. Expansion overseas begins.

364-146 BCE Punic Wars against Carthage end with Roman control of Spain and North Africa, and the destruction of Carthage.

71 BCE Slaves revolt, led by Spartacus.

52 BCE Gaul (France) conquered by Julius Caesar.

44 BCE Caesar assassinated.

27 BCE Augustus becomes first emperor.

43 CE Claudius conquers Britain.

117 CE Empire reaches its greatest size.

284 CE Empire splits into two halves.

410 CE Visigoths sack Rome.

476 CE Western part of the Empire falls.

THE ROMAN EMPIRE
At its height the Roman Empire stretched from the Middle East to Britain. The inhabitants were of many different races and spoke many different languages.

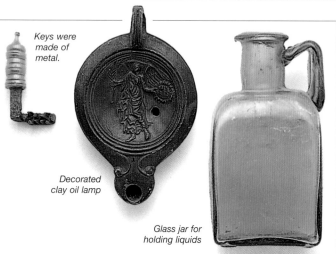

TECHNOLOGY AND CRAFTS

The Romans were highly skilled engineers and craftworkers. Their towns had water supplies and drains, and rich people lived in centrally heated houses. The houses often had detailed mosaics on the floors. Artisans worked with glass, metals, bone, and clay to make beautiful objects that have lasted to this day.

Keys were made of metal.

Decorated clay oil lamp

Glass jar for holding liquids

HADRIAN'S WALL
The emperor Hadrian ordered a wall to be built across northern Britain to defend Roman lands from the fierce, unconquered tribes who lived in the mountains of Scotland. The wall, parts of which can still be seen today, was 120 km (75 miles) long, and studded with forts. The army built defensive ditches, fortress bases, and signal towers along it.

Find out more
BARBARIANS
BYZANTINE EMPIRE
CAESAR, JULIUS
EUROPE, HISTORY OF
ITALY

FRANKLIN DELANO
ROOSEVELT

1882 Born Hyde Park, New York.

1907 Passed New York State Bar law exam.

1910 Elected to New York state senate.

1913-20 Assistant secretary of the navy.

1920 Runs for vice president.

1921 Afflicted by polio.

1928 Elected governor of New York.

1932 Elected president of the United States.

1933 Institutes New Deal.

1936, 1940, 1944 Re-elected president.

1941 United States enters World War II after Japanese bomb Pearl Harbor, Hawaii.

1945 Roosevelt dies just before the end of the war.

IN 1932 THE UNITED STATES was at one of its lowest points in history. Thirteen million people – nearly one third of the country's work force – were unemployed. Then a new president was elected with a mission to make Americans prosperous again. When Franklin Delano Roosevelt was disabled by polio in the summer of 1921, it appeared to be the end of a promising political career. But Roosevelt was a fighter and, helped by his wife, Eleanor, he regained the partial use of his legs. In 1928 he was elected governor of New York, then ran for president in 1932. He won a landslide victory, and for 13 years – the longest time any United States president has ever served – Roosevelt worked to overcome the effects of unemployment and poverty, telling Americans that "the only thing we have to fear is fear itself". He launched the New Deal – a series of social reforms and work programmes. During World War II, Roosevelt proved to be an able war leader, and with his Soviet and British allies he did much to shape the postwar world.

NEW DEAL

During the Depression of the 1930s, Roosevelt promised a New Deal. The government provided jobs for the unemployed and tried to return the country to prosperity. New laws were passed that provided better conditions for workers and pensions for retired workers.

The New Deal as seen by a cartoonist of the time.

FIRESIDE CHATS
President Roosevelt was an expert communicator who used the then new medium of the radio to explain his controversial policies to the nation. These informal "fireside chats" established firm links between the President and the American people.

ELEANOR ROOSEVELT
Throughout her life President Roosevelt's wife, Eleanor (1884-1962), was a tireless campaigner for human rights. After 1945 she represented her country in the United Nations.

YALTA CONFERENCE

In February 1945, President Roosevelt, Winston Churchill, the British prime minister (far left), and Joseph Stalin, Soviet premier (far right), met in the Soviet resort of Yalta. They decided which European countries would lie in the US and Soviet spheres of influence.

Find out more
CHURCHILL, SIR WINSTON
DEPRESSION of the 1930s
UNITED NATIONS
UNITED STATES, HISTORY OF
WORLD WAR II

RUSSIAN FEDERATION

THE LARGEST NATION in the world is the Russian Federation. Also called Russia, it consists of 20 autonomous (self-governing) republics, and more than 50 other regions. It covers one-tenth of the earth's land area – one-third of Asia, and two-fifths of Europe. Russia has a very varied climate and a landscape that ranges from mountains in the south and east to vast lowlands and rivers in the north and west. The population is varied too, although most of the 140 million people are of Russian origin and speak the Russian language. The Russian Federation came into being in 1991 after the break up of the Soviet Union, or U.S.S.R. After 1991, the Russian people experienced greater political freedom but also economic hardship as their country changed from a state-planned to a free-market economy. The Russian Federation has vast agricultural resources. It is also rich in minerals, and has considerable industry. Although many people in Russia are very poor, the country now has some of the world's richest billionaires.

The Russian Federation stretches from eastern Europe in the west across the entire width of Asia to the Pacific Ocean in the east, and from the Arctic Circle in the north to Central Asia in the south.

MODERN RUSSIA
Large Russian cities look similar to cities elsewhere in the world, but the bright lights hide economic problems. Both luxury and essential goods are often in short supply. Lining up for food (above) is a daily occupation, and clothes and consumer goods are scarce and often of poor quality. Most homes are rented from the government, but housing is in limited supply, which means that overcrowding is common.

MOSCOW
The capital city of the Russian Federation is Moscow. It was founded during the 12th century. At the city's heart, on the banks of the Moscow river, lies the Kremlin. This is a walled fortress housing all the government buildings. Within these walls lies the impressive Red Square. The stunning St. Basil's Cathedral stands at the southern end of the square. It was built in the 16th century to celebrate a military victory.

Nevsky Prospect is St Petersburg's busiest shopping street.

RUSSIAN ORTHODOX CHURCH
The chief religion in Russia is the Russian Orthodox Church. Under Communism, all religions were persecuted. In the late 1980s, freedom of worship returned to Russia, and today millions of people worship without fear (above). The Russian Federation also contains many Muslims, Jews, and Buddhists.

ST. PETERSBURG
The second-largest city in the Russian Federation, St. Petersburg has a population of 4.2 million. Before 1917, St. Petersburg (called Leningrad from 1924 to 1991) was the capital of Russia. It still contains many beautiful, historical buildings, such as the Hermitage Art Gallery, once the summer palace of the czars.

AGRICULTURE

Most agriculture in the Russian Federation takes place on the fertile Russian plain that stretches from the western border into Central Asia. Here, farmers produce wheat and other cereals, meat, dairy products, wool, and cotton. The Russian Federation is one of the world's biggest cereal producers, but often fails to grow enough food to feed its own population and has to import grain.

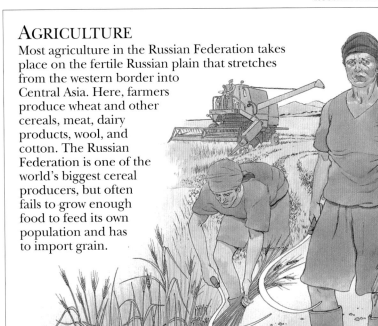

Agriculture in the Russian Federation is mainly confined to the southern and western regions due to the cold climate in the northern margins.

RUBLES AND KOPECKS

The unit of Russian money is the ruble, which is divided into 100 kopecks. Following the break up of the Soviet Union in 1991, Russia moved from a state-planned to a free-market economy. This led to economic instability and fluctuating exchange rates. In recent times the currency has begun to stabilise.

RUSSIAN PEOPLE

Most people in the Russian Federation are Russian in origin. But there are at least 100 minority groups, including Tatars, Ukrainians, Bashkirs, and Chukchis. Some, such as the Yakut hunters, shown here in traditional clothing, are Turkish in origin; other groups are Asiatic. The population is not spread evenly through this vast nation. About 75 per cent live west of the Ural Mountains; less than 25 per cent live in Siberia and the far east of the country.

The Yakut (left) are distributed across a large area centred on the Lena river. The economy of the more southerly Yakut is based on the husbandry of cattle and horses, while the Yakut further north engage in hunting, fishing, and herding.

The Bolshoi Theatre, home of the Bolshoi Ballet

BOLSHOI BALLET

The world-famous Bolshoi Ballet dance company was founded in Moscow in 1773. It became famous touring the world with performances of Russian folk dances and classic ballets such as *Swan Lake*. Other Russian art forms did not enjoy the same freedom of expression under the old Soviet regime. Artists opposed to the Communist government worked in secret. For example, the novels of Aleksandr Solzhenitsyn (born 1918) were banned for many years. His most famous works, such as *The Gulag Archipelago*, were smuggled in from Europe or retyped by readers and circulated secretly.

Ленингра́д

RUSSIAN LANGUAGES

In the Russian Federation more than 112 languages including Tatar, Ukrainian, and Russian are spoken. Russian is the primary language of the majority of people in Russia, and is also used as a second language in other former republics of the Soviet Union. Russian writers use the Cyrillic alphabet, shown here.

TECHNOLOGICAL ACHIEVEMENTS

As part of the Soviet Union, Russian science developed unevenly. Today, the Russian Federation leads the world in some medical techniques, particularly eye surgery (right), but lags far behind Western Europe and the United States in areas such as computers. In the field of space research, the Soviet Union led the world, launching the first satellite in 1957, and putting the first man in space, Yuri Gagarin, in 1961. More recently, the Russians have launched the first paying passengers into space.

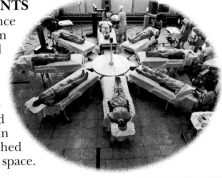

SIBERIA

The vast region of Siberia is in the northeast of the Russian Federation, and stretches from the Ural Mountains in the west to the tip of Alaska in the east. Although Siberia occupies nearly 80 per cent of the land area of the Russian Federation, it is thinly populated. Most Siberian people live close to the route of the Trans-Siberian Railway, which runs for 9,438 km (5,864 miles) between Moscow and Vladivostok. Much of northern Siberia lies inside the Arctic circle, and during the summer months the sun never sets, but simply dips close to the horizon at night.

RIVER VOLGA

Russia contains Europe's longest river, the River Volga. Flowing 3,531 km (2,194 miles) from the Valdai Hills to the Caspian Sea, it is the country's leading waterway, and of great economic importance. Large boats transport oil, wheat, timber, and machinery across the country. Canals link the river to the Baltic and White Seas. The river itself is a rich source of fish, particularly sturgeon. Sturgeon's roe is pickled to make the delicacy caviar.

LAKE BAIKAL

With an area of 31,468 sq km (12,150 sq miles), Lake Baikal is the largest freshwater lake in the world. It is also the world's deepest lake, reaching depths of 1,940 m (6,367 ft). In recent years, logging and chemical industries have polluted the water, prompting a major campaign to protect its fragile environment.

Lake Baikal is known as the "blue eye of Siberia", and contains more than 20 per cent of the world's entire supply of fresh water.

TRANS-SIBERIAN RAILWAY

The Trans-Siberian Railway links European Russia with the Pacific coast across Siberia. It is the world's longest continuous rail line, starting at Moscow and ending 9,297 km (5,777 miles) away in the Pacific port of Vladivostok. Construction of the railway enabled Siberia's mineral wealth to be exploited, and large cities have developed along its route. The journey takes eight days, and crosses eight time zones. Only one passenger train runs each way daily, but freight trains run every five minutes, day and night.

Founded in 1893, where the Trans-Siberian Railway crosses the river Ob', Novosibirsk, 3,183km (1,978 miles) east of Moscow, has developed into an important commercial centre.

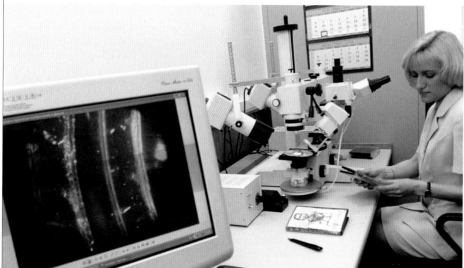

Scientist working in a laboratory to detect pirate CDs.

FEMALE WORKFORCE

Many more Russian men than women died during World War II and in the labour camps set up by the Soviet leader Stalin. As a result, women had to go out to work and many took up physical jobs traditionally done by men. In the Soviet period, good child care enabled women with children to go out to work. Today, more women in Russia hold jobs in science, technology, and engineering than in the rest of Europe, but very few reach the top jobs in these fields.

Find out more

COLD WAR
COMMUNISM
RUSSIAN REVOLUTION
SOVIET UNION, HISTORY OF
WORLD WAR II

| Volcano | Mountain | Ancient monument | Capital city | Large city/town | Small city/town |

STATISTICS

Area: 17,075,400 sq km (6,592,812 sq miles)
Population: 140,041,000
Capital: Moscow
Languages: Russian
Religions: Russian Orthodox
Currency: Ruble
Main occupations: Engineering, research, agriculture
Main exports: Oil, natural gas, electricity, vodka
Main imports: Cars, machinery

SPACE PROGRAMME

Russia's space programme began with the launch of the Sputnik satellite in 1957. In 1965, the Russian cosmonaut Aleksei Leonov became the first person to walk in space. In 1969, the Russians lost the race with the US to land a spacecraft on the Moon. The world's most successful space station (permanent spacecraft in orbit round the Earth) was the Russian craft Mir, which orbited the earth from 1986 to 2001. It was made up of modules that were added to the station at different dates. Astronauts stayed on board for lengthy periods of time, as supplies were delivered by visiting spacecraft.

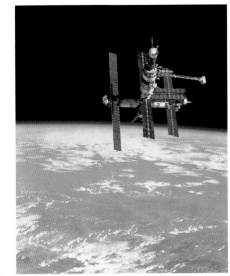

RUSSIAN LACQUERS
Lacquered boxes have been made in the Moscow region for the last four centuries. The papier mâché boxes are decorated with miniature paintings of folk stories, rural scenes, dances, forests, and fairy tales, and are then lacquered.

CAVIAR
Caviar, an expensive delicacy, is made from the tiny black eggs of the *beluga* sturgeon, a type of fish that lives in the Black and Caspian Seas. Tins of caviar are exported worldwide.

LADA

In 1965, the Russians signed a deal with the Italian car company Fiat to manufacture an economy car called the Lada in the Soviet Union. Today, Ladas, which are based on the Fiat, are exported to the West. Relatively few Russians own a car; however, the demand for luxury western cars is growing.

SCALE BAR
0   500   1000   km
0   500   1000   miles

447

RUSSIAN REVOLUTION

IN 1917, THE PEOPLE OF RUSSIA staged a revolution that was to change the course of modern history. The Russian people were desperate for change. Russia was suffering serious losses against Germany in World War I. Food and fuel were scarce. Many people were starving. Czar Nicholas II, ruler of Russia, was blamed for much of this. In March 1917 (February in the old Russian calendar) a general strike broke out in Petrograd (today St. Petersburg). The strike was in protest against the chaos caused by the war. Nicholas was forced to give up his throne, and a group of revolutionaries, called the Mensheviks, formed a provisional government. This government soon fell, because it failed to end the war. In November, the Bolsheviks, a more extreme revolutionary group, seized power. They ended the war with Germany and, led by Vladimir Lenin, set up the world's first Communist state. They declared the country a Soviet republic. This revolution was the first Communist takeover of a government. It inspired more to follow.

1905 REVOLUTION
In 1905 unarmed workers marched on Nicholas II's Winter Palace in St. Petersburg. The czar's troops fired on the crowd. Nicholas set up an elected parliament, or Duma. But the Duma had no real power, so distrust of the czar grew.

OCTOBER REVOLUTION
What is known as the October Revolution broke out on 7 November 1917 (25 October in the old Russian calendar used before the revolution). The cruiser *Aurora* fired blanks across the River Neva at the headquarters of the Menshevik government in the Winter Palace. The Bolsheviks also attacked other important buildings in Petrograd.

LENIN

Vladimir Lenin (1870-1924), founder of the Bolshevik party, believed in the ideas of the German writer Karl Marx. He lived mostly in exile from Russia, until the October Revolution. He was a powerful speaker whose simple slogan of "Peace, land, and bread" persuaded many Russians to support the Bolsheviks. He ruled Russia as dictator.

NICHOLAS II
Russia's last czar, Nicholas (1868-1918), was out of touch with his subjects. They blamed him for the Russian defeats in World War I (1914-18), where he fought at the front. His sinister adviser, a monk named Rasputin, was widely hated and feared. After Nicholas gave up the throne, he and his family were arrested. The Bolsheviks shot them all the following year.

RUSSIAN REVOLUTION

1914 Russia joins World War I against Germany and Austria.

1916 One million Russian soldiers die after German offensive. Prices in Russia rise.

1917 March International Women's Day march in Petrograd turns into bread riot. The Mensheviks set up a provisional government. The Bolsheviks organize another government made up of committees called soviets.

July Lenin flees Russia.

October Lenin returns to Petrograd.

7 November Armed workers seize buildings in Petrograd.

15 November Bolsheviks control Petrograd.

Find out more
COMMUNISM
HUMAN RIGHTS
RUSSIAN FEDERATION
SOVIET UNION, HISTORY OF
WORLD WAR I

SATELLITES

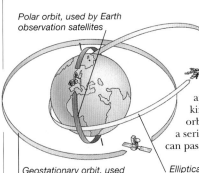

Polar orbit, used by Earth observation satellites

Geostationary orbit, used by communications satellites

Elliptical orbit, used by spy satellites

SATELLITE ORBITS
A communications satellite takes exactly 24 hours to orbit the Earth, so it appears to remain fixed over one spot. This kind of orbit is called geostationary. A polar orbit allows a satellite to see the whole Earth in a series of strips. In an elliptical orbit, a satellite can pass low over a selected part of the Earth.

Solar panels generate electricity from sunlight to power the satellite.

Radar altimeter provides data on wind speed, ocean currents, and tides.

WHEN AIRCRAFT and balloons first took to the skies, the people in them were amazed at their new view of the world. From hundreds of metres up they could see the layout of a large city, the shape of a coastline, or the patchwork of fields on a farm. Today, we have an even wider view. Satellites circle the Earth, not hundreds of metres, but hundreds of kilometres above the ground. From this great height, satellites provide a unique image of our planet. Some have cameras that take photographs of land and sea, giving information about the changing environment on Earth. Others plot weather patterns or peer out into space and send back data (information) about planets and stars. All of these are artificial satellites that have been launched into space from Earth. However, the word satellite actually means any object that moves around a planet while being held in orbit by the planet's gravity. There are countless natural satellites in the universe: the Earth has one, which is the Moon.

Infra-red scanner measures water vapour in the atmosphere and the temperatures of seas and cloud tops.

Earth observation satellite ERS-2

Antenna for transmitting data back to Earth

ARTIFICIAL SATELLITES
There are many types of artificial satellite. Weather satellites observe rain, storms, and clouds, and measure land and sea temperatures. Communications satellites send radio and television signals from one part of the Earth to another. Spy satellites observe military targets from low altitudes and send back detailed pictures to ground stations. Earth observation satellites monitor vegetation, air and water pollution, population changes, and geological factors such as mineral deposits.

MAPPING THE EARTH
Resources satellites take pictures of the Earth's surface. The cameras have various filters so they can pick up infra-red (heat) radiation and different colours of light. Vegetation, for instance, reflects infra-red light strongly, showing up forests and woodlands. Computer-generated colours are used to pick out areas with different kinds of vegetation and minerals.

Satellite map image of San Francisco Bay, California. Clearly visible are two bridges: the Golden Gate Bridge on the left and the Bay Bridge on the right.

SPUTNIK 1
On 4 October 1957, the Soviet Union launched *Sputnik 1*, the world's first artificial satellite. *Sputnik 1* carried a radio transmitter that sent signals back to Earth until it burned up in the atmosphere 92 days later.

NATURAL SATELLITES
There are around 200 known natural satellites, or moons, in the solar system. Most of these orbit (move around) the four giant outer planets: Jupiter, Saturn, Uranus, and Neptune. The largest moons are bigger than Mercury, the smallest planet; the smallest moons are only a few kilometres across and have irregular, potato-like shapes.

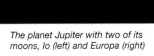

The planet Jupiter with two of its moons, Io (left) and Europa (right)

Find out more
ASTRONOMY
GEOLOGY
NAVIGATION
SPACE FLIGHT
TELEPHONES
TELEVISION

SCANDINAVIA

AT THE FAR NORTH of Europe are the countries of Scandinavia, which have much in common yet in some ways could not be more different. Their economies are closely linked, but each uses its own currency. They are all independent nations; but in times past, several of them have been bound together in a single union. Each country has its own language, yet strong cultural ties exist between the nations. Landscapes are different, however. Denmark is flat – the biggest hill is only 173 m (567 ft) high – and most of the country is very fertile; but both Norway and Iceland are mountainous with little farmland. Sweden and Finland are dotted with lakes – more than 180,000 in Finland alone. Greenland is almost entirely covered in ice and snow. Politically, the different countries co-operate through the Nordic Council, which aims to strengthen ties between the nations. Denmark, Finland, and Sweden are members of the European Union, a trade alliance of European nations. Most Scandinavians enjoy a high standard of living and an active cultural life. Norway and Sweden award the annual Nobel Prizes for sciences, literature, and peace.

Cross country skiing is a popular sport in many parts of Scandinavia.

Geographically, Scandinavia consists of the Norway and Sweden peninsula. But the name is also used widely to include Denmark and Finland. The Faeroe Islands, Iceland, and Greenland are often associated with Scandinavia.

The frozen north of Scandinavia, called Lapland, is the home of 60,000 Lapps. Many of them live by herding reindeer for their hide and meat.

FINLAND

Although Finland is part of Scandinavia, it is closely tied to the Russian Federation, and the two countries share a long frontier. Until 1917, Finland was a province of the old Russian empire. Today Finnish trade is still conducted with the Russian Federation. Forests cover two-thirds of Finland, and the paper industry dominates the economy. Shipbuilding and tourism are also important. Finland is one of the world's most northern countries, and throughout the winter months only the southern coastline is free of ice.

The Swedish capital of Stockholm is built on numerous islands.

SWEDEN

The biggest of the Scandinavian countries, Sweden is also the wealthiest. Over the years, the Swedes have developed a taxation and social welfare system that has created a good standard of living for everybody. As a result, few people in Sweden are either very rich or very poor. The population is slightly more than 9 million, most of whom live in the south and east of the country; the mountainous north lies within the Arctic Circle and is almost uninhabited.

NORWAY

Shipping, forestry, and fishing were the traditional Norwegian industries. But in 1970, oil was discovered in the Norwegian sector of the North Sea, and the country's fortunes were transformed. Today, almost 4.7 million Norwegians enjoy a high standard of living, low taxes, and almost no unemployment. But Norway has almost no natural resources apart from oil and timber. The wooded country is mountainous and indented with numerous inlets, or fjords, from the North Atlantic Ocean. These fjords make communications difficult between the cities in the south and the more sparsely populated regions in the north.

Deep-sea fishing is a major occupation throughout Scandinavia.

FISHING

The north Atlantic Ocean provides a rich marine harvest for Scandinavian fishermen. High-quality cod and mackerel are caught in the cold, nutrient-rich waters. Fish-farming, especially in the fjords, is on the increase in Norway, the world's largest salmon producer.

NORTH SEA OIL

Discoveries of oil and natural gas beneath the North Sea seafloor began in 1959, when a seaward extension of a major natural-gas field in the northeastern part of the Netherlands was identified. Within two decades, natural-gas production sites were located along a 100-mile band stretching from the Netherlands to eastern England. Farther north, Norway's first offshore oil field went into production in 1971. Today Norway's economy largely depends on its abundant natural resources and the country is Europe's largest oil producer. Norway is self sufficient in natural gas and oil.

North Sea oil, produced on oil rigs such as the one pictured above, is exported globally. Norway is a world leader in the construction of drilling platforms.

FJORDS

During the ice age, glaciers carved steep-sided valleys in the rocks along Norway's coast. As the ice melted, the North Sea flowed in, creating fjords. Glaciers have cut hundreds of fjords into Scandinavia's Atlantic coastline. Fjords are usually deeper in their middle and upper reaches than at the seaward end. The water in these inlets is calmer than in the open sea.

SAUNAS

Finland is home to the sauna which has become a national institution. The Finns have used the steam bath for centuries as a way of cleansing and relaxing the body, and today most houses in Finland have one. A sauna is a small, very warm room which is filled with steam. The steam is produced by throwing water over hot stones periodically. As the water crackles and spits, the air fills with clouds of steam. Cooling off under a cold shower or a plunge in an icy pool (left) follows a session in the sauna, and completes the process. Saunas are traditionally fuelled by wooden logs, however they are increasingly powered by electricity, especially in Finland's cities.

This man is cooling off in an icy pool of water after a session in a sauna.

COPENHAGEN

Copenhagen (right) is the capital of Denmark, and about one quarter of all Danish people live in and around the city. Copenhagen is on the east coast of Zealand, the largest of 482 islands that make up about 30 per cent of Denmark. The low-lying Jutland peninsula to the west makes up the rest of the land area.

FARMING IN SWEDEN

The fertile soil in southern Sweden makes this area the most productive farming area in the country, with pig farming, dairy-farming and crops such as wheat, barley and potatoes. Many Swedish farmers belong to agricultural cooperatives which process and distribute their crops.

The farming regions close to the Gulf of Bothnia are best known for dairy produce.

The tranquil waters of a Norwegian fjord. Fjords often reach great depths. The great weight of the glaciers which formed them eroded the bottom of the valley far below sea-level. The best farming land is found in the lowland areas around fjords.

Find out more

ANTARCTICA
ARCTIC
EUROPE
OIL

GREENLAND
Area: 2,175,600 sq km
(839,780 sq miles)
Population: 58,000

ICELAND
Area: 103,000 sq km
(39,770 sq miles)
Population: 307,000

FAEROE ISLANDS
(DENMARK)
Area: 1,399 sq km
(540 sq miles)
Population: 49,000

DENMARK
Area: 43,069 sq km
(16,629 sq miles)
Population: 5,501,000
Capital: Copenhagen

FINLAND
Area: 338,130 sq km
(130,552 sq miles)
Population: 5,250,000
Capital: Helsinki

NORWAY
Area: 323,900 sq km
(125,060 sq miles)
Population: 4,661,000
Capital: Oslo

SWEDEN
Area: 449,960 sq km
(173,730 sq miles)
Population: 9,060,000
Capital: Stockholm

Volcano   Mountain   Ancient monument   Capital city   Large city/town   Small city/town

452

SCIENCE

THERE ARE MANY FORMS OF SCIENCE, and together they study the nature and behaviour of the universe and everything in it. Science comes from the Latin word for "to know". Scientists find out what they want to know by practical methods. They observe, take measurements, make experiments, and write down the results. There are four main categories (types) of science: natural sciences, physical sciences, technological sciences, and social sciences. Natural sciences include the life sciences, such as biology and botany, and earth sciences, such as geology. Physical sciences include physics and chemistry. Technological science includes engineering, and uses information discovered by scientists to make or build things in the real world. Social sciences study people, and include anthropology and psychology. All the sciences depend on mathematics.

A glass rod in a beaker of water looks bent because light waves travel slower through water than through air.

PHYSICS

Physics is the study of matter and energy, and how they work together. Because there are many different kinds of matter and forms of energy, there are many different branches of physics. Optics, for example, looks at the different way light waves can behave. For instance, they travel at different speeds through space, air, glass, or water.

SCIENTIFIC METHOD

Scientific method involves using observation and hypotheses (theories) to explain things, and then testing these hypotheses with experiments. To be sure that their results are accurate, scientists always follow strict rules when making an experiment. In an experiment only the conditions under test must change, everything else must be kept the same. In this way, differences in results should only be caused by the experimenter's deliberate changes.

A simple experiment to find out how much salt can be dissolved in water

A measured amount of salt is mixed in to a measured amount of water.

More salt is added to the water until the salt no longer dissolves, but sinks to the bottom of the jar. This is called the saturation point.

EARTH SCIENCES
Geography and geology are earth sciences. Earth scientists study the structure of our planet and the way it changes. The study of rocks and fossils can tell us a lot about the way the planet and its life have evolved. Since Earth is a living planet, the earth sciences are linked to the life sciences.

Geologists study rocks and crystals.

Chrysocolla

Cyanotrichite

Shoot grows up towards the sun.

Bean shoot

LIFE SCIENCES
Any of the sciences that study living things is called a life science. Biology is the study of life of all kinds, botany is the study of plants, and zoology is the study of animals. Because animal and plant life depend on each other, scientists also study them together. Ecology is the study of the relationships between living things of all kinds and how they fit in with and affect their environments.

SOCIAL SCIENCES
The sciences that study people are called social sciences. There are various kinds. Anthropology is the study of life and culture of the whole of humanity. Sociology studies the way humans behave together in groups; it looks at how families work, how society is made up, what makes it change, and how the changes affect people. Psychology is also a social science, but it looks at how people behave as individuals.

Roots absorb water and nutrients.

Find out more
BIOLOGY
CHEMISTRY
EARTH
PHYSICS
ROCKS AND MINERALS

HISTORY OF
SCIENCE

SPACE TRAVEL, computers, and reliable medical care are just a few of the things that owe their existence to scientists and inventors. Scientists study the natural world, from distant galaxies to tiny atoms, and try to explain what they see. The work of a scientist is based on a cycle of experiment, observation, and theorization (making theories). For instance, in the 17th century, English scientist Isaac Newton experimented with sunlight passing through a prism. From the spectrum (bands of colours) that he observed, he suggested the theory that white light is a mixture of colours. Inventors are people who think of a new idea that can be put into practice. An invention may be the result of a scientific discovery, such as the laser, which Theodore Maiman (born 1927) built because of his knowledge of light and atoms. However, this is not always the case. Early people invented the lever before they knew how it worked. Whatever their chosen fields, scientists and inventors have one thing in common: they are people of rare insight who make discoveries new to the world.

ANCIENT TIMES

Early people first invented tools about 2 million years ago. About 10,000 years ago, people began to settle in communities and started farming and building. The first civilizations grew up in the Middle East, Africa, India, and China. There, people studied the Sun and stars, built simple clocks, developed mathematics, and discovered how to make metals and pottery.

This stone blade was used about 200,000 years ago in Egypt.

The wheel was invented in about 3500 BCE.

The plough was invented in about 4000 BCE.

The pump was invented in the 2nd century BCE.

Hero of Greece built the first simple steam engine in the 1st century CE.

GREEKS AND ROMANS

From about 600 BCE, the Greeks began to study their world. Great philosophers (thinkers) such as Pythagoras developed the "scientific method" – the principle of observation and experiment that is still the basis of science today. The Greeks studied mathematics and astronomy and invented simple machines. At around the same time, the Romans used Greek scientific ideas to help them build great structures.

ARCHIMEDES
Greek scientist Archimedes (287-212 BCE) explained how levers and pulleys work and discovered how things float. This idea is said to have come to him while he was in his bath.

A balloon first carried people in 1783.

Archimedes's screw was a device for raising water.

In 1608, Dutch optician Hans Lippershey invented the telescope.

ISAAC NEWTON
In 1687, Isaac Newton (1642-1727) published the daring idea that gravity is a universal force, keeping planets and moons in their orbits as well as causing things to fall to the ground. Newton also put forward the famous laws of motion, and found that white light is composed of the colours in the rainbow.

LEONARDO DA VINCI
The great Italian artist and inventor Leonardo da Vinci (1452-1519) designed many machines, including a parachute and a helicopter. However, these machines were never built.

1000-1600 CE

During this period, Arabic civilizations made several discoveries, particularly about the nature of light. After about 1000 CE, people in Europe began to use the scientific method of the Ancient Greeks. Polish astronomer Nicolaus Copernicus (1473-1543) suggested that the Earth orbits the Sun, and Andreas Vesalius (1514-64), a Flemish doctor, made discoveries about human anatomy.

In 1438, Johannes Gutenberg of Germany (c.1398-1468) invented the modern printing process.

1600-1800

Italian scientist Galileo Galilei (1564-1642) made discoveries about force, gravity, and motion. Modern astronomy began in 1609 when German astronomer Johannes Kepler (1571-1630) discovered the laws of planetary motion and Galileo built a telescope to observe the heavens. During the 1700s, the first engines were built by inventors such as James Watt (1736-1819) of Scotland. Chemistry advanced as scientists discovered how everything is composed of chemical elements such as oxygen and hydrogen.

1800-1900

The invention of the battery by Italian Alessandro Volta (1745-1827) led to discoveries about electricity and magnetism by scientists such as Englishman Michael Faraday (1791-1867) and many electrical inventions such as electric light. Englishman John Dalton (1766-1844) and other scientists found out that everything is made of tiny atoms. Frenchman Louis Pasteur (1822-1895) showed that bacteria cause disease, which led to better health care. Transport advanced with the invention of locomotives, powered ships, and cars.

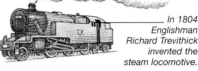

The telephone was invented by a Scottish-American, Alexander Graham Bell, in 1876.

In 1804 Englishman Richard Trevithick invented the steam locomotive.

THOMAS EDISON

Thomas Edison (1847-1931) was one of the world's most successful inventors. He made more than 1,000 inventions, including the record player (patented 1878) and a system for making motion pictures. Edison was also one of the inventors of the electric light bulb.

In 1895 Italian scientist Guglielmo Marconi invented radio transmission.

1900 TO THE PRESENT

Scientists delved into the atom, finding electrons and the nucleus, and then studied the nucleus itself. This led to the invention of nuclear power and to the science of electronics, which brought us television and the computer. Scientists also explored living cells and found new ways of fighting disease. Astronomers studied stars, planets, and distant galaxies. The invention of aircraft and space flight allowed people to travel into the air and out into space.

WRIGHT BROTHERS

In 1903, the world watched in wonder as Orville Wright (1871-1948) and his brother Wilbur (1867-1912) made the first powered aeroplane flight.

Several scientists developed television during the 1920s. The first public television service started in the 1930s.

WILLIAM SHOCKLEY

Computers, televisions, and other electronic devices depend on the transistor, invented in 1948 by a team of scientists headed by William Shockley (born 1910). Now millions of transistors can be packed into a tiny microchip.

Theodore Maiman and Charles Townes invented the first working laser in 1960.

Artificial satellites were first launched in 1957.

In 1946 a team of American scientists built the first fully electronic computer.

ALBERT EINSTEIN

In 1905 and 1915, the German scientist Albert Einstein (1879-1955) proposed his theories of relativity. They showed that light is the fastest thing in the universe, and that time would slow down, length would shorten, and mass would increase if you could travel at almost the speed of light. The Sun's source of energy and nuclear power, and how black holes can exist in space are explained by his discoveries.

MAX PLANCK

In about 1900, German scientist Max Planck (1858-1947) published his quantum theory, which explained the nature of energy and led to many new ideas. For example, although we usually think of light as waves, quantum theory explains how light sometimes seems to behave as tiny particles called photons.

HISTORY OF SCIENCE

5000 BCE Metal objects first made in Middle East.

400 BCE Greek scientist Democritus suggests that all things are made of atoms.

105 CE Chinese inventor Ts'ai Lun makes paper.

650 CE Persians invent the windmill.

1000 CE Chinese use gunpowder in warfare.

1657 Dutchman Christiaan Huygens constructs pendulum clock.

1712 English engineer Thomas Newcomen builds first practical steam engine.

1775 Englishman Joseph Priestley discovers oxygen.

1789 French scientist Antoine Lavoisier explains chemical reactions.

1803 English scientist John Dalton explains existence of atoms.

1826 Frenchman Joseph Niépce takes first photograph.

1879 Thomas Edison (US) and Englishman Joseph Swan invent electric light bulb.

1885 German engineer Karl Benz builds first car.

1888 German scientist Heinrich Hertz discovers radio waves.

1898 French-Polish scientist Marie Curie discovers radium.

1911 English scientist Ernest Rutherford discovers nucleus of the atom.

1924 US astronomer Edwin Hubble discovers galaxies and, in 1929, the expansion of the universe.

1942 Italian scientist Enrico Fermi builds first nuclear reactor.

1959 Soviet Union launches first space probe.

1969 ARPANET (first version of the Internet) goes live.

1993 The World Wide Web developed.

Find out more

BIOLOGY
CHEMISTRY
MEDICINE, HISTORY OF
PHYSICS
RENAISSANCE
SCIENCE
TECHNOLOGY

SCOTLAND

ST. ANDREW'S CROSS
The cross of St. Andrew, patron saint of Scotland, is called the saltire.

FROM EDINBURGH TO THE HIGHLANDS, the Scottish people are proud of their unique culture. Scotland is part of the United Kingdom, but has kept some of its independence. Scottish banks print their own pound notes, the legal system is different to that of England and Wales, Scottish university courses last four years, not three as in England, and Scottish students sit Higher Still examinations, not A-levels. Since 1999, Scotland has also regained its parliament. Because it is so far north, Scotland has short days in winter, but long hours of daylight in summer. The old industries have declined, but new jobs have been created in service industries and through North Sea oil.

Scotland and its islands are the most northerly parts of the United Kingdom.

HIGHLANDS
The north of Scotland contains the Highlands, a rugged but beautiful mountainous region that includes Ben Nevis, the highest mountain in Britain, and spectacular lochs (lakes). Scotland covers an area of 78,742 sq km (30,394 sq miles). Of its population of about 5.1 million people, most live further south in the so-called Lowlands, near the cities of Glasgow and Edinburgh.

EDINBURGH
The capital of Scotland is the city of Edinburgh. The kings of Scotland used to rule the country from Edinburgh, and the newly created Scottish parliament has its home there. The volcanic crag at the centre is topped by Edinburgh Castle, and dominates the city's skyline. Every year, Edinburgh hosts an internationally renowned arts festival.

Sporran

HIGHLAND GAMES
The champions of Scotland's traditional sports compete at the annual Highland Games. The Games have a long history, and include events such as putting the shot and throwing the hammer. It also includes a unique event – tossing the caber. For this, athletes compete with each other to pick up and toss (throw) the caber – a large tree trunk – as far as possible.

KILTS AND SPORRANS
Tartan and kilts are unique to Scottish culture. A kilt is like a skirt and is made from tartan, a checked woollen material. Traditionally, the kilt is worn with the sporran, special shoes, and sometimes a dagger tucked into a sock. There are many different tartans. Each belongs to a special clan, or tribe.

WHISKY
Scotland is famous for its whisky. Many different distilleries across the country produce hundreds of malt whiskies varying in taste and colour. Traditional Scottish dishes include porridge, and haggis, made from spiced sheep's innards mixed with oats.

Find out more
STUARTS
UNITED KINGDOM
UNITED KINGDOM, HISTORY OF

SEASHORE WILDLIFE

SEASIDE DANGERS
Most of these baby turtles, hatching from eggs buried by their mother in the sand, will die. They are food for gulls, crabs, lizards and other hunters. Humans also steal the eggs. Conservation efforts are now being made to protect turtles.

Gulls hover over the sea looking for fish, while waders hunt around the shore.

A SEASHORE is formed wherever the land meets the sea, and can be a polar ice cliff or a tropical beach. The endless motion of the waves, and the tide going in and out, means the shore changes constantly with time. Each seashore has its own selection of plant and animal life that is specially adapted to an environment governed by the rhythm of the tides. Inhabitants of the seashore must survive pounding waves, salty sea water, fresh rainwater, drying winds, and hot sunshine. Plants thrive along rocky coasts and in some muddy areas, providing food and shelter for creatures, but they cannot grow on shifting sand or pebbles. Here the inhabitants depend on the tide to bring new supplies of food, in the form of particles floating in the water. Successful seashore animal groups include molluscs and crustaceans, both of which are protected by hard casings.

Seagull

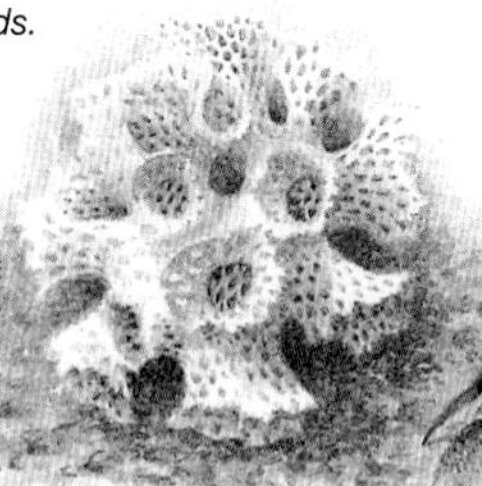

Lace coral can survive harsh rubbing by the wave-washed sand grains. It provides a refuge for animals in its lacy folds.

Many sea birds patrol the coast, searching for food or scavenging on the dead bodies of cast-up sea creatures.

Common starfish

SANDY BEACHES
Waves roll and tumble the tiny grains of sand on the beach. Plants cannot get a firm hold on this type of shore, so they usually grow higher up. Although the sandy beach often looks deserted, dozens of creatures are just below the surface. Sand makes an ideal hiding place for burrowing creatures. Many filter food from the sea water when the tide is in or digest tiny edible particles in the sand.

WADING BIRDS
Waders probe into sand or mud with their long, narrow bills to find shellfish and worms. Large species with the longest bills, such as the curlew (above), reach down several centimetres for deeply buried items. Smaller waders, such as the black-bellied dunlin, take food from just below the surface.

GHOST CRAB
There are hundreds of kinds of shore crabs along the world's coastlines. They are the seashore's "cleaners"; they can consume almost anything edible – living or dead. The ghost crab (above right) takes its name from its ghostly pale colour.

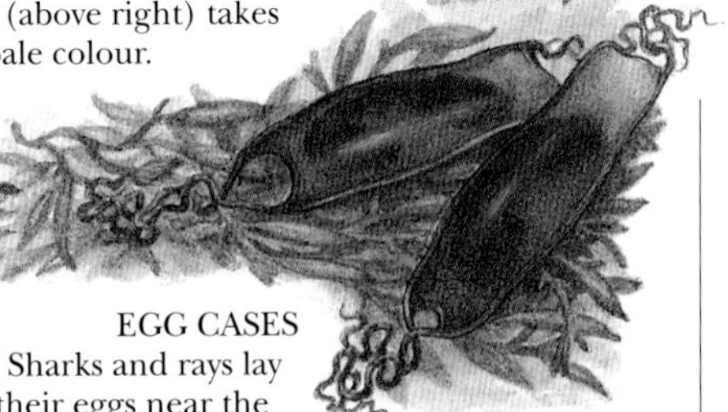

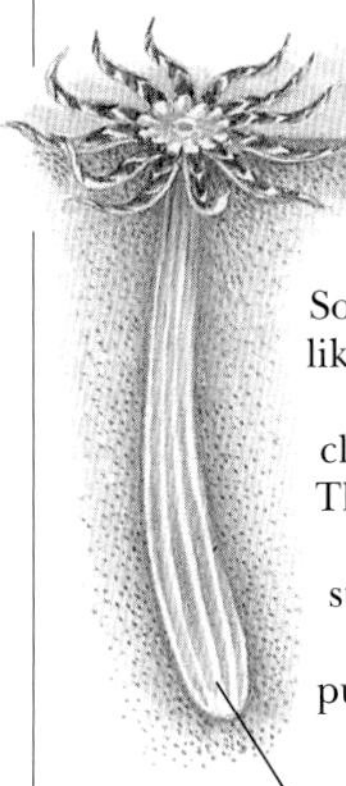

RAZOR CLAM
So called because it looks like an old-fashioned cut-throat razor, the razor clam has a hinged shell. The mollusc inside digs quickly by pushing its strong, fleshy foot into the sand and then pulling the shell down.

The burrowing sea anemone's arms spread out to sting and catch small prey. Its stalk, up to 30 cm (12 in) long, is used to hold on to the sand.

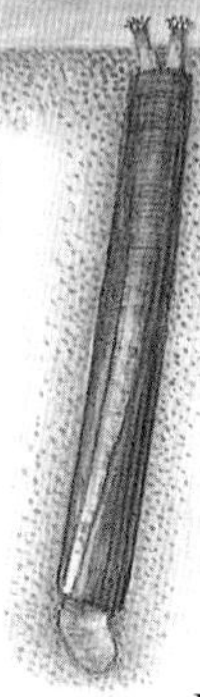

SAND HOPPER
Sand hoppers are crustaceans which feed on rotting vegetation. They swarm over seaweed which has washed up on shore and, when in danger, leap away on their strong back legs, hence their name.

EGG CASES
Sharks and rays lay their eggs near the shore, anchored to seaweeds or rocks by clinging tendrils. When the young fishes hatch, the egg cases, known as "mermaid's purses", come free and are often washed up on the shore.

WEEVER FISH
The weever lies half buried in the sand, waiting to gobble up small fishes, crabs, and shrimps. It has poisonous spines on its fins, which give a nasty sting if the fish is stepped on.

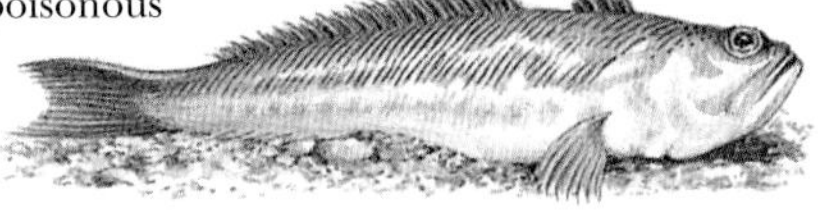

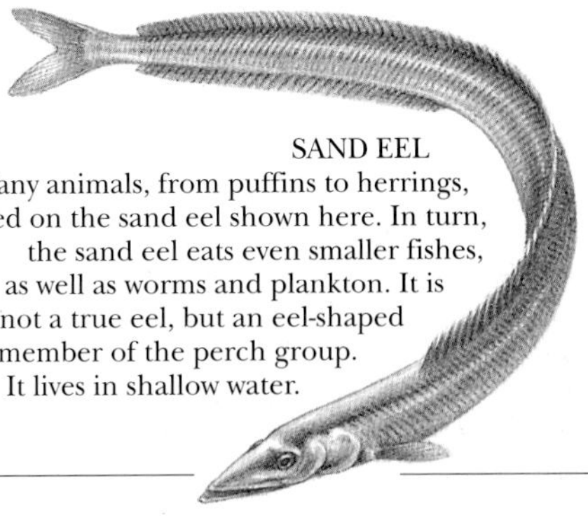

SAND EEL
Many animals, from puffins to herrings, feed on the sand eel shown here. In turn, the sand eel eats even smaller fishes, as well as worms and plankton. It is not a true eel, but an eel-shaped member of the perch group. It lives in shallow water.

SALT MARSHES

Salt marshes form at the back of the shore, where the tide floods flat areas of land near a river's mouth. Plants such as cordgrass, glasswort, eelgrass, sea club rush, and sea starwort are able to survive in the salt that builds up in the soil. Birds such as geese, gulls, and terns can feed on salt marshes all year round, especially in winter, when inland areas are frozen hard. Some birds use salt marshes as summer breeding grounds, some as stop-overs while migrating.

Some large seaweeds are called kelps, such as sugar kelp and oarweed.

CLIFFS

Only a few very agile land animals, such as snakes, can reach precarious cliff ledges. So the ledges are safe nesting sites for a variety of birds, from gannets to gulls, razorbills, and cormorants. A few plants, like thrift ("sea pink"), also gain a foothold, provided they can withstand strong winds and salty spray.

SEAWEED

There are three main kinds of rocky-shore seaweeds, also known as algae: brown, red, and green. They do not have roots, stems, or leaves. Instead, most anchor themselves to the rocks by structures called holdfasts. The larger brown and red weeds have stem-like stipes, ending in leaflike blades known as laminae or fronds.

Periwinkles seal themselves to the rock with mucus as the tide retreats, to keep them from losing water and drying out.

ROCKY SHORES

Rocks provide a firm surface for seaweeds, and many creatures shelter among the fronds. But the weeds still face problems. Waves smash them against the hard stony surface, and they are regularly submerged by salt water, then left high and dry at low tide. Shellfish cling to the rocks, and a variety of fishes and crabs adapt themselves to the ever-changing conditions, hiding from predators in holes and crevices.

WHELKS

These rocky-shore scavengers hunt for dead or dying animals. They are relatives of land snails and find prey by "smelling" the water, which they draw in through a periscope-like siphon.

CHITON

Chitons are also called "coat of mail shells" because they look like chainmail armour. Each chiton has an eight-part shell set into its broad, fleshy body. It can grip a rock very firmly. These molluscs feed on small algae from the rock surface.

ANEMONES

These jellyfish relatives use their tentacles to sting small fishes, shrimps, and other creatures, and draw them into the body cavity through the mouth. When the tide goes out, the tentacles fold inwards for protection.

Barnacle

MANTIS SHRIMP

The mantis shrimp, a crustacean, hides in a hole waiting for prey. When a fish or other victim approaches, the shrimp stuns it by a lightning blow from its club-shaped second "leg".

Branching holdfast provides shelter for small animals

Red seaweed

SEA STAR

The biscuit sea star feeds on shellfish, sea squirts, corals, sponges, and other animals. It glides along on dozens of tiny, sucker-tipped hydraulic tube feet located on its underside.

WILLIAM SHAKESPEARE

THE GREATEST PLAYWRIGHT of all time was probably the Englishman William Shakespeare. He was born in Stratford-upon-Avon, where he went to school, and later married. When he was in his 20s, he went to London to work as an actor, and a playwright. His plays were very successful, and 37 of them survive. Some, such as *Hamlet,* are tragedies, that end with the death of the hero or heroine. Others, such as *Twelfth Night,* are comedies, full of amusing characters who get into terrible difficulties that are eventually sorted out. Shakespeare also wrote histories that are based on real-life situations, such as *Henry IV.* Most of Shakespeare's plays are written in an unrhymed verse form called blank verse. They are famous worldwide for their use of language, fascinating characters, and wide appeal.

1564 Born, Stratford-upon-Avon, England.

1582 Marries Anne Hathaway.

1592 Writes his first plays in London.

1594-99 Produces early comedies, and many history plays.

1599 Globe Theatre constructed.

1600-08 Writes many of his greatest tragedies.

1616 Dies in Stratford-upon-Avon.

THE GRAMMAR SCHOOL
With its rows of wooden desks, the old grammar school still stands in Stratford. Shakespeare was probably educated here.

Henry Wriothesley

POETRY
Shakespeare was a fine poet, and wrote a series of 14-line love poems called sonnets. They are addressed to two different people, "a dark lady" and Mr. W.H. Some scholars believe that Mr. W.H. may have been Henry Wriothesley, the Third Earl of Southampton, who was Shakespeare's patron.

Male actors played female roles.

The audience stood around the stage.

KING'S MEN
In the 1590s, Shakespeare joined a troupe of actors called the Lord Chamberlain's Men, and became their resident writer. When James I came to the throne in 1603, they gained his support and became known as the King's Men. They had their own theatre, the Globe, near the River Thames in London.

WAS IT BACON?
In the 19th century, some people thought that the learned writer Francis Bacon (1561-1626) had written Shakespeare's plays, because Shakespeare had not gone to university. But there is no real evidence that proves this.

English actress, Maggie Smith, in a performance of A Midsummer Night's Dream.

A MIDSUMMER NIGHT'S DREAM
One of Shakespeare's most popular plays, *A Midsummer Night's Dream,* is a comedy. The play has a huge cast of characters, including two young couples who fall in and out of love, a group of workmen, and the king and queen of the fairies, who create hilarious confusion with their magic.

Find out more
ELIZABETH I
LITERATURE
THEATRE
TUDORS

SHARKS AND RAYS

A PERFECT SHAPE FOR SPEED, an incredible sense of smell, and a mouth brimming with razor-sharp teeth make sharks the most fearsome fish in the sea. Sharks have existed for 350 million years, and their basic shape has hardly changed at all during this time. As adults, they have no predators and fear nothing in the ocean. The great white shark is the largest predatory fish, at more than 9 m (27 ft) in length and 2.7 tonnes (2.7 tons) in weight. Dozens of huge teeth line its jaws. The great white shark prowls the ocean, eating any kind of meat, alive or dead, and often swallows its prey in one gulp. Sharks have to keep moving in order to take in enough oxygen, and the great white travels more than 500 km (300 miles) in a day. Most fish have bony skeletons, but sharks and their relatives, the rays, have skeletons made of a substance called cartilage.

Rays are flat-bodied, with a wide mouth on the underside and blunt teeth for crushing clams and other shellfish. Rays live close to the seabed and move gracefully by flapping their huge wings.

Good sense of smell for hunting

Long tail used for rounding up fish in the water

The thresher shark lashes the water with its tail to sweep fish into a group. Then, with its mouth open, the shark charges through, gobbling them up.

Excellent eyesight for spying prey

THRESHER SHARK
This shark measures 6 m (20 ft) in length. It lives mainly in the warm coastal waters of the Atlantic and Pacific oceans but sometimes strays north in summer.

FIN
A shark's dorsal (back) fin cuts the sea's surface as the shark circles before attacking. The dolphin's fin is more crescent-shaped.

Stingrays have a poison spine on the tail.

STINGRAY
There are about 100 kinds of stingrays – the biggest measures 4 m (12 ft) across.

Huge wings

Shark tooth

TEETH
Sharks have many rows of teeth. As they grow, the teeth move from inside the mouth to the outside edge, where they are used for tearing flesh. Eventually the teeth wear away or break off, only to be replaced by the teeth behind.

Sharks' teeth have a serrated edge so they can saw through flesh.

SKIN
Shark skin is covered with toothlike scales, and has a texture like sandpaper.

Dorsal fin

Dorsal fin

Nostrils are excellent at detecting the smell of blood in the water.

WHALE SHARK
The harmless whale shark cruises slowly through the tropical oceans, feeding by filtering tiny floating animals (plankton) from the water. It is a peaceful creature and is the biggest fish of any kind, at 15 m (50 ft) long.

Upper lobe of caudal fin (tail)

Pectoral fin

SWIMMING MACHINE
The shark's swimming power comes from its tail. The larger upper lobe drives it down with each stroke and helps keep the body level; otherwise the creature's weight would tilt its head down. A shark cannot swivel its fins to stop quickly. It must veer to one side instead.

A human can swim safely with the gentle whale shark, the biggest fish in the sea.

HAMMERHEAD
The eyes and nostrils of the hammerhead shark are on the two "lobes" of its head. Hammerheads prey on stingrays, unharmed by the poison in their spines.

Find out more
ANIMALS
ANIMAL SENSES
FISH
OCEAN WILDLIFE

SHELLS AND SHELLFISH

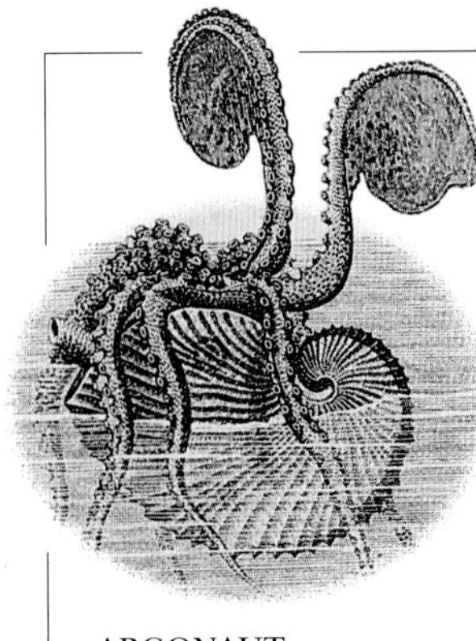

ALL THE WONDERFUL SHELLS you find on the seashore were once the homes of soft-bodied sea creatures. These creatures are commonly known as shellfish, although they are not fish at all, but molluscs, like slugs and snails. There are thousands of different kinds of shellfish living in the sea, including mussels, oysters, and clams. Many, such as the winkle, have small, delicate shells; others, such as the queen conch, have big, heavy shells. The shell itself is like a house, built by the shellfish. As it feeds, the shellfish extracts calcium carbonate from the water. This mineral is used by the shellfish to build up layers of shell, little by little. As the creature grows bigger, its shell grows bigger too. Some shellfish live in a single, coiled shell; others, known as bivalves, have a hinged shell with two sides that open and close for feeding.

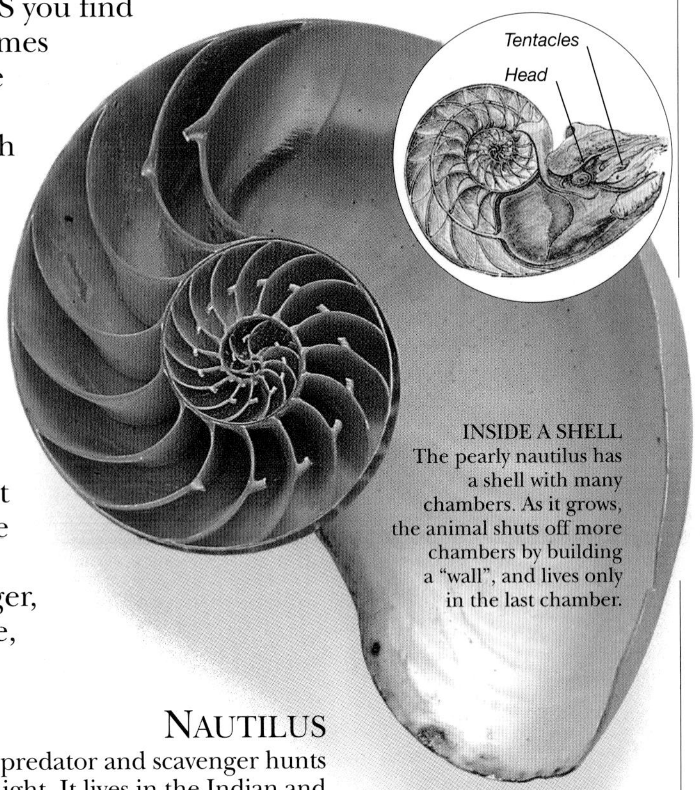

ARGONAUT
The paper nautilus is a type of octopus which makes a thin shell to keep its eggs in. It is also known as the argonaut, after the sailors of Greek legend, because people believed they used its papery shell as a boat.

Tentacles
Head

INSIDE A SHELL
The pearly nautilus has a shell with many chambers. As it grows, the animal shuts off more chambers by building a "wall", and lives only in the last chamber.

NAUTILUS
This predator and scavenger hunts at night. It lives in the Indian and Pacific oceans, and has more than 30 tentacles for catching prey.

HOW SHELLS GROW
Shellfish hatch as larvae from eggs, then develop shells. Creatures with single coiled shells, such as this triton, grow by adding layers of shell-building material (calcium carbonate) to the open end. Hinged-shell creatures, such as cockles, add calcium carbonate to the rounded edges, in the form of coils called growth rings.

Growth rings on adult triton shell

Larva has a smooth shell.

Eggs

Young shells are tiny and have few coils.

Growth rings are slowly added to the open end.

HINGED SHELLS
The two sides of a hinged shell (bivalve) are held together by a tough ligament. Powerful muscles keep the valves closed for protection. The valves open slightly to allow the creature to breathe and feed.

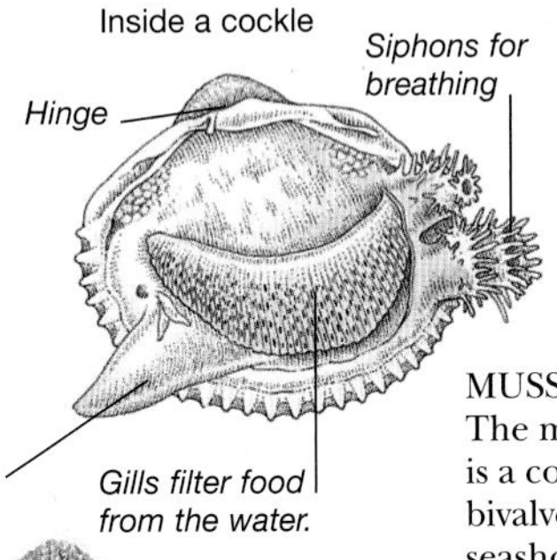

Inside a cockle

Siphons for breathing

Hinge

Foot

Gills filter food from the water.

COCKLE SHELL
The ridged cockle buries itself in sand and feeds when the tide comes in.

MUSSEL
The mussel is a common bivalve on many seashores.

SCALLOP
The scallop is able to swim by "flapping" its two valves. By snapping the two sides shut, it can shoot through the water to escape from a predator.

Inside a scallop

HOW A PEARL IS MADE
If a piece of grit gets lodged in an oyster's shell, the oyster covers it with mother-of-pearl (nacre), a substance lining its shell.

Tiny piece of grit irritates oyster.

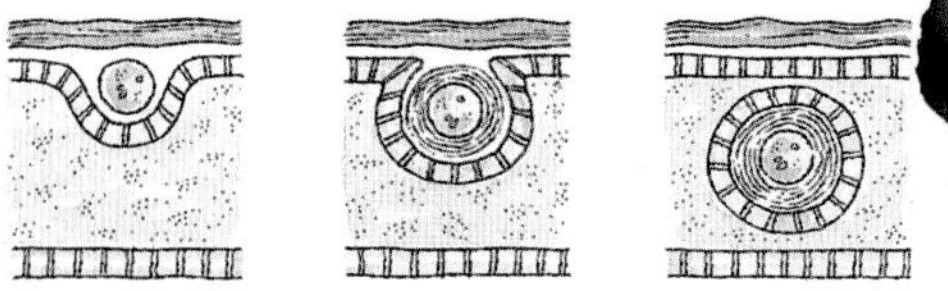

Mother-of-pearl (nacre) forms over grit.

Pearl comes free, removing the irritation.

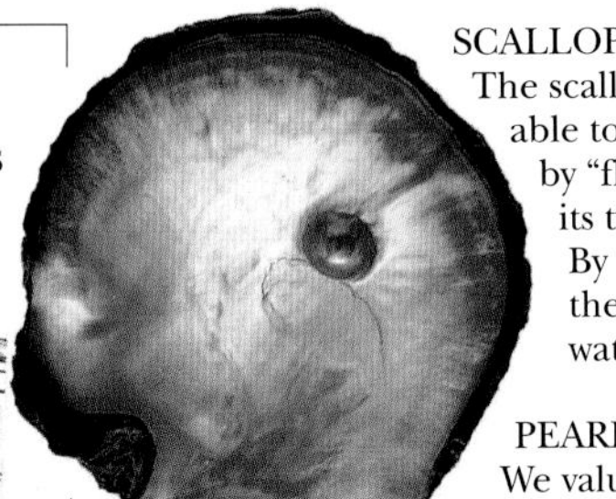

PEARL
We value oyster pearls highly because of their white, shiny appearance, but other kinds of shellfish make pearls too. The Caribbean conch makes pink pearls, and some shellfish make orange ones. The pearl shown here is a "blister pearl" on a black-lipped oyster shell.

Find out more
ANIMALS
ANIMAL SENSES
ECOLOGY AND FOOD WEBS
OCEAN WILDLIFE
SEASHORE WILDLIFE

SHIPS AND BOATS

EVER SINCE OUR EARLIEST ancestors discovered that wood floats on water, ships and boats have played a major part in human history. The first boats helped people cross streams and rivers and carried hunters into shallow waters so they could go fishing. Better ways of building ships and boats began to develop when people left their homes to explore new territories. Since more than two thirds of the Earth is covered by water, these early explorers had to go out to sea to discover new lands, and they needed vessels that could make long voyages. Ships and boats changed and improved over thousands of years as distant nations began to trade and opposing navies fought battles at sea. Today, there are thousands of different types of ships and boats. Ships are seagoing vessels; boats are generally smaller and travel on coastal or inland waters.

Traditional craft such as this Chinese junk are still used in some parts of the world.

SHIPBUILDING
Modern ships are built of steel plates welded together. Ship builders make all the parts separately and finally assemble the ship in the shipyard. After months of sea trials to check its safety, the ship is ready for service.

The captain commands the ship from the bridge, which houses the steering wheel and navigation instruments such as compasses, radar equipment, and charts.

A crane (called a derrick), driven by steam or electricity, is used to load and unload cargo.

Weight of ship pushing downwards

Upthrust from water pushing upwards

HOW SHIPS FLOAT
Although metal is very heavy, a ship contains large spaces filled with air. The hull (main body) of a ship pushes water out of the way, and the water pushes back on the ship with a force called upthrust. The upthrust balances the weight of the ship and keeps it afloat.

Propeller

Rudder

RUDDER AND PROPELLER
A rotating propeller forces the ship through the water, and the rudder steers the ship. When the rudder twists, the weight of water thrusting against it turns the ship.

A powerful diesel engine drives one or more propellers at the stern (back) of the ship.

Cabins for crew to sleep in when not on duty

Main body of the ship is called the hull.

The front end of a ship is called the bow.

CARGO SHIP
Every year, cargo ships carry millions of tonnes of goods across the world's oceans. Some cargo ships, called container ships, carry huge loads piled up in large, steel boxes that stack together like building blocks. The largest ships of this kind carry more than 10,000 such containers.

KINDS OF SHIPS
There are many kinds of ships. They range from passenger vessels to cargo ships that carry goods of all types to and from the world's ports.

Cargo is stored in a large compartment below the deck, called a hold. Large modern cargo vessels may have 12 or more holds. Ships that carry fresh food have refrigerated holds.

FERRY
Ferries take people and goods across a stretch of water. Large ferries carry cars, trucks, and trains as well as people.

OIL TANKER
Oil is transported at sea in huge tankers. The engines and bridge are at the stern to give more storage space.

CRUISE LINER
Liners are large ships that carry passengers on scheduled routes. Most liners are like floating hotels and take tourists on lengthy cruises.

TRAWLER
Trawlers are engine-powered fishing boats that drag a net (the trawl) along the sea bed in order to catch fish that swim near the bottom of the sea.

HISTORY OF SHIPS AND BOATS

The development of ships began more than 6,000 years ago with rafts and reed boats, and continues today with the introduction of nuclear-powered ships and boats made of light, strong plastics.

HIDE BOAT

About 6,000 years ago the Ancient Egyptians used boats made of a wicker framework covered with animal skins. In about 3200 BCE the Egyptians invented sails.

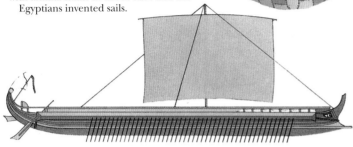

TRIREME

The Greeks invented the trireme (above) in about 650 BCE. It had sails and lines of rowers to carry it along at speed. The Romans built similar ships for trade and war.

Groups of rowers were positioned on two levels.

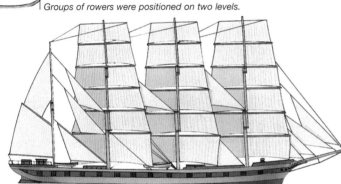

CLIPPER

Fast sailing ships called clippers (above) appeared during the 19th century, the height of the age of sailing. They carried many sails and had sleek lines to increase speed. Clippers were used mainly for trade.

STEAMSHIPS

Oceangoing steamships (below) took to the seas early in the 19th century. The earliest vessels had paddles connected to the engine and sails to gain extra speed in high winds. Ships with propellers entered service during the 1840s.

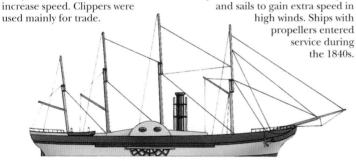

KINDS OF BOATS

Different boats have different uses. Many boats, such as yachts, are pleasure craft; tugs and fishing boats, however, are the workhorses of coastal waters.

POWERBOAT

Powerboats are small, fast boats driven by powerful petrol or diesel engines. They are used either for pleasure or for racing.

TUGBOAT

Tugs tow larger vessels, guiding them through difficult or shallow waters at sea or on inland waterways such as canals.

YACHT

Yachts are pleasure boats. They have engines or sails. Racing yachts are built purely for speed and are made of strong, light materials.

HYDROFOIL

A boat's engine has to work hard to overcome the resistance of the water. Light, fast boats called hydrofoils avoid this problem because they rise up on skis at high speeds. With the hydrofoil travelling so rapidly, water behaves as if it were a solid, so the hydrofoil skims over the water surface just like an aeroplane wing in air.

Any force can be divided into two parts at right angles to each other. The part along the length of the boat drives the boat forwards.

Air rushing past the sail produces a force that tends to move the boat at right angles to the wind.

Wind rushing past sail

Wind pushing on sail

HOW A BOAT SAILS

Modern sailing boats do not need the wind behind them to move – they can travel in almost any direction. In the same way that air rushing over the wings of an aeroplane produces an upward force called lift, wind moving past a sail produces a force at right angles to the sail. Adjusting the sail makes the boat move in different directions.

Centreboard prevents boat from drifting with the wind and stops the boat from capsizing.

With the wind behind the boat, the sail is stretched out across the boat.

Direction of wind

Direction of movement

A sailing boat cannot travel directly into the wind. Instead, it must follow a zigzag path. This is called tacking.

The boat heads into the wind with the sail drawn in as tightly as possible.

With the wind to the side of the boat, the sail is drawn in more tightly. The boat travels fastest with the wind in this position.

Direction of movement

Find out more

NAVIGATION
OCEANS AND SEAS
PORTS AND WATERWAYS
SUBMARINES
TECHNOLOGY
WIND

SKELETONS

INSIDE THE HUMAN BODY, hundreds of bones link together like scaffolding to form the skeleton. Without a skeleton, the body would collapse. The skeleton holds the body rigid and gives shape to all the softer parts. It also protects the organs – the skull surrounds the brain, and the ribs act as a protective cage around the lungs and heart. The skeleton is also an anchor for the muscles, which move the different parts of the body. Bone is made of living cells surrounded by a framework of minerals, particularly calcium and phosphate, and tough fibres of a substance called collagen. In a newborn baby, many of the bones are made of a soft, rubbery substance called cartilage. As a baby grows, the cartilage is gradually replaced by hard bone. Our wrists and ankles are among the last to become bone. In later life, bones gradually become more fragile and brittle, and break more easily.

INTERNAL SKELETONS

Humans and other mammals, fish, birds, and reptiles all have an inner skeleton, or endoskeleton, made up of many separate bones. The central part of the skeleton is the spine (vertebral column or backbone). The spinal joints can move only a little, but the spine as a whole is very flexible. Some creatures, such as worms, have no bones. Instead the pressure of fluid inside their bodies helps them keep their shape. They are said to have a hydrostatic skeleton.

Lizard has an internal skeleton, like other vertebrates.

JOINTS

Bones are linked together at joints. There are several types of joints, including fixed, hinge, and ball-and-socket joints. Fixed joints, such as those between the separate bones in the skull, cannot move. Hinge joints, such as those in the elbow, allow movement in one direction only. Ball-and-socket joints, such as the hip, allow the bones to swing in two directions and also to twist.

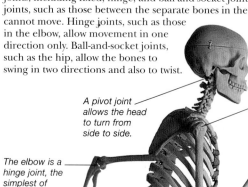

The shoulder and the hip are both ball-and-socket joints and allow the greatest range of movement.

A pivot joint allows the head to turn from side to side.

The elbow is a hinge joint, the simplest of joints, and moves mainly back and forth.

The wrist is formed by an ellipsoidal joint which can be flexed or extended and moved from side to side.

HUMAN SKELETON

There are 206 bones in the human skeleton, including 28 in the skull, 26 in the spine, 30 in each arm, 30 in each leg, and 25 in the chest. The largest bone is in the thigh, and the smallest ones are the ossicles, which are three tiny bones inside each ear.

Skull

Maxilla (upper jaw)

Mandible (lower jaw)

Cervical (neck) vertebrae

Clavicle (collarbone)

Scapula (shoulder blade)

Sternum (breastbone)

12 pairs of ribs

Humerus (upper-arm bone)

Lumbar (lower back) vertebrae

Ulna (forearm bone)

Radius (forearm bone)

Carpals (wrist bones)

Metacarpals (palm bones)

Phalanges (finger bones)

Hip joint

Pelvic (hip) girdle

Femur (thighbone)

Patella (kneecap)

Tibia (shin bone)

Fibula (calf bone)

Tarsals (ankle bones)

Metatarsals (foot bones)

Phalanges (toe bones)

Soft, spongy bone inside

Hard, compact bone outside

Medullary cavity

Thin, tough outer layer called the periosteum

BONE

Living bone is tough and slightly flexible – only dead bone is white and brittle. Blood vessels pass through small holes in the bone's surface, and carry a steady supply of blood to the bone. Some bones contain a jelly-like substance called red bone marrow, which makes blood cells.

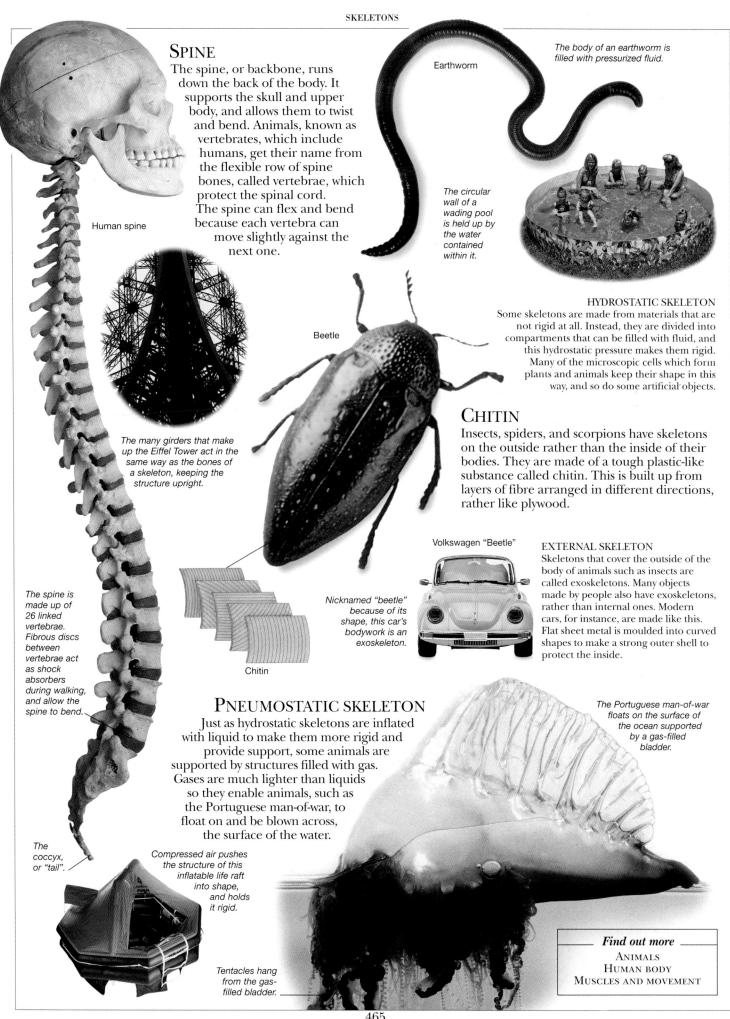

SPINE

The spine, or backbone, runs down the back of the body. It supports the skull and upper body, and allows them to twist and bend. Animals, known as vertebrates, which include humans, get their name from the flexible row of spine bones, called vertebrae, which protect the spinal cord. The spine can flex and bend because each vertebra can move slightly against the next one.

Human spine

The many girders that make up the Eiffel Tower act in the same way as the bones of a skeleton, keeping the structure upright.

The spine is made up of 26 linked vertebrae. Fibrous discs between vertebrae act as shock absorbers during walking, and allow the spine to bend.

The coccyx, or "tail".

Earthworm

The body of an earthworm is filled with pressurized fluid.

The circular wall of a wading pool is held up by the water contained within it.

HYDROSTATIC SKELETON

Some skeletons are made from materials that are not rigid at all. Instead, they are divided into compartments that can be filled with fluid, and this hydrostatic pressure makes them rigid. Many of the microscopic cells which form plants and animals keep their shape in this way, and so do some artificial objects.

CHITIN

Insects, spiders, and scorpions have skeletons on the outside rather than the inside of their bodies. They are made of a tough plastic-like substance called chitin. This is built up from layers of fibre arranged in different directions, rather like plywood.

Beetle

Chitin

Volkswagen "Beetle"

Nicknamed "beetle" because of its shape, this car's bodywork is an exoskeleton.

EXTERNAL SKELETON

Skeletons that cover the outside of the body of animals such as insects are called exoskeletons. Many objects made by people also have exoskeletons, rather than internal ones. Modern cars, for instance, are made like this. Flat sheet metal is moulded into curved shapes to make a strong outer shell to protect the inside.

PNEUMOSTATIC SKELETON

Just as hydrostatic skeletons are inflated with liquid to make them more rigid and provide support, some animals are supported by structures filled with gas. Gases are much lighter than liquids so they enable animals, such as the Portuguese man-of-war, to float on and be blown across, the surface of the water.

The Portuguese man-of-war floats on the surface of the ocean supported by a gas-filled bladder.

Compressed air pushes the structure of this inflatable life raft into shape, and holds it rigid.

Tentacles hang from the gas-filled bladder.

Find out more
ANIMALS
HUMAN BODY
MUSCLES AND MOVEMENT

SLAVERY

FIVE THOUSAND YEARS AGO the Sumerians put their prisoners to work on farms as slaves. The workers had no rights and no pay, and their masters regarded them as property. In ancient Greece and Rome, slaves produced most of the goods and also worked as household servants. During the 16th century, European nations began to colonize the Americas, and imported thousands of Africans to work as slaves on their plantations and silver mines. Between 1500 and 1800, European ships took about 12 million slaves from their homes to the new colonies. By the 19th century, those against slavery set up movements in the United States, and Britain, to end it. Slavery was formally abolished in the British Empire and the United States in the mid-1800s. Sadly, it continues today in many parts of the world, most often affecting children and immigrants.

ROMAN SLAVES
Most wealthy Roman citizens owned slaves. Some slaves lived as part of the family; others were treated very badly. Some earned manumission (a formal release from slavery) through loyalty to a master.

TRIANGLE OF TRADE

The British trade in slaves was known as the triangular trade. Ships sailed from British ports laden with goods such as guns and cloth. Traders exchanged these goods with African chiefs for slaves on the west coast of Africa. The slave ships then carried their cargo across the Atlantic to the Americas and the Caribbean. Here, slaves were in demand for plantation work, so the traders exchanged them for sugar, tobacco, rum, and molasses. The ships then returned to Britain carrying this cargo, which was sold at huge profits.

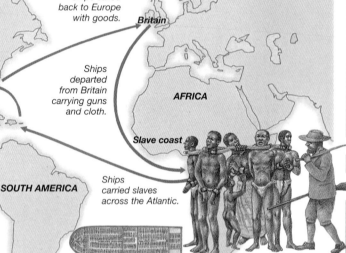

Ships sailed back to Europe with goods.

NORTH AMERICA

Tobacco

Ships departed from Britain carrying guns and cloth.

Britain

AFRICA

Slave coast

Ships carried slaves across the Atlantic.

SOUTH AMERICA

Rum, sugar, and molasses

Slave ship

SLAVE SHIPS
Slavers (slave traders) packed their ships with Africans to sail on what was known as the middle passage across the Atlantic. The slaves were chained and kept below deck for most of the voyage. Unclothed and underfed, thousands of Africans died on the Atlantic crossing.

SLAVE REBELLIONS
Many Africans fought against slavery. In 1791, one of the most famous rebellions began in the French colony of Haiti. A slave named Toussaint L'Ouverture led an army of slaves against the French soldiers in a rebellion that lasted 13 years. L'Ouverture was captured and died in prison in 1803. In 1804, Haiti gained independence and became the world's first black republic.

SLAVE MARKET

Once the slaves reached the West Indies or the southern states of America, they were auctioned at a slave market. Here, they were treated like animals. Families were sometimes separated, and people were sold singly to plantation owners. Slaves were put to work on cotton, sugar, and tobacco plantations. Many received cruel treatment, and severe whipping was a common punishment for slaves who tried to escape.

SLAVERY AND WEALTH

England dominated the slave trade, and some British cities became very rich as a result. Bristol and Liverpool, for instance, imported goods such as sugar and tobacco produced by slaves in the West Indies. Ships from both cities carried slaves from Africa to American plantations.

Ships in Bristol harbour

COTTON

African slave labourers were made to grow sugar in Brazil and the Caribbean. Later, tobacco was also grown. By the late 1700s there were huge cotton plantations in North America, and the British textile industry began to flourish, stimulating the Industrial Revolution. Cotton was made into cloth in Glasgow and Manchester

AM I NOT A MAN & A BROTHER

GRANVILLE SHARP

In 1772, British clerk Granville Sharp defended a black immigrant named James Somerset in a legal case known as the Somerset Case. This established that slavery was not recognized in Britain, and a slave who stepped on British soil was automatically free. The ruling was seen as officially abolishing slavery in England.

OLAUDAH EQUIANO

Africans themselves played a part in the anti-slavery movement. One of the best-known African anti-slavery campaigners was Olaudah Equiano (1745-97). Born in Nigeria, he was captured with his sister when he was eleven, and taken to Britain as a servant. His autobiography was influential and is one of the earliest important works by an African written in English.

ABOLITIONISTS

On both sides of the Atlantic, Quakers, evangelical Christians, and liberal thinkers fought to abolish slavery. In Britain, Granville Sharp, and William Wilberforce (1759-1833), formed the Anti-Slavery Society in 1787-88. Members campaigned for the abolition of slavery and the freeing of all slaves. As part of the campaign, pottery owner Josiah Wedgwood produced a special medal. In 1833, the Slavery Abolition Act freed slaves in the British Empire.

ANTI-SLAVERY MOVEMENT
In 1840, a World Anti-Slavery Convention took place in London, with delegates from the United States. Women took an active part in the abolition movement, often linking their situation with that of slaves. American feminists Lucretia Mott (1793-1880) and Susan B. Anthony (1820-1906) were leading campaigners.

> ### Find out more
> AFRICA, HISTORY OF
> AMERICAN CIVIL WAR
> INDUSTRIAL REVOLUTION
> TUBMAN, HARRIET
> UNITED STATES, HISTORY OF

SNAILS AND SLUGS

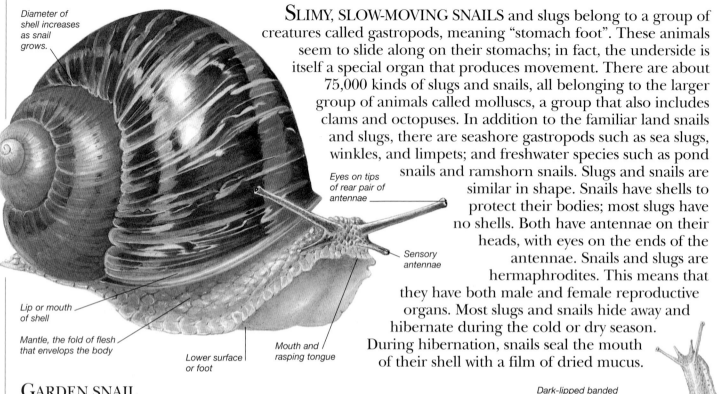

Diameter of shell increases as snail grows.

Eyes on tips of rear pair of antennae

Sensory antennae

Lip or mouth of shell

Mantle, the fold of flesh that envelops the body

Lower surface or foot

Mouth and rasping tongue

SLIMY, SLOW-MOVING SNAILS and slugs belong to a group of creatures called gastropods, meaning "stomach foot". These animals seem to slide along on their stomachs; in fact, the underside is itself a special organ that produces movement. There are about 75,000 kinds of slugs and snails, all belonging to the larger group of animals called molluscs, a group that also includes clams and octopuses. In addition to the familiar land snails and slugs, there are seashore gastropods such as sea slugs, winkles, and limpets; and freshwater species such as pond snails and ramshorn snails. Slugs and snails are similar in shape. Snails have shells to protect their bodies; most slugs have no shells. Both have antennae on their heads, with eyes on the ends of the antennae. Snails and slugs are hermaphrodites. This means that they have both male and female reproductive organs. Most slugs and snails hide away and hibernate during the cold or dry season. During hibernation, snails seal the mouth of their shell with a film of dried mucus.

GARDEN SNAIL

The snail's shell protects the animal from predators and prevents the soft, moist body from drying out. The shell is made of calcium carbonate and other minerals. As the snail grows, it adds more material to the mouth of the shell, making it larger. The snail's tongue is called a radula. It is small and file-like, with as many as 150,000 tooth-like denticles for rasping at plant food.

Dark-lipped banded snail has dark band around shell mouth.

YOUNG
After mating, the snail or slug lays eggs, either singly or in batches, in mucus. The young snails and slugs hatch from their eggs after about two to four weeks.

SLIME
Snails and slugs make several types of slime. As the slug crawls along, it lays down one kind of slime in patches. Another kind of slime is given off when the creature is attacked by a predator. A slug crawls by waves of muscle contractions passing along its foot.

SLUG

Slugs are unpopular with gardeners because some do serious damage to plants and vegetables. Most slugs have no shells; some have a very small shell embedded in the back. Slugs avoid drying out by living in damp places and emerging only at night or after rain.

SEA SLUG
There are many beautifully coloured sea slugs in the shallow coastal waters of the world, particularly around coral reefs. Many have feathery or tufted gills for absorbing oxygen from the water. Sea slugs are predators, feeding mainly on sponges, barnacles, sea mats, and sea anemones.

TOPSHELL
The purple topshell snail lives close to the high-tide mark.

Find out more

OCEAN WILDLIFE
SEASHORE WILDLIFE
SHELLS AND SHELLFISH

SNAKES

LONG, LEGLESS, SCALY, and slithering, snakes are a very successful group of reptiles. They are found everywhere except the coldest regions, highest mountain peaks, and a few islands. Most snakes can swim and climb well. All snakes are hunters. Some, such as pythons and boa constrictors, squeeze and suffocate their prey to death; others, such as cobras, paralyse their victims with a poisonous bite. Fast-moving snakes such as sand snakes hunt down insects, small birds, and mammals. Blind snakes are burrowers that eat ants and termites. More than 400 kinds of snakes are venomous (poisonous), but only some can give a fatal bite to humans. Deadly poisonous snakes include cobras, boomslangs, and mambas.

FANGS
The pair of hollow teeth at the front of the upper jaw are called fangs. The fangs lie flat along the jaw and swing forward when the snake strikes. Muscles pump venom from glands down the fangs into the victim.

RATTLE
Rattlesnakes are so named because they shake the tip of the tail (the rattle) to scare off predators. The rattle consists of a row of hollow tail segments which make a noise when the snake shakes them.

Rattle at tip of tail

SNAKE CHARMING
This is an ancient entertainment in Africa and Asia. Snake charmers fascinate snakes with movements that make the snakes sway to the music.

RATTLESNAKE
At more than 2 m (7 ft) long, the eastern diamondback is the largest rattlesnake, and the most poisonous snake in North America. The rattlesnake feeds mainly on rats, rabbits, and birds. Unlike many other snakes, which lay eggs, the rattlesnake gives birth to about 10 live young in late summer.

Snake's long belly has large scales called ventral scutes which overlap like tiles on a roof.

Emerald tree boa constricts or squeezes its prey.

MILK SNAKE
The non-venomous milk snake shown left is found all over North America, down to the north of South America. It looks similar to the poisonous coral snake, but the milk snake has yellow bands bordered by black, whereas the poisonous coral snake has black bands bordered by yellow. The milk snake hunts small mammals, birds, and other reptiles, including rattlesnakes. It coils around its prey and chokes it to death.

YOUNG SNAKES
Some snakes are described as viviparous, because they give birth to fully formed young. Others lay eggs in a burrow or under a log, leaving the young to hatch and fend for themselves. Certain kinds of pythons coil around the eggs and protect them until they hatch.

CONSTRICTOR
Boas and pythons are called constrictors because they constrict or coil around their prey and suffocate it. There are 72 kinds of boas and pythons; they include some of the largest snakes on Earth. Anacondas are boas of the Amazon region in South America. These massive snakes reach more than 8 m (25 ft) in length and weigh 225 kg (500 lbs).

The sea snake's body follows S-shaped curves, pushing sideways and backwards.

Young grass snake hatches from its egg head first and flicks its tongue to sense its surroundings.

SEA SNAKE
There are more than 60 kinds of sea snakes – the yellow-bellied sea snake shown left is the most common. It measures up to 80 cm (32 in) in length, preys on fish, and gives birth to about five young at sea. Sea snakes spend their lives swimming in the warm waters of the Indian Ocean, around Southeast Asia and Australia, and in the western Pacific.

Find out more
ANIMALS
DESERT WILDLIFE
FOREST WILDLIFE
REPTILES
SPIDERS AND SCORPIONS

SOIL

IF YOU REACH DOWN and pick up a handful of soil, you will be holding one of the Earth's most basic and valuable resources. Soil teems with life. A plot of earth the size of a small garden may contain millions of insects and micro-organisms, plus organic matter from dead or dying plants and animals. Soil provides the foundation for roots, a source of food for plants, and a home not only for burrowing animals, such as moles, but also for millions of spiders and centipedes.

There are many different types of soil, from thick silt and loose sand to waterlogged mud and dry desert. Soil is formed from the wearing down of rocks and takes many years to develop. Each 6.5 sq cm (1 sq in) of soil, for instance, may take 100 to 2,000 years to form. The quality of soil varies from region to region. In hot places, such as Africa and Australia, where there is little rain, the soil is very dry. In temperate regions such as Europe and North America, much of the soil is rich and fertile. But soil can be destroyed in just a fraction of the time it takes to form. Overfarming the land, for example, has led to soil erosion in many parts of the world.

FERTILIZER
Farmers add fertilizers to poor soil. The fertilizer is rich in minerals that help the crops to grow.

TYPES OF SOIL
Soil may be black, brown, red, yellow, orange, or cream in colour, depending on the minerals it contains. Rich, dark, peaty soil is ideal for garden plants.

Peaty soil

Clay soil

Chalky soil

Sandy soil

SOIL EROSION
In overfarmed areas, or where natural vegetation is removed, soil is no longer protected from rain or held in place by roots. Winds blow away the loose soil particles as dust, and rains wash them away as mud. The land becomes infertile and cannot support life. Today, soil erosion affects more than 513,000 sq km (198,000 sq miles) in the United States alone.

SOIL LAYERS
Soil is formed from several different layers that merge into one another. On top is a layer of humus, consisting of dead and rotting leaves. Underneath this layer is the topsoil where decayed plant and animal matter is broken down and recycled by insects, fungi, and bacteria. The subsoil layer, which contains less organic matter, lies below the topsoil and above a loose layer of partly weathered rock. A hard layer of solid bedrock lies below all the other layers.

HUMUS
Humus is the layer of decaying leaves and other plant material in the soil.

TOPSOIL
Topsoil is full of burrowing bugs, worms, and other creatures. It also gives anchorage to plants with shallow root systems.

COMPOST
Fungi, bacteria, worms, and insects thrive in a compost heap, helping the contents to decay and be recycled.

RECYCLING
All living things eventually rot away, back into the soil. The compost heap is a valuable recycler. In time, it turns domestic organic rubbish such as apple peelings, banana skins, eggshells, and grass cuttings into humus, a food supply for the soil. In this way, valuable resources are recycled.

Moles tunnel in the upper metre of rich soil, where there are many worms to eat.

Slug

Beetle

Snail

Caterpillar

Earthworm

Beetle

Centipede

Potato tuber

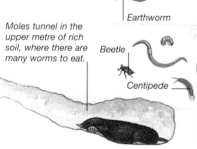

SUBSOIL
The subsoil layer is reached only by deep-rooted plants such as trees.

PARTLY WEATHERED ROCK ZONE
This layer of rocks has weathered and crumbled into loose chunks, and contains no organic matter.

POTATO
All plants, including the potato, use the energy in sunlight, mineral nutrients in the soil, water, and carbon dioxide from the air to grow. The potato plant stores its food reserves in the potatoes that we eat.

Tree roots reach into subsoil layer.

Find out more
FLOWERS AND HERBS
MUSHROOMS
toadstools, and other fungi
PLANTS
TREES

SOUND

WE LIVE IN A NOISY WORLD. The roar of city traffic, the music from a piano, the bark of a dog, all come to our ears as sound waves travelling through the air. Sound is generated when a disturbance sets air moving; for example, when someone plucks a guitar string. We hear sounds when sound waves – tiny vibrations in the air – strike our eardrums. Sound waves need a substance to travel through. This substance may be a liquid, such as water; a solid, such as brick and stone; or a gas, such as air.

Sounds such as musical notes have a certain pitch. A high-pitched sound makes the air vibrate backward and forward more times each second than a low-pitched sound. The number of vibrations per second is called the frequency of the sound and is measured in hertz (cycles per second). Humans cannot hear sounds with frequencies above about 20,000 hertz, or below about 30 hertz.

LOUDNESS AND DECIBELS
The sound of a train is louder than the sound of a whisper because the train produces larger vibrations in the air. The loudness of sound also depends on how close you are to its source. Loudness is measured in decibels (dB). A jet airliner taking off is rated at about 120 dB; the rustling of leaves is about 33 dB.

ECHOES
If you shout in a large hall or near mountains, you can hear your voice echo back to you. An echo occurs when a sound bounces off a surface such as a cliff face and reaches you shortly after the direct sound. The clarity of speech and music in a room or concert hall depends on the way sounds echo inside it.

The distance from one region of highest pressure to the next is called the wavelength of the sound. The higher the pitch, or frequency, of the sound, the shorter the wavelength.

Region of high-pressure air

Region of low-pressure air

The noise of the boat's engine sends sound waves through the water.

SPEED OF SOUND
Sound travels in air at a speed of about 1,224 km/h (about 760 mph). It travels more slowly when the temperature and pressure of the air are lower. In the thin, cold air 11 km (7 miles) up, the speed of sound is about 1,000 km/h (620 mph). In water, sound travels at 5,400 km/h (about 3,350 mph), much faster than in air.

SOUND WAVES
A sound wave consists of air molecules vibrating backward and forward. At each moment the molecules are crowded together in some places, producing regions of high pressure, and spaced out in others, producing regions of low pressure. Waves of alternately high pressure and low pressure move through the air, spreading out from the source of the sound. These sound waves carry the sound to your ears.

HARMONICS
In a musical note, secondary frequencies, called harmonics, are mixed with the main frequency. Harmonics are characteristic of different instruments, which is why a note played on a piano sounds different from the same note played on a violin. Harmonics bring life to the sound of musical instruments: an electronically produced sound of a single pure frequency sounds artificial and dull.

RESONANCE
An object such as a glass gives out a musical note when struck because it has its own natural frequency of vibration. If you sing a musical note of this frequency, the object vibrates at its natural frequency, pushed by the sound waves that hit it. This is called resonance. A very loud sound can make a glass resonate so strongly that it shatters.

Find out more
EARS
MUSIC
MUSICAL INSTRUMENTS
RADIO

SOUTH AFRICA

AFRICA'S SOUTHERNMOST LAND, South Africa is immensely rich in natural resources, with a varied landscape and diverse animal species. In the 17th century, the Cape Town region was settled by Dutch colonists, who were soon followed by the British. From the 1830s, the Dutch (or Boers) began to penetrate the interior. Here, they clashed with the black majority, particularly the Zulus, a disciplined and effective fighting force. In the 20th century, South Africa was dominated by the white minority. The black population was deprived of the vote until 1994, when South Africa held its first multiracial, democratic elections. South Africa's diverse economy is based on mining and agriculture. It is just beginning to exploit its tourist potential. Two independent countries, Lesotho and Swaziland, marooned within South Africa, are economically dependent on their neighbour.

Situated at the southern tip of the African continent, South Africa is bordered by both the Atlantic and Indian Oceans. Much of the country consists of a broad plateau, bordered in the northeast by the arid Namib and Kalahari Deserts, and in the south by mountains and a sandy, coastal plain.

CAPE TOWN
Cape Town, home to the South African parliament, is situated along the southwestern shores of Table Bay. The town is dominated by the distinctive shape of Table Mountain, which rises to 1,005 m (3,300 ft). Cape Town was the first place to be settled by Dutch colonists in the 17th century. It was strategically placed on the main shipping routes between Europe and Asia. Today, it is still a major port and commercial centre.

SERVING FOOD
Wooden vessels are used throughout the African continent. Bowls like this one from Lesotho are traditionally carved from a single block of wood.

THE DRAKENSBERG
The Drakensberg, or Dragon Mountains are a large range in the southeast of South Africa. They form a steep escarpment, reaching the height of 3,482 m (11,424 ft), which rises out of South Africa's central plateau. Much of South Africa's interior is dominated by tableland. This is an area of dry, rolling grassland (*veld*), with scattered trees. In places it is more than 1,200 m (3,900 ft) above sea level. It is grazed by both sheep and cattle.

TOWNSHIPS
Until 1994, the "apartheid" system enforced the separation of the black majority from the ruling, white minority. Many black people were forced to live in purpose-built "townships", and still live there today. Soweto is a sprawling group of townships with a population of about two million. It is situated outside Johannesburg, where most of its inhabitants work, forcing them to travel long distances each day.

MINERALS
South Africa is the world's largest gold producer. It also exports large quantities of diamonds, manganese, chromium, and platinum.

A FERTILE LAND
South Africa, with its fertile soils and warm climate, is ideally situated for agriculture. The main crops grown for export are wheat, sugar cane, potatoes, peanuts, citrus fruits, and tobacco. Sheep and cattle graze the *veld*. European settlers brought vines to South Africa in the 17th century. The Cape province is a major wine-producing area, and South African wine is exported all over the world.

Find out more
AFRICA
AFRICA, HISTORY OF
ELEPHANTS
FARMING
NATIONAL PARKS

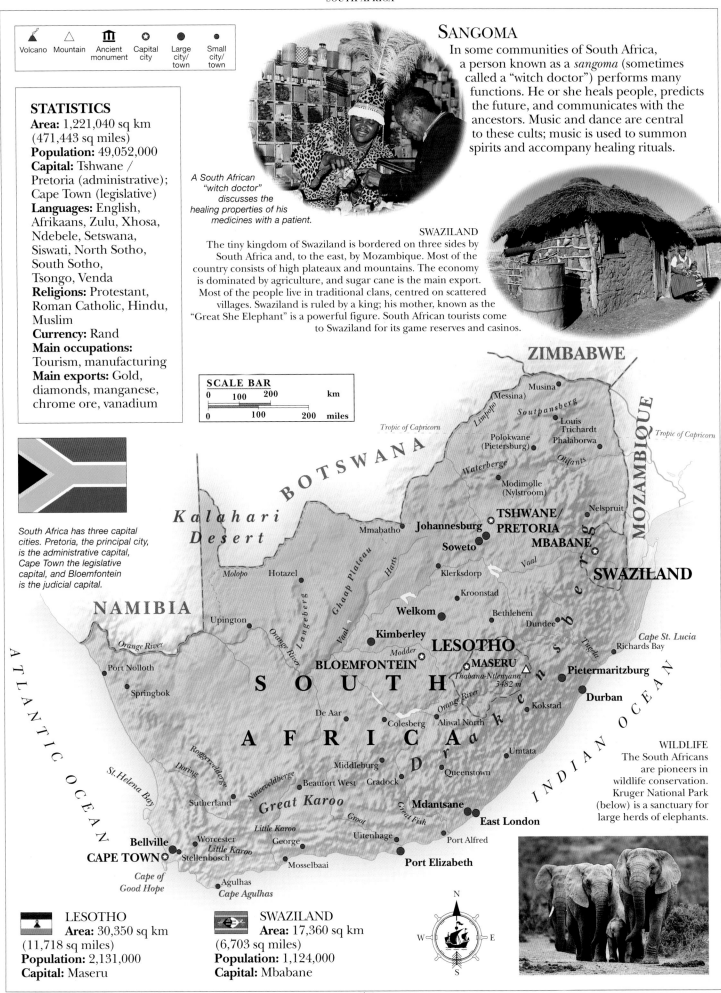

| Volcano | Mountain | Ancient monument | Capital city | Large city/town | Small city/town |

STATISTICS
Area: 1,221,040 sq km (471,443 sq miles)
Population: 49,052,000
Capital: Tshwane / Pretoria (administrative); Cape Town (legislative)
Languages: English, Afrikaans, Zulu, Xhosa, Ndebele, Setswana, Siswati, North Sotho, South Sotho, Tsongo, Venda
Religions: Protestant, Roman Catholic, Hindu, Muslim
Currency: Rand
Main occupations: Tourism, manufacturing
Main exports: Gold, diamonds, manganese, chrome ore, vanadium

South Africa has three capital cities. Pretoria, the principal city, is the administrative capital, Cape Town the legislative capital, and Bloemfontein is the judicial capital.

SANGOMA
In some communities of South Africa, a person known as a *sangoma* (sometimes called a "witch doctor") performs many functions. He or she heals people, predicts the future, and communicates with the ancestors. Music and dance are central to these cults; music is used to summon spirits and accompany healing rituals.

A South African "witch doctor" discusses the healing properties of his medicines with a patient.

SWAZILAND
The tiny kingdom of Swaziland is bordered on three sides by South Africa and, to the east, by Mozambique. Most of the country consists of high plateaux and mountains. The economy is dominated by agriculture, and sugar cane is the main export. Most of the people live in traditional clans, centred on scattered villages. Swaziland is ruled by a king; his mother, known as the "Great She Elephant" is a powerful figure. South African tourists come to Swaziland for its game reserves and casinos.

SCALE BAR
0   100   200   km
0   100   200   miles

WILDLIFE
The South Africans are pioneers in wildlife conservation. Kruger National Park (below) is a sanctuary for large herds of elephants.

LESOTHO
Area: 30,350 sq km (11,718 sq miles)
Population: 2,131,000
Capital: Maseru

SWAZILAND
Area: 17,360 sq km (6,703 sq miles)
Population: 1,124,000
Capital: Mbabane

SOUTH AMERICA

THREE VERY DIFFERENT TYPES of landscape dominate the triangular continent of South America. Along the western coast the towering Andes Mountains reach to more than 6,900 m (22,600 ft) in height. Dense rain forest covers the hot and humid northeastern area. Further south are great open plains of grass and scrub. There are huge mineral deposits and rich farming lands. Despite this, some of the 12 nations which make up the continent are under-developed.

Until about 170 years ago, Spain and Portugal ruled almost all of South America. Most people still speak Spanish or Portuguese. The population is made up of three groups: those descended from European settlers; Native Americans; and people of mixed ancestry. Many people are desperately poor and can barely afford to buy food. Large sections of the population are uneducated and cannot read or write. Many South American governments are insecure or unstable. Most have borrowed large sums of money from wealthier nations. The cost of repaying these debts makes it hard for some countries to develop. But Brazil and Argentina are emerging as major economic powers.

South America lies south of the isthmus of Panama, between the Atlantic and Pacific oceans. It covers 17.8 million sq km (6.9 million sq miles).

Care of the Argentine cattle is the job of cowboys called gauchos.

USING THE LAND

Large herds of beef cattle roam the grasslands of the Pampas, supporting the meat-packing trade in Argentina, Uruguay, and Paraguay. Corn (maize) is grown as a staple crop right across the continent. Coffee is grown as a cash crop in Brazil and Colombia, while coca plants grown in Bolivia, Peru, and Colombia, provide most of the world's cocaine, an illegal drug.

ANDES MOUNTAINS
Stretching the entire length of the continent, the Andes mountain chain is 47,250 km (4,500 miles) long. As well as mineral deposits, the Andes have rich farming land in mountain valleys and on the Altiplano, a large plateau in Peru and Bolivia.

Roads crossing the Andes follow routes through the few low passes.

PERU
With a population of more than 29 million, Peru is one of the larger South American countries. It includes a long stretch of the Andes and part of the rain forest. Many people live on mountain farms and are very poor. Others work on plantations growing coffee, sugar, and cotton for export. Oil has recently been discovered and is bringing some wealth to Peru.

Coffee is still picked by hand in parts of South America.

LAKE TITICACA
In the Andes mountains on the border between Peru and Bolivia, Lake Titicaca is the highest large lake in the world. The lake's surface is 3,812 m (12,507 ft) above sea level. Some parts are 180 m (600 ft) deep. Although large ships operate on the lake, the local people still use reed to build their traditional fishing boats.

BOLIVIA

The mountain nation of Bolivia has no coastline. Its only links with the rest of the world are railways and roads running through Peru and Chile. Although there are large deposits of oil, tin, and silver in the high Andes, the nation remains very poor. About 70 per cent of the population are Aymara or Quechua Native Americans who grow just enough food in the mountains to feed themselves. Some farmers make extra money by growing the coca plant, which is processed to make the illegal drug cocaine.

A woman from Bolivia in traditional dress

SOCCER

Supported passionately, soccer is a favourite sport in most South American countries. Argentina, Brazil, and Uruguay have been very successful in international competitions. In 1930, Uruguay became the first country to host the World Cup. Uruguay also managed to win the tournament in the same year. World Cup victories in 1958, 1962, 1970, 1994, and 2002 mean that Brazil has won this fiercely contested event more times than any other country in the world.

Argentinian football fans parade the streets, demonstrating support for their national soccer team. Argentina won the Fédération Internationale de Football Association (FIFA) World Cup in 1978 and 1986.

The Native Americans of South American forests live in large huts shared by many families. They sleep in hammocks hung between the posts of the huts.

NATIVE AMERICANS

The first peoples of South America were Native Americans. In the lowlands, Native Americans lived in small villages and gathered food from the forest, but in the Andes they built great civilizations. The arrival of European explorers destroyed these great cultures, and today only a few remote tribes still live in the forest as their ancestors did. However, the destruction of the rain forest for farming and mining threatens to eliminate these last traces of Native American society.

FALKLAND ISLANDS

Located in the Atlantic Ocean, the Falkland Islands were discovered by the English navigator John Davis, in his ship *Desire* in 1592. In 1690, the islands were named after Viscount Falkland, treasurer of the British navy. Islas Malvinas, the Argentinian name, comes from "Les Malouines", the name given to the islands by French sailors in the 1700s. The islands were occupied at various times by England, Spain, France, and Argentina.

Rockhopper, Magellanic, and Gento penguins are common on the Falkland Islands.

AMAZON

The longest river in South America is the Amazon, which rises in the Andes and flows 6,516 km (4,050 miles) to the Atlantic. For most of its length the river flows through a rain forest which covers 6.5 million sq km (2.5 million sq miles). In recent years much of the rain forest has been cut down to provide farmland. Although the destruction continues, it is now beginning to slow down.

Find out more

ARGENTINA
BRAZIL
COLOMBIA
FOOTBALL AND RUGBY
INCAS

MINERALS IN CHILE

Copper is Chile's largest export. Chuquicamata (above) is the country's most productive copper mine. Metallic minerals are plentiful along the length of the Andes mountains. They are formed over thousands of years by pressure and heat during mountain-building processes. The Atacama Desert in the northern third of the country stores copper, silver, gold, and abundant deposits of sodium nitrate.

* Countries covered on other pages.

ARGENTINA *
Area: 2,766,890 sq km (1,068,296 sq miles)
Population: 40,914,000
Capital: Buenos Aires

BOLIVIA
Area: 1,098,580 sq km (424,162 sq miles)
Population: 9,775,000
Capital: Sucre, La Paz
Languages: Spanish, Quechua, Aymará
Religions: Roman Catholic
Currency: Boliviano
Main occupations: Subsistence farming, mining, trading
Main exports: Gold, silver, zinc, lead, tin, oil, natural gas

BRAZIL *
Area: 8,511,970 sq km (3,286,472 sq miles)
Population: 198,739,000
Capital: Brasília

CHILE
Area: 756,950 sq km (292,258 sq miles)
Population: 16,601,000
Capital: Santiago
Languages: Spanish, Amerindian languages
Religions: Roman Catholic, non-religious
Currency: Chilean peso
Main occupations: Mining, agriculture
Main exports: Copper, fresh fruit, fishmeal, salmon, wine, lithium, molybdenum, gold

COLOMBIA *
Area: 1,138,910 sq km (439,733 sq miles)
Population: 45,644,000
Capital: Bogotá

ECUADOR
Area: 283,560 sq km (109,483 sq miles)
Population: 14,573,000
Capital: Quito
Languages: Spanish, Quechua, other Amerindian languages
Religions: Roman Catholic, Protestant, Jewish
Currency: U.S. dollar
Main occupations: Oil production, agriculture, fishing
Main exports: Oil, bananas, fish

FRENCH GUIANA
Area: 83,533 sq km (32,252 sq miles)
Population: 221,500
Capital: Cayenne
Status: French department

GUYANA
Area: 214,970 sq km (83,000 sq miles)
Population: 772,000
Capital: Georgetown
Languages: English Creole, Hindi, Tamil, Amerindian languages, English
Religions: Christian, Hindu, Muslim
Currency: Guyana dollar
Main occupations: Subsistence farming, mining, forestry
Main exports: Gold, sugar, bauxite, diamond, timber, rice

PARAGUAY
Area: 406,750 sq km (157,046 sq miles)
Population: 6,996,000
Capital: Asunción
Languages: Guaraní, Spanish
Religions: Roman Catholic
Currency: Guaraní
Main occupations: Agriculture
Main exports: Energy, cotton, oilseeds, soya

PERU
Area: 1,285,220 sq km (496,223 sq miles)
Population: 29,547,000
Capital: Lima
Languages: Spanish, Quechua, Aymará
Religions: Roman Catholic
Currency: Nuevo sol
Main occupations: Subsistence farming, fishing, manufacturing
Main exports: Oil, fish, cotton, coffee, textiles, copper, lead, coca leaves, sugar

SURINAM
Area: 163,270 sq km (63,039 sq miles)
Population: 481,000
Capital: Paramaribo
Languages: Pidgin English (Taki-Taki), Dutch, Hindi, Javanese, Saramacca, Carib
Religions: Christian, Hindu, Muslim
Currency: Surinam dollar
Main occupations: Agriculture, forestry, mining, fishing
Main exports: Bauxite, gold, oil, rice, bananas, citrus fruits, shrimp, aluminium

URUGUAY
Area: 174,810 sq km (67,494 sq miles)
Population: 3,494,000
Capital: Montevideo
Languages: Spanish
Religions: Roman Catholic, Protestant, Jewish, non-religious
Currency: Uruguayan peso
Main occupations: Agriculture, tourism, manufacturing
Main exports: Wool, meat, rice

INCA TERRACES
These terraces near Cuzco, Peru, were built by the Incas to enable cultivation of the hillside. They are still farmed by descendants of the Inca people today.

VENEZUELA
Area: 912,050 sq km (352,143 sq miles)
Population: 26,815,000
Capital: Caracas
Languages: Spanish, Amerindian languages
Religions: Roman Catholic, Protestant
Currency: Bolivar
Main occupations: Mining, agriculture, oil production
Main exports: Coal, bauxite, iron, gold, bitumen fuel, steel, aluminium, oil, coffee

At a height of 979 m (3,212 ft), the majestic Angel Falls in Venezuela (above), is the highest uninterrupted waterfall in the world. It was named after bush pilot Jimmy Angel.

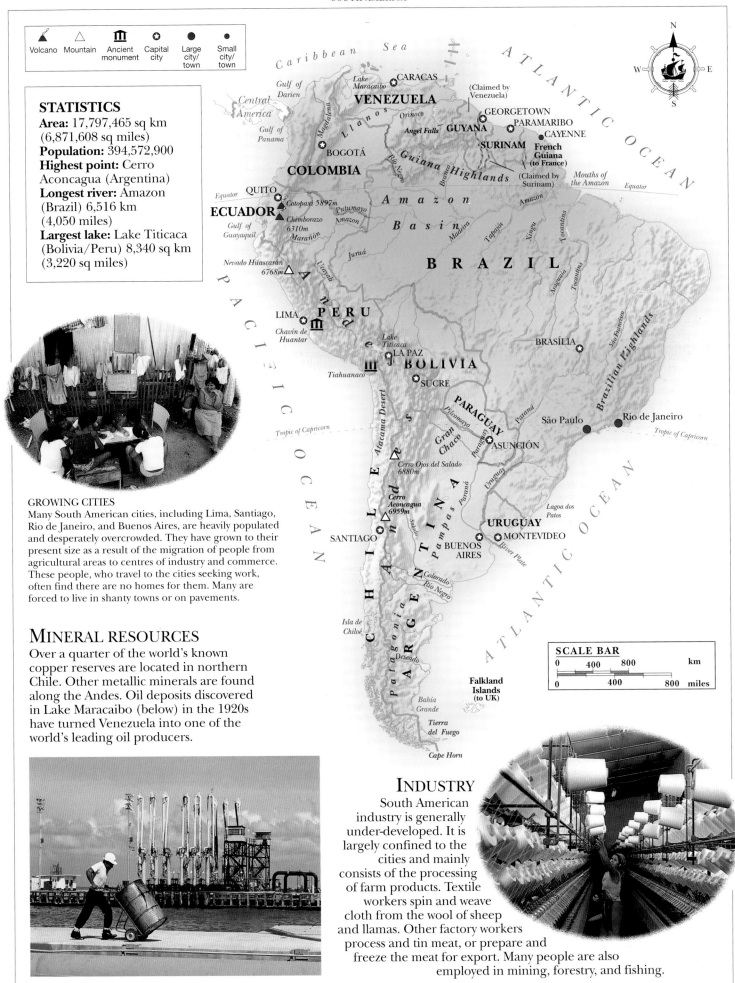

Volcano	Mountain	Ancient monument	Capital city	Large city/ town	Small city/ town

STATISTICS
Area: 17,797,465 sq km
(6,871,608 sq miles)
Population: 394,572,900
Highest point: Cerro
Aconcagua (Argentina)
Longest river: Amazon
(Brazil) 6,516 km
(4,050 miles)
Largest lake: Lake Titicaca
(Bolivia/Peru) 8,340 sq km
(3,220 sq miles)

Caribbean Sea

ATLANTIC OCEAN

Gulf of Darien

Lake Maracaibo
CARACAS

Central America

VENEZUELA
(Claimed by Venezuela)

Gulf of Panama

Llanos
Orinoco

GEORGETOWN
PARAMARIBO
GUYANA
SURINAM
CAYENNE
French Guiana
(to France)

Magdalena
Angel Falls
Rio Negro
Guiana Highlands
Branco

BOGOTÁ
COLOMBIA

(Claimed by Surinam)
Mouths of the Amazon

Equator
QUITO
Cotopaxi 5897m
Equator

Amazon
Amazon

ECUADOR
Chimborazo 6310m
Marañón
Putumayo
Amazon

Amazon Basin

Gulf of Guayaquil

Madeira
Tapajós
Xingu
Tocantins

Juruá

B R A Z I L

Nevado Huascarán 6768m
Ucayali

P E R U

LIMA
Chavín de Huantar

Lake Titicaca
LA PAZ

BRASÍLIA

São Francisco

Brazilian Highlands

Tiahuanaco
BOLIVIA
SUCRE

Atacama Desert
Tropic of Capricorn

PARAGUAY
Pilcomayo
Paraguay
Gran Chaco
Paraná
Paraguay
ASUNCIÓN

São Paulo
Rio de Janeiro
Tropic of Capricorn

Cerro Ojos del Salado 6880m

Uruguay

Lagoa dos Patos

A n d e s

Cerro Aconcagua 6959m

A R G E N T I N A

URUGUAY
MONTEVIDEO

C H I L E

SANTIAGO

Pampas
Salado
BUENOS AIRES

River Plate

Colorado
Rio Negro

Patagonia

Isla de Chiloé

Deseado

SCALE BAR

0	400	800	km

| 0 | 400 | 800 | miles |

Bahía Grande

Falkland Islands (to UK)

Tierra del Fuego

Cape Horn

PACIFIC OCEAN

ATLANTIC OCEAN

N
W E
S

GROWING CITIES
Many South American cities, including Lima, Santiago,
Rio de Janeiro, and Buenos Aires, are heavily populated
and desperately overcrowded. They have grown to their
present size as a result of the migration of people from
agricultural areas to centres of industry and commerce.
These people, who travel to the cities seeking work,
often find there are no homes for them. Many are
forced to live in shanty towns or on pavements.

MINERAL RESOURCES
Over a quarter of the world's known
copper reserves are located in northern
Chile. Other metallic minerals are found
along the Andes. Oil deposits discovered
in Lake Maracaibo (below) in the 1920s
have turned Venezuela into one of the
world's leading oil producers.

INDUSTRY
South American
industry is generally
under-developed. It is
largely confined to the
cities and mainly
consists of the processing
of farm products. Textile
workers spin and weave
cloth from the wool of sheep
and llamas. Other factory workers
process and tin meat, or prepare and
freeze the meat for export. Many people are also
employed in mining, forestry, and fishing.

HISTORY OF
SOUTH AMERICA

Attendants, uniformly dressed, carry the dead king on a bier.

Gold mask

Dead Chimu king is prepared for burial in a sitting position.

Chimu burial ceremony

CHIMU EMPIRE

The Chimu empire centred on the vast capital city of Chan Chan, in what is now northern Peru. The empire covered much of the Pacific coast of South America and reached the height of its power in the 15th century. Around 1470, the Incas conquered the Chimu empire, and Chan Chan fell into ruin. The Chimu are remembered as a highly civilized society. The royal dead were buried with a wealth of funeral offerings.

SOUTH AMERICA

200 BCE-600 CE Nazca empire in Peru.

600 City-states of Tiahuanaco and Huari in Peru.

1000-1470 Chimu empire in Peru.

1200 Inca empire in Bolivia, Chile, Ecuador, and Peru.

1494 Treaty of Tordesillas divides New World between Spain and Portugal.

1499-1510 Amerigo Vespucci explores coast of South America; the continent is named after him.

1530 Portuguese colonize Brazil.

1532-33 Spanish led by Francisco Pizarro conquer Inca empire.

1545 Silver discovered in Peru.

1808-25 Liberation wars: Spanish and Portuguese colonies

1822-89 Empire of Brazil

1879-84 Border wars between Peru, Chile, and Bolivia.

1932-35 War between Paraguay and Bolivia over disputed territory.

1946 Juan Perón becomes president of Argentina.

1967 Che Guevara killed in Bolivia.

FOR THOUSANDS OF YEARS, the continent of South America developed independently from the rest of the world. Great cultures rose and fell, among them the Nazcas, Chimus, and Incas, all of which developed highly advanced civilizations of great wealth and achievement. In 1532 the Spaniards invaded the Inca empire and within a few years ruled over most of the continent. The Portuguese established control over Brazil. Soon Spanish and Portuguese became the main languages of South America, and for the next 300 years the affairs of South America were decided in Europe. The native peoples were almost wiped out by disease and ill treatment. When Spain and Portugal became involved in the Napoleonic wars in Europe, the South Americans seized the chance to win their independence. Afterwards, the new countries were ruled by European families who had settled in South America. Many more Europeans arrived during the 19th and early 20th centuries. The nations of South America have only recently begun to control their destinies.

Line of demarcation 1494

Portuguese territories

Spanish territories

TREATY OF TORDESILLAS
In the 1494 Treaty of Tordesillas, Spain and Portugal divided the non-European world between them. They drew a rough line down the South American continent, giving Spain the lands to the west and Portugal the lands to the east of the line.

SPANISH DOMINATION
From 1532 to 1810, Spain controlled the whole of South America apart from Portuguese-owned Brazil. The vast Spanish Empire there was divided into three viceroyalties – New Granada in the north, Peru in the centre, and Rio de la Plata in the south. On the right is Santiago, the patron saint of Spanish soldiers.

NATIVE AMERICANS
The Native Americans were put to work as slaves in the silver mines. They were also forced to labour in the big plantations of sugar and other crops that were exported to Europe. Most Native Americans died of poor conditions, overwork, and European diseases they had no immunity against.

SIMÓN BOLÍVAR

In 1808, Spain was involved in a war with French emperor Napoleon Bonaparte; the South American colonies took this opportunity to declare their independence. Led by Simón Bolívar (1783-1830) and José de San Martín (1778-1850), the colonies fought against Spanish control; all gained their freedom by 1825. Bolívar hoped to unite all of South America, but many disliked his dictatorial approach. In 1822, Brazil declared its independence from Portugal, leaving only Guiana in the north under European control.

ROMAN CATHOLIC CHURCH

When the Spanish arrived in South America, they brought the Roman Catholic religion with them. Catholic priests tried to stamp out local religions and convert the Native Americans to their faith. In the end the priests were forced to include parts of the old Native American religions in their services. In some places, the priests tried to protect the Native Americans against Spanish rulers who were cruel to them, but most priests upheld the Spanish colonial government. During the 20th century the Catholic Church began to take a more active role in supporting the poor against powerful landlords and corrupt governments.

Bolívar leads soldiers into battle

BRAZILIAN EMPIRE

From 1822 to 1889 Brazil was an empire. Under Emperor Pedro II (1825-1891) roads and railways were built, and the coffee and rubber industries began to prosper. Thousands of immigrants poured into the country from Italy, Portugal, and Spain. In 1888, the African slaves who had been brought over to work the plantations were freed. This angered many landowners, as they had been using the slaves as cheap labour. The landowners withdrew their support from Pedro, and in 1889 the army took over the empire and a republic was declared.

Stamp bearing a portrait of Pedro II

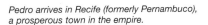

Pedro arrives in Recife (formerly Pernambuco), a prosperous town in the empire.

ERNESTO "CHE" GUEVARA

One of the most popular heroes of the 20th century, Che Guevara (1928-1967) was born into a rich Argentinian family. Guevara was a doctor before choosing to spend his life supporting revolutions against oppressive South American governments. In 1959, he helped Fidel Castro overthrow the Cuban government. Guevara served under Castro until 1965. In late 1966 he moved to Bolivia, where he based himself in the countryside among peasants. In 1967, he was killed by the Bolivian army. His death made him a hero for revolutionaries everywhere. In 1997, he was reburied in Cuba.

JUAN PERÓN

From 1946 to 1955, Argentina was ruled by President Juan Perón (1895-1974). Poor people living in the cities supported Perón and his wife, Eva. He introduced many reforms but did not allow anyone to oppose him. After the economy weakened in the early 1950s, and after Eva died (1952), Perón was much less popular. In 1955, the army overthrew him. In 1973, he again held power but died the following year. His third wife, Isabel Martínez de Perón, succeeded him as president.

Find out more

CENTRAL AMERICA
CONQUISTADORS
INCAS
SOUTH AMERICA

SOUTHEAST ASIA

AT ITS SOUTHEAST CORNER, the continent of Asia extends far out into the sea, in two great peninsulas and a vast chain of islands. In this region, which is called Southeast Asia, more than 592 million people live in 11 independent countries. The area has a rich and varied culture, and music and dancing are particularly important. Their performance is often governed by strict rituals and rules, some of them religious. There are several different religions in the area: most people on the mainland are Buddhist; Indonesia is chiefly Muslim; and Christianity is the religion of the Philippines. For much of this century the lives of many Southeast Asian people have been disrupted and destroyed by wars. The fighting made normal trade, agriculture, and industry impossible and turned Laos and Cambodia into the two poorest nations on Earth. Conflict between the government and Islamists in the southern Philippines continues to claim lives. Other Southeast Asian countries, such as Singapore, have become more peaceful and prosperous.

Southeast Asia is the part of Asia to the south of China, and east of India. The mainland portion has an area of 1.6 million sq km (640,000 sq miles). The region continues to the south as a chain of islands that separate the Pacific and Indian oceans. The island of Sumatra is 1,720 km (1,070 miles) long; other islands are tiny.

THAILAND
There are 65.9 million people in Thailand, and the country is among the wealthiest in the region. Most people in the cities work in mining and industry; in the countryside most are farmers, growing rice, sugar, and rubber trees. The country's rich heritage includes ritual temple dances and beautiful architecture.

Singapore City began as a small British trading station; today giant skyscrapers dominate the skyline.

Sap is extracted by tapping – cutting or shaving the bark with a sharp knife.

Plantation workers drain the sticky sap from the trees in the morning when the flow of sap is fastest.

RUBBER
One of the most important products of Southeast Asia is rubber. The industry began about a century ago when British traders brought rubber trees to the region from Brazil. The sap of the trees is collected, then mixed with acid to form solid sheets of latex, which are hung out to dry.

SINGAPORE
The tiny island state of Singapore occupies just 620 sq km (239 sq miles) off the coast of Malaysia. The nation is highly industrialized and very rich. Most of Singapore's 4.6 million people earn their living from industries such as textiles and electronics.

The Borobudur Temple was built with about 56,600 cubic m (2,000,000 cubic ft) of gray volcanic stone.

JAVA
The country of Indonesia is made up of 13,677 islands. Java is the most populated island, with 121 million people. Many are farmers producing large quantities of rice. The capital city, Jakarta, is a centre for the textile industry. The island has much unique wildlife, including species of tiger and rhinoceros found nowhere else.

BOROBUDUR TEMPLE
A massive Buddhist monument in Java, the Borodubur Temple was constructed between 778 and 850 CE. From about 1000 BCE it was buried under volcanic ash until its discovery by the English lieutenant governor Thomas Stamford Raffles in 1814. A team of Dutch archaeologists restored the site during 1907-11, and a second restoration was completed by 1983.

Protected by law, orangutans still face hunting, and destruction of their rainforest habitat. Orangutan is the Malaysian for "person of the forest".

VIETNAM

Vietnam is a mountainous land which occupies the eastern part of the Indo-China peninsula in Southeast Asia. Its population, which is mainly rural, mostly lives in the lowland deltas of the Red and Mekong rivers. More than half of its people work in agriculture. Rice takes up more land area than all other crops produced in Vietnam put together. Other crops include rubber, maize, sugar, bananas, coconuts, pepper, tea, tobacco, and sweet potatoes. Northern Vietnam is more industrialized than the agricultural south. It has mineral resources, which include coal, salt, tin, and iron. Farmers often work in salt farms (left) to supplement their earnings from agriculture.

ORANGUTAN

The orangutan is a large humanlike ape that is now restricted to lowland swamp forests in Borneo and a small part of Sumatra. Orangutans once lived in the jungles of mainland Southeast Asia as well, but numbers have been depleted by human hunters. With its short, thickset body, long arms, and short legs, the orangutan displays many physical similarities to gorillas and chimpanzees. However, a shaggy, reddish coat, and an even greater disproportion between arm and leg lengths, sets the orangutan apart from its related primates. The male orangutan may be about 1.37 m (4.5 feet) tall and weigh about 85 kg (185 lbs) when mature, while females usually weigh about 40 kg (90 lbs).

DAO PEOPLE

Ethnic minorities make up about 14 per cent of Vietnam's population. One of these groups is the Dao, who live in the northern regions. The Dao can also be found in the neighbouring countries of China, Laos, and Thailand. The origins of the first Dao groups in Vietnam are uncertain, but it would appear that they emigrated from their native provinces of southern China in the 18th and 19th centuries.

BURMA (MYANMAR)

Burma gained independence from British colonial control in 1948 and immediately adopted a policy of political and economic isolation. Once a rich nation, the country was subsquently reduced to one of the world's poorest despite its plentiful natural resources. The Irrawaddy river basin occupies most of the country and provides rich farming land. Burma has in recent years been ruled by a military government which has excluded all foreign influences. About three out of four people are Buddhists, but in the countryside many still worship the *nats* – ancient spirits of the forest and mountains. Devotees of Buddhism pray at temples such as the Shwedagon Pagoda (below) in Yangon.

ELEPHANT SCHOOL

Elephants in Thailand are trained to work for a living. They have proved themselves to be far more cost-efficient than modern tractors. They need little fuel and do not rust or need spare parts. Tractors last for about six years, an elephant lives for 30. In addition, elephants are less harmful to the environment. They move timber and take tourists for rides in the rainforest.

BRUNEI
Area: 5,770 sq km (2,228 sq miles)
Population: 389,000
Capital: Bandar Seri Begawan
Languages: Malay, English, Chinese
Religions: Muslim, Buddhist, Christian
Currency: Brunei dollar

BURMA (MYANMAR)
Area: 676,550 sq km (261,200 sq miles)
Population: 48,138,000
Capital: Rangoon (Yangon)
Languages: Burmese, Karen, Shan, Chin, Kachin, Mon, Palaung, Wa
Religions: Buddhist, Christian, Muslim, Hindu
Currency: Kyat

CAMBODIA
Area: 181,040 sq km (69,000 sq miles)
Population: 14,494,000
Capital: Phnom Penh
Languages: Khmer, French, Chinese, Vietnamese, Cham
Religions: Theravada Buddhist
Currency: Riel

EAST TIMOR
Area: 15,007 sq km (5,794 sq miles)
Population: 1,131,000
Capital: Dili
Languages: Tetum, Bahasa Indonesia, Portuguese
Religions: Roman Catholic
Currency: US dollar

INDONESIA
Area: 1,904,570 sq km (735,555 sq miles)
Population: 240,272,000
Capital: Jakarta
Languages: Javanese, Madurese, Sundanese, Bahasa Indonesia, Dutch
Religions: Muslim, Protestant, Roman Catholic, Hindu, Buddhist
Currency: Rupiah

LAOS
Area: 236,800 sq km (81,428 sq miles)
Population: 6,834,000
Capital: Vientiane
Languages: Lao, Miao, Yao, Vietnamese, Chinese, French
Religions: Buddhist, Animist
Currency: New kip

MALAYSIA
Area: 329,750 sq km (127,317 sq miles)
Population: 25,716,000
Capital: Kuala Lumpur
Languages: Malay, Chinese, Tamil
Religions: Muslim, Buddhist, Chinese faiths, Christian, traditional beliefs
Currency: Ringgit

PHILIPPINES
Area: 300,000 sq km (115,831 sq miles)
Population: 97,977,000
Capital: Manila
Languages: Filipino, Cebuano, Hiligaynon, Samaran, Ilocano, Bikol, English
Religions: Roman Catholic, Protestant, Muslim, Buddhist
Currency: Philippine peso

SINGAPORE
Area: 620 sq km (239 sq miles)
Population: 4,658,000
Capital: Singapore City
Languages: Chinese, Malay, Tamil, English
Religions: Buddhist, Christian, Muslim
Currency: Singapore dollar

THAILAND
Area: 513,120 sq km (198,116 sq miles)
Population: 65,906,000
Capital: Bangkok
Languages: Thai, Chinese, Malay, Khmer, Mon, Karen, Miao
Religions: Theravada Buddhist, Muslim, Christian
Currency: Baht

VIETNAM
Area: 329,560 sq km (127,243 sq miles)
Population: 86,968,000
Capital: Hanoi
Languages: Vietnamese, Chinese, Thai, Khmer, Muong, Nung, Miao, Yao, Jarai
Religions: Buddhist, Christian, non-religious
Currency: Dông

PHILIPPINES

Most of the islands in the Philippines are mountainous and forested. The Filipino people live in towns and villages on the narrow coastal plains, or on plateaus between the mountain ranges. The volcanic cone of Mount Mayon, 320 km (200 miles) southeast of Manila, is one of the most beautiful in the world. However, its beauty hides its dangerous character. The volcano is still active, and past eruptions have destroyed parts of the nearby city of Albay.

The magnificent, golden-domed Omar Ali Saifuddin mosque, Brunei

BRUNEI

Lying on the northwestern coast of the island of Borneo, Brunei is ruled by a sultan. Since gaining independence from Britain in 1984, the country has become increasingly influenced by Islam. Its interior is mostly rainforest and the nation's abundant oil and gas reserves have brought its citizens one of the highest standard of living in the world.

INDONESIA

Although more than 13,500 islands make up the Republic of Indonesia, only about 6,000 are inhabited. Most Indonesian people live in the countryside and work on farms. However, some cities are densely populated. For example, the city of Yogyakarta (left), on the southern coast of the heavily populated island of Java, has a population of about 600,000.

The bustling city of Yogyakarta lies at the foot of a volcano.

Find out more
ISLAM
VIETNAM WAR
VOLCANOES

Volcano | Mountain | Ancient monument | Capital city | Large city/town | Small city/town

STATISTICS

Area: 4,477,761 sq km (1,728,157 sq miles)
Population: 592,483,000
No. of independent countries: 11
Religions: Buddhism, Islam, Taoism, Christianity, Hinduism
Largest city: Jakarta (Indonesia) 8,792,000
Highest point: Hkakabo Rasi (Burma) 5,885 m (19,309 ft)
Longest river: Mekong 4,184 km (2,600 miles)
Main occupation: Farming
Main exports: Sugar, fruit, timber, rice, rubber, tobacco, tin
Main imports: Machinery, iron and steel products, textiles, chemicals, fuels

POPULATION
The population on mainland Southeast Asia is concentrated in the river valleys, plateaux, or plains. The population of maritime Southeast Asia is unevenly distributed; Java is densely settled while other islands are barely occupied.

MAINLAND SOUTHEAST ASIA

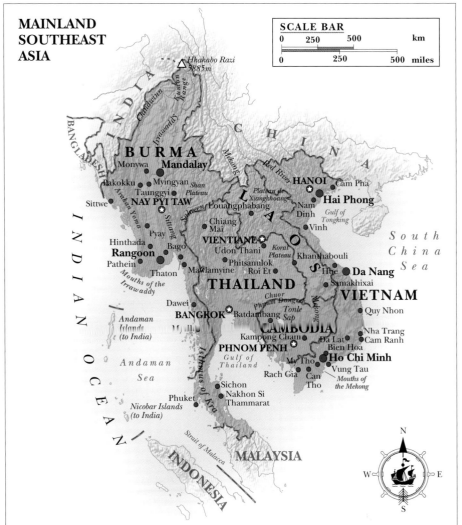

SCALE BAR
0 250 500 km
0 250 500 miles

MARITIME SOUTHEAST ASIA

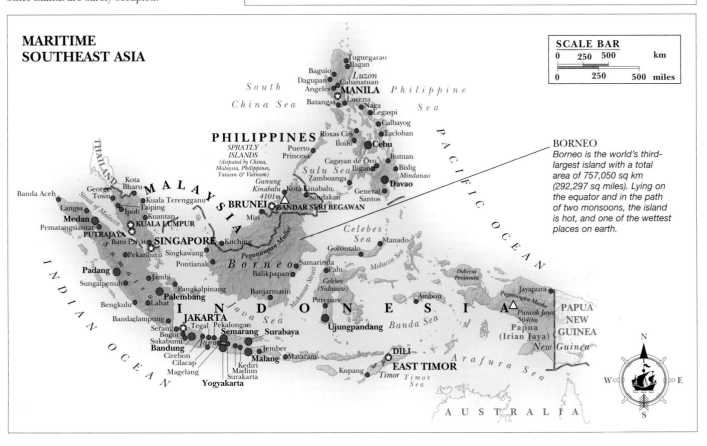

SCALE BAR
0 250 500 km
0 250 500 miles

BORNEO
Borneo is the world's third-largest island with a total area of 757,050 sq km (292,297 sq miles). Lying on the equator and in the path of two monsoons, the island is hot, and one of the wettest places on earth.

CENTRAL
SOUTHEAST EUROPE

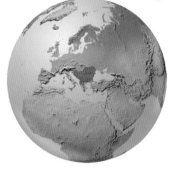

THE NOBLE DANUBE RIVER cuts central Southeast Europe in half, providing fertile farmland along its lower course, in the heart of the region. This area of flatland, called the Danubian Plain, is surrounded by mighty mountain systems, including the Carpathians to the north, and the Balkans and Rhodope mountains in the south. Following World War II, the countries of central Southeast Europe were governed for more than 50 years by strict communist regimes, until the collapse of the Soviet Union in the early 1990s. Serbia was once part of federal Yugoslavia. The collapse of this federation led to civil war in 1991, after which five separate states emerged. Kosovo, an area in southern Serbia inhabited by Muslim Albanian-speakers declared itself an independent country in 2008.

Lying to the south of the Alps, the west of the region is mountainous with deep wooded valleys. The western border is formed by the rocky coast of the Adriatic Sea. To the east lie the flat plains of the Danube, which drains into the Black Sea, and rolling steppelands.

BULGARIAN TOBACCO
Bulgaria has fertile soils and a mild climate, and a wide range of crops is grown there, including cereals, sunflower seeds, grapes, and tomatoes. High-quality red wine, made from grapes grown on the Danubian plain, is exported. In the south of the country, Turkish-style tobacco is grown; it is processed in factories around the town of Plovdiv. Here, women can be seen stringing the harvested tobacco leaves together. They are then left to cure in the heat of the sun before being graded by size and colour.

A Romanian gypsy makes a living by selling berries

RURAL MOLDOVA

Once a part of Romania, Moldova became a Soviet state in 1940. In 1991, with the break-up of the Soviet Union, Moldova became independent. This small country is dominated by fertile rolling steppes. Most of the population works in agriculture. Warm summers and even rainfall provide ideal conditions for growing vegetables, fruits and grapes, and Moldova is internationally famous for its wines. Although the Soviets mechanized state-owned farms, there are now many small-scale farmers, who cultivate their land using traditional methods.

GYPSIES
Romania has the largest gypsy (or Romany) population in Europe. Gypsies, who have a distinct language and culture, are thought to have originated in India, and moved to Europe via the Middle East. Traditionally, they wandered from place to place, selling goods, repairing metal utensils, and dealing in horses and livestock. They have suffered many centuries of persecution from the countries in which they settled, who found it difficult to understand their different customs and ways of life.

TRANSYLVANIA

The Romanian region of Transylvania is a high plateau, surrounded by the Carpathian Mountains. To the east and south the mountains form an impassable barrier. The region, with its rugged scenery and dramatic castles, has had a colourful history, passing from Hungarian to Ottoman Turkish to Habsburg (Austrian) rule. Amongst its tyrannical rulers was the 15th-century prince, Vlad the Impaler, notorious for his cruelty. When the author Bram Stoker wrote *Dracula* in 1897, he borrowed from Slavic and Hungarian legends. His blood-sucking vampire is based on Vlad the Impaler.

ROSES
Vast fields of roses are grown in Bulgaria. Petals are picked at dawn to produce attar, the essential oil of roses.

Find out more

COMMUNISM
DANCE
EUROPE
FLOWERS AND HERBS
MOUNTAINS

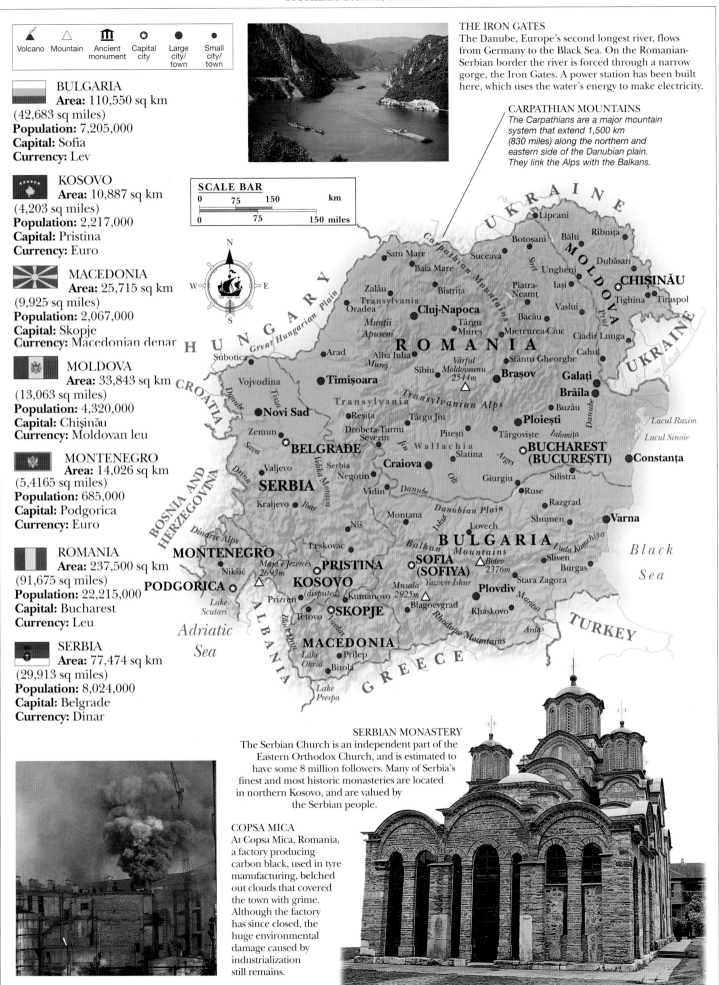

Volcano Mountain Ancient monument Capital city Large city/town Small city/town

BULGARIA
Area: 110,550 sq km (42,683 sq miles)
Population: 7,205,000
Capital: Sofia
Currency: Lev

KOSOVO
Area: 10,887 sq km (4,203 sq miles)
Population: 2,217,000
Capital: Pristina
Currency: Euro

MACEDONIA
Area: 25,715 sq km (9,925 sq miles)
Population: 2,067,000
Capital: Skopje
Currency: Macedonian denar

MOLDOVA
Area: 33,843 sq km (13,063 sq miles)
Population: 4,320,000
Capital: Chişinău
Currency: Moldovan leu

MONTENEGRO
Area: 14,026 sq km (5,4165 sq miles)
Population: 685,000
Capital: Podgorica
Currency: Euro

ROMANIA
Area: 237,500 sq km (91,675 sq miles)
Population: 22,215,000
Capital: Bucharest
Currency: Leu

SERBIA
Area: 77,474 sq km (29,913 sq miles)
Population: 8,024,000
Capital: Belgrade
Currency: Dinar

THE IRON GATES
The Danube, Europe's second longest river, flows from Germany to the Black Sea. On the Romanian-Serbian border the river is forced through a narrow gorge, the Iron Gates. A power station has been built here, which uses the water's energy to make electricity.

CARPATHIAN MOUNTAINS
The Carpathians are a major mountain system that extend 1,500 km (830 miles) along the northern and eastern side of the Danubian plain. They link the Alps with the Balkans.

SCALE BAR
0   75   150   km
0   75   150 miles

SERBIAN MONASTERY
The Serbian Church is an independent part of the Eastern Orthodox Church, and is estimated to have some 8 million followers. Many of Serbia's finest and most historic monasteries are located in northern Kosovo, and are valued by the Serbian people.

COPSA MICA
At Copsa Mica, Romania, a factory producing carbon black, used in tyre manufacturing, belched out clouds that covered the town with grime. Although the factory has since closed, the huge environmental damage caused by industrialization still remains.

MEDITERRANEAN
SOUTHEAST EUROPE

Mediterranean Southeast Europe is largely mountainous. Ranges including the Dinaric Alps run from the north to the south, parallel to the western coast. The western shores of the region are washed by the Adriatic Sea, an arm of the Mediterranean Sea.

THE LANDSCAPE of Mediterranean Southeast Europe is composed of rugged mountains, rocky coasts, and isolated valleys. The region has experienced many centuries of conflict and invasions from both Europe and Asia. Croatia, Bosnia and Herzegovinia, and Albania were once part of the Turkish Ottoman Empire. Slovenia was annexed by the Habsburg and Austria-Hungarian Empires, and the cultural influences of these two dynasties remain. After World War II, most of Southeast Europe became part of the Communist bloc. In 1990, Slovenia elected a non-communist government which led to civil strife and the final breakup of the Yugoslavian Federation. Slovenia joined the European Union in 2004 and Croatia is a candidate for future EU membership.

SARAJEVO

The capital of Bosnia and Herzegovina, which straddles the River Miljacka, has a strongly Muslim character, with mosques, wooden houses and an ancient Turkish market place. In 1992, when Bosnia declared independence from Yugoslavia, Sarajevo became the focus of a civil war. Thousands of Muslims were driven from the countryside by the fighting, and fled to Sarajevo. The city suffered terrible damage in 1993, when it was surrounded by Serb forces and bombarded.

Slovenian dancers wear leather trousers and dirndl skirts

SLOVENIAN TOURISM

Slovenia is an increasingly popular tourist destination, especially for people from the German-speaking countries. More than 1.3 million tourists visit each year to see the Adriatic coastal resorts, historic spa towns, and the mountains, where they can enjoy skiing, hiking, boating and fishing. Lake Bled (above), at the foot of the Julian Alps is a popular resort, famous for bathing in summer and as a winter sports centre.

SLOVENIAN DANCERS

Slovenia shares a long history with its northern neighbour, Austria. Culturally, Slovenia has more in common with its Alpine neighbours, Switzerland and Austria, than the countries to the south. Cultural traditions are kept alive through music and dance. National costumes are distinctly Alpine.

ZAGREB

The Croatian capital is a major commercial centre. Vegetables and fruit produced by local farmers are sold in markets in the town's squares. Much of the city dates to the 19th century, although there are some medieval buildings dating from the 13th century. Zagreb is Croatia's main industrial centre, specializing in manufacturing, textiles and chemicals.

DUBROVNIK

The most picturesque city on the Adriatic coast, Dubrovnik has a history which dates back 1,000 years. With its steep and twisting narrow streets, ancient city walls and historic fortifications, Dubrovnik was once one of Croatia's main tourist attractions. In 1991, this beautiful city came under fire as a result of Croatia's independence struggle. The tourist industry has now recovered from the effects of civil war.

Volcano	Mountain	Ancient monument	Capital city	Large city/town	Small city/town

ALBANIA
Area: 27,400 sq km (10,579 sq miles)
Population: 3,639,000
Capital: Tirana
Currency: Lek

BOSNIA & HERZEGOVINA
Area: 51,130 sq km (19,741 sq miles)
Population: 4,613,000
Capital: Sarajevo
Currency: Marka

CROATIA
Area: 56,538 sq km (21,829 sq miles)
Population: 4,489,000
Capital: Zagreb
Currency: Kuna

SLOVENIA
Area: 20,250 sq km (7,820 sq miles)
Population: 2,006,000
Capital: Ljubljana
Currency: Euro

TIRANA

The capital of Albania was founded by Turks in the 17th century. Strategically situated at the junction of several trade routes, it became an important commercial centre. The city became capital of Albania in 1920. In the 1930s, Italian architects were employed to re-plan its centre. From 1946, communist Albania received aid from both Russia and China. The Soviets built the Palace of Culture, which flanks Tirana's central square. Today, Tirana is Albania's main industrial centre. The city specializes in glass, porcelain, metal working, tractor-repairs, and food-processing.

Under Communist rule, there were few cars in central Tirana. Car ownership was then banned.

Watermelons grow well during Albania's blazing hot summers.

ALBANIAN AGRICULTURE

Half the Albanian population is employed in agriculture, and the number of privately-owned farms is now expanding. Although only a quarter of this rugged land can be farmed, the country is self-sufficient in nearly all its main crops. It grows wheat, corn, sugar beets, cotton, sunflower seeds, tobacco, potatoes, and fruit. Yet Albania's vast agricultural potential is hindered by very traditional methods of farming.

LAKE OHRID

Lake Ohrid, on the Macedonian-Albanian border is Macedonia's main tourist attraction. Visitors come to the lake for fishing and swimming, and to visit the town of Ohrid, on its northeastern shore. Ohrid has many historic buildings including this medieval church (right), which stands on the shores of the lake just outside the town. Macedonia is dominated by Slavs, who make up about two-thirds of the population, and are followers, like Serbia, of the Eastern Orthodox Church. However, about 23 percent of the Macedonian population is Albanian and Muslim. This situation is causing some tension within the country, especially as the Albanian population is growing very rapidly.

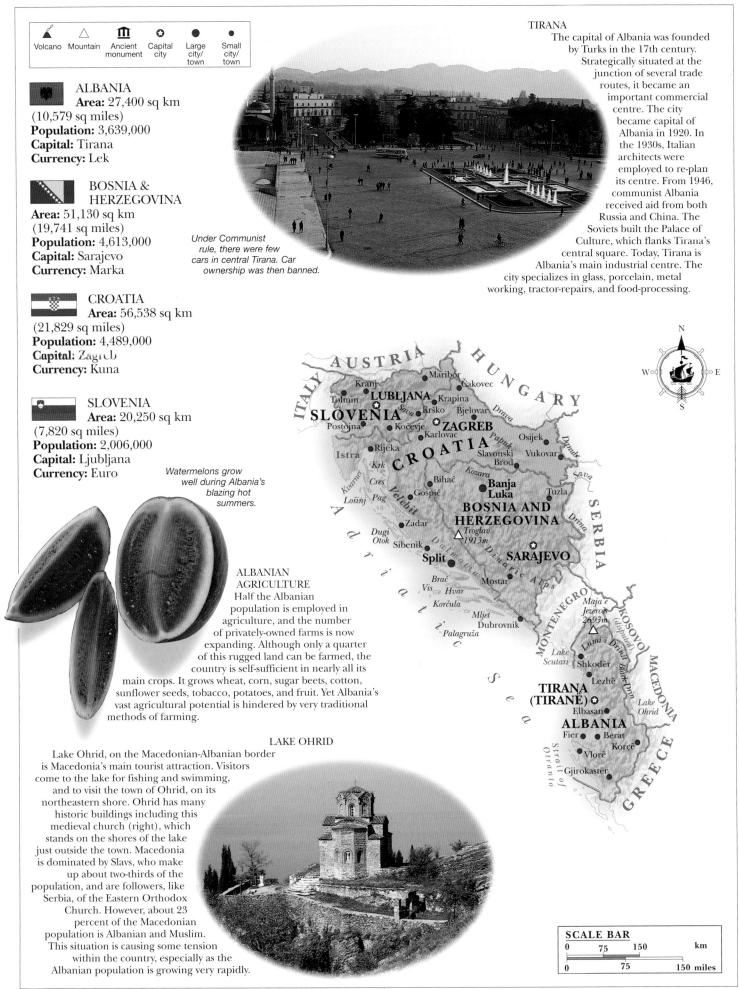

SCALE BAR

0   75   150   km

0   75   150 miles

SOUTHERN AFRICA

THE COUNTRIES OF SOUTHERN AFRICA are dominated by dry savannah and woodland, with humid subtropical forests in the north and, to the centre and west, the Kalahari and Namib Deserts. Traditionally, agriculture has been the mainstay of these countries' economies, but rich mineral deposits, in particular diamonds, uranium, copper and iron, are being discovered and exploited, especially in Namibia, Zambia, and Botswana. Economically, the region is dominated by South Africa, with its well-developed mining industries and large cities. Zimbabwe has reserves of coal, gold and nickel, but the country's economy has been brought close to collapse by drought and misgovernment. Both Angola and Mozambique, former Portuguese colonies, have been devastated by civil wars since independence and are only now beginning to re-build their shattered economies.

Bordered on the west by the Atlantic Ocean and on the east by the Indian Ocean, much of southern Africa lies within the tropics. The landscape includes the Namib and Kalahari Deserts. Madagascar, the fourth largest island in the world, lies to the east.

DESERT NOMADS
The nomadic San of the Kalahari in Botswana live by gathering fruit and vegetables and hunting springbok and wildebeest.

URANIUM WEALTH

The largest open pit uranium mine in the world is located at Rössing in the Namib Desert. The mine was opened in 1976 by a group of British, South Africa, French, and Canadian companies. As well as being the world's largest uranium producer, Namibia also has extensive reserves of tin, lead, zinc, copper, silver, and tungsten, and produces 30 per cent of the world's diamond output.

GOLD CITY

Founded in 1886, Johannesburg was the centre of South Africa's gold-mining industry for nearly a century, and remains the country's chief industrial, commercial, manufacturing, and financial centre. Greater Johannesburg is one of Africa's largest cities, the heart of an expanding motorway system and the South African rail network.

VICTORIA FALLS

Located on the Zambezi River, on the border between Zimbabwe and Zambia, the Victoria Falls are 1,700 m (5,500 ft) at their widest point, and fall to a maximum depth of 108 m (354 ft) in the chasm below. The huge volume of plummeting water creates a mighty roar, known to locals as "the smoke that thunders", which can be heard 40 km (25 miles) away. From the chasm, the river carves a narrow gorge before plunging into a deep pool known as the Boiling Pot.

NAMIB DESERT
The Namib Desert extends up to 160 km (100 miles) inland along the coast of southwest Africa. Sand dunes can reach heights of 240 m (800 ft). Moisture from coastal fogs supports some vegetation.

Find out more
AFRICA
AFRICA, HISTORY OF
DESERT WILDLIFE
SOUTH AFRICA

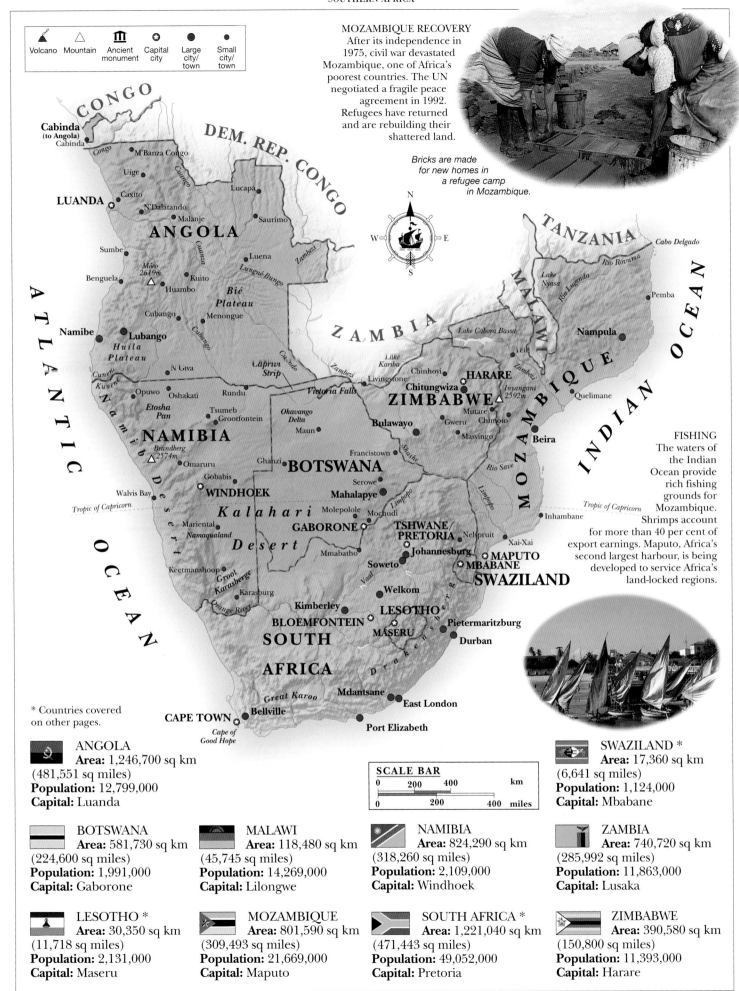

Volcano | Mountain | Ancient monument | Capital city | Large city/town | Small city/town

MOZAMBIQUE RECOVERY
After its independence in 1975, civil war devastated Mozambique, one of Africa's poorest countries. The UN negotiated a fragile peace agreement in 1992. Refugees have returned and are rebuilding their shattered land.

Bricks are made for new homes in a refugee camp in Mozambique.

FISHING
The waters of the Indian Ocean provide rich fishing grounds for Mozambique. Shrimps account for more than 40 per cent of export earnings. Maputo, Africa's second largest harbour, is being developed to service Africa's land-locked regions.

* Countries covered on other pages.

ANGOLA
Area: 1,246,700 sq km (481,551 sq miles)
Population: 12,799,000
Capital: Luanda

BOTSWANA
Area: 581,730 sq km (224,600 sq miles)
Population: 1,991,000
Capital: Gaborone

MALAWI
Area: 118,480 sq km (45,745 sq miles)
Population: 14,269,000
Capital: Lilongwe

NAMIBIA
Area: 824,290 sq km (318,260 sq miles)
Population: 2,109,000
Capital: Windhoek

SWAZILAND *
Area: 17,360 sq km (6,641 sq miles)
Population: 1,124,000
Capital: Mbabane

ZAMBIA
Area: 740,720 sq km (285,992 sq miles)
Population: 11,863,000
Capital: Lusaka

LESOTHO *
Area: 30,350 sq km (11,718 sq miles)
Population: 2,131,000
Capital: Maseru

MOZAMBIQUE
Area: 801,590 sq km (309,493 sq miles)
Population: 21,669,000
Capital: Maputo

SOUTH AFRICA *
Area: 1,221,040 sq km (471,443 sq miles)
Population: 49,052,000
Capital: Pretoria

ZIMBABWE
Area: 390,580 sq km (150,800 sq miles)
Population: 11,393,000
Capital: Harare

SCALE BAR
0   200   400   km
0   200   400   miles

HISTORY OF THE
SOVIET UNION

IN 1922, A NEW NATION came into being. The Union of Soviet Socialist Republics, or the Soviet Union, was the new name for Communist Russia, led by Vladimir Lenin (1870-1924). The years following the 1917 Revolution were difficult. Civil war between Communists and anti-Communists had torn Russia apart. More than 20 million people had died. When Lenin died, Joseph Stalin took over as dictator. In a reign of terror, he eliminated all opposition to his rule. He started to transform the Soviet Union into a modern industrial state. The huge industrial effort made the Soviet Union strong. It survived German invasion in 1941, although World War II (1939-1945) cost the nation many lives. After 1945 the Soviet Union became a superpower, but it still had difficulty providing enough goods for its people. In 1985, Mikhail Gorbachev came to power. He introduced reforms and began a policy of openness with the West. In 1991, the Communist Party was declared illegal, and the Soviet Union broke up.

INDUSTRIALIZATION
Stalin introduced a series of Five-Year Plans to increase production of coal, steel, and power. The plans were successful for the country, but workers had little reward for their efforts and many were used as slave labour.

Posters showing muscular workers encouraged people to work hard.

This shows how collective farms were organized under Stalin. The collective included a school where children were educated, a factory, and a hospital. The collective had to send fixed deliveries of crops to the State.

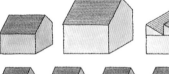

School, hospital, and factory

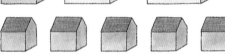

Workers' homes

Private plots for fruit, vegetables, and poultry

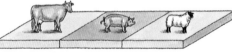

Grazing land for pigs, sheep, and cattle

Land for growing crops

JOSEPH STALIN
Born in poverty in Georgia, in the south-west of the Russian Empire, Joseph Stalin (1879-1953) was a follower of Lenin. After Lenin's death, Stalin seized power and destroyed his opponents. He formed a secret police force to arrest, torture, and execute millions of suspected enemies. These ruthless "purges" enabled Stalin to remain unchallenged as Soviet leader until his death.

COLLECTIVE FARM
Stalin wanted to get rid of all the old-fashioned peasant farms and increase productivity. He reorganized the land into *kolkhozy* (giant collective farms), controlled by the government. The government took the land and livestock of millions of *kulaks* (richer peasants); those who protested were sent to work in prison labour camps. Most of the collectives' products were exported, or sent to the government to feed the city workers.

ALEXANDRA KOLLONTAI
Communism was supposed to introduce equality into Soviet society. However, while women worked alongside men in heavy industry, they were not allowed to hold real power. But a woman named Alexandra Kollontai (1872-1952) did become a member of Stalin's government. She made many important speeches and wrote several articles about peace and women's rights.

WORLD WAR II

In 1941, German armies invaded the Soviet Union and reached the gates of Moscow, the capital. The Soviets resisted heroically. Stalingrad and Leningrad survived long and bitter sieges. New factories in the east began to produce advanced weapons, such as the T-34 tank, in large numbers. In 1943, Soviet armoured forces, led by Marshal Zhukov, fought and won the largest tank battle ever. But the Soviets paid a high price for victory. They suffered more military casualties than any other country in the war. More than 20 million people died.

SOVIET UNION

1917 Russian Revolution

1922 Soviet Union formed.

1924 Lenin dies and is replaced by Stalin.

1941-45 More than 20 million Soviets die in World War II.

1955 Warsaw Pact, an alliance of Communist states, created.

1962 Soviet Union builds missile bases on Cuba. US Navy blockades island. Soviet Union removes missiles.

1980 Soviet invasion of Afghanistan.

1988 Soviet troops withdraw from Afghanistan.

1991 Soviet Union breaks up as Lithuania, Latvia, and other republics declare their independence.

CHERNOBYL

In 1986 there was a major disaster at Chernobyl, near Kiev. A nuclear power plant exploded, killing at least 30 people and injuring hundreds more. Radioactive dust and smoke blew all over Europe and exposed thousands of people to contamination. Instead of keeping this disaster secret, the Soviets followed their new policy of *glasnost*, or openness, and warned the rest of the world of the danger.

SPACE RACE

On 4 October 1957, the whole world listened in amazement to a strange beeping sound that came from space. The Soviet Union had launched the first satellite, called *Sputnik 1*, into orbit around Earth. It was followed four years later by Yuri Gagarin (left), the first human in space.

COLLAPSE OF COMMUNISM

After his appointment in 1985, Soviet premier Mikhail Gorbachev introduced policies of *glasnost* (openness) and *perestroika* (economic reform) to improve the poor state of the Soviet economy. People under Soviet control began to demand more freedom. The Communist Party ceased to be the only political party. In Romania, the Communist dictator, Nicolae Ceausescu, was overthrown and executed in 1989. In the Soviet Union, anti-Communist demonstrations took place. People destroyed statues of Lenin and other Communist leaders. In Moscow, the statue of Felix Dzerzhinsky, head of the hated KGB, or security police, was toppled.

GORBACHEV AND YELTSIN

Throughout the late 1980s, Soviet people suffered from terrible economic hardship. Many thought that the changes brought about by Gorbachev's policy of *perestroika* were too slow. Mikhail Gorbachev (right) resigned in 1991. Boris Yeltsin (left) became the leader of the new Russian Federation. The Soviet Union broke up as the republics formed their own governments. Yeltsin resigned in 1999, and was replaced by Vladimir Putin who served as president until 2008.

Find out more

CAUCASUS REPUBLICS
COLD WAR
COMMUNISM
RUSSIAN REVOLUTION
WOMEN'S RIGHTS
WORLD WAR II

SPACE FLIGHT

SPACE SHUTTLE

Between 1981 and 2010, America's space shuttles made more than 130 flights to Earth orbit, carrying a crew of several astronauts. They took off like rockets, but landed like aircraft. Their cargo bay was large enough for a satellite. Two shuttles were destroyed in accidents – *Challenger* in 1986, and *Columbia* in 2003.

The booster rockets broke away at a height of about 47 km (29 miles). They were recovered from the ocean and used again.

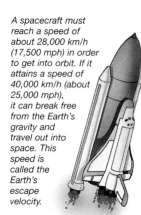

A spacecraft must reach a speed of about 28,000 km/h (17,500 mph) in order to get into orbit. If it attains a speed of 40,000 km/h (about 25,000 mph), it can break free from the Earth's gravity and travel out into space. This speed is called the Earth's escape velocity.

A large fuel tank fed the main engines. It broke away at a height of 110 km (70 miles), just eight minutes after launch.

Smaller engines guided the shuttle into orbit.

UNTIL THE MIDDLE OF last century stories about space flight were found only in science fiction books. Today, rockets blast off regularly. They place satellites in Earth orbit, send astronauts and cargo to the International Space Station, and launch spacecraft to explore the solar system. Space flight became a reality after the development of powerful rocket engines, capable of giving a spacecraft or satellite the speed it needs to reach Earth orbit. For its journey from Earth into space, a spacecraft is attached to the top of a launch vehicle (rocket), which is powered by rocket engines and carries huge amounts of fuel. The exploration of the solar system is one of the most exciting aspects of space flight. Humans have only travelled as far as the Moon, a journey of just three days. However, robotic spacecraft have travelled for years to explore the distant planets, returning amazing images and information collected by their cameras and instruments.

SPACE ROCKET
Spacecraft are carried into space by launch vehicles, or rockets. The launch rocket consists of several parts called stages, each with its own rocket engine. Each stage breaks away as it uses up its fuel, eventually leaving only the spacecraft to fly in space. Spacecraft that return to Earth use a small engine to slow them down until they fall out of orbit.

At the launch pad, a tall gantry enabled astronauts to enter the shuttle. The shuttle's rocket engines fired, and the spacecraft lifted off to begin its journey into space.

SOYUZ SPACECRAFT
The Russian Soyuz spacecraft can carry three cosmonauts. It is launched on a rocket and is used to ferry people to and from the International Space Station. The habitable parts are the Orbital Module and the Descent Module. The cosmonauts travel back to Earth in the Descent Module. The Orbital and Service modules separate from the Descent Module and burn up in the atmosphere.

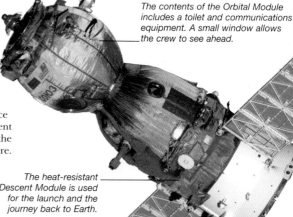

The contents of the Orbital Module includes a toilet and communications equipment. A small window allows the crew to see ahead.

The heat-resistant Descent Module is used for the launch and the journey back to Earth.

As the spacecraft rotates, the solar panels point toward the Sun.

The Service Module houses the temperature control systems, an electric power supply, and long-range radio telecommunications.

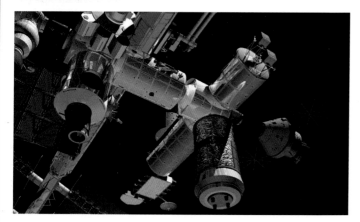

ORION SPACECRAFT
The Orion spacecraft is expected to take its first astronauts into space in about 2014. It is NASA's replacement for the Space Shuttle and will be launched by an Ares rocket. At first, it will be used to go to and from the International Space Station. It is pictured here about to dock on the right. Later it may take astronauts as far as the Moon.

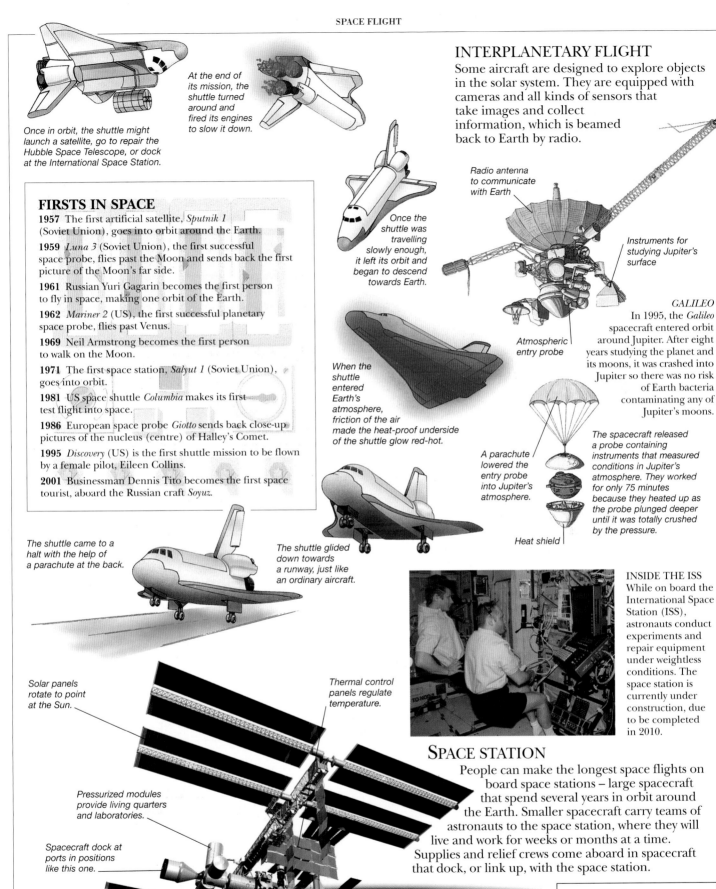

Once in orbit, the shuttle might launch a satellite, go to repair the Hubble Space Telescope, or dock at the International Space Station.

At the end of its mission, the shuttle turned around and fired its engines to slow it down.

INTERPLANETARY FLIGHT

Some aircraft are designed to explore objects in the solar system. They are equipped with cameras and all kinds of sensors that take images and collect information, which is beamed back to Earth by radio.

Once the shuttle was travelling slowly enough, it left its orbit and began to descend towards Earth.

Radio antenna to communicate with Earth

Instruments for studying Jupiter's surface

GALILEO
In 1995, the *Galileo* spacecraft entered orbit around Jupiter. After eight years studying the planet and its moons, it was crashed into Jupiter so there was no risk of Earth bacteria contaminating any of Jupiter's moons.

Atmospheric entry probe

When the shuttle entered Earth's atmosphere, friction of the air made the heat-proof underside of the shuttle glow red-hot.

A parachute lowered the entry probe into Jupiter's atmosphere.

The spacecraft released a probe containing instruments that measured conditions in Jupiter's atmosphere. They worked for only 75 minutes because they heated up as the probe plunged deeper until it was totally crushed by the pressure.

Heat shield

FIRSTS IN SPACE

1957 The first artificial satellite, *Sputnik 1* (Soviet Union), goes into orbit around the Earth.

1959 *Luna 3* (Soviet Union), the first successful space probe, flies past the Moon and sends back the first picture of the Moon's far side.

1961 Russian Yuri Gagarin becomes the first person to fly in space, making one orbit of the Earth.

1962 *Mariner 2* (US), the first successful planetary space probe, flies past Venus.

1969 Neil Armstrong becomes the first person to walk on the Moon.

1971 The first space station, *Salyut 1* (Soviet Union), goes into orbit.

1981 US space shuttle *Columbia* makes its first test flight into space.

1986 European space probe *Giotto* sends back close-up pictures of the nucleus (centre) of Halley's Comet.

1995 *Discovery* (US) is the first shuttle mission to be flown by a female pilot, Eileen Collins.

2001 Businessman Dennis Tito becomes the first space tourist, aboard the Russian craft *Soyuz*.

The shuttle came to a halt with the help of a parachute at the back.

The shuttle glided down towards a runway, just like an ordinary aircraft.

INSIDE THE ISS
While on board the International Space Station (ISS), astronauts conduct experiments and repair equipment under weightless conditions. The space station is currently under construction, due to be completed in 2010.

Solar panels rotate to point at the Sun.

Thermal control panels regulate temperature.

SPACE STATION

People can make the longest space flights on board space stations – large spacecraft that spend several years in orbit around the Earth. Smaller spacecraft carry teams of astronauts to the space station, where they will live and work for weeks or months at a time. Supplies and relief crews come aboard in spacecraft that dock, or link up, with the space station.

Pressurized modules provide living quarters and laboratories.

Spacecraft dock at ports in positions like this one.

International Space Station

Radiators turn edge-on to the Sun to lose excess heat.

Remote sensing instruments look down on Earth.

Find out more
ASTRONAUTS
and space travel
COMETS AND METEORS
GRAVITY
MOON
PLANETS
ROCKETS AND MISSILES

SPAIN

Spain is situated on the Iberian Peninsula in the southwest corner of Europe. France and the Bay of Biscay are to the north, the Mediterranean Sea to the east, the Strait of Gibraltar and Africa are to the south, and Portugal is to the west.

SPAIN SHARES THE IBERIAN PENINSULA with Portugal. It is the fourth largest country in Europe, and both its landscape and its people are varied. The centre of Spain is a hot, dry plateau with snowcapped mountain ranges to the north and south. The southern region of Spain contains Europe's only desert. Spain has some large minority groups, including Catalans in the north-east, Galicians in the north-west, and Basques in the north-centre. Most of the rest are Castilian Spanish. The country was torn apart by a vicious civil war from 1936-39, and right-wing dictators ruled Spain for much of the 20th century. However, in the mid-1970s the country formed democratic governments. This change allowed Spain to join the European Community, now known as the European Union (EU), in 1986 and to benefit from the higher standard of living in the rest of Europe. Once reliant on farming and fishing for its income, Spain has experienced economic growth since joining the EU. The economy is now dominated by tourism.

In many parts of Spain the donkey cart is still a common form of transport.

FLAMENCO
Flamenco music and dance was developed by gypsies in Andalucia, in the south of Spain. Flamenco songs deal with the entire range of human emotion, from despair to ecstasy. Dancers dress in traditional costume and are usually accompanied by guitars and their own hand-held percussion instrument called castanets. The men's steps are intricate, with toe and heel clicking; women's dancing depends on the grace of the hands and body, rather than on footwork.

TOURISM
More than 50 million tourists from all over the world visit Spain. Tourism employs 10 per cent of the work-force and is a major source of income. Tourists come to enjoy the sun, as the climate is mild in the winter and hot in the summer. The country boasts fine beaches, and its old towns are full of interesting buildings and fine works of art.

In Spain, bullfighting is a national sport. It is very popular, but many people consider it to be unnecessarily cruel. This bullfighter is shown wearing a typically elaborate costume.

RELIGION
The Roman Catholic Church plays an important part in the lives of most Spanish people. Nearly everybody is a member of the church and attends mass on Sundays. The priest is an influential member of the community, and the church is a centre of local activities.

BULLFIGHTING
In Spain, men fight with bulls to entertain crowds. The matador, or bullfighter, stands in the bullring and teases the bull into a rage by waving a red cape. When the bull charges, the matador sticks long, pointed barbs into the bull's shoulders. Once it is exhausted, the matador uses a sword to kill the bull. It is still difficult for women to break into the sport.

Old-fashioned horse-drawn carriages ferry tourists around a number of Spanish cities. These carriages (left) are pictured in the Plaza de España, Seville.

KING JUAN CARLOS

The Spanish Civil War of 1936-39 resulted in a dictatorship by General Franco. In 1975 Franco died and was succeeded by King Juan Carlos, grandson of the last Spanish king. Under his rule, Spain became a multi-party democracy, and attained membership of the EU.

Juan Carlos and Princess Sophia of Greece (right) were married in Athens on May 14, 1962.

SEVILLE

Seville is a major port as well as an important industrial, cultural, and tourist centre. With the discovery of the New World, Seville entered its greatest period of prosperity, being the chief port of trade with the new colonies until 1718 when it was superseded by Cádiz. The city is the capital of bullfighting in Spain and a centre of the Andalusian gypsies, famed for their songs and dances.

Regional dishes include salt-cured ham (above), Spanish omelette (left), and mussels in an onion and garlic sauce (below).

The splendid gardens and architecture of the Moorish palace in Granada

GRANADA

North African Muslims, known as the Moors, once ruled most of Spain. The town of Granada was the capital of their kingdom, and the Alhambra fortress overlooking the town enclosed a magnificent Moorish palace which remains to this day. The palace and its gardens (left) gradually fell into ruin after the Moors were defeated in 1492, but they have since been restored to their former glory.

SPANISH GUITAR

The guitar originated in Spain in the 16th century. It plays a central role in flamenco, traditionally accompanying the singer. The flamenco guitar developed from the modern classical guitar, and evolved in Spain in the 19th century. Flamenco guitars have a lighter, shallower construction and a thickened plate below the soundhole, used to tap rhythms. Today, flamenco guitarists often perform solo.

The classical guitar is Spain's national instrument.

REGIONAL FOOD

Spain boasts a variety of regional dishes, the most famous of which are paella and tapas. Paella is a classic dish from the Valencia region, where rice is grown. It consists of a variety of meat, fish, fresh vegetables, and saffron-flavoured rice. Tapas, sometimes known as pinchos, are small snacks that originated in Andalusia in the 19th century to accompany sherry. Stemming from a bartenders' practice of covering a glass with a saucer or tapa (cover) to keep out flies, the custom progressed to food being placed on a platter to accompany a drink. Tapas range from cold meats or cheeses to elaborately prepared hot dishes of seafood, meat, or vegetables. A tapa is a single serving, whereas a *ración* serves two or three.

The climax of Pamplona's (left) annual fiesta, Los Sanfermines, is when bulls stampede through the city.

FIESTAS

More than 3,000 fiestas take place each year in Spain. On any day of the year there is a fiesta happening somewhere - usually more than one. Fiestas are a means for a village, town, or city to honour either its patron saint, the Virgin Mother, or the changing seasons. Fiestas can take the form of processions, bull-running (above), fireworks, re-enacted battles, some ancestral rite, or a mass pilgrimage to a rural shrine. Whatever the pretext, a fiesta is a chance for everybody to take a break from normal life and let off steam, with celebrations going on around the clock.

PAINTING

Many great artists lived and worked in Spain. Diego Velasquez (1599-1660) was famous for his pictures of the Spanish royal family. Several modern painters, including Pablo Picasso (1881-1973) and Salvador Dali (1904-89), were born in Spain.

Velasquez included himself as the painter in his picture The Maids of Honour.

INDUSTRY

Farming and fishing were once the basis of the Spanish economy. The country has now developed additional industries including textiles, metals, shipbuilding, car production, and tourism. Iron, coal, and other minerals are mined in the Cordillera Cantabrica in the north of Spain. In the 1980s, many foreign-owned electronics and high-tech industries began to locate in the country. Major agricultural products include cereals, olives, grapes for wine, and citrus fruits, especially oranges from around Seville.

In the coastal towns of Spain many people work in fishing or in the related industries of boatbuilding and netmaking.

BARCELONA

The city of Barcelona lies on the Mediterranean coast of eastern Spain. It is the second largest city in the country (Madrid is the largest) and is a bustling port of almost two million people. Barcelona is the capital of the province of Catalonia. It lies at the heart of a large industrial area and was the site of the 1992 Olympic Games. Its people speak Catalan, a language that sounds similar to Spanish but has many differences. The city is renowned for its beautiful architecture and many historic buildings.

The cathedral of Sagrada Familia in Barcelona was designed by Antonio Gaudi and begun in 1882. It is still not finished today.

GIBRALTAR

Spain claims that Gibraltar, at its southern tip, is Spanish. However, since 1713 this rocky outcrop has been a British colony. Gibraltar is just 6.5 sq km (2.5 sq miles) in area. Most of the 28,000 inhabitants work in tourism.

The Rock of Gibraltar towers over the entrance to the Mediterranean Sea.

OLIVES

The deep fertile soils and warm climate of southern and eastern Spain are ideal for olive cultivation. The country is one of the world's leading olive producers. Most of the crop is made into olive oil.

Find out more

EUROPEAN UNION
EUROPE, HISTORY OF
PAINTERS
TRADE AND INDUSTRY

Madrid

Spain's largest city, Madrid, lies at the centre of the country, surrounded by a broad plain. Madrid has been Spain's capital city since the 16th century. Recently it has become an important centre for commerce and industry. The Gran Via (Great Way), shown here, highlights some of the city's most beautiful architecture, and is also a bustling street with many shops, hotels, and theatres.

Volcano	Mountain	Ancient monument	Capital city	Large city/town	Small city/town

POPULATION
In the first half of the 20th century, most of the Spanish population lived in villages or small towns, scattered around the country. Today, tourism and industry have drawn most of the population to the cities and the coastal areas.

STATISTICS
Area: 499,440 sq km (192,834 sq miles)
Population: 40,525,000
Capital: Madrid
Languages: Spanish, Catalan, Galician, Basque
Religions: Roman Catholic
Currency: Euro
Main Occupations: Manufacturing, shipbuilding, fishing, agriculture
Main Exports: Textiles, chemicals, ships, cars, fish, fruit and vegetables
Main Imports: Oil, natural gas

CORDILLERA CANTABRICA
These rugged, forested mountains rise on Spain's Atlantic coast. They form the northern edge of the Meseta.

MESETA
Much of this vast plateau of ancient rock is covered with dry, dusty high plains. It has thin soils and is mainly used to graze sheep.

PYRENEES
These majestic mountains form a natural boundary with France.

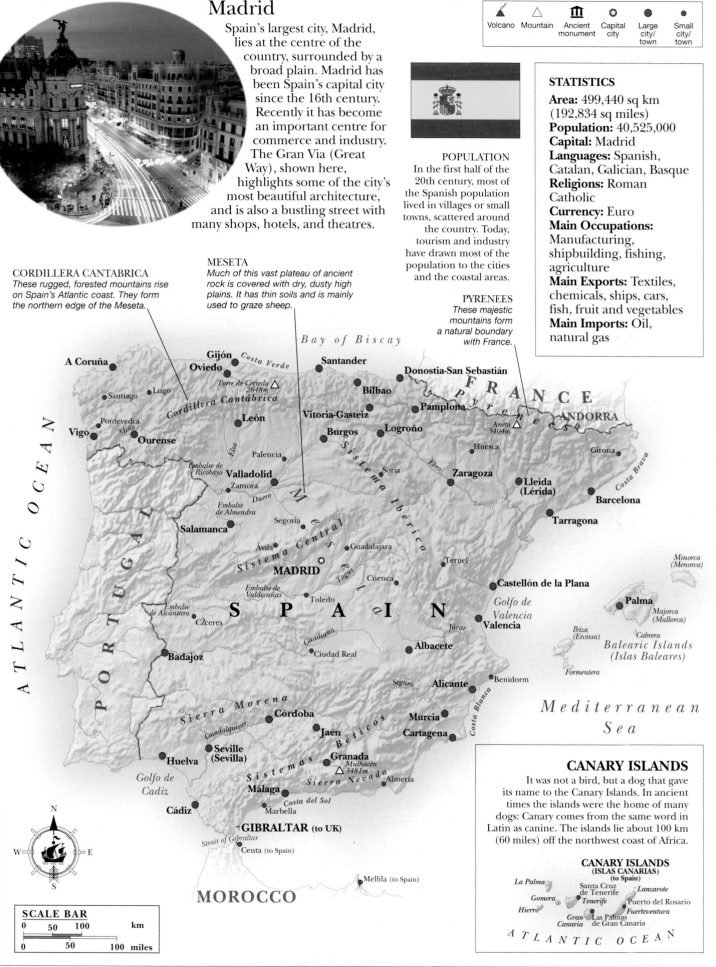

CANARY ISLANDS
It was not a bird, but a dog that gave its name to the Canary Islands. In ancient times the islands were the home of many dogs: Canary comes from the same word in Latin as canine. The islands lie about 100 km (60 miles) off the northwest coast of Africa.

CANARY ISLANDS
(ISLAS CANARIAS)
(to Spain)

La Palma · Santa Cruz de Tenerife · Lanzarote
Gomera · Tenerife · Puerto del Rosario
Hierro · Gran Canaria · Fuerteventura
Las Palmas de Gran Canaria

ATLANTIC OCEAN

Map labels

A Coruña · Gijón · *Costa Verde* · Santander · Donostia-San Sebastián · *Bay of Biscay* · FRANCE
Santiago · Lugo · Oviedo · *Torre de Cerredo 2648m* · Bilbao · Pamplona · ANDORRA
Vigo · Pontevedra · *Miño* · León · Vitoria-Gasteiz · Logroño · *Aneto 3404m* · Huesca · Girona
Ourense · *Cordillera Cantábrica* · *Esla* · Burgos · Soria · *Sistema Ibérico* · Zaragoza · Lleida (Lérida) · *Costa Brava*
Palencia · *Ebro* · Barcelona
Embalse de Ricobayo · Valladolid · *Duero* · Tarragona
Zamora · *Meseta*
Embalse de Almendra · Segovia
Salamanca · *Sistema Central* · Ávila · Guadalajara · Teruel · *Minorca (Menorca)*
MADRID · *Tagus* · Cuenca · Castellón de la Plana · Palma
Embalse de Valdecañas · Toledo · *Golfo de Valencia* · *Majorca (Mallorca)*
Embalse de Alcántara · Cáceres · *Ibiza (Eivissa)* · *Cabrera*
SPAIN · *Balearic Islands (Islas Baleares)*
Guadiana · Ciudad Real · Albacete · *Júcar* · Valencia · *Formentera*
Badajoz
Segura · Alicante · Benidorm
Sierra Morena · Córdoba · *Béticos* · Murcia · *Costa Blanca* · *Mediterranean Sea*
Guadalquivir · Jaén · *Sistemas* · Cartagena
Seville (Sevilla) · Granada · *Mulhacén 3481m*
Huelva · *Sierra Nevada* · Almería
Golfo de Cadiz · Málaga · *Costa del Sol*
Cádiz · Marbella
GIBRALTAR (to UK)
Strait of Gibraltar · Ceuta (to Spain)
MOROCCO · Mellila (to Spain)
PORTUGAL · ATLANTIC OCEAN

SCALE BAR
0 50 100 km
0 50 100 miles

N · W · E · S

SPIDERS AND SCORPIONS

FEW ANIMALS ARE MORE FEARED but less understood than spiders and scorpions. We often call these scurrying little creatures insects, but they really belong to the group of animals called arachnids, along with ticks and mites. Insects have six legs; spiders and other arachnids have eight legs. There are about 40,000 kinds of spiders and 1,400 kinds of scorpions. All are carnivorous (meat eaters). Scorpions hunt down their prey and kill it with their pincers. If the prey is big, or struggles, the scorpion uses the sting in its tail. Many spiders capture insects by spinning a silken web. The silk of some webs is stronger than steel wire of the same thickness. Not all spiders spin webs, however; some catch their prey by dropping a net of silk onto it. A few spiders, such as the trap-door spider, rush out at their victim from a burrow. Some scorpions and several spiders are dangerous to humans, including the Australian funnel web spider and the Durango scorpion of Mexico.

WEB
Spiders make webs with a special silken thread from glands at the rear end of the body. Tubes called spinnerets squeeze out the thread like toothpaste. The silk hardens as the spider's legs pull it out.

GARDEN SPIDER

Thousands of spiders live in our houses and gardens, feeding on flies, gnats, and moths. The common garden spider spins a beautiful, complicated web called an orb web, often between the stems of plants. Some spiders lie in wait for their prey in the centre of the web; others hide nearby. Many orb-web spiders spin a new web almost every day.

The female black widow has a deadly bite.

SPIDERLINGS
Young spiders are called spiderlings. They hatch from eggs inside a silken cocoon and feed on stores of yolk in their bodies. After a few days, weeks, or months, depending on the weather, they cut their way out of the cocoon and begin to hunt for food.

BLACK WIDOW
The female black widow spider is so named because it sometimes kills its mate. This spider is also one of the few spiders that can kill humans. The female black widow shown here is standing near its eggs, which are wrapped in a silken egg sac or cocoon.

TARANTULA
True tarantulas are shy spiders which live mainly in burrows. False tarantulas, such as the big spider shown here, include various large, hairy hunting spiders from North and South America. They are also called bird or monkey spiders. Their bite is painful to humans, but it is less poisonous than the bite of smaller spiders such as the black widow.

FOOD
Spiders eat animal prey. Their most common victims are insects, worms, sow bugs, and other spiders. The spider's venom subdues or paralyses the prey while the spider wraps it up in a silk bag to eat later.

YOUNG SCORPIONS
Scorpions are born fully formed. At first the female scorpion carries the young on its back, where they are well protected from predators. After the young have moulted (shed their skin) for the first time, they leave their mother to fend for themselves.

Scorpion's large pincers are called pedipalps. They seize, crush, and tear the prey, then pass it to the jaws.

Mother carries the young on her back.

Imperial scorpion

The sting is connected to twin poison glands at the end of the tail.

SCORPION

Scorpions live mainly in warm regions, lurking beneath rocks or in cracks or burrows. Most feed at night, ambushing or hunting down their prey. They feed mainly on insects and spiders. The scorpion uses the sting at the end of the tail in self-defence, as well as to subdue its prey.

Find out more
ANIMALS
DESERT WILDLIFE
SNAKES

SPORTS

EVERYONE WHO takes part in a sport does so for his or her own individual reasons. Early-morning joggers feel good by keeping fit and trying to beat a personal best time. Backpackers enjoy the fresh air and like to learn outdoor survival skills. And in a sports competition, no experience can match the sensation of winning. Sports are games and activities that involve physical ability or skill. Competitive sports have fixed rules and are organized so that everyone has an equal opportunity to succeed.

Many of today's sports developed from activities that were necessary for survival, such as archery, running, and wrestling. Some sports, such as basketball and volleyball, are modern inventions. And as the equipment improves, the rules change to ensure that no competitor has an advantage. Sponsorship and television are now major influences on sports. Leading players become millionaires, and most popular events have huge international audiences.

Many ancient sports are still played today but some, such as foot-wrestling, have long been forgotten.

Officials make sure each game lasts the same time.

Players must wear special sports shoes to avoid slipping on the floor.

EQUIPMENT AND UNIFORMS
Uniforms are important in team sports. They help players and spectators quickly recognize fellow team members and tell them apart from the opposing side. Underneath the basic shirt and shorts or jersey and trousers, players wear protective gear, especially in games such as football and hockey. Shoes are designed to suit the playing surface – rubber-soled for a basketball court, for example, and cleated (spiked) for grass. Other equipment includes a standard ball and, for some sports, bats or rackets.

FIELD
The rules of every team sport include standard sizes for the field or court, its markings, and other features such as goal posts. There may be more than one standard if the game is played by both adults and young people. For example, the dimensions of the free-throw lane and the backboard are different for high school, college, and professional basketball. The rules of some sports, such as baseball and soccer, give the largest and smallest sizes allowed for the playing area.

The ring of the basket stands 3 m (10 ft) above the floor.

Basketball court

TEAM SPORTS
In a team sport such as basketball, everybody must co-operate, or work together, in order to win. The stars in a team sport are usually the attacking players who score points or kick for a goal. However, if every player tried to be a star, there would be no one to play a defensive role and prevent the opposing team from scoring. So every player on the team has a special job, and each plays an equal part in a successful game.

Basketball hand signals

Personal foul

One free throw

Time out

RULES
Each team sport has its own rules so that everyone taking part knows how to play the game. Referees, umpires, or other judges stand at the edge of the playing area and make sure that the players obey the rules. In some sports, they use a loud whistle to stop and start play. They also signal with their hands or with flags to let the players know their decisions.

COMPETITION

In individual competition, contestants compete alone. Some try to beat a record; some measure their performance against other contestants. Players compete "one-on-one" in sports such as fencing, judo, and tennis. Several contestants compete together in racing sports such as horse racing or the 100-metre dash. In some sports, such as alpine skiing and archery, contestants compete separately to record the best timing or scores. In other sports, such as diving or gymnastics, judges decide the scores.

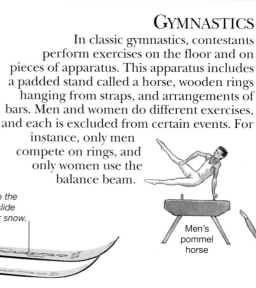

Skis enable the wearer to slide swiftly over snow.

GYMNASTICS

In classic gymnastics, contestants perform exercises on the floor and on pieces of apparatus. This apparatus includes a padded stand called a horse, wooden rings hanging from straps, and arrangements of bars. Men and women do different exercises, and each is excluded from certain events. For instance, only men compete on rings, and only women use the balance beam.

Men's rings

Men's pommel horse

Women's balance beam

Women's uneven parallel bars

Men's horse vault

Men's parallel bars

Women's floor exercises

COMBAT SPORTS

Modern combat sports originated in the fighting sports of Ancient Greece, although people wrestled for sport 15,000 years earlier. Various styles of unarmed combat evolved – boxing and wrestling in the West and jujitsu in the East. The martial arts, such as judo, karate, aikido, and tae kwon do, come from jujitsu.

Archery target

TARGET SPORTS

Firing at targets began with archery, or bow-and-arrow practice, about 500 years ago. In modern archery, competitors shoot a series of arrows at a target from a range of distances. They score ten points for arrows that hit the centre, or bull, and get lower scores the closer the arrow is to the edge of the target. Another target sport is shooting, in which competitors fire rifles or pistols at targets.

WHEEL SPORTS

Competitions on wheels include everything from roller-skating to Grand Prix automobile racing. Physical skill and fitness are most important in unpowered wheel sports such as skateboarding, cycling, and bicycle motocross.

AIR SPORTS

Flying, gliding, and skydiving provide some of the greatest thrills in sport. Pilots race aeroplanes and, in aerobatics, perform manoeuvres. Glider, balloon, and hang glider pilots use warm air currents to move around without power. Skydiving parachutists "free fall" for thousands of metres, linking hands in formation before opening their parachutes to land safely.

In parasailing, a tow vehicle lifts the participant into the air with the aid of a special parachute.

ANIMAL SPORTS

Greyhounds, pigeons, camels, and sled dogs compete in races, but horse racing is the best-known animal sport. Horse racing takes place over jumps as well as on flat ground. In harness racing, the horse pulls its driver around a track in a two-wheeled "sulky", like the chariot of ancient times. Other horse sports include show jumping, eventing, dressage, and polo.

> **Find out more**
> CRICKET
> DANCE
> FOOTBALL AND RUGBY
> HEALTH AND FITNESS
> LUNGS AND BREATHING
> OLYMPIC GAMES

STARS

IF YOU LOOK AT THE SKY ON A CLEAR dark night, it is possible to see up to about 3,000 of the billions of stars in our galaxy. Although they appear as tiny dots, they are, like our closest star the Sun, huge, hot balls of gas, deep in space. Some stars are gigantic – if placed in the centre of our solar system, they would stretch beyond the Earth's orbit. Others are far smaller, about the size of our planet, and give off only faint light. Stars are unimaginably distant. Light from even our nearest star (apart from the Sun) takes more than four years to reach us.

Ancient skywatchers noticed that stars seem to form patterns in the sky. They imagined that the shapes represented pictures called constellations. These constellations, such as the Great Bear, are still useful for learning the positions of the stars. Astronomers identify the brightest stars with individual names, or by their constellation combined with a Greek letter, such as alpha, beta, or gamma. For instance, the second brightest star in the constellation of Cygnus (the Swan) is Beta Cygni, or Albireo.

BLACK HOLE
The remains of a very massive star may collapse into a tiny volume, forming a black hole. The gravitational pull of a black hole is so strong that matter and radiation, such as light, cannot escape from it.

NEUTRON STAR
A supernova may leave a neutron star – a spinning ball with a mass greater than the Sun's, yet only about 16 km (10 miles) across. As a neutron star spins, it sends out a powerful beam of radiation.

SUPERNOVA
When a massive star dies, it collapses in less than one second. This is followed by a colossal explosion called a supernova. The explosion produces other substances which scatter through space in an expanding gas cloud.

RED SUPERGIANT
Some dying stars grow into huge, cool stars called red supergiants, which can be up to 1,000 times the diameter of the Sun. A red supergiant contains many substances formed by nuclear reactions.

Temperature at centre of red supergiant is about 10 billion°C (18 billion°F).

A group of growing stars in a cluster.

The gas and dust in a mini-globule pack closer together, and it spins faster and gets hotter. The mini-globule has become a protostar (a young star).

Death of a massive star

STAR STARTS TO SHINE
When the centre of the protostar reaches about 10 million°C (18 million°F), nuclear reactions begin which slowly change hydrogen into helium. The protostar begins to shine, and has become a true star.

The planetary nebula survives only for a few thousand years.

White dwarf

NEBULA
Stars are born from great clouds of dust particles and hydrogen gas, called nebulae. The word nebula (plural nebulae) comes from the Latin for "mist".

BIRTH OF A STAR
Gravity pulls parts of a nebula into blobs called globules. These get smaller and spin faster, finally breaking up into a few hundred "mini-globules". Each of these will eventually become a star.

Death of a star about the size of the Sun

RED GIANT
As a sunlike star runs low in hydrogen, it swells into a cooler, larger star called a red giant. This will happen to our own Sun in about 5,000 million years.

LIFE AND DEATH OF A STAR
Throughout the universe, new stars form and old stars die. The birthplaces of stars are clouds of gas and dust scattered through space. Stars the size of the Sun shine for about 10 billion years. The most massive stars (which contain 100 times as much matter as the Sun) shine very brightly, but live for a shorter time – only about 10 million years.

PLANETARY NEBULA
At the end of its life, a red giant blows off its outer layers of gas. These make a glowing shell called a planetary nebula, which eventually disperses. At the centre is a white dwarf, a tiny hot star that is the burned out core of the red giant. It will outlast the nebula by billions of years.

TWINKLING STARLIGHT
Nuclear reactions inside a star heat the star up from the centre, causing it to emit light and heat from its surface. A star appears to flicker or twinkle because its light passes through the Earth's atmosphere, which is a constantly shifting blanket of gases. Seen from a travelling spacecraft, stars shine steadily because there is no surrounding atmosphere to disturb the path of the light.

STAR BRIGHTNESS
A star's brightness is called its magnitude. The brightest magnitudes are the smallest numbers, so magnitude 1 stars are brighter than magnitude 2 stars. How bright a star looks depends on its distance and how much light it emits.

VARIABLE STARS
Many stars, called variable stars, appear to vary in brightness. Some stars constantly swell and shrink, becoming alternately fainter and brighter. Other variables are really two stars that circle each other and block off each other's light from time to time.

Double stars circle around each other. When one star is in front of the other, the brightness dims. When both stars can be seen, the brightness increases.

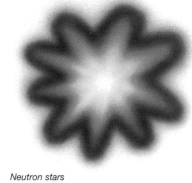

Some variable stars are produced by exploding stars. The explosion makes the star appear much brighter than usual for a period that can last from a few days to a few years.

Neutron stars (pulsars) are the smallest stars. They have about the same mass as the Sun, but are only about 16 km (10 miles) in diameter.

White dwarfs are small stars at the end of their life; some are smaller than the Earth.

Yellow dwarfs, or medium-sized stars, are about the same size as the Sun.

CONSTELLATIONS
Modern astronomers group stars into 88 constellations. Each has a Latin name, such as Ursa Major (the Great Bear) or Corona Australis (the Southern Crown). The "sun signs" of astrology have the same names as the 12 constellations of the zodiac – the band of sky along which the Sun and planets appear to pass during the course of a year.

When the constellation of Orion (above) is in the night sky, it can be seen from anywhere on Earth.

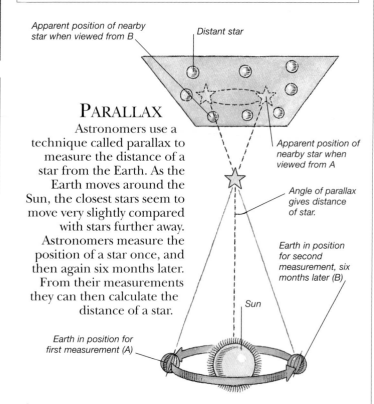

Apparent position of nearby star when viewed from B

Distant star

PARALLAX
Astronomers use a technique called parallax to measure the distance of a star from the Earth. As the Earth moves around the Sun, the closest stars seem to move very slightly compared with stars further away. Astronomers measure the position of a star once, and then again six months later. From their measurements they can then calculate the distance of a star.

Apparent position of nearby star when viewed from A

Angle of parallax gives distance of star.

Earth in position for second measurement, six months later (B)

Sun

Earth in position for first measurement (A)

STAR QUALITIES
The colour of a star's light corresponds to the surface temperature of the star: red stars are the coolest, blue stars are the hottest. A star's brightness (the amount of energy it gives out) is linked to its mass (the amount of material it contains): heavier stars are brighter than lighter stars. Astronomers can use the colour and brightness of the light emitted from a star to help calculate its size and distance from the Earth.

Giants have diameters between 100 and 1,000 times larger than that of the Sun.

Supergiants are the largest stars, with diameters up to 1,000 times that of the Sun.

Find out more
ASTRONOMY
BLACK HOLES
GRAVITY
NAVIGATION
PLANETS
SUN
TELESCOPES
UNIVERSE

STATUE OF LIBERTY

ON A BRONZE PLAQUE inside the base of the Statue of Liberty are the words of a poem written by Emma Lazarus in 1883. Part of it reads: "Give me your tired, your poor,/ Your huddled masses yearning to breathe free./ The wretched refuse of your teeming shore./ Send these, the homeless, tempest-tost to me./ I lift my lamp beside the golden door!" The "masses" were the people fleeing poverty and oppression in Europe; the "golden door", the opportunity to start a new life in the United States. The French historian Edouard de Laboulaye planned the statue in 1865 to symbolize liberty and to commemorate the friendship of France with the United States. It was designed by Frédéric Auguste Bartholdi and built by the company owned by Alexandre Gustave Eiffel, whose famous Eiffel Tower dominates the skyline of Paris.

STATUE OF LIBERTY

Supported by four steel columns with a framework of iron, the copper-covered Statue of Liberty represents a woman dressed in a long classical robe, standing 46 m (151 ft) high. The head measures 3 m by 5 m (10 ft by 17 ft) the right arm holding the torch is 13 m (42 ft) long. The torch at the top of the statue is 93 m (305 ft) above the water.

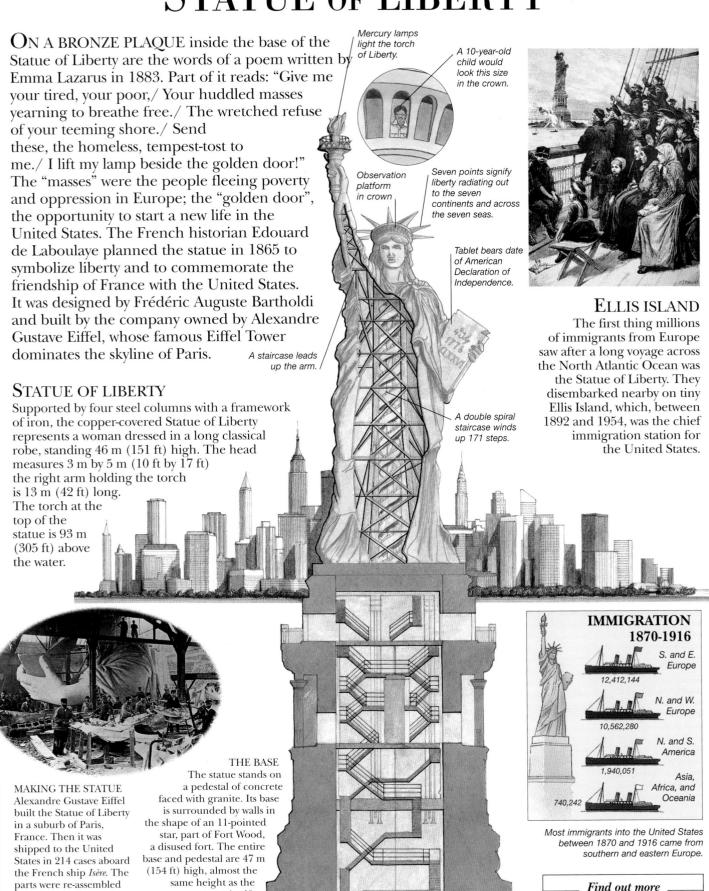

Mercury lamps light the torch of Liberty.

A 10-year-old child would look this size in the crown.

Observation platform in crown

Seven points signify liberty radiating out to the seven continents and across the seven seas.

Tablet bears date of American Declaration of Independence.

A staircase leads up the arm.

A double spiral staircase winds up 171 steps.

ELLIS ISLAND

The first thing millions of immigrants from Europe saw after a long voyage across the North Atlantic Ocean was the Statue of Liberty. They disembarked nearby on tiny Ellis Island, which, between 1892 and 1954, was the chief immigration station for the United States.

THE BASE

The statue stands on a pedestal of concrete faced with granite. Its base is surrounded by walls in the shape of an 11-pointed star, part of Fort Wood, a disused fort. The entire base and pedestal are 47 m (154 ft) high, almost the same height as the statue itself.

Visitors enter here and take a lift to the base of the statue.

MAKING THE STATUE

Alexandre Gustave Eiffel built the Statue of Liberty in a suburb of Paris, France. Then it was shipped to the United States in 214 cases aboard the French ship *Isère*. The parts were re-assembled in New York.

IMMIGRATION 1870-1916

S. and E. Europe	12,412,144
N. and W. Europe	10,562,280
N. and S. America	1,940,051
Asia, Africa, and Oceania	740,242

Most immigrants into the United States between 1870 and 1916 came from southern and eastern Europe.

Find out more

UNITED STATES OF AMERICA
UNITED STATES, HISTORY OF

STONE AGE

MORE THAN TWO MILLION YEARS AGO, stone was the most valuable raw material known to people. They made stone tools and weapons, usually from flint. These early people were called hominins, and were more apelike than us. They gradually learned to make specialized implements, such as knife blades. Stone Age people moved constantly, looking for hunting areas and setting up camps in small groups. A few groups lived in caves during the coldest seasons. They gathered fruits, berries, and roots, and hunted wild animals. By the start of the Mesolithic Age (Middle Stone Age; 15,000 years ago) many types of larger animals had died out. Mesolithic people, who were "modern people" (*Homo sapiens*) like us, used new stone-edged tools to fish and hunt deer and wild pigs. About 10,000 years ago some Neolithic (New Stone) Age people learned how to domesticate animals and grow crops. They settled on farms.

c. 2,500,000 BCE Palaeolithic Age begins.

c. 2,000,000 BCE Hominins make the first stone tools.

c. 1,500,000 BCE First hand axe.

c. 125,000 BCE Ice Age retreats; people return to Europe, hunt large animals.

c. 75,000 BCE People use fire and bury their dead.

c. 20,000 BCE Spear thrower invented. Also harpoon, bow and arrows, sewing, and cave painting.

c. 12,500 BCE Mesolithic Age.

c. 9500 BCE Neolithic Age.

c. 3000 BCE Metal tools and weapons replace stone.

Mammoth has been lured into a pit trap covered in branches.

Hunters killed prey with sharp stone weapons.

MAMMOTH HUNT

From about 50,000 years ago, "modern people" hunted wild animals. By co-operating in groups and using their superior brainpower, they could kill creatures much larger than themselves. They sometimes slaughtered large numbers of deer and similar creatures by driving whole herds over cliffs. Elephant-like woolly mammoths were popular game; they are now extinct.

Stretching hide to make clothing.

Woman cooks a hare on a spit over the fire.

Dwelling places made from animal hides and mammoth bones kept out the cold wind.

Man is using a bone hammer to chip away at a flint core.

MAKING FLINT TOOLS AND WEAPONS

2 Later tools were much better. The toolmaker prepared a flint core by skillful chipping.

HAND AXE
The hand axe was the first deliberately shaped tool made by humans. It was gripped at the rounded end and used to cut meat or dig roots. Popular for over a million years, it was used longer than any other tool.

This flint hand axe was found in a desert area near Thebes, Egypt.

1 The first flint implements were crude. People used the sharp edge of a broken rock as a cutting tool.

3 Hitting the core with a bone hammer made flakes, each one a special tool.

Find out more
ARCHAEOLOGY
BRITAIN, ANCIENT
EVOLUTION
PREHISTORIC PEOPLES

STORMS

TORNADOES

The most violent storms are tornadoes, or whirlwinds. A twisting column of rising air forms beneath a thunder cloud, sometimes producing winds of 400 km/h (250 mph). The air pressure at the centre is very low, which can cause buildings to explode. A waterspout is a tornado over water, formed when water is sucked up into the funnel of air. Dust devils are tornadoes which have sucked up sand over the desert.

Severe storms build up as moist air, heated by warm land or sea, rises. Storm clouds develop as the rising air cools and rain forms. Air rushes in to replace the rising air, and strong winds begin to blow.

ABOUT 2,000 thunderstorms are raging throughout the world at this very moment, and lightning has struck about 500 times since you started reading this page. Storms have enormous power: the energy in a hurricane could illuminate more light bulbs than there are in the United States. A storm is basically a very strong wind. Severe storms such as thunderstorms, hurricanes, and tornadoes all contain their own strong wind system and blow along as a whole. Certain areas, such as the region around the Gulf of Mexico, are hit regularly by severe storms because of the local conditions. Storms can cause great damage because of the force of the wind and the devastating power of the rain, snow, sand, or dust which they carry along. One of the most destructive forces of a hurricane is a storm surge. The level of the sea rises because of a rapid drop in air pressure at the centre of the storm. This rise combines with the effect of the wind on the sea to create a huge wall of water which causes terrible damage if it hits the coast.

The base of the tornado is fairly narrow – about 1.5 km (1 mile) across.

The rising air spirals up the column, sucking up dirt and objects as heavy as trucks from the ground.

DESTRUCTION AND DEVASTATION
Winds of 320 km/h (200 mph) leave a trail of destruction (below) when the hurricane strikes the shore. The strongest winds are in a belt around the calm eye.

THUNDER AND LIGHTNING
Thunder clouds often form on hot, humid days. Strong air currents in the cloud cause raindrops and hailstones to collide, producing electric charges. Lightning flashes in giant sparks between the charges, and often leaps to the ground. A burst of heat from the flash makes the air nearby expand violently and produces a clap of thunder.

HURRICANES
When warm, moist air spirals upward above tropical oceans, it forms a hurricane – a violent storm which is also called a typhoon or a cyclone. The spin of the Earth causes the storm winds to circle around a calm centre called the eye. The eye usually moves along at about 25 km/h (15 mph). It can measure as much as 800 km (500 miles) across.

Negative charges in the bottom of the cloud attract positive charges in the ground. Eventually, a huge spark of lightning leaps from the cloud to the highest point on the ground.

Buildings are protected by lightning rods – strips of metal on the roof which attract the lightning and lead the electricity safely to the ground.

Find out more
CLIMATES
RAIN AND SNOW
WEATHER
WIND

STUARTS

IN 1603, THE LAST TUDOR MONARCH – Elizabeth I – died without leaving an heir. Her cousin, James Stuart, already James VI of Scotland, took over the English throne as well, becoming James I of England. The Stuarts united England and Scotland peacefully, but there were deep differences between King and Parliament over the power of the monarch. In 1642, these differences led to civil war. James I's son, Charles I, was executed in 1649, and England became a republic under Cromwell. In 1660, the Stuarts were restored (brought back to power) under Charles II. However, when his Catholic brother James II came to the throne in 1685, people resented his religion and his harsh laws. He was banished to Scotland and his son-in law, the Protestant William of Orange, became king. The last Stuart was Queen Anne, James II's second daughter.

COAT OF ARMS
The Stuart coat of arms included the English and Scottish lions, the Irish harp, and the French fleur-de-lys.

JAMES I
A vain man, James I believed God had made him ruler, and he ignored Parliament for much of his reign. Instead, he relied on the advice of favourites, and this weakened his government. However, James did achieve peace with Spain, England's old enemy. He also ordered an important new English translation of the Bible.

Headdress with stiffened frill

Dark coat over brocade vest

Fitted bodice trimmed with bows

Noblewoman of the Stuart period

Upper-class man from about 1670

Felt hat

Leather shoes with buckles

RESTORATION
After Oliver Cromwell's death, parliamentary leader George Monck (1608-70) negotiated with the exiled Charles II, and Britain became a monarchy again. During what historians call the Restoration, Charles II led a pleasure-seeking life, quite different to the Puritanism of Cromwell and his followers.

STUARTS

1603-25 Reign of James I.

1605 Gunpowder Plotters try to blow up parliament.

1625-49 Reign of Charles I.

1642-49 English Civil War.

1649-60 England becomes a republic.

1660 Monarchy restored.

1660-85 Reign of Charles II.

1666 Great Fire of London.

1685-88 Reign of James II.

1688 "Glorious Revolution" brings William of Orange to Britain.

1689-1702 Reign of William and Mary.

1702-14 Queen Anne rules, the last of the Stuart dynasty.

QUEEN ANNE
The last Stuart ruler was Queen Anne (1665-1714), She had a troubled life, and her reign was also difficult, as England waged a long war against France. However, British forces under John Churchill, Duke of Marlborough, gained victories which made England more powerful overseas. The decorative arts, such as furniture-making, flourished during Anne's reign.

Queen Anne table with cabriole legs

GLORIOUS REVOLUTION
In 1688, British leaders opposed to James II's Catholicism, invited Protestant Dutch King William of Orange to rule Britain. William, who reigned jointly with his wife, Mary, agreed a Bill of Rights forbidding the introduction of laws or taxes without Parliament's approval. Known as the "Glorious Revolution", this marked the start of modern constitutional monarchy, by which Parliament has greater powers than the king or queen.

Find out more
CROMWELL, OLIVER
ENGLISH CIVIL WAR
FIRE OF LONDON
UNITED KINGDOM, HISTORY OF

SUBMARINES

THE GREAT POWER of a submarine lies in its ability to remain hidden. It can travel unseen beneath the waves, carrying its deadly cargo of missiles and torpedoes, and remain underwater for long periods. However, the submarine had humble beginnings; legend states that during the siege of Tyre (Lebanon) in 332 BCE, Alexander the Great was lowered into the sea inside a glass barrel. Aided by the invention of the electric motor for underwater propulsion and the torpedo for attacking ships, modern submarines developed into powerful weapons during the two world wars of the 20th century. Today's submarines are powered either by a combination of diesel and electric motors or by nuclear-powered engines. There are two main types: patrol submarines, which aim to seek and destroy ships and other submarines, and missile-carrying submarines. Small submarines called submersibles are used mainly for non-military purposes, such as marine research.

NUCLEAR SUBMARINE
The most powerful of all weapons is the nuclear missile-carrying submarine. Its nuclear-powered engines allow it to hide underwater almost indefinitely without coming up for air, and it carries sufficient nuclear missiles to destroy several large cities.

Propeller drives the submarine through the water.

Diesel-electric engines are specially designed to make as little noise as possible.

The conning tower stands clear of the water when the submarine is on the surface.

Periscope and communication antennas

Torpedoes ready for firing

Small movable wings called the bow planes, and rudders in the tail, steer the submarine.

Tubes for launching torpedoes

HUNTER-KILLER SUBMARINE
A diesel engine powers this hunter-killer submarine when it travels on the surface, and an electric motor when it is underwater. Buoyancy tanks fill with water to submerge the submarine; to surface again, compressed air pushes the water out of the tanks.

Crew's living quarters are usually cramped. Some submarines carry a crew of more than 150.

Control room, from where the captain commands the submarine

Anti-submarine helicopter trails active sonar system in the water.

SONAR
Helicopters, ships, and hunter-killer submarines are equipped with sonar (sound navigation and ranging) for detecting submarines. Passive sonar consists of microphones, which pick up the sound of the submarine's engines. Active sonar sends out ultrasonic sound pulses which are too high-pitched to be heard but bounce off a hidden submarine and produce a distinctive echo.

Hunter-killer submarine uses active sonar to detect enemy submarine.

The missile-carrying submarine will dive to escape its attackers.

Submarine captain sees helicopter through periscope.

TORPEDOES
Torpedoes are packed with explosives and have their own motors to propel them to their targets. They are launched by compressed air from tubes in the nose and rear of the submarine.

PERISCOPE
Submarine captains traditionally used a periscope, a tube containing mirrors and lenses, to see above the surface while the submarine was submerged. The latest submarines have digital imaging systems instead of periscopes to relay pictures from the surface.

Find out more
NAVIGATION
OCEANS AND SEAS
ROCKETS AND MISSILES
SHIPS AND BOATS
WATER

507

SUMERIANS

THE WORLD'S FIRST CITIES were built on the banks of the Tigris and Euphrates rivers in what is now Iraq. About 5,000 years ago, the people of Sumer, the area of southern Iraq where the two rivers flow together, began to build what would become great, bustling cities. They made bricks from the riverside mud to build houses and massive temples. The Sumerians also developed one of the world's earliest writing systems, by making marks in soft tablets of clay, which they left in the sun to harden. Their earliest cities, such as Ur and Uruk, became famous all over the Middle East as Sumerian merchants travelled abroad trading food grown in the fertile local fields. The Sumerians flourished until about 2000 BCE, when desert tribes invaded.

MESOPOTAMIA
The land between the Tigris and Euphrates rivers is known as Mesopotamia. The home of the Sumerians was in southern Mesopotamia and Ur was one of their greatest cities.

GILGAMESH
The Sumerians created the earliest written story that has survived to modern times. Written on clay tablets, the story tells of Gilgamesh, King of Uruk and the son of a goddess and a man. Gilgamesh begins as a cruel king, but be becomes a hero when he kills two fearsome monsters. Later, Gilgamesh visits the underworld to try to search for immortal life.

Cuneiform script consisted of wedge-shaped marks made with a reed writing-stylus.

ZIGGURAT
At the centre of each Sumerian city was a stepped tower called a ziggurat, topped by a temple. By building their ziggurats high, the Sumerians believed that they were reaching up to the heavens, so that each temple could become a home for one of Sumer's many gods and goddesses. Only priests were allowed to worship in the temples.

SUMER

The land between the two rivers was fertile but dry. Farmers dug canals to bring water to their fields, and found that this meant they could produce huge harvests – there was usually enough to sell. The Sumerians found other useful resources near the rivers. They used reeds for boat-building and simple houses, and clay for making bricks and pottery.

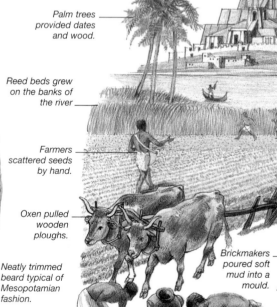

Mud-brick ziggurat towered over the city.

Palm trees provided dates and wood.

Reed beds grew on the banks of the river

Farmers scattered seeds by hand.

Oxen pulled wooden ploughs.

Brickmakers poured soft mud into a mould.

Sumerians travelled along the rivers in boats made from local reeds. Fishermen used similar boats.

Reed huts were common in southern Mesopotamia.

Bricks were left to bake dry in the hot sun.

Neatly trimmed beard typical of Mesopotamian fashion.

SARGON
Originally the servant of a king of Kish, in Akkad, north of Sumer, Sargon rose to become Akkad's ruler. In around 2325 BCE, he conquered Sumer, Mesopotamia and the eastern territory of Elam. He made Mesopotamia into a united country for the first time. Sargon was a powerful king who protected merchants, and built up flourishing trade.

Workers dug up clay to make bricks.

Find out more
ALPHABET
BRONZE AGE
WHEELS

508

SUN

THE NIGHT SKY is full of stars, so distant that they are mere points of light. The Sun is also a star, but we are closer to it than to any other star. Along with the other planets of the solar system, the Earth moves around the Sun, trapped in orbit by the force of gravity. The Sun sustains nearly all life on Earth with its light and heat. The Sun is a ball of glowing gases, roughly three-quarters hydrogen and one-quarter helium, along with traces of other elements. Within its hot, dense core, hydrogen particles crash together. This produces nuclear reactions that release enormous amounts of energy, keeping the core of the Sun very hot. The energy travels outwards and leaves the Sun's surface mainly as light, and infrared and ultraviolet radiation. Energy sources that humans use to provide power originate from the Sun. For example, coal is the remains of ancient plants, which trapped the Sun's energy.

Energy travels outwards in the form of heat and electromagnetic waves such as infrared, light, and radio waves.

Relatively cool and dark areas, called sunspots, form on the surface of the Sun. Sunspots develop in places where the Sun's magnetic field becomes particularly strong.

Great streamers of glowing hydrogen gas, called prominences, frequently soar up from the Sun. Prominences are often about 60,000 km (more than 37,000 miles) long.

Light from the Sun takes about eight minutes to reach the Earth.

STORY OF THE SUN
The Sun formed just under 5,000 million years ago from a cloud of hydrogen, helium, and dust, which contracted under its own gravity. The contraction heated the cloud until nuclear reactions began, converting hydrogen into helium. At this point the Sun began to shine steadily. It is believed that the Sun will continue to shine for another 5,000 million years before it runs out of hydrogen fuel and begins to die.

SOLAR FLARES
Huge explosions on the Sun's surface, called solar flares, fire streams of electrically charged particles into space.

CORONA AND SOLAR WIND
The corona is a thin atmosphere of gases that extends for millions of kilometres around the Sun. A blast of electrically charged particles, called the solar wind, blows out from the corona at a rate of millions of tonnes each second. The Earth is protected from these particles by its magnetic field, but they can damage spacecraft and satellites. Coronal Mass Ejections are sudden blasts of great clouds from the corona. These are thought to cause auroras – coloured lights in the sky above the Earth's poles – and magnetic storms.

Core extends to about 175,000 km (about 110,800 miles) from the Sun's centre.

The hot, glowing surface of the Sun is called the photosphere (sphere of light). It is about 400 km (250 miles) deep.

A glowing red layer of hydrogen gas called the chromosphere (sphere of colour) lies above the photosphere. The chromosphere is a few thousand kilometres deep.

Warning: Never look at the Sun, either directly or through dark glasses. The intense light could seriously damage your eyesight.

The Sun's diameter is 109 times that of the Earth. More than 1,300,000 globes the size of the Earth could fit into the Sun.

SOLAR ENERGY
Electronic devices called solar cells convert sunlight into electricity. Solar cells power satellites and produce electricity in experimental houses and cars. In 2003, the solar-powered *Nuna II* car (below) drove across Australia at an average speed of 96.8 km/h (60 mph).

Umbra is the centre of the moon's shadow, where the Sun is completely hidden.

Penumbra is the outer part of the moon's shadow, where part of the Sun can be seen.

SOLAR ECLIPSES
When the Moon passes between the Earth and the Sun, the Sun is hidden. This is called a solar eclipse. A total solar eclipse occurs at places on the Earth where the Sun appears to be completely hidden (although prominences, chromosphere, and corona can be seen). Elsewhere the eclipse is partial, and parts of the Sun can be seen.

SUN FACTS

Earth–Sun distance	149.6 million km (92.9 million miles)
Diameter at equator	1,392,000 km (864,950 miles)
Time to rotate once	25.4 days
Temperature at surface	5,500°C (10,000°F)
Temperature at centre	15,000,000°C (27,000,000°F)

Find out more
ASTRONOMY
ENERGY
STARS

SWITZERLAND

A LAND OF HIGH MOUNTAINS and isolated valleys, the 26 provinces (cantons) of Switzerland have been a united confederation since 1291. With access to the north via the Rhine river and control of the Alpine passes to the south, Switzerland has dominated Europe's north-south trade routes for many centuries. The country lacks natural resources, but has become a wealthy financial, banking and commercial centre, with a worldwide reputation for precision engineering, especially watch-making. Although mountains cover nearly three-quarters of the land, dairy farming is very important, and the Swiss export a wide range of cheeses and milk chocolate. Liechtenstein, a tiny mountainous country on Switzerland's eastern border, is also an important financial and manufacturing centre.

Switzerland is a land-locked country at the heart of Europe. The Alps create a major barrier to the south. To the north the Jura Mountains form its border with France. Lake Geneva, on the French border, is formed by the Rhône river.

LIECHTENSTEIN
Area: 160 sq km (62 sq miles)
Population: 35,000
Capital: Vaduz
Languages: German, Alemannish dialect, Italian
Religions: Roman Catholic, Protestant
Currency: Swiss franc

SWITZERLAND
Area: 41,290 sq km (15,940 sq miles)
Population: 7,604,000
Capital: Bern
Languages: German, Swiss-German, French, Italian, Romansch
Religions: Roman Catholic, Protestant, Muslim, non-religious
Currency: Swiss franc

ALPINE PASTURES
Most Alpine villages are clustered at the base of mountain slopes and in valley plains. These locations provide fertile soil, adequate water and temperate weather. Vines can even be grown on south-facing slopes. Swiss dairy farmers keep their cattle in the valleys during the winter. In summer they are taken up to lush, green Alpine meadows to graze.

WINTER SPORTS

Over 100 million visitors a year come to the Swiss Alps to enjoy climbing, hiking and winter sports. Alpine skiing has been included in the Olympic Games since 1936. Mountain resorts, with chair lifts, ski runs, and ski instructors, cater for winter visitors. But tourism is having a dangerous impact. Trees are cleared to make way for ski runs. Without these natural barriers, there is a much greater risk of avalanches.

LAKE GENEVA
Picturesque villages line the shores of Europe's largest Alpine lake, especially to the north, where the soil is fertile. Geneva, at the southwest of the lake, is a major banking and insurance centre. Many international organizations, such as the Red Cross, are based in the city.

SCALE BAR
0   50 km
0   30 miles

Volcano Mountain Ancient monument Capital city Large city/ town Small city/ town

Find out more
EUROPE, HISTORY OF
MOUNTAINS
MOUNTAIN WILDLIFE
SPORTS

TECHNOLOGY

THE INVENTION OF STONE TOOLS more than two million years ago marked the beginning of technology. For the first time in history, people found that cutting or chopping was easier to do with tools than with bare hands. Technology is the way in which people use the ideas of science to build machinery and make tasks easier. Although technology began in prehistoric times, it advanced rapidly during and after the Industrial Revolution, beginning in the 18th century. Since that time technology has dramatically changed our world. It has given us fast, safe transport, materials such as plastics, increased worldwide communications, and many useful daily appliances. Perhaps the greatest benefits of technology are in modern medicine, which has improved our health and lengthened our lives. Advances in technology have been mainly beneficial to humans and our lifestyle. However, increased technology has a negative side, too – it has produced weapons with the power to cause death and destruction. Technology and development have caused many environmental problems such as ozone depletion, and is often dependent on non-renewable resources, such as oil, which has a limited life. Governments and other organizations are now trying to use new technology to find solutions to these problems.

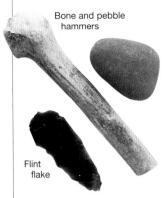

EARLY TECHNOLOGY
Humans living during the Stone Age developed a variety of tools for everyday purposes. They used rounded pebbles and bones as hammers to form cutting tools from a strong stone called flint. Flint was chipped and flaked to produce a sharp cutting edge like a blade.

Bone and pebble hammers

Flint flake

COMPUTERS

The development of computers has been one of the most important recent advances in technology. The invention of the microchip (right) changed the emphasis of producing goods from mechanical to electronic. This meant that many tasks which had previously been done manually were now automated. Computers perform many different tasks and are used in banking, architecture, manufacturing, and a range of other businesses. Computers also aid new technology, because they can help develop new machines.

Microchips lie at the heart of a computer. These tiny devices store and process huge amounts of information at high speed.

Threshing machines help farmers separate the heads from the stalks of rice plants. Previously, this job had to be done by hand.

SMALL-SCALE TECHNOLOGY

People in poorer countries cannot afford to buy the technological goods that are common in richer parts of the world such as North America and Europe. Their primary concern is feeding and housing their families, and they tend to use smaller, simpler machines, such as windmills that drive pumps for irrigation.

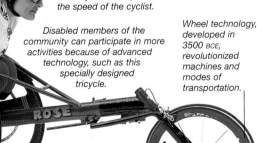

Synthetic clothing materials are lightweight, machine-washable, and allow ease of movement.

The cyclist's helmet is made from plastic and polystyrene. It has an aerodynamic shape to increase the speed of the cyclist.

Disabled members of the community can participate in more activities because of advanced technology, such as this specially designed tricycle.

Wheel technology, developed in 3500 BCE, revolutionized machines and modes of transportation.

LIFESTYLE
In the western world, technology has generally made daily life easier. Washing machines, cars, and cash machines all make daily tasks more convenient, providing more time for leisure, hobbies, and sports. People also now have the time and means to travel to other countries to experience different cultures and environments.

MEDICAL TECHNOLOGY
Inventions such as x-ray machines and brain scanners help doctors to detect and treat illness. Doctors can transplant organs, implant tiny electronic pacemakers to keep a heart beating, and repair damaged tissue with plastic surgery. Medical technology, such as glasses, contact lenses, or hearing aids, also helps to improve the daily lives of many people affected by impaired vision or hearing. Prosthetic (artificial) limbs are also being improved and now allow their users more movement and flexibility.

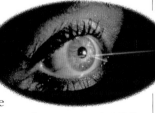

Laser surgery can correct many eye defects without needing to cut the eye.

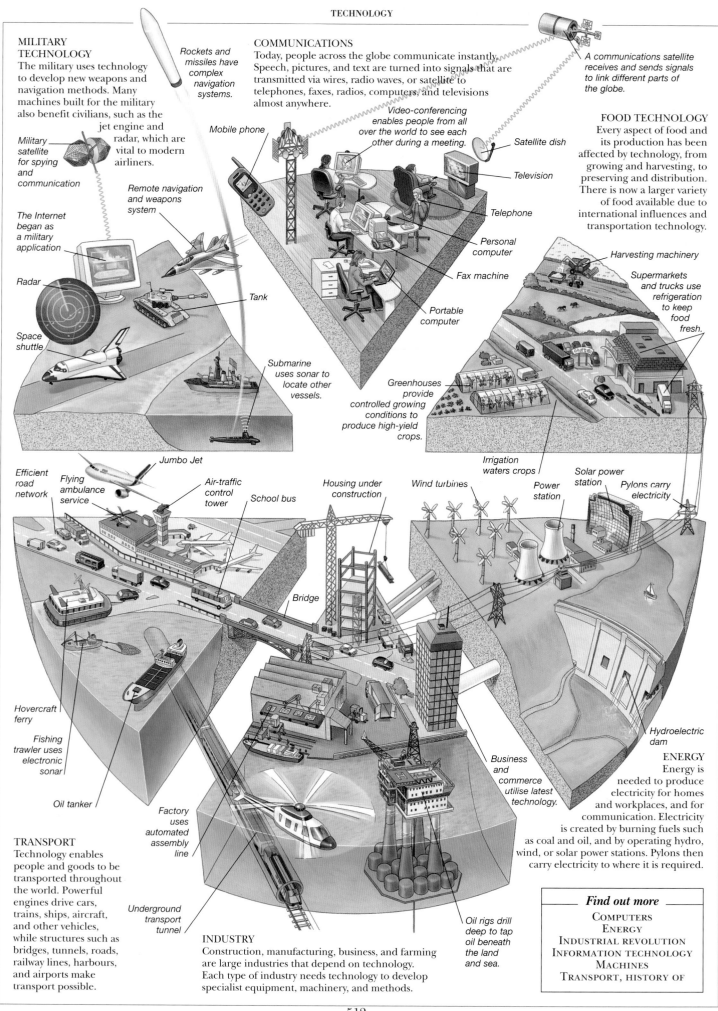

MILITARY TECHNOLOGY

The military uses technology to develop new weapons and navigation methods. Many machines built for the military also benefit civilians, such as the jet engine and radar, which are vital to modern airliners.

Rockets and missiles have complex navigation systems.

Military satellite for spying and communication

The Internet began as a military application

Radar

Space shuttle

Remote navigation and weapons system

Tank

Submarine uses sonar to locate other vessels.

COMMUNICATIONS

Today, people across the globe communicate instantly. Speech, pictures, and text are turned into signals that are transmitted via wires, radio waves, or satellite to telephones, faxes, radios, computers, and televisions almost anywhere.

Mobile phone

Video-conferencing enables people from all over the world to see each other during a meeting.

A communications satellite receives and sends signals to link different parts of the globe.

Satellite dish

Television

Telephone

Personal computer

Fax machine

Portable computer

FOOD TECHNOLOGY

Every aspect of food and its production has been affected by technology, from growing and harvesting, to preserving and distribution. There is now a larger variety of food available due to international influences and transportation technology.

Harvesting machinery

Supermarkets and trucks use refrigeration to keep food fresh.

Greenhouses provide controlled growing conditions to produce high-yield crops.

Irrigation waters crops

Efficient road network

Flying ambulance service

Jumbo Jet

Air-traffic control tower

School bus

Housing under construction

Wind turbines

Power station

Solar power station

Pylons carry electricity

Bridge

Hovercraft ferry

Fishing trawler uses electronic sonar

Oil tanker

Factory uses automated assembly line

Business and commerce utilise latest technology.

Hydroelectric dam

ENERGY

Energy is needed to produce electricity for homes and workplaces, and for communication. Electricity is created by burning fuels such as coal and oil, and by operating hydro, wind, or solar power stations. Pylons then carry electricity to where it is required.

TRANSPORT

Technology enables people and goods to be transported throughout the world. Powerful engines drive cars, trains, ships, aircraft, and other vehicles, while structures such as bridges, tunnels, roads, railway lines, harbours, and airports make transport possible.

Underground transport tunnel

INDUSTRY

Construction, manufacturing, business, and farming are large industries that depend on technology. Each type of industry needs technology to develop specialist equipment, machinery, and methods.

Oil rigs drill deep to tap oil beneath the land and sea.

Find out more
COMPUTERS
ENERGY
INDUSTRIAL REVOLUTION
INFORMATION TECHNOLOGY
MACHINES
TRANSPORT, HISTORY OF

TEETH

EVERY TIME WE EAT we use our teeth to bite, chew, crunch, and grind food. Teeth enable us to break up food into small pieces so that our bodies can digest it and use it. A tooth has three main parts – the crown of the tooth, which shows above the gum; the neck, which shows at gum level; and the root, which is hidden in the jawbone. The root of the tooth is fixed securely in the jaw by a substance called cementum. A tooth has three layers – creamy white enamel on the outside (the hardest substance in the body); a layer of dentine beneath; and the pulp cavity in the centre. The pulp contains many nerves, which connect to the jawbone. There are four main kinds of teeth; each kind is shaped for a different job. Chisel-like incisors at the front of the mouth cut and slice food; longer, pointed canines tear and rip food; and flat, broad premolars and molars crush and grind it. During our lives, we have two sets of teeth – milk teeth as children, and a second set of teeth as adults.

HEALTHY TEETH
It is important to take care of your teeth to keep them healthy. Teeth should be cleaned with a toothbrush and toothpaste at least twice a day. Dental floss should be used regularly. Sugary foods are damaging to teeth and cause tooth decay.

Enamel

Pulp cavity

Dentine

Gum

Blood vessels

Root

Jawbone

Cementum

Nerve

Cross-section of a molar

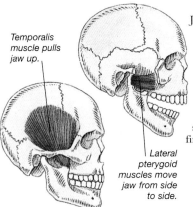

Temporalis muscle pulls jaw up.

Lateral pterygoid muscles move jaw from side to side.

JAWS
The upper jaw is fixed to the skull and does not move. Powerful muscles in the cheeks and the side of the head pull the lower jaw up towards the upper jaw, so that the teeth come together with great pressure for biting. Other muscles pull the lower jaw sideways, so that we can chew with both up-and-down and side-to-side movements. Teeth are an important first step in the process of digesting food.

DENTISTS
Dentists use X-rays (right) to see the roots of teeth and to identify any cavities. In the past, dentists extracted decaying teeth, but now only the affected parts are removed and the hole is filled with hard artificial materials. The white areas on this X-ray are fillings and two crowns on posts.

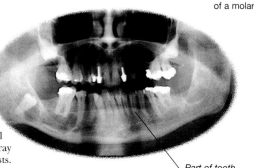

Part of tooth shows below the gum line.

STRUCTURE OF A TOOTH
Teeth have one, two (like this molar), three, or occasionally four roots, which anchor them securely in the jawbone and withstand the pressure of biting and chewing. Blood vessels which carry nutrients and oxygen, and nerves which transmit sensation, pass out through tiny holes in the base of each root.

MILK TEETH AND ADULT TEETH
Children have 20 milk teeth which gradually fall out and are replaced by a second set of permanent adult teeth. Adults have 32 teeth in total. Each jaw has 4 incisors, 2 canines, 4 premolars, and 6 molars (2 of which are wisdom teeth). Wisdom teeth grow when a person is about 20, although some may never push through the gum.

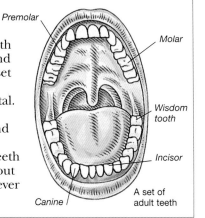

Premolar

Molar

Wisdom tooth

Incisor

Canine

A set of adult teeth

TUSKS
Animals use their teeth for more than just eating food. Large teeth help to defend against enemies, or when battling with rivals during the mating season. The warthog's tusks shown here are huge canine teeth – like the tusks of a walrus. Tusks are used to frighten off predators and, sometimes, to dig up food.

Find out more
FOOD AND DIGESTION
HUMAN BODY
SKELETONS

TELEPHONES

Earpiece

A loudspeaker, called the receiver, contains a thin metal disc that vibrates, converting electric signals into sound waves.

Silicon chip

Electronic circuits generate signals corresponding to each button as it is pressed. They also amplify (boost) incoming electric signals and send them to the receiver.

WITH THE PUSH of a few buttons on the telephone, it is possible to talk to someone nearly anywhere else in the world. By making instant communication possible, the telephone has done more to "shrink" the world than almost any other invention. A telephone signal can take several forms on its journey. Beneath the city streets it travels in the form of electric currents in cables, or as light waves in thin glass fibres. Telephone signals also travel as radio waves when they beam down to other countries via satellites, or when they carry messages to and from mobile phones. Many electronic devices "talk" to each other by sending signals via telephone links. Computers exchange information and programs with one another, and fax machines use telephone lines to send copies of pictures and text to other fax machines across the world within seconds.

TELEPHONE HANDSET
A small direct (one-way) electric current flows in the wires connected to a telephone handset. Signals representing sounds such as callers' voices, computer data, and fax messages consist of rapid variations in the strength of this current.

The electric cable connects to the telephone network, allowing access all over the world.

Microphone

Soundwaves of the user's voice strike a microphone called the transmitter, creating an electrical signal that is sent down the telephone cable.

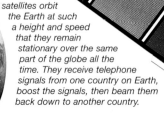

Communication satellites orbit the Earth at such a height and speed that they remain stationary over the same part of the globe all the time. They receive telephone signals from one country on Earth, boost the signals, then beam them back down to another country.

TELEPHONE NETWORK
Computer-controlled telephone exchanges make the connections needed to link two telephones. When a person dials a telephone number, automatic switches at the local exchange link the telephone lines directly. International calls travel along undersea cables or, in the form of radio waves, by way of satellites.

Words and pictures printed by a fax machine have jagged edges because they are made up of thousands of dots.

Fibre-optic cables use light waves to carry thousands of phone calls at one time.

FAX
A facsimile, or fax, machine scans a page by measuring its brightness at thousands of individual points. It then sends signals along the telephone wire, each representing the brightness at one point. A printer inside the receiving fax machine prints a dot wherever the original picture is dark, making a copy. Today, email is increasingly replacing the fax.

ALEXANDER GRAHAM BELL
The inventor of the telephone was a Scottish-American teacher named Alexander Graham Bell (1847-1922). In 1875, Bell was experimenting with early telegraph systems. For this he used vibrating steel strips called reeds. He found that when a reed at one end of the line vibrated, a reed at the other end gave out a sound. In 1876, Bell patented the world's first practical telephone.

PORTABLE PHONES
A cordless telephone has a built-in radio transmitter and receiver. It communicates with a unit connected to a telephone line in a home. Mobile phones (left) work with the aid of powerful relay stations such as cellular exchanges. Mobile phones are becoming increasingly versatile. Many now also function as cameras and can connect to the Internet.

Find out more
INTERNET
RADIO
SATELLITES
TECHNOLOGY

TELESCOPES

FROM FAR AWAY, a person looks like a tiny dot. But with a telescope, you can see a clear, bright image that reveals all the details of that person's face. Large modern telescopes make it possible for astronomers to make images of extremely faint objects in the universe, such as galaxies billions of light years away, or small icy worlds at the edge of the solar system. Less powerful telescopes are important too: they are valuable tools for mapmakers, sailors, and bird watchers. Telescopes have helped scientists make some of the greatest discoveries about the universe. In 1609, the Italian scientist Galileo first turned a telescope to the skies. His observations led him to suggest that the Earth moved around the Sun and was not the centre of the universe, as people believed at that time. Since then, astronomers have continued to build ever bigger and better telescopes and to make new and unexpected discoveries with them.

OPERA GLASSES
Opera glasses are the simplest kind of binoculars. They consist of two small telescopes placed side by side.

Eyepiece lenses are adjustable to match the strength of each eye.

Prisms "fold up" the light inside the binoculars, whIch magnifies objects as much as a long telescope.

A prism is a triangular-shaped piece of glass.

BINOCULARS
Binoculars are more complex than opera glasses. They contain a system of lenses and prisms that makes them powerful yet small in size.

Light enters the front of the binoculars.

The Keck telescope, right, does not use lenses, like binoculars, but a large primary mirror made up of smaller segments. Each segment is adjusted by a computer to an accuracy 25,000 times smaller than a human hair.

REFLECTING TELESCOPE
Most astronomers use reflecting telescopes, the best telescopes for picking up the faint light from distant stars. A large curved mirror catches the light and concentrates it to form an image. For observing directly by eye, a smaller mirror then carries the image to a lens called the eyepiece. In large telescopes used by professional astronomers, the light goes into an electronic instrument or camera and the observations are stored in a computer.

The secondary mirror bounces light back down to tertiary mirror.

The structure keeps all parts in same relative positons as telescope turns and tilts.

The tertiary mirror reflects light to cameras and scientific instruments.

Cameras and scientific instruments.

The primary mirror is made from 36 small hexagons that work like a single mirror. Together, these segments collect light and reflect it to focus on the secondary mirror.

RADIO TELESCOPES
Stars and other objects in space give out invisible radio waves as well as light. Astronomers study the universe with radio telescopes, which are large dish-shaped antennas that pick up radio waves from space. Radio astronomy has led to the discovery of dying stars and distant galaxies that would not have been seen from their light alone.

The eyepiece lens focuses the image into the observer's eye.

The objective lens is a convex lens which concentrates the light to form an image.

The middle lens turns the image the right way up.

REFRACTING TELESCOPE
A large lens at the front of a refracting telescope refracts, or bends, the light to form an image of a distant object. The eyepiece lens is at the back. Some refractors have a third lens in the middle. Without this lens, the telescope would produce an upside-down image.

Find out more
ASTRONOMY
LIGHT
MICROSCOPES
SCIENCE, HISTORY OF

TELEVISION

SINCE ITS INVENTION early in the 20th century, television has become one of the world's most important sources of opinion, information, and entertainment. Television gives us the best seats in the theatre, at a rock concert, or at the Olympic Games. It also beams us pictures of war and disaster, the conquering of space, and other world events as they happen. Television programmes are actually electronic signals sent out as radio waves by way of satellites and underground cables. A television set converts the signals into sound and pictures. People can watch pre-recorded films and record broadcast programmes to play at a later time using optical discs (DVDs) or a personal video recorder (PVR). Lightweight video cameras can also be used to make home movies. Closed-circuit (nonbroadcast) television cameras are used to guard shops and offices, monitor traffic conditions, and survey crowds at sports events.

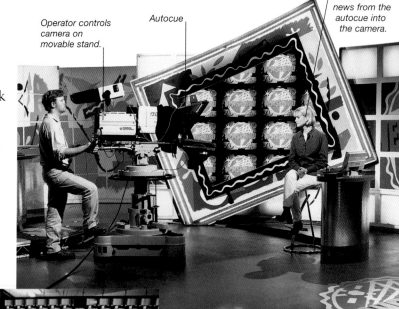

Operator controls camera on movable stand.

Autocue

Presenter reads the news from the autocue into the camera.

TELEVISION STUDIO

Within the space of a few hours, a studio might be used for a game show, a play, a variety show, and a panel discussion, so studio sets have to be changed very rapidly. Presenters and people working behind the cameras receive instructions from the control room via headphones. Most programmes are recorded, sometimes months before they are broadcast.

CONTROL ROOM

The director and vision mixer sit in the control room (shown above) in front of a bank of screens showing pictures from several sources, such as from cameras at various angles in the studio and at outside broadcast locations, from digital recording machines, and from satellites. Other screens show still photographs, captions, and titles. The vision mixer is instructed by the director which image to broadcast on screen and for how long. Sound is also mixed in at the same time. The producer has overall control of the final programme.

AUTOCUE
The presenter reads the script from an autocue. The words are displayed on a monitor screen and reflected in a two-way mirror in front of the camera lens. An operator on the studio floor controls the speed at which the words move.

OUTSIDE BROADCAST
Outside broadcast teams use portable cameras when mobility is important, as in a news report, and large, fixed cameras for events such as football games. The pictures are recorded on videotape or beamed back to the studio via a mobile dish antenna.

Sound is recorded through a sound boom.

Sections of digital recording are cut, edited, and reordered.

The editor watches the original recordings and puts together the final programme.

EDITING SUITE
When a programme is not broadcast live, an editor gathers all the material recorded from each camera and selects the best sections and edits them together in the right order. This is done in an editing suite (left) with specialist equipment. Editing allows filming to be done out of sequence, and from many different angles. Smooth editing can be crucial to the flow and final cut of a programme.

TELEVISION RECEIVER

A television receiver picks up signals broadcast by television stations and converts them to moving pictures on a screen. Images appear to move because 25-60 pictures appear each second. The most common type of screen is the LCD (Liquid Crystal Display). LCDs are made up of millions of tiny dots of light called pixels. Each pixel contains a red, a green, and a blue subpixel – different combinations of these three colours can produces all the colours that make up a picture. The subpixels are controlled by groups of liquid crystals. Electronic circuits in the TV work out which pixels need to be switched on to make a picture. They pass electric signals through the liquid crystals, which act like tiny light switches to turn each subpixel on or off.

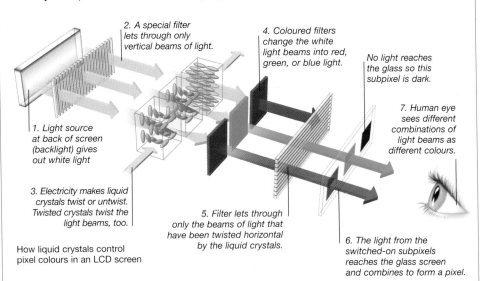

2. A special filter lets through only vertical beams of light.

4. Coloured filters change the white light beams into red, green, or blue light.

No light reaches the glass so this subpixel is dark.

1. Light source at back of screen (backlight) gives out white light

7. Human eye sees different combinations of light beams as different colours.

3. Electricity makes liquid crystals twist or untwist. Twisted crystals twist the light beams, too.

5. Filter lets through only the beams of light that have been twisted horizontal by the liquid crystals.

6. The light from the switched-on subpixels reaches the glass screen and combines to form a pixel.

How liquid crystals control pixel colours in an LCD screen

TELEVISION TRANSMISSION

Television signals can reach a viewer by several routes. Usually, transmitters broadcast television signals directly to homes as ultrahigh frequency (UHF) radio waves. Alternatively, the signals are sent up to a satellite, which transmits them over a larger region. Individual homes receive the satellite broadcast via dish antennas (right). In other cases, a ground station picks up the signals and sends them out along cables.

Satellite television sends signals from the TV station to homes via a satellite.

Television station

House aerial picks up UHF signals.

Cable television

Cable feeds the signal into the house to the receiver.

The horn collects concentrated incoming waves

NEW TECHNOLOGIES

Today's widescreen TV sets have flat plasma screens or liquid crystal displays, but these will be replaced by ultra-thin organic LED displays (OLED). High Definition (HD) broadcasts and screens use more pixels to give better picture quality. At home, personal video recorders (PVRs) store video on computer hard disc drives. Movies and TV shows can now be downloaded from the Internet, too. Digital broadcasting uses binary code to carry TV signals with better quality sound and pictures. And with interactive television, viewers can select what to watch and when from a wide range of options.

Pocket digital video player

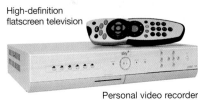

High-definition flatscreen television

Personal video recorder

INVENTION

In 1926, Scottish engineer John Logie Baird (1888-1946) gave the first public demonstration of television. At about the same time, the Russian American engineer Vladimir Zworykin (1889-1982) invented the electronic camera tube, which was more sophisticated than Baird's system and is the basis of today's television sets. In 1956 the U.S. company Ampex first produced videotape; videocassette recorders appeared in 1969, produced by Sony of Japan.

VIDEO CAMERAS

Today's video cameras or "camcorders" are tiny in comparison with the giant studio cameras used in the early days of TV. They fit easily in the palm of one hand. Most are now digital and record high-quality video sequences – including stereo sound as well – in the form of binary code stored on magnetic tape, optical DVD discs, memory cards, or a hard disc drive built into the camera.

Camcorder

Find out more
CAMERAS
ELECTRONICS
INFORMATION TECHNOLOGY
RADIO
SOUND

THEATRE

AT THE HEART OF ALL THEATRE lies the excitement of watching a live performance. Bringing a play to life involves many people. The words of the dramatist, or playwright, the ideas of the director, and the actors' skill combine to make an audience believe that what is happening on the stage – the drama – is real. Early theatre grew out of religious festivals held in Greece in honour of the god Dionysus, and included singing and dancing as well as acting. The different forms of theatre that emerged in India, China, and Japan also had religious origins. In medieval Europe people watched "miracle plays", which were based on religious stories. Later, dramatists began to write about all aspects of life, and companies of actors performed their plays in permanent theatres. Theatre changes to suit the demands of each new age for fantasy, spectacle, or serious drama.

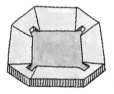

WILLIAM SHAKESPEARE
This most famous of all playwrights was born in Stratford-upon-Avon, but moved to London as young man. He wrote more than 37 plays, including tragedies such as *Hamlet*, comedies such as *As You Like It*, and history plays such as *Henry V*. He died in 1616 at the age of 52.

The theatre's curved shape amplified sounds for the audience.

OPEN-AIR THEATRE
Ancient Greek theatre made use of landscapes like this one at Delphi. Actors wore exaggerated masks so that characters could be recognized from afar.

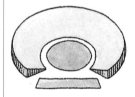

GREEK THEATRE
The audience sat in a semicircle of steplike seats. There was a circular orchestra – a space for dancing and singing – and a low stage for actors.

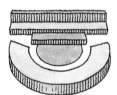

ROMAN THEATRE
Based on Greek theatres, the Roman theatre was usually open to the sky and enclosed on three sides. A permanent wooden roof sheltered the raised stage.

THE OPEN STAGE
Some modern theatres have an open stage without a curtain. The actors can address the audience more directly, as if holding a conversation.

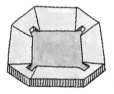

THEATRE-IN-THE-ROUND
Here the audience surrounds the cast on all four sides, bringing everyone close together. The actors enter through aisles between the seats.

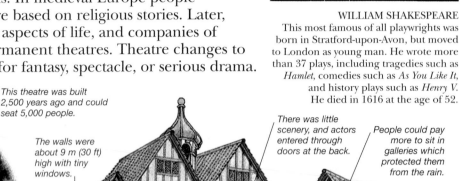

This theatre was built 2,500 years ago and could seat 5,000 people.

The walls were about 9 m (30 ft) high with tiny windows.

There was little scenery, and actors entered through doors at the back.

People could pay more to sit in galleries which protected them from the rain.

The yard audience stood very close to the actors on stage.

GLOBE PLAYHOUSE

Shakespeare was an actor and a writer at this famous theatre on the south bank of the River Thames in London. There was room for more than 2,000 people in the round wooden building. The audience stood in the open yard or sat in the enclosed gallery to watch a performance. In 1995, the Globe was rebuilt at a nearby site in London.

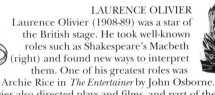

LAURENCE OLIVIER
Laurence Olivier (1908-89) was a star of the British stage. He took well-known roles such as Shakespeare's Macbeth (right) and found new ways to interpret them. One of his greatest roles was Archie Rice in *The Entertainer* by John Osborne. Olivier also directed plays and films, and part of the Royal National Theatre in London is named after him.

DRAMA AND DRAMATISTS

Playwrights often use drama to convey a message about life. Watching the downfall of characters in a tragedy helps us to understand more about life. Comedy makes us laugh, but some dramatists, such as George Bernard Shaw, used it to say serious things about society. Modern dramatists, such as Samuel Beckett and Bertolt Brecht, have experimented with words and characters to push the boundaries of drama even further.

THE PICTURE FRAME
Clever use of scenery and a sloping stage helps to change the audience's view through the proscenium arch (the frame of the stage) and makes the stage look deeper.

PROFILE-SPOT
Stagehands control this light from the rear of the upper circle. They use the strong beam to pick out and follow an actor in a pool of brilliant light.

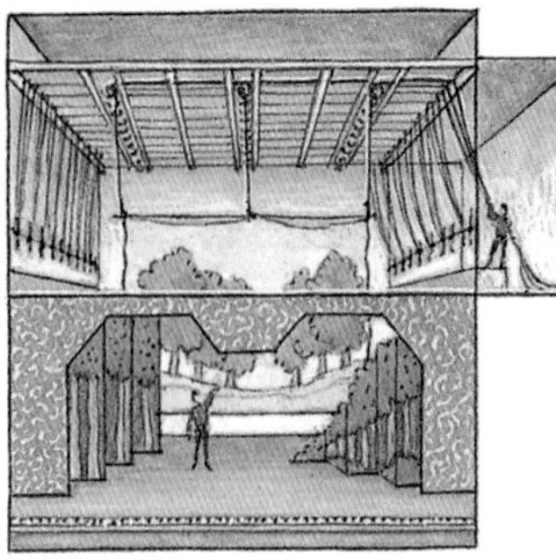

UP IN THE FLIES
High above the stage there is "fly" space in which scenery and equipment hang. A system of pulleys makes it possible to lower scenery.

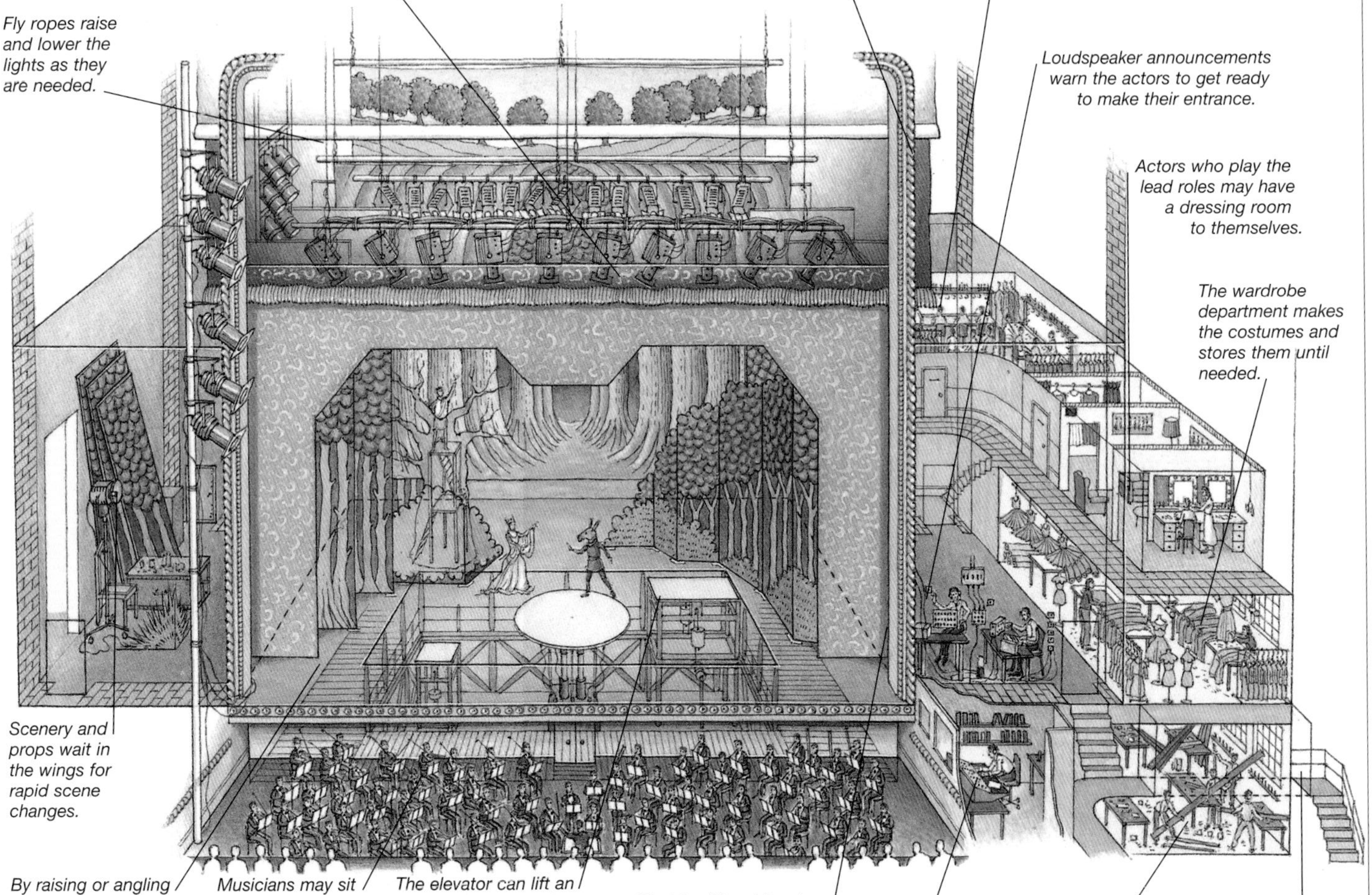

Lowering the curtain, or tabs, hides the stage while stagehands change scenery.

The flameproof safety curtain seals off the stage from the auditorium if fire breaks out.

Some of the actors share a dressing room where they put on makeup and change into costume.

Fly ropes raise and lower the lights as they are needed.

Loudspeaker announcements warn the actors to get ready to make their entrance.

Actors who play the lead roles may have a dressing room to themselves.

The wardrobe department makes the costumes and stores them until needed.

Scenery and props wait in the wings for rapid scene changes.

By raising or angling the stage slightly the designer can change the audience's view.

Musicians may sit in an orchestra pit below the front of the stage.

The elevator can lift an actor or prop onto the stage in a split second.

Most traditional theatres have a "picture frame" stage – the play takes place under a proscenium arch.

The busy carpentry department builds the sets. Props, such as furniture, are stored here when not in use.

Actors enter and leave the theatre by the stage door.

From the lighting control board or console, the operator can dim or brighten any light in the theatre. A lighting change can alter the mood of a play in seconds.

SOUND EFFECTS
Sound effects must happen at exactly the right moment. If an actor falls down before the sound of a gunshot, the whole scene is ruined. The sound operator listens and watches carefully for each cue.

Find out more
COMPOSERS
DANCE
LITERATURE
MUSIC
SHAKESPEARE, WILLIAM

TIME

HOUR FOLLOWS HOUR as time passes. Time always flows steadily in the same direction. Behind us in time lies the past, which we know. Ahead lies the future, which we cannot know. We cannot change time, but we can measure it. People first measured time in days and nights, which they could easily see and count. They also measured time in months, by watching the phases of the Moon, and in years, by watching the cycle of the seasons. Today, we have clocks and watches that can measure time in fractions of a second.

In 1905, German physicist Albert Einstein proposed the scientific theory of relativity. This says that time is not constant, but that it would pass more slowly if you could travel very fast (near the speed of light), or in strong fields of gravity. Scientists believe that time may even come to a stop in black holes deep in space.

HOURGLASS
Sand draining through an hourglass shows the passing of time. It takes one hour for the sand to run from the top to the bottom bulb.

7 a.m. in New York City, USA

The Earth spins counterclockwise when looking down at the North Pole. It goes clockwise viewed from above the South Pole.

UNITS OF TIME
One full day and night is the time in which the Earth spins once. This is divided into 24 hours: each hour contains 60 minutes, and each minute contains 60 seconds. The Babylonians fixed these units about 5,000 years ago, using 24 and 60 because they divide easily by 2, 3, and 4.

9 a.m. in Rio de Janeiro, Brazil

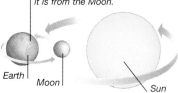

In reality, the Earth is 400 times further away from the Sun than it is from the Moon.

Earth | Moon | Sun

YEARS AND MONTHS
A year is based on the time the Earth takes to go once around the Sun, which is 365.26 days. Months vary from 28 to 31 days. They were originally based on the time between full moons, which is about 29.5 days.

The International Date Line is at 180 degrees longitude.

3 p.m. in Moscow, Russian Federation

INTERNATIONAL DATE LINE
The western side of the International Date Line is one day ahead of the eastern side. When you cross the line, the date changes.

12 noon in London, Britain

TIME ZONES
The world is divided into 24 regions, called time zones, each with a different time of day. This was done to avoid having several time differences within one area, and to ensure that all countries have noon during the middle of the day.

2 p.m. in Cairo, Egypt

UNIVERSAL TIME
The time at the prime meridian is used as a standard time known as Universal Time (UT) or Greenwich Mean Time (GMT).

The prime meridian is at 0 degrees longitude.

DAYS AND NIGHTS
The Sun lights up one half of the Earth, where it is day. The other half, away from the Sun, is dark, and there it is night. Days and nights come and go because the Earth spins once every 24 hours. But the day and night may last different lengths of time because the Earth is tilted at an angle to the Sun.

The Hindu calendar is based on lunar months. Diwali, the Festival of Lights, marks the start of the new year, which falls in October or November.

CALENDARS
The date is fixed by the calendar, which contains 12 months with a total of 365 days. Every fourth year is a leap year which has one extra day, February 29. Leap years are years that divide by four, such as 2008 and 2012. The calendar contains leap years because the Earth takes slightly longer than 365 days to go once around the Sun. Prehistoric peoples may have used monuments such as Stonehenge, in southern England (below), to measure the Sun's position and find the exact length of the year.

Twice a year the Sun is overhead the Equator at 12 noon.

Find out more
CLOCKS AND WATCHES
EARTH
EINSTEIN, ALBERT
PHYSICS
SCIENCE
STARS
UNIVERSE

TRADE AND INDUSTRY

WITHOUT TRADE AND INDUSTRY, people would have to create everything they needed to live. If you wanted a loaf of bread you would have to grow wheat, grind the wheat to make flour, mix the dough, and bake it in an oven. You would also need to build the mill and make the oven! Industry organizes the production of bread, so that just a few farmers, millers, and bakers can make bread for everyone. Similarly, industry supplies us with most other essential and luxury goods, from fresh water to cars. Trade is the process of buying and selling. Trade gets the products from the people who make them to the people who need them. And through trade, manufacturers can buy the raw materials they need to supply their factories and keep production going. Together, the trade and industry of a nation are sometimes called the economy.

SILK ROAD
Trade between different regions and peoples goes back to ancient times. The Silk Road was one of the earliest and most famous trade routes. Traders led horses and camels along this route between 300 BCE and 1600 CE, carrying silk from China to Europe.

India exports cotton textiles to Europe.

India exports tea to the Russian Federation.

India imports cars from Japan.

India imports oil from the Middle East.

India exports rice to Australia.

Imports

Exports

INTERNATIONAL TRADE
Goods move around the world by sea, land, and air. This international trade takes materials such as oil from the countries that have a surplus to those that have no or insufficient oil deposits. International trade is also necessary because goods do not always fetch a high price in the country where they are made. For example, many clothes are made by hand in countries where wages are low. But the clothes are sold in another country where people are richer and can pay a high price. Money earned this way helps less rich countries pay for their imports.

IMPORTS AND EXPORTS
Goods that are traded internationally are called imports and exports. Goods that one country sells to another are called exports; imports are goods that a country buys from another. In most nations, private businesses control imports and exports. But in others, the government imposes strict controls on what can be bought and sold.

TRADE AGREEMENTS
Some countries sign trade agreements in order to control trade between them. The agreement may simply fix the price at which the two countries buy and sell certain goods, such as tea and wheat. The European Union (EU) has a complicated network of trade agreements which allow free exchange of goods between member countries. The EU also restricts trade with countries that are not members of the Union. This helps encourage industry within the Union.

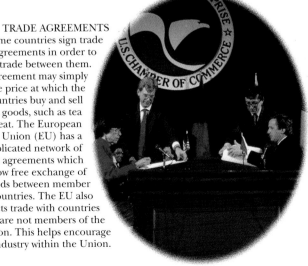

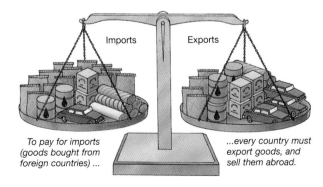

Imports

Exports

To pay for imports (goods bought from foreign countries) ...

...every country must export goods, and sell them abroad.

BALANCE OF PAYMENTS
Each country pays for imports with the money it earns by selling goods in other countries. This balance between imports and exports is called the balance of trade, or the balance of payments. Countries that do not export enough must borrow money from abroad to pay for imports.

FACTORIES

Some industry takes place in people's homes, but workers in factories make most of the products that we buy. In a factory each person has a small task in the manufacturing process. He or she may operate a large machine or assemble something by hand. No one person makes an entire product. This process of mass production makes manufacturing cheaper and quicker. Most factories are owned by large companies; a few factories are owned by governments or by the people who work in them.

The restaurant industry provides the service of cooking and serving food.

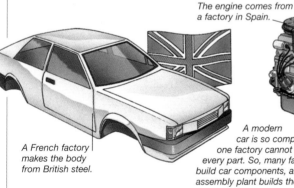

SUPPLY AND DEMAND

Companies set up factories to produce goods that they think people will want to buy. They sell the goods at a price that allows the company to make a profit. As long as there is a demand for the goods, the factory will continue to supply them. When fewer people buy the goods that the factory makes, prices drop to try to attract buyers, and workers in the factory may lose their jobs.

A factory starts by making a small number of umbrellas.

Shops put a few umbrellas on sale at a high price.

Many people need umbrellas and buy them, increasing demand.

The factory employs more people to make more umbrellas.

When everyone has an umbrella, demand for umbrellas falls.

Prices drop, and the factory needs fewer umbrella workers.

SERVICE INDUSTRIES

Not all industries make objects for sale. Some industries provide a service in return for money. A garage, for instance, might charge a fee to adjust a car so that it runs more efficiently. People pay for this service rather than do the work themselves.

The engine comes from a factory in Spain.

A French factory makes the body from British steel.

A modern car is so complex that one factory cannot make every part. So, many factories build car components, and an assembly plant builds the vehicle.

The transmission is made in Germany.

Final assembly of the car may take place in Spain.

TRADE UNIONS

During the 19th century, workers began to form trade unions in order to obtain better pay and conditions for their members. If a union cannot achieve its aims, its members may go on strike – stop work – until their demands are met.

The successful strike of women workers in a London match factory in 1888 encouraged other workers to join unions.

MANUFACTURING

The basic form of industry is manufacturing. This means working on materials to manufacture, or make, a finished product. Almost everything we use is the product of manufacturing, and most manufacturing takes place in large factories. However, craftsworkers manufacture goods alone or in small groups. Some goods go through many stages of manufacturing. For example, workers making cars assemble manufactured components or parts which, in turn, have been made in many other factories, often in other countries.

Find out more
DEPRESSION OF THE 1930s
INDUSTRIAL REVOLUTION
MACHINES
MONEY
PLASTICS
PORTS AND WATERWAYS

TRAINS

WHEN THE FIRST RAILWAYS were built more than 150 years ago, many people said they were the most wonderful of all inventions. Others said the snorting, smoking steam engines were like ugly, metal monsters. Trains and railways certainly changed our world. Not only did embankments and cuttings alter the landscape, but also, for the first time, people and goods could be carried long distances in vast quantities – and at speeds undreamed of. Railways also allowed cities to grow more than ever before. Today, large networks of railways stretch through many countries. If the tracks of the world's main rail routes were laid end to end, they would circle the Earth more than 34 times. Trains are an efficient method of transport. They use less fuel and produce less pollution than cars and trucks because they carry large cargoes in a single journey. Because of the damage road vehicles do to our environment, many people believe trains are the best form of transport for the future.

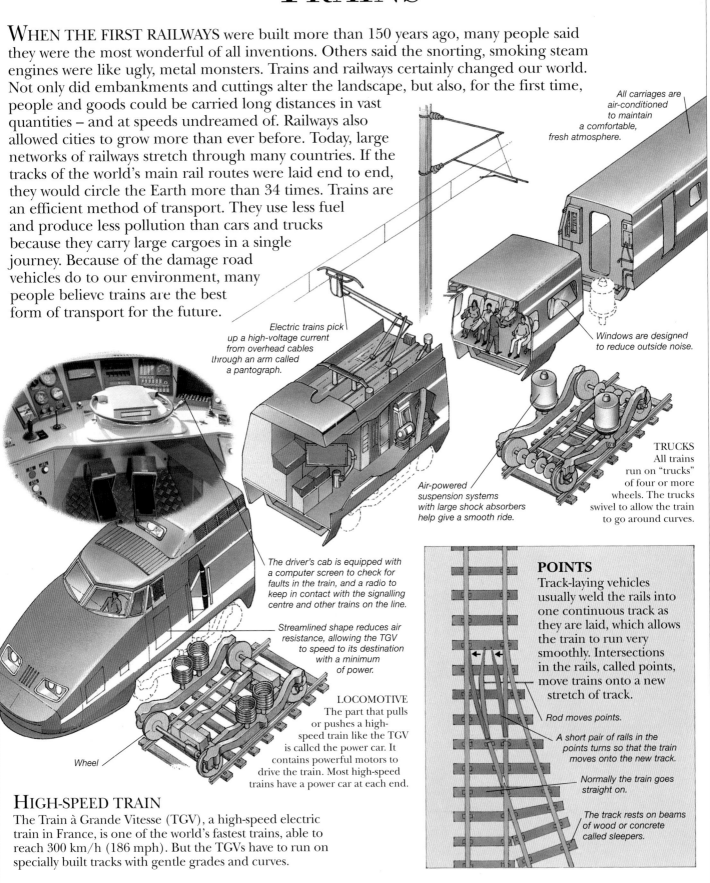

All carriages are air-conditioned to maintain a comfortable, fresh atmosphere.

Electric trains pick up a high-voltage current from overhead cables through an arm called a pantograph.

Windows are designed to reduce outside noise.

Air-powered suspension systems with large shock absorbers help give a smooth ride.

TRUCKS
All trains run on "trucks" of four or more wheels. The trucks swivel to allow the train to go around curves.

The driver's cab is equipped with a computer screen to check for faults in the train, and a radio to keep in contact with the signalling centre and other trains on the line.

Streamlined shape reduces air resistance, allowing the TGV to speed to its destination with a minimum of power.

LOCOMOTIVE
The part that pulls or pushes a high-speed train like the TGV is called the power car. It contains powerful motors to drive the train. Most high-speed trains have a power car at each end.

Wheel

POINTS
Track-laying vehicles usually weld the rails into one continuous track as they are laid, which allows the train to run very smoothly. Intersections in the rails, called points, move trains onto a new stretch of track.

Rod moves points.

A short pair of rails in the points turns so that the train moves onto the new track.

Normally the train goes straight on.

The track rests on beams of wood or concrete called sleepers.

HIGH-SPEED TRAIN

The Train à Grande Vitesse (TGV), a high-speed electric train in France, is one of the world's fastest trains, able to reach 300 km/h (186 mph). But the TGVs have to run on specially built tracks with gentle grades and curves.

RICHARD TREVITHICK

In 1804, a steam locomotive (right) built by Englishman Richard Trevithick ran on rails for the first time. Trevithick thought that steam power had a future, and bet that his steam engine could haul 9 tonnes (9 tons) of iron 15 km (9.5 miles) along a mine railway in Wales. Trevithick won his bet; the engine carried not only the iron but also 70 cheering coal miners who climbed aboard.

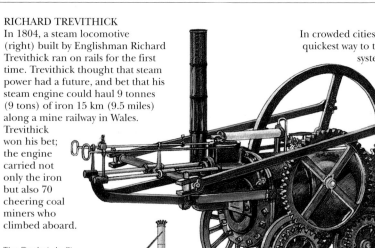

The Rocket, built by English engineer George Stephenson in 1829, was a new design that heralded the age of the passenger train.

A front truck was introduced on early American locomotives to give a smoother ride around curves.

During the mid-1800s, England's railway system developed into a large network.

Engines could reach 200 km/h (126 mph) by the 1930s – the peak of the steam age.

Steam locomotives of the1930s were very sophisticated compared to the first engines.

UNDERGROUND TRAINS

In crowded cities, underground trains are the quickest way to travel. The first underground system was opened in London in 1863. Now many cities have their own network. The Metro in Paris is one of the most efficient underground systems in the world.

STEAM RAILWAYS

Railways date back 4,000 years to the Babylonians, who pushed carts along grooves. But the age of railways really began in the early 1800s when steam engines first ran on rails. In 1825, the first passenger line opened in England; 30 years later, vast railway systems stretched across Europe and North America. By the 1890s, steam engines could reach speeds of more than 160 km/h (100 mph).

SIGNALS AND SAFETY

Trackside signals tell the driver how fast to go and when to stop. In the past, signals were mechanical arms worked by levers in the signal box. Nowadays they are usually sets of coloured lights controlled by computers that monitor the position of every train.

MAGLEVS AND MONORAILS

One day we may be whisked along silently at speeds of 480 km/h (300 mph) on trains that glide a small distance above special tracks, held up by magnetic force – which is why they are called maglevs (for magnetic levitation). Some countries, such as China, already have maglev lines. Other new designs include monorail trains, which are electric trains that run on, or are suspended from, a single rail.

The Shanghai maglev

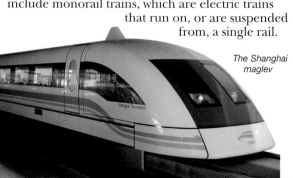

ORIENT EXPRESS

Some trains have become famous for their speed, some for their luxury, and others for the length of their route. From 1883, the *Orient Express*, for example, provided a first-class service from Paris to Constantinople (Istanbul), Turkey. It still travels part of this route today. The world's longest train route is the *Trans-Siberian Express*, which runs 9,438 km (5,864 miles) across Siberia.

Find out more

ENGINES
INDUSTRIAL REVOLUTION
TECHNOLOGY
TRANSPORT, HISTORY OF

HISTORY OF
TRANSPORT

WE LIVE IN AN AGE when people can fly across the Atlantic Ocean in less than three hours. Straight roads link city to city across the world. Yet 7,000 years ago the only way that people could get from one place to another was by walking. In around 5,000 BCE people began to use donkeys and oxen as pack animals, instead of carrying their goods on their backs or heads. Then, 1,500 years later, the first wheeled vehicles developed in Mesopotamia. From around 1500 CE, deep-sea sailing ships developed rapidly as Europeans began to make great ocean voyages to explore the rest of the world. During the 1700s, steam power marked another milestone in transport. Steam engines were soon moving ships and trains faster than anyone had imagined. During the next century the first cars took to the road and the first flying machines took to the air.

STAGECOACH
So called because they stopped at stages on a route to change horses, stagecoaches were the most popular type of public land transport during the 17th and 18th centuries. Coaching inns sprung up along popular stagecoach routes.

Railways began to appear in the United States in the 1820s. Trains could carry more goods and people than any other kind of transport.

LAND TRAVEL
Land travel is the most common kind of transport. It all began with walking. Two thousand years ago the Romans built a network of superb roads over which people travelled by foot or by horse-drawn cart. It was only in the 1800s that steam power took the place of horse power. Steam locomotives provided cheap long-distance travel for ordinary people. In the early years of this century, engine-powered cars, trucks, and buses were developed.

CARS
Cars are now the most popular form of private transport. They were invented towards the end of the 19th century.

JUNK
One of the world's strongest sailing ships, the junk has been used in Asia for thousands of years. Mainly a trading vessel, it has large, highly efficient sails made of linen or matting.

BARGE
A barge is a sturdy boat which transports cargo, such as coal, from place to place along canals and rivers.

SEA TRAVEL
Floating logs led to the first watercraft, the simple raft. In around 3500 BCE the Sumerians and the Egyptians made fishing boats out of reeds from the riverbank. They also built watertight wooden ships with oars and a sail, for seagoing voyages. In the 19th century, steel replaced wood, and steam engines gradually took over from sails. Today's engine-powered ships can carry huge loads of cargo at speeds never reached under sail.

Ocean liners (below) are used as floating hotels. They take passengers on cruises and call at different resorts along the way.

AIR TRAVEL

In 1783 the Frenchmen Pilâtre de Rozier and the Marquis d'Arlandes made the first human flight in a hot air balloon. Then, in 1903, to everyone's amazement, brothers Orville and Wilbur Wright built and flew the first powered plane near Kitty Hawk, North Carolina, U.S.A. Aircraft developed rapidly in the two world wars that followed. In 1918, the U.S. Post Office began the first airmail service. Today, it is hard to imagine a world without aircraft.

BALLOONS

Long before aeroplanes were invented, people flew in balloons – bags filled with hot air or a lighter-than-air gas. In 1783, the Montgolfier brothers of France built the first balloon to lift humans into the air. Balloons were used by the French emperor Napoleon as flying lookout posts, and later, balloons were used during the Civil War and World War I. Today, ballooning is a popular sport.

In the early days of flying, airline companies used colourful posters to encourage people to fly with them.

AEROPLANES

Today, millions of people depend on aeroplanes for both business and pleasure. But the golden age of aeroplane development occurred only 80 years ago, when daring pilots took great risks in testing aeroplanes and flying long distances. Jet-powered passenger aeroplanes appeared in the 1950s. A supersonic airliner, *Concorde*, was in service from 1976 to 2003. At 2,500 km/h (1,550 mph), it travelled faster than the speed of sound.

The Apollo II spacecraft

SPACE TRAVEL

Not content with the sky, humans wanted to explore space and distant planets as well. In 1957, the Soviets fired the first satellite, *Sputnik*, into orbit (a path around the Earth). In 1968, the United States sent the first manned craft around the Moon. Then, in 1969, astronaut Neil Armstrong became the first person to walk on the Moon.

POLLUTION-FREE TRANSPORT

Many of today's forms of powered transport pollute the environment because their engines send out dangerous gases. Cars, in particular, upset the natural balance of the atmosphere. Lead-free petrol helps reduce the amount of poison which cars release into the air. The transport systems that cause the least pollution are those using natural power, such as wind. On land, people can help preserve our planet by walking, bicycling, or using animals to pull wheeled vehicles. At sea, large loads can be moved in sailing ships powered only by the wind.

Rollerblading

Skateboarding

Walking

Cycling

Find out more
AIRCRAFT
CARS
SHIPS AND BOATS
TECHNOLOGY
TRAINS

TREES

WITHOUT PLANTS such as trees there could be no life on Earth. Trees take in carbon dioxide from the air and give off oxygen by the process of photosynthesis, so maintaining the balance of the atmosphere. Tree roots stabilize the soil so it is not washed away by the rain, and their leaves give off vast amounts of water vapour, which affects the balance of the world's weather. Forests cover about 39 million sq km (15 million sq miles) of the planet's surface. Trees vary greatly in size, from towering redwoods to dwarf snow willows, that are only a few centimetres high. They supply food for millions of creatures, and produce wood to make buildings, furniture – even the pages of this book.

Giant sequoia trees are the largest living things – more than 84 m (270 ft) high, and 2,000 tonnes (1,970 tons) in weight; an elephant weighs about 5 tonnes (5 tons).

Leaves

English oak tree in spring and autumn

Buds

Oak bark

Acorns are the fruits of the oak tree; they develop from the pollinated female flowers during autumn.

CONIFEROUS TREES

Pines, firs, cedars, and redwoods are called coniferous trees, or conifers, because they grow their seeds in hard, woody cones. The long, narrow leaves, called needles, stay on the tree all winter. These trees are also called evergreens, because they stay green all year.

CONES
Each tree has its own type of cone, which develops from the fertilized female flowers.

Larch cone

Scots pine needles grow in pairs.

Pine cone

Arolla pine needles

Conifer roots usually spread out sideways.

Sitka spruce cone turns brown as it ripens.

NEEDLES
Every conifer has distinctively shaped needles that grow in a certain pattern. Sitka spruce needles are long and sharp.

Needle

Sitka spruce is an evergreen coniferous tree often seen in forest plantations.

BROAD-LEAVED TREES

Oaks, beeches, willows, and many other trees are called broad-leaved because their leaves are broad and flat, unlike the sharp needles on coniferous trees. Some broad-leaved trees are also called deciduous, because their leaves die and drop off in autumn.

The roots of a deciduous tree may reach out sideways to the same distance as the tree's height.

LEAVES
Broad-leaved trees can be recognized by the shape of their leaves and the pattern in which the leaves grow on the twigs. In winter, you can identify a bare tree by its bark, buds, and overall shape.

Leaves of the holly tree are spiky.

Japanese maple leaves have deep notches.

The gingko tree has fan-shaped leaves.

Rowan or mountain ash trees have compound leaves.

Sweet chestnut leaves have a jagged edge.

GROWTH

All trees grow from small seeds inside their fruit. Each seed contains a food store and a tiny embryo tree. The seed begins to grow when the temperature and moisture of the soil are suitable. A young tree is called a sapling.

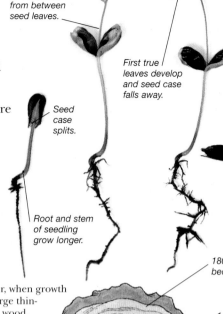

Shoot grows from between seed leaves.

First true leaves develop and seed case falls away.

Seed case splits.

Beech seed (or beechnut) is contained in hard seed case.

Root begins to emerge.

Root and stem of seedling grow longer.

New leaves develop each spring.

SEASONAL GROWTH

In temperate regions, where there are definite seasons each year, trees grow during spring and summer. Growth occurs mainly at the ends of the tree, the tips of the branches, and the roots. The twigs lengthen, and flowers and leaves appear from the buds. Root tips grow longer and push their way through the soil. The roots and branches thicken, as does the tree trunk, so that the tree's girth, or waistband, also increases in size.

Twig tips grow.

Trunk and branches thicken.

Roots become fatter.

Root tips lengthen.

TREE TRUNK

During spring and early summer, when growth is rapid, tree trunks thicken. Large thin-walled cells form light-coloured wood. Slower growth during the rest of the year produces thick-walled cells that make darker-coloured wood. One light-coloured ring plus one dark ring indicates one year's growth. Some tropical trees grow all year round; they have faint rings or none at all.

Bark cambium (growing area) of young tree

INSIDE A TREE

Counting the rings on a section of trunk can tell us the age of a tree. This is a section of a very old giant sequoia tree.

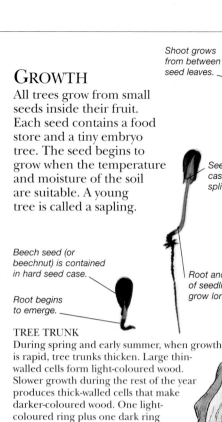

Young bark is smooth.

Bark grows from the inside and pushes the older bark outwards.

Old bark cracks and flakes.

1800 CE Washington, D.C., becomes U.S. capital.

1400 CE Joan of Arc burned at the stake.

800 CE Charlemagne crowned emperor.

Native Americans used the smooth bark of birch trees to make canoes.

BARK

The tree's bark is its skin. It shields the living wood within, stops it from drying out, and protects it from extreme cold and heat. Bark prevents damage from moulds, but some animals, such as deer and beavers, eat the bark, and a few wood-boring beetles can tunnel through. A tree with no leaves can be identified by the colour and texture of its bark.

The rough bark of the cork tree is stripped off every eight to 10 years; it is used to make bottle stoppers and floor tiles.

Coconut palm tree

PALM TREES

The 2,700 kinds of palm tree are found in warm Mediterranean and tropical regions. These tall, straight trees provide many products, including palm oils, dates, and coconuts from the coconut palm.

The outer husk of the coconut is used to make coconut matting (above). Coconuts are a valuable source of milk, edible fats, and animal food.

Native Americans carved whole tree trunks to create totem poles.

WOOD

Each year we use thousands of tonnes of wood for building, as fuel for cooking and heating, and to make tools, furniture, and paper. As the world's population grows, vast areas of forest are cut down, particularly in South America, where much of the tropical rain forest has been destroyed.

Whole tree trunks are used to make telephone poles.

In the past, loggers had to float logs to the sawmill.

Find out more

FOREST WILDLIFE
FRUITS AND SEEDS
PLANTS
SOIL

HARRIET TUBMAN

c. 1820 Born into slavery.

1849 Escapes from slavery via the Underground Railroad.

1850 Fugitive Slave Act makes it a crime to help runaway slaves. Tubman makes her first trip as a "conductor".

1850-61 Leads over 300 people to freedom.

1857 Leads her parents to freedom in Auburn, New York.

1861-65 Serves as nurse, scout, and spy for the Union Army.

1913 Dies.

BLACK AMERICANS OWE MUCH to the bravery and determination of Harriet Tubman. Between 1850 and 1861, she led more than 300 black American slaves to freedom on what was known as the "Underground Railroad". Her courageous work earned her the nickname "General Moses", after the Biblical figure Moses who led the Jews out of slavery in Egypt. Tubman was born into slavery and like many other slaves experienced brutal treatment at the hands of her white masters. In 1849, she escaped from a Maryland plantation and made her way to Philadelphia. She vowed to go back and rescue other slaves, and a year later, she returned to Maryland to help members of her family escape. In all, she made 19 journeys back to the South, risking capture, and possible death. During the American Civil War (1861-65), she worked for the Union Army in South Carolina. After slavery was abolished, she continued to fight for black rights, setting up schools for black children, and a home for elderly black Americans.

VALUABLE GANG OF YOUNG NEGROES
By JOS. A. BEARD.
Will be sold at Auction,
ON WEDNESDAY, 25TH INST.
At 12 o'clock, at Banks' Arcade,
17 Valuable Young Negroes, Men and Women, Field Hands. Sold for no fault; with the best city guarantees.
Sale Positive and without reserve!
TERMS CASH.
New Orleans, March 24, 1840.

SLAVES FOR SALE
Slaves had no rights. They were bought and sold as property. By law, they were not allowed to own anything, assemble in groups of more than five, or even learn to read and write.

UNDERGROUND RAILROAD

The "Underground Railroad" was not really a railway, but an elaborate network of escape routes that was described using railway terms. Runaway slaves, known as "freight" or "passengers", were helped to flee secretly at night. Guides called "conductors" led them from one "station", or stopping place, to the next. The escape routes stretched all the way from the states of the South to the North and Canada. During the day, helpers hid fugitives in barns and haylofts. Thousands of anti-slavery campaigners – both black and white, and many of them women – risked their lives to operate the "railroad".

CANADA
Ogdensburg
Kingston
Montpelier
L. Ontario
Toronto
Oswego
Rochester
Buffalo
Syracuse Albany
L. Eyrie
Eyrie
Jamestown
Elmira
UNITED STATES
Appalachian Mountains
New Haven
Boston
Atlantic Ocean
New York
Philadelphia

Map of Underground Railroad escape routes

STOPPING PLACE
Every 15–30 km (10–20 miles) along the route was a "station", or safe house, where the "passengers" could rest or hide in safety. This sign (right) commemorates a "station" of 1821.

The GOODWIN SISTER'S HOUSE ELIZABETH & ABIGAIL UNDERGROUND RAILWAY 1821

Harriet Tubman (far left) with a group of freed slaves

GENERAL MOSES

Harriet Tubman was a brave woman who believed that God gave her courage and strength. She was so successful a "conductor" that angry plantation owners offered a huge reward for her capture. She travelled during winter, meeting runaway slaves about 15 km (10 miles) from their plantations and then leading them to safety. She escaped capture more than once, and never lost a slave on her escape missions.

$150 REWARD
RANAWAY from the subscriber, on the night of the 2d instant, a negro man, who calls himself Henry May, about 22 years old, 5 feet 6 or 8 inches high, ordinary color, rather chunky built, bushy head, and has it divided mostly on one side, and keeps it very nicely combed; has been raised in the house, and is a first rate dining-room servant, and was in a tavern in Louisville for 18 months. I expect he is now in Louisville trying to make his escape to a free state. On all probability he will try to get employment on a steamboat. He is a good cook, and is handy in any capacity as a house servant. Had on when he left a dark cassinett coatee, and dark striped cassinett pantaloons, new also had other clothing. I will give $50 reward if taken in Louisville, 100 dollars if taken one hundred miles from Louisville in this State, and 150 dollars if taken out of the State, and delivered to me, or secured in any jail so that I can get him again.
WILLIAM BURKE
Bardstown, Ky, September 2d, 1838.

RUNAWAY SLAVES
Northern states banned slavery in the 1780s, but it remained legal in the South until 1865. Laws passed in 1793 and 1850 made it a crime to help runaway slaves.

Find out more
AMERICAN CIVIL WAR
HUMAN RIGHTS
KING, MARTIN LUTHER
SLAVERY
UNITED STATES, HISTORY OF

TUDORS

HENRY VII
The first Tudor king was Henry VII (r. 1485-1509). His name was Henry Tudor, and the dynasty (ruling house) took its name from him. A member of the House of Lancaster, he married Elizabeth of York to unite their two houses. He kept other noble families under control, banning their armies, and defeating two rivals to the throne.

THE TUDORS CAME TO the throne in 1485. Before that, there had been years of civil war between two rival ruling family groups, the House of York and the House of Lancaster. But during the Tudor period, which ended in 1603, England enjoyed a time of lasting peace. Rulers such as Henry VII, who united the warring houses, and Elizabeth I, improved the economy, making the country a richer place. It was also a golden age for the arts, with major poets, great playwrights, and fine composers creating important works. However, there were damaging disputes over religion, with the official faith of England changing repeatedly until Elizabeth I became queen. Under her, the Protestant Church of England became established as the national religion.

THE TUDORS

1485 Battle of Bosworth: Henry Tudor defeats Richard III. He rules as Henry VII.

1497 Henry supports voyages to America by John and Sebastian Cabot.

1509-47 Henry VIII reigns.

1534 Henry VIII rebels against the pope and becomes head of the Church of England.

1547-53 Edward VI reigns.

1553-58 Reign of Mary I.

1554 Mary marries Philip of Spain, creating an alliance between the two countries.

1558-1603 Reign of Elizabeth I, last of the Tudors.

DAILY LIFE
In Tudor times, most people lived in the countryside, and there was much poverty. Many country people had a difficult life, working hard and earning little. A few made money farming sheep and exporting the wool to Europe. In the towns, merchants and craftworkers could make a good living. Some of their houses still survive.

Gaps between timbers filled in with wattle (thin strips of wood) and daub (mud or clay).

Framework made of strong oak timbers

Roof covered with baked clay tiles

Overhang, or "jetty", gave more room on the upper floor.

This house, belonging to a wealthy Tudor merchant, had two storeys. Its central hall reached up through both levels.

Fireplace had a brick chimney, to keep heat away from the timbers.

Large central hall provided living space for the family.

Lute

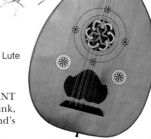

MARY TUDOR
England was a Protestant country when Mary Tudor (r. 1553-58) became queen. Mary married Philip II of Spain, and made England Catholic again. She ordered that Protestants who refused to change their faith were to be burned at the stake, for which she earned the nickname "Bloody Mary".

Protestants being burned at the stake.

MUSIC AND ENTERTAINMENT
The Tudors enjoyed good food and drink, dancing, and music. Some of England's greatest composers lived during the Tudor period. They included Thomas Morley and John Dowland, who wrote songs and music for the lute, and Thomas Tallis and William Byrd, who composed choral music.

Find out more
ELIZABETH I
HENRY VIII
STUARTS

TURKEY

MARKET PRODUCE
Street markets are an important part of every Turkish town. Stalls sell a variety of produce, from olives, spices and vegetables to clothing and household goods. This woman is wearing traditional Turkish clothes – loose, baggy trousers and a printed headscarf – which are still widely worn, especially in the countryside.

TURKEY LIES in both Asia and Europe; today it is on the verge of becoming part of modern Europe, yet retains many elements of its Asian history. Western Turkey was an important part of both the Greek and Roman worlds. The invasion of Turkish nomads (Ottomans) from the east in the 15th century brought the Islamic religion and the nomadic culture of Central Asia. Turkey became a republic in 1923, and rapidly entered the 20th century. Islam is no longer the state religion, although it is widely practised. A wide range of manufacturing and textile industries have strengthened Turkey's growing economic links with Europe. With its warm climate and fertile soils, Turkey is able to produce all its own food – even in the arid southeast huge dams on the Euphrates river are used to water the land. The west and south coasts are visited by increasing numbers of tourists.

Turkey lies at the western edge of Asia, and extends into the south-eastern tip of Europe. It is bounded on three sides by the Black, Mediterranean and Aegean Seas.

Bodrum's St. Peter's castle (right) is a fine example of Crusader architecture.

ISTANBUL

Turkey's largest city and sea port straddles the continents of Europe and Asia, which are separated by the Bosporus Strait. Founded by Greeks in the 8th century BCE, later to become capital of the Eastern Roman Empire, Istanbul fell to the Ottoman Turks in 1453. The Ottomans beautified the capital with mosques, and built the sumptuous Topkapi Palace, the home of the sultan and his many wives. Today Istanbul is a sprawling, bustling city with a population of more than 10 million.

The Library of Celsus at Ephesus was built in the 2nd century CE for a Roman consul.

TURKISH TOURISM

Turkey's warm climate, beautiful coastline and rich history attract many tourists from northern Europe. Most of the tourists travel to the Aegean and Mediterranean coasts where picturesque harbours, such as Bodrum (above), are accessible to beautiful beaches. There are some worries that the fast pace of development is spoiling the landscape.

ANKARA
Ankara became capital of the new Turkish republic in 1923 – a break with the Ottoman past. Ankara's history dates back to the 2nd millennium BCE. It was an important Ottoman cultural and commercial centre, located on the main caravan routes. Today, the modern city centre is the headquarters of the government.

CLASSICAL RUINS
The Aegean coast was colonized by Greeks by the 7th century BCE, and western Turkey was an important part of the Greek, and subsequently, the Roman worlds. Many well preserved classical cities attract both archaeologists and tourists to Turkey. Ephesus was the home of the Temple of Artemis, one of the Seven Wonders of the ancient world.

Find out more
ASIA, HISTORY OF
GREECE, ANCIENT
OTTOMAN EMPIRE
ROMAN EMPIRE
WONDERS
of the ancient world

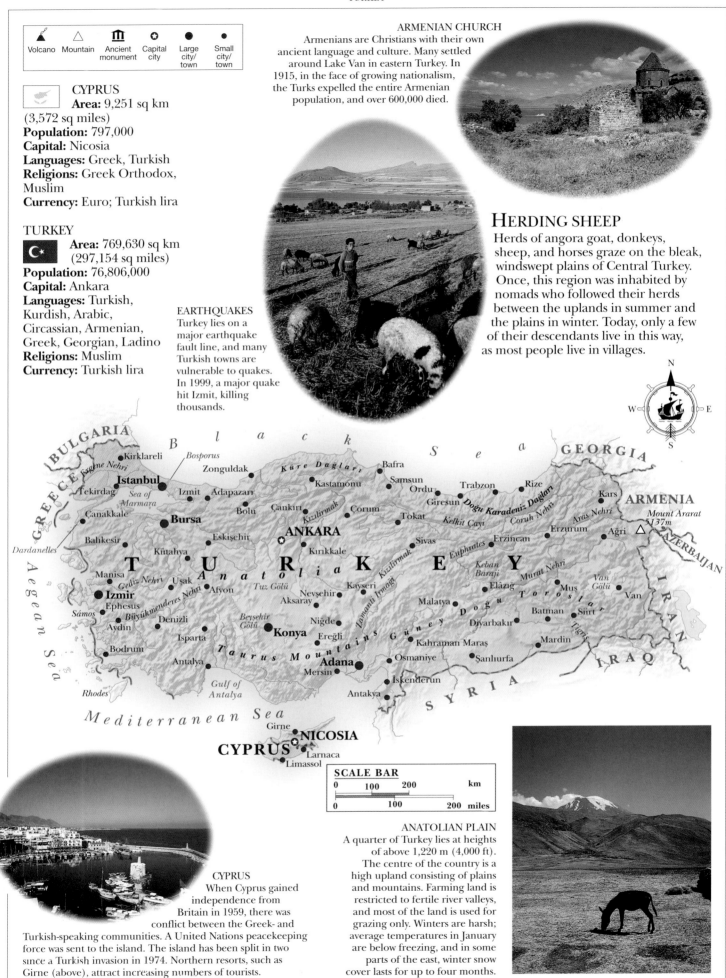

Volcano | **Mountain** | **Ancient monument** | **Capital city** | **Large city/town** | **Small city/town**

CYPRUS
Area: 9,251 sq km (3,572 sq miles)
Population: 797,000
Capital: Nicosia
Languages: Greek, Turkish
Religions: Greek Orthodox, Muslim
Currency: Euro; Turkish lira

TURKEY
Area: 769,630 sq km (297,154 sq miles)
Population: 76,806,000
Capital: Ankara
Languages: Turkish, Kurdish, Arabic, Circassian, Armenian, Greek, Georgian, Ladino
Religions: Muslim
Currency: Turkish lira

ARMENIAN CHURCH
Armenians are Christians with their own ancient language and culture. Many settled around Lake Van in eastern Turkey. In 1915, in the face of growing nationalism, the Turks expelled the entire Armenian population, and over 600,000 died.

HERDING SHEEP
Herds of angora goat, donkeys, sheep, and horses graze on the bleak, windswept plains of Central Turkey. Once, this region was inhabited by nomads who followed their herds between the uplands in summer and the plains in winter. Today, only a few of their descendants live in this way, as most people live in villages.

EARTHQUAKES
Turkey lies on a major earthquake fault line, and many Turkish towns are vulnerable to quakes. In 1999, a major quake hit Izmit, killing thousands.

CYPRUS
When Cyprus gained independence from Britain in 1959, there was conflict between the Greek- and Turkish-speaking communities. A United Nations peacekeeping force was sent to the island. The island has been split in two since a Turkish invasion in 1974. Northern resorts, such as Girne (above), attract increasing numbers of tourists.

SCALE BAR
0 — 100 — 200 km
0 — 100 — 200 miles

ANATOLIAN PLAIN
A quarter of Turkey lies at heights of above 1,220 m (4,000 ft). The centre of the country is a high upland consisting of plains and mountains. Farming land is restricted to fertile river valleys, and most of the land is used for grazing only. Winters are harsh; average temperatures in January are below freezing, and in some parts of the east, winter snow cover lasts for up to four months.

UKRAINE

Volcano	Mountain	Ancient monument	Capital city	Large city/town	Small city/town

UKRAINE HAS BEEN an independent republic since 1991, when the Soviet Union collapsed. The country is dominated by rolling flat grasslands, rich in fertile soils, and is crossed by major rivers such as the Dnieper, Donets, and Bug. The year-round warm climate and sandy beaches of the Crimean peninsula attract many tourists, especially from Russia and Germany. With its fertile land and mild climate, Ukraine is a major cereals producer, once called the "bread-basket" of the Soviet Union. In the east, the basin of the River Donets is rich in deposits of coal, iron ore, manganese, zinc, and mercury. It is the centre of a major industrial heartland. In 1986, a radiation leak in Chernobyl, one of Ukraine's nuclear power stations, caused panic in Europe. Much of the land around the plant is still contaminated, and towns stand desolate and empty. In 2004, when the people elected a president who favoured close ties with the West, relations between Ukraine and Russia became more strained and disputes occurred.

The Carpathian Mountains form Ukraine's western border. To the south lies the Black Sea. The Crimean peninsula extends into the Black Sea, forming the Sea of Azov to the east. Ukraine's flat steppes are bisected by the Dnieper river, which drains into the Black Sea.

STATISTICS
Area: 603,700 sq km (223,090 sq miles)
Population: 45,700,000
Capital: Kiev
Languages: Ukrainian, Russian, Tatar
Religions: Ukrainian Orthodox, Roman Catholic, Protestant, Jewish
Currency: Hryvnia
Main occupations: Agriculture, mining
Main exports: Coal, titanium, iron ore, manganese ore, steel
Main imports: Oil, natural gas

INDUSTRIAL HEARTLAND
Eastern Ukraine, with its rich reserves of iron, coal, gas, and oil, is a major centre of industry. Ukraine is one of the world's top steel producers, and large iron and steel works dominate the landscape. Ukraine also manufactures mining and transport equipment, trucks, cars, railway locomotives, ships, and turbines.

KIEV
Kiev is one of Eastern Europe's oldest towns. It is believed to have existed as a commercial centre in the early 5th century.

SCALE BAR
0   50   100   km
0   50   100   miles

KIEV
The capital of Ukraine lies on the Dnieper river, 952 km (591 miles) from the river's mouth in the Black Sea. Kiev was founded in the 8th century as the capital of the state of Kievan Rus. The focus of the city is the ancient Upper Town where historic buildings still survive despite the damage done during World War II. The Church of Saint Sophia (left), founded in the 11th century, is a famous landmark of the Eastern Orthodox faith.

Find out more
EUROPE
EUROPE, HISTORY OF
IRON AND STEEL
NUCLEAR ENERGY
SOVIET UNION, HISTORY OF

UNITED KINGDOM

THE UNITED KINGDOM of Great Britain and Northern Ireland was formed under the Act of Union of 1801. It is made up of England, Wales, and Scotland, which together form the island of Great Britain, and the province of Northern Ireland. In the late 1990s, the British government devolved power to regional governments by creating new parliaments in Northern Ireland, Scotland and Wales. The English countryside is famed for its gently sloping hills and rich farmland. Wales and Scotland are mostly wild and mountainous. Much of Northern Ireland is low-lying and marshy. In Wales and parts of Scotland, many of the people speak a language of their own. Britain is a multicultural country, for the English, Scots, Welsh, and Irish are all separate peoples. In the last 100 years refugees and immigrants from Europe, Africa, Asia, and the Caribbean have settled in Britain, bringing with them their own languages and religions. Britain once controlled a vast empire that stretched around the world. In recent years its economy has declined, but the discovery of oil in the North Sea has helped to make the country self-sufficient in energy.

The United Kingdom is just off the northwest coast of Europe. To its east lies the North Sea. The Atlantic Ocean washes its northern and western coasts. The English Channel separates the country from mainland Europe.

Distinctive red double-decker buses and black taxis ferry Londoners around their city.

LONDON

When the Roman armies invaded Britain almost 2,000 years ago, they built a fortified town called Londinium to safeguard the crossing over the River Thames. By 1100, the city of London had grown in size to become the capital of the entire country. Today, London is a huge city of more than 7 million people and is the political, financial, and cultural centre of Britain. Tourists come from all over the world to admire the historic buildings, particularly the Tower of London (left), an 11th-century fortress.

CITY OF LONDON

The ancient heart of London is called the City. London is one of the world's leading financial centres, and most of the nation's banks and businesses have their headquarters here. The modern building shown on the left is the Lloyd's Building, where the world's shipping is registered and insured.

Cricket began in Britain, and is the country's national sport. Many villages have their own teams.

ENGLAND

The biggest and most populated part of the United Kingdom is England. Many people live in large towns and cities, such as London, Birmingham, and Manchester. Parts of the southeast and the north are very crowded. The English countryside is varied, with rolling farmland in the south and east and hilly moors in the north and west. England is dotted with picturesque villages where old houses and shops are often grouped around a village green.

The rose is the national flower of England.

JERSEY AND GUERNSEY

The Channel Islands of Jersey and Guernsey are closer to France than they are to Britain. The French coast is just 24 km (15 miles) away from Jersey, the largest island. Close to Jersey and Guernsey are some smaller islands that are also part of the Channel Islands group. All of the islands have a mild climate, so one of the principal occupations is the growing of vegetables. The warm weather and ample sunshine also attract holidaymakers, who in the summer months swell the islands' usual population of 150,000.

Thousands of colourful flowers are used to decorate floats for Jersey's "Battle of the Flowers" festival.

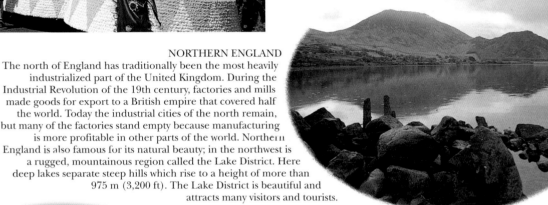

NORTHERN ENGLAND

The north of England has traditionally been the most heavily industrialized part of the United Kingdom. During the Industrial Revolution of the 19th century, factories and mills made goods for export to a British empire that covered half the world. Today the industrial cities of the north remain, but many of the factories stand empty because manufacturing is more profitable in other parts of the world. Northern England is also famous for its natural beauty; in the northwest is a rugged, mountainous region called the Lake District. Here deep lakes separate steep hills which rise to a height of more than 975 m (3,200 ft). The Lake District is beautiful and attracts many visitors and tourists.

"Mad Sunday" motor cyclist on the Isle of Man

ISLE OF MAN

The Isle of Man is part of the United Kingdom but enjoys a certain amount of independence. The Manx people, as islanders are called, have their own government, called the Tynwald, which makes many decisions about how the island is run. There is also a Manx language, though it is now used only for formal ceremonies. Manx independence has a long history, and between 1405 and 1765 the island was a kingdom separate from England.

FISHING INDUSTRY

The waters of the northeast Atlantic are among the world's richest fishing grounds. But EU regulations, designed to reduce catches and conserve fish stocks, are causing widespread discontent amongst fishermen.

The United Kingdom has many fishing ports, like this one in Scotland.

PEOPLE

The United Kingdom is densely populated, with most of the people living in urban areas, particularly in the southeast of England. Almost 10 per cent of the total population of the country lives in London. The southeast is also the most prosperous area. Other parts of the country are less crowded. For example, the Highlands in Scotland have less inhabitants today than 200 years ago.

SHETLAND AND ORKNEY

To the northeast of Scotland, two groups of islands form Britain's most northerly outposts. Orkney and Shetland comprise about 170 islands in all, but only the larger islands are inhabited. The landscape is bleak and there are few trees. The land is too poor to make farming profitable, and the traditional local industry is fishing. The islands are also famous for their hand-knitted wool clothes: Fair Isle has given its name to a distinctive knitting pattern.

A Welsh village has the longest placename in the United Kingdom.

LLANFAIRPWLLGWYNGYLLGOGERYCHWYRN-DROBWLLLLANTYSILIOGOGOGOCH

WALES

Farming, forestry, and tourism are the most important occupations in the rural regions of Wales. Farms tend to be small and average 40 hectares (16 acres) in size. Farmers in the upland regions keep cattle and sheep. Wales was once one of the main coal-producing areas in the world. There were 630 collieries in the region in 1913. However, the coal industry declined in the years after the first World War.

PUBLIC HOUSES

Public houses, more usually called pubs, developed from inns which offered travellers food, drink, and shelter. The pub played a part in British culture, too. In the *Canterbury Tales* by Geoffrey Chaucer (1340-1400), pilgrims on their way to Canterbury in southeast England rest at pubs and tell each other tales. Many of the plays of William Shakespeare (1564-1616) were performed in the yards of London pubs. Today the pub is a social centre where adults meet to discuss the events of the day. Pubs often entertain their customers with music or poetry, and many British rock bands began their careers playing in a pub.

The leek is the Welsh National emblem.

By custom, the first son of the British king or queen becomes Prince of Wales, and wears a gold crown.

EISTEDDFOD

Every year a festival of poetry, music, and drama celebrates and promotes the Welsh language. This National Eisteddfod began in the 7th century. Today colourful choirs and orchestras compete for awards at the event.

SCOTTISH TOURISM

Tourism is an important source of income for Scotland. People are lured to the region by its beautifully wild Highland scenery. Scotland is steeped in history and visitors often take the opportunity to visit its many ancient castles. For centuries, Scotland was dominated by struggles between rival families, known as clans. Today one of the most popular tourist souvenirs is tartan – textiles woven in the colours of the clans.

Most of Scotland consists of high mountains and remote glens or valleys.

The Scottish emblem is the thistle.

The Irish shamrock emblem

NORTHERN IRELAND

Prior to the the 1960s, the economy of Northern Ireland was based on manufacturing, engineering, shipbuilding, and textiles. Heavy industry was concentrated in Belfast where shipbuilding (above) was the largest employer. However, civil disorder after 1968 had a detrimental effect on the economy and, as across the whole of the UK, the manufacturing industry has been in decline since then.

Find out more

ENGLAND
NORTHERN IRELAND
SCOTLAND
WALES

Volcano Mountain Ancient monument Capital city Large city/town Small city/town

STATISTICS

Area: 244,880 sq km
(94,550 sq miles)
Population: 61,634,000
Capital: London
Languages: English, Welsh, Scottish Gaelic, Irish Gaelic
Religions: Anglican, Roman Catholic, Presbyterian, Muslim, Methodist
Currency: Pound sterling
Main occupations: Finance, engineering, oil and gas production, manufacturing, agriculture
Main exports: Oil, natural gas, chemicals, electronics, cars, aircraft
Main imports: Machinery, fruit and vegetables, metals, raw materials

ENGLAND
Area: 130,423 sq km
(50,356 sq miles)
Population: 51,456,000
Capital: London

SCOTLAND
Area: 78,133 sq km
(30,167 sq miles)
Population: 5,169,000
Capital: Edinburgh

WALES
Area: 20,766 sq km
(8,017 sq miles)
Population: 2,980,000
Capital: Cardiff

NORTHERN IRELAND (no official flag)
Area: 14,695 sq km
(5,674 sq miles)
Population: 1,759,000
Capital: Belfast

SHETLAND ISLANDS

SCALE BAR
0 50 100 km
0 50 100 miles

ENGLISH CHANNEL
British people call the narrow stretch of sea that separates their country from France the English Channel; but the French call it La Manche, which means "The Sleeve".

NORTH SEA OIL
The discovery of oil under the North Sea greatly benefitted the British economy from the 1980s. Construction and operation of the oil drilling platforms provided many jobs, and money from oil sales allowed the British government to cut taxes.

CHANNEL ISLANDS

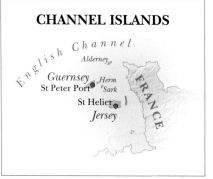

HISTORY OF THE
UNITED KINGDOM

In 1801, THE UNITED KINGDOM came into being with the Act of Union. Before that there had been four separate nations: England, Wales, Scotland, and Ireland. However, England had begun taking over the government of Wales in the 1000s, Ireland in the 1100s, and had shared a joint monarchy with Scotland since 1603. The United Kingdom is a small country, but by 1850 it had become the richest and most powerful nation in the world, controlling the largest empire in history. Even today, the Commonwealth includes more than 40 independent countries that were once British colonies. The United Kingdom has often been forced to fight long and bitter wars, but has survived and prospered because of its island position and its strong navy. The British system of laws and government by Parliament has become a model which many other nations have copied.

PALAEOLITHIC SETTLERS
A quarter of a million years ago, during mild conditions between two Ice Ages, people began to settle in Britain. They walked across the bridge of land which joined Britain to Europe at the time.

BATTLE OF HASTINGS

In 1066, a battle changed the course of English history. A Norman army led by William the Conqueror defeated an English king, Harold of Wessex, at Hastings, in southern England. William's descendants have ruled the country ever since. As king, he built castles in his new kingdom and gave land to powerful barons. They in turn give land to local lords for agreeing to fight for them. Peasants farmed the land of the local lord, and paid rent in produce and money. This system was called feudalism.

HENRY VIII
A truly multitalented king, Henry VIII was an expert at many things, from jousting and archery to lute-playing and languages. His impact on England was tremendous. In 1541, he forced the Irish Parliament to recognize him as king of Ireland. He also broke from the Roman Catholic Church, in order to divorce his wife, and became head of a new Church of England. Henry was an absolute ruler who executed anyone who displeased him, including two of his six wives.

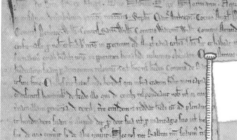

MAGNA CARTA
The Magna Carta (Great Charter) of 1215 was an agreement between the king and the nobles of England. The charter promised that the king would not abuse his royal power to tax the nobles. This important moment in English history was the start of the belief that even kings must obey certain laws of the land.

UNITED KINGDOM

43 CE Ancient Romans, under Claudius, invade Britain and make it part of their empire.

411 Romans leave Britain.

c. 500 Christian missionaries arrive in Britain and preach Christianity to the people.

UNION FLAG
The flag of the United Kingdom is made up from the red crosses of St. George of England and St. Patrick of Ireland, plus the white St. Andrew's cross of Scotland, on a blue background. Wales has its own flag.

c. 870 Viking conquest of Britain begins.

1066 Normans invade Britain.

1215 Magna Carta agreement between the king and the nobles of England.

1282 Edward I, king of England, conquers Wales.

1485 Battle of Bosworth. Henry VII becomes the first Tudor king.

1534 Parliament declares Henry VIII head of the Church of England.

1588 English navy defeats the Spanish Armada (fleet) sent by Philip II, king of Spain.

CHARLES II
The Parliamentary army defeated and executed King Charles I during the English Civil War (1642-51). For nine years Oliver Cromwell (1599-1658), a member of Parliament, and his army ruled the country as a republic. In 1660, Charles' son returned from travels abroad (above) and claimed the throne as King Charles II. The nation, weary of the republic, welcomed him.

ADMIRAL NELSON
The most famous and daring commander of the British Royal Navy was Admiral Horatio Nelson (1758-1805), who defeated the Spanish and French at the Battle of Trafalgar (1805). Before the battle he said "England expects every man to do his duty". Nelson was fatally wounded in the battle.

CHARTISTS
During the 19th century, British people fought for the right to vote. Groups such as the Chartists (1837-48) organized demonstrations demanding a fairer system with representation for all, a secret voting system, and regular elections. Above is a Chartist riot being crushed by the police.

IMMIGRATION
The United Kingdom has become a multiracial and multicultural society, with immigration mainly from Commonwealth countries in the Caribbean, and from many of the Asian nations. This picture, taken in the 1960s, shows new arrivals from Jamaica receiving meals at a hostel set up to provide support for immigrants.

WELFARE STATE
In 1945, following the end of World War II, a Labour government came into power and introduced a welfare state and universal free education. This placed most hospitals under public control. It also provided welfare for people "from the cradle to the grave", including free medical treatment under the National Health Service.

European Parliament building in Strasbourg, France

CONSTITUTIONAL CHANGES
In 1973 Britain joined the European Community (now the European Union). Gradually, more power over matters such as trade has moved from the British parliament in London to European institutions in Brussels. In 1907 Scotland and Wales voted for "devolution", decentralizing power away from London to local institutions, including a Scottish parliament in Edinburgh.

UNITED KINGDOM

1642-51 Civil War between the King and Parliament.

1660 Charles II becomes King of England.

1707 Act of Union unites England, Wales, and Scotland.

1801 Ireland united with Great Britain.

1900 Britain is the strongest, richest country in the world.

1914-18 Britain fights in World War I.

1931 Commonwealth of Nations is established.

1939-45 Britain fights in World War II.

1945 Welfare state introduced.

1973 Britain becomes a member of the European Community (now the EU).

1997 Scotland votes in favour of its own parliament.

Find out more
ENGLISH CIVIL WAR
ELIZABETH I
EUROPEAN UNION
INDUSTRIAL REVOLUTION
NORMANS
UNITED KINGDOM
VICTORIANS

REGIONAL HISTORY OF
UNITED KINGDOM

FOR MUCH OF ITS HISTORY, the United Kingdom has been anything but united. England, Wales, Scotland, and Ireland were all once separate countries and have often split into rival kingdoms themselves. Since the 1100s, England has tried to unite the countries of the British Isles under its rule. In 1171 England invaded Ireland, although it failed to win control; a century later, England conquered Wales. Until the 1600s, Scotland and England were deadly enemies. They were only united when a Scottish king inherited the English throne. The United Kingdom as we know it came into being in 1801, when the final Act of Union was passed between Ireland and the rest of the country, athough most of Ireland left the union in 1922. Today, the separate parts of the country are regaining control of their affairs from London.

ALFRED THE GREAT
Known as the "Great", Alfred was the grandson of Ecgberht of Wessex (r. 829-39), the first person to unite England.

Conwy Castle was built during the 1200s. Conwy is on the north coast of Wales.

Melrose Abbey

SCOTLAND

The first true king of Scotland was Kenneth MacAlpin, who united the country north of the River Forth in 843. By 1018 the country was united within roughly its present borders. For the next 200 years Scottish kings fought a long series of border wars with England. They built many stone castles, as well as several abbeys, such as Melrose.

INVASION OF WALES
In 1277, the English King Edward I demanded that the Welsh Prince Llywelyn Yr Ail accept him as the ultimate ruler of Wales. Llywelyn refused and so Edward invaded. After the death of Llywelyn in 1282, Wales became part of England. In order to keep control, Edward built 10 great stone castles throughout the principality.

Robert the Bruce

Hero of Scottish independence, Robert the Bruce led 30,000 men to victory against an English army of 100,000 under King Edward II at the Battle of Bannockburn.

DECLARATION OF ARBROATH
After their victory at Bannockburn, the Scots expected the English to leave them alone. This did not happen, so in 1320 the Scottish lords and bishops met at Arbroath to draw up a petition to Pope John XXII, asking him to recognize Scottish independence. In 1328, the English finally recognized Scotland as an independent nation.

The Declaration of Arbroath

BANNOCKBURN
In 1290 Margaret, the young queen of Scotland, died without an heir. The Scottish lords asked Edward I of England to choose a successor, but in 1296 he took direct control of Scotland. William Wallace (c. 1274-1305) – Braveheart – rose in revolt against English rule but was executed in 1305. Robert the Bruce (1274-1319) continued the fight, finally defeating the English army at Bannockburn in 1314.

INVASION OF IRELAND

In 1155, Pope Adrian IV authorized King Henry II to bring the Irish Church into line with the Catholic Church in Rome. Henry invaded in 1171, forcing the Irish bishops to submit to Rome at the Rock of Cashel. The invasion marked the start of English involvement in Ireland.

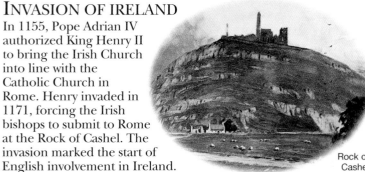

Rock of Cashel

UNION OF ENGLAND AND SCOTLAND

In 1603, Elizabeth I of England died. Her heir was her distant cousin, James VI of Scotland. He also took over the English throne as James I, so uniting the two countries. Scotland kept its own parliament, Church, and judicial system until 1707, when the Act of Union united the two parliaments in London. In 1999, Scotland once again had its own parliament.

James I of England and VI of Scotland

BATTLE OF THE BOYNE

In 1688, Catholic King James II was forced off the English throne. Irish Catholics objected and started a rebellion. They asked James to lead them, and he brought troops from France. However, in 1690, the Protestant English King William III defeated the Catholics at the Battle of the Boyne.

CULLODEN

After Queen Anne died in 1714, the British throne went to the German King George I. Many Scots believed that Catholic James Edward Stuart (1688-1766), son of James II, should be king. In 1715, they rose in revolt. The rebellion failed, but in 1745, the Scots tried again under Charles Edward Stuart (1720-88), known as Bonnie Prince Charlie. They were defeated at Culloden Moor in 1746.

NORTHERN IRELAND

During the 19th century, Irish Catholics campaigned for Home Rule for Ireland. Northern Irish Protestants objected to this. In 1920-22 the British government divided Ireland, setting up separate states in northern and southern Ireland, each with its own parliament. Many Northern Irish Catholics, continue to campaign for a united Ireland free of British rule.

GOOD FRIDAY

In 1972 the Northern Ireland parliament was closed because it could not keep the peace between Protestants and Catholics. Eventually, US senator George Mitchell and the British minister Mo Mowlam worked out an agreement to share power between all political parties. It was signed on Good Friday, 10 April, 1998. However, there have been problems making power-sharing work.

DEVOLUTION

For some years, many people in Scotland and Wales have wanted devolution, the passing of power from England to their own parliaments. In 1998, the British government held a vote on devolution in both countries. A Scottish parliament and a Welsh Assembly were then set up. They both met for the first time in 1999.

Many football fans, such as this young Scot, paint their country's flag on their faces in support of their national team.

THE REGIONS OF THE UNITED KINGDOM

871-899 Alfred rules England.

1018 Malcolm II unites Scotland.

1171 Henry II invades Ireland.

1200s Wales united.

1277-84 England conquers Wales.

1296 Edward I of England rules Scotland.

1314 English defeated at Bannockburn and driven out of Scotland.

1320 Scottish lords draw up Declaration of Arbroath.

1536 Act of Union between England and Wales.

1603 Scottish and English crowns unite.

1690s Protestants take complete control of Ireland.

1707 Act of Union between Scotland and England.

1746 Scots defeated at Culloden.

1801 Act of Union between Britain and Ireland.

1920-22 Ireland divided into north and south.

1999 Scotland and Wales get devolved government.

Find out more

ENGLAND
NORTHERN IRELAND
SCOTLAND
WALES

UNITED NATIONS

IN 1945, AT THE END of World War II, the nations that opposed Germany, Italy, and Japan decided that such a war must never be repeated. They set up the United Nations, with the aim of preventing future conflicts, and drew up the United Nations Charter. The United Nations (UN) met for the first time in San Francisco in 1945. Today, 192 nations belong to the UN. The UN consists of six main organs: the General Assembly, the Security Council, the Secretariat, the Economic and Social Council, the Trusteeship Council, and the International Court of Justice. Each is concerned with world peace and social justice. The UN also has agencies which deal with global issues such as health. Each member nation of the UN has a seat in the General Assembly; 15 nations sit on the Security Council. The UN is not without problems. Its members often disagree, and it suffers financial difficulties.

LEAGUE OF NATIONS
In 1919, the victors of World War I including Great Britain, founded the League of Nations to keep peace. But in 1935 the League failed to prevent Italy from invading Ethiopia. In 1946, the League's functions were transferred to the UN. Haile Selassie, emperor of Ethiopia, is seen addressing the League, above.

UNITED NATIONS
The headquarters of the UN in New York City, United States, is where the General Assembly and Security Council meet, as well as many of the specialist agencies of the organization. Politicians from every member nation come to New York to address the UN, and many international disputes and conflicts are settled here.

SECURITY COUNCIL

The aim of the Security Council is to maintain peace in the world. It investigates any event which might lead to fighting. The council has five permanent members – Britain, the United States, the Russian Federation, France, and China – and 10 members elected for two years each.

UN SYMBOL
The symbol of the United Nations (above) consists of a map of the world surrounded by a wreath of olive branches, symbolizing peace.

UNICEF

The United Nations Children's Fund (UNICEF) is one of the most successful agencies of the UN. UNICEF was originally founded to help child victims of World War II. The fund now provides education, health care, and medical help for children across the world, particularly in areas devastated by war or famine. Much of its work takes place in the poorer countries of Africa and Asia.

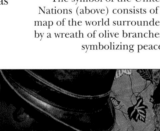

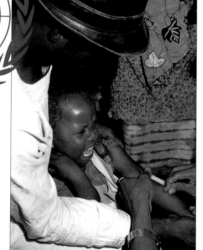

Children in underdeveloped countries are immunized against disease, thanks to UNICEF.

PEACEKEEPING
The UN is sometimes called on to send a peacekeeping force to a country in order to prevent war. In 1989, a UN force was sent to Namibia, southern Africa, to supervise the elections that led to Namibia's independence. More recently, a UN peacekeeping mission was established to help uphold a peace agreement in Darfur, southern Sudan.

Find out more

EUROPE, HISTORY OF
GOVERNMENTS AND POLITICS
WORLD WAR I
WORLD WAR II

UNITED STATES OF AMERICA

ON THE FLAG OF the United States, 50 identical stars represent the country's 50 states. But the states themselves could not be more different. If the stars showed their areas, the largest, for Alaska, would be nearly 500 times bigger than the star for the smallest state, Rhode Island. If the stars showed population, Alaska's star would be the smallest, and the star for California, which has the most people, would be more than 50 times larger. The states vary in other ways, too. The Rocky Mountains in the western states reach more than 4,400 m (14,400 ft) in height, but flat plains extend for hundreds of kilometres across the country's centre. At Barrow, Alaska, the most northerly town, the average temperature is just -13°C (9°F), yet in Arizona temperatures have reached 57°C (134°F). Since 1945, the USA has played a leading role in world affairs. The nation is the most powerful in the Western world. American finance, culture, and politics have spread outward from the United States. Products made in the United States are available in every country. Decisions made by American politicians affect the lives of many people throughout the world.

The United States covers much of the continent of North America. It reaches from the Atlantic to the Pacific oceans and from the Mexican border to Canada. The nation covers a total of 9.37 million sq km (3.68 million sq miles).

NASA

The United States is a world leader in technology, particularly in space research. The National Aeronautics and Space Administration (NASA) spends millions of dollars every year on satellites and spacecraft. In 1969, Neil Armstrong, commander of NASA's *Apollo 11*, became the first man to walk on the moon. One of NASA's recent successes is the space shuttle, a reusable spacecraft.

Operatives monitor data in a NASA space shuttle control centre.

STATE AND FEDERAL GOVERNMENT

The United States is a democracy and has a written constitution which sets out how government works. State governments, which meet in the state capital, have the authority to make laws affecting their own residents. The states were once nearly self-governing, but today the federal, or national, government has more power. It makes decisions on foreign policy and can pass laws which affect the entire country.

NEW YORK CITY

At the mouth of the Hudson River on the east coast of the United States is New York City, the country's biggest city. It is also one of the oldest. New York was founded in the 1620s and is now an urban area with 8 million people. The city is the financial heart of the nation and houses the offices of many large companies and dozens of theatres, museums, and parks. Skyscrapers more than 300 m (1,000 ft) tall dominate the city centre, Manhattan.

Manhattan, the centre of New York City, is built on a rocky island between the Hudson and East rivers.

HAWAII AND ALASKA

Hawaii, a group of tropical islands in the Pacific Ocean, became the fiftieth US state in 1959. The islands produce pineapples, sugar, and coffee. Polynesians first settled Hawaii in the 700s, and many native Polynesians still live here. Alaska lies outside the main part of the United States, too, separated from the other states by Canada.

The Sugar Train on the Hawaiian island of Maui

CALIFORNIA

In 1848 gold was discovered in California, and many people rushed to the region to prospect for it. California is still the state with the most inhabitants. About 36 million people live there. Most of the state has a mild, sunny climate and produces vast amounts of fruit. Many towns in California have become resorts. Modern industries have started up in California; the so-called Silicon Valley, for example, is a centre for the computer business.

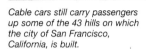

Cable cars still carry passengers up some of the 43 hills on which the city of San Francisco, California, is built.

AMERICAN PEOPLE

Native Americans, the original Americans, now make up only a small part of the total population of more than 307 million. Most people are the descendants of settlers from overseas and speak English. They live in the same neighbourhoods and mingle in everyday life. Their cultures have also mingled, producing a new form of English different from that spoken in England. Some groups, such as the Chinese and the Italians, also keep their own traditions and language alive in small, urban communities.

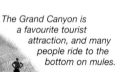

The Grand Canyon is a favourite tourist attraction, and many people ride to the bottom on mules.

BASEBALL

Baseball is the USA's top sport, and was first played between two organized teams in 1846.

HOLLYWOOD

Hollywood, in Los Angeles, was founded in 1887 as a community for Christians. Today, it is the centre of America's film industry. Many movie studios are based here, and actors, actresses and other celebrities live and work nearby. The area is a big tourist attraction. Visitors come to spot the stars and to take photos of the Hollywood sign (right) in the Hollywood Hills.

BLUES

During the 17th, 18th, and 19th centuries thousands of Africans were brought to America as slaves. Slavery was outlawed in 1865, and since then black writers, artists, and musicians have made their mark on American culture. The popular music known as blues originated among slaves in the southern states of America.

Famous blues singer B.B. King (born 1925) has played his guitar, named Lucille, in concerts all over the world.

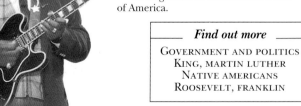

GRAND CANYON

There are many natural wonders in the United States; one of the most impressive is the Grand Canyon in Arizona. The Colorado River took thousands of years to cut the canyon by natural erosion through solid rock. It is 29 km (18 miles) wide in places and more than 1,800 m (6,000 ft) deep.

Find out more

GOVERNMENT AND POLITICS
KING, MARTIN LUTHER
NATIVE AMERICANS
ROOSEVELT, FRANKLIN

SEAT OF GOVERNMENT

 DISTRICT OF COLUMBIA
Area: 159 sq km (61sq miles)
Population: 592,000
Capital: Washington

STATES, with date of admission to Union

 ALABAMA 1819
Area: 133,906 sq km (51,705 sq miles)
Population: 4,661,000
Capital: Montgomery

 ALASKA 1959
Area: 1,530,572 sq km (591,000 sq miles)
Population: 686,000
Capital: Juneau

 ARIZONA 1912
Area: 295,237 sq km (114,000 sq miles)
Population: 6,500,000
Capital: Phoenix

 ARKANSAS 1836
Area: 137,744 sq km (53,187 sq miles)
Population: 2,856,000
Capital: Little Rock

 CALIFORNIA 1850
Area: 411,017 sq km (158,706 sq miles)
Population: 36,757,000
Capital: Sacramento

 COLORADO 1876
Area: 269,575 sq km (104,091 sq miles)
Population: 4,939,000
Capital: Denver

 CONNECTICUT 1788
Area: 12,996 sq km (5,018 sq miles)
Population: 3,501,000
Capital: Hartford

 DELAWARE 1787
Area: 5,296 sq km (2,045 sq miles)
Population: 873,000
Capital: Dover

 FLORIDA 1845
Area: 151,928 sq km (58,664 sq miles)
Population: 18,328,000
Capital: Tallahassee

 GEORGIA 1788
Area: 152,565 sq km (58,910 sq miles)
Population: 9,686,000
Capital: Atlanta

HAWAII 1959
Area: 16,759 sq km (6,471 sq miles)
Population: 1,288,000
Capital: Honolulu

 IDAHO 1890
Area: 216,414 sq km (83,564 sq miles)
Population: 1,523,000
Capital: Boise

 ILLINOIS 1818
Area: 145,922 sq km (56,345 sq miles)
Population: 12,902,000
Capital: Springfield

 INDIANA 1816
Area: 93,712 sq km (36,185 sq miles)
Population: 6,377,000
Capital: Indianapolis

 IOWA 1846
Area: 145,740 sq km (56,275 sq miles)
Population: 3,003,000
Capital: Des Moines

 KANSAS 1861
Area: 213,081 sq km (82,277 sq miles)
Population: 2,802,000
Capital: Topeka

 KENTUCKY 1792
Area: 104,654 sq km (40,410 sq miles)
Population: 4,269,000
Capital: Frankfort

 LOUISIANA 1812
Area: 123,678 sq km (47,752 sq miles)
Population: 4,411,000
Capital: Baton Rouge

 MAINE 1820
Area: 86,150 sq km (33,265 sq miles)
Population: 1,316,000
Capital: Augusta

 MARYLAND 1788
Area: 27,089 sq km (10,460 sq miles)
Population: 5,634,000
Capital: Annapolis

 MASSACHUSETTS 1788
Area: 21,454 sq km (8,284 sq miles)
Population: 6,498,000
Capital: Boston

 MICHIGAN 1837
Area: 151,573 sq km (58,527 sq miles)
Population: 10,003,000
Capital: Lansing

 MINNESOTA 1858
Area: 218,584 sq km (84,402 sq miles)
Population: 5,220,000
Capital: St. Paul

 MISSISSIPPI 1817
Area: 123,505 sq km (47,689 sq miles)
Population: 2,939,000
Capital: Jackson

 MISSOURI 1821
Area: 180,501 sq km (69,697 sq miles)
Population: 5,912,000
Capital: Jefferson City

 MONTANA 1889
Area: 380,820 sq km (147,046 sq miles)
Population: 967,000
Capital: Helena

 NEBRASKA 1867
Area: 200,334 sq km (77,355 sq miles)
Population: 1,783,000
Capital: Lincoln

 NEVADA 1864
Area: 286,331 sq km (110,561 sq miles)
Population: 2,600,000
Capital: Carson City

 NEW HAMPSHIRE 1788
Area: 24,031 sq km (9,279 sq miles)
Population: 1,316,000
Capital: Concord

 NEW JERSEY 1787
Area: 20,167 sq km (7,787 sq miles)
Population: 8,683,000
Capital: Trenton

 NEW MEXICO 1912
Area: 314,902 sq km (121,593 sq miles)
Population: 1,984,000
Capital: Santa Fe

 NEW YORK 1788
Area: 127,180 sq km (49,108 sq miles)
Population: 19,490,000
Capital: Albany

 NORTH CAROLINA 1789
Area: 136,402 sq km (52,669 sq miles)
Population: 9,222,000
Capital: Raleigh

 NORTH DAKOTA 1889
Area: 183,104 sq km (70,702 sq miles)
Population: 641,000
Capital: Bismarck

OHIO 1803
Area: 107,036 sq km (41,330 sq miles)
Population: 11,485,000
Capital: Columbus

 OKLAHOMA 1907
Area: 181,076 sq km (69,919 sq miles)
Population: 3,642,000
Capital: Oklahoma City

 OREGON 1859
Area: 251,400 sq km (97,073 sq miles)
Population: 3,790,000
Capital: Salem

 PENNSYLVANIA 1787
Area: 117,339 sq km (45,308 sq miles)
Population: 12,448,000
Capital: Harrisburg

 RHODE ISLAND 1790
Area: 3,139 sq km (1,212 sq miles)
Population: 1,051,000
Capital: Providence

 **SOUTH CAROLINA** 1788
Area: 80,576 sq km (31,113 sq miles)
Population: 4,480,000
Capital: Columbia

 SOUTH DAKOTA 1889
Area: 199,715 sq km (77,116 sq miles)
Population: 804,000
Capital: Pierre

 TENNESSEE 1796
Area: 109,145 sq km (42,144 sq miles)
Population: 6,215,000
Capital: Nashville

 TEXAS 1845
Area: 690,977 sq km (266,807 sq miles)
Population: 24,327,000
Capital: Austin

 UTAH 1896
Area: 219,871 sq km (84,899 sq miles)
Population: 2,736,000
Capital: Salt Lake City

 VERMONT 1791
Area: 24,898 sq km (9,614 sq miles)
Population: 621,000
Capital: Montpelier

 VIRGINIA 1788
Area: 105,578 sq km (40,767 sq miles)
Population: 7,769,000
Capital: Richmond

 WASHINGTON 1889
Area: 176,466 sq km (68,139 sq miles)
Population: 6,549,000
Capital: Olympia

 WEST VIRGINIA 1863
Area: 62,756 sq km (24,232 sq miles)
Population: 1,814,000
Capital: Charleston

 WISCONSIN 1848
Area: 145,425 sq km (56,153 sq miles)
Population: 5,628,000
Capital: Madison

 WYOMING 1890
Area: 253,306 sq km (97,809 sq miles)
Population: 533,000
Capital: Cheyenne

Legend

Volcano	Mountain	Ancient monument	Capital city	Large city/town	Small city/town

STATISTICS

Area: 9,372,610 sq km
(3,681,760 sq miles)
Population: 307,212,000
Capital: Washington, DC
Languages: English,
Spanish, Italian, German,
French, Polish, Chinese,
Tagalog, Greek
Religions: Protestant,
Roman Catholic, Jewish,
non-religious
Currency: US dollar
Main occupations:
Research, manufacturing,
agriculture
Main exports: Energy, raw
materials, food, electronics,
cars, coal
Main imports: Oil

MIDWEST

The United States is the world's
largest exporter of wheat and
produces nearly half of the corn on
Earth. This enormous quantity of
food is grown on the open plains
that cover the Midwest between the
Mississippi River and the Rockies.
Grain farming is highly mechanized,
with giant machines operating in fields
hundreds of hectares in size. The United
States also produces one quarter of the
world's oranges, one seventh of the world's nuts,
and half of the world's soya beans.

*The seemingly endless wheat
fields of the Midwest*

INDUSTRY

Most of the industries in the
United States are the largest and most
profitable of their type in the world.
America has abundant mineral
deposits, raw materials, and energy
sources. The most economically
important industries in the US include
car manufacturing, food processing,
textile and clothing manufacture, and
the computer industry. "Silicon Valley"
in California is a world centre for
micro-electronics. New York City is
the nation's financial capital while
Washington has an important
aerospace industry.

BORDER
*The border between Canada and the
USA is the world's longest land
border between any two countries.*

SCALE BAR
| 0 | 250 | 500 | km |
| 0 | 250 | 500 | miles |

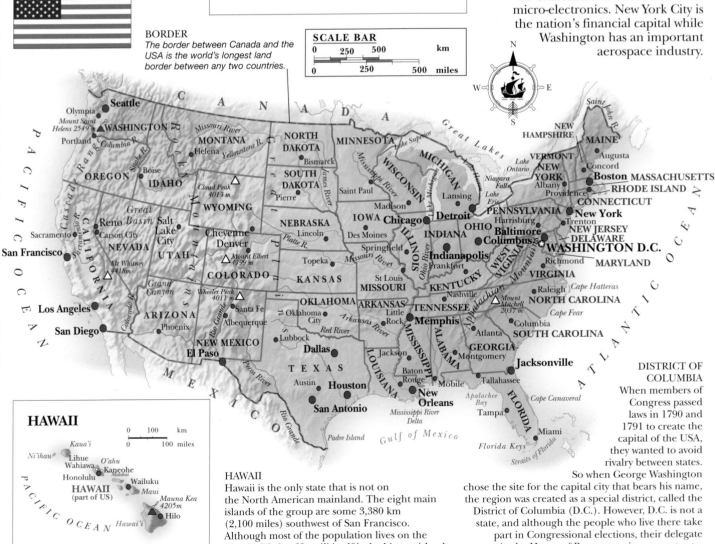

HAWAII
Hawaii is the only state that is not on
the North American mainland. The eight main
islands of the group are some 3,380 km
(2,100 miles) southwest of San Francisco.
Although most of the population lives on the
island of Oahu, Hawai'i itself is the biggest island.

DISTRICT OF COLUMBIA
When members of
Congress passed
laws in 1790 and
1791 to create the
capital of the USA,
they wanted to avoid
rivalry between states.
So when George Washington
chose the site for the capital city that bears his name,
the region was created as a special district, called the
District of Columbia (D.C.). However, D.C. is not a
state, and although the people who live there take
part in Congressional elections, their delegate
in the House of Representatives cannot vote.

546

HISTORY OF THE
UNITED STATES

TODAY, THE UNITED STATES OF AMERICA is the most powerful nation on Earth. Yet, just 230 years ago the United States was a new and vulnerable nation. It occupied a narrow strip of land on the Atlantic coast of North America and had a population of only about four million people. Beyond its borders lay vast areas of unclaimed land. Throughout the 19th century, American settlers pushed the frontier westwards across that land, fighting the Native Americans for control. At the same time, millions of immigrants from Europe were arriving on the East Coast. By 1900, the nation's farms and factories were producing more than any other country. That wealth and power led to its involvement in international affairs and drew it into two world wars. But the country continued to prosper. Since 1945 the system of individual enterprise that inspired the founders of the United States has made its people among the world's richest. American business, influence, and culture have spread to every other nation in the world.

FOUNDING FATHERS
The United States originally consisted of 13 states, each with its own customs and history. In 1787 George Washington and other leaders, sometimes called the Founding Fathers, drew up the United States Constitution, a document that established a strong central government. The Constitution, which also safeguards the rights of the states and those of their people, has been in force since 1789.

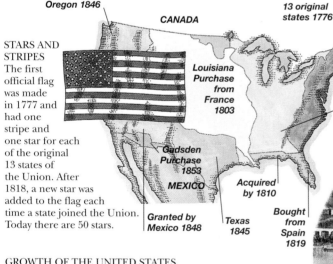

Map labels:
- Oregon 1846
- CANADA
- 13 original states 1776
- Louisiana Purchase from France 1803
- Acquired by 1783
- Gadsden Purchase 1853
- MEXICO
- Acquired by 1810
- Granted by Mexico 1848
- Texas 1845
- Bought from Spain 1819

STARS AND STRIPES
The first official flag was made in 1777 and had one stripe and one star for each of the original 13 states of the Union. After 1818, a new star was added to the flag each time a state joined the Union. Today there are 50 stars.

GROWTH OF THE UNITED STATES
The 13 original colonies on the East Coast gained their independence from Britain in 1783, and acquired all the land as far west as the Mississippi River. In 1803 the vast area of Louisiana was bought from France, and by 1848 the United States had reached the Pacific Ocean.

FALL OF THE SOUTH
The Civil War ended in 1865, leaving the South in ruinous poverty. The hatred and bitterness caused by the war lasted for many years as the central government took temporary control of the defeated southern states.

SPREAD OF THE RAILWAY
In 1860 there were more than 48,000 km (30,000 miles) of railways in the eastern United States, but almost none had been built west of the Mississippi River. On 10 May 1869, the first continental railway was completed, and the two coasts of America were joined for the first time. A ceremony was held at Promontory Point in Utah to mark the occasion. The growth of the national railway network helped unify the country.

IMMIGRATION

During the 19th century many Europeans crossed the Atlantic in search of new freedoms and opportunities. The United States welcomed Irish people escaping famine, eastern European Jews fleeing persecution, and countless others. By 1890, half a million immigrants were arriving each year in the United States. As a result, the country became a mixture of many different cultures and religions.

INDUSTRY

The United States offered an endless supply of raw materials to 19th-century industrialists, who soon took advantage of these resources. Manufacturers such as Ransom Olds pioneered mass production of cars and many other goods. In the Olds Motor Works, cars moved along a production line, with workers at intervals each performing a single task. This technique made assembly faster, and Henry Ford and other manufacturers quickly adopted it.

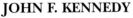

Immigrants arriving in the United States were examined at a reception centre on Ellis Island, New York.

THE UNITED STATES AT WAR

Until the United States entered World War I in 1917, its armed forces had rarely fought overseas. After the war ended the United States tried once again to stay out of conflicts abroad. But in 1941 the Japanese attacked Pearl Harbor naval base in Hawaii, bringing the U.S. into World War II. Since 1945, the U.S. has fought in several overseas wars, notably in Korea (1950-53) and Vietnam (1961-73).

The Iwo Jima monument in Arlington National Cemetery is a memorial to Americans who died in World War II. It shows Marines raising the flag on Iwo Jima Island in the Pacific. Many US soldiers died in the battle for the island.

JOHN F. KENNEDY

In 1960, John F. Kennedy (1917-63) became the youngest man ever elected president. In 1961, Kennedy approved the invasion of Communist Cuba by US-backed Cuban exiles. The invasion, at the Bay of Pigs, was a disaster, and Kennedy was severely criticized. In 1962 the Soviets stationed nuclear missiles on the island. For one week, nuclear war seemed unavoidable, but Kennedy persuaded the Soviet Union to remove the missiles and averted the war. Kennedy's presidency ended tragically on 22 November 1963, when he was assassinated during a visit to Dallas, Texas, United States, after serving for exactly 1,000 days in office.

CHICAGO DAILY NEWS

PRESIDENT IS KILLED

Texas Sniper Escapes; Johnson Sworn In

Story Begins on Next Page

UNITED STATES

1783 The 13 colonies win their freedom from Britain.

1787 Constitution is drafted.

1789 George Washington becomes the first president.

1790-1800 A new capital, Washington, D.C., is built on the Potomac River.

1803 Louisiana Purchase doubles size of the country.

1845 Texas joins the Union.

1848 US defeats Mexico and acquires California and other territories.

1861-65 Civil War ends slavery

1869 First transcontinental railroad is completed.

1917-1918 US fights in World War I.

1929 Economic depression.

1941 United States enters World War II.

1963 President Kennedy assassinated.

1969 Neil Armstrong walks on the moon.

1991 US leads United Nations forces against Iraq in the Gulf War.

2001 Islamic terrorists destroy the World Trade Center.

2003 US invades Iraq.

EQUAL OPPORTUNITIES

Since 1789, the US Constitution has guaranteed every citizen equal rights. In reality, many minority groups are only now starting to achieve equality. The photograph shows Barack Obama, the United States' first African American president.

UNIVERSE

THE VAST EXPANSE OF SPACE that we call the universe contains everything there is. It includes the Sun, the planets, the Milky Way galaxy, and all other galaxies too. The universe is continually growing, and each part is gradually moving further away from every other part. We know about the universe by using powerful telescopes to study light, radio waves, x-rays, and other radiations that reach Earth from space. Light travels nearly 9.5 billion km (6 billion miles) in a year. We call this distance a light-year. The light from a distant star that you can see through a telescope may have travelled thousands of years to reach us. Most scientists believe that the universe was created by a massive explosive event that happened billions of years ago. This idea is called the Big Bang theory. Many scientists now believe that visible matter makes up only 7 per cent of the universe and that the rest is dark matter and dark energy.

Milky Way has a halo of stars and gas.

MILKY WAY
The Sun is just one of 100 billion stars in the large spiral galaxy we call the Milky Way. Like most other spiral galaxies, the Milky Way has curved arms of stars radiating from a globe-shaped centre. The Milky Way is 100,000 light-years across, and the Sun is 30,000 light-years from its centre.

GALAXIES
Galaxies, which contain gas, dust, and billions of stars, belong to one of three main groups – elliptical, irregular, or spiral. Most galaxies are elliptical, ranging from sphere shapes to egg shapes. A few galaxies are irregular. Others, such as the Milky Way, are spirals. The universe consists of billions of galaxies of all types.

Pieces of paper represent clusters of galaxies.

GALAXY CLUSTERS
Most galaxies belong to groups called clusters, which may contain thousands of galaxies of all types. These clusters form "walls" with great voids in between, so that the universe is like a foam.

In this image the galaxies are yellow and red, and the blue haloes around them represent dark matter.

Balloon expands in the same way that the universe is expanding.

THE EXPANDING UNIVERSE
You can get an idea of how the universe is expanding by imagining several small pieces of paper glued onto a balloon. Each piece represents a cluster of galaxies. As you blow up the balloon, all the paper pieces move further away from one another. In the same way, galaxy clusters are moving further away from one another. The further a cluster is, the faster it travels away from us.

THE INVISIBLE UNIVERSE
When scientists estimate the mass of a galaxy cluster, the figure usually turns out to be much more than the mass of the visible galaxies alone. The extra, invisible matter is called dark matter, and no-one knows what it is. Dark matter and ordinary matter together account for only 30% of the universe. Scientists call the remaining 70% dark energy. Dark energy is like a force that acts against gravity and pushes the galaxies apart. It is causing the expansion of the universe to speed up.

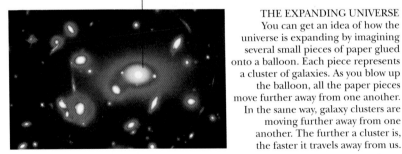

Dinosaurs lived on Earth 65–215 million years ago.

LOOKING BACK IN TIME
If you look through a telescope you can see galaxies millions of light-years away. You are not seeing them as they are now but as they were long ago, when their light first set out on its journey – so in a sense, you are looking into the past.

Galaxy is 100 million light-years away. Light left this galaxy when the dinosaurs lived on Earth.

Find out more
BIG BANG
BLACK HOLES
COMETS AND METEORS
EARTH
LIGHT
MOON
PLANETS
STARS
SUN
TELESCOPES

QUEEN
VICTORIA

IN 1837, A YOUNG WOMAN called Victoria became Queen of Britain. She was only 18, but was determined to rule wisely and well. She reigned for 64 years, longer than any other British monarch. During her rule, Britain went through huge social, economic, and political changes, becoming the world's first industrial nation and creating a vast empire. Parliament made political decisions and governed the country, but Victoria involved herself closely in state affairs. Her dignified appearance and family life came to symbolize that period of British history, so historians call her reign the Victorian Age.

1819 Born at Kensington Palace, London.

1837 Becomes Queen after the death of her uncle, William IV.

1838 Coronation at Westminster Abbey, London.

1840 Marries her German cousin, Prince Albert.

1861 Albert dies; Victoria retires from public life.

1897 Diamond Jubilee: Victoria celebrates 60 years on the throne.

1901 Dies, aged 81.

PENNY BLACK
Issued in 1840, the penny black was the first postage stamp. Victoria's head was printed on it.

Through her children's marriages, Victoria was related to every major European royal family.

Prince Albert

Queen Victoria

Victoria and Albert had nine children.

ALBERT
When Victoria was 20 she married her German cousin, Prince Albert. She adored him, and he advised her on political matters. He was also enthusiastic about education and industrial progress. Albert, who introduced the decorated Christmas tree into Britain, was a devoted father.

BENJAMIN DISRAELI
Politicians advised Victoria on political matters. During her long reign, there were 10 prime ministers. A great favourite was Benjamin Disraeli, prime minister in 1868, and from 1874-80. Victoria was interested in the British Empire, and it was Disraeli who brought India directly under British rule. In 1876, Disraeli persuaded Parliament to make Victoria "Empress of India".

DEATH OF THE MONARCH
During the last 25 years of her reign, Victoria involved herself in matters such as housing for the poor, and her popularity soared. When she died in the first year of the 20th century, thousands of people lined London's streets to watch her funeral procession.

BALMORAL
Victoria and Albert created a much-loved family home at Balmoral in the Scottish Highlands, which is used by the royal family today. In 1861, Albert died of typhoid and Victoria was grief-stricken. She went into deep mourning and retired from public duties, spending time at Balmoral in the company of a household servant, John Brown. Her absence from public life made the British people angry, and for some years she was very unpopular.

Find out more

BRITISH EMPIRE
INDUSTRIAL REVOLUTION
UNITED KINGDOM, HISTORY OF
VICTORIANS

VICTORIANS

UNDER THE RULE OF QUEEN VICTORIA, the British people enjoyed a long period of prosperity. Profits gained from the Empire overseas, as well as from industrial improvements at home, allowed a large, educated middle-class to develop. Great advances were made in the arts and sciences. In the cities, department stores were opened for the convenience of those with cash to spend. Domestic servants were employed in many homes, although vast numbers of people remained poor and lived in slums. Public transport, police forces, clean water supplies, and sewage treatment were introduced to ease conditions in the new towns. Like Victoria, middle-class people set high moral standards, and devised programmes to "improve" the lives of the poor. The Victorians thought themselves the most advanced society in the world.

QUEEN VICTORIA
Victoria (1819-1901) is best remembered dressed all in black and in mourning for her husband Albert, who died in 1861. Queen Victoria had great dignity and was highly respected by her subjects.

CRYSTAL PALACE
In 1851, a new building was erected in Hyde Park, London, to house the Great Exhibition. It was made entirely of glass and cast iron. Joseph Paxton designed it so it could be moved later and rebuilt in south London.

VICTORIAN STYLE
Victorians loved elaborate decoration. Almost all Victorian objects, from lamp posts to teaspoons were covered in carvings, patterns, and other ornamentation. Large houses and public buildings, such as St. Pancras station, London (right), were built in the style of ancient castles, cathedrals, and palaces.

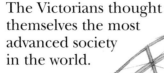

St. Pancras station

THE GREAT EXHIBITION
In 1851, Prince Albert organized the first international exhibition in Britain. More than 6 million people visited the Crystal Palace (above) to celebrate the industrial age. The 14,000 exhibits included a 24-ton lump of coal, a railway engine, the Koh-i-noor diamond from India, and a stuffed elephant.

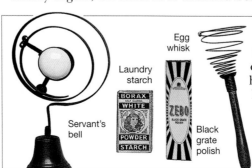

Egg whisk

Laundry starch

BORAX
WHITE
POWDER
STARCH

ZEBO
BLACK GRATE POLISH

Servant's bell

Black grate polish

DOMESTIC LIFE
Servants were a feature of every upper- and middle-class household. Maids worked long hours for little or no pay, sometimes only for board and lodging. In 1871, more than $\frac{1}{3}$ of British women aged 12-20 were "in service".

MUSIC HALLS

Working people went to music halls for cheap and popular entertainment. Audiences could eat and drink while enjoying melodramas, acrobats, comedians, and singers. Sentimental songs were especially popular.

Acrobats performed exciting feats on stage in music halls.

The Martini-Henry rifle appeared around 1871. It had a range of 275 m (300 yards).

EMPIRE BUILDING

During Victoria's reign, there were dozens of small-scale wars as the various European nations carved out empires in Africa and Asia. The people who already lived in these places stood little chance against trained troops equipped with rifles and automatic guns.

The Gatling gun fired bullets at a rate of 1,000 rounds per minute.

IRONCLAD BATTLESHIPS

Britain kept a huge navy to protect and control an empire which spanned the world. Fast gunboats and powerful battleships – with armour-plated wooden hulls for protection – sailed to areas where there was trouble, defending British political and commercial interests wherever these were threatened.

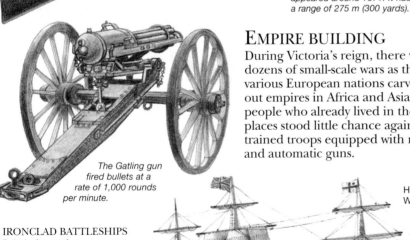

HMS Warrior

SOCIAL REFORM

In Victorian times, a new industrial era resulted in a wealthy middle class. However, it also created a vast working class who often suffered terrible living and working conditions. Some boys worked as chimney sweeps in wealthy homes (above). Their plight was publicized by Charles Kingsley's novel *Water Babies*, and reformers such as Lord Shaftesbury campaigned for new labour laws.

Find out more

BRITISH EMPIRE
INDUSTRIAL REVOLUTION
TRANSPORT, HISTORY OF
UNITED KINGDOM, HISTORY OF

VIETNAM WAR

BETWEEN 1956 AND 1975 Vietnam was the scene of one of the most destructive wars in modern history. In 1954, Vietnam defeated French colonial forces and was divided into two countries – a Communist North and a non-Communist South Vietnam. The Viet Cong (Vietnamese Communists) rebelled against the South Vietnamese government and, helped by North Vietnam under Ho Chi Minh, fought to reunite the country. This brought in the United States, which believed that if Vietnam fell to the Communists, nearby countries would fall too. During the 1960s the United States poured troops and money into Vietnam, but found itself in an undeclared war it could not win. Despite intensive bombing and the latest military technology, the Viet Cong were better equipped and trained for jungle warfare. Casualties in Vietnam were appalling, and strong opposition to the war developed in the United States. A cease-fire was negotiated, and in 1973 all American troops were withdrawn. Two years later North Vietnam captured Saigon, capital of South Vietnam, and Vietnam was united as a Communist country.

VIETNAM
Vietnam is in Southeast Asia. The war was fought in the jungles of South Vietnam and in the skies above North Vietnam. Viet Cong fighters received supplies from the North along the Ho Chi Minh trail. At the end of the war, the country was reunited with its capital at Hanoi. Saigon, the southern capital, was renamed Ho Chi Minh City.

VIETNAM WAR

1859 France begins to colonize Vietnam.

1954 Vietnamese defeat French.

1956 Viet Cong lead rebellion against South Vietnamese government.

1961 United States sends advisers to train South Vietnamese army.

1964 Gulf of Tongkin clash between North Vietnamese and US naval craft leads to war.

1965 United States begins bombing of North; first US combat troops arrive in South.

1968 Tet (Vietnamese New Year) offensive by Viet Cong

1968 American troops massacre My Lai villagers.

1968 Antiwar protests in the US

1973 Cease-fire signed in Paris; American troops leave Vietnam.

1975 Vietnam reunited under Communist control.

TROOPS
The first American military personnel arrived in Vietnam during 1961 to advise the South Vietnamese government. By 1969 there were about 550,000 American troops in Vietnam.

DESTRUCTION
The lengthy fighting had a terrible effect on the people of Vietnam. Their fields were destroyed, their forests stripped of leaves, and their houses blown up, leaving them refugees. Thousands were killed, injured, or maimed.

COSTS
It is unlikely that the exact cost of the Vietnam war will ever be known, but in terms of lives lost, money spent, and bombs dropped, it was enormous. Both sides suffered huge casualties and emerged with seriously damaged economies.

The United States spent $150 billion on the war; there are no figures for what North Vietnam spent.

Four times as many bombs were dropped by the American Air Force on Vietnam than were dropped by British and American bombers on Germany during the whole of World War II.

More than one million South Vietnamese and between 500,000 and one million North Vietnamese died in the war; over 58,000 American soldiers and nurses lost their lives.

The US Air Force bombed the jungle with chemicals to strip the leaves off the trees. Much of Vietnam is still deforested today.

Find out more

COMMUNISM
SOUTHEAST ASIA
UNITED STATES, HISTORY OF

VIKINGS

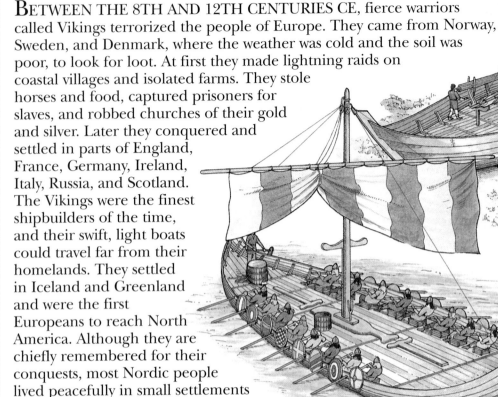

Viking knorr

BETWEEN THE 8TH AND 12TH CENTURIES CE, fierce warriors called Vikings terrorized the people of Europe. They came from Norway, Sweden, and Denmark, where the weather was cold and the soil was poor, to look for loot. At first they made lightning raids on coastal villages and isolated farms. They stole horses and food, captured prisoners for slaves, and robbed churches of their gold and silver. Later they conquered and settled in parts of England, France, Germany, Ireland, Italy, Russia, and Scotland. The Vikings were the finest shipbuilders of the time, and their swift, light boats could travel far from their homelands. They settled in Iceland and Greenland and were the first Europeans to reach North America. Although they are chiefly remembered for their conquests, most Nordic people lived peacefully in small settlements and worked as farmers, merchants, and craftsworkers.

Villagers loaded up the knorrs with farm produce, for trading purposes.

LONGSHIP AND KNORR

The Vikings depended on ships for transportation, because their lands were surrounded by the sea and covered with dense forests, which made travel difficult. They built magnificent longships out of wood cut from the vast Scandinavian forests. A longship carried about 80 warriors, who rowed and sailed the ship and also fought battles when they reached land. The Vikings also built smaller ships called knorrs, which they used for trading and transporting goods.

Viking longship

WARRIORS

Viking warriors usually fought with swords and battle axes, although some used spears, and bows and arrows. They carried wooden shields, and some wore armour made of layers of thick animal hides. Viking chieftains often wore metal helmets and chainmail armour.

Swedish helmet (7th century)

A warrior used both hands to swing the long-handled battle axe at an enemy.

The sword was among the fearsome weapons carried by the Vikings.

BURIALS

Important Vikings were buried with their ships. Relatives placed the body in a wooden cabin on the deck. Sometimes, dogs, horses, cattle, and slaves were buried with their owners. The body of a great warrior might be burned on a pile of wood or placed on the deck of a longship which was then set alight.

Relatives have surrounded the body with the dead person's most treasured possessions, including his horse.

VIKING FAMILIES

Some Vikings lived in bustling trading towns, such as York, England. But most lived in isolated farming settlements. Everything the family needed had to be made or grown on the farm. Viking women had more rights than many other European women of the time. For instance, they were allowed to get divorced if they wished.

Find out more

NORMANS
SCANDINAVIA

VOLCANOES

LIVING IN THE SHADOW of a volcano can be a source of constant fear. An active volcano can erupt with little warning: smoke and hot ash billow from the crater at the volcano's summit, and red-hot lava flows down the slopes, setting fire to everything in its path. Volcanoes are caused by the movement of vast slabs of rock, called plates, in the Earth's surface. When the plates collide or spread apart, molten rock from deep underground is forced to the surface, at or near the place where the plates meet. There are about 850 active volcanoes in the world. Most lie in a belt called the Ring of Fire, which surrounds the Pacific Ocean. Volcanoes also occur in the ocean, where they form underwater mountains or islands, such as Hawaii.

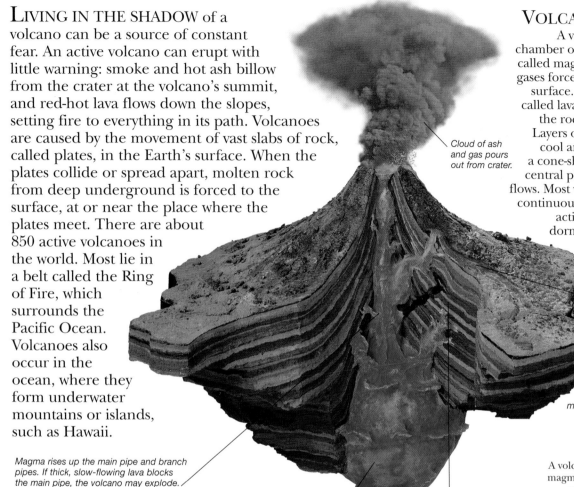

Cloud of ash and gas pours out from crater.

Red-hot lava flows down side of volcano.

Earth's crust is formed of layers of different kinds of rock. Close to the centre of the Earth, the intense heat melts the rock.

Magma rises up the main pipe and branch pipes. If thick, slow-flowing lava blocks the main pipe, the volcano may explode.

Magma chamber forms deep underground.

Volcano builds up with layers of ash and solidified lava.

VOLCANIC ERUPTIONS

A volcano lies over a deep chamber of red-hot, molten rock, called magma. Pressure from hot gases forces the magma up to the surface. The molten rock, now called lava, melts a hole through the rock above and flows out. Layers of lava and volcanic ash cool and solidify, building up a cone-shaped mountain with a central pipe through which lava flows. Most volcanoes do not erupt continuously. Between eruptions, active volcanoes are called dormant. Extinct volcanoes are those that are no longer active.

MAGMA
A volcano's shape depends on the magma it produces. Thick magma produces a steep cone; runny magma results in a flattened, shieldlike volcano. Some volcano cones are made only of ash.

LAVA
Molten rock which has escaped to the Earth's surface is called lava. A bubbling lake of molten rock fills the crater of the volcano, and fountains of fiery lava leap high into the air. Glowing streams of lava pour out of the crater and flow down the sides of the volcano like rivers of fire. The lava has a temperature of about 1,100°C (2,000°F), which is hot enough to melt steel.

PUMICE
Lava containing bubbles of gas hardens to form a rock called pumice, which is peppered with tiny holes. The holes make pumice very light; it is the only rock that can float in water.

GEYSERS
A jet of boiling water which suddenly shoots up from the ground is called a geyser. Hot rock deep below the surface heats water in an underground chamber so that it boils. Steam forces the water out in a jet. When the chamber refills and heats up, the geyser blows again.

POMPEII
In 79 CE, Mount Vesuvius in Italy erupted. Clouds of ash shot into the air, while pyroclastic flows (clouds of hot ash and air) swept down the mountain, burning all in their paths. Archaeologists have uncovered much of Pompeii, where the bodies of the victims left hollows in the ash. The plaster cast below is made from such a hollow and shows the last moments of a person killed by a pyroclastic flow. Vesuvius last erupted in 1944. It could erupt again at any time. Another volcanic disaster occurred on the island of Krakatoa, Indonesia, in 1883.

Find out more
CONTINENTS
EARTHQUAKES
GEOLOGY
MOUNTAINS
ROCKS AND MINERALS

WALES

FROM THE WILDS OF ITS NORTHERN mountains to the industrial valleys of the south, Wales covers an area of 20,761 sq km (8,014 sq miles). It has a population of almost 3 million and is the smallest country in the United Kingdom. Wales has been under English control since the late 13th century, although in 1999 a Welsh Assembly was introduced, giving Wales limited self-government. Until recently, coal mining was a major industry, particularly in the south, but by the 1990s most mines had closed, causing widespread unemployment. Sheep and cattle farming have remained economically important. Wales has a strong national identity, with its own language and a long tradition of music and song. Welsh choirs are famous worldwide.

WELSH DRAGON
The Welsh flag carries a red dragon, the national symbol of Wales.

Wales lies on a peninsula (land jutting into the sea) in western Great Britain. It is bordered by England on its eastern border and the Irish Sea to the west.

CARDIFF

Located on the south coast of Wales, Cardiff is the country's capital and the largest city. It is also the headquarters of the new Welsh Assembly. For many years Cardiff was a major port, exporting coal from the valleys in the south. The port has declined, but the city is still an administrative and business centre.

WELSH COUNTRYSIDE
Much of Wales is extremely beautiful, particularly around St. David's Bay on the Pembrokeshire coast in the west. Welsh landscape is varied. Snowdonia, in the north of the country, has spectacular mountain scenery, and is a national park. Green hills cover mid-Wales. The southeast is industrial.

PRINCE OF WALES
Edward I of England conquered Wales in 1284, but told the Welsh he would find them a prince who had never spoken English. He then held up his baby son as Prince of Wales at Caernarfon (Caernarvon) Castle. The title passes to the heir to the British throne. Today, Prince Charles is the Prince of Wales.

RUGBY
The national sport of Wales is Rugby Union. The game plays an important part in daily life and Welsh teams play at national and international level. The Millennium Stadium in Cardiff is the world's finest.

Neil Jenkins, Welsh rugby star

KEEP WALES TIDY
PLEASE TAKE YOUR LITTER HOME
EWCH Â'CH SBWRIEL GYDA CHI.
CADWCH GYMRU'N DACLUS
MAX PENALTY £1000 COSB UCHAF

WELSH LANGUAGE
Wales is bilingual, that is two languages – Welsh and English – are officially recognized. Road signs are in Welsh and English, and many people in the north speak Welsh as a first language. Teaching Welsh in schools has revived interest in traditional Welsh culture. Poets, speakers, and choirs compete at traditional festivals called *eisteddfods*.

Find out more
FOOTBALL AND RUGBY
UNITED KINGDOM
UNITED KINGDOM, HISTORY OF

GEORGE
WASHINGTON

1732 Born in Westmoreland, Virginia.

1759-74 Member of the Virginia parliament

1775-81 Leads Continental forces in the Revolution.

1787 Helps draft the Constitution of the United States of America.

1789 Chosen as first president of the United States.

1793 Elected to second term as president.

1797 Retires as president.

1799 Dies at Mount Vernon.

"THE FATHER OF HIS COUNTRY" was a nickname that George Washington earned many times over. First, he led the American forces to victory against the British in the Revolution, then he served the American people again as the first president of the United States. As a military leader, he was capable and strong-willed. Even when the British seemed set to win the war, Washington did not give up hope and continued to encourage the American troops. As president, he was an energetic leader who used his prestige to unite the new nation. Yet, despite his many personal strengths, Washington was an unlikely figure to lead a revolution. He was born into a wealthy family and trained as a surveyor before serving in the local militia. He could have had a brilliant military career, but at the age of 27 he returned to farming in Virginia. He did the same at the end of the Revolution, and only went back to national politics in 1787 because he felt the country needed his help once more.

VICTORY AT TRENTON

On Christmas night, 1776, George Washington led his troops across the icy Delaware River and attacked the British in Trenton, New Jersey, before they had time to prepare themselves for battle. The surprise attack did much to increase American morale at the start of the Revolution.

Troops had to break the ice in order to make their way across the river.

CONTINENTAL CONGRESS

In 1774, the 13 British colonies in North America set up a Continental Congress to protest against unfair British rule. George Washington was one of the delegates from Virginia. Although the Congress favoured reaching an agreement with Britain, fighting broke out between the two sides in 1775. The Congress raised an army under Washington and on 4 July 1776, issued the Declaration of Independence. Peace was declared in 1781 and the Congress became the national government of the newly formed United States of America. In 1789 it was abolished and a new government structure was established.

MOUNT VERNON
Built in 1743, Mount Vernon was the home of George Washington for more than 50 years. The wooden house overlooks the Potomac River near Alexandria, Virginia, and is now a museum dedicated to Washington.

Find out more

AMERICAN REVOLUTION
UNITED STATES OF AMERICA
UNITED STATES, HISTORY OF

WATER

WE ARE SURROUNDED by water. More than 70 per cent of the Earth's surface is covered by vast oceans and seas. In addition, 10 per cent of the land – an area the size of South America – is covered by water in the form of ice. However, little new water is ever made on Earth. The rain that falls from the sky has fallen billions of times before, and will fall billions of times again. It runs down the land to the sea, evaporates (changes into vapour) into the clouds, and falls again as rain in an endless cycle. Water has a huge effect on our planet and its inhabitants. All plants and animals need water to survive; life itself began in the Earth's prehistoric seas. Seas and rivers shape the land over thousands of years, cutting cliffs and canyons; icy glaciers dig out huge valleys. Water is also essential to people in homes and factories and on farms.

The force of surface tension holds water molecules together so that they form small, roughly spherical drops.

SURFACE TENSION
The surface of water seems to be like an elastic skin. You can see this if you watch tiny insects such as water striders walking on water – their feet make hollows in the surface of the water, but the insects do not sink. This "skin" effect is called surface tension. It is caused by the attraction of water molecules to each other. Surface tension has another important effect: it causes water to form drops.

Molecules at the surface have other molecules pulling on them only from below. This means there is a force pulling on this top layer of molecules, keeping them under tension like a stretched elastic band.

In the body of the liquid, each water molecule is surrounded by others, so the forces on them balance out.

WATER FOR LIFE
All plants and animals, including humans, are made largely of water and depend on water for life. For instance, more than two thirds of the human body is water. To replace water lost by urinating, sweating, and breathing, we must drink water every day to stay healthy. No one can survive more than four days without water.

STATES OF WATER
Pure water is a compound of two common elements, hydrogen and oxygen. In each water molecule there are two hydrogen atoms and one oxygen atom; scientists represent this by writing H_2O. Water is usually in a liquid state, but it can also be a solid or a gas. If left standing, water slowly evaporates and turns into water vapour, an invisible gas. When water is cooled down enough, it freezes solid and turns to ice.

ICE
Water freezes when the temperature drops below 0°C (32°F). Water expands, or takes up more space, as it freezes. Water pipes sometimes burst in very cold winters as the water inside freezes and expands.

WATER
Salty water boils at a higher temperature and freezes at a lower temperature than fresh water, which is why salt is put on roads in winter to keep ice from forming.

WATER VAPOUR
Water boils at 100°C (212°F). At this temperature it evaporates so rapidly that water vapour forms bubbles in the liquid. Water vapour is invisible; visible clouds of steam are not water vapour but are tiny droplets of water formed when the hot vapour hits cold air.

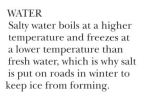

Water falls as rain and is collected in lakes and artificial reservoirs.

Water is cleaned in a treatment plant.

Water tank stores clean water.

Once the water is treated, it is pumped up into a high tank, ready to be used.

With the water high above the ground, the tap can be opened and the water runs out.

WATER TREATMENT

Water in a reservoir is usually not fit to drink. It must pass through a treatment centre which removes germs and other harmful substances. Chlorine gas is often dissolved into the water to kill bacteria and viruses. In addition, the water is stored in huge basins so that pieces of dirt sink to the bottom; filters made of stones and sand remove any remaining particles.

Water can provide an unlimited supply of power, unlike the underground resources such as coal and gas.

SOLUTIONS

Pure water is rarely found in nature because water dissolves other substances to form mixtures called solutions. For example, sea water is salty because there are many minerals dissolved in it. Water solutions are vital to life; blood plasma, for instance, is a water solution.

Sugar dissolves in water, making a sweet-tasting sugar solution.

The sugar disappears when it is completely dissolved.

HYDROELECTRIC POWER

People have used water as a source of power for more than 2,000 years. Today, water is used to produce electricity in hydroelectric (water-driven) power stations. Hydroelectric power stations are often built inside dams. Water from a huge lake behind the dam flows down pipes. The moving water spins turbines which drive generators and produce electricity. Hydroelectric power produces electricity without causing pollution or using scarce resources.

If three identical holes are drilled in the side of a water-filled container, water spurts out much further from the lowest hole because of the weight of the water above.

WATER PRESSURE

Water rushes out of a tap because it is under pressure; that is, it is pushed from behind. Pressure is produced by pumps that force water along using pistons or blades like those on a ship's propeller. Water pressure is also created by the sheer weight of water above. The deeper the water, the greater the pressure. If you dive into a pool, you can feel the water pressure pushing on your eardrums.

POLLUTION AND DROUGHT

In many places, such as East Africa, there is insufficient rain and constant drought. Plants cannot grow, and people and animals must fight a constant battle for survival. Fresh, clean water can also be difficult to obtain even in places with lots of rain. This is because waste from cities and factories pollutes the water, making it unsafe to drink.

Fire fighters connect their hoses to fire engines which contain powerful pumps. The pumps increase the pressure so that the water can reach flames high up in buildings.

Deep underground water stores exist below the surface of the Earth. After a drought, these stores dry out; it may take years for them to be refilled.

Find out more

ELECTRICITY
HEAT
LAKES
OCEANS AND SEAS
RAIN AND SNOW
RIVERS

WEATHER

The air over the Sahara Desert is so stable and dry that rain seldom falls.

Clouds hang over the hot and rainy tropics of Central Africa.

WEATHER DESCRIBES CONDITIONS, such as rain, wind, and sunshine, that occur during a short period of time in a particular place; climate is the overall pattern of weather in a region. From one moment to the next the weather can change. A warm, sunny day can be overtaken by a violent storm. Dark clouds form, high winds blow, and rain lashes the ground, yet it may be only a few minutes before the sunny weather returns. However, in some parts of the world, such as in parts of the tropics, the weather barely changes for months at a time. There it is always hot, and heavy rains fall. Meteorologists are scientists who measure and forecast the weather. They do this by studying clouds, winds, and the temperature and pressure of the Earth's atmosphere. But despite the use of satellites, computers, and other technology in weather forecasting, weather remains a force of nature that is hard to predict.

Swirls of cloud mark patterns of winds.

Snow and ice cover the cold Antarctic continent.

WORLD WEATHER
The Sun is the driving force for the world's weather. The heat of the Sun's rays produces wind and evaporates water from the seas, which later forms clouds and rain. The direct heat above the equator makes the weather hot, while the poles, which get less of the Sun's heat, are cold and cloudy.

A scale of hours on the recorder shows at what times the Sun was shining.

MEASURING THE WEATHER
Several thousand weather stations on land, ships, and aircraft measure weather conditions around the world. The stations contain instruments that record temperature, rainfall, the speed and direction of wind, air pressure, and humidity (the amount of water vapour in the air). Balloons called radiosondes carry instruments to take measurements high in the air. Weather satellites in space send back pictures of the clouds.

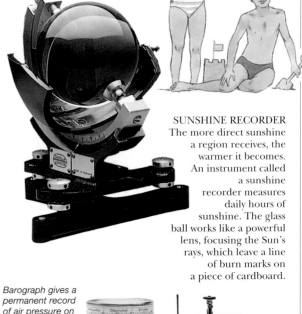

SUNSHINE RECORDER
The more direct sunshine a region receives, the warmer it becomes. An instrument called a sunshine recorder measures daily hours of sunshine. The glass ball works like a powerful lens, focusing the Sun's rays, which leave a line of burn marks on a piece of cardboard.

The wind spins the cups, and the wind speed is shown on a dial.

Rain pours through a funnel into a container. After every 24 hours the collected water is poured into a measuring cylinder that gives a reading of the day's total rainfall.

Barograph gives a permanent record of air pressure on a chart.

ANEMOMETER
The Sun's heat produces winds – moving currents of air that flow over the Earth's surface. Meteorologists use anemometers to measure wind speed, which shows the rate of approaching weather.

RAIN GAUGE
Droplets of water and tiny ice crystals group together to form clouds, and water falls from the skies as rain and snow. Meteorologists measure rainfall, which is the depth of water that would occur if the rain did not drain away.

BAROGRAPH
A barograph measures air pressure. This is important in weather forecasting because high pressure often brings settled weather; low pressure brings wind and rain.

CLOUDS

Low-lying clouds at the top of a hill cause the air to become cold, foggy, and damp. This is because the clouds contain many tiny droplets of water. Clouds form in air that is rising. The air contains invisible water vapour. As the air ascends, it becomes cooler. Colder air cannot hold so much vapour, and some vapour turns to tiny droplets or freezes to ice crystals, forming a cloud. Slow-rising air produces sheets of cloud. Air that is ascending quickly forms clumps of cloud.

CLOUD FORMATION

There are three main kinds of clouds, that form at different heights in the air. Feathery cirrus clouds float highest of all. Midway to low are fluffy cumulus clouds. Sheets of stratus clouds often lie low in the sky; grey stratus bears rain. Cumulonimbus cloud, a type of cumulus cloud, towers in the sky and often brings thunderstorms.

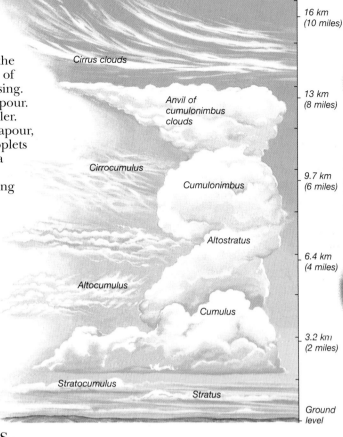

Cirrus clouds

16 km (10 miles)

Anvil of cumulonimbus clouds

13 km (8 miles)

Cirrocumulus

9.7 km (6 miles)

Cumulonimbus

Altostratus

6.4 km (4 miles)

Altocumulus

Cumulus

Stratocumulus

3.2 km (2 miles)

Stratus

Ground level

CIRRUS CLOUDS

Cirrus clouds form high in the sky so they contain only ice crystals. Cirrocumulus (above) and cirrostratus also form at high altitudes.

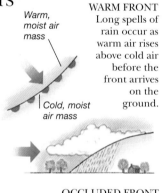

CUMULUS CLOUDS

Separate masses of cloud are called cumulus clouds. Altocumulus is medium-high patchy cloud, and low stratocumulus contains low, dense clumps of cloud.

AIR MASSES AND FRONTS

Huge bodies of air, called air masses, form over land and sea. Air masses containing warm, cold, moist, or dry air bring different kinds of weather as they are carried by the wind. A front is where two air masses meet. The weather changes when a front arrives.

Warm, moist air mass

WARM FRONT

Long spells of rain occur as warm air rises above cold air before the front arrives on the ground.

Cold, moist air mass

COLD FRONT

Cold air moves in under warm air, bringing heavy rain followed by showers.

Cold air mass

Warm air mass

OCCLUDED FRONT

A cold front overtakes a warm front, lifting warm air above it. Rain also falls along an occluded front.

Cold air mass

Warm air mass

Cold air mass

WEATHER FORECASTING

The weather centres in different countries receive measurements of weather conditions from satellites and observers around the world. They use this data to forecast the weather that lies ahead. Supercomputers do the many difficult calculations involved and draw charts of the weather to come. Forecasters use the charts to predict the weather for the next few days, producing weather reports for television, newspapers, shipping, and aircraft.

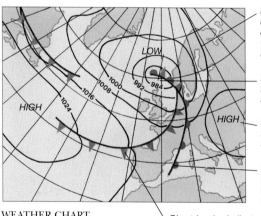

Lines called isobars give the air pressure, which is measured in millibars.

LOW indicates regions of lowest air pressure.

HIGH indicates regions of highest air pressure.

Red semicircles indicate the advancing edge of a warm front.

Blue triangles indicate the advancing edge of a cold front.

LOW

1000

992

984

1016

HIGH

1024

HIGH

WEATHER CHART

A weather forecaster predicts the day's weather using a chart showing air pressure and fronts over a large region. Lines called isobars connect regions with the same atmospheric pressure. Tight loops of isobars of decreasing pressure show a low, where it is windy and possibly rainy. Isobars of rising pressure indicate a high, which gives settled weather.

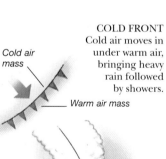

HIGHS AND LOWS

The pressure of the air varies from time to time and from place to place. Regions of low pressure are called cyclones or lows. The air rises and cools, bringing clouds and rain. An anticyclone, or high, is a region of high pressure. The air descends and warms, bringing clear, dry weather. Winds circle around highs and lows, as can be seen in this satellite picture of a cyclonic storm.

Find out more

ATMOSPHERE
CLIMATES
EARTH
RAIN AND SNOW
STORMS
WIND

WEIGHTS AND MEASURES

HOW FAR AWAY is the moon? How deep are the oceans? How tall are you? How hot is it on Mars? It is possible to measure all of these things and many more. Every day we need to make measurements. In cooking, for example, a recipe requires the correct weight of each ingredient, and once mixed, the ingredients have to be cooked at a certain temperature. We make measurements using measuring instruments. For example, a thermometer measures temperature, a ruler measures distance, and a clock measures time. All measurements are based on a system of units. Time, for example, is measured in units of minutes and seconds; length is measured in metres or feet. Precise measurements are very important in science and medicine. Scientists have extremely accurate measuring instruments to determine everything from the tiny distance between atoms in a piece of metal, to the temperature of a distant planet, such as Neptune.

Scale pan carries fixed weights in units of grams or ounces.

WEIGHT
Weighing scales measure how heavy things are. They compare the weight of an object in one pan to a known weight that sits in the other pan.

VOLUME
Volume measures the amount of space that an object or liquid takes up. A measuring jug measures the volume of a liquid. By reading the level of the liquid against a scale of units, you can find the volume of the liquid in the jug.

Thermometers measure temperature.

LENGTH AND AREA
Tape measures and rulers indicate length. They can also be used to calculate area, which indicates, for example, the amount of land a football field takes up or the amount of material needed to make a coat.

We can also measure things that we cannot see. This digital meter measures the strength of an electric current in amperes (A).

UNITS OF MEASUREMENT
When you measure something, such as height, you compare the quantity you are measuring to a fixed unit such as a metre or a foot. Scientists have set these units with great precision, so that if you measure your height with two different rulers, you will get the same answer. The metre, for example, is defined (set) by the distance travelled by light in a specific time. This gives a very precise measure of length.

TIME
Time is measured in hours, minutes, and seconds. A digital stopwatch can measure the time of a race to the nearest hundredth of a second.

METRIC SYSTEM
A system of measurement defines fixed units for quantities such as weight and time. Most countries use the metric system, which was developed in France about 200 years ago. Then the metre was fixed as the 10 millionth part of the distance between the North Pole and the equator. The metre is now fixed using the speed of light.

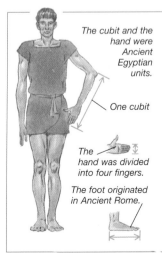

The cubit and the hand were Ancient Egyptian units.

One cubit

The hand was divided into four fingers.

The foot originated in Ancient Rome.

BODY MEASUREMENTS
The earliest systems of units were based on parts of the human body, such as the hands or feet. Both the Ancient Egyptians (about 3000 BCE) and the Romans (from about 800 BCE) used units of this kind. However, body measurements present a problem. They always give different answers because they depend on the size of the person making the measurement.

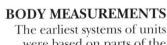
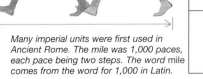

Many imperial units were first used in Ancient Rome. The mile was 1,000 paces, each pace being two steps. The word mile comes from the word for 1,000 in Latin.

IMPERIAL SYSTEM
Units of the imperial system include inches and feet for length, pints and gallons for volume, and pounds and tons for weight. The imperial system is used mainly in the United States.

Find out more
CLOCKS AND WATCHES
EGYPT, ANCIENT
MATHEMATICS
ROMAN EMPIRE

WEST AFRICA

THE VARIED CLIMATES, landscapes, and resources of the countries of West Africa have attracted both traders and colonizers. Arabs operated trading caravans across the Sahara Desert, while the Europeans sought both West African slaves and gold. Today, most of the countries in this region are desperately poor, their problems made worse by corrupt governments, debt, and occasional civil wars. The vast majority of people live by farming. Coffee, cocoa, and oil palms are all cultivated in the humid tropical lowlands of the west and south, while cattle, sheep, and goats are herded by the nomads of the Sahel. Vast reserves of oil have been found in the Niger Delta and off Ivory Coast, and there is mineral wealth in both Mauritania and Sierra Leone, but these resources are still not having an impact on most people's daily lives.

PLANTAINS
Plantains are members of the banana family. They are cooked and mashed to make a staple food in many parts of tropical West Africa.

FISHING IN MAURITANIA
Two-thirds of Mauritania is covered by the Sahara Desert. Only one per cent of the land, the area drained by the Senegal River, can be cultivated. However, Mauritania has some of the richest fishing grounds in the world. Many other nations fish there. Catches are sold through the state fishing company, and fishing provides over half of Mauritania's export earnings.

Most of the countries of this region border the Atlantic Ocean. The northern countries lie on the fringes of the Sahara Desert and the Sahel, a vast area of semi-desert. The tropical rainforests of the west and south are irrigated by three major rivers – the Niger, Volta, and Senegal.

A Mauritanian fisherman uses a pole to carry his nets to the water's edge. Local fishing is small-scale and traditional.

SAHARA DESERT
The Sahara is spreading south, turning much of Mauritania, Mali, and Niger into desert. In Mauritania, 75 per cent of grazing land has been lost in the past 25 years. Drought, cutting down trees for fuel, and over-grazing are all contributing to this process. When soil has no roots to cling to, the wind blows it away. Windbreaks of trees and shrubs are being planted in order to halt the desert's advance.

ISLAM
Many of the countries of West Africa are Islamic. The religion was spread by Arab traders, who controlled the great caravan trading routes across the Sahara from the 8th century. The rulers of the West African kingdoms adopted Islam from the 13th century. The Grand Mosque at Djenne, in Mali, is the largest mud-brick building in the world. It dates to the 14th century, but requires constant rebuilding.

The streets of Senegal's capital, Dakar, are lined with market stalls and street sellers. This busy, expanding port has a population of more than two million.

FARMING
Throughout West Africa, most people live by small-scale farming. In Senegal, the main crops that are grown for export include groundnuts, cotton, and sugar-cane. Rice, millet, and sorghum are staple foods. Many farmers travel regularly into local towns, or even Dakar, the capital city, to sell their excess produce. Most farmers rely on the flooding of the Senegal river to water their land. The damming of the river is disrupting this natural cycle.

The Wodaabe are nomadic cattle herders, who only come into towns for trading and festivals.

The main dye used in this cloth is indigo, a blue colour produced by pulping the leaves of the indigo vine.

WODAABE PEOPLE

The nomadic Wodaabe people graze their herds along the Nigerian-Niger borderlands. Every year they hold a beauty contest, where the men compete for wives. Under the careful scrutiny of the women, they parade themselves in make-up which emphasizes their eyes and teeth.

NIGERIAN TEXTILES
The Yoruba and Hausa are the main ethnic groups in Nigeria. The Hausa are found in the north of the country, the traditionally city-dwelling Yoruba in the southwest. Both groups produce patterned textiles, hand-dyed using natural plant extracts.

DOWNTOWN LAGOS

Lagos is Nigeria's largest city, chief port, and until 1991, the country's capital. It developed as a major Portuguese slave centre until it fell under British control in 1861. The city sprawls across the islands and sandbars of Lagos lagoon, linked by a series of bridges. Most of the population is concentrated on Lagos Island. The southwest of the island, with its striking high-rise skyline, is the commercial, financial, and educational centre of the city. Lagos is Nigeria's transport hub; it is served by a major international airport, and is also the country's main outlet for exports. Lagos suffers from growing slums, traffic congestion, and overcrowding. Pollution is also a major problem.

BAMBUKU HEAD
In many parts of West Africa, traditional beliefs are still very much alive. Ancestors are worshipped, or called upon to cure sickness and help people in difficulties. Spirits are worshipped at rituals and ceremonies. In eastern Nigeria, the fierce expression on this Bambuku head is used to frighten away evil spirits. It is left in a small shelter at the entrance to the village.

NIGERIAN OIL

Since the 1970s, Nigeria has become dependent on its vast oil reserves in the Niger Delta. It is the tenth largest producer in the world, and oil accounts for 90 per cent of its exports. The Nigerian government has become over-dependent on oil; the country was once a major exporter of tropical fruits, but agriculture has declined. When world oil prices declined in the 1980s, Nigeria was forced to rely on financial assistance from the World Bank. There are also growing concerns about the pollution problems caused by the oil industry in the Niger Delta. Protesters have attacked Shell, one of the main companies operating in Nigeria.

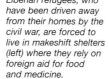

AFRICAN GOLD

The gold of West Africa is found underground, or as a fine dust, obtained by sifting soil in shallow river beds. In the 19th century, African gold produced great wealth for European traders. In Asante, Ghana, goldsmiths were a privileged class. They created this magnificent head, taken as loot by the British in 1874.

The use of modern equipment (left) in the logging industry in Ivory Coast is speeding up the process of deforestation.

LOGGING IN IVORY COAST

The tropical rain forests in the moist, humid interior of Ivory Coast have suffered considerable damage. Many trees have been cut down in order to grow more profitable cocoa trees which thrive in the tropical conditions. Cocoa beans are transported to factories along the coast where they are made into cocoa butter, an ingredient in chocolates and some cosmetics. Exports are sent through the port of Abidjan, once the capital and now West Africa's main port.

The yield of cocoa trees (right) is very low. An average fully grown tree bears only 20 cocoa pods.

COCOA BEANS

Cocoa beans were first discovered by the Aztec peoples of Mexico. They used the seeds to make a drink called *chocolatl*, which was exported to Europe by Spanish and Portuguese colonists, where it became an instant success. West Africa now produces over half the world's supply of cocoa beans. Seeds are sun-dried, fermented, roasted, and ground to make cocoa butter.

TOURISM IN GAMBIA

Gambia is a narrow country, clinging to the banks of the Gambia River, and almost entirely surrounded by Senegal. Most people live off the land, but increasing numbers are moving to the coast. Here, sandy beaches and mild winters are attracting many visitors from northern Europe. Tourism is Gambia's fastest-growing industry.

Liberian refugees, who have been driven away from their homes by the civil war, are forced to live in makeshift shelters (left) where they rely on foreign aid for food and medicine.

LIBERIAN REFUGEES

Liberia has never been colonized, making it the oldest independent republic in Africa. It was founded by the USA in the 1820s as a refuge for Africans who had been freed from slavery. The name Liberia means "freed land". Descendants of the American slaves mixed uneasily with the majority native population. For many years, Liberia was a devastated war zone, the result of violent conflict between the country's ethnic groups, which include the Kpelle, Bassa, and Kru peoples. Homeless victims of the fighting were forced to live in vast refugee camps, where disease and food shortages were common. In 2003, UN peacekeepers entered the country, and the armed groups have now largely been disbanded.

LAKE VOLTA

One of the largest man-made lakes in the world, Lake Volta was formed by the building of the Askosombo Dam on Ghana's Volta River in 1965. Some 78,000 people, living in 740 villages, were resettled when the dam was built. The lake is a major fishing ground, and also supplies water for farmers. The hydroelectric dam generates most of Ghana's power.

Find out more

AFRICA
AFRICA, HISTORY OF
DESERT WILDLIFE
OIL
VOLCANOES

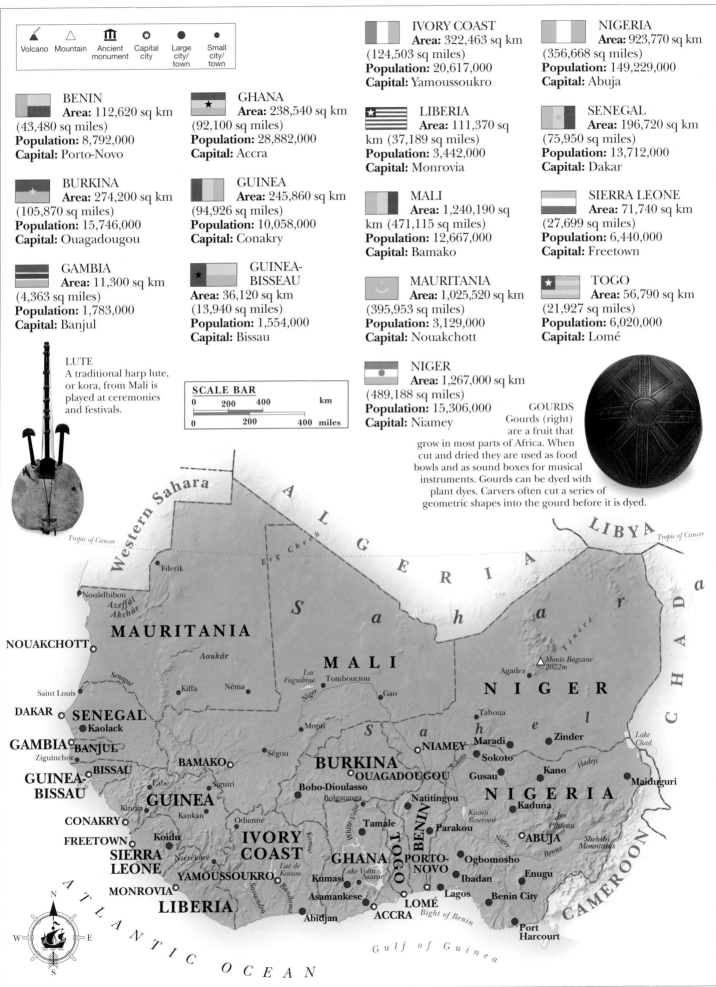

Volcano 🌋	**Mountain** △	**Ancient monument** 🏛	**Capital city** ✪
Large city/town ●	**Small city/town** ●		

IVORY COAST
Area: 322,463 sq km (124,503 sq miles)
Population: 20,617,000
Capital: Yamoussoukro

NIGERIA
Area: 923,770 sq km (356,668 sq miles)
Population: 149,229,000
Capital: Abuja

BENIN
Area: 112,620 sq km (43,480 sq miles)
Population: 8,792,000
Capital: Porto-Novo

GHANA
Area: 238,540 sq km (92,100 sq miles)
Population: 28,882,000
Capital: Accra

LIBERIA
Area: 111,370 sq km (37,189 sq miles)
Population: 3,442,000
Capital: Monrovia

SENEGAL
Area: 196,720 sq km (75,950 sq miles)
Population: 13,712,000
Capital: Dakar

BURKINA
Area: 274,200 sq km (105,870 sq miles)
Population: 15,746,000
Capital: Ouagadougou

GUINEA
Area: 245,860 sq km (94,926 sq miles)
Population: 10,058,000
Capital: Conakry

MALI
Area: 1,240,190 sq km (471,115 sq miles)
Population: 12,667,000
Capital: Bamako

SIERRA LEONE
Area: 71,740 sq km (27,699 sq miles)
Population: 6,440,000
Capital: Freetown

GAMBIA
Area: 11,300 sq km (4,363 sq miles)
Population: 1,783,000
Capital: Banjul

GUINEA-BISSAU
Area: 36,120 sq km (13,940 sq miles)
Population: 1,554,000
Capital: Bissau

MAURITANIA
Area: 1,025,520 sq km (395,953 sq miles)
Population: 3,129,000
Capital: Nouakchott

TOGO
Area: 56,790 sq km (21,927 sq miles)
Population: 6,020,000
Capital: Lomé

NIGER
Area: 1,267,000 sq km (489,188 sq miles)
Population: 15,306,000
Capital: Niamey

LUTE
A traditional harp lute, or kora, from Mali is played at ceremonies and festivals.

SCALE BAR
0   200   400   km
0   200   400   miles

GOURDS
Gourds (right) are a fruit that grow in most parts of Africa. When cut and dried they are used as food bowls and as sound boxes for musical instruments. Gourds can be dyed with plant dyes. Carvers often cut a series of geometric shapes into the gourd before it is dyed.

WHALES AND DOLPHINS

TEN MILLION YEARS before humans first lived on Earth, whales were swimming in the oceans. Whales are among the most intelligent of all creatures. They are also the largest living animals, and among the gentlest and most graceful. Whales, dolphins, and porpoises make up a fascinating group of mammals. They are warm-blooded, but unlike seals, they have no fur; a thick layer of fatty blubber under the skin keeps them warm. The whale group is divided into those with teeth (toothed whales) and those without teeth (baleen whales). There are dozens of different toothed whales, including the friendly bottle-nosed dolphin and the ferocious killer whale, which eats almost anything in the sea. Toothless or baleen whales include the humpback and blue whales, which feed by sieving small sea creatures, such as krill, into their mouths. Since all whales and dolphins breathe air, they must swim to the surface of the water regularly. Whales and dolphins swim by moving their tails up and down; fish move their tails from side to side. Whales have suffered greatly from hunting by humans, and 21 kinds are on the official lists of endangered species. Today, whaling is not allowed, in the hope that the population of whales will increase.

Dorsal (back) fin

Blowhole (nostrils)

Baleen plates for feeding

Throat pleats

Tail fluke

THE SOCIABLE DOLPHIN
One of the most playful creatures in the world is the dolphin. This sociable animal lives in "schools" of up to 1,000. They race through the waves, and sometimes can be seen scooting along in front of boats.

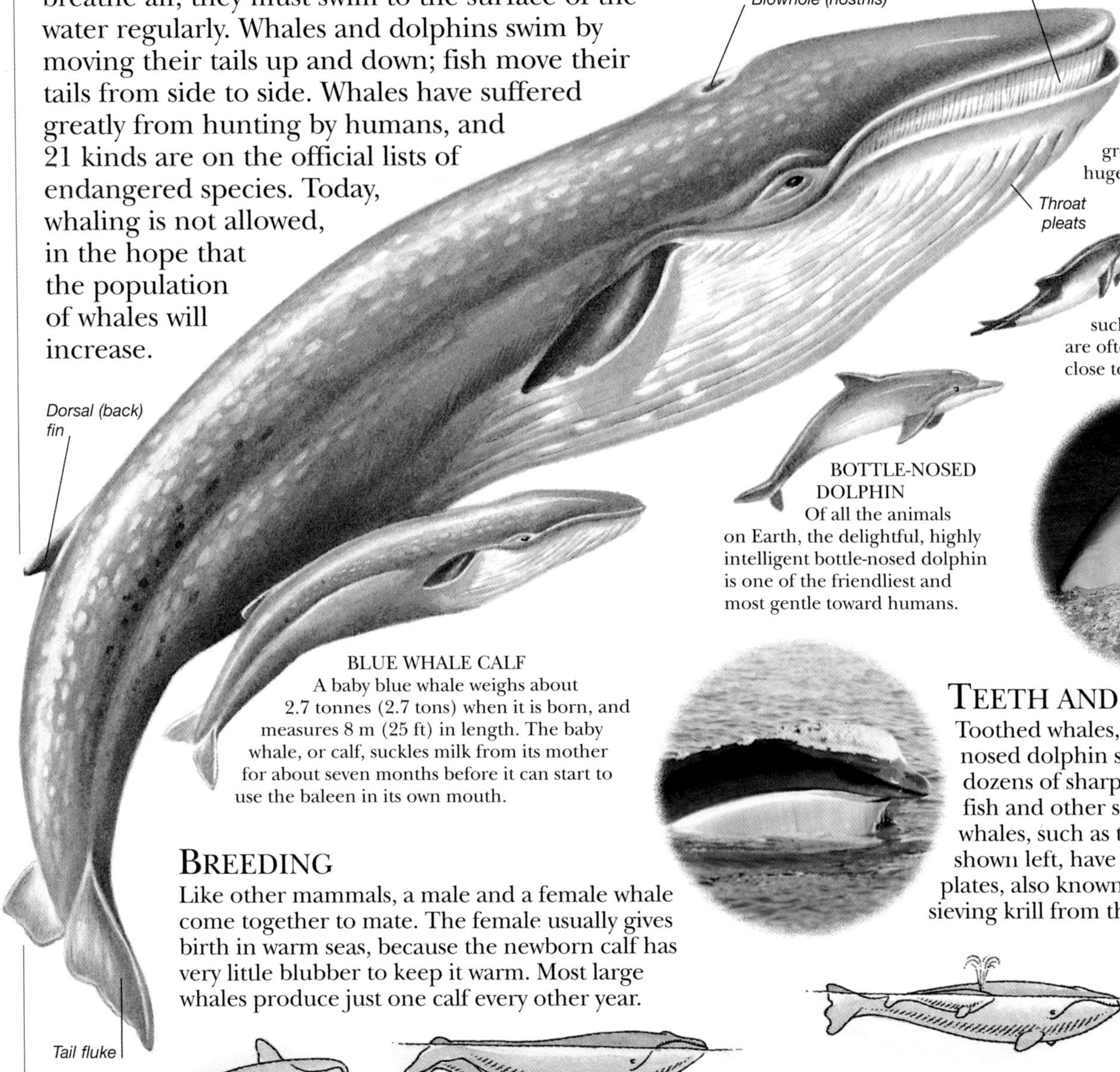

BLUE WHALE
The blue whale is the largest animal that is alive today, and it roams all oceans. Blue whales can live to 80 years of age. The skin on the blue whale's throat has many grooves, and expands hugely as the whale feeds.

PORPOISE
There are six different kinds of porpoise. Common, or harbour, porpoises such as the one shown here are often seen in shallow water close to harbours and beaches.

BOTTLE-NOSED DOLPHIN
Of all the animals on Earth, the delightful, highly intelligent bottle-nosed dolphin is one of the friendliest and most gentle toward humans.

BLUE WHALE CALF
A baby blue whale weighs about 2.7 tonnes (2.7 tons) when it is born, and measures 8 m (25 ft) in length. The baby whale, or calf, suckles milk from its mother for about seven months before it can start to use the baleen in its own mouth.

BREEDING
Like other mammals, a male and a female whale come together to mate. The female usually gives birth in warm seas, because the newborn calf has very little blubber to keep it warm. Most large whales produce just one calf every other year.

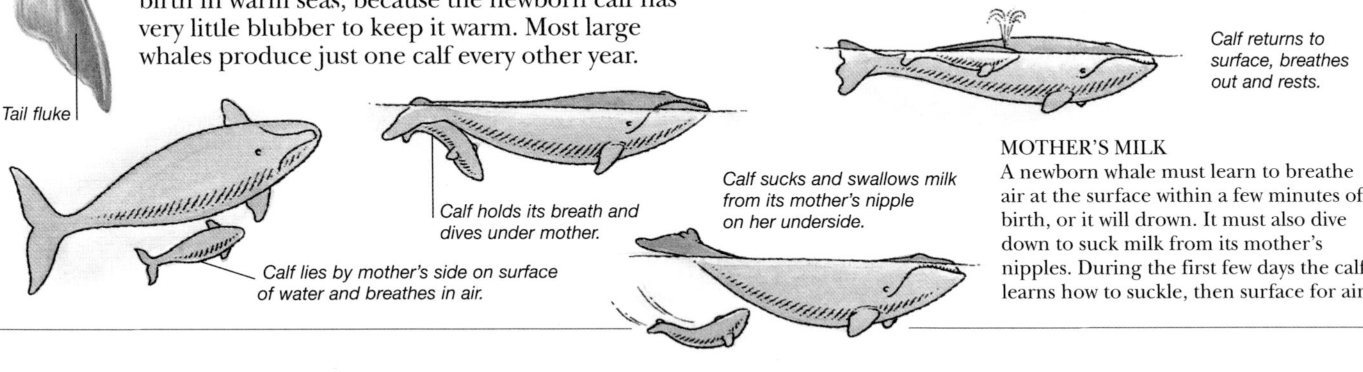

TEETH AND BALEEN
Toothed whales, such as the bottle-nosed dolphin shown above, have dozens of sharp teeth for gripping fish and other slippery prey. Baleen whales, such as the right whale shown left, have comb-like baleen plates, also known as whalebone, for sieving krill from the sea.

Calf returns to surface, breathes out and rests.

MOTHER'S MILK
A newborn whale must learn to breathe air at the surface within a few minutes of birth, or it will drown. It must also dive down to suck milk from its mother's nipples. During the first few days the calf learns how to suckle, then surface for air.

Calf sucks and swallows milk from its mother's nipple on her underside.

Calf holds its breath and dives under mother.

Calf lies by mother's side on surface of water and breathes in air.

SPERM WHALE

The impressive sperm whale is the deepest diving sea mammal known to us. It swims down to at least 600 m (2,000 ft), holding its breath for more than an hour. Measuring more than 15 m (50 ft) in length, it is the largest of the toothed whales and has enormous teeth on its lower jaw – up to 25 cm (10 in) long. The sperm whale feeds on squid and fish deep down near the seabed. In the past, so many sperm whales were killed to make products from their fatty blubber, flesh, and the oil in their foreheads (spermaceti) that very few of these great creatures now exist.

THE LARGEST BRAIN
The brain of the sperm whale is the biggest of any animal, weighing more than 9 kg (20 lb).

The sperm whale's enormous forehead is filled with a waxy, oily substance called spermaceti, which helps keep the whale upright in the water.

Up to 50 teeth in lower jaw

BLOWHOLES
After a dive, whales rise to the surface to blow out warm, moist air from their lungs. As this air mixes with the cold ocean air, the moisture condenses (like your breath on a cold winter morning). This is what makes the watery-looking spout.

Blue whale

Right whale

Humpback whale

Sperm whale

WHALE SOUNDS
Whales make a variety of sounds, including squeals, groans, yips, and wails, which carry many kilometres through the water. Each male humpback whale has its own song, lasting for up to 35 minutes, which it sings over and over again. Dolphins in a group "talk" constantly to each other as they play and feed.

Shark is detected by dolphin.

Outgoing clicking sound and returning echoes

Melon organ in forehead

ECHOLOCATION
In addition to using their sight and hearing, dolphins are able to sense other creatures nearby by means of a special organ in their forehead called the "melon". By making a loud clicking sound which bounces off objects and makes echoes, the dolphin can tell the size and distance of another creature in the water. It can then warn other dolphins of any danger.

MIGRATION
Many whales spend the winter in warm seas and summer in colder waters, travelling great distances from ocean to ocean. Grey whales travel south to give birth to one calf in winter near California. Then the mother and baby begin a long journey up the coast toward the Bering Sea and the Arctic Ocean.

Bering Sea

CANADA

UNITED STATES

California

WHALES OF THE WORLD
All whales and most dolphins live in the sea; four kinds of dolphins live in rivers. Some whales, such as the humpback whale, inhabit all oceans; others, such as the narwhal and the beluga whale, live only near the Arctic region.

Humpback whale 16 m (50 ft), 26 tonnes (26 tons)

BIGGEST ANIMAL EVER
Blue whales are larger than the dinosaurs were – up to 30 m (100 ft) in length. They are the heaviest animals ever, weighing 136 tonnes (134 tons) – about as heavy as 2,000 people.

Killer whale (orca) 8 m (25 ft), 3.5 tonnes (3.5 tons)

Beluga, 1.5 tonnes (1.5 tons)

Pacific white-sided dolphin, 90 kg (200 lb)

STRANDINGS
Whales sometimes swim too close to the land and are stranded. Without water to support their bodies, they cannot breathe, and soon die.

Human diver, 2 m (6 ft) in length. Blue whale 30 m (100 ft) in length.

Ganges river dolphin, 90 kg (200 lb)

Narwhal, 1.5 tonnes (1.5 tons)

Find out more
ANIMALS
ANIMAL SENSES
MAMMALS
MIGRATION, ANIMAL
OCEAN WILDLIFE

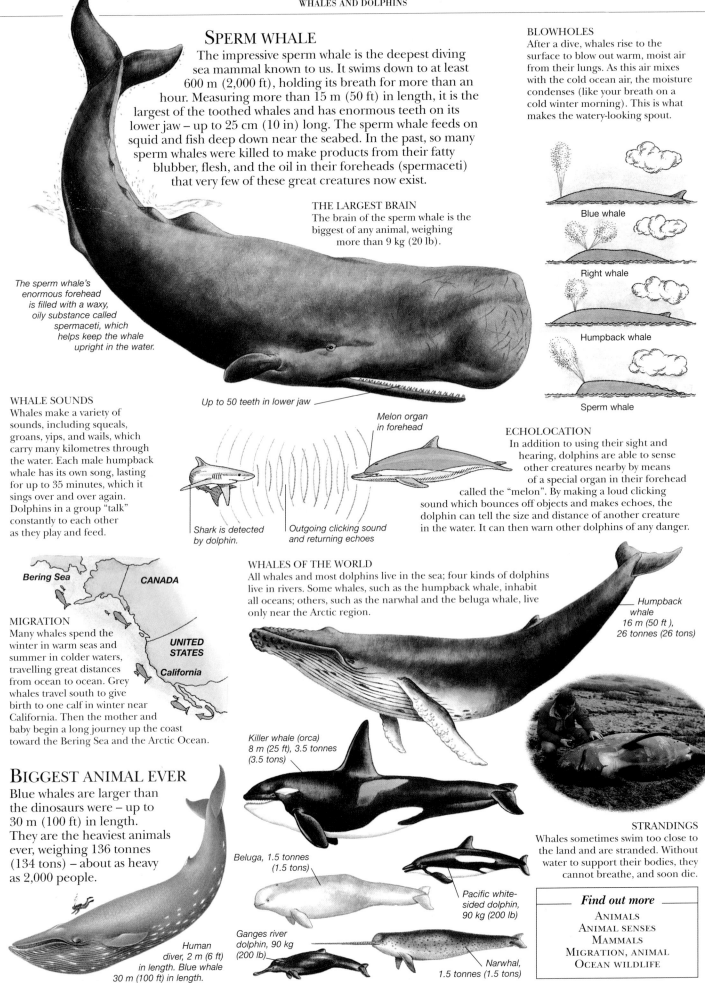

WHEELS

SOMETIMES THE SIMPLEST INVENTIONS are the most important. Although no one is sure exactly who invented the first wheel, the earliest records go back to about 5,500 years ago. The wheel has made possible a whole range of machines, from photocopiers to jet engines, that we take for granted today. Wheels have a unique characteristic – they are circular, without corners, enabling them to roll or spin evenly. This allows almost all forms of land transportation – bicycles, cars, trains, and trams – to roll smoothly along roads, rails, and rough ground. In addition, the circular motion of a wheel means that it can transmit power continuously from an engine. Many more inventions are based on wheels. The crane, for example, relies on pulleys (grooved wheels around which a rope is passed), which reduce the effort needed to lift heavy weights; gears multiply or reduce the speed and force of a wheel and are essential in countless other machines.

AXLE AND BEARINGS
A wheel spins on a shaft called an axle. Wheels often have ball bearings – several small steel balls that run between the axle and the wheel, allowing it to turn smoothly. Without bearings, the great weight of a Ferris wheel (above) would squeeze the wheel against the axle and prevent it from turning.

Before wheels were invented, people had to push or drag heavy loads over the ground. Perhaps watching a smooth rock roll down a hill gave people the idea of using wheels for transport.

About 4,500 years ago, the Ancient Egyptians built great triangular pyramids as tombs and temples. Gangs of workers dragged huge blocks of stone with the aid of log-rollers.

The first vehicle wheels used for carts were solid wood. They were made of two or three planks of wood fixed together and cut into a circle. They first appeared in about 3200 BCE.

INVENTING THE WHEEL
The first recorded use of a wheel dates back to around 3500 BCE. This was the potter's wheel, a simple turntable used in southwest Asia by Mesopotamian pottery workers to make smooth, round clay pots. About 300 years later, the Mesopotamians fitted wheels to a cart, and the age of wheeled transportation began.

GYROSCOPES
A gyroscope is a rotating wheel mounted on a frame. When the wheel spins, its momentum makes it balance like a spinning top. Once a gyroscope is spinning, it always tries to point in the same direction. Aircraft, ships, and missiles use gyroscopes to navigate, or direct themselves, to their destinations.

Bibendum, the famous symbol of the French tire company Michelin

Wheels with spokes developed in about 2000 BCE. Spoked wheels are lighter and faster than solid wheels and were fitted to war chariots.

The gear wheels are connected by teeth that interlock (fit exactly) into each other. Their mutual positions decide how the force changes.

Wheels held together by wire spokes appeared in about 1800. They are very light and strong, and were first used for cars, bicycles, and early airplanes. In the 1950s, metal wheels replaced wire wheels on cars.

TIRES
Car and bicycle wheels have rubber tires filled with air. They give a comfortable ride and all, except those of racing cars, have a tread (a pattern of ridges) to help them grip the road. Scottish engineer Robert W. Thomson invented the first air-filled tire in 1845.

GEARS
Sets of interlocking toothed wheels are called gears. Gears transfer movement in machines and change the speed and force of wheels. For example, a large gear wheel makes a small gear wheel rotate faster, but the faster moving wheel produces less force. Gears can also change the direction of the motion.

Find out more

CARS
PLASTICS
TRANSPORT, HISTORY OF

WIND

AS A GENTLE BREEZE or a powerful hurricane, wind blows constantly around the world. Winds are belts of moving air that flow from one area to another, driven by the Sun's heat. Warm air is lighter than cold air, so warm air rises as it is heated by the Sun, and cold air flows in to take its place. This sets up a circular current of air which produces winds. Light, warm air exerts less pressure on the Earth than cold air, creating an area of low pressure toward which cold air flows. Similarly, cold air sinks and produces an area of high pressure from which air flows outward. The greater the difference in pressure between two areas, the stronger the winds. Weather forecasters use the Beaufort scale to measure the speed of wind. It runs from 0 to 12: for example, force 2 is a light breeze; force 12 is a hurricane. The size and shape of areas of land and water affect local winds, which are often given special names, such as the chinook in North America and the sirocco in Italy.

WIND DIRECTION
A wind is often named according to the direction from which it is coming. For example, a wind which comes from the west is called a westerly. Windsocks (above) and vanes are used to show wind direction.

At the equator, the Sun's heat warms the air. In this area, the air rises, causing a belt of calm air called the doldrums.

Horse latitudes
Path of air
Doldrums

When the air has risen very high, it cools and sinks back to the Earth in the horse latitudes.

Doldrums
Path of air
Horse latitudes

Polar easterlies

Westerlies

Horse latitudes
NE trade winds

Equator

SE trade winds

Horse latitudes
Westerlies

The westerlies are warm winds which blow away from the horse latitudes in the direction of the poles.

The trade winds flow from the horse latitudes toward the equator.

In between the westerlies and the trade winds is an area of calm called the horse latitudes. The name may refer to the many horses that died on ships that were becalmed in this region.

The polar easterlies are cold winds which blow away from the poles.

WORLD WINDS

Besides local and seasonal winds, there are certain winds that always blow. These are called prevailing winds. There are three main belts of prevailing winds on each side of the equator. They are called the trade winds, the westerlies, and the polar easterlies. The direction they blow in is affected by the spin of the Earth. They are angled toward the left in the southern hemisphere and toward the right in the northern hemisphere.

MONSOONS

Seasonal winds that blow in a particular direction are called monsoons. For example, during the summer in southern Asia, the wind blows from the Indian Ocean toward the land, bringing heavy rains. In winter, the wind blows in the opposite direction, from the Himalayas towards the ocean.

WIND TURBINES

The earliest ships used wind power to carry them across the sea. Wind also powers machines. Windmills were used in Iran as long ago as the 7th century for raising water from rivers, and later for grinding corn. Today huge windmills, or wind turbines, can produce electricity; a large wind turbine can supply enough electricity for a small town. Wind turbines cause no pollution but they are large and noisy and take up huge areas of land.

A wind farm in the United States uses 300 wind turbines to produce electricity.

Find out more
CLIMATES
ENERGY
STORMS
WEATHER

WOMEN'S RIGHTS

WORKING WOMEN
In the United States about 43 per cent of workers are women. But few hold important positions, and most earn less than men doing the same jobs.

UP UNTIL TWO HUNDRED YEARS AGO women had few rights. They were not allowed to vote, and were considered the property of their fathers or husbands. By the middle of the 19th century, women were demanding equality with men. They wanted suffrage – the right to vote in elections – and an equal chance to work and be educated. They demanded the right to have their own possessions, to divorce their husbands, and to keep their children after divorce. The fight for women's rights was also called feminism. The first organized demand for the vote occurred in the United States in 1848. By the 1920s, women had won some battles, particularly for the vote and greater education. In the 1960s, women renewed their call for equal rights. This new wave of protest was named the women's liberation movement, and led to laws in many countries to stop discrimination against women. Yet today, in a few countries, women are still denied full voting rights.

EMILY DAVISON
In 1913 British suffragette Emily Davison leaped under the king's horse at a race and died. Her protest drew attention to the Votes for Women campaign.

SUSAN B. ANTHONY
One of the leaders of the suffrage movement in the United States, Susan B. Anthony (1820-1906) helped launch *Revolution,* the first feminist newspaper.

FORCE FEEDING
In 1909, suffragettes in prison refused to eat. Warders fed them by pouring food down tubes that they forced through the women's noses and into their stomachs. It was painful and seriously injured some women. Force-feeding ended in 1913.

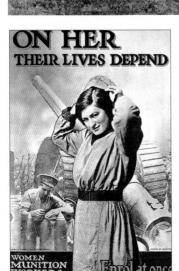

WOMEN AT WAR
During World War I (1914-18), women in Britain worked to keep factories going while the men fought. They proved that women were just as capable as men. In 1918, British women over 30 got voting rights. Two years later, all American women also gained the vote.

SUFFRAGETTES

In 1905, a British newspaper used the word suffragette to insult women who were fighting for the vote. However, the suffragettes themselves were delighted. People have used the name ever since. Many suffragettes broke the law and went to prison for their beliefs. Women who used peaceful means to obtain the vote were called suffragists.

Suffragettes publicized their campaign by chaining themselves to the railings of famous buildings.

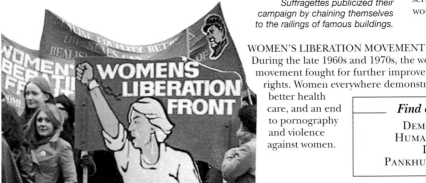

WOMEN'S LIBERATION MOVEMENT
During the late 1960s and 1970s, the women's liberation movement fought for further improvements in women's rights. Women everywhere demonstrated for equal pay, better health care, and an end to pornography and violence against women.

> *Find out more*
> DEMOCRACY
> HUMAN RIGHTS
> LAW
> PANKHURST FAMILY

WONDERS
OF THE ANCIENT WORLD

TWO THOUSAND YEARS AGO Ancient Greek and Roman tourists visited the world's great landmarks just as we do today. Ancient "travel agents" compiled lists of amazing things that travellers should see. These "wonders" were outstanding examples of human artistic or engineering achievement. The seven most commonly listed monuments to human endeavour are called the Seven Wonders of the Ancient World. They all had qualities that made them stand out from the rest. Some were the most beautiful statues, others the largest structures of the day. Of the seven wonders, only one, the Great Pyramids, can still be seen today. The Hanging Gardens, the Temple of Artemis, the Statue of Zeus, the Mausoleum, the Colossus, and the Lighthouse at Pharos have all vanished or are in ruins.

PYRAMIDS
Three pyramids were built at Giza, Egypt, in about 2600 BCE as tombs for three Egyptian kings. The largest, made from more than two million huge blocks of limestone, stands 147 m (482 ft) high.

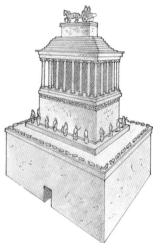

MAUSOLEUM
The Mausoleum at Halicarnassus (in modern Turkey) was a huge marble tomb built for Mausolus, a rich governor. It stood 41 m (135 ft) high, with a base supporting 36 columns, under a stepped pyramid. An earthquake destroyed most of the mausoleum.

LIGHTHOUSE
The Greek architect Sostratos designed the world's first lighthouse. It was built around 304 BCE on the island of Pharos, Alexandria, Egypt. It stood about 134 m (440 ft) high. A fire burned at the top to mark the harbour entrance.

HANGING GARDENS
In 605 BCE Nebuchadnezzar II, king of Babylon, built the Hanging Gardens in his kingdom. He planted many exotic plants on a brick terrace 23 m (75 ft) above the ground. Machines worked by slaves watered the plants.

COLOSSUS
The bronze statue of the sun god Helios towered 37 m (120 ft) over the harbour entrance on the island of Rhodes in the Aegean Sea. Built in 292 BCE, it was about the same size as the Statue of Liberty in New York.

TEMPLE OF ARTEMIS
This, the largest temple of its day, was dedicated to Artemis, goddess of the moon and hunting. Built almost entirely of marble by the Greeks at Ephesus (in modern Turkey), it burned down in 356 BCE, leaving only a few broken statues.

ZEUS
The great Statue of Zeus, king of the Greek gods, stood 12 m (40 ft) high at Olympia, Greece. Phidias, a famous Greek sculptor, created the statue in about 435 BCE. The god's robes and ornaments were made of gold, and the skin was of ivory.

Olympia

Ephesus
Halicarnassus

Rhodes

Alexandria

Giza

Babylon

LOCATION OF THE WONDERS
The map shows the location of the Seven Wonders of the Ancient World. Travellers visited many of them by ship. Most of the wonders were destroyed by earthquakes or fire, but some remains can still be seen in the British Museum in London, England.

___ *Find out more* ___
ALEXANDER THE GREAT
BABYLONIANS
EGYPT, ANCIENT

WORLD WAR I

BETWEEN 1914 AND 1918, a terrible war engulfed Europe. The war was called the First World War, or the Great War, because it affected almost every country in the world. It began because of the rivalry between several powerful European countries. Fighting started when the empire of Austria and Hungary declared war on Serbia. Soon, other countries joined the war. They formed two main groups: the Allies, composed of Britain, France, Italy, Russia, and the United States, versus the Central Powers – Germany, Austria-Hungary, and Turkey. In the beginning everyone thought the war would be short and glorious. Young men rushed to join the armies and navies. But it soon became clear that none of the opposing armies was strong enough to win a clear victory. Thousands of troops died, fighting to gain just a few hundred feet of the battlefield. In the end, the war, which some called the "war to end all wars", had achieved nothing. Within a few years a worse war broke out in Europe.

ARCHDUKE FERDINAND
On 28 June 1914, a Serbian terrorist shot Franz Ferdinand, heir to the throne of Austria and Hungary. Germany encouraged Austria to retaliate, or fight back, by declaring war on Serbia. A month after the assassination, World War I had begun.

COUNTRIES AT WAR
The war involved nearly 30 countries – more countries than any previous war. There was fighting in the Middle East, Africa, and the Pacific. However, most of the war was fought in Europe. The western front in northern France was a line of trenches that stretched from Switzerland to the English Channel. Soldiers on the eastern front fought in what is now Poland. Fighting took place on land, at sea, and in the air.

Allied countries are green, Central Powers are pink, and neutral countries are shown in beige.

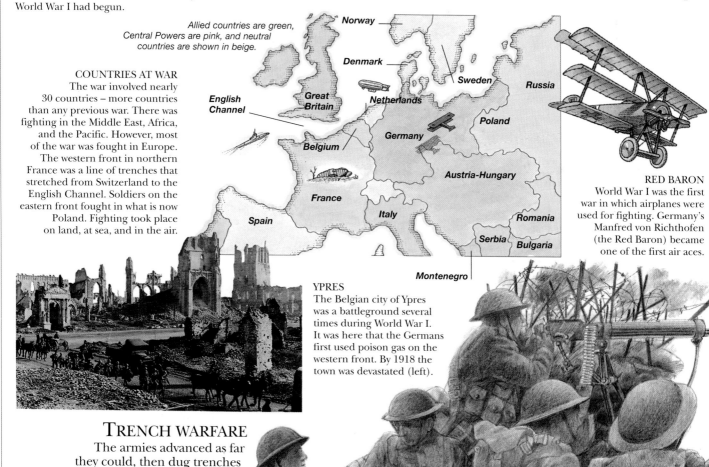

Norway
Denmark
Sweden
Russia
English Channel
Great Britain
Netherlands
Poland
Germany
Belgium
Austria-Hungary
France
Italy
Spain
Romania
Serbia
Bulgaria
Montenegro

RED BARON
World War I was the first war in which airplanes were used for fighting. Germany's Manfred von Richthofen (the Red Baron) became one of the first air aces.

YPRES
The Belgian city of Ypres was a battleground several times during World War I. It was here that the Germans first used poison gas on the western front. By 1918 the town was devastated (left).

TRENCH WARFARE
The armies advanced as far they could, then dug trenches for shelter. Life in the trenches was miserable. Soldiers were often up to their knees in mud. Lice and rats added to their discomfort. When soldiers left the trenches to advance further, the enemy killed them by the millions with machine guns. Each side also had artillery – guns that fired huge shells – which killed many more and churned up the battlefield into a sea of mud.

U-BOATS
German submarines called underwater boats, or U-boats, sank many cargo ships in the Atlantic, causing food shortages in Britain.

LUSITANIA
On 7 May 1915, a German U-boat torpedoed the British passenger liner *Lusitania*. More than 100 American passengers drowned, some of whom were very rich and famous. This angered many Americans and turned them against Germany. The sinking helped to bring the United States into the war on the Allied side.

WORLD WAR I
June 1914 Assassination of Archduke Franz Ferdinand

July 1914 Austria-Hungary declares war on Serbia.

August 1914 Germany declares war on Russia and France and invades Belgium. Britain declares war on Germany and Austria-Hungary.

May 1915 Italy joins Allies.

July 1916 Allies use tanks for the first time in France.

April 1917 United States enters the war.

March 1918 Russia signs treaty with Germany. Germany's final huge attack at Marne fails.

September 1918 Allies begin their final attack.

November 1918 Germany signs armistice, ending the war.

PROPAGANDA
Wartime posters and newspapers aimed to persuade people that the enemy was evil and that war must go on. The message of this propaganda, or government-controlled news, was that everyone should help by fighting, working, raising money, and making sacrifices. The poster (left) shows a frightening image of Germany with its hands on Europe.

WOMEN WORKERS
As thousands of men went off to war, women took over their jobs in the factories. Most women worked long hours, and many had dangerous jobs, such as making ammunition. Their efforts disproved the old idea that women were inferior to men, and eventually led to women gaining the right to vote. But when the troops returned after the war, there was massive unemployment, and women lost their jobs.

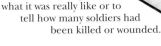

COMMUNICATION
People at home had little idea of the real conditions of the war. Officers read mail from soldiers and censored, or cut out, information that told the true story. Troops returning home were often too sickened by life in the trenches to explain what it was really like or to tell how many soldiers had been killed or wounded.

GERMANS
Until 1918, it looked as if Germany and her allies might win. But they were outnumbered, and when the British navy blocked the ports and cut off supplies of food and vital war materials, the German people rioted. They demanded food and peace, and the Kaiser – the German emperor – gave up his throne. Germany then made a peace treaty called the Treaty of Versailles with the Allied forces. The Germans lost much land and took the blame for starting the war.

DEATH TOLL
Germany and Russia each lost nearly two million soldiers in the war. Britain lost nearly one million. In all, 10 million died.

Find out more
DEPRESSION OF THE 1930s
WOMEN'S RIGHTS
WORLD WAR II

WORLD WAR II

IN 1939, GERMAN TANKS and bombers attacked Poland, and the bloodiest war in history began. Like World War I, World War II was a global war and was fought on the ground, in the air, and at sea. The war was a result of the rise to power of the German National Socialist or Nazi party, led by Adolf Hitler. The Nazis wanted to wipe out the memory of defeat in World War I. Within a year, German armies, with help from Italy, had occupied much of Europe. Only Britain opposed them. In 1941, Hitler invaded the Soviet Union. But the Soviet people fought hard and millions died. In the Pacific, the Japanese formed an alliance, called the Axis, with Germany and Italy. Japanese warplanes bombed the American naval base at Pearl Harbor, in Hawaii. This brought the United States into the war, and they joined the Soviet Union and Britain to form the Allies. By May 1945, Allied forces had defeated the Nazis in Europe; Japan surrendered in August. When the war ended, 45 million people had died and much of Europe was in ruins. Two new "superpowers" – the Soviet Union and the United States – began to dominate world politics.

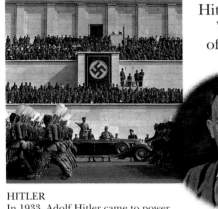

HITLER

In 1933, Adolf Hitler came to power in Germany as leader of the Nazi party. The Nazis were fascists: they were against Communism and believed in strong national government. The Nazis ruthlessly crushed anyone who opposed them. They enslaved and murdered Jews, gypsies, and other minorities, whom they blamed for all of Germany's problems, from defeat in World War I to unemployment and inflation.

British Spitfire

German Messerschmitt

The growth of Nazi Germany

Norway

Sweden

Dunkirk

Britain

Soviet Union

Poland

France

Nazi Germany

Czechoslovakia

Austria

Hungary

INVASION

In 1938, Hitler took control of Austria and parts of Czechoslovakia. Britain and France did not oppose him, and he went on to invade Poland. Britain and France then declared war on Germany. German troops smashed into France in 1940, sweeping aside the armies of Britain and France. Fleets of fishing boats and pleasure steamers from the southern coast of England helped the Royal Navy to rescue the retreating Allied soldiers from the beaches at Dunkirk, on the coast of France.

BLITZ

Between August and October 1940, the British Royal Air Force fought the Luftwaffe – the German air force – in the Battle of Britain, and finally won. Without control of the skies, Hitler could not invade Britain. His bombers began to bomb British cities during the night. This "blitzkrieg" or blitz, killed 40,000 people, mostly civilians.

EVACUATIONS

During the bombing of major cities, such as London, thousands of British children were evacuated to country towns and villages where they were much safer.

MIDWAY

Japan conquered many Pacific islands and invaded mainland Asia. However, the United States fleet defeated the Japanese at the Battle of Midway, which took place between 4-7 June 1942. The battle turned the Pacific war in favour of the Allies.

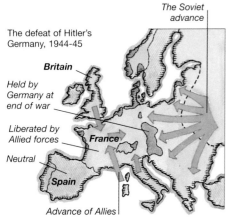

The defeat of Hitler's Germany, 1944-45

The Soviet advance

Britain

Held by Germany at end of war

Liberated by Allied forces

France

Neutral

Spain

Advance of Allies

RESISTANCE

Many people in Europe hated the Nazi occupation of their countries. So they formed secret resistance movements to spy on and fight the enemy. They used hidden radios (above) to work behind the battle lines. Resistance workers risked torture and death if they were discovered.

PEACE IN EUROPE

By the spring of 1945, the Allies had recaptured most of occupied Europe and began to cross the Rhine River into Germany. In the east, the Soviet army swept toward Berlin, Germany's capital. Crushed between these two powerful forces, the German armies surrendered. Hitler committed suicide, and the biggest and most expensive war in human history ended.

D-DAY

In June 1944, Allied troops invaded occupied Europe in the greatest seaborne landing ever mounted. Invasion day was code-named D-day. The D stood for deliverance. After a bitter struggle, and aided by resistance fighters, the Allied forces broke through, and the German soldiers retreated or were taken as prisoners.

VE DAY

On May 8, 1945, the Allies celebrated VE (Victory in Europe) Day. However, there were still another three months of bitter fighting in the Pacific. In August 1945, US planes dropped two atom bombs on Japan, destroying the cities of Hiroshima and Nagasaki. This was done to force Japan to surrender quickly and so save Allied lives that would be lost if the Allies invaded Japan. Within a few weeks the Japanese surrendered and the war ended.

CONCENTRATION CAMP

After Germany surrendered, Allied troops discovered horrifying concentration (prison) camps throughout Europe, where the Nazis had imprisoned up to 26 million people they considered "undesirable", including millions of Jews. The prisoners were starved and tortured, and many were eventually gassed to death.

Find out more

CHURCHILL, SIR WINSTON
EUROPE, HISTORY OF
HOLOCAUST
ROOSEVELT, FRANKLIN DELANO
WORLD WAR I

WORMS

WE DESCRIBE MANY long, slender, soft, legless creatures as worms. There are thousands of different kinds, ranging from the tiny hookworm to the much larger bootlace worm. The word worm is a fairly general term, and there are a number of distinct groups. Annelids, or segmented worms, include leeches, earthworms, and ragworms. Nematodes, or roundworms, have long tubelike bodies without segments. There are at least 20,000 kinds of roundworms. Some, including hookworms, cause serious diseases in humans such as river blindness and elephantiasis. Flatworms, or playhelminths, make up a third group. There are more than 17,500 kinds, and they include the parasitic flukes and tapeworms that infest sheep, pigs, and other animals.

Ragworm lives in sand and under rocks.

Undigested sand comes out of the worm's rear end and forms a worm cast on the surface.

Entire body may be more than 9 m (30 ft) long.

Proglottis (single segment)

Scolex (pin-sized head) has hooks.

Lugworm eats sand at head end.

TAPEWORM
These long worms are parasitic; they live in the digestive systems of animals such as cats and dogs. A cat, for example, becomes infected when it eats a mouse that has eaten a plant coated with tapeworm eggs. The eggs hatch into larvae inside the mouse, then develop into tapeworms once inside the cat. When waste matter passes out of the cat, tapeworm eggs also pass out.

Tapeworm grows in segments. These segments grow from the head in a long, widening ribbon. Each segment contains a full set of reproductive organs.

SEASHORE WORMS
Ragworms are active predators that seize prey such as smaller worms. Their name comes from the flaps along the body that make the animal look like a strip of torn rag. Large ragworms can bite through human skin and draw blood. Lugworms live in U-shaped burrows under the surface of the sand, digesting the nutrients from them.

POND WORMS
Even a small pond contains many worms, such as leeches and bloodworms. Leeches have 33 body segments. They suck the blood or fluids of other animals, including mammals and fish. The leech can swim by flapping its body, which has a sucker at each end. Bloodworms, or tubifex worms, show deep red blood through their thin skin.

Worm's tiny bristles grip the soil particles.

Intestine *Upper main blood vessel* *Hearts*

Mouth

Reproductive organs *Main nerve*

INSIDE AN EARTHWORM
Although earthworms are annelids, with a body divided into many similar segments, not all the segments are the same. A digestive tube runs along the worm's body. The main nerves come together at the head end of the body to form a simple brain. The blood vessels in the worm's body sometimes form five pairs of hearts.

Tubifex (bloodworm)

Medicinal leech

EARTHWORM
There are more than 3,000 kinds of earthworm. These long-bodied animals are responsible for the health of the soil. As the earthworms push their way along, they take in soil at the head end, digesting nutrients in the soil particles. The undigested remains that come out at the rear end form a worm cast. By burrowing in the earth, worms mix the soil layers, and their burrows allow air and water to soak downward, generally increasing the fertility of the soil.

Fat part of body is called the saddle.

BLOODWORM TAILS
Pond-dwelling bloodworms, or tubifex worms, wave their rear ends in the water to gather oxygen. Their heads are buried in the mud, taking in nutrients.

Find out more
ANIMALS
MEDICINE, HISTORY OF
SOIL

WRITERS AND POETS

A READER'S IMAGINATION can be excited by the way in which writers and poets use words. Writers create fantasy worlds for readers to explore. Historical novelists and science fiction writers transport us back to the past or into the distant future. Others writers, such as journalists, write in a way that creates a lifelike picture of real events they have experienced. Poets arrange words into patterns or rhymes that bring pleasure just by their sound or their shape on the page. A writer is anyone who expresses facts, ideas, thoughts, or opinions in words. Most writers hope or expect that their work will be published – printed in books or magazines and read by thousands of people. But some writers, including diarists such as the Englishman Samuel Pepys (1633-1703), write for their own pleasure. They do not always expect their work to be published. Poets are people who write in verse, or poetry. Poets make sure the lines of their poems form a regular pattern, so that, unlike prose, or ordinary writing, the poem has a rhythmic sound.

HOMER
One of the world's first writers was the Ancient Greek poet Homer, who lived about 2,700 years ago. He wrote long epic verses called *The Iliad* and *The Odyssey*. In *The Odyssey* the beautiful singing of the bird-like sirens lures sailors to their death, by shipwreck on the rocky coast.

WRITING
Even a short novel has more than 50,000 words, so writing can be hard work. To make it easier, most writers organize their work carefully. Writing methods are quite individual. Many authors use computers, while some still prefer pen and paper. American Raymond Chandler (1888-1959), who wrote detective novels, had a favourite way of writing throughout his working life.

Like any author, Chandler would have used maps to check his hero's movements around Los Angeles, the setting for many of his novels.

Chandler typed the first draft, or version, of his books on yellow paper. He used half-size sheets because he made changes by retyping, not by changing words with a pen. Retyping a whole sheet would have taken longer.

Books such as J. S. Hatcher's Textbook of Pistols gave Chandler the accurate information he needed to make his stories seem lifelike and real.

Chandler's secretary typed a clean version of the finished draft on white paper.

Chandler smoked a pipe and drank coffee as he worked. At times he also drank a lot of alcohol.

MANUSCRIPT
A writer's original typed or handwritten version of a work is called a manuscript. The editor writes instructions to the printer on the manuscript, and may also make changes and revisions to improve the writing. For example, F. Scott Fitzgerald (1896-1940) was bad at spelling, and his publisher corrected these errors.

The manuscript for this page, with the publisher's corrections

ANNE FRANK
During World War II, the German Nazi government persecuted millions of European Jews. To escape, Anne Frank (born 1929) and her Jewish family hid in a secret attic in a Netherlands office. The diary that Anne wrote while in hiding was later published. It is a deeply moving and tragic account of her ordeal. Anne died in a prison camp in 1945.

CHAUCER

Geoffrey Chaucer (c.1340-1400) was an English government official. He wrote poems in English at a time when most English writers were writing in French and Latin. Chaucer began his most famous work, the *Canterbury Tales*, in about 1386. It is a collection of stories told by pilgrims travelling from London to Canterbury. The stories tell us much about 14th-century life and are often very amusing.

HARRIET BEECHER STOWE

Uncle Tom's Cabin is a powerful anti-slavery novel written by Harriet Beecher Stowe (1811-96) in 1852. It became extremely popular all over the world, even in some southern states of America, where printing a copy was illegal at the time.

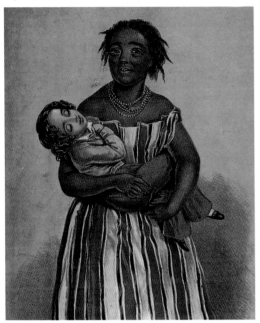

DICKENS

Some of the greatest novels in the English language are the work of Charles Dickens (1812-70). He wrote colourful and exciting novels, such as *Oliver Twist, Nicholas Nickleby,* and *David Copperfield,* which also drew attention to the poverty and social injustices of 19th-century England.

LONGFELLOW

During his lifetime, Henry Wadsworth Longfellow (1807-82) was the most popular poet in the United States. His *Song of Hiawatha*, which was published in 1855, sold more than a million copies while Longfellow was still alive. The poem tells the story of a Native American tribe before America was colonized by Europeans. Longfellow wrote on many subjects and in many styles, but he is best remembered for his romantic "picture poems" about American life.

NEIL SIMON

Playwright Neil Simon was born in New York City on 4 July 1927. He has written more than 25 plays and musicals, many of which have been made into films. Most of his plays deal with aspects of ordinary American life. However, the writer's insight and sense of humour ensure that his plays appeal to people of all nationalities.

The Goodbye Girl, one of Neil Simon's best-loved films, is set in New York.

LITERARY FILE

c. 2400 BCE Ancient Egyptian writers create the world's first literature: *The Pyramid Texts.*

c. 600 BCE Greek poet Sappho writes early lyric poetry (poetry with music).

c. 500 BCE Greek poet Aeschylus (525-456 BCE) writes the earliest dramas.

c. 100 CE Greek writer Plutarch (46-120 CE) writes *The Parallel Lives*, a collection of biographies.

1420 Zcami Motokiyo (1363-1443), the greatest writer of Japanese Noh dramas, writes *Shikadosho* (Book of the Way of the Highest Flower).

1740-42 Englishman Samuel Richardson (1689-1761) writes one of the first English novels, *Pamela, or, Virtue Rewarded.*

1765 Horace Walpole (1717-97), an Englishman, writes a ghost story, *The Castle of Otranto.*

1819-20 American Washington Irving (1783-1859) publishes one of the first books of short stories, which includes *The Legend of Sleepy Hollow* and *Rip Van Winkle.*

1841 American writer Edgar Allan Poe (1809-49) publishes *The Murders in the Rue Morgue*, the first detective story.

1847 English novelist Charlotte Brontë writes *Jane Eyre* under the false name Currer Bell, because it is still unacceptable for "respectable" women to write fiction.

1864 Jules Verne (1828-1905), a Frenchman, writes the first science fiction story, *Journey to the Center of the Earth.*

1956 The performance of *Waiting for Godot* by Irish-French dramatist Samuel Beckett (1906-89) opens the way for modern drama.

1993 American novelist Toni Morrison (born 1931), author of *Song of Solomon* and *Beloved*, becomes the first black American to win the Nobel Prize for Literature.

Find out more

BYRON, LORD
DICKENS, CHARLES
FILMS
LITERATURE
SLAVERY
THEATRE

X-RAYS

To the early pioneers of medicine, the thought of looking through the body of a living person would probably have seemed like magic. But today it is routine for doctors and dentists to take pictures of their patients' bones and teeth with an x-ray camera. X-rays are invisible waves, like light or radio waves. They can travel through soft materials just as light passes through glass. For example, x-rays can travel through flesh and skin. But hard materials such as bone and metal stop x-rays, so bone and metal show up as a shadow on an x-ray picture. X-rays have many uses: scientists use them to probe into the molecular structure of materials such as plastics, and engineers make x-ray scans of aircraft to find cracks that could cause mechanical failure. In addition, the Sun, stars, and other objects in space produce x-rays naturally.

WILHELM ROENTGEN
The German scientist Wilhelm Roentgen (1845-1923) discovered x-rays in 1895. Roentgen did not understand what these rays were, so he named them x-rays.

Scanner is lined with lead to prevent x-rays from escaping.

Array of photodiodes – electronic detectors that produce electrical signals when x-rays hit them

Conveyor belt carries suitcases into the scanner.

A metal object such as a pistol does not allow x-rays to pass through it, so the pistol shows up on screen.

Computer receives electrical signals from the photodiodes and converts them into an image of the case.

X-ray tube produces x-rays.

X-RAY TUBE
Like a light bulb, an x-ray tube is filled with an inert (non-reacting) gas, but produces x-rays instead of light.

A strong electric current heats a wire. The energy from the electric current knocks some electrons out of the atoms in the wire.

Monitor screen displays contents of case to security guards.

As the electrons crash into the target, atoms of the metal produce the x-ray beam.

A powerful electric field pulls electrons at high speed toward the metal target.

BAGGAGE SCANNER
Airports have x-ray scanners (left) to check baggage for weapons and other dangerous objects. An x-ray tube produces a beam of x-rays, and a conveyor belt carries each suitcase into the path of the beam. Electronic detectors pick up the x-rays once they have passed through the case. A computer uses signals from the detectors to build up a picture of the contents of the case.

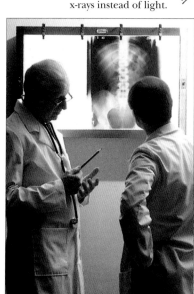

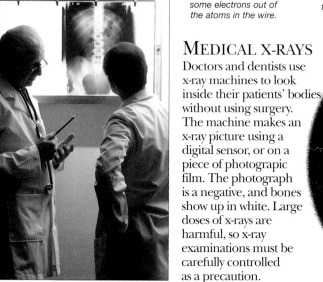

MEDICAL X-RAYS
Doctors and dentists use x-ray machines to look inside their patients' bodies without using surgery. The machine makes an x-ray picture using a digital sensor, or on a piece of photograpic film. The photograph is a negative, and bones show up in white. Large doses of x-rays are harmful, so x-ray examinations must be carefully controlled as a precaution.

X-RAYS IN SPACE
Satellites containing x-ray telescopes orbit the Earth. The telescopes detect x-rays coming from the Sun and stars, and from objects such as black holes. The satellites send x-ray pictures back to Earth. Astronomers use these pictures to discover and understand more of the universe.

> *Find out more*
> Atoms and molecules
> Machines
> Medicine, history of
> Science
> Stars

ZOOS

PEOPLE BEGAN TO KEEP animals in zoological gardens, or zoos, more than 3,000 years ago, when rulers in China established a huge zoo, called the Gardens of Intelligence. Today, most cities have a zoo, wildlife park, or aquarium, which provide a chance to observe and study hundreds of different animals. However, many people do not agree on the value of zoos. Zoo supporters say that zoos give people the opportunity to be close to animals, which they would never otherwise experience; zoos help us appreciate the wonder of the natural world; and zoo staff carry out scientific research and important conservation work, such as breeding rare species. Zoo critics believe that it is wrong to keep animals in captivity; the creatures behave unnaturally, and in poorly run zoos they suffer because of stress, unsuitable food, dirty conditions, and disease.

EARLY ZOOS
In early zoos, animals such as elephants were taught to perform for the visitors, as shown in this picture. Animals are no longer trained to perform for the public. The purpose of a zoo is to enable people to see how wild animals behave in their natural surroundings. The ideal solution is to save wild areas, with their animals and plants, and allow people to visit these, but this is not always possible.

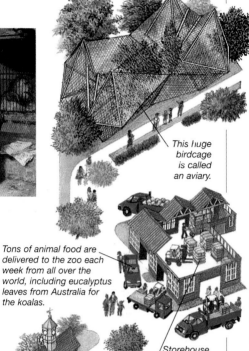

This huge birdcage is called an aviary.

Tons of animal food are delivered to the zoo each week from all over the world, including eucalyptus leaves from Australia for the koalas.

Storehouse, where food is stored. Zoo trucks take food from here to the animals.

Display boards and guide books full of information provide education.

Gardeners take care of the zoo grounds and look after all of the plants.

Signposts around the zoo direct visitors to different areas.

Thousands of school-children visit zoos each year with their teachers.

Zoo vans collect dirty straw from each of the animal houses.

Zookeeper delivering straw to animals

Zoos have restaurants and cafés, where visitors can eat, drink, and relax.

Visitors can buy souvenirs in the zoo shop.

Zookeepers hose down the animal houses every day with water.

HOW ZOOS ARE RUN
A zoo employs zookeepers to look after the animals, zoologists (scientists who study animals), veterinarians, accountants, architects, cooks, gardeners, builders, and many other people. The zoo manager must keep all of these people organized because there are many jobs to do, such as ordering the correct food for each animal and running the souvenir shop and the restaurants. Visitors have to pay an entrance fee toward the upkeep of the zoo, but most zoos also need government funds.

MODERN ZOOS
In some zoos, such as the San Diego Zoo, United States, (left), animals range free in large enclosures with trees and other natural features. People view the animals through glass panels rather than iron bars. You can even see the animals from an open-topped bus. In most countries, inspectors can arrive unannounced to check the welfare of the creatures. A few zoos still treat their captives badly, and organizations such as Zoo Check work toward ensuring better conditions in zoos.

Find out more
ANIMALS
CONSERVATION
and endangered species

INDEX

Page numbers in **bold** type have most information in them.

D · E

K · L · M

GAZETTEER

A

Abu Dhabi United Arab
Emirates **346**
Abuja Nigeria **566**
Acapulco Mexico **341**
Accra Ghana **566**
Addis Ababa Ethiopia **171**
Adelaide Australia **57**
Aden Yemen **346**
Adriatic Sea *sea*
Mediterranean Sea **291**
Aegean Sea *sea*
Mediterranean Sea **245**
Afghanistan *country* C Asia
113
Africa *continent* **12**
Alabama *state* USA **546**
Alaska *state* USA **546**
Albania *country* SE Europe
487
Alberta *province* Canada **95**
Alexandria Egypt **377**
Algeria *country* N Africa **377**
Algiers Algeria **377**
Alicante Spain **497**
Alice Springs Australia **57**
Alps *mountains* C Europe **191**
Amazon *river* Brazil/Peru **79**
Amazon Basin *basin* South
America **79**
American Samoa *dependency*
Pacific Ocean **395**
Amman Jordan **346**
Amsterdam Netherlands **321**
Andes *mountains* S America
477
Andorra *country* SW Europe
224
Andorra la Vella Andorra **224**
Angola *country* SW Africa **489**
Anguilla *dependency* West
Indies **98**
Ankara Turkey **532**
Antananarivo Madagascar **272**
Antarctica *continent*
Antarctica **29**
Antigua and Barbuda *country*
West Indies **98**
Antwerp Belgium **321**
Appennines *mountains*
Italy/San Marino **291**
Arabian Peninsula *peninsula*
SW Asia **345**
Arabian Sea *sea* Indian Ocean
43
Arctic Ocean *ocean* **36**
Argentina *country* S South
America **38**
Arizona *state* USA **546**
Arkansas *state* USA **546**
Armenia *country* SW Asia **105**
Aruba *dependency* West Indies
98
Ascension Island *dependency*
Atlantic Ocean **51**
Ashgabat Turkmenistan **113**
Ashmore and Cartier Islands
dependency Indian Ocean
272
Asia *continent* **43**
Asmara Eritrea **171**
Astana Kazakhstan **43**
Asunción Paraguay **477**
Atacama Desert *desert* Chile
477
Athens Greece **245**

Atlantic Ocean *ocean* **51**
Atlas Mountains *mountains* N
Africa **377**
Auckland New Zealand **372**
Australia *country* Oceania **57**
Australian Capital Territory
territory Australia **57**
Austria *country* W Europe **60**
Ayers Rock *see* Uluru
Azerbaijan *country* SE Asia **105**

B

Baffin Bay *bay* Atlantic Ocean
95
Baghdad Iraq **346**
Bahamas *country* West Indies
98
Bahrain *country* SW Asia **346**
Baku Azerbaijan **105**
Balearic Islands *islands* Spain
497
Baltic Sea *sea* Atlantic Ocean
191
Bamako Mali **566**
Bandar Seri Begawan Brunei
483
Bangalore India **270**
Bangkok Thailand **483**
Bangladesh *country* S Asia **270**
Bangui Central African
Republic **109**
Banjul Gambia **566**
Barbados *country* West Indies
98
Barcelona Spain **497**
Basel Switzerland **510**
Basseterre Saint Kitts and
Nevis **98**
Bavarian Alps *mountains*
Austria/Germany **60**
Beijing China **119**
Beirut Lebanon **346**
Belarus *country* E Europe **63**
Belfast UK **537**
Belgium *country* NW Europe
321
Belgrade Serbia **485**
Belize *country* Central
America **111**
Belmopan Belize **111**
Belo Horizonte Brazil **79**
Ben Nevis *mountain* UK **537**
Bengal, Bay of *bay* Indian
Ocean **270**
Benin *country* W Africa **566**
Bering Strait *strait* Russian
Federation/USA **546**
Berlin Germany **236**
Bermuda *dependency* Atlantic
Ocean **51**
Bern Switzerland **510**
Berner Alpen *mountains*
Switzerland **510**
Bethlehem West Bank **288**
Bhutan *country* S Asia **270**
Birmingham UK **537**
Biscay, Bay of *bay* Atlantic
Ocean **497**
Bishkek Kyrgyzstan **113**
Bissau Guinea-Bissau **566**
Black Forest *physical region*
Germany **236**
Black Sea *sea* Atlantic Ocean
191
Blackpool UK **537**

Blanc, Mont *mountain*
France/Italy **291**
Bloemfontein South Africa **473**
Bogotá Colombia **128**
Bohemian Forest *mountains*
C Europe **236**
Bolivia *country* W South
America **477**
Bombay *see* Mumbai
Bonn Germany **236**
Bordeaux France **224**
Borneo *island* SE Asia **483**
Bosnia and Herzegovina
country SE Europe **487**
Boston USA **546**
Botswana *country* S Africa **489**
Bouvet Island *dependency*
Atlantic Ocean **51**
Brahmaputra *river* S Asia **119**
Brasília Brazil **79**
Bratislava Slovakia **191**
Brazil *country* C South
America **79**
Brazzaville Congo **109**
Bridgetown Barbados **98**
Brisbane Australia **57**
Bristol Channel *inlet* UK **537**
British Columbia *province*
Canada **95**
British Indian Ocean
Territory *dependency*
Indian Ocean **272**
British Virgin Islands
dependency West Indies **98**
Bruges Belgium **321**
Brunei *country* SE Asia **483**
Brussels Belgium **321**
Bucharest Romania **485**
Budapest Hungary **191**
Buenos Aires Argentina **38**
Bujumbura Burundi **171**
Bulgaria *country* SE Europe
485
Burkina *country* W Africa **566**
Burma *country* SE Asia **483**
Burundi *country* C Africa **171**

C

Cabinda *province* Angola **109**
Cádiz Spain **497**
Cairo Egypt **377**
Calais France **224**
Calcutta *see* Kolkata
Calgary Canada **95**
California *state* USA **546**
California, Gulf of *gulf*
Pacific Ocean **341**
Cambodia *country* SE Asia **483**
Cameroon *country* W Africa
109
Canada *country* N North
America **95**
Canary Islands *islands* Spain
497
Canberra Australia **57**
Cape Town South Africa **473**
Cape Verde *country* Atlantic
Ocean **51**
Caracas Venezuela **477**
Cardiff UK **537**
Cardigan Bay *bay* Atlantic
Ocean **537**
Caribbean Sea *sea* Atlantic
Ocean **381**
Cartagena Colombia **128**

Casablanca Morocco **377**
Castries Saint Lucia **98**
Cayenne French Guiana **477**
Cayman Islands *dependency*
West Indies **98**
Central African Republic
country C Africa **109**
Central America *geopolitical
region* **111**
Chad *country* C Africa **109**
Channel Islands *islands* W
Europe **537**
Chennai India **270**
Chicago USA **546**
Chile *country* SW South
America **477**
China *country* E Asia **119**
Chisinau Moldova **533**
Christchurch New Zealand **372**
Christmas Island *dependency*
Indian Ocean **272**
Cocos Islands *dependency*
Indian Ocean **272**
Cologne Germany **236**
Colombia *country* N South
America **128**
Colombo Sri Lanka **270**
Colorado *state* USA **546**
Comoros *country* Indian
Ocean **272**
Conakry Guinea **566**
Congo *country* C Africa **109**
Congo Basin *basin* C Africa
109
Congo, Democratic Republic
of *country* C Africa **109**
Connecticut *state* USA **546**
Cook Islands *dependency*
Pacific Ocean **395**
Copenhagen Denmark **452**
Corfu *island* Greece **245**
Cork Ireland **284**
Corsica *island* France **224**
Costa Rica *country* Central
America **111**
Crete *island* Greece **245**
Crimea *peninsula* Ukraine **533**
Croatia *country* SE Europe
487
Cuba *country* West Indies **98**
Cyprus *country*
Mediterranean Sea **43**
Czech Republic *country*
C Europe **191**

D

Dakar Senegal **566**
Dallas USA **546**
Damascus Syria **346**
Danube *river* C Europe **236,
485**
Darwin Australia **57**
Dead Sea *salt lake*
Israel/Jordan **288**
Delaware *state* USA **546**
Delhi India **270**
Denmark *country* N Europe
452
Detroit USA **546**
Dhaka Bangladesh **270**
Dijon France **224**
Dili East Timor **483**
Dingle Bay *bay* Atlantic
Ocean **284**
Djibouti *country* E Africa **171**

Djibouti Djibouti **171**
Dodecanese *islands* Greece
245
Dodoma Tanzania **171**
Doha Qatar **346**
Dominica *country* West Indies
98
Dominican Republic *country*
West Indies **98**
Donegal Bay *bay* Atlantic
Ocean **284**
Dordogne *river* France **224**
Douro *river* Portugal/Spain
420
Dubai United Arab Emirates
346
Dublin Ireland **284**
Durban South Africa **473**
Dushanbe Tajikistan **113**
Düsseldorf Germany **236**

E

East Timor *country* SE Asia
483
Ecuador *country* NW South
America **477**
Edinburgh UK **537**
Egypt *country* NE Africa **377**
Eiger *mountain* Switzerland
510
El Salvador *country* Central
America **111**
Elburz Mountains *mountains*
Iran **282**
England *national region* UK
537
English Channel *channel*
France/United Kingdom
191
Equatorial Guinea *country*
C Africa **109**
Erie, Lake *lake* Canada/USA
546
Eritrea *country* E Africa **171**
Estonia *country* NE Europe **63**
Ethiopia *country* E Africa **171**
Etna, Monte *volcano* Italy **291**
Euphrates *river* SW Asia **532**
Europe *continent* **191**
Everest, Mount *mountain*
China/Nepal **270**

F

Faeroe Islands *dependency*
NW Europe **452**
Falkland Islands *dependency*
Atlantic Ocean **38**
Fiji *country* Pacific Ocean **395**
Finland *country* N Europe
452
Florence Italy **291**
Florida *state* USA **546**
Florida Keys *islands* USA **546**
France *country* W Europe **224**
Frankfurt am Main Germany
236
Freetown Sierra Leone **566**
French Guiana *dependency* N
South America **477**
French Polynesia *dependency*
Pacific Ocean **395**

G

Gabon *country* C Africa **109**
Gaborone Botswana **489**
Galilee, Sea of *lake* Israel **288**
Galway Bay *bay* Atlantic Ocean **284**
Gambia *country* W Africa **566**
Ganges *river* S Asia **270**
Garda, Lago di *lake* Italy **291**
Garonne *river* France **224**
Gaza Strip *disputed region* Gaza Strip **288**
Geneva Switzerland **510**
Geneva, Lake *lake* France/Switzerland **510**
Genoa Italy **291**
Georgetown Guyana **477**
Georgia *country* SW Asia **105**
Georgia *state* USA **546**
Germany *country* N Europe **236**
Ghana *country* W Africa **566**
Gibraltar *dependency* **497**
Glasgow UK **537**
Gothenburg Sweden **452**
Grampian Mountains *mountains* UK **537**
Gran Chaco *lowland plain* South America **38**
Grand Canyon *canyon* USA **546**
Great Barrier Reef *reef* Australia **57**
Great Bear Lake *lake* Canada **95**
Great Lakes *lakes* Canada/USA **546**
Great Wall of China *Ancient monument* China **119**
Great Plains *plains* Canada/USA **95**
Great Rift Valley *depression* Asia/Africa **171**
Great Slave Lake *lake* Canada **95**
Greater Antilles *islands* West Indies **98**
Greece *country* SE Europe **245**
Greenland *dependency* NE North America **452**
Grenada *country* West Indies **98**
Grenoble France **224**
Guadeloupe *dependency* West Indies **98**
Guam *dependency* Pacific Ocean **395**
Guatemala *country* Central America **111**
Guatemala City Guatemala **111**
Guernsey *island* Channel Islands **537**
Guinea *country* W Africa **566**
Guinea-Bissau *country* W Africa **566**
Gulf, The *gulf* SW Asia **346**
Guyana *country* N South America **477**

H

Haifa Israel **288**
Haiti *country* West Indies **98**
Halifax Canada **95**
Hamburg Germany **236**
Hamilton New Zealand **372**
Hanoi Vietnam **483**

Hanover Germany **236**
Harare Zimbabwe **489**
Havana Cuba **98**
Hawaii *state* USA **546**
Hebrides *islands* UK **537**
Hebron Israel **288**
Helsinki Finland **452**
Himalayas *mountains* S Asia **270**
Hindu Kush *mountains* Afghanistan/Pakistan **113**
Hiroshima Japan **294**
Hô Chi Minh Vietnam **483**
Hobart Australia **57**
Hokkaido *island* Japan **294**
Honduras *country* Central America **111**
Hong Kong *former UK dependency* China **119**
Honshu *island* Japan **294**
Houston USA **546**
Hudson Bay *bay* Atlantic Ocean **95**
Hungary *country* C Europe **191**

I · J

Ibiza *island* Spain **497**
Iceland *country* NW Europe **452**
Idaho *state* USA **546**
Illinois *state* USA **546**
India *country* S Asia **270**
Indian Ocean *ocean* **272**
Indiana *state* USA **546**
Indianapolis USA **546**
Indonesia *country* SE Asia **483**
Indus *river* S Asia **270**
Innsbruck Austria **60**
Iowa *state* USA **546**
Iran *country* SW Asia **282**
Iranian Plateau *plateau* Iran **282**
Iraq *country* SW Asia **346**
Ireland *country* NW Europe **284**
Irian Jaya *province* Indonesia **483**
Irish Sea *sea* Atlantic Ocean **284**
Islamabad Pakistan **270**
Isle of Man *dependency* NW Europe **537**
Israel *country* SW Asia **288**
Istanbul Turkey **532**
Italy *country* S Europe **291**
Ivory Coast *country* W Africa **566**
Jakarta Indonesia **483**
Jamaica *country* West Indies **98**
Japan *country* E Asia **272**
Java *island* Indonesia **483**
Jersey *island* Channel Islands **537**
Jerusalem Israel **288**
Johannesburg South Africa **473**
Jordan *country* SW Asia **346**
Jutland *peninsula* Denmark **452**

K · L

K2 *mountain* China/Pakistan **270**
Kabul Afghanistan **113**
Kalahari Desert *desert* S Africa **489**

Kamchatka *peninsula* Russian Federation **447**
Kampala Uganda **171**
Kansas *state* USA **546**
Kathmandu Nepal **270**
Kazakhstan *country* C Asia **43**
Kentucky *state* USA **546**
Kenya *country* E Africa **171**
Khartoum Sudan **171**
Khyber Pass *pass* Afghanistan/Pakistan **270**
Kiev Ukraine **533**
Kigali Rwanda **171**
Kilimanjaro *volcano* Tanzania **171**
Killarney Ireland **284**
Kingston Jamaica **98**
Kingstown Saint Vincent and the Grenadines **98**
Kinshasa Congo, Dem. Rep. of **109**
Kiribati *country* Pacific Ocean **395**
Kisangani Congo, Dem. Rep. of **109**
Kobe Japan **294**
Kolkata India **270**
Kosovo *country* SE Europe **485**
Kuala Lumpur Malaysia **483**
Kuwait *country* SW Asia **346**
Kuwait Kuwait **346**
Kyoto Japan **294**
Kyrgyzstan *country* C Asia **113**
Kyushu *island* Japan **294**
La Paz Bolivia **477**
Laâyoune Western Sahara **377**
Lahore Pakistan **270**
Laos *country* SE Asia **483**
Latvia *country* NE Europe **63**
Lausanne Switzerland **510**
Le Havre France **224**
Lebanon *country* SW Asia **346**
Leeds UK **537**
Leeward Islands *islands* West Indies **98**
Lesbos *island* Greece **245**
Lesotho *country* S Africa **473**
Lesser Antilles *islands* West Indies **98**
Liberia *country* W Africa **566**
Libreville Gabon **109**
Libya *country* N Africa **377**
Libyan Desert *desert* N Africa **12**
Liechtenstein *country* C Europe **191**
Liffey *river* Ireland **284**
Lille France **224**
Lilongwe Malawi **12**
Lima Peru **477**
Limoges France **224**
Lisbon Portugal **420**
Lithuania *country* NE Europe **63**
Liverpool UK **537**
Ljubljana Slovenia **487**
Llanos *physical region* Colombia/Venezuela **477**
Loire *river* France **224**
Lomé Togo **566**
London UK **537**
Los Angeles USA **546**
Louisiana *state* USA **546**
Luanda Angola **489**
Lusaka Zambia **12**
Luxembourg *country* NW Europe **321**
Luxembourg Luxembourg **321**
Lyon France **224**

M

Maastricht Netherlands **321**
Macedonia *country* SE Europe **485**
Madagascar *country* Indian Ocean **272**
Madras *see* Chennai
Madrid Spain **497**
Maine *state* USA **546**
Majorca *island* Spain **497**
Málaga Spain **497**
Malabo Equatorial Guinea **109**
Malawi *country* S Africa **12**
Malaysia *country* SE Asia **483**
Maldives *country* Indian Ocean **272**
Male Maldives **272**
Mali *country* W Africa **566**
Malta *country* S Europe **291**
Managua Nicaragua **111**
Manama Bahrain **346**
Manchester UK **537**
Manila Philippines **483**
Manitoba *province* Canada **95**
Maputo Mozambique **489**
Marrakech Morocco **377**
Marseille France **224**
Marshall Islands *country* Pacific Ocean **395**
Martinique *dependency* West Indies **98**
Maryland *state* USA **546**
Maseru Lesotho **473**
Massachusetts *state* USA **546**
Massif Central *plateau* France **224**
Matterhorn *mountain* Italy/Switzerland **510**
Mauritania *country* W Africa **566**
Mauritius *country* Indian Ocean **272**
Mayotte *dependency* Indian Ocean **272**
Mbabane Swaziland **473**
Mediterranean Sea *sea* Atlantic Ocean **191**
Mekong *river* SE Asia **119**
Melbourne Australia **57**
Memphis USA **546**
Mexico *country* Central America **341**
Mexico City Mexico **341**
Mexico, Gulf of *gulf* Atlantic Ocean **381**
Michigan *state* USA **546**
Micronesia *country* Pacific Ocean **395**
Midway Islands *dependency* Pacific Ocean **395**
Milan Italy **291**
Minnesota *state* USA **546**
Minorca *island* Spain **497**
Minsk Belarus **63**
Mississippi *state* USA **546**
Mississippi River *river* USA **546**
Missouri *state* USA **546**
Mogadishu Somalia **171**
Moldova *country* SE Europe **533**
Mombasa Kenya **171**
Monaco *country* W Europe **224**
Mongolia *country* E Asia **43**
Monrovia Liberia **566**
Montana *state* USA **546**
Montenegro *country* SE Europe **485**
Montevideo Uruguay **477**
Montserrat *dependency* West Indies **98**

Morocco *country* N Africa **377**
Moroni Comoros **272**
Moscow Russian Federation **447**
Mozambique *country* S Africa **489**
Mumbai India **270**
Munich Germany **236**
Muscat Oman **346**
Myanmar *see* Burma

N

Nagasaki Japan **294**
Nairobi Kenya **171**
Namib Desert *desert* Namibia **489**
Namibia *country* S Africa **489**
Naples Italy **291**
Nassau Bahamas **98**
Nauru *country* Pacific Ocean **395**
Navassa Island *dependency* West Indies **98**
Nazareth Israel **288**
Ndjamena Chad **109**
Nebraska *state* USA **546**
Negev *desert* Israel **288**
Nepal *country* S Asia **270**
Netherlands *country* NW Europe **321**
Nevada *state* USA **546**
New Brunswick *province* Canada **95**
New Caledonia *dependency* Pacific Ocean **395**
New Delhi India **270**
New Hampshire *state* USA **546**
New Jersey *state* USA **546**
New Mexico *state* USA **546**
New Orleans USA **546**
New South Wales *state* Australia **57**
New York USA **546**
New York *state* USA **546**
New Zealand *country* Oceania **372**
Newcastle upon Tyne UK **537**
Newfoundland *province* Canada **95**
Niagara Falls *waterfall* Canada/USA **95, 546**
Niamey Niger **566**
Nicaragua *country* Central America **111**
Nice France **224**
Nicosia Cyprus **43**
Niger *country* W Africa **566**
Niger *river* W Africa **566**
Nigeria *country* W Africa **566**
Nile *river* N Africa **12**
Niue *dependency* Pacific Ocean **395**
North America *continent* **381**
North Carolina *state* USA **546**
North Dakota *state* USA **546**
North European Plain *plain* N Europe **191**
North Geomagnetic Pole *pole* **36**
North Island *island* New Zealand **372**
North Korea *country* Asia **302**
North Pole *pole* **36**
North Sea *sea* Atlantic Ocean **191**
Northern Ireland *political division* UK **537**
Northern Mariana Islands *dependency* Pacific Ocean **395**

ACKNOWLEDGEMENTS

Contributors Simon Adams, Neil Ardley, Norman Barrett, Gerard Cheshire, Judy Clark, Chris Cooper, Margaret Crowther, John Farndon, Will Fowler, Adrian Gilbert, Barbara Gilgallon, Peter Lafferty, Margaret Lincoln, Caroline Lucas, Antony Mason, Rupert Matthews, Dan McCausland, Steve Parker, Steve Peak, Theodore Rowland-Entwistle, Sue Seddon, Marilyn Tolhurst, Marcus Weeks, Philip Wilkinson, Frances Williams, Tim Wood, Elizabeth Wyse
Additional editorial assistance from Helen Abramson, Sam Atkinson, Jane Birdsell, Lynn Bresler, Azza Brown, Liza Bruml, Caroline Chapman, Claire Gillard, Matilda Gollon, Carl Gombrich, Samantha Gray, Sudhanshu Gupta, Prita Maitra, Caroline Murrell, Pallavi Narain, Connie Novis, Louise Pritchard, Ranjana Saklani, Jill Somerscales
Additional design assistance from Sukanto Bhattacharjya, Tina Borg, Duncan Brown, Darren Holt, Shuka Jain, Ruth Jones, Sabyasachi Kundu, Johnny Pau, Clare Watson, Simon Yeomans
Illustration Coordinator Ted Kinsey
Picture Research Maureen Cowdroy, Diane LeGrand, Samantha Nunn, Deborah Pownall, Louise Thomas, Bridget Tily, Emma Wood
Cartographers Pam Alford, Tony Chambers, Ed Merritt, Rob Stokes, Peter Winfield
DTP Harish Aggarwal, Georgia Bryer, Siu Chan, Nomazwe Madonko, Pankaj Sharma, Claudia Shill
Photography Stephen Oliver
Index Jackie Brind
Proofreader Lee Wilson
Gazetter Sylvia Potter
Additional Production Chris Avgherinos

ADVISORS AND CONSULTANTS

Chemistry and Physics
Ian M. Kennedy BSc
Jeff Odell BSc, MSc, PhD
David Glover
Dr. Jon Woodcock

Culture and Society
Iris Barry
Peter Chrisp MA
Margaret Cowan
John Denny B.Mus.Hons
Dr. Peter Drewett BSc, PhD, FSA, MIFA
Dr. Jamal, Islamic Cultural Centre
Miles Smith-Morris
Brian Williams BA
The Buddhist Society

Earth Resources
April Arden Dip.M
Hedda Bird BSc
Conservation Papers Ltd.
Peter Nolan, British Gas Plc
Stephen Webster BSc, M. Phil
Earth Conservation Data Centre

Earth Sciences
Erica Brissenden
Alan Heward PhD
Keith Lye BA, FRGS
Rodney Miskin MIPR, MAIE
Shell UK Ltd.
Christine Woodward
The Geological Museum, London
Meteorological Office

Engineering
Karen Barratt
Jim Lloyd, Otis Plc
Alban Wincott
Mark Woodward MSc, DICC.Eng

History
Reg Grant
Dr. Anne Millard BA, Dip Ed, PhD
Philip Parker MA
Ray Smith
The Indian High Commission
Campaign for Nuclear Disarmament

Medicine and the Human Body
Dr. Sue Davidson
Dr. T. Kramer MB, BS, MRCS, LRCP
Richard Walker
Dr. Frances Williams MB, BChir, MRCP

Music
Simon Wales BA, MBA,
London Symphony Orchestra

Natural History
Kim Bryan
Wendy Ladd and the staff of the Natural History Museum
London Zoo

Space Science
NASA
Neil MacIntyre MA, PhD, FRGS
Dr. Jacqueline Mitton
John Randall BSc, PGCE
Christian Ripley BSc, MSc
Carole Stott BA, FRAS

Sport
Brian Aldred
David Barber
Lance Cone
John Jelley BA
International Olympic Committee

Technology
Alan Buckingham
Jeremy Hazzard BISC
Paul Macarthy BSc, MSc
Cosson Electronics Ltd.
Robert Stone BSc, MSc,
C. Psychol, AFBsF, M.ErgS,
Advanced Robotic Research Ltd.
Stuart Wickes B. Eng

Transport
Ian Graham
Doug Lloyd, Westland Helicopters
John Pimlott BA, PhD
Tony Robinson
Wing Commander Spilsbury, RAF
M. J. Whitty GI Sore.E

In addition, Dorling Kindersley would like to thank the following people and organizations for their assistance in the production of this book:

Liz Abrahams, BBC; Alan Baker; All England Tennis Club; Alvis Ltd.; Amateur Swimming Assoc.; Apple UK Ltd.; Ariane Space Ltd.; David Atwill, Hampshire Constabulary; Pamela Barron; Beech Aircraft Corp; Beaufort Air Sea Equipment; Bike UK Ltd.; BMW; Boeing Aircraft Corporation; BP Ltd.; British Amateur Athletics Assoc.; British Amateur Gymnastics Assoc.; British Antarctic Survey; British Canoe Union; British Coal Ltd.; British Forging Industry Assoc.; British Foundry Assoc.; British Gas Ltd.; British Museum; British Paper and Board Federation; British Parachuting Assoc.; British Post Office; British Ski Federation; British Steel; British Sub-Aqua Club; British Telecom International Ltd.; Paul Bush; Michelle Byam; Karen Caftledine, Courtauld Fibres; Martin Christopher, VAG Group; Citroen; CNHMS; Colourscan, Singapore; "Coca-Cola" and "Coke" are registered trade marks which identify the same products of The Coca-Cola Company; Commander Richard Compton-Hall; Lyn Constable-Maxwell; Cottrell & Co Ltd.; Geoffrey Court; Sarah Crouch, Black & Decker Ltd.; F. Darton and Co. Ltd.; Department of Energy, Energy Conservation Support Unit; Adrian Dixon; DRG Paper Ltd.; Patrick Duffy, IBA Museum; Earth Observation Data Centre; Electronic Arts; Embassy of Japan, Transport Department; Esso Plc; Eurotunnel Ltd.; Ford UK Ltd.; Sub Officer Jack Goble, London Fire Brigade; Julia Golding; Brian Gordon; Paul Greenwood, Pentax Cameras Ltd.; Patrick and Betty Gunzi; Hamleys, Regent Street, London; Helmets Ltd.; Jim Henson Productions Ltd.; Alan Heward, Shell UK Ltd.; cartoon frames taken from "Spider in the Bath", reproduced by permission from HIBBERT RALPH ENTERTAINMENT © and SILVEYJEX PARTNERSHIP ©; Hoover Ltd.; Horniman Museum; House of Vanheems Ltd.; IAL security products; ICI Ltd.; Ilford Ltd.; Imperial War Museum; Institute of Metals; Institution of Civil Engineers; Janes Publications Ltd.; Nina Kara; Jonathan Kettle, Haymarket Publishing; Julia Kisch, Thorn EMI Ltd.; Kite Shop, London; Sarah Kramer; Krauss-Maffei GMBH; Lambda Photometrics Ltd.; Sandy Law; Richard Lawson Ltd.; Leica GmbH; Leyland Daf Ltd.; London Transport Museum; London Weather Centre; The Lord Mayor of Westminster's New Year Parade; Lyndon-Dykes of London; Joan MacDonnell, Sovereign Oil and Gas Ltd.; Neil MacIntyre; Marconi Electronic Devices Ltd., Lincoln; Paul McCarthy, Cosser Electronics Ltd.; McDonnell Douglas Aircraft Corporation; Philip Mead; Mercedes; The Meteorological Office, London; Ruth Milner, Comark Ltd.; A. Mondadori Editore, Verona; Mysteries New Age Centre, London; National Army Museum; National Grid Company Ltd.; National Physical Laboratory; National Remote Sensing Centre, Farnborough; Nautilus Ltd.; Newcastle Hindu Temple; Helene Oakley; Olympus Ltd.; The Ordinance Survey; Osel Ltd.; Otis PLC; Gary Palmer, Marantz Ltd.; Personal Protection Products; Pilkington Glass Ltd.; Pioneer Ltd.; Philips Ltd.; Porter Nash Medical; Powell Cotton Museum; John Reedman Associates; Renaissance Musée du Louvre; Robertson Research Ltd.; Tony Robinson; Rockware Glass Ltd.; Rod Argent Music; Rolls Royce Ltd.; Liz Rosney; Royal Aircraft Establishment; Royal Astronomical Society, London; Royal Military Academy, Sandhurst; SNCF; Andrew Saphir; Malcolm Saunders, Simon Gloucester Saro Ltd.; Seagate Ltd.; Sedgewick Museum; Shell UK Ltd.; Skyship International Ltd.; Dennis Slay, Wessex Consultants Ltd.; Amanda Smith, Zanussi Ltd.; Ross Smith, Winchcombe Folk Police Museum; Sony Ltd.; Rachael Spaulding, McDonald's Restaurant Ltd.; Stanfords Map Shop, London; Steelcasting Research and Trade Assoc.; Stollmont Theatres Ltd.; Swatch Watches Ltd.; Tallahassee Car Museum; Texaco Ltd.; The Theatre Museum, Covent Garden, London; Toyota; Trafalgar House, Building and Civil Engineering; Trevor Hyde; Wastewatch; Jim Webb; Westland Helicopters Ltd.; Westminster Cathedral; Malcolm Willingale, V Ships, Monaco; Wiggins Teape Ltd.; Howard Wong, Covent Garden Records, London; Woods Hole Oceanographic Institute; Yarrow Shipbuilders Ltd.; The YHA Shop, London.

PICTURE SOURCES

The publisher would like to thank the following for their kind permission to reproduce their photographs:

Abbreviations: a = above, b = below, c = centre, f = far, l = left, r = right, t = top.

A

Architectural Association: Joe Kerr 353cl.
Action Plus: Glyn Kirk 144tl, 556bl.
Courtesy of Akai Professional: 363br
AKG London: 259bc, 430bl; Michael Teller 259c.
Alamy Images: Helene Rogers 348crb; Keith Dannemiller 348bl; Images Etc Ltd 254tr; North Wind Picture Archives 389bl; Oleksiy Maksymenko 280cb; Realimage 424clb; Simon Kotowicz 205cb.
Album: 205t.
Bryan And Cherry Alexander Photography: 327bc.
Max Alexander: 372br.
Alvis Ltd: 437br.
Allsport: 79cl; Ben Bradford 97cl; Howard Boylan 536cl; Shaun Botterill 371bl.
Amtrak: 184br.
Ancient Art & Architecture Collection: 18cl, 81bl, 88tl, 275tl, 308tl, 308bc; Charles Tait 81tr; N.P.Stevens 175tr; Ronald Sheridan 81cr, 157tl, 246cla, 275bl, 295crb, 399bl, 431ca, 508tl, 540tl, 540bl.
Animal Photography: Sally Anne Thompson 402bl.
Animals Unlimited: Patty Cutts 402cr.
Courtesy of Apple: 135b; 517tr.
Ardea London Ltd: 142tr; Francies Gohier 140bc.
The Art Archive: 88cl, 114bc, 146bl, 193cl, 193bl, 296cr, 329bl; Chateau Malmaison 194cla.
Ashmolean Museum, Oxford: 18tr, 174bc.
Associated Press Ap: 191cr, 298crb, 491crb.
Australian Tourist Commission: 54bl.
National Archaelogical Museum: 84cl.
Neil Audley: 49bl.
Australian Overseas Information Services, London: 59bl.
Axiom: Chris Bradley 376c; Chris Caldicott 376cl, 377tr, 429br.

B

Barnaby's Picture Library: 520bl.
N.S. Barrett: 215tr.
Beech Aircraft Corporation: 413clb, 413bc.
Belkin.com: 136fcrb.
Bite Communications Ltd.: 280cl, 280c.
BMW: 184cb.
The Boeing Company: 15ca.
D. C. Brandt, Joyce and Partners: 33cb, 34clb.
Bridgeman Art Library, London / New York: *Catherine, Mulatte of the Bradeo* portrait by A. Durer, 1521 69br; *Greeks under Seige* by Eugene Delacroix 88br, 133tl, 181tr, 203cla; *King James I of England* by Paul Van Somer 248cla, 256clb, 319br, 321tr; *William Morris,* photographic portrait by Hollyer, 1884 353tl, 397bc; *Henry Wrothesley 3rd Earl Southampton* 459cl; *Sir Francis Bacon* bust by Roubillac 459cr, 467tr, 506br, 581tr; *Belvoir Castle Henry VIII* by Hans Holbein younger 256tr; Berger Collection, Denver Art Museum *Oliver Cromwell* c1649 146tr; Bibliotheque Nationale, Paris 396c; Bonhams *Samuel Pepys* portait by John Riley 206tr; Bristol City Museum Art Gallery *Bristol Harbour 1785,* by Nicholas Pocock 467tl; British Library 22bc; St. Cuthbert from Bede 8th century 23clb, Queen Mary Psalter, bailiff berating peasants 401bc; British Museum 19cb, Benin sword 69cl; British Museum London, *Nineveh Epic of Gilgaresh* (clay tablet 7th Century BC) 508tl; British Museum, London 53cb, 334cl, 396tl; Cairo Museum/Giraudon 32clb; Christies, London 421tr; City of Bristol Museum Art Gallery 295tl; Eton College, Windsor 334cr; Fabbir 90cb; Fine Art Society *Seige at Droghedon* 1641 146bc; Forbes Magazine Collection 365crb; Galleria Degli Uffizi 541tl; Galleria dell Accademia Firenze 431bl; Hertford Cathedral 330tl; Hever Castle 256crb; Lambeth Palace Library collection, burning of Thomas Cranmer from the *Foxe's Book of Martyrs* 1563 (woodcut), 530bl; Lauros Girandon Musée de la Ville de Paris; *Leeds Museum and Gallery Kirkstall Abbey* by George Alexander 256bl; Louvre, Paris 246bc, 427bc; Mozart Museum, Salzburg, Austria, *Mozart and his sister Maria-Anna,* ivory by Eusebius Johann Alphen 60c; Musée d'Orsay, Paris (© DACS) 397cr; National Portrait Gallery 181tl; New Zealand High Commission, London 372cl; *Henry VIII,* portait, Philip Mould 256tl; Phillips Fine Art Auctioneers 530tl; Prado, Madrid 495tr; Sherlock Holmes 319br, 547cr; Rafael Valls

Gallery, London 146cl; Richard Philip 22br; Roy Miles Gallery *Lord Byron* by Sir William Allan 88bc; Royal Albert Memorial Museum *Olandah Equiano* portrait 1780's 467bc; Sante Maria delle Grazie, Milano 295bl; *Self Portrait with Gloves,* 1498 (panel) by Albrecht Durer, Prado, Madrid, Spain 235tr; *Snow White and the Seven Dwarves,* c.1912 (block print), English School. Stapleton Collection, UK. 235b; Staaliche Museen zu Berlin 107bc; T.U.C. London 274cb; Tate Gallery, London 62bc; Wallace Collection, London, *Oliver Cromwell* (portrait) 146tl; Wilberforce House Museum, Hull *The Kneeling Slave* 13th century, England (painting) 467cl.
British Film Institute: Stills, Posters and Designs 205tr.
British Library, London: 23tl, 74cra, 74crb, 84bl, 337bl, 337bc, 373clb; Stuart 506tr.
British Museum, London: 61cl, 84br, 332bc; British Museum 23bc; Museum of Mankind 332tl.
British Airways Archive Museum Collection: 254cra, 526tr.
British Steel: 286cl, 286crb.
Britstock-ifa: 248bc.
British Tourist Authority: 534bl.

C

Casio: 517tr.
Bruce Coleman Ltd: 76crb, 110cr, 116cr, 118tl, 142bl, 142br, 165bl, 166tl, 180clb, 223cl, 228bc, 260tr, 286clb, 300cl, 361cr, 370cl, 394bc, 394bcr, 412crb, 518cl, 528br, 544bl, 548bc; Jack Dermid 458tl; A.J. Deane 267br; Bernol Thies 458cla; Bob and Clara Calhoun 66clb; Brian and Cherry Alexander 450tr; Brian Coates 73bl, 394bcl; C.B. & D.W. Frith 85c; C.B. Frith 161tl, 161tl, 261tr; Charles Henneghein 124bc, 304tr, 494bl; Chris Hollerbeck 229bl, 544tl; Colin Moyneux 519c; David C. Houston 269bl; David Davies 436bc; David Hughes 457tl; Dieter & Mary Plage 570crba; Dr. Echart Pott 312bc, 416bl; Dr. Frieder Sanct 342c; Eric Crichton 213cb; Fitz Prenzel 52bl; Frans Lanting 368crb; G. D. Plage 260cl, 314cl, 261c; Gene A. Ahrens 543tl; Gerald Cubitt 40bc, 139cr, 200clb, 238tl, 258bc, 271c, 326bl, 398tl; H. Rivarola 67cl, 68cl; Hans Reinhardt 103tr, 190bl; 326cb; Hans Richard 178tr; Inigo Everson 415tc, 415cr; Jane Burton 27bc, 173bc, 243cl, 341bc, 359crb; Jaroslav Poncar 559cla; Jeff Foott 27c; Jeff Simon 304clb; Jen and Des Bartlett 313tr; Joe Van Wormer 415bl; John Markhom 74clb; John Shaw 167c, 170cl, 346clb, 426br; John Topham 223tr; Jonathan Wright 385tl, 463tr; Keith Gunner 355cl; Kim Taylor 179bc, 196cl, 359cra, 572tl; L.C. Marigo 201ca; Leonard Lee Rue III 513br; M. Timothy O' Keefe 435tr; Michael Fogden 404br; Michael Freeman 121br, 258clb, 363bc; Michael Klinec 125tr, 126bl; Michel Viard 359tl; N.A.S.A. 166cr, 172tl, 352bl; Neville Fox-Davies 354clb; Norbert Rosig 190tr; Norbert Schwertz 555crb; Norman Myers 351bl, 416tr; Norman Owen Tomalin 26tr, 350crb, 436cra, 542cra; Norman Plyers 314tr; R. Campbell 220crb; R.I.M. Campbell 32ca, 32cl; Robert Perron 404cr; Rod Williams 87bc, 351cl; Ron Cartnell 313br; Udo Hirsch 266cl; Vatican Museums and Galleries, Rome 396clb; Walter Lankinen 304cl, 257cb, 257bl, 52bc; Werner Stoy 166c, 555clb.
Collections: Bill Wells 384bc; Brian Keen 536cr; Brian Shuel 283cr, 284bl, 307tc; Gena Davies 556cla; Geoff Howard 307crb; John Miller 307bl; Nigel Hawkins 186bl; Sandra Lousada 536br; Select 382bc; Yuri Lewinski 23cr.
Collection Viollet: 296tl.
Colorific!: Joe McNally/Wheeler Pics 238cra; Roger de la Harpe 488tr.
Columbia Pictures: 149bl.
Corbis UK Ltd.: Adrian Wilson / Beateworks 516c; Andy Rain / EPA 240bl; Archivo Iconografico S.A. 533bl; Bill Nation / Sygma 99cb; Car Culture 99cb; Dean Conger 112b, 446b, 533cl; Earl and Nasima Kowall 113br; E.M. Pasieka / Science Photo Library 76crb; Hervé Hughes / Hemis 497tl; Hulton-Deutsch Collection 425bl; Karen Kasmauski 427bl; Keith Hunter / Arcaid 241cr; John Noble 35b; Lawrence Manning 419crb; Michael St Maur Sheil 320bc; Michael Rosenfeld / Science Faction 164bl; Moodboard 311tc; Murat Taner 539c; Nik Wheeler 496br; Peter Beck 301cl; Reuters 409br; Rolf Vennenbernd / EPA 100c; Stephanie Maze 451tc; Frederic Larson/San Francisco Chronicle 168clb; Ariel Skelley 280crb; Tom Wagner 277tl.

D

James Davis Travel Photography: 50cr, 419b, 531bl, 532br.
Duncan Brown: 444tr, 444c, 444br.
Dickens House Museum: 157tr, 157bl.
DK Images: NASA 493bl; Stephen Oliver 164br.

Dominic Photography: Zoe Dominic 459bl.

E

Earth Satellite Corporation: 330crb.
Empics Ltd: 216cr, 391tr; 305198 216cr; Tony Marshall 216tl.
The English Heritage Photo Library: Down House 150bl; Jonathan Bailey, Down House 150tl.
T. Malcolm English: 255bc.
Environmental Images: Steve Morgan 241ca; Toby Adamson 231bl.
European Space Agency: 49cra, 419cra.
European Parliament Photolibrary: 192cl, 192bl.
Mary Evans Picture Library: 14tl, 14tr, 16br, 31tr, 32bc, 53tr, 53bl, 59tl, 59cl, 65tl, 80cr, 89clb, 96crb, 107tl, 120c, 122tr, 125tl, 125cl, 137cr, 137bl, 137br, 147cr, 147bl, 147bl, 149tl, 150bc, 153tr, 153cl, 164tr, 167bv, 178bl, 185cb, 187tr, 187cb, 187bl, 195tl, 197ce, 198cla, 203clb, 206tl, 209tr, 225tl, 231tc, 232bl, 239tl, 239br, 240tl, 247clb, 248tr, 248cra, 249bl, 274tl, 274clb, 274bc, 295bc, 296bc, 307tl, 312cl, 319tl, 334bl, 334br, 335cb, 335bc, 364clb, 364bl, 365bl, 367tr, 369cra, 374bl, 389tl, 391c, 392bc, 400bl, 401clb, 404tr, 404clb, 412cr, 412cr, 424tr, 424bc, 426tr, 430br, 448tr, 448cb, 454ca, 454bc, 455tl, 455ca, 466clb, 467cr, 467bl, 479cl, 499tr, 514bc, 515tl, 518tr, 520tl, 521tr, 522bl, 524cr, 524cr, 528cr, 528bc, 540cra, 540br, 541tr, 548tl, 550ca, 550crb, 550bl, 551tl, 551cl, 551cl, 552cr, 556br, 571c, 574tl, 574tc, 574cla, 575ca, 578tl, 579tc, 579ca, 579cl, 579cb, 580tr; Explorer 134cla, 134cl, 225cl; Illustrazione 194tr; Spencer 401tr.
Eye Ubiquitous: David Foreman 532bl; Helen A. Lisher 536tl; Mike Southern 50tl; P. Maurice 532tc; Tim Durham 419cb.

F

Family Life Picture Library: Angela Hampton 276c, 280br.
FLPA – Images of Nature: 505clb; Roger Wilmshurst 36ctr; W.S. Clark 380tl.
Michael & Patricia Fogden: 214cr.
Werner Forman Archive: 46tr, 364bc, 441tr, 554bl; British Museum 46clb.
Format Photographers: Karen Robinson 182cl; Mo Wilson 241tl; Sasha Lefreund 241cl.
Fortean Picture Library: Allen Kennedy 193tl.
French Railways: 523cl.
Courtesy of Fuji Film: 2-3b; 91tr.
John Frost Historical Newspapers: 576tl.

G

General Motors Corporation: 509bl.
Geoscience Features: 106bc, 168bl, 232tr, 402crb.
German National Tourist Office: 234b.
Getty Images: AFP 344bc; Andreas Pollok / Photodisc 280bc; Chip Somodevilla / Getty Images News 538bc; ColorBlind / The Image Bank 524bc; Enamul Hoque / Photographer's Choice 136cla; Hulton Archive 316bl; Iconica 405br; Image Source 500cb; Macduff Everton 425bl; Michael Kelley / Stone+ 389crb; OTHK / Asia Images 524bl; PNC / Photodisc 134bl; Photographer's Choice 379br; Sajjad Hussain / AFP 99crb; Sean Sullivan 425clb; Stone 94cr, 404cr; Taxi 409br; The Bridgeman Art Library 167bl; Thomas Collins / Photographer's Choice 164br; Tim Sloan / AFP 548bc; Tim Sloan / AFP 21clb; Tom Raymond 361tl.
Photographie Giraudon: 337ca; Lauros 365cl.
Google: 280cl.
Greenpeace Inc: 138tl.

H

Sonia Halliday Photographs: 89bc, 193cr, 223b, 300cra, 392tl; James Wellard 203tc; R.H.C. Birch 246tr.
David Hamilton: 534cl.
Robert Harding Picture Library: 12tr, 28bc, 37cr, 37bc, 49cr, 95tc, 111tc, 117tl, 117cr, 128cl, 222cl, 222b, 282bl, 282br, 290bl, 343cr, 371br, 371tl, 376br, 377br, 378tr, 472tr, 476tr, 480tr, 482cl, 564cl, 565cl; Adam Woolfit 485bc, 486tr; C. Bowman 380cr; David Hughes 192bc; F.J. Jackson 35cl; Frans Lanting 117c; Fraser Hall 472bc; G. P. Corrigan 34tl; G. Renner 29tc; G.Boutin 376bc; G.M. Wilkins 473tc; G.R. Richardson 233bl; Gavin Hellier 60br, 472ct; Goldstrand 485cr; James Strachan 112tr; Jeff Greenberg 63cr; Jeremy Lightfoot 245c; J.H.C. Wilson 269cl; Julia Thorne 420bl; Michael Jenner 293br, 345b; Mitsuaki Iwago 29tr; Paul van Riel 291br; Phil Robinson 484br; R. Ashworth 282tl; R. Cundy 380ct; Rob Cousins 95cr; Robert Cundy 472clb; Robert Francis 56cl; Robert

Frerck/Odyssey 380cl; Roy Rainford 378bl; I. van Goubergen 320tc; T. Waltham 381tr; Thierry Borridon 221bl; Victor Engelbert 565cr; Weisbecker 268cr.
Hewlett Packard: 136br; 136c.
Kaii Higashiyama: 397tr.
The Historical Society of Pennyslvania: 557bl.
© Michael Holford: 62tl, 62clb, 114c, 402cb, 403cr, 408br; British Library 130cr; British Museum 360tr.
Holt Studios International: Duncan Smith 202bl; Richard Anthony 511cr.
Hulton Getty: 18tl, 45tr, 59cb, 70tl, 75tr, 82cl, 82cr, 82cb, 82bl, 83tr, 88tr, 122tl, 122bl, 127tl, 127bl, 132bc, 154bc, 157crb, 176tl, 176tr, 182bc, 185tr, 192tl, 203bc, 259tr, 312tl, 400cl, 400CB, 400crb, 425tr, 443tl, 455crb, 455bl, 491cl, 506bc, 571bc, 573clb, 575bl, 576c, 576clb, 576cb, 578bl; Bettmann Archive 33cl, 127cr, 407bc; Bettmann/UPI 80cr; Douglas Miller 182cr; Ernst Haas 176c.
Jacqui Hurst: Robert Aberman 344br.
Hutchison Library: 37cl, 44tl, 44br, 45br, 77cl, 78tr, 78ctl, 108cr, 128bl, 132bl, 269c, 271cl, 272tr, 288br, 399tr, 470c, 474cl, 475tr, 476tl, 563cl, 565bl; B. Regent 403bc, 565tl; Bernard Regent 470tl; Bernard Regent 108bl, 108bc; Carlos Freste 267bc; Christina Dodwell 271bl; Christine Pemberton 45tl; Crispin Hughes 169bl, 486tc, 563cr, 565ctr; Eric Lawrie 475tl; F. Greene 45c; Felix Greene 329cr; H.R. Dorig 334tl, 478crb; Jeremy Horner 44crb, 117cl; John Downman 381br; John G. Egan 487cr; Juliet Highey 268tl; Kerstin Rodseps 571bl; Leslie Woodhead 564tl; M. Friend 484cl; M. Jeliffe 109tr; Mary Jeliffe 376tr; Maurice Harvey 446clb; Melanie Friend 487b; N. Durrell McKenna 119tr; Nick Haslam 63tr, 63bl, 446cr, 485tr; Nigel Sitwell 78cr; P. Moszynski 164cr; Philip Wolmuth 182crb; R. Ian Lloyd 301bc; Richard Howe 77br; Robert Aberman 531br; Robert Francis 44cra; Sarah Erinngton 12c, 109bc, 116br, 161bc, 161bc, 169tl, 201bl, 202tl, 489br, 564br; Timothy Beddow 169c; Titus Moser 113tr; Trevor Page 132bl, 112cl; V. Ivleva 112cr; Vanessa S. Boeye 44bl.

I.A.L. Security Products: 580cr.
Illustrated London News Picture Library: 525br.
Image Bank: 41tr, 43br, 56tl, 56br, 61crb, 93c, 93bc, 94c, 97tr, 97bl, 97br, 111br, 118cr, 118bl, 126cl, 137tr, 140bl, 205bc, 217tl, 224bl, 229bc, 238bc, 288tl, 288bl, 293bl, 344cl, 349bc, 349bc, 358tl, 395cr, 474cl, 474b, 477cl, 477br, 480bc, 499tl, 505bl, 507tl, 513tl, 522tl, 524tr, 525bc; Alan Beeker 525ca; Alex Hamilton 323bc; Andrea Pistolesi 439tl; Ben Rose 404c; Bernard van Berg 224tr; Brett Frooner 209bc; Colin Molyneux 253tl; David Hiser 304ca; David Martin 323tr; David W. Hamilton 102tc, 544tr; Don Klumpp 343b, 345tr; Erik Leigh 369crb; Francis Hildago 266bc; Francisco Ontanon 495bl; Frank Roiter 62crb; Fulvio Roiter 244bc; G. A. Wilton 159tr; G. Gundberg 451br; G. Rontmeester 537bc; Gary Gladstone 522tl; Georgina Bowater 234t; Gianalberto Cigolini 121tl; Giulliano Colliva 93bl; Guido Alberto Rossi 494bc, 94c, 289cl, 495bl; Harold. Sand 339cr, 546tr; Hank Delespinesse 499cl; J. Bryson 91bl; Jean Pierre Pienchat 426bl; Joe Azzara 569tr; Joseph B. Brignolo 344tr, 418crb; Kaz Mori 166cr; Kodansha Images 462tr; Lou Jones 471bc; Luis Castaneda 191bl; M. Melford 338bc; Marc Solomon 217br; Marvin E. Newman 450cl; Michael Melford 424cla; Michael Salas 58tr; P. & G. Bower 102tc; Paul Kleuenz 480cr; Peter Thomann 126cl; Robert Holland 393crb; Robert Phillips 418bl; Ronald R. Johnson 292tl, 494cr; Steve Dunwell 348bl; Steve Niedorf 333ca; Stockphotos 325cr; Thomas R. Rampy 67crb; Toyotumi Mori 293c; Trevor Wood 536tr.
Imperial War Museum: 83cla, 571clb, 574cl.
Innes Photo Library: Ivor Innes 80cl, 80clb; John Blackburn 80bl.
Intercity: 184crb.
iStockphoto.com: Julián Rovagnati 280crb.

JET Joint Undertaking: 383tl.

Barnabas Kindersley: 293tl, 293clb, 293crt; 116bl.
David King Collection: 132tr.
Kobal Collection: 54br, 157c, 204cra, 205bl, 265cb, 269tl, 361bc, 437tl, 579bl.
Courtesy of **Kodak:** 405tr.

Lada: 447bl.
Leitz: 233br.
Link Picture Library: 328cb; Greg English 328br; Orde Eliason 328cl, 328bl.

London Features International: 363crb.
Lotus Cars Ltd: 238cb.
Lupe Cunha: 250cl, 333ce.

Magnum: 491bc.
Mansell/Time Inc: 133br.
Mansell Collection: 31bc, 59cr, 90cl, 573tl.
Mercedes Benz: 99clb.
The Metropolitan Museum of Art: Rogers Fund 1904 296clb.
Michelin: 569clb.
William Morris Gallery: 353tr, 353bl, 353bc.
Museum Of London: 31br, 146crb, 206bc.

N.A.S.A.: 47cl, 49 cla, 49 cr, 49 fcra, 49tr, 49 cla, 52cr, 131c, 352cb, 393bl, 419c, 425bc, 437bl, 492bl, 492crb, 500cr, 526cl, 526br, 549clb, 560tl, 561bl; Finlay Holiday Films 238cr; John Hopkins University Applied Physics Laboratory / Carnegie Institution of Washington 409bl; N.A.S.A 75c.
The National Archives of Scotland: 540cb.
National Gallery, London: 397tl, 51tl.
National Trust Photographic Library: Ian Shaw 366bc; Jennie Woodstock 366c; Martin Trelawny 556c.
National Maritime Museum, London: 141tl, 193bc, 392bl; James Stevenson 117br.
National Portrait Gallery, London: 88cr, 550tl.
The Natural History Museum, London: 30tl, 220cr.
Network Photographers Ltd.: 110br; Gideon Mendel 328tl, 328cr; Louise Gubb 328c.
Peter Newark's Pictures: 20cl, 20cr, 122cr, 154c, 154br, 312tr, 367crb, 367bc, 368tl, 368cl, 408bc, 466bc, 478br, 503tr.
N.H.P.A.: 38cl, 57tr, 78bc, 475br, 476br; Bill Wood 435tc; Brian and Cherry Alexander 35tr, 35c, 378cl; Daryl Balfour 171tr; J. H. Carmichael 387cra; Jerry Sauvanet 219tl; John Shaw 380b; Manfred Danegger 356tr; Martin Harvey 481br; Phillipa Scot 318cla; Roger Tidney 156tl; Stephen Dalton 65c; Stephen Krasemann 170t.
Nokia: 136cb, 514br.
Novosti (London): 445br, 448bl, 490tr, 490crb, 490bc; Vladimir Vyatkin 446bl.

Olympic Co-ordination Authority: 391tr.
Ordnance Survey © Crown Copyright: 330c.
Christine Osborne: 40bl, 333tl.
Oxford Scientific Films: 468bc, 469bc, 475bl; Animals Animals, M. Austerman Fran Allen 260cr; Fran Allen 261cr; B.G. Murray/JR Garth Scenes 426c; G.I. Bernard 210bc, 425crb; J.A.L. Cooke 30bc, 279tl; JAL Cooke 468clb; John Paling 27clb; Kathie Atkinson 326tl; Kim Westerskov 152tc; Lawrence Gould 208cl; Pam & Willy Kemp 173tl; Raymond Blythe 68tl; Ronald Toms 570bl; Stan Osolinksi 145c; Sue Trainer 230bc.

Palace of Versailles: 319cra. **Panasonic:** 91cl.
Panos Pictures: 37bl, 563br; Alfredo Cadeno 78bl; B. Klass 270b; Caroline Penn 477bl; Chris Stowers 485c; Dermot Tatlow 429bc; Dominic Harcourt-Webster 169cr; Giacomo Pirozzi 473 ctr; 108tr, 108cl; Gregory Wrona 105tl; Heidi Bradner 485bl; Howard Davies 487tl; Jean-Leo Dugast 481bc; Jeremy Hartley 563br; John Miles 78cl; Liba Taylor 170bl; N. Durrell Mc Kenna 488c; Neil Cooper 489tr; Pietro Cenini 169br; Trgve Bolstad 488cl.
PA News Photo Library: 239bl.
Patankar, Aditya: 364ct.
Photofusion: Sam Tanner 374br.
Pictor International: 239cr, 245cl, 245cr, 289cr, 290tr, 379br, 419cr, 419cr, 451bl, 484tr, 484c, 485tl, 496tl, 534tr.
Picture Mate: 91cr.
Planet Earth Pictures: 36bl, 460bl, 473br, 581bl; Adam Jones 378cr, 379cl; Anup Shah 170br, 481tl; Brian and Cherry Alexander 35cr; Christin Petron 32cr; David Phillips 354bc; Doug Perrine 379tl; Gary Bell 57c; John Downer 488bl; Jonathan Scott 170cr; Joyce Photographics 28cr; Mary Clay 379cr; Paul Cooper 209crb; Peter David 151tr, 151bc; Peter Lillie 488br; Tom Walker 268bl, 378br; Warren Williams 383ca; William Smithey 152c.
Richard Platt: 178bc, 324crb, 330cl.
Popperfoto: 14cl, 14c, 45cb, 122cl, 122br, 194tc, 194cl, 194cb, 298bl, 355tr, 385bl, 391br, 397clb, 443bl, 443br, 455c, 479cl, 479bl, 542tl, 553cl, 553cr; Bilderberg 541br; David Crosling, Reuters 83crb; Dmitri Messinis 194cb; Dylan Martinez, Reuters 83crb; Michael Stephens, Reuters 248bl; Reuters 176bc, 240ca, 541cl.

Powerstock Photolibrary / Zefa: 186ca, 262tl, 297bl, 412tr, 522cr; D.H. Teuffen 31tl; Geoff Kalt 471tr; Hales 520bc; Ingo Seiff 99tl; S. Palmer 580bl; T.Schneider 114tl.
Press Association Picture Library: 541bc.
Public Record Office Picture Library: 375cb.

Quadrant Picture Library: Mark Wagner 186crb.

Redferns: Mick Hutson 382cr; Steve Grillett 361tl.
Reuters: 509bl.
Rex Features: 41tl, 50br, 188tla, 188tlb, 236t, 250cl, 329tl, 372bc, 377bl; Chat 307cb; David Pratt 113bl; Fotex 451tl; J. Sutton-Hibbert 231c; James Fraser 241cr; Julian Makey 241bc; Richard Gardner 307cl; Steve Wood 496tr; Wheeler 183tl.
Ann Ronan Picture Library: 131bc, 203c, 336tl.
Cliff Rosney: 544bc. **Rover Group:** 188cr.
The Royal Collection (© 1999 Her Majesty Queen Elizabeth II): 133tr, 308crb.
The Royal Mint (Crown copyright): 348tl.

Scala: 396br, 454crb; Museo Nazionale Athenai 84cb.
Science Photo Library: 410bl, 515bl, 524bl; Alan Hart-Davies 253br; Alexander Isiaras 383clb, 511br; Alta Greenberg 543cr; Astrida Hans Frieder Michler 511c; CAIDA 280tr; Chris Bjornberg 161bl; Chris Butler 410br; CNRI 158bc, 161cl, 161cr; David Parker 600 Group 437c; David Parker/Max Planck/ Institut for Aeronomie 131c; David Wintraub 381tl; Dr Fred Espenak 502tl; Dr. Gerald Schatten 250br; Dr. Jeremy Burgess 342tl, 342bl; Earth Satellite Corp. 449ca; Earth Satellite Corporation 379cl; Eckhard Slawik 502cla; Edward Kinsman 158crb; E.W. Space Agency 409bcl; Frank Espanak 49cra; Kenneth Eward / Biografx 158bc; Ian Boddy 250cr; Jane Stevenson 432tl; Jim Stevenson 90tl; John Bavosi 158bl; John Sanford 131bl, 352tl; Ken Briggs 183bl; Lawrence Migoale 161bl; M.I. Walker 342cl; N.A.S.A. 49cl, 306br, 409bl, 409bc, 410bc, 410 bl, 410bcl, 410bcr, 417tl, 580bc; N.I.B.S.C. 252bl; N.R.A.O. 49v; Pasieka 161crb; Philippe Plailly 333cb; Philippe Reilly 306bl; Professor Harold Edgerton 404cra; Proffessor R. Gehz 49ca; R.E. Litchfield 342bc; Rich Treptow 425clb; Royal Greenwich Observatory 125bc; Simon Fraser 124tr; Smithsonian Institute 49tc; St. Mary's Hospital Medical School 335c; Takeshi Takahara 524bl; Tim Malyon 306tr; US Geological Survey 409br; W. Crouch & R.Ellis/NASA 549cb; William Curtsinger 28tr; Yves Bauken 277cb.
National Museum of Scotland: Mayan bowl 332crb.
Scottish Highland Photolibrary: R. Weir 456cra.
Shakespeare Globe Trust: 459tr. **Shell UK:** 390bc.
Ronald Sheridan: 375t. **Silkeborg Museum:** 32tl.
SKR Photos: LFI 360bl. **Sky TV:** 517crb.
South American Pictures: 479cra; Tony Morrison 61bc.
Spectrum Colour Library: 148br; E. Hughes 535cl.
Frank Spooner Pictures: 12bl, 96bl, 222tr, 292bc, 521bl; Bartholomew Liaison 153cr; Chip Hines 153bc; Eric Bouver 14bc; G. Nel Figaro 373cl; Gamma 117tr, c, 301tl, 344bl, 438cr; Gamma/V. Shone 168tr; Jacques Graf 406crb; John Chiason 39br; L. Novovitch-Liaison 548bc; Novosti/Gamma 491ca.
Sporting Pictures (UK) Ltd: 215cr, 223tl, 289bl, 391cl, 393tl, 500cl.
Still Pictures: 417c; Edward Parker 417clb; Mark Edwards 417br.
The Stock Market: 297cb; Zefa 433br.
Tony Stone Images: 51tr, 77bl, 79br, 190br, 271br, 277tr, 277cla, 277cl, 277bl, 321bl, 456cl, 456crb, 481bl, 522cl; Bob Thompson 380tr; Demetrio Carrasco 428cra; Doug Nausbaum 235tl; Doug Armand 235tl; Gary Yeowell 531tl; Glen Allison 378c; Hugh Sitton 290bc, 531c; James Balog 510c; John Beatty 36tl, 50cl; John Callahan 272cr; John Lamb 272bl; Jon Gray 522cl; Manfred Mehlig 60bl, 510bl; Martin Puddy 271tr; Michael Busselle 186clb; Nigel Hillier 531cr; Nigel Snowdon 56tr; Peter Cade 659tr; Ragnar Sigurdsson 50bc; Randy Wells 379tc; Robert Everts 484bl; Rohan 320bl; Seigfreid Layda 235c; Shaun Egan 290tl; Stephen Studd 510tr; Stuart Westmoreland 54cr; Tom Parker 535bl; Tom Walker 36tc.
Survival Anglia Photo Library: 139cl, 139c; Jeff Foott 139cl.
Don Sutton: 382cla, 382bl; DS17633 382br.
Syndication International: 503bl.

Tass News Agency: 237clb, 493cl.
© Tate Gallery, London: 353cr.

Ron & Valerie Taylor: 389clb.
Telegraph Colour Library: 453cl; Jason Childs 54cl.
Thames & Hudson Ltd: *The Complete Architecture Works* 123bc.
Louise Thomas: 481cr.
Topham Picturepoint: 298cl, 516bl, 517bl, 539cb, 575tl; Image Works.
Toy Brokers Ltd: 465tr.
Toyota (GB) PLC: 184bl.
Art Directors & TRIP: B. Vikander 532tr; G. Spenceley 487cl.

U

Unicef: 542bc.
United Nations: 542cl.
University of Manchester: Barri Jones, Department of Archaeology 32tr.

V

La Vie Du Rail: 524.
View Pictures: Dennis Gilbert 259br.
Virginia Museum of Fine Arts: gift of Col. & Mrs Edgar W. Garbisch 547tr.

W

National Museum of Wales: 535cra.
The Wallace Collection: 397c.
John Walmsley Photo Library: 71tr, 429ca, 556bc.
John Watney: 283c.
Reg Wilson: 168.
Winchester City Council: 18crb.
Harland and Wolf: 535cr.

X

Xinhua News agency: 492tl.

Y

Jerry Young: 211bl.

Z

Zefa Picture Library: 43bl, 56bl, 92cl, 98c, 106tl, 111cr, 118bc, 188bc, 234cr, 234bl, 249bc, 284t, 287bc, 289tr, 290c, 340cr, 340bl, 386cl, 428bc, 446tl, 482cr, 496cl, 505c, 522cr, 535tl, 536bl, 557br, 558c, 559crb; Abril 436c; B. Croxford 344cr; B. Keppelmeyer 222cr; Colin Kaket 270tr; Damm 344tl, 482bc; Dr. David Conker 74bl; Dr. R. Lorenz 399tl; Fritz 373bc; G. Hunter 94bl; Groebel 445cr; H. Grathwohl 340tr; Heilman 201tl, 202bc; Helbig 66tr; J.

Zittenzieher 268br; K. Goebel 174tl, 235cr, 343cl; K. Keith 497tl; Kohler 234cl; Leidmann 269tr; Messershmidt 123tr; O. Langrand 237bc; Orion Press 85tr; Praedel 451cr; R.G. Everts 237crb; Starfoto 268cl; UWS 314cr; W. Benser 268c; W. F. Davidson 120tl; W. Mole 360br; W.F. Davidson 555bc; Werner H. Muller 121cr.

All other images © Dorling Kindersley
For further information see: www.dkimages.com

Additional thanks to: Max Alexander; Peter Anderson; Tony Barton Collection; Geoff Brightling; Jane Burton; Peter Chadwick; Joe Cornish; Andy Crawford; Geoff Dann; Tom Dobbie, Philip Dowell; Niel Fletcher; Bob Gathany; Frank Greenaway; Steve Gorton; Alan Hill; Chas Howson; Colin Keates; Barnabas Kindersley; Dave King; Bob Langrish; Liz McAulay; Andrew McRobb; Ray Moller; Tracey Morgan; Stephen Oliver; Susannah Price; Rob Reichenfeld; Tim Ridley; Kim Sayer; Karl Shone; Steve Shott; Clive Streeter; Harry Taylor; Kim Taylor; Wallace Collection; Matthew Ward; Francesca Yorke, Jerry Young.

Every effort has been made to trace the copyright holders and we apologise in advance for any unintentional omissions. We would be pleased to insert the appropriate acknowledgments in any subsequent edition of the publication.

ILLUSTRATION CREDITS

Abbreviations: a = above, b = below, c = centre, l = left, r = right, t = top.

A

Graham Allen: 350
David Ashby: 99cl, tl, tr; 206c; 274; 365cl; 466c; 547; 548r; 491tl; 466cr

B

Stephen Biesty: 15; 16; 99cr; 101; 102; 255t; 507c; 515; 519c; 519tl
Rick Blakely/Studio Art and Illustration: 177cl; 254; 306; 322c; 352; 438c; 449tl; 462c; 463t, c; 492; 493b, l; 522; 580
Peter Bull Art Studio: 91tr; 185bc; 237c; 275c, bc; 384cl, cr; 425bl; 561
Christopher Butzer: 308c

C

Julia Cobbold: 106; 299b; 355c; 416; 436; 534br; 535tr
Stephen Conlin: 33t; 34c; 123; 342cr; 431cl; 543b
John Crawford-Fraser: 149cr; 364cr

D

William Donahue: 89c; 441c, bl; 523; 554t; 572
Richard Draper: 49

E

Angelika Elsebach: 24t, c; 25c; 30; 65; 68; 163cr; 196; 200; 201; 218 except tl; 219; 227cl, br; 228; 279; 314tl, c, b; 327; 468; 498; 527tl; 567c
Angelika Elsebach/David Moore: 527tr, bl
Gill Elsebury: 155; 156; 226; 370; 469

G

L.R. Galante: 17cl; 46cr; 144cr; 198bc; 249cl; 262c, cr; 263c; 265c; 319cr; 401c
Tony Gibbons: 462b; 463b

H

Nick Hall: 166; 167c; 421; 422; 512
Nicholas Hewetson: 8cr; 9c; 9bl; 31c, bc; 40r; 41; 47t, b; 61t; 62cl; 85; 93tr, bl, cr; 97cr; 110tr; 116cl, tr; 94tl; 132cl;

134; 141c, br; 153bl; 160cr; 174; 175b, tl; 281 tl, bl; 205tl; 221c; 223c; 234; 239tr; 244bl; 246c; 247cl; 249tl, cl; 250; 253b; 258; 266; 267c; 283br; 292b; 296; 297; 299tl, cl; 310bl; 315; 319br; 324bl; 329tr; 335tl; 341cr; 349; 361tr; 362; 372tl, cr; 373tl, cr; 375cl, cr; 391; 392cl, br; 394; 423tr, b; 430c; 435cl; 437cl; 440b; 443cr; 445; 450tl, br; 471bc; 474cl; 475; 478; 479; 480cl; 494cl; 500; 503c; 539tl; 544; 549cr, bl; 551; 554bl; 560; 562bl, br; 571tr
Adam Hook/ Linden Artists: 22cl; 23c; 46cr; 150cl; 367c; 400cr; 506cl

J

Kevin Jones Associates: 383

K

Aziz Khan: 17cr; 18cr, c, bl; 45l; 69tr, bl; 83c, bl; 130tr; 137cr; 147cl; 150bl; 165c; 182bl; 186tr; 192cr; 192br; 194br; 198cr; 231br; 241bl; 259bl; 265tr, bl; 275tr; 321cr; 332tr; 365cr; 366br; 382tr; 407tl; 429bc; 456tr; 466c; 506tl, bl; 508tr; 530tr; 541bl; 556tr
Steven Kirk: 160tl; 434; 435tl, b

L

Jason Lewis: 126; 185tl; 255r; 367tc
Richard Lewis: 131; 167t; 183; 217; 253c; 406; 424; 437bl; 449tr; 471tc, bl; 505t; 509; 521
Ruth Lindsay: 67; 86; 104; 162cr; 213tl; 214; 242; 243; 257; 261; 278; 318; 341l; 356 except cl; 568bl
Mick Loates/Linden Artists: 26; 27b; 66; 138; 139; 151; 152; 172; 195; 302; 303; 313; 389; 409; 410

M

Kathleen McDougall: 400tl
Coral Mula: 504tl, bl

Q

Sebastian Quigley/Linden Artists: 145; 148t, bl; 300bl; 338; 355b; 413cr

R

Eric Robson/Garden Studios: 457; 458
Jackie Rose: 300r, b
Simon Roulstone: 70c, bl, bc; 75tl, cl; 99c; 125c, cr; 135c; 176cl; 178tl, cr, c; 184tl; 185cl; 232c; 253cr; 280tr; 286cr; 369bl; 424c; 512

S

Sergio: 76; 165; 199; 252; 262cl, bl; 358; 432; 433
Rodney Shackell: 17c; 33b; 34b; 46br; 71cl; 115; 179; 198c (insets); 281tr; 209cl; 246b; 267bl; 247bc; 322tc; 323br; 396; 397; 398b; 399tl; 403tr; 429; 454; 455tc; 466tl; 502tr; 534bl; 535ct, cb, cr
Rob Shone: 20; 28bl; 120; 121; 140br; 304; 310r, cl; 311; 364cr; 393; 423tl, cr; 426; 439c; 440cr; 442t, cl; 505br; 553
Francesco Spadoni: 147tl, bc, br; 349cl; 407tc, cr, bl
Francesco Spadoni/Lorenzo Cecchi: 130cl, tr, bl, br
Clive Spong/Linden Artists: 229
Mark Stacey: 18bl; 81cl; 82tr, br; 90cr; 114cr; 137cl; 304cl; 312cr; 332c; 459c; 530c

T

Eric Thomas: 13cr; 14br; 21; 58; 59bl; 64c; 72bl, br; 74; 96tr, cl, bc; 99tc; 107; 181bl; 187cl; 188cl; 190; 225; 233c; 283tr; 285; 287; 321c; 336r; 337; 359; 362; 321cl; 403c; 408; 427tl, cl; 448; 494tr; 504c; 518bl; 524tl, cl; 538cr; 552; 557c; 573br; 574bl; 581

V

François Vincent: 493tr

W

Richard Ward/Precision: 13tr; 47c; 52t; 53t; 59tl; 62tr; 64cr; 89tl; 114br; 124; 127c; 129; 166cr; 140t, bl; 151cr; 168c, cr, b; 173; 198t; 210bl; 218tl; 221tl; 232; 244t; 367bl; 368bl; 314b (maps); 322br; 323tl, bl; 325bl; 329c; 330bc; 346; 347; 356cl; 385; 386; 402bcl, bl; 414tl; 503br; 507b; 520; 549t, c; 558tc; 569br; 570
Craig Warwick/Linden Artists: 390
Phil Weare: 411; 470bl; 577
David Webb/Linden Artists: 27t; 72bc; 142; 207bl, tl; 210tc, tr, bc, br; 211bl; 326br; 383; 387; 414b; 415; 568t, bc
Ann Winterbotham: 92br; 207r; 354c; 460
Gerald Wood: 46bl; 202; 204; 205br; 209cr; 215br; 402tlc; 418; 499br; 517bc; 526tl, cr; 525; 569c; 575
John Woodcock: 9cr; 19cb; 52c; 73tl, c; 178; 161; 164b; 177c; 208bl; 247r; 249tr, br; 260; 273b; 325tl, c, cr; 333l; 335br; 342cl; 375bc; 392tr; 411cr; 431r; 441br; 449bl; 455r; 461cl, bl; 499bl; 502cr; 518cl; 518bc; 528; 538b; 539b; 542; 490; 491tr; 559; 567b; 568cl, tr, c; 573c, cr; 574tr, br; 576; 579
Dan Wright: 103; 210c; 351

JACKET CREDITS

Key: a-above; b-below/bottom; c-centre; l-left; r-right; t-top.

Jacket images: *Front:* **Corbis:** Burstein Collection br; Pablo Martinez Monsivais / Pool / CNP fbl. **Dorling Kindersley:** Egyptian Museum, Cairo c. **Getty Images:**

David Maitland fbr; Michael J P Scott cl; naturepl.com: Michele Westmorland bl. **Science Photo Library:** Susumu Nishinaga bc; Pekka Parviainen cr; Tek Image fcl. *Back:* **Getty Images:** Harvey Lloyd ftl. **Science Photo Library:** Tony Craddock tl; B.W.Hoffman / AGStockUSA tr; Mehau Kulyk tc; Rafael Macia ftr. *Spine:* **Getty Images:** Caroyl La

Barge bl; John Lund clb; Hiroyuki Matsumoto cl; Nacivet br; Nicholas Rigg crb; Manoj Shah cra; Sightseeing Archive cla; SMC Images cr.

All other images © Dorling Kindersley
For further information see: www.dkimages.com